KEY TO MAP PAGES

Key to Regions

- South West England
- South East England
- London
- Wales
- West Midlands
- East Midlands
- East of England
- North West England
- Yorkshire
- North East England
- Scotland

Key to this map

- 236-237 — Road maps
- Birmingham — Urban area maps
- Oxford — City / Town centre plans

Seasonal symbols

- Spring
- Summer
- Autumn
- Winter
- Rainy day

For a full list of tourist symbols please refer to page 142

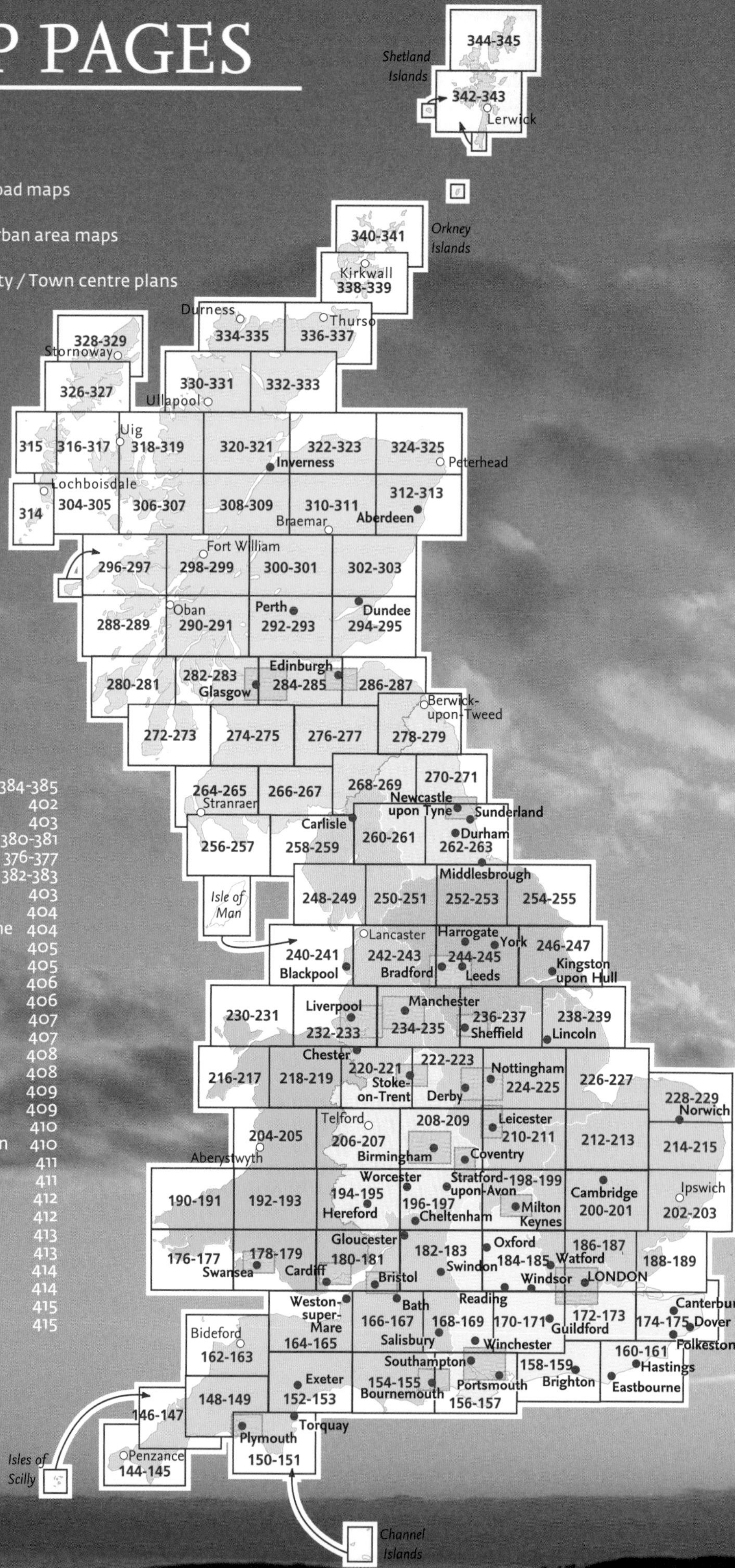

City & town centre plans

Urban area maps

DISCOVER BRITAIN

Britain is a beguiling group of islands, packed with mountains, moors, rivers, lakes and forests, brimming over with plants and wildlife, and enclosed by miles and miles of beautiful coastline.

This Touring Atlas and Guide identifies, locates and describes many of the best places to visit within Britain and gently reminds us that getting out and about is not exclusively a summer activity.

Britain is open 24 hours a day and 365 days a year and this book can be the inspiration for travel, entertainment and adventures whatever the season.

Gairloch sunset

CONTENTS

The country is split into the following regions within which you will find information for over 1300 places to visit. If you know the name of the attraction you are looking for, use the index to find its details. Each description has a map reference for you to locate it and wherever applicable a phone number and website. Where appropriate there are also symbols to advise if an attraction is suited to a rainy day and if it is especially appealing during a particular season.

As well as helping you plan your journey, this mapping also shows the location of 200 'Outstanding' tourist features.

Over 1300 tourist features are highlighted on detailed road mapping.

Avebury stone

Sarsen Stones

In the dry valleys these boulders litter the landscape; they are the famous 'Sarsen' stones, used by stone age man to build Avebury stone circle and other prehistoric monuments.

Symbols

- Spring
- Summer
- Autumn
- Winter
- Rainy day

For a full list of tourist symbols please refer to page 142.

Portmeirion Village 217 E4

This unique, if eccentric 'village' was created during the mid 20th century by the architect Clough Williams-Ellis in a flamboyant, Mediterranean style on his privately-owned peninsula on the beautiful Tremadoc Bay.

☎ 01766 770000 www.portmeirion-village.com

All attractions are referenced to the largest scale mapping.

Within the attraction descriptions there are 200 'Outstanding' features which are highlighted yellow.

Any description with an empty symbol ☐ can be found as a place or area name on the map.

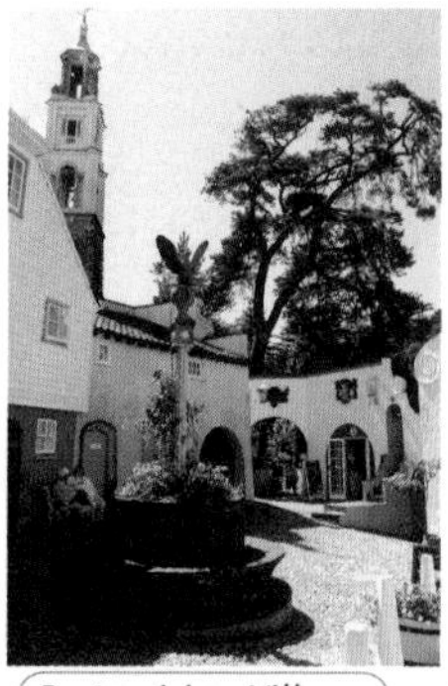

Portmeirion Village

Route planning map

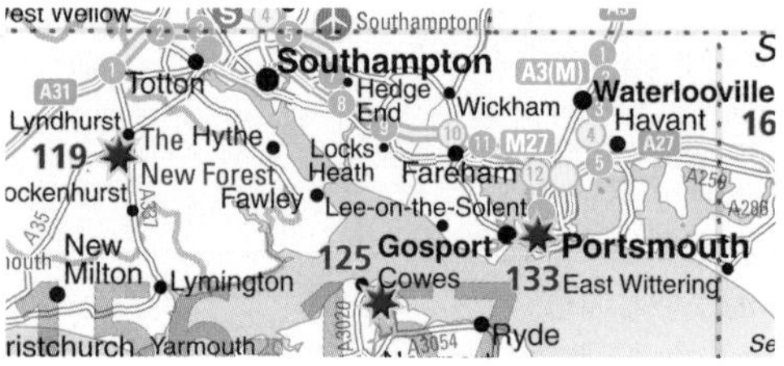

Road mapping

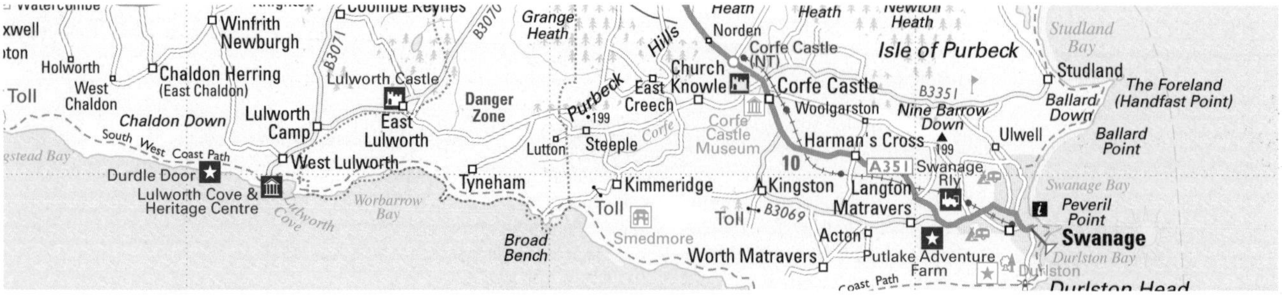

Urban area maps 346-375

These maps help you navigate through the suburbs of Britain's major cities.

Urban area maps

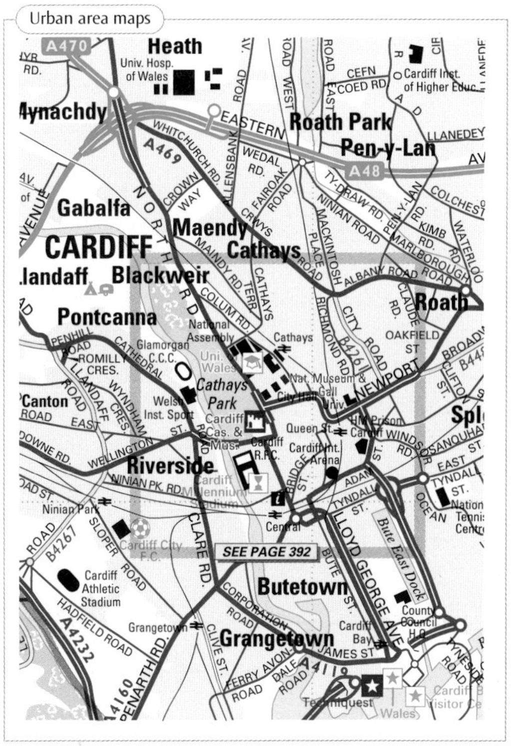

Central city maps 376-387

Six of Britain's busiest city centres are mapped in great detail to enable you to find your destination with ease.

Central city maps

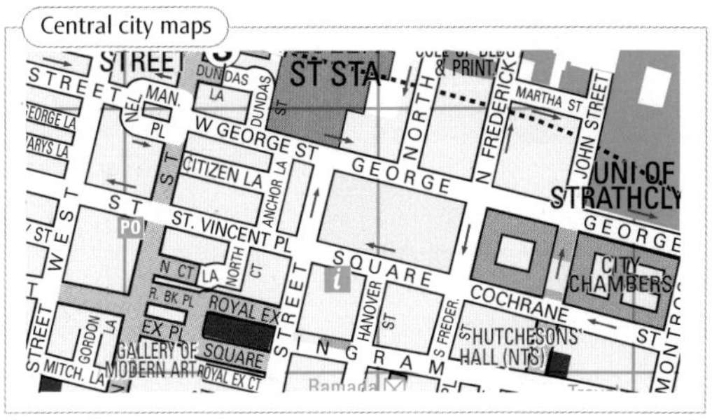

Town and city plans 388-415

Layouts of Britain's diverse towns and cities provide an overview of each location and a brief guide aids exploration.

Town and city plans

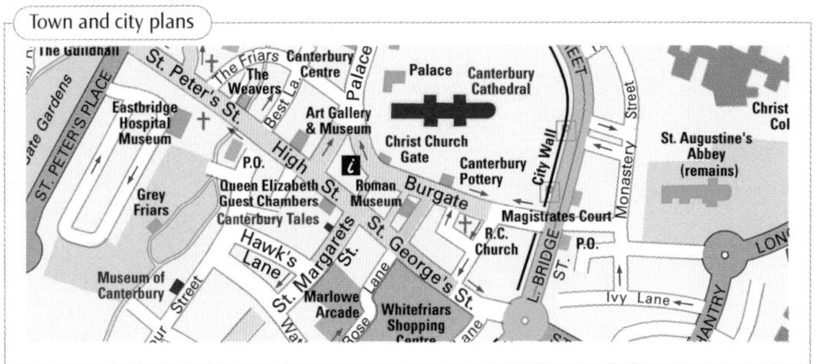

Wast Water

The rich tapestry of Britain's landscape looks permanent and immovable; in fact it is constantly changing and what we see today is just a tiny moment in time. Mountains the size of the Himalayas, vast lava flows, tropical seas, huge ice sheets and animals the size of several London buses have come and gone over the millennia and the legacy of these can be seen in the current landscape. Here in Britain, the earth is quieter now, the changes less dramatic than at times in the past, but they are still going on in the form of weathering and gradual changes in sea level, and every now and again a small tremor is a reminder of the stresses at work beneath the surface.

Since the very end of the last Ice Age, a mere 10,000 years ago, the flora and fauna we know today managed to gain a foothold and have developed over the years. Britain's landscape diversity has led to a wide variety of habitats, from the rocky and sometimes barren Scottish Highlands to the lush wooded valleys of southern England. Man, naturally adaptable, has left many marks on the face of the land, some ephemeral, but some extend back into the mists of time.

The next few pages give a brief insight into the 'hows' and 'whys' of Britain's landscape; its formation, natural history and the changes wrought by the hand of man. Look differently at the view. Take time to appreciate the beauty.

GUIDE TO GEOLOGY

SEDIMENTARY ROCKS (S)

Formed from sediments, of various sizes, deposited and slowly compacted into solid rock.

There are two types:

Transported sediments are bits of existing rocks which fall down hillsides, eventually being washed into streams. They are worn down further by rolling along the stream bed, eventually being carried into lakes or the sea, where the largest and heaviest are dropped first (they can also be blown there or deposited by ice). As further debris accumulates on top of them, they are compacted into solid rock, the size of the original particles defining the type of eventual 'sedimentary rock'. Conglomerates form from pebbles, and mudstones from the tiniest particles.

Non-transported sediments in Britain, are limestone and chalk. These are formed from the shells and skeletons of sea creatures and corals. As the creatures die, they sink to the floor, eventually being compressed into rock.

ROCK AGES

The time period during which a rock was formed is given a name in geology. These names have not been used in the text for the sake of simplicity but as an example, a sedimentary rock formed 300 million years ago would be called a 'Carboniferous sedimentary rock', however, if it had been formed 100 million years ago, it would be a 'Cretaceous sedimentary rock' and so on. Refer to any geology book for the full table.

SEDIMENTARY ROCKS
- Unconsolidated Sands & Shell Banks
- Clay
- Chalk
- Limestone
- Sandstone
- Greywacke and Slate (metamorphic)
- Mixed Hard Sediments including sandstone, shale, mudstone, greywacke, slate and limestone

IGNEOUS ROCKS
- Igneous (Extrusive/intrusive)

METAMORPHIC ROCKS
- Gneiss, Schist, Quartzite etc

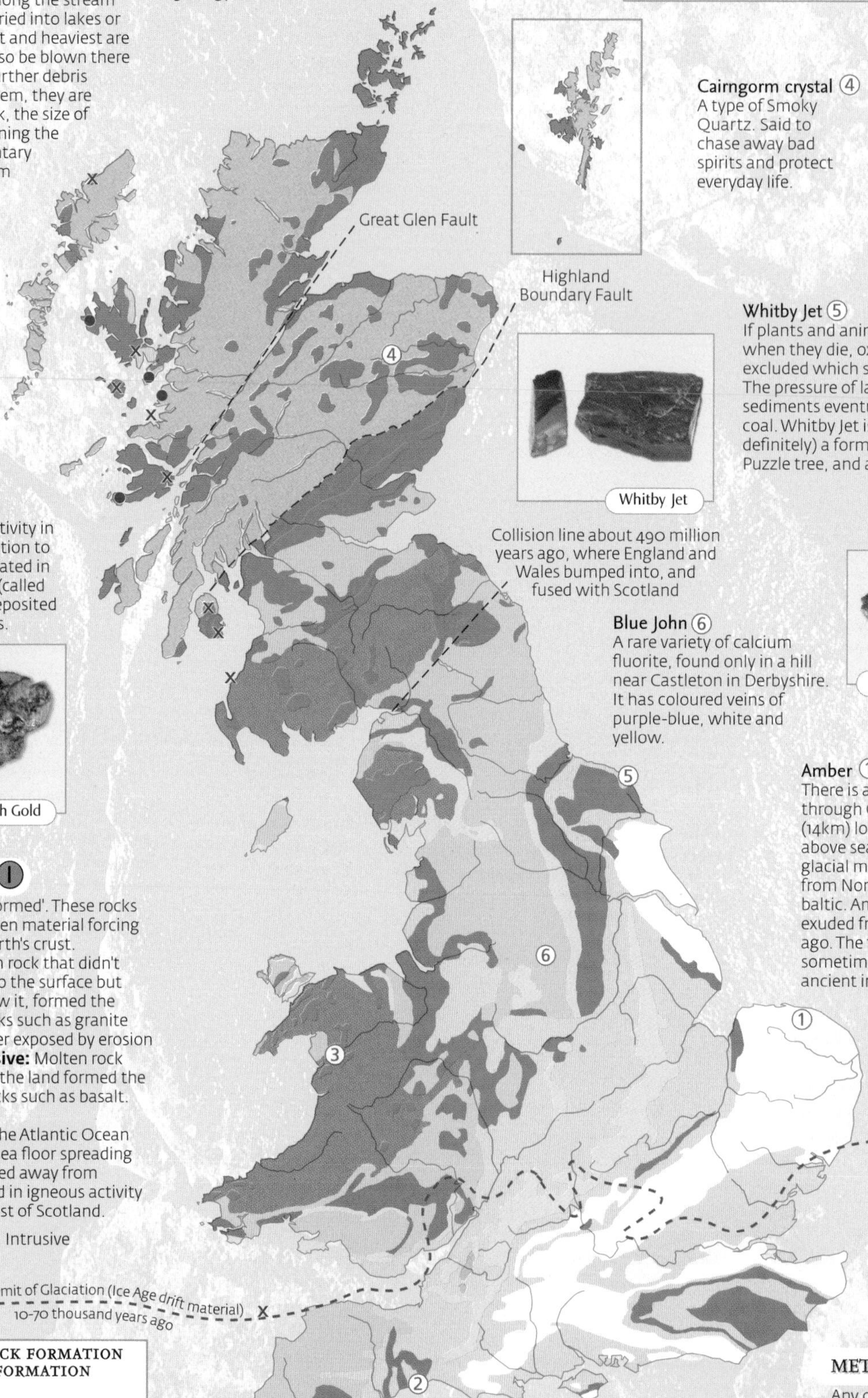

Cairngorm crystal (4)

A type of Smoky Quartz. Said to chase away bad spirits and protect everyday life.

Cairngorm crystal

Whitby Jet (5)

If plants and animals are covered quickly when they die, oxygen and bacteria are excluded which stops their decomposition. The pressure of layer upon layer of these sediments eventually compresses them into coal. Whitby Jet is probably (but not definitely) a form of fossilised Monkey Puzzle tree, and a form of coal.

Whitby Jet

Welsh Gold (3)

Very basically, volcanic activity in Wales caused gold in solution to be forced into fissures created in earlier, solidified magma (called Greenstone). Gold was deposited along with quartz in veins.

Welsh Gold

Blue John (6)

A rare variety of calcium fluorite, found only in a hill near Castleton in Derbyshire. It has coloured veins of purple-blue, white and yellow.

Blue John

Amber (1)

There is a gigantic ridge running through Cromer in Norfolk, 8.7 miles (14km) long and up to 290 feet (90m) above sea level. It is the remains of a glacial moraine and contains rock from Norway and amber from the baltic. Amber started life as resin exuded from trees millions of years ago. The final hard, translucent stone sometimes contains remains of ancient insect species.

Amber

IGNEOUS ROCKS (I)

Igneous means 'fire-formed'. These rocks were made from molten material forcing its way up into the Earth's crust. **Intrusive:** The molten rock that didn't quite break through to the surface but cooled in a mass below it, formed the 'intrusive' igneous rocks such as granite and gabbro, often later exposed by erosion at the surface. **Extrusive:** Molten rock that poured out onto the land formed the 'extrusive' volcanic rocks such as basalt.

60 million years ago the Atlantic Ocean was born, caused by sea floor spreading when Greenland moved away from Scotland. This resulted in igneous activity all along the west coast of Scotland.

● Volcanic   x Intrusive

CYCLE OF ROCK FORMATION AND RE-FORMATION

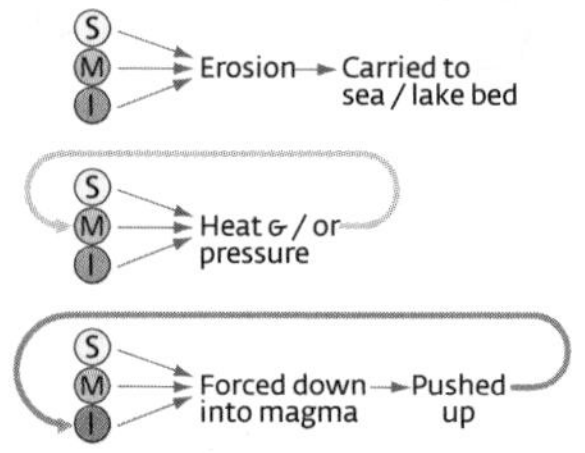

Ammonites (2)

The rocks in Lyme Regis were laid down in a fairly deep tropical sea. Large ammonites, up to 24 inches (60cm) across, are scattered all over Monmouth beach and small ones can often be found where they have been washed out of the cliffs. Have a look in the wonderful fossil shop. Note: Do not dig in the cliffs.

Ammonite

METAMORPHIC ROCKS (M)

Any of the three rock groups, subsequently altered by intense heat and/or pressure, during periods of major upheaval, into another rock type. Limestone can become marble, mudstones can turn into slate and gemstones can be formed.

UNDERSTANDING THE LANDSCAPE

GUIDE TO THE PROTECTED AREAS OF BRITAIN

PROTECTED AREAS

Areas of England, Wales and Scotland are recognised as being Nationally or even Internationally important for the habitats and flora and fauna they support. Certain areas of the countryside have therefore been given designations affording them some protection against inappropriate development and destruction.

NATIONAL PARKS

Landscapes managed to conserve and enhance the wildlife, natural beauty and cultural heritage of an area, and to inform and involve the public in this process. Most of the land is privately owned, with the various National Park Authorities working with the owners to conserve these special areas.
For more information see: www.anpa.gov.uk

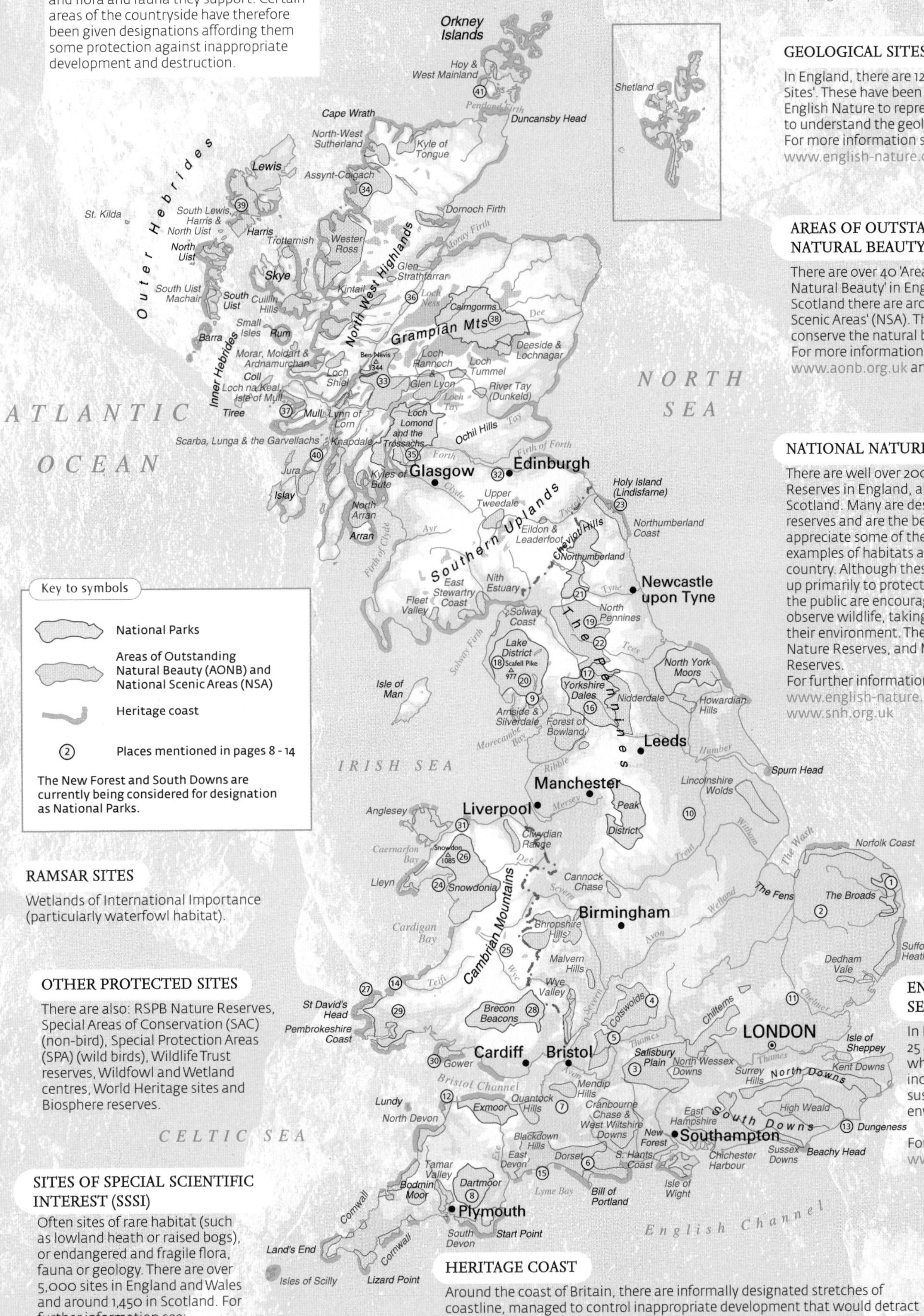

GEOLOGICAL SITES

In England, there are 1200 'Geological Sites'. These have been chosen by English Nature to represent key places to understand the geology of England. For more information see: www.english-nature.org.uk

AREAS OF OUTSTANDING NATURAL BEAUTY (AONB)

There are over 40 'Areas of Outstanding Natural Beauty' in England and Wales. In Scotland there are around 40 'National Scenic Areas' (NSA). The principle is to conserve the natural beauty of these areas. For more information see: www.aonb.org.uk and www.snh.org.uk

NATIONAL NATURE RESERVES (NNR)

There are well over 200 National Nature Reserves in England, and around 73 in Scotland. Many are designated as 'Spotlight' reserves and are the best places to appreciate some of the most important examples of habitats and wildlife in the country. Although these areas have been set up primarily to protect the flora and fauna, the public are encouraged to visit them and observe wildlife, taking care not to disturb their environment. There are also Local Nature Reserves, and Marine Nature Reserves.
For further information see: www.english-nature.org.uk and www.snh.org.uk

RAMSAR SITES

Wetlands of International Importance (particularly waterfowl habitat).

OTHER PROTECTED SITES

There are also: RSPB Nature Reserves, Special Areas of Conservation (SAC) (non-bird), Special Protection Areas (SPA) (wild birds), Wildlife Trust reserves, Wildfowl and Wetland centres, World Heritage sites and Biosphere reserves.

ENVIRONMENTALLY SENSITIVE AREAS (ESA)

In England and Wales, over 25 areas have been chosen where farmers are offered incentives to farm in a sustainable and environmentally friendly way.

For more information see: www.defra.gov.uk

SITES OF SPECIAL SCIENTIFIC INTEREST (SSSI)

Often sites of rare habitat (such as lowland heath or raised bogs), or endangered and fragile flora, fauna or geology. There are over 5,000 sites in England and Wales and around 1,450 in Scotland. For further information see: www.english-nature.org.uk and www.snh.org.uk

HERITAGE COAST

Around the coast of Britain, there are informally designated stretches of coastline, managed to control inappropriate development that would detract from their natural beauty. So far, there are in the region of 46 along the coasts of England and Wales and many under consideration in Scotland. Here they are called 'Preferred Conservation Zones' - (PCZ) For further information see: www.countryside.gov.uk and www.ccw.gov.uk and www.snh.org.uk

EAST ANGLIA

Grimes Graves (2)

Hundreds of saucer shaped hollows on the surface are evidence of Neolithic flint mining. Around 2300 BC, early man excavated flint and made axes with which to chop down trees and cultivate the land. The poor soils were soon spent, so the people moved on. An early example of 'slash and burn'.

Map ref. 213 G4

Grimes Graves

Norfolk Broads

Photo: Mike Page

(1) Norfolk Broads

This peaceful landscape of meandering waterways looks timeless. In fact, the retreating glaciers left a huge reed swamp over East Anglia, which gradually became woodland. By the early middle ages several inundations by the sea had left a patchwork of marsh, fen, woodland and swamp, the latter covering what is now the Broads. Centuries of vegetation had grown and died, creating thick layers of peat. After the Norman conquest, Norwich was developing quickly and needed fuel; peat was perfect and over the next 350 years this valuable resource was dug out by hand, until Mother Nature caused the sea level to rise once more, flooding the peat workings to create the tranquil waterways of the Broads.

Map ref. 229 E4

Flint is:

Liquid silica, fused with limestone or other sediments. This forms a hard, brittle, fine-grained rock and can be found as nodules within limestones and shales.

Flint building detail

Flint wall

Flint was used as a building material where little else was available.

CHALK DOWNS

Marlborough Downs

The smooth rounded Marlborough Hills are typical of a chalk landscape. They are divided by 'dry' valleys, probably formed when water in the chalk was frozen and glacial surface streams eroded the rock. Sometimes, steep scarps have formed, demonstrating the varying hardness of the chalk layers. Most of the downlands are waterless due to the very porous nature of chalk and spring lines are common where the water meets the impermeable clays beneath. Lower down the slopes the soil is richer, here you will find woodlands, meadows and orchards.

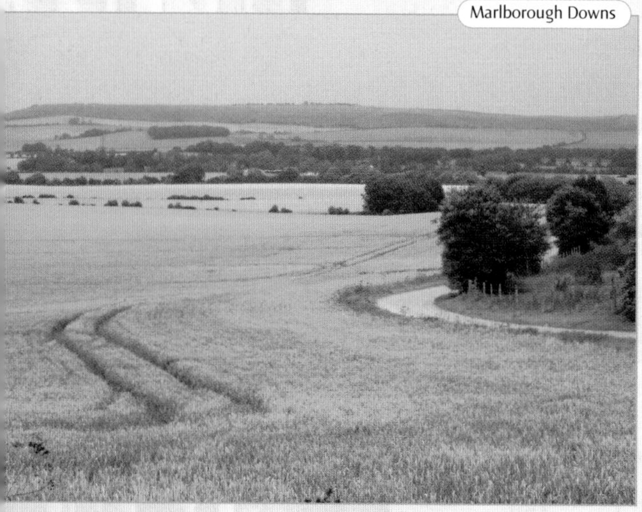
Marlborough Downs (3)

Map ref. 182 D5

Chalk is:

The purest and whitest form of limestone. It contains a large proportion of tiny plates called Coccoliths. Chalk is very porous and relatively soft, forming rounded ridges. Water seeps down and accumulates as large underground reservoirs.

Avebury – standing stone

Map ref. 168 C1

(3) Sarsen Stones

The chalk layers were overlaid with sandstone, most of which has weathered away. However, in places, the sandstone was cemented together with silica to form hard blocks. In the dry valleys these boulders litter the landscape; they are the famous 'Sarsen' stones, used by stone age man to build Avebury Ring and other prehistoric monuments.

COTSWOLDS

Cotswolds

The rolling Cotswold Hills are the result of an event that took place 180 million years ago. A bulge formed under the North Sea and as a consequence, a shallow warm sea formed over an area from Somerset to The Midlands. In the Cotswolds, Oolites (see 'Limestone is:' below for description) settled on the bottom forming the characteristic limestone of the area. This sedimentary rock has been gently folded and eroded into the hills and valleys we see today. Sheep have always been the mainstay of this rural landscape; the Saxon meaning of 'Cotswolds' actually means 'Hills of the Sheepfolds'.

(4) Roof tiles

Harder blocks of limestone were quarried underground, and then left on the surface. The action of frost shattered them into thin sheets, which were used for roof tiles.

Map ref. 197 D5

Lower Slaughter – Roof tiles

Limestone is:

Bits of shells and sea creatures, which fall to the bottom in areas of shallow warm water, eventually compressing into rock. 'Oolitic' Limestone is a special type and comprises tiny round pellets formed by the particles being rolled around on the watery bed first, building up layers of calcium, then being cemented together. Stand on the Cotswold Hills and you're on what was once the bed of a tropical sea or lake.

Cotswold Water Park

Map ref. 182 C3

(5) Cotswold Water Park

A beautiful area of over 114 lakes and ponds form the water park, the result of gravel extraction dating from the 1920s. Cotswold Oolitic Limestone underlies the park, covered in a layer of clay. On top of this, repeated glaciations dumped up to eight metres of sand and gravel. The high water table soon causes the newly dug gravel pits to fill with water. As it filters up through the limestone it becomes crystal clear, pure and alkaline; ideal for wildlife and water sports. The Thames starts just to the west of the area, water flowing into it through the lakes.

FIELDS

Fields - Ridge & Furrow

Ancient Field Systems

Ever since man first picked up a seed and planted it in the earth, there have been fields of a sort. In the Bronze Age, low banks of stone in narrow parallel lines with short cross divisions ran for miles across Dartmoor; the Dartmoor 'reaves'. Fields of the Iron Age were nothing more than small pastures separated by large stony banks, clustered around a settlement. The Romans probably had fields in the Fens and the Anglo-Saxons invented large 'open' field systems. The commonest patterns we see in the fields today are post-Norman Conquest; rows of 'humped' strips, around 11 yards (10m) wide, formed by the method of ploughing used; this was the 'ridge and furrow' field system which reached its peak in the mid 1300s. It is most typically found in The Midlands, North-East England and Central Scotland, and is distinguished by having no formal divisions of hedges or walls. Hedges used to enclose fields are a relatively modern invention.

Hedges were gradually planted between the 13th and 17th centuries. Then between the early 1700s and mid 1800s, the infamous 'Enclosure Acts' replaced Medieval ridge and furrow fields with new areas bounded by hedges. Similar reorganisation produced straight stone walls in Scotland. With mechanisation and the internal combustion engine, came bigger agricultural machinery which resulted in the removal of many hedgerows from the mid 20th century.

Portable, woven wooden hurdles were used to enclose stock before permanent settlements came into being.

Between 1750 and 1850 Oliver Rackham estimated that over 200,000 miles (320,000km) of hedges were planted.

HEDGEROWS

Ancient Hedgerows

Medieval England was full of hedges but not often around 'fields'. There are hedges described in the Anglo-Saxon 'perambulations', as boundary markers. So how do you know if you are looking at an ancient hedge? Look for clues: if a hedgerow crosses rows of wide ridge and furrow it's probably post-1700; if it follows a parish boundary or large earth bank it could be Saxon. If it has woodland flora underneath, it was possibly part of a woodland edge, and if it is on top of an earth bank, again it could be ancient. There is no exact science to tell the age of a hedge, although some can be identified on old maps. A rough estimation can be made by counting the number of species of shrubs and trees in any 90 foot (27.5m) length and multiplying it by 100 to give the number of years. For example, if a 90 foot (27.5m) stretch contains several Dog Rose, some Hawthorn and Elder, then three multiplied by 100 will give an age of 300 years. This only works south of Derbyshire and has many other pitfalls but it is fun and might amuse the children for a while.

The New Agricultural Landscape

Farming is entering a new age. There have always been farmers helping wildlife but now they are being encouraged to do so as the emphasis is shifting from intensive production to environmentally friendly schemes. In arable areas you may well see a large, bushy hedgerow with a permanent 6½ foot (2m) wide strip of tussocky grass next to it. This is a 'Field Margin' left unploughed and unsprayed to provide habitat for over-wintering wildlife. Next to this there might well be a wide strip of temporarily uncropped ground, this is 'Set Aside' land, again good for wildlife. In some areas, the first few metres of the crop might look rather weedy, this area is a 'Conservation Headland' and has been left free from herbicides to encourage some of our rare arable flowers to flourish. Don't be surprised to see wooden boxes put up for owls, bats, birds and even dormice.

Field margin

PREHISTORY

Glastonbury Tor

Map ref. 166 C4

(7)

Glastonbury Tor

Hard sandstone caps the Tor, protecting the softer layers of limestones and clays underneath from erosion. However, the terracing on its slopes is still a cause for controversy. Are they the result of natural differential erosion of the rock layers, medieval strip farming for grain or vines, or a Neolithic maze pattern carved into the hill to form a ritual pathway to the top?

(6)

Maiden Castle

This chalk hilltop was inhabited from the late Stone Age through to Roman times. The original village can no longer be seen on the surface.

Maiden Castle

Map ref. 154 C4

Dartmoor – Bowerman's Nose

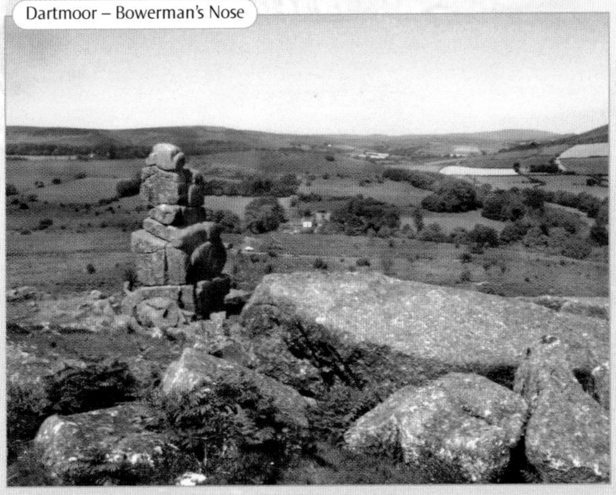

Map ref. 152 A4

(8)

Dartmoor

280 million years ago, a mass of molten rock was pushed up underneath the sedimentary rocks covering Dartmoor, during a period of intense folding. The magma cooled slowly deep within the Earth, forming granite, which was exposed by weathering millions of years later. Around the edges, the intense heat and pressure metamorphosed surrounding material into slate and produced deposits of tin and copper ores. The impermeable granite supports a large mire and bog; the source of many Devon rivers and local legends. Above this mire the bare rock has been shaped into dramatic tors by wind, water and ice. These rocky landmarks have names like 'Bowerman's Nose'.

Grimspound

Beneath Hookney Tor you can make out a walled enclosure of about 4 acres (1.6 ha). It dates from the Bronze Age and contains circles of granite boulders or 'hut circles'. The wall was probably once topped with a wooden palisade.

WOODLAND

Ancient woodland
When the ice retreated and the climate started to get warmer, about 10,000 years ago, plants began to colonise the land. By the time the sea level rose to cut Britain off from mainland Europe, around 6,000 years ago, thirty or so types of trees and shrubs had established themselves here; these we call our 'native' species. Since that time, many other species have arrived, most deliberately introduced by man. Some of these reproduce quite happily and are called 'naturalised' species; others are still classed as 'exotic'. Of the original 'wildwood' nothing now remains, and most of our woodlands are a complex mix of old and new, natural and planted. There are pockets of 'Ancient Semi-Natural Woodland', the most precious of which are those descended from woodlands known to have been in existence from at least AD1600, having been managed in some way by man. It is difficult to date a woodland, but ancient woodland will probably have a large, wide ditch and bank or large stone wall exactly following a sinuous woodland edge. Other signs include 'indicator' species such as Herb Paris.

Coppiced Woodland

Management of deciduous woodland
In the past, a woodland 'stayed if it paid'; this is how many have survived. Where trees were **coppiced**, the stem was cut off at ground level to produce multiple stems for fencing and charcoal, some trees were left to develop into tall 'standards' between the coppice, and then felled for timber. This cycle allows light into the woodland, allowing flowers and shrubs to flourish, so that butterflies, dormice and birds are encouraged. Trees in some woods were **pollarded**; the same as coppicing but the stem is cut off above the browsing line so that animals could graze underneath but not eat the new wood shoots. Today, these methods are being reintroduced; new markets are opening up for woodland products with environmental schemes helping to fund them.

Pollarded tree

Veteran trees
Britain has many very old individual trees, unlike the rest of Europe. They are sometimes mentioned as boundary markers in the Anglo Saxon perambulations and support precious wildlife, such as the endangered Stag Beetle. In a veteran tree, the growth rate has slowed, but this does not mean it is dying. Some veterans are even hollow but still perfectly healthy. There is a register of over 126,000 ancient and rare trees growing in the British Isles today. Have a look at the Tortworth Chestnut in Gloucestershire, The Silver Fir at Strone, Argyll or the Holker Hall Great Lime, Cumbria.

Veteran tree

Stag Beetle

Holker Hall Great Lime

(9) ***Map ref. 249 E5***

(10) Sherwood Forest
Not an area of dense forest but open heathland with pockets of woodland. A 'forest' was simply an unfenced area where someone powerful could keep deer.

Map ref. 224 B1

Hatfield Forest

(11) Hatfield Forest
A rare example of a Royal Forest as it was in Medieval England. It includes areas of coppice and old pollards.

Map ref. 187 E1

Native pine woodland
Caledonian Pines are a subspecies unique to Scotland and form several ancient semi-natural woodlands there. Their management has to be entirely different to that for deciduous woodland, as they do not coppice. To allow natural regeneration, the main requirement is for deer, stock and rabbit proof fencing. Occasionally, it might be necessary to clear the ground in some way, as the trees are natural colonisers of disturbed ground. Otherwise, they can be left to themselves. These precious woods are a vital habitat for many of Scotland's endangered species.

Upper Loch Torridon – Caledonian Pines

Map ref. 319 E4

BRITAIN'S COASTLINE

Britain's coastline
Britain has approximately 12,100 miles (19,500km) of coastline, including all the islands, and one of the most extreme tidal ranges in the world. (In spring, the tidal range at Chepstow can be 40 feet (12.2m)). This, along with constant pounding from the Atlantic and North Sea and scouring by wind, rain and the ice age, has left a coastline of great diversity and character.

(12)

Mortehoe coastline

Map ref. 163 E1

Winchelsea Beach

Map ref. 161 E2

(13)

Pembrokeshire – Sand dunes

(14) ***Map ref. 191 D4***

Pembrokeshire Coastal Path

Charmouth

(15) ***Map ref.153 G3***

YORKSHIRE DALES

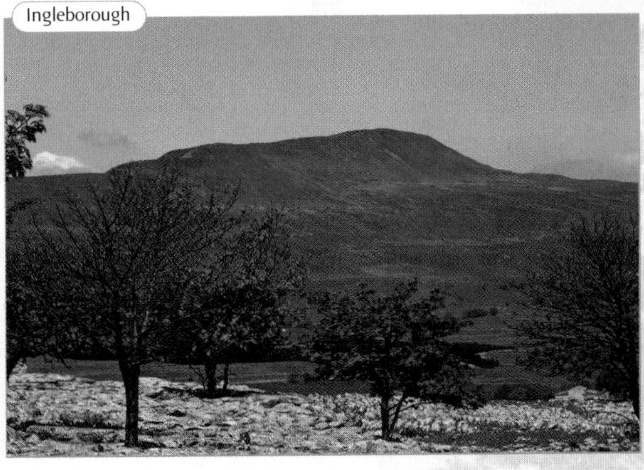

Ingleborough

Yorkshire Dales & Hills

Sandwiches of shales, hard sandstones and limestones topped with Millstone Grit overlie almost horizontal layers of very old limestone. Differential erosion of these layers gives the characteristic 'stepped' appearance of the hills of Pen-y-Ghent and Ingleborough. Evidence of glaciation is everywhere, many valleys show the classic 'U' shape and around Ribblehead is an amazing landscape of rounded hummocks, 'drumlins'; material dumped and moulded by glaciers. Villages tend to be restricted to the valleys, with their rivers and walled fields. The slopes and moors are mostly grazed by sheep, arable farming never having been very successful here. The whole area has a feeling of timelessness and peace. Sit back and listen to the song of the skylark.

Limestone pavement

Rainwater seeps into the natural vertical cracks (joint planes) of this rock, gradually dissolving it and widening the joints (grykes) leaving large blocks (clints) between them; hence 'limestone pavements' are formed. Good examples can be seen around Ingleborough and Malham. The grykes can be several feet wide and deep and harbour some rare native alpine plants.

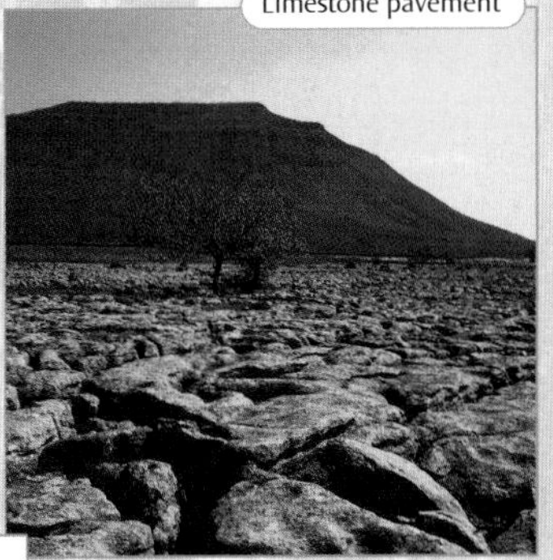

Limestone pavement

Malham Cove

(16) ***Map ref.* 243 E1**

Malham Cove

A river once cascaded into the valley from the top of the cliff, but it has long since found a way through the porous rock further upstream and now appears at the base.

Gaping Ghyll

Water runs off the moors and tops, over the harder layers, then disappears underground through the porous limestone rock into 'swallow holes'. Gaping Ghyll is such a hole, 350 feet (91.5m) deep with the highest known waterfall in England.

(17)

Austwick – Norber Stones

Norber stones

Sandstone blocks were carried here by glaciers and abandoned on the limestone plateau when the ice melted. Limestone erodes more quickly than sandstone; the result is a bizarre landscape of dark, hard sandstone boulders perched precariously on small pedestals of white limestone.

NORTH PENNINES

(19) Great Whin Sill, North Pennines

Under the sedimentary rocks is an almost horizontal layer of dolerite, an igneous rock forced up and between the beds of sandstone. In places, millions of years of erosion by weather and ice have exposed it at the surface. This is the Great Whin Sill, which, on average, is 100 feet (30.5m) thick. It extends for 100 miles (160km) from Upper Teesdale to the Northumberland coast. On the Pennine escarpment and in Teesdale, the outcrops of dolerite appear as craggy, dark, vertical columns of rock; High Cup Nick and Cronkley Fell are good examples. Where the hot molten rock came into contact with surrounding limestone, the latter changed into a coarse grained marble called 'sugar limestone', which is home to many rare Teesdale plants.

North Pennines

Hadrian's Wall

(21) Hadrian's Wall

The Romans took advantage of the northern escarpment of the hard Great Whin Sill, using it as a base on which to build Hadrian's Wall.

Teesdale – High Force

High Force waterfall

The River Tees tumbles over the exposed hard dolerite, gradually quarrying away the softer rock beneath. Eventually, the overhang becomes too heavy and crashes down. Over time therefore, the waterfall is slowly retreating upstream.

***Map ref.* 261 E5**

(22)

Lindisfarne – Holy Island

(23) Farne Islands

The pounding action of the North Sea waves wore away the sandstone protecting the dolerite here on the coast. The hard igneous rocks were left as isolated, craggy islands in the sea.

***Map ref.* 279 F2**

LAKE DISTRICT

Lake District

A landscape full of variety, from precipitous, craggy fells to gently wooded valleys and lakes. The underlying geology is complex but basically volcanic, changed by heaving, folding, heat, pressure and glaciation. In places the mountains are the remains of lavas and ashes metamorphosed to varying degrees; the softer ones and overlying sedimentary rocks having been eroded away. The main volcanic area is in the centre, with the high craggy peaks of Sca Fell, Helvellyn and the Langdale Pikes. Underneath these volcanic rocks lies a large mass of granite, pushed up in the distant past, and exposed by erosion in areas such as Ennerdale and Shap. In the north, Skiddaw is made from the oldest rocks of the Lake District, originally fine sedimentary material, altered by heat and pressure into the 'Skiddaw Slates', then eroded into smooth but steep mountains. The lakes themselves owe their existence to the glaciers. The ice over-deepened the valleys, which slowly filled with water, giving the final touch to this beautiful landscape.

Lake District – Wast Water

(18) ***Map ref.* 248 C2**

Langdale – Blea Tarn

(20) Blea Tarn

Blea Tarn was formed in the hollow left by a small glacier.

***Map ref.* 249 D2**

Wales

A land of spectacular and varied scenery, resulting from a highly complex geological past and several inundations by the sea. The coastline has everything from wide sandy bays to spectacular cliffs. Inland, there are mountain peaks, rolling hills, valleys and lakes.

(31) Great Orme

Once an island of hard limestone; sand and alluvial deposits built up to join it to the mainland. Llandudno sits on these deposits.

Gwaun Valley

Formed by meltwater flowing beneath a glacier under extreme pressure, this beautiful sheltered wooded valley is a valuable habitat with SSSI (Site of Special Scientific Interest) status.

Cambrian Mountains

(25)

Central Wales

Smooth, flat-topped hills characterise this area, although the uniformity of the plateau is somewhat of a mystery. The rocks consist of much folded and faulted sandstones, mudstones and slates, so why are the tops flat? One theory suggests that having been inundated by the sea several times after the folding process, the peaks were eroded flat by strong currents carrying sand and stones.

(26) ***Map ref. 217 F2***

Llanberis Pass

(29)

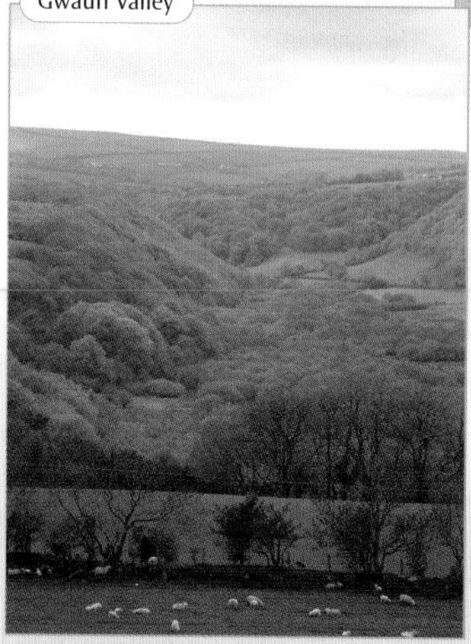
Gwaun Valley

Map ref. 190 D4

(24) Sarn Badrig

A shallow subtidal reef, (one of several) which extends for about 15 miles (24km) from Mochras Island into Cardigan Bay. It was formed from the detritus of a glacial terminal moraine when sea levels were much lower and this was dry land; some of it can still be seen at a very low tide and you can walk out along it (check tide tables). Legends of a 'lost land' are associated with it.

Llanberis Pass

A classic glaciated valley, carved from volcanic rocks. Along it, older mudstones have been turned into high quality slate by heat and pressure. These are famous for their ability to cleave into thin, strong sheets, as a result, vast slate quarries scar the landscape.

(27)

Pillow Lava

Strumble Head

Another volcanic area but of a different sort. Here the lava erupted under the sea and cooled very quickly into typically rounded 'pillow' shapes. This happened several times before the sea level fell leaving these strange shapes exposed on the headland.

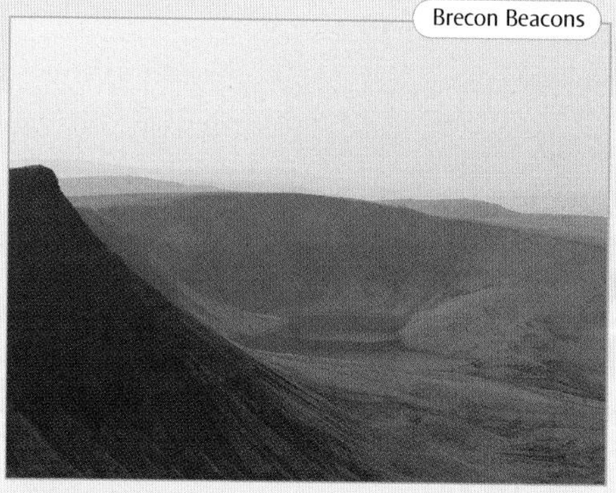
Brecon Beacons

Snowdonia

(26) Snowdon

Snowdon is actually made up of volcanic material which erupted on the floor of an ancient sea. It was later uplifted to become dry land, and this is why you will find fossilised shells on the top.

Map ref. 217 F2

(28) Brecon Beacons

These mountains have been carved from a massive block of Old Red Sandstone, glaciers having scooped out the northern slopes.

Map ref. 193 G1

Teifi Valley

Today, the river Teifi between Llechryd and Cardigan has an uneven bed of slate debris. This is due to 19th century slate extraction in the gorge. Tons of slate waste was dumped in the river, almost choking it. Eventually, the waste had to be disposed of on Rosehill Marsh, as large boats could no longer travel upriver. This slate debris now forms one of the many habitats in the Welsh Wildlife Centre. It is thought that the original Teifi followed a more westerly course but during the last ice age, material dumped around the Welsh coast by the glacier that formed over Ireland, blocked it, forcing the river to carve a new, deeper gorge.

Cenarth – River Teifi

(30)

Gower – Rhossili Beach

Gower

A quiet and lovely peninsula, the whole area has been designated as an 'Area of outstanding Natural Beauty' (AONB). The high ridge of Cefn Bryn, which runs across the middle of the plateau, is made of hard Old Red Sandstone, uplifted and folded. The Rhossili Downs are made from the same rock and give rise to the spectacular 200 foot (61m) high cliffs of Rhossili Bay. The southern part is tough limestone, forming cliffs with beautiful bays where the sea has exploited weaknesses in the rock.

Map ref. 178 A4

SCOTLAND

THE BIRTHPLACE OF GEOLOGY

Edinburgh Castle

(32)

Map ref. 397 E1

Edinburgh Castle and the Royal Mile

Somewhere around 380 million years ago, the volcano underneath what is now Edinburgh Castle stopped pouring out lava. It cooled into a basalt 'plug'. Time passed, the surrounding sedimentary rocks were slowly worn away. Then less than two million years ago, ice sheets moved past the remains of the volcano, plucking off the rest of the softer rock and dumping it in a long tail to the east of the plug. On this ridge was built the 'Royal Mile'. To the north of the tail, the glacier carved out a gorge now occupied by Princess Street gardens and to the south, a similar hollow is the location for Grassmarket.

The Royal Mile

(32)

Map ref. 397 E2

(33)

Rannoch Moor

Map ref. 299 F4

Rannoch Moor

Robert Louis Stevenson picked out this landscape for his novel 'Kidnapped'. Some call it desolate: blanket bog formed on impermeable rock, treacherous to cross on foot. The underlying rock is granite, usually associated with mountains, so why is the moor flat? It was once a granite mountain, but the rock is coarse and crumbles. Erosion plus several passes of ice have plucked and scraped the surface flat, leaving the surrounding mountains (which are made of even harder metamorphic rocks) resembling an amphitheatre. It is a true wilderness, one of the few left in Britain.

Loch Lomond

If you look at the pattern of Scottish Lochs to the north of Loch Lomond, you will see that they form a radial pattern. The loch was bulldozed out only ten and a half thousand years ago by a glacier, which was based somewhere in the centre of this pattern. The ice followed the line of a major crack in the land called the 'Highland Boundary Fault' plucking out the already loose rocks along the fault line and gouging out a trough with the rocks it carried. When the ice melted, the empty chasm filled with water. Today, the sea is kept at bay by debris dumped at the side of the ancient glacier. To the south of the Loch, the line of the fault can be seen clearly, running along the islands and Conic Hill.

(35)

Loch Lomond

Map ref. 283 E1

Loch Ness

(36)

Loch Ness lies in the Great Glen Fault, the dividing line that runs from Fort William to Inverness. In the distant past, the land to the north of this fault moved south-west, then back again, the total displacement being around 80 miles (130km). Along this classic 'wrench' fault, travelled ice, plucking out the rock debris to such a depth that the Loch holds around three times the volume of water as Loch Lomond, although its surface area is much less. Significant earth tremors associated with continuing movement of the Great Glen Fault, normally occur three times a century; the last one was in 1901!

Loch Ness

Map ref. 309 E2

Gneiss is:
When subjected to heat and pressure, sandy shales become gneiss. This type of rock has distinctive bands of light and dark minerals.

Suilven

Sutherland boasts some of the most spectacular and ancient, if not highest, mountain landscape in Scotland. Suilven is a monolith of almost horizontally banded hard Torridonian sandstone in a flat expanse of ancient Lewisian gneiss, itself around 2,900 million years old. Roughly 4.5 miles (7km) of sediments from the rivers of Greenland (to which Scotland was joined) were laid on top of the already eroded Lewisian gneiss about 900 million years ago, when the whole area was basking in the sun at around 15 degrees north. Earth movements and sea level changes eventually allowed the area to become dry land and millions of years of erosion have subsequently left the 'hard cores' of the sedimentary layers standing proud.

Suilven

Map ref. 331 D3

(34)

Loch Lomond is the largest freshwater loch in Scotland at 27.5 sq miles (71.1 sq km)

Staffa – Fingal's Cave

(37)

Staffa, Fingal's Cave

Off the west coast of Mull, the tiny island of Staffa exhibits some of the most amazing geological scenery in the world. For centuries man thought the regular basalt columns of 'Fingal's Cave' could not possibly be natural. Sixty million years ago, Greenland and North America were torn away from Scotland by the birth of the Atlantic Ocean, and lava poured out along this tear. The top slaggy crust on Staffa is the result of lots of bubbles, holes and minerals in the lava. The central part cooled to produce columns which have a polygonal structure. The base cooled more slowly, producing a denser texture and solid base.

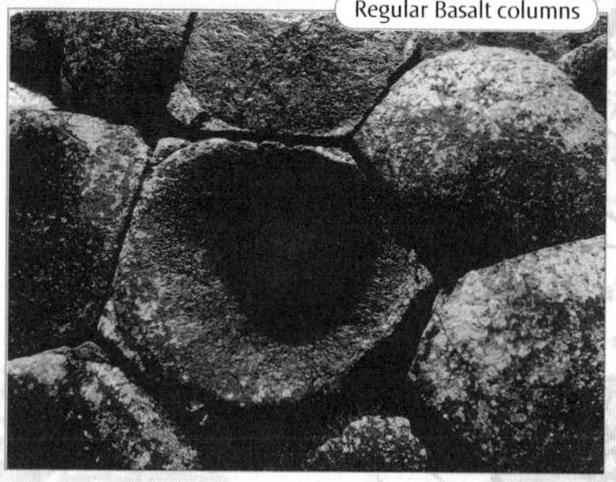
Regular Basalt columns

Map ref. 288 C1

The Atlantic Ocean is named after the giant Atlas, who held up the sky on his shoulders. His father was the Titan Iapetus - after which the Iapetus Ocean was named.

When they were first uplifted, around 400 million years ago, the Caledonian Mountains were taller than the Himalayas are now.

Map ref. 326 C3

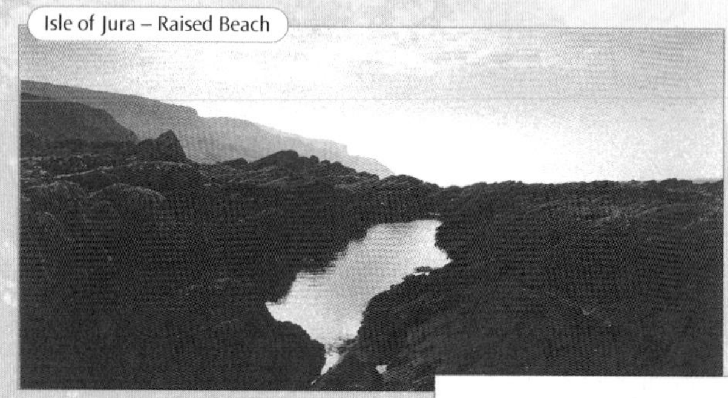
Isle of Jura – Raised Beach

(40)

Scotland has 790 islands but only about 1/6th are inhabited.

Taransay – Machair

(40)

Isle of Jura – Isolated sea eroded arch

Isle of Jura

Another phenomenon of the west coast can be seen on the western beaches of Jura. When the land was covered in ice, sea level fell (as it was locked in solid form). When it melted, not only did sea level rise once more, but so did the land, having been physically pushed down by the weight of ice. The land mass is still rising today; this is called 'isostatic uplift'. To further complicate matters, the whole of Britain is tilting down in the southeast and up in the northwest. As a consequence, the beaches formed at the end of the glaciation have been raised in stages, forming 'raised beaches'.

(39)

Taransay, Machair

The Outer Hebrides face the full force of the Atlantic. This position, combined with the geology, has produced a unique landscape called 'Machair'. The beach is mainly wave pounded shells and sand, blown inland onto the low-lying marshes to produce a rich, alkaline soil. Easily damaged, modern farming techniques would destroy it, so it is treated gently and as a consequence, the grassland contains many rare flowers.

Rackwick Bay

Once a continuous plateau of sandstone, the sea level rose after the last ice age and created this archipelago of over 70 individual islands, collectively known as the Orkney Islands. Around 500 million years ago, a huge igneous mass pushed up under the sea from the depths of the Earth. Over the years, this was covered by layers and layers of sediments, the youngest of which were eroded away during periods of uplift and glaciation. On Hoy, the banding in the cliffs shows strata of tough, pebbly sandstones, unique in the Orkneys. Rackwick Bay is an excellent example, with massive sea-smoothed boulders up to 10 feet (3m) across littering the beach.

The longest river in Scotland is the River Tay at 120 miles (193km).

Cairngorms & Loch Morlich
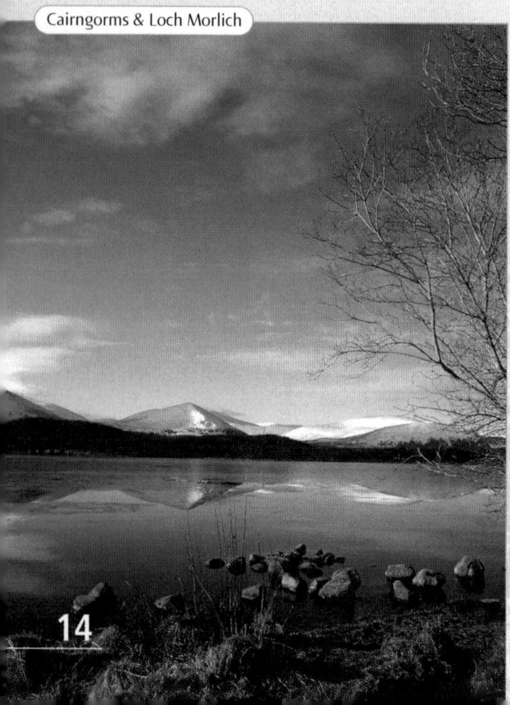

(38)

Cairngorms

Until 420 million years ago, Scotland and England were on different continents, separated by the Iapetus Ocean. Both were in the southern hemisphere and moving north (Scotland much more slowly). At the Tropic of Capricorn, they collided, fusing into one landmass in a seamless join roughly along the line of Hadrian's Wall. Over millions of years, the force of the collision buckled the surface rocks, forming the Central Highlands. Deep below, granite was pushing its way up underneath the folding mountains, forming the infant Cairngorms. The rose-coloured granite, deeply buried for so long, is now exposed at the surface.

Map ref. 310 B4

(41)

Orkney Islands – Rackwick Bay

Map ref. 338 B3

UNDERSTANDING NATURAL HISTORY

The following habitats are home to many species of the flora and fauna found in Britain today.

Use Collins Gems, Wild Guides and Nature Guides for good general information. Field Guides for detail or Complete British Wildlife for everything you need in one book.

DECIDUOUS WOODLAND

Common Dormouse

Look for gnawed hazelnuts, smooth on the inside, teeth marks on surface. Has fluffy tail and ginger colour. Purrs and snores.

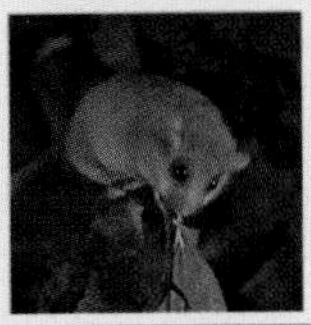

(*Muscardinus avellanarius*)

Ramsons
(*Allium ursinum*)
Smells of garlic.

Tree creeper

Climbs up tree trunks, often in a spiral pattern. Has a long, thin, downcurved bill.

(*Certhia familiaris*)

Great Spotted Woodpecker

Drums on tree trunks in spring. Distinctive black and white markings. The male has a red nape. Likes large mature trees with holes for nesting.

(*Dendrocopos major*)

Royal Society for the Protection of Birds
www.rspb.org.uk

Hazelnut

Tawny Owl

Small owl the size of a pigeon. Likes large trees with nesting holes. Call is "Hoo hoo hoo hoooo". Pellets under trees will contain bones of small mammals.

(*Strix aluco*)

Blue tit

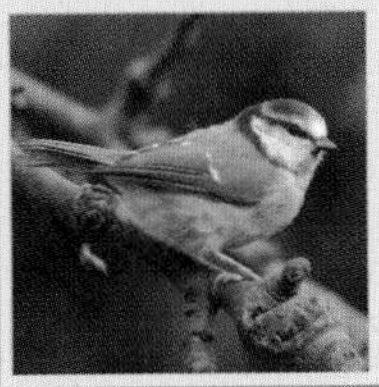

Particularly likes oak trees which provide it with hundreds of caterpillars for babies in spring. Often hangs upside down on the ends of branches to reach food.

(*Parus caeruleus*)

Ragged robin
(*Lychnis flos-cuculi*)

Badger

Extensive system of large holes with freshly dug earth outside. Distinctive footprints (front and back different).

(*Meles meles*)

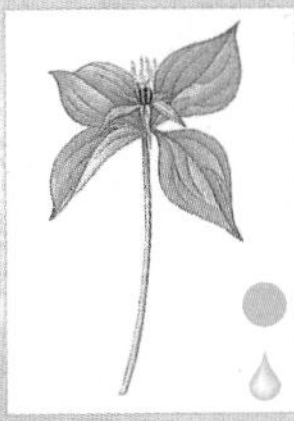

Herb paris
(*Paris quadrifolia*)
Indicator of old woodland.

Silver-washed fritillary

Silver sheen on underside of hind wings. Likes Bramble flowers. Caterpillars feed exclusively on violets.

(*Argynnis paphia*)

Wood anemone
(*Anemone nemorosa*)
In the sun, will raise their heads and open petals.

MOUNTAIN

Ptarmigan

Turns white in winter. Summer colouring of grey brown and black makes it difficult to see. Call is a croaking noise.

(*Lagopus mutus*)

Don't be surprised to see wallabies hopping about in the Peak District, wild boar roaming Kent woodlands or even black panthers in the Forest of Dean.

Golden eagle

Second largest bird in the UK. Tends not to like forests, preferring open areas.

(*Aquila chrysaetos*)

Crowberry
(*Empetrum nigrum*)
Winter food for moorland and mountain birds.

Mountain hare

Black tipped ears. Often turns white in winter. Small tracks going directly up slopes, doesn't zig-zag.

(*Lepus timidus*)

Mountain avens
(*Dryas octopetela*)

HEDGEROWS

Natural History Museum
www.nhm.ac.uk

Wren

Tiny bird with tail held almost vertically. Loud ringing song and loud, persistent 'tik tik tik' when alarmed.

(*Troglodytes troglodytes*)

Bird song varies according to geographical region.

Common shrew

High pitched 'twitters' coming from the grass, especially in March/April.

(*Sorex aranaeus*)

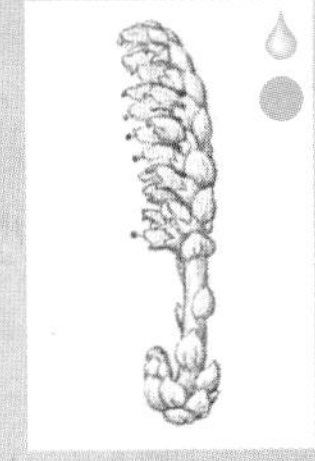

Toothwort
(*Lathraea squamaria*)
Parasitic plant, especially on hazel.

The pygmy shrew is Britain's smallest mammal. It weighs less than a 1op coin and must eat this weight of food every day to survive.

Lords-and-Ladies
(*Arum maculatum*)

Holly blue

Flies higher than other blues. Found near Holly in spring and Ivy in late summer.

(*Celastrina argiolus*)

Pignut
(*Conopodium majus*)
Pigs love the roots, hence the name.

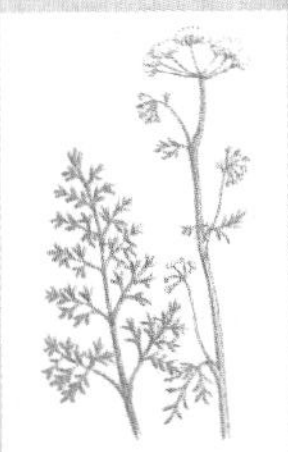

Song thrush

Dark brown spots underneath. Repeats phrases when singing. Uses a stone to smash open snail shells.

(*Turdus philomelos*)

Glow worm

Green glow at night from the wingless female. Snails are a large part of the larvae's diet and the snails preferred are found in chalk and limestone areas.

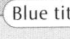

(*Lampyris noctiluca*)

Symbols

Status (fauna) - This has been generalised to give an indication of sensitivity and rarity. Where this cannot be definitely established, no symbol is given. For more information, see www.jncc.gov.uk

Not endangered — Of concern — Endangered — Identification clues — Nocturnal — Hibernates

Soil (flora) - Symbols are only shown for plants that will only grow in specific conditions.

Acid (peaty) soil — Alkaline (chalky) soil — Damp soil — Dry soil

GRASSLAND

Eyebright
(Euphrasia officinalis)
Pretty but parasitic plant.

Wild parsnip
(Pastinaca sativa)

Orange tip

Only males have orange tips. Prefers damp areas.

(Anthocharis cardamines)

Common field grasshopper

Listen for 6 to 10 half-second chirps, evenly spread over 12 seconds.

(Chorthippus brunneus)

Common blue

Males are bright blue. Likes Fleabane. Usually seen in groups. Rests head down on stems.

(Polyommatus icarus)

The stoat has a black tip to its tail. The weasel, with no 't' in its name, doesn't.

Cuckoo flower
(Lady's smock)
(Cardamine pratensis)
Flowers when the cuckoo calls.

Cowslip
(Primula veris)
Food plant of Duke of Burgundy Fritillary caterpillar.

Stoat

Larger than a weasel with black tip on tail. In the north, some will turn white in winter. Tend to run along boundaries such as hedges, don't like to be in the open.

(Mustela erminia)

Cinnabar moth

Caterpillars eat Ragwort, which makes them poisonous.

(Tyria jacobaeae)

Harebell
(Campanula rotundifolia)
Called Bluebells in Scotland.

The Mammal Society
www.abdn.ac.uk

Lapwing

Black crest. Call 'kee-ee-wit'. Breeds on farmland, usually in short spring sown crops and pasture.

(Vanellus vanellus)

Quaking grass
(Briza media)
Makes a lovely rattling sound in the wind.

LOWLAND HEATH

Adder

z z

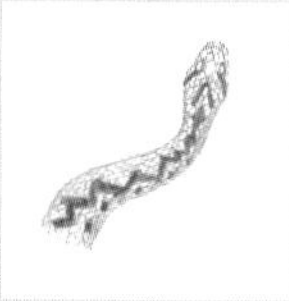

Black or brown zig-zag marking down back – but colours and pattern can vary. Poisonous but not usually deadly. Basks in sun.

(Vipera berus)

Bell heather
(Erica cinerea)

Stonechat

Male has black head, red chest, white on side of neck. Song sounds like pebbles being knocked together 'wee tak tak'.

(Saxicola torquata)

Common cudweed
(Filago vulgaris)
Once given to cows as medicine.

Gorse
(Ulex europaeus)

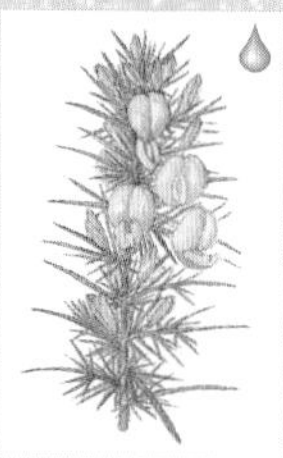

Hobby

Under parts have dark streaks. Has a white neck. Wings are swept back in flight. Takes prey on the wing. Migrates in winter.

(Falco subbuteo)

Heath spotted orchid
(Dactylorhiza maculata)

Clouded Buff Moth

Day flying in June/July. Males have one reddish spot on each yellow forewing.

(Diacrisia sannio)

MOORLAND & BOG

Exmoor pony

Usually dark brown, with a broad face and back and short legs.

(Equus caballus)

Red deer

Russet coloured coat with no white spots on adults. Largest of the British deer with branching antlers which are shed in late winter.

(Cervus elaphus)

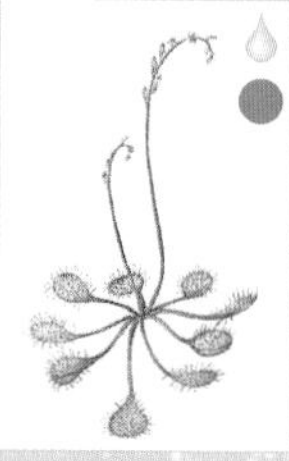

Round leaved sundew
(Drosera rotundifolia)
Carnivorous plant. 'Dew' is really 'glue'.

Mountain ringlet

Usually found above 1600 feet (500m). Likes to feed on Tormentil flowers.

(Erebia epiphron)

Bog asphodel
(Narthecium ossifragum)

Merlin

Smallest bird of prey. Long, square-ended tail.

(Falco columbarius)

Cranberry
(Vaccinium oxycoccus)

Golden plover

The male is gold and brown above, black underneath with a white dividing line in summer. Typically stands still, feeds, runs a bit, stops, feeds and so on.

(Pluvialis apricaria)

URBAN

An adult hedgehog has around 5000 spines.

Hedgehog

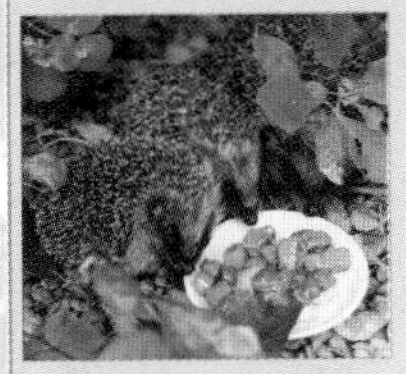

The only spiny British mammal. Listen for noisy grunting sounds at dusk in spring. Often hibernates in piles of wood meant for bonfires, check before lighting.

(*Erinaceus europaeus*)

Habitat

The place where a species lives. The species shown here often move from one habitat to another for different parts of their life cycle. For example toads can breed in ponds, forage in long vegetation and hibernate in stone walls.

Butterfly Bush
(*Buddleia davidii*)
Garden escapee. Loved by butterflies and bees.

Mason bee

Little piles of mortar at the base of walls are a clue to the nest of this solitary bee.

(*Osmia rufa*)

House cricket

Native of warmer climes, found in warm buildings. Sometimes mistaken for a cockroach.It has a lovely song.

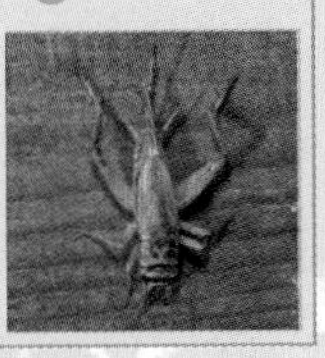

(*Acheta domesticus*)

The tiny pipistrelle bat can eat up to 3000 insects in one night.

The Bat Conservation Trust
www.bats.org.uk

Rosebay willowherb
(*Epilobium angustifolium*)
Also called 'fireweed' as it grows where fire has been.

House martin

White rump and a forked tail. Mud nest below house eaves. Summer migrant. Attractive, twittering song.

(*Delichon urbica*)

Peacock butterfly

The 'eyespots' on this butterfly supposedly confuse birds and deter other predators. Loves Buddleia.

(*Inachis io*)

Fox

Reddish brown, tail bushier in winter. Footprints fall in one line. Mainly seen at dawn and dusk.

(*Vulpes vulpes*)

CONIFEROUS WOODLAND

Crested tit

Distinctive black and white crest. Often hangs upside down on thin branches looking for seeds and insects.

(*Parus cristatus*)

Yellow birds nest
(*Monotropa hypopitys*)
No green parts.

A flock of goldfinches is called a 'charm'.

Wild cat

(mainly)

Looks like a large tabby with a thicker, blunt tail. Needs areas of varied habitat. Solitary and shy. Only found in Scotland.

(*Felis sylvestris*)

Pinewood mushroom
(*Agaricus silvaticus*)

Injured creatures

If you find an injured creature, phone the RSPCA 0870 55 55 999 or SSPCA (Scotland) 0870 73 77 722

Capercaillie

Very large woodland bird. Males are black. Needs ground flora of short berrying shrubs. Confined to a few native Scottish pinewoods.

(*Tetrao urogallus*)

Giant wood wasp

HARMLESS! Flies May to August.

(*Urocerus gigas*)

Ling
(*Calluna vulgaris*)

Pine marten

(mainly)

Dark brown/reddish coat with orange/yellow throat/chest. Might be seen chasing red squirrels in trees.

(*Martes martes*)

Red squirrel

Thick bushy tail, large ear tufts in winter. Usually orange to red/chestnut fur. Nests high in trees using twigs and a lining of moss and grass.

(*Sciurus vulgaris*)

Biodiversity

The number of different species on Earth.

ARABLE FARMLAND

Yellowhammer

Yellow with black streaks and red/orange rump. Song 'a little bit of bread and no cheese'. Likes open areas with bushy hedgerows.

(*Emberiza citrinella*)

Harvest mouse

Makes nest of woven shredded grass (still attached to the stalk) within the stalks of grasses and reeds.

(*Micromys minutus*)

Ivy-leaved speedwell
(*Veronica hederifolia*)

Common poppy
(*Papaver rhoeas*)
One plant can produce up to 500 flowers.

Skylark

Males ascend and sing a beautiful warbling song in spring and summer. Has a small crest. Prefers open areas with low hedges and no trees.

(*Alauda arvensis*)

Brown hare

Long black tipped ears. Rests in a scrape in the ground (doesn't burrow). Boxing hares are a male and a female.

(*Lepus europaeus*)

Field forget-me-not
(*Myosotis arvensis*)

Wild pansy
(*Viola tricolor*)

The common dormouse can spend up to 3/4 of its life asleep.

Grey Partridge

Plump bird with orange face. Look particularly along hedgerows where there is a wide grassy margin.

(*Perdix perdix*)

Barn owl

White heart shaped face and pure white underneath. Completely silent in flight. Call is a loud shriek. Owl pellets on ground will contain bones of small mammals.

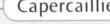

(*Tyto alba*)

FEN & MARSH

Common fleabane
(Pulicaria dysenterica)
Once burnt to get rid of fleas.

Swallowtail

Likes thistles and ragged robin. Caterpillars only feed on milk parsley. Only in East Anglia.

(Papilio machaon)

Raft spider

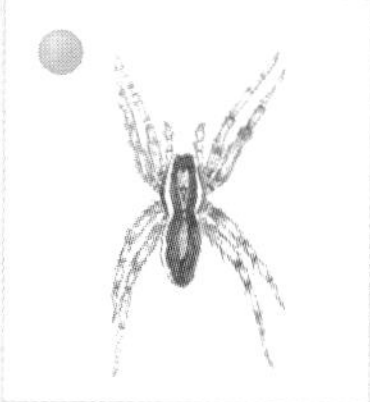

Britain's largest spider. Female's body can be almost an inch (22mm) long. Sits at boggy pool edges with legs on water.

(Dolomedes fimbriatus)

Yellow wagtail

Tail has white edges which it wags up and down. Black legs. Runs a lot. Summer visitor.

(Motacilla flava)

Marsh Harrier

Long tail. Wings held in a 'V' shape. Spring courtship involves aerial acrobatics.

(Circus aeruginosus)

Devil's-bit scabious
(Succisa pratensis)

Butterfly Conservation
www.butterfly-conservation.org

Marsh fritillary

Sheen to underside of wings. Likes devil's-bit scabious the caterpillars spinning a fine web in its leaves.

(Euphydryas aurinia)

Redshank

Long red legs and orange base to bill. Male yodels in flight "tu-udle".

(Tringa totanus)

The 'exploding' bombardier beetle has not been seen in Britain since 1928.

STILL WATER & REEDBEDS

Pintail

Male has long pointed tail feathers, brown head with white foreneck.

(Anas acuta)

Marsh marigold
(Caltha palustris)

Water vole

Rat-sized but longer fur, blunt nose and tiny ears. Creates a 'lawn' of shorter grass around banks. Shiny black droppings. 'Ratty' of 'Wind in the Willows' fame.

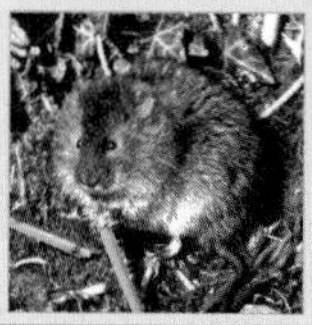

(Arvicolla terrestris)

Emperor dragonfly

Largest wingspan of any British dragonfly. Dark line runs full length of back. Male sky blue, female greenish.

(Anax imperator)

Reed bunting

Male in summer has black head and throat with distinctive white stripe between the two. Tail feathers are white and deeply forked.

(Emberiza schoeniclus)

Common reed
(Phragmites australis)
Stems used for thatching.

Common newt

Only seen in ponds in spring when breeding. At this time, male has an undulating crest with spotted flanks. The underside is often bright orange with spots.

(Triturus vulgaris)

Bittern

Rare. Try RSPB reserves in spring, where there are reedbeds. May hear its booming call, almost like a foghorn.

(Botaurus stellaris)

A toad can live for 40 years.

Yellow water lily
(Nuphar lutea)
Pods shaped like brandy bottles.

Common toad

Dry warty skin. Prefers to walk rather than hop. Only seen in ponds in spring when breeding. Lays long strings of spawn rather than clumps.

(Bufo bufo)

English Nature
www.english-nature.org.uk

Great crested grebe

Black crest. Courtship display facing each other and moving heads quickly from side to side, usually with a bill full of water plants. Strange grating bark call.

(Podiceps cristatus)

General advice

Do not disturb wildlife or damage their habitats.

RIVERS & STREAMS

Atlantic Salmon

Best seen when travelling upstream to spawn, jumps out of the water to traverse waterfalls.

(Salmo salar)

Banded demoiselle

Male has distinctive 'thumbprint' on wings and a wingspan of 2.5 inches (60mm).

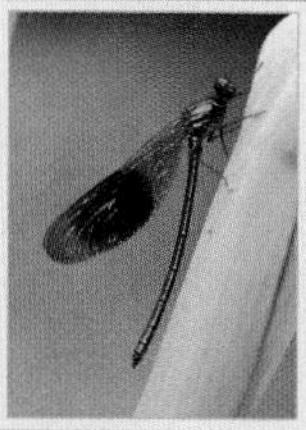

(Calopteryx splendens)

Kingfisher

Brilliant colouring. Makes tunnel in river bank. Often perches on branch over water.

(Alcedo atthis)

Watercress
(Nasturtium officinale)
Don't eat - may have liver fluke eggs on.

Water crowfoot
(Ranunculus aquatilis)

Daubenton's bat

Flies very low over water to catch prey. If you have a bat detector, listen at 35-85kHz.

(Myotis daubentonii)

Otter

Brown fur, large whiskers and white chest. Can be 36 inches (90cm) long. Five-toed, webbed feet.

(Lutra lutra)

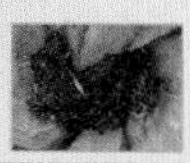

Spraint (Otter poo). Black, full of tiny fish bones.

SEA CLIFFS & BEACH

Sanderling

Runs backwards and forwards with the waves. Winter visitor and passage migrant in autumn and spring.

(*Calidris alba*)

Green shore crab

Usually greenish but can have considerable patterning. Up to 2.5 inches (60mm) long. Tolerant of low salinity so can be found far up in estuaries.

(*Carcinus maenas*)

Puffin

Unmistakable markings. Prefers high sea cliffs and offshore islands. Occasionally nest in old rabbit burrows.

(*Fratercula arctica*)

Thrift
(*Armeria maritima*)

Sea gooseberry

Lights run along body. Gets trapped in rock pools.

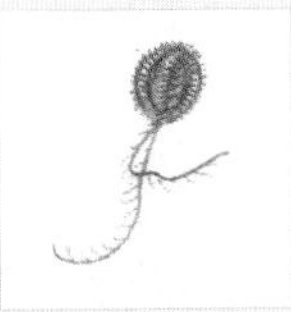

(*Pleurobrachia pileus*)

Common brittlestar

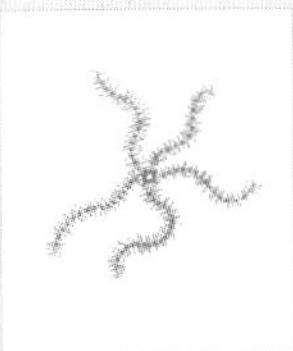

Five thin spiny arms around a disc of about 0.75 inches (20mm). Has five jaws.

(*Ophiothrix fragilis*)

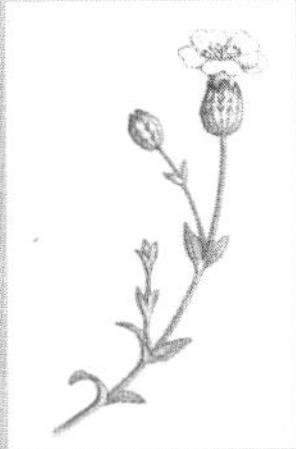

Sea campion
(*Silene maritima*)

Fulmar

Yellow/blue bill. Skims waves with stiff wings. If disturbed when nesting they spit a greenish oil.

(*Fulmarus glacialis*)

Gem anemone

Rock pools. Up to 3 inches (80mm) tall. Up to 48 green 'tentacles'.

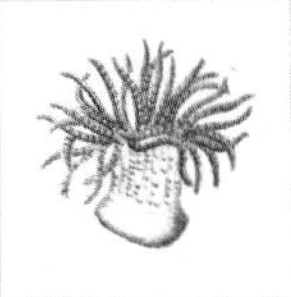

(*Bunodactis verrucosa*)

Sheep's-bit scabious
(*Jasione montana*)
Often eaten by sheep.

Chough

Looks like a crow but has red bill and legs. Only on west coasts.

(*Pyrrhocorax pyrrhocorax*)

SAND DUNES

Common lizard

Black stripe along back. Basks in sun in spring. Can shed its tail if caught, then grow a new one.

(*Lacerta vivipara*)

Sea holly
(*Eryngium maritimum*)

Green tiger beetle

Green with two creamy yellow spots, one on each wing case. 0.625 inch (16mm) long.

(*Cicindela campestris*)

Yellow horned poppy
(*Glaucium flavum*)
Pods can grow up to 30cm long.

Sandwich Tern

Black cap with short crest and long black bill with yellow tip. Call is a rasping "kirrick". Summer visitor.

(*Sterna sandvicensis*)

Common milkwort
(*Polygala vulgaris*)
Was once thought to increase milk production in cows.

ESTUARY & SALT MARSH

Curlew

Long down curved bill. Distinctive, haunting call, 'cooor-li'.

(*Numenius arquata*)

Sea aster
(*Aster tripolium*)

Golden samphire
(*Inula crithmoides*)

Oystercatcher

Long orange bill, long pink legs. Black and white plumage. Eats cockles.

(*Haematopus ostralegus*)

Common sea lavender
(*Limonium vulgare*)

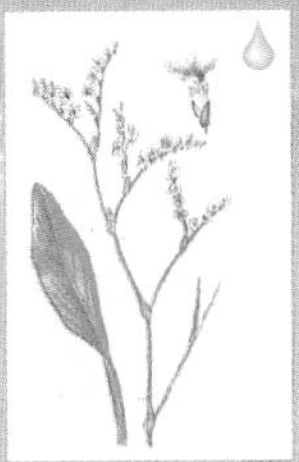

Sea wormwood
(*Artemisia maritima*)
Aromatic leaves.

Shelduck

Large red bill with bump on the top. Chestnut/orange band around chest in the breeding season.

(*Tadorna tadorna*)

Research has shown that some birds dream the song they are going to sing in the morning.

COASTAL WATERS

Thornback Ray

Diamond-shaped flat fish with spines along its long tail. Egg cases found on the beach called 'Mermaid's purses'.

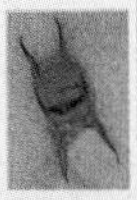

(*Raja clavata*) Egg case

Grey seal

Flat head and 'Roman' nose, unlike round head of Common seal. Also longer than Common. Pups born on shore late summer and autumn.

(*Halichoerus grypus*)

Bottle nosed dolphin

Very social, usually in groups. Has short 'snout'. Worth going on a boat trip to see, will often swim in front or at the side of the boat.

(*Tursiops truncatus*)

TRANSPORT

Canals

Canal building in Britain goes back thousands of years - short stretches were excavated to link rivers. Car Dyke, which stretched 56 miles (89km) across the Fens, was built by the Romans and can still be seen today. However, canals as we know them came into being because of the Industrial Revolution. Before the mid 1700s, goods were transported slowly and in small quantities by horse and cart on poor roads, or by sea, at great expense. With the discovery that coke could be used to smelt iron ore, huge quantities of coal were needed for this and associated industries. The first canal to be built was commissioned by the 3rd Earl of Bridgewater to transport coal from his mines to Manchester. The Bridgewater Canal opened in 1761 and was a huge success; 30 tons could be carried in a single load. By the 1830s there were over 4000 miles (7000km) of canals. However, the developing railways sounded the death knell for canal haulage. Even when wages were cut so far that boatmen had to house their families on board, railways were still more profitable and much faster. Other European countries had modernised and widened their canals, so that loads of 2,000 tons could be carried, but investment for canals here was not forthcoming. Many were abandoned and by the 1960s their numbers had halved. Luckily, at about this time, working people were taking more holidays and had more disposable income; the 'boating holiday' era had begun. Today, many miles have been restored, their narrow width making them almost unique in Europe and an historical treasure. Towpaths are being upgraded for cycling, walking and fibre-optic cableways. There is even a small revival for goods haulage due to congestion on the roads. Full circle, we might say.

Shropshire Union Canal

www.visitheartofengland.com

Burnley – Weavers Triangle

Map ref. 243 E4

Railways

The world's first steam locomotive was built by Richard Trevithick in 1803. After that, several engineers built steam engines and in 1830 the Liverpool to Manchester line became the world's first main line railway to carry passengers and freight on a double track line of metal rails, using steam locomotives built by George and Robert Stephenson. Over the next 20 years, over 6000 miles (9650 km) of public railways were built in Britain. When World War I broke out in 1914, there were 20,053 miles (32,265km) of track and 23,000 locomotives. However, their heyday was over and by the 1960s, for various organisational and political reasons, the railways were in financial trouble and the inevitable hatchet fell. Over 2,000 stations were closed and railway lines were ripped up. It has taken many years but the value of these disused tracks is at last being realised. Many footpaths and cycleways are being created enabling us to enjoy the flora and fauna along these corridors, which escaped the chemical persecution of their arable and pastoral cousins; without the railways, we might have lost many of them.

Tyseley – railway track

Brampton Valley Way

Map ref. 210 C4

ENERGY

Coal

It was coal that fired the Industrial Revolution. Wherever coal could be transported, industry would spring up. Iron foundries, glass works, potteries and brickworks. However, as with any finite resource, supply eventually became a problem and cheaper foreign coal made it uneconomic to dig the deeper pits needed to access our own. Worries about global warming prompted the 1992 Earth Summit in Rio de Janeiro, where the search for alternative energy supplies started in earnest.

Rhondda Valley – colliery

Map ref. 179 F3

Short Rotation Coppice (SRC)

Look for fields of 'shrubs' or unfamiliar tall grasses; 'biofuels' grown to be burnt in pollution free, high-tech converters, producing heat, or power, or both. Around 100 acres (40ha) of 'short rotation willow coppice' (willow cut every two or three years), could keep a village of about 50 houses warm *ad infinitum*. This growing system is excellent for wildlife, soaks up pollutants and is resistant to most pests and diseases. Classed as 'carbon neutral' it only releases carbon taken up by the plant during its short growing cycle.

Wind farms

Evidence of alternative energy sources are appearing all over the landscape of Britain. Wind farms are probably the best known, taking pure energy from the air. They already supply enough power for around 400,000 households.

Map ref. 204 D4

Llywernog – wind farm

Other

In the future we may see solar panels lining motorways to power lights and signs, barrages in estuaries collecting energy from the tides and small, privately owned water mills capturing the energy of streams once more, this time to drive turbines instead of grinding stones. You may even fill your car with methane from landfill sites.

Field of short rotation Willow coppice

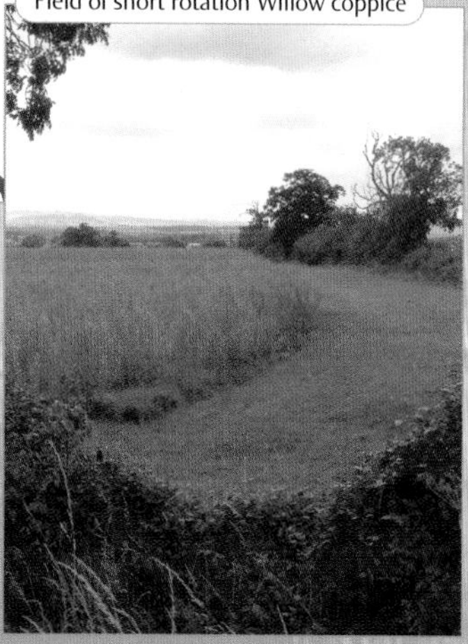

TEXTILES

Map ref. 234 C1

Rochdale – derelict mill

Until the mid 1700s, spinning and weaving was a domestic industry, but various inventions speeded up the process. In 1771, Richard Arkwright established the world's first successful water-powered cotton spinning mill at Cromford in Derbyshire, and became known as the 'father of the factory system'. Cotton production became centred in Lancashire and the west of Scotland, wool in West Yorkshire and south-west England, silk and linen in northern England. In 1912, cotton manufacture peaked at 8 billion yards (7.25 billion metres). All was well until World War I. It was no longer possible to export cloth, so countries such as Japan set up their own factories and never looked back. Between the two world wars, 800 mills closed. Although there was a slight revival in the 1950s, by the 1980s textile production in the north-west had all but ceased. Hundreds of mills lay derelict and many were pulled down. Today, the potential of the remaining fine buildings has been recognised; several are now World Heritage Sites. At Saltaire, West Yorkshire, the old mill buildings house galleries, a restaurant, antiques and other ventures. New Lanark on the banks of the Clyde has been restored to a working community and is a huge tourist attraction. Other less famous mills have found new uses - Ebley Mill in Stroud, Gloucestershire has been given a new lease of life as the District Council building.

Stroud – Ebley Mill

Map ref. 182 A2

SHIPBUILDING

Britain has always been a seafaring nation and with the developments in sail and the invention of the compass. Ships were built for trade and exploration from as early as the 14th century. During the 18th century, the Navigation Acts (requiring all British trade to be carried by British ships), and the growth of the British Empire stimulated shipbuilding further; by the 19th century the British shipbuilding industry was the largest in the world. Eventually iron replaced wood and steam replaced sail. In 1914, the tonnage from British shipyards was more than the rest of the world put together; employment reached around 300,000. However, for various economic reasons, shipbuilding here started to decline. In the 1970s South Korea moved into shipbuilding, assisted by the World Bank, this was the final straw. British construction methods were outdated and none of the 'rescue packages' instigated by the government worked. 1977 saw nationalisation of the industry; 1983 saw privatisation. Warship yards survived but those producing merchant shipping all but disappeared. All is not doom and gloom however. British shipyards still produce around 27 ships a year (although we have the capacity to produce twice that number) and Britain is a world leader in ship repairs, building warships and small specialist ships, marine equipment manufacture and ship conversions. Derelict dockyards, like those at Hartlepool, have been revived with the building of a huge new marina and some of the old buildings house new industries and tourist attractions. A similar story is told of Cardiff Docks, hit in particular by the decline in the coal and steel industries, the whole area has seen a remarkable regeneration (the second largest in Europe) with a visitor centre and various tourist attractions. Many new media and IT based industries have been attracted to the revamped and new business parks.

Cardiff Bay

Map ref. 180 A5

Cranes in disused docks

FORESTRY

Trees are a significant part of the landscape, they give it character. They can be used for screening unsightly developments, as sound barriers, for stabilising banks and spoil heaps, but mostly we see them as woodlands. After World War II, the government instigated mass planting of conifers to ensure reserves for the future. At that time, issues of wildlife and aesthetics were unheard of. Blocks and lines of conifers were planted in mostly upland areas all over the country; Kielder Forest is a prime example. Those forests are now reaching maturity but instead of chopping them all down and replanting in the same way, different methods are being used, to enhance conservation and amenity value. Landscaping and conservation now work hand in hand with commercial timber production. Trees are being removed in groups over a longer time scale so that stream sides are cleared or archaeological features enhanced, hill contours are followed and biodiversity increased. Some upland moorland is being allowed to revert to woodland (its natural state) by fencing out livestock. Within the woodlands themselves, rides are widened to let more light in, benefiting flora and fauna. This also helps access for forestry equipment, as the ground is drier.

Scotland – block conifer plantation

Glades and rides within a woodland provide a microclimate for wildlife - and somewhere to stack timber. When planting today, valuable habitats such as lowland heath are left alone, straight lines are avoided, trees are planted to blend in with the surrounding landscape character and contours of the land and a mix of broadleaved and coniferous trees are used. This has led to forests being areas for recreation as well as timber production, for example there are sculpture trails in the Forest of Dean. The new National Forest is being planted in the English midlands, it covers three counties and 200 square miles (518 sq km). The aim is to make one third of the area woodland (commercial and conservation), incorporating learning and recreational facilities. Over four million trees have been planted to date.

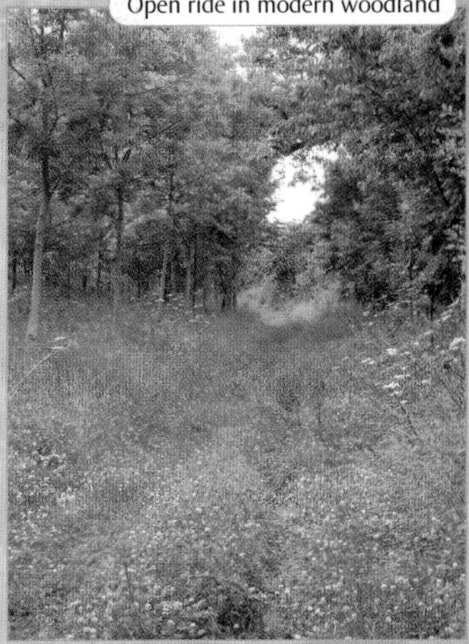

Open ride in modern woodland

Forest of Dean – Sculpture Trail

Map ref. 181 F1

MYTHS AND LEGENDS

GIANTS

Where did giant tales come from? One story says they were descendents of Ham, the 'bad' son of Noah. Another, that they were the result of a union between the banished daughters of a King of Greece and demon spirits. In practice, people probably believed that the easiest explanation for monuments such as Stonehenge was that huge giants must have built them.

Callanish giants 9

Thirteen giant people were reputedly turned to stone when they refused to let St Kieran build a church here or be baptised by him. The Gaelic name for Callanish is "na Fir Bhreign", meaning 'the false men'.

Callanish Stones

Fairy Flag of Dunvegan 6

Still kept in Dunvegan Castle is a fragile scrap of cloth. Legend says it is part of a flag given to a previous chief by his fairy wife. When unfurled, it gives victory to the MacLeod Clan in battle, makes their marriages fruitful and magically charms the herrings in the loch into the nets.

Dunvegan Castle

FAIRIES

Stories of folk existing in 'another dimension' to our own occur all over the world. In Britain they are best known as 'fairies'. They can be good (like the 'Brownies' who will do your housework for you), seem to be friendly towards farmers wives and always pay for anything they take. They can be spiteful, taking human babies and putting strange 'changelings' in their place. Mostly, they are seen as mischievous. The origins of these tales in Scotland seem to relate to the ancient Pictish people and in England and Wales, perhaps to the Bronze Age people, superseded by Iron Age (fairies are said to have a deep loathing of iron).

SAINTS

Many legends surround the making of Saints, often involving birds and animals or miraculous events.

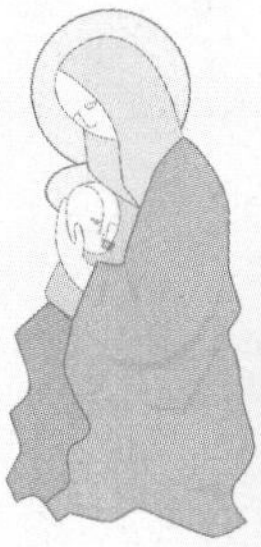

St. Brynach 7

St. Brynach journeyed to Nevern, where an angel appeared and told him to look for a white sow. The sow showed him where to build a church and this he did. In the churchyard stands a Celtic cross. On the seventh day of April, the Saint's day, a cuckoo is said to perch here and sing for the first time in the year.

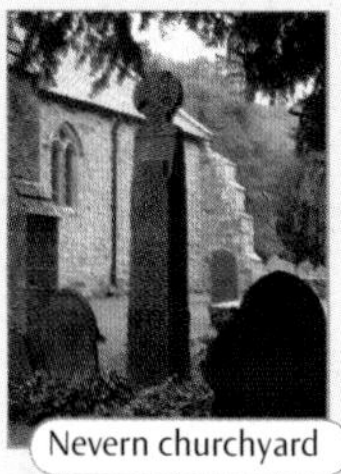

Nevern churchyard

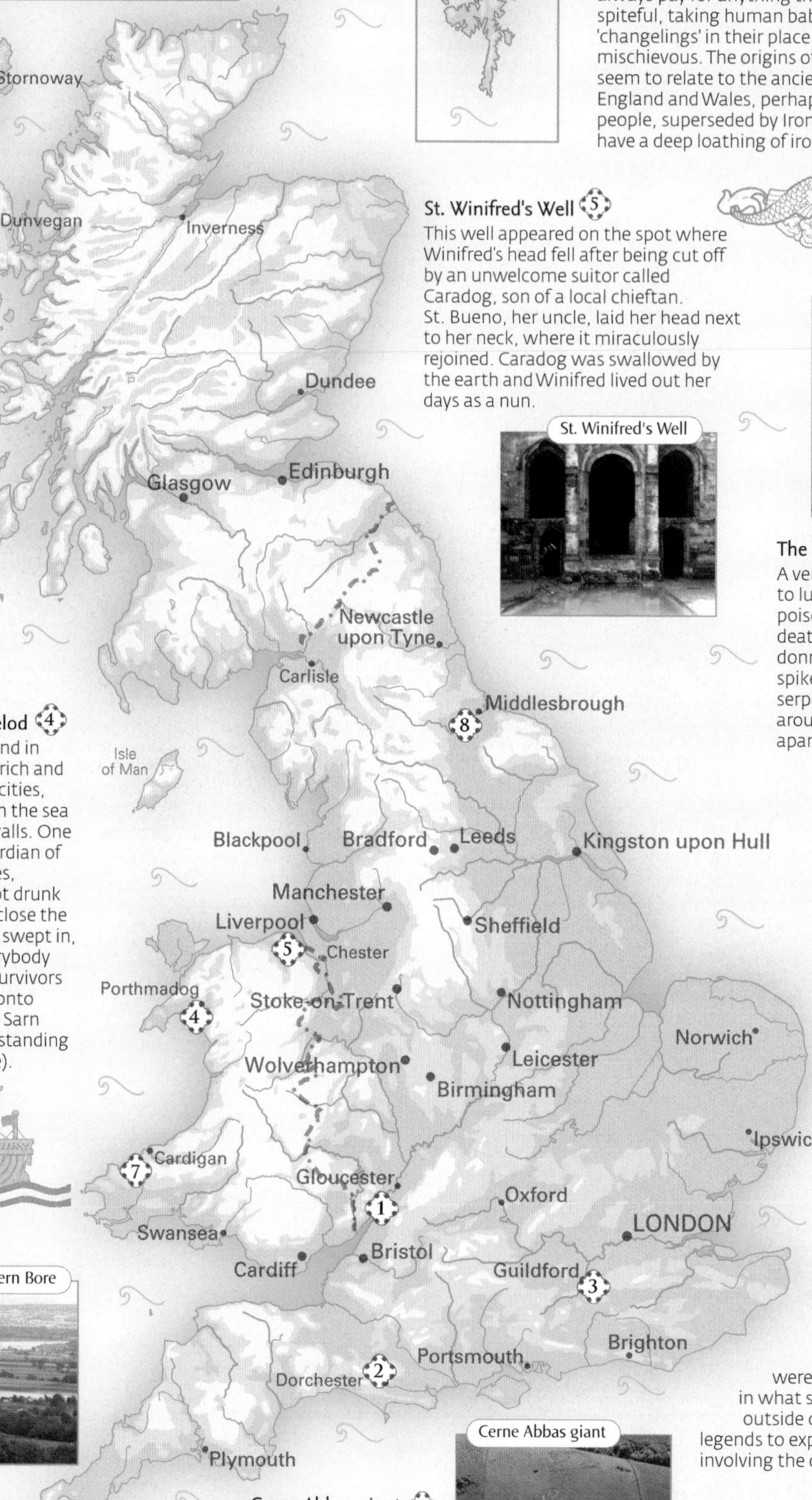

St. Winifred's Well 5

This well appeared on the spot where Winifred's head fell after being cut off by an unwelcome suitor called Caradog, son of a local chieftan. St. Bueno, her uncle, laid her head next to her neck, where it miraculously rejoined. Caradog was swallowed by the earth and Winifred lived out her days as a nun.

St. Winifred's Well

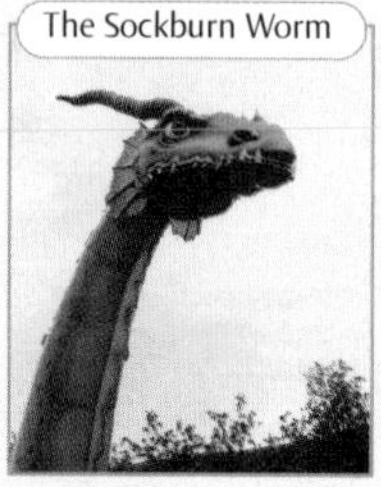

The Sockburn Worm

The Sockburn Worm 8

A venomous serpent was said to lurk in the river Tees, poisoning it and causing death and disease. A knight donned armour covered in spikes and wrestled the serpent, so that it coiled itself around him and ripped itself apart.

Cuckoo

In order to be allowed to live in this world and the Land of Eternal Youth, the cuckoo had to promise never to build a nest in either world and so never bring up or know her own children.

Cuckoo

Cantre'r Gwaelod 4

There was a land in Cardigan Bay, rich and fertile with 16 cities, protected from the sea by great sea walls. One night, the guardian of the sluice gates, Seithennin, got drunk and forgot to close the gates. The sea swept in, drowning everybody except a few survivors who escaped onto Snowdon (see Sarn Badrig, Understanding the Landscape).

Cowslip

St. Peter was said to have dropped the keys to Heaven and the first Cowslip sprang up from where they fell.

Cowslip

LOST LANDS

The legend of Cantre'r Gwaelod and others relating to submerged lands could stem from actual inundations by the sea, when Neolithic man was around to witness them.

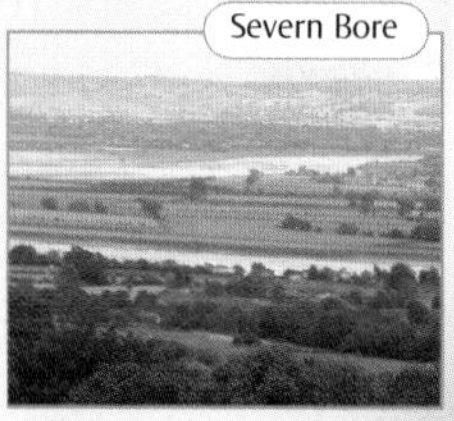

Severn Bore

WATER

Water, the giver of life, has always been associated with spirits and deities. Holy wells are often places previously used for pagan worship.

MOVING CHURCHES

In an attempt to Christianise pagan sites of worship, many churches were built on them, sometimes in what seemed like strange places, outside of a village. There are many legends to explain these locations, often involving the devil or the building stones themselves moving.

Cerne Abbas giant

Sabrina 1

The river Severn is, according to legend, inhabited by an ancient British river spirit 'Sabrina'. One story relates that when the Roman army attempted to cross the river and attack the British leader Caractacus, and the Druids, the priests called on Sabrina and she drove the bore up the river, drowning the whole Roman army.

Cerne Abbas giant 2

A Danish giant was terrorising the people of Dorset. One day, he ate too many sheep and became sleepy, so he lay down. While he slept, the villagers crept up on him and cut off his head. As a warning to other giants, they carved his outline into the chalk.

Dunsfold church 3

According to legend, this church is half a mile from the village because the stones to build it kept moving to this site when they were left overnight.

Dunsfold church

SOUTH WEST ENGLAND

The long, tapering finger of land that forms the far south west is favoured with a temperate climate and endowed with soft, timeless beauty. The pretty coastline, sometimes rugged, other times gentle, and the green, upland expanses of Dartmoor, Exmoor and the Cotswolds, together with an abundance of charming chocolate-box villages, all merit exploration. Echoes of bygone times lie scattered through the region, adding a hint of legend and mysticism in contrast to today's more up-to-the-minute attractions.

Mevagissey Harbour

A La Ronde (NT) — 152 D4

A remarkable 16-sided house built in the late 18th century on the instructions of two cousins, Jane and Mary Parminter, on their return from a Grand Tour of Europe. Many items on show were collected by the ladies during their tour and amongst the more unusual features of internal decoration are a feather frieze and a gallery encrusted by shells.

☎ 01395 265514 www.nationaltrust.org.uk

Abbotsbury Swannery & Sub-Tropical Gardens — 154 B4

A sheltered coastal location behind Chesil Beach provides a distinctive microclimate which has allowed this 20 acre (8ha) woodland garden to flourish. There are magnificent spring displays of camellias, magnolias and rhododendrons, exotic species such as bamboos, palms and bananas, and themed areas like the Mediterranean, Himalayan and New Zealand gardens.

Down on the shore, in the lee of Chesil Beach, there has been a swannery for over 600 years, established by Benedictine monks in the 14th century. Up to 1000 swans may be in residence at any one time, and between late May and late June it is possible to walk amongst the swans and observe newborn cygnets close up.

☎ 01305 871387 (Gardens) www.abbotsbury-tourism.co.uk
☎ 01305 871858 (Swannery)

Alice in Wonderland Family Park — 347 C2

A 7 acre (2.5ha) theme park based on the books of Lewis Carroll, the focal point being one of Europe's largest hedge mazes with over 5000 bushes trained to form shapes of characters from the Alice books. Other attractions include rides, particularly for younger children, indoor and outdoor play areas and a theatre giving short shows based on the Alice characters.

☎ 01202 483444 www.aliceinwonderlandpark.co.uk

American Museum — 167 E1

An early 19th century manor house which, since the late 1950s, has been home to a museum illustrating American history, culture and way of life. 18 rooms have been decorated and furnished to depict the evolution of American homes and their fashions from the 17th to 19th centuries and there are also collections of quilts and textiles, Folk Art and Native American Art. The attractive grounds contain a re-created piece of George Washington's garden at Mount Vernon.

☎ 01225 460503 www.americanmuseum.org

Antony House (NT) — 150 A2

On the Lynher River estuary, north-west of Torpoint, this fine example of an 18th century manor house contains collections of paintings, textiles and furniture. The grounds, landscaped by Humphrey Repton, contain the National Collection of Hemerocallis.

☎ 01752 812191

Avebury Ring

Arlington Court (NT) — 163 G1

An early 19th century house on the site of two previous buildings. The 3000 acre (1200ha) estate was home to the Chichester family for over 500 years, and the house contains many of the diverse and exotic acquisitions of the last owner, Miss Rosalie Chichester. There are extensive formal and informal gardens, delightful woodland walks, a small carriage museum and a bat cave where a large colony of lesser horseshoe bats can be observed by closed-circuit television.

☎ 01271 850296 www.nationaltrust.org.uk

Ashton Court Estate — 352 A3

A magnificent estate of 850 acres (340ha) designed by Humphrey Repton and comprising woods and parkland, red and fallow deer herds, and outstanding views over Bristol and beyond. A diversity of natural habitats makes this an important wildlife site, of great interest to naturalists, while for the more physically active there are mountain bike, orienteering and horse riding trails, and golf courses. The site is also host to a range of events, notably the Bristol International Balloon Festival held every year in August.

The 19th century mansion houses a visitor centre and café but is not otherwise open to the public.

☎ 0117 963 9174 www.bristol-city.gov.uk

At-Bristol — 391 C1

Three separate attractions housed in a new complex close to the waterfront in the centre of Bristol, providing a fascinating range of educational entertainment.

'Wildwalk' is a stroll through plant and animal evolution using displays and interactive exhibits.

'Explore' is an imaginative, interactive science exhibition divided into four themes related to the brain, engineering and technology, global communications, and the Curiosity Zone which explores the oddities of the physical environment.

The IMAX theatre is a four-storey high screen with surround sound, making the viewer feel part of the action. A range of short films can be seen each day, with the emphasis on science and wildlife.

☎ 0845 345 1235 www.at-bristol.org.uk

Athelhampton — 155 D3

A splendid 15th century manor house with impressive Grade I gardens. The central feature of the house is the Great Hall, built in 1493 by Sir Robert Martyn, a former Lord Mayor of London.

The 20 acre (8ha) garden was designed by Inigo Thomas in the late 19th century and, in addition to the world famous topiary pyramids, there are eight walled gardens inspired by the Renaissance, fountains, pavilions and a 16th century dovecote.

☎ 01305 848363 www.athelhampton.co.uk

Auk Walk — 147 E1

A clifftop walk near Trevalga which, between April and July, overlooks the nesting sites of puffins, guillemots and razorbills.

Avebury Ring & Alexander Keiller Museum (NT) — 168 C1

Around 4500 years old, this is possibly the largest stone circle in Europe, the surviving sarsen stones being enclosed by a substantial earthwork almost 1 mile (1.6km) in circumference. Within this there were two smaller stone circles, though little remains of the more northerly.

Information about Avebury Ring can be found in the Alexander Keiller Museum (for which there is a charge), named after the former owner of the site who endeavoured to restore the area following the plunder and removal of stones which took place, particularly in medieval times. The museum gives an excellent overview of the site, explains the known history and displays artefacts uncovered during archaeological excavations.

☎ 01672 539250 www.nationaltrust.org.uk
www.english-heritage.org.uk

Babbacombe Model Village — 151 F1

An ingenious miniature English landscape set in 4 acres (1.5ha) of beautiful gardens with over 400 models built on a scale of 1:12. Originally intended to represent the archetypal English village and its rural surroundings, the project has expanded to incorporate a comprehensive range of buildings, with particular emphasis on domestic architecture. The setting is enhanced by the many attractive water features flowing through the gardens, and is particularly enchanting in summer when illuminated at dusk.

☎ 01803 315315 www.babbacombemodelvillage.co.uk

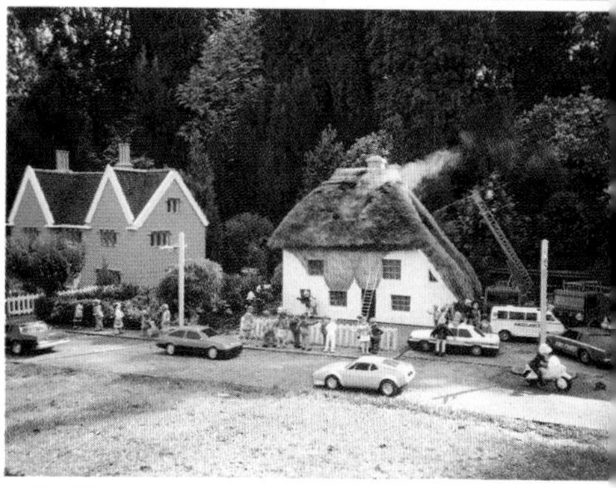

Babbacombe Model Village

Barrington Court (NT) — 153 G1

A lovely Elizabethan manor house owned by the National Trust but let as showrooms for antique furniture. The gardens, influenced by Gertrude Jekyll, are a notable feature, consisting of a series of walled, themed 'rooms' such as the White Garden, Lily Garden and Kitchen Garden.

☎ 01460 241938 www.nationaltrust.org.uk

Bath — 167 E1

The only hot springs in the country are the source of Bath's name and of its importance as a fashionable resort and tourist attraction. This in turn generated the wealth which enabled the construction of the wonderful Georgian buildings which have helped to give Bath its World Heritage Site status.

Even before the Romans arrived and built the amazing baths complex, the hot springs were a site of veneration for local Celtic tribes. However, following the Romans' departure, interest was lost in the springs and it was not until the early 18th century that it attained its position as the epitome of fashionable society. This was due largely to the efforts of Richard 'Beau' Nash, who transformed Bath from provincial town to unrivalled centre of fashion. Sea bathing eventually superseded spas as the fashionable cure, but Bath was left with a splendid architectural heritage with masterpieces such as the Circus, Royal Crescent, Assembly Rooms and Pulteney Bridge.

www.visitbath.co.uk

Bath Abbey 388 E2

Built between 1499 – 1616, this is one of England's last great medieval churches, known by the Elizabethans as the 'Lantern of the West' because of the abundance of stained glass. The most impressive example is the great East Window, illustrating 56 scenes from the life of Christ.

Externally, the most remarkable feature is the west front, carved angels commemorating a dream of the founder, Bishop Oliver King. A small but informative museum in the vaults traces the abbey's history.

☎ 01225 422462

Batsford Arboretum 197 D4

Overlooking the Evenlode Valley, at 55 acres (22 ha) this is one of the largest collections of trees and shrubs in the country with over 1500 species. The park dates back to the 17th century when the original gardens were more formal than those seen today. This transition took place in two stages – towards the end of the 19th century by Algernon Freeman-Mitford who created the wild garden, and after World War II when the wild garden had fallen into neglect and the 2nd Lord Dulverton set about creating the arboretum. Some of the features of the original wild garden are still present – the Japanese Rest House and Buddha, Rockeries and the Hermits Cave.

☎ 01386 701441 www.batsarb.co.uk

Bennetts Water Garden 154 C4

An 8 acre (3ha) area of landscaped lakes, formerly clay pits from the local brickworks. With 150 varieties of waterlily flowering in summer, this is one of the best displays in the country, and there are connections with Monet's Garden at Giverny. There is also a small museum devoted to local village life and the history of the site.

☎ 01305 785150 www.waterlily.co.uk

Berkeley Castle & Gardens 181 F3

Completed in 1153 by Lord Maurice de Berkeley for Henry II in order to guard the Severn Estuary, the layout of the castle has changed little since the end of the 14th century. It is England's oldest inhabited castle and is still home to the Berkeley family after 25 generations. The cell where King Edward II was held captive for 18 months before his murder in 1327 can be seen, as can the 30ft (9m) deep dungeon. The extensive grounds feature a butterfly house, lily pond and the bowling alley where Elizabeth I played bowls with her courtiers.

☎ 01453 810332 www.berkeley-castle.com

Bath – Royal Crescent

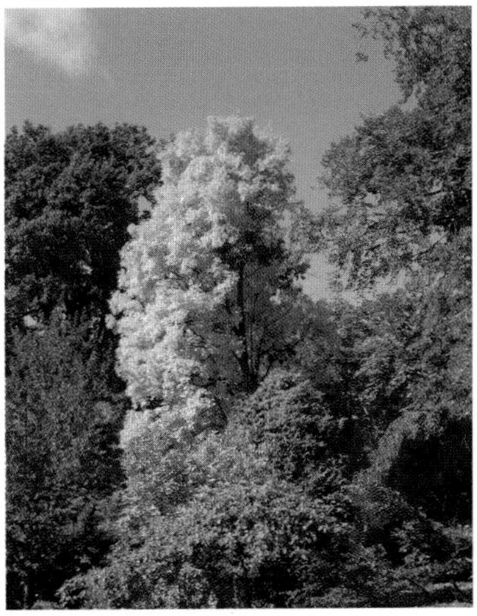

Batsford Arboretum

Berry Pomeroy Castle 151 E1

With a reputation as one of the most haunted castles in England, this decidedly atmospheric ruin is splendidly located on a crag above a wooded valley. The oldest part is thought to date from the 14th century, but the main building, a large mansion, was built between 1548 – 1613 and was subsequently abandoned later in the 17th century.

☎ 01803 866618 www.english-heritage.org.uk

Bicton Park Gardens 153 D4

Delightful gardens and parkland covering 63 acres (25ha) featuring an amazing 19th century domed Palm House, arguably one of the world's most beautiful garden buildings. Other highlights include the Italian Garden and Pinetum. For the less horticulturally inclined, there is a rural life museum, a 1.5 mile (2.5km) narrow-gauge railway and adventure playground.

☎ 01395 568465 www.bictongardens.co.uk

Big Sheep, The 163 E3

Innovative attraction combining traditional sheep-related activities such as shearing, lambing, feeding and sheepdog trials, with more unusual enterprises such as Ewetopia, an adventure play area, sheep racing, complete with knitted jockeys, and duck trials.

☎ 01237 478800 www.thebigsheep.co.uk

Birdland 197 D5

Birdland opened in 1957 and moved to its present 7 acre (3ha) natural setting in 1989. There are over 500 birds with more than 50 aviaries for parrots, hornbills and toucans, amongst many other species. The River Windrush winds through the park creating a natural habitat for flamingos, pelicans and storks. The penguins are always popular, especially at feeding time.

☎ 01451 820480 www.birdland.co.uk

Blaise Castle House Museum 352 A1

A late 18th century castle folly in beautiful grounds designed by Humphrey Repton. The museum has a fine social history collection including an excellent range of domestic equipment, a Victorian toy room including model trains, period costumes and paintings.

☎ 0117 903 9818 www.bristol-city.gov.uk

Bodmin & Wenford Railway 147 E3

Operating from Bodmin General station, this is Cornwall's only standard-gauge steam railway. It consists of two lines, one interchanging with the main line at Bodmin Parkway. Most trains are steam-hauled over 6.5 miles (10km) of track.

☎ 0845 125 9678 www.bodminandwenfordrailway.co.uk

Bodmin Moor 147 F2

A large expanse of granite moorland dotted with tors in the north and many Bronze Age and Neolithic sites, particularly in the south. Brown Willy, Cornwall's highest point at 1377ft (420m), is located here in the bleaker northern part of the moor. Daphne du Maurier's famous novel 'Jamaica Inn' is set on the moor around Altarnun and Bolventor.

Bowood House & Gardens 167 G1

Built in the early 18th century, but partly demolished in 1955, Bowood is an elegant Georgian mansion. Its most notable features are Robert Adam's magnificent library, the laboratory where Joseph Priestley discovered oxygen, the Orangery, now a picture gallery, and the Sculpture Gallery. The 2000 acre (800ha) grounds, however, are arguably Bowood's chief attraction. Landscaped by Lancelot 'Capability' Brown, complete with elegant parkland, Cascade Waterfall, Hermit's Cave and a Doric temple by the tranquil lake, they make a splendid backdrop to the house. For six weeks in spring the magnificent rhododendron gardens are open, with thousands of flowering bulbs elsewhere in the grounds. For children there is an excellent adventure playground and soft play area.

☎ 01249 812102 www.bowood.org

Bradley Manor 152 B5

A small 15th century manor house in a tranquil setting of woodland and open fields. The Great Hall is a particularly interesting feature.

☎ 01626 354513 www.nationaltrust.org.uk

Brewers Quay 154 C5

A converted harbourside brewery housing a range of shops, activities and attractions.

'The Timewalk' depicts 600 years of Weymouth's history as seen through the eyes of the brewery cat and her predecessors. 'Brewery Days' looks at the area's brewing heritage through interactive displays and audiovisual presentations. 'Discovery' is a hands-on science centre with over 60 interactive items.

☎ 01305 777622 www.brewers-quay.co.uk

Bristol City Museum & Art Gallery 352 B2

One of the largest museums in the south west, housed in an impressive Edwardian Baroque building. There are detailed displays relating to local geology, archaeology and natural history, interesting temporary exhibitions and some unusual art exhibits.

☎ 0117 922 3571 www.bristol-city.gov.uk

Bristol Industrial Museum 391 C1

Located in the Floating Harbour in a converted goods transit shed, the museum is home to a wide range of exhibits relating to Bristol's industrial heritage. The port's history is told through models, paintings and memorabilia, and there are exhibitions on the printing and packaging industry, and Bristol's part in the infamous slave trade triangle.

☎ 0117 925 1470 www.bristol-city.gov.uk

Bristol Zoo
352 B2

For a generation brought up on safari parks, Bristol Zoo might seem a rather modest establishment, but there is plenty to see. It comprises a 12 acre (5ha) site with delightful gardens providing a colourful backdrop to over 300 fascinating species with a particular emphasis on conservation of wildlife and its natural habitats. There are zoo trails and a good adventure playground for children.

☎ 0117 973 8951 www.bristolzoo.org.uk

British Empire & Commonwealth Museum
391 C3

A fascinating museum detailing the history of the British Empire and subsequent development of the Commonwealth, from the voyage of John Cabot in 1497 to the present day. There are 20 themed galleries devoted to exploration, trade and conquest, illustrated by a wide selection of artefacts, costumes, photographs and film clips, with an imaginative variety of interactive exhibits.

☎ 0117 925 4980 www.empiremuseum.co.uk

Brownsea Island
155 G4

Located in the sheltered waters of Poole harbour, this 500 acre (200ha) island boasts a wide range of natural habitats such as saline lagoon, heathland and freshwater lakes. This haven for wildlife is home to such rarities as red squirrels, glow worms, water voles, dragonflies and over 20 species of butterfly. There are hides to observe both breeding colonies and migrant birds, and a boardwalk through reed beds passes near the heronry.

Historically, the island is chiefly famous as the site of Lord Baden-Powell's first camp in 1907 which led to the formation of the Scout movement.

Access is by pedestrian ferry from the mainland, and away from the reserve there are woodland walks with delightful views.

☎ 01202 707744 www.nationaltrust.org.uk

Buckfast Abbey
150 D1

This was originally founded in 1018, but was abandoned after the Dissolution of the Monasteries until 1882 when Benedictine monks took over the site and rebuilt the abbey in a traditional Anglo-Norman style with some particularly striking stained glass work. There is an informative exhibition on the site and shops selling a variety of produce from Benedictine monasteries across Europe. Physic, Sensory and Lavender gardens have been re-created in the grounds.

☎ 01364 645500 www.buckfast.org.uk

Buckland Abbey (NT)
150 A1

Originally a 13th century monastery overlooking the Tavy valley, this was subsequently converted to a family home, initially owned by the sea-faring Grenville family. In 1581 the property was bought by Sir Francis Drake and it remained in his family until 1942. Features include the fine, oak-panelled Great Hall, exhibitions on Drake's achievements and adventures, Elizabethan gardens and craft workshops.

☎ 01822 853607 www.nationaltrust.org.uk

Cadhay
153 D3

An attractive Tudor manor house approached through an avenue of lime trees. The fine 15th century timbered roof of a previous dwelling has been incorporated into the Great Hall.

☎ 01404 812432 www.eastdevon.net

Caen Hill Locks
168 A1

An impressive flight of 29 locks on the Kennet and Avon Canal at Devizes, raising the water level 240ft (73m) in 2.5 miles (4km)

Canonteign Falls
152 B4

Located in a natural hillside gorge landscaped 160 years ago, this claims to be England's highest waterfall at almost 220ft (66m). After being neglected for years, the site has been restored to reveal striking rock formations, lakes and waterfalls. Additional features include a Victorian fern garden, wetland nature reserve, children's play areas and adventure playground.

☎ 01647 252434 www.canonteignfalls.com

Carnewas & Bedruthan Steps
146 C3

Spectacular coastal scenery of cliffs and rocky beach. Access to the beach is via a stairway from the clifftop at Carnewas, where a National Trust shop is housed in a former mine office. The Steps are a series of rock stacks along the beach, produced as a consequence of marine erosion.

☎ 01637 860563 www.nationaltrust.org.uk

Castle Drogo (NT)
152 A3

Contrary to appearances, this is an early 20th century building designed by Sir Edwin Lutyens and built in an outstanding position above the Teign valley. Constructed of specially quarried granite, the foundations were cut into the hillside, and in some rooms the exposed rock can be seen. Overall, it presents a striking combination of medieval style with modern comfort.

Outside, established formal gardens provide a colourful setting in spring and summer, and there are lovely woodland walks, some providing magnificent views over the Teign valley.

☎ 01647 433306 www.nationaltrust.org.uk

Chambercombe Manor
163 F1

Located in a tranquil valley, Chambercombe was mentioned in the Domesday Book, though the present house dates from the 12th century. Eight rooms are on display, with period furniture from Elizabethan to Victorian times. Very atmospheric, and rumoured to be haunted.

☎ 01271 862624 www.chambercombemanor.co.uk

Cheddar Gorge & Caves
166 B2

Cheddar Gorge is the most dramatic natural feature of the Mendip area, a mile (1.6km) long chasm with cliffs, almost vertical in places, around 400ft (120m) high. A drive through the gorge, for which access is free, is a breathtaking experience, more so when taken out of season as, not surprisingly, this is a popular attraction and can be crowded in summer. For walkers, there is a 3 mile (5km) clifftop circular walk which provides fine views, and which can be accessed by Jacob's Ladder, 274 steps up the side of the gorge.

The lower end of the gorge in Cheddar village has succumbed to commercial tourist pressure, but the caves offer visitors the chance to see some amazing stalactite and stalagmite formations in the dramatic Gough's Cave. Cox's Cave nearby is smaller, with narrow passages and some striking coloured formations. There is also an exhibition on the life of cave-dwelling man, based on remains discovered in the caves dating from Palaeolithic times.

☎ 01934 742343 www.cheddarcaves.co.uk

Chedworth Roman Villa (NT)
182 C1

Discovered in 1864 and now owned by the National Trust, the Villa sits at the head of a small valley overlooking the River Colne. It would have been one of the grandest houses in the Cotswolds at the time it was built, with evidence of 32 rooms, and there are still substantial remains including two Roman baths and some extremely well-preserved mosaic flooring. There are audiovisual demonstrations and a museum within the grounds.

☎ 01242 890256 www.nationaltrust.org.uk

Chesil Beach

Chesil Beach
154 B4

An 18 mile (29km) shingle ridge running from Burton Bradstock to Portland, effectively tying the island to the mainland. South of Abbotsbury the ridge is detached from the coast, enclosing The Fleet, a brackish lagoon and setting for J. Meade Faulkner's definitive smuggling story 'Moonfleet'.

An interesting feature of the beach is the increase in size of its component flint and quartzite stones, from pea size in the west to fist size at Portland, where the ridge can be up to 45ft (14m) high. This is a popular site with sea anglers, but powerful offshore currents, probably a factor in the feature's formation, make it very dangerous for bathers.

Chettle House
155 F1

A delightful Queen Anne manor house providing an excellent example of English Baroque architecture. Complemented by 5 acres (2ha) of attractive gardens. Limited opening.

☎ 01258 830858

Christchurch Priory
347 D3

Considered to be the longest parish church in Britain at over 300ft (90m), this splendid medieval monastic building is noted for its exceptional interior carvings. Access to the tower, via 120 steps up a spiral staircase, is sometimes available for a small charge, and is worth it for the splendid views.

☎ 01202 485804 www.christchurchpriory.org

Chysauster Ancient Village
144 B3

A late Iron Age courtyard village believed to have been inhabited at least up until the Roman occupation. The settlement consisted of eight or more oval stone houses, each surrounding a courtyard, and a stone wall enclosed the whole complex. Within the houses some rooms were for human occupation, others for animals or food storage.

☎ 01831 757934 www.english-heritage.org.uk

Cleeve Abbey
164 D3

A late 12th/early 13th century Cistercian abbey particularly noted for its well preserved cloisters, considered amongst the finest in England. Other distinctive features include the remarkable timber roof in the refectory and medieval wall paintings.

☎ 01984 640377 www.english-heritage.org.uk

Cleeve Common 196 B5

Cleeve Common is the high spot of the Cotswold Hills, rising to 1083ft (330 m) above sea level, with, on a clear day, far-reaching views across to the Malvern Hills and the Brecon Beacons in South Wales. The Common is protected by the Wildlife and Countryside Act and is a Site of Special Scientific Interest. The area was cleared of forest over 10,000 years ago and has been used for livestock grazing ever since. Rock climbing is popular on Cleeve Cloud and the public golf course is a test on the exposed hilltop.

☎ 01242 522878 www.cleevecommon.freeserve.co.uk

Clevedon Court (NT) 180 D5

Surviving virtually intact from its construction in 1320, the house incorporates parts of older buildings including a 12th century tower and 13th century hall. The contents include fine collections of glass, Eltonware and furniture, and there are sketches by William Makepeace Thackeray who wrote much of 'Vanity Fair' here. There are attractive terraced gardens giving good sea views.

☎ 01275 872257 www.nationaltrust.org.uk

Clouds Hill (NT) 155 E3

A tiny, rather isolated cottage which formed a retreat for T.E. Lawrence (Lawrence of Arabia) following his desert achievements. The four rooms on display contain memorabilia and an exhibition on his life. Open only part of each week.

☎ 01929 405616 www.nationaltrust.org.uk

Clovelly 162 D3

Cars are prohibited from this unique village where a steep cobbled street lined with delightful, flower-covered, whitewashed houses runs down to a tiny harbour. As the streets are too steep for motor transport, donkeys were formerly used for conveying heavy loads and, although now superseded by hauled sledges, are still on hand for children's rides in summer.

The harbour and distinctive quay are the most memorable features and, although fishing is no longer of major importance, it is still a feature of village life. This, together with sympathetic management, ensures the village retains its character whilst proving a popular attraction.

☎ 01237 431781 www.clovelly.co.uk

Coleridge Cottage (NT) 165 E3

For three years from 1797, this was home to the poet Samuel Taylor Coleridge where he wrote, amongst other works, 'The Rime of the Ancient Mariner'. Part of the cottage containing his memorabilia is open to the public.

☎ 01278 732662 www.nationaltrust.org.uk

Coleton Fishacre (NT) 151 F2

Built in the Arts and Crafts style of the late 19th century for the D'Oyly Carte family, this house is distinguished for its internal decoration influenced by the Art Deco movement.

The garden is particularly noted for its range of tender and exotic plants which thrive in the sheltered, moist environment. The terrace gardens are delightful with their range of colour and diversity in summer, whilst woodland pathways through the less formal stream-fed valley lead to coastal walks with panoramic views.

☎ 01803 752466 www.nationaltrust.org.uk

Combe Martin Wildlife & Dinosaur Park 163 G1

A 25 acre (10ha) parkland, ideal for children, with a range of animals and birds including falconry displays, butterfly house, otter pool, sea lions, snow leopards, wolves and a large meerkat enclosure. The dinosaur museum houses not only fossils but also models animated by computer technology, the star being a full-size Tyrannosaurus Rex. There are also botanical gardens containing subtropical plants, and a range of indoor activities.

☎ 01271 882486 www.dinosaur-park.com

Compton Acres 347 B3

The attractive 10 acre (4ha) gardens were devised around 1920 by Thomas Simpson who wanted to create a series of separate garden 'rooms', each illustrating a specific national garden style. National styles include Japanese, Egyptian, Italian, Indian, Canadian, Spanish and Scottish, each with appropriate plants and statuary. The result is a series of delightful gardens in a location giving stunning views over Poole Harbour and surrounding hills.

☎ 01202 700778 www.comptonacres.co.uk

Compton Castle (NT) 151 E1

Built between the 14th and 16th centuries, this fortified manor house has been the Gilbert family home almost continuously for the last 600 years. The original buildings, dating from 1350 and fortified in Henry VIII's reign, have remained unaltered since.

☎ 01803 875740 www.nationaltrust.org.uk

Cookworthy Museum 150 D3

Opened in 1971, this fascinating museum, housed in the Old Grammar School, displays items associated with rural life and social history in the Kingsbridge area, particularly in the 19th and early 20th centuries.

☎ 01548 853235 www.devonmuseums.net

Corfe Castle (NT) 155 F4

A hilltop ruin which dominates the surrounding countryside. Built by the Normans in the late 11th century to replace an earlier Saxon structure which had been the site of the murder of King Edward the Martyr in AD978, the castle controlled the route through the Purbeck Hills. It was used as a prison, and subsequently as a treasury and hunting lodge by King John in the early 12th century, whilst Henry III added further walls, towers and gatehouses.

The last owners were the Bankes family, Lady Mary Bankes holding the castle against Parliamentary attack for a long period during the Civil War. The steep hillside and thick walls made the castle almost impregnable, and it required the treachery of one of the besieged officers for it to be taken.

Subsequently, the destruction of the castle was ordered, and it is a credit to the soundness of the original construction that it took several months to reduce it to the ruin that can be seen today. The rubble was not wasted; much of it was used to build Corfe Castle village.

☎ 01929 481294 www.nationaltrust.org.uk

Cornish Cyder Farm, The 146 B4

Guided tours round probably the largest Cornish cider maker in Cornwall. The farm also produces liqueurs and other fruit products. Admission to the farm is free.

☎ 01872 573356 www.thecornishcyderfarm.co.uk

Cornish Engines (NT) 145 D2

Local engineer Richard Trevithick developed the high pressure steam system which originally powered these two impressive beam engines. Their purpose was to operate the winding gear to transport men and ore through the mineshafts and to pump out water from depths of around 1800ft (550m). The Industrial Discovery Centre on the same site provides an absorbing perspective on Cornwall's industrial heritage.

☎ 01209 315027

Cornish Seal Sanctuary 145 E4

On the Helford Estuary, just east of Gweek. One of Europe's leading marine animal rescue centres, comprising a hospital and rehabilitation pools, and caring for around 50 abandoned or injured seals and otters. Feeding demonstrations take place throughout the day.

☎ 01326 221361

Cotehele (NT) 150 A1

On the River Tamar just west of Calstock. Originally a medieval manor house, improved and enlarged by Sir Richard Edgcumbe and his son between 1490 and 1520. Subsequent alterations have not substantially affected their work, making this one of the least altered medieval houses in the country. The gardens provide all year round colour and are crossed by a network of woodland and riverside walks.

☎ 01579 351346

Cotswold Farm Park 196 D5

The park has a wide variety of animals including rare breeds, pets and working animals such as oxen and sheepdogs. The tractor school gives 3 to 12 year olds the chance to learn to drive battery and pedal powered tractors, and the Touch Barn enables visitors to get close to the smaller animals. There are daily and seasonal demonstrations such as milking, lambing and shearing.

☎ 01451 850307 www.cotswoldfarmpark.co.uk

Corfe Castle

Cotswold Hills 182 A3

The Cotswolds, an Area of Outstanding Natural Beauty, run for 60 miles (96km) from Bath north eastwards to the Warwickshire border and eastwards towards Oxford. The hills are not particularly high – the high point of 1083ft (330m) is on Cleeve Common near Cheltenham – but the landscape is rich and varied, from rolling hills to steep sided valleys. The picturesque towns and villages are frequently busy, especially in the north, but there are many quiet and peaceful areas to be found. The 100 mile (160km) Cotswold Way winds its way from Chipping Campden in the north, southwards to Bath. Passing such places of interest as Hailes Abbey, Woodchester Mansion, the Tyndale Monument and the Stone Age long barrows of Belas Knap and Hetty Pegler's Tump, the walk is always interesting and takes in some of the country's finest countryside. The belt of limestone that stretches across central England gives the Cotswolds much of their character in the buildings and drystone walls that help to blend the towns and villages seamlessly with the open countryside.

☎ 01242 522878 www.cotswoldsaonb.com

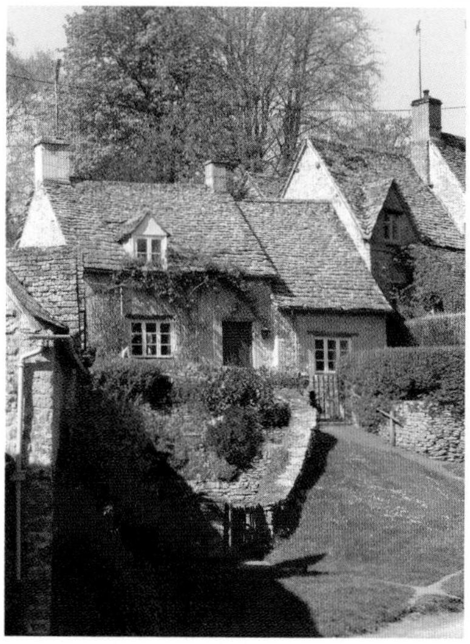

Cotswold village – Bibury

Cotswold Water Park 182 C3

With 133 lakes formed as the result of gravel extraction and covering over 2000 acres (809ha), this is considered Britain's largest water park. The lakes provide a variety of associated watersports including angling, sailing, canoeing, water-skiing and windsurfing, but there are also land-based activities on offer. There are several nature reserves with public access within the country park areas, the bird life being of special interest. Opportunities abound for walking, cycling and adventure activities, and a bathing beach is open in summer. Access is free, but there is a charge for activities.

☎ 01285 862962 www.waterpark.org

Crealy Adventure Park 152 D3

A good day out for families with children, having activities suitable for all ages and interests. These include adventure playgrounds, farm animals, a variety of rides and lakeside walks.

☎ 01395 233200 www.crealy.co.uk

Dartington Crystal 151 D1

Guided tours of the factory enable visitors to learn about glass production, from the initial stage of blowing the molten glass through to the finishing process of completed items. A visitor centre traces the history of glass production and holds live demonstrations of glass-making skills, whilst the activity centre provides hands-on family entertainment. There is a large factory shop on site.

☎ 01805 626242 www.dartington.co.uk

Dartmoor 149 F2

A National Park, perhaps the last untouched wilderness of southern England, this is an extensive, bare upland area of granite with clusters of rocky summits or tors of between 1000-2000ft (300-600m). Scenery ranges from almost featureless tracts of open moorland in the north, to the wooded valleys of the Teign and Dart in the south.

The more remote areas of high moorland have a rather forbidding reputation, enhanced in part by its use as an atmospheric setting for Sir Arthur Conan Doyle's story 'The Hound of the Baskervilles'. In good weather the area is outstanding walking country, with a mixture of old rail tracks (a legacy of former mineral extraction) and ancient footpaths. Possibly due to a more favourable past climate, there are around 2000 prehistoric sites on the moor, the Bronze Age village of Grimspound being perhaps the best example, and the area is considered one of the most significant locations for Bronze Age relics in Europe. The more wooded and hospitable moorland fringes are home to the many fast flowing streams tumbling down from the uplands, particularly attractive spots being Lydford Gorge and Becky Falls.

Dartmouth Castle 151 E2

The first to be designed with specific respect to artillery use, this 15th century castle has a superb location on the narrow entrance to the Dart estuary. A contributor to the coastal defence system over the last 500 years, the building is still in good repair. Informative displays recount the castle's history.

☎ 01803 833588 www.english-heritage.org.uk

Dean Heritage Centre 181 F1

Set around a restored corn mill and millpond, the centre looks at various aspects of the Forest of Dean – geology, hunting, crafts, the industrial heritage including iron and coal mining.

☎ 01594 822170 www.deanheritagemuseum.com

Dinosaur Museum 154 C3

Devoted entirely to dinosaurs and their world, this museum has a range of imaginative and interactive exhibits. It is possible to handle some of the actual fossil bones and life-size reconstructions, and there is a wealth of factual information for visitors. There is a well-stocked shop.

☎ 01305 269880 www.dinosaur-museum.co.uk

Dobwalls Family Adventure Park 147 G3

A theme park based on the miniature railway hobby of John Southern, a local farmer. Around 10 steam and diesel trains based on the American style railroads travel along 2 miles (3km) of track. Additional attractions include an impressive adventure playground, children's driving school and wildlife art gallery.

☎ 01579 320325

Dunster Castle & Gardens (NT) 164 C3

Dating from at least Norman, and possibly Saxon times, the castle has a magnificent site on a wooded hill above the village of Dunster. The chief medieval relic is the 13th century gatehouse, while the main building, dating from 1617, was substantially remodelled for domestic use in Victorian times.

The 28 acre (11ha) gardens are equally interesting with unusual and subtropical plants, including the National Collection of Arbutus (strawberry trees), probably England's oldest lemon tree, camellias, magnolias and a fine display of spring bulbs. There are extensive views across Exmoor, the Quantock Hills and the Bristol Channel.

☎ 01643 821314 www.nationaltrust.org.uk

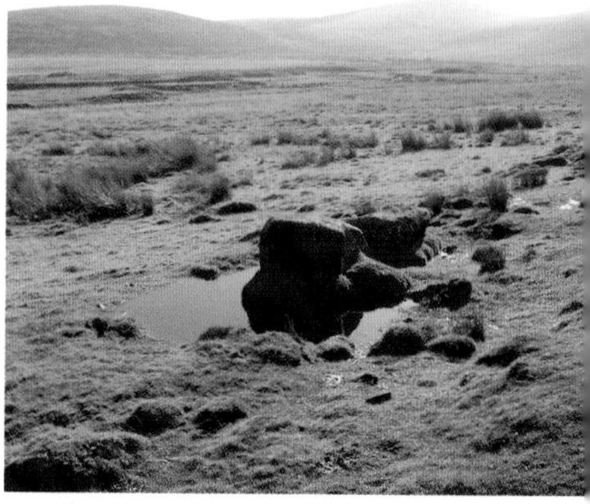

Dartmoor

Dunster Watermill 164 C3

There was mention of a mill on this site in the Domesday Book, but the current building dates from the 18th century and has been restored. Visitors can watch the milling process and there is a collection of old-fashioned agricultural machinery, and a tearoom.

☎ 01643 821759 www.nationaltrust.org.uk

Durdle Door 155 E4

This is a natural sea arch composed of Portland limestone formed where marine erosion has exploited an area of weakness in the rock. A short but energetic and breathtaking hike of just over 1 mile (1.6km) west along the cliffs from Lulworth Cove brings the walker to this fascinating feature. Cheats can park at the nearby holiday park for a small fee and stroll to the coast.

Dyrham Park (NT) 181 G5

Impressive and little altered late 17th century house set in 268 acres (105ha) of deer park, built for William Blathwayt, a minister in William III's government. It contains some fine furnishings, paintings and a collection of Delftware, popular at the time in deference to the king's Dutch origins. Park and ride access is arranged to preserve the original setting.

☎ 0117 937 2501 www.nationaltrust.org.uk

East Lambrook Manor 154 A1

Delightful Grade I cottage style garden created in the mid 20th century by Margery Fish and portrayed in her popular book 'We Made a Garden'. Established with the conservation of endangered species in mind, the garden was neglected in the 1970s but has since been sympathetically restored to provide a wealth of colour and scent, including the National Collection of Geraniums. The house is not open to the public, but the 17th century malthouse is used for art exhibitions.

☎ 01460 240328 www.eastlambrook.com

East Somerset Railway
167 D3

Also known as the Strawberry Line, steam trains run along the 2.5 mile (4km) track which includes a 1 in 56 gradient, one of the steepest for an English preserved railway. It was founded by the wildlife artist David Shepherd and the station complex includes an art gallery, as well as an engine shed and workshops. It is advisable to phone in advance for train times.

☎ 01749 880417 www.eastsomersetrailway.org

Eden Project
147 E4

This has been described as 'the world's largest greenhouse' but that is a gross oversimplification of the botanical diversity contained within.

Opened in 2001 and still undergoing further development, the Eden Project was devised by Tim Smit (who also redeveloped the Lost Gardens of Heligan). Its purpose is to illustrate how the human race depends on plants, and aims to provide levels of interest appropriate to all ages and scientific abilities.

The site was originally a vast clay pit 200ft (60m) deep and 35 acres (14ha) in area. It comprises two biomes constructed from transparent hexagonal plastic on a galvanized steel tubing framework. Each of these has its own controlled environment designed to replicate conditions in one of the world's major climatic regions. Outside can be found plants from temperate climates such as the prairies, Himalayas and western Europe. Displays in each area show how man interacts with these environments and the uses to which the plants are put.

A deservedly popular attraction, which at peak times may be closed to prevent overcrowding.

☎ 01726 811911 www.edenproject.com

Eden Project

Edmondsham House
155 G1

Delightful Tudor manor house with later Georgian additions set in an attractive 6 acre (2ha) garden with lovely spring bulbs, unusual trees and an organic walled garden. There is also an interesting octagonal Victorian dairy and the remains of a medieval cock fighting pit. Limited opening.

☎ 01725 517207

Escot
153 D3

220 acres (88ha) of parkland designed by Lancelot 'Capability' Brown and containing a wide range of animals and related activities including falconry displays, bear enclosures, otters, an extensive collection of tropical and freshwater fish, maze and wetland conservation area. There are also children's activities and pleasant walks through the colourful gardens and parkland. Access to the aquatic centre and wetlands area is free.

☎ 01404 822188 www.escot-devon.co.uk

Exeter Cathedral
398 B2

Miraculously escaping major structural damage during the World War II bombing of Exeter, the cathedral and its close provide an historic retreat amidst the post-war rebuilding of the city centre. Evidence of Christian worship on this site dates from the 5th century, but the oldest features of the current building are the twin Norman towers dating from the early 12th century. Much of the cathedral was rebuilt during the late 13th and 14th centuries, building materials being local stone from Beer and Purbeck limestone, and this provides perhaps England's finest example of Decorated Gothic architecture. Other notable aspects are the 14th century minstrels' gallery, the bishop's throne which dates from 1312 and is one of the finest examples of wood carving surviving from this period, the elaborate choir stalls with 13th century misericords and the 500 year old astronomical clock. Of more recent interest are the Exeter Rondels, delightfully embroidered cushions on the north and south walls of the nave depicting, in around 14 million stitches, scenes of local and national history.

☎ 01392 255573 www.exeter-cathedral.org.uk

Exmoor
164 A3

Unlike the other moorlands of the south-west peninsula, Exmoor is composed of sandstone rather than granite, a feature reflected in its scenery which is less bleak than its neighbours. Acidic soils give rise to a typical high moorland flora of heathers interspersed with bilberry, though on the fringes are pleasant wooded river valleys which provide a greater diversity of wildlife than the upland plateau.

There are many attractive places to visit, including the area around Oare and Badgworthy Water (setting for the novel 'Lorna Doone'), Tarr Steps, and the little towns of Dulverton, Dunster, Porlock and Washford. Dunkery Beacon, the highest point at 1703ft (519m), provides views as far as the Brecon Beacons to the north and the Mendips to the east. The moor ends abruptly at the coast with a series of headlands and cliffs, the latter being amongst the highest in England. Minehead is the chief coastal resort, but Watchet, Blue Anchor and Porlock Weir are well worth a visit. Over 600 miles (960km) of foot and bridlepath cross the moor, making it a popular area for walking and riding.

Farleigh Hungerford Castle
167 E2

Extensive ruins of a 14th century castle built by Sir Thomas Hungerford. The chapel has undergone major conservation work and contains particularly fine wall paintings, stained glass and tombs of the Hungerford family.

☎ 01225 754026 www.english-heritage.org.uk

Finch Foundry (NT)
149 G1

Opened in 1814, this water-powered forge produced hand tools for the agricultural and mining industries until 1960. Regular demonstrations show the three waterwheels driving the massive tilt hammers and grindstone.

☎ 01837 840046 www.nationaltrust.org.uk

Flambards Village Theme Park
145 D4

A theme park combining historical re-creations with the more characteristic adventure rides such as roller coaster and log flume.

The Victorian Village comprises shops and houses furnished and equipped with original items, while 'Britain in the Blitz' is an authentic representation of a street blitzed in World War II.

☎ 01326 573404

Fleet Air Arm Museum
166 C5

A museum dedicated to the history of maritime aviation and in particular the Royal Naval Air Service. There are around 40 historic aircraft on display, together with a range of exhibits – a particular highlight is the Carrier Hall which contains a representation of a 1970s aircraft carrier. The Restoration Hangar has a viewing window for visitors to observe ongoing projects. For younger visitors there is an adventure playground and a flight simulator.

☎ 01935 840565 www.fleetairarm.com

Forde Abbey
153 G2

In a superb location on the banks of the River Axe, this former Cistercian monastery, founded in 1140, became a private home in 1649. The beautifully furnished rooms have splendid plaster ceilings, and a particular treasure is the set of Mortlake Tapestries of designs originally drawn for the Sistine Chapel.

The 30 acre (12ha) gardens are considered amongst the best in England, with borders displaying vivid colour, an impressive rockery, wonderful bog garden with drifts of Asiatic primulas and a background of sweeping lawns and mature specimen trees.

☎ 01460 221900 www.fordeabbey.co.uk

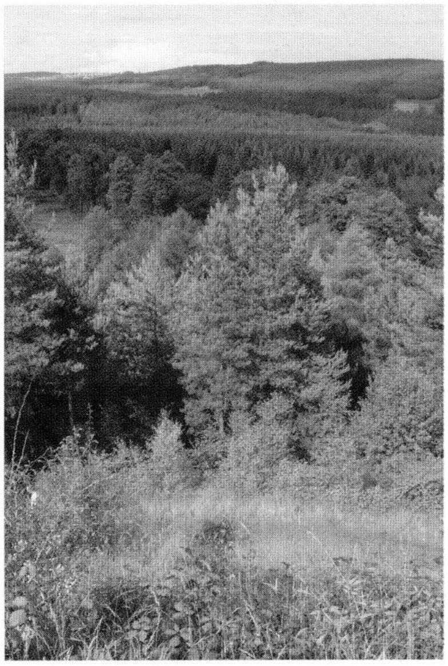

Forest of Dean

Forest of Dean
181 F1

Lying between the Rivers Wye and Severn, this former royal hunting forest has the largest area of 150 year old oak trees in Britain. Ponds, streams, an arboretum and nature reserve make this an area where peace and tranquilty can be enjoyed along with a rich cultural and industrial heritage which can be investigated through several themed trails. Speech House is now a hotel and conference centre but was built in 1676 as a hunting lodge for Charles II. It later becoming a meeting place for the locals and is still a focal point for the entire forest. Amongst the diverse flora and fauna are rare birds, wild boar and even an occasional polecat. There is ample opportunity for outdoor pursuits – canoeing, caving, climbing, cycling and horse riding or just a leisurely stroll around one of the many lakes and ponds.

☎ 01594 812388 www.forestofdean.gov.uk

Geevor Tin Mine
144 A3

A working tin mine until 1990, this is one of the largest mining history sites in the country. The mine's surface buildings have been restored and visitors can look round the processing plants where the ore was crushed. A highlight is an underground tour of an adit, or horizontal passage, which gives the merest hint of the former working conditions. A small museum has a model of the site plan and describes the method of tin production.

☎ 01736 788662 www.geevor.com

Glastonbury Abbey
166 B4

Magnificent ruins of an historic abbey whose foundation by Saxon kings in the 7th century probably predates the town. The repeated target of Viking attacks in the 8th and 9th centuries, the abbey's fortunes were revitalised by St Dunstan's appointment as abbot in AD940, and the building was considerably enlarged. A devastating fire in 1184, and the subsequent need for rebuilding funds, led to the Arthurian legend when the monks fortuitously 'discovered' the bodies of Arthur and Guinevere buried in the graveyard.

The abbey did not survive the Dissolution of the Monasteries, but the remains, together with an interpretation area, clearly indicate its wealth and importance in medieval times. The Glastonbury Thorn, legendary off-shoot of Joseph of Arimathea's staff, still grows in the grounds.

☎ 01458 832267 www.glastonburyabbey.com

Glastonbury Tor
166 C4

This solitary mound of Triassic rock rises 518ft (158m) above the southern edge of the Somerset Levels in an area subject to tidal inundations as recently as the early 17th century. The tor was settled in Neolithic times with a lake village at its base. The summit tower has been re-opened after structural repairs and the tor can be reached by a park and ride bus from the abbey, for which there is a small charge.

Goonhilly Satellite Earth Station

Glendurgan (NT)
145 E4

Located at the mouth of the Helford Estuary, this splendid 40 acre (16ha) valley garden was created in 1820. It contains many fine specimen trees, including a poplar which grew 79ft (24m) in 14 years, and an interesting laurel maze. In spring there is an outstanding display of magnolias, camellias and wild flowers.

☎ 01326 862090 www.nationaltrust.org.uk

Gloucester Cathedral
399 B2

Christian worship has taken place on this site since AD679 though the present building was started in 1089 and consecrated in 1100. King Henry III was crowned here, the only monarch to have been crowned outside Westminster since the Norman conquest. The 14th century fan vaulted cloisters are amongst the earliest and finest in the world. There are frequent exhibitions and guided tours to the top of the tower (for which there is a charge), reached by climbing 269 steps.

☎ 01452 528095 www.gloucestercathedral.org.uk

Gloucestershire & Warwickshire Railway
196 C5

Originally part of the Great Western main line from Cheltenham to Birmingham which closed in 1960, this steam and diesel railway passes through picturesque Cotswold scenery during a 20 mile (32km) round trip from Toddington to Cheltenham Racecourse. There is a static display of locomotives and rolling stock at Toddington station.

☎ 01242 621405 www.gwsr.plc.uk

Godolphin House
144 C3

Dating from around 1475, this delightful Tudor/Stuart mansion was for generations home to the Godolphin family whose fortune was founded on tin. The house contains some fine 16th and 17th century English oak furniture and paintings, and there are interesting formal medieval gardens and a wagon collection in the Elizabethan stables.

☎ 01736 763194 www.godolphinhouse.com

Golden Cap
154 A3

This sea cliff, the highest on the south coast at 626ft (191m), is named and formed from a sandstone outcrop weathered to a golden brown. There are spectacular views from the summit, particularly the panorama from Start Point in the west to Portland in the east.

www.nationaltrust.org.uk

Goonhilly Satellite Earth Station
145 E4

Located on the barren uplands of the Lizard peninsula, this is one of the world's largest satellite communications centres, with a site comprising more than 60 satellite dishes. The main dish, measuring 108ft (33m), has listed building status. The station deals with huge numbers of television broadcasts, international telephone calls and e-mails via satellite equipment and fibre optic cables.

The informative visitor centre is host to a range of activities including its interactive exhibition area with high speed internet access and virtual imaging. A guided tour of the site, which is a National Nature Reserve, is also available.

☎ 0800 679593 www.goonhilly.bt.com

Great Chalfield Manor (NT)
167 F1

Built in the late 15th century and sensitively restored in Edwardian times, this delightful moated manor house has beautiful oriel windows and the original Great Hall, complete with minstrels' gallery.

☎ 01225 782239 www.nationaltrust.org.uk

Hailes Abbey (NT)
196 C4

This Cistercian abbey was founded in 1246 and in 1270 was gifted a phial containing what was said to be the blood of Christ. After the 1539 Dissolution, parts of the site survived as a mansion house but fell into disuse in the 18th century. Excavation of the heavily overgrown site took place in the late 19th century. Little is left of the buildings apart from the remains of the cloister arches.

☎ 01242 602398 www.nationaltrust.org.uk

Hardy Monument
154 C4

Standing 770ft (240m) above sea level on the highest point of Black Down Hill, this 70ft (21m) monument was erected in memory of Thomas Masterman Hardy, captain of the *Victory* at the Battle of Trafalgar. 121 stone steps lead to the top from where there are magnificent views.

Hardy's Cottage
154 D3

A small cob and thatch cottage with delightful garden, birthplace of the novelist Thomas Hardy in 1840 and built by his great grandfather. Two of Hardy's books were written here and set in the local area.

☎ 01305 262366 www.nationaltrust.org.uk

Hartland Quay
162 C3

An isolated hamlet at the end of a toll road (charge in summer only), dwarfed by dramatic cliffs whose contorted structure provides evidence of former massive earth movements. Reduced now to a few cottages and tourist facilities, including a museum depicting the area's history, Hartland Quay was once a thriving little port supplying this remote area. Walks on the surrounding cliffs provide breathtaking views of this austere coastline.

www.elmscott.freeservers.com

Hay Tor Granite Tramway
152 A5

A relic of the former granite quarrying industry, these tracks, constructed of the stone they were built to carry, run from the flanks of Hay Tor to Stover Canal some 10 miles (16km) away.

Hestercombe
165 F5

Three centuries of garden history are contained in this 50 acre (20ha) Grade I garden.

The Georgian landscape garden, designed in the late 1750s by Coplestone Warre Bampfylde whose family owned the estate from 1391 – 1872, comprises lakes, pleasant woodland walks and temples set in 40 acres (16ha). The Victorian garden was created for Viscount Portman in the late 19th century, and in summer the formal bedding provides an exuberance of colour. However, Hestercombe is best known for its Edwardian garden, designed by Sir Edwin Lutyens and planted by Gertrude Jekyll in what is considered to be their finest collaboration.

☎ 01823 413923 www.hestercombegardens.com

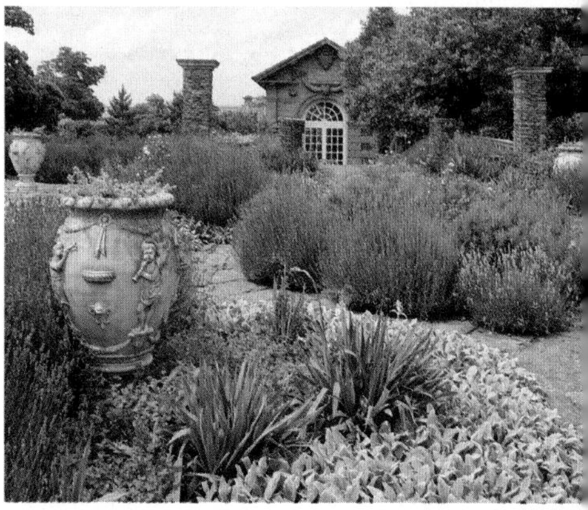

Hestercombe

Hidcote Manor Gardens (NT)
197 D3

The Hidcote estate was bought by a wealthy American widow in 1907. The garden was created by her son, Lawrence Johnston, who took a keen

interest in gardening which grew to a point where his designs were to have influences on many other gardens, for example Sissinghurst. The garden is arranged as a series of outdoor 'rooms', creating many different moods as a journey through the garden is taken. The garden is now in the ownership of the National Trust.

☎ 01386 438333

Hidcote Manor Gardens

Holnicote Estate (NT) — 164 C3

Given to the National Trust in 1944 by Sir Richard Acland, the estate consists of more than 12,000 acres (5042ha) of varied scenery, ranging from moors and woodlands, to cliffs and beaches. It includes the high points of Exmoor at Dunkery and Selworthy Beacons, with their sensational views, and a 5 mile (8km) stretch of coastline. The village of Selworthy, one of the prettiest on the moor, was built by the Acland family for their estate workers.

☎ 01643 862452 www.nationaltrust.org.uk

Horton Court (NT) — 181 G4

The remains of a 12th century rectory, probably the oldest in England, consisting of a Norman hall and a particularly good example of an ambulatory.

☎ 0117 937 2501 www.nationaltrust.org.uk

Iford Manor — 167 E2

Delightful Grade I early 20th century garden in a hillside setting by the River Frome, formerly owned by the architect and landscape gardener Harold Peto. It was designed in an Italianate style, complete with terraces, colonnade, cloisters, statuary and fountains, but there is also a lovely meadow of naturalised bulbs, notably martagon lilies. There are magnificent views of the local countryside.

☎ 01225 863146 www.ifordmanor.co.uk

Jurassic Coast — 153

This stretch of East Devon and Dorset coastline, between Exmouth in the west and Studland in the east, has been designated a World Heritage Site. Its outstanding geological and palaeontological locations, coupled with stunning and varied coastal scenery, make a visit almost compulsory to appreciate this fine example of the natural landscape.

www.jurassiccoast.com

Kennack Sands — 145 E5

Two sheltered, sandy beaches, considered amongst the cleanest in Britain, located in an Area of Outstanding Natural Beauty.

Killerton (NT) — 152 C2

A hillside garden of around 20 acres (8ha) landscaped by John Veitch. The garden is particularly lovely in spring, although attractive throughout the year. The 18th century house contains period furniture and is home to a significant costume collection which changes annually. The extensive surrounding parkland provides delightful walks.

☎ 01392 881345 www.nationaltrust.org.uk

Kingston Lacy (NT) — 155 F2

Designed in the 17th century for the Bankes family following the slighting of Corfe Castle, and later restyled by Sir Charles Barry, this mansion is home to a wealth of treasures. These include paintings by Titian, Rubens and Raphael, an impressive marble staircase from Italy and a striking Spanish room decorated in gilded leather.

The formal garden is surrounded by 250 acres (100ha) of wooded parkland with waymarked walks, or there are longer walks along ancient trackways that can be taken through the 8795 acre (3520ha) estate.

☎ 01202 883402 www.nationaltrust.org.uk

Kingston Maurward Park — 154 C3

Gardens and parkland of 35 acres (14ha) surrounding a delightful Georgian mansion which is now an agricultural college. The restored Edwardian Garden is divided into a series of outdoor 'rooms' and there is an attractive rose garden, colourful herbaceous borders and drifts of spring bulbs, while the National Collections of Penstemons and Salvias are also kept here. A small farm park provides interest for children.

☎ 01305 215000 www.kmc.ac.uk

Knightshayes Court (NT) — 152 C1

Designed by William Burges, this elaborate Victorian Gothic house features ornate interior decoration including painted ceilings and a minstrels' gallery.

The 50 acre (20ha) gardens, amongst the finest in the county, are of interest throughout the year and contain both formal and informal plantings.

☎ 01884 254665 www.nationaltrust.org.uk

Knoll Gardens — 347 B1

A garden of 6 acres (2.5ha) with interesting water features and over 6000 well-labelled plants from around the world in colourful themed gardens. It includes the National Collection of Mahonias and a developing retail nursery.

☎ 01202 873931 www.knollgardens.co.uk

Lacock Abbey (NT) — 168 A1

Founded in 1232, but converted to a country house around 1540 following the Dissolution of the Monasteries. The cloisters, chapter house, sacristy and monastic rooms have been preserved, while an octagonal tower was built in the Tudor period, and further work in the 18th century included a fine Gothic entrance hall. The grounds have lovely displays of spring flowers, a Victorian woodland garden and restored botanic garden. A converted 16th century barn houses the Fox Talbot Museum of Photography, which commemorates the work of the pioneering photographer who lived here.

☎ 01249 730277 www.nationaltrust.org.uk

Land's End — 144 A4

Traditionally considered the south west extremity of the British mainland, this is a granite headland with spectacular cliff scenery. Although commercialisation with a theme park is considered by some to have spoiled the area, a short walk along the cliffs provides an escape from the crowds to a more natural environment.

Lanhydrock (NT) — 147 E3

This imposing residence originally dates from the 17th century but was largely rebuilt following a devastating fire in 1881. 50 rooms are open to the public, including state rooms and nurseries, sculleries and kitchens, containing state-of-the-art Victorian furniture and equipment, and the house provides a fascinating insight into the 'Upstairs, Downstairs' way of life. However, the centrepiece is the impressive 96ft (30m) Long Gallery, chief relic of the 17th century building, with its splendid plasterwork ceiling depicting scenes from the Old Testament.

The 900 acre (364ha) estate, extending down to the banks of the River Fowey, includes both formal and woodland areas as well as parkland, and contains some exceptional specimen trees from a collection started in the early 17th century. Magnificent spring displays of magnolias, camellias and rhododendrons give way in summer to colourful herbaceous borders and annual bedding in the formal garden.

☎ 01208 265950 www.nationaltrust.org.uk

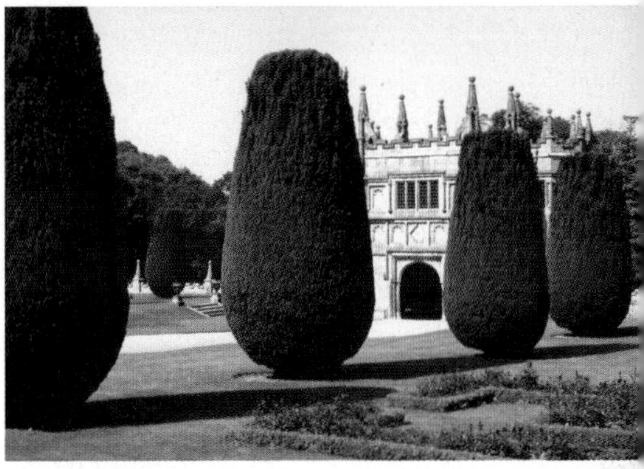

Lanhydrock

Lappa Valley Railway — 146 C4

This 15 inch (38cm) narrow-gauge railway was originally a mineral line running between Newquay and East Wheal Rose. A short section, passing through a scenic valley, has been restored. The surrounding parkland includes woodland walks and play areas.

☎ 01872 510317 www.lappavalley.co.uk

Launceston Castle — 148 D2

Located in a commanding position above the town where it formerly controlled the main route into Cornwall, this is now a medieval castle ruin built on the motte of the original Norman stronghold.

Launceston Steam Railway — 147 G1

This narrow-gauge steam railway links Launceston with the little village of New Mills, a distance of 2.5 miles (4km). The carriages are hauled by Victorian steam locomotives through scenic countryside and there are a range of walks that can be taken from both stations. The railway workshops in Launceston are open to visitors.

☎ 01566 775665

Lizard Peninsula — 145 E4

The coastal scenery of the Lizard peninsula is a striking combination of headlands, coves, cliffs and stacks cut out of the distinctive red and green serpentine rock which is typical of this area. Particularly attractive are Mullion Cove, Kynance Cove and Cadgwith village, while more dramatic

locations include the west coast cliffs and the collapsed cavern which forms the Devil's Frying Pan. The peninsula culminates in Lizard Point, a headland forming the southerly tip of the British mainland.

Longleat House 167 F3

A magnificent Elizabethan mansion set in 900 acres (360ha) of rolling park landscaped by Lancelot 'Capability' Brown.

The house, built for Sir John Thynne, and still belonging to his descendants, was completed in 1580. Inside, it has been sumptuously decorated with gilded, painted Italianate ceilings designed by John Dibblee Crace in the 1870s and 1880s. Furniture ranges from 16th century English pieces to splendid French work of the 17th and 18th centuries, together with some unusual Italian examples. Many other treasures have been accumulated by the family over the centuries, including a fine collection of paintings by English, Dutch and Italian masters, 16th and 17th century Flemish tapestries and 40,000 books housed in seven libraries.

The grounds, bordered by woodland, include formal gardens, plantings of rhododendrons and a handsome lake.

☎ 01985 844400 www.longleat.co.uk

Longleat House

Longleat Safari Park 167 F3

Set in the magnificent grounds of Longleat House, the Park was opened in 1966, the first of its kind in the country. Since then, an amazing range of attractions has been added, though lions, tigers, elephants, giraffes and many other animals can still be seen in the drive-through Safari Park. The grounds boast several mazes and labyrinths, including arguably the world's largest yew hedge maze, further animal attractions, a permanent Dr Who exhibition, narrow-gauge railway, boat trips, simulator rides and children's play areas. A passport ticket is available for the attractions package.

☎ 01985 844400 www.longleat.co.uk

Lost Gardens of Heligan 145 G2

This is one of Europe's largest garden restoration projects. Originally developed by the Tremayne family in the late 18th century, the 57 acres (23ha) of gardens gradually descended into an apparent wilderness when the house was taken over as a military hospital in World War I, and most of the workforce of 22 gardeners enlisted. Little was done to remedy the situation until the early 1990s, when the structure of the original magnificent garden was uncovered, largely at the instigation of Tim Smit who inspired the Eden Project.

The estate, including gardens and parkland, totals about 200 acres (80ha), with palm trees, tree ferns and bamboos giving it a subtropical atmosphere. Extensive flower and vegetable gardens are now back in production. Visitors can bear witness to the estate's return to productivity by sampling the results in the garden's restaurant.

☎ 01726 845100 www.heligan.com

Lulworth Castle 155 E4

A 17th century hunting lodge badly damaged by fire in 1929 and subsequently restored. Features include a reconstructed kitchen, dairy, cellar and laundry. The adjacent Roman Catholic chapel was the first to be built after the Reformation, its design reflecting George III's stipulation that its identity should be disguised before he gave permission.

☎ 01929 400352 www.lulworth.com

Lulworth Cove & Heritage Centre 155 E4

An accident of geology, where the sea has breached resistant coastal limestone rocks to erode the softer clay and sand deposits inland, has led to the development of this striking, circular cove. Elsewhere in the area exposed rocks bear witness to massive earth movements millions of years ago, a particularly memorable example being at Stair Hole just west of the cove's mouth.

The focal point of the Heritage Centre is a rock display tracing the geological history of the area. A video shows how the power of the sea has directly influenced the development of this amazing natural scenery.

☎ 01929 400587 www.lulworth.com

Lundy Island 162 B1

A granite island, 3 miles (5km) north to south and 0.5 miles (1km) east to west, located at the entrance to the Bristol Channel 11 miles (17km) north-north-west of Hartland Point. Noted particularly for its scenery and wildlife, most of the island has been designated a Site of Special Scientific Interest, while the surrounding sea area is currently England's only Marine Nature Reserve.

The island rises to a height of 400ft (120m), the exposed west coast having the more dramatic scenery, whilst exposure to salt spray ensures a maritime flora including thrift and sea campion. Trees are restricted to the more sheltered east coast which is home to the Lundy Cabbage, found only on the island. 35 different breeding species of bird nest here, notably the puffin; Lundy means 'puffin island' in Norse. The surrounding coastal waters are home to sea anemones, sponges and corals, some brightly coloured, and also to seals and basking sharks. Access is by the *Oldenburg*, the island's own boat which sails from Bideford three times a week in summer and twice weekly in winter.

☎ 01271 863636 www.lundyisland.co.uk

Lost Gardens of Heligan

Lydford Gorge (NT) 149 E2

Dramatic and awe-inspiring gorge carved into slate from the Upper Devonian period, a less durable rock than the granite traditionally associated with Dartmoor. The force of the water carried along rocks and boulders which have carved out sizeable potholes in the river bed, the most striking of these being the Devil's Cauldron which forms a breathtaking whirlpool.

The gorge is 1.5 miles (2.5km) long, up to 200ft (70m) deep and includes the 100ft (35m) White Lady Waterfall. A circular walk descends through woodland to the White Lady then follows a delightful route through the gorge itself and is particularly attractive in Autumn. In places the path can be narrow and slippery.

☎ 01822 820320 www.nationaltrust.org.uk

Lydiard Mansion 182 C4

A beautifully restored Georgian mansion now under council ownership, former home of the Bolingbroke family and still containing their furniture and paintings. The surrounding parkland with its lawns, lakes and woodland offers pleasant walks, and there are children's play areas. Access to the grounds is free.

☎ 01793 770401 www.swindon.gov.uk

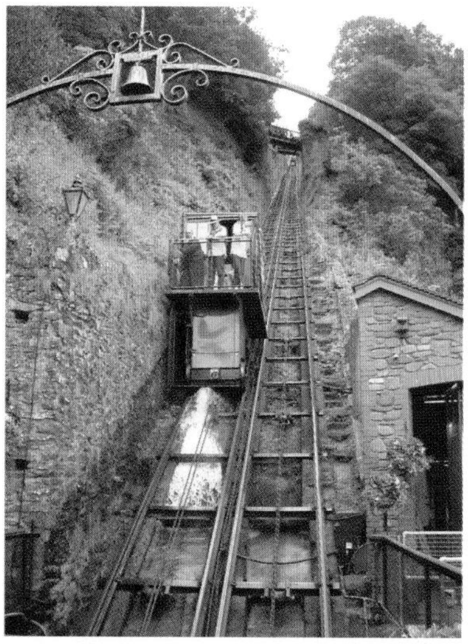

Lynton & Lynmouth Cliff Railway

Lynton & Lynmouth Cliff Railway 164 A3

Funded by Sir George Newnes (the wealthy London publisher of 'Tit Bits' and 'The Strand') and completed in 1890, the cliff railway is a magnificent example of Victorian engineering and ingenuity. At the time, it greatly enhanced the tourist potential of this picturesque area, by giving visitors easy access from Lynmouth, where the boats docked, to Lynton, at the top of the 500ft (152m) cliff.

Open to the public at specific times; a trip on this 'green' listed monument is a must.

Lytes Cary Manor (NT) 166 C5

Delightful manor house, with 14th century chapel, dating mainly from the 15th century when the Great Hall was built, but extended in the 16th century. The house was restored in the 20th century and furnished in period style, while the garden was also replanted in a series of 'rooms' with topiary and colourful, well-stocked herbaceous borders.

☎ 01458 224471 www.nationaltrust.org.uk

Lydford Gorge

Maiden Castle
154 C4

The name deriving from the Celtic 'Mai Dun', or Great Hill, this is one of the largest Iron Age hillforts in Europe, first developed in Stone Age times around 3000BC. Bronze Age burials have been discovered in one area, but the site was increased to its current size of 47 acres (19ha) in the Iron Age, around 450 – 300BC. Around AD43 the fort was taken by the Romans. The foundations of a Roman temple built in the 4th century can still be seen. The fort was later abandoned, but even today remains a hugely impressive site.

www.english-heritage.org.uk

Mapperton
154 B3

A delightful terraced garden around a 17th century manor house (limited opening). The upper garden is Italianate, with topiary and formal borders, and steps leading down to fish ponds.

☎ 01308 862645 www.mapperton.com

Marwood Hill
163 F2

A privately owned, colourful 20 acre (8ha) garden including three small lakes. The extensive collection of plants comprises, amongst others, alpines, clematis, camellias, rhododendrons and fine tree species such as eucalyptus.

☎ 01271 342528

Mendips
166 B2

A ridge of Carboniferous limestone stretching some 25-30 miles (40-48km) roughly between Weston-super-Mare and Shepton Mallet. Although the landscape consists mainly of rounded summits, with a high point of 1068ft (325m) at Black Down, the hills rise quite sharply from the surrounding lowlands, particularly in the north west, and provide extensive views across Exmoor, the Bristol Channel, Somerset and Wiltshire.

The most dramatic scenery can be seen in the famous Cheddar Gorge, a mile (1.6km) long ravine exposing steep cliffs (see page 26). A smaller, unspoilt version can be found at Ebbor Gorge near Wookey Hole. Evidence of prehistoric settlement is common in the area, with Neolithic, Bronze Age and Iron Age remains. From Roman times until the 19th century, lead mining was important, and abandoned mine workings can still be seen on the plateau.

Milton Lodge
166 C3

Attractive Grade II terraced gardens on a hillside overlooking Wells, providing magnificent views of the cathedral. Highlights include naturalised spring bulbs, a variety of climbers, old fashioned and shrub roses and a 7 acre (3ha) arboretum.

☎ 01749 672168

Minack Theatre
144 A4

The location on the granite cliffs above Porthcurno beach gives this open-air theatre a spectacular and atmospheric setting. A 17-week summer season includes a wide range of productions which are cancelled only in extreme weather conditions. The visitor centre explains the theatre's history and evolution.

☎ 01736 810181 www.minack.com

Minterne
154 C2

Formality has not been a consideration in these 20 acres (8ha) of lovely gardens landscaped in the 18th century. A chain of small lakes and streams provides a home for moisture-loving and water plants, whilst major collections of rhododendrons, cherries and acers provide magnificent spring colour and splendid autumn foliage.

☎ 01300 341370

Monkey World
155 E4

A spacious rescue and rehabilitation centre for primates, set in a delightful area of Dorset heath and woodland. The unspoilt 65 acre (26ha) site is home to more than 150 animals of 15 different species, including over 50 chimpanzees, probably the largest group outside Africa.

☎ 0800 456600 www.monkeyworld.co.uk
☎ 01929 462537

Moors Valley Country Park
156 A2

A 750 acre (300ha) park providing a range of leisure and recreational facilities in a pleasant countryside setting of lakes and woodland. Attractions include an adventure playground, steam railway, golf course, cycle hire and high ropes course. There is an extensive network of foot and cycle paths, and nature trails.

☎ 01425 470721 www.moors-valley.co.uk

Morwellham Quay Museum
149 E3

Important since the 12th century as the nearest river port to Tavistock, Morwellham became particularly significant following the discovery of rich copper veins in the locality in the 1840s. The mines closed in the late 19th century and Morwellham was abandoned until 1970 when work was started on an open-air museum. This museum has carefully and accurately re-created the port and associated industrial and domestic buildings to provide a fascinating insight into the life of what was once one of Europe's major copper ports.

☎ 01822 832766 www.morwellham-quay.co.uk

Mount Edgcumbe
346 A3

Superbly located on a hill overlooking Plymouth Sound, this was the family home of the Edgcumbes, built in the 16th century to replace the residence at Cotehele. Following bomb damage in World War II the house was restored by Adrian Gilbert Scott and is furnished with the family's possessions, including Regency furniture, paintings and 16th century tapestries.

☎ 01752 822236 www.gardensincornwall.co.uk

Mount Edgcumbe Country Park
346 A3

The grounds of Mount Edgcumbe House were developed in the late 18th century to create Cornwall's first landscaped park. The site covers 865 acres (346ha), and as well as the parkland there is a formal area comprising English, French and Italian gardens with the addition of two new gardens to celebrate the family's past links with Australia and America. The park also holds the National Collection of Camellias. There are attractive pathways through the grounds with fine sea views.

☎ 01752 822236 www.gardensincornwall.co.uk

Museum of Costume
388 D1

A sumptuous display, arguably one of the best in the world, of more than 150 figures in original costumes and accessories, from the 16th century to the present day. Housed in the grandly decorated Assembly Rooms (to which entry is free), there is an excellent audio guide to the museum.

☎ 01225 428126 www.museumofcostume.co.uk

National Marine Aquarium
407 C3

Displayed on three floors, the visitor is taken through a range of reconstructed habitats, from the start of a moorland stream through estuarine and coastal environments to the ocean depths. An engrossing array of aquatic species can be seen, from the bizarre to the beautiful, and there are displays, talks and presentations providing information on the species themselves and the environments, sometimes threatened, that they inhabit.

A new venture has been the sinking of the ex-Royal Navy frigate, *HMS Scylla*, in Whitsand Bay to form an offshore reef. The aim is to study its colonisation by marine life and this can be viewed via underwater camera technology from the aquarium.

This is an exceptionally well-thought-out attraction designed to inform the public about marine habitats.

☎ 01752 600301 www.national-aquarium.co.uk

National Marine Aquarium

National Maritime Museum Cornwall
145 F3

In a striking building which dominates the quayside, this museum is devoted to the sea, boats and their importance in people's lives, with particular emphasis on Cornwall.

☎ 01326 313388 www.nmmc.co.uk

National Maritime Museum

National Waterways Museum
399 B1

200 years of Britain's waterway heritage is exhibited over 3 floors of this historic listed warehouse built in 1873. There are many interesting displays, as well as trips along the canal. The entrance to the museum is in the form of a replica lock chamber complete with dripping water.

☎ 01452 318200 www.nwm.org.uk

Newark Park (NT)
181 G3

A Tudor hunting lodge originally built in around 1550 which was converted into a castellated house by James Wyatt at the end of the 18th century. Limited opening from April to October, but also open weekends in February for an impressive display of snowdrops.

☎ 01453 842644 www.nationaltrust.org.uk

Newquay Zoo
146 C3

The chance to see a wide range of exotic species, housed where possible in natural enclosures. Traditional zoo activities such as feeding displays and children's farm are combined with a special emphasis on wildlife conservation and the associated breeding programme for endangered species.

☎ 01637 873342 www.newquayzoo.co.uk

No. 1 Royal Crescent
167 E1

The first to be built in Royal Crescent in 1768, this imposing Palladian town house has been meticulously restored complete with authentic furnishings and pictures.

☎ 01225 428126 www.bath-preservation-trust.org.uk

Owlpen Manor
182 A3

Bought by the Mander family in 1974, since when the 16th century manor house and estate have been revived and restored. The formal gardens comprise seven hanging terraces dating back to the 16th and 17th centuries and the estate has walks through beech and bluebell woods. The house contains wall paintings, family portraits and Cotswold arts and crafts. There is also a resident ghost, Queen Margaret of Anjou, wife of Henry VI, who stayed here prior to his defeat at Tewkesbury.

☎ 01453 860261 www.owlpen.com

Paignton & Dartmouth Steam Railway
151 E2

A delightful 7 mile (11km) trip from Paignton to Kingswear which gives breathtaking views of Lyme Bay and the Devon coast before passing through woodland along the Dart estuary. It is possible to turn this into a day excursion by taking the passenger ferry from Kingswear to Dartmouth followed by a river trip to Totnes and bus back to Paignton. A 'Round Robin' ticket is available for this.

☎ 01803 555872 www.paignton-steamrailway.co.uk

Paignton Zoo
151 E2

Set in 75 acres (30ha) of attractive surroundings with the emphasis on natural habitats and endangered species conservation, this well organised zoo is home to over 1300 animals and birds. A range of feeding activities and other events takes place every day and in addition there is a miniature railway, playground and animal education centre.

☎ 01803 697500 www.paigntonzoo.org.uk

Painswick Rococo Garden
182 A1

Restoration of the heavily overgrown garden in the 1980s was inspired by a painting by local artist Thomas Robins which showed the 6 acre (2.5ha) site in its original 18th century layout. February sees a spectacular display of snowdrops.

☎ 01452 813204 www.rococogarden.co.uk

Pencarrow
147 E2

A grand, family-owned Georgian mansion with splendid collections of furniture, porcelain and pictures. The 50 acre (20ha) grounds comprise fine formal and woodland gardens with waymarked walks and over 700 varieties of rhododendron giving a spectacular display in spring. The woodland contains a large number of Monkey Puzzle trees – the name is said to have originated here after a guest scraped his hand on one and commented: 'It would puzzle a monkey.'

☎ 01208 841369 www.pencarrow.co.uk

Pendennis Castle
145 F3

This formed part of the coastal defences set up by Henry VIII in response to the threat of war from France and Spain following his divorce from Catherine of Aragon. Occupying a superb site on a headland overlooking the entrance to Carrick Roads, the castle consists of a round tower and gate surrounded by a lower curtain wall. A further outer defence was added by Elizabeth I, but the castle was only attacked during the Civil War when it was besieged by Parliamentarians for five months. A Discovery Centre incorporates interactive displays on the castle's history.

☎ 01326 316594 www.english-heritage.org.uk

Plymouth Dome
407 C2

A visitor centre using multimedia technology to trace the city's history and maritime connections, with breathtaking views of Plymouth Sound from the observation galleries.

☎ 01752 603300 www.plymouthdome.info

Porthcurno Sands
144 A4

A beautiful stretch of clean, silvery sand makes this amongst the best of Cornwall's beaches. Exhilarating walks along the coastal path to the east lead to Treryn Dinas, one of the most spectacular of the Cornish headlands, crowned by the precarious Logan Stone.

Portland Castle
154 C5

A well preserved example of Henry VIII's coastal fortresses overlooking Portland Harbour. Although not seeing action until the 17th century, when it was seized by both Parliamentarians and Royalists, the castle has always had a significant role in coastal defence, being a seaplane station in World War I and heavily involved in D-Day preparations in World War II.

☎ 01305 820539 www.english-heritage.org.uk

Powderham Castle
152 C4

Home to the Courtenay family since 1390, the castle lies in a beautiful setting in a 4000 acre (1600ha) estate on the River Exe estuary. The state rooms are richly decorated and furnished and the marble hall is also of interest, containing a 13ft (4.5m) long case clock.

The grounds provide a variety of activities, including woodland walks, working blacksmith and wheelwright, and children's secret garden.

☎ 01626 890243 www.powderham.co.uk

Prinknash Abbey & Park
182 A1

Around 30 monks live at the abbey which was not completed until 1972. The abbey buildings extend to over 300 acres (120ha) and include the workshops and the old abbey of St Peter's Grange. The surrounding Bird and Deer Park has a children's castle, a Tudor wendy house, aviaries, ponds and lakes, and an abundance of deer, geese, cranes and peacocks.

☎ 01452 812066 www.prinknash-bird-and-deerpark.com

Prior Park (NT)
167 E1

A magnificent location on a hillside to the south of Bath provides the 18th century mansion of Prior Park with splendid panoramic views of the city and surrounding countryside. The delightful landscape garden was created by local businessman Ralph Allen, with input from the poet Alexander Pope and Lancelot 'Capability' Brown. The house is now a school and not open to the public. There is no parking, but a frequent bus service runs from the city centre.

☎ 01225 833422 www.nationaltrust.org.uk

Putlake Adventure Farm
155 F5

An unpretentious farm attraction particularly suitable for younger children, hosting a whole range of activities.

☎ 01929 422917 www.putlakefarm.co.uk

Quince Honey Farm
164 A5

One of the largest honey farms in Britain, with over 1500 hives spread across Devon and Exmoor. In the exhibition area honey bees can be observed at close range, nesting in a variety of man-made and natural habitats as well as in state-of-the-art observation hives.

A wide range of honey-based products is available at the centre's shop.

☎ 01769 572401 www.quincehoney.co.uk

Red Lodge
391 B1

Elizabethan house dating from 1590, substantially modernised around 1730 and now furnished to represent both periods. The highlight is the Great Oak Room with its magnificent oak panels and splendid carved stone chimneypiece.

☎ 0117 921 1360 www.bristol-city.gov.uk

Ridgeway, The

This ancient trackway, formerly used by drovers, traders and occasionally invaders, has been in use for at least 5000 years. There is much evidence of prehistoric occupation in the surrounding area in

the form of burial mounds and hill forts, and there is a particularly memorable stretch taking in Wayland's Smithy, Uffington Castle and the adjacent White Horse. The track runs from Overton Hill near Avebury along the north edge of the Marlborough and Berkshire Downs, crosses the Thames at Goring and continues along the west edge of the Chiltern Hills to Ivinghoe Beacon. The plant life is of special interest as, in some areas, the characteristic, and increasingly rare chalk grassland can still be seen. The bird and insect life is also worthy of note.

Roche Chapel
147 D3

Remains of a 14th century chapel perched on a rocky outcrop on the site of what is thought to be an early Christian hermit's cell.

Roman Baths & Pump Room
388 E2

One of the outstanding Roman sites in Britain, founded in the first century AD for pilgrims visiting the sacred hot springs of the temple to Sulis Minerva. After the Romans left, the site fell into disrepair although the town continued to grow, but by the early 17th century the springs were again attracting interest. A visit in 1702 by Queen Anne further encouraged this interest and by 1720 the town was becoming a highly fashionable spa. Further development in the 19th century led to the uncovering and preservation of the Roman site.

As far back as 10,000 years ago the hot springs had generated human attention as a source of healing. The magnificent Roman complex used lead pipes to conduct the water to a series of bathing rooms which have now been excavated and can be visited, together with the temple remains, hypocausts and cold plunges, aided by an audio guide.

The elegant Pump Room (free entry) was the headquarters of fashionable 18th century society and the visitor can emulate this by taking the waters, or less adventurously, morning coffee or afternoon tea.

☎ 01225 477785 www.romanbaths.co.uk

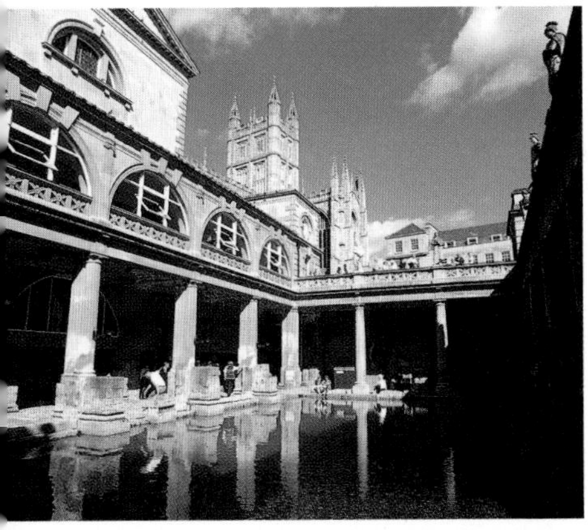

Roman Baths & Pump Room – Bath

Rosemoor
163 F4

A regional centre for the Royal Horticultural Society (RHS), second only to the gardens at Wisley in importance. Originally 8 acres (3ha), the garden was given to the RHS and a further 32 acres (13ha) was added. The surrounding woodland has been purchased to provide an attractive natural backdrop.

Many rare and interesting plants flourish here, and the woodland garden is considered to be particularly lovely. Other areas of interest include the Rose Garden with 2000 roses in around 200 varieties, stream and bog gardens, colour theme gardens and a kitchen garden.

☎ 01805 624067 www.rhs.org.uk

Russell-Cotes Art Gallery & Museum
389 F2

This museum houses a combination of the exotic and eclectic in a rather extravagant Italianate villa, built as a testament to the worldly success of Sir Merton Russell-Cotes, who gave it to the town of Bournemouth in 1922, complete with artworks and a notable collection of late 19th century furniture.

☎ 01202 451858 www.russell-cotes.bournemouth.gov.uk

S.S. Great Britain
352 B3

Built in Bristol by Isambard Kingdom Brunel in 1843, this is the world's first (and only surviving) ocean-going, iron hulled steam ship driven by a screw propellor. Designed as a passenger vessel for the North Atlantic crossing, she subsequently carried 15,000 migrants to Australia, 40,000 troops to the Crimea, and coal to California, but ended up abandoned in the Falkland Islands. In 1970 she was returned to Bristol, to the same dry dock where she was built. The dockside museum tells the history of this remarkable ship.

☎ 0117 926 0680 www.ss-great-britain.com

St Just in Roseland
145 F3

Although architecturally the church is not of special interest, it has an enchanting waterside setting and a steeply sloping graveyard described by John Betjeman as 'Perhaps the most beautiful churchyard on Earth' with its profusion of palms and subtropical shrubs.

St Mawes Castle
145 F3

Located on a headland on the east side of the Carrick Roads, this castle was built to defend against a possible French and Spanish invasion following Henry VIII's divorce from Catherine of Aragon and is an excellent example of Tudor military architecture. Captured by Parliamentarians in 1646, with far less trouble than its neighbour Pendennis, it was not re-fortified until the early 20th century, when it formed part of the coastal defences for World Wars I and II.

☎ 01326 270526 www.english-heritage.org.uk

St Michael's Mount (NT)
144 C3

Dramatic granite island accessible on foot via a causeway at low tide and by ferry at other times. Although generally accepted as a place of spiritual significance, the original settlement on the island may have been a late Iron Age port. The 5th century saw the start of the mount's importance as a place of pilgrimage, when legend has it that a group of fishermen had a vision of St Michael. A Benedictine monastery was founded on the summit in 1135, and following the Dissolution of the Monasteries by Henry VIII the ruins of the building were incorporated into a castle.

The steep slopes of the mount are clothed in subtropical vegetation, and a unique maritime garden of some 20 acres (8ha) has been developed on terraces. The 200ft (60m) ascent to the castle via the cobbled Pilgrims' Steps is quite steep in places, but is well worth it for the spectacular views. The castle itself contains displays of weaponry and other militaria, period furniture, paintings and miniatures.

☎ 01736 710507 www.nationaltrust.org.uk

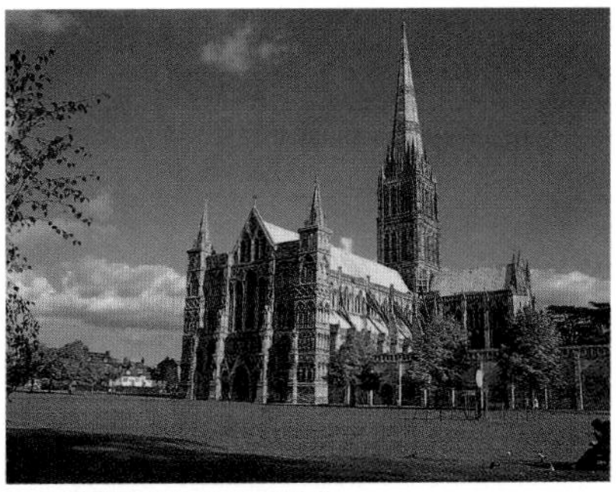

Salisbury Cathedral

Salisbury Cathedral
408 F2

At Salisbury, one of the world's most celebrated spires soars above an Early English masterpiece of a cathedral, the whole comprising a singularly beautiful medieval building which inspired the famous painting by John Constable. Raised between 1220 – 1258, and with the spire added between 1285 – 1315, this comparatively rapid construction led to a remarkable conformity of style, characterised by slender Purbeck marble pillars, narrow pointed arches and high vaulting.

Inside, the cathedral is relatively austere following a sprucing up by James Wyatt in the 18th century. Treasures include one of the world's oldest working clocks dating from the 14th century, and the largest cloisters in England lead to the beautiful octagonal chapter house which contains one of the four surviving original versions of Magna Carta, considered the best preserved.

The exceptional spire, at 404ft (123m) the tallest in Britain, rests on foundations only 6ft (2m) deep. Guided tours take visitors 332 steps up the tower to the base of the spire and give splendid views over the city.

The cathedral is set in a delightful, large Close which itself contains some memorable buildings, many dating from the 18th century.

☎ 01722 555120 www.salisburycathedral.org.uk

Saltram House (NT)
346 B2

A former Tudor house redeveloped as a splendid Georgian mansion set in a landscaped park overlooking the Plym estuary. Many of the original contents remain and there are significant pieces by Chippendale and Wedgwood as well as several portraits by Sir Joshua Reynolds, who lived locally. There is some notable work by Robert Adam, and a magnificent 18th century Axminster carpet. There is also an interesting period kitchen, formal gardens and woodland walks.

☎ 01752 333500 www.nationaltrust.org.uk

Sherborne Castle
154 C1

A splendid Tudor mansion built by Sir Walter Raleigh in 1594 and subsequently extended in the 17th and 18th centuries by the Digby family who have owned it since 1617. The state rooms show a range of decorative styles from the 16th to 19th centuries and there are excellent collections of furniture and fine arts.

The grounds are considered to be amongst the finest to be created by Lancelot 'Capability' Brown, with a 50 acre (20ha) lake and magnificent specimen trees. The 20 acre (8ha) garden has delightful drifts of spring bulbs, colourful summer borders and striking autumn colour. Within the grounds are the remnants of a Norman castle destroyed in the Civil War.

☎ 01935 813182 www.sherbornecastle.com

Silbury Hill
168 B1

Constructed around 2500BC, probably using some of the chalk rubble excavated from Avebury, this is thought to be the highest man-made mound in Europe at 130ft (40m). It is estimated that it would have taken 1000 men 10 years to build. No archaeological excavations have ever discovered anything of significance in the mound and its purpose has never been satisfactorily explained.

Unfortunately, continuous wear and tear by people climbing the mound has meant that access is now prohibited.

Slimbridge Wildfowl & Wetlands Trust
181 G2

Originated in 1946 by Sir Peter Scott, Slimbridge is the centre of the Wildfowl and Wetlands Trust (WWT) and has become one of the most important wildfowl and wetland conservation centres in the world. 800 acres (320ha) contain species from all over the world, including the rare Hawaiian Goose (Ne Ne) which has been returned to its native habitat because of the success of the breeding project at Slimbridge. The informative visitor centre gives an insight into the birds that make Slimbridge their home, including the largest collection of ducks, geese and swans in the world. There are also sculpture trails, an art gallery and events throughout the year. Winter sees thousands of wild geese feeding in the Severn Estuary which can be viewed from the observation tower.

☎ 01453 890333 www.wwt.org.uk

Slimbridge Wildfowl & Wetlands Trust

Snowshill Manor (NT)
196 C4

In 1919 Charles Wade bought the ruined manor with its 14 acres (5.5ha) of land which he set about restoring using traditional skills. The renovated manor was used as a storage area for the enormous variety of artefacts collected from all over the world. Wade actually lived in the small cottage in the grounds. The tranquil organic gardens give lovely views across the surrounding Cotswold countryside.

☎ 01386 852410 www.nationaltrust.org.uk

South Devon Railway
151 D1

This scenic steam railway winds its way along 7 miles (10.5km) of the Dart valley between Buckfastleigh and Totnes on a former Great Western Railway branch line. On site at Buckfastleigh there is a small museum and the chance to see the restoration of some of the rolling stock. There are also model railway exhibits, a children's play area and riverside walks.

☎ 01364 643338 www.southdevonrailway.org

Stapehill Abbey Crafts & Garden
347 B1

A 19th century Cistercian abbey, now used for a variety of craft workshops. The attractive 30 acre (12ha) gardens are home to many rare and unusual species and include a striking Japanese Garden.

The Countryside Museum has exhibits on social and agricultural history and an assortment of village shops, and Home Farm has a selection of farm animals to be viewed.

☎ 01202 861686

STEAM Museum of the Great Western Railway
412 A1

A fascinating museum on the restored site of the former Swindon Railway Works, as much concerned with the lives of the thousands of employees and passengers of the Great Western Railway (GWR) as with the locomotives themselves. Hands-on exhibits and ingenious displays trace the history of the GWR and give an insight into the skills and dedication of the railway workers in every aspect of the enterprise, from Isambard Kingdom Brunel's initial inspiration onwards.

☎ 01793 466646 www.steam-museum.org.uk

Stembridge Tower Mill (NT)
166 B4

Located in a prominent position overlooking the Somerset Levels, this is the last remaining thatched windmill in England. It was built in 1822 and remained in operation until 1910.

☎ 01458 250818 www.nationaltrust.org.uk

Stoke sub Hamdon Priory (NT)
154 A1

A group of buildings, the remains of a chantry built for a provost and four chaplains in the 14th century by the Beauchamp family. The complex consists of a Great Hall, the only part open to the public, private rooms and a range of outbuildings.

☎ 01985 843600 www.nationaltrust.org.uk

Stonehenge
168 C3

An awe-inspiring prehistoric monument constructed in stages between about 5000 and 3000 years ago, now designated a World Heritage Site. The original purpose is uncertain, but suggestions include an astronomical observatory, temple or other sacred site.

Stonehenge was originally a simple bank and ditch excavated by tools made of antler, wood and bone. Some centuries later an inner stone circle was added, though not completed, using bluestones from the Prescelly Mountains in Pembrokeshire. Subsequent modification led to the central altar stone being surrounded by an inner horseshoe of rearranged bluestones and an outer sarsen horseshoe. The final, and major building phase around 1500BC brought massive sarsen stones of up to 50 tons (56 tonnes) from the Marlborough Downs 20 miles (32km) away. These were erected and capped by stone lintels to make a continuous outer ring. The central axis aligns with the point of sunrise on Midsummer Day, giving credence, without supporting evidence, to the idea of Stonehenge as an astronomical calendar.

Today, Stonehenge is effectively an impressive ruin, stones having fallen or been used in the past as a surreptitious resource for other local building projects. Visitors cannot generally walk among the stones, but the site is very atmospheric and views of the stones, particularly near dawn or dusk, are breathtaking.

☎ 01980 624715 www.english-heritage.org.uk

Stourhead (NT)
167 E4

Unlike most estates, where the house takes pride of place, here the 2600 acres (1052ha) of grounds are by far the superior draw, providing an exceptional example of the English landscape garden.

The house, built in 1721 by Colen Campbell for the banker Henry Hoare, is an elegant example of Palladian architecture and contains some good early Chippendale furniture and choice paintings.

Henry Hoare's son, also Henry, designed the garden after returning from a Grand Tour in 1741, his purpose being to emulate scenes from paintings by Poussin and other European landscape artists. The centrepiece, a magnificent lake, was formed by damming the River Stour. The rhododendrons, for which the garden is famed in spring, were a later addition.

King Alfred's Tower, the 150ft (46m) red brick folly at the far end of the estate, provides magnificent views across the grounds and surrounding countryside (open summer afternoons only).

☎ 01747 841152 www.nationaltrust.org.uk

Stuart Line Cruises
152 D4

A family run firm based in Exmouth offering a variety of cruises either in the sheltered Exe estuary or along the coast to Sidmouth, Teignmouth or Torbay. A great opportunity to view the unique south Devon coastal scenery from the sea.

☎ 01395 222144 www.stuartlinecruises.co.uk

Studland Heath (NT)
155 G4

This National Nature Reserve on the Isle of Purbeck covers around 1500 acres (631ha) and supports a variety of habitats including heathland, bog and sand dunes. A central feature is the Little Sea, an acidic freshwater lake around which are four hides to observe wintering wildfowl. Another significant area to the west of the reserve is Godlingston Heath, a large tract of lowland heath with populations of all six British species of reptile and the rare Dartford Warbler. Wading birds can be seen on coastal sites and the area is notable for its insect population, particularly dragonflies and butterflies. Footpaths, nature trails, birdwatching hides and leaflets provide access and information for the visitor. There is a parking charge.

☎ 01929 450259 www.nationaltrust.org.uk

Sudeley Castle
196 C5

Once owned by Ethelred the Unready, and more famously home to Katherine Parr, the sixth wife of Henry VIII, Sudeley was a victim of Cromwell's destruction and lay derelict for over 200 years until the ambitious restoration project was started in 1837. There are themed exhibitions, impressive furniture and paintings from such artists as Rubens, Van Dyck and Turner. Ten distinct gardens covering 14 acres (5.5ha) surround the castle and feature a ruined 15th century Tithe Barn. The tomb of Katherine Parr lies in the 15th century St Mary's Church.

☎ 01242 602308 www.sudeleycastle.co.uk

Stonehenge

Swanage Railway 155 G5

A 6 mile (10km) stretch of standard-gauge steam railway running between Swanage and Norden on a trip lasting 25 minutes. The route passes through lovely countryside, including the spectacular ruins of Corfe Castle. A variety of special events takes place throughout the year.

☎ 01929 425800 www.swanagerailway.co.uk

Tank Museum 155 E4

With exhibits ranging from 'Little Willie', the first tank ever built in 1915, to the British Army's most recent 'Challenger 2', this museum contains one of the world's most impressive collections of armoured fighting vehicles. In school holidays, 'Tanks in Action!' displays take place.

☎ 01929 405096 www.tankmuseum.co.uk

Tate St Ives 144 C2

In a splendid location above Porthmeor beach, this art gallery displays work by modern British artists in both permanent and temporary exhibitions. The building itself is quite distinctive and has received several awards for its architecture.

☎ 01736 796226 www.tate.org.uk

Tintagel Castle 148 A2

A dramatic clifftop location gives this extensive, ruined medieval castle spectacular views along the north Cornish coast. Situated on a promontory approached via a narrow neck of land, such an excellent defensive site is likely to have been in use from much earlier times, and Iron Age, Celtic and Roman occupations have been suggested. This lengthy history of occupancy, coupled with the windswept, romantic atmosphere, has helped enhance the idea of Tintagel as the legendary castle of King Arthur.

☎ 01840 770328 www.english-heritage.org.uk

Tintagel Old Post Office 147 E1

Delightful 14th century manor house in the village centre, one room of which was used as a post office in the 19th century.

☎ 01840 770024 www.nationaltrust.org.uk

Tintinhull House (NT) 154 B1

Lovely, colourful formal garden of 1.5 acres (0.5 ha) developed around a 17th century manor house by Phyllis Reiss between 1933 – 61. The planting scheme, influenced by the style of Hidcote, is divided into seven 'rooms', each with its own theme but integrating sympathetically with the others. The house is not open to the public.

☎ 01935 822545 www.nationaltrust.org.uk

Tiverton Castle 152 C1

Although Norman in origin, only the tower and gatehouse remain; the remainder has been much altered, depicting a range of architectural styles. There are attractive gardens and an especially good collection of Civil War arms and armour. Limited opening outside July and August.

☎ 01884 253200 www.tivertoncastle.com

Tiverton Museum 152 C1

A mid 19th century school houses what is probably the largest social history collection in the south west.

☎ 01884 256295 www.tivertonmuseum.org.uk

Torre Abbey 412 E1

Founded in 1196, but partly destroyed during the Dissolution of the Monasteries in 1539, only fragments of the original buildings remain, including the medieval barn and gatehouse. It was converted to a country house and then substantially remodelled in the 19th century and now belongs to the local council, serving in part as a museum and art gallery. There are collections of silver, glass, maritime paintings, Pre-Raphaelite and 20th century art and a room devoted to Agatha Christie memorabilia. Access is free to the grounds which include palm and cactus houses.

☎ 01803 293593 www.torre-abbey.org.uk

Trebah Garden 145 E4

A subtropical garden of 25 acres (10ha) developed in a steep, wooded ravine which conjures up a jungle atmosphere. It is particularly noted for its tree ferns and palms, blue and white hydrangeas and 100 year old rhododendrons. The gardens descend over 200ft (60m) to a private beach on the Helford River estuary.

☎ 01326 250448 www.trebah-gardens.co.uk

Trelissick (NT) 145 F3

A lovely woodland park of around 370 acres (148ha) with magnificent views across the Fal estuary. As with many Cornish coastal gardens, tender and exotic plants flourish, but Trelissick is especially noted for its magnolias, camellias and hydrangeas. The house is not open to the public.

☎ 01872 862090 www.nationaltrust.org.uk

Trengwainton (NT) 144 B3

A garden of interest throughout the year, but especially in spring and early summer, with splendid displays of magnolias, camellias and rhododendrons. Many of the plants found here were brought back from Frank Kingdom Ward's plant hunting expedition in the 1920s. A series of walled gardens contain unusual species particularly suited to the mild climate, and the stream garden in particular is a feast of colour with its primulas, lysichitums and lilies. Superb coastal views can be seen from the restored terrace over Mounts Bay and the Lizard.

☎ 01736 363148 www.nationaltrust.org.uk

Trerice (NT) 146 C4

An attractive Elizabethan manor house considered to be something of an architectural gem with its detailed plaster ceilings, splendid fireplaces and distinctive gabling following the Dutch style. Furnishings include a range of oak and walnut furniture, unusual clocks, embroideries and paintings. The pleasant grounds are planted with an eye for colour and foliage, and the former stables house a small museum tracing the development and history of the lawnmower.

☎ 01637 875404 www.nationaltrust.org.uk

Tresco Abbey Gardens 146 A1

From acacias to agaves, and palms to proteas, these marvellous subtropical gardens, located on the site of a former abbey founded in AD964, contain an amazing variety of plants. The garden was developed between 1843 – 72 by Augustus Smith, who enhanced the naturally mild climate by building tall windbreaks to shelter the site from the worst of the weather.

The site also incorporates the Valhalla Museum of ships' figureheads.

☎ 01720 424105 www.tresco.co.uk

Trewithen 146 D5

Outstanding woodland garden created by George Johnstone in the first half of the 20th century. Covering around 30 acres (12ha), the gardens are particularly famous for their splendid collections of magnolias, camellias and rhododendrons. The attractive, early Georgian house is open to the public for a limited period in summer.

☎ 01726 883647 www.trewithengardens.co.uk

Truro Cathedral 146 C5

The first cathedral in Britain to be consecrated since the Reformation, this beautiful neogothic building was designed by John Loughborough Pearson and completed in 1910. It was built on the site of St Mary's Parish Church (consecrated in 1259), and part of the old building was incorporated into the new cathedral which has a commanding central location in the city. The Victorian stained glass windows are considered amongst the finest in the world, and other notable features include the Father Willis organ and an excellent collection of Victorian embroidery.

☎ 01872 276782 www.trurocathedral.org.uk

Tyntesfield (NT) 181 E5

A splendid Victorian house built in the Gothic Revival style, with lots of towers and turrets. The interior has been little altered, and there is an extensive collection of Victorian decorative arts plus a range of domestic offices and a family chapel. The unspoilt 500 acre (200ha) estate comprises parkland, lovely formal gardens with superb views from the terrace, and a delightful kitchen garden. This is a recent acquisition by the National Trust, and is undergoing extensive renovation. Admission is by pre-booked guided tour. It will be some years before the house is fully open. Access is by a park and ride service from Nailsea.

☎ 0870 458 4500 www.nationaltrust.org.uk

Ugbrooke 152 B5

Home to the Clifford family for the past 300 years, this former Tudor mansion was substantially rebuilt by Robert Adam in 1750, the chapel and library wing being particularly characteristic of Adam's style. The house fell into some disrepair in the mid 20th century but has been handsomely and meticulously restored and contains fine displays of furniture, paintings, embroideries and a rare military collection.

The parkland was landscaped by Lancelot 'Capability' Brown and contains many fine specimen trees, while the formal gardens include a box parterre, Spanish garden and lakeside walks.

☎ 01626 852179

Watermouth Castle 163 F1

Built in 1825, this castellated mansion is now a popular family destination with a great range of attractions including mechanical music demonstrations, a maze, cider making and dairy exhibits, and a wide selection of children's rides and play activities.

☎ 01271 863879 www.watermouthcastle.com

Watersmeet House (NT) 164 A3

Former fishing lodge built in 1832 in a beautiful wooded valley at the confluence of Hoar Oak Water and the East Lyn River. It now houses a National Trust information centre and shop, serving as a focus for the many delightful walks in the area.

☎ 01271 850887 www.nationaltrust.org.uk

Wells Cathedral
166 C3

Dominating the centre of Wells, England's smallest city, this has been the site of a religious building since the 8th century. The present cathedral was founded in 1180, but was built in phases over the following 400 years, thus incorporating several different architectural styles. However, the original Saxon font was retained and is still used for baptisms.

The splendid west front, one of the most outstanding façades in the country, was completed in 1250 and accommodates nearly 300 pieces of statuary. Within the magnificent Gothic interior are unusual scissor-shaped arches, constructed as additional support when the combined weight of tower and spire proved too much for the lower stage of the tower. The upper tower and spire were subsequently destroyed by fire and not rebuilt; the lower tower was rebuilt to a height of 182ft (55m), the highest in the county.

Other highlights include the 14th century clock, amongst the oldest in the world, mid 20th century colourful embroideries in the choir, medieval stained glass, and probably the longest medieval library building (168ft, 51m) in England, containing documents which date from the 10th century.

☎ 01749 674483

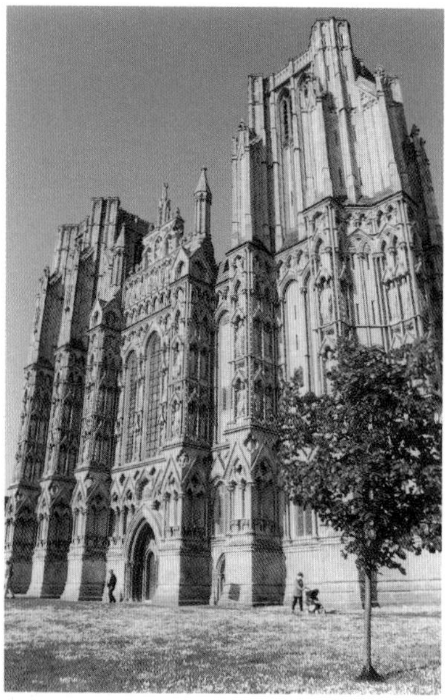

Wells Cathedral

West Kennet Long Barrow
168 C1

Possibly England's finest burial mound, this Neolithic chambered tomb was the site of around 50 burials. Measuring 343ft (105m) by 76ft (23m), the mound's entrance is protected by massive sarsen stones and it is possible to walk into the stone burial chamber a short way into the mound.

www.english-heritage.org.uk

West Somerset Railway
165 E4

At 20 miles (32km), this is one of the longest stretches of preserved steam railway in Britain. It runs along the north Somerset coast from Minehead to Watchet, then continues inland via several small stations to Bishop's Lydeard. The original line continued to Taunton, and there is a bus link for those wishing to complete the journey.

☎ 01643 704996 www.west-somerset-railway.co.uk

Westbury Court (NT)
181 G1

This water garden originated between 1696 and 1705 and was the National Trust's first garden restoration. It is the earliest Dutch water garden remaining in the country and has been planted with species dating back to before 1700. A restored pavilion sits at the head of a long canal bordered by yew hedges, and in the grounds are a walled garden and a Holm oak, said to be the oldest in the country.

☎ 01452 760461 www.nationaltrust.org.uk

Westbury White Horse
167 F2

The chalk downs of central Wiltshire are ideal for these massive hill carvings which are not, as generally assumed, particularly ancient. The Westbury horse is considered the oldest in the county and is perhaps the best sited. It is thought to date from the late 17th century, replacing an earlier one, possibly of Saxon origin. Above the horse is a large Iron Age fort with excellent views.

www.wiltshirewhitehorses.org.uk

Westonbirt – The National Arboretum
182 A3

The Arboretum is now in the care of the Forestry Commission but originates from 1829 when Robert Holford decided to extend his father's estate at Westonbirt. There are 18,000 trees and shrubs from all over the world, many of them rare or endangered, and some of which date back to the original planting, making this one of the finest tree collections in the world. Covering 600 acres (240 ha), it is not only the trees that make Westonbirt special but also the wild flowers, fungi, birds and animals that can be enjoyed along 17 miles (27km) of paths and trails. The displays of rhododendrons, azaleas, magnolias and the wild flowers in the Silk Wood are at their best in May, while autumn sees a spectacular change of colour throughout the gardens. The International Festival of Gardens takes place from June to September.

☎ 01666 880220

Wheal Martyn
147 E4

A fascinating look at the history of the china clay industry on a 26 acre (10ha) site dating from the 1870s and restored in the 1970s. Some areas of the site are still in active production and can be seen from a viewing platform. The visitor centre has displays and exhibits on both the raw materials and finished products of the industry and a trail takes the visitor round the old clay works. The site also contains a nature trail and adventure play area.

☎ 01726 850362 www.wheal-martyn.com

Wilton House
168 B4

Following the Dissolution of the Monasteries, the Benedictine site and land at Wilton were granted by Henry VIII to William Herbert, who incorporated the abbey ruins into a Tudor mansion. After a fire in 1647, Inigo Jones and John Webb redesigned and rebuilt the house in the Palladian style. The chief features of this rebuilding are the state rooms, particularly the Single and Double Cube rooms, so-called because of their precise dimensions, and renowned for their outstanding painted ceilings and elaborate plasterwork. The Double Cube room, arguably the foremost surviving example of a 17th century state room in England, was designed for the exhibition of family portraits by Van Dyck, and these can still be seen in their original setting. Elsewhere in the house there are paintings by Reynolds, Rembrandt, Brueghel, Rubens and Poussin, amongst others, making a collection which is considered one of the finest in Europe.

The 21 acre (8.5ha) grounds, bounded by the Rivers Nadder and Wylye, contain both formal gardens and landscaped parkland. Fine specimen trees can be seen on the woodland walks and there are architectural features such as the well-known Palladian Bridge. Other additions include the Millennium Water Feature and, for younger visitors, an adventure playground.

☎ 01722 746729 www.wiltonhouse.com

Woodchester Mansion
182 A2

A highly unusual place to visit, the mansion was abandoned before completion in 1870 and is in virtually the same state now. Much of the impressive craftsmanship of the time can be seen, something that would not have been possible if the mansion had been finished. Endangered lesser and greater horseshoe bats live in the roof spaces which can be observed by closed-circuit cameras. The mansion is open at weekends during the summer months.

☎ 01453 750455 www.woodchestermansion.org.uk

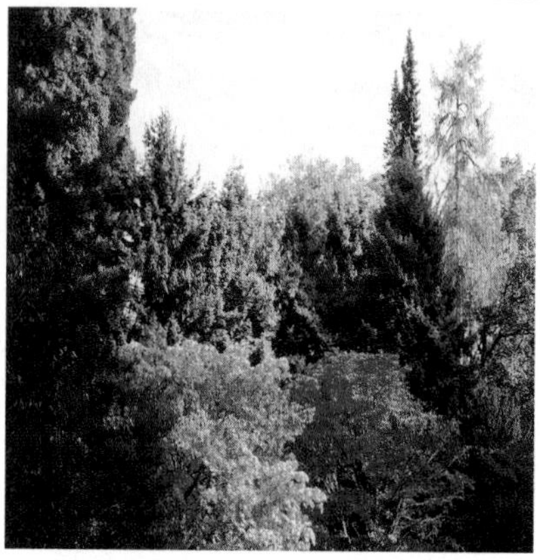

Westonbirt – The National Arboretum

Woodlands Leisure Park
151 E2

One of the biggest indoor activity complexes in the country, including the three-floor Ice Palace, specifically designed for the under sevens. Outdoors comprises 60 acres (24ha) of rides and activities in a wooded valley.

☎ 01803 712598 www.woodlandspark.com

Wookey Hole Caves & Papermill
166 C3

Spectacular caves carved out where underground streams have percolated through carboniferous limestone, gradually dissolving the rock over millions of years. Later precipitation of this dissolved limestone has resulted in striking formations of stalactites and stalagmites, some of which resemble human figures, most notably the Witch of Wookey. The dramatic nature of the caves is emphasised by skilful lighting.

Excavations have demonstrated that the caves were inhabited as long as 30,000 years ago, and tools have been discovered together with bones from species such as woolly rhinoceros, cave lions, mammoths and hyenas. Occupation is thought to have continued until Roman times.

The emerging underground River Axe at Wookey Hole has, in the past, been harnessed to provide water power, initially for woollen mills and subsequently for paper making. Visitors can see this traditional paper making process at the restored paper mill.

☎ 01749 672243 www.wookey.co.uk

SOUTH EAST ENGLAND

This appealing corner of England is alive with attractive market towns, quaint villages, historical stately homes, beautiful gardens and huge, strategically sited castles. Here, the wooded Weald and the green sward of the South Downs lead down to the Channel coast with its small traditional harbours and large bustling shipping ports. From Europe this is often the gateway to England, giving visitors the opportunity to acquaint themselves with the foibles and idiosyncrasies of Britain in one of its most pleasant and verdant regions.

Bodiam Castle

Alfriston Clergy House (NT) 160 A3

A thatched, half-timbered 14th century Wealden Hall House with a pretty cottage garden. It was the first historic building acquired by the National Trust in 1896, purchased for a nominal £10. The house is oak framed and infilled with wattle and daub. One of the beams has a carving of an oak leaf which some believe gave rise to the adoption of the National Trust's famous logo.

☎ 01323 870001 www.nationaltrust.org.uk

Amberley Museum 158 C2

This 36 acre (14.5ha) open-air museum, occupying a former chalk quarry, is dedicated to south east England's industrial past, also featuring various craftspeople demonstrating their skills. Visitors can travel around the site by vintage bus and narrow-gauge railway.

☎ 01798 831370 www.amberleymuseum.co.uk

Arundel Castle 158 C3

Situated on a hill with views over the River Arun and out to sea, this castle is an impressive sight, dominating the nearby town with its towers and battlements. The castle began life at the end of the 11th century with the building of the motte. The gatehouse dates from 1070, but most of the rest is 19th century.

Arundel Castle is the ancestral home of the Dukes of Norfolk, who have played an important role in English history, the third duke being the uncle of both Anne Boleyn and Catherine Howard, wives of Henry VIII.

Within the castle there are fine collections of paintings by Van Dyck, Gainsborough, as well as 16th century furniture, tapestries, clocks and armour. The magnificent grounds include a Victorian kitchen and flower gardens. The Fitzalan Chapel is worth a visit.

☎ 01903 882173 www.arundelcastle.org

Arundel Castle

Ascott (NT) 199 D5

This was formerly a half-timbered 17th century farmhouse but was much altered and enlarged when it came into the ownership of the de Rothschild family in 1876. The outstanding art collection contains paintings by Gainsborough, Rubens, Hogarth and some of the Dutch masters, whilst there is also some notable Chinese porcelain and Chippendale furniture. Outside the grounds extend to some 260 acres (104ha) with fine specimen trees, herbaceous borders, a Dutch garden and an unusual topiary sundial.

☎ 01296 688242 www.nationaltrust.org.uk

Ashdown House (NT) 183 E4

Built in the 1660s in an isolated location high up on the Berkshire Downs, this is an unusual Dutch style house constructed from local dressed chalk blocks. It was probably designed by William Winde who spent his formative years in Holland with Royalist exiles, and who may well have been influenced by the French architect Francois Mansart who built a strikingly similar chateau in Normandy.

Public access is restricted to the hall, the impressive staircase and the cupola leading on to the roof, from where there are wonderful views. There are attractive woodland walks on the estate.

☎ 01793 762209 www.nationaltrust.org.uk

Ashmolean Museum 406 B2

Claiming to be Britain's first museum, the Ashmolean opened in 1683, displaying a collection of natural history specimens assembled by the Tradescant family. Although chiefly famed for their horticultural expertise, the Tradescants were wide-ranging and idiosyncratic collectors, their acquisitions including not only natural history items but, amongst many others, a picture made from feathers, the Passion of Christ carved on a plum stone and a hat band of snake bones. The collection was transferred to the ownership of Elias Ashmole who presented it to Oxford University. In the late 19th century, it was rehoused in the magnificent neoclassical building which is its present home. It was subsequently merged with the university's art collection.

☎ 01865 278000 www.ashmol.ox.ac.uk

Basildon Park (NT) 184 B5

Handsome late 18th century Palladian mansion with impressive classical façade, built of Bath stone and salvaged from neglect in the mid 20th century. The richly decorated interior contains some fine plasterwork, the Shell Room, with its unusual collection of sea shells, and a striking Octagon Room. Waymarked walks can be taken through the 400 acres (160ha) of attractive parkland and there are small but colourful formal gardens.

☎ 0118 984 3040 www.nationaltrust.org.uk

Bateman's (NT) 160 B1

This attractive 17th century stone-built house was home to Rudyard Kipling from 1902 to 1936, with many of the rooms kept as Kipling left them. The delightful gardens contain a water mill.

☎ 01435 882302 www.nationaltrust.org.uk

Battle Abbey 160 C2

Partially ruined abbey on the site of the Battle of Hastings, traditionally said to have been founded by William the Conqueror in 1070 to atone for the terrible loss of life incurred during the conquest of England. The gatehouse, built circa 1338, is the best preserved part of the abbey. Supposedly, the altar was located on the very spot where Harold II died.

☎ 01424 773792 www.english-heritage.org.uk

Bayham Abbey 173 F5

Now an impressive ruin, located in a pretty wooded valley, Bayham Abbey was founded around the turn of the 12th century, and built from local golden sandstone. During the 18th century the site was landscaped to create the effect of a 'romantic' ruin.

☎ 01892 890381

Beachy Head 160 A4

Forming an abrupt termination of the South Downs, the 535ft (163m) high chalk cliffs at Beachy Head are an awe-inspiring sight, dwarfing the lighthouse on the rocks below. Spectacular panoramic views are on offer.

Beale Park 184 B5

Gilbert Beale had a passion for birds, to the extent that his favourite peahen would accompany him round the estate in his Rolls Royce. Now, nearly 50 years later, this superb collection of birds has grown considerably and the park has an impressive record with rare species, both with breeding and returning them to the wild.

The site, on the banks of the River Thames, covers around 400 acres (160ha) of parkland and ancient watermeadow, and boasts a remarkable array of aviaries. There are also rare breeds of farm animals, adventure play areas, a deer park, meerkat enclosure, maze and narrow-gauge railway. Boat trips can be taken on the river, and special events take place in school holidays.

☎ 0118 984 5172 www.bealepark.co.uk

Beaulieu Abbey 348 A4

The name 'Beaulieu' is thought to derive from the Saxon 'beo ley' or bee meadow, subsequently interpreted as 'beau lieu' or beautiful place by the Norman scribes of the Domesday Book. The Cistercian abbey was founded here by King John in 1204 and built with stone brought in from the Isle of Wight and Caen in Normandy. The estate of 10,000 acres (4000ha) was a wealthy one and consequently a magnificent abbey was built. This was subsequently ruined during the Dissolution of the Monasteries, the monks' refectory being converted to form the parish church. The cloister is the best preserved part of the abbey, while the Domus, or lay brothers' dwelling, remained entire and now houses an excellent exhibition on life in the medieval abbey. The remaining stone was removed to build coastal defences at Southsea Castle.

☎ 01590 614604 www.beaulieu.co.uk

Beaulieu Palace House 348 A4

Following the Dissolution of the Monasteries, Beaulieu Abbey estate was sold to the Earl of Southampton, an ancestor of the current owner, Lord Montagu. The Palace House was built in the 19th century around the abbey gatehouse, producing a curious combination of 14th century Gothic, as seen in the fan vaulted ceilings, and Baronial style Victorian architecture. Inside can be seen family portraits and other treasures of the Montagu family.

☎ 01590 614604 www.beaulieu.co.uk

Bedgebury National Pinetum 173 G5

Covering 320 acres (129.5ha) in an attractive landscaped valley setting, the pinetum has over 6000 trees including vulnerable and endangered species. The pinetum was first established as the National Conifer Collection in 1925.

☎ 01580 211044 www.bedgeburypinetum.org.uk

Bekonscot Model Village 185 E3

This is a 1930s re-creation of Britain in miniature. A pleasantly landscaped site of more than 40,000sq ft (3716sq m) boasts scaled down models of villages, farms, churches, castles, and even a zoo and a racecourse, together with a working coal mine, fishing port and steam fair. There is also a model railway with 7000ft (2100m) of track.

☎ 01494 672919 www.bekonscot.com

Bembridge Windmill (NT) 157 F4

Built around 1700 and in use until 1913, this is the only surviving windmill on the Isle of Wight. It contains a complete set of restored wooden machinery, most of it original.

☎ 01983 873945 www.nationaltrust.org.uk

Bentley Wildfowl & Motor Museum 159 G2

The Bentley estate is centred on a Palladian style mansion containing some fine furnishings and paintings. Surrounding the house are formal gardens using yew hedging to create 'outside rooms', and a large waterfowl collection including ducks, geese, swans and flamingos in an attractive natural setting of trees, lakes and ponds. The motor museum has over 100 exhibits including veteran, vintage and classic cars, and motorcycles.

☎ 01825 840573 www.bentley.org.uk

Birdworld 170 D3

Sufficient birds of all shapes, sizes, colours and habits for even the most demanding of ornithologists, displayed in 26 acres (10ha) of carefully designed grounds. There is an established breeding programme, particularly with the Humboldt penguins, making the peak of the breeding season in May and June a good time to visit, but there is plenty to see at other times, including Underwater World with aquarium and alligator swamp.

☎ 01420 22140 www.birdworld.co.uk

Bishop's Palace 157 E1

The impressive ruins of the medieval seat of the Bishops of Winchester, set in wooded grounds. The palace was built in 1136 by Henry de Blois, brother of King Stephen, and was subsequently enlarged in the 14th century by William of Wykeham before being reduced to its present state by Parliamentary forces in 1644. The remains of the Great Hall can be seen, together with the three-storey tower. The ground floor of the Dower House has been restored as a 19th century farmhouse.

☎ 01489 892460 www.english-heritage.org.uk

Blackgang Chine 157 D5

Originally developed in the 1840s as a scenic garden for Victorian tourists, this clifftop site of around 40 acres (16ha) has gradually evolved into a family leisure park.

The park endeavours to provide a mix of entertainment and education, the former catered for by a variety of attractions such as the water chute, roller coaster, gentler rides for younger children and nursery rhyme scenes. More informative displays can be seen in the maritime museum on the restored quayside and at the replica Victorian saw mill, complete with working engines.

☎ 01983 730330 www.blackgangchine.com

Blenheim Palace 183 G1

A stunning example of English Baroque architecture, Blenheim Palace was built for John Churchill, 1st Duke of Marlborough, following his victory at the Battle of Blenheim.

The palace was designed by Sir John Vanbrugh and built between 1705 – 22. The building itself covers 14 acres (5.5ha), whilst the grounds, landscaped by Lancelot 'Capability' Brown in the 1760s, extend to over 2000 acres (800ha).

Internally, the palace is sumptuously and elaborately decorated and furnished; there are gold leaf ceilings by Nicholas Hawksmoor, marble and stone carvings by Grinling Gibbons, frescoes by Louis Laguerre and portraits by Reynolds, Romney and Van Dyck. The ceiling of the Great Hall, 67ft (20m) high, has a painting depicting Marlborough's victory at Blenheim and the Long Library, a particularly impressive 183ft (56m), has a magnificent stucco ceiling.

The palace was also the birthplace of Sir Winston Churchill. Five rooms, including his birth room, are devoted to the Churchill Exhibition, with memorabilia tracing his life and work.

The grounds were originally designed by Henry Wise, Queen Anne's gardener, but now only the walled garden remains, and much of the later work, including the splendid lake, was by Lancelot 'Capability' Brown, while the Italian Garden and Water Terraces were designed by Achille Duchene in the early 20th century. The parkland provides hours of pleasant walking, and there is also a maze, adventure playground and butterfly house.

☎ 01993 811091 www.blenheimpalace.com

Bletchley Park Museum 353 C3

A Victorian mansion, formerly Britain's World War II code breaking headquarters, now housing a fascinating museum devoted to cryptography and computing. During the war, around 12,000 people worked here, their greatest success was to crack the German Enigma code. Guided tours are included in the entry fee.

☎ 01908 640404 www.bletchley park.org.uk

Bluebell Railway 159 F1

The Bluebell Railway, named after the profusion of bluebells seen beside the line in spring, is the only all-steam, standard-gauge, preserved railway in the country. It extends for 9 miles (14.5km) from Sheffield Park in the south, via Horsted Keynes, to Kingscote in the north.

British Railways closed the line in March 1958 as a cost cutting exercise; two years later 4 miles (6.5km) to the north of Sheffield Park were reopened by a group of enthusiasts. Since then, a further 5 miles (8km) have been added. There are plans to extend the track as far as East Grinstead where it will connect with the main line.

The railway's headquarters and locomotive department are situated at Sheffield Park station where an impressive selection of engines can be found. Some older locos date from the 1870s, with the newest built as late as the 1950s. There is also a museum of small exhibits, a model railway, a shop, a restaurant and a real ale bar at this station. The restoration and maintenance of carriages and wagons takes place at Horsted Keynes where work in progress can be seen from a viewing gallery.

☎ 01825 720800 www.bluebell-railway.co.uk

Bocketts Farm Park 171 G2

This is a working farm with a variety of farm animals and crops, set in scenic downland countryside. Features include tractor rides, children's play areas, pig races, plus seasonal events such as lambing and harvesting.

☎ 01372 363764 www.bockettsfarm.co.uk

Bodiam Castle

Bodiam Castle (NT) 160 C1

Everyone's favourite; a picture book castle with massive sandstone walls and towers rising from a broad moat, spiral staircases, battlement walks and hidey-holes to explore. Today, only a small part of the interior survives.

Bodiam was built in the late 14th century by Sir Edward Dalyngrigge, who had amassed considerable wealth in the wars against France, as a defensive stronghold protecting the Rother Valley from the French. It was intended to be a comfortable home as well as a defensible castle and symbolized the movement from traditional castle to comfortable manor house.

The castle was left partially ruined after attack in 1645 during the Civil War. Repairs to the building commenced in the 19th century, and during the early 20th century the castle was sympathetically restored by its then owner Lord Curzon who bequeathed it to the National Trust in 1926.

In addition to the castle, visitor attractions include a museum containing objects found during the restoration by Lord Curzon, plus a restaurant.

☎ 01580 830436 www.nationaltrust.org.uk

Borde Hill 159 F1

A large, mainly informal garden, created at the turn of the 19th century, set in 200 acres (80ha) of Grade II* parkland. The formal gardens, situated by

Blenheim Palace

the house (not open to the public) include walled, rose and herbaceous gardens; and restored Victorian greenhouses. Many of the rare trees and shrubs were introduced from the Himalayas as seed by plant hunters. Seasonal interest includes rhododendrons and magnolias in the spring, roses and herbaceous plants in the summer, and impressive autumn colours.

☎ 01444 450326 www.bordehill.co.uk

Box Hill Country Park (NT) 171 G2

One of the best known summits of the North Downs; an area of natural beauty comprising woodland, with abundant box trees, and chalk downland with impressive views to the south. Near the summit there is an information centre, shop and a fort dating from the 1890s.

☎ 01306 885502 www.nationaltrust.org.uk

Breamore 156 A1

A red brick Elizabethan manor house, constructed in the characteristic E-shape of the period, set in beautiful parkland in the Avon valley. It is still a family home, and contains fine collections of furniture, porcelain and tapestries, whilst the wood-panelled Great Hall displays 16th and 17th century portraits. A carriage museum in a converted stable block contains the last operational stage coach in England, and there is an informative countryside museum in the old, farmyard. An adventure playground and maze provide additional entertainment for children.

☎ 01725 512468 www.breamorehouse.com

Broadlands 169 E5

Originally a 16th century house, remodelled in the 18th century to create a handsome Palladian mansion, Broadlands is beautifully set in sweeping lawns bordered by the River Test and in grounds landscaped by Lancelot 'Capability' Brown.

A particular feature of the house is the magnificent Saloon with its white and gold plaster ceiling. Many of the fine furnishings, paintings and sculptures were originally acquired by the family of Lord Palmerston, noted Victorian prime minister whose birthplace this was and whose life is remembered in an exhibition here. A more recent resident was Lord Mountbatten of Burma, and an interesting and informative exhibition on his life and times has been staged by his grandson, Lord Romsey, the present owner.

Open from mid June to late August.

☎ 01794 505010 www.broadlands.net

Brooklands Museum 171 F1

This motoring and aviation museum is situated on the site of the world's first motor racing circuit. Not only is it steeped in motor racing history, but it was also the site of the first powered flight by a Briton in a British aeroplane in 1908. Today the museum contains over 30 aircraft and part of the steeply banked, original racing circuit.

☎ 01932 857381 www.brooklandsmuseum.com

Broughton Castle 197 G4

A medieval manor house built around 1300 and set on an island surrounded by a 3 acre (1ha) moat. Much of the original building remains, but it was greatly enlarged in the late 16th century, adding splendid decorative plasterwork, panelling and fireplaces. The castle was a secret meeting place for Parliamentarians during the Civil War, and at one stage it was besieged and captured by Royalists. There is an interesting display of arms and armour from this period in the Great Hall. The grounds contain colourful herbaceous borders, roses, climbers and a formal walled garden. Not open every day; it is advisable to telephone in advance.

☎ 01295 276070 www.broughtoncastle.demon.co.uk

Buckinghamshire County Museum 184 D1

An interesting collection which uses interactive displays to recount the cultural, social and natural history of the county. Exhibits include information on woodlands, farming, fossils, Celts and Romans, and there is also a programme of temporary exhibitions and an art gallery.

The museum building is also home to the Roald Dahl Children's Gallery, a hands-on exhibition where characters from Roald Dahl's books bring to life aspects of history, natural history, science and technology. Entry is by timed ticket. There is a charge for the Dahl Gallery but the museum is free.

☎ 01296 331441 www.visitbuckinghamshire.org

Buckinghamshire Railway Centre 184 C1

This is a working steam museum boasting one of the biggest collections of locomotives, wagons and carriages in the country. As well as the opportunity to ride on steam-hauled trains, there is a good-sized miniature railway and the chance to see restoration work in progress.

☎ 01296 655450 www.bucksrailcentre.org.uk

Buckler's Hard Maritime Museum 348 A4

Buckler's Hard is a delightful, unspoilt 18th century village located on the Beaulieu River. Proximity to timber from the New Forest and a depth of water sufficient to launch substantial warships combined to create a shipbuilding industry here during the 18th century. Two rows of terraced Georgian cottages housed the workforce, and some have been reconstructed to depict the lives of the workers and their families. The Maritime Museum traces the story of this local industry. River trips are available in the summer.

☎ 01590 616203 www.bucklershard.co.uk

Burnham Beeches 185 E4

A splendid Chilterns beech wood of around 574 acres (232ha) which has been a protected public open space since 1880. The woods are home to a diversity of wildlife, including rare plants, insects and fungi, and are known for their striking autumn colour.

Buscot Park (NT) 183 E3

An 18th century Palladian mansion with a remarkable collection of paintings and furniture belonging to the Faringdon Collection Trust. Paintings include works by Rembrandt, Rubens, Murillo and Reynolds, some particularly notable Pre-Raphaelite pieces and contemporary items, and there is furniture designed by Thomas Hope and Robert Adam.

The landscaped park features an Italianate water garden created by Harold Peto in the early 20th century.

☎ 08453 453387
☎ 01367 240786 www.buscot-park.com

Canterbury Cathedral 392 B2

The cathedral was founded in AD597 by St Augustine, a missionary from Rome, and has been the centre of the English church ever since. Today, the impressive cathedral, along with nearby St Martin's Church and St Augustine's Abbey, is a World Heritage Site.

The architectural styles of the cathedral range from Norman to Perpendicular. The large crypt is the oldest part of the present building and dates from the 11th century. Rebuilt after a fire, the 12th century Quire features beautiful stained glass windows depicting miracles and stories associated with Thomas Becket. Famously murdered here in 1170, he is one of the cathedral's most notable archbishops. Two years later he was made a saint. As a result of his martyrdom the cathedral became one of the world's most important centres of pilgrimage.

The magnificent nave, comprising tall columns and vaulted arches, was built in the 14th century and took 28 years to complete. Visitors can see medieval tombs within the cathedral including those of King Henry IV and Edward, the Black Prince.

To get the most out of a visit to this remarkable building, guided and audio tours are available.

☎ 01227 762862 www.canterbury-cathedral.org

Canterbury Cathedral

Canterbury Tales, The 392 B2

A series of superb reconstructions of medieval streets and Thomas Becket's shrine set inside the historic St Margaret's Church. It tells of Chaucer's famous characters on their journey from the Tabard Inn in London to Canterbury Cathedral, bringing them all very much to life.

☎ 01227 479227 www.canterburytales.org.uk

Carisbrooke Castle & Museum 157 D4

Such an obvious defensive site almost demanded the construction of a castle, and there is evidence that people complied, certainly from Saxon times and probably before. The present castle dates from around 1100, and still retains the typical motte and bailey outline, but was considerably enlarged in the late medieval period. Following the Armada in 1588 it was further fortified, and the wellhouse and its tread wheel were added so that water could be drawn more easily from the 161ft (49m) well in the event of siege.

Carisbrooke's chief claim to fame is as the place of imprisonment of Charles I prior to his trial and execution.

The museum is housed in the Great Hall of the Constable's Lodgings and contains memorabilia on Charles I, as well as general information on the Isle of Wight's history.

☎ 01983 522107 www.english-heritage.org.uk

Chartwell (NT) 173 D3

The family home of Winston Churchill for over 40 years, he purchased it in 1924 because he fell in love with the impressive views over the Weald. The large brick built house is still full of many of his

personal possessions. Churchill also left his mark on the attractive gardens, creating lakes, garden walls and rockeries.

☎ 01732 868381 www.nationaltrust.org.uk

Chastleton House (NT) 197 E5

One of the most outstanding Jacobean properties in England, Chastleton has been continuously occupied by one family since its construction in the early 17th century. Particular treasures include elaborate plasterwork, Florentine tapestries and delightful glassware. Entry is by timed ticket and it is advisable to book in advance.

☎ 01608 674355 www.nationaltrust.org.uk

Chatham Historic Dockyard & World Naval Base 173 G2

The history of the dockyards extends back over 400 years. Nelson's famous flagship the *Victory* was built here in 1765. Today, on an 80 acre (32.5ha) site, visitors can see vessels including a World War II destroyer *H.M.S. Cavalier*, the modern submarine *Ocelot*, and *H.M.S. Gannet* which is the last surviving Victorian navy sloop. The site also contains a museum and an exhibition on the Royal National Lifeboat Institution.

☎ 01634 823807 www.chdt.org.uk

Chenies Manor House 185 F3

Queen Elizabeth slept in this 15th century manor house on several occasions, and the building still contains reminders of this period in its furniture and tapestries. Additionally, there is an interesting collection of antique dolls, while the restored 16th century pavilion in the grounds houses various exhibitions.

The delightful gardens are well known for their tulip display, and there are themed areas including a Tudor sunken garden, white garden, herbaceous borders, physic garden and kitchen garden.

☎ 01494 762888 www.visitbuckinghamshire.org

Chichester District Museum 158 A3

Local history museum housed in an 18th century corn store. Includes artefacts excavated from around Chichester.

☎ 01243 784683 www.chichester.gov.uk/museum/

Chiltern Open Air Museum 185 F3

Over 30 historic buildings have been constructed on this attractive 45 acre (18ha) park and woodland site. Most of the buildings were rescued from destruction and have been carefully dismantled and moved from their original locations to create this museum. The diverse display includes re-creations of a Victorian farmyard, complete with animals, a 1940s fully furnished 'prefab' and an Iron Age enclosure. There is even an Edwardian Public Convenience.

There are also demonstrations of traditional skills and information on the methods and materials used to make the buildings. There are plenty of hands-on activities and, throughout the year, there are various special events.

☎ 01494 871117 www.coam.org.uk

Chilterns 184 C4

The chalk downland which makes up the Chilterns extends from Luton in the north-east and runs south-west through Buckinghamshire and Oxfordshire to the southern edge at the River Thames. The open nature of the countryside, dotted with beech hangers and attractive villages, makes this delightful walking country, and part of the Ridgeway, a prehistoric track, runs through the area. Splendid views can be seen from vantage points such as Coombe Hill, with a height of 853ft (260m), Ivinghoe Beacon, and the windmill above Turville village.

Clandon Park (NT) 171 F2

Impressive Palladian mansion built circa 1731 for the 2nd Lord Onslow. Notable for its imposing two-storey marble entrance hall with magnificent Italian plasterwork ceiling. The house contains the Gubbay collection of furniture and porcelain, along with tapestries and the Ivo Forde Meissen collection of Italian comedy figures. The gardens, designed by Lancelot 'Capability' Brown in 1781, include a grotto, Maori house and parterre.

☎ 01483 222482 www.nationaltrust.org.uk

Claremont Landscape Garden (NT) 171 G1

One of the earliest examples surviving today of a 'landscape' garden. Dating from circa 1715, many of the great names in landscape gardening played a part including Charles Bridgeman, Sir John Vanbrugh, William Kent and Lancelot 'Capability' Brown. Extending to 49 acres (20ha) the garden includes a lake, impressive grass amphitheatre and grotto.

☎ 01372 467806 www.nationaltrust.org.uk

Claydon (NT) 198 C5

A charming, mainly 18th century house belonging to the Verney family until the mid 20th century. The unassuming exterior hides a wealth of extravagance in interior decoration. This was carved in the rococo style by Luke Lightfoot and the house contains some of the most remarkable decorative carving in the country, seen at its most outstanding in the Chinese Room. The saloon, library and stairwell boast some beautiful plasterwork, whilst the stairs are decorated with mahogany, ebony and ivory parquetry.

Florence Nightingale was a frequent visitor after her sister's marriage to Sir Henry Verney, and there is a display of memorabilia relating to her life and work.

☎ 01296 730349 www.nationaltrust.org.uk

Chiltern Open Air Museum

Cliveden (NT) 185 E4

A splendid 400 acre (160ha) estate in a magnificent location 200ft (60m) above the River Thames. The impressive house, designed by Sir Charles Barry and former home to the Astor family, is now an hotel with limited public access (telephone for opening times), but the principal attractions are the gardens and views. Planting has been designed to give colour and interest throughout the year.

☎ 01628 605069 www.nationaltrust.org.uk

Cobham Hall 173 F2

Large, attractive red brick mansion dating from 1584, set in 150 acres (61ha) of parkland landscaped by Humphrey Repton. The interior features a notable hall by James Wyatt in the Gothic style and a granite staircase dating from 1602. The house is currently an independent school and opening times are therefore restricted to the Easter and summer holidays.

☎ 01474 824319

Coombe Hill 185 D2

At 853ft (260m), this is one of the highest points on the Chiltern Hills, with magnificent views over the surrounding countryside. The monument on the summit is dedicated to the men of Buckinghamshire who were killed during the Boer War.

Cotswold Wildlife Park 183 E2

Set in 140 acres (56ha) of attractive gardens and parkland surrounding a 19th century mansion, the Wildlife Park is home to a wide range of animals. As well as the usual large animal attractions there are also endangered species such as the giant tortoise, red panda, and Asiatic lion.

There is a children's farmyard with domestic animals and a good adventure playground. A regular programme of events and talks takes place, particularly in summer.

☎ 01993 823006 www.cotswoldwildlifepark.co.uk

Cowper & Newton Museum 199 D2

Orchard Side, one of a pair of Georgian houses which now make up the museum, was the former home of the poet and hymn-writer William Cowper. Visitors can see his manuscripts and memorabilia, together with some belonging to his friend, the local curate John Newton who composed 'Amazing Grace'. There are also local history displays and an interesting textile exhibition.

☎ 01234 711516 www.mkheritage.co.uk

Danebury Ring 169 E4

An Iron Age hill fort, dating from about 500BC, with substantial defensive earthworks enclosing a 13 acre (5ha) site. Its name comes from 'dun', meaning hill, and 'bury', meaning fort.

The earliest evidence for occupation is Neolithic artefacts but the hill fort itself was not built until around 475BC and was abandoned around 100BC.

The site has been extensively excavated to reveal evidence for 75 roundhouses and many more rectangular storage buildings, and many of the finds can be seen at the Museum of the Iron Age in Andover. The isolated site has magnificent views over the surrounding downland.

www.hants.gov.uk

Deal Castle 175 F3

Coastal defensive fort built in 1539 during the reign of Henry VIII to protect England from France and Spain. Constructed in the shape of a Tudor Rose, the walls were deliberately built low and rounded to avoid enemy fire from the sea. Visitors can explore the underground passages and see the 53 gunports.

☎ 01304 372762 www.english-heritage.org.uk

Denbies Wine Estate 171 G2

Extending to 265 acres (107ha) on the slopes of the North Downs, this is the largest vineyard in Britain. Visitors can tour the working winery, experience guided wine tasting, and take the vineyard train up to the North Downs Way where there are excellent views.

☎ 01306 876616 www.denbiesvineyard.co.uk

Denmans — 158 B3

Richly and artistically planted, Denmans extends to approximately 4 acres (1.5ha) and is owned by garden writer and designer John Brookes. Highlights include an attractive walled garden and a glass area for the more tender species.

☎ 01243 542808 www.denmans-garden.co.uk

Dickens House Museum — 175 F2

The museum commemorates Charles Dickens' association with Broadstairs. It is said that Mary Pearson Strong, who once lived here, was the inspiration for the character of Betsey Trotwood, in Dickens' famous book 'David Copperfield'. Memorabilia and personal items such as the author's own letters are on display.

☎ 01843 861232 www.dickenshouse.co.uk

Dorney Court — 185 E5

A timber-framed, brick infilled 15th century building with a magnificent great hall and gallery, considered to be one of the finest examples of a Tudor manor house in England. Home to the Palmer family for over four centuries, the house contains many family portraits, fine furniture and heirlooms. The pleasant gardens have a particular claim to fame – here was grown the first pineapple to be cultivated in England. Opening is limited so it is advisable to telephone in advance.

☎ 01628 604638 www.dorneycourt.co.uk

Dover Castle — 395 E2

Well preserved Norman castle, on the site of a Roman fortress which in turn occupied that of an Iron Age Fort. Situated 375 feet (114m) above sea level, the castle has played a key role in the defence of the realm: William the Conqueror saw its importance and strengthened the castle shortly after the Battle of Hastings. However, much of the castle as we see it today dates from the reign of Henry II when the impressive four-storey keep, the distinctive inner bailey and part of the outer walls were built, creating a concentric fortress. Just prior to the death of King John the castle was damaged by a French siege and his son, Henry III, was quick to carry out strengthening work completing the outer bailey. The castle maintained its defensive role right up to and including World War II, when the tunnels under the castle became the headquarters from which the evacuation of Dunkirk was directed. Exhibitions and displays highlight key events in the castle's chequered and well documented history. A walk along the battlements gives the visitor a commanding view over the harbour.

☎ 01304 201628 www.english-heritage.org.uk

Dover Castle

Druidstone Park — 174 D2

In 12 acres (5ha) of attractive gardens and woodland, visitors can see a variety of animals including owls, deer, wallabies and various wildfowl. The open-air art park features sculptures in a variety of media, some by well-known artists. Children can also explore the farmyard with its pigs, llamas, donkeys and ponies.

☎ 01227 765168 www.druidstone.net/

Drusillas Park — 160 A3

Ideal for children, this small zoo primarily features the smaller species of animal housed in naturalistic environments. Over 100 species can be seen, such as meerkats, monkeys and penguins. There is also a walk-through bat enclosure and a wide range of play and hands-on activities.

☎ 01323 874100 www.drusillas.co.uk

Eastbourne Pier — 397 B3

Built in the 1870s, this 1000 ft (305m) long pier was designed by Eugenius Birch, using an ingenious method whereby the legs that support the pier sit on special cups allowing it to move from side to side in bad weather. Attractions include a restored Victorian Camera Obscura, bars, restaurant, café, amusement arcades and night club.

☎ 01323 410466 www.eastbournepier.com

Emmetts (NT) — 173 D3

Bequeathed to the National Trust in 1965, this mainly informal hillside garden dates from 1860 - 70. In about 1900, it was extended to 5 acres (2ha). Emmetts is particularly attractive in the spring with a profusion of daffodils and, later on, bluebells.

☎ 01732 751509 www.nationaltrust.org.uk

Exbury Gardens — 348 A4

A magnificent 250 acre (100ha) woodland garden set on the east side of the Beaulieu River. It is particularly famed for its rhododendron collection, started in the 1920s by the banker Lionel de Rothschild, who imported more than 1000 varieties and bred from these to produce 400 more, providing sensational colour from April to June. There are also good collections of magnolias and camellias, while the daffodil meadow, rock garden, rose garden and herbaceous borders greatly extend the garden's period of interest. Pleasant walks can be taken in the woodlands, and a 12.5 inch (30cm) narrow-gauge railway runs through part of the grounds.

☎ 023 8089 9422 www.exbury.co.uk

Finkley Down Farm Park — 169 E3

A great variety of farm animals, domestic pets and poultry can be seen on this working farm. Adventure playground and informative countryside museum.

☎ 01264 324141 www.finkleydownfarm.co.uk

Firle Place — 159 G3

A Tudor house remodelled in the 18th century, in an attractive setting at the foot of the South Downs. It has been home to the Gage family for over 500 years and houses collections of Old Master paintings such as Reynolds and Gainsborough, fine furniture and porcelain.

☎ 01273 858335 www.firleplace.co.uk

Fishbourne Roman Palace — 158 A3

Discovered in 1960, the remains of the north wing of this 1st century palace are enclosed by a modern building. The largest collection of in-situ Roman mosaics in Britain can be seen, along with remains of a bath suite, courtyards, corridors and hypocausts. A museum displays artefacts from excavations on and around the site and there is a Roman garden that has been replanted to its original plan.

☎ 01243 785859 www.sussexpast.co.uk

Fisher's Farm Park — 171 F5

Family attraction with farmyard animals including ducks, sheep, goats, shire horses and Shetland ponies. There are also adventure play areas which include a 25ft (7.5m) climbing wall, merry-go-round and trampolines.

☎ 01403 700063 www.fishersfarmpark.co.uk

Fort Brockhurst — 157 F2

A 19th century fort, one of several in the area built for the protection of Portsmouth. It has remained essentially unaltered, particular features being the moated keep, parade ground and gun ramps. Opening is limited so it is advisable to telephone in advance.

☎ 023 9258 1059 www.english-heritage.org.uk

Fort Victoria Country Park — 156 C4

The remains of Fort Victoria, which was built to protect the western entry to the Solent, now house a variety of attractions. These include a fascinating aquarium concentrating on local marine life, one of the largest model railway layouts in the country, a marine heritage exhibition and planetarium. The surrounding 50 acres (20ha) of grounds provide woodland and seashore walks. There is a cost for attractions but entry to the park is free.

☎ 01983 823893 www.fortvictoria.co.uk

Godstone Farm — 172 C3

This popular farm park features indoor and outdoor play areas as well as farm animals, chipmunks and llamas.

☎ 01883 742546 www.godstonefarm.co.uk

Great Coxwell Barn (NT) — 183 E3

A substantial medieval barn built in the 13th century as part of a Cistercian cell under the control of Beaulieu Abbey. It is constructed chiefly from Cotswold stone, with the original doors still in place on the east and west walls. Internally the roof is supported by the original oak posts and trusses, though most of the rafters have been replaced.

☎ 01793 762209 www.nationaltrust.org.uk

Great Dixter — 160 D1

A beautiful Tudor house built circa 1460 and restored in 1910 by Edwin Lutyens. It has one of the largest timber framed halls in the country and is home to gardening writer Christopher Lloyd. The 5 acre (2ha) garden, also designed by Lutyens, has been developed by Lloyd, producing a combination of historical design and contemporary and adventurous planting. The garden contains clipped topiary, wild meadow flowers, mixed borders including the famous 'long border' which is some 200ft (60m) long, ponds, walls, stone steps and paths.

☎ 01797 252878 www.greatdixter.co.uk

Great Tew — 197 F5

This could be described as a quintessential English village, with terraces of Cotswold stone cottages, most built in the 1630s for Lord Falkland's estate workers. The cottages are a mixture of thatched and stone-roofed, and a pub and village green complete the picture.

Grey's Court (NT) 184 C4

An unusual 14th century house, rebuilt in the 16th century and subsequently modified but still retaining one of the original towers. A distinctive feature is the Tudor wheelhouse where donkeys turned the wheel which brought water up from a 200ft (61m) well.

The 8 acre (3ha) gardens are a particularly attractive aspect, set among the ruins of the 14th century building. Telephone in advance to check for opening times.

☎ 01494 755564 www.nationaltrust.org.uk

Groombridge Place Gardens 173 E5

The walled, formal gardens were designed in the 17th century by John Evelyn and are set against a delightful moated manor house (not open to the public) of the same age. The grounds extend to 200 acres (80ha) and feature herbaceous borders, pools, woodland and rose garden. There is also the 'enchanted forest' to explore.

☎ 01892 863999 www.groombridge.co.uk

H.M.S. Victory 407 D1

Now lying in dry dock, the *Victory* is the oldest commissioned warship in the world and the flagship of the Second Sea Lord, though she is of course best known as Lord Nelson's flagship at the Battle of Trafalgar in 1805. Commissioned in 1778, her excellent sailing qualities caused several admirals to choose her as their flagship, and although her active career ended in 1812 it was agreed that she should be preserved as a memorial to Nelson and this distinguished period of the Royal Navy's history. Tours are not available from July to the end of school summer holidays due to pressure of numbers, but guides are on hand to answer visitors' questions.

☎ 023 9272 2562 www.hms-victory.com

H.M.S. Warrior 407 E1

Launched in 1860, *H.M.S. Warrior* was the world's first iron-hulled, armoured battleship and was then considered the most formidable ever seen. She was powered both by sail and steam, and has now been restored to her original launch condition. Visitors are able to explore the four large decks which illustrate life in the Victorian navy.

☎ 023 9272 2562 www.hmswarrior.org

Hammerwood Park 172 D5

This neoclassical house was built in 1792 by Benjamin Latrobe who was later responsible for the Capitol, and the porticos of the White House in Washington D.C. It was converted into flats after World War II and owned by the pop group Led Zeppelin in the 1970s. It gradually fell into disrepair until rescued in 1982 by the present owners who give guided tours and tell of the continuing process of restoration.

☎ 01342 850594 www.hammerwoodpark.com

Haslemere Educational Museum 171 E4

This family museum was founded in 1888 and opened to the public in 1895. Permanent galleries include: geology, natural history and human history. There are interactive displays, interesting collections and even a real Egyptian mummy.

☎ 01428 642112 www.haslemeremuseum.co.uk

Hastings Castle (Ruins) 400 F2

Originally built by William the Conqueror in 1066 as a wooden fort on an earth motte, it was rebuilt in stone in 1070 as the first permanent Norman castle in the country. It is now a ruin commanding panoramic views of Hastings. Visitors to the castle can see an audiovisual show 'The 1066 Story' about the Battle of Hastings and the history of the castle.

☎ 01424 781111

Hatchlands (NT) 171 F2

An 18th century brick built mansion set in a 430 acre (174ha) park designed by Humphrey Repton. The interior contains early examples of work by Robert Adam as well as a fine collection of keyboard instruments once owned, or played by famous composers including J.C. Bach, Beethoven, Chopin, Mozart and Purcell.

☎ 01483 222482 www.nationaltrust.org.uk

Herstmonceux Castle 160 B2

Beautiful parkland, woodland and well kept Elizabethan gardens extending to 550 acres (220ha) are centred on a brick built 15th century moated castle (not open to the public). There is a children's woodland play area and nature trail. The estate is also the site of the Observatory Science Centre, former home of the Royal Greenwich Observatory (separate entry fee).

☎ 01323 833816 www.herstmonceux-castle.com

Hever Castle 173 D4

This romantic, double-moated, 13th century castle was the childhood home of Anne Boleyn, and later owned by Anne of Cleves. The castle contains prayer books inscribed and signed by Anne Boleyn. There are also Tudor portraits, furniture, tapestries and a collection of miniature houses with period decoration and furnishings.

The spectacular gardens were constructed between 1904 and 1908. Features include a 35 acre (14ha) lake, Italian gardens with statuary and sculptures, a 360ft (110m) herbaceous border and herb garden. There are two mazes: a traditional yew hedge maze and an unusual water maze.

☎ 01732 865224 www.hevercastle.co.uk

High Beeches 172 B5

20 acres (8ha) of Grade II* listed woodland, water and wild flower garden dating from the early 20th century. It contains a varied and extensive collection of plants and is particularly colourful in spring and autumn.

☎ 01444 400589 www.highbeeches.com

Highclere Castle 169 F2

This former Georgian mansion, set in magnificent parkland landscaped by Lancelot 'Capability' Brown, was extravagantly refurbished both internally and externally by Sir Charles Barry in the 1840s. The lavishly decorated rooms embrace a variety of styles including Gothic, Moorish and rococo, which somehow combine to form a splendid example of High Victorian architecture.

The castle is the ancestral home of the Earls of Carnarvon, and there is an exhibition of Egyptian artefacts brought back by the 5th Earl following the Tutankhamen excavations in the 1920s.

The 7th Earl was the Queen's racing manager, and there is an exhibition on horse racing history.

Opening times are limited.

☎ 01635 253210 www.highclerecastle.co.uk

Hinton Ampner (NT) 169 G5

Considered to be one of the great gardens of the 20th century, designed on the basis of a Victorian garden by Ralph Dutton, the 8th Lord Sherborne. The house stands on a ridge with magnificent views over downland scenery. The terraced gardens are a transformation of a Victorian remnant into a masterpiece of formal and informal plantings using predominantly pastel shades. Only open on certain days of the week in summer.

☎ 01962 771305 www.nationaltrust.org.uk

Hop Farm Country Park 173 F4

Once a working hop farm, this large group of Victorian oast houses forms the setting for this family attraction. Amongst the entertainments are shire horse displays, an animal farm, children's play areas, a military vehicle display as well as a visit to the 'Hop Story' museum.

☎ 01622 872068 www.thehopfarm.co.uk

Horton Park Farm 171 G1

Situated within the Horton Country Park, this popular attraction features a wide range of farm animals to feed and cuddle. There are also rare breeds, an adventure playground, indoor play area, a maze and tractor rides.

☎ 01372 743984 www.hortonpark.co.uk

Howletts Wild Animal Park 175 D3

Founded by the late John Aspinall, this wild animal park is set in mature parkland and has the largest breeding colony of gorillas in captivity. It is notable for encouraging bonding between the keepers and their animals as Aspinall believed that this improved the emotional wellbeing of the animals and has led to successful breeding programmes. Other animals include the largest herd of African elephants in the UK, tigers, leopards, deer and rare monkeys.

☎ 01303 264647 www.howletts.net

Hughenden Manor (NT) 185 D3

The home of former prime minister, Benjamin Disraeli, from 1847 – 71, and extensively restyled during this period by the Victorian Gothic architect E.B. Lamb. The interior has been left much as Disraeli would remember it, with his books, furniture, pictures and other memorabilia of his life. The 5 acre (2ha) gardens were designed by Disraeli's wife, Mary Anne. There are colourful herbaceous borders and formal annual bedding, woodland walks and an orchard with old varieties of apples and pears. Limited opening so it is advisable to telephone in advance.

☎ 01494 755573 www.nationaltrust.org.uk

Ightham Mote (NT) 173 E3

A very attractive moated manor house dating from 1330 surrounded by a lovely garden with lakes and woodland. The interior of the house has a rich history, with the Great Hall dating from the 1340s, a 14th century crypt, a Tudor chapel and a Jacobean fireplace.

☎ 01732 810378 www.nationaltrust.org.uk

Isle of Wight Pearl 156 D4

An extensive collection of all types of pearl jewellery. Visitors can learn how pearls are cultivated, see a replica of the world's largest pearl and learn how the jewellery is made.

☎ 01983 740352 www.isle-of-wight-pearl.com

Isle of Wight Zoo 157 F4

Specialising in big cats, the zoo is home to around 20 tigers, many actually born here, and there is plenty of opportunity to observe the animals and learn more about them and their conservation. Other big cats are represented: lions, leopards,

jaguars and panthers, and there is also a fascinating lemur enclosure, snakes, insects and a good display of tarantulas. There is a regular programme of informative talks about the animals.

☎ 01983 403833 www.isleofwightzoo.com

Jane Austen's House 170 C4

An unpretentious 17th century red brick house where Jane Austen lived from 1809 – 17 and where she wrote or revised her six famous novels. The house is furnished in period style and contains many items associated with the author and her family, including letters and papers, furniture and first editions of the novels.

☎ 01420 83262 www.janeaustenmuseum.org.uk

Kent & East Sussex Railway 160 D1

Preserved steam and diesel engines run along this attractive standard-gauge line which runs for 10.5 miles (17km) from Tenterden to Bodiam (a short distance from the medieval castle). The line was built as the first light railway in Britain. At Tenterden, the headquarters, there is a museum plus the carriage and wagon workshop.

☎ 01580 765155 www.kesr.org.uk

Knole (NT) 173 E3

This enormous Tudor mansion, made of Kentish ragstone and set in a 1000 acre (405ha) deer park with 26 acre (10.5ha) landscaped grounds, was built in the mid 15th century for the Archbishop of Canterbury, Thomas Bourchier. It later passed to Henry VIII and then in 1603 it was gifted by Elizabeth I to her cousin Thomas Sackville, 1st Earl of Dorset. Extensive alterations and additions were made by the 1st Earl up to 1608 which transformed the house dramatically, particularly the interior. Today the house is notable for its 365 rooms – one for each day of the year, 52 staircases – one for each week of the year, and its 7 courtyards – one for each day of the week.

Knole contains an impressive collection of 17th century furniture started by the 1st Earl and continued by his descendents, most notably the 6th Earl who was Lord Chamberlain to William III. Later, the 3rd Duke, great-grandson of the 6th Earl, continued the collection by adding many valuable paintings.

☎ 01732 462100 www.nationaltrust.org.uk

Knole

Lamb House (NT) 161 E1

This brick fronted house, set in a one acre (0.5ha) walled garden in the centre of Rye, was built by James Lamb in 1723, the year he became mayor of Rye. George I stayed here in 1726 and acted as godfather to Lamb's son. The American novelist Henry James lived at Lamb House from 1898 to 1916 and the house is primarily devoted to mementoes of his time here.

☎ 01372 453401 www.nationaltrust.org.uk

Leeds Castle & Gardens 174 A3

Set on two islands in the middle of a large artificial lake, this beautiful castle was constructed in the 12th century as an impregnable stronghold, the barbican being built during the reign of Edward I. Six of the medieval queens of England have occupied the castle including Eleanor and Margaret, the wives of Edward I. Converted into a royal palace by Henry VIII, it has been restored and now contains a magnificent collection of medieval furnishings, French and English furniture and fabrics, tapestries and paintings by Degas, Pissarro, and Vuillard. Inside are also the Queen's Gallery, Banqueting Hall and Chapel. There are 500 acres (202ha) of parkland and gardens to explore, within which are an aviary, a maze and a grotto. The Woodland Garden provides a display of narcissi and daffodils in spring.

☎ 01622 765400 www.leeds-castle.com

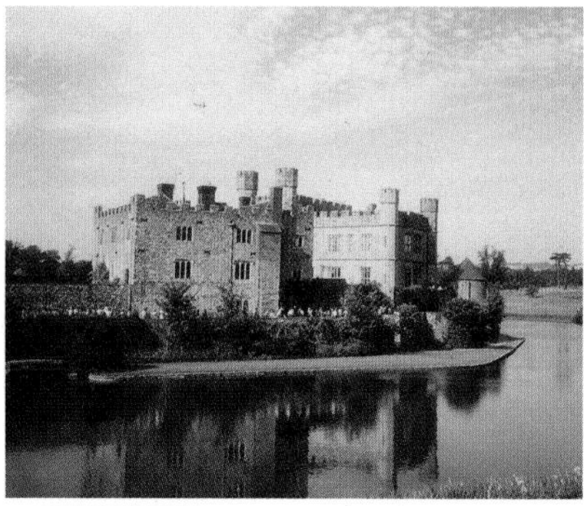

Leeds Castle

Legoland 185 E5

Every small child's dream come true, Legoland is aimed at the 4-12 age group, with a mixture of incredible models, toned down theme park rides and special activities.

Particular highlights include the Rat Trap, an intricate arrangement of slides, climbing nets and walkways, The Dragon roller coaster, the water chute at Pirate Falls, and for the younger children, Duplo Land. The Mindstorms workshops will appeal more to older children, with the chance to construct robots, while visitors of all ages should appreciate Miniland, where 50 million Lego bricks have been used to re-create miniature versions of Europe's capital cities.

☎ 08705 040404 www.legoland.co.uk

Leonardslee Gardens 159 E1

This spectacular 240 acre (97ha) woodland garden is a riot of colour in May and June when the rhododendrons and azaleas are in flower. Located in a valley with seven lakes (originally used in iron smelting to provide power) this garden was acquired in 1889 by Sir Edmund Loder who set about an ambitious planting programme. Other attractions include an alpine house, bonsai exhibition, Victorian motor car collection and a herd of semi-wild wallabies that were first introduced over 100 years ago.

☎ 01403 891212 www.leonardslee.com

Lewes Castle 159 G2

This ruined castle dates from around 1069 and is unusual in having two mottes. The shell keep dates from the early 12th century and two semi-octagonal towers were built in the 13th century along with a range of buildings inside the shell wall. The impressive barbican, one of the best preserved castle barbicans in England, was added in the 14th century. There are magnificent views from the towers of the town of Lewes and the surrounding countryside.

☎ 01273 486290 www.sussexpast.co.uk

Living Rainforest 184 A5

This unique rainforest conservation project, with its thousands of weird, wonderful and, in some cases, endangered species, has been constructed under 20,000sq ft (1836sq m) of glass deep in rural Berkshire. There are two distinct regions represented, Amazonia and Lowland Tropical, each with its characteristic climate and flora. Of particular note is the splendid collection of orchids and the 8ft (2.5m) lily pads on view between June and October.

☎ 01635 202444 www.livingrainforest.org

Look Out Discovery Park 171 D1

Very much a hands-on attraction, this interactive science and nature exhibition will have a particular appeal to children. Themed zones look at topics such as light and colour, body and perception, and woodland and wildlife.

The centre is set in 2600 acres (1040ha) of Crown Estate woodland and there are plenty of nature trails and walks, and a 70ft (22m) tower providing views over the surrounding countryside.The Coral Reef swimming pool with its Wild West Rapids is also across the way.

☎ 01344 354400 www.bracknellforest.gov.uk

Loseley House 171 E3

Beautiful Elizabethan mansion set in the 1400 acre (566ha) Loseley Park. The house, dating from 1562, was built with stone from the ruins of Waverley Abbey and contains many fine works of art and panelling from Henry VIII's Nonsuch Palace. The estate comprises a formal 2.5 acre (1ha) walled garden (which is subdivided into five themed components), managed woodland and agricultural land. The well known Loseley ice cream and other dairy products are produced from the estate's herd of Jersey cows.

☎ 01483 304440 www.loseleypark.com

Legoland

Lullingstone Castle 173 E2

Situated in the lovely Darenth valley, this historic family mansion, first built in the late 15th century, was extensively altered during the reign of Queen Anne who was a frequent visitor to Lullingstone. The Tudor gatehouse was one of the earliest in England to be built entirely of bricks. There are fine state rooms, the impressive Great Hall, the grand staircase and library. Outside is the church of St Botolph containing a fine Tudor rood screen.

☎ 01322 862114

Lullingstone Roman Villa
173 E2

Discovered in 1939, the site has been preserved within a modern building. The villa is thought to have been built during the 1st and 2nd centuries, although much of what can be seen today dates from the 4th century and includes well preserved floor mosaics, frescoes and a bathing complex. There is also the remains of one of the earliest Christian chapels.

☎ 01322 863467 www.english-heritage.org.uk

Mapledurham House & Mill
184 B5

An attractive H-shaped red brick house built in the late 16th century and set in pleasant parkland on the banks of the River Thames. Within the house are fine plasterwork ceilings and an impressive oak staircase, while a private family chapel designed in 'Strawberry Hill' Gothic with original elaborate plasterwork was added in 1797. There are literary connections with Alexander Pope, John Galsworthy and Kenneth Grahame.

An interesting feature in the grounds is a 15th century water mill restored to full working order and producing flour and bran.

Opening mainly restricted to weekends in the summer season.

☎ 0118 972 3350 www.mapledurham.co.uk

Marwell Zoo
169 G5

A well designed and carefully laid out zoo specialising in the conservation of endangered species but also with plenty of established favourites. Animals are housed in large, open enclosures and can be viewed via special walkways or road and rail trains. For children there is the Encounters Village where animals can be handled. There are regular special events during school holidays.

☎ 01962 777407 www.marwell.org.uk

Mary Rose
407 D1

Built around 1510, the *Mary Rose* was quite innovative for her time in that she could fire a broadside using heavy cannon. Prior to this, ships engaged at close quarters for hand-to-hand fighting.

A favourite ship of Henry VIII, the *Mary Rose* sank in 1545; the king was watching from Southsea Castle as he took part in a skirmish with the French. She was not seen again above water until 1982 and is now on display in the Ship Hall.

A short walk away, the *Mary Rose* Museum displays over 1200 artefacts retrieved from the wreck and surrounding sea bed. In addition there is information on how the wreck was raised.

☎ 023 9272 2562 www.maryrose.org

Michelham Priory
160 A3

Sitting on an island surrounded by the longest water-filled medieval moat in England, the building dates from 1229. Originally an Augustinian Priory until the Dissolution in 1537, it then became a country house. Exhibits include furniture, tapestries and artefacts. The gardens are in a variety of historic and contemporary styles and include a physic garden, cloister garden and orchard. There is also a working water mill.

☎ 01323 844224 www.sussexpast.co.uk

Mid Hants Railway
170 B4

Delightful steam railway nicknamed 'The Watercress Line' as it was formerly used to transport fresh watercress to market. Ten miles (16km) of track have been restored between Alresford and Alton, passing through lovely countryside – including watercress beds. The stations are restored to give a pre-war atmosphere and there is a visitor centre at Alresford. A programme of special events runs throughout the year.

☎ 01962 733810 www.watercressline.co.uk

Milton's Cottage
185 E3

Timber-framed 16th century cottage where the poet John Milton brought his family in 1665 to escape the Great Plague in London. Here he completed 'Paradise Lost' and commenced 'Paradise Regained'. The building houses first editions and other memorabilia, and has delightful cottage gardens.

☎ 01494 572313 www.miltonscottage.org

Modern Art Oxford
406 C2

This was established in 1965 and is arguably one of the foremost displays of contemporary art outside London, with exhibits from around the world including works by Ed Ruscha, Yoko Ono, Louise Bourgeois, Tracey Emin, David Goldblatt and Marina Abramovic. Work on display encompasses a variety of art forms; painting, sculpture, photography, design, film, video and architecture. Housed in a refurbished Victorian brewery, the museum also has a wide ranging programme of regular talks, events and children's workshops.

☎ 01865 722733 www.modernartoxford.co.uk

Monk's House (NT)
159 G3

Small country home of novelist Virginia Woolf and her husband Leonard, purchased by them in 1919. The rooms contain mementoes of the life and times of the famous 'Bloomsbury Group' of which they were key players. Extracts of Virginia's diaries and a display of her photographs can be seen in the garden room where she used to write.

☎ 01372 453401 www.nationaltrust.org.uk

Mottisfont Abbey Gardens (NT)
169 E5

The 12th century priory at the centre of this 20,000 acre (800ha) estate became a private house after the Dissolution of the Monasteries. However, the site's chief claim to fame, its walled rose garden designed by Graham Stuart Thomas, was only created in 1972, and is home to the National Collection of Old Fashioned Roses. Although these only have a short flowering period in June, elsewhere the gardens have been planted for interest throughout the season. The 'font' or spring, from which the place name is derived, is in the grounds.

☎ 01794 340757 www.nationaltrust.org.uk

Museum of Canterbury
392 B1

Part of the museum is housed in what was once a hospital for poor priests dating from the 13th century. There are a wide range of exhibits, including archaeological finds and historical collections dating from pre-Roman to the present day.

☎ 01227 452747 www.canterbury-museums.co.uk

Museum of Oxford
406 B2

Housed in the historic Town Hall, this museum traces the history of Oxford and the university. There is a particularly fine medieval collection, fascinating reconstructed interiors of city buildings from the 16th century onwards, paintings, furniture and many other items connected with the city and university.

☎ 01865 815559 www.oxford.co.uk

National Motor Museum
348 A4

In 1952 Lord Montagu of Beaulieu inherited five historic vehicles and started the museum as a tribute to his father who had been a pioneer of motoring in Britain. The initially small display proved so popular that, in 1972, a purpose-built museum was developed in the park surrounding Lord Montagu's home at Beaulieu. This now houses over 250 historically important vehicles, a magnificent collection of motoring memorabilia including film, books, photographs and permanent displays. Highlights of the collection include some of the world's oldest cars such as Fiats and Renaults, record breakers such as Golden Arrow and Bluebird, a motorsport gallery celebrating Grand Prix racing and rallying, and a James Bond experience with cars and boats from the films. Visitors can travel round the grounds by monorail or open-topped replica 1912 London bus.

☎ 01590 612345 www.beaulieu.co.uk

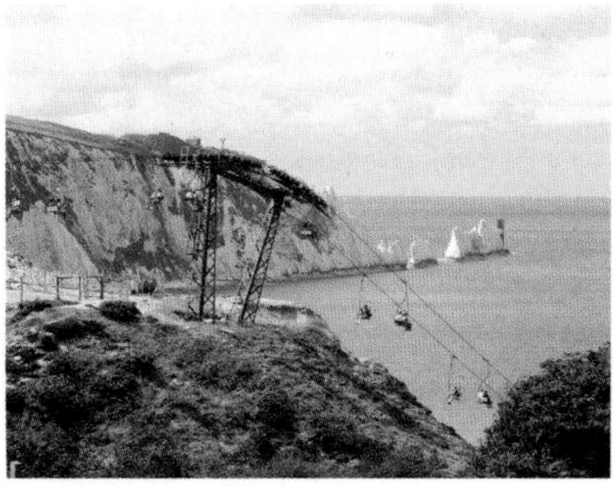

Needles Pleasure Park

Needles Pleasure Park
156 C4

A spectacular chairlift ride provides unique views of the striking coloured sands of the Alum Bay cliffs and across to The Needles and lighthouse. There are also boat trips, children's rides and games, tours round the Isle of Wight Sweet Factory and glass blowing demonstrations at Alum Bay Glass.

A short walk along the cliffs is a 19th century fort, Needles Old Battery. As well as an exhibition on the site's history, a 200ft (60m) tunnel leads to a viewpoint with unrivalled views across to the Needles, three distinctive jagged, eroded remnants of the former chalk cliffs.

☎ 0870 458 0022 www.theneedles.co.uk

New Forest
156 B1

Contrary to expectation, much of this 150 square mile (388sq km) Area of Outstanding Natural Beauty is not actually still forested; rather it is a mixture of woodland and heath, poor sandy soils giving little incentive for cultivation. The Forest was designated a royal hunting preserve by William the Conqueror in 1079 and, at this time, punishment for trespass included mutilation and even death; now around 8 million people visit the area each year.

Although close to large centres of population, once away from the main roads there is a distinct feeling of having 'got away from it all'. The Forest itself is relatively sparsely settled, with only Lyndhurst and Brockenhurst of any significant size. However, the high visitor numbers in recent years have called for practical measures, such as the 40mph (64kph) speed limit throughout the Forest, to protect the environment, the wildlife, the ponies and other grazing animals.

The harsh penalties meted out in the 11th century were later rescinded and the local owner-

occupiers, or Commoners, were granted certain rights, such as the freedom to graze livestock or more obscurely, turbary (peat cutting). These rights are administered by the Verderers, and the Verderers Court, which is held every two months, is considered to be the oldest court of law in England. The distinctive Forest landscape, with its free-grazing ponies, cattle and sheep, is a consequence of these ancient laws.

The remoter parts of the Forest, particularly the wetland areas, are home to some of Britain's rarest plant, animal and insect species, whilst the open heathland is of particular interest to birdlovers. The scenery, although not dramatic in terms of relief, makes for pleasant walking and cycling country.

New Forest

New Forest Museum & Information Centre 156 C2

The place to visit for all the background information on the Forest and its inhabitants. There are interactive displays on the area's geology, and specific exhibits on wildlife, history and culture. The famous New Forest Embroidery is on display and there is a regular programme of temporary exhibitions.

☎ 023 8028 2269 www.newforestmuseum.org

Nymans (NT) 159 E1

This beautiful 30 acre (12ha) garden set on the side of a sheltered valley was created by three generations of the Messel family dating from 1890. The garden originally surrounded a 14th century manor house which was largely destroyed by fire in 1947, and the ruins give an atmospheric backdrop to the planting. The garden is designed as a series of 'rooms' with hedges, walls and trees providing shelter for rare and exotic plants.

☎ 01444 400321 www.nationaltrust.org.uk

Osborne House 157 E3

This was the rural retreat for Queen Victoria and her family, away from the pressures of ceremonial life. The house was designed by Prince Albert with technical input from Thomas Cubitt. The Prince was an admirer of Italian art and architecture and his design was based on the style of an Italian villa, complete with towers and terraces. As a widow, Victoria was a frequent visitor until her death in 1901, and many of the apartments have been preserved with little change since then, in keeping with her wishes.

The interior design of Osborne House is equally lavish. The Grand Corridor is lined by marble sculptures, and there are portraits and frescoes which underline the family's links with Europe and the Empire. Particularly sumptuous is the Durbar Room, built in the early 1890s to celebrate the Queen's role as Empress of India.

Within the grounds, 'Swiss Cottage', the royal equivalent of a Wendy House, was built with Prince Albert's intention of providing his children with the basics of housekeeping and cookery. There is also the ultimate boys' toy, Victoria Fort, which the royal princes helped to construct.

The pleasant gardens were laid out by Prince Albert in Italianate terraces, with beautiful views across the Solent, and there is a restored walled garden.

☎ 01983 200022 www.english-heritage.org.uk

Owl House, The 173 F5

This 16th century timber-framed house (not open to the public) was purchased by Lady Dufferin in 1952. The gardens, extending to 16 acres (6.5ha), were created during her time here and include expansive lawns, woodland walks and sunken water gardens.

☎ 01892 890230 www.owlhouse.com

Oxford 406

Originally an important Saxon town, thanks to its strategic position where the Rivers Thames and Cherwell meet, the key date in Oxford's development as a major university town was 1167 when all Anglo-Norman students were expelled from the Sorbonne and selected Oxford as a suitable alternative. The first three colleges, Balliol, Merton and University, were built in the 13th century and others followed slowly over time so that now the university has around 15,000 students and 39 colleges. The city centre is dominated by the attractive college buildings, many of which are open to the public. Of particular interest are Christ Church, with its splendid Great Hall, Magdalen, with its riverside gardens, and Merton. Some of the colleges charge admission and access may be limited in term time. Other impressive buildings are the Bodleian Library, Ashmolean Museum and Sheldonian Theatre, an early design by Sir Christopher Wren. The city's cathedral, the smallest in England, is in Christ Church College, where it doubles as the college chapel. Famous literary, scientific and theological associations abound, and the museums contain major historical, natural history and scientific collections. Oxford is essentially a medieval city, and is best visited by public transport. The centre is compact and there is an excellent park and ride system.

www.visitoxford.org

Oxford Story 406 B2

A time car ride through the history of Oxford University in carriages designed as desks. The associated audiovisual presentation provides information both on the development of the university and the many influential people who have passed through its doors.

☎ 01865 790055 www.oxfordstory.co.uk

Osborne House

Oxfordshire Museum, The 183 G1

Located in a fine town house in Woodstock, this illuminating museum has plenty of information on the social history of the county, permanent displays tracing the story of the inhabitants, landscapes, buildings and industries from earliest times to the present day. There is also a special gallery for children and a purpose-built gallery for temporary exhibits.

☎ 01993 811456 www.oxfordshire.gov.uk

Palace Pier 390 F3

Opened on 20th May 1899, this 1722ft (525m) long pier (Grade II* listed) features filigree ironwork arches and some of the original kiosks. Over the years, these basic attractions have been joined by a huge array of modern-day amusements such as a funfair, arcades, night club, bars and restaurants.

☎ 01273 609361 www.brightonpier.co.uk

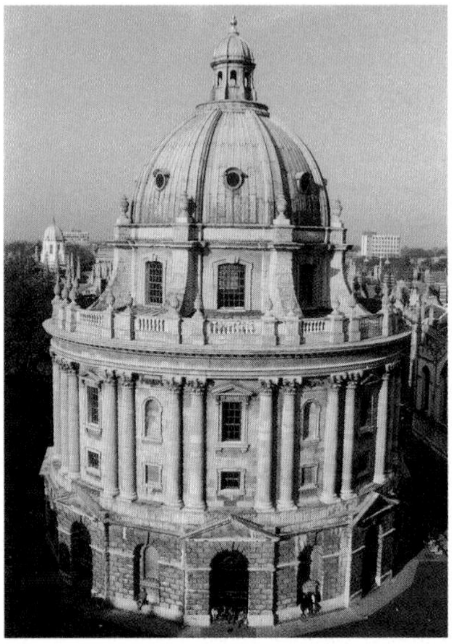

Oxford – Radcliffe Camera

Paradise Park 159 G3

This varied attraction, set in colourful themed gardens, is ideal for children. It focuses on the local area's history and includes life-size moving dinosaurs, a model village featuring Sussex landmarks, a collection of fossils, crazy golf and a miniature railway.

☎ 01273 512123 www.paradisepark.co.uk

Parham House 158 C2

This 'E' shaped Elizabethan house, built in 1577 with later additions, has panelled rooms hung with portraits and 17th century furniture, some of which is still covered with the original needlework. Parham is surrounded by extensive grounds including a deer park and an attractive 11 acre (4.5ha) garden featuring a brick and turf maze and a 4 acre (1.5ha) walled garden, the flowers from which are used to adorn the house.

☎ 01903 744888 www.parhaminsussex.co.uk

Paulton's Park 156 C1

A leisure park of 140 acres (56ha) particularly suitable for families, with over 50 rides and activities, including a log flume and roller coaster. In addition there is a good collection of exotic birds and wildfowl in aviaries and ponds, a 19th century working waterwheel, 10 acre (4ha) lake and Romany Museum providing insight into traditional gipsy life.

☎ 023 8081 4455 www.paultonspark.co.uk

Penshurst Place — 173 E4

Built of local sandstone, this impressive castellated manor house dates from the 14th century and has been occupied by the Sidney family since 1552. The house is notable for its outstanding medieval Barons Hall built in 1341 with its 60ft (18m) high chestnut-beamed roof. The State Rooms contain a collection of paintings from the 15th to 17th centuries, furniture, tapestries and armour. The vast 10 acre (4ha) walled garden, created between 1570 and 1666, is formed into a series of garden rooms divided by a mile of yew hedging. The variety of planting gives all year round interest. Also of interest is the deer park and toy museum.

☎ 01892 870307 www.penshurstplace.com

Petworth House (NT) — 171 E5

Situated on the edge of a 700 acre (283ha) landscaped deer park and adjacent to the town of Petworth, this magnificent 17th century mansion was built around an older manor house owned by the Earls of Northumberland. The park, landscaped in the mid 18th century, is considered to be one of Lancelot 'Capability' Brown's finest and is home to Europe's largest herd of fallow deer.

The house contains the National Trust's largest and finest collection of pictures, the foundations of which were laid by Charles Seymour, 6th Duke of Somerset, when he acquired the house in 1690 on his marriage to the Earl of Northumberland's daughter. On the Duke's death the house passed by marriage to the Wyndham family. Charles Wyndham, the 2nd Earl of Egremont, added to the existing collection of Italian, French and Dutch Old Masters and acquired ancient sculpture from Rome and Greece. The 3rd Earl of Egremont continued the tradition. He collected contemporary British paintings. Interestingly, he was a patron of Turner, providing a studio for him at Petworth and many of Turner's paintings can be seen in the house. The 3rd Earl also acquired work from Gainsborough and Reynolds.

Following alterations to the house in the 1870s only two of the original 17th century interiors remain: a baroque chapel and a marble hall with black and white checked floor.

☎ 01798 343929 www.nationaltrust.org.uk

Petworth House

Pevensey Castle — 160 B3

Dating from Roman times, and occupied by the Normans in 1066, the castle's location as a possible invasion point led to several sieges during its history. It eventually became uninhabited by the 16th century and fell into ruin. A gun emplacement was built there during the Spanish Armada and the castle was again used during World War II. Pillboxes from that time can still be seen. There are towers, battlements and dungeons to explore.

☎ 01323 762604 www.english-heritage.org.uk

Pitt Rivers Museum — 406 A2

A unique collection of objects from all over the world, with something of interest for everyone.

The museum was founded in 1884 when Lt-Gen Pitt-Rivers, a prominent figure in the world of anthropology and archaeology, donated his collection of over 18,000 items to Oxford University. This collection has now been considerably enlarged to comprise over half a million objects, displayed according to function.

☎ 01865 270927 www.prm.ox.ac.uk

Polesden Lacey (NT) — 171 G2

Attractive Regency house in a beautiful setting on the North Downs. It was the home for many years of society hostess, Mrs Ronald Greville, who was a friend of Edward VII. It contains sumptuous interiors and is especially renowned for its paintings. The future George VI and Queen Elizabeth spent part of their honeymoon here in 1923. The gardens have lovely views and extend to 30 acres (12ha), including lawns, walled garden and herbaceous borders.

☎ 01372 452048 www.nationaltrust.org.uk

Port Lympne Wild Animal Park — 174 D5

The park was created in 1973 when John Aspinall bought the Port Lympne estate. It comprises a 350 acre (140ha) reserve where the animals can roam in relatively unconstrained conditions. Aspinall supported an ethos of bonding between keepers and animals that has resulted in successful breeding programmes. At the park visitors can see a large group of black rhinos, Asian elephants, tigers and lions, amongst others. Also open to the public is the house, built during World War I, with its 15 acre (6ha) formal garden.

☎ 01303 264647 www.howletts.net

Portchester Castle — 349 E3

One of England's oldest fortifications, Portchester was originally built in the 3rd century AD by the Romans as part of a chain of fortresses known as the Saxon Shore forts, built in response to Saxon raids. The massive walls, 20ft (6m) high and 10ft (3m) thick, are amongst the finest surviving examples of this period in northern Europe. Subsequently occupied almost continuously until the 19th century, the site was initially a walled settlement with an impressive Norman keep, part of which still stands, then respectively a castle, royal palace, military hospital and a gaol for French prisoners during the Napoleonic Wars.

☎ 023 9237 8291 www.english-heritage.org.uk

Portsmouth Cathedral — 407 F1

Formerly the parish church of Portsmouth, cathedral status was granted in 1927 when the diocese of Portsmouth was created. The original building dates from the 12th century, and the transept and sanctuary still remain, combined with a 17th century nave and tower, rebuilt following Civil War damage. A cupola was added in 1703 and the modern nave and aisles in the mid 20th century, producing an unusual fusion of style with a central tower. Internally, there are several interesting features including the Navy Aisle, with its maritime connections, the remains of a 13th century wall painting, a fine 16th century Florentine majolica plaque and a 20th century bronze statue of John the Baptist.

☎ 023 9282 3300 www.portsmouthcathedral.org.uk

Portsmouth Historic Dockyard — 407 E1

The development of the dockyard at Portsmouth was initiated by Richard I in the 1190s and evolved over succeeding centuries. It became the construction centre for Henry VIII's fleet and received Royal Dockyard status in 1670 when Charles II founded the Royal Navy. By 1800 the navy had nearly 700 ships and the dockyard was considered the largest industrial complex in the world. Apart from a blip at the end of the Napoleonic Wars, expansion was almost continuous throughout the 19th century. In the 20th century the dockyard was vital to Britain's successes in both World Wars, but since then has been in decline due to defence cuts and streamlining of the armed services. The Naval Base remains the premier home port for the Royal Navy, but the title of Royal Dockyard has gone.

The historic Georgian part of the dockyard is now open to the public and this provides a unique opportunity to experience 500 years of the Royal Navy's history, from the remains of the 16th century ship *Mary Rose*, to Action Stations, which uses interactive technology to illustrate the role of the modern navy. In between, a visit to *H.M.S. Victory* reveals the privations suffered by sailors in Nelson's fleet, the scrupulously restored *H.M.S. Warrior* displays a state of the art mid-19th century warship, the Royal Naval Museum gives a detailed history of the service from the 18th century onwards, while Warships by Water harbour tours give a glimpse of the modern operational fleet.

☎ 023 9272 2562 www.flagship.org

H.M.S. Victory – Portsmouth Historic Dockyard

Pulborough Brooks RSPB Nature Reserve — 158 C2

Created in 1989, this 420 acre (170ha) reserve primarily consists of an area of wet grassy meadows which flood in winter. Thousands of water birds such as swans, ducks, geese and wading birds visit the site, especially as winter migrants. There is a visitor centre housed in a converted barn and a 2 mile (3.2km) circular trail.

☎ 01798 875851 www.rspb.org.uk

Quebec House (NT) — 173 D3

General James Wolfe, who led the British to victory over the French in the Battle of Quebec in 1759, lived here as a boy. Named after the battle, this gabled red brick house dating from the 16th century, contains an exhibition paying tribute to his life and the victory that made his name.

☎ 01732 868381 www.nationaltrust.org.uk

Richborough Castle 175 F2

Now a ruin, this fort is thought to date from the Roman invasion in AD43 and, with Watling Street starting at its east gate, became their main entry point into Britain en route to London. Today, flint walls rising to 25ft (7.5m) high can be seen and the foundations of a triumphal arch that was originally over 80ft (24m) high. There is a museum containing artefacts found on site and an exhibition on Roman life.

☎ 01304 612013 www.english-heritage.org.uk

River & Rowing Museum 184 C4

A museum dedicated to rowing and the River Thames, and to Henley, the town where they are inextricably linked.

There are three themed galleries – the Rowing Gallery, the Thames Gallery and the Henley Gallery.

An additional walk-through attraction, particularly aimed at children, re-creates the characters and settings of Kenneth Grahame's 'Wind in the Willows'.

☎ 01491 415600 www.rrm.co.uk

Robin Hill Country Park 157 E4

The 88 acres (35ha) of this country park combine nature trails and woodland walks with theme park rides and adventure playgrounds.

☎ 01983 527352 www.robin-hill.com

Rockbourne Roman Villa 156 A1

Discovered in 1942 by a farmer digging out a ferret, this extensive villa was occupied from the 2nd century AD until the end of Roman rule in Britain in the 5th century AD. Although much of the area has been excavated, part has been backfilled for protection since the site is not under cover. However, the outlines are marked out, and mosaic floors and underfloor heating systems can be viewed. A museum displays artefacts found on the site, including pottery, jewellery and a large hoard of coins.

☎ 01725 518541 www.hants.gov.uk

Romney Marsh 174 C5

This fertile, flat landscape (once under the sea) was reclaimed from marshland in medieval times, and is protected from flooding by a shingle bank. Running along the landward side of the marsh is the 23 mile (37km) long Royal Military Canal, which was built during the Napoleonic wars. The Marsh, as well as being home to the longwool Romney sheep, is also rich in flora and fauna, and is a favourite spot for birdwatchers.

Romney, Hythe & Dymchurch Railway 174 D5

Originally opened in July 1927 to transport the public, this 15 inch narrow-gauge railway now covers a distance of 13.5 miles (22km) from the Cinque Port of Hythe to Dungeness. The line travels through the seaside resort of Dymchurch, and also New Romney where there is a Toy and Model Railway museum.

☎ 01797 362353 www.rhdr.org.uk

Rousham House 197 G5

An unspoilt 17th century house, later extended and remodelled by William Kent in the style of a Gothic Tudor mansion. However, the original staircase and some 17th century panelling still remain, together with Kent's painted parlour containing some of his furniture and painted ceiling.

The landscape garden at Rousham, started by the royal gardener Charles Bridgeman, was further developed and elaborated on by Kent. It remains almost as he left it, with many 18th century water features and temples still in existence. There is also an attractive walled garden with colourful herbaceous border, parterre and pigeon house.

The house opens two days a week in summer, but the garden is open all year. No children under 15.

☎ 01869 347110 www.rousham.org

Rousham House

Royal Navy Submarine Museum 349 E4

A fascinating museum tracing the history and explaining the principles of submarine technology and warfare. Visitors can see *Holland I*, the Royal Navy's first submarine, recovered from the sea bed almost 70 years after sinking on her way to the breakers yard and now fully restored. This can be compared to *H.M.S. Alliance*, preserved fully equipped from when she ended service in 1973 and now in dry dock.

☎ 023 9252 9217 www.rnsubmus.co.uk

Royal Pavilion 390 F2

With its 'Hindu Style' domes and minarets, this Regency Palace is one of the most distinctive and unusual buildings in Britain. Originally a farmhouse, it was transformed for the notoriously profligate Prince Regent (later George IV). In 1787 Henry Holland was commissioned to enlarge the property; further alterations and additions were made by John Nash between 1815 and 1822 . The result was the extravagant Indian and Chinese influenced palace that we see today. The Pavilion has undergone a substantial programme to restore it to its former glory, and stands in restored Regency gardens which have been replanted to Nash's original 1820s design.

The lavish interior features impressive and unusual rooms; notably the Entrance Hall with its Chinese motif wall decorations and the 162ft (49m) Long Gallery, also with a distinctly Chinese décor. The Banqueting Room is stunning with a 45ft (14m) high painted ceiling, with the huge one ton crystal chandelier suspended from a carved dragon. In 1820, the King's Apartments were finally finished, coinciding with George IV's accession and today contain much of the original furniture. After the death of George IV in 1830, the palace was used by William IV and then Queen Victoria who sold it on to the town council in 1850.

☎ 01273 290900 www.royalpavilion.org.uk

Royal Victoria Country Park 348 B3

Located on the site of a former military hospital, the park covers over 100 acres (40ha) of landscaped grounds, woodlands, marsh and beach, and there are nature trails, walks, a narrow-gauge railway and, in summer, a programme of events. A Sensory Garden has also been developed here, designed for scent, sound, colour and texture. The only remaining feature of the hospital is the chapel, which houses a museum of the hospital's history.

☎ 023 8045 5157 www.hants.gov.uk

Rycote Chapel 184 B2

A 15th century chapel retaining the original furniture, with outstanding carved and painted woodwork, two roofed pews and a musicians' gallery.

☎ 023 9258 1059 www.english-heritage.org.uk

St Mary's House 159 D3

Originally built as a pilgrims' inn, this timber-framed house dates from 1470. Features of the house include an Elizabethan staircase, Gothic fireplaces along with 16th century marquetry and furniture. The gardens have unusual animal topiary, herbaceous borders and a rose garden.

☎ 01903 816205

Sandham Memorial Chapel (NT) 169 F1

A red brick chapel built in the 1920s as a memorial to Lieutenant H.W. Sandham, who died following the Macedonia campaign. Inside, the chapel walls are lined with a dramatic series of murals by Stanley Spencer who had been an orderly on the campaign.

☎ 01635 278394 www.nationaltrust.org.uk

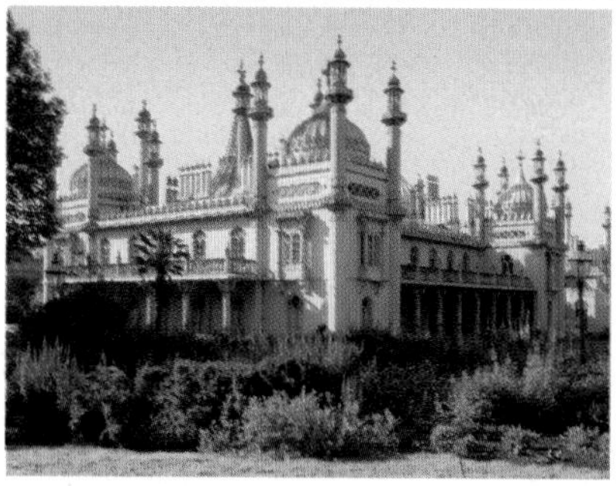

Royal Pavilion – Brighton

Savill Garden 185 E5

Beautiful 35 acre (14ha) garden set within Windsor Great Park comprising woodland, a formal rose garden and herbaceous borders. Named after Eric Savill (deputy surveyor of Windsor Park and Woods) who began work on it for George V in 1932. The garden has a magnificent display of rhododendrons and azaleas giving it superb colour in the spring, although it is worth a visit at any time of year.

☎ 01753 847518 www.savillgarden.co.uk

Scotney Castle Garden (NT) 173 F5

Surrounding the ruins of a 14th century moated castle are picturesque 19th century gardens created by Edward Hussey. The rich planting includes rhododendrons and azaleas giving superb spring colour, plus many Japanese maples, tulip trees and liquidambers which give a splendid display in autumn.

☎ 01892 891081 www.nationaltrust.org.uk

Sea Life Centre 390 F3

Aquarium in a Victorian building with superb ocean tunnel display where visitors can 'walk' through the ocean amongst sharks, rays and giant turtles. There is also a giant Pacific octopus and touch tanks where visitors can hold crabs and feed rays.

☎ 01273 604234 www.sealifeeurope.com

Seven Sisters Country Park 160 A4

The country park lies within an Area of Outstanding Natural Beauty and is a designated Site of Special Scientific Interest. It was established in 1971 and encompasses 700 acres (283ha) either side of the River Cuckmere. The site comprises a wide range of habitats including the beautiful chalk downland with its unique flora and fauna, wetland, coastal and marine environments. The park takes its name from the famous Seven Sisters white cliffs formed where the chalk of the South Downs meets the sea.

There are a number of 18th century flint barns within the park, one of those in Exceat has been converted into a visitor centre. As well as enjoying the area on foot, visitors can also hire bicycles and canoes.

☎ 01323 870280 www.sevensisters.org.uk

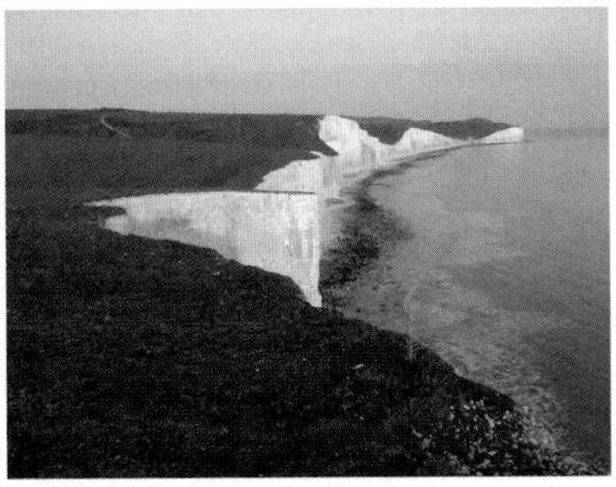

Seven Sisters Country Park

Sheffield Park (NT) 159 G1

With their wide range of rare and unusual trees and shrubs, these beautiful gardens have the character of a landscaped arboretum. They were created for the first Earl of Sheffield in the late 18th century by Lancelot 'Capability' Brown and Humphrey Repton, and extend to 120 acres (48.5ha). In 1909 the estate was acquired by Arthur G. Soames who, over the next 25 years, was responsible for refining the overall design and introduced much of the varied and exotic planting we see today.

Four large lakes form the centrepiece of the garden. Waterfalls and a 25ft (7.5m) cascade connect the lakes together and are spanned by attractive ornamental bridges. In the spring there are magnificent displays of bluebells and daffodils, then later on, rhododendrons and azaleas make an impressive splash of vibrant colour. In summer, red, white and pink water lily flowers add colour to the lakes.

☎ 01825 790231 www.nationaltrust.org.uk

Sir Harold Hillier Gardens & Arboretum 169 E5

A unique collection of shrubs and trees which is one of the largest of its kind in the world. The gardens were established by Sir Harold Hillier in 1953, and extend to over 180 acres (70ha). The collection comprises over 42,000 plants from the world's temperate regions, grown in themed gardens which are designed so that there is colour and interest throughout the year. The Visitor and Education Pavilion describes the purpose and background history of the gardens.

☎ 01794 368787 www.hilliergardens.org.uk

Sissinghurst Castle (NT) 174 A5

These world famous gardens created in the 1930s by writer and poet Vita Sackville-West and her husband, diplomat and writer Sir Harold Nicolson, were first opened to the public in 1938. He was the designer who liked formality and clean lines, and she was the romantic plantswoman who liked profusion and surprise; two gifted people whose talents blended perfectly. Much of the garden's charm is due to the backdrop provided by the Elizabethan buildings, the focal point of which is a four-storey red brick tower, to one side of which is a moat.

The garden extends to 6 acres (2.5ha) and is comprised of a series of 10 'outdoor rooms' divided by hedges of rose, hornbeam and yew, as well as walls. This stunning garden has had an important influence on garden design and planting in the late 20th century.

☎ 01580 710700 www.nationaltrust.org.uk

Smallhythe Place (NT) 174 A5

Early 16th century half-timbered farmhouse, once home to Victorian actress Dame Ellen Terry who lived here from 1899 until her death in 1928. The house contains various mementoes from Terry and her theatrical contemporaries, including a letter from Oscar Wilde.

☎ 01580 762334 www.nationaltrust.org.uk

Southampton Maritime Museum 409 F2

Housed in a 14th century warehouse with impressive timber roof, built for the wool trade, the museum recounts the story of the Port of Southampton. There are models of the great passenger liners, a panoramic layout of the docks, and interactive exhibits showing how the ships and docks function.

☎ 023 8022 3941 www.southampton.gov.uk

Southsea Castle & Museum 157 F3

Built in 1544 as part of Henry VIII's coastal defences, and said to have been designed by the king himself. Its initial purpose was to protect the large fleet of warships based in Portsmouth Harbour, including the flagship *Mary Rose* which sank in front of the castle in 1545.

The building remained an active military base until 1960. During the preceding 400 years it was captured by Parliamentarians in 1642, suffered major damage from an explosion in 1759, was renovated and enlarged in the early 19th century and used as a military prison in Victorian times.

☎ 023 9282 7261 www.southseacastle.co.uk

Spitfire & Hurricane Memorial, R.A.F. Manston 175 F2

The permanent home of two original examples of World War II fighter aircraft along with associated memorabilia. Visitors can see a prototype of the 'Dambusters' bouncing bomb plus a display telling the story of combat over Kent during the war.

☎ 01843 821940 www.spitfire-museum.com

Sissinghurst Castle

Squerryes Court 172 D3

An attractive brick-built 17th century manor house, home to the Warde family since 1731. The interior of the house contains tapestries dating from 1720, 17th century paintings, as well as furniture and porcelain. The 20 acre (8ha) garden includes a lake, herbaceous borders, and a formal garden which has been restored using the original plans.

☎ 01959 562345 www.squerryes.co.uk

Standen (NT) 172 C5

Built between 1892 and 1894, the house was designed by Philip Webb, a lifelong friend and colleague of William Morris, and is a fine showpiece of the Arts and Crafts movement. It contains furniture, tapestries and paintings of the period, along with Morris textiles and wallpapers. There are lovely views from the beautiful 10 acre (4ha) hillside garden.

☎ 01342 323029 www.nationaltrust.org.uk

Staunton Country Park 157 G1

Extending to over 1000 acres (400ha), this was created by Sir George Staunton in the early 18th century as a Regency Pleasure Garden, and is now one of the few remaining Regency parks in the country. Sir George was a noted botanist and authority on China, and the park was inspired by his travels in the Far East.

The tropical glasshouses, rebuilt to Sir George's original designs, contain unusual plants from rainforest environments. There is also a yew maze, puzzle garden, play area, ornamental lake and range of unusual follies.

☎ 023 9245 3405 www.hants.gov.uk

Stoneacre (NT) 173 G3

An attractive half-timbered house dating from 1480 and restored in the 1920s. It features a Great Hall spanned by impressive timberwork. Outside is a 20th century cottage garden.

☎ 01622 862157 www.nationaltrust.org.uk

Stonor Park 184 C4

The red brick Tudor façade disguises a building dating originally from the 12th century and extended in the 14th century, set in a lovely wooded valley on the slopes of the Chilterns. Internally, the rooms are decorated in 18th century Gothic style and there are some interesting paintings and Mortlake tapestries. There is also an exhibition on the life and work of St Edmund Campion, who sought refuge here at the time of the Reformation.

The attractive hillside gardens have displays of daffodils, narcissi, irises and roses, and there are good views over the surrounding deer park.

☎ 01491 638587 www.stonor.com

Stowe School 198 B4

One of the finest Georgian landscape gardens (NT) in the country, covering 350 acres (140ha) of parkland, valleys, views, lakes and rivers, laid out between 1713 – 25. There are over 30 temples dotted around the grounds, designed by well-known architects of the day such as William Kent and Sir John Vanbrugh, and many of these have been restored. The Temple family, who owned Stowe at this time, were fortunate to have the successive services of three of the great landscape gardeners of the time, Charles Bridgeman, William Kent and Lancelot 'Capability' Brown.

The magnificent house at the centre of the park is

now a public school, with access limited mainly to school holidays, but the park is open on a more regular basis.

☎ 01280 822850 (Garden) www.nationaltrust.org.uk
☎ 01280 818282 (House) www.stowe.co.uk

Tangmere Military Aviation Museum — 158 B3

Tangmere, one of Britain's earliest airfields, was operational between 1917 – 1970, and the museum, which started in 1982, traces the history of flight-based warfare, emphasising Tangmere's links with the Royal Air Force and Battle of Britain.

☎ 01243 775223 www.tangmere-museum.org.uk

Thorpe Park — 171 F1

This popular theme park covers over 500 acres (200ha) and is located on the site of former gravel pits which have been landscaped into a series of lakes. This watery location has been used to set the main theme of the park, that of water rides.

The park is divided into a number of areas. These include, amongst others, 'Ranger Country', 'Lost City', 'Neptune's Kingdom', 'Canada Creek' and 'Octopus Garden'. Elsewhere in the park is Nemesis Inferno, a feet-free roller coaster – a real 'white knuckle' experience.

In addition to all the rides there is also a traditional 1930s farm where children can stroke the sheep, pigs and cows.

☎ 01932 562633 www.thorpepark.co.uk

Thorpe Park

Tonbridge Castle (Ruins) — 173 E4

Remains of a Norman motte and bailey castle set in 14 acres (5.5ha) of grounds. Within the impressive 13th century gatehouse visitors can experience castle life through interactive displays and an audio tour.

☎ 01732 770929 www.tonbridgecastle.org

Tunbridge Wells Museum & Art Gallery — 173 E5

Museum of local and natural history, plus an art gallery, which has frequently changing art and craft exhibitions.

☎ 01892 554171 www.tunbridgewells.gov.uk/museum

Uffington Castle & White Horse (NT) — 183 E4

Belying its name, Uffington Castle has no connection with medieval fortifications but is an imposing Iron Age hill fort covering 8 acres (3ha) close to the Ridgeway, an ancient track.

The White Horse, cut into the chalk of the hillside to the east of the castle, is 374ft (114m) long and rather stylised in appearance. Tests indicate a Bronze Age origin, and the figure is thought to represent Epona, a horse goddess, though it will come as no surprise that many legends have developed around this feature.

www.english-heritage.org.uk

Uppark (NT) — 157 G1

A late 17th century house in an attractive setting high on the South Downs. The estate, extending to 50 acres (20ha), was designed by Humphrey Repton. The interior is Georgian and includes paintings, furniture, textiles and ceramics, and an 18th century dolls' house with its original contents. The servants' quarters can also been seen.

☎ 01730 825857 www.nationaltrust.org.uk

Valley Gardens — 171 E1

These beautiful gardens with their impressive displays of rhododendrons, azaleas, magnolias, camellias and carpeting of daffodils cover an area of 200 acres (80ha) within Windsor Great Park. As well as the amazing spring colour, they are very attractive in the autumn.

☎ 01753 847518 www.crownestate.co.uk

Ventnor Botanic Gardens — 157 E5

One of the youngest botanical gardens in the country, started in 1970 on the site of a former hospital. The potential of the location, with its mild climate, was recognised by the late Sir Harold Hillier, the famous plantsman, and the 22 acre (9ha) garden was designed and planted with help from his nurseries, tender plants flourishing in the sheltered environment. Unfortunately a combination of harsh winters and stormy weather in the 1980s destroyed a large number of species, and the replacements have only recently become established.

☎ 01983 855397 www.botanic.co.uk

Vyne, The (NT) — 170 B2

A splendid red brick Tudor mansion built for Henry VIII's Lord Chamberlain, Lord Sandys. Subsequent modifications in the 17th century include the first classical portico of its kind in the country, and there were some further 18th century alterations. Notable features include the Long Gallery, a sweeping Palladian staircase, and the Tudor chapel. The garden has some good herbaceous border displays, and the estate consists of a further 500 acres (200ha) of park and woodland, providing attractive walks.

☎ 01256 881337 www.nationaltrust.org.uk

Waddesdon Manor (NT) — 184 C1

The external appearance of this late Victorian building owes more to the style of a 16th century French chateau than a conventional English country house. It was built for Baron Ferdinand de Rothschild, its primary purpose being to display his splendid collection of French decorative arts. There are also paintings by Gainsborough, Reynolds, Romney, and Dutch and Flemish masters. The wine cellars contain a collection of over 15,000 bottles, some dating back to 1868.

The late 19th century formal gardens surrounding the house are amongst the finest Victorian gardens in Britain, and include a magnificent, colourful parterre, carpet bedding, rose garden, specimen trees, fountains and an extensive collection of French, Dutch and Italian statuary. The centrepiece is the ornate, cast iron rococo aviary which has an interesting collection of exotic birds.

☎ 01296 653226 www.waddesdon.org.uk

Wakehurst Place (NT) — 172 C5

The setting of Wakehurst Place is superb, with fine views across the Sussex Weald. The gardens, which comprise a mixture of walled gardens, woodland, water gardens and lakes, a Himalayan glade, plus more formal planting, surround a 16th century sandstone mansion (not owned by the Trust) and extend to 170 acres (70ha). Much of the impressive collection of trees and shrubs were originally planted by Gerald Loder, 1st Lord Wakehurst, between 1903 and 1936 and then by Sir Henry Price who bequeathed the garden to the National Trust in 1963. Two years later the Royal Botanic Gardens leased the gardens from the Trust to complement their work at Kew.

The wide variety of native and exotic trees give rise to impressive autumn colours when the maples, American beech and larch come into their own. In spring the woodland floors are scattered with bluebells, and later on, rhododendrons create a superb sight.

Wakehurst Place is also home to the Millennium Seed Bank, an ambitious project to safeguard over 24,000 plant species from around the world. An exhibition allows visitors to see the ongoing seed preservation and research in progress.

☎ 01444 894066 www.nationaltrust.org.uk

Walmer Castle & Garden — 175 F4

Tudor castle built 1539 – 40 as a coastal artillery fortress for Henry VIII. In 1708 the castle became the residence of the Lords Warden of the Cinque Ports, some of the most famous encumbents being the Duke of Wellington, Sir Winston Churchill and the Queen Mother. Visitors can enjoy the attractive gardens and see the room where Wellington died.

☎ 01304 364288 www.english-heritage.org.uk

Waterperry — 184 B2

An 80 year old garden with a fine collection of alpines, herbaceous plants, shrubs and trees.

The herbaceous borders are a particularly attractive feature, carefully planted to ensure that colour is continuous from May through to October. There are also delightful formal rose gardens, raised beds of alpines, a knot garden and riverside walks.

A fascinating collection of agricultural and horticultural tools is housed in an 18th century granary in the grounds.

☎ 01844 339226 www.waterperrygardens.co.uk

Weald & Downland Open Air Museum — 158 A2

Almost 50 historic buildings dating from the 13th to the 19th century have been rebuilt on this attractive 50 acre (20ha) parkland site in the lovely South Downs countryside. The buildings were rescued from destruction and have been carefully dismantled and moved from their original locations to create this museum. The site illustrates traditional rural life in an inspiring way.

☎ 01243 811363 www.wealddown.co.uk

Wellington Country Park — 170 C1

A good range of activities in this 350 acres (140ha) of woodland, parkland and lakes. For younger children there is an adventure playground, small breeds farm and miniature railway, while other options include fishing on the lake, nature trails, and camping and caravanning facilities. There are events taking place throughout the year.

☎ 0118 932 6444 www.wellington-country-park.co.uk

Wakehurst Place

West Berkshire Museum 169 F1

Two of Newbury's most historic buildings, the 17th century Cloth Hall and 18th century Granary, are now home to an absorbing museum of local history. There are specific galleries devoted to the Kennet and Avon Canal, traditional local industries, costume and local history. The Civil War is also a major theme, two battles of the period having taken place locally. There is a programme of special exhibitions.

☎ 01635 30511 www.westberks.gov.uk

West Dean Gardens 158 A2

In an attractive setting at the foot of the South Downs, this 35 acre (14ha) garden contains specimen trees, herbaceous planting and a Victorian walled kitchen garden with 16 restored glasshouses and frames. A notable feature of the garden is a 300ft (100m) pergola by Harold Peto dating from 1911. Over recent years extensive planting of bulbs has taken place resulting in spectacular spring displays. The garden holds two National Collections, that of the Tulip Tree and Horse Chestnut.

☎ 01243 818210 www.westdean.org.uk/site/gardens/

West Wycombe Park (NT) 184 D3

Extravagant 18th century Italianate mansion with the external appearance of a classical temple. Inspired by Grand Tours, there are splendid painted ceilings, and furniture, paintings and sculpture dating from the mid 18th century ownership of Sir Francis Dashwood, who founded the notorious Hell Fire Club. Club members were drawn from the upper echelons of society, and local mythology had them indulging in Satanic rites, though reality was probably wine, women and a spot of free thinking. Sir Francis also created the beautiful rococo landscape garden in the 300 acres (150ha) of parkland surrounding the house.

An unusual addition to the grounds are the Hell Fire Caves. Again the inspiration of Sir Francis, the existing caves were greatly extended in the 1750s by a remarkable feat of engineering. Although providing a suitably atmospheric meeting place for the Hell Fire Club, Sir Francis's motives were partly altruistic in that the work provided employment for local villagers following a series of failed harvests. The caves are privately owned and there is an additional entry fee.

☎ 01494 533739 www.nationaltrust.org.uk

Winchester Cathedral 414 B2

One of the great cathedrals of England, and perhaps one of the best examples of Gothic Perpendicular architecture to be found.

The original minster was built by King Cenwalh of Wessex in AD643 and was the royal Saxon cathedral, burial place of kings. The foundations can still be seen adjacent to the West Door but this building was replaced by Bishop Walkelin, the first Norman bishop, who laid the foundations of the present cathedral in 1079, building materials including stone from the Isle of Wight and local timber. The cathedral was completed within 14 years, but over the following centuries underwent much modification, particularly between 1350 – 1450 when the original Romanesque nave was transformed to the English Gothic style, mainly due to the efforts of Bishop William of Wykeham. The nave measures 556ft (170m), making Winchester the longest medieval church in Europe. The whole building is an ecclesiastical and architectural treasure house.

Within the cathedral is a statue to William Walker, a deep sea diver who could be said to have single-handedly saved the cathedral from collapse at the beginning of the 20th century. He spent five years working underwater in complete darkness replacing the decaying timber of the ancient foundations.

☎ 01962 857200 www.winchester-cathedral.org.uk

Windsor Castle 414 D3

Strategically placed above the River Thames and a day's march from London, William the Conqueror selected Windsor as the site for a fort to protect the western approach to the capital. Since then it has become the largest and oldest occupied castle in the world.

William's original building was a wooden motte and bailey fort constructed in 1079, Henry II replacing this with stone outer walls and a round tower in 1165. In the succeeding centuries monarchs have enlarged and modified the castle, militarily if necessary, or decoratively in more peaceful times, and the building today occupies a site of 12 acres (5ha).

The magnificent State Rooms contain outstanding pictures from the Royal Collection including works by Holbein, Rembrandt and Canaletto, fine furniture, painted ceilings and carvings by Grinling Gibbons. These rooms are used for ceremonial and state occasions and may be closed when the Queen is in residence. In the winter months the richly decorated Semi State Rooms can also be viewed. The Drawings Gallery houses changing exhibitions of material drawn from the Royal Library and other treasures.

Within the precincts is St George's Chapel, built in the late 15th century and one of Britain's finest examples of Gothic architecture. It contains the tombs of 10 monarchs and the great battle sword of Edward III hangs on one of the walls.

Outside the castle, one of the best known of British ceremonies, the Changing of the Guard, takes place throughout the year. It is advisable to telephone in advance to check days and times.

It is important to note that this is a working palace, and that some areas may be closed off at short notice.

☎ 01753 869898 www.the-royal-collection.org.uk

Wisley R.H.S. Gardens 171 F2

Home to the Royal Horticultural Society since its donation by Sir Thomas Hanbury in 1903, this garden was first established by George Wilson in 1878, a scientist and keen gardener, with the aim of growing difficult plants successfully.

The gardens extend to 204 acres (97ha) along the banks of the River Wey and are of interest to both keen horticulturalists and those who are just after a visual treat. Visitors can wander amongst the model gardens which give ideas that can be easily applied at home. The gardens also feature glasshouses, sweeping lawns, 420ft (128m) long herbaceous borders, an impressive rock garden and the Jubilee arboretum.

In front of the half-timbered Tudor-style building, which is used as a laboratory and offices, is a formal canal which is an impressive sight when the water lilies are in flower. The gardens look spectacular all through the year; in spring the Alpine meadow is stunning, with its carpet of yellow daffodils, the rose gardens and herbaceous borders are a riot of colour in the summer, the large number of trees provide autumn colour and in winter the heated glasshouses come into their own with their colourful exotics.

☎ 01483 224234 www.rhs.org.uk/gardens/wisley/

Witley Common Information Centre (NT) 171 E3

Located on Witley Common, an area of lowland heath and woodland with a wide variety of plant and animal life, this purpose-built education and information centre houses a countryside exhibition explaining the area's importance and management.

☎ 01428 683207 www.nationaltrust.org.uk

Worthing Museum & Art Gallery 158 D3

The museum has an emphasis on local history and is housed in an Edwardian building. It contains collections of ceramics, toys, textiles, geology, a variety of temporary exhibitions and a sculpture garden.

☎ 01903 239999 ext 1140 www.worthing.gov.uk/leisure/museumartgallery/
☎ 01903 221150 (Saturdays)

Yarmouth Castle 156 C4

Completed in 1547, this was the final castle to be built in Henry VIII's coastal defence system, following a French invasion of the Isle of Wight in 1545. It is of a fairly simple design, consisting of a basic square with no central tower. Bounded by the sea to the north and east, the south and west walls were protected by a moat, filled in at the end of the 17th century. Around 1600 a large gun battery was built in the north part of the courtyard, while domestic buildings filled the south side. The gun platform now provides splendid views across the harbour and Solent.

☎ 01983 760678 www.english-heritage.org.uk

Wisley R.H.S. Gardens

LONDON

England's multi-cultural capital vibrates with round-the-clock reminders of its long and prestigious history. 'Old Father Thames' washes through a panorama of imposing buildings old and new, offering tastes of English tradition, cultural opportunities, avant-garde events and shopping galore. London is the definitive twenty-four hour city where the leisure facilities, entertainment, sporting venues and diversity of events are amongst the best in the world.

Houses of Parliament

Bank of England Museum
356 B3

An interesting insight into the role of finance, from the foundation of the bank in 1694 by Royal Charter to the high-tech world of modern banking. Besides displays of gold and banknotes, there is also a Roman mosaic floor (uncovered during rebuilding work in the 1930s) plus a variety of interactive displays.

☎ 020 7601 5491 www.bankofengland.co.uk/museum

Britain At War
356 B3

A re-creation of what life was like for the ordinary people of London during the Blitz. There are realistic reconstructions, including an underground air-raid shelter, an Anderson shelter and a BBC studio. Through the use of sights, sounds and special effects, visitors can get a real feel for the atmosphere of war-torn London.

☎ 020 7403 3171 www.britainatwar.co.uk

British Museum
376 J3

This is the oldest public museum in the world and was founded in 1753 when Sir Hans Sloane bequeathed his considerable collection of artefacts, along with his library and herbarium, to the nation in return for paying his heirs £20,000. George II and the Parliament of the time, led by the Speaker, Arthur Onslow, were persuaded to accept the gift and a public lottery was held to raise the necessary funds. The next year Montagu House was acquired in order to house the collection which has since increased to over six million objects. Over the years the building has had to expand to accommodate this huge collection, and the bulk of the neoclassical building which visitors see today, including the impressive south front, dates from 1852.

The museum houses the world's greatest collection of antiquities including the national collections of archaeology and ethnography, with treasures from all over the globe. Highlights include the Rosetta Stone, the Elgin Marbles and the Sutton Hoo treasure. There are also Egyptian mummies, which include not only humans but cats, baboons and even crocodiles, and the 2000 year old peat-preserved Lindow Man. The exhibits are so rich and varied that to attempt to see them all in a single visit would be impossible.

☎ 020 7323 8299 www.thebritishmuseum.ac.uk

British Museum

Buckingham Palace
376 D11

Built in 1705, and originally called Buckingham House, it was purchased by George III for his wife Queen Charlotte in 1761. Over the years it has been remodelled and extended a number of times, firstly by George IV with the assistance of his architect John Nash. A new suite of rooms was added and the north and south wings were rebuilt, with the Marble Arch as a centrepiece to the courtyard. The arch was later removed and now stands near the north east corner of Hyde Park. Queen Victoria made further alterations and additions, most notably the East Front which was designed by architect Edward Blore in 1847. Due to the deterioration of the stone, this was subsequently refaced in 1913 creating the familiar façade that we see today. Soon after Queen Victoria's accession in 1837, it became the monarch's official London residence.

The palace is open during August and September with visitors able to see 19 of the state rooms. These include the Throne Room, the Blue Drawing Room, the impressive White Drawing Room and the 150ft (46m) Picture Gallery. The huge Ballroom can also be seen; at 122ft (37m) long and 60ft (18m) wide, it is used for State banquets and can accommodate 150 guests. Treasures that can be seen within the palace include paintings by artists such as Rembrandt and superb examples of English and French furniture.

☎ 020 7766 7300 www.royal.gov.uk/output/page555.asp

Buckingham Palace

Cabinet War Rooms
376 H10

An intriguing underground suite of rooms used by Winston Churchill and his war cabinet as a meeting, planning and information centre during World War II. On display are the soundproofed Cabinet War Room, a Map Room, the original hot-line and scrambler used by Churchill when communicating with President Roosevelt, Churchill's private quarters and the desk from which he made some of his famous wartime broadcasts.

☎ 020 7930 6961 www.iwm.org.uk/cabinet/

Chessington World of Adventures
171 G1

This popular attraction, covering 65 acres (27ha), combines the original zoo with a modern theme park. The zoo has a wide range of animals including a family group of West Lowland gorillas, sea lions, penguins and a variety of big cats such as lions, tigers and leopards. A gentle monorail allows visitors to travel over the animal enclosures for a superb bird's-eye view.

The theme park is divided into a number of areas and has all the usual thrill rides, along with those more suitable for younger children. 'The Forbidden Kingdom' has the white-knuckle ride Rameses' Revenge which revolves riders through a full 360° and blasts them with water; 'Transylvania' features The Vampire, Britain's first hanging roller coaster which also swings riders from side to side; 'Toytown' is ideal for the little ones as they can wear themselves out on Toadie's Crazy Cars and Berry Bouncers; 'Mystic East' features Dragon Falls, a traditional log flume, which has the usual plunge at the end, and Samurai where riders are spun round – not for those with delicate stomachs! Visitors can also enjoy 'Beanoland', where foam-filled balls can be catapulted, and 'Pirates Cove' where the Black Buccaneer pirate ship rocks riders from side to side. The sheer variety of attractions means that there is something for everyone.

☎ 01372 729 560 www.chessington.co.uk

Chiswick House
186 B5

This fine 18th century domed villa, designed by Lord Burlington in 1728, was modelled on Palladio's Villa Rotonda at Vicenza. The William Kent interiors, particularly the reception rooms which include a domed saloon and velvet room, are sumptuous. Many have painted ceilings and gilded decorations, and feature period furnishings. Kent, alongside royal gardener Charles Bridgeman, was also responsible for the design of the gardens where he continued the Italianate theme with Doric columns, statues and obelisks, plus a cascade.

☎ 020 8995 0508 www.english-heritage.org.uk

Covent Garden
377 K6

Once the site of the famous fruit and flower market, this area is now a fashionable pedestrianised piazza. The arcades are lined with small specialist shops and there are plenty of places to eat and drink. The atmosphere is lively, with street entertainers a real highlight. The Jubilee Hall plays host to a variety of markets, including antiques, arts and crafts. Surrounding the piazza, visitors can also see St Paul's church, built by Inigo Jones and completed in 1633, London's Transport Museum, the Theatre Museum and the Royal Opera House.

Cutty Sark
357 C4

This famous tea clipper, built in 1869, was the fastest in the tea race from China and subsequently, when used in the Australian wool trade, she consistently set new speed records. Visitors can explore the ship and see where the sailors ate, slept and worked, and there is also an impressive collection of carved figureheads to be seen.

☎ 020 8858 3445 www.cuttysark.co.uk

Dulwich Picture Gallery
357 B5

Much of the collection was put together by French art dealer Noël Desenfans and Sir Francis Bourgeois between 1790 and 1795, for the king of Poland. Due to the king's abdication they took over responsibility for the collection and it was left in Sir Francis's will to Dulwich College in 1811, with the stipulation that the paintings should go on public display. A purpose built gallery designed by Sir John Soane houses the pictures, which include works by Claude, Cuyp, Rembrandt, Rubens, Van Dyck, Gainsborough and Canaletto.

☎ 020 8693 5254 www.dulwichpicturegallery.org.uk

Eltham Palace
186 D5

A 1930s mansion constructed around a Great Hall, built for Edward IV in the 1470s. The house was commissioned by Stephen Courtauld, millionaire patron of the arts, and his wife Virginia. It had all the latest electrical gadgets including a centralised

vacuum cleaner and sound system. The interior exhibits superb examples of Art Deco styling, for example, the dining room has black and silver doors, an aluminium ceiling and maple walls. The bathroom features onyx and gold mosaic. The gardens extend to 19 acres (7.5ha) and include a moat, rose garden and pergola.

☎ 020 8294 2548 www.english-heritage.org.uk

Fenton House (NT) 186 B4

A late 17th century house containing collections of fine porcelain, early keyboard instruments and Georgian furniture. Outside is a walled garden with roses, orchard and a kitchen garden.

☎ 020 7435 3471 www.nationaltrust.org.uk

Geffrye Museum 356 B3

The museum is housed in several 18th century almshouses, with attractive gardens. Through a series of period rooms, the changing style of domestic interiors and furniture of the English middle classes from 1600 to the present day are shown.

☎ 020 7739 9893 www.geffrye-museum.org.uk

Greenwich – Old Royal Observatory

Greenwich 357 C4

Situated on the River Thames and a designated World Heritage Site, Greenwich is of international significance. It has a long and interesting history with strong royal and maritime links. Greenwich Park, which affords superb views, is the oldest royal park in London. The 17th century Royal Naval College, designed by Sir Christopher Wren, is built on the site of the Royal Palace of Greenwich. As the primary royal residence from the 15th to 17th centuries, it was the birthplace of Henry VIII and Elizabeth I. Alongside the river are the *Cutty Sark*, the fastest tea clipper of her time, and *Gipsy Moth IV*, on which Sir Francis Chichester was the first person to circumnavigate the globe single-handedly in 1967. The National Maritime Museum, which includes the Palladian style Queen's House designed by Inigo Jones, can also be visited.

The Old Royal Observatory, built by Wren in 1675, is the home of Greenwich Mean Time and the world's Prime Meridian – Longitude 0°, where the eastern and western hemispheres meet. The brass meridian line can be seen set into the ground, and you can stand with a foot in each hemisphere. The building contains a collection of time keeping, astronomical and navigational objects. Also of interest are the 19th century Ranger's House and St Alfege Church.

☎ 0870 608 2000 www.greenwichwhs.org.uk

H.M.S. Belfast 356 B3

Launched in 1938, this was the Royal Navy's largest cruiser of World War II. It participated in the sinking of the German battle cruiser *Scharnhorst* in 1943 and remained in Navy service until 1965. Most of the ship can be visited, including the engine room, boiler room and the bridge. There are displays depicting life on board during the war.

☎ 020 7940 6300 www.iwm.org.uk/belfast

Ham House (NT) 186 A5

An outstanding 17th century house, built in 1610 and enlarged in the 1670s, containing an impressive collection of paintings, furniture and textiles. The formal 17th century gardens have been restored to their original form.

☎ 020 8940 1950 www.nationaltrust.org.uk

Hampton Court Palace & Garden 355 A6

Located on the banks of the River Thames, this impressive building, covering approximately 6 acres (2.5ha), was originally built by Cardinal Thomas Wolsey, and dates from the early 16th century. He presented it to Henry VIII in 1528 to try and regain favour after he failed to annul the king's marriage to Catherine of Aragon. After becoming a royal palace, it was rebuilt and extended a number of times. Henry was responsible for the construction of the magnificent hammerbeamed hall and the vast kitchens. In the 1690s William and Mary commissioned Sir Christopher Wren to rebuild the palace, but due to a lack of time and money much of the Tudor palace survived. The two differing architectural styles can be seen clearly today. At this time the interior was decorated by some of the best artists and craftsmen of the day – Tijou, Grinling Gibbons, Laguerre and Verrio.

Visitors can enjoy the magnificent state apartments which contain furniture, tapestries and paintings from the Royal Collection. Other attractions include a rare 'real tennis' court on which Henry VIII once played. The grounds include 60 acres (25ha) of beautiful gardens. There is a 1 mile (1.6km) - long canal, extensive radiating avenues of limes and clipped yews, an orangery, and the famous maze. The privy garden, an attractive parterre, to the south of the palace, dates from William and Mary's reign and, after many years of neglect, was restored to its former glory during the 1990s.

☎ 0870 752 7777 www.hrp.org.uk

Horniman Museum 357 B5

An eccentric and eclectic international collection of arts, crafts and artefacts housed in a purpose-built museum set in 16 acre (6ha) grounds. Originally collected by tea merchant and world traveller Frederick J Horniman, the exhibits cover a remarkable range, from torture devices, Egyptian mummy cases and masks, musical instruments to an enormous stuffed walrus. An ideal family attraction.

☎ 020 8699 1872 www.horniman.ac.uk

Houses of Parliament 377 K11

Also known as the Palace of Westminster and home to the main seat of Government. The original palace was built in the first half of the 11th century by Edward the Confessor and remained the main residence of the monarch until the first half of the 16th century when it moved to Whitehall. The Lords, however, continued to meet at Westminster. In 1834 the building was badly damaged by fire and all but the crypt, Jewel Tower and Westminster Hall survived. The hall, which is 240ft (73m) by 60ft (18m) has a magnificent hammerbeam oak roof. Most of the present building was constructed in Gothic Revival style between 1840 and 1888 by Charles Barry and Augustus Pugin and contains 1100 rooms, 100 staircases and over 2 miles (3km) of passages.

Situated on the River Thames, the building is an impressive sight with its two towers, one at each end. The Victoria Tower on the south west corner, on which the Union Jack flies when parliament is sitting, rises to a height of 336ft (102m). St Stephens clock tower (commonly known as Big Ben), to the north, is 316ft (96m) high and is famous the world over. It has four clock faces, each 23ft (7m) in diameter and contains the 13 ton bell, 'Big Ben', cast in 1858.

The Houses of Parliament are worth a visit, just to see the exterior, but visitors can also take a guided tour of the palace during the summer recess and see the impressive interiors.

☎ 020 7219 4272 www.parliament.uk

Imperial War Museum 377 P13

The museum has displays covering warfare from World War I to the present day and majors on Britain and the Commonwealth. Natural light from the domed atrium illuminates an impressive collection of tanks and weapons including a V2 rocket and also a Spitfire. Not only does it include conventional hardware of war but also interesting exhibits relating to war's impact on the population at large. For example there are displays on rationing, morale-boosting, censorship and there is also an exhibition on the Holocaust. The arts associated with wartime can also be seen, such as photographs, letters, paintings and poetry, and there are also old newsreels and period music.

☎ 020 7416 5320 www.iwm.org.uk

Houses of Parliament

Kensington Palace
354 D3

Built by Sir Christopher Wren and bought by William III in 1689. Queen Victoria was born here in 1819 and on her 70th birthday the State Apartments were opened to the public. It was home to Diana, Princess of Wales, and is currently the residence of several members of the Royal Family. The Royal Ceremonial Dress Collection, dating from the 18th century, is on display, including some of Diana's dresses.

☎ 0870 751 5170 www.hrp.org.uk

Kenwood House
354 D2

This impressive neoclassical mansion, adjacent to Hampstead Heath, was remodelled by Robert Adam between 1764 and 1773. The house contains an outstanding collection of paintings with works by Turner, Gainsborough, Rembrandt, Vermeer, Van Dyck and Reynolds. The landscaped grounds, laid out by Humphrey Repton, are often the venue for lakeside open air concerts in the summer.

☎ 020 8348 1286 www.english-heritage.org.uk

London Aquarium
377 L10

Located in the cellars of County Hall (previously home to the now defunct Greater London Council) on the banks of the River Thames, this is one of the largest aquaria in Europe. At the centre of the aquarium there are two huge tanks extending over two floors, one displaying the sealife of the Pacific and one of the Atlantic. Visitors can see large 6ft (2m) long sharks, conger eels, stingrays and also the daily feeding of the fish by divers. Elsewhere there are slightly smaller tanks with themed areas displaying varying aquatic habitats, such as coral reefs and tropical rivers with piranha fish. There is a display of unusual and beautiful sea horses and also touch tanks where children are encouraged to touch the rays, crabs and starfish.

☎ 020 7967 8000 www.londonaquarium.co.uk

London Aquarium

London Dungeon
356 B3

In the vaults under London Bridge Station, this horror museum houses a gruesomely realistic exhibition of sacrifices, tortures, plagues, murders and executions. It is not recommended for the nervous or squeamish as the reconstructions and atmosphere of the place make for quite a scary experience.

☎ 020 7403 7221 www.dungeons.co.uk

London Eye
377 L10

Opened in 2000 as part of the millennium celebrations, at 450ft (135m) this observation wheel is the world's highest. It has become one of London's most recognisable landmarks comprising 32 capsules, each holding up to 25 people. The slow, gentle ride takes 30 minutes and gives visitors plenty of time to take in the splendid views.

Conceived and designed by architects David Marks and Julia Barfield, it is positioned in a prime location on the south bank of the River Thames and overlooks many of London's famous and impressive landmarks such as the Houses of Parliament, Westminster Abbey, St Paul's Cathedral and Buckingham Palace. On a clear day views of up to 25 miles (40km) can be seen.

To get the most from the experience it is worthwhile studying a map and the photoguide to help pick out key landmarks. These can be purchased at the London Eye shop.

☎ 0870 500 0600 www.londoneye.com

London Eye

London Zoo
356 A3

Founded in 1828, this was the world's first scientific zoo. In many ways the zoo was pioneering; in 1849 it introduced a reptile house – the first in the world, then the first public aquarium and the first insect house were built in 1853 and 1881 respectively.

Covering an area of 36 acres (14.5ha), it houses over 650 species of animals and participates in breeding programmes for over 140 of them. Visitors can follow a recommended route to ensure that they do not miss anything; this is marked by use of green footprints on the ground.

All the usual zoo animals, and more, are present, such as lions, apes, elephants and a variety of birdlife. Ever popular, the giraffes live in style within a neoclassical residence designed by Decimus Burton. Within the same hoofed animal area, extravagantly marked okapi, tapir and bongoes can be found. The children's zoo is in a farmyard setting and contains domesticated animals from around the world. These include camels, llamas and reindeer, as well as the more familiar sheep, cows, pigs, hens and ducks. Other attractions include the huge walk-through aviary, designed by Lord Snowdon, and Moonlight World, where nocturnal creatures can be seen. The Millennium Conservation Centre, with its advanced low-energy design, houses the Web of Life Exhibition; this is well worth a visit. Biodiversity is the focus, the extraordinary range of life on earth is explored, showing adaptation to different environments.

☎ 020 7722 3333 www.londonzoo.co.uk

London Zoo - Rhino Iguana

London's Transport Museum
377 K6

Telling the story of the world's largest urban passenger transport system, the museum contains gleamingly preserved survivors from the first cabs to trolleybuses and modern day tube trains. There are lots of hands-on exhibits where visitors can try out the controls. The museum, which was opened in 1980, is housed in the attractive old Covent Garden flower market building.

☎ 020 7379 6344 www.ltmuseum.co.uk

Lord's Cricket Ground & Museum
354 D3

The ground at Lord's is the headquarters of English cricket and the official home of the Marylebone Cricket Club (MCC). Guided tours are available, and include visits to the grounds, the futuristic-looking media centre, the players' dressing room, and, when not in use, the Long Room with its portraits of famous cricketers. The tour also includes a visit to the world's oldest sporting museum, the MCC Museum, where, among other exhibits, the famous Ashes urn is on show.

☎ 020 7616 8656 www.lords.org

Madame Tussaud's & the Planetarium
376 A1

This famous waxwork collection started out as a small touring exhibition in 1802, brought from France by Madame Tussaud. Over the years the collection has grown and diversified enormously, and in recent years topical interactive activities have been introduced. Today, visitors can see amazingly life-like and life-sized waxwork figures of villains and heroes, politicians and royalty, popstars and film stars, from the past and present; mingle with sporting and media stars, sing and dance with celebrities and learn football tips from England team members.

'The Chamber of Horrors' is probably the best known and most notorious part of the exhibition: Dr Crippen stares out from behind bars; grim and bloodthirsty punishments and a reconstruction of Jack the Ripper's London, with its eerie atmosphere,

Madame Tussaud"s

can be seen. In the 'Grand Hall', many world leaders and royalty, from past and present, are gathered together. 'Premiere Night' brings together stars of the silver screen from 1914 to the present day. To finish, a ride on the 'Spirit of London' is a must, where visitors travel on small black cabs through London's turbulent history.

The Planetarium is next door and can also be visited on the same ticket. There are interactive exhibits and scale models as well as a fascinating show that takes visitors on a voyage of discovery into the solar system and beyond. Both educational and entertaining, it gives a great feel for the vastness and beauty of the universe.

☎ 0870 400 3000 www.madame-tussauds.co.uk

Monument, The 356 B3

Designed by Sir Christopher Wren and his colleague Dr Robert Hook, it was built between 1671 and 1677 to commemorate the Great Fire of London and to celebrate the subsequent rebuilding of the city. Made from Portland stone and standing 202ft (61.5m) tall, it is the tallest free-standing stone column in the world. Its height is significant as it is exactly 202ft away from the site of the baker's shop in Pudding Lane where the fire started in 1666. It has a spiralled, cantilevered staircase with 311 steps. The climb is worthwhile as the view from the top is superb.

☎ 020 7626 2717

Morden Hall Park (NT) 355 D6

The parkland, with the River Wandle flowing through it, extends to over 125 acres (50ha) and was once a deer park. It comprises meadows, wetlands and a superb rose garden planted in a random design with over 2000 plants. Other attractions include independently-run craft workshops, a city farm and garden centre.

☎ 020 8545 6850 www.nationaltrust.org.uk

Museum in Docklands 356 C3

Located in a converted Georgian warehouse on West India Quay, the museum traces the history of London's docks and river from Roman times, through its heyday, its post-war decline, and on to its recent regeneration. There are 12 galleries over five floors, and the exhibits include artefacts, paintings and photographs, accompanied by interactive displays.

☎ 0870 444 3856 www.museumindocklands.org.uk

Museum of Childhood 356 B3

Housing the children's section of the Victoria and Albert Museum, this museum contains an impressive collection of toys and childhood artefacts, the national collection of children's costume, plus a gallery telling the story of childhood in London's East End.

☎ 020 8980 2415 www.museumofchildhood.org.uk

Museum of Garden History 377 L13

The museum is housed in the former church of St Mary-at-Lambeth in whose churchyard are the graves of the two John Tradescants, father and son, who were royal gardeners during the reigns of Charles I and II. The museum tells the story of gardening through the ages. Part of the churchyard has been laid out as a garden in the style characteristic of the Tradescants' time, including a replica of a 17th century knot garden, along with some of the well-known plants they brought back from their travels, such as the Tulip Tree.

☎ 020 7401 8865 www.cix.co.uk/~museumgh

Museum of London 377 S3

Over 2000 years of London's history are on display, divided into seven permanent and well laid out galleries. These range from the Iron Age 'London before London', through Roman, Tudor and Stuart times, to 'World City' (1789 to 1914) when London became the world's first metropolis. Exhibits include over 1.1 million objects and there are attractive reconstructions of streets and interiors. The River Thames is shown to have a key role in the development and life of the city through the ages.

☎ 0870 444 3852 www.museumoflondon.org.uk

National Army Museum 355 D4

Tells the story of the British Army over the last 500 years, from Agincourt to the present day. It chronicles all the major British campaigns and has a large 400 sq ft (37 sq m) model of the battle of Waterloo, containing over 70,000 model soldiers. Other exhibits include the skeleton of Napoleon's horse, a reproduction of a World War I trench and a lamp used by Florence Nightingale.

☎ 020 7730 0717 www.national-army-museum.ac.uk

National Gallery 376 H7

In a commanding position on the north side of Trafalgar Square, the gallery is where the nation's major collection of historical paintings is housed. Founded in 1824, the collection has grown over the years, often due to the generosity of wealthy benefactors, and now numbers over 2300 Western European paintings, mostly dating from 1260 to 1900.

The gallery is divided into four wings. The Sainsbury Wing, opened in 1990, contains some of the earlier Renaissance paintings, including those by Van Eyck, Botticelli, Leonardo da Vinci and Raphael; the West Wing takes us from 1500 to 1600 with works by, amongst others, Titian, Holbein and Michelangelo. In the North Wing, works by Rubens, Van Dyck, Rembrandt and Vermeer are on show, taking us from 1600 to 1700; and finally the East Wing exhibits paintings dating from 1700 to 1900 and features works by Gainsborough, Constable, Monet, Cezanne and Van Gogh. To do justice to the collection it is best not to try and see everything in one visit.

☎ 020 7747 2885 www.nationalgallery.org.uk

National Maritime Museum 357 C4

Housed in architecturally important buildings including The Queen's House by Inigo Jones, the museum tells the story of Britain and the sea; its navy, merchants and explorers. A nautical enthusiast's paradise, there are some 20 galleries with exhibits including models of ships, clocks and watches, contemporary and historic paintings, carved figureheads, weapons and fine silver collections. There are also plenty of hands-on activities.

☎ 020 8858 4422 www.nmm.ac.uk

National Portrait Gallery

National Portrait Gallery 376 H7

Founded in 1856 by historian Philip Stanhope as a gallery of original portraits to commemorate British history. Today, visitors can see over 1000 works which are arranged chronologically within the gallery, from medieval times to the present day. The focus of the collection is the subjects of the paintings rather than the painters themselves. The full portrait collection, the largest in the world, contains over 10,000 pictures in a variety of media: oils, watercolours, sculptures, caricatures, miniatures, photographs and also silhouettes. Paintings of kings, queens, politicians, musicians, artists and poets, ranging from the likes of Shakespeare to Madonna are on display. In addition to the permanent galleries there is a varied programme of temporary exhibitions throughout the year.

The well stocked shop and rooftop restaurant offering excellent views of London are worth a visit.

☎ 020 7306 0055 www.npg.org.uk

National Gallery

Natural History Museum 355 D4

In 1856 Professor Richard Owen, the Superintendent of the Natural History section of the British Museum, campaigned for more space to display the exhibits. A site in South Kensington was purchased and a new, purpose-built museum was constructed, opening to the public in 1881. Lavishly decorated with plants and animals, the resulting 4 acre (1.5ha) museum building is a masterpiece. The main entrance consists of a dramatic series of recessed arches on decorated columns leading to the imposing Central Hall, which contains a huge 85ft (26m) skeleton of a dinosaur – Diplodocus.

The collection is vast and varied, covering all aspects of the natural world, both as traditional exhibits and interactive displays. The Darwin Centre allows visitors to take a look behind the scenes and see scientists working on the collection. A real favourite, especially with the children, is the Dinosaur Exhibition, where there is an animatronic Tyrannosaurus Rex, skeletons and plenty of touch screens. The Earth Galleries, entered through a giant globe, feature displays on the origins of the universe and there is an earthquake simulator where visitors can experience this phenomenon. Other exhibits worth a visit are the huge, life-sized model of a blue whale and the creepy crawlies. The museum is enormously enjoyable as well as educational and there really is too much to see in one visit.

☎ 020 7942 5000 www.nhm.ac.uk

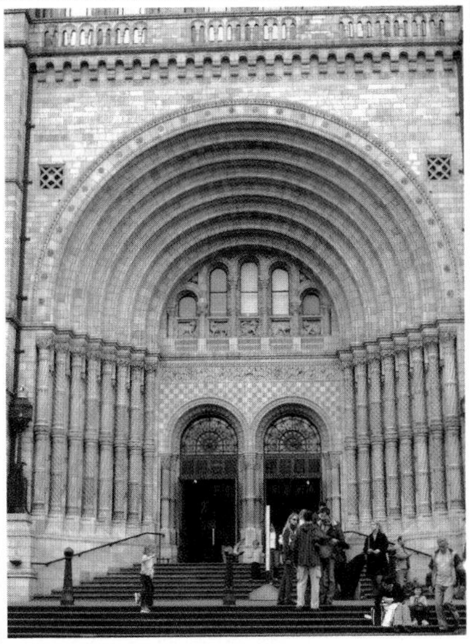

Natural History Museum

Osterley Park & House (NT) 355 A4

Set in extensive parkland, the original Tudor mansion was transformed in the 18th century into a neoclassical villa by Robert Adam. Considered by many to be some of his finest work, it features superb plasterwork, carpets and furniture.

☎ 020 8232 5050 www.nationaltrust.org.uk

Royal Academy of Arts 376 E7

Founded in 1768, the Royal Academy holds major temporary public exhibitions throughout the year. Sir Joshua Reynolds – who was the first president – Gainsborough, Turner and Constable all studied and have exhibited here. Located in Burlington House, a superb early 18th century mansion, one of the few surviving in the West End, the academy is probably most famous for its inspirational annual Summer Exhibition, which displays thousands of works by living artists for view and sale. In addition to the wide range of temporary exhibitions, a suite of rooms, restored to their former 18th century grandeur, houses highlights from the permanent collection. Entry to this is free. The full collection comprises mainly British art from the last 200 years and includes at least one work by all past and present members of the academy.

☎ 020 7300 8000 www.royalacademy.org.uk

Royal Air Force Museum 354 C1

Located on the former airfield at RAF Hendon, and opened in 1972, the museum, housed in five huge buildings, contains a collection of over 100 full-sized aircraft, along with artefacts and other memorabilia. 'Milestones of Flight' covers the history of flight, from the earliest attempts to modern day supersonic jet fighters. For younger visitors the Aeronauts Gallery has plenty of interactive exhibits where they can test their piloting skills.

☎ 020 8205 2266 www.rafmuseum.org.uk

Royal Botanic Gardens, Kew 355 B4

This superb 300 acre (121.5ha) botanic garden was founded by Princess Augusta (mother of George III) in 1759, and in July 2003 it was afforded World Heritage Site status. Kew's reputation as the foremost botanical institution in the world was originally developed by its first two directors, Sir William Hooker (appointed in 1841) and his son Sir Joseph (who succeeded his father in 1865).

The gardens have one of the largest and most diverse collections of plant species in the world; over 60,000 species of plant are displayed in both formal and informal settings, and in the many greenhouses, which themselves cover an area of 4 acres (1.5ha). Within the grounds are the Queen's Garden, which has been laid out in 17th century style, the grass garden and the herbaceous garden. The lake, aquatic garden and ten-storey pagoda were designed by Sir William Chambers in 1760. Major features of Kew are the magnificent curved glass Palm House (built in 1848) and the Temperate House (completed in 1868), designed by Decimus Burton and Richard Turner. In more recent years the Princess of Wales Conservatory was constructed and has a variety of climatic areas, from the humid tropics through to desert conditions. There is plenty of interest to keep everyone happy, both botanical experts and those just wanting to absorb the beauty of the grounds.

☎ 020 8332 5655 www.rbgkew.org.uk

Royal Mews, Buckingham Palace 376 D12

Built in 1825 to a design by John Nash, the Mews give an insight into the work of the Royal Household department that provides transport for the Royal Family, both horse-drawn and motor. The Royal Mews are home, for most of the year, to 30 or so horses used in official and ceremonial duties. Visitors can also see the remarkable state carriages, most notably the Gold State Coach made in 1761 and the Irish State Coach bought by Queen Victoria in 1852 and used for the state opening of parliament.

☎ 020 7766 7302 www.royal.gov.uk/output/page556.asp

St Martin-in-the Fields Church 376 J7

Overlooking Trafalgar Square, this church was designed by James Gibbs and was consecrated in 1726. With its attractive spire and portico, its design has been much copied throughout the world, especially in the United States. Among the notable events to have taken place here are the christening of Charles II in 1630 and the burials of Nell Gwynne, William Hogarth, Sir Joshua Reynolds and Thomas Chippendale.

The church hosts lunchtime and evening concerts and has a brass rubbing centre. It also has a long history of work with the homeless.

☎ 020 7766 1100 www.stmartin-in-the-fields.org

St Paul's Cathedral

St Paul's Cathedral 377 S5

Designed by Sir Christopher Wren, the current St Paul's rises to a height of 365ft (111m) and is the fifth cathedral to stand on the site. It was built between 1675 and 1710, the previous cathedral having been destroyed during the Great Fire of London. Its design was revolutionary and Wren

Royal Botanic Gardens, Kew

encountered opposition from the Dean and Chapter who wanted a more traditional church. Fortunately, Wren's vision and determination won through, resulting in the masterpiece of design and engineering that we see today; the magnificent dome providing one of the best known London landmarks.

After St Peter's in Rome, St Paul's dome is the second largest in the world and has three viewing galleries. The Whispering Gallery runs around the interior and has unusual acoustics – a whisper against its walls is audible on the opposite side. Encircling the outside at 173ft (53.5m) is the Stone Gallery, and at 280ft (85.5m) is the Golden Gallery which runs around the highest point of the dome, from which the views across the city are superb. To reach here, visitors need to climb 530 steps.

The enormous scale and grandeur of the interior is breathtaking, with massive arches and lofty ceilings. The decoration is extravagant, richly gilded throughout and with brightly coloured mosaics in the Quire, which were originally planned by Wren, but not installed until 1891 – 1904. The interior also features carving by Grinling Gibbons, decorative metal work by Jean Tijou, sculpture by Henry Moore and the magnificent organ, which has been played by both Handel and Mendelssohn. Among the cathedral's 300 memorials is one to the Duke of Wellington whose body lies in the crypt, alongside the tombs of Admiral Nelson and Sir Christopher Wren.

☎ 020 7236 4128 www.stpauls.co.uk

Science Museum 355 D4

Opened in 1857, on land purchased with the profits from the Great Exhibition of 1851, the museum comprises over 40 galleries spread over seven floors. The huge collection, with over 10,000 items on show, focuses on science and scientific advances over the last 300 years, not only from Britain but also from around the world. The exhibits range from steam power, where visitors can see Stephenson's *Rocket*, to space exploration with the surprisingly small *Apollo 10* command module on display. There are a diverse range of galleries, with topics spanning computing, printing, nuclear power, flight, marine engineering and food, seen in a social as well as purely scientific light. The Wellcome Wing concentrates on contemporary science, medicine and technology and has an IMAX 3D cinema (for which there is a charge). Throughout the museum there are a vast number of interactive and hands-on displays, which really help to illustrate scientific principles, not only for the children, but for the adults too.

☎ 0870 870 4868 www.sciencemuseum.org.uk

Science Museum – Space Auditorium

Shakespeare's Globe Theatre 377 S7

The current Globe Theatre, officially opened in 1997, is a careful reconstruction of the original, which was built nearby in 1599, and for which Shakespeare wrote some of his greatest plays. The reconstruction was the dream of American actor-director Sam Wanamaker, who, sadly, never lived to see its completion. In its construction, techniques and materials as close to the original as possible have been used. It is open to the elements in the centre and has a thatched roof; as a consequence, when it rains, the 'groundlings' (the audience standing in front of the stage) get wet, just as they did in Shakespeare's day. During performances, which take place between May and September, the whole atmosphere is designed to be just as it was 500 years ago; there is no hi-tech lighting or wizardry and the crowd is encouraged to participate by shouting, cheering and jeering.

In a space beneath the theatre is the UnderGlobe where there is an exhibition of Shakespeare's life and times, with displays on the original as well as the current Globe. The exhibition includes a range of live demonstrations and interactive displays. There are also interesting tours of the whole site when there are no plays in progress.

☎ 020 7902 1500 www.shakespeares-globe.org

Somerset House 377 L6

The building, dating from the 1770s, now houses three major art collections (for which there is a charge). The Courtauld Gallery features a collection of paintings by artists such as Michelangelo, Monet and Van Gogh. The Gilbert Collection contains mainly decorative arts including jewel-encrusted gold snuffboxes. The Hermitage Rooms provide a splendid setting for varied exhibitions often featuring collections loaned from the State Hermitage Museum in St Petersburg. Areas on free public view include the Nelson Staircase, the Seamen's Waiting Hall and the King's Barge House with multimedia presentations telling the building's story. Outside a central courtyard features an impressive 55 jet fountain which is converted to an ice rink during the winter.

☎ 020 7845 4600 www.somerset-house.org.uk

Syon House 355 B4

This 16th century house, standing in 40 acre (16ha) grounds landscaped by Lancelot 'Capability' Brown, has been home to the Dukes of Northumberland since 1594. Catherine Howard, Henry VIII's fifth wife, was imprisoned here before her execution in 1542 and Lady Jane Grey began her 9-day reign here after Edward VI's death. Robert Adam made many alterations from 1762 – 1769, creating imaginative and elegant interiors – the variety of each room is exceptional.

☎ 020 8560 0881 www.syonpark.co.uk

Tate Britain 357 A4

Overlooking the River Thames, the gallery dates from 1897 and was built on the site of the Millbank Penitentiary, a former prison, to house the collection of 19th century art given to the nation by the sugar magnate, Sir Henry Tate. The permanent collection has grown enormously over the years, and today the gallery holds the largest collection of British art in the world, with works dating from 1500 to the present day. Temporary shows include the controversial Turner Prize Exhibition.

Visitors can see work by artists such as Gainsborough, Stubbs, Blake, Constable, Bacon, Hirst, Hockney and Hepworth. The adjoining Clore Gallery houses the Turner bequest, comprising thousands of paintings and studies, left to the nation by Turner on condition that they remained together.

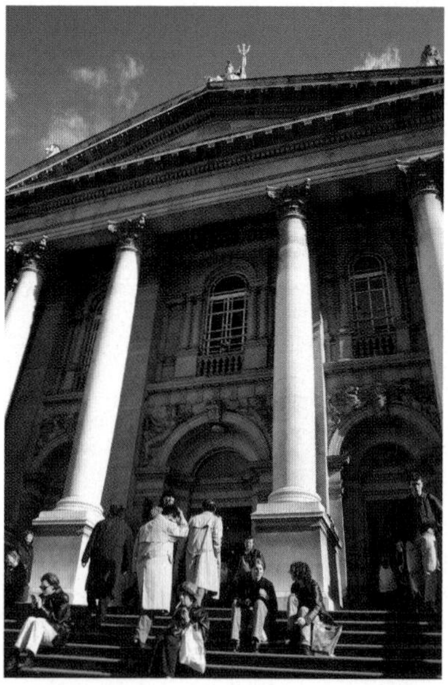

Tate Britain

☎ 020 7887 8000 www.tate.org.uk/britain

Tate Modern 377 R8

The gallery, situated on the south bank of the River Thames opposite St Paul's Cathedral, was opened in May 2000 and features international modern art from 1900 to the present day. It is housed in the vast, former Bankside Power Station, designed by Sir Giles Gilbert Scott (designer of the red telephone box) in 1947. The sheer scale of the building creates a superb setting in which to exhibit. The vast hall, once occupied by the power station turbines, allows huge works of art to be displayed.

The permanent exhibits are arranged thematically into four main areas: Still life/Object/Real Life; Nude/Action/Body; History/Memory/Society; and Landscape/Matter/Environment. Works by Picasso, Matisse, Dali, Warhol, Monet and Bacon, amongst many others, can be seen. Throughout the year there are also a series of temporary exhibitions including three major loan exhibitions.

☎ 020 7887 8000 www.tate.org.uk/modern

Tate Modern

Thames Barrier Visitor Centre 357 D4

The visitor centre has multimedia presentations, models and displays describing the construction and operation of this movable flood barrier, which, at 1700ft (520m) long, is the world's largest. It was officially opened in 1984.

☎ 020 8305 4188

Theatre Museum 377 K6

Located in specially converted premises in Covent Garden, this museum is dedicated to artefacts associated with the performing arts, ranging from theatre to puppetry. The collection includes over a million theatre programmes and playbills (not all on display).

☎ 020 7943 4700 www.theatremuseum.vam.ac.uk

Tower Bridge Experience 356 B3

Tower Bridge has been a distinctive London landmark since 1894. Its fascinating history and the story of how it was built is told in the Tower Bridge Experience through the use of interactive displays. Visitors can see the engine rooms and climb up to the 140ft (42.5m) high walkways from which there are superb views of London.

☎ 020 7403 3761 www.towerbridge.org.uk

Tower of London 356 B3

Dating back to the 11th century, the Tower has been part of London's history for over 900 years. During this time it has had many roles, serving as a royal palace, an arsenal, royal mint, jewel house, royal menagerie (the ravens are now the only survivors) and, most notoriously, as a jail and place of execution. There are many different things for the visitor to see, either independently, or with the help of the distinctively dressed Yeoman warders (Beefeaters), who are happy to combine their traditional ceremonial role with that of tourist guide.

The oldest part is the massive rectangular 90ft (27.5m) high White Tower. Originally built as a fortress and residence providing accommodation for the king, today visitors can see a wide range of arms and armour. The Bloody Tower is associated with the deaths of the two princes in 1483. Sir Walter Raleigh was also imprisoned here for 13 years. The scaffold site on Tower Green is where seven famous prisoners were executed including Anne Boleyn, Catherine Howard and Lady Jane Grey, their bodies being buried in the adjacent Chapel of St Peter ad Vincula. Prisoners often entered the Tower from the Thames through Traitor's Gate. Be sure not to miss the Crown Jewels, a glittering and well laid out array which mainly date from the Restoration in 1660, when Charles II ascended the throne. Also worth a visit is the Medieval Palace which comprises a series of rooms shown as they may have looked during the reign of Edward I. All in all, there is a vast range of things to see, with Britain's rich and turbulent royal history evident at every turn.

☎ 020 7709 0765 www.tower-of-london.org.uk

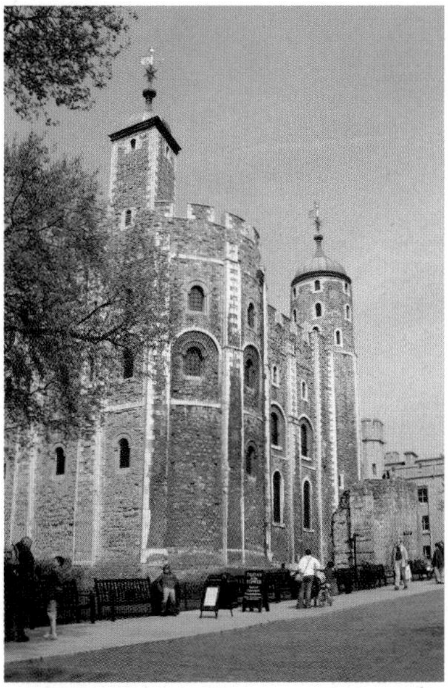

Tower of London

Victoria & Albert Museum

Victoria & Albert Museum 355 D4

Established in 1852 with profits from the Great Exhibition, and originally called the Museum of Manufactures, then the South Kensington Museum, it was finally renamed the V&A in 1899. This national museum of art and design has exhibits from all over the world, spanning over 2000 years. It is vast and labyrinthine, with four floors and over 145 galleries covering an area of 10 acres (4ha).

The collection is immense and wide-ranging with over 4 million objects as diverse as the carved oak Great Bed of Ware, made in 1590, which measures 12ft (3.6m) square, and the tiny Indian miniature paintings. Other exhibits include Oriental ceramics, Chippendale and Art Nouveau furniture, Italian Renaissance sculpture, and a significant collection of paintings by John Constable. The museum also contains Indian film posters, photographs and around 500,000 watercolours, engravings and etchings. The British Galleries are a popular destination with exhibits dating from the 16th to 20th centuries, encompassing works by famous designers such as William Morris, Charles Rennie Mackintosh and Robert Adam.

With 7 miles (11km) of galleries to explore it is impossible to see everything in one visit.

☎ 020 7942 2000 www.vam.ac.uk

Westminster Abbey 376 J12

Steeped in history, the abbey is the coronation church of all the crowned sovereigns since William the Conqueror, whose coronation took place in the original Norman building in 1066. Very little of the Norman structure remains; most of the magnificent Gothic building seen today was built by Henry III between 1245 and his death in 1272. After his death, progress was slow and the nave, which at 102ft (31m) is the highest in England, was not completed until 1517. The famous west towers, which rise to a height of 225ft (69m) were a much later addition and were completed in 1745.

Both architecturally and historically, the abbey is an absolute feast with an impressive array of tombs and memorials to some of Britain's most important figures. Within the chapel of St Edward the Confessor is his great shrine along with the tombs of Henry III, Edward I, Edward III, Richard II and Henry V. Nearby is the Coronation Chair, upon which all England's monarchs (except Edward V and Edward VIII) have been crowned since 1308. Henry VII's Chapel is magnificent, with an intricately detailed fan vaulted ceiling. It is the final resting place of Henry VII, Mary I and Elizabeth I. Within the nave can be seen the tomb of the unknown warrior whose body was laid here as a memorial to the thousands who died in World War I. The octagonal Chapter House, which between 1253 and 1547 was one of the regular meeting places of Parliament, still contains its original coloured tile floor and medieval wall paintings. Visitors can also see the Cloisters and the museum which is situated in the Norman undercroft.

☎ 020 7222 5152 www.westminster-abbey.org

Westminster Abbey

Westminster Cathedral 376 E13

Completed in 1903, this is the principal Roman Catholic church in England. The neo-Byzantine style, with its distinctive red brickwork and horizontal white stone stripes, is eyecatching. The spacious interior has the broadest nave in England and is richly decorated with multicoloured mosaics and marble.

☎ 020 7798 9055 www.westminstercathedral.org.uk

WEST MIDLANDS

Famous as the traditional 'Black Country', for so long the powerhouse of British manufacturing and forever associated with the famous makes of motor vehicles that it designed and built. Yet, outside of this cluster of throbbing industrial towns and cities, with their lively culture and retail attractions, the surrounding counties seem to have deliberately distanced themselves from this influence. Here quaint historic charm and rural calm appear to continue unchallenged.

New Place Garden, Stratford-upon-Avon

Acton Scott Working Farm Museum — 207 D4

This museum re-creates the working practices of early 20th century farming. The land is worked using horses and machinery in use at the time and there are traditional demonstrations of the skills of the blacksmith, carpenter, wheelwright and farrier along with butter making, milking by hand, lambing, shearing and cider making. Amongst the wide variety of animals are Tamworth pigs, Longhorn cattle and Shropshire sheep.

☎ 01694 781306

Alton Towers Leisure Park — 222 B3

A family day out, or maybe two days as there is so much to fit into one day. Set around the historic 19th century Gothic mansion and its landscaped gardens which date back to 1860, the theme park features exotically named rides such as Nemesis, Oblivion, the Flume and Spinball Whizzer. The famous Corkscrew is situated in UG Land which has a prehistoric theme and features virtual reality games. There are themed areas for younger children such as Cred Street, Old MacDonald's Farmyard and Adventure Land. Unfortunately it is necessary to queue for most of the rides though some have a time slot booking system. There is disabled access to most of the rides though some enforce height restrictions for safety reasons.

☎ 08705 204060 www.alton-towers.co.uk

Ancient High House — 221 G5

Built in 1595 by John Dorrington, this Tudor building is the largest timber-framed town house in England. King Charles and his nephew Prince Rupert stayed here in 1642 at the beginning of the Civil War and, when overrun by the Parliamentarians the following year, it became a prison for Royalist prisoners. Extensive renovations by the Borough Council has enabled the building to be opened to the public, and exhibits of period furniture, wallpapers and costumes can be enjoyed. It is also home to the Staffordshire Yeomanry Museum.

☎ 01785 619131

Anne Hathaway's Cottage — 197 D2

The pre-marital home of the wife of William Shakespeare, and of her descendants until the late 19th century. It is a Tudor 12-roomed thatched farmhouse, parts of which date back to the 15th century. Recent additions to the lovely garden are the Shakespeare Tree Garden, which has many of the trees mentioned in his plays, and a maze, the design of which dates from the Elizabethan era.

☎ 01789 292100

Arbury Hall — 209 F4

The original house is Elizabethan but it was transformed in the 18th century into one of the finest examples of Gothic Revival architecture in the country. Home to the Newdegate family since the 16th century, many of the superb rooms are open to the public. There are superb vaulted ceilings and displays of art, glass, porcelain and antique furniture. The house is surrounded by fine landscaped gardens with lakes and woodland walks.

☎ 024 7638 2804

Ash End House Children's Farm — 359 F1

A small, family run farm where the visitor can get close to the animals, many of which are under cover in case of bad weather. There is wheelchair access throughout the farm.

☎ 0121 329 3240 www.ashendhouse.fsnet.co.uk

www.visitheartofengland.com

Alton Towers Leisure Park

Attingham Park (NT) — 207 E1

A late 18th century mansion with magnificent interiors, built originally for the 1st Earl of Berwick, now owned by the National Trust. Guided tours are available which give an insight into life up and downstairs, as the kitchens and servants quarters are open to the public. The picture gallery was designed by John Nash who constructed the curved ceiling out of iron and glass. Surrounding the house are mature gardens, deer park, woodland and riverside walks, and in the walled garden is a children's adventure playground.

☎ 01743 708162 www.nationaltrust.org.uk

Avoncroft Museum of Historic Buildings — 196 B1

An unusual museum which has over 25 historical buildings from the last 700 years, painstakingly dismantled and rebuilt on a site of 25 acres (10ha). Originally the aim was to rescue and restore only timber-framed buildings, but such has been the success of the venture that all manner of buildings are now on show, including a 1946 prefab, a working windmill, church and gaol.

☎ 01527 831363 www.avoncroft.org.uk

Baddesley Clinton (NT) — 209 D5

This moated house sits in grounds of 120 acres (48ha) and has been largely unchanged for almost 400 years. The original building dates from the 15th century and stayed in the family of its owner, the Under Treasurer of England, John Broome, until it was acquired by the National Trust in 1981. The house has three priest's holes which were installed in the late 16th century by Henry Ferrers, a staunch Roman Catholic. The gardens include ponds and lakeside walks, a walled garden and nature trail.

☎ 01564 783294 www.nationaltrust.org.uk

Baggeridge Country Park — 358 A1

This was largely developed by the District Council after the closure of the mineworks in 1968. It is the northern part of the park that was once one of the largest and most modern coal mines in the world. Trees have been planted to augment those that have developed naturally since the closure of the mine, and meadows have been created which now include a visitor centre and caravan park. The southern part of the park features ponds and streams, and was designed by Lancelot 'Capability' Brown for the Earl of Dudley.

☎ 01902 882605

Benthall Hall (NT) — 207 F2

A 16th century sandstone house which was given a more Gothic look in the 18th century. The magnificent interior has fine oak panelling and a carved oak staircase, while the plasterwork is equally stunning. The 3 acre (1.2ha) grounds include a restored plantsman's garden as well as a rock garden, rose garden and terraces. There is also a 17th century Restoration church which holds services on alternate Sundays.

☎ 01952 882159 www.nationaltrust.org.uk

Berrington Hall (NT) — 195 E1

This elegant house was designed and built in the late 18th century by Henry Holland while the parkland was designed by his father-in-law, Lancelot 'Capability' Brown. The main feature is a 14 acre (5.6ha) lake, which has sweeping views down the valley to the Brecon Beacons. The exterior sandstone walls from which the house is built give it a severe first impression, but the interior is delicate with beautifully detailed ceilings and a spectacular staircase hall.

☎ 01568 615721 www.nationaltrust.org.uk

Biddulph Grange Garden (NT) — 221 F2

These 15 acre (9ha) gardens were the conception of James Bateman in the mid 19th century in order to display his wide ranging and extensive plant collection from all over the world – a common practice for Victorian gardens. The gardens are laid out as a series of smaller themed gardens, including Egyptian and Chinese gardens, pinetum and rock garden, all connected by pathways, steps and tunnels (making access difficult for wheelchairs and pushchairs). The gardens fell into disuse during World War I when the Grange was used as a hospital, and since its acquisition by the National Trust has been, and continues to be, extensively restored. There is a quiz and trail for children.

☎ 01782 517999 www.nationaltrust.org.uk

Birmingham Botanical Gardens — 378 C14

Founded in 1832, these 15 acres (6ha) of beautiful gardens have a variety of interest including exotic flora, play areas and aviaries. Many different types of habitat are on display – an alpine yard, winter garden, wetlands, pinetum and cottage garden to name but a few.

There are four glasshouses with themes of tropical, subtropical, Mediterranean and arid. It is also home to the National Bonsai Collection.

☎ 0121 454 1860 www.birminghambotanicalgardens.org.uk

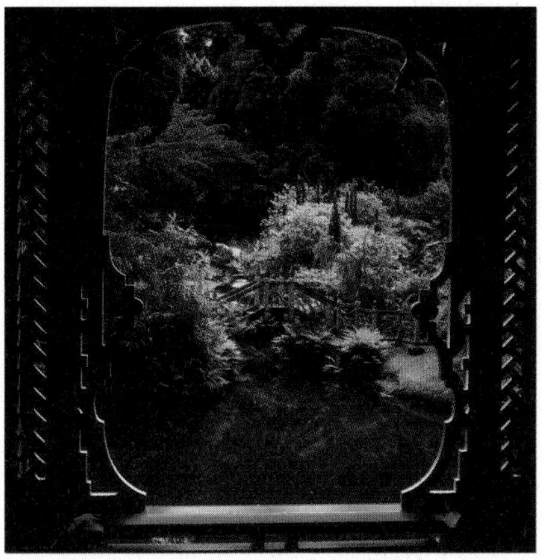

Biddulph Grange Garden

Black Country Living Museum

Black Country Living Museum — 358 B2

A faithful reproduction of a village dating from the turn of the 20th century is the centrepiece of this museum which focuses on the industrial heritage of the West Midlands. There are even caverns and an underground coal mine. Guides in period costume are on hand to demonstrate traditional skills – there is a forge, foundry, colliery, cobbler – and there is plenty to occupy the children. Most of the museum is set outdoors but there is also an interactive exhibition hall, gift shop and tearoom.

☎ 0121 557 9643 www.bclm.co.uk

Bredon Tithe Barn (NT) — 196 B4

This 14th century Tithe Barn is built of local Cotswold stone and was lovingly restored after a fire in 1980. It is around 140ft (44m) in length with an aisled interior giving it a distinctly ecclesiastical feel. It also features a remarkable stone chimney cowling.

☎ 01684 855300 www.nationaltrust.org.uk

Buildwas Abbey — 207 F2

Founded by the Savignacs in 1135 and merged with the Cistercian Order soon after, the abbey changed little until the Dissolution and is unusual in that the cloister is situated north of the main church. Parts of the original tiled floor of the Chapter House still exist and, apart from the roof, the building is still virtually intact. Research has uncovered evidence of water channels and fishponds, most probably used as a source of food by the monks.

☎ 01952 433274 www.english-heritage.org.uk

Burford House Gardens — 195 E1

7 acres (3ha) of beautiful gardens on the banks of the River Teme, originally designed by John Treasure in 1952 to complement the Georgian Burford House. Home to the National Clematis Collection, of which there are over 300 varieties, there is also a clematis maze. Wisteria Burford cascades down the rear wall of the house and is a beautiful sight when it flowers in May. The house has a contemporary art gallery which is open during the summer months and there is a garden centre, gift shop and licensed café.

☎ 01584 810777 www.burford.co.uk

Cadbury World — 359 D4

A visitor centre devoted entirely to chocolate and designed to be of particular interest to children, but with plenty to interest all. Learn the process of chocolate manufacture, experience imaginative rides through a world of chocolate. There are also television adverts from the last 40 years and a 1930s sweet shop. It is advisable to book tickets in advance, especially during the summer holidays.

☎ 0121 451 4159 www.cadburyworld.co.uk

Cannock Chase Country Park — 208 B1

One of the largest country parks in Britain, covering 4000 acres (1600ha) which lies within one of the smallest Areas of Outstanding Natural Beauty, Cannock Chase. There are many designated Sites of Special Scientific Interest and the visitor centre is the starting point for many of the well-signposted walks running through the park.

☎ 01543 876741

Cannon Hill Park — 359 D3

One of the most popular parks in Birmingham, with a variety of landscapes including flowerbeds, lakes, a wild flower meadow and woodland, which is part of a conservation area. There are plenty of facilities – canoeing, tennis courts, bowling and putting greens and a tearoom which is housed inside the Midland Arts Centre.

☎ 0121 442 4226

Carding Mill Valley & Long Mynd (NT) — 206 D3

Stretching across an area 10 miles (16km) long and 2 to 4 miles (3.5 to 6.5km) wide south of Shrewsbury, the Long Mynd holds much of interest, including several prehistoric barrows and earthworks, and is ideal walking country. Carding Mill Valley is a steep-sided valley offering a good, though strenuous route onto the ridge. There is a National Trust information centre and tearoom next to the car park.

☎ 01694 723068 www.nationaltrust.org.uk

Charlecote Park (NT) — 197 E2

A 16th century house visited by both Queen Victoria and Elizabeth I – the entrance porch still has the coat of arms of Elizabeth I to commemorate her stay of two nights in 1572. All of the rooms are luxuriously furnished, the dining room and library having particularly exquisite ceilings in the Elizabethan Revival style. The formal gardens open out onto 250 acres (100ha) of parkland designed by Lancelot 'Capability' Brown where, allegedly, Shakespeare was once caught poaching deer.

☎ 01789 470277 www.nationaltrust.org.uk

Commandery, The — 415 C2

An historic timber-framed building which was the headquarters of Charles II during the Civil War, though its origins date back much further than that, possibly to the 11th century. Most of the current building dates from the 15th century and has undergone many changes to reflect the style of the period.

☎ 01905 361821 www.worcestercitymuseums.org.uk

Coors Visitor Centre — 222 D5

Formerly the Bass Museum, the Coors Visitor Centre tells the story of the long and distinguished history of brewing in Burton and also in Britain in general. There is a visitor centre, frequently changing exhibitions and a computerised journey around Burton in 1881 which will be of interest to children, as will the magnificent shire horses.

☎ 0845 600 0598 www.coorsvisitorcentre.co.uk

Coughton Court (NT) — 196 C1

The house has been in the Throckmorton family since 1409 and has remained relatively unchanged since the Tudor gatehouse was built in 1530. There are exhibits relating to Mary, Queen of Scots, including the chemise she was wearing when she was executed, and also a Gunpowder Plot exhibition – at the time the house was rented out to one of the plotters, Sir Everard Digby. The grounds include one of the country's finest walled gardens and also a lake, riverside walk, bog garden and orchard.

☎ 01789 400777 www.coughtoncourt.co.uk

Coventry Cathedral — 394 E2

The old Cathedral was famously bombed in November 1940 during the devastation of Coventry and the remains have been incorporated into the new Cathedral which was consecrated in 1962. A new chapel was added to celebrate the millennium, and the visitor centre has many displays showing the history of the Cathedral and the city of Coventry.

☎ 01203 227597 www.coventrycathedral.org.uk

Coventry Transport Museum — 394 D2

The largest collection of British vehicles in the world, at the birthplace of the British motor industry. The collection includes cars, vans, trucks, bicycles and motorbikes from the present day back to 1896 when the first factory was established. Famous marques such as Daimler, Maudsley, Triumph, Jaguar, Riley and Humber are represented.

☎ 024 7683 2425 www.transport-museum.com

Croft Castle (NT) — 194 D1

This impressive country manor house has fine Georgian interiors and furniture while the curtain wall and round towers at each corner date from the 14th and 15th centuries. Apart from a break of 177 years in the 18th and 19th centuries, the Croft family have lived on this site since the Norman conquest though the castle is now maintained by the National Trust. The grounds include an avenue of 350 year old Spanish chestnuts, and adjacent to the castle are the remains of the earthworks of the original fort.

☎ 01568 781246 www.nationaltrust.org.uk

Dorothy Clive Garden, The
221 E4

Set amongst lovely hilly countryside, the garden has a variety of landscapes in its 8 acres (3ha) – woodland, alpine, a water garden and summer borders. The garden has been extended into an old quarry which is now the rhododendron garden, shaded with trees and also featuring a waterfall.

☎ 01630 647237 www.dorothyclivegarden.co.uk

Drayton Manor Park
209 D2

A 250 acre (96ha) theme park with such evocative named rides as Pandemonium, Excalibur and Apocalypse. Gentler rides can be taken in Splash Canyon, or on Excalibur where fire-breathing dragons are encountered on a journey through medieval England. Height restrictions are enforced for safety on some rides. As well as the rides there is a zoo covering 15 acres (6ha) with over 100 species, a rare breeds farm, exotic animal reserves and a museum showing the history of Drayton Manor.

☎ 08708 725252 www.draytonmanor.co.uk

Dudley Zoo & Castle
358 B2

A magnificent location for a zoo, being set in the grounds of the ruins of Dudley Castle – the route through the zoo has cleverly been designed to take in the old castle walls. The 40 acres (16ha) is home to more than 200 species, many endangered. There is a visitor centre which also concentrates on the archaeological excavations which have been carried out locally.

☎ 01384 215313 www.dudleyzoo.co.uk

Dudmaston (NT)
207 G4

This 17th century house has exhibits of the flower paintings of Francis Derby dating from the same time, as well as modern and botanical art. The grounds include rock, rose and bog gardens and are especially impressive in the spring with collections of rhododendrons and azaleas. There are also woodland and lakeside walks in the 300 acre (120ha) parkland.

☎ 01746 780866 www.nationaltrust.org.uk

Eastnor Castle
195 G4

Built by the 1st Earl Somers in 1820, and extensively restored after 1949, the castle is still privately owned by his descendants – the Hervey-Bathurst family. Much of the original work of the interior, designed by Robert Smirke, is still in evidence, particularly in the Staircase Hall, Dining Room and Red Hall, which has a magnificent collection of armour moved here in 1989 from the Great Hall. The grounds are magnificent, comprising an arboretum, lake and deer park in which there are mazes and nature trails.

☎ 01531 633160 www.eastnorcastle.com

Fleece Inn, The (NT)
196 C3

Owned by the National Trust, this half-timbered, medieval house has been used as an inn since 1848. It has remained largely unchanged since then, but was originally in use as a farmhouse and animal shelter.

☎ 01386 831173 www.nationaltrust.org.uk

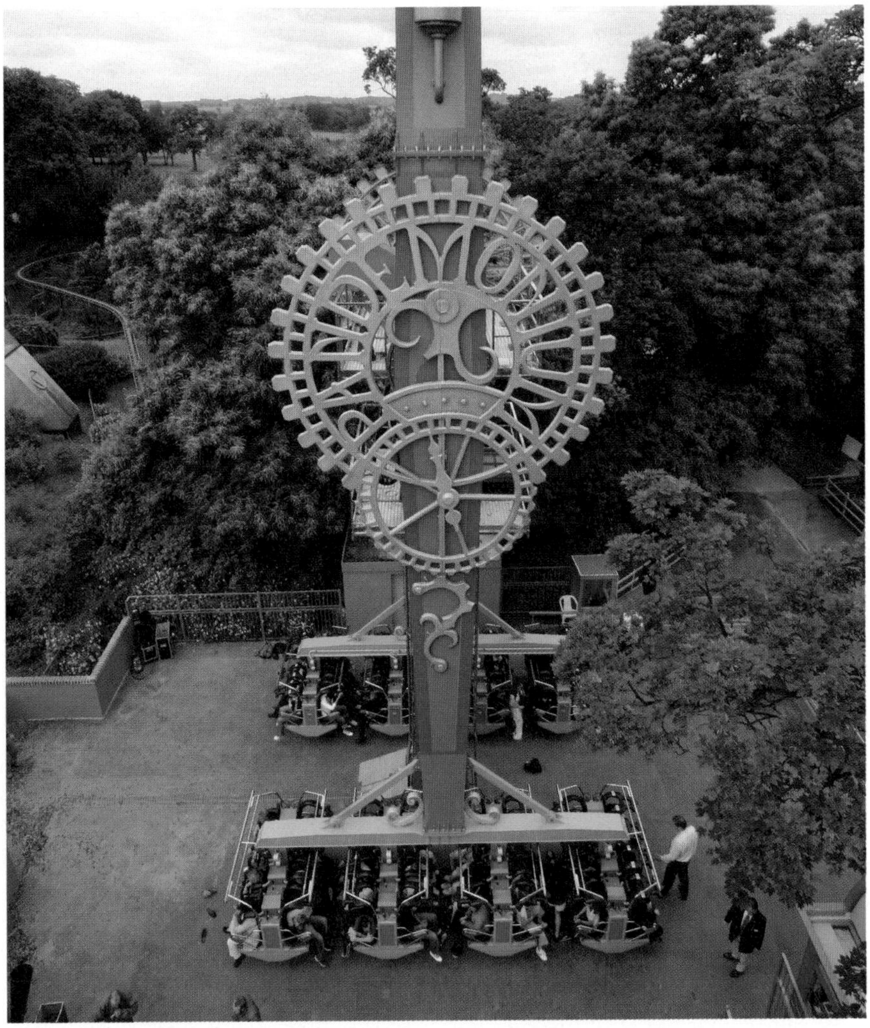

Drayton Manor Park – Pandemonium Ride

Goodrich Castle
195 E5

Guarding an ancient crossing point of the River Wye, this well-preserved 12th century ruin is constructed out of the red sandstone on which it sits. Despite seeing action during the Civil War, much of the castle is complete, including the three-storey keep as well as archways, pillars and passageways, giving a good idea of the castle as it was. There are outstanding views across the Wye Valley and the surrounding countryside.

☎ 01600 890538 www.english-heritage.org.uk

Greyfriars, The (NT)
415 C2

Built in 1480 by Thomas Greene, this timber-framed merchant's house was added to in the 17th and 18th centuries, and was rescued from demolition during World War II. None of the original 15th century furnishings survive but there is Georgian wallpaper and 16th and 17th century tapestries and furniture. The large double doors open out to a cobbled passageway and a small walled garden.

☎ 01905 23571 www.nationaltrust.org.uk

Hagley Hall
358 A4

The home of Lord and Lady Cobham was originally built between 1756 and 1760 by the 1st Lord of Lyttelton at a cost of £25,000, twice the original estimate. In 1925 a fire destroyed parts of the house, including the library and some of the extensive art collection, though it was subsequently restored to its former glory. There is fine plasterwork by Francesco Vassali, Chippendale furniture, and family portraits amongst the art collection which includes works by Van Dyck, Reynolds and Lely. The Hall is surrounded by a 350 acre (135ha) deer park.

☎ 01562 882408 www.hagleyhall.info

Hall's Croft
410 F2

Once the home of John Hall, a physician, who married Shakespeare's eldest daughter, Susanna, in 1607. The hall and parlour are the oldest parts of this timber-framed house, which dates from the early seventeenth century, and is furnished as it would have been at the time. The grounds include a herb garden containing herbs that Hall would have used in his practice.

☎ 01789 204016 www.shakespeare.org.uk

Hanbury Hall (NT)
196 B1

A William and Mary style country house built in 1701 which features splendid painted ceilings and an impressive staircase. There is a collection of porcelain on display as well as exhibitions on the family and local history. The grounds include a 20 acre (8ha) garden which is surrounded by parkland covering 400 acres (160ha). Amongst the many interesting features are an orangery, mushroom house, ice house and an 18th century bowling green.

☎ 01527 821214 www.nationaltrust.org.uk

Harvard House
197 E2

This impressive timber-framed building was built in 1596 by Thomas Rogers and has remained unchanged since then. His grandson, John Harvard, emigrated to America in 1647 and died only a year later. It was a bequest in his will that helped to establish Harvard University in Cambridge, Massachusetts. The Museum of British Pewter is housed within the building.

☎ 01789 204507 www.shakespeare.org.uk

Harvington Hall
208 A5

The largest number of priest's holes in Britain are to be found in this Elizabethan manor house which was originally built in 1580 and is now owned by the Roman Catholic Archdiocese of Birmingham. Many of the original wall paintings still adorn the walls, having been discovered beneath a layer of whitewash in 1936. Large numbers of birds are attracted by the moat and the two lakes in the gardens, which also include a Georgian chapel and a malt house.

☎ 01562 777846 www.harvingtonhall.com

Hatton Country World
197 E1

Comprises two separate attractions – Hatton Shopping Village and Hatton Farm Village. The shopping village comprises arts and craft shops, alongside antique outlets and larger retailers, set amongst converted Victorian farm buildings.

The Farm Village is set in open countryside and has plenty for children – sheep racing, a guinea pig village, play areas, a maze along with demonstrations and exhibitions of farm craft. There is a charge to pay for entry.

☎ 01926 843411 www.hattonworld.com

Haughmond Abbey
207 E1

Once part of a thriving and prosperous community, this ruined Augustinian Abbey is now in the care of English Heritage. The medieval beamed ceiling in the Chapter House is impressive, as is its 12th century entrance. Work on the surrounding fields has revealed that the abbey ruins were incorporated into the grounds of the now demolished 18th century Sundome House.

☎ 01743 709661 www.english-heritage.org.uk

Hawkstone Park
220 C5

Restored after years of neglect, this 18th century parkland covers an area in excess of 100 acres (40ha) and is now a Grade 1 listed landscape. Intricate archways, a ruined medieval castle, winding pathways, tunnels, passageways and an underground grotto give the visitor a fascinating, though at times strenuous, 3 to 4 hour round trip of the grounds.

☎ 01939 200611 www.hawkstone.co.uk

Hereford Cathedral
401 B2

Standing on the banks of the River Wye, much of the original 12th century cathedral still survives today although extensive restoraton took place in the 18th and 19th centuries. It is probably most famous for the Chained Library and Mappa Mundi exhibitions housed in the New Library building. Mappa Mundi dates from around 1300 and is the most complete and largest medieval world map still in existence. There is also an interactive exhibition which makes use of both original artefacts and the latest computer technology. Entry to the Cathedral is free but there is a charge for the exhibitions.

☎ 01432 359880 www.herefordcathedral.org

Hergest Croft Gardens
194 B2

The estate dates back to 1267 but this garden of wooded valleys and glades, flower beds and open grassland was created in 1912 when the estate was bought by the Banks family. There are over 4000 shrubs and trees in four distinct areas of the garden covering over 50 acres (20ha) – the Kitchen Garden, Park Wood, the Azalea Garden and the Edwardian House which has an old rockery and croquet lawn.

☎ 01544 230160 www.hergest.co.uk

Hodnet Hall Gardens
220 D5

60 acres (24ha) of magnificent gardens in the ownership of the Heber-Parcy family. The design has changed over hundreds of years to match the three different sites of the homes of the family and their ancestors. There is a variety of shrubs and plants designed to give colour to the gardens throughout the summer, as well as woodland walks and a chain of ornamental pools. The 17th century tearoom is well worth a visit.

☎ 01630 685786

Ironbridge Gorge
207 F2

The Iron Bridge, the first bridge in the world to be constructed completely of iron, is the focal point of the 'Valley of Invention' which was at the centre of the industrial revolution in Britain. Now a World Heritage Site, ten museums tell the story of the industrial revolution and the part this area played in it. The Blists Hill Victorian Town is an open-air re-creation of a late 19th century working community where even old money can be bought at the bank and used in the local shops and pubs. On some Saturdays there are re-enactments of a Victorian wedding ceremony. The Museum of the Gorge looks at the effects of the revolution on the beautiful gorge itself, and the Broseley Pipeworks, which closed in 1957, is presented as if it were still a working factory. There is also a Museum of Iron, China Museum and Tile Museum, as well as the Bridge and Tollhouse where there is an exhibition and souvenir shop. A passport ticket can be bought to give access to all ten museums and, as they cover an area of around 6 square miles (15 sq km), a shuttle bus runs between them at weekends and on bank holidays.

☎ 01952 884391 www.ironbridge.co.uk

Kenilworth Castle
360 A3

An impressive 11th century ruined castle which has been radically altered and extended since then. John Dudley acquired the castle in the 16th century but was executed for his part in the plot to place Lady Jane Grey on the throne. His son, Robert Dudley, created formal gardens where he entertained Queen Elizabeth I on several occasions. Now in the care of English Heritage, some of the 12th century buildings in the inner courtyard survive, as does the Tudor gatehouse.

☎ 01926 852078 www.english-heritage.org.uk

Letocetum Roman Baths & Museum (NT)
208 D2

The remains of a Roman bathhouse and an inn have been excavated at this site which was an overnight halt on Watling Street, the main road from London to North Wales. A museum exhibits many of the artefacts that have been discovered on the site and gives the historical background to the site.

☎ 01543 480768 www.nationaltrust.org.uk

Lichfield Cathedral
208 D1

Situated in a peaceful close surrounded by half-timbered buildings, this Gothic cathedral dates from the 14th century. With three spires, known as the 'Ladies of the Vale', it is unique amongst medieval cathedrals. The Lichfield Gospels, an 8th century manuscript, is on display in the Chapter House, which dates from 1249 and is one of the most beautiful parts of the cathedral. There is a visitor centre and a licensed restaurant situated in an elegant 18th century house next to the cathedral.

☎ 01543 306240

Little Malvern Court
195 G3

Home to the Berington family since the Dissolution of the Monasteries in 1539 and comprising the 14th century Prior's Hall and the Victorian Manor House. The interior features paintings by the family along with many examples from Europe, and there is a fine collection of 18th and 19th century needlework. Lovely views can be taken from the gardens covering 10 acres (4ha) which once belonged to the 12th century priory that stood on the site.

☎ 01684 892988

Ludlow
207 E5

A 12th century market town, with 500 listed buildings, which retains its original grid-like layout. Amongst the listed buildings are the 17th century Feathers Hotel, the Broadgate, which is the only surviving gate from the old city walls, and the medieval Reader's House with its three-storey Jacobean porch. The Church of St Lawrence has the grandeur of a cathedral and shows, in one of its stained glass windows, the life of St Lawrence, Ludlow's patron saint. The geology of the area and the town's local history are the main themes of the museum in the Assembly Rooms.

☎ 01584 875053 www.ludlow.org.uk

www.visitheartofengland.com

Ironbridge Gorge

Ludlow Castle
207 E5

Built in the late 11th century to repel Welsh marauders, the castle has much that is original, including the keep, chapel and some of the doorways. It became a royal palace under Edward IV, and home of the Council of the Marches, responsible for the government of Wales and the borders. There are many exhibitions, displays and events throughout the year.

☎ 01584 873355 www.ludlowcastle.com

Malvern Hills
195 G3

Stretching for 9 miles (15km) with a high point of 1380ft (425m) at Worcestershire Beacon, the Malvern Hills divide the counties of Herefordshire and Worcestershire. Easily accessible either from the towns on the flanks of the hills or from the numerous car parks that are dotted around the entire length. This is a designated Area of Outstanding Natural Beauty which can be extremely busy in good weather though quieter spots can be found even during the busiest periods.

☎ 01684 560616 www.malvernhillsaonb.org.uk

Mary Arden's House
197 D2

Glebe Farm is the home of William Shakespeare's mother, Mary Arden – for years it was thought that the adjacent timber-framed Palmer's Farm was her home but it has only recently been discovered not to be so.

The Shakespeare Countryside Museum is housed in the outbuildings which include a dovecote, smithy, cider press and workshop containing a variety of Elizabethan farm implements. There are frequent displays of falconry.

☎ 01789 204016 www.shakespeare.org.uk

National Sea Life Centre
378 G8

Set in the rejuvenated canalside area of Birmingham, one of the many highlights is the completely transparent tunnel giving the impression that the visitor is completely surrounded by all manner of sea creatures, including sharks and rays. Conservation is an important part of the centre's activities and is part of the SOS (Save Our Seas) scheme which works with many worldwide conservation groups. The seahorse breeding and conservation centre allows visitors to see work normally carried on behind the scenes.

☎ 0121 643 6777 www.sealifeeurope.com

Packwood House (NT)
209 D5

This 16th century house was extensively restored between the two World Wars by Graham Baron Ash and donated to the National Trust in 1941. It played host to Henry Ireton, Cromwell's general, before the Battle of Edgehill in 1642, and also to Charles II after his defeat at Worcester in 1651. There is a large number of sundials and clocks adorning the walls while the impressive gardens include yew trees with a theme of the 'Sermon on the Mount'.

☎ 01564 783294 www.nationaltrust.org.uk

Potteries Museum & Art Gallery
410 A2

A local history museum examining all aspects of the area, from the world famous pottery industry through to community, wildlife and geology. The centrepiece of the wartime section of the museum is a Spitfire designed by Reginald Mitchell who was educated in Hanley and served his apprenticeship in Fenton before going on to design the Spitfire. He died in 1937 before he saw it enter full service.

☎ 01782 232323

RAF Museum
207 G2

Formerly the Aerospace Museum, the RAF Museum has a collection of over 70 aircraft from Britain, Germany, Argentina, America and Japan. There are also air force vehicles, missiles and engines, and ever-changing exhibitions. The aircraft are mainly housed in three hangars with themes of transport and training, warplanes, research and development. The restoration work which is ongoing at the museum can be observed from the viewing gallery, and the annual air show is always popular.

☎ 01902 376200 www.rafmuseum.org.uk

Ragley Hall
196 C2

The family home of the Marquess and Marchioness of Hertford, this magnificent Palladian house was built in 1680 and stands in grounds of over 400 acres (160ha) designed by Lancelot 'Capability' Brown. The Great Hall has superb baroque plasterwork by James Gibbs and included in the fine art collection is the mural 'The Temptation' by Graham Rust. The grounds include woodland walks, a maze, adventure playground and rose garden.

☎ 01789 762090

Ryton Organic Gardens
360 C3

10 acres (4ha) of totally organic gardens covering all aspects of organic gardening – composting, pest control, flower, fruit and vegetable production amongst many others. A natural area includes trees, wild flower meadow and lake. The Paradise Garden is dedicated to the late Geoff Hamilton, the popular presenter of 'Gardeners World'. It is also home to the headquarters of the Henry Doubleday Research Association which promotes organic gardening and farming.

☎ 024 7630 3517 www.hdra.org.uk

Severn Valley Railway
207 G3

This standard-gauge steam railway runs for a distance of 16 miles (26km) from Bridgnorth to Kidderminster and passes through beautiful Severn Valley countryside, including a trip across a 200ft (60m) single span bridge. The station at Bewdley has a model railway and workshops where restoration work on one of the largest collections of locomotives and rolling stock in the country can be viewed.

☎ 01299 403816 www.svr.co.uk

Shakespeare's Birthplace
410 D2

A half-timbered house bought by the Bard's father, John Shakespeare, in the mid 16th century, a few years before Shakespeare's birth in 1564, and which remained in the family until 1806. 16th and 17th century furniture adorn the interior and, of particular interest, are the signatures of famous visitors engraved into a window in the Birth Room. The visitor centre has a multitude of original exhibits and displays, and there is a lovely traditional English garden.

☎ 01789 204016 www.shakespeare.org.uk

Shugborough Estate (NT)
222 A5

This Georgian mansion is the ancestral home of Lord Lichfield and has exhibitions of period silver, furniture, paintings and china. Amongst the many events throughout the summer are craft, weaving and gardening weekends and also a fully working water mill where milling demonstrations take place. The 900 acres (360ha) of gardens and parkland include a yew tree which is thought to be the widest tree in the country.

☎ 01889 881 388 www.nationaltrust.org.uk

Spetchley Park
196 A2

Surrounding the 19th century mansion (not open to the public) these gardens have been owned by the Berkeley family since 1605. Formal clipped hedges, fountain gardens, herbaceous borders and winding paths offer so much of interest in this 30 acre (19ha) garden (not open to the public on Saturdays). The 110 acre (70ha) Deer Park is not open during June.

☎ 01453 810303 www.spetchleygardens.co.uk

Stafford Castle
221 G5

There is plenty to see and do at this 900 year old castle originally built by William the Conqueror but largely destroyed during the Civil War. The visitor centre has displays of finds made in archaeological excavations. Historical re-enactments and Shakespeare theatrical productions are a feature of the summer months, for which there is an admission charge. There is also a herb garden which was originally planted for medicinal purposes.

☎ 01785 257698

Stokesay Castle
206 D4

This 13th century fortified manor house, now in the care of English Heritage, is one of England's finest and is set in beautiful countryside amongst the Shropshire Hills, not far from the Welsh border. Many parts of the castle are original, including the Great Hall in which the roof timbers are soot blackened from the open hearth. The solar chamber has a magnificent Jacobean fireplace and the delightful 17th century gatehouse is probably more ornamental than strategic.

☎ 01588 672544 www.english-heritage.org.uk

Symonds Yat
181 E1

A large loop in the River Wye has Symonds Yat Rock at its narrowest point. This impressive wooded gorge is a nesting place for the rare peregrine falcon which can be observed from the RSPB information area at the top of the rock during the summer months. A steep descent from the large car park, for which there is a charge, leads to Symonds Yat East where there is a popular inn and café, while an unusual hand pulled ferry crosses the Wye to Symonds Yat West, where there is a visitor and heritage centre.

☎ 01600 713899

Tamworth Castle
209 E2

A Norman motte and bailey castle dating from the 12th century, with numerous additions since then, including the medieval Banqueting Hall. 15 rooms are open to the public with displays from throughout the castle's history. There are many events including ghost vigils and tours in search of the many ghosts allegedly seen in the castle. There are also frequent Shakespearian plays. Beneath the castle are the pleasure grounds with floral terraces, play areas, tennis courts, crazy golf and a café.

☎ 01827 709629 www.tamworthcastle.freeserve.co.uk

Thinktank
379 Q7

One of the largest millennium projects, with a wide range of different things to do and see for all the family. Science and nature are brought to life by displays, many of which are interactive, in ten different galleries. Local history is featured, as is nature, medicine, a vision of the future and the oldest working steam engine in the world, designed by James Watt.

☎ 0121 202 2222 www.thinktank.ac

Warwick Castle

Tutbury Castle 222 D5

This 11th century castle has played host to many royal guests including giving safe harbour to Charles I and his nephew Prince Rupert during the Civil War. Because of this, Cromwell ordered the castle to be dismantled though it was rebuilt in 1662. Mary, Queen of Scots was imprisoned here and, of all the places she was imprisoned, it is said that she had a special loathing for Tutbury. There is also a secret staircase, privy garden and herbery.

☎ 01283 812129 www.tutburycastle.com

Upton House (NT) 197 F3

This 17th century house has wonderful collections of 18th century furniture, tapestries, art and porcelain. The house was bought by Walter Samuel, the Chairman of Shell, in 1927. He carried out extensive modifications to both interior and exterior and gave the house and his collections to the National Trust in 1948. This included his splendid art collection of works by El Greco, Canaletto, Stubbs and Hogarth. There are 31 acres (12.5ha) of terraced garden containing herbaceous borders, fruit and vegetable gardens.

☎ 01295 670266 www.nationaltrust.org.uk

Viroconium Roman Town 207 E2

With a population of over 6000, Viroconium (Wroxeter) was once the fourth largest city in Roman Britain. The remains are extensive and include city walls and the fully excavated public baths. Beneath these are timber buildings dating from the early part of the first century when a garrison was stationed here before it was moved to Chester and Viroconium became an important trading centre. A visitor centre explains the history of the town as well as exhibiting many of the artefacts discovered on the site.

☎ 01743 761330

Warwick Castle 197 E1

Set on the banks of the River Avon, this is one of the finest examples of 14th century fortifications in Britain. Real-life characters help to bring the castle to life and life-sized waxworks add detail to many of the displays, which include an accurate re-creation of the visit of the Prince of Wales, later to become Edward VII, in 1898. The macabre dungeon and torture chamber are reached down a narrow flight of stairs – the writings of a Royalist held during the Civil War can still be seen on the wall. The Great Hall is amongst the luxuriously decorated state rooms which has Oliver Cromwell's death mask on display and also paintings by masters such as Van Dyck and Rubens.

The grounds were designed by Lancelot 'Capability' Brown and include walks along the Avon, an 18th century conservatory and Victorian Rose Garden. There is also a restored mill and engine house which was used to produce the electricity of the household at the turn of the 20th century. There are many events throughout the year including fireworks concerts, medieval festivals and birds of prey displays. A good day out for all the family.

☎ 0870 442 2000 www.warwick-castle.co.uk

Wedgwood Story Visitor Centre 364 C3

Wedgwood Pottery was founded in 1759 by Josiah Wedgwood and his legacy can be seen during a tour of the state-of-the-art factory that includes hands-on demonstrations. Film and interactive displays are used to tell the story of the company and exhibits from all periods of its history are on display. The shop sells exclusive designs as well as seconds and discontinued lines.

☎ 01782 282986 www.thewedgwoodstory.com

West Midland Safari Park 208 A5

A 4 mile (6km) drive through the 150 acre (94ha) park gives access to all manner of exotic animals including elephants, lions, tigers, rhinoceros, bison, llama, antelope. Home to the country's only pride of white lion, of which there are only around 70 remaining worldwide, and white tigers, of which there are only around 150. There are also shows planned out at different times of the day – sea lion shows and hippo feeding, and chances to get close to animals such as snakes and crocodiles.

☎ 01299 400700 www.wmsp.co.uk

Weston Park 208 A2

Mentioned in the 11th century Domesday Book, though the present house was built in 1671. There are nine elegant rooms, including a library with over 3000 books, and the magnificent dining room which has a large collection of art by Van Dyck. The expansive grounds, designed by Lancelot 'Capability' Brown, are formal around the house and include a restored terrace garden as well as parkland including lakes, pools and the deer park. There is plenty for children with a miniature railway, animal centre and adventure playground.

☎ 01952 852100 www.weston-park.com

Wightwick Manor (NT) 208 A3

Built by the Mander family at the end of the 19th century to designs influenced by the Arts and Crafts movement, and decorated with original William Morris materials, Kempe glass and Pre-Raphaelite art. Descendants of the family still live in part of the manor. The 17 acre (7ha) garden is a delight with topiaries, terraces and ponds.

☎ 01902 761108 www.nationaltrust.org.uk

Wilderhope Manor (NT) 207 E3

On the edge of Wenlock Edge stands this Elizabethan manor house. It is now in use as a youth hostel and, as such, it is largely unfurnished which allows the skill of the craftsmen who created the oak spiral staircase, timber-framed walls and plaster ceilings to be appreciated to its full extent. Limited opening.

☎ 01694 771363

Worcester Art Gallery & Museum 415 A2

In an historic Victorian building which also houses the city library, this local museum focuses on the history, geology and natural history of the area. A fully stocked 19th century chemist shop is amongst the exhibits of interest, as is the section of the museum devoted to the Worcestershire Regiment and Yeoman Cavalry. The art gallery has frequently changing contemporary art exhibitions from local and national artists.

☎ 01905 25371 www.worcestercitymuseums.org.uk

Worcester Cathedral 415 C2

The Cathedral stands on the site of an ancient Saxon monastery which was largely destroyed in 1041. Rebuilding started in 1064 and, after a series of problems including a fire and collapse of the tower, was all but complete by the time of its dedication in 1218. Time took its toll on the cathedral and it was not until the Victorians undertook a massive restoration programme that it took on the form that we see today. The richly decorated tombs of Prince Arthur and King John can be found near the High Altar.

☎ 01905 28854 www.cofe-worcester.org.uk/cathedral

Wyre Forest 207 G5

Once a popular hunting ground with an area of 4200 acres (1680ha) but which used to cover most of the West Midlands. Forest clearance for agriculture started during Neolithic times and continued through to the 16th century when the demand for both timber products and also charcoal was at its height. The visitor centre is south-west of Bewdley at Callow Hill and is the starting point for many trails. It also has a restaurant, gift shop and information on all aspects of the forest.

☎ 01299 266944 www.wyreforest.net

EAST MIDLANDS

In the south lie the misty, fertile fens, with their regimented rows of salads and brassicas. Then to the north are the rolling chalky wolds, shimmering with acres of gently whispering cereal crops. This region is truly Britain's kitchen garden. Further east the restless waves of the North Sea pound the chalky coastline and here, for generations, the windswept sandy beaches have played host to the skilled workers and families of the large midland cities in an ageless seaside tradition.

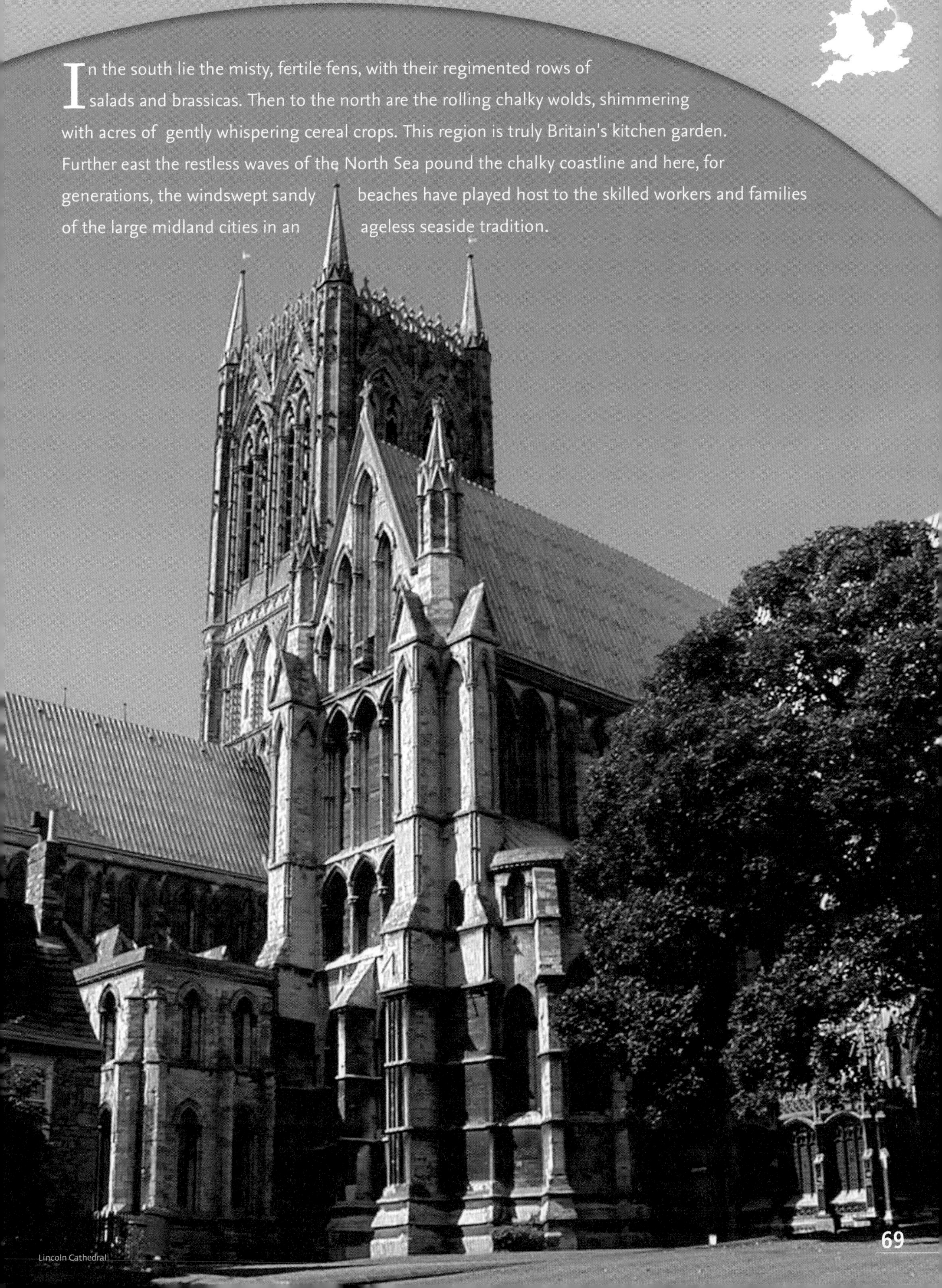

Lincoln Cathedral

Althorp House
198 B1

Since 1508, Althorp House has been home to the Spencer family. The classically-styled house in its typically English parkland was thrust into the limelight by the tragic death in 1997 of Diana, Princess of Wales, herself a member of the family. She now rests in peace on an island in the centre of the lake. Although there is no public access to the island, there is an excellent exhibition about Diana housed in the former stable block. Audiovisual displays relate her life and work, with poignant memorabilia such as school reports and her beautiful wedding dress. Diana's involvement with various charities is well known and the Diana, Princess of Wales Memorial Fund, set up to continue this work, gets a high profile; all proceeds from the entrance fees go to this fund.

The house itself contains many treasures, which can be viewed by the public. In particular, there is an exceptional collection of portraits by artists such as Gainsborough, Van Dyck and Rubens.

Open July to September only.

☎ 0870 167 9000 www.althorp.com

Althorp House

American Adventure Theme Park
223 F3

Right on the edge of the glorious Derbyshire Peak District and set around a 32 acre (13ha) lake (once an opencast mine), this exciting theme park includes the tallest Skycoaster in Europe, a 200ft (61m) high face-first, free-fall, white-knuckle experience. Try the Motion Master, which synchronises a seat with what is happening in an action packed film. Then there is Nightmare Niagara, a triple drop log flume, and The Missile, a roller coaster with six completely circular loops. Tiny tots and the faint-hearted are also catered for, and the management promise that with over 100 rides, there will be 'no unacceptably long queues'.

☎ 0845 330 2929 www.americanadventure.co.uk

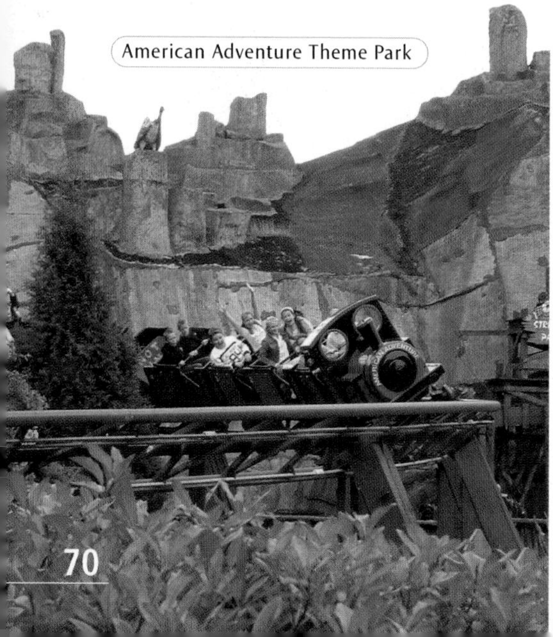

American Adventure Theme Park

Barnsdale Gardens
211 E1

Built over several years by gardener Geoff Hamilton, all the 35-plus model gardens from the various TV series can be seen here. Plant nursery and excellent coffee shop.

☎ 01572 813200 www.barnsdalegardens.co.uk

Battle of Britain Memorial Flight Visitor Centre
226 A2

Exhibition and guided tours of the maintenance hangar containing the Memorial Flight aircraft, including an Avro Lancaster, Chipmunks, Dakota, Hurricanes and Spitfires.

☎ 01526 344041 www.lincolnshire.gov.uk

Beacon Hill Country Park
361 A1

Part of Charnwood Forest, and now included as part of the new National Forest, the network of paths running through the 335 acres (135ha) of grassland, mixed woodland and heath, make the park ideal for walking and picnics. Beacon Hill itself (at 802ft (245m) the second highest point in Leicestershire) was once home to Bronze Age people and remains of their Hill Fort can still be seen. It now sports a toposcope, pointing out interesting features in the surrounding landscape.

☎ 01509 890048 www.leics.gov.uk

Belton House (NT)
225 E4

Built in the Restoration style for Sir John Brownlow in the late 1600s, this sumptuous country house is well worth a visit for the wealth of elaborate woodcarving and plasterwork, not to mention the fine furniture, silverware and tapestries. A magnificent Orangery graces the formal gardens and the substantial landscaped parkland includes a lake; perfect for a leisurely stroll. If the children get bored, head for the Adventure Playground and Wildlife Discovery Centre. The Stables Restaurant also includes a children's menu.

☎ 01476 566116 www.nationaltrust.org.uk

Belvoir Castle
224 D4

For 1000 years Belvoir has been home to the Dukes of Rutland. Meaning 'beautiful view', the name is actually pronounced 'beaver' and the view is right across the glorious Vale of Belvoir. The present castle was built in the early 1800s after a fire destroyed the previous one, and it contains many fine paintings and sculptures along with French furniture, tapestries and porcelain. There is also a fascinating museum dedicated to the history of the Queens Royal Lancers. Outside, the sloping lawns lead to the terraced formal gardens and the secluded Duchess' Spring Gardens.

☎ 01476 871000 www.belvoircastle.com

Bestwood Lodge Country Park
363 E1

Just four miles (6km) north of Nottingham, this 650 acre (263ha) park was once part of the ancient Sherwood Forest. 20 miles (32km) of footpaths now wind through a remarkable range of habitats, from reedbeds to woodland and heath. Over 150 species of birds inhabit the park.

☎ 0115 927 3674 www.nottinghamshire.gov.uk

Bolsover Castle
236 B5

Looking like a 'proper' castle, this 'Little Castle' is really a 17th century mansion house built to represent the romantic ideal of chivalry and elegance. Walking around, an imaginative audiovisual presentation re-creates the atmosphere of the time. The huge Riding House, originally built by William Cavendish to train horses in the art of manege, has been converted into a Discovery Centre and the restored garden boasts a fountain with 23 new statues. There is a visitor centre, café, and picnics are allowed in the grounds.

☎ 01246 822844 www.english-heritage.org.uk

Boughton House

Boughton House
211 E4

The 'English Versailles', so called because of the French-style changes made to the original 1500s Tudor monastic building. Home to the Dukes of Buccleuch, the interior is richly furnished and the ceilings are decorated with delightful mythical scenes. The Buccleuch collection of fine art is world renowned, including works by Van Dyck and Caracci. There is a superb armoury and ceremonial coach, and the grounds house a tearoom, play area and walled garden with plant centre. House open August only. Grounds open May to August.

☎ 01536 515731 www.boughtonhouse.org.uk

Bradgate Park
361 A2

Leicestershire's largest country park is famous for its large deer herd and Lady Jane Grey (queen of England for nine days). The ruins of Bradgate house, her birthplace, lie amongst the granite outcrops. However, the chapel has survived and houses a small museum. The tower folly 'Old John' stands on the ridge and is a famous local landmark. Excellent for walking.

☎ 0116 236 2713 www.leics.gov.uk

Buxton Museum & Art Gallery
235 E5

Follow the time line of the Peak District through seven rooms of geology, archaeology and history. Exhibitions feature work by local artists.

☎ 01298 24658 www.derbyshire.gov.uk

Calke Abbey (NT)
223 E5

An interesting example of a baroque country house captured in its state of decline. The last baronet died here in 1924 and left splendidly decorated rooms, where the family had lived, along with deserted, run-down areas, abandoned due to lack of servants. Little restoration work has been done, in order to preserve the remarkable social history it portrays. There is an extensive natural history collection, wonderful parkland, café and shop, and a walled garden with Auricula theatre.

☎ 01332 863822 www.nationaltrust.org.uk

Canons Ashby
198 A2

The house takes its name from an Augustinian Priory, the church surviving on a hilltop in the grounds. Home to the Dryden family since it was built in the mid 1500s, it has remained virtually the same since 1710. The Jacobean plasterwork is exceptional and the Elizabethan wall paintings have been superbly restored. The formal gardens have been brought back to their 18th century glory.

☎ 01327 861900 www.nationaltrust.org.uk

Carsington Water 223 D1

This 741 acre (300ha) reservoir was originally designed to collect water at times of high rainfall and release it back into the River Derwent in times of drought. It has also proved to be an excellent centre for water sports, fishing, walking, cycling and picnicking. The extensive modern visitor centre has an interactive display explaining how the reservoir was constructed, as well as shops, restaurant and a café. Half a million trees and shrubs were planted to landscape the area and provide habitat for wildlife and there are two hides from which to observe the many birds in the Wildlife Centre. The Watersports Centre will hire out canoes, dinghies and windsurfers, and provide instruction on how to use them, or you can take your own craft. A network of waymarked footpaths and bridleways allow for walking, horse riding and cycling (bikes can be hired). For younger children, there is a large adventure playground and families can cook their own food in the designated barbeque areas. Facilities for the less able are particularly good.

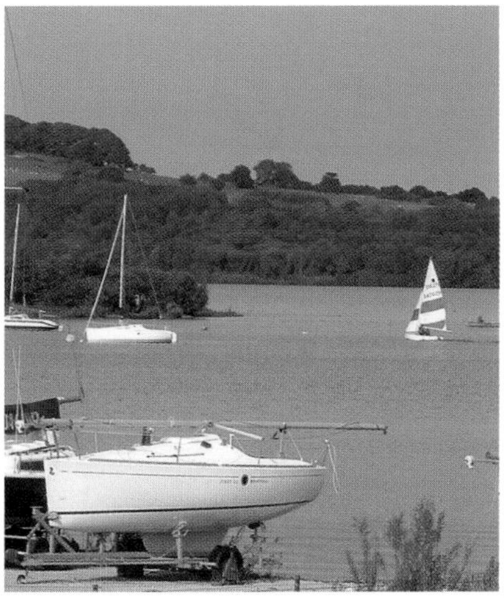

Carsington Water

Chatsworth House 235 G5

In the heart of the Derbyshire Peak District stands one of Britain's best loved stately homes, the residence of the Duke and Duchess of Devonshire. The magnificent house has over 25 beautifully decorated and furnished rooms, containing some of the finest treasures to be found in a private collection.

There are over 100 miles (161km) of walks through the 1000 acres (405ha) of Lancelot 'Capability' Brown designed parkland, which includes a lovely 100 acre (41ha) garden and the famous gravity fed waterworks, which power spectacular fountains and a waterfall cascading down a long flight of stone steps. Chatsworth has never rested on its laurels; the estate has been developed to provide a first-class adventure playground, with 'commando' style rope walks down to safe water and sand play areas for tiny tots. A working farmyard allows children to get really close to the animals and a 28-seat trailer provides tours of the woods and parkland. The maze is a challenge, and for shopaholics there is a farm shop selling Estate and local produce as well as one selling everything from furniture to porcelain. There are brass band concerts on a Sunday and events throughout the year. Truly a top-class family day out.

☎ 01246 565300 www.chatsworth-house.co.uk

Chatsworth House

Church Farm Museum 227 D1

Just outside Skegness town centre is a restored farmyard, showing life as it was in rural Lincolnshire around the turn of the 20th century. Besides the farmhouse, there is a 'mud and stud' thatched cottage and various farm buildings, all with period exhibitions. Outside, the orchard has old apple tree varieties and a herd of Lincolnshire Longwool sheep graze the paddock. There are always things going on, such as baking and threshing, and refreshments are available.

☎ 01754 766658 www.lincolnshire.gov.uk

Clumber Country Park (NT) 236 D5

Lovely country park of over 3800 acres (1537ha) with heath, woods and farmland. There is a serpentine lake and an avenue of lime trees (reputedly the longest in Europe) as well as a superb chapel in the Gothic Revival style, temples, a classical bridge and a walled kitchen garden with magnificent glasshouses. Excellent for walking and cycling (bikes can be hired) with refreshments in the stable block.

☎ 01909 476592 www.nationaltrust.org.uk

Coton Manor Wildlife Garden 210 B5

Ten acre (4ha) garden with a wide range of interesting and unusual plants. Five acre (2ha) bluebell wood, which is a real picture in spring, as well as an orchard and wild flower meadow. Plant nursery and excellent tearoom.

☎ 01604 740219 www.cotonmanor.co.uk

Denby Pottery 223 E3

Get messy and have a go at making a plate or a frog. Daily tours, excellent factory shop, cookery demonstrations, museum, garden, Dartington Crystal and gift shops, restaurant and children's play area.

☎ 01773 740799 www.denbyvisitorcentre.co.uk

Derby Industrial Museum 395 A2

The site of the world's oldest factory (the silk mills, built in the early 1700s) is appropriately the location for this museum. It tells the story of Derby's industrial heritage; mining, pottery, foundry work, railway engineering and a major exhibition of Rolls Royce aero-engines form the backbone of the museum. There are regularly changing displays and events.

☎ 01332 255308 www.derby.gov.uk

Doddington Hall 237 F5

This beautiful Elizabethan mansion, gatehouse and family church were completed in 1600 and the exterior has remained unchanged. However, the interior is a surprise, having been completely redecorated and furnished in the Georgian style in the mid-1700s. The wonderful array of textiles, paintings and artefacts collected since give it a very 'lived in' air.

Outside, the lovely gardens occupy 6 acres (2.4ha), most of which are walled, with formal topiary and herbaceous planting. There is also a wild garden and intriguing turf maze. Refreshments are served in the Gatehouse.

☎ 01522 694308 www.doddingtonhall.com

Donington Grand Prix Collection 223 F5

Five halls contain the world's largest collection of Grand Prix cars (over 130), from the oldest to the newest. Also helmets, veteran and vintage cars and much more. Gift shop selling models, videos, books and other merchandise.

☎ 01332 811027 www.doningtoncollection.com

Dove Dale 222 C2

The River Dove flows along a limestone gorge, giving its name to the area of Dovedale, arguably the most beautiful of the Derbyshire Dales. The river itself is excellent for trout fishing and has been immortalised by Isaac Walton in his book 'The Compleat Angler'. Classified as an Area of Outstanding Natural Beauty, the valley runs for over two miles (3.2km) and there are beautiful walks both along it and in the surrounding hills, which are the remains of ancient coral reefs.

Dove Dale

Elvaston Castle Country Park 362 B3

The first country park in Britain, Elvaston includes 200 acres (81ha) of grounds containing formal gardens, woodland, nature trails, an ornamental lake and estate museum. Refreshments and shop.

☎ 01332 571342 www.derbyshire.gov.uk

Eyam Museum 235 G5

The rat weather vane gives a clue to the theme of this museum; the 1665 outbreak of the Bubonic Plague. The story of this community is told from its beginnings in prehistory, through the tragedy of the plague (the villagers isolated themselves so as not to spread the disease), to its recovery and regrowth through the Industrial Revolution and beyond.

☎ 01433 631371 www.eyammuseum.demon.co.uk

Fantasy Island 227 D1

Rides are classified as 'Extreme Thrill' (with names such as 'Absolutely Insane' and 'The Beast') and 'Family Fun' (Europe's largest ferris wheel, for example, and a train ride through the world of the Jellikins for the little ones). Most of the rides are inside and with over 15 places to eat, a huge market and over 30 shops in the Mall, the weather is largely irrelevant.

☎ 01754 874668 www.fantasyisland.co.uk

Foxton Locks

Foxton Locks 210 C4

Located on the Grand Union Canal, Foxton Locks were built to solve the problem of raising boats the 75ft (22.5m) between Market Harborough and the hill summit a few miles north. Ten locks were constructed between 1810 and 1814 to form the 'Foxton Staircase' and it takes 45 minutes and 25,000 gallons (113,650l) of water for one boat to negotiate all ten; the water passing into side ponds, where it is stored. At the start of the 20th century, in order to speed up the passage of boats in an attempt to compete with the railways, the famous 'Inclined Plane' was built. Considered one of the 'Seven Wonders of the Waterways', the structure was designed by Gordon Cale Thomas and built by Gwynne of London. It consisted of two tanks, each filled with water, large enough to carry two narrow boats or a barge. A 25 horsepower engine enabled the tanks to travel up and down the slope in 12 minutes, also saving many thousands of gallons of water. However, due to lack of improvements on the rest of the canal and the success of the railways, the Inclined Plane lift was uneconomic and only operated for about ten years before being abandoned and eventually sold for scrap in 1928. The museum on the site tells the story and shows the plans for rebuilding it. The towpaths and surrounding area are lovely for walks and there is a pub and café at the locks.

☎ 01162 792657 www.fipt.org.uk

Gainsborough Old Hall 237 F4

Over 500 years old, this timber framed medieval manor house has a superb Great Hall, medieval kitchen and interesting furniture. Audio tours available.

☎ 01427 612669 www.english-heritage.org.uk

Gibraltar Point 227 D2

An internationally important National Nature Reserve, this 1000 acre (430ha) site contains many constantly changing coastal habitats, namely sand dunes, saltmarsh, freshwater marsh, sandbanks and mudbanks. Stretching from Skegness to the Wash, this is a haven for overwintering and breeding birds, and footpaths and hides have been constructed to enable visitors to observe but not disturb them.

☎ 01754 762677 www.lincstrust.org.uk

Great Central Railway 210 A1

Britain's only main line double track steam railway offers rides from Loughborough to Leicester stations. Dine in style, drive an engine, enjoy a 'themed' ride (such as a 'who dunnit') or try a Santa Special. Museum, engine sheds and shop at the Loughborough end.

☎ 01509 230726 www.gcrailway.co.uk

Grimsthorpe Castle 225 F5

Dating from the 13th century, this castle with its impressive baroque frontage has an interesting collection of tapestries, paintings and fine furniture, including thrones from the House of Lords. Surrounded by 3000 acres (1213ha) of parkland, there is a family cycle trail, a Woodland Adventure Playground, a tour with the Park Ranger (who will point out the wealth of wildlife), a shop and a café.

☎ 01778 591205 www.grimsthorpe.co.uk

Gunby Hall (NT) 226 C1

Lovely red brick 18th century house with fine oak panelling and period furnishings. Nine acres (3.6ha) of beautiful gardens with traditional flowers, fruit and vegetables.

☎ 01909 486411 www.nationaltrust.org.uk

Haddon Hall 222 D1

Parts of the hall date back to 1170, when the illegitimate son of William the Conqueror held it. However, it was not until 200 years later that the building was completed. Remarkably well preserved, it has featured in many period dramas and films.

Home of the Manners family since 1567, areas of interest include the Medieval Banqueting Hall, with Minstrels Gallery, the Great Chamber, which has many fine tapestries, and the Long Gallery, of early 17th century lineage, where the Elizabethan gentry and their ladies could take gentle walking exercise in inclement weather.

The beautiful gardens were brought back from a derelict state by the 9th Duchess of Rutland, who created a romantic garden with herbaceous borders and terraced rose gardens. The 17th century stable block houses a licensed restaurant and there is a gift shop.

☎ 01629 812855 www.haddonhall.co.uk

Haddon Hall

Harborough Museum 210 C4

The history of this planned medieval market town (many medieval yards still exist) is told through displays in this museum. The story of Market Harborough's famous corset making industry is explained with old photographs and models, including a steam former used to shape the corsets. There is a reconstruction of a bootmaker's workshop, many photographs and texts from the town as it was, and archaeological finds, including artefacts from the nearby Drayton Roman Villa and Naseby battlefield.

☎ 01858 821085 www.leics.gov.uk

Hardwick Hall (NT) 223 F1

Designed by Robert Smythson for the wealthy Bess of Hardwick, no expense was spared to build this magnificent example of Elizabethan grandeur. Imposing symmetrical towers and acres of glittering glass windows give a stunning first impression. Hardwick Hall displays the National Trust's most important collection of textiles in the country, including the Gideon Tapestries, which hang in the Long Gallery and cover the 167ft (50m) long wall. Other items of interest include period furniture, portraits and armour.

Before living here, Bess lived in Hardwick 'Old' Hall (now managed by English Heritage), the remains of which can be seen on the hilltop next to the 'New' Hall. It was the wealth accumulated from her four husbands that enabled her to move!

Outside, a herb garden, orchard and formal flower beds are enclosed by courtyards, and surrounding this is a country park containing rare breeds of sheep and cattle. There is also a stonemasons centre, which can be visited.

☎ 01246 850430 www.nationaltrust.org.uk

Hardwick Hall

Heights of Abraham
223 E2

The journey of discovery starts with a spectacular ride in a cable car over the River Derwent and Matlock Bath village, to the summit. At the top there is an old lead mine, the Great Rutland Cavern Nestus Mine, and the Great Masson Cavern to explore, the latter including a film presentation on how it was formed. Climb the Prospect Tower for magnificent views. There are two adventure playgrounds, woodland walks, the 'Who, Why, What' story of the Estate, excellent gift shops, and refreshments in The Terrace café, Woodlanders restaurant and the Tavern.

☎ 01629 582365 www.heights-of-abraham.co.uk

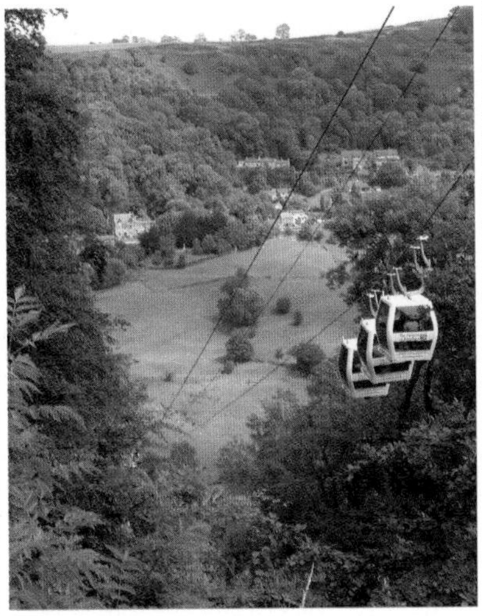

Heights of Abraham

Kedleston Hall (NT)
362 A2

A mansion in the neoclassical style with a remarkable array of Robert Adam interiors. The state rooms still have their original furniture, and an amazing display of Indian artefacts (collected by Lord Curzon, Viceroy of India in the early 1900s) can be seen in the Eastern Museum. The mansion is surrounded by parkland, which includes a restored 18th century garden. There is a shop and restaurant.

☎ 01332 842191 www.nationaltrust.org.uk

Lincoln Castle
403 B2

Built in 1068, this impressive and massive early Norman castle on its hilltop houses one of the four surviving copies of the Magna Carta, sealed by King John in 1215. There are still many original features to see, and a walk along the walls outside provides superb views across the surrounding countryside.

☎ 01522 511068 www.lincolnshire.gov.uk

Lincoln Cathedral
403 B2

Sharing the central hill with Lincoln Castle, this magnificent cathedral is one of the finest medieval buildings in Europe. Originally built in 1072 from local limestone, it was consecrated in 1092 and has been a place of worship ever since. It was damaged by fire in 1141 and an earthquake in 1185 caused considerable collapse. Rebuilt by the Bishop of Lincoln (St Hugh), he incorporated huge flying buttresses on the outside so that fewer supporting structures were needed on the inside. This allowed large windows to be installed and gave the inside an open and airy feel. In 1237 the central tower collapsed, which was not replaced for several years. By 1549 there were three towers, each with a spire; the central one blew down and the others were eventually removed, being considered unsafe!

The cathedral library contains many important manuscripts, including one written by the Venerable Bede in the late tenth century. The medieval library often exhibits books and manuscripts and there are guided roof and floor tours daily (except Sundays).

☎ 01522 544544 www.lincolncathedral.com

Lyddington Bede House
211 D3

Originally built as a wing of a medieval palace, owned by the Bishops of Lincoln, it was seized by the Crown in 1547 and given to Lord Burghley. He converted it into small rooms, almshouses, for the poor, with the condition that they learn a craft and attend church. Audio tour of the rooms.

☎ 01572 822438 www.english-heritage.org.uk

Lyveden New Bield (NT)
211 E4

Designed in the shape of a cross, Sir Thomas Tresham built (but did not complete) this Elizabethan 'Lodge' to show his religious convictions. It has remained almost unchanged since 1605. The layout of the water garden is also original, containing terraces and fascinating spiral mounds.

☎ 01832 205358 www.nationaltrust.org.uk

Mam Tor
235 F4

Known locally as 'shivering mountain', the summit of Mam Tor stands high above Hope and Edale. Popular with walkers, several well-maintained paths reach the top and along its ridgeway, where there are impressive views. Traces of an Iron Age fort can be found on the summit.

Melbourne Hall & Gardens
223 E5

Two Prime Ministers and Lady Caroline Lamb (the mistress of Lord Byron) have lived here. Originally built in the 12th century, most of the building was demolished and rebuilt in the 17th century. It now contains a fine collection of furniture and paintings and is the home of Lord and Lady Kerr. The formal gardens are beautifully laid out in the French style, with delightful fountains and an intriguing yew tunnel. House open in August only.

☎ 01332 862502

Melton Carnegie Museum
210 C1

Through displays of local archaeology, art, industry and rural pursuits, the museum tells the story of the market town of Melton Mowbray and the surrounding area.

☎ 01664 569946 www.leics.gov.uk

Museum of Lincolnshire Life
403 A1

Two centuries of social history are explored in this museum, which occupies the old barracks of the Loyal North Lincoln Militia; interactive displays tell the story of the Regiment. The fascinating history of local crafts is told and there are impressive collections representing agricultural and industrial heritage.

☎ 01522 528448 www.lincolnshire.gov.uk

National Space Centre
361 B3

Follow the brown signs with the rocket logo to this amazing centre covering all aspects of space research. For the over 5s, the Space Theatre shows amazing films about different worlds, how the universe was born and the edge of the known universe; under 5s can be treated to a 'Sunshine Show'. There are lots of buttons to push on hands-on displays in the five galleries. The first gallery looks at astronauts, the second is about our exploration of the universe to date, the third investigates our own solar system and the fourth examines how the huge advances in technology, due to space research, affect our lives on Earth. The final gallery takes a peek into the possible future. The silver 135ft (41m) rocket-shaped building contains a glass lift, which enables observation of the huge Blue Streak and Thor Able rockets. A truly inspiring and exciting day out.

☎ 0116 261 0261 www.nssc.co.uk

National Tramway Museum
223 E2

Set in a restored period village, including shops, cafés, a pub and a museum (which holds the largest national collection of electric trams). One ticket allows all day rides up and down the street on trams from all over the world. A workshop enables observation of 'work in progress' on trams being restored.

☎ 0870 758 7267 www.tramway.co.uk

Lincoln Cathedral

Newstead Abbey 223 G2

A 'must see' for Byron devotees, Newstead houses mementoes of one of England's most notorious poets. Originally built as an Augustinian priory, it was converted into a country house by the Byron family in the mid 1500s. Although much of the Abbey is now a ruin, there are beautifully furnished period rooms – although look out for the 'White Lady' ghost!

The walled garden, lake and exquisite Japanese gardens are set within the 300 acre (121.5ha) estate.

☎ 01623 793557 www.newsteadabbey.org.uk

Nine Ladies Stone Circle 222 D1

On Stanton Moor, a circle of nine evenly-spaced stones stand in a 33ft (10m) diameter circle in a large, open woodland glade. The tallest stone stands at 2.3ft (0.7m) and there is one outlier, the King Stone. An atmospheric reminder of the mysterious past.

☎ 01629 816200 www.english-heritage.org.uk

Northampton Central Museum 198 C1

Fascinating museum concentrating on Northampton's boot and shoe industry. The collection of footwear is one of the largest in the world, featuring every aspect of shoe design and manufacture. There are also impressive displays of oriental and British ceramics, and Italian paintings.

In another section of the museum, the history of the county of Northamptonshire is explained with exhibits from the surrounding area.

☎ 01604 838111 www.northampton.gov.uk

Nottingham Castle Museum & Art Gallery 405 F1

The original Nottingham Castle was built in the early 1100s but was completely demolished in 1651. A new one was built on the same site by the Duke of Newcastle, which was gutted by fire in 1831. The shell was restored in 1878 to house a museum, which now displays a superb collection of fine art, ceramics, metalwork and glass. With children in mind, there are hands-on exhibitions and the 'Look Out' playground includes watch towers and a medieval barn. Tours of the city caves are available from the museum, and there is a café and shop.

☎ 0115 915 3700 www.nottinghamcity.gov.uk

Oakham Castle 211 D2

The superb Great Hall remains from the original 12th century castle. It contains fine sculptures and an amazing collection of horseshoes, mounted on the walls, the oldest of which probably dates from 1470. The custom was that every visiting peer of the realm had to give a horseshoe to the Lord of the Manor on his or her first visit. HRH The Princess Royal gave one of the latest in 1999.

☎ 01572 758440 www.rutnet.co.uk

Peak Cavern 235 F4

This huge cavern has the largest natural cave mouth in Britain. A complete village once existed here, making ropes for the local lead mining industry. The guided tour passes various awe inspiring features, including the Great Cave which measures 150ft (45m) by 90ft (27m).

☎ 01433 620285 www.peakcavern.co.uk

Peak District 235 F3

Essentially separated into the rugged sandstone Dark Peak and gentler limestone White Peak areas, the Peak District is very much a product of man, through farming, mining and quarrying. It has been inhabited since the end of the last Ice Age.

Peak District – Monsal Head

The first National Park, the Peak District displays an amazing variety of habitats on its uplands and in its sheltered Dales, making it very pleasant walking country. The villages are picturesque and welcoming. Look out for the floral art of 'Well Dressing' in many villages, a custom largely confined to this area, and try the famous 'Bakewell Puddings' (not tarts) in the town of Bakewell. Visit the many caverns (with a guide) or relax in one of the many teashops or traditional pubs.

☎ 01629 816200 www.peakdistrict.org

Peveril Castle 235 F4

Built in the 11th century to guard the King's Manor, this castle, on its high vantage point, offers superb views across the Peak District of Derbyshire.

☎ 01433 620613 www.english-heritage.org.uk

Pickfords House Museum 395 B1

The former home of Joseph Pickford (architect), this Grade 1 listed Georgian town house is furnished in period style; even down to the housekeeper's cupboard. It shows vividly how an ordinary professional gentleman and his servants would have lived at the time. There are also displays of toys and toy theatres, textiles and costumes. Outside, the garden has been re-created in the style of the period.

☎ 01332 255363 www.derby.gov.uk

Poole's Cavern 235 E5

The subterranean Wye Brook has dissolved the limestone rock here over millennia to form this magnificent cavern. Neolithic man sheltered here, Celts and Romans worshipped here, a robber called Poole is said to have hidden here in the 15th century, and people have visited it to marvel at its wonders since the 1600s. There are some fantastic formations fashioned from the slowly dripping limestone rich water; stalactites, stalagmites, rimstone pools, flowstones and curtain features, some of which have been coloured by minerals leaching out from the hills above. The entrance was once quite restricted, so in the late 1800s, the owner used dynamite to enlarge it (destroying some large features in the process). In this era, the cavern held a bandstand, museum and monkey house and was illuminated by large candelabra. Luckily, the caves are now appreciated solely for their natural beauty and today's guides will not threaten abandonment at the end of the passage without further pay!

Research has shown that the cave system stretches for around one and a half miles (2.4km) beyond the boulder rubble at the current end. The visitor centre at the entrance has information on the so far unseen caves, tells the history of the cavern and has an exhibition of artefacts found in it.

☎ 01298 26978 www.poolescavern.co.uk

Renishaw Hall & Gardens 236 B5

The grounds of Renishaw Hall contain lakeside walks, a sculpture trail, yuccary, a host of traditional and exotic plants and a café. The stable houses art galleries and a museum, which includes an exhibition of clothing from the last 150 years. Guided tours available.

☎ 01246 432310 www.sitwell.co.uk

Rutland County Museum 211 D2

The rural history of England's smallest county is told in a building originally designed as an indoor riding school for the Rutland Fencible Cavalry. Further buildings house galleries, local crafts, a café and shop.

☎ 01572 758440 www.rutnet.co.uk

Poole's Cavern

Sherwood Forest Country Park 224 B1

Natural sandy heathland and ancient oaks have produced a fascinating ecosystem, represented in this 450 acre (182ha) country park, part of the former Royal Hunting Forest. The famous hollow 'Major Oak', where the legendary Robin Hood supposedly hid, can be found here and there are many waymarked woodland trails to explore. The excellent visitor centre illustrates the legends and natural history of the Forest, with displays and videos; it also houses two shops and a café.

☎ 01623 824490 www.nottinghamshiretourism.co.uk

Sherwood Pines Forest Park 224 B1

With over 2960 acres (1200ha) of heath and woodland, this is an excellent area for safe cycling (cycles can be hired), walking, horse riding and picnics. For young children, there is an adventure playground.

☎ 01623 822447 www.forestry.gov.uk

Shipley Country Park 223 F3

This 600 acre (243ha) country park includes woodlands, lakes and two large, flat, open areas popular for kite flying. There are many walks and cycle tracks, a sculpture trail, bird hide, adventure playground, visitor centre, shop, picnic site and coffee shop.

☎ 01773 719961 www.derby.gov.uk

Snibston Discovery Park 209 G1

This former 100 acre (40.5ha) colliery site has been transformed into a unique museum and discovery centre for science and technology. Ride on the colliery railway and have a go on over 90 experiments to discover the wonders of science. Ex-miners give guided tours of the old colliery and, by contrast, the Science Alive gallery is full of state of the art interactive games illustrating scientific principles in fun ways. There is a separate gallery for under 8s and under 5s. Good restaurant and excellent access for the less able.

☎ 01530 278444 www.leics.gov.uk

Speedwell Cavern 235 F4

This is a former lead mine incorporating several naturally formed chambers and an amazing underground canal. 105 steps lead down to the waterway, where a boat will take visitors on a guided tour of this atmospheric 200 year old mine. At the end is an awesome, massive cavern, with a 65.5ft (20m) waterfall. The roof disappears into blackness, too high to be seen and the water is so deep it was believed to be bottomless.

☎ 01433 620512 www.speedwellcavern.co.uk

Springfields Outlet Shopping Village & Festival Gardens 226 A5

25 acres (10ha) of beautiful plants to delight gardeners and florists alike. Bulbs plus trees, shrubs, herbaceous plants, a semi-tropical greenhouse and display gardens. For shopaholics, there is a factory outlet shopping village.

☎ 01775 724843

Stainsby Mill 236 A5

On the Hardwick Estate is a water-powered mill. Producing flour as far back as the 13th century, the machinery was replaced in the mid 1800s. Now restored, flour is ground regularly and can be purchased here.

☎ 01246 850430 www.nationaltrust.org.uk

Stanford Hall 210 A5

Lovely 17th century house in grounds alongside the River Avon. Beautifully furnished with a fine collection of Tudor and Stuart paintings and a magnificent library. The former stables house a motorcycle museum with racing and vintage machines, and there is a full scale replica of the early 'Hawk' flying machine. The grounds include a rose garden, nature trail and, of course, tearooms.

☎ 01788 860250 www.stanfordhall.co.uk

Stoke Bruerne Waterways Museum 198 C2

A former cornmill in the lovely village of Stoke Bruerne was chosen to house this fascinating museum, which recalls 200 years of the inland waterways. The busy Grand Union Canal is immediately outside, with boat trips available along it. Refreshments can be found in the village.

☎ 01604 862229 www.thewaterwaystrust.org

Sudbury Hall (NT) 222 C4

Richly decorated late 17th century house with a very elaborate Great Staircase. Interesting mythological decorative paintings, Grinling Gibbons woodcarvings and magnificent plasterwork. Shop, tearoom and picnic site.

☎ 01283 585337 www.nationaltrust.org.uk

Sudbury Hall Museum (NT) 222 C4

The National Trust Museum of Childhood is housed in a service wing of the main Hall. Everything about children from the 1700s to the present day. Toys and games along with a re-created Victorian schoolroom and examples of child employment. There is a treasure hunt to play and, at Christmas, tea with Santa.

☎ 01283 585337 www.nationaltrust.org.uk

Sulgrave Manor 198 A3

Beautiful Tudor House where George Washington's ancestors lived. Guided tours are given around the furnished rooms, gardens and George Washington Exhibition. Café and shop.

☎ 01295 760205 www.stratford.co.uk

Tales of Robin Hood 405 E1

Travel back to Sherwood Forest in the time of Robin Hood. Experience the sights, sounds and smells of the age from a guided carriage. Opportunities to try archery and brass rubbing or listen to a storyteller. Falconry demonstrations at weekends.

☎ 0115 948 3284 www.robinhood.uk.com

Tattershall Castle (NT) 226 A2

Imposing and impressive 15th century tower, one of the first to be built of red brick. Fortified and moated, it was restored in the early 1900s and has four storeys of huge rooms with massive Gothic fireplaces, stained glass windows and brick vaulting.

☎ 01526 342543 www.nationaltrust.org.uk

Treak Cliff Cavern 235 F4

One of the first 'Blue John' mines, where the beautifully coloured mineral was extracted. Amazing stalactites and stalagmites can be seen on the guided tour.

☎ 01433 620571 www.bluejohnstone.com

Twycross Zoo 209 F2

Twycross covers 40 acres (16ha) of countryside and is famous for its collection of primates. These include man's closest relative, the bonobo, along with the smallest pygmy marmosets, through orang-utans, chimpanzees, gibbons and mountain gorillas. Baby animals are always arriving and are a popular attraction, as is feeding time in the sealion pen. Other animals include lions, giraffes, flamingos, the rare Mhorr gazelle, penguins, seals, snakes, crocodiles and elephants, to name but a few. For younger children there is 'Pets Corner' and an adventure playground. Three quarters of the 1000-plus animals here are classified as endangered and one of the main functions of the zoo is as a captive breeding centre to help in their conservation; information on this and other aspects of the zoo are available through the various exhibitions and information boards.

☎ 01827 880250 www.twycrosszoo.com

Twycross Zoo – Lion Cub

Wicksteed Park 211 D5

Opened in the 1920s, Wicksteed was one of the first big amusement parks; it still has a less 'frantic' air than some others. The large boating lake, gardens, pitch and putt and quite magical miniature railway are a welcome breath of quieter days, whereas the roller coaster, twin pirate ship and twin-seat racing cars cater for those seeking thrills. There is a huge, free playground for younger children and plenty of places to shop and eat. A very pleasant day out catering for all.

☎ 01536 512475 www.wicksteedpark.co.uk

Woolsthorpe Manor (NT) 225 E5

Birthplace and home of Sir Isaac Newton, this small, 17th century manor house contains a 'Young Newton' exhibition and an early edition of his 'Principia' work. In the barn is a Science Discovery Centre and café, and a descendant of the apple tree, under which Newton is said to have discovered the principles of gravity, grows in the orchard.

☎ 01476 860338 www.nationaltrust.org.uk

Ye Olde Pork Pie Shoppe 210 C1

Still made to the original recipe, pork pies have been baked by Dickinson & Morris in this shop since 1851. Next door they have opened a sausage shop, and both shops offer demonstrations.

☎ 01664 562341 www.porkpie.co.uk

EAST OF ENGLAND

Wide, pastel-hued skies, reedy flat fens, secluded nature reserves, river estuaries and delightful coastal towns characterise this area. East of Norwich, the interconnecting waterways of the Broads offer a unique area for leisure and recreation. Few hills rise to interrupt the distant views of cathedral cities and timeless villages, with their rich historic stories. This is the home of artists and musicians and also one much favoured by boatlovers, birdwatchers, equestrians and antiquarians.

Wicken Fen National Nature Reserve

Alby Crafts & Gardens
228 D2

Working craft centre in converted brick and flint farm buildings surrounded by 4 acres (1.5ha) of attractive gardens.

☎ 01263 761590 www.albycrafts.co.uk

Aldenham Reservoir Country Park
186 A3

Comprising 175 acres (70ha) of woodland and parkland with a 65 acre (26ha) reservoir. There are plenty of things to do and see including fishing, sailing, a rare breeds farm, children's adventure play area, nature trails and a re-creation of Winnie the Pooh's 100 Aker Wood. There is a charge for parking.

☎ 020 8953 9602 www.hertsdirect.org/aldenham

Anglesey Abbey (NT)
200 D1

This attractive Jacobean house was built on the site of an earlier Augustinian priory. Much of what visitors see today is the legacy of Huttleston Broughton, 1st Lord Fairhaven, who bought the house in 1926 and, over the next thirty years, accumulated a large collection of paintings, books, furniture, tapestries and clocks. He also landscaped the superb gardens which extend to 98 acres (40ha), and comprise both formal and informal designs. The lawns and avenues of trees combine with more structured planting to provide colour all year round and are enhanced by Lord Fairhaven's fine collection of statuary. Within the grounds is Lode Mill, an 18th century working water mill.

☎ 01223 810080 www.nationaltrust.org.uk

Audley End

Audley End
200 D4

This magnificent Jacobean mansion was built between 1603 and 1614 by Thomas Howard, the 1st Earl of Suffolk, on the site of a former abbey. At the time, it was the largest house in England. In 1668, it briefly became a royal palace when it was purchased by Charles II for £50,000, for his use when visiting the races at Newmarket. Between 1708 and 1753 a large part of the house was demolished; the building we see today is just a small part of the original.

In the 1760s much of the interior was remodelled by Robert Adam and, today, visitors can see over thirty rooms containing attractive period furnishings. Adam's work can also be seen in the extensive grounds where he created ornamental garden buildings to enhance the superb landscape park laid out by Lancelot 'Capability' Brown in 1762. There are fine Victorian gardens featuring a parterre, originally laid out in 1830 and re-created in 1993, a rose garden, as well as a walled garden of approximately 10 acres (4ha) within which is an impressive 170ft (52m) long vine house.

☎ 01799 522399 www.english-heritage.org.uk

Banham Zoo
214 B3

Opened in 1968 and set in 35 acres (14ha) of beautiful parkland and gardens, this attractive zoo features over 1000 animals, including big cats, reptiles, penguins and kangaroos. Visitors can tour the site on the Safari Roadtrain, which gives an excellent overview of the animals.

☎ 01953 887771 www.banhamzoo.co.uk

Bedford Museum
199 F3

Housed in the former Higgins & Sons Brewery, the collection of this local museum focuses on Bedfordshire's social and natural history, geology and archaeology.

☎ 01234 353323 www.bedfordmuseum.org

Beth Chatto Gardens, The
202 B5

In 1960 Beth and Andrew Chatto took 4 acres (1.5ha) of inhospitable wasteland and decided to create a garden. It seemed like an impossible task, with its sunbaked, sandy slopes and boggy areas, but the colourful gardens visitors can see today are a testament to their horticultural skill. On the site are four main areas: the scree, gravel, woodland and water gardens, each with their own gardening challenges.

☎ 01206 822007 www.bethchatto.co.uk

Blickling Hall (NT)
228 C3

An impressive sight, Blickling Hall is an early 17th century Jacobean mansion built mainly of red brick and limestone. Highlights within the house include the spectacular 125ft (38m) Long Gallery with its superb plaster ceiling, a library, an oak staircase and fine collections of paintings, furniture and tapestries. The parkland surrounding the house was landscaped in the 18th century and includes an artificial lake and 600 acres (243ha) of woodland. Unusually, within the grounds there is a burial pyramid.

☎ 01263 738030 www.nationaltrust.org.uk

Bourne Mill (NT)
202 B5

Originally built as a fishing lodge in 1591, this Grade I listed building, with attractive 'Dutch' gables, was converted to a mill in the 19th century. It has a 4 acre (1.5ha) mill pond and much of the machinery, including the waterwheel, is in working order.

☎ 01206 572422 www.nationaltrust.org.uk

Bressingham Steam Museum & Gardens
214 B3

Created by horticulturalist Alan Bloom, visitors can see main line locomotives, traction engines and an elaborate Victorian steam roundabout against a lovely backdrop of colourful landscaped gardens. Not to be missed are rides on the working narrow gauge railways that run for more than 5 miles (8km) around the gardens, lake and woods. For garden lovers, the 6 acre (2.5ha) Dell Garden, featuring 47 island beds of perennials, provides a superb show of colour in the summer. There is also a 'Dad's Army' exhibition.

☎ 01379 686900 www.bressingham.co.uk

Burghley House
211 F2

This superb Tudor mansion was built between 1565 and 1587 by William Cecil (later Lord Burghley), who was Elizabeth I's Lord Treasurer and principal advisor. It is set in a 300 acre (120ha) deer park landscaped in 1756 by Lancelot 'Capability' Brown. Externally, the mansion remains virtually unchanged and is considered by many to be one of the finest examples of late Elizabethan architecture. The interior was extensively remodelled in the late 17th century and contains the work of Antonio Verrio, Grinling Gibbons and Louis Laguerre. The beautiful interiors are a marvellous showcase for the house's impressive collection of art, which was amassed largely by the 5th and 9th Earls of Exeter (Lord Burghley's descendants) who were both avid collectors.

☎ 01780 752451 www.burghley.co.uk

Cambridge
200 C2

Situated on the banks of the River Cam, Cambridge is a combination of narrow medieval streets and magnificent buildings. Flanking the river are The Backs, a picturesque mixture of lawns, formal gardens and open spaces.

The fairly compact city centre is dominated architecturally by the historic University, the hi-tech industries that have developed in recent years tending to be confined to the outskirts. There are 31 colleges, rich both historically and architecturally. The first college, Peterhouse, was founded in 1284 by the Bishop of Ely. Queens' College is notable for its unusual wooden Mathematical Bridge – built originally without the use of nails. Perhaps the most famous of the colleges is the 15th century King's College whose chapel has an outstanding fan vaulted ceiling and exceptional stained glass windows. Other colleges include Magdalene College, where the fellows still dine by candlelight, and the most recent, Robinson College, which was founded in 1974 by a local millionaire. Many of the good and great studied at the University – luminaries include Sir Isaac Newton, Samuel Pepys, Archbishop Thomas Cranmer, Oliver Cromwell, William Wordsworth and, more recently, the likes of Stephen Hawking and the 'Pythons' John Cleese, Eric Idle and Graham Chapman. Guided walks around the city and colleges leave from the Tourist Information Centre daily throughout the year and, especially if time is short, they are a good way to get a feel for what there is to see.

Cambridge also offers a fine range of museums to visit: the Fitzwilliam Museum has an eclectic collection of art and artefacts, the Sedgwick Museum of Geology has a lovely gem collection, and the Cambridge University's Museum of Zoology has a fascinating collection of animals; visitors can see a giant ground sloth, now extinct, that was collected in Victorian times.

☎ 0906 586 2526 (60p/min) www.visitcambridge.org

Cambridge – Pembroke College

Cambridge American Military Cemetery & Memorial
200 B2

A beautiful and moving tribute to the American servicemen and women who lost their lives in World War II. The peaceful site, with over 3800 headstones, extends to 30.5 acres (12ha) and is framed on two sides by woodland. There is a memorial building made of Portland stone within which the museum room contains a superb 30ft by 18ft (9m x 5.5m) map: 'The Mastery of the Atlantic – The Great Air Assault'.

☎ 01954 210350 www.abmc.gov

Cambridge University Botanic Gardens
391 F2

This attractive 40 acre (16ha) garden was founded by Professor John Stevens Henslow (who was Charles Darwin's teacher) in 1831. It was opened to the public in 1846 and today contains thousands of plant species in lovely landscaped settings, including nine National Collections.

☎ 01223 336265 www.botanic.cam.ac.uk

Castle House (Sir Alfred Munnings Art Museum)
202 B4

From 1919 to 1959 Castle House was home to Sir Alfred Munnings, artist and past president of the Royal Academy, famous for his equestrian paintings. The house, a mixture of Tudor and Georgian architecture, and surrounded by 40 acres (16ha) of land, is presented much as it was when Munnings lived in it and includes his furniture and many of his paintings.

☎ 01206 322127 www.siralfredmunnings.co.uk

Cecil Higgins Art Gallery
199 F3

Originally home to the Higgins family, who were wealthy Bedford brewers, this Victorian mansion is furnished as it would have been in the late 19th century. An adjoining gallery was added in 1976, which has changing exhibitions of paintings, prints and drawings. Artists include Gainsborough, Constable, Turner, Rembrandt and Picasso. Also on display are collections of silver, glass, ceramics and the Thomas Lester lace collection.

☎ 01234 211222 www.cecilhigginsartgallery.org

Clacton Pier
189 E1

The pier, which dates from 1871, was a catalyst for the development of Clacton as a seaside resort. Originally it was a landing pier, but soon became popular with day-trippers from London and for promenading. The first pier was quite a humble affair; only 160 yards (146m) long and 4 yards (3.5m) wide. The pier now covers an area of 6.5 acres (2.5ha) and is packed with fairground rides, a Seaquarium and all the usual pubs, restaurants and side stalls.

☎ 01255 421115 www.clactonpier.co.uk

Colchester Castle Museum
202 A5

Housed in the largest Norman keep in Britain, the museum has a wide range of exhibits spanning 2000 years of British History. There is a superb display on the siege of Colchester during the English Civil War, and various Roman relics. Visitors can also take a tour of the Roman vaults which still lie under the present castle – it was built on the foundations of the Roman Temple of Claudius.

☎ 01206 282 939 www.colchestermuseums.org.uk

Colchester Zoo
202 A5

This superb zoo, which has over 200 rare and endangered species, is set in 60 acres (24ha) of attractive parkland. The enclosures have been designed to replicate the natural environments of the animals as closely as possible. The rich animal life of Africa has several enclosures including the 'Kingdom of the Wild', which houses many of the grazing animals of the African savannah such as zebras, ostriches, pygmy hippos and white rhinos. 'Elephant Kingdom' features the zoo's breeding herd of African elephants, and 'Chimp World' is always popular. 'Playa Patagonia' is well worth seeing; an impressive 26 yard (24m) long tunnel allows visitors to view sea lions swimming above their heads. The zoo is also home to one of the best large cat collections in Europe, including the rare white tiger.

Daily displays allow visitors to get closer to the animals; the penguin parade is always a favourite and visitors even get a chance to feed the elephants and giraffes.

☎ 01206 331292 www.colchester-zoo.com

Colchester Zoo – White Tiger

Cressing Temple Barns
201 F5

There are two timber-framed barns on the site: the Barley Barn built in the early 13th century and the Wheat Barn built in the mid to late 13th century. Both barns have been rebuilt over the years but some of the original constructions remain. Also to be seen are a blacksmith's shop, a bakehouse and a reconstructed Tudor garden.

☎ 01376 584903

Cromwell Museum
212 A5

Following the execution of Charles I in 1649, Oliver Cromwell came to power and ruled the country until his death in 1658. This museum, situated in the old Huntingdon Grammar School where he was a pupil, houses memorabilia and possessions relating to his life.

☎ 01480 375830 edweb.camcnty.gov.uk/cromwell

Denny Abbey & Farmland Museum
200 C1

Originally founded in 1159, this Benedictine abbey features superb Norman interiors and displays telling the story of the abbey through the centuries. Over the years it has housed the Knights Templars and the Poor Clares (nuns of the Franciscan order), eventually becoming a farmhouse.

The Farmland Museum looks at the rural history of the local area and farming over the years. Attractions include a village shop, a traditional farmer's cottage and a 17th century stone barn.

☎ 01223 860988 www.dennyfarmlandmuseum.org.uk

Docwra's Manor Gardens
200 B3

An attractive series of enclosed gardens, designed to display differing characteristics. The gardens are divided by walls, hedging and farm buildings surrounding a Queen Anne farmhouse.

☎ 01763 261473

Dunstable Downs (NT)
199 F5

This popular location for kite-flying comprises 510 acres (206ha) of beautiful chalk grassland and farmland with superb views over the Vale of Aylesbury. There are circular walks, a picnic area and a countryside centre with interpretive displays and a shop.

☎ 01582 608489 www.nationaltrust.org.uk

Dunwich Heath (NT)
203 F1

A beautiful area of lowland heath on the Suffolk coast. The terrain, which covers 215 acres (87ha), includes large tracts of purple heather, as well as gorse, woodland, sandy cliffs and a mile (1.6km) long sandy beach. The heath is rich in insect and birdlife and is home to the now rare ant-lion and nightjar. An information centre is housed in converted coastguard cottages.

☎ 01728 648501 www.nationaltrust.org.uk

East Anglia Transport Museum
215 F2

A reconstructed 1930s style street and attractive woodland area are the perfect setting for visitors to enjoy a trip on beautifully preserved vehicles from the first half of the 20th century. These include trams, buses, trolleybuses, cars, steamrollers and a variety of other light commercial vehicles.

☎ 01502 518459 www.eatm.org.uk

Easton Farm Park
203 D2

Set in 35 acres (14ha) of lovely countryside, this farm park has lots of things for children to see and do. There are plenty of farm animals including Suffolk Punch horses, goats, sheep, rabbits, hens and cows. Children can also ride the Shetland ponies and will be fascinated by watching chicks hatch in the Chick Nursery and by Mildred, a wooden cow who moos and can also be milked. There is also an adventure play area, and the River Deben provides lovely river walks.

☎ 01728 746475 www.eastonfarmpark.co.uk

Elton Hall
211 F3

Dating from Tudor times, this romantic house is a combination of medieval, Gothic and classical architectural styles and has been home to the Proby family for over 350 years. The house has superb furniture, porcelain and some outstanding paintings by Constable, Gainsborough and Reynolds. The Library has over 12,000 books including Henry VIII's prayer book, complete with his writing. The beautiful gardens are especially good in the summer; the herbaceous borders are a riot of colour and the rose garden, which includes highly scented old fashioned roses, is stunning. There is also a sunken garden, a knot garden and a Gothic orangery, as well as an arboretum.

☎ 01832 280468

Ely Cathedral
212 D5

This magnificent cathedral dates from the late 11th century and was originally built as a monastic church, gaining cathedral status in 1109. It still retains several monastic outbuildings. After the Dissolution it continued to exist as a cathedral except for a brief period in the 17th century when Oliver Cromwell used it as a stable for his cavalry horses. The architecture is unusual with a 248ft (75.5m) long Norman nave and a remarkable 14th century Octagon Tower.

☎ 01353 667735 www.cathedral.ely.anglican.org

Epping Forest
186 D3

This 6000 acre (1800ha) remnant of a vast medieval forest has large tracts that are recognised as Sites of Special Scientific Interest. It is part open space, part woodland and has been owned by the Corporation of London since 1878. There are some lovely walks including part of the long distance footpath, the Forest Way. In Tudor times the forest was used for hunting, and Elizabeth I's timber-framed hunting lodge can still be seen. An information centre has interesting displays on the forest.

☎ 020 8532 0188

Fairhaven Gardens
229 E4

Delightful woodland and water garden covering an area of 180 acres (73ha) which includes South Walsham Inner Broad. There are 3 miles (5km) of lovely walks, and boat trips are available on the broad at an extra cost. There are superb displays of primroses and candelabra primulas in the spring, and marvellous autumn colours afforded by the numerous mature trees.

☎ 01603 270449 www.norfolkbroads.com/fairhaven

Fairlands Valley Park
200 A5

The park extends to 120 acres (48.5ha) and includes an 11 acre (4.5ha) lake where watersports are available. It is also home to a variety of wildlife.

☎ 01438 353241 www.stevenage-leisure.co.uk/fairlands

Felbrigg Hall (NT)
228 C2

This magnificent 17th century house is set in an estate of over 1700 acres (690ha). The house contains superb 18th century furniture and paintings collected by William Windham II (who inherited the house in 1749) when on his Grand Tour. The parkland has lovely waymarked walks taking visitors past some very ancient trees. There is also a 500 acre (200ha) wood and a walled garden which includes a combination of decorative planting and a traditional kitchen garden.

☎ 01263 837444 www.nationaltrust.org.uk

Fitzwilliam Museum
391 F2

The museum owes its foundation to the bequest of Richard, the 7th Viscount Fitzwilliam of Merrion in 1816, who left his collection along with funds to house them, to the University of Cambridge. The current collection, which has grown considerably over the years, is superb, including paintings by Titian, Rubens, Canaletto, Gainsborough, Monet and Picasso, antiquities from Ancient Egypt, Rome, China and Greece, medieval manuscripts, sculpture, furniture, coins and medals.

☎ 01223 332900 www.fitzmuseum.cam.ac.uk

Flag Fen Bronze Age Centre
212 A3

Flag Fen is one of the most important Bronze Age sites in Europe. Visitors can see 3000 year old timber that was once part of a wooden structure that crossed a shallow lake, and is contained within a purpose built preservation hall. Reconstructed Iron Age and Bronze Age round houses can be seen and, within the visitor centre, there is a museum containing artefacts found on the site. During the summer archaeologists can often be seen at work.

☎ 01733 313414 www.flagfen.com

Flatford Mill & Bridge Cottage (NT)
202 B4

The 18th century mill, made famous by landscape artist John Constable (1776 – 1837) and once owned by his father, is itself not open to the public but there are organised walks (at a charge) during the summer months pointing out the locations illustrated in his work. Just upstream from the mill is the 16th century thatched Bridge Cottage which features a Constable exhibition.

☎ 01206 298260 www.nationaltrust.org.uk

Framlingham Castle
203 D1

This 12th century castle, surrounded by grass-covered earthworks, has crenellated towers topped with Tudor chimneys linked by impressive 43ft (13m) high curtain walls. The wall walk along the top is open to visitors and commands excellent views. Within the walls, the visitor centre now occupies what was once a poor house dating from 1729. This is one of a number of uses the castle has been put to over the years; it has also served its time as a prison and a school.

☎ 01728 724189 www.english-heritage.org.uk

Fritton Lake Countryworld
229 F5

Many activities are available, all centred around a 150 acre (61ha) lake. Attractions include a children's farm, heavy horse stables, formal Victorian gardens, falconry centre, adventure playground, 9 hole golf course and 18 hole putting green, a miniature railway, fishing and boating on the lake, cycle trails and lovely woodland walks.

☎ 0871 2224244 www.frittonlake.co.uk

Gainsborough's House
201 G3

This 16th century townhouse, with 18th century brick façade, is the birthplace of the artist Thomas Gainsborough (1727 - 88). The house contains a large collection of his paintings, drawings and prints along with 18th century furniture and objects. There is also a changing programme of contemporary exhibitions throughout the year.

☎ 01787 372958 www.gainsborough.org

Grafham Water
199 G1

This large water park, extending to 1500 acres (600ha), has a variety of activities including sailing, fishing, cycling, and a nature reserve with trails and hides. There is a charge for car parking.

☎ 01480 812154

Grime's Graves
213 G4

These fascinating Neolithic flint mines date from 4000 to 5000 years ago. Visitors can descend 30ft (10m) by ladder into one of the shafts and see the radiating galleries where ancient man worked the high quality flint with antler picks.

☎ 01842 810656 www.english-heritage.org.uk

Hamerton Zoo Park
211 G5

Established as a wildlife conservation sanctuary in 1990 and set in 15 acres (6ha) of parkland, the zoo specialises in rare, endangered and unusual animals with species totalling over 100. Animals that can be seen include wolves, porcupines, snakes, giant millipedes and African land snails, as well as monkeys, sloths and an array of colourful birds.

☎ 01832 293362 www.hamertonzoopark.com

Harrold-Odell Country Park
199 E2

This attractive 144 acre (58ha) park, situated beside the River Great Ouse, with its lakes, water meadows, woodland and nature reserve, is a haven for wildlife. It is worth taking binoculars as the site attracts large numbers of wildfowl, especially in winter. There is a hide, and an information centre with café.

☎ 01234 720016 www.ivelvalley.co.uk

Hatfield Forest (NT)
187 E1

There are some delightful walks and nature trails around this rare surviving example of a medieval royal hunting forest. Extending to over 1000 acres (400ha) of ancient woodland and pasture, it supports a wide variety of flora and fauna including 400 year old pollarded oaks and hornbeams, fallow deer, and, in the summer, cattle can be seen grazing. There are also two ornamental lakes and a grotto called the Shell House, both dating from the 18th century.

☎ 01279 874040 www.nationaltrust.org.uk

Hatfield House
186 B2

This superb Jacobean house, set in 4000 acres (1600ha) of parkland, was built in 1611 by Robert Cecil, 1st Earl of Salisbury, who was Chief Minister to James I. It has remained in the Cecil family ever since. The luxurious interior exhibits superb examples of Jacobean craftsmanship, such as the magnificent carved oak staircase and long gallery. There are also impressive paintings by Reynolds, Hilliard and Mytens, an armoury and fine 16th, 17th and 18th century furniture and tapestries.

The house was built on the site of an earlier 15th century palace which was home to Elizabeth I for much of her childhood. Most of the old Tudor red bricked palace was destroyed to build the new house but one wing, including the great

banqueting hall, where Elizabeth held her first Council of State on her accession in 1558, still survives in the grounds of the current mansion.

The beautiful 42 acre (17ha) gardens situated adjacent to the house were originally laid out by John Tradescant the Elder, who was employed by the 1st Earl. Tradescant was a great plant hunter and he brought huge quantities of plants from Europe. Over the years the layout of the gardens has changed many times, most notably in the 18th century when the fashion for landscape gardening resulted in much of the earlier Jacobean formality being swept away. Today, the gardens are totally organic and have been restored to display much of their varied history, with a knot garden, lime walk, privy garden with yew hedges and a wilderness garden.

☎ 01707 287010 www.hatfield-house.co.uk

Hatfield House – Long Gallery

Henry Moore Foundation 186 D1

Seventy acre (28ha) estate, gifted to the foundation by Henry Moore, with sculpture gardens and fields. There is an ever changing display of his work. Visits by appointment only.

☎ 01279 843333 www.henry-moore-fdn.co.uk

Holkham Hall 227 G3

This impressive Palladian mansion was built on the site of an earlier manor house between 1734 and 1764 for the 1st Earl of Leicester, Thomas Coke, and is based on designs by William Kent. During his Grand Tour of Europe the 1st Earl had amassed a vast collection of valuable art and artefacts and he wanted a suitably grand house in which to display them. The resulting mansion, built of sand-coloured local brick, with its pedimented portico, square corner towers and side wings, has been little altered over the years, but unfortunately the 1st Earl never saw the finished building as he died in 1759, five years before it was completed.

The interior of the house is superb, the pink marble and alabaster entrance hall, designed by the 1st Earl in collaboration with Lord Burlington, being particularly impressive. Stairs from the hall lead to the elaborate state rooms on the first floor with their superb collections of statuary, furniture, tapestries and splendid paintings by Gainsborough, Van Dyck, Rubens, Claude Lorraine and Poussin.

The 3000 acre (120ha) landscaped grounds surrounding the house were set out by Lancelot 'Capability' Brown and include a mile-long lake and thousands of trees. Today the park is home to a large herd of fallow deer and the lake has many species of wildfowl. There is no charge to enter the grounds and there are lovely walks around the lake and, in the summer, boat trips.

Other attractions include the Holkham Bygones Collection, the nursery garden, the Holkham Pottery and a history of farming exhibition.

☎ 01328 710227 www.holkham.co.uk

Horsey Windpump (NT) 229 F3

Restored five-storey windpump built in 1912. From the top there are marvellous views across Horsey Mere.

☎ 01493 393904 www.nationaltrust.org.uk

Houghton Hall 227 F5

This superb Palladian house, surrounded by 350 acres (142ha) of parkland and gardens, was built between 1722 and 1735 for Britain's first Prime Minister, Sir Robert Walpole. Designed by James Gibbs, and later refined by Colen Campbell, the whole house was built to impress; the main block features magnificent corner towers topped by domes, and is connected to service blocks by curved colonnades.

Houghton Hall

The extravagant interiors were designed and furnished by William Kent and include the highly ornamented Stone Hall, which features a bust of Sir Robert and lavish ornamentation and sculptures by Rysbrack. The Great Staircase is made of carved mahogany and rises to the full height of the house. The rooms are a magnificent showcase for the impressive collection of pictures, sculptures, china and tapestries. Visitors can also see the huge Model Soldier Collection, amassed during the lifetime of the 6th Marquess of Cholmondeley, the current owner's father.

The beautiful grounds include extensive parkland, home to a large herd of white fallow deer, and a 5 acre (2ha) walled garden which is divided into areas devoted to fruit and vegetables, a 400ft (120m) long herbaceous border, a formal rose garden with over 150 varieties, glass houses and a croquet lawn.

☎ 01485 528569 www.houghtonhall.com

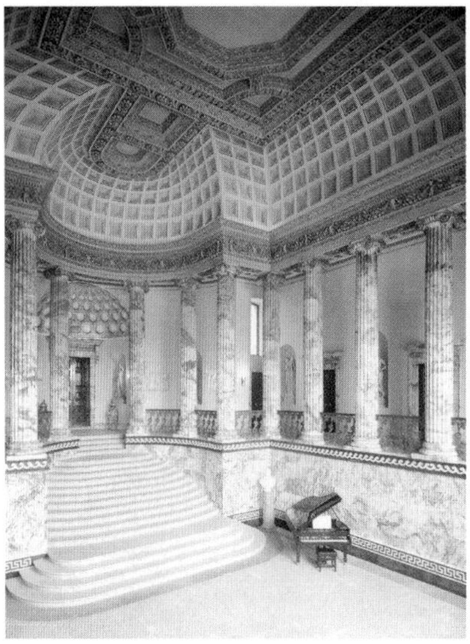

Holkham Hall – Marble Hall

Houghton Mill (NT) 212 A5

Set in a picturesque spot on an island in the Great Ouse, this weather-boarded working water mill dates from the 18th century. There are milling demonstrations on Sunday afternoons (water levels permitting), working models, interactive displays, an art gallery and lovely riverside walks.

☎ 01480 301494 www.nationaltrust.org.uk

Hyde Hall 187 G3

A lovely 24 acre (9.75ha) hilltop garden acquired by the Royal Horticultural Society in 1993. There is year round colour: highlights include lovely herbaceous borders, ornamental ponds, a large collection of roses, the National Collection of Viburnum and the acclaimed Dry Garden.

☎ 01245 400256 www.rhs.org.uk

Ickworth (NT) 201 G1

This unusual house dates from 1795 and was built to display the collection of art accumulated by Frederick Hervey, Bishop of Derry and later 4th Earl of Bristol, during his Grand Tour. The Italianate house is dominated by a massive oval 98ft (30m) high rotunda, with curved corridors leading to two wings. Many of the descendants of the 4th Earl were also great collectors and today the house has a superb array of paintings, including works by Gainsborough, Titian and Velàzquez. The Hall is set in a 1800 acre (73ha) Lancelot 'Capability' Brown landscaped park which features some magnificent ancient specimen trees. There are lovely gardens laid out in formal Italianate style dating from the 19th century, situated to the south of the house.

☎ 01284 735270 www.nationaltrust.org.uk

Imperial War Museum (Duxford) 200 C3

Built during World War I, the aerodrome at Duxford was one of the earliest RAF stations in the country and saw action during World War II. It is now home to one of the world's largest collections of preserved civil and military aircraft and is Europe's premier aviation museum. The 7 acres (2.8ha) of exhibition space include some two hundred planes. A free road train runs at regular intervals to take visitors around the site.

Original World War I hangars contrast with the award-winning American Air Museum building designed by Lord Foster. Housed within this superb modern structure is an impressive collection of American combat aircraft.

In the Land Warfare Hall is a huge collection of tanks, military vehicles and artillery. Other hangars contain naval helicopters and midget submarines, a Battle

of Britain exhibition and a British aircraft collection.

Duxford is one of the largest centres for aircraft restoration in the world and visitors can view the work in progress. Most weekends during the summer there is an opportunity to experience a flight over Duxford in a 1930s passenger bi-plane and several air shows take place during the year.

☎ 01223 835000 www.iwm.org.uk/duxford

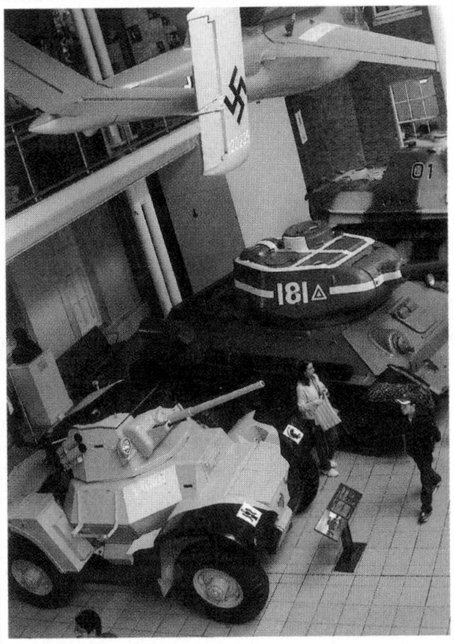

Imperial War Museum

Kentwell Hall 201 G3

This beautiful red brick moated Tudor mansion, dating from the mid 16th century, is approached by a three-quarter mile (1.2km) long lime-tree avenue. The interior of the house was remodelled in 1825 and contains a large collection of 16th century artefacts. On selected weekends visitors can enjoy re-creations of everyday Tudor life. In the courtyard there is a superb brickwork maze in the shape of a Tudor rose, and the grounds contain clipped yews, a fine walled garden with original 17th century layout, and a rare breeds animal farm.

☎ 01787 310207 www.kentwellhall.co.uk

Knebworth House 200 A5

Home to the Lytton family since 1490, the original red brick Tudor manor house underwent extensive remodelling in the 19th century. This resulted in the rather eccentric Gothic appearance we see today with its extravagant façade of turrets, domes and gargoyles.

Within the house visitors can see the superb Jacobean Banqueting Hall with early 17th century oak screen and minstrels' gallery, the Victorian-Gothic state drawing room and the armoury.

The house is situated within 250 acre (101ha) grounds which include a deer park and lovely woodland areas. There are 25 acres (10ha) of gardens designed by Sir Edwin Lutyens who married Lady Emily Lytton, sister of the 2nd Earl of Lytton, in 1897. Features of the garden include an attractive formal rose garden, twin pleached lime avenues, herbaceous borders and a maze. Other attractions include a giant children's adventure playground, a three-quarter mile (1.2km) miniature railway and a dinosaur trail with 72 life-size fibreglass dinosaurs. Knebworth is also famous for its rock concerts and as a film location.

☎ 01438 812661 www.knebworthhouse.com

Lavenham Guildhall (NT) 202 A3

This early 16th century timber-framed building overlooks Lavenham's market place and was built by one of the Guilds who regulated the local wool trade. Over the years it has been used for many different purposes: prison, town hall, workhouse and for housing evacuees during World War II. Inside there are exhibitions on the medieval woollen cloth trade, local history, farming, industry and a replica of the Guildhall at the time it was built.

☎ 01787 247646 www.nationaltrust.org.uk

Layer Marney Tower 188 C1

This 16th century Tudor gatehouse is the tallest in Britain at some 80ft (24m) tall. It was originally planned as a large palace by Henry, 1st Lord Marney, Henry VIII's keeper of the Privy Seal, but he died in 1523, followed two years later by his son, leaving no male heirs and an unfinished building.

The gatehouse has superb Italianate terracotta decoration and fine brickwork, and is set in formal gardens. There are exhibitions within the tower including a model of the palace as it may have looked had it been completed. Other attractions include a rare breeds farm and a medieval barn.

☎ 01206 330784 www.layermarneytower.co.uk

Leighton Buzzard Light Railway 199 E5

Originally built in 1919 to connect the many sand quarries in the area, this 2ft (610mm) narrow-gauge railway now runs for 3 miles (4.8km) giving a 70-minute round trip. It houses one of the largest collections of steam and diesel narrow-gauge locomotives in the United Kingdom.

☎ 01525 373888 www.buzzrail.co.uk

Linton Zoo 201 D3

Set in 16 acres (6.5ha) of gardens, a visit to this zoo provides an enjoyable day out. There is a focus on conservation, education and breeding programmes, with the animals being housed in enclosures resembling their natural habitats as closely as possible. Big cats, giant tortoises and tarantula spiders are among the animals to be seen.

☎ 01223 891308 www.lintonzoo.com

Knebworth House

Lodge RSPB Nature Reserve, The 199 G3

The gardens surrounding this 19th century Tudor-style house (the house is the RSPB's UK headquarters and is not open to the public) are run by organic methods and include formal gardens, a wildlife area, herbaceous border and large specimen trees. There is also a nature reserve which is a mixture of sandy heath and woodland. When the bluebells are in flower in the spring, the woods are a lovely sight. In the reserve there are over 3 miles (5km) of paths to explore and a variety of birds such as woodpeckers, warblers, woodlarks and hobby may be seen.

☎ 01767 680541 www.rspb.org.uk/reserves/guide/t/thelodge/index.asp

Mangapps Railway Museum 188 C3

A standard-gauge working museum giving a three-quarter mile (1.2km) ride through pleasant countryside. Restored stations and signal boxes from various sites around East Anglia can be seen, as well as 10 locomotives and over 80 carriages and wagons. There are also impressive collections of railway signalling equipment and railway relics.

☎ 01621 784898 www.mangapps.co.uk

Melford Hall (NT) 201 G3

Queen Elizabeth I was entertained in this red brick Tudor mansion in 1578. The exterior has changed little since then and is notable for its six octagonal towers with pepper-pot roofs and tall chimneys.

The interior features a panelled banqueting hall, Regency library, an 18th century drawing room and a display of watercolours by Beatrix Potter. Outside is an attractive garden with lawns and trees.

☎ 01787 880286 www.nationaltrust.org.uk

Mole Hall Wildlife Park 201 D4

Twenty acres (8ha) of gardens and grounds surrounding a moated manor house (closed to the public). A variety of animals can be seen including otters, chimps, deer, owls and wildfowl. There is also a tropical butterfly pavilion, pets corner and a water maze.

☎ 01799 540400 www.molehall.com

Mountfitchet Castle 200 D5

A Norman castle destroyed in 1215 with only fragments of masonry remaining. In the early 1980s an earth and timber castle was constructed along with a village of thatched buildings, including a smithy, a brew house and a dovecote, where visitors can learn about life in Norman England. The scene is completed with animals such as chickens and sheep wandering about.

☎ 01279 813237 www.mountfitchetcastle.com

Muckleburgh Collection, The 228 C1

Set on the site of an anti-aircraft artillery range from World War II, the museum, located in the old NAAFI building, has Britain's largest working military collection, with over 120 vehicles including 16 working tanks and 3000 other exhibits. On Sundays visitors can usually see a tank in action and take a ride on a US armoured personnel carrier, the Gama Goat.

☎ 01263 588210 www.muckleburgh.co.uk

Museum of East Anglian Life 202 B2

This 70 acre (28ha) open-air museum has a variety of historic buildings including the 13th century Abbot's Hall tithe barn. Many of the other buildings have been moved from their original settings and reconstructed on the site, such as the attractive working Alton Water Mill, Edgar's Farmhouse and Eastridge Windpump. There are also various rare breed farm animals to see including Suffolk Punch horses, Suffolk sheep and Red Poll Cattle, as well as working steam engines.

☎ 01449 612229 www.eastanglianlife.org.uk

National Horseracing Museum
201 E1

The museum is full of interest even to the novice, with displays on horses and courses, famous jockeys and trainers. There are trophies, portraits and paintings as well as films of classic races.

☎ 01638 667331 www.nhrm.co.uk

Nene Valley Railway
211 G3

A standard-gauge 7.5 mile (12km) railway which runs between Yarwell and Peterborough. It is home to a fine collection of steam locomotives, both British and continental, as well as rolling stock. There is also a small museum and, for children, Thomas the Tank Engine has his own little branch line.

☎ 01780 784444 www.nvr.org.uk

Norfolk Broads
229 E4

Made up of rivers, lakes and fens, this nationally important wetland provides a unique, but delicate environment for a wide range of wildlife. Three principal rivers: the Thurne, Yare and Waveney, flow through the area, occasionally opening out into wide lakes called 'broads'. These were created by peat cutting dating back to about the 9th century. In the 13th to 14th centuries the sea level rose, flooding the peat pits.

This rare wetland habitat is a haven for a wide range of flora and fauna, including some endangered insects such as the beautiful Swallowtail butterfly and the Norfolk Hawker dragonfly which are unique to the area. The tranquil waterways are alive with ducks, swans, coots, moorhens, herons, kingfishers and the exotic-looking Great Crested Grebe who can be seen carrying their humbug-striped young on their backs in the spring. There are over 190 miles (300km) of footpaths, and bicycles can be hired to explore the peaceful country lanes, but, without a doubt, the best way to get around is by boat. Take a leisurely journey along the 125 miles (200km) of navigable lock-free waterways and Broads, and the stress of civilisation feels like it is a million miles away.

☎ 01603 610734 www.broads-authority.gov.uk

Norfolk Broads

Norwich Castle Museum & Art Gallery
405 B2

The museum and art gallery is housed within a magnificent Norman keep, originally part of a royal palace, situated on a mound overlooking the city. Visitors can see collections of fine art, natural history, archaeology, silverware and ceramics. In addition to the permanent displays there are also regular temporary exhibitions.

☎ 01603 493625 www.museums.norfolk.gov.uk

Norwich Cathedral
405 B2

Founded in the 11th century, with many later changes and additions, the present cathedral has a tall elegant spire, and, at 315ft (96m), it is second only in height to Salisbury. The 180ft (55m) square monastic cloisters, which feature intricate fan vaulting, date from the 14th and 15th centuries and are the largest in England. The cathedral is also notable for the large number of attractive, brightly painted, roof bosses in the nave and cloisters.

☎ 01603 218321 www.cathedral.org.uk

Orford Castle
203 F3

This unusual 90ft (27m) high multi-sided keep was built in the mid to late 12th century by Henry II and was once part of a larger castle. Spiral stairs lead to a maze of rooms. A climb to the top is rewarded by views over the surrounding countryside.

☎ 01394 450472 www.english-heritage.org.uk

Orford Ness
203 F3

This is the largest vegetated shingle spit in Europe. It was taken over by the military in 1913 and was a secret test site until the mid-1980s. It is now a National Nature Reserve and its variety of habitats, including mudflat, shingle, salt marsh and brackish lagoons, make it an important site for flora and fauna, in particular breeding and overwintering birds. Access is by ferry and visitors can follow a fascinating 5.5 mile (8.8km) route, that can be walked in total or in part.

☎ 01394 450900 www.nationaltrust.org.uk

Oxburgh Hall (NT)
213 F2

This magnificent red brick moated manor house was built by the Bedingfeld family and dates from 1482. It has an unusual appearance with its ornate stepped gables and tall, twisted chimney stacks. Although remodelled extensively during the mid 19th century, the Gatehouse, with its octagonal turrets rising to 80ft (24m), remains relatively unaltered. Within the hall can be seen finely carved oak furniture, some original Victorian wallpapers and fine textiles, including needlework by Mary, Queen of Scots and Bess of Hardwick. Outside there are walled and kitchen gardens, a Victorian French parterre and woodland walks.

☎ 01366 328258 www.nationaltrust.org.uk

Paradise Wildlife Park
186 C2

Ideal for children with a variety of animals including pandas, large cats, tapirs, meerkats, camels and zebra, as well as the more familiar farmyard animals. There is also a funfair, amusements, crazy golf and a woodland railway.

☎ 01992 470490 www.pwpark.com

Paycocke's (NT)
201 G5

Dating from around 1500, this timber-framed house was built for cloth merchant John Paycocke as a wedding present for his son Thomas. It contains fine wood panelling and carving as well as a display of Coggeshall lace. Outside there is an attractive cottage garden leading to a small river.

☎ 01376 561305 www.nationaltrust.org.uk

Peckover House & Garden (NT)
212 C2

This Georgian brick-built town house dates from about 1722 and has some fine rococo decoration in plaster and wood. It is the former home of Quaker banker Jonathon Peckover. Within the house there is a restored Victorian library and collections of decorative and applied art. The house sits within a lovely 2 acre (0.8ha) walled Victorian garden with mature trees, croquet lawn, herbaceous borders and an orangery.

☎ 01945 583463 www.nationaltrust.org.uk

Peterborough Cathedral
211 G3

This magnificent Norman cathedral dates from 1118 and has a dramatic 13th century west front with three enormous arches. The interior is equally impressive with a rare 13th century painted wooden nave ceiling and exquisite fan vaulting in the retro-choir dating from about 1500. The cathedral is the burial place of Henry VIII's first wife, Catherine of Aragon.

☎ 01733 343342 www.peterborough-cathedral.org.uk

Peterborough Museum & Art Gallery
211 G3

This impressive town house dating from 1816 became the home of the museum and art gallery in the 1930s. It has displays of local history and archaeology including many Roman relics. There are also bone models and straw marquetry made by Napoleonic prisoners of war.

The art collection contains works dating from the 1600s to the present day including paintings by Van Huysum, Sickert and Turner.

☎ 01733 343329 www.peterboroughheritage.org.uk

Pleasure Beach
229 G5

Set on the seafront at Great Yarmouth, this amusement park has all the familiar rides, such as roller coasters, dodgems and carousels. All ages are catered for, with the thrill factor ranging from extreme white knuckle to gentle children's merry-go-rounds. Rides can be paid for individually by tokens, or wristbands can be purchased.

☎ 01493 844585 www.pleasure-beach.co.uk

St Albans Cathedral
186 A2

The cathedral, which dates from the 11th century, has had numerous additions over the years including the opening of a new Chapter House in 1982. It has a long low appearance, extending 550 ft (168m) east to west with a squat sturdy looking tower. The Norman part of the building was begun in 1077 using Roman bricks and tiles salvaged from the ruins of the nearby Roman town of Verulamium. These can be seen today in the walls of the tower.

The cathedral is well known as a site of national pilgrimage as it contains the shrine of St Alban, the first British Christian martyr, who was executed on this site in AD209. Also to be seen are medieval wall paintings and decorated ceilings.

☎ 01727 860780 www.stalbanscathedral.org.uk

St George's Guildhall (NT)
227 E5

Constructed between 1410 and 1420, this is the largest surviving English medieval guildhall. The impressive Great Hall, situated on the upper floor, with its original open timber roof, is 101ft by 29ft

(30m x 8m). Other 15th century features which survive intact are the five large buttresses supporting the north wall. The building has now been converted into an arts centre and is generally closed on performance days.

☎ 01553 765565 www.nationaltrust.org.uk

Sandringham House 227 E5

The current house dates from 1870 and was built for the Prince of Wales (later Edward VII) in Neo-Elizabethan style from red brick with pale stone dressings. It has been passed down through the generations as a private royal residence and is used by the present Queen as her country retreat. The main ground floor rooms, which are still used regularly by the royal family, can be seen. Many objects collected by Queen Alexandra and Queen Mary are on show, and in the Ballroom there is an exhibition of the Duke of Edinburgh's collection of wildlife art. Outside in the coach and stable block there is a museum displaying many family possessions as well as some of the gifts given to the royal family over the years.

The house sits in beautiful 60 acre (24ha) gardens with lakes, glades and an abundance of trees. The acid soil allows the growth of stunning rhododendrons and azaleas, making it particularly attractive in the spring. There is also a 600 acre (243ha) country park, which is free, and which has some lovely woodland and heath areas with nature trails and a visitor centre.

☎ 01553 772675 www.sandringhamestate.co.uk

Shaw's Corner (NT) 186 A1

This red brick Edwardian house was the home of the Irish playwright George Bernard Shaw from 1902 until his death in 1950. The rooms are still set out as he left them, with his personal effects providing a fascinating insight into his life. The 3.5 acre (1.4ha) richly planted gardens have lovely views over the local countryside and contain the revolving hut where Shaw used to write.

☎ 01438 820307 www.nationaltrust.org.uk

Shepreth Wildlife Park 200 B3

Situated in a lovely countryside setting with three lakes, the centre started out as a wildlife sanctuary, and one of the park's aims is to raise money for its rescued and unwanted animals and its hospital. There are plenty of animals to see: terrapins live in Combat Lake, whilst meerkats and squirrel monkeys live on Combat Island. Mountain lions, tigers and lynx can be seen in the Big Cat House, and Waterworld and Bug City provide a home to insects and invertebrates. Just as popular are the horses, goats, ducks and geese which can be hand fed.

☎ 09066 800031 (25p/min) www.sheprethwildlifepark.co.uk

Shrine of Our Lady of Walsingham 228 A2

This has been a centre for pilgrimage since 1061, when Richeldis de Faverches, a local noblewoman, had a vision in which she was told by the Virgin Mary to build a replica of the Holy House in Nazareth. Today, a 20th century red brick church sits on the site of the shrine.

☎ 01328 820239 www.walsingham.org.uk

Somerleyton Hall & Gardens 215 F2

This extravagant Victorian mansion was built between 1844 and 1851 for the railway entrepreneur Sir Morton Peto. No expense was spared; lavish carving is evident throughout, both in wood and stone, there are sumptuous state rooms and an impressive entrance hall. The clock on the stable block is of particular interest as it was originally designed by Vulliamy for the Houses of Parliament.

The superb gardens extend to 12 acres (4.8ha) and include a yew hedge maze planted in 1846, a walled garden and glasshouses by Sir Joseph Paxton (designer of the Crystal Palace).

☎ 0871 2224244 www.somerleyton.co.uk

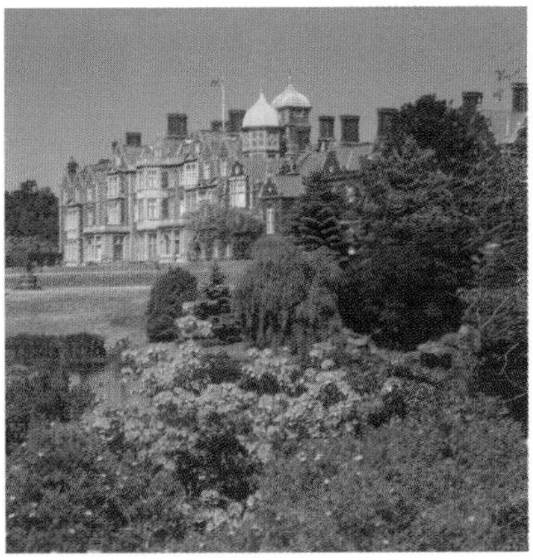

Sandringham House

Southend Pier 188 B4

The present iron pier first opened in 1889 and was extended to its current length in 1929. At 2360 yards (2158m) it is the longest pleasure pier in the world. A train service runs the length of the pier. At the shore end is a museum (admission charge) with exhibits giving an insight into the pier's history. At the pier head sea fishing is popular; there are also pleasure boat trips, a lifeboat station and information centre to visit.

☎ 01702 215620 www.southendpier.co.uk

Standalone Farm 200 A4

This 170 acre (68ha) model farm provides visitors with an opportunity to learn about rural life and farming. There are daily milking demonstrations, exhibits of farm machinery and natural history. Animals that can be seen include sheep, cows, donkeys, shire horses, rabbits and guinea pigs. There is also an arboretum containing 35 species of newly planted trees.

☎ 01462 686775 www.letchworthgardencity.net/standalone

Suffolk Wildlife Park 215 G3

Set in 80 acres (32ha) of coastal parkland, visitors can see a wide variety of mainly African animals, including big cats, giraffes, zebras, white rhinos, buffalo and snakes. There is a safari road train to take visitors around the site.

☎ 01502 740291 www.suffolkwildlifepark.co.uk

Swiss Garden 199 G3

Created in the early 19th century by Lord Ongley, this is a lovely 10 acre (4ha) example of a Swiss picturesque garden centred around a pretty thatched cottage. There are walks and vistas, a grotto, networks of ponds and islands with ironwork bridges, some fine conifers, shrubs and woodland glades.

☎ 01767 626236

Thetford Forest Park 213 F3

This working forest is the largest lowland pine forest in Britain. The varied habitat, which also includes broadleaf woodland and areas of heathland, supports a rich variety of wildlife; there is a chance of seeing crossbills and nightjars and red deer might even be spotted.

Scattered around the forest there are a number of picnic sites where visitors can relax and explore, and at its heart is the High Lodge Forest Centre which provides a variety of activities. Bikes are available for hire and there are a number of cycle trails: gentle ones suitable for families and a black route for the more experienced and adventurous riders. For those aged 10 and over there is an exciting rope course in the tree tops high above the forest floor and an adventure playground suitable for the smaller children. Other attractions include a large maze and a giant sculpture trail which includes a huge red squirrel. There is also a shop and restaurant.

☎ 01842 810271 www.forestry.gov.uk

Tilbury Fort 187 F5

Situated in a strategic position on the north bank of the River Thames, this late 17th century fort was designed to withstand heavy artillery fire; low lying, with double moats and brick-fronted earth embankments. There are exhibitions showing how the fort protected London from seaborne attack. Nearby, Elizabeth I gave a speech rallying her forces on the eve of their battle against the Spanish Armada.

☎ 01375 858489 www.english-heritage.org.uk

Titchwell Marsh 227 F3

This wetland nature reserve on the Norfolk coast, with reed bed and shallow lagoon habitats, is managed especially for birds by the RSPB. It is an important site for breeding avocets and, in the summer, marsh harriers can be seen. The cold weather sees the arrival of migrant and overwintering birds in the lagoons including large numbers of ducks and geese. There are three easily accessible hides for the use of visitors.

☎ 01485 210779 www.rspb.org.uk/reserve/guide/t/titchwell/

Verulamium Museum 186 A2

This museum contains re-creations of Roman scenes, showing everyday Roman life. There are also displays of interesting local finds including wall paintings, jewellery and some superb mosaics. During excavations nearby in 1989, a coffin and the remains of a Roman man were found. The museum has called him 'Postumus' and a video tells the fascinating story of the associated excavation and conservation work.

☎ 01727 751810 www.stalbansmuseums.org.uk/verulamium_museum.htm

Thetford Forest Park

Verulamium Roman Town
186 A2

At the height of the Roman occupation, Verulamium, now St Albans, was the third largest town in Britain. Set within a park are sections of the boundary wall, hypocaust and the remains of a theatre built about AD140. This is the only known example in Britain of a Roman theatre with a stage, rather than an amphitheatre. The remains of some of the Roman buildings were used in the construction of St Albans Cathedral.

☎ 01754 768837 www.verulamium.co.uk

Waltham Abbey
186 C2

It is said that King Harold II left from here to face William of Normandy at the Battle of Hastings in 1066, his body being returned to the abbey for burial. Outside the present abbey church are two inscribed stones marking the spot where King Harold's body is believed to lie. Following the Dissolution, the abbey was partly demolished and the remains that can be seen today include a late 14th century gatehouse that was once part of the cloisters, and part of the Norman abbey nave which was incorporated into the present Waltham Abbey Church. Within the nave can be seen striking spiral and zig-zag patterned columns and a superb painted ceiling.

☎ 01992 767897 www.english-heritage.org.uk www.walthamabbeychurch.co.uk

West Stow Country Park
213 F5

Set on the southern edge of the Breckland in the Lark Valley, this 125 acre (50ha) country park comprises heath, lake and woodland. Nature trails and bird hides enable visitors to enjoy the wide variety of flora and fauna that thrive in the park as a result of this habitat diversity.

An added attraction within the park is a reconstruction of an Anglo-Saxon village, built using original tools and techniques. This is located on the site of an original settlement and finds from the site are displayed in an interpretation centre.

☎ 01284 728718 www.stedmunds.co.uk/west_stow.html

Whipsnade Wild Animal Park
185 F1

Opened to the public in 1931, this is now one of Europe's largest wildlife conservation parks. It is set in nearly 600 acres (242ha) with over 3000 animals including hippos, rhinos, giraffe, vultures, cheetahs, bison, bears, tigers and much, much more. Visitors can travel around the large site using the free safari tour bus or on the narrow-gauge Great Whipsnade Railway. There is an impressive 17 acre (6.8ha) elephant paddock, the Splashzone where visitors can see the sea lions being fed, a children's farm and adventure playground, and a discovery centre where there is almost everything from seahorses to giant centipedes.

☎ 01582 872171 www.whipsnade.co.uk

Wicken Fen National Nature Reserve (NT)
212 D5

A haven for wildlife, and almost the last remnant of the extensive fen landscape that once covered eastern England. There are numerous paths enabling visitors to explore this fascinating area, as well as several hides, a restored Fenman's cottage and the last working windpump in the fens. The William Thorpe Visitor Centre has displays telling the story of the fen and its wildlife.

☎ 01353 720274 www.nationaltrust.org.uk

Wimpole Hall (NT)
200 B2

This magnificent 18th century house, the largest in Cambridgeshire, has a striking domed yellow drawing room by Sir John Soane and a library and chapel by James Gibbs; the chapel features a trompe l'oeil painting by Sir James Thornhill.

The landscaped grounds, with lakes and Gothic folly, are equally impressive: they extend to 360 acres (145ha) and were landscaped by the foremost practitioners of the time, namely Charles Bridgeman, Lancelot 'Capability' Brown and Humphrey Repton. The formal gardens around the house include parterres, a rose garden and a walled vegetable garden. The estate was purchased by Rudyard Kipling's daughter, Elsie Bambridge, who left it to the National Trust in 1976.

☎ 01223 207257 www.nationaltrust.org.uk www.wimpole.org

Wimpole Home Farm (NT)
200 B3

This 'model' farm, built in 1794 by Sir John Soane, an agricultural and farming enthusiast, features thatched farm buildings and the Great Barn which is now home to a museum of farming methods and equipment. A variety of animals including many rare breeds of cattle, sheep, pigs and poultry can be seen, as well as a Victorian dairy.

☎ 01223 207257 www.nationaltrust.org.uk www.wimpole.org

Woburn Abbey
199 E4

Woburn has been home to the Earls and Dukes of Bedford for nearly 400 years. The current Palladian style mansion, built on the site of a 12th century Cistercian monastery, is set in a 3000 acre (1200ha) deer park. In the 17th century the 4th Earl built a new wing on the site of the old abbey church. This contains an intriguing grotto with elaborately carved stonework resembling stalactites and seaweed, as well as 18th century furniture carved in the shape of sea shells with dolphins supporting the seats and table tops. The 4th Duke commissioned the west wing in 1747 which includes the grand series of state rooms.

Within the house there are over 250 paintings dating from as early as the 16th century, including works by Van Dyck, Gainsborough, Reynolds and Velázquez. The Venetian Room has 21 views of Venice by Canaletto, commissioned by the 4th Duke during his Grand Tour. There is also some excellent 18th century furniture, silver pieces by renowned Huguenot silversmiths, and some superb porcelain, including the Sèvres dinner service presented to the 4th Duchess by Louis XV in 1763.

The grounds were landscaped by Humphrey Repton at the beginning of the 19th century and are home to ten species of deer, including the rare Père David Chinese deer. Repton's Red Book, showing his plans for the grounds, can be seen in the Library. There is a hornbeam maze, masses of rhododendrons and a lake.

Within the estate is the famous Safari Park where visitors can enjoy seeing the animals wandering freely (additional charge).

☎ 01525 290666 www.woburnabbey.co.uk

Wood Green Animal Shelter
200 A1

The shelter at Godmanchester is one of three, the first of which was founded in Wood Green, London in 1924. At 50 acres (20ha), this is the largest and welcomes visitors who are interested in rehousing or learning about the animals, or who just want to look around. In addition to the animals there are charity, gift and pet accessory shops, water gardens, a wind turbine and a playground.

☎ 08701 904090 www.woodgreen.org.uk

Woodbridge Tide Mill
203 D3

A restored, Grade I listed working tide mill driven by the water held in a pond that is filled twice daily by the incoming tide. There are demonstrations at low tide.

☎ 01473 626618 www.tidemill.org.uk

Woodside Farm
185 F1

There are hundreds of animals to see here: monkeys, llamas, flamingos and giant tortoises, as well as the usual farm animals, all within a 7 acre (2.8ha) site. Children are encouraged to help feed and handle the animals. Other attractions include an adventure play area and an 18 hole crazy golf course.

☎ 01582 841044 www.woodsidefarm.co.uk

Wrest Park
199 F4

The magnificent gardens, which extend to some 90 acres (36ha), were originally laid out in the early 18th century, and are the main attraction here. There are woodland walks, avenues, a canal, a formal parterre, marble fountains, an orangery and a fine pavilion by Thomas Archer. The 19th century house, built in the style of an 18th century French chateau, has a few ornately plastered rooms open to visitors.

☎ 01525 860152 www.english-heritage.org.uk

Wroxham Barns
229 E3

Traditional and contemporary craftsmen and women can be seen at work in this rural craft centre located in 18th century restored farm buildings. There is also a children's farm in a farmyard setting and a funfair.

☎ 01603 783762 www.wroxham-barns.co.uk

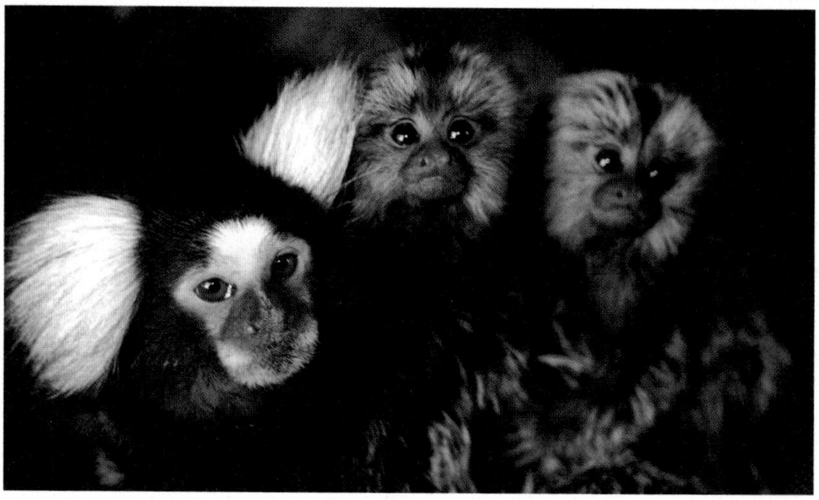

Woburn Safari Park – Marmosets

YORKSHIRE

This vast historic area encompasses all that is best within Britain.

From the south the huge, bustling conurbations gradually surrender to the individual barren moors intermingled with the beautiful dales. Then, north east, over the mighty A1(M), passing through dozens of picturesque towns and villages, are the wild, scenic moors and forests of North Yorkshire. These end abruptly at the east coast where the traditional seaside resorts with their faded gentility still provide the quintessential English holiday experience.

View from hillside, Yorkshire

1853 Gallery — 244 A4

The 1853 Gallery is housed in a Grade II listed textile mill that was built in 1853. Featured within its three art galleries are hundreds of works by Bradford-born artist David Hockney. The gallery exhibits his lithographs, etchings, home made prints, photo collages and oil paintings, along with his early drawings. Displays of historical old mill items and objets d'art can also be viewed amongst the pictures.

☎ 01274 531163 www.saltsmill.org.uk

Aysgarth Falls & National Park Centre — 251 F4

The River Ure forms this magnificent triple flight of waterfalls as it descends over limestone rock ledges through Wensleydale. The Upper Fall featured in the film 'Robin Hood, Prince of Thieves'. Enjoy a riverside walk linking the Upper, Middle and Lower Falls, for stunning views and scenery, and discover how the Aysgarth Falls were created, by visiting the Aysgarth Falls National Park Centre.

☎ 01969 663424

Bagshaw Museum — 371 E3

Step back in time at Bagshaw Museum, housed within this enchanting Gothic mansion, complete with imposing copper tower. As well as admiring the interior Gothic décor, find out about the social and local history of Batley and what it was like to live in the area in the 19th century. Additionally, gain a fascinating insight into Ancient Egyptian life, view the Oriental decorative arts and encounter the enchanting world of the tropical rainforest.

☎ 01924 326155

Bempton Cliffs — 255 E5

The chalk cliffs from Flamborough Head to Bempton provide a sanctuary for over 200,000 nesting birds. An RSPB reserve, this is the largest seabird colony in England. From the specially provided viewing areas, puffins, gannets, kittiwakes, guillemots, razorbills, fulmars and herring gulls can be seen. Most rewarding if visited during the breeding season between April and August.

☎ 01262 851179 www.rspb.co.uk

Beningbrough Hall (NT) — 245 E2

This grand Georgian mansion was built in 1716. It now houses numerous 18th century treasures, including over 100 portraits loaned from the National Portrait Gallery. Its impressive Baroque interior boasts outstanding woodcarving and plasterwork, an unusual central corridor spanning the entire length of the house, and a fully equipped Victorian laundry. Outside is a wonderful walled garden, interesting wood sculptures, potting shed, wilderness play area and 7 acres (3ha) of parkland to be enjoyed.

☎ 01904 470666 www.nationaltrust.org.uk

Bolling Hall — 370 C2

Much of this splendid period house dates back to the 1600s and was once home to the Bolling family. The Hall displays a variety of period furnishings and oak furniture, together with stained-glass windows depicting Coats of Arms in the central hall. The house also contains a medieval tower to the 18th century wing.

☎ 01274 723057

Bolton Abbey Estate — 243 G2

Belonging to the Duke and Duchess of Devonshire since the 1750s, this Yorkshire country estate encompasses 30,000 acres (12,200ha) of parkland beside the River Wharfe. Central to the estate, and near to the village of Bolton Abbey, is the 12th century Bolton Priory. Explore the medieval buildings and enjoy some of the 80 miles (130km) of moorland, woodland and riverside paths, including Strid Wood, the largest remaining acidic woodland in Yorkshire.

☎ 01756 718009 www.boltonabbey.com

Bolton Castle — 251 F3

Bolton Castle is an enormous 14th century fortress, with walls 9ft (3m) thick and towers rising 100ft (30m). In 1568, Mary, Queen of Scots, was imprisoned within its walls and Royalists were besieged here during the Civil War. Within the castle, tableaux portray life here during the 15th century. Outside, there is a medieval garden and walled herb garden, together with a vineyard, rose gardens, a maze and an orchard.

☎ 01969 623981 www.boltoncastle.co.uk

Bradford Industrial Museum — 371 D1

Originally a 19th century spinning mill, this museum depicts industrial life as it was back then. The complex is complete with the mill owner's house, back-to-back cottages, working shire horses, stables, and mill machinery.

☎ 01274 435900

Bramham Park — 244 D3

This French-inspired garden was created in the early 18th century. Its water gardens, cascades and geometric avenues, designed by Robert Benson, First Lord Bingley, remain virtually unaltered since their formation. There are 66 acres (27ha) of impressive vistas, long pathways lined with tall beech hedges leading to surprising views, temples, ornamental ponds, cascades, and a fine rose garden. The fine Queen Anne house is open to the public by appointment only.

☎ 01937 846000 www.bramhampark.co.uk

Brontë Parsonage Museum — 243 G4

Formerly home to the famous Brontë family, this Parsonage has been carefully preserved into a museum. On show are eleven rooms furnished as they were in the mid 1850s, including the dining room, the kitchen, Mr Brontë's study, Charlotte's room and the children's study. Throughout are displays of the siblings' books and manuscripts, letters to friends and their personal possessions.

☎ 01535 642323 www.bronte.info

Burton Constable Hall — 247 D4

On show inside this stately Elizabethan mansion are 30 wonderfully preserved rooms in 18th and 19th century fashion. They are styled with fine furniture, paintings and sculptures. There is a 'Cabinet of Curiosities' containing an intriguing collection of fossils, natural history and scientific instruments and a library containing 5000 books. Within the stable block is a riding centre, and there are 200 acres (80ha) of parkland, landscaped by Lancelot 'Capability' Brown.

☎ 01964 562400 www.burtonconstable.com

Cannon Hall Country Park — 235 G2

Meander around over 70 acres (30ha) of parkland and formal gardens, first landscaped in the 1760s. The historic walled garden contains over 40 varieties of pear trees, first grown in the 18th century, along with peaches and nectarines. In one of the greenhouses is the Cannon Hall vine, grown from a seed brought back from the continent in 1802. The Hall contains a museum displaying fine paintings, glassware, pottery, furniture and a collection of military items set in period rooms.

☎ 01226 790270

Captain Cook Memorial Museum — 254 C1

From 1746, James Cook lodged in the attic of this 17th century harbourside house, whilst an apprentice to Captain John Walker. In commemoration of the great explorer, the museum recounts Cook's Whitby years and his later achievements. There are models, maps and manuscripts, letters, ship plans, original paintings and drawings, as well as artefacts from his voyages.

☎ 01947 601900 www.cookmuseumwhitby.co.uk

Castle Howard — 253 G5

A magnificent stately home, built in 1699 by the architect Sir John Vanbrugh. Castle Howard, with its famous dome, can be found in the Howardian Hills, between Malton and Thirsk. The castle continues to be home to the Howard family, where they have resided since it was built. Inside are exceptional collections of art, including paintings by Canaletto, Holbein, Gainsborough and Reynolds, and furniture by Chippendale and Sheraton. There are also impressive antique sculptures and a splendid collection of porcelain and china. Furthermore, costumed characters take on the role of historic personalities to re-enact life as it used to be in this stately home.

More can be seen outside, in over 1000 acres (400ha) of gardens and parklands. There are also exceptional temples, lead statues and monuments, lakes, waterways and fountains. All of which makes a trip to Castle Howard a wonderful day out.

☎ 01653 648333 www.castlehoward.co.uk

Castle Howard

Colour Museum
390 B1

Interactive galleries look at the history, development and technology aspects of colour. The perceptions, use and effects of light and colour, as well as the progress of dying techniques and textile printing, can all be explored.

☎ 01274 390955

Dalby Forest Drive
254 B4

Dalby Forest Drive extends for 9 scenic miles (15km) across hills, through valleys, past lakes and over streams. Stop along the way to enjoy one of the many walks to access stunning views and scenery. Encounter the northern edge of the plateau and dales, ancient earthworks created before the Dark Ages, Jurassic rock formations, ravines and the valley lake. Much of the extensive woodlands comprise spruces and pines, although along the valleys there are oak, ash and alder trees, some of which are descendants of the ancient forest. In addition to the diverse plant life and outstanding landscape, wildlife, such as roe deer, crossbills and nightjars, can also be found in abundance.

The visitor centre is located 1 mile (1.5km) along the drive from the Thornton Dale entrance. Here, information about Dalby, together with maps and booklets relating to the various trails, can be obtained.

☎ 01751 472771 www.forestry.gov.uk/dalbyforest

Duncombe Park
253 F4

Duncombe Park provides a classic example of an 18th century landscaped garden, surrounding a Baroque mansion, now home to Lord and Lady Feversham. There are 35 acres (15ha) of fine terraces, lawns, trees, temples and a scented 'secret garden'. Wonderful views extend over the valley and distant moors. Beyond the gardens are over 400 acres (160ha) of parkland. Half is now a National Nature Reserve with enjoyable waymarked walks.

The house, containing 18th century portraits and period furniture, can be accessed by guided tour only.

☎ 01439 770213 www.duncombepark.com

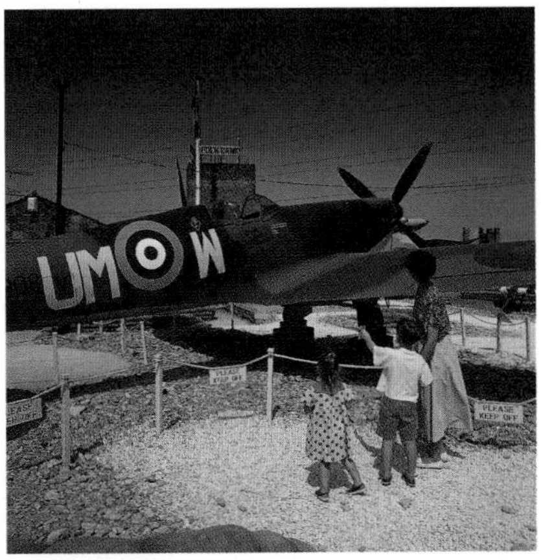

Eden Camp

Eden Camp
253 G5

Wartime Britain is magnificently brought to life at this award winning museum. Constructed within a former prisoner of war camp, the huts re-enact life during World War II. The sights, sounds and smells of everyday life during the war can be truly experienced.

Each hut conveys a different aspect of the war, including the rise of the Nazi Party, the outbreak of war, rationing, evacuees, propaganda, women at war, the Blitz, animals at war, the munitions factories, the rescue services and much more. Additional huts depict military and political events of World War II from a worldwide perspective, including scenes such as the Dambusters and The Great Escape. Another covers conflicts experienced by British forces since 1945 and yet another looks at World War I, incorporating a re-created trench.

The Eden Camp music hall is of particular interest to children, where puppets, representing some of the great entertainers of the time, perform well-known wartime songs. There is also an assault course, a number of military vehicles and a large collection of artillery.

☎ 01653 697777 www.edencamp.co.uk

Elsham Hall Country & Wildlife Park
238 A1

In the grounds of Elsham Hall is a unique venture, a combination of wildlife, arts and crafts. There is a theatre, craft centre, exhibition gallery, carp feeding jetty, butterfly garden walkway, adventure playground, arboretum, falconry centre and much more.

☎ 01652 688698 www.elshamhall.co.uk

Eureka! Museum for Children
370 B3

This is an interactive museum, designed especially for children aged 3-12 years. Over 400 hands-on exhibits can be explored, touched, listened to and smelt, based around 4 main themes: Me and My Body; Invent, Create, Communicate; Living and Working Together; and Our Global Garden. Everything has been developed to inspire.

☎ 01422 330069 www.eureka.org.uk

Flamingo Land Theme Park
253 G4

Set in 375 acres (152ha), this theme park is packed full of fun for all the family. Eight white-knuckle roller coasters and six other thrilling rides are key attractions. Ride on Wall's Magnum Force, Europe's only triple looping coaster, Cliff Hanger, Europe's tallest tower ride, or Terroriser, The Bullet, Corkscrew and Top Gun.

Another attraction is the large zoo with over 1000 animals, from around the world, including Siberian tigers, meerkats, Humboldt penguins, exotic birds and the UK's largest flock of pink flamingos. There is a water ride that travels through the Lost Kingdom – a themed area that incorporates part of the zoo, past the hippos, rhinos and giraffes. There are plenty of rides for younger children and a children's zoo. A number of family shows, too, are performed throughout the day.

☎ 01653 668287 www.flamingoland.co.uk

Fountains Abbey & Studley Royal Water Garden (NT)
244 B1

This amazing 800 acres (325ha) World Heritage Site, situated in the valley of the River Skell, shelters the ruins of over 10 historic buildings. One of these ruins is the imposing remains of a 12th century Cistercian Abbey, with its 15th century tower rising 170ft (52m). There is also an Elizabethan mansion, with two rooms open for viewing and a Victorian church, with fine stained-glass windows and ornate interior. Three floors of the 12th century monastic water mill, once used to produce flour for the monks, can be explored, too.

The wonderful landscaped gardens contain an 18th century water garden, ornamental lakes with temples, statues and cascades, all of which can be enjoyed and admired. Additionally, hundreds of red, sika and fallow deer roam in the medieval deer park.

☎ 01969 640382 www.fountainsabbey.org.uk

Flamingo Land Theme Park

Harewood House
244 C3

Renowned for its wonderful architecture and interiors by Robert Adam, this exceptional stately home belongs to the Earl of Harewood. Collections include exquisite Chippendale furniture, fine porcelain, and 18th century and Italian renaissance works of art. There are also royal photographs and memorabilia, from the 1930s to 1960s, when HRH Princess Mary lived here.

The impressive grounds, landscaped by Lancelot 'Capability' Brown, include lakeside and woodland walks. Alternatively, take a boat trip across the lake.

A visit to the Bird Garden is a must, with over 100 rare and exotic birds from around the world, including threatened species from Africa, America and Australia. There is also an excellent adventure playground.

☎ 0113 218 1010 www.harewood.org

Harlow Carr
244 B2

These botanical gardens, owned by the Royal Horticultural Society, cover 68 acres (30ha) in which the suitability of growing plants in the northern climate is assessed. Of particular interest are the scented garden, the streamside garden, flower and vegetable trial gardens, the rock garden, herbs and ornamental grasses, to name just a few. There is also an arboretum, model village and plant centre.

☎ 01423 565418 www.rhs.org.uk

Fountains Abbey

Helmsley Castle (Ruins) 253 F4

The dramatic ruins of Helmsley Castle include the 12th century keep and Tudor mansion. Two deep ditches cut down into the solid rock around the castle to form impressive earthworks.

☎ 01439 770442

Huddersfield Narrow Canal & Standedge Experience 235 E2

The Huddersfield Narrow Canal, which runs for 23 miles (40km), is split in two by Standedge Tunnel. At 3.25 miles (5km) long and 645ft (200m) above sea level, it is Britain's highest, longest and deepest canal tunnel. The Standedge Visitor Centre, with its interactive exhibition and guided boat trip through part of the tunnel, provides a remarkable account of how it was engineered in the 18th century.

☎ 01484 844298 www.standedge.co.uk

Jorvik 415 E2

Viking history is re-created using the well-preserved remains discovered on the site on which the museum now stands. Journey back over 1000 years to AD975 and experience the Viking way of life through the reconstructed streets, complete with sights, sounds and smells. Visitors travel in 'time-capsule' viewing cars to be taken past and through two-storey dwellings and over backyards and rooftops. From the archaeological finds, the houses and shops are laid out exactly as they were, and even the faces of the people on exhibition have been reconstructed from actual Viking skulls.

Also on display are over 800 items found during the archaeological dig, including a wonderfully preserved 8th century Anglo Saxon helmet. Special exhibitions throughout the year feature hands-on activities, artefacts and new academic research based around themes such as seafaring, craft skills, bones and warfare.

☎ 01904 543403 www.jorvik-viking-centre.co.uk

Jorvik

Jorvik Glass 245 G1

Located within the splendid grounds of Castle Howard, Jorvik Glass Centre provides workshop demonstrations of glass-blowing. A variety of glassware is available in the gift shop.

☎ 01653 648555

Kirklees Light Railway 235 G1

Take a 50 minute return trip on this steam train, admiring the beautiful scenery whilst travelling through two of the South Pennine valleys. This fifteen inch gauge railway runs 4 miles (6km) from Clayton West and into the longest tunnel on this gauge of line. There is also a visitor centre, children's play area, and steam models on display.

☎ 01484 865727

Kirkstall Abbey 244 B4

Situated on the River Aire in attractive parkland, Kirkstall Abbey is one of the UK's best preserved Cistercian monasteries. The Abbey was built between 1152 and 1182 and much of it has survived up to eaves level including the church, part of the 16th century tower, the transept, cloisters and the Chapter House.

☎ 0113 230 5492 www.kirkstall.org.uk/abbey

Leeds City Art Gallery & Museum 384 J5

This excellent art gallery displays a variety of fine art collections from the 19th and 20th centuries. Find outstanding English watercolours, traditional prints, Pre-Raphaelite paintings and Henry Moore sculptures, along with contemporary works. Entry is free.

☎ 0113 247 8248 www.leeds.gov.uk/artgallery

Lightwater Valley Park

Lightwater Valley Park 252 B5

Thrills, excitement and pleasurable family entertainment can all be found at this fun-packed theme park, set in 175 acres (71ha) of parkland. For the adventurous, there are several white-knuckle rides, including the Ultimate Beast, Europe's longest coaster at 1.5 miles (2.5km), and the Sewer Rat built 40ft (12m) underground. There is also the Black Widow's Web giant ferris wheel, the Beaver Rapids log flume and the Wave giant swing boat. Younger children, too, are well catered for, with specially designed mini amusements, including the Ladybird roller coaster and Spinning Teacups.

Recover at a gentler pace with a number of more leisurely attractions. Tour the park on the Lightwater Express steam train or enjoy the boating lake. Additional amusements include go-karting and a children's farm.

☎ 0870 458 0040 www.lightwatervalley.co.uk

Lotherton Hall 245 D4

An Edwardian country home, formerly owned by the Gascoigne family. On display are fine collections of pottery, paintings, sculpture, furniture, jewellery, ceramics, silver, oriental art and British costume. The surrounding grounds and parkland boast a re-created Edwardian garden, a medieval deer park and a 12th century chapel. The Bird Garden houses over 200 species, many of which are rare and endangered, including flamingos, snowy owls and hornbills.

☎ 0113 281 3259 www.leeds.gov.uk/lothertonhall

Magna Centre 365 B1

This Science Adventure Centre is set in a splendidly converted former steelworks. Inside are hands-on, interactive experiences based around the four main elements used to make steel. The Fire Pavilion examines the advantages of fire and its explosive possibilities, while the Air Pavilion is in an airship structure, hovering above the floor. Be prepared to get wet in the Water Pavilion, by shooting water cannons, launching a water-powered rocket or creating a hot geyser. In the Earth zone, manoeuvre a JCB or explode a rock face.

☎ 01709 720002 www.visitmagna.co.uk

Malham Cove 243 E1

This huge, curved rock face, rising up around 260ft (80m), is formed of natural limestone. The top of the cove provides an excellent example of limestone pavement, pitted with deep cracks and crevices as a result of the weathering of such terrain.

Manor House 244 A3

This Elizabethan manor house is built on the site of a former Roman fort. The museum recounts Ilkley's local history with exhibits from Roman through to Victorian times, when the area became a spa town. In the gallery are displays of works from local artists and craftspeople.

☎ 01943 600066

Merchant Adventurers Hall 415 E2

Built in the mid 14th century, this Guildhall is York's largest timber-framed building and is believed to be one of the finest medieval halls in Europe. In addition to the Great Hall, where merchants conducted their business, there is the Undercroft, or hospital, and the Chapel. On display are fine collections of furniture, portraits, silver and jewellery, together with information about the lives of the merchants during medieval times.

☎ 01904 654818 www.theyorkcompany.co.uk

Middleton Railway 244 C5

Of great historical importance, this is the oldest working railway in the world, having been established by an Act of Parliament in 1758. It was also the first to succeed commercially with steam locomotives in 1812, as well as being the first standard gauge railway to be operated by volunteers in 1960. View the collection of industrial steam and diesel engines or travel on the railway for a family day out at Middleton Park, with woodland, nature trails, picnic area and lake.

☎ 0113 271 0320 www.middletonrailway.org.uk

National Museum of Photography, Film & TV

National Railway Museum

Millennium Galleries & Winter Gardens

409 B3

Housed within a modern and stylish complex are four galleries, showcasing visual arts, crafts and design by contemporary designers and past masters. The Metalwork Gallery exhibits decorative metalwork and silverware, and recounts the history of the city's metalworking trade. John Ruskin's collection of paintings, manuscripts, papers, books and architectural plastering are also on display and there are special collections from places including the Victoria and Albert Museum and the Tate. Adjacent are the Winter Gardens, in a stunning temperate glasshouse, containing 2500 plants and 150 different species.

Admission into the galleries and Winter Gardens is free; charges apply for the special exhibitions.

☎ 0114 278 2600

Mount Grace Priory (NT)

252 D3

Built in the late 14th century, these ruins are better preserved than any of the other ten Carthusian monasteries in England. The Carthusian monks lived a hermit's life in small two-storey cells with a garden. One of these has been reconstructed to replicate how the monks lived and worked. In spring, the grounds are awash with daffodils, making it a particularly attractive place to visit. Adjacent is a 17th century manor house, built on the site of the monastery guesthouse, housing an exhibition and arts and crafts.

☎ 01609 883494 www.nationaltrust.org.uk

National Museum of Photography, Film & TV

390 C2

The museum's interactive galleries provide a fascinating insight into the world of photography, film and television, both past and present. Among over three million items on display are the world's first negative, the earliest television footage, and Louis Le Prince's 1888 film of Leeds Bridge, regarded as the first example of moving pictures. Explore the history of popular photography and discover the digital age of computers, special effects and virtual reality. Learn how television cameras work, discover how animation is created, read the news, see the cameras used on 'James Bond' films, or find the toys from 'Play School'.

Alongside these galleries is the five-storeys-high IMAX screen, which regularly features 3D and other films, as well as two other conventional cinemas, which show films from around the world.

The permanent galleries are free to visit, whilst there are admission charges for the cinemas and some special exhibitions.

☎ 0870 701 0200 www.nmpft.org.uk

National Railway Museum

415 E1

Over 200 years of railway history is celebrated in style, providing a terrific family day out – for free. Complete with sounds and smells, the atmosphere of steam and rail travel is wonderfully re-created. A splendid collection of locomotives can be found on display in the Great Hall, recounting the story of the railway from Rocket to Eurostar. Inspect the Mallard, the world's fastest steam locomotive, explore Queen Victoria's luxurious royal carriage and examine the Japanese Bullet Train, in conjunction with a short video presentation. There are millions of railway artefacts, too, including models, silver and crockery, nameplates, clocks and watches, tickets, photographs, workshop tools, posters, engineering drawings, and even a lock of Robert Stephenson's hair.

The Working Railway demonstrates how signals work, the technology behind them and their development over time. Children will enjoy the Interactive Learning Centre where hands-on exhibits explain the workings of trains and the railway. Engineers and craftspeople can be watched in the Works Wing while they carry out conservation work, and children can also build their own model train here.

Rides on the miniature railway are available most weekends and school holidays, and on the steam train during school holidays.

☎ 01904 621261 www.nrm.org.uk
☎ 01904 686286 (24hr info line)

Normanby Hall Country Park & Farming Museum

237 G1

A mansion built in the Regency style, with a rural museum, Victorian walled garden, beautiful grounds with woodland, deer park and nature trails. For children there is an adventure playground and miniature railway. Tearoom and plant nursery.

☎ 01724 720588 www.northlincs.gov.uk

North Bay Miniature Railway

254 D4

Two trains operate on this miniature railway, which runs from Peasholm Gap in North Bay. Each train can carry up to 100 people, travelling almost a mile (1.6km), complete with a tunnel, bridges, signals, stations and gradient boards all reproduced to scale.

☎ 01723 373333

North York Moors

253 F2

The vast, heather-clad moorlands, breathtaking open landscape, extensive woodlands and serenity are what make the North York Moors National Park special. Extending east of the A19, from the A170 in the south to the A171 in the north, the Moors are bounded on the eastern side by ragged cliffs and untouched coastline, overlooking the North Sea. There are over 1400 miles (2253km) of paths and tracks to follow, including the Cleveland Way National Trail.

A journey through Dalby Forest, or a steam train trip on the North Yorkshire Moors Railway, provides a wonderful way to explore the stunning and varied countryside. The area's historic heritage includes magnificent ruined abbeys, besieged castles, period buildings and gardens, and informative museums. Rievaulx Abbey, Whitby Abbey, Captain Cook Memorial Museum, Duncombe Park and Mount Grace Priory all warrant a visit. The coastal fishing villages and ancient towns of Whitby and Scarborough are popular places, whilst Robin Hood's Bay offers fossil hunting.

Many television and film makers have valued the area, having featured some of the unspoilt villages and stations of the North York Moors in 'Heartbeat', 'Harry Potter and the Philosopher's Stone', 'Brideshead Revisited', 'Poirot' and 'Sherlock Holmes', to name just a few.

www.moors.uk.net

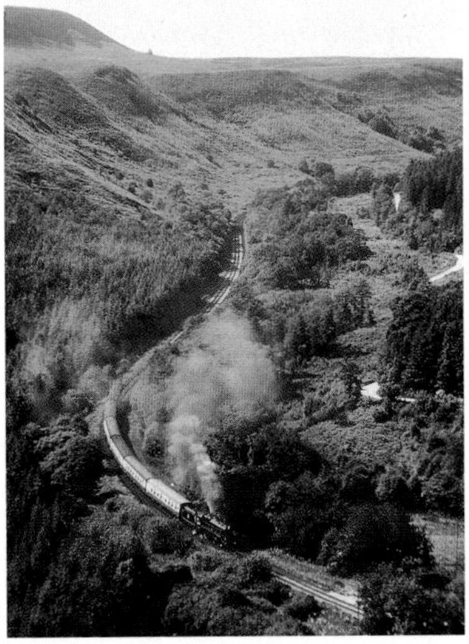

North Yorkshire Moors Railway

North Yorkshire Moors Railway

254 B4

Travel on a steam train across the North Yorkshire Moors National Park on one of the earliest and most historic lines in the North of England. Stretching 18 miles (29km) from Pickering to Grosmont, the journey passes through beautiful countryside, charming villages and authentically restored stations. George Stephenson originally built the railway line, which includes one of the steepest rail gradients in the country between Goathland and Grosmont.

The railway and its stations have regularly featured in a variety of television programmes and films, including 'Heartbeat', 'Harry Potter and the Philosopher's Stone', 'Brideshead Revisited', 'Poirot', 'Sherlock Holmes' and 'All Creatures Great and Small'. Stop off along the way to enjoy the attractions and pleasant walks in the area. The Locomotive Shop and engine sheds can be accessed at Grosmont.

☎ 01751 472508 www.northyorkshiremoorsrailway.com
☎ 01751 473535 (Talking Timetable)

North York Moors – Goathland

Pleasure Island Theme Park 238 D2

Six white-knuckle terror rides, lots of family rides, fun rides for the little ones, and superb classic rides on restored machines, including a 1920s 'Flying Chair' and a 1905 Carousel. Entertainment galore and lots of places to eat.

☎ 01472 211511 www.pleasure-island.co.uk

Pugneys Country Park 371 F4

One of the two lakes in this country park caters for non-powered watersports, including fishing, canoeing, windsurfing and sailing. Equipment is available for hire if required. The other smaller lake is a nature reserve with two bird hides.

☎ 01924 302360

Richmond Castle 252 A2

High on the cliffs above the River Swale stands the imposing Richmond Castle. Built by William the Conqueror to control the north, some of its original 11th century walls remain. The rectangular keep, rising 100ft (30m) with walls 11ft thick (3.5m), was built in the 12th century and remains almost intact. There is also an exhibition centre displaying some of the artefacts excavated from the site, where the castle's history can be explored.

☎ 01748 822493 www.english-heritage.org.uk

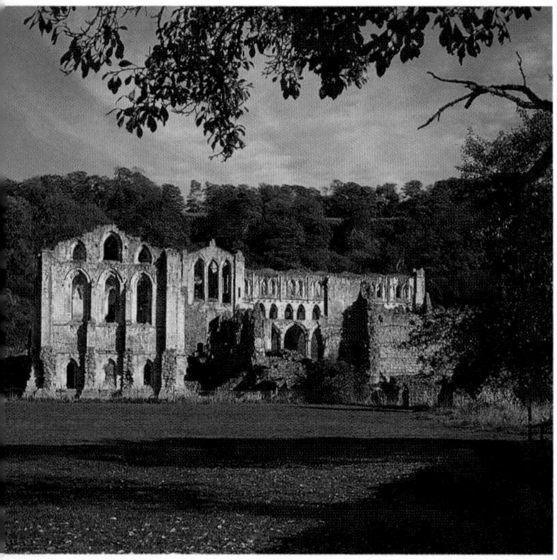

Rievaulx Abbey

Rievaulx Abbey 253 E4

Set amongst the wooded hills of Rye Dale are the majestic ruins of this once powerful Cistercian monastery. Founded in 1132, this impressive abbey was built unconventionally, being hampered by the terrain, with its central aisle laid north to south, rather than the usual east to west direction.

The nave dates from 1135, whilst the towering presbytery, which is virtually intact, was rebuilt in the 13th century. Several outbuildings can also be identified, some standing to a good height. The monks' refectory is clearly evident with its wonderful arched lancet windows, along with the spectacular remains of the 13th century choir.

There is a visitor centre and a fascinating museum with interactive exhibits exploring the site's history.

☎ 01439 798228 www.english-heritage.org.uk

Ripley Castle 244 B1

Home to the Ingilby family since the early 1300s, discover 700 years of political, military, religious and social history. Most of the current building dates from the 16th century, including the three-storey, fortified tower complete with a priest's secret hiding hole. On display are fine paintings, furniture, books and china, and the tower houses a collection of Royalist armour. The delightful gardens include a walled garden, which contains the National Hyacinth Collection, the kitchen garden, with rare vegetables, and the hot houses are filled with tropical plants. There is also a deer park and lakeside walks.

☎ 01423 770152 www.ripleycastle.co.uk

Royal Armouries Museum 385 N9

Housing a fascinating collection of arms and armour, the museum covers 3000 years of history with over 8000 exhibits. The five galleries spectacularly explore the themes of war, tournaments, hunting, self-defence and oriental warfare. Complementing the exhibits are many interactive touch-screen demonstrations, enjoyable films, costumed demonstrations and dramatised interpretations. More fun can be discovered outside, weather permitting, including jousting, falconry and horsemanship. The craft of gun making and leather working can also be observed, along with the falcons, hunting dogs and other animals in the Menagerie. Entrance for the main museum collection is free; charges apply for special themed events such as the shooting galleries.

☎ 0113 220 1999 www.armouries.org.uk

Scarborough Art Gallery 254 D4

Displayed within this Italianate villa are fine art collections by local artists and by those who painted in Scarborough, such as Grimshaw, H.B. Carter and Lord Leighton. The paintings feature Scarborough's wonderful seascapes and views. The gallery is particularly appealing to a family audience. There are hands-on displays, pictures and paintings depicting Scarborough's history from fishing village to popular seaside resort. Children can also dress up in costumes and masks as one of the characters from the paintings.

☎ 01723 374753

Scarborough Castle 255 D4

Towering above the town and harbour, Scarborough Castle stands on a headland 300ft (91m) above sea level. The castle was built in the 12th century and has endured numerous Civil War sieges and bombardment during World War I. Explore the remains of the imposing, three-storey keep, built in the 12th century, medieval chapels, the curtain walls, and 13th century barbican. The site also provides evidence of earlier Iron Age settlements and remains of a Roman signal station.

☎ 01723 372451 www.english-heritage.org.uk

Sewerby Hall & Gardens 247 E1

Sewerby Hall is set in 50 acres (20ha) of parkland with fabulous coastal views over Bridlington Bay. This stylish Georgian house contains the East Yorkshire Museum featuring local history, archaeology, photography, and contemporary arts and crafts. One of the rooms is dedicated to the record-breaking aviator, Amy Johnson, displaying her souvenirs and mementoes. The gardens offer woodland walks, a delightful Old English Garden, pleasure gardens, children's zoo, adventure playground, 19th century Orangery, pitch and putt golf and putting green.

☎ 01262 673769 www.sewerby-hall.co.uk

Shandy Hall 253 E5

This authentically restored house belonged to the amusing parson, Laurence Sterne. It is where he completed his two novels, 'Tristram Shandy' and 'A Sentimental Journey', in the 1760s. Two acres (1ha) of lovely gardens surround the house, complete with old fashioned roses and unusual cottage garden plants. The shop sells Sterne's books and unusual plants.

☎ 01347 868465

Shibden Hall 370 B3

Shibden Hall is an impressive, half-timbered manor house, dating back to 1420. Different rooms portray varying styles of architecture and furnishings associated with a particular era. Explore the 15th century kitchen, the 17th century dining room or the 16th century housebody. Its 17th century barn houses a folk museum with a notable collection of horse-drawn vehicles, while its reconstructed workshops display 19th century craft tools. The surrounding 90 acres (36ha) of parkland provide woodland walks, miniature railway, boating lake and play area.

☎ 01422 352246

Skipton Castle 243 F2

A wonderfully preserved, fully roofed, medieval castle, having survived a three-year siege during the Civil War. Inspect the banqueting hall, the kitchen, bedchamber and privy, climb to the top of the Watch Tower and back down to the dungeons below. Furthermore, unwind in the Chapel Terrace overlooking the town and surrounding woodland, or in the cobbled Tudor courtyard complete with a yew tree planted in the 17th century.

☎ 01756 792442 www.skiptoncastle.co.uk

Spurn Head 239 E1

Spurn Head, curling at the mouth of the Humber Estuary, marks the southernmost point of the Yorkshire Coast. The sandy peninsula extends for about 3.5 miles (5.5km) with a rough track passable by cars almost to its end (best to check the tide times). A rather uninhabited place, but its mudflats and saltmarsh attract thousands of birds and migrating species, including rare varieties such as yellow-browed warblers and wrynecks.

Temple Newsam 244 C4

Displayed within their original room settings in this wonderful Tudor-Jacobean mansion are extensive collections of fine paintings, furniture, silver, porcelain and Leeds pottery. Amongst the furniture collection are some excellent Chippendale masterpieces. The surrounding parkland, and gardens designed by Lancelot 'Capability' Brown, extend 2 sq miles (518ha) and incorporate a woodland garden, an Italian garden and a walled garden. Additionally, there is a Rare Breeds Centre, with over 400 animals.

☎ 0113 264 7321 www.leeds.gov.uk/templenewsam

Thorp Perrow Arboretum 252 B4

The 85 acres (35ha) of woodland contain one of the largest and finest collections of trees and shrubs in the north of England. There are four national collections of ash, lime, walnut and laburnum, as well as oaks, ornamental cherries, willows and hazels. The arboretum is attractive throughout the year with thousands of daffodils in spring, tree blossom, bluebells and wild flowers in summer, and spectacular colours in autumn. Enjoy woodland walks, tree trails, nature trails, children's trail, lake and 16th century Spring Wood. The falconry centre provides demonstrations and hands-on experience of birds of prey.

☎ 01677 425323 www.thorpperrow.com

Tropical World
244 C4

This attraction houses the largest tropical plant collection outside Kew Gardens. The Amazon rainforest, the African and American deserts and the North Sea waters are all captivatingly re-created. Discover over 30 varieties of butterflies, along with nocturnal owl monkeys, Egyptian fruit bats and bush babies, tropical fish and birds, terrapins and reptiles, all living amongst the tropical environments.

☎ 0113 266 1850

Wakefield Cathedral
244 C5

First built in the 14th century and much restored in the 19th century, Wakefield Cathedral boasts the tallest spire in Yorkshire. Inside, it also features a 17th century font, 15th century masonry and carvings, and excellent Victorian stained-glass windows by Kempe.

☎ 01924 373923 www.wakefield-cathedral.org.uk

Whitby Abbey

Whitby Abbey
254 C1

High on the cliff above the harbour stand the dramatic ruins of Whitby Abbey. Founded by Abbess St Hilda in AD657, the abbey was destroyed by the Vikings and rebuilt by the Normans in the 13th century. Amongst the ruins is the Benedictine Church, dating from the 13th and 14th centuries, complete with an impressive three-tiered choir and north transept. The abbey's 2000 year history is interactively re-created with computer-generated images, audiovisual displays and activities in the visitor centre, housed in the remains of a 17th century house. There are also displays of archaeological artefacts from the site and a restored 17th century stone garden.

This is a wonderful place to visit and has been an inspirational site for many, from saints to writers, including Bram Stoker, author of 'Dracula'.

☎ 01904 603568 www.english-heritage.org.uk

White Scar Cave
250 C5

The guided tour of White Scar Cave, one of the longest and most spectacular natural caves in Britain, covers 1 mile (1.6km) and takes about 80 minutes. Underground streams, waterfalls, stalactites, stalagmites, and other natural limestone formations can all be seen. There is also a massive cavern formed during the Ice Age containing thousands of stalactites and several prehistoric mud pools.

☎ 01524 241244 www.whitescarcave.co.uk

York
415

The city of York is rich in history, splendour and variety. The Romans, who founded the city in AD71, the Vikings, the Normans, and the Georgians have all left their mark. The medieval walls, which include remnants of the Roman fortress walls, still surround the city, within which are narrow medieval streets and alleyways, including the infamous 'Shambles'. Visit the many museums that recount the site's changing times and display various archaeological finds, including York Castle Museum, Jorvik Viking Centre, the Yorkshire Museum and the more chilling York Dungeon.

York Minster is England's largest medieval Gothic church and the Merchants Adventurers' Hall is evidence of York's prospering times, during the Middle Ages, as a trading city operating under Guilds. With the Victorian Age came an economic revival for York through the railways, and the National Railway Museum celebrates over 200 years of railway history.

There are also interesting shops, wonderful parks and gardens, river and bus trips, bars, cafés and guided walks, including an evening 'Ghost Walk'.

www.york-tourism.co.uk

York Castle Museum
415 E2

Over 400 years of social history are revealed within the walls of what was once the city's old prison. The museum displays a remarkable collection of over 100,000 everyday items including period costumes, jewellery, arms, armour and toys. Encounter prison life 200 years ago by peering into cells, one of which housed the notorious highwayman, Dick Turpin, and read the graffiti still on the walls. The re-created cobbled streets, lined with replica shops, and reconstructed living rooms, provide a fascinating insight into how the Victorians lived.

☎ 01904 687687 www.yorkcastlemuseum.org.uk

York Dungeon
415 E2

Encounter the more gruesome side of York's history to discover the chilling aspects of superstition, torture, death and pain experienced over the last 2000 years. Tour round York's 14th century plague-ridden streets, meet Guy Fawkes as he is tortured to unveil the gunpowder plot and its conspirators, hear the infamous highwayman, Dick Turpin, recount his tales before being hanged. Then there are the Witchcraft trials, the ferocious Viking invaders, and the local woman crushed to death by stones – all have a story to tell.

☎ 01904 632599 www.thedungeons.com

York Minster
415 E2

York Minster is a stunning medieval Gothic cathedral and the largest in northern Europe. Building began in the 13th century, but it took until the 15th century to be completed. The numerous, beautiful stained-glass windows are a key feature. Admire the Norman stained-glass windows in the nave, the Five Sisters Window in the north transept containing 100,000 pieces of glass, and the Great East Window with 27 panels. The Chapter House reveals fine carvings and the north transept is styled with polished stone columns.

In the Undercroft, Treasury and Crypt there is a museum that relates the cathedral's varied history over the last 2000 years. A climb to the top of the central tower is well worth the effort for magnificent views.

☎ 01904 557216 www.yorkminster.org

Yorkshire Dales
250 D4

Outstanding beauty, spectacular natural landscapes, diverse habitats and a tranquil environment can all be used to describe the Yorkshire Dales, 1700 sq miles (4400 sq km) of which make up the Yorkshire Dales National Park.

The dramatic limestone and gritstone landscape, particularly in the southern dales (including Malhamdale and Airedale), provides stunning scenery with the rocky limestone cliffs and pavements, dramatic waterfalls and many caves. Bolton Abbey, White Scar Cave and Malham Cove are popular attractions, while the towering Three Peaks (Pen-y-Ghent, Ingleborough and Whernside) provide fabulous viewpoints.

Less rugged countryside and valleys depict the more northern and eastern dales, with wild flower and hay meadows, heather topped moors, woodland and picturesque villages. There are also many castles, abbeys, museums and gardens to explore including Constable Burton Hall, Bolton Castle, Thorp Perrow Arboretum, Fountains Abbey, and Aysgarth Falls.

The Pennine Way, Dales Way footpath, Coast to Coast Walk and the Settle to Carlisle Railway all pass through the Dales. The area, with its striking surroundings and picturesque rural villages, has also provided the backdrop to many television programmes and films, including 'Emmerdale', 'Robin Hood: Prince of Thieves', 'All Creatures Great and Small' and 'Calendar Girls'.

www.yorkshiredales.org.uk

Yorkshire Dales – Conistone

Yorkshire Museum
415 D1

Packed full of archaeological, Roman, Viking, Anglo-Saxon and medieval finds, the museum reveals a host of historic treasures. Amongst the collections are ancient fossils, medieval jewellery, including the spectacular Middleham Jewel, fine pottery and decorative arts. Outside, 10 acres (4ha) of botanical gardens can be explored, where there are also some interesting buildings including the ruins of the Benedictine St Mary's Abbey, a 14th century hospitium, a preserved section of a Roman fortress and a working observatory.

☎ 01904 687687 www.yorkshiremuseum.org.uk

Yorkshire Sculpture Park
235 G1

Artistically arranged within 500 acres (202ha) of pleasant 18th century landscaped parkland are major modern and contemporary sculptures. Exhibits from well-known names include those by Henry Moore, Elizabeth Frink and Barbara Hepworth. There are also two indoor galleries, a regularly changing programme of exhibitions and a visitor centre.

☎ 01924 830302 www.ysp.co.uk

NORTH WEST ENGLAND

Today the dark industrial images of the past are consigned to history and the busy urban sprawl of Manchester and Liverpool offer some of the very best in city design and culture. But nowhere in the country is the stark contrast between urban and rural life more apparent than in this region. Just a short distance up the M6 is the misty, dreamy Lake District, England's most popular national park. Here sixteen major lakes and England's highest mountains are packed into an area approximately thirty miles long and thirty miles across.

Jetty on Derwent Water

Abbot Hall Art Gallery & Museum of Lakeland Life
249 G3

Within the Georgian house of Abbot Hall there is a fine collection of British art from the 18th century onwards, including works by Ruskin, Constable and Romney. Exhibitions of national interest are held here and sculpture, arts, crafts and 18th century objets d'art also feature.

The Museum of Lakeland Life illustrates 250 years of Cumbrian history and has re-created period rooms, workshops and shops. There are personal effects and exhibits relating to 'Swallows and Amazons' author Arthur Ransome, and collections of Victoriana and costume.

☎ 01539 722464 www.abbothall.org.uk www.lakelandmuseum.org.uk

Acorn Bank (NT)
260 C5

A walled garden with a large collection of culinary herbs, medicinal plants, shrubs, roses, herbaceous borders and orchards of old English fruit trees. A path through the ancient oak woodland leads to a restored water mill on Crowdundle Beck. Lovely displays of daffodils and wood anemones in spring.

☎ 017683 61893 www.nationaltrust.org.uk

Adlington Hall
234 D4

Originally built as a hunting lodge in 1040 by the Legh family, the present structure incorporates parts of the original building as well as Tudor, Elizabethan and more modern additions. The Hall is home to the largest 17th century organ in the country. The gardens were landscaped in the 18th century in the style of Lancelot 'Capability' Brown and now also include a maze and rose garden. Only open on selected days during the summer.

☎ 01625 820875 www.adlingtonhall.com

Adrian Sankey Glass Makers
249 E2

Visitors may view unique contemporary glass being made by craftspeople using the traditional methods of glass-blowing and hand finishing.

☎ 015394 33039 www.glassmakers.co.uk

Aira Force (NT)
260 A5

70ft (21m) waterfall set amongst woodland on the west side of Ullswater, spanned by a small arched stone bridge.

www.nationaltrust.org.uk

Anderton Boat Lift
234 A5

The boat lift is the only one of its kind in the UK, and when it was built in 1875 it was the first anywhere in the world. Boats enter one of two counterbalanced water-filled tanks which then pass each other mostly by the process of gravity. The rise is 50ft (15m) between two sections of the Trent and Mersey Canal. A visitor centre explains the processes fully and there are trips up and down the lift on a specially built glass-bottomed boat.

☎ 01606 786777 www.andertonboatlift.co.uk

Aquarium of the Lakes
249 E4

An award winning aquarium with more than 30 habitat exhibits of the creatures living in and around the streams, rivers and lakes of the Lake District. These include otters, ducks, trout, eels, pike, perch, and also the giant crabs, sharks and rays of Morecambe Bay. Imaginatively themed to follow the journey of a Lakeland river from its source to the sea, with interactive displays and a cinema presentation of life above and below the surface of Lake Windermere.

☎ 015395 30153 www.aquariumofthelakes.co.uk

Arley Hall
234 A4

The hall is set in superb gardens which are considered by many to be among the best in Europe. There are fine double herbaceous borders, two walled gardens, a shrub rose garden and yew topiary. The present day hall dates from between 1832 and 1845, although parts of the original Tudor building remain. The hall has fine wood panelling, plasterwork, porcelain and a wonderful library.

☎ 01565 777353 www.arleyhallandgardens.com

Astley Hall Museum & Gardens
233 G1

Dating back to Elizabethan times, this country house has textile, art, glassware and ceramic collections and a unique display of furniture. The house is set in extensive woodland and gardens.

☎ 01257 515555 www.astleyhall.co.uk

Beacon Fell Country Park
242 B3

The Fell lies within the Forest of Bowland Area of Outstanding Natural Beauty and the majority of its 185 acres (75ha) are covered by coniferous forest. There are panoramic views from the top of Beacon Fell where a triangulation pillar marks the site of the original warning beacon. A number of walks and cycle paths are clearly marked and a visitor centre is open during the summer.

☎ 01995 640557 www.lancashire.gov.uk/environment/countryside/sites/beaconf.asp

Beatles Story
380 D10

Charting the history of the rise to fame of the four boys from Liverpool. There is a replica of The Cavern Club, a walk-through Yellow Submarine, and displays of Beatles memorabilia.

☎ 0151 709 1963 www.beatlesstory.com

Beeston Castle (Ruins)
220 C2

There are stunning views to be seen from this 13th century ruined castle which stands tall on sandstone crags overlooking the Cheshire Plains – it is well worth the steep climb to the top. The Castle of the Rock exhibition outlines the history of the site, from prehistoric times to the Civil War when the castle was eventually destroyed by the Parliamentarians in 1646.

☎ 01829 260464 www.english-heritage.org.uk

Birdoswald (Banna)
260 C1

In a commanding position overlooking the River Irthing, this well-preserved Roman fort was one of 16 along Hadrian's Wall. Parts of the walls and gateways remain and the fort is linked to Harrow's Scar Milecastle by an impressive section of the Wall. Excavations have revealed a basilica and granaries, and the site has an interactive visitor centre and self-guided trail. Birdoswald continued to be used after the Roman departure up until the 17th century and a farmhouse dating to that period remains.

☎ 016977 47602 www.birdoswaldromanfort.org.uk

Blackpool Piers
241 G4

Blackpool has three piers, each with its own style of entertainment. The North Pier is the oldest, built in 1863 and now a listed building, and is the quietest of the piers with the more genteel attractions. Central Pier is great for the children with a traditional funfair including a Big Wheel which gives superb views along the coastline. The South Pier is the place for adrenaline junkies to head to with various opportunities to jump, be thrown, tossed or swung out over the sea. Entrance to all the piers is free although there is a charge for amusements.

☎ 01253 343097 www.blackpoollive.com

Blackpool Pleasure Beach
241 G4

There are over 140 rides and attractions at this hugely popular amusement park on Blackpool's Promenade, founded in 1896. As well as a large selection of modern white-knuckle rides like The Big One, Europe's tallest (235ft, 72m) and fastest (85mph) roller coaster, and the Avalanche, based on a bobsleigh run, there are a selection of much older wooden roller coasters; the Big Dipper dates from 1923 and the twin track Grand National (two cars racing against each other on parallel tracks) from 1935. Valhalla is a truly spectacular ride in the dark with fire and lots of water. For younger children there is Beaver Creek, a theme park within a theme park, with its own selection of rides and amusements. There are a number of musical and dance shows performed daily and there are over 50 places to eat and drink as well as all the usual gift shops and traditional seaside entertainments. The rides vary in price, usually based on their 'scare' value, and tickets can be bought individually, in books or the cheaper option of a wristband if a whole day's visit is planned.

☎ 0870 444 5566 www.bpbltd.com

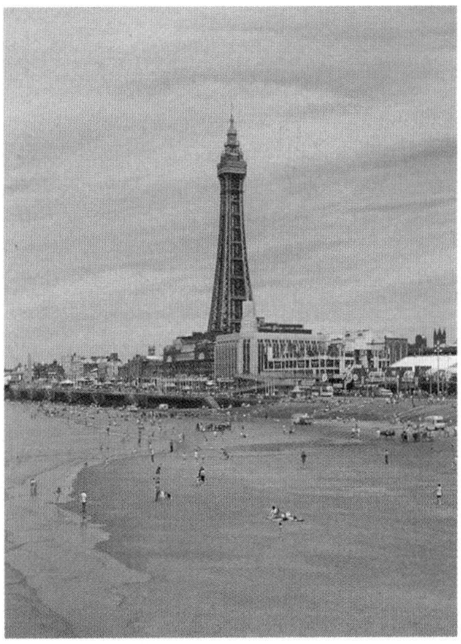

Blackpool Tower

Blackpool Tower
389 C1

The tower was opened in 1894 as the town's very own version of the Eiffel Tower in Paris, and was originally to be called the Blackpool Eiffel Tower. Just 30 years later it was considered for demolition as the steel used in its construction had become corroded, but instead, over a period of three years, the entire structure was replaced and the tower is now one of the town's most well-known attractions. It stands 518ft (158m) tall and is a spot of elegance on Blackpool's crowded seafront. An all-inclusive entry fee gives access to the Tower Circus, the Ballroom, the Aquarium, Jungle Jim's adventure playground and, of course, a trip to the top of the tower. There has been a circus here, between the legs of the tower, since the early days although the shows are now always entirely animal free. The Edwardian Ballroom is home to a mighty Wurlitzer organ on which Latin and old-time dance music is played. Visitors can take to the dance floor themselves or simply participate in high tea whilst others twirl past them. At the top of the tower the Walk of Faith is not for the faint-hearted, as a glass floor allows visitors the chance to look straight down onto the promenade far below.

☎ 01253 622242 www.blackpooltower.co.uk

Blackpool Zoo
241 G4

This 32 acre (13ha) zoo has a collection of over 400 animals including gorillas, lions, tigers and elephants. Gorilla Mountain allows visitors to get up close to the inhabitants and the Swimulator gives the opportunity for visitors to experience the thrill of riding with dolphins without getting wet! There are also keeper talks, animal feeding times, a miniature railway and a Children's Zoo where young children can feed and stroke many domestic animals.

☎ 01253 830830 www.blackpoolzoo.org.uk

Blackwell The Arts & Crafts House
249 F3

In a beautiful position overlooking Lake Windermere, Blackwell was designed by M.H. Baillie Scott between 1897 and 1900 as a holiday home for a wealthy Manchester brewer. It is a wonderful example of the architecture of the Arts and Crafts Movement. Much of the original interior decoration, including stained glass and carved panelling, remains intact and is complemented with furniture, paintings, arts and crafts. Changing exhibitions of historic and contemporary applied arts and crafts are held in upstairs galleries.

☎ 015394 46139 www.blackwell.org.uk

Blue Planet Aquarium
233 F5

Britain's largest aquarium attraction has two floors of exhibits, interactive displays and, for those with diving experience, a chance to swim with sharks. There is sealife on display from all over the world in imaginative displays which re-create varying water environments. Krakatoa has deadly species from the Indo-Pacific swimming amongst submerged temples and statues. The Underwater Safari conveys visitors through the longest (233ft, 71m) underwater viewing tunnel in the world where they are surrounded by sharks and other temperate fish from around the world, as well as 16,000 tons of water! Piranhas, stingrays and electric eels can be seen in the Amazonia display, and children can get their hands on starfish, rays, urchins and sea anemones in the touch pools. The knowledgeable staff are on hand to answer questions and give talks throughout the day. There is a large Caribbean-themed restaurant and a gift shop.

☎ 0151 357 8800 www.blueplanetaquarium.com

Bolton Museum, Art Gallery & Aquarium
234 B2

A good local museum with displays on Egyptology, natural and local history, geology and archaeology. The art gallery has some fine 20th century sculpture and there is a small aquarium with some rare fish species.

☎ 01204 332211 www.boltonmuseums.org.uk

Blue Planet Aquarium

Brantwood
249 E3

Standing on the east side of Coniston Water, with fine views of the lake and mountains beyond, Brantwood was the home of thinker, writer and artist John Ruskin from 1872 – 1900. Originally built in 1797, some rooms are much as Ruskin left them, and contain his art collection, own paintings, furniture, books and personal items. Extensive woodland and themed gardens created by Ruskin surround the house.

☎ 015394 41396 www.brantwood.org.uk

Bridgemere Garden World
221 E3

This huge garden nursery reputedly grows more plants, in more varieties, than anywhere else in Britain, and has over 5000 species on site at any time. 7 acres (3ha) of the nursery have been developed into a series of gardens designed to inspire customers. Many of the gardens are reconstructions of Chelsea Flower Show gold medal winners and range in style from country cottage to modern day patio gardens.

☎ 01270 520381 www.bridgemere.co.uk

Brookside Garden Centre & Miniature Railway
234 D4

This half-mile (1km) circuit makes its way around the garden with authentic signals, signal box and a replica of a West Country station. There are five locomotives in all, three steam and two diesel. The addition of a high level bridge and 65ft (20m) tunnel add to the interest. Passengers sit astride the train in the open and therefore the running of the train is weather dependent.

☎ 01625 872919 www.brookside-miniature-railway.co.uk

Camelot Theme Park
233 G1

The five magical lands at this Arthurian themed park are filled with rides, shows and other attractions which means that there is something here for all the family. The scariest rides are to be found in Land of the Brave, with the spinning roller coaster Whirlwind a popular attraction. King's Realm is filled with rides for all the family and for smaller members there is Merlin's Playland. Young children will also love Squire Bumpkin's Friendly Farm where there are plenty of animals to pat and stroke. Finally, Knight's Valley is the land of the shows – the half-hour jousting tournament is well worth a look.

☎ 01257 453044 www.camelotthemepark.co.uk

Carlisle Castle
393 B2

An imposing Norman fortress with a fascinating and eventful history due in no small part to its proximity to the English and Scottish border. Mary, Queen of Scots was imprisoned here in 1568 after her abdication from the Scottish throne, and the castle also featured in the Wars of the Roses and the Jacobite Rising.

The impressive 12th century keep still stands, as does the inner gatehouse with portcullis known as the Captain's Tower. 'Licking stones' found in a room used as a dungeon are grim testimony to the conditions of those imprisoned here. The King's Own Royal Border Regiment Museum is located within the castle.

☎ 01228 591922 www.english-heritage.org.uk

Carlisle Cathedral
393 B2

Originally founded in 1122, the cathedral today is notable for the large east window which contains some 14th century stained glass, the choir with distinctive 14th century barrel-vaulted blue starry ceiling, a 16th century carved Flemish altarpiece (Brougham Triptych) and medieval carving and paintings. Cathedral and diocesan silver is displayed in the Treasury.

☎ 01228 548151 www.carlislecathedral.org.uk

Cartmel Priory
249 E5

This fine Augustinian priory church, founded in 1188, reflects many periods of ecclesiastical architecture and is still in use today. It contains notable stained glass and carved choir stalls. Also remaining is the original priory gatehouse (National Trust) which is used as the Cartmel Heritage Centre.

☎ 015395 36874 www.nationaltrust.org.uk

Castlerigg Stone Circle
259 F4

Megalithic circle of 38 stones in a beautiful setting surrounded by Lakeland fells. Dating from about 3000 years ago, the circle is 100ft (30m) in diameter and encloses a smaller rectangle of ten stones. The site is thought to have been used as a tribal gathering place, although the precise use is unknown.

www.english-heritage.org.uk

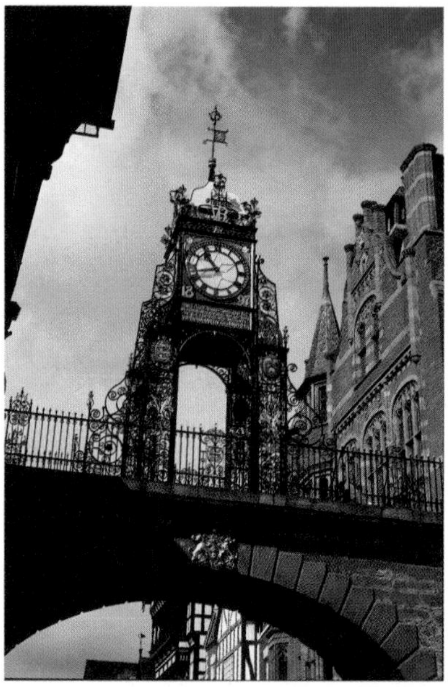

Chester – Eastgate Clock

Chester
394

Chester has a rich history that covers nearly 2000 years. In AD79 the Romans built their largest known fortress here, named Deva after the river Dee. The Dewa Roman Experience and the Grosvenor Museum both have good insights into life in Chester during Roman times. There are various relics of Roman structures scattered around the town, including a partially excavated amphitheatre which would once have held 7000 spectators. Chester has the most complete city walls of anywhere in Britain and it is possible to walk the whole way around, a distance of about 2 miles (3km), although in a number of places the walls are not much higher than the current street height. The centre of Chester has a Tudor look to it with lots of black and white architecture. The four main streets are lined with the Rows, two-storey open galleried half-timbered arcades, some of which are thought to be 700 years old. The most picturesque of these are along Eastgate Street which is also home to the Eastgate Clock, erected to celebrate Queen Victoria's Diamond Jubilee. It is

reputedly the most photographed timepiece after Big Ben. Alongside the River Dee are the Groves, a great place for riverside walks, and there are lovely views from one of the many boat trips.

Chester Cathedral 394 B2

There has been Christian worship on the site of the cathedral since the 10th century, when a Benedictine monastery dedicated to St Werburgh was founded. During the 13th century work began on a new church on the site, built in the Gothic style. It was constructed around the original Norman church which was then taken down from the inside. Parts of this Norman building are still in evidence, for example in the refectory which now houses the cafeteria. The Gothic style church took around 250 years to complete and this long history of worship has led to all architectural styles being represented in the building. In 1541, following the dissolution of the monasteries, the church was dedicated as the Cathedral Church of Christ and the Blessed Virgin Mary. Over many years the church became neglected until, in the late 19th century, Sir George Gilbert Scott masterminded a major restoration project. Of particular note are the intricate medieval carvings above the choir stalls featuring dragons, angels and monsters. It was here that Handel first rehearsed 'The Messiah' and a copy of his annotated score is on display. Digital audio tours are available using hands-free equipment. Admission charges have now been introduced.

☎ 01244 324756 www.chestercathedral.org.uk

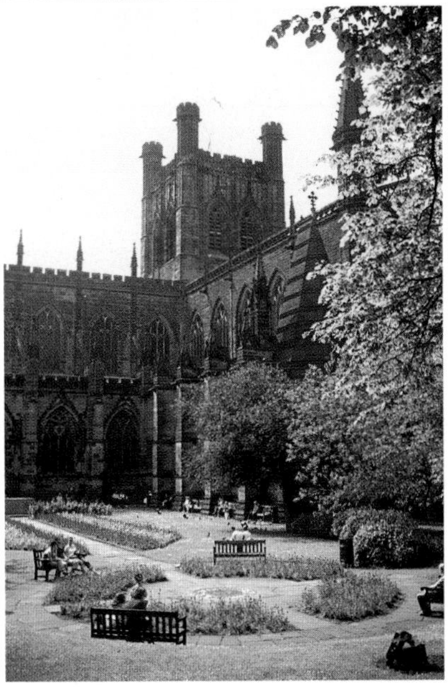

Chester Cathedral

Chester Zoo 233 F5

Without doubt one of the best zoos in Europe, with a well-respected history of conservation work, Chester Zoo is the largest garden zoo in Britain, covering over 110 acres (50ha). Over 7000 animals can be seen, from around 500 different species, at least half of which are rare or endangered and many of which are part of successful breeding programmes. When the zoo was founded by George Mottershead in 1934 he wanted it to be a zoo without bars and he achieved this by creating large enclosures with natural barriers. The 11 miles (17km) of footpath wind their way around the award winning gardens and, if this seems too much to do on foot, hop on the Zoofari overhead railway or the waterbus. The Monkey Islands exhibit is home to the largest colony of chimpanzees in the country and the Twilight Zone bat cave has free-flying bats. There are over 60 species of mammals from tiny harvest mice to the giant Asian elephants, as well as reptiles, birds, fish and amphibians. A series of short, fun and informative talks take place at various enclosures throughout the day and there is a full programme of feeding sessions. Refreshments are readily available and there is a gift shop.

☎ 01244 380280 www.chesterzoo.org.uk

Chester Zoo

Cholmondeley Castle Gardens 220 C2

Romantically landscaped gardens, pretty in any season, are set in the grounds of the Gothic style Cholmondeley Castle (not open to the public). The parkland has an ancient private chapel, rare breeds of animals, including llamas, and lakeside and woodland walks.

☎ 01829 720838

Dalton Castle (NT) 248 C4

A rectangular 14th century tower which houses a local history exhibition.

☎ 01524 701178 www.nationaltrust.org.uk

Dock Museum 241 E1

The museum illustrates Barrow's history from the earliest times with particular emphasis on the 19th century industrial development through iron and steel, then shipbuilding and engineering. There is a collection of ships' models and computer access to the Vickers Photographic Archive of the workings of the Barrow Shipyard. There are also displays of archaeology, geology, natural history, and an art gallery. The museum is in a modern building over a Victorian dry dock.

☎ 01229 894444 www.dockmuseum.org.uk

Dove Cottage 249 E2

Home of the poet William Wordsworth from 1799 – 1808, where he wrote much of his greatest poetry. Home, too, of his sister Dorothy, his wife Mary (whom he married in 1802) and three eldest children. Originally built in the 17th century as an inn, the small two-storey house has oak panelling and Westmoreland slate floors, and is little changed from Wordsworth's day. It also has a delightful cottage garden and orchard.

The adjoining Wordsworth Museum illustrates the life of the poet and his circle with rare books, personal memorabilia, portraits, paintings of Grasmere, and a unique collection of original manuscripts (including a selection of Wordsworth's poems and Dorothy Wordsworth's 'Grasmere Journals').

☎ 015394 35544 www.wordsworthlakes.co.uk

Dunham Massey Hall, Park & Gardens (NT) 368 B4

An early Georgian manor house that was extensively remodelled in the early 20th century, resulting in sumptuous Edwardian interiors. Over 30 rooms are open to the public, including the refurbished kitchen, laundry and servants' quarters. Of particular note is the 18th century walnut furniture, the silver collection of the 2nd Earl of Warrington, and some fine paintings. The house is set in 250 acres (101ha) of wooded deer park with formal avenues of trees, an orangery and a working 17th century mill.

☎ 0161 941 1025 www.nationaltrust.org.uk

Ellesmere Port Boat Museum 233 F5

The canal basin and historic dock where the Shropshire Union Canal meets the River Mersey is home to what claims to be the world's largest collection of traditional canal craft. The museum owns over 5000 items, ranging from large boats to canal company buttons, although not all are on display. Indoors there are exhibits of industrial heritage, waterways objects, working steam machinery and a series of dock workers' cottages re-creating scenes from domestic life between the 1840s and 1950s. Most of the boats on display can be stepped onto to give an insight into life aboard a small narrowboat. There are daily canal boat cruises with live commentary around this once busy port, now redeveloped with craft workshops.

☎ 0151 355 5017 www.boatmuseum.org.uk

Fell Foot Park (NT) 249 E4

Restored 18 acre (8ha) Victorian park on the south shore of Windermere with trails, picnic sites and rowing boats for hire. Well suited to families with children. Lovely displays of daffodils in spring, followed by rhododendrons.

☎ 01539 531273 www.nationaltrust.org.uk

Formby Red Squirrel Reserve (NT) 233 D1

The reserve at Formby is an unspoilt stretch of coastline with miles of walks through pine woods and sand dunes. It is one of the only places left in this country where it is possible to see red squirrels. There is a charge for car parking.

☎ 01704 878591 www.nationaltrust.org.uk

Furness Abbey 248 D5

The extensive red sandstone ruins of this medieval abbey are found in a peaceful setting in a wooded valley. Founded in 1123 by Stephen, later King of England, Furness became one of the richest Cistercian abbeys in England. The visitor centre has some interesting stone carvings from the abbey and an exhibition about the life of the monks.

☎ 01229 823420 www.english-heritage.org.uk

Gawthorpe Hall (NT) 243 E4

Gawthorpe was the home of the Shuttleworth family and there is a fine display of needlework, lace and costume collected by the last family member to live here. Built in 1600, this imposing house was restored in the middle of the 19th century, creating the opulent interiors on display today. There are a number of society portraits, on loan from the National Portrait Gallery, hanging in the long gallery. In summer, there are pleasant walks in the riverside grounds.

☎ 01282 771084 www.nationaltrust.org.uk

Grizedale Forest Park 249 E3

This extensive area of mixed woodland between Coniston Water and Windermere is a centre for recreational activities, including walking and cycling, with picnic areas and around 100 sculptures set within the forest. The visitor centre has a forest exhibition and keeps guide maps for all the waymarked trails. Bike hire is available and there is a high-ropes aerial adventure course.

☎ 01229 860010 www.grizedaleforestpark.co.uk

H.M. Customs & Excise National Museum 380 D9

The museum, located on the ground floor of the Merseyside Maritime Museum, tells the exciting story of the continual battle between smugglers and duty men from 1700 to the present day. See displays of some of the strange seizures made by customs, such as a guitar made from turtle, and learn about the techniques used to combat current day smugglers.

☎ 0151 478 4499 www.customsandexcisemuseum.org.uk

Holker Hall

Hare Hill (NT) 234 C5

This garden is particularly impressive in spring when the rhododendrons and azaleas are in flower. At the heart of the woodland garden is a walled garden with a pergola and wire sculptures.

☎ 01625 584412 www.nationaltrust.org.uk

Harris Museum & Art Gallery 242 B5

Large collections of British paintings, ceramics, glass and costume are displayed in this impressive Greek revival building. The history of the town is brought to life in the Story of Preston Gallery and there is a lively series of contemporary art and social history exhibitions.

☎ 01772 258248 www.visitpreston.com/whats_on/museums/harris/htm

Heaton Hall 369 D1

Heaton Hall is a fine neoclassical country house set in 650 acres (263ha) of public parkland. Many of the building's original features have been retained, such as the ornate scrolling plasterwork, the classically inspired paintings and the unusual Pompeiian Cupola room. The principal rooms in the house have been restored and furnished to reflect life here as it was in the late 18th and early 19th centuries.

☎ 0161 773 1231 www.manchestergalleries.org.uk

High Cup Nick 260 D5

A dramatic curved rocky basalt cliff at the head of a well-defined V-shaped valley in the North Pennines – an inspiring panorama for the determined walker.

Hill Top (NT) 249 E3

This 17th century farmhouse owned by Beatrix Potter remains virtually unchanged, with furniture and china ornaments just as she left them. Beatrix Potter bought Hill Top in 1905 from the proceeds of the sale of her first books, which included 'The Tale of Peter Rabbit'. Although she did not live here all the time, the house was her inspiration and appears in the pictures and stories in many of her later books. Usually very busy in summer when entrance numbers are controlled.

☎ 015394 36239 www.nationaltrust.org.uk

Holker Hall 249 E5

The Cavendish family stately home originally dates from the 17th century but has many later additions and alterations. The pink sandstone Victorian west wing, open to the public, was rebuilt in Elizabethan style after a fire in 1871. The interior is richly furnished and decorated with ornate plaster ceilings, linenfold panelling, silk wall hangings, marble fire surrounds and a carved oak staircase. Paintings grace the walls and there is a collection of Wedgwood Jasper Ware.

Holker Hall is surrounded by a deer park and 25 acres (10ha) of award-winning formal and woodland gardens, with ornamental ponds and fountains and also a wild flower meadow. Rhododendrons, magnolias and azaleas are spectacular in spring and there is a National Collection of Styracaceae. The Great Holker Lime, probably planted in the early 17th century, has an enormous fluted trunk measuring 26ft (8m) across.

The Lakeland Motor Museum, housed in the former stables, has an extensive collection of transport and motoring memorabilia, and includes a display illustrating the record-breaking speed exploits of the Campbell family. There is a full size replica of Bluebird. A number of special events are held at Holker including an annual garden festival.

☎ 015395 58328 www.holker-hall.co.uk

Hutton-in-the-Forest 260 A4

Home of Lord Inglewood's family since 1605, this 17th century house is built around a medieval pele tower. Altered in the 18th and 19th centuries, Hutton-in-the-Forest now reflects a wide variety of architectural and decorative styles but retains its classical façade. The house contains fine furnishings, paintings and ceramics while the grounds include a walled garden dating from 1730, topiary terraces and a woodland walk.

☎ 017684 84449 www.hutton-in-the-forest.co.uk

Jodrell Bank Observatory & Arboretum 234 B5

Jodrell Bank is a leading radioastronomy facility and the huge attraction is the 200ft (76m) Lovell Radio telescope, the second largest in the world. An observational footpath allows visitors to get up close to the telescope and view it from all angles. There is a small exhibition about the work of the observatory, and a state-of-the-art visitor centre is under construction. The 35 acre (14ha) arboretum has over 2000 species of tree and shrub and there are a number of nature trails to help explore this colourful area.

☎ 01477 57133 www.jb.man.ac.uk

Knowsley Safari Park 367 D1

When the park opened in 1971 it was the first to have drive-through animal enclosures. There are now 5 miles (8km) of roads to drive, which allow visitors to view the wild animals, including lions, elephants, giraffes and buffalo, in natural settings. There is a bypass route for those too wary to take their cars into the baboon enclosure, where the animals can be viewed from a safe distance. The entrance fee also includes admission to Lake Farm, a children's farm, the Reptile House, the information centre and a chance to view the sealion show. There is a small amusement park, for which an additional charge is made.

☎ 0151 430 9009 www.knowsley.com/safari

Lady Lever Art Gallery 366 A3

Set in the garden village created by William Hesketh Lever for the workers at his soap factory, this gallery was founded in 1922 and dedicated to his wife. It has a superb collection of Victorian paintings including Turner and the pre-Raphaelite Rossetti, a large collection of Wedgwood, and a host of memorabilia relating to Lord Leverhulme's fascination with Napoleon.

☎ 0151 478 4136 www.ladyleverartgallery.org.uk

Lake District 248 D2

An inspiration to writers and painters, and a mecca for walkers and climbers, the Lake District is one of the most beautiful parts of Britain. It was glacial action that led to the development of the distinctive landscape of rounded mountain summits with ribbon lakes. The area is designated as a National Park, covering 885 square miles (2292 sq km) and containing over 1800 miles (2897 km) of footpaths. It encompasses England's longest and deepest lakes – Windermere and Wast Water respectively – and England's highest mountain, Scafell Pike.

The variety of scenery is breathtaking. Each of the lakes has an individual character and the mountains are broken up by crags, ridges, tarns and streams. Sheep farming has long been the agricultural heritage of the area and the fells are sheep cropped and dotted with small farms and dry stone walls. Picturesque villages and vibrant market towns complete the picture.

With unprecedented access to the countryside, walking and climbing are the most popular leisure activities but there are countless opportunities and facilities for cycling, boating, angling and other outdoor pursuits. Museums, heritage centres, historic houses and gardens, family attractions and the many literary associations of the area, most notably with Wordsworth, are also a draw to visitors. The Lake District can be very busy in the summer, Windermere in particular being a hive of activity, but the National Park and other organisations work hard to maintain the balance between preserving the unique natural beauty of the area and catering for the many visitors.

Lake District Visitor Centre at Brockhole 249 E2

Interactive exhibitions and special events are designed to give visitors of all ages an insight into the Lake District National Park and how the unique landscape is cared for. The centre is housed in a late 19th country house set within 30 acres (12ha) of landscaped gardens on the shores of Windermere.

Visitors are encouraged to enjoy the grounds and there are lakeside walks, an adventure playground and cruises on the lake.

☎ 015394 46601 www.lake-district.gov.uk

Lakeside & Haverthwaite Railway 249 E4

Three and a half miles (6km) of track with steep gradients running through the scenic Leven Valley from Haverthwaite to Lakeside at the south end of Windermere. Both steam and diesel locomotives are in service with a daily timetable operating between April and October.

☎ 01539 31594

Lancaster City Museum 242 A1

Based in a grand Georgian former town hall built in 1873, this museum illustrates the city's history, from Neolithic times to the present day.

☎ 01524 64637 www.lancaster.gov.uk/council/museums

Leighton Hall 249 F5

This neogothic mansion is home to the furniture-making Gillow family, and is set in 1550 acres (627ha) of landscaped parkland. The hall has early and rare examples of Gillow furniture, fine paintings, a 19th century walled garden, and a small collection of birds of prey which fly daily. The hall is open to the public from May to September.

☎ 01524 734474 www.leightonhall.co.uk

Levens Hall 249 F4

An imposing grey stone Elizabethan mansion built round a large square medieval pele tower which has been lived in by the Bagot family for centuries and is still a family home. The house has fine ceiling plasterwork, oak panelling, carved oak chimney pieces, embossed leather wall coverings and notably contains a collection of Jacobean furniture and some early English patchwork.

It is for the yew topiary gardens, however, that Levens is world-renowned. The gardens were designed around 1694 by a Frenchman, Guillaume Beaumont, who had previously laid out the gardens at Hampton Court. Beaumont's original design at Levens remains unchanged today. A huge number and variety of shapes have been clipped out of the common and golden yew and there are also impressive box and beech hedges. Each year it takes from August to December for all the hedges to be clipped. The hedging provides a wonderful backdrop to seasonal bedding and herbaceous borders. Levens also has parkland with a herd of fallow deer, and a working steam engine collection.

☎ 015395 60321 www.levenshall.co.uk

Levens Hall – Topiary Gardens

Little Moreton Hall (NT) 221 F2

Arguably Britain's finest timber-framed manor house, which has an exterior virtually unchanged since it was built in 1580. The interior is unfurnished but the wainscotted long gallery, cobbled courtyard and 17th century knot garden are well worth a look.

☎ 01260 272018 www.nationaltrust.org.uk

Liverpool Cathedral 380 J11

Nothing about this cathedral has been done on a small scale. It is the largest Anglican cathedral in Europe and the fifth largest cathedral in the world. It has the largest working organ with over 9700 pipes, the highest and heaviest church bells, and the highest Gothic arches ever built. This neogothic structure looks much older than it really is – it was only completed in 1978, 74 years after it was designed by Giles Gilbert Scott. It is well worth a climb up the tower, two consecutive lifts followed by 108 steps, as there are panoramic views over Liverpool and towards the Welsh Hills. Part of the way up the tower is the Elizabeth Hoare Embroidery Gallery where there is a sumptuous display of Victorian and Edwardian ecclesiastical embroidery. The gallery also gives fine views over the interior of the cathedral from some 100ft (30m) above the floor level. Although entrance to the cathedral is free, visitors are requested to make a donation towards the running costs of this beautiful building. There is a charge for climbing the tower, and for viewing the embroidery display.

☎ 0151 702 7217 www.liverpoolcathedral.org.uk

Liverpool Museum 380 G5

This museum has hugely varied collections of exhibits covering just about every imaginable topic – from Egyptian tombs, to the night sky, via the Amazonian rainforests. There are fascinating exhibits on dinosaurs, the natural and physical sciences, an award winning hands-on Natural History exhibition, a Space and Time gallery. The Planetarium (there is a small fee) has half-hour shows including the solar system, space exploration and stunning images from the Hubble telescope. Besides the permanent displays, there is an ever-changing programme of special events and attractions.

☎ 0151 478 4399 www.liverpoolmuseum.org.uk

Lake District – Tarn Hows

Lowry, The 368 C2

This shimmering building of metal and glass at the redeveloped Salford Quays houses the largest public collection of works by L.S. Lowry. There are some 350 paintings and drawings on display, including many of his well-known industrial scenes with their stylised matchstick men, as well as his lesser-known mountain and seascapes. There are changing exhibitions, combining works from the collection with those borrowed from other institutions, and private collections as well as paintings, sculptures and photographs by other local artists. ArtWorks is an interactive exhibition designed to encourage the creativity of visitors. There are also two theatres which offer a variety of performances including ballet, drama, opera and comedy. On a warm day it is possible to sit on the quayside with refreshments from one of the cafés or bars.

☎ 0161 876 2000
☎ 0870 787 5780 www.thelowry.com

The Lowry

Lyme Park (NT) 235 D4

This country estate covers nearly 1400 acres (567ha) of wild moorland and parkland which are home to red and fallow deer. The property at its centre combines Elizabethan, Georgian and Regency architecture, together with an Italianate interior. The state rooms have Mortlake tapestries, Grinling Gibbons wood carvings and a fine collection of English clocks. Back outside, the hall is surrounded by 17 acres (7ha) of Victorian gardens boasting a flowering sunken garden, Jekyll-style herbaceous borders and a reflection lake. The house featured as Pemberley in the BBC's adaptation of Jane Austen's 'Pride and Prejudice'.

☎ 01663 762023 www.nationaltrust.org.uk

Manchester Art Gallery 383 K7

There are over 2000 items on display in this city centre gallery. The collection is particularly known for its 19th century British paintings and includes works by some of the great pre-Raphaelites. There is also an exceptional collection of decorative art and craft work, from ancient Greek pottery to contemporary furniture. The Manchester Gallery houses work from local

artists, including Lowry, and the Interactive Gallery aims to open children's minds to art. Audio tours of the collection are available.

☎ 0161 235 8888 www.manchestergalleries.org.uk

Martin Mere 233 F1

This Wildfowl and Wetland Trust site teems with wild geese, swans, ducks and flamingos, and is a year-round attraction. In the landscaped waterfowl gardens it is possible to feed some of the world's rarest and most endangered species of bird by hand. The visitor centre is excellent and explains the need for conserving the wetlands as well as hosting exhibitions and special events.

☎ 01704 895181 www.wwt.org.uk

Mersey Ferries 380 B8

One of the best ways to see Liverpool's landmark Liver building is from the equally famous Mersey Ferry. As well as the regular commuter ferry for Birkenhead and Wallasey, there is a 50-minute river explorer cruise which incorporates a lively commentary on the history of Liverpool and Europe's oldest ferry.

☎ 0151 330 1444 www.merseyferries.co.uk

Merseyside Maritime Museum 380 D9

This huge museum in Liverpool's Albert Dock is the second largest of its kind in the country and tells the story of one of the world's greatest ports. There are a number of fascinating exhibitions including one that explores the role of Liverpool in the transatlantic slave trade and another, the Emigrant Gallery, that allows the visitor to share in the experiences of those who left Liverpool for the New World. There are numerous objects associated with nautical archaeology, maritime paintings, ships' models, and galleries about the Titanic and the Lusitania. During the summer it may be possible to board one of the preserved ships in the dock outside.

☎ 0151 478 4499 www.merseysidemaritimemuseum.org.uk

Mirehouse 259 F4

In a wonderful setting near to Bassenthwaite Lake and beneath Skiddaw, this 17th century house is still used as a family home. Wordsworth, Tennyson, Carlyle and Southey all visited Mirehouse and some of their letters are on display, together with a collection of Francis Bacon manuscripts. In front of the house is a wild flower meadow, there are adventure playgrounds in the woods, an orchard with regional fruit varieties, a bee garden and lakeside walk. The house has limited opening but the grounds are open daily from April to October.

☎ 017687 72287 www.mirehouse.com

Muncaster Castle 248 C3

Situated in a remote part of Cumbria, Muncaster is a 19th century castle incorporating parts of earlier buildings including the medieval pele tower. It has been in the same family since the 13th century and is said to be haunted. The elegant rooms, including the Great Hall and Octagonal Library, display a great number of treasures collected over the centuries.

There are 77 acres (31ha) of gardens and woodland to explore with walks overlooking Eskdale. In late spring there are carpets of bluebells and many species of rhododendrons in flower. An Owl Centre in the grounds has owls, buzzards, kestrels and red kites, and is the headquarters of the World Owl Trust. The centre has flying displays and video footage from cameras placed in nesting boxes.

☎ 01229 717614 www.muncaster.co.uk

Museum of Liverpool Life 380 C9

This museum celebrates Liverpool's people, their culture, achievements and contribution to life in this country over the last century. A varied range of displays looks at all aspects of Liverpool life. The City Soldiers gallery tells the story of the King's Regiment, the River Room concentrates on life around the Mersey, and the Mersey Culture section looks at popular music, home-grown soap operas, football and the Grand National.

☎ 0151 478 4080 www.museumofliverpoollife.org.uk

Museum of Science & Industry 382 F8

An impressive museum that provides enough entertainment for a whole day out. It is based in the buildings of the world's oldest passenger railway station. George Stephenson's Rocket arrived here in 1830 on its inaugural journey from Liverpool. There are 13 galleries in all; there is a reconstruction of a Victorian sewer with all the appropriate smells, a Power Hall which has huge working engines and locomotives, and a hands-on science centre called Xperiment, all of which help to bring the industrial and scientific past to life. The newest gallery looks at the contribution that Manchester scientists past and present have made to the modern world, as well as featuring some recent developments such as odourless socks!

☎ 0161 832 2244 www.msim.org.uk

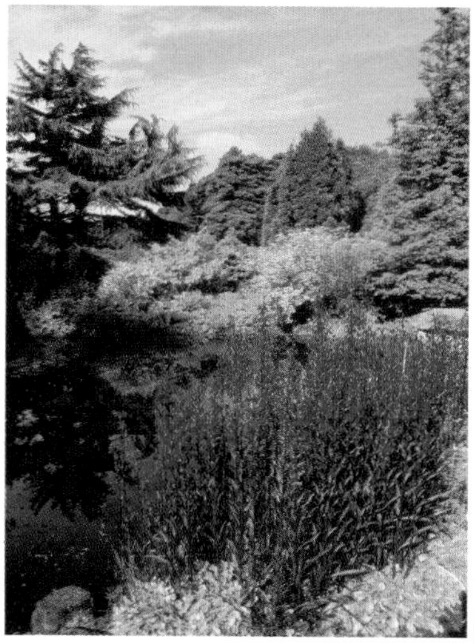

Ness Botanic Gardens

Ness Botanic Gardens 233 E5

Ness Botanic Gardens were founded by the Liverpool cotton merchant Arthur Kilpin Bulley in 1898. Bulley was interested in introducing new plant species from abroad, and in particular he believed that Himalayan and Chinese mountain plants would grow well in this country. When Bulley died the garden was gifted to the University of Liverpool who has since maintained and developed the gardens with an emphasis on research, conservation and education. There are now 62 acres (25ha) of gardens, greenhouses and experimental grounds, with an extensive collection of specimen trees and shrubs which include many rhododendrons and azaleas. There are also renowned rock, rose, heather and water gardens. The gardens have a number of interest trails, a visitor centre, gift shop, tearoom and children's play areas.

☎ 0151 353 0123 www.nessgardens.org.uk

Quarry Bank Mill & Styal Estate

Nether Alderley Mill (NT) 234 C5

This restored 15th century water mill has working Victorian machinery and is powered by overshot (the water flows over the wheel rather than under it) tandem wheels. Flour grinding demonstrations occasionally take place, water supplies permitting.

☎ 01625 584412 www.nationaltrust.org.uk

Ordsall Hall 369 D2

A fine black and white half-timbered manor house in the incongruous surroundings of Salford city centre. There is a fully restored and furnished Great Hall, a bedroom and Tudor kitchen to be explored, as well as a chance of spotting The White Lady, Ordsall Hall's ghost. Closed on Saturdays.

☎ 0161 872 0251 www.salford.gov.uk/ordsallhall

Pleasureland Amusement Park 233 E1

Originally opened in 1920 with just a helter skelter and a roller coaster, Pleasureland has now expanded to have over 100 rides and attractions. There are a few big white-knuckle rides such as the Traumatizer, a suspended coaster, and Space Shot which launches riders 120ft (37m) into the air, as well as more traditional roller coasters, a log-flume and ghost train. There is also an area with rides especially for young children. Admission to the park is free although the rides themselves are not. Visitors can purchase a wristband which will give unlimited rides all day.

☎ 08702 200204 www.pleasureland.uk.com

Quarry Bank Mill & Styal Estate (NT) 234 C4

Situated in 384 acres (155ha) of the beautiful countryside of Styal Country Estate, this museum is a fantastic place to learn about the social and industrial history of this country. Quarry Bank Mill is a fully preserved and working example of a Georgian cotton mill powered by the largest working water wheel in Europe. Cotton is still spun and woven here and is available for sale in the shop. Inside the mill there are hands-on displays, demonstrations from hand spinning to large-scale factory weaving, and an 1840s steam-powered beam engine which is worked daily. The Apprentice House was built in 1790 to house pauper children who worked at the mill. The conditions in which these children lived and worked is now brought to life with the aid of enthusiastic guides in period costume who engage visitors in conversation and discussion. Visitors are encouraged to ask questions, test the straw filled beds, touch all the

objects in the house and pump water from the well in the yard. Styal village was a tiny hamlet before the mill arrived but by 1840 it was a thriving village with most of its inhabitants working at the mill. It claims to be the least altered factory colony in this country with well-preserved workers' cottages, chapel, school and shop, and the whole village has an idyllic rural atmosphere. The estate land around the village and mill has some wonderful riverside and woodland walks.

☎ 01625 527468 www.quarrybankmill.org.uk

Railway Age, The 221 E2

A wide range of electric, steam and miniature locomotives, a model railway and an impressive collection of signalling equipment.

☎ 01270 212130 www.therailwayage.co.uk

Ravenglass & Eskdale Railway 248 B3

A narrow-gauge railway running 7 miles (11km) from the coast at Ravenglass to Dalegarth Station near Boot in Eskdale, with a journey time of around 40 minutes. Small steam locomotives pull passengers through spectacular scenery with the Scafell range of mountains in view for much of the time. There is a choice of open and covered carriages, and the service is often used by walkers and cyclists to get into the heart of Lakeland. 'La'al Ratty', the water vole mascot for the railway, keeps children amused, sometimes acting as guard, train driver or stationmaster. The railway was first opened in 1875 to transport iron ore, and at Ravenglass Station there are displays of memorabilia and photographs illustrating the line's history.

☎ 01229 717171 www.ravenglass-railway.co.uk

Ravenglass & Eskdale Railway

Rheged – the Village in the Hill 260 A5

A vast purpose-built family attraction named after Cumbria's Celtic Kingdom of Rheged and designed to blend in with the landscape. It is built into a disused limestone quarry and has a grass covered roof, the largest in Europe. Although the building covers 85,000 square feet (719 sq m) on five different levels, the glass atriums and windows provide ample light and spectacular views. A stream runs through the building and there are small lakes outside.

Apart from the unique construction, the main draw is a giant cinema screen the size of six double-decker buses. Spectacular epic films are shown each day including features on Cumbrian myths and legends, the Lakeland landscape, the underwater world, and the ascent of Everest.

Rheged is also home to the National Mountaineering Exhibition which celebrates Britain's mountaineering heritage. Exhibits include clothing, equipment, photographs and film. Additionally, there is a children's indoor play area, local food, craft and gift shops, restaurant, art exhibitions and a full programme of special events. Free car parking and entry to the building.

☎ 01768 868000 www.rheged.com

Ribchester Roman Fort & Museum 242 C4

This museum is built on the site of a Roman fort occupied from AD78 and is dedicated to the history of Bremetenacum Veteranorum, the Roman name for Ribchester. There are some interactive exhibits, Roman replicas like the Ribchester Parade Helmet, and collections of weaponry, jewellery, coins and pottery. The external remains of the Roman granary can also be seen by visitors.

☎ 01254 878261 www.ribchestermuseum.org

Rydal Mount 249 E2

Little has changed at Rydal Mount since William Wordsworth lived here with his family from 1813 until his death in 1850. The house was originally a 16th century farm cottage but was made much larger in the 18th century. Furnished as it would have been in Wordsworth's day, the house has some of his poetry, personal possessions and family portraits on display.

The extensive picturesque terraced gardens were designed by Wordsworth and there are wonderful views of Rydal Water, Windermere and the surrounding fells. Rydal Mount was beloved by all Wordsworth's family and was a source of inspiration to the poet.

☎ 015394 33002 www.wordsworthlakes.co.uk

Salford Museum & Art Gallery 382 B4

Lark Hill Place is a re-created Victorian shopping street with original shop fronts and authentic period rooms. LifeTimes focuses on real people and events to tell the story of Salford over the last 200 years. The Victorian Gallery has a permanent collection of paintings and sculpture, and hosts temporary exhibitions of work by local and national artists.

☎ 0161 736 2649 www.salford.gov.uk/leisure/museums/salfordmuseum.htm

Salt Museum 234 A5

Cheshire has been a large producer of salt for over 2000 years. It is the only place in Britain where it is still produced on a large scale, and this interesting museum at Northwich explains the vital importance of salt to human life, as well as describing the production process.

☎ 01606 41331 www.saltmuseum.org.uk

Silk Museum & Paradise Mill 234 D5

Macclesfield was one of Britain's main silk spinning and weaving centres during the late 18th and early 19th centuries. Paradise Mill is now an award winning museum where knowledgeable guides, many of them former silk workers, take visitors around the restored jacquard handlooms and demonstrate the intricate processes involved in silk work. The Silk Museum, housed in what was once the Macclesfield School of Art, has displays on the properties of silk, the textile industry and the social history of the area.

☎ 01625 612045 www.silk-macclesfield.org

Sizergh Castle & Gardens (NT) 249 F4

Originally built in the 14th century by the Strickland family, who still live here, the massive fortified tower developed into a manor house with the addition of a Great Hall in the 15th century and two long wings during the Elizabethan period. There are some remarkable oak-panelled rooms, most notably the bedroom known as the Inlaid Chamber, and fine Elizabethan carved wooden chimneypieces. The house contents include period oak furniture, family portraits, china and Jacobite relics.

Sizergh has an impressive limestone rock garden with a large collection of hardy ferns, a Dutch garden with flowering cherries and a rose garden underplanted with bulbs. Specimen trees and shrubs provide wonderful autumn colour. Extensive walks with views of the Lakeland fells and Morecambe Bay are to be enjoyed in the 1600 acre (638ha) estate.

☎ 015395 60070 www.nationaltrust.org.uk

South Lakes Wild Animal Park 248 D5

Opened in 1994, this is now a major conservation zoo park. Animals from many parts of the world are kept in mixed groups in natural surroundings, and others are free to roam the park. Among around 100 species of animals are kangaroos, bears, rhinos, giraffes, antelope, lemurs, cheetahs, lions, primates and rare Amur and Sumatran tigers. Animal hands-on sessions are held with the zoo keepers providing a wealth of information. Feeding sessions include the spectacle of the tigers climbing tall poles for their meat, a device designed to exercise their muscles. A miniature railway operates in summer.

The park takes part in coordinated breeding programmes and works to conserve natural habitats all over the world to save endangered species. It is also home of the Sumatran Tiger Trust which works in Sumatra to protect the remaining wild tigers.

☎ 01229 466086 www.wildanimalpark.co.uk

South Tynedale Railway 260 D3

This is England's highest narrow-gauge railway. Restored steam and diesel locomotives run for over two miles (3km) from the station at Alston through the beautiful South Tyne valley to Kirkhaugh in the North Pennines. The return journey takes 50 minutes but passengers may spend time at Kirkhaugh and return on a later train.

☎ 01434 381696 www.strps.org.uk

Stagshaw Garden (NT) 249 E2

A hillside woodland garden overlooking Windermere with rhododendrons, azaleas and camellias. A beck runs through the garden with several small waterfalls. Open April to June only, at other times by appointment

☎ 015394 46027 www.nationaltrust.org.uk

Stapeley Water Gardens & Palms Tropical Oasis 221 D2

Stapeley is the country's largest and best regarded water garden centre, with hundreds of water plants displayed, and for sale, in pools. The water lilies are particularly impressive between June and September. The Palms Tropical Oasis, for which there is a fee, has palm trees, parrots, reptiles, monkeys and creepy-crawlies in heated glasshouses.

☎ 01270 623868 www.stapeleywatergardens.com

Tabley House
234 B5

This is the only 18th century Palladian house in the north west. The son of the original owner was the first patron of British art and built up quite a collection of paintings, including works by Turner and Reynolds, many of which are still on display in the locations they were originally intended for. The house is also home to a collection of fine furniture, including pieces by Gillow and Chippendale.

☎ 01565 750151 www.tableyhouse.co.uk

Tate Liverpool
380 C9

Home to the national collection of modern art in the north of England, Tate Liverpool has four floors of contemporary art. There are exhibitions of art from the Tate Collection and special exhibitions of work from other public and private collections, including some from overseas. There are free talks and guided tours daily. There is a charge for some special exhibitions.

☎ 0151 702 7400 www.tate.org.uk

Tatton Park (NT)
234 B4

This is one of the most complete historic estates open to visitors, and there is plenty here to occupy for a whole day. There are two historic houses, 1000 acres (400ha) of parkland containing some magnificent gardens, and a working farm. The opulent mansion was built at the end of the 18th century and gives a wonderful glimpse into how the original owners, the Egerton family, lived. The state and family rooms still contain many of the original furnishings, contents and paintings, including two Canalettos. The fully restored servants' quarters are a stark contrast. The second house is the Tudor Old Hall – downstairs paints a realistic picture of medieval life, whilst upstairs the rooms are styled as they would have been in the early 1600s. The final room of the tour is a re-creation of an estate worker's cottage from 1958. The gardens, perhaps the best feature of the estate, are extensive and incorporate many different styles. There is a walled garden, a beech maze, a fernery, an Italianate garden and one of the finest examples of a Japanese garden in Europe. Home Farm is always popular with children, especially when the piglets are just being born, and the adjacent fields have sheep, cattle and chickens. The farm works as it did during the 1930s, with vintage farm implements and rare breeds of animal. All of this is set in open parkland where herds of fallow deer roam freely.

☎ 01625 534400 www.tattonpark.org.uk

Tegg's Nose Country Park
234 D5

Tegg's Nose is a distinctive hill with open heather moorland, meadows and woodland. A series of well-marked footpaths take visitors to some tremendous views over the Cheshire countryside towards North Wales. There is an excellent visitor centre.

☎ 01625 914279 www.cheshire.gov.uk/countryside/outandabout/teggs_nose_country_park

Tullie House
393 B2

With collections of archaeology, history, wildlife, geology and fine and decorative arts, this modern museum has many hands-on and audiovisual exhibits, and provides interest and entertainment for all ages. The troubled history of the Borders area, from prehistory through to medieval times and beyond, is illustrated with the use of sight, sound and smell in the 'Border Galleries'. The growth of Carlisle as a main railway centre is featured and there are changing contemporary art exhibitions. Tullie House, the Jacobean House which gave the museum its name, stands within the grounds.

☎ 01228 534781 www.tulliehouse.co.uk

Ullswater Steamers
259 G5

Three traditional Victorian vessels cruise the eight miles (13km) of Ullswater all year round. Steamer services started on the lake in 1859 and a passenger service has continued ever since, although the ships are now oil powered. Ullswater is unspoilt, and from the lake there are dramatic views of Helvellyn, England's second highest mountain. Passengers may travel between any of the piers at Glenridding, Howtown and Pooley Bridge or buy a round trip ticket.

☎ 017684 82229 www.ullswater-steamers.co.uk

Walker, The
380 G5

This gallery houses one of the country's finest collections of artwork outside London. There is European art from the 14th century right up to the present day, including works by Rembrandt, Poussin and Degas. The speciality of this gallery however is British art, including a major collection of Victorian paintings and pre-Raphaelite work. 20th century art is represented by Cezanne, Monet, Lucien Freud and David Hockney, whilst two temporary exhibition galleries show contemporary work.

☎ 0151 478 4199 www.thewalker.org.uk

Walton Hall Gardens
367 F3

A heritage centre in the gardens tells the story of the Walton Estate, of Lewis Carroll and his connections with Walton Hall (not open to the public) and the local natural history. There are ornamental gardens, spacious lawns, picnic areas, a children's zoo and woodland trails, as well as a number of waymarked trails from the gardens leading out into the surrounding countryside.

☎ 01925 601617 www.warrington.gov.uk/entertainment/parks/walton

Whinlatter Forest
259 E4

An upland forest park with waymarked trails through the forest, routes to the top of the surrounding fells, a permanent orienteering course, adventure playground and picnic areas. The first trees were planted here in 1919 and the Forestry Commission Visitor Centre at the top of Whinlatter Pass has displays about the forest. From May to September there are CCTV pictures at the visitor centre of osprey chicks being reared in local nests. Viewpoints throughout the park afford spectacular vistas of the Lake District and across to Scotland.

☎ 017689 78469 www.whinlatterforestpark.co.uk

Whitworth Art Gallery
369 D2

The Whitworth is home to a collection of British watercolours, including paintings by Turner, modern art and sculpture, and the largest collection of textiles and wallpapers outside of the Victoria and Albert Museum in London. The works are grouped and displayed in themes which change once or twice a year.

☎ 0161 275 7450 www.whitworth.man.ac.uk

Windermere Lake Cruises
249 E3

Traditional and modern launches carry over a million passengers each year between Waterhead (Ambleside), Bowness and Lakeside on Windermere. The oldest boat in the fleet is *The Tern*, a railway steamer built in 1891. Daily services operate all year and circular cruises of the lake, the longest in England, or shorter sightseeing trips are available. Traditional rowing boats and self-drive motor boats may also be hired.

☎ 015395 31188 www.windermere-lakecruises.co.uk

Windermere Steamboat Museum
249 F3

A fascinating collection of historic steam and motor boats moored in a covered wet dock, with launch trips if the weather is fair. Among the vintage boats is the steam launch *Dolly*, reputedly the oldest mechanically powered boat in the world, built around 1850 and restored to her former glory after spending 67 years on the bed of Ullswater. Among other attractions at the museum are model boats and a model boats pond, 'Swallows and Amazons' exhibition, Beatrix Potter's rowing boat, and displays about how Windermere has been used for transport since Roman times.

☎ 015394 45565 www.steamboat.co.uk

World of Beatrix Potter Attraction
249 F3

The 'Tales of Beatrix Potter' are brought to life in an amazingly detailed re-creation of the scenes inhabited by her characters using sounds, music, lighting effects and even smells. Of great appeal to children and all lovers of Beatrix Potter's books.

☎ 015394 88444 www.hop-skip-jump.com

Tatton Park

NORTH EAST ENGLAND

The evocative ruin of Hadrian's Wall stretches like a ribbon across this remotely beautiful border country. Yet, in stark contrast to the armed conflicts of the past the industrial revolution brought a different type of struggle to the area. Coal, steel, railways and shipbuilding helped create dozens of 'boom' settlements. Over the years these have mellowed into towns and cities of real character bustling with residents who are genuinely proud of their heritage and unrivalled in their hospitality.

Hadrian's Wall

Alnwick Castle & Garden
279 F5

Just to the north of Alnwick town centre and rising impressively above the River Aln, the castle has been home to the Percys, ancestral family of the Duke of Northumberland, since 1309. It is the second largest lived-in castle in England (after Windsor).

The exterior view of this austere and striking medieval fortress, with its life-size stone figures standing guard on the battlements, is in stark contrast to the sumptuous state rooms furnished in Italian Renaissance style. Adam ceilings and fireplaces are the legacy of restoration by the first Duke of Northumberland in the 18th century and there are fine paintings and porcelain.

The Regimental Museum of the Northumberland Fusiliers is housed in the Abbots Tower. Archaeological exhibits, the Percy coach, dungeon, gun terrace and landscaped grounds by Capability Brown are among other attractions. Often used as a film location, scenes from the 'Harry Potter' films have been filmed at the castle.

The Alnwick Garden (separate charge) is a project underway to transform the former 18th century sloping walled garden into a modern, innovative garden and notably features The Grand Cascade.

☎ 01665 511350 www.alnwickcastle.com www.alnwickgarden.co.uk

Alnwick Castle & Gardens

Arbeia Roman Fort & Museum
372 D1

In a commanding position at the mouth of the River Tyne, the Roman stone fort of Arbeia was the supply base for Hadrian's Wall. Reconstructed buildings, including the impressive West Gate, and a varied display of archaeological finds from weapons to jewellery, present a picture of life on the northern frontier of Roman Britain. Archaeologists may be seen at work on excavations and children will enjoy Time Quest, for which there is a charge, an opportunity to find out what it is like to be an archaeologist.

☎ 0191 456 1369

Auckland Castle
262 B4

The official residence of the Bishop of Durham, dating back over 800 years, with state rooms and the magnificent 12th century St Peter's Chapel. Limited opening. Unusual 18th century Deer House in adjoining parkland.

☎ 01388 601627 www.auckland-castle.co.uk

BALTIC The Centre for Contemporary Art
404 F3

Opened in 2002, the Baltic is housed in the former grain warehouse of a 1950s flour mill. It is a vast and imposing building close to the Tyne Bridge on the south bank of the river. There is no permanent collection but a changing programme of exhibitions displayed in five galleries with facilities to cater for all art media. Envisaged as an 'Art Factory', there are artists' studios and work is created through commissions and by the work of artists-in-residence. The centre has a rooftop restaurant with excellent views of Tyneside.

☎ 0191 478 1810 www.balticmill.com

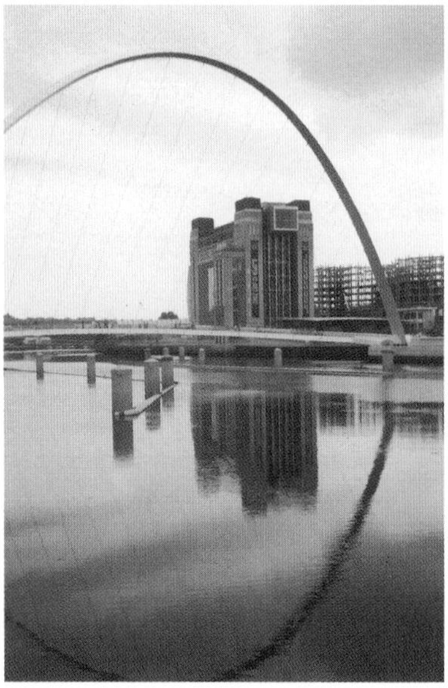

BALTIC The Centre for Contemporary Art

Bamburgh Castle
279 F3

Formidable Norman castle dominating the seaside village of Bamburgh, much restored in the 18th and 19th centuries but still retaining the original large square keep. The castle is stunningly situated on a rocky outcrop above a long white sandy beach with views seawards of the Farne Islands and Holy Island.

Bamburgh withstood many sieges but fell into disrepair after sustaining severe damage during the Wars of the Roses in 1464. The first Lord Armstrong, inventor, engineer and industrialist, carried out major restoration and refurbishment in the 19th century, and Bamburgh is still the home of the Armstrong family today.

Paintings, furniture, tapestries, china and glassware are displayed in the fine King's Hall and Cross Hall. The old laundry building houses an Aviation Artefact Museum with many parts from crashed World War II aircraft, while the Armstrong Museum portrays the life of the first Lord Armstrong through his work as an engineer. There is an impressive collection of armour and a dungeon.

☎ 01668 214515 www.bamburghcastle.com

Beamish, North of England Open Air Museum
262 B2

Celebrating the industrial, rural and social heritage of the north-east, Beamish shows how people lived and worked in the 1800s and early 1900s. A town, colliery village and railway station have been re-created with many authentic buildings being dismantled elsewhere and brought to the site. Staff in period costume are a wealth of information.

Visitors may go shopping in the town shops, and there is also a bank, dentist and newspaper office in the main street. Guided tours of the drift mine take visitors underground. The colliery village includes tiny pit cottages, a chapel and a school where playing with traditional toys in the playground is a popular activity. Cheese is made on a working farm, nearby is a manor house and, by way of contrast, there is a Victorian fairground.

Trams link the various areas, and replica buses and horse-drawn vehicles provide other means of transport. Covering over 300 acres (120ha), Beamish provides a full day out for all the family. Winner of both British and European Museum of the Year awards.

☎ 0191 370 4000 www.beamish.org.uk

Bede's World
372 C2

Dedicated to the 8th century monk, the Venerable Bede, who chronicled the ecclesiastical history of the time, this is an absorbing day out for all the family. Bede's World incorporates the monastic site of St Paul's, a museum, an Anglo-Saxon demonstration farm and herb garden. Many fascinating archaeological finds are displayed in the interactive exhibition which explores early medieval life and Christian heritage.

☎ 0191 489 2106 www.bedesworld.co.uk

Belsay Hall, Castle & Gardens
270 C4

30 acres (12ha) of picturesque landscaped gardens surround 19th century neo-classical Belsay Hall and a ruined Jacobean manor house with 14th century tower house. All were owned by the Middleton family for 600 years. Notable for a quarry garden, rhododendrons and many exotic species of plants. A winter garden ensures Belsay is worth a visit in any season.

☎ 01661 881636 www.english-heritage.org.uk

Bamburgh Castle

Beamish, North of England Open Air Museum

Brinkburn Priory
270 D2

The Augustinian priory of Brinkburn, founded around 1135, is set amongst woodland beside the River Coquet. On a fine day the priory grounds are a lovely place for a picnic. Restored in the 19th century, the church of the original monastery survives intact and contains some striking wooden contemporary sculptures by Fenwick Lawson. Venue for the Brinkburn Music Summer Festival. Standing nearby is a Gothic style manor house.

☎ 01665 570628 www.english-heritage.org.uk

Captain Cook Birthplace Museum
253 E1

Learn about the life of Captain James Cook and his voyages of exploration in this interesting hands-on museum that will appeal to adults and children alike. Located in the landscaped grounds of Stewart Park, close to where Cook was born.

☎ 01642 311211

Cragside (NT)
270 C1

Aptly named, the Victorian home of the first Lord Armstrong is built on a crag surrounded by rock gardens. Contains many original contents and fascinating gadgets invented by Armstrong. In the 1880s Cragside enjoyed central heating, hot and cold running water and, most remarkably, was lit by hydro-electricity using the man-made lakes in the grounds. Well-known for rhododendrons in late spring, the extensive and varied landscaped woodland estate can be explored by car or on foot.

☎ 01669 620333 www.nationaltrust.org.uk

Dunstanburgh Castle (NT)
279 G4

Extensive and dramatic ruins of a 14th century castle on headland cliffs. Reached by coastal footpath from Craster or Embleton.

☎ 01665 576231 www.english-heritage.org.uk/ www.nationaltrust.org.uk

Durham Cathedral

Durham Cathedral
396 E2

Dominating the Durham city skyline, this awe-inspiring cathedral, with three massive towers, stands high above and in an almost complete loop of the River Wear. The present cathedral was largely built between 1093 and 1133 and is considered to be the greatest piece of Romanesque architecture in Britain. The nave, however, has pointed arches which makes it unique for this period.

The cathedral contains the tomb of Cuthbert, 7th century Bishop of Lindisfarne, and of the Venerable Bede who wrote about the life of St Cuthbert. Exhibitions tell the story of the cathedral and how it was built and 'The Treasures' in the 13th century undercroft displays St Cuthbert's cross and fragments of his coffin. The medieval Monk's Dormitory has a wonderful hammer-beam oak roof and houses part of the cathedral library. Visitors may climb the 325 steps of the tower.

Together with Durham Castle (built 1072), which is now part of the university, the cathedral is designated a World Heritage Site.

☎ 0191 386 4266 www.durhamcathedral.co.uk

George Stephenson's Birthplace (NT)
262 A1

A small 18th century stone tenement where railway engineer George Stephenson was born in 1781. Typical of those built for mining families at that time, with whole families living in just one room, it is furnished as it may have been in Stephenson's day.

☎ 01661 843276 www.nationaltrust.org.uk

Hadrian's Wall 261 G1

The wall is a well preserved and impressive Roman frontier fortification, built between AD122-128 on the orders of Emperor Hadrian at the height of the Roman Empire. It extends 73 miles (118km) from Bowness-on-Solway to Wallsend. No doubt intended as a symbol of Roman power, it was used to control trade and the movement of people in the region. It is now a designated World Heritage Site.

The original height of the wall was around 15ft (5m) and was bounded on the north by a defensive ditch and on the south by a ditch between turf ramparts. It included turret watch towers, milecastles and forts. The wall is all the more dramatic for much of it being built on ridges and crags and set amidst beautiful countryside. Numerous car parks on the B6318 give walkers access to the paths alongside the wall.

At the east end of the wall is Segedunum, the remains of a fort once holding a garrison of 600 soldiers, and now an award-winning museum. It includes a reconstructed section of wall and Roman baths, while nearby is 88yds (80m) of original wall.

www.hadrians-wall.org www.english-heritage.org.uk

Hamsterley Forest 261 G5

A beautiful area of mixed woodland between Weardale and Teesdale, extending over 5000 acres (2000ha) with waymarked walks, horse riding trails and cycle routes. The Visitor Centre is the starting point of a 4 mile (6.5km) forest drive (toll charge).

☎ 01434 220242

Hancock Museum 404 D2

A small natural history museum with a wealth of exhibits, live animals and interactive displays showing how the planet and the animal and plant kingdoms evolved. A great place for children to visit, the Hancock also features the 'Land of the Pharaohs' gallery with two Egyptian mummies and a varied programme of touring exhibitions.

☎ 0191 222 6765

Hartlepool Historic Ships 263 E4

The lively Historic Quay is a reproduction of an 18th century seaport complete with shops, houses and a quayside littered with barrels, carts, anchors and ropes. Exhibitions in the quayside buildings give visitors a taste of seafaring at the time of Nelson, and there is an interactive children's maritime adventure centre. Staff in period costume add to the atmosphere.

Afloat in the dock is the restored *HMS Trincomalee*, a frigate built in 1817 by the East India Dock Company at Bombay (separate entry fee). Moored outside the nearby Museum of Hartlepool (free) is the paddle steamer *PSS Wingfield*, a former Humber ferry.

☎ 01429 860077

High Force 261 E5

Spectacular 70ft (21m) waterfall, said to be England's largest, in upper Teesdale. Reached by a pretty woodland walk.

Holy Island 279 F2

Holy Island is accessible by a causeway passable at low tide and is set within the Lindisfarne National Nature Reserve. Founded in the 7th century by St Aidan, the monastery at Lindisfarne became an important centre of Christian learning and the beautiful illuminated Lindisfarne Gospels were written here.

The ruined 12th century Benedictine priory has a rainbow arch still standing over the nave, and the museum contains notable Anglo-Saxon carvings and illustrates how the monks lived.

With stones taken from the priory, the formidable looking Lindisfarne Castle was built in the 16th century to protect the island from the Scots. Converted into a private home in 1903 by architect Edwin Lutyens, the castle contains a fine collection of early 17th century oak furniture and has a small walled garden designed by Gertrude Jekyll. Also on the island is a Heritage Centre and St Aidan's Winery, where Lindisfarne Mead is made. Entry to the island is free but there are charges for the attractions.

☎ Priory: 01289 389200 www.english-heritage.org.uk
☎ Castle: 01289 389244 www.nationaltrust.org.uk
☎ Heritage Centre: 01289 389044 www.lindisfarne-heritage-centre.org

Housesteads (Vercovicium) (NT) 261 D1

The best-preserved Roman fort in Britain, Housesteads was one of sixteen bases along Hadrian's Wall. Built around AD124 to house 800 infantry soldiers, it was in use until the end of the Roman occupation of Britain in the early 5th century. The fort contains the headquarters building, commander's house, barracks, hospital, latrines and granaries. There is a site museum.

☎ 01434 344363 www.english-heritage.org.uk www.nationaltrust.org.uk

Howick Hall Gardens 279 G5

This was once the home of British Prime Minister Earl Grey, for whom the tea was blended to suit the water at Howick. Surrounding the 18th century house (not open) there are terraces, herbaceous borders and notably a woodland garden planted with rhododendrons, azaleas, camellias and magnolias. Lovely displays of snowdrops in February are followed by other spring bulbs. From the garden a path leads to a sandy cove at Howick Haven.

☎ 01665 577285 www.howickgarden.org.uk

Hadrian's Wall, Housesteads

Kielder Forest — 269 E2

In the remotest part of the Northumberland National Park, close to the Scottish border, Kielder Forest covers an area of 153,000 acres (62,000ha) with mainly Sitka spruce. There is estimated to be 150 million trees in the forest. Timber production is ongoing and an increasing diversity of trees is being planted. The forest is home to deer, red squirrels and many birds of prey, and surrounds Kielder Water, the largest man-made lake in Europe. Ideal for walking, cycling, boating and fishing, the area has three visitor centres and numerous tourist facilities. Sculpture trails and public art are also among the attractions in the Kielder area.

☎ 01434 220643 www.kielder.org

Laing Art Gallery — 404 E2

Internationally renowned watercolours hang in a dedicated gallery and the extensive collection of oil paintings include works by John Martin, Joshua Reynolds, Thomas Gainsborough, Holman Hunt, Burne Jones and a growing number of contemporary paintings. With the emphasis on locally produced decorative art, the Laing also has collections of silver, glass and ceramics. 'Art on Tyneside' illustrates the history of the region's art and craft traditions and there is a gallery specifically aimed at young children.

☎ 0191 232 7734

Life Science Centre — 404 F1

Interactive and entertaining educational centre which illustrates some of the mysteries of life. In innovative ways, such as a motion simulator ride and a sound and light show in a theatre modelled as a brain, the centre takes a look at evolution, the basics of DNA, what all living things have in common and what goes on in the human mind. Housed in a striking modern building next to Newcastle main line rail station.

☎ 0191 243 8223 www.lifesciencecentre.org.uk

National Glass Centre — 411 A3

An innovative metal and glass building on the north bank of the River Wear, dedicated to the use of glass in the fields of design and technology, and as contemporary art. Exhibitions and interactive galleries look at the centuries-old tradition of glassmaking in Sunderland, and illustrate the many and surprising ways in which glass is used today. Visitors may walk along the glass roof and watch students from the University of Sunderland in the glass factory. Master craftspeople also give regular demonstrations of glassmaking.

☎ 0191 515 5555 www.nationalglasscentre.com

Ormesby Hall (NT) — 253 E1

Set in an attractive garden, this 18th century Palladian mansion has some notable interior plasterwork and carved wood decoration. There is an impressive stable block still in use and a restored Victorian laundry and kitchen with scullery and game larder. Also of interest is a model railway exhibition.

☎ 01642 324188 www.nationaltrust.org.uk

Queen Elizabeth II Country Park — 271 E3

Once the site of one of the largest colliery spoil heaps in Europe, this landscaped country park features maturing woodland, a 40 acre (16ha) lake and a variety of wildlife. Ideal for picnics and walks. A cycle path runs around the lake where canoeing, windsurfing and fishing are popular. The Woodhorn Colliery Museum, on the edge of the park, is housed in former colliery buildings, and a narrow gauge railway runs for 0.6 miles (1km) linking the museum to the lakeside.

☎ 01670 856968

Raby Castle — 262 A5

An impressive medieval castle set in a 200 acre (80ha) deer park, Raby was built by the Nevills and has been home to Lord Barnard's family for over 350 years. The interior chambers provide many historical insights and range from the Barons' Hall, where 700 knights gathered to plot the 'Rising of the North', to the medieval kitchen which was used until 1954. Many of the rooms date from the 18th and 19th centuries and contain works of art and fine furniture. Visitors can also enjoy the grounds which include a large walled garden, rose garden and old yew hedges.

☎ 01833 660202 www.rabycastle.com

Seaton Delaval Hall — 271 F4

A splendid Palladian mansion designed by Sir John Vanbrugh in 1718, after he had already completed Blenheim Palace and Castle Howard. The central turreted block has a grand portico and is flanked by two substantial wings which creates a vast forecourt. A fine parterre, pond and fountain created in the 20th century complements the house and there are impressive stables in the east wing. Limited opening.

☎ 0191 237 1493

Shipley Art Gallery — 372 A2

An arts and crafts museum with a renowned collection of contemporary furniture, textiles, metalwork, ceramics, glass and jewellery. By way of contrast, there are some old masters paintings and an exhibition illustrating the history of Gateshead.

☎ 0191 477 1495

South Shields Museum & Art Gallery — 372 D1

This museum brings to life the 20th century social history of South Tyneside and illustrates the dramatic changes which have taken place during that time. Also features the story of popular novelist Catherine Cookson who was born locally in 1906 and whose writing reflects the life and times of the area. Alongside the museum's art collection, the interactive art gallery gives visitors the opportunity to explore the techniques and materials used by artists.

☎ 0191 456 8740

Teesdale Hay Meadows, Forest-in-Teesdale — 261 E5

The rich grasslands of the North Pennines provide a wonderful display in summer when the hay meadows are awash with a striking variety and abundance of tall grasses. Additionally, a vast assortment of wild flowers, including wood anemone, frog orchid, adder's tongue fern and ragged robin will be found blossoming amongst the grasses. The area also attracts nesting farmland birds such as redshank, skylark and meadow pipit.

Vindolanda (Chesterholm) Roman Fort — 261 D1

The remains of a Roman fort (AD127) and surrounding civilian settlement about 2 miles (3km) south of Hadrian's Wall. There are ongoing excavations and archaeologists have revealed a succession of forts on the site. The well-preserved artefacts in the museum include armour, boots, shoes, jewellery and coins. Among the most significant finds have been letters and documents written in ink on wood; photographs of these tablets are on display. A section of Hadrian's Wall has been reconstructed in timber and stone to its original height and there are full-scale replicas of a Roman temple, shop, house and a Northumbrian croft.

☎ 01434 344277 www.vindolanda.com

Wallington (NT) — 270 C3

Built in 1688, Wallington was for generations home to the Blackett and Trevelyan families. The house contains fine rococo plasterwork and the central hall is decorated in Pre-Raphaelite style with pictures reflecting Northumbrian history. There are paintings and porcelain as well as a collection of dolls' houses. The extensive grounds include a beautiful walled garden and Edwardian conservatory, woodland and a path along the banks of the River Wansbeck.

☎ 01670 773600 www.nationaltrust.org.uk

Warkworth Castle — 271 E1

Standing on a hill above the River Coquet, the well-preserved ruins dominate the town of Warkworth. The castle was once home to the powerful Percy family and was the setting for several scenes in Shakespeare's 'Henry IV'. Dating mainly from the 12th to the 14th centuries, the remains include a magnificent eight-towered keep, chapel, great hall and decorated lion tower. Special events for visitors are regularly staged here.

☎ 01665 711423 www.english-heritage.org.uk

Wildfowl & Wetlands Trust Washington — 372 C3

Many species of waterbirds can be enjoyed in any season in this area of ponds and woodland. It provides a stopping place and wintering habitat for migratory birds after their flight across the North Sea. Large numbers of curlew and redshank roost here and there is a breeding colony of heron. The site is easily accessible with well laid out paths. It has hides and an excellent visitor centre.

☎ 0191 416 5454

Yeavering Bell — 278 D4

This hill at the edge of the Cheviots is crowned by the largest Iron Age hillfort in Northumbria covering 14 acres (6ha) with a stone rampart enclosing much of the summit. A steep path leads to the top, from where there are spectacular views over the surrounding landscape.

WALES

Dwelling in the "Land of Song", the Welsh nation treasures a proud culture based on Europe's oldest language which is still very much alive today. Three sides of the predominantly rural principality are fringed with beckoning shorelines. Sparkling water tumbles down the rugged mountainsides into beautiful lakes which act as mirrors for the stunning scenery and ever changing sky. Experience the grandeur and wildness of three national parks with all their varied natural glory and absorb the Welsh history glimpsed in her castles, crafts and Celtic heritage.

Llynnau Mymbyr and Snowdon

Aberconwy House (NT) 231 F5

A 14th century merchant's house within the town of Conwy containing furnished rooms and an audiovisual presentation. Displays depict scenes of daily life from nearly six centuries.

☎ 01492 592246 www.nationaltrust.org.uk

Aberdulais Falls (NT) 350 D1

Natural waterfalls in the Vale of Neath provide the energy for a fascinating industrial site with a unique hydroelectric scheme. Over four centuries, a waterwheel provided the power for the production of copper and tin goods. Today the Turbine House contains an interactive computer, fish pass, display panels and an observation window with good views of the falls.

☎ 01639 636674 www.nationaltrust.org.uk

Aberglasney Gardens 192 B5

Restored in recent years to reveal Jacobean origins, the 10 acres (4ha) of colourful gardens lie in a valley east of Carmarthen. Known as 'The Garden Lost in Time', the area features pools, a yew tunnel, walled gardens, an ancient cloister garden and woodland, as well as collections of rare plants.

☎ 01558 668998 www.aberglasney.org.uk

Abergwesyn Pass 193 E2

A scenic, remote 14 mile (22km) drive crosses the Cambrian Mountains following an old drovers' route. The lower forests give way to high, deserted moorland providing a taste of wild Wales.

Afan Argoed Country Park 179 E3

Deep in the Afan valley, inland from Port Talbot, the Forest Park covers 25 tranquil square miles (10 ha) with trails for walking and cycling, orienteering, picnic areas, camping, pony trekking and educational visits. The visitor centre features the history and wildlife of the area, including historical remains from early settlements and the South Wales Miners' Museum created by ex-colliers. Charge for car parking in summer.

☎ 01639 850564 www.neath-porttalbot.gov.uk

Anglesey Sea Zoo 217 D1

A varied collection of local marine life is housed in Wales' largest marine aquarium, on the shores of the Menai Strait. The Sea Zoo has a walk-through shipwreck, lobster hatchery and discovery pools, as well as a shark pool and fish forest. Tropical displays are also included and conservation is an important aspect of the work of the zoo. Outside is an adventure playground, boating lake and seasonal crab fishing.

☎ 01248 430411 www.angleseyseazoo.co.uk

Barry Island Pleasure Park 165 E1

Occupying a promontory south of Cardiff, the Park has over 50 rides and attractions including the popular Log Flume, Viper Rollercoaster, Sea Ray Pirate Ship and Galloping Horses. The Park is surrounded by shops and catering facilities.

☎ 01446 732844 www.barryisland.com

Beaumaris Castle 231 E5

The castle sits in the town of Beaumaris, on the shores of the Menai Strait, and offers fine views across to the mountains of Snowdonia. This was the last and largest of King Edward's edifices, erected to establish his authority over the Welsh. Beaumaris Castle was started in 1295 and, although never fully completed, it remains remarkably intact and is a designated UNESCO World Heritage Site.

Here is an impressive example of military architecture, having an outer moat and perfectly symmetrical double concentric walls within. The fortified dock has moorings for ships of considerable size. The high walls, gatehouses and strong towers were intended as stout defences, but the castle never came under attack. The inner buildings accommodated a Great Hall, luxurious rooms, kitchens, stables and a chapel. Visitors can also explore the fascinating interior passageways found inside the walls of the inner ward.

☎ 01248 810361 www.cadw.wales.gov.uk

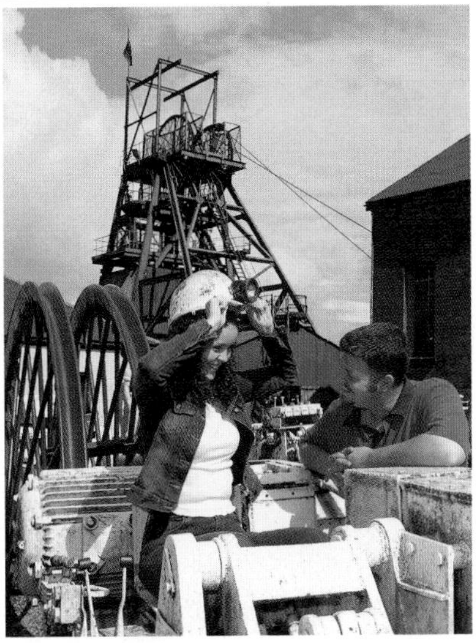

Big Pit Mining Museum

Big Pit Mining Museum 180 B2

Overlooking a traditional mining valley at Blaenavon, Big Pit had been a working coal mine for over 200 years until its closure in 1980. The present tour guides are all former miners. On the surface are colliery workings, reconstructed buildings and the old pit-head baths to explore, but the main attraction is the 300ft (90m) descent in the pit cage; hard hat and lamp are provided. The hour-long guided tour recalls life at the coal face and leads through underground roadways, air doors and stables to the shafts and coal faces. Warm clothing and appropriate footwear are advised and restrictions apply to young children going underground. The whole experience merits two to three hours and catering is supplied by the original miners' canteen. Education packs are available and special events are arranged throughout the season.

☎ 01495 790311 www.nmgw.ac.uk/bigpit

Beaumaris Castle

Bodnant Gardens (NT) 231 G5

Renowned for the dazzling springtime and early summer blooms, these 80 acres (32.5ha) of magnificent gardens overlook the river Conwy and distant Snowdonia. An array of colours is provided, especially by the collections of rhododendrons, camellias and magnolias and a vibrant laburnum arch. The garden has been developed over its hundred year history by generations of the Aberconway family and includes a succession of terraces featuring a water lily pond, roses, a croquet lawn, a canal and magnolias. A woodland valley garden, known as The Dell, provides an attractive contrast to the formal plantings of the Italianate terraces.

At the end of the formal garden sits the Pin Mill, an early 18th century lodge which became a pin factory, then a tannery, before being transported from the west of England to its present site.

The botanical collections nurtured at Bodnant are world famous, but beauties also abound which require little knowledge of plants. The gardens are planted on a hillside and run right down to the river.

☎ 01492 650460 www.nationaltrust.org.uk

Bodnant Gardens

Brecon Beacons 193 G5

Four distinct upland ranges lie within the beautiful national park which extends over 520 sq m (837 sq km) in the heart of southern Wales. The picturesque landscape is characterised not only by gentle, grassy hillsides and light woodlands, but also by steep craggy mountains. Central are the prominent Beacons themselves, rising to 2906ft (886m) at the summit of Pen-y-Fan. In the west are the rolling hills of Fforest Fawr with their deep valleys and ancient hunting forest and also the solitary, wild Black Mountain. The range known as the Black Mountains lies at the eastern edge of the park towards the English border. The most southerly region offers a landscape of caves and waterfalls amongst the limestone pavements.

Prehistoric sites have been identified within the park and later structures follow the progress of history through the ambitious days of castle building after the Norman conquest.

Within its five visitor centres, the park authorities promote a large variety of attractions for all ages, including museums, theatres and family activity

centres. In the open air are a wealth of opportunities for walking, cycling, horse-riding, caving, gliding, watersports, golf and fishing. Expert tuition is available for trying new skills and there are facilities for hiring and purchasing appropriate equipment.

☎ 01874 624437 www.breconbeacons.org

Brecon Beacons

Brecon Beacons Visitor Centre 193 F5

At an altitude of 1100ft (335m), amidst the grandeur of the Brecon Beacon mountains, the purpose-built centre houses resource material, souvenirs, a model and displays of the area, as well as a café. The centre is surrounded by open hillside, giving wide views across the valley to the distinctive summit of Pen y Fan, the highest peak in South Wales. Informative staff and printed guides describe local points of interest and suggest a fine variety of walks, graded from easy to moderate.

☎ 01874 623366 www.breconbeacons.org

Brecon Mountain Railway 179 G1

This narrow-gauge railway, starting at Pant Station just north of Merthyr Tydfil, follows a scenic 3.5 mile (5km) track into the Brecon Beacon mountains. The all-weather observation coaches are hauled by a vintage steam locomotive; the return journey takes just over an hour. Panoramic views abound from the end station where there are many opportunities for walks and a picnic site. Special events are organised at certain times of year and the train can be hired for parties.

☎ 01685 722988 www.breconmountainrailway.co.uk

Caernarfon Castle

Cadair Idris 204 C1

Steeped in Celtic legends, the beautiful 11 mile (17km) ridge of Cadair Idris, on the southern flank of the Snowdonia National Park, comprises five peaks, with the highest point, Penygadair, at almost 3000ft (900m). A variety of tracks, varying in difficulty, lead to the ridge, and all give breathtaking views of the surrounding countryside and the distant coast.

Caerleon Roman Fortress, Baths & Amphitheatre 351 D1

North of Newport stand the substantial remains of a Roman fortress, including the baths, barrack blocks, fortress wall and 5000-seater amphitheatre, together with an imaginative Roman legionary museum. This is the site of the significant 50 acre (20ha) Roman fortress of Isca, encompassing a complete town dating from AD75, with much still on view. The museum shows how the Romans lived and fought, with interactive displays and special events suitable for all ages, sufficient for several hours' visit.

☎ 01633 423134 www.nmgw.ac.uk

Caernarfon Castle 217 D1

Built on a promontory projecting out into the Menai Strait, this UNESCO World Heritage Site castle dominates the town of Caernarfon and has survived in fine condition. Construction was started by Edward I in 1283 as part of his ring of castles intended to control Welsh uprisings, and it was planned as a royal residence and seat of government. The building was completed by Edward II in 1322. Massive walls run between the 11 great polygonal towers, topped by battlemented wall walks, giving the castle formidable defences. Also incorporated into the scheme were drawbridges, heavy doors and six portcullises. Each of the towers is different and one included a water gate enabling supplies to be brought by sea.

The Queen's Tower houses the regimental museum of the Royal Welch Fusiliers. An audiovisual presentation explains the history and customs associated with the castle. Continuing a tradition established by Edward I, the castle is the venue for the investiture of the Prince of Wales, as was the scene in 1969 when Prince Charles was presented to the people here.

☎ 01286 677617 www.cadw.wales.gov.uk

Caerphilly Castle 351 A1

Right in the town centre, Caerphilly is the largest castle in Wales, but was never a royal residence. It

Caerphilly Castle

was built by Red Gilbert de Clare to defend the territory of Henry III against Welsh Prince Llywelyn the Last. The medieval fortress, started in 1268, occupies a strategically important 30 acre (12ha) site, having a complex design of massive gatehouses, water defences and stout concentric walls. The most unusual feature of the castle is one of the towers which leans outwards at an angle ten degrees from vertical – the result of subsidence.

An extensive water system provided the first point of defence around the castle, followed by a rectangular enclosure with robust outer and inner walls. The latter contain two great gatehouses and the remains of the hall. In the heart of the castle are the living areas, together with kitchens, a chapel and domestic quarters.

Over the past 200 years the complex has undergone much restoration. Visitors can watch an audiovisual display and see replica siege engines in the visitor centre.

☎ 029 2088 3143 www.cadw.wales.gov.uk

Cardiff Castle & Museum 392 E2

The castle is situated in the heart of the city and was commissioned in Victorian times by the 3rd

Marquess of Bute in an elaborate neogothic style. Highly decorative, fantasy adornments abound, particularly in the clock tower, fountains and lavish interiors. The Welsh Regiment Museum is situated within the castle grounds.

☎ 029 2087 8100 www.cardiffcastle.com

Carew Castle 176 D2

The substantial ruins of Carew Castle stand on river meadows between the village and an ancient tidal mill. The castle was built between the 13th and 16th centuries and was the site of the Great Tournament of 1507. Firstly a Norman stronghold, then an elegant royal Elizabethan residence, it displays many fine architectural features. A circular walk links the castle, mill, causeway, millpond, 11th century Celtic cross and medieval bridge.

☎ 01646 651782 www.carewcastle.com

Carreg Cennen Castle 178 C1

These old ruins, high on a crag near Trapp in the Black Mountains, were rebuilt in the 13th and 19th centuries. Visitors can explore prehistoric caves, battlements and vaulted passageways, and enjoy the outlook from the grassy hilltop.

☎ 01558 822291 www.cadw.wales.gov.uk

Castell Dinas Bran (Ruins) 219 F3

Both a hillfort and medieval castle, the ruins stand high above Llangollen. It is reputedly the final hiding place of the Holy Grail, a treasured Christian relic. Access is by public footpath taking some 20 minutes each way.

☎ 01938 553670

Celtica 204 D3

This multimedia presentation focusing on the Celts is housed in Y Plas, a 17th century mansion just outside Machynlleth. The lively experience provides information on the heritage and culture of the Celts by way of an hour-long audio tour through eight themed galleries. Topics range from culture and beliefs to life as a tribe member, and are located within areas described, for example, as the Vortex, the Foundry, the Roundhouse and The Forest.

☎ 01654 702702 www.celticawales.com

Centre For Alternative Technology 205 D2

Situated in the hills north of Machynlleth, the Centre for Alternative Technology has been operating for over 25 years by a charity raising awareness of environmental concerns in daily living. The gardens and visitor centre provide information on renewable energy, environmental building, energy efficiency and organic cultivation in a captivating and educational way. Seven acres (3ha) of the site are on public display and can be accessed in summer by a water-balanced cliff railway. Attractions and resources are suitable for all ages.

☎ 01654 702400 www.cat.org.uk

Ceredigion Museum 204 B4

A restored Edwardian theatre is home to this museum of local history from the Stone Age to modern times. Displays include items of archaeology, folk life, agriculture, crafts, industry and art.

☎ 01970 633088 www.ceredigion.gov.uk

Chepstow Castle 181 E3

Strategically set overlooking a Wye Valley gorge, Chepstow was one of the first stone castles to be built in Britain. Construction was commenced in 1068 as a stronghold for the Norman conquest of south-east Wales and is unusual in having no early timber base. Over successive centuries the defences were enlarged and in the 12th century the impressive edifice was divided into four separate, connecting sections. Towering over the present-day entrance is the gatehouse containing a prison in one of its round towers. Further additions included a second hall, tower, gatehouse and comfortable living quarters with well-equipped kitchens and storerooms.

The castle came under siege twice during the Civil War and now visitors can see exhibitions on the history of its construction. Life-sized models of the medieval lords who occupied the castle, and a dramatic Civil War battle scene illustrate the changing role of Chepstow Castle through the Middle Ages. Outdoor evening theatre is often performed here in summer.

☎ 01291 624065 www.cadw.wales.gov.uk

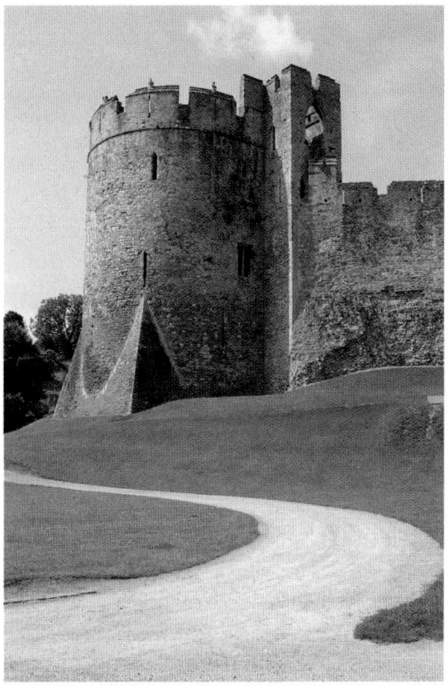

Chepstow Castle

Chepstow Museum 181 E3

An elegant town house has been transformed into a museum describing the town's colourful history in imaginative settings. Displays and artistic interpretations show the development of Chepstow as a fortified stronghold and busy port.

☎ 01291 625981 www.chepstow.co.uk

Chirk Castle (NT) 219 F4

The castle, to the west of Chirk, still has the original 14th century high walls and drum towers and has been continuously occupied for over 400 years. The state rooms contain fine items of furniture, tapestries and portraits. The formal gardens adjoining the castle contain superb yews, roses and climbing plants, whilst further away lie a hawk house, rock garden and shrub garden with pool. Parkland surrounds the estate and particularly noteworthy are the wrought iron entrance gates.

☎ 01691 777701 www.nationaltrust.org.uk

Colby Woodland Garden (NT) 177 E2

The garden is set in 8 acres (3ha) of beautiful woodland in a sheltered valley leading to the south Pembrokeshire coast at Amroth. The colourful bluebells, rhododendrons and azaleas are at their best in late spring, but at other times plants also feature around a themed sculpture trail, a walled kitchen garden and a Gothic-style gazebo.

☎ 01834 811885 www.nationaltrust.org.uk

Conwy Castle 231 F5

Occupying an imposing location over the river in the centre of Conwy town, the castle is one of the most important examples of military architecture in Europe. It was built for Edward I in 1283-9 by 1500 craftsmen, with supplies brought in by sea. Eight huge drum towers with pinnacled battlements dominate the two wards of the castle. The large outer ward was accessed from the town, whereas the inner ward, with the royal apartments, was approached only by water. The Middle Gate connected the two sections. The building remains in an excellent state of preservation, despite having suffered attacks during the Civil War and later.

An exhibition portrays Edward I and his campaign of castle building. The panoramic views from the top of the turrets stretch to the distant mountains and out across the sea, but the castle itself is best viewed from the far side of the estuary.

☎ 01492 592358 www.cadw.wales.gov.uk

Cosmeston Country Park 165 E1

Old quarries just west of Cardiff have been transformed into a 200 acre (81ha) landscaped park, featuring two lakes with watersports, facilities for children, orienteering courses, a forest school, bridleways, a sculpture trail and a maths trail. Woodland, grassland and wetlands support conservation areas. Within the park lies a 14th century reconstructed medieval village which hosts special events throughout the year and which can be toured on payment of an entrance charge.

☎ 029 2070 1678 www.valeofglamorgan.gov.uk

Criccieth Castle 217 E4

Overlooking Tremadog Bay, the ruins include the inner wall, impressive gatehouse and original wall walk dating from the 13th century. A cartoon video shows the story of Gerald of Wales and other Welsh princes.

☎ 01766 52227 www.cadw.wales.gov.uk

Conwy Castle

Denbigh Castle 219 D1

The ruins of this Norman fortification overlook Denbigh town. It retains a large gatehouse, three towers, a steep barbican and an ancient, weathered statue, probably of Edward I.

☎ 01745 813385 www.cadw.wales.gov.uk

Erddig

Dinefwr Park (NT) 192 C5

Pleasant walks cross this wooded parkland just outside Llandeilo. Deer have been a feature of the estate for over one thousand years and Lancelot 'Capability' Brown designed the landscape around a medieval castle and Newton House.

☎ 01558 823902 www.nationaltrust.org.uk

Dolaucothi Gold Mine (NT) 192 C3

At Pumsaint, in deepest Wales, the Romans discovered gold deposits in the river Cothi and evidence remains of their sophisticated and ingenious tunnels, aqueducts and caverns. A second gold rush followed in the late nineteenth century and now visitors, equipped with miners' lamps and helmets, can tour the workings, hear the history and try gold panning for themselves. Waymarked paths lead through the surrounding wooded hillsides.

☎ 01558 825146 www.nationaltrust.org.uk

Elan Valley Visitor Centre 192 F1

Four artificial lakes were created in the valley in the early 20th century to provide water for Birmingham. The Visitor Centre is approached from Rhayader and contains an exhibition and interactive resources on the history and nature of the area, renowned for its birdlife. Walks lead around the reservoirs in the peaceful Cambrian mountains, giving good vantage points of the dams and drowned valleys. The area is particularly attractive in autumn.

☎ 01597 810880 www.elanvalley.org.uk

Electric Mountain 217 E1

A fascinating view inside the Dinorwig hydroelectric station near Llanberis includes interactive exhibitions and art galleries. Visitors can book an underground minibus tour deep inside the mountain to see the enormous turbines in action. The natural science theatre offers a presentation on the natural history of the Snowdonia area.

☎ 01286 870636 www.electricmountain.co.uk

Erddig (NT) 220 A3

Dating from the 18th century, this impressive estate near Wrexham was the home of the Yorke family, whose generosity towards their staff can be appreciated by viewing the large house. The grand 'upstairs' state rooms boast fine collections of furniture and original artefacts, whilst 'below stairs' the servants' quarters give fascinating glimpses into the lives of the workers. An extensive range of outbuildings are also of considerable interest and include a display of vintage vehicles in the stable yard. There is much to attract all ages, and regular event days are planned throughout the season, including horse-drawn carriage rides.

Walks lead through the garden areas into a large park with woodland. The gardens feature an array of speciality fruit trees, the national collection of ivies, a Victorian parterre and yew walks.

As most rooms have no electric lighting, it is advisable to visit on bright days to fully appreciate the pictures and textiles.

☎ 01978 315151 www.nationaltrust.org.uk

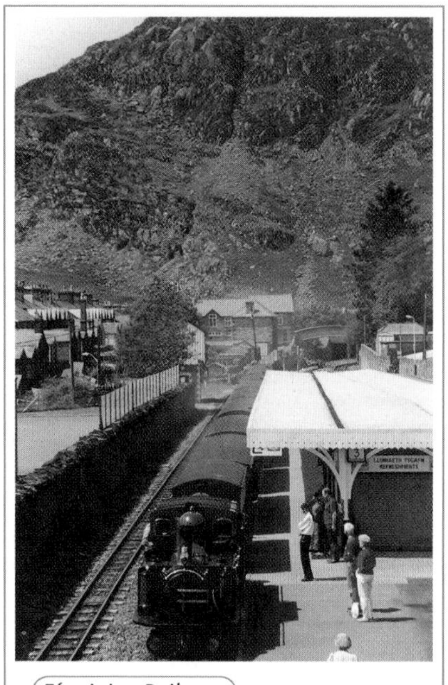

Ffestiniog Railway

Ffestiniog Railway 217 F3

The 13.5 mile (20km) narrow-gauge railway links Blaenau Ffestiniog with the harbour at Porthmadog. Now it is a quaint passenger ride, but it was first opened in 1836 as a means of carrying slate from the quarries. The high demand for slate brought steam power to the line, which is one of its main attractions. Interesting feats of engineering can be observed on the journey, including the Cob, a substantial embankment across the river estuary, and, higher up near Tanygrisiau, the only spiral on a public railway in Britain.

Not only is the railway, with its original rolling stock, appealing to enthusiasts, but the location amidst the glorious scenery of Snowdonia makes the route highly popular with all visitors. It is possible to leave the train at a number of stations en route and the situation of Tan-y-Bwlch station makes it an ideal starting point for beautiful walks. Blaenau Ffestiniog station is now linked with the standard gauge line from Llandudno Junction. Shops can be found at three of the stations, with displays and stocks of railway memorabilia and souvenirs. The railway runs to a set timetable and offers special 'Guest Driving' days.

☎ 01766 516024 www.festrail.co.uk

Glynn Vivian Art Gallery & Museum 411 E2

The gallery contains examples of fine art, decorative and applied art, costume, textiles and archives. Of special interest is the collection of porcelain and Swansea china, in addition to the contributions from contemporary Welsh artists.

☎ 01792 516900 www.swansea.gov.uk

Gower 178 A4

The peninsula of Gower, west of Swansea, is 15 miles (24km) long and about 6 miles (10km) wide with many historical features. Gower is also an Area of Outstanding Natural Beauty thanks to both its coastal and inland environments. The shoreline follows cliffs, dunes, beaches, marshes and river estuaries, whilst the interior comprises pleasant hills, valleys, woods, heaths, caves and commons. Gower Heritage Centre at Parkmill contains a crafts and rural life museum based around a working medieval water mill.

www.swansea.gov.uk

Great Aberystwyth Camera Obscura 204 B4

High on Constitution Hill at the north end of town, and accessed by a cliff railway, this is the world's biggest Camera Obscura. The huge 14 inch (35cm) lens focuses on over 1000 square miles (400 ha) of land and seascape, all reflected onto a circular screen in the viewing gallery below.

☎ 01970 617642 www.cardiganshirecoastandcountry.com

Great Orme Country Park 231 F4

The imposing headland to the west of Llandudno is 2 miles (3km) long and can be accessed by footpaths, road, bus, Victorian Tramway or cabin lift. Of interest are the geology, rich wildlife, archaeology and landscape of the peninsula, in addition to a visitor centre, gardens, a copper mine, and leisure facilities such as a ski slope and a programme of events on land and water.

☎ 01492 874151 www.conwy.gov.uk

Harlech Castle 217 E4

This rugged castle was built on the rocks above Cardigan Bay, once lapped by waves, but now overlooking sand dunes where the sea has retreated. Construction began during Edward I's second campaign in Wales from 1283, and its protected position, walls and artillery platforms made the castle stoutly defensible. It was taken by Owain Glyndwr in the siege of 1404, in the last great uprising of the Welsh against the occupying English, and was held by him for four years.

The castle is concentric, with strong outer walls. The inner walls contained the main living quarters, and the imposing twin-towered gatehouse, with its residential apartments, is one of the main features of the castle. The massive eastern façade, the guardroom and the castle's wide round towers, designed to intimidate attackers, are all impressive. The entrance is at the position of a second drawbridge which

Harlech Castle

used to lower onto towers, of which only the foundations remain. The mighty structure commands superb views out to sea and to the mountains of Snowdonia.

☎ 01766 780552 www.cadw.wales.gov.uk

Kidwelly Castle 178 A2

The substantial and well preserved remains of Kidwelly Castle, south of Carmarthen, are set within the site of an earlier earth and timber ringwork. The massive, concentric castle was started in the mid 13th century and developed impressively over three centuries, eventually becoming a judicial court. The entrance is guarded by a large gatehouse and visitors can climb the round towers, walk on the extensive walls and explore the dungeons.

☎ 01554 890104 www.cadw.wales.gov.uk

Lamphey Palace 176 D2

Just east of Pembroke, the ruins of this medieval bishop's palace remain an impressive sight, surrounded by fishponds, orchards and parkland. Of particular note are the shell of the Great Hall and the chapel.

☎ 01646 672224 www.pembroke-wales.uk.com

Llanberis Lake Railway 217 E1

This scenic narrow-gauge railway skirts Lake Padarn, near Llanberis, with great views of Snowdon. Steam locomotives haul the tourist carriages and the return trip of 5 miles (8km) takes about an hour, including stops.

☎ 01286 870549 www.lake-railway.freeserve.co.uk

Llanerchaeron (NT) 192 A2

This little-changed 1790s gentleman's estate comprises a carefully restored, Nash-designed house with outbuildings, now operating as an organic farm. Produce is on sale and walks lead through the wooded valleys.

☎ 01558 825147 www.nationaltrust.org.uk

Llansteffan Castle (ruins) 177 G1

The castle ruins sit on a steep ridge overlooking Carmarthen Bay and are witness to its expansion since its Norman origins. Visible now are two baileys surrounded by thick walls and a Tudor gatehouse.

☎ 01267 241756 www.cadw.wales.gov.uk

Llanthony Priory (ruins) 194 B5

Hidden in a remote valley in the Black Mountains, the substantial ruins of this ancient Cistercian priory form a striking picture against the green surrounding hillsides. The priory was built in the 12th century and includes examples of both Gothic and Norman architecture. The monastic foundation was soon abandoned and the buildings fell into disuse. However, today there is a small inn and hotel built into the part of the priory where the abbot would once have lived.

☎ 029 2082 6185 www.cadw.wales.gov.uk

Llechwedd Slate Caverns 218 A3

Tours of the massive slate caverns in Blaenau Ffestiniog include underground rides, sound and light shows, and a hard hat walk bringing to life the days of the Victorian miners. The Deep Mine tour descends steeply by railway car and the Miners' Tramway focuses on the historical details of the industry. On the surface stands the original Llechwedd village with facilities for visitors.

☎ 01766 830306 www.llechwedd-slate-caverns.co.uk

Manorbier Castle 177 D3

Accessed by a delightful narrow lane, Manorbier Castle overlooks a sandy bay in south Pembrokeshire. Once a Norman stronghold, today's structure dates from the 12th century and is in remarkably good condition. The castle has many interesting features, including a baronial hall, stout gatehouse, state apartments, gardens and a chapel. The family of the current owners have lived here for over 300 years and it was the birthplace, in 1146, of Giraldus Cambrensis who wrote extensively of his travels around Wales.

☎ 01834 871394

Museum of Welsh Life 180 A5

A fascinating open-air museum covering 100 acres (40ha) near Cardiff illustrates the rich heritage of Wales, showing lifestyles, buildings and traditions through five hundred years of folk history. Original buildings have been transported here from many parts of Wales and painstakingly reconstructed, including craftsmen's workshops, a school, cottages, shops, a mill, farmhouse and a chapel. Demonstrations of many crafts enliven a visit and hands-on opportunities are available for visitors to try their skills. Produce from the farm, mill and other sources on the site are often on sale.

The museum is situated in the grounds of the impressive St Fagans castle which is also open, as are the surrounding gardens. Purpose-built, large indoor galleries house exhibits of costume, daily life and farming implements. Traditional festivals, music and dance events are staged regularly throughout the year. To do justice to the whole enterprise, which has no entrance charge, and to allow time to explore the extensive grounds, at least a half day visit is recommended.

☎ 029 2057 3500 www.nmgw.ac.uk

National Botanic Garden of Wales 178 B1

The Millennium showpiece Garden of Wales lies in the Tywi Valley, upstream from Carmarthen in a peaceful 18th century park of 568 acres (230ha). With the aim of raising awareness of the natural and manmade world, it focuses on conservation, horticulture, science, the arts, leisure and education.

The centrepiece of the garden is the impressive Great Glasshouse, designed by Norman Foster to hold 1000 panes and containing plants from the world over in their natural climates. Outside, the landscape has been built with a deep ravine, rock terraces, waterfalls and lakes to display a multitude of different plantings. Separate sections include a genetic garden and a physic garden. Visitors are encouraged to enjoy the sights, taste the country, experience the sounds, and smell the seasonal scents.

The Gallery in the Garden has a changing schedule of exhibitions on themes such as arts and science, botanical illustration, photography, traditional and contemporary art. Educational programmes are geared to all ages using state-of-the-art technology, and the Garden has become an internationally renowned centre for botanical science.

☎ 01558 668768 www.gardenofwales.org.uk

National Museum & Gallery 392 E2

Found in the heart of Cardiff, this lively museum covers the fascinating 4600 million year history of Wales up to the present day. It is well known for its art treasures, particularly the fine collection of French Impressionist works, but also covers science and natural history through interactive hands-on exhibits. Special events are staged for families, and temporary exhibitions merit further enquiry.

☎ 029 2039 7951 www.nmgw.ac.uk

National Showcaves Centre for Wales 178 B1

An awesome series of natural caves under the Brecon Beacons at Dan-yr-Ogof offers a variety of attractions suitable for the whole family. Self-guided tours lead through the skilfully illuminated chambers of the huge Cathedral showcave and the Bronze Age Bone cave, accompanied by commentaries. It is advisable to wear warm clothing and stout shoes. Other areas are devoted to an Iron Age farm, dinosaur park, museum, shire horse centre and farmyard.

☎ 01639 730801 www.showcaves.co.uk

National Woollen Museum 191 G4

A former, busy woollen mill in northern Carmarthenshire has been transformed into a

National Botanic Garden of Wales

museum on the history of the industry. Working exhibitions demonstrate the technical process of 19th century production from the fleece to the fabric. Within the grounds are craft workshops and also Melin Teifi, a fully working mill.

☎ 01559 370929 www.nmgw.ac.uk

Newborough Warren 216 D1

This long stretch of dunes to the south-west of Anglesey is part of a nature reserve, giving distant views to Snowdonia. Natural life abounds and footpaths also give access to a pine forest.

Oakwood Leisure Park 177 D1

Well signposted in south Pembrokeshire, Oakwood is a major theme park with some of the fastest, tallest and wettest rides in the country. Children are catered for with age-appropriate attractions, including the KidzWorld play area. In summer holidays the park stays open until 10pm for a spectacular fireworks and waterscreen light show.

☎ 01834 891373 www.oakwood-leisure.com

Oystermouth Castle (ruins) 350 A3

Although ruined, Oystermouth Castle, on its mound at the west of Swansea Bay, is well preserved. Of note are its late 13th century decorated windows, gatehouse, chapel and Great Hall.

☎ 01792 368732 www.cadw.wales.gov.uk

Pembrey Country Park 178 A2

A 500 acre (202ha) wooded park, Pembrey lies on a sandy stretch of coast south of Carmarthen. The 8 mile (13 km) long Cefn Sidan beach is noted for its swimming and fishing. Other facilities provided (some with entrance charges) are crazy golf, dry ski slope, forest walks, nature trails, horse riding and a small railway.

☎ 01554 833913 www.carmarthenshire.gov.uk

Pembroke Castle 176 C2

Its defensive situation above the river in Pembroke enhances the grandeur of this largely intact castle. The birthplace of Henry VII, the first Tudor king, it has a remarkable history dating back 800 years. The stronghold survived ferocious attacks during the Civil War, but still much remains, including the enormous 80ft (24m) high round keep, thick ramparts, a gatehouse, barbican, Great Hall and dungeon tower. There is an interpretive centre, brass rubbing and special living history days in summer.

☎ 01646 681510 www.pembrokeshirecoast.org

Pembrokeshire Coast National Park 176 B3

Britain's only truly coastal national park covers 240 sq m (620 sq km) of spectacular landscape around Wales' south-western shore. It is renowned for its beautiful scenery, prolific variety of wildlife and historic significance.

The 200 mile (320km) coastal path can be strenuous in parts, but many stretches provide gentler walks. Nowhere in the park is further than 10 miles (16km) distant from the sea. The landscape ranges from steep cliffs to expansive beaches, wooded slopes and inland hills, all supporting special habitats for many rare and endangered plants, birds and animals. Grey seals, porpoises and dolphins may be glimpsed off shore, and some of the maritime islands are home to huge, protected colonies of seabirds. Inland areas are also worth exploring to discover rare plants and insects in the woodlands, heath and marsh areas.

Signs of human activity across the centuries are found in the shape of tombs, burial cairns, castles, crosses, cottages, quarries and quays. The many Iron Age forts, Norman castles and monuments are reminders of the people who lived here over the centuries and of the area's place in history.

☎ 01437 764636 www.pembrokeshirecoast.org

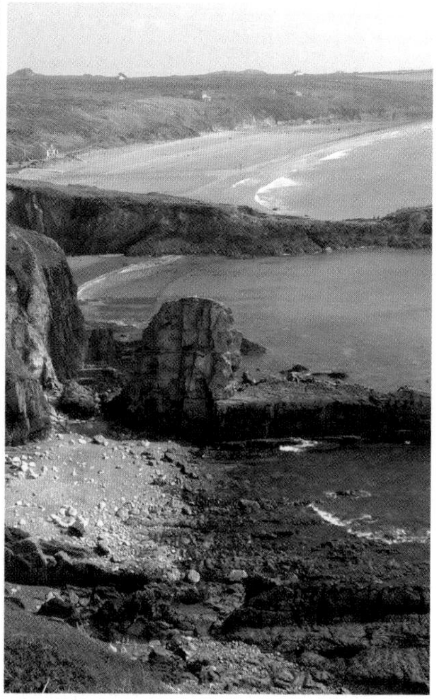

Pembrokeshire Coast

Penhow Castle 180 D3

This is reputedly Wales' oldest lived-in castle, spanning 860 years. Once the home of medieval knights, it is now the ancestral home of the Seymour family. Tours lead from the drawbridge through the historic periods, visiting the battlements, Norman keep and bedchamber, Great Hall with a minstrels' gallery, the Victorian housekeeper's room and kitchens. The entrance fee includes a choice of themed audio tours, such as musical, domestic history, cooks, young adventurer or, in the evening, a candlelight tour.

☎ 01633 400800 www.penhowcastle.com

Penmon Priory (ruins) 231 E4

The ruins of the 12th century priory lie at the eastern edge of Anglesey, alongside the old St Seiriol's Well, church and ancient dovecot. The rocky coastline provides views of the Puffin Island seabird colonies.

Penrhyn Castle (NT) 231 E5

This imposing 19th century castle outside Bangor was built in Norman style and contains remarkably luxurious furnishings, artworks and decor. The kitchen and service rooms have been restored to their 1894 state, ready prepared for a banquet for the Prince of Wales. Outbuildings house a railway museum and a doll museum. The 45 acres (18ha) of grounds include a walled garden, special plant collections and parkland overlooking the Menai Strait.

☎ 01248 371337 www.nationaltrust.org.uk

Pistyll Rhaeadr 219 D4

The highest waterfall in England and Wales cascades down 240ft (74m) and is known as the 'Hidden Pearl of Wales', located in the heart of the principality. It is a spectacular sight, especially after rainfall.

☎ 01691 780392 www.pistyllrhaeadr.co.uk

Plantasia 411 E3

This giant hothouse garden pyramid is found in Swansea's Parc Tawe and houses rare and exotic plants from around the world. Butterflies, insects, reptiles, fish, monkeys and birds also inhabit the three climate zones, providing visitors with a colourful and authentic atmosphere.

☎ 01792 474555 www.swansea.gov.uk

Plas Newydd, Llangollen 219 F3

Renowned as the home of the two 'Ladies of Llangollen' from 1780 to 1831, Plas Newydd is an impressive Gothic black and white house. It is noted not only as the Regency home of the independent, eccentric spinsters, but also for its interior furnishings and fittings and newly-restored, peaceful gardens.

☎ 01824 708250 www.denbighshire.gov.uk www.llangollen.com/plas/html

Plas Newydd, Anglesey (NT) 217 E1

Splendidly set on the Anglesey coast of the Menai Strait, this 18th century stately mansion, enjoying spectacular views to Snowdonia, was the former home of the Marquess of Anglesey. The house combines classical and Gothic architecture and featured inside are paintings by Rex Whistler, including his largest work. The cavalry museum in the servants' quarters commemorates the Battle of Waterloo and displays various campaign relics.

Expansive gardens offer informal walks among fine collections of flowering trees and shrubs, with many exotic plants thriving in the mild climate. In addition to the spring garden, there is a summer terrace, Australasian arboretum, a formal Italianate garden, a woodland area and an

Plas Newydd

adventure play trail. The rhododendron garden, situated some way from the house, is only open from April to early June during flowering time. Autumn, too, brings its own seasonal colours to the grounds.

A marine walk leads along the shore, and historical boat trips are available from the jetty in good weather.

☎ 01248 715272 www.nationaltrust.org.uk

Plas-yn-Rhiw (NT) 216 B5

Originating in the 16th century, this small manor house is situated towards the end of the Lleyn Peninsula, affording breathtaking sea views. Once fallen into disrepair, the attractive house has been restored and 50 acres (20ha) of gardens reclaimed, reaching down to the shoreline. The house contains much of the original furniture and utensils. Subtropical shrubs, box hedges and grass paths divide the ornamental gardens; a stream and waterfall cascade down to the sea, and snowdrop woods provide a backdrop to the house.

☎ 01758 780219 www.nationaltrust.org.uk

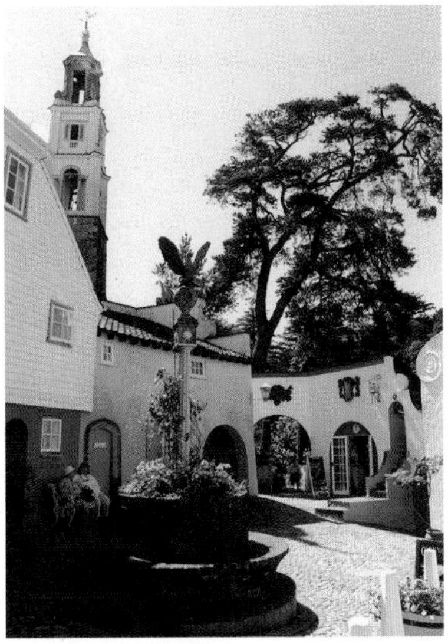

Portmeirion Village

Portmeirion Village 217 E4

This unique, if eccentric 'village' was created during the mid 20th century by the architect Clough Williams-Ellis in a flamboyant, Mediterranean style on his privately-owned peninsula on the beautiful Tremadog Bay. The 175 acres (70 ha) were transformed from a neglected wilderness into a fantasy of pastel-washed cottages, classical towers and lodges, piazzas and archways, façades and fountains, stairways and shops, grottoes and colonnades. Restaurants and hotels form an integral part of the village, as do a range of shops, including the popular Portmeirion Pottery. Here Noel Coward wrote 'Blithe Spirit', and it has been the haunt of many artists, writers and composers of world renown; the village is also well known as the location for the TV series 'The Prisoner'.

The surrounding gardens benefit from the warm influence of the Gulf Stream, enabling many subtropical plants to flourish, in addition to substantial groves of rhododendrons, azaleas and hydrangeas, and a variety of impressive evergreen trees. The woodlands enclose two lakes and reach down to sandy areas of beach and an elegant quayside. Portmeirion has a charm of its own which can only be fully experienced by allowing generous time for a visit.

☎ 01766 770000 www.portmeirion-village.com

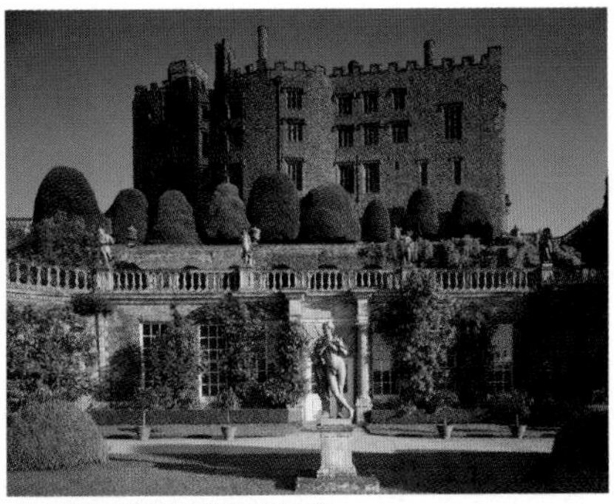

Powis Castle & Garden

Powis Castle & Garden (NT) 206 B2

Both the house and gardens of this property near Welshpool are of particular interest. The medieval castle was built on a prominent rock by Welsh princes, and over the course of later centuries was endowed with fine collections of artwork and furniture by the Herbert and Clive families. Of special note are the Clive Museum with beautiful treasures from India, and the 19th century state coach and livery in the coach house.

The castle overlooks 55 acres (22ha) of world-famous terraced gardens designed in Italian and French styles with sumptuous plantings, statues, an orangery and an aviary. Rare and tender plants are sheltered by large yew hedging; the terrace walls and herbaceous beds exude colour, and containers display imaginative arrangements of plantings. In the lower gardens can be found pyramidal apple trees, a vine tunnel and roses. An informal area of woodland was laid out in the 18th century on the ridge opposite the formal gardens and specimen trees are planted on the grassland slopes.

☎ 01938 551944 www.nationaltrust.org.uk

Raglan Castle 180 D2

Situated in central Monmouthshire, Raglan Castle is a fine example of a medieval fortress palace. Building commenced in 1435 and it developed more as a luxurious Tudor residence than a military base, although it was subjected to siege during the Civil War and was greatly damaged by Cromwell's troops. Raglan was further ransacked after the Restoration and by the 19th century had become very much a ruin. The oldest remaining structure is known as the Yellow Tower of Gwent, named after the colour of the stone from which it was built. The tower was surrounded by more walls and a moat. Later additions included the Pitched Stone Court, the Great Gatehouse and Fountain Court, the rather grand living quarters. The Great Hall is positioned between two courtyards and dates mainly from Elizabethan times.

Today's ruins give an insight into the lavish way of life of its former occupants, and hints of a French influence in elements of the architecture. The changing history of the castle is explained by displays in the closet tower and two rooms of the gatehouse.

☎ 01291 690228 www.cadw.wales.gov.uk

Rhuddlan Castle & Twt Hill 232 B5

Just south of Rhyl stand the stone remains of Edward I's 13th century stronghold. Today the most prominent structures are the gatehouse, walls and towers, as well as the decorative fireplaces of the drawing room. The grounds contain formal gardens, woodlands and ponds. Limited opening in summer only.

☎ 01745 590777 www.cadw.wales.gov.uk

St David's Cathedral & Bishop's Palace 190 A5

Situated in the heart of the charming, small city of St David's, the Cathedral has been a dominant presence since the 12th century. It was built in Norman transitional style and has undergone many transformations under successive bishops. The nearby ruins of the Bishop's Palace date from the 14th century. Many notable features adorn the cathedral, and the surrounding gardens are an additional attraction. There is a bookshop and guided tours; an annual classical music festival takes place in late spring.

☎ 01437 720517 www.stdavidscathedral.org.uk

St David's Head 190 A5

A dramatically beautiful coastline within easy walking distance from Whitesands also provides access to a ruined ancient fort. Offshore lie the islands known as The Bishops and Clerks, best viewed by boat.

Segontium Roman Museum 217 D1

The museum depicts the significant Roman occupation of the area, dating back to AD77. Excavated finds from the nearby Roman fort are displayed, plus records of this remote Roman regiment.

☎ 01286 675625 www.nmgw.ac.uk

Raglan Castle

Snowdon Mountain Railway
217 E2

Starting from Llanberis, the dramatic 4.5 mile (7km) ride to the summit of Snowdon on this Victorian rack and pinion railway takes two and a half hours return and ascends 3200ft (980m).The narrow-gauge line affords breathtaking views of Snowdonia and beyond, traversing woodlands, a viaduct and then the open mountainside with an average gradient of 1 in 8. Three of the four coal-fired steam locomotives date from the late 19th century. The trip allows half an hour at the summit station.

☎ 0870 458 0033 www.snowdonrailway.co.uk

Snowdonia National Park
217 F1

Named after the highest mountain in Wales, the national park covers 827 sq m (2142 sq km) in the counties of Gwynedd and Conwy. It is primarily a wild area of great natural beauty – a landscape of majestic mountains, lush valleys and glittering lakes, surrounded by unspoilt coastlines. The rivers of Snowdonia tumble down the mountains as rushing streams, and arrive at the sea in wide estuaries, providing, along their way, ideal habitats for a huge diversity of plants and wildlife. The area holds much appeal for the naturalist, the mountaineer, the rambler, the artist and the water lover, as well as to those who simply appreciate its stunning scenery.

The Park's study centre is located at Plas Tan y Bwlch near Maentwrog and a Welcome Centre is situated in Betws-y-Coed at one of the park gateways. The main industry of Snowdonia is still hill farming, but tourism is also a major contributor to the economy. Walking and climbing are the most popular pursuits for visitors who have over 2000 miles (3400km) of delightful footpaths to explore. The great majority of the local population regard Welsh as their first language and signs of Welsh history and culture abound, from castles to cottages and from song to sheepdog trials.

☎ 01766 770274 www.snowdonia-npa.gov.uk

South Stack Cliffs
230 A4

Bird watching and lighthouse viewing make the journey to this far tip of Holy Island well worthwhile. The spectacularly located lighthouse sits on a rocky promontory, but it is accessible only on foot via a steep descent of over 400 steps. Spring and early summer are the best times to observe the multitude of seabirds, including shearwaters, skuas, guillemots, razorbills and puffins, wheeling around the dramatic cliffsides. The visitor centre contains exhibitions on the bird life and the natural environment, plus the history of the lighthouse.

☎ 01407 762181

Strata Florida Abbey
193 D1

Cistercian monks built the abbey in the 12th century on the banks of the river Teifi in mid Wales, but only the ruined church and cloister survive from this once-important centre of learning.

☎ 02920 500200 www.cadw.wales.gov.uk

Swallow Falls
218 A2

The Welsh name Rhaeadr Ewynnol (foamy rapids) aptly describes these rushing torrents above Betws-y-Coed. A pedestrian walkway overlooks the wild river, as it carries the waters of Snowdonia towards the sea. A spectacular sight, especially after rain.

Talyllyn Railway
204 C2

The historic, narrow-gauge Talyllyn steam railway dates from 1865 and runs 7 miles (11.5km) from Tywyn on the west coast, inland to Nant Gwernol. The authentically restored rolling stock chugs through beautiful wooded countryside, with stops en route to admire dramatic waterfalls, particularly from Dolgoch station. The round trip takes just over two hours, but there are also opportunities to explore extensive forest walks in the unspoilt Fathew Valley. For real enthusiasts, Footplate Experience Courses and special events can be arranged.

☎ 01654 710472 www.talyllyn.co.uk

Techniquest
180 A5

Located in the Cardiff Bay redevelopment area, this educational and fun discovery centre is suitable for the whole family. Techniquest aims to promote understanding and appreciation of science. On offer are 160 stimulating hands-on exhibits, puzzles and challenges in the shape of a Planetarium, a laboratory, a discovery room, a hi-tech science theatre and other enjoyable and accessible environments. Facilities are also available for groups and school tours. Allow at least two hours for a visit.

☎ 029 2047 5475 www.techniquest.org

Tintern Abbey (Ruin)
181 E3

Once a favoured site for artists and poets including William Wordsworth, the graceful ruins of the 13th century Cistercian Abbey overlook the beautiful Wye valley north of Chepstow. Much of the Abbey is preserved and it offers a fascinating glimpse into the life and times of the medieval monks.

☎ 01291 689251 www.tintern.org.uk

Tredegar House
351 C2

For more than five centuries this imposing mansion near Newport was home to the powerful Morgan family. Some 30 rooms are open to the public and the interior is furnished sumptuously with original pieces. Costumed guides lead tours describing life 'upstairs' and 'below stairs'. Outside are 90 acres (37ha) of landscaped gardens and parkland with lakes, carriage rides and craft workshops.

☎ 01633 815880 www.newport.gov.uk

Tretower Castle & Court
194 A5

The stone keep of this castle in the Brecon Beacons was built as a fortification in the 13th century. The nearby Court was added in the following century to serve as a comfortable residence. Various stages in the development of both buildings can be seen, including the detailed craftsmanship of the Court. The re-created 15th century garden is at its best in early summer.

☎ 01874 730279 www.cadw.wales.gov.uk

Tudor Merchant's House (NT)
177 E3

A late 15th century prosperous merchant's house near Tenby harbour has been furnished to depict lifestyles from Tudor days onwards. Interesting features include original frescoes, a Flemish chimney and small herb garden.

☎ 01834 842279 www.nationaltrust.org.uk

Tŷ Mawr Wybrnant (NT)
218 A2

Tucked away in a beautiful, peaceful valley, this small stone house holds a special significance in the history of the Welsh language. Here in the 16th century the entire Bible was first translated into Welsh by Bishop William Morgan. Restoration work has returned the house to its probable original state and it now contains a display of Welsh bibles and related exhibits.

☎ 01690 760213 www.nationaltrust.org.uk

Upton Gardens
176 D2

Overlooking the waters of Milford Haven, the landscaped gardens cover 35 acres (14ha) and offer secluded, inclined woodland walks. The main planting contains over 250 species of trees and shrubs, including some exotic varieties.

☎ 01646 651782 www.pembrokeshirecoast.org.uk

Vale of Rheidol Railway
204 C5

Starting from Aberystwyth main line station, this narrow-gauge steam train climbs steeply upwards along a spectacular 12 mile (19km) track and requires 3 hours for the round trip (allowing an hour at the beauty spot of Devil's Bridge). The original engines and carriages, built in 1902 to transport passengers and lead, are still in use. Highlights of the trip are three historic bridges at the summit spanning the Devil's Punchbowl whirlpool. Walks abound amid the rugged, wooded landscape.

☎ 01970 625819 www.rheidolrailway.co.uk

Welsh Slate Museum
217 E2

The vast, old Dinorwig slate quarry in the Padarn Country Park near Llanberis has been transformed into an imaginative museum of the bygone industry. Exhibitions, demonstrations, multimedia presentations, restored buildings, children's activities and tours bring to life the work of the quarrymen. The museum offers a fascinating, free day out for the whole family.

☎ 01286 870630 www.nmgw.ac.uk

Snowdonia

SCOTLAND

From the grassy hills of the Borders to the desolate Cuillin Ridge of Skye, the landscape of Scotland is breathtaking in its variety. Lonely glens, sparkling lochs and ever-changing skies give the land a challenging character, which is reflected in the qualities of the Scottish people. Tough and self-reliant, they have produced some of Britain's finest soldiers, its boldest explorers and most astute industrialists.

Kilchurn Castle, Loch Awe

Abbot House
285 F1

This restored 15th century house was originally the residence of the Abbot of Dunfermline. It is steeped in history and even survived the great fire of 1624. Exhibits and audiovisual displays trace Scotland's story from Pictish to modern times and recount details about King Robert the Bruce, St Margaret and other figures who played a role in the history of Scotland's most ancient capital.

☎ 01383 733266 www.abbothouse.co.uk

Abbotsford House
277 G2

Sir Walter Scott, the novelist, bought a farmhouse here in 1811, replacing it with a castellated and turreted mansion in the Scottish Baronial style and naming it Abbotsford in memory of the Melrose Abbey monks who forded the River Tweed here. He gleaned architectural ideas from many sources, including Melrose Abbey, Linlithgow Palace and Rosslyn Chapel. Internally the house is little altered and visitors can see the author's personal possessions, 9000 volume library and eclectic collection of historic relics such as a lock of Bonnie Prince Charlie's hair and Mary, Queen of Scots' crucifix. The armoury bristles with historic weapons and the entrance hall is festooned with the skulls of elk and wild cattle.

☎ 01896 752043

Aberdeen Art Gallery
388 B2

An elegant building opened in 1885 that houses one of the finest art collections in the UK. It includes 18th century portraits, paintings by many well known Impressionists and important works by modern British artists such as Nash, Nicholson and Bacon. The gallery also has a collection of Aberdeen silver and other arts and crafts.

☎ 01224 523700 www.aagm.co.uk

Aberdour Castle
285 F1

Overlooking the harbour is a 13th century fortified residence. There are also the ruins of the 14th century keep along with other buildings built and extended in later centuries. One of these is still roofed and contains a gallery on the first floor, complete with painted ceiling, illustrating how it was furnished in 1650. There is also a restored walled garden with a fine circular dovecot and terraced garden.

☎ 01383 860519 www.historic-scotland.gov.uk

Angus Folk Museum (NTS)
302 B5

The museum is within Kirkwynd Cottages, a row of six reconstructed early 18th century cottages with stone-slabbed roofs. The interiors display one of the finest folk collections of domestic relics in Scotland. There is also an agricultural collection in the farm steading opposite, including a restored 19th century horse-drawn hearse, providing an insight into rural livelihoods over the last 200 years.

☎ 01307 840288 www.nts.org.uk

Antonine Wall
284 C2

This Roman fortification stretched 38 miles (61km) from Bo'ness on the Forth to Old Kilpatrick on the Clyde. Built circa AD142 – 3, it consisted of a turf rampart on stone foundation behind a ditch 12ft (3.7m) deep and 40ft (12m) wide. Forts were positioned approximately every 2 miles (3km) and linked by a cobbled road. It was probably abandoned around AD163. Remains are best preserved in the Falkirk/Bonnybridge area.

☎ 0131 668 8800 www.historic-scotland.gov.uk

Aonach Mòr Mountain Gondola & Nevis Range Ski Centre
299 D2

Britain's only mountain gondolas take passengers up Aonach Mòr, beside Ben Nevis, to 2150ft (655m). Enjoy spectacular views of the Highlands and Islands and walks through forest tracks. The gondola also provides access to Britain's largest downhill mountain bike track. During the winter season, the Nevis Range provides Scotland's highest winter ski and snowboard area, with ski school and ski hire. There is a mountain restaurant, bar and shop at 2150ft (655m).

☎ 01397 705825 www.nevisrange.co.uk

Arbroath Abbey
303 E5

The substantial ruins of a Tironesian monastery founded by William the Lion in 1178. The Abbey is most notably associated with the signing of the Declaration of Arbroath in 1320, which asserted Scotland's independence from England. There is also a herb garden, exhibits about life in the Abbey and the Declaration, and a visitor centre.

☎ 01241 878756 www.historic-scotland.gov.uk

Ardkinglas Woodland Garden
291 D3

Overlooking Loch Fyne is one of the finest collections of conifers in Britain. Within the woodland garden is one of Europe's mightiest conifers, a 250 year old silver fir with a girth of 31ft (9.6m), and one of Britain's tallest trees, a grand fir over 200ft (61m) tall. There is also a spectacular display of rhododendrons and a gazebo containing a 'scriptorium' themed around a collection of literary quotes.

☎ 01499 600261 www.ardkinglas.com

Arduaine Gardens (NTS)
289 G4

A 20 acre (8ha) garden on a promontory with fine views overlooking Loch Melfort. Noted particularly for rhododendrons, azaleas, magnolias and other interesting trees and shrubs, which flourish in the warm sheltered climate created by the North Atlantic Drift.

☎ 01852 200366 www.nts.org.uk

Auchindrain Township Open Air Museum
290 C4

Auchindrain is an original West Highland township of great antiquity and the only communal tenancy township in Scotland to have survived on its centuries-old site. The conserved township buildings are furnished and equipped as they would have been at the end of the 19th century and provide a fascinating glimpse of Highland life.

☎ 01499 500235 www.auchindrainmuseum.org.uk

Bachelors' Club (NTS)
274 C3

A 17th century thatched house with period furnishings where Robert Burns and his friends formed a debating club in 1780. Burns also attended dancing classes and was initiated as a Freemason here.

☎ 01292 541940 www.nts.org.uk

Balmacara Estate & Lochalsh Woodland Garden (NTS)
307 E2

Traditional crofting is still carried out on this beautiful Highland estate. There are wonderful views of Skye and Applecross, and the woodland garden provides sheltered lochside walks among pines, ferns, fuchsias, hydrangeas and rhododendrons. Amongst the villages on the estate is Plockton, an outstanding conservation area and location for the television series 'Hamish Macbeth'. A small visitor centre is located at Balmacara Square. Charges apply for the garden.

☎ 01599 566325 www.nts.org.uk

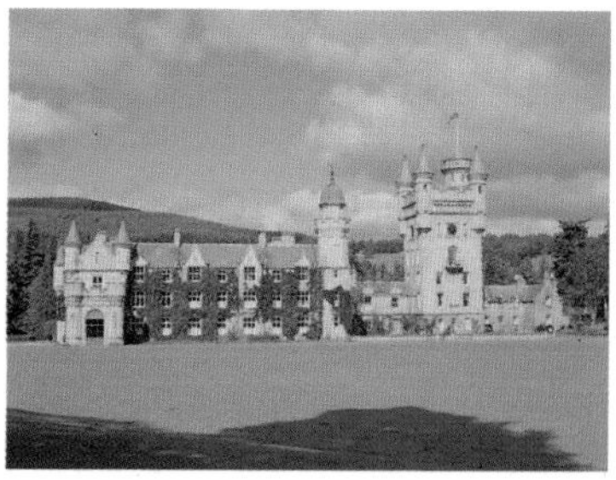

Balmoral Castle

Balmoral Castle
311 E5

Situated on the south side of the River Dee, Balmoral has been the Highland holiday home of the Royal Family since 1852. The present castle was designed by Aberdeen City architect William Smith under the keen eye of Queen Victoria's husband, Prince Albert, who considered the castle they previously leased on the site too small. The pale colour of the granite stone used in the building is quite distinctive and was quarried from nearby Glen Gelder.

The only part of the castle open to the public is the ballroom which has items from within the castle on display; paintings, porcelain and the Balmoral Tartans and Tweeds collection. In the stables there are carriages on view, while in the carriage hall there is a display of commemorative china and an exhibition about the Balmoral Estate.

Three acres (1ha) of formal gardens include a conservatory and Victorian glasshouses, kitchen garden and water garden, and there are waymarked walks along the river and through the woods. Guided ranger walks, land rover safaris and pony trekking are also available. Balmoral is only open to the public between April and July.

☎ 013397 42534 www.balmoralcastle.com

Bannockburn 1314
292 D5

This is the site of the famous battle in 1314 when Robert the Bruce, King of Scots, defeated the English Army of Edward II. The Heritage Centre stages a colourful exhibition, with life-size figures of Bruce and William Wallace, heraldic flags and an audiovisual presentation on the Battle of Bannockburn.

☎ 01786 812664 www.nts.org.uk

Barry Mill (NTS)
294 D1

A working 19th century meal mill. There are full demonstrations on weekend afternoons, and displays outline the history of the mill.

☎ 01241 856761 www.nts.org.uk

Baxters Highland Village
323 F3

The story of Baxters, the Scottish food company, began in 1868 when George Baxter opened a small grocery store in Fochabers. At the Highland Village there is a presentation of the Baxters story, cookery demonstrations and the re-creation of George Baxter's original shop.

☎ 01343 820393 www.baxters.com/village

Bealach na Ba
319 D5

Scotland's highest road, between Loch Kishorn and Applecross, provides a spectacular drive, climbing to the summit at 2056ft (625m). Bealach na Ba translates to 'Pass of the Cattle', denoting its original

purpose. The challenging drive is well rewarded and there are parking areas to enjoy the fabulous views. Beyond the summit, the road descends to Applecross, a peaceful fishing village.

Beecraigs Country Park
285 D2

Nestled high in the Bathgate Hills, Beecraigs covers an area of 915 acres (370ha) and offers a wide range of leisure and recreational pursuits. There are various walks and trails as well as a well-stocked fishery, a deer farm which sells its own venison, and the opportunity to participate in archery, orienteering, abseiling and skiing. There is a charge for some of these activities.

☎ 01506 844516 www.beecraigs.com

Ben Lawers National Nature Reserve (NTS)
292 B1

Located north-east of Killin is Perthshire's highest mountain, Ben Lawers, rising 3984ft (1214m). It is noted for its rich variety of mountain plants and bird population, including raven, ring-ouzel, ptarmigan, dipper and curlew. There is a nature trail and ranger-guided walks in summer.

☎ 01567 820397 www.nts.org.uk

Ben Nevis
299 D2

At 4406ft (1344m), this is Britain's highest mountain and is popular for both rock climbing and hill walking. Ben Nevis is best seen from the north approach to Fort William, or from the Gairlochy Road, across the Caledonian Canal. At the top are the ruins of the Mountain Top Observatory, where Victorian scientists collected data, whatever the weather.

To the south, the Water of Nevis plummets through a steep wooded gorge. Glen Nevis offers wonderful gorge walks and the visitor centre provides information on the fascinating history, geology, flora and fauna of Ben Nevis and Glen Nevis. There are ranger guided walks during June, July and August.

Ben Nevis

Blackhouse
329 E3

A traditional Hebridean thatched and chimneyless house dating from the 1870s with byre, attached barn and stackyard. It is fully furnished and a peat fire burns in the hearth. Opposite is a furnished 1920s crofthouse, or whitehouse, which replaced the blackhouse dwellings. The visitor centre provides informative displays.

☎ 01851 710395 www.historic-scotland.gov.uk

Blackness Castle
285 E1

A 15th century stronghold, once one of the most important fortresses in Scotland and one of four castles the Articles of Union left fortified. Shaped like a ship with three sides surrounded by water, it has served as a royal castle, a state prison in Covenanting times and a powder magazine in the 1870s. More recently, it has been a film location for the BBC production of 'Hamlet'. Visitors can explore inside, walk the walls and climb the central tower.

www.historic-scotland.gov.uk

Blacksmith's Shop
268 B5

Built around 1712, this became a world famous centre for runaway marriages when Scottish law permitted marriage at 16 without parental consent, while English law did not. Gretna Green was the closest place to the border for eloping couples and an exhibition traces the history of these runaway weddings which took place in the Blacksmith's Shop, the nearest building to the stagecoach stop.

☎ 01461 338441 www.gretnagreen.com

Blair Castle
301 D3

This white turreted baronial castle, set within magnificent grounds, was the traditional seat of the Dukes and Earls of Atholl. The oldest part, Cumming's Tower, dates back to 1269. Over 30 rooms convey more than 700 years of history. Discover fine collections of furniture, portraits, lace, china, costumes, arms, armour, Jacobite relics and Masonic regalia. Explore the deer park, restored 18th century walled garden, woodland, riverside and mountain walks.

☎ 01796 481207 www.blair-castle.co.uk

Bonawe Iron Furnace
290 C1

The restored remains of this charcoal-fuelled furnace, once used for iron smelting, is the most complete example of its type. Established in 1753, it functioned until 1876. Displays illustrate the iron-making process. Open from end of April to September only.

☎ 01866 822432 www.historic-scotland.gov.uk

Bo'ness & Kinneil Railway
285 D1

Savour the nostalgia of the railway age and travel by steam train from Bo'ness to visit Birkhill Fireclay Mine. The scenic 7 mile (11km) round trip passes via the south shore of the Firth of Forth, through woodlands, and crosses the Antonine Wall. Regular timetable during the summer, plus special events.

☎ 01506 822298 www.srps.org.uk

Bothwell Castle
375 E3

Regarded as the finest 13th century stronghold in the country, Bothwell Castle was much fought over by the Scots and English during the Wars of Independence. Substantial ruins of this red sandstone castle remain today in a picturesque setting alongside the River Clyde.

☎ 01698 816894 www.historic-scotland.gov.uk

Bowhill House
277 F3

A splendid Georgian mansion in impressive woodland setting, containing a remarkable collection of French furniture designed by Andre Boulle, paintings by Canaletto, Gainsborough, Reynolds and Van Dyck, tapestries and fine porcelain. There are some interesting historical exhibits including letters from Queen Victoria and proof copies of Sir Walter Scott's books.

There are walks and an adventure playground in the grounds. The house is only open in July; check in advance for opening times of grounds.

☎ 01750 22204

Branklyn Gardens (NTS)
293 G2

Started in 1922 on the site of a former orchard, Branklyn is an outstanding 2 acre (0.8ha) garden with rhododendrons, alpines, herbaceous and peat garden plants. These are predominantly from China, Tibet, Bhutan and the Himalayas, and include the blue Himalayan poppy.

☎ 01738 625535 www.nts.org.uk

Britannia
373 C1

Launched in 1953 onto the Clyde, the Royal Yacht served the Queen and royal family for state visits, diplomatic functions and royal holidays for 44 years. Today *Britannia* is moored in Leith Docks alongside the Ocean Terminal shopping centre. The tour begins in the visitor centre where the history of the yacht and its royal connections are explained. Five decks of the ship are then open for exploration including the bridge, admiral's quarters, the officers' mess, the state rooms, the engine room and some of the living quarters used privately by the Queen and Prince Philip.

☎ 0131 555 5566 www.royalyachtbritannia.co.uk

Britannia

British Golf Museum
294 C3

Touch screen and audiovisual displays, together with a fascinating collection of memorabilia, trace the history of golf from the Middle Ages through to the present day.

☎ 01334 460046 www.britishgolfmuseum.co.uk

Brodick Castle (NTS)
273 F2

An imposing, originally 13th century red sandstone castle on a site occupied initially by Irish and later by Vikings. Extended in the 17th and 19th centuries, the pleasant interior belies the somewhat forbidding exterior.

Brodick's greatest treasures are its gardens; the woodland garden, started in 1923, is home to one of Europe's finest rhododendron collections, magnificent in spring, whilst the walled garden contains tender and exotic plants encouraged by the mild climate.

Set at the foot of Goat Fell, the estate provides scenic trails, abundant wildlife and an adventure playground.

☎ 01770 302202 www.nts.org.uk

Brodie Castle (NTS)
322 B4

The oldest parts of Brodie Castle are 16th century, although the Brodie family owned land here as early as the 12th century. The well-furnished castle interior contains fine French furniture, porcelain, and a major art collection of modern British and French paintings. There are some impressive ornate plasterwork ceilings, a large library and fully equipped Victorian kitchen.

The grounds are famous for the spring display of daffodils, many of them specialist varieties, and there are woodland walks and a four acre (2ha) pond with wildlife observation hides. The park also contains a notable carved Pictish stone.

☎ 01309 641371 www.nts.org.uk

Broughton House (NTS) 266 A5

Delightful 18th century town house, home between 1901 – 33 to the artist Edward Hornel, who helped establish an artists' colony in Kirkcudbright. Some of his paintings hang in the gallery here, later ones influenced by visits to Japan.

The 2 acre (1ha) garden consists of distinct compartments including Hornel's Japanese-style garden. Check in advance for opening times.

☎ 01577 330437 www.nts.org.uk

Burg (NTS) 288 D2

Covering an area of 1405 acres (569ha), this is a spectacular and remote part of Mull. The high, volcanic cliffs are known as 'The Wilderness', denoting the area's wild terrain. MacCulloch's Fossil Tree, engulfed by lava 50 million years ago, can be reached by a steep iron ladder down to the beach at low tide. There is no vehicular access to Berg; it is reached by a 6 mile (10km) walk from Kilfinichen Bay.

www.nts.org.uk

Burns National Heritage Park 274 B4

Set up in 1995, this embraces several sites in the Alloway area closely connected with Robert Burns, considered Scotland's national poet.

The whitewashed Burns Cottage is the poet's birthplace, a small, dark, gloomy building giving a good impression of impoverished 18th century rural existence. Adjacent is the Museum, tracing Burns' life and displaying his manuscripts and memorabilia. A short distance away is the modern Tam O' Shanter Experience with entertaining audiovisual presentations on the poet's life and a re-enactment of his famous poem, 'Tam O' Shanter'. The ruined Alloway Kirk across the road is the burial place of Burns' father and one of the settings for 'Tam O' Shanter', as is the nearby stone arch Brig O' Doon. The neoclassical Burns Monument, decorated with characters from the poems, has pleasant, well-tended gardens.

☎ 01292 443700 www.burnsheritagepark.com

Burns National Heritage Park

Burrell Collection 374 B3

This award winning purpose-built museum houses a magnificent collection gifted to the city of Glasgow in 1944 By Sir William Burrell, a shipping magnate, and his wife, Constance. Visitors can see ancient artworks from China, Egypt, Greece and Rome including Egyptian alabaster and Chinese jade. There are remarkable collections of tapestries, oriental rugs, medieval metalwork, stained glass and paintings by Manet, Degas and Rembrandt, as well as modern sculpture including works by Rodin and Epstein. A number of rooms from Burrell's home, the 16th century Hutton Castle, have been perfectly re-created. The building itself is light and airy and its woodland setting within Pollok Country Park ensures all the objects on display are shown at their very best. Free guided tours are available and there is a good tearoom and restaurant on the lower floor.

☎ 0141 287 2550 www.glasgowmuseums.com

Caerlaverock Castle 267 E4

A splendid moated, triangular 13th century castle, with a substantial keep gatehouse at the northern apex, entered by a footbridge. Its impregnable appearance is reinforced by the desolate surroundings of the Solway coast, though the castle was captured on several occasions. Capture invariably resulted in damage, and the castle is consequently a mixture of building styles, both externally and internally. It was finally abandoned in 1640 when it was wrecked by the Covenanters.

☎ 01387 770244 www.historic-scotland.gov.uk

Caerlaverock Wildfowl & Wetlands Trust 267 E4

A splendid 1350 acres (546ha) of protected saltmarsh and mudflat bordering the Solway Firth. Well designed observation towers and hides provide visitors with exceptional views of migratory wildfowl, notably the Barnacle Geese of Svalbard, most of whom overwinter here. There is still plenty of bird life in summer, and there are nature trails through the meadows and knowledgeable to staff to answer the inevitable questions.

☎ 01387 770200 www.wwt.org.uk

Cairn Gorm Mountain 310 B4

This granite mountain mass of rounded summits includes some of Scotland's highest peaks. It is a popular area for hill walkers, climbers and skiers. The Cairngorms are Britain's only example of Arctic tundra vegetation and the area provides a habitat for populations of red deer, mountain hare, snow buntings and ptarmigans. Cairn Gorm summit, at 4086ft (1245m), provides fantastic views of the lochs, forests and surrounding mountains.

www.cairngormmountain.com

Cairngorms National Park 310 B5

The Cairngorms National Park stretches 1400 sq miles (3800 sq km), making it Britain's largest national park area. Aviemore is the commercial centre for the area. In winter, the village is a mecca for skiers and snowboarders and in summer there are facilities for pony trekking, mountain biking, fishing, sailing, windsurfing and canoeing. Whilst the peaks are popular with climbers, there are also forest and river treks to follow, as well as walks around and through the villages, including Newtonmore and Boat of Garten.

The funicular railway, Scotland's only mountain railway, takes visitors on a spectacular and comfortable journey to Ptarmigan Station on Cairn Gorm, 490ft (150m) below the summit. The Ski Centre can be found 9 miles (14km) south-east of Aviemore. Other attractions include the Cairngorm Reindeer Centre and Cairngorm Sled-dog Adventure Centre.

☎ 01479 861261 www.cairngorms.co.uk

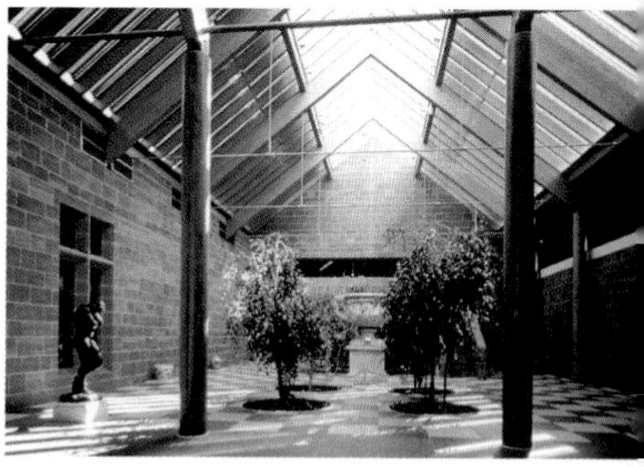

Burrell Collection

Calderglen Country Park 284 A4

The park covers an area of 440 acres (180ha) and is made up of grassland, wooded gorge and several fine waterfalls. There are over 8 miles (13km) of nature trails through the woods and alongside the River Calder. The visitor centre has information about the park. There is also an ornamental garden, children's zoo, play area, shop and café.

☎ 01355 236644

Caledonian Railway 303 E4

From the unique Victorian terminus at Brechin, board a steam train and journey back in time as you travel the falling grade to Bridge of Dun, where the Royal Trains used to stop. From here, enjoy a scenic walk along the River South Esk and visit the bird sanctuary, Montrose Basin. Back at Brechin, there is a static display of model trains. Steam hauled trains run at weekends from the end of May to beginning of September.

☎ 01356 622992 www.caledonianrailway.co.uk

Callanish Standing Stones 328 D4

A unique cruciform setting of megaliths, second in importance only to Stonehenge, which were erected about 3000BC. An avenue of 19 monoliths leads north from a circle of 13 stones, with rows of more stones fanning out to the south, east and west. Inside the circle is a small, chambered tomb. There is a visitor centre, including an audiovisual presentation about the stones (for which there is a small charge).

☎ 01851 621422 www.historic-scotland.gov.uk

Callendar House 284 C2

Callendar House encapsulates 600 years of Scotland's history, from medieval times to the 20th century. Great historical visitors of the house include Mary, Queen of Scots, Cromwell and Bonnie Prince Charlie. Permanent attractions include displays on the story of Callendar House, and on the Falkirk area during the great social revolution of 1750 – 1850.

☎ 01324 503770 www.falkirkmuseums.demon.co.uk

Cardoness Castle 265 G5

An excellent example of a fortified tower house, this late 15th century stronghold is now a well preserved ruin. The four-storey building still retains the original staircase, vaulted basement and elaborate fireplaces, and has views over the Water of Fleet to Fleet Bay.

☎ 01557 814427 www.historic-scotland.gov.uk

Carlyle's Birthplace (NTS) 267 F3

Thomas Carlyle, the author, historian and social reformer, was born in 1795 in the unpretentious, whitewashed Arched House built by his father and uncle. It is now a tiny museum featuring his personal memorabilia. True to his roots, Carlyle refused burial in Westminster Abbey and his grave can be found in the churchyard behind the cottage.

☎ 01576 300666 www.nts.org.uk

Castle Campbell 293 E5

Once known as Castle Gloom, the castle is set high on a promontory above Dollar Glen. Built towards the end of the 15th century by the 1st Earl of Argyll, it was burned by Cromwell in the 1650s. The original tower, however, is well preserved along with its courtyard and Great Hall. The 60 acres (24ha) of woodland in the glen make an attractive walk to the castle.

☎ 01259 742408 www.historic-scotland.gov.uk

Castle Fraser (NTS) 312 C3

A magnificent castle completed in 1636 and one of the most sophisticated Scottish buildings of the period. It has a notable Great Hall with tall windows and a high ceiling, striking in its simplicity. Castle Fraser also contains a wealth of historic portraits, curtains, carpets and bedhangings. There is a formal walled garden in the grounds.

☎ 01330 833463 www.nts.org.uk

Castle Menzies 300 D4

This imposing 16th century castle presents a fine example of the transition between a Z-plan clan stronghold and a later mansion house. Seat of the clan chiefs for over 400 years, Castle Menzies was involved in a number of historic occurrences, which are recounted in the museum.

☎ 01887 820982

Castle of Mey 337 E1

Originally the seat of the earls of Caithness, 16th century Mey Castle became the Scottish summer holiday retreat of Her late Majesty Queen Elizabeth, The Queen Mother, between 1952 and 2002. It was built to a Z-plan, characteristic of its era, with towers and corbelled turrets. The Great Wall of Mey, standing 12ft (3.7m) high, protects the attractive walled garden from the strong winds and salt spray.

☎ 01847 851473 www.castleofmey.org.uk

Cawdor Castle 322 A4

Cawdor Castle is the name romantically associated with Shakespeare's Macbeth, and dates originally from the 14th century. The medieval tower and drawbridge are still intact and generations of art lovers and scholars are responsible for the eclectic collection of paintings, books, tapestries and porcelain found in the castle. There are three beautiful gardens, five nature trails, a nine-hole golf course, putting green, and gift shop.

☎ 01667 404615 www.cawdorcastle.com

Corrieshalloch Gorge (NTS) 320 A2

Here is one of the finest examples of a box canyon in Britain, forming a spectacular 200ft (61m) deep, mile-long (1.6km) gorge. A viewing platform stretched across the gorge looks up towards the magnificent Falls of Measach.

☎ 01445 781200 www.nts.org.uk

Craigievar Castle (NTS) 312 A4

Completed in 1626, Craigievar is an excellent example of Scottish baronial architecture although it was built for a merchant, William Forbes. It is like the castles of fairytales with the seven storeys topped with turrets, gables and corbels. The interior has original ornate plasterwork ceilings and a fine collection of 17th and 18th century furniture. The grounds have woodland walks.

☎ 013398 83635 www.nts.org.uk

Craigmillar Castle 373 C2

The oldest part of the castle is the L-shaped tower built in the early 1400s which was later surrounded by an embattled double curtain wall. By the end of the 16th century it was a comfortable residence and today, partially ruined, the castle still retains a strong sense of the mighty fortress it once was. Mary, Queen of Scots, has close links with the castle. She fled here following the murder of Rizzio, and the murder of her second husband was plotted here.

☎ 0131 661 4445 www.historic-scotland.gov.uk

Crathes Castle (NTS) 312 C5

An impressive 16th century tower house with remarkable original painted ceilings and a collection of Scottish furniture and family portraits. It was the home of the Burnett family for more than 350 years until it was given to the National Trust in 1951. The walled garden, originally the kitchen garden, was divided in the 20th century into eight separate themed gardens with many herbaceous plants. Several waymarked trails lead through the mixed woodland of the Crathes Estate.

☎ 01330 844525 www.nts.org.uk

Crichton Castle 286 A3

A large castle built around a medieval tower house to create an elegant interior courtyard. The arcaded range erected by the Earl of Bothwell between 1581 and 1591 has a façade of faceted stonework in an Italian Renaissance style.

☎ 01875 320017 www.historic-scotland.gov.uk

Crossraguel Abbey 274 A5

The substantial remains of a 13th century Cluniac monastery founded by the Earl of Carrick. The chapter house and gatehouse are amongst the best preserved and visitors can view the abbey precincts and surroundings from the top of the latter. The abbey was abandoned during the Reformation in the late 16th century.

☎ 01655 883113 www.historic-scotland.gov.uk

Cruachan Power Station Visitor Centre 290 C2

A guided tour takes visitors 0.5 miles (1km) inside Ben Cruachan to a huge cavern to see a reversible pumped storage scheme where water power is converted into electricity. The visitor centre houses touch screen and computer video technology to explain how electricity is produced.

☎ 01866 822618 www.visitcruachan.co.uk

Cuillin Hills 306 A2

The Cuillin Hills form a major sight on the Isle of Skye, their jagged summits of volcanic rock and granite evident from most parts of the island. Several peaks reach over 3000ft (914m), suitable for only the experienced climber. The mountains, however, can still be enjoyed on many walks, particularly from Elgol, Sligachan and the Glenbrittle road near Carbost.

Cuillin Hills

Culloden (NTS) 321 G5

Site of the fierce battle on 16 April 1746, when the Hanoverian Army defeated the forces of Bonnie Prince Charlie, thereby ending the Jacobite uprising. Turf and stone dykes have been reconstructed on their original spot. The Graves of the Clans, the Well of the Dead, the Memorial Cairn, the Cumberland Stone and the Field of the English can also be seen. The visitor centre houses a Jacobite exhibition.

☎ 01463 790607 www.nts.org.uk

Culross Palace (NTS) 285 D1

Built in 1597–1611 for local entrepreneur Sir George Bruce, the palace features its original decorative interiors and period 17th and 18th century furnishings. The restored 17th century garden contains rare herbs and perennials of the period. Elsewhere in Culross village, discover the remains of a Cistercian Abbey founded in 1217, the eastern part of which forms the present parish church. The Town House provides an exhibition of the area's history.

☎ 01383 880359 www.nts.org.uk

Culzean Castle (NTS) 274 A4

A dramatic clifftop location and splendid design by Robert Adam in the late 18th century makes Culzean (pronounced Cullane) one of the most impressive of Scotland's stately homes. Replacing the original 15th century structure, the exterior, with arrow slits and battlements, evokes the

medieval period, but the elegant interior exemplifies the classical designs favoured by Adam. The spectacular Oval Staircase is considered one of his finest achievements, while the sumptuous Circular Saloon makes a striking contrast to the surrounding natural scenery.

The 565 acre (233ha) estate, now a country park, provides woodland, clifftop and seashore walks, deer park, aviary and swan pond. The 30 acre (12ha) gardens include a large, colourful walled garden.

☎ 01655 884455 www.nts.org.uk

Dallas Dhu Distillery 322 C4

A picturesque small distillery established in 1899. Although no longer in production, Dallas Dhu is maintained in working order to enable visitors to take a close look at every part of the traditional distilling process and see exactly how whisky is made.

☎ 01309 676548 www.historic-scotland.gov.uk

David Livingstone Centre (NTS) 375 E4

Scotland's famous explorer and missionary was born here in 1813. He spent his childhood in a one-room tenement, which remains much as it was in Livingstone's day. The rest of the tenement block now houses a museum on the life of the great explorer, with many of his personal belongings on display.

☎ 01698 823140 www.nts.org.uk

Dean Castle 274 C2

A splendid collection of restored buildings comprising a 14th century fortified keep with a 15th century palace, dungeon, battlements, banqueting hall, kitchens and minstrels' gallery. The museum contains a significant collection of arms and armour, medieval musical instruments, tapestries and some Robert Burns manuscripts. Entry to the castle is by guided tour only.

The surrounding 200 acre (80ha) country park provides a variety of attractions including formal gardens, nature trails and a ranger service offering guided walks. There is a varied programme of events in summer.

☎ 01563 522702 www.deancastle.com

Dean Gallery 373 B1

This impressive neoclassical building was originally an orphanage but now houses a huge collection of work by the distinguished Scottish sculptor Eduardo Paolozzi. The gallery is also home to the Dada and Surrealist collections from the Gallery of Modern Art across the road.

☎ 0131 624 6200 www.natgalscot.ac.uk

Deep Sea World 285 F1

Enjoy a spectacular diver's eye view of the marine environment by travelling along a moving walkway through a long transparent viewing tunnel. Come face to face with sand tiger sharks and watch divers hand feed them. Touch the live exhibits in the large rock pools. Visit the stunning Amazonian Experience, which features ferocious piranhas, poisonous golden dart frogs, electrifying eels and the deadly stonefish.

☎ 01383 411880 www.deepseaworld.co.uk

Dirleton Castle & Gardens 286 C1

The oldest part of this romantic castle dates from the 13th century and, although the castle was destroyed in 1650, there are still large parts of the original masonry in evidence. The gardens dating from the 16th century are well worth a look.

☎ 01620 850330 www.historic-scotland.gov.uk

Discovery Point & R.R.S. Discovery 396 C2

Centred on the Royal Research Ship *Discovery*, Captain Scott's famous polar exploration ship, this visitor centre vividly re-creates her historic voyages. Spectacular exhibits, interactive displays and special effects bring to life the story of the ship and a short dramatic film re-enacts the Antarctic expedition and its rescue.

Combine a visit with nearby Verdant Works, a restored 19th century jute works surrounding a cobbled courtyard.

☎ 01382 201245 www.rrsdiscovery.com

R.R.S. *Discovery*

Dornoch Cathedral 332 C5

This small, well maintained cathedral was founded in 1224 by Gilbert, Archdeacon of Moray and Bishop of Caithness. Partially destroyed by fire in 1570 and restored in 1835 – 37, and again in 1924, the fine 13th century stonework is still visible. There are 27 magnificent stained glass windows and impressive woodwork.

☎ 01862 810357

Drum Castle (NTS) 312 C4

The 13th century tower of Drum is one of the three oldest tower houses in Scotland. Jacobean and Victorian extensions made the house into a fine mansion and it contains notable portraits and furniture, much from the 18th century. Drum was the home of the Irvine family for more than 650 years and a room displays family memorabilia. The extensive grounds include a collection of historic roses established by the National Trust in 1991, an arboretum and the ancient oak woodland of the 'Old Wood of Drum'.

☎ 01330 811204 www.drum-castle.org.uk www.nts.org.uk

Drumlanrig Castle 266 C1

A sweeping drive through a wooded avenue leads to an imposing late 17th century castle built of local pink sandstone. Originally a 15th century castle, it was converted, complete with turrets, towers and cupolas, for the 1st Duke of Queensberry. The state rooms have splendid oak panelling, Louis XIV furniture and paintings by Holbein, Murillo, Rembrandt and Brueghel.

The 40 acres (16ha) of formal and informal gardens are being restored according to the original plans, and new rhododendron areas are being created using seed collected from the wild. The adjacent Drumlanrig Country Park has waymarked trails, wildlife including red squirrels and otters, and some magnificent specimen trees. There is a visitor centre and a ranger service offers a programme of guided walks.

☎ 01848 330248 www.buccleuch.com

Drummond Castle Gardens 293 D3

This is one of Scotland's largest formal gardens with magnificent early Victorian parterre, fountains, terracing and topiary. It is laid out in the form of a St Andrew's cross, centred around a multi-faceted 17th century sundial, carved by John Milne, master mason to Charles I.

☎ 01764 681257 www.drummondcastlegardens.co.uk

Drummond Castle Gardens

Drumpellier Country Park 375 E2

The park covers an area of 500 acres (202ha) of open grassland, mixed woodland, lowland heath and two natural lochs, one of which is a Site of Special Scientific Interest. A diverse range of wildlife can be seen by visitors and a network of paths makes all areas of the park accessible. There is a visitor centre and café, a road train, play area, and boat hire and fishing on the lochs.

☎ 01236 422257 www.northlan.gov.uk/leisure+and+tourism

Dryburgh Abbey 277 G2

Founded in the 12th century in a delightful location on the banks of the River Tweed, the pink sandstone abbey remains demonstrate several architectural styles as the buildings were frequently assailed by the English, until 1545 when they were abandoned. Even so, Dryburgh is the most complete of the Border abbeys, the barrel vaulted chapter house being particularly impressive. Sir Walter Scott is buried here, as is Field Marshal Earl Haig, the World War I leader.

☎ 01835 822381 www.historic-scotland.gov.uk

Duart Castle 289 G1

This is one of Scotland's oldest inhabited castles and home to the 28th Chief of Clan Maclean. The keep, built in 1360, adjoins the original courtyard. Used as a garrison for Government troops after the 1745 Rising, it then fell into ruin but was restored by Sir Fitzroy Maclean in 1911.

☎ 01680 812309 www.duartcastle.com

Duff House 324 B3

Designed by William Adam for the first Earl of Fife in 1735, Duff House is one of the best examples of Georgian baroque architecture in Britain, and houses paintings, furniture and tapestries from the collections of the National Galleries of Scotland.

Duff House is surrounded by parkland and there are woodland walks by the River Deveron. The grounds are free and open all year.

☎ 01261 818181 www.duffhouse.org.uk

Duncansby Head 337 F1

Duncansby Head is located at the north-eastern edge of the Scottish mainland, beyond John o' Groats. Its lighthouse commands a fine view of Orkney, the Pentland Skerries and the east coast headlands.

Slightly to the south are the Duncansby Stacks, three huge stone needles in the sea, along with the sandstone cliffs, severed with deep crevices (geos), one of which is bridged by a natural rocky arch.

Dundee Contemporary Arts 396 C1

Centre for contemporary art and film with five floors containing two galleries, cinema, print studio, craft shop, visual research centre and activity room. Admission to the galleries and exhibitions is free, with a charge for the cinema.

☎ 01382 606220 www.dca.org.uk

Dunfermline Abbey & Palace 285 E1

The remains of the great Benedictine abbey founded by Queen Margaret in the 11th century. The foundations of her church are under the present 12th century Romanesque style nave. Robert the Bruce is buried in the choir, now the site of the present parish church. Of the monastic buildings, the ruins of the refectory, pend and guesthouse remain.

☎ 01383 739026 www.historic-scotland.gov.uk

Dunnottar Castle 303 G1

A spectacular ruin 160ft (48.5m) above the North Sea, recognisable to many film buffs as the setting of Franco Zeffirelli's film 'Hamlet' which starred Mel Gibson. Situated on a flat-topped promontory with sheer cliffs on three sides, and linked to the mainland by a narrow neck of land, Dunnottar's dramatic defensive position ensured a rich and colourful history.

Between the 9th and 17th centuries the castle was fought over many times and for over three hundred years was held by the Keiths, who were Earls Marischal of Scotland, the most powerful family in Scotland. In 1297 William Wallace attacked the English garrison and burnt the wooden castle here, and Mary, Queen of Scots was a visitor in 1562 and 1564. Most famously, in 1652 the Scottish crown jewels, the Honours of Scotland, were hidden here safely for eight months during a siege by Cromwell's army.

Today several buildings from different periods remain, including the 14th century tower house. Access is by means of a steep path and steps.

☎ 01569 762173 www.dunechtestates.co.uk

Dunrobin Castle 333 D4

Overlooking the sea and set within magnificent formal gardens, Dunrobin Castle has belonged to the Earls and Dukes of Sutherland for centuries. It was originally a square keep, built in the 13th

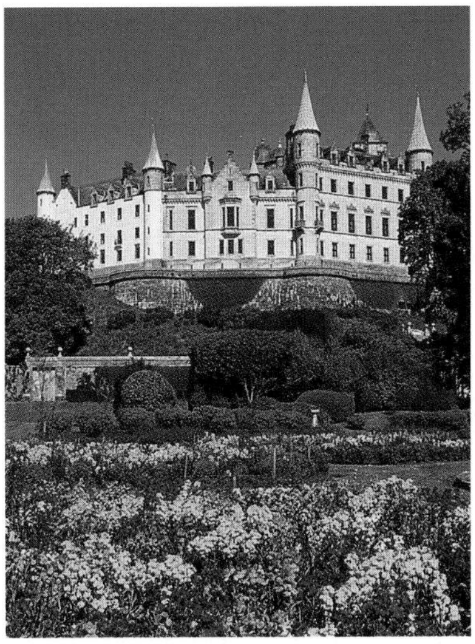

Dunrobin Castle

century by Robert, Earl of Sutherland, after whom it was named Dun Robin. Its turreted, chateau-style appearance resulted after extensive modifications by Sir Charles Barry during the 1840s, after he had completed the new Houses of Parliament. As Scotland's most northerly great house, the castle is also its largest, with 189 rooms, and its oldest continuously-inhabited home.

Period rooms display fine paintings, furniture, family memorabilia and even a steam-powered fire engine.

The sheltered gardens, with their formal parterres, were first laid in 1850 and were inspired by those of Versailles. There are falconry demonstrations and a Victorian museum includes an exceptional collection of Pictish stones.

☎ 01408 633177

Duthie Park & David Welch Winter Gardens 313 E4

This popular 50 acre (20ha) park with boating lake and Winter Gardens was first laid out in the late 19th century. It is just a short walk from Aberdeen city centre, next to the River Dee. The world-renowned David Welch Winter Gardens, renamed in recognition of the work of a former Aberdeen Parks Director, covers two acres (1ha) and is one of the largest covered gardens in Europe.

Eas a' Chual Aluinn 331 E2

This is Britain's tallest waterfall, dropping 658ft (200m) at the head of Loch Glencoul. Seals and the occasional elusive otter may be seen on the loch.

Easdale Island Folk Museum 289 G3

The Island of Easdale was once the centre of the slate industry. This museum, set amongst former quarriers' cottages, provides a fascinating account of industrial and domestic life on the island during the 18th and 19th centuries.

☎ 01852 300370 www.slate.org.uk

Edinburgh 285 G2

Edinburgh is a superb city for visitors and with most of the interesting features so close together it is great for exploring on foot. The city grew up around the castle and it still dominates the skyline today. The Royal Mile, consisting of mostly medieval buildings, runs east from the castle to the

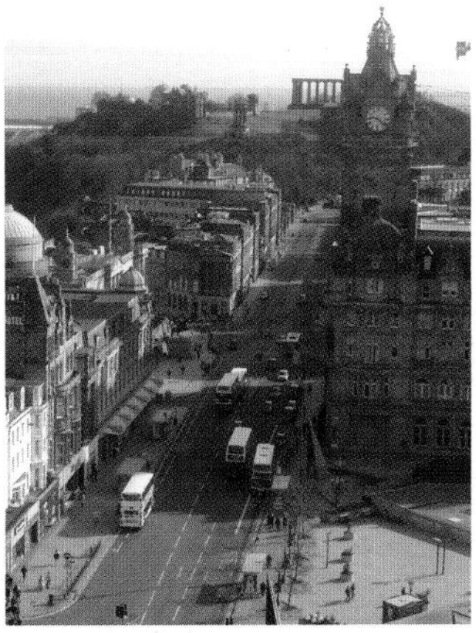

Edinburgh – Princes Street

Palace of Holyroodhouse, through the heart of the Old Town. Numerous narrow street and alleys lead off it, many with fascinating architecture to explore. The New Town is immediately to the north, separated only by the beautiful Princes Street Gardens. In stark contrast to the Old Town, it is full of spacious terraces and crescents that are some of the finest examples of Georgian town planning in Europe. The Water of Leith walkway takes visitors to the unspoilt Dean Village. To the east of the main city centre is Holyrood Park, a 650 acre (263ha) oasis of peace with hills, crags, moorlands, marshes and lochs. Arthur's Seat, within the park, is the core of an extinct volcano (822ft, 251m high) and it is worth a walk to the top for superb views over the entire city and the Firth of Forth. Each August the city really comes to life as, over a period of three weeks, the Festival takes place. It is a combination of theatre, dance, music and comedy with performances at all hours of the day and night.

Dunnottar Castle

Edinburgh Castle
397 E1

The castle rises from an extinct volcanic outcrop and dominates the city that has grown up around it. There has been some kind of fortress up on the hill since the 7th century although the oldest part of the present castle, St Margaret's Chapel, was built during the 12th century. In its early years the castle was a royal residence but has assumed an increasingly military role over time, and today still houses an important garrison for the Scottish regiments. The Scottish crown jewels are on display alongside the Stone of Destiny. In the castle vaults, once used as cells for military prisoners, is Mons Meg cannon, a 15th century siege gun which could fire a 500 pound stone a distance of 2 miles (3km). The Royal Apartments inside the palace have been sensitively restored to their 16th century splendour and the chamber where Mary, Queen of Scots gave birth to James VI (James I of England) are especially worth a look. Each day at one o'clock a gun is fired from the castle, originally for the benefit of ships in the Firth of Forth, a tradition that has continued unbroken since the 17th century. Knowledgeable guides lead frequent tours of the castle although it is also possible to wander freely. Each August the grounds play host to the Military Tattoo with massed bands, pipes, drums and display teams from around the world.

☎ 0131 225 9846 www.historic-scotland.gov.uk

Edinburgh Castle

Edinburgh Zoo
373 A2

Established in 1913 by the Royal Zoological Society of Scotland, and set in 80 acres (32ha) of beautiful parkland on the side of Corstorphine Hill. The zoo has over 1000 animals, many of them rare or threatened in the wild, ranging in size from the tiny blue poison arrow frogs to the giant white rhinos. The zoo is best known for its penguins, which swim in the world's largest penguin pool and participate in the Penguin Parade, to the delight of children of all ages.

☎ 0131 314 0300 www.edinburghzoo.org.uk

Edinburgh Zoo

Edzell Castle & Garden
303 D3

The castle is a late medieval, red stoned tower house incorporated into a 16th century courtyard mansion. There is a splendid walled garden, laid out by Sir David Lindsay in 1604. Its walls incorporate a wonderful display of heraldic and symbolic sculptures, alternating with recesses filled with flowers and bird's nests. At its far corners, find a well preserved, two-storey summerhouse and the remains of a bathhouse.

☎ 01356 648631 www.historic-scotland.gov.uk

Eilean Donan Castle
307 E2

Situated on an islet in Loch Duich, this picturesque and inhabited castle dates back to 1214. It passed into the hands of the Mackenzies of Kintail, who became the Earls of Seaforth, was garrisoned by Spanish Jacobite troops in 1715 and blown up by the English. During the 20th century, the castle was fully restored.

☎ 01599 555202 www.eileandonancastle.com

Elgin Cathedral (Ruins)
323 E3

The magnificent and substantial ruin of the 13th century cathedral known as the 'Lantern of the North' and regarded by many as the most beautiful in Scotland. Interesting features include the 15th century octagonal chapter house with vaulted ceiling and a Pictish cross-slab in the choir. Spectacular views of the cathedral and surrounding area are possible from a platform at the top of one of the massive towers.

☎ 01343 547171 www.historic-scotland.gov.uk

Elgin Museum
323 E3

Internationally renowned for its fossils and Pictish stones, the museum houses unique collections of natural history, geology, archaeology, art, ethnography and the social history of the Moray area.

☎ 01343 543675 www.elginmuseum.org.uk

Fair Isle
342 A5

Situated between Orkney and Shetland, Fair Isle is one of Britain's most isolated inhabited islands. Most famous for the intricately patterned knitwear which bears its name, this craft continues today. It is important, too, for its birdlife and there are many opportunities for ornithological studies, including the Bird Observatory. The island's archaeology provides much interest and traditional crofting is also still in evidence.

www.fairisle.org.uk
www.nts.org.uk

Falkirk Wheel
284 C1

A spectacular wheel reconnects the Union Canal up 82ft (25m) to the Forth and Clyde Canal. Weighing 1300 tonnes (2205 pounds), it is equivalent in height to a nine-storey block of flats and is the world's only rotating boat lift. The visitor centre provides information about the construction of the wheel and the restoration of the canal.

☎ 01324 619888 www.thefalkirkwheel.co.uk

Falkland Palace (NTS)
294 A4

Built in the 1500s, Falkland Palace formed the country residence of the Stewart Kings and Queens. Restored period rooms on view include the Chapel Royal, the King's Bedchamber and the Queen's Room. The fine gardens contain the original royal tennis court, built in 1539 and the oldest still in use in Britain today.

☎ 01337 857397 www.nts.org.uk

Falls of Clyde Wildlife Reserve & Visitor Centre
284 C5

The reserve covers almost 150 acres (59ha) of ancient woodland along both sides of the gorge alongside the River Clyde. The Clyde flows over four waterfalls within the reserve, the largest of which, Corra Linn, features an 84ft (26m) drop. The reserve, run by the Scottish Wildlife Trust, has recorded sightings of over 100 species of bird and in spring and summer it is possible to catch sight of breeding peregrine falcons. The visitor centre, housed in the old Dye House at New Lanark, has information on all the wildlife that make the reserve their home.

☎ 01555 665262 www.swt.org.uk

Fife Folk Museum
294 B3

The local museum is housed in a 17th century tollbooth and 18th century weavers' cottages overlooking the Ceres Burn. The collection illustrates the social, economic and cultural history of rural Fife.

☎ 01334 828180 www.fifefolkmuseum.co.uk

Finlaystone House Gardens
283 E2

140 acres (57ha) of woodland, waterfalls and gardens surround the 14th century Finlaystone House (not open to the public). The family-run estate overlooks the River Clyde and there are spectacular views across the Firth. The extensive gardens were originally laid out in 1900 and are considered to be among the finest in Scotland. The whole estate can be explored via a number of trails leading to picnic sites and adventure play areas. There is also a visitor centre.

☎ 01475 540505 www.finlaystone.co.uk

Floors Castle
278 B3

Thought to be Scotland's largest inhabited castle, this magnificent, castellated Georgian mansion was designed by William Adam although the more flamboyant turrets and cupolas were added in Victorian times. The public apartments display an outstanding collection of 17th and 18th century French furniture, together with magnificent Brussels tapestries, paintings by Matisse and Augustus John, and European and Chinese porcelain.

The herbaceous borders in the walled garden are splendidly colourful in summer, while the extensive parkland which overlooks the River Tweed offers a range of woodland walks.

☎ 01573 223333 www.floorscastle.com

Floors Castle

Fort George
321 G4

A vast site of one of the most outstanding artillery fortifications in Europe, having been planned in 1747 as a base for George II's army and completed in 1769. It continues to serve as a barracks and remains virtually unaltered. There is much to see, including the Queen's Own Highlanders Regimental Museum.

☎ 01667 462777 www.historic-scotland.gov.uk

Fyvie Castle (NTS)
312 C1

Adorned with turrets, gables and towers, Fyvie is one of the finest examples of Scottish baronial architecture. The five towers were reputedly built by, and named after, each of the families who owned the castle in succession – Preston, Meldrum, Seton, Gordon and Leith. The oldest part dates from the 13th century and there are ghosts and legends associated with the castle. The interior has some original 17th century plaster ceilings, an impressive decorated wheel staircase and collections of portraits, arms and armour, and 17th century tapestries. In the landscaped parkland visitors can enjoy a variety of scenic lochside walks. Traditional Scottish fruits and vegetables are grown in the old walled garden.

☎ 01651 891266 www.nts.org.uk

Gallery of Modern Art
387 M7

Opened in 1996 and housed in an elegant neo-classical city centre building, this popular gallery shows contemporary artwork by British artists. There is also a wide range of temporary exhibitions and a programme of events including music, drama and dance.

☎ 0141 229 1996 www.glasgowmuseums.com

Georgian House (NTS)
397 E1

The north side of Charlotte Square has been referred to as Robert Adam's masterpiece and is perhaps the finest example of neoclassical architecture in the country. The Georgian House at number 7 has had three floors elegantly restored to reflect the way the house would have looked during its ownership by the Lamont Family who bought the house in 1796.

☎ 0131 226 3318 www.nts.org.uk

Gladstone Court Museum
276 B2

A reconstructed Victorian street which brings to life small town life as it was during the second half of the 19th century. The town of Biggar has more museums per head of population than anywhere else in Scotland – others are Greenhill Covenanters' House, the Gasworks Museum, the Puppet Theatre and Moat Park Heritage Centre.

☎ 01899 221573 www.biggar-net.co.uk/museums

Gladstones Land (NTS)
397 E2

A superb example of a 17th century tenement house, this six-storey mansion has been wonderfully restored to indicate what life was like here in the 1600s. Particularly impressive are the decorated ceilings and wall friezes of the Painted Chamber.

☎ 0131 226 5856 www.nts.org.uk

Glamis Castle
302 B5

Originally a 14th century, three-storey keep, the present turreted castle was modified in the 17th century. One of the oldest parts is Duncan's Hall, legendary setting for Shakespeare's 'Macbeth'. Family home to the Earls of Strathmore, it was the late Queen Mother's childhood home and birthplace of Princess Margaret. On display are fine collections of china, paintings, tapestries and furniture.

☎ 01307 840394 www.glamis-castle.co.uk

Glasgow Botanic Garden
374 B2

Since 1842 these gardens have been a tranquil oasis in Glasgow's bustling West End. The gardens have long been known for their glasshouses and the largest is the huge Kibble Palace erected in 1873 and home to tree ferns from Australia and New Zealand, and plants from Africa, the Far East and the Americas. Other specialist plant collections include cacti, orchids and begonias.

☎ 0141 334 2422

Glasgow School of Art
386 J5

The work of Charles Rennie Mackintosh (1868 – 1928) has become synonymous with Glasgow. He blends organic forms with linear and geometric designs to create fabulous architecture, furniture and art work. Mackintosh was a student at the Glasgow School of Art before winning a competition to design a new building to house the school. Built between 1897 and 1907, the building is today considered to be his finest example of work and is the earliest example of a complete art nouveau building in the country. The only way to see the interior of the building is on a student-led guided tour.

☎ 0141 353 4526 www.gsa.ac.uk

Glasgow Science Centre
386 A8

A stunning titanium-clad building alongside the Clyde. The site is made up of three attractions – the IMAX theatre, the three-storey Science Mall and the Glasgow Tower. The IMAX has a cinema screen larger than a five-a-side football pitch and shows 2D and 3D films. The Science Mall has hundreds of hands-on exhibits, workshops and a planetarium. The Glasgow Tower, which at 328ft (100m) is the highest free-standing structure in Scotland and the only 360 degree rotating structure in the world, has information on past and future developments in Glasgow as well as superb views from the top. Tickets can be purchased for single attractions or there is a double ticket allowing entrance to two attractions.

☎ 0141 420 5000 www.gsc.org.uk

Glencoe
298 D4

This is a highly dramatic and historic glen. It has been the scene of numerous feudal clashes, particularly between the MacDonald and Campbell clans, and is probably best known for the 1692 massacre of part of the MacDonald clan by soldiers of King William. In fact, its name translates as 'Valley of Weeping'.

Its steep-sided mountains offer superb walking and climbing. Geologically, they also provide an example of a collapsed volcano. Red deer, wildcats, golden eagles and rare arctic plants can be seen among the breathtaking peaks and spectacular waterfalls. There are many walks, some more challenging than others.

☎ 01854 811307 www.nts.org.uk

Glencoe Visitor Centre (NTS)
298 D4

The visitor centre buildings have been laid out as a 'clachan' or small settlement and have fascinating interactive displays and exhibits about the history, geology and conservation of the area. A video recording recounts the massacre of part of the MacDonald clan by soldiers of King William in 1692. The Glencoe Lookout Station shows web cam images and the 'Living on the Edge' exhibition includes information about the history of mountaineering.

☎ 01855 811307 www.nts.org.uk

Glenfiddich Distillery
323 F5

Situated close to the river Fiddich, the distillery produces the only Highland single malt whisky that is distilled, aged and bottled at the same site. Glenfiddich is the world's biggest selling single malt and visitors can tour the distillery where production first started on Christmas Day 1887. Although the tour is free, there is a charge for a much longer connoisseur's tour and tasting.

☎ 01340 820373 www.glenfiddich.com

Glenfinnan Monument (NTS)
298 B1

Set amid superb Highland scenery at the head of Loch Shiel, Glenfinnan monument was erected in 1815 in tribute to the clansmen who died for the Jacobite cause. It is sited where Bonnie Prince Charlie raised his standard in 1745. The information centre recounts the Prince's campaign with displays and an audiovisual programme. Nearby is the Glenfinnan Viaduct, a spectacular railway viaduct with 21 arches, built in 1901.

☎ 01397 722250 www.nts.org.uk

Glenluce Abbey (NTS)
264 C5

Founded in 1192, the Cistercian monks' diligence in draining the surrounding marshes to create productive land ensured the abbey's survival. The chapter house, built around 1500, has endured almost intact with unusual decorative carvings and a ribbed vault ceiling providing splendid acoustics. More prosaic, but equally interesting are the well preserved clay drains and waterpipes laid by the monks. A small museum displays artefacts relating to the abbey, which was finally abandoned in 1560.

☎ 01581 300541 www.historic-scotland.gov.uk

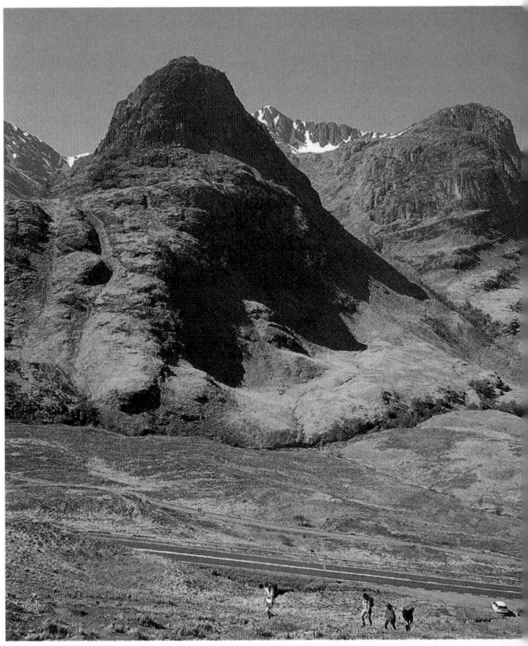

Glencoe

Glenturret Distillery
293 D2

Whisky is still produced in the traditional manner at Scotland's oldest Highland malt distillery (established in 1775). Set in a picturesque location, enjoy free tasting as well as the Famous Grouse Experience in the interactive visitor centre.

☎ 01764 656565 www.glenturret.com

Gordon Highlanders Regimental Museum 313 E4

Striking exhibits from a unique collection, recalling 200 years of service of the regiment which largely recruited soldiers from north east Scotland. The medal display includes 12 Victoria crosses. Interactive screens and an audiovisual theatre serve to dramatise the history of this famous regiment which was amalgamated to form The Highlanders (Seaforth, Gordons and Camerons) in 1994.

☎ 01224 311200 www.gordonhighlanders.com

Grampian Transport Museum 312 A3

An extensive collection of historic road vehicles, many of them rare and unusual, which illustrates the history of road travel and transport in north-east Scotland. Among the items is the Craigievar Express, a steam powered tricycle built in 1895. With working exhibits, video presentations and the opportunity to climb aboard many vehicles, including a snow plough, it is a lively museum with lots to do.

☎ 019755 62292 www.gtm.org.uk

Greenhill Covenanters' House 276 B2

A 17th century farmhouse, rescued from 10 miles down the road and rebuilt here piece by piece. The museum returns the visitor to troubled times when James VI, Charles I and II, and James VII tried to rule against the wishes of the majority of the population and the Kirk of Scotland. The tale is simply, but comprehensively, told through the life of Lady Greenhill, the then owner of the farmhouse.

☎ 01899 221752 www.biggar-net.co.uk/museums

Grey Mare's Tail (NTS) 276 C4

Spectacular 200ft (61m) waterfall tumbling from the corrie containing Loch Skene down a rocky gorge into Moffat Water. Reached by a path that is precipitous in places.

☎ 01556 502575 www.nts.org.uk

Haddo House (NTS) & Country Park 313 D1

Haddo House is an elegant Georgian mansion designed by William Adam in 1732 for the 2nd Earl of Aberdeen, while much of the splendid interior decoration is Adam Revival style dating from the 1880s. Haddo has a beautiful library and contains some fine furniture and an extensive art collection. The formal garden includes terracing with rose beds.

Adjacent is Haddo Country Park, open all year, with waymarked trails, 3 miles (5km) of surfaced paths and wildlife hides.

☎ 01651 851440 www.nts.org.uk

Hermitage Castle 268 C2

A vast, eerie ruin of a forbidding fortress in a bleak moorland setting, dating from the 14th and 15th centuries and consisting of four towers and connecting walls. The imposing medieval exterior is deceptive as certain features resulted from a Victorian restoration, and inside the structure is little more than a ruin.

☎ 01387 376222 www.historic-scotland.gov.uk

Hermitage, The (NTS) 301 E5

Interesting walks in mixed woodland, containing one of Britain's tallest Douglas fir trees. The focus is a delightful 18th century folly, Ossian's Hall, set above a wooded gorge of the River Braan.

☎ 01796 473233 www.nts.org.uk

Highland Folk Museum 309 G4

An open-air museum, partly housed in an 18th century shooting lodge, illustrating the social history of people in the Highlands. There is another site at Newtonmore.

☎ 01540 661307 www.higlandfolk.com

Highland Wildlife Park 310 A4

Discover Scottish wildlife, from native species to creatures long extinct, in 180 acres (73ha) of parkland. Encounter enormous bison, ancient breeds of sheep and one of the world's rarest mammals, the Przewalski's Horse, by driving through the main reserve (staff will drive those without a car). Special themed events are held at weekends.

☎ 01540 651270 www.highlandwildlifepark.org

Hill House (NTS) 283 D1

Charles Rennie Mackintosh designed this house for the publisher Walter Blackie in 1904. A masterpiece of domestic architecture synthesizing traditional Scottish style with avant-garde innovation, this extraordinary building still looks modern today. Mackintosh, with his wife Margaret, also designed the interiors and most of the furniture.

☎ 01436 67900 www.nts.org.uk

Hill of Tarvit Mansion House & Garden (NTS) 294 B3

Sir Robert Lorimer designed this fine Edwardian house to provide a setting for his important collection of French, Chippendale style and vernacular furniture. Superb paintings, Flemish tapestries and Chinese porcelain and bronzes adorn the interiors. Lorimer also designed the formal gardens.

☎ 01334 653127 www.nts.org.uk

Hopetoun House

Hopetoun House 285 E2

Set in 100 acres (40ha) of magnificent parkland on the shores of the Firth of Forth, this house is one of Scotland's finest stately homes. It is the work of William Bruce, the architect who designed Holyroodhouse, and was later extended by William Adam. The magnificent state rooms feature the original 18th century furniture, remarkable paintings including works by Gainsborough, Raeburn and Canaletto, rococo ceilings, 17th century Aubusson tapestries, Meissen porcelain and some spectacular chandeliers in the Ballroom. The extensive parkland has woodland and riverside walks, a deer park and a walled garden.

☎ 0131 331 2451 www.hopetounhouse.com

House of Dun (NTS) 303 E4

Overlooking the Montrose Basin is this beautiful Georgian house, designed in 1730 by William Adam and containing superb contemporary plasterwork. Home during the 19th century to Lady Augusta Kennedy-Erskine, daughter of William IV, many of her belongings remain, as well as her wool work and embroidery.

☎ 01674 810264 www.nts.org.uk

House of the Binns (NTS) 285 E2

Built between 1612 and 1630 by Thomas Dalyell, the house reflects the change in style of Scottish homes during the 17th century, from fortified stronghold to spacious mansion. Four of the main rooms have elaborate plasterwork ceilings and there is some fine furniture dating mostly from the late 18th and early 19th centuries. Outside there are woodland walks to a panoramic viewpoint over the Firth of Forth. The house is only open from June to September.

☎ 01506 834225 www.nts.org.uk

Hugh Miller's Cottage (NTS) 321 G3

The famous stonemason, geologist, writer and church reformer, Hugh Miller (1802 – 56), was born in this furnished thatched cottage, built around 1698. His life and work can be explored through exhibits of his belongings, including his fine fossil collection, his writings and video footage.

☎ 01381 600245 www.nts.org.uk

Huntingtower Castle 293 F2

Known as Ruthven Castle until 1600, Huntingtower Castle is a 15th century castellated mansion. A 17th century range links its two fine and complete towers. A key feature is the outstanding painted ceiling. Noteworthy historic events include a visit by Mary, Queen of Scots, the capture of King James the VI, and the birth of the Jacobite commander, Lord George Murray.

☎ 01738 627231 www.historic-scotland.gov.uk

Hutchesons' Hall (NTS) 387 N7

Built between 1802 and 1805, this elegant building replaced a 17th century hospice, and statues of George and Thomas Hutcheson, taken from the original building, have been incorporated into the frontage. A major rebuild in 1876 heightened the hall and made the way for an impressive staircase. The hall now houses a National Trust for Scotland shop and visitor centre and an exhibition entitled Glasgow Style displaying works by young Glasgow designers.

☎ 0141 552 8391 www.nts.org.uk

Inveraray Castle 290 C4

The Duke of Argyll's family, the senior branch of the Campbell Clan, moved here in the early 15th century. The present building, in the style of a castle, was erected between 1745 and 1790, replacing a previous fortified keep. Explore the grand staterooms, and some of the former bedrooms, and view the famous collections of armour, French tapestries, paintings, and fine Scottish and European furniture. The Clan Room contains a genealogical display. Gardens are open by appointment only.

☎ 01499 302203 www.inveraray-castle.com

Inveraray Jail 290 C4

This award winning attraction re-creates prison life in the 1800s. There are fascinating exhibitions, such as 'Torture, Death and Damnation', where the crank machine, whipping table and hammocks can all be tested first-hand, along with the sounds and smells of everyday life locked in the cells.

☎ 01499 302381 www.inverarayjail.co.uk

Inverewe Gardens (NTS) 319 E1

A world-famous garden created from a once barren peninsula on the shore of Loch Ewe by Victorian gardener Osgood Mackenzie. Exotic plants from many countries flourish here in the mild climate created by the warm currents of the North Atlantic Drift. Find Himalayan rhododendrons, Tasmanian eucalypts, and other subtropical plants from New Zealand, Chile and South Africa.

Much of the garden's structure is original, with work having been started in 1863 and continued by Mackenzie's daughter, until she handed over the estate to the Trust. There is also a visitor centre and access to the wider estate.

☎ 01445 781200 www.nts.org.uk

Iona (NTS) 288 B2

St Columba began to spread the gospel here in AD563, from where Christianity spread throughout Scotland and beyond. Explore the abbey, home to the Iona Community, with a beautiful interior and carvings, the 13th century priory, the oldest cemetery in Scotland, containing the graves of many kings and chiefs, the restored St Oran's Chapel, and the 10th century St Martin's Cross. There are also superb long sandy beaches, turquoise seas and unrivalled views.

☎ 01631 570000 (National Trust Office) www.nts.org.uk

Italian Chapel 339 D2

Italian prisoners of war, whilst constructing the Churchill Barriers in World War II, transformed two corrugated iron Nissen huts into this ornate chapel. Its beautiful interior is the result of their ingenuity and craftsmanship. The painting of Madonna and Child is by Domenico Chioccetti.

☎ 01865 781279

J.M. Barrie's Birthplace & Camera Obscura (NTS) 302 B4

J.M. Barrie, creator of 'Peter Pan', was born in this two-storey weaver's cottage in 1860. The upper floors have been furnished to reflect the era and an exhibition about Barrie's literary and theatrical work is housed next door. Camera Obscura, found within the cricket pavilion on Kirrie Hill, was presented to Kirriemuir by the author.

☎ 01575 572646 www.nts.org.uk

Jarlshof Prehistoric & Norse Settlement 343 G5

A complex of ancient settlements within 3 acres (1.2ha) can be found on this extraordinarily important site. The oldest is a Bronze Age village of oval stone huts. Above this is an Iron Age broch and wheelhouses, and even higher still is an entire Viking settlement. A house, built around 1600, sits on the crest of the mount. Displays in the visitor centre explain Iron Age life and the history of the site.

☎ 01950 460112 www.historic-scotland.gov.uk

Inveraray Jail

Inverewe Gardens

Jedburgh Abbey 278 A5

Dominating the skyline in Jedburgh's centre, this red sandstone abbey was founded by David I in the 12th century, probably on the site of a 9th century church. The remarkably complete abbey church is mostly Romanesque and early Gothic in design, with a fine rose window and richly carved Norman doorway. Cloister remnants have been uncovered and artefacts found are on display at the visitor centre, together with an excellent exhibition on life in the monastery.

Jedburgh suffered various assaults during border warfare and was abandoned in 1560, though the church was used for another three centuries.

☎ 01835 863925 www.historic-scotland.gov.uk

Kelburn Castle & Country Centre 282 D4

Family home of the Earls of Glasgow, comprising a Norman keep within a 16th century castle with later additions, all surrounded by spectacular natural scenery. Activities include assault and adventure courses, horse riding, soft play and, for the less energetic, pets corner, delightful gardens and woodland walks through the Secret Forest. Ranger service and special weekend events.

☎ 01475 568685 www.kelburncountrycentre.com

Kellie Castle (NTS) 294 D4

The oldest part of Kellie Castle dates from 1360, but most of the present building was completed around 1606. It was sympathetically restored by the Lorimer family, who lived here in the 1870s. Inside, there are splendid painted ceilings and panelling, as well as excellent furniture designed by Sir Robert Lorimer. The extensive grounds include a lovely organic Victorian walled garden.

☎ 01333 720271 www.nts.org.uk

Kelso Abbey 278 B3

The largest of the Border abbeys founded by David I in 1128, Kelso was a fine example of Romanesque architecture. Little now remains of this once wealthy and powerful establishment; English raids in the first half of the 16th century focused on the abbey and destruction was completed in 1545 when 100 defenders were slaughtered. All that remains is part of the north-west transept, tower and a fragment of the nave.

☎ 0131 668 8800 www.historic-scotland.gov.uk

Kilchurn Castle 290 D2

A substantial ruin based on a square tower built by Colin Campbell of Glenorchy, circa 1550. It was much enlarged in 1693 by Ian, Earl of Breadalbane, whose arms are over the gateway with those of his wife. The castle incorporates the first purpose-built barracks in Scotland and commands spectacular views down Loch Awe. Open during summer only.

☎ 0131 668 8800 www.historic-scotland.gov.uk

Kildalton Church & Crosses 280 C5

The Old Church at Kildalton is the site of the finest intact High Cross in Scotland. Carved in the late 8th century, the Celtic cross stands 9ft (2.7m) high. There are also several other fine carved gravestones in the churchyard.

☎ 0131 668 8800 www.historic-scotland.gov.uk

Killiecrankie 301 E3

Just north of Pitlochry is the site of the battle of Killiecrankie in 1689, won by the Highland Jacobites under Bonnie Dundee. On the edge of the wooded gorge is the Pass of Killiecrankie Visitor Centre, which relates the fierce encounter. From here, a path leads to 'Soldiers Leap', where a fleeing government soldier made a spectacular jump over the River Garry during the battle.

☎ 01796 473233 www.nts.org.uk

Kilmartin House Museum 290 A5

Within a six-mile (10km) radius of Kilmartin Valley, over 350 ancient monuments can be found, including 150 that are prehistoric. This award-winning archaeological museum examines the relationship between Scotland's richest prehistoric landscape and its people. Artefacts from ancient monuments, reconstructions and interactive audiovisual displays make a fascinating exhibition.

☎ 01546 510278 www.kilmartin.org

Kintail Estate & Morvich (NTS) 307 G3

This west Highland estate is home to the Falls of Glomach, an impressive 370ft (113m) high waterfall, and the Five Sisters of Kintail, four of which are over 3000ft (915m). The site of the Battle of Glen Shiel, which took place in 1719, is also within this area, 5 miles (8km) from Morvich. The best access to the mountains is from the Countryside Centre at Morvich.

☎ 01599 511231 www.nts.org.uk

Kirkcaldy Museum & Art Gallery 294 A5

Located in the attractive War Memorial Gardens, the gallery contains fine and decorative arts of local and national importance. There is an outstanding collection of 18th to 20th century Scottish paintings, and probably the largest public collection of works by William McTaggart and the Scottish colourist, S.J. Peploe, outside the National Galleries of Scotland.

☎ 01592 412860

Lennoxlove — 286 C2

Lennoxlove House is the seat of the Duke of Hamilton and there are fine collections of furniture and family portraits belonging to the Hamilton family. The earliest part of the house, the rectangular keep, was built well before 1400 and there have been extensions and additions during every century since. The various owners of the house have associations with the Stewarts and there are a number of mementoes belonging to Mary, Queen of Scots, including her death mask.

☎ 01620 823720 www.lennoxlove.org

Lighthouse, The — 387 L8

Scotland's Centre for Architecture, Design and the City is the long-term legacy of Glasgow being the UK City of Architecture and Design in 1999. This Charles Rennie Mackintosh-designed building, once owned by the Herald newspaper, has a distinctive tower at one corner which gives it the name the Lighthouse. It houses the Mackintosh Interpretation Centre which features plans, photos and models of his work, and there are great views over the city skyline from the top of the tower.

☎ 0141 221 6362 www.thelighthouse.co.uk

Linlithgow Palace — 285 E2

The ruin of a great 15th century Palace on the edge of Linlithgow Loch which is associated with many of Scotland's best known historical figures; James V and Mary, Queen of Scots, were both born here. The palace was damaged by fire in 1746 and it has been a roofless ruin ever since. The chapel is worth a look and the galleried Great Hall is magnificent. The quadrangle courtyard has a richly-carved 16th century fountain.

☎ 01506 842896 www.historic-scotland.gov.uk

Linn of Tummel (NTS) — 301 E3

Follow a riverside nature trail, from Garry Bridge, through mixed woodland to the meeting place of the Rivers Garry and Tummel. The Linn of Tummel, which translates as 'pool of the tumbling stream', comprises a series of rocky rapids in a beautiful setting.

☎ 01796 473233 www.nts.org.uk

Loch an Eilein Visitor Centre & Forest Trail — 310 A4

An island in Loch an Eilein harbours the remains of a 15th century castle. An ancient pine forest surrounds the loch, with some species dating back to the era of Bonnie Prince Charlie. There is a waymarked forest trail and a visitor centre.

Loch Lomond & The Trossachs National Park — 291 F4

In 2002, Loch Lomond and the Trossachs were inaugurated as Scotland's first National Park. The park stretches from Arrochar to Callander, west to east, and from Balloch to Crianlarich, south to north. It is an area of contrasts, depicted by the lochs, wooded hills and lowlands in the south to the rugged and dramatic Highland mountains in the north. Ben Lomond towers over Loch Lomond, Britain's largest expanse of fresh water, and visitors can enjoy the wild glens and unspoilt lochs of the Trossachs. The Breadalbane area boasts numerous mountains over 3000ft (915m), including Ben More, Ben Lui, Ben Challum and Ben Vorlich, whilst the Argyll Forest in the west is overlooked by the Arrochar Alps and bounded by sea lochs.

Loch Lomond Shores visitor centre in Balloch provides the main gateway into the National Park.

☎ 01389 722600 www.lochlomond-trossachs.org

Loch Ness Monster Exhibition Centre — 309 E2

The story of Loch Ness, the monster and other mysteries of the area are presented in a wide-screen cinema. Find out about the sightings of 'Nessie' and the various search expeditions, view the account of John Cobb's world water speed record attempt in 1953 on Loch Ness and hear about the 18th century mysterious 'footprints'.

☎ 01456 450342 www.lochness-centre.com

Lochore Meadows Country Park — 293 G5

Green and pleasant countryside reclaimed from coal mining wasteland in the 1960s, set around a large lake. Find a variety of activities within the 1200 acres (486ha), including golf, fishing, sailing, windsurfing, walking and horse riding. There is also a nature reserve with a bird-watching hide and ancient historical remains, such as Lochore Castle. Admission to the park is free, with charges for the activities.

☎ 01592 414300 www.lochore-meadows.co.uk

Logan Botanic Garden — 256 A2

The exceptionally mild climate, courtesy of the Gulf Stream, makes this one of Scotland's most exotic gardens, allowing a colourful array of tender plants to thrive. Many specimens are of wild origin, particularly representing the temperate regions of the Southern Hemisphere. The peat garden comprises a delightful collection of meconopsis, primulas, trilliums and dwarf rhododendrons. The walled garden has spring interest with magnolis, camellias, rhododendrons and a splendid collection of half-hardy perennials for summer colour. The woodland garden boasts mature eucalyptus and unusual, colourful southern hemisphere shrubs. Recent introductions are a result of plant hunting trips to Chile. There is also a Discovery Centre informing visitors of the work of the National Botanic Gardens of Scotland.

☎ 01776 860231 www.rbge.org.uk

Maes Howe — 340 B5

This chambered cairn is the finest megalithic (Neolithic) tomb in the British Isles. It consists of a large mound 115ft (35m) in diameter covering a stone-built passage and a large burial chamber with cells in the walls. Vikings and Norse crusaders carved the runic inscriptions in the walls. Admission, shop and tearoom are at the nearby 19th century Tormiston Mill.

☎ 01856 761606 www.historic-scotland.gov.uk

Manderston — 287 F4

Manderston could well be described as a celebration of opulence; a relatively modest 18th century house transformed by architect James Kinross into an extravagant, neoclassical Edwardian mansion.

Luxurious rooms boast intricate plasterwork, silk and velvet wall hangings, panelling and fine furniture. Marble abounds, from inlaid floors to the magnificent, probably unique staircase with its silver-plated balustrade. For contrast, the 'below stairs' element is also on view, together with a large collection of Blue John pieces and a biscuit tin museum.

Similarly, no expense was spared on the 56 acre (22ha) grounds. There are four splendid formal Edwardian terraces overlooking a lake and informal woodland gardens, while the walled gardens combine colourful plantings with fountains and statuary.

☎ 01361 883450 www.manderston.co.uk

McManus Galleries — 396 B2

Contained within this Victorian Gothic building, designed by Sir George Gilbert Scott, are some remarkable collections of national importance. The galleries feature local history, costume, natural history, archaeology, decorative arts and a superb Scottish Victorian art collection. Do not miss the magnificent Albert Hall with its fine stained glass window and vaulted roof.

☎ 01382 432350 www.dundeecity.gov.uk/mcmanus

Meigle Sculptured Stones — 302 A5

This is one of the most notable collections of Dark Age sculpture in Western Europe. There are 26 carved stones, the largest over 8ft (2m) tall.

☎ 01828 640612 www.historic-scotland.gov.uk

Loch Lomond

Mellerstain

Mellerstain
278 A3

A superb Georgian mansion representing some of the best architectural work of William Adam, who began the building in 1725, and his son, Robert, who completed it some 50 years later, giving a wonderful opportunity to compare their styles. The Robert Adam interior decoration is an outstanding feature of Mellerstain, the exquisite ceilings preserved in the original colours being particularly remarkable. Interior decoration is matched by the furnishings; pieces by Chippendale, Hepplewhite and Sheraton, and paintings by Van Dyck, Gainsborough and Aikman.

The gardens are formal, comprising Italianate terraces with magnificent views of the Cheviot Hills whilst the grounds, designed by William Adam in the style of Lancelot 'Capability' Brown, make a splendid backdrop to the house.

☎ 01573 410225 www.mellerstain.com

Melrose Abbey
277 G2

A Cistercian abbey founded in 1136 by David I, noted for its elegant and elaborate masonry. Largely demolished by the English in 1385, it was rebuilt in the Gothic style but was finally destroyed in 1545. It is considered the most beautiful of the great Border abbeys, delicately carved stonework giving an intimation of its former splendour. The outer shell of the abbey church is still extant, with its magnificent east window.

An embalmed heart, thought to be that of Robert the Bruce, was found here. On his express wish it was taken for burial in the Holy Land, but the courier was killed in Spain and the heart returned to Scotland.

☎ 01896 822562 www.historic-scotland.gov.uk

Mount Stuart
282 C4

A spectacular Victorian Gothic house, Mount Stuart is the ancestral home of the Marquess of Bute. Its splendid interiors and architecture include a mix of astrological designs, stained glass and marble. In the 300 acres (121ha) of grounds and gardens there is a mature Victorian pinetum, arboretum and exotic gardens.

☎ 01700 503877 www.mountstuart.com

Mousa Broch
343 D5

This is the finest surviving Iron Age broch tower, standing over 40ft (12m) high. The stairs can be climbed to the parapet.

☎ 01466 793191 www.historic-scotland.gov.uk

Museum of Childhood
397 E3

Devoted to the history of childhood, this is an enchanting, colourful and extremely noisy place! Children love this museum for the sheer quantity of dolls, trains, models, games and books from all over the world, and adults love it for its nostalgia factor.

☎ 0131 529 4142 www.cac.org.uk

Museum of Flight
286 C2

There are around 50 complete aircraft, 80 engines and 5000 items of aircraft related equipment on display at Scotland's national aviation museum. The planes range from the oldest, the Hawk glider of 1896, to modern passenger airlines, supersonic jet fighters and Concorde. There are special exhibitions on space flight, early aviation and air traffic control. An annual airshow gives visitors the chance to see many planes in flight.

☎ 01620 880308 www.nms.ac.uk/flight

Museum of Scotland
397 E2

Scotland's national museum is housed in a striking, modern sandstone building completed in 1998. The museum traces the history and achievements of Scotland and its people, from the country's geological beginnings right up to the present day. The lower floors cover the period up to about 1700 with displays of rocks and fossils, Roman, Pictish and Gaelic artefacts. Two floors are devoted to Industry and Empire and tell of how the Scots pioneered many aspects of heavy engineering. The top floor covers the 20th century and is based around items that Scottish people thought best represented their country, which has resulted in displays on Irn-Bru and football strips, amongst others. There are free themed tours at regular intervals throughout the day and audio guides are available.

☎ 0131 247 4422 www.nms.ac.uk

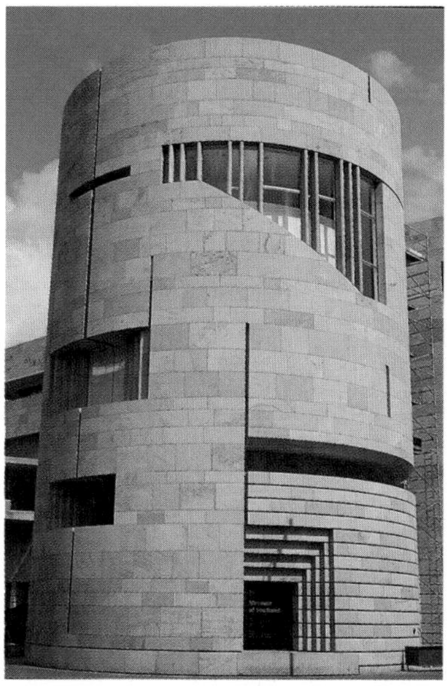

Museum of Scotland

Museum of Scottish Lead Mining
275 G4

Set in Wanlockhead, Scotland's highest village in the dramatic Lowther Hills, the museum traces 300 years of local lead mining history. A walk-through exhibition in the excellent visitor centre explains mining and extraction processes, and there is a good display of local minerals, including galena, chalcopyrite and sphalerite. A village trail includes a guided tour round Lochgell Lead Mine, together with restored miners' cottages.

☎ 01659 74387 www.leadminingmuseum.co.uk

National Gallery of Scotland
397 E2

This fine Greek temple style building was designed by William Henry Playfair and opened to the public in 1859. It houses Scotland's greatest collections of European paintings and sculpture from the Renaissance to post-impressionist periods. There are works by Raphael, Titian, El Greco, Turner, Degas and Van Gogh as well as a superb collection of Scottish art featuring important works by Wilkie, Raeburn and Ramsay.

☎ 0131 624 6200 www.natgalscot.ac.uk

National Wallace Monument
292 D5

The National Wallace Monument takes visitors back 700 years to the days of Scotland's first struggle for independence. The story of William Wallace, freedom fighter and national hero, is told along with events that shaped this period of history. Climb the 246 steps to the top of the 220ft (67m) high tower for superb views.

☎ 01786 472140 www.stirling.co.uk/attractions/wallace.htm

Neidpath Castle
276 D2

A rare example of a 14th century castle converted to a 17th century tower house, in a spectacular setting above the River Tweed. Massive walls, some 12ft (3.5m) thick in places, withstood Civil War bombardment longer than any other castle in the area, while inside is a pit prison cut out of the rock. The Great Hall hosts an exhibition of beautiful batik wall hangings depicting the life of Mary, Queen of Scots. Check in advance for opening times.

☎ 01721 720333

New Lanark World Heritage Site
284 C5

New Lanark is a superb example of a restored industrial village with plenty to keep a family busy for most of the day. Founded in 1785 by David Dale and Richard Arkwright as a centre for cotton spinning, the elegant sandstone buildings sit alongside the River Clyde in a remarkable rural setting. Dale's son-in-law, Robert Owen, took over the management of the site in 1798 and his belief in looking out for the welfare of his workers led to him setting up a cooperative store, a nursery to allow mothers with young children to work, adult education facilities, decent housing and a social centre for the community of 2500 people. Owen's 'social experiment' was viewed with scorn by all of his competitors but his beliefs soon proved fruitful and the business was greatly improved. The Institute for the Formation of Character now houses the award winning visitor centre and the Millennium Experience, an innovative ride which explains Owen's aspirations and ideas for a better future. Visitors can also look around the village store, Owen's house and mill workers' cottages. A passport ticket gives access to all of these attractions.

☎ 01555 661345 www.newlanark.org

New Lanark World Heritage Site

North West Highlands – Suilven

North West Highlands 320 A5

The North West Highlands provides a stunning and dramatic landscape of rugged mountains, hidden glens, moorlands, pine forests, secluded sandy beaches and sea lochs.

In Torridon, find mountain peaks towering over 3000ft (914m), whilst Ullapool is a thriving fishing village. Other remote villages along the north-west coast include Lochinver and Kinlochbervie. In Poolewe, find Inverewe Gardens, formed from a once barren peninsula on the shore of Loch Ewe, where exotic plants flourish in the warm climate created by the North Atlantic Drift. Alternatively, drive on Scotland's highest road, Bealach na Ba, climbing to the summit at 2056ft (625m) for spectacular views.

There are many natural features to look out for, too. Eas a' Chual Aluinn is Britain's tallest waterfall, and Corrieshalloch Gorge is one of Britain's finest examples of a box canyon. From here, a viewing platform stretched across the gorge looks up towards the magnificent Falls of Measach. Smoo Cave, in Durness, is an impressive limestone cave which has formed at the head of a narrow coastal inlet. The wild surroundings are also home to a variety of wildlife including red deer, eagles, otters and seals.

Old Man of Hoy 338 A2

Standing off the magnificent cliffs of north-west Hoy is this prominent, isolated sea stack. Comprised of red sandstone, it stands at 450ft (137m) high. The Old Man of Hoy can also be seen from the Scrabster to Stromness ferry.

Our Dynamic Earth 397 E3

This is a great family attraction based in a tented futuristic looking dome. Ten themed areas make use of dramatic special effects, stunning imagery and state-of-the-art interactive displays to take the visitor on a journey of discovery from the very beginning of time to our unknown future. Visitors begin their journey in the time machine elevator which takes them back to the creation of the universe before moving through a series of galleries that explain how the earth and continents were formed, how life has developed on earth and all about the seas and oceans.

☎ 0131 550 7800 www.dynamicearth.co.uk

Paisley Museum & Art Galleries 374 A3

The Paisley Pattern is a well-known fabric design of swirling teardrops or pine cones. Paisley Museum has the world's largest collection of Paisley shawls, as well as the looms on which these intricately patterned garments were created. There is also a nationally important collection of ceramics and many fine 19th century Scottish paintings.

☎ 0141 889 3151 www.renfrewshire.gov.uk

Palace of Holyroodhouse 397 E3

Largely a 17th century building, the north-west tower was built in 1501 for James IV. Holyroodhouse is the Queen's official residence in Scotland and it is used for state ceremonies. The Great Gallery occupies the whole of the first floor of the north wing, and in it hang 89 portraits of real and legendary kings of Scotland. The state apartments reflect the changing tastes of successive monarchs and are renowned for their fine stucco ceilings. Mary, Queen of Scots' chambers can be viewed in the west corner tower. The Queen's Gallery, for which there is a separate charge, hosts a programme of changing exhibitions from the Royal Collection, focusing primarily on works from the Royal Library at Windsor Castle.

☎ 0131 556 5100 www.royal.gov.uk

Our Dynamic Earth

Paxton House 287 G4

Superb 18th century Palladian mansion, designed by John and James Adam and further embellished by brother Robert, providing an interesting contrast in styles. As well as the notable interior decoration, this is essential viewing for furniture enthusiasts, with one of the greatest Chippendale collections in Scotland and fine Regency furniture by William Trotter of Edinburgh. The large art gallery, an out-station for the National Galleries for Scotland, has a programme of temporary exhibitions.

The 80 acres (32ha) of parkland surrounding the house offer walks along the banks of the River Tweed and an adventure playground.

☎ 01289 386291 www.paxtonhouse.com

People's Story Museum 397 E3

A lively museum, in the picturesque Canongate Tolbooth which was built in 1591. It uses oral history, reminiscence and written sources to tell the story of the lives, work and leisure of the ordinary people of Edinburgh, from the late 18th century to the present day.

☎ 0131 529 4057 www.cac.org.uk

Pitmedden Garden (NTS) 313 D2

A 17th century walled garden, notable for the Great Garden which is made up of four parterres of elaborate designs in boxwood hedging. These are filled with colourful annual bedding in summer. Interest is also provided by large herbaceous borders, roses, espalier fruit trees, roses and an herb garden. On the surrounding 100 acre (40ha) estate there is the Museum of Farming Life.

☎ 01651 842352 www.nts.org.uk

Pollok House (NTS) 374 B3

The Pollok Estate has been the home of the Maxwell family since the 13th century and the current house, an impressive Edwardian country mansion, was built in 1740. Sir William Stirling Maxwell (1818 – 1878) was an authority on the art and history of Spain and his collection of works by Goya and El Greco is superb. There is also a fine collection of the work of English poet and artist William Blake, as well as silverware and furnishings from the Edwardian period. The gardens are also worth a look with a collection of over 1000 species of rhododendron. Entrance is free from November to March.

☎ 0141 616 6410 www.nts.org.uk

Preston Mill & Phantassie Dovecot (NTS) 286 C2

A picturesque 18th century grain mill that was used commercially up until 1959. Today the mill no longer produces grain but visitors can see and hear the machinery and water wheel in action. There is an exhibition on milling and a display on the history of Preston Mill. It is a short scenic walk to the Phantassie Dovecot which once held 500 birds.

☎ 01620 860426 www.nts.org.uk

Priorwood (NTS) 277 G2

A specialist garden with varied and colourful herbaceous borders, plants being especially selected for drying qualities. This takes place on the premises where visitors can learn about the art of dried flower arranging. The garden also has an organic orchard growing historic apple varieties.

☎ 01896 822493 www.nts.org.uk

Queensferry Museum
285 F2

Traces the history of the people of Queensferry, the historic ferry crossing to Fife, the building of the Forth road and rail bridges, and the wildlife in the Forth estuary.

☎ 0131 331 5545 www.cac.org.uk

Rannoch Moor
299 F4

A wild, remote and fairly level area of around 50 sq miles (130 sq km), at an altitude of 1000ft (305m) surrounded by mountains. It is predominantly covered in a mixture of heather, peat bogs, rocks, and numerous lochs and streams. From the moor, enjoy fine views of Black Mount, Glencoe and the Grampians.

Rannoch Station can be found at the end of the B846, from where the only way to cross east to west is by foot. The main roads travel along its outer edges, while the West Highland Railway crosses it from south to north. Both the north and the south shores of the 10 mile (16km) long Loch Rannoch can be travelled along, with the south being the more scenic. The Blackwood of Rannoch, situated on the southern shore, is one of the last remaining examples of ancient Caledonian Forest and an important source of Scots Pine seed. An ancient burial ground of St Michael's can also be found. Loch Ericht lies to the north, accessed via a tunnel aqueduct.

There are plenty of scenic walks to enjoy on the moor. The lochs are also popular for trout fishing, while their sandy shores and islands attract many birds such as black-throated divers and goosander.

Ring of Brogar
340 A5

The Ring of Brodgar (also known as the Ring of Brogar) is a magnificent circle of upright stones, dating back to the Neolithic period. A ditch encloses the stones and is spanned by entrance causeways.

☎ 01855 841815 www.historic-scotland.gov.uk

Rosslyn Chapel
285 G3

A mysterious 15th century chapel that is thought to be just part of a much larger once-planned collegiate church whose foundations have been excavated. The carvings on the exterior and inside are outstanding; there are botanically accurate plants and leaves as well as biblical, pagan and masonic symbology.

☎ 0131 440 2159 www.rosslynchapel.org.uk

Royal Botanic Garden

Rannoch Moor

Royal Botanic Garden
373 B1

The Botanics are acknowledged to be some of the finest gardens in the world and the beautifully landscaped gardens cover an area of over 70 acres (28ha). The amazing Glasshouse Experience, a series of ten themed glasshouses with five different climatic zones to suit plants from all over the world, is home to giant water lilies and amazing orchids. There is an elegant 1850s glass topped Palm House, which is Britain's tallest and houses a 200 year old palm tree. Other spectacular areas are the Chinese Hillside, the renowned Rock Garden, the Scottish Heath Garden and an arboretum with over 200 species of tree. Guided tours are available between April and September for a fee.

☎ 0131 552 7171 www.rbge.org.uk

Royal Museum of Scotland
397 E2

Thirty-six galleries of varying sizes present artefacts from around the globe, natural history specimens, and engines and other industrial machinery. The Main Hall, with its elegant Victorian bird-cage design, is flooded with natural light and provides a great sense of space and tranquility with fountains and fish ponds.

☎ 0131 247 4219 www.nms.ac.uk

Royal Scots Regimental Museum, The
397 E1

Housed in a 1900 Drill Hall, this museum contains paintings, artefacts, silver and medals illustrating the Regiment's illustrious history from its formation in 1633.

☎ 0131 310 5016 www.theroyalscots.co.uk/museum

St Abb's Head (NTS)
287 G3

A 200 acre (80ha) National Nature Reserve on a dramatic, isolated promontory of black volcanic rock. Between April and August sheer 300ft (91m) cliffs provide nest sites for seabird colonies including kittiwakes, guillemots, razorbills and fulmars, while puffins tunnel into the clifftop. The visitor centre's remote camera link allows observation of the birds during the nesting season (entry fee). The headland provides splendid coastal views while the offshore waters are part of Scotland's first voluntary marine nature reserve.

☎ 01890 771443 www.nts.org.uk

St Andrews Cathedral
294 D3

The remains of one of the largest cathedrals in Scotland and the associated domestic ranges of the priory. The museum houses an outstanding collection of early Christian and medieval monuments, and other objets trouvés. St Rules Tower, in the precinct, is part of the first church of the Augustinian canons at St Andrews, built early in the 12th century. A climb up 150 steps is rewarded with fabulous views at the top. Combine a visit with St Andrews Castle.

☎ 01334 472563 www.historic-scotland.gov.uk

St Bride's Church
275 G2

The oldest structure in the village of Douglas, this church was built during the late 14th century. Originally the parish church of Douglas, it later became the mausoleum of the Black Douglas family. The restored choir, which contains three canopied monuments to the Douglas family, and the south side of the nave remain. Access to the church can be arranged by contacting the key keeper, details of which are on the church gate.

☎ 01555 851657 www.historic-scotland.gov.uk

St Giles Cathedral
397 E2

Not strictly a cathedral, as it was only the seat of a bishop on two brief occasions in the 17th century, but the historical title seems to have stuck. The basic structure of the church is late 15th century, although parts of the early 12th century Norman chapel still remain. The cathedral is renowned for its Victorian and 20th century stained glass, Reiger organ and beautiful Thistle Chapel.

☎ 0131 225 9442 www.stgiles.net

St Magnus Cathedral
338 D2

The cathedral was founded by Jarl Rognvald and dedicated to his uncle, St Magnus. The remains of both men are in the massive east choir piers. The original building dates from 1137 – 1200, but sporadic additional work went on until the late 14th century. It contains some of the finest examples of Norman architecture in Scotland, with small additions in transitional styles and some early Gothic work. A charge applies to tour the tower and upper areas, and should be booked in advance.

☎ 01856 874894

Scone Palace
293 G2

A castellated palace, enlarged and embellished in 1803, incorporating the 16th century and earlier palaces. Notable for its grounds and pinetum, and its magnificent collection of porcelain, furniture, ivories, 18th century clocks and 16th century needlework. From the 9th century, Moot Hill at Scone was the site of the famous Coronation Stone of Scone (the Stone of Destiny), and crowning place of Scottish Kings. In 1296 the English seized the Stone and took it to Westminster Abbey. Returned to Scotland's Edinburgh Castle in 1997, a replica now stands on Moot Hill.

☎ 01738 552300 www.scone-palace.co.uk

Scottish Crannog Centre
300 C5

A unique re-creation of an Iron Age loch dwelling, or crannog, this timbered and thatched house, standing on stilts within Loch Tay, has been authentically built using evidence obtained from underwater archaeological excavations of crannogs preserved in the loch.

☎ 01887 830583 www.crannog.co.uk

Scottish Fisheries Museum
295 D4

Housed in 16th to 19th century buildings, the museum describes the history of fishing in Scotland up to the present day.

☎ 01333 310628 www.scottish-fisheries-museum.org

Scottish Maritime Museum
274 B2

An informative museum on the harbourside at Irvine, with sailing and working boats, lifeboats and a collection of documents, photographs and artefacts interpreting Scotland's maritime history.

Indoor exhibits are based in the huge Linthouse Engine Shop which was dismantled and relocated from the Linthouse Shipyard in Govan in 1992. Nearby is a restored tenement flat, typical home to a 1920s shipyard worker. The floating exhibits are moored by the quay. In addition, there is ongoing restoration work on a variety of vessels.

☎ 01294 278283 www.scottishmaritimemuseum.org

Scottish National Gallery of Modern Art
373 B1

Set in beautiful parkland, the gallery has a superb collection of 20th century paintings, graphic art and sculpture amounting to almost 4000 pieces. There are fine examples of work by Lichtenstein, Matisse and Picasso and an unrivalled collection of Scottish art including works by Charles Rennie Mackintosh. The sculpture garden in the grounds has work by Barbara Hepworth, Eduardo Paolazzi and Henry Moore.

☎ 0131 624 6200 www.natgalscot.ac.uk

Scottish National Portrait Gallery
397 D2

Provides a unique visual history of Scotland, told through portraits of the figures who shaped it: royals and rebels, poets and philosophers, heroes and villains. The portraits are all of Scots although not all are by Scots; there is work by Rodin, Van Dyck and Gainsborough. The gallery is also home to the Scottish National Photographic Collection.

☎ 0131 624 6200 www.natgalscot.ac.uk

Scottish Seabird Centre
286 C1

Visitors can watch live pictures, via remote cameras, of the sea birds that make the islands in the Firth of Forth their home. Amongst the estimated 150,000 sea birds are gannets, thought to be the largest colony in the world, terns, guillemots and puffins, as well as seals and dolphins. There is also a cinema showing films on the wildlife, interactive displays and boat trips out to the islands themselves. There are superb views of Bass Rock and the other islands in the Firth of Forth from the roof terrace.

☎ 01620 890202 www.seabird.org

Seton Collegiate Church
286 B2

The chancel and apse of a lovely 15th century church with a transept and steeple added in 1513. Much of the church is in good condition and is full of interesting detail. The grounds of the church have the remains of a number of buildings thought to be priests' houses and there is a display of stonework from Seton Palace, destroyed in 1715.

☎ 01875 813334 www.historic-scotland.gov.uk

Skara Brae
340 A5

This site contains the best preserved group of Stone Age houses in Western Europe. A storm in 1850 lifted the sand covering the area to reveal the remains of this former fishing village. Ten one-roomed houses can be found, joined by covered passages, and contain their original stone furniture, hearths and drains. They provide a remarkable illustration of life in Neolithic times.

☎ 01856 841815 www.historic-scotland.gov.uk

Smith Art Gallery & Museum
292 C5

Displays and exhibitions encapsulate the history of Stirling through a wonderful collection of fine art and natural history. Some unusual pieces on view include the world's oldest dated curling stone, ancient tartans, prehistoric whalebones and the world's oldest football.

☎ 01786 471917 www.smithartgallery.demon.co.uk

Stirling Castle – Robert the Bruce statue

Smoo Cave
334 D2

This impressive limestone cave has formed at the head of a narrow coastal inlet. An easy and safe access path leads into the cave from the road above. At 100ft (30m) wide and 50ft (15m) high, this is arguably one of the largest cave entrances in Britain. A wooden pathway extends into the second inner chamber, where Allt Smoo falls from an opening in the roof. A small boat provides access to the third chamber. The outer cave contains an ancient midden, indicating that Stone Age man once lived there. The cave is free to enter on foot, whilst a charge applies to enter by boat.

☎ 01971 511259 www.smoocave.org

Souter Johnnie's Cottage (NTS)
274 A5

A thatched cottage, home to souter (cobbler) John Davidson, a drinking companion of Robert Burns, and inspiration for Souter Johnnie in Burns' poem 'Tam O' Shanter'. The cottage contains Burns memorabilia and a reconstructed cobbler's workshop.

☎ 01655 760603 www.nts.org.uk

Staffa (Fingal's Cave) (NTS)
288 C1

This romantic, uninhabited island is famed for its extraordinary basaltic column formations. The best known of these is Fingal's Cave, 227ft (69m) deep and 66ft (20m) high. This cathedral-like structure, constantly pounded by the sea, was the inspiration for Mendelssohn's Hebrides overture. The cave can be viewed from a boat, which lands on the island if weather conditions permit. A colony of puffins can also be found nesting during spring and summer.

☎ 01631 570000 www.nts.org.uk

Stewartry Museum
266 A5

A purpose-built Victorian building opened in 1893 providing a home for a fascinating and quirky range of exhibits depicting the social and natural history of the Solway coast. There are also works by local artists, temporary exhibitions and a family and local history information service.

☎ 01557 331643

Stirling Castle
292 C5

Considered by many as Scotland's grandest castle, it is certainly one of the most important. Most of the building dates from the 15th and 16th centuries, when it became a popular Royal residence. The castle architecture is outstanding. The Great Hall and the Gatehouse, built by James IV, the magnificent Renaissance palace, built by James V, and the Chapel Royal, rebuilt by James VI, are amongst the key highlights. Mary, Queen of Scots was crowned here in 1543 and narrowly escaped death by fire in 1561. The medieval kitchens have been re-created, complete with models of cooks preparing a banquet in the 16th century.

Stirling Castle is set high on a volcanic outcrop, and commands stunning views, including the battlefields of Stirling Bridge and Bannockburn, Ben Lomond and the Trossachs.

☎ 01786 450000 www.historic-scotland.gov.uk

Storybook Glen
313 D5

A delight for children of all ages, this 20 acre (8ha) unusual theme park has over 100 models of fairytale and nursery rhyme characters set in beautiful landscaped gardens.

☎ 01224 732941 www.storybookglenaberdeen.co.uk

Strathclyde Country Park
375 F4

1000 acres (404ha) of woodland, rough wetlands, wildlife refuges and neat open parkland surround the 200 acre (80ha) man-made Strathclyde Loch. The park offers a huge variety of recreational activities (many of which have a fee) including watersports, horse riding, fishing, orienteering and cycling as well as numerous way-marked trails, sports pitches, sandy beaches and picnic areas. The visitor centre has information on the natural history and wildlife of the park. Within the park are the remains of Bothwellhaugh Roman Fort and Bathhouse. The park is also home to Scotland's largest theme park, M & D's, which has more than 40 rides and a large indoor entertainment complex.

☎ 01698 266155 www.northlan.gov.uk/leisure+and+tourism

Strathisla Distillery 323 G4

The oldest working distillery in the Highlands, established in 1786, and home to Chivas Regal blended Scotch whisky in which Strathisla single malt is predominant. The distillery takes water from the Broomhill Spring which Dominican monks used to make beer in the 13th century. There is a comprehensive self-guided tour of the distillery and whisky tasting.

☎ 01542 783044 www.chivas.com

Strathnaver Museum 335 G2

The former parish church of Farr was converted into this local museum and shows the story of the Strathnaver Clearances and the Clan Mackay.

☎ 01641 521418

Strathspey Railway 310 B3

A trip on this steam railway, reopened in 1978, runs 5 miles (8km) from Aviemore to Boat of Garten. The line now extends to Broomhill, also known as Glenbogle in the BBC TV series 'Monarch of the Glen'.

It operates mainly throughout the summer, but also on other occasions, so it is advisable to check the timetable.

☎ 01479 810725 www.strathspeyrailway.co.uk
☎ 01479 812220 (talking timetable)

Summerlee Heritage Park 375 F2

Said to be Scotland's noisiest museum, Summerlee Heritage Park preserves and interprets the history of the steel and engineering industries that were once dominant in the surrounding area. Spread over 25 acres (10ha), there is plenty to see including a reconstructed Miners Row where the living conditions of the miners from the 1840s to the 1960s can be experienced, and a re-created mine where their working conditions can be examined.

☎ 01236 431261 www.northlan.gov.uk/leisure+and+tourism

Sweetheart Abbey 267 D4

Splendid late 13th/early 14th century ruin founded by Devorgilla, Lady of Galloway, in memory of her husband John Balliol, and named because she was buried with her husband's embalmed heart which she carried with her in a casket after his death.

The 30 acre (12ha) site is dominated by the shell of the abbey church with its substantial central tower and lofty arched nave, but the most interesting feature is the great precinct wall. While not perhaps a professional defensive work, it was sufficiently formidable to deter raiding gangs.

☎ 01387 850397 www.historic-scotland.gov.uk

Strathclyde Country Park

Tantallon Castle 286 C1

This formidable castle has a majestic setting on cliffs overlooking the Firth of Forth and Bass Rock. A stronghold of the Douglas family, it was built at the end of the 14th century but after a number of sieges it was finally destroyed by Cromwell in 1651. The massive 50ft (15m) high curtain wall is all that remains intact.

☎ 01620 892727 www.historic-scotland.gov.uk

Thirlestane Castle 286 C5

Originally a 14th century fortress converted to a home by William Maitland, Secretary of State to Mary, Queen of Scots. Further restyling in the 17th century by Sir William Bruce created state rooms with arguably some of the finest plasterwork ceilings in Britain. Paintings include works by Gainsborough, Romney and Hopper, whilst the nursery wing contains a large collection of historic toys. The Border Country Life Museum is located here, and there are woodland walks and an adventure playground in the grounds.

☎ 01578 722430 www.thirlestanecastle.co.uk

Threave Castle 266 B4

Set on an island in the River Dee, access is by ferry following a 0.5 mile (1km) walk across fields.

Though probably settled here as far back as AD500, the present structure, a massive 5-storey keep, was built by Archibald the Grim in the 1370s. The castle had a turbulent history as home of the 'Black' Douglas clan, and was extended in the 15th century with substantial artillery fortification during a significant disagreement with James II. Besieged by the Covenanters, it was slighted and abandoned in 1640, but was briefly used to house Napoleonic prisoners of war.

☎ 0131 668 8800 www.historic-scotland.gov.uk

Threave Gardens (NTS) 266 B4

Gardens of around 60 acres (24ha), developed as a horticultural training centre by the National Trust for Scotland and maintained by students. Well worth visiting at almost any time, with spectacular springtime displays of nearly 200 varieties of daffodil, complemented by rhododendrons and other early flowering shrubs, extensive herbaceous colour in summer, striking trees and heathers in autumn, and rock, peat, walled and formal gardens.

☎ 01556 502575 www.nts.org.uk

Torosay Castle 289 G1

This Victorian family home contains furniture, pictures, china, family albums and scrapbooks dating from Edwardian times. The surrounding 12 acres (5ha) of gardens include formal terraces and a statue walk set amidst fuchsia hedges. There are also woodland and water gardens, a eucalyptus walk, oriental garden and rockery. Extensive views past Duart Castle and the Sound of Mull to the mountains of Arran and Lorne.

☎ 01680 812421 www.holidaymull.org/members/torosay.html

Torridon (NTS) 319 F4

Around 16,000 acres (6475ha) of some of Scotland's finest mountain scenery whose peaks rise over 3000ft (914m). Of major geological interest, Liathach and Beinn Alligin are formed of red sandstone, some 750 million years old, and their summits of white quartzite, some 600 million years old. The visitor centre, at the junction of the A896 and Diabaig road, has an audiovisual presentation on the local wildlife. There is also a deer museum and deer park, and ranger-led walks in season.

☎ 01445 791221 www.nts.org.uk

Traquair House 277 E2

Dating from the 12th century, and originally a royal hunting lodge, this is considered the oldest continuously inhabited house in Scotland, visited by 27 Scottish and English monarchs. Presenting a striking, whitewashed façade, internally many original features remain, including vaulted cellars, a medieval staircase and priest's hole. Furniture, fittings and memorabilia bear a fascinating testimony to the vagaries of Scottish political and domestic life over the centuries. There is also an 18th century working brewery with tastings in summer, maze, trails and adventure playground.

☎ 01896 830323 www.traquair.co.uk

Urquhart Castle 309 E2

The ruins of one of the largest castles in Scotland are found on the shores of Loch Ness. First built in the 1230s on the site of a vitrified fort, the castle fell into decay after 1689 and was blown up in 1692 to prevent it being occupied by Jacobites. Many of the remains are 14th century and the Grant Tower is 16th century.

☎ 01456 450551 www.historic-scotland.gov.uk

Vikingar! Experience, The 282 D3

A multimedia display on local Viking history, from the earliest raids to their defeat at the Battle of Largs in 1263. The adjacent leisure complex houses a swimming pool, cinema and play area.

☎ 01475 689777 www.vikingar.co.uk

Weaver's Cottage (NTS) 283 F3

The village of Kilbarchan was, in 1830, home to over 800 weavers' looms. Today, the last remaining hand loom can be seen in this typical 18th century weaver's cottage. There are displays of local and historical weaving interest, an attractive cottage garden where plants are grown to make natural dyes and a presentation explaining the village's links with the famous Paisley patterned shawls.

☎ 01505 705588 www.nts.org.uk

West Highland Line 298 D2

Travel from Fort William to Mallaig on the West Highland Line, either on Scotrail or on the Jacobite Steam Train, which leaves in the morning and returns late afternoon. The round trip covers 84 miles (135km) and tours through magnificent Highland scenery.

Cross the 100ft (30m) high Glenfinnan Viaduct, and go past Loch Shiel and the monument commemorating where Bonnie Prince Charlie raised his standard. Travel through Arisaig, the UK's most westerly main line railway station, then via Loch Morar, which, at 1077ft (328m), is Britain's deepest loch. Enjoy great views en route of the Isles of Rum, Eigg, Muck and Canna, and the southern tip of Skye.

The journey stops at Glenfinnan and there is plenty of time to explore Mallaig and its harbour before returning.

☎ 01463 239026 www.steamtrain.info
www.scotrail.co.uk

Whithorn Priory 257 E2

St Ninian founded a church here around AD400, and this site is considered the cradle of Christianity in Scotland. The ruined priory, once the cathedral church of Galloway, was built in the 12th century as his tomb had become a place of pilgrimage. The ecclesiastical history of the site is complex, and finds from the ongoing archaeological work, including some fine Celtic crosses, are on display in the museum.

☎ 01988 500508 www.historic-scotland.gov.uk

Key to route planning map pages

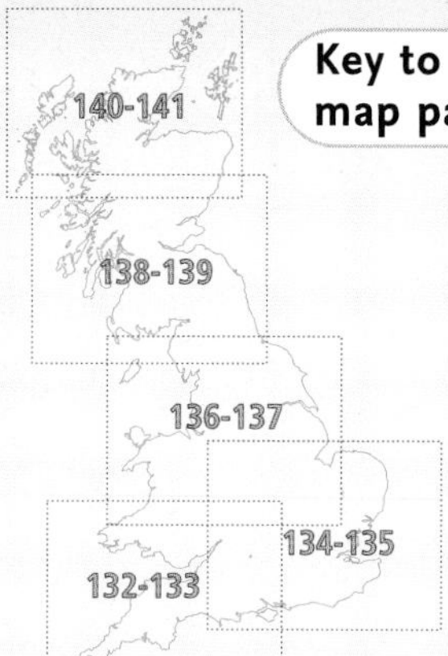

Outstanding attractions

star number on this map		described on page
2	Althorp House	70
7	Avebury Ring & Alexander Keiller Museum (NT)	24
8	Babbacombe Model Village	24
12	Bath	25
13	Batsford Arboretum	25
18	Big Pit Mining Museum	107
22	Blenheim Palace	41
27	Brecon Beacons	107
33	Caerphilly Castle	108
39	Cheddar Gorge & Caves	26
40	Chepstow Castle	109
41	Chesil Beach	26
49	Corfe Castle (NT)	27
50	Cotswold Hills	28
53	Dartmoor	28
63	Eden Project	29
65	Exeter Cathedral	29
66	Exmoor	29
70	Forest of Dean	29
74	Goonhilly Satellite Earth Station	30
83	Hestercombe	30
84	Hidcote Manor Gardens (NT)	30
97	Lanhydrock (NT)	31
104	Longleat House	32
105	Lost Gardens of Heligan	32
107	Lydford Gorge (NT)	32
108	Lynton & Lynmouth Cliff Railway	32
110	Museum of Welsh Life	111
111	National Botanic Garden of Wales	111
112	National Marine Aquarium	33
113	National Maritime Museum Cornwall	34
117	Needles Pleasure Park	47
119	New Forest	47
125	Osborne House	48
126	Oxford	48
128	Pembrokeshire Coast National Park	112
133	Portsmouth Historic Dockyard	49
136	Raglan Castle	113
141	Roman Baths & Pump Room	35
143	Rousham House	50
152	St. Michael's Mount (NT)	35
145	Salisbury Cathedral	35
150	Slimbridge Wildfowl & Wetlands Trust	36
154	Stonehenge	36
155	Stourhead (NT)	36
162	Warwick Castle	68
164	Wells Cathedral	38
165	Westonbirt - The National Arboretum	38
167	Wilton House	38

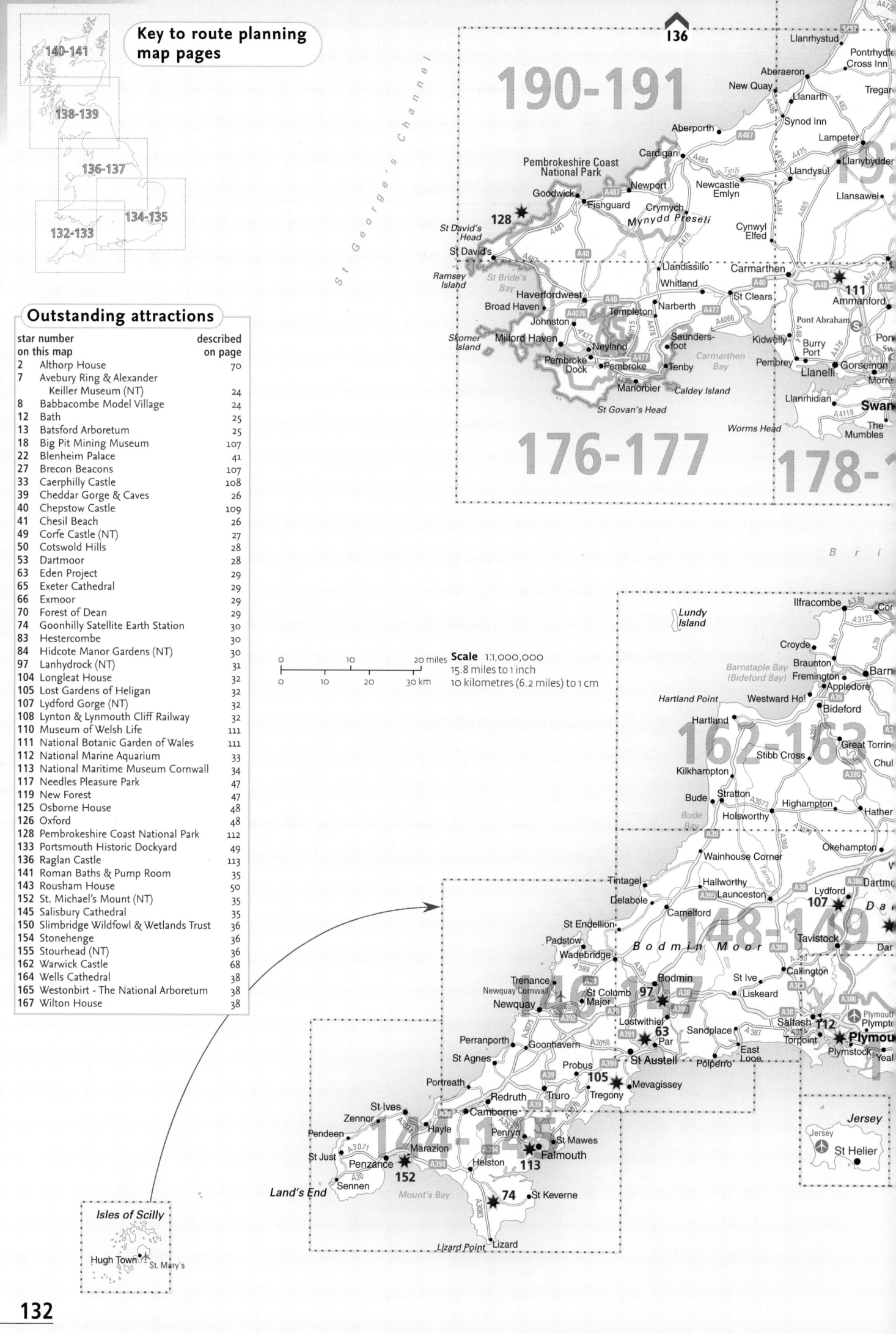

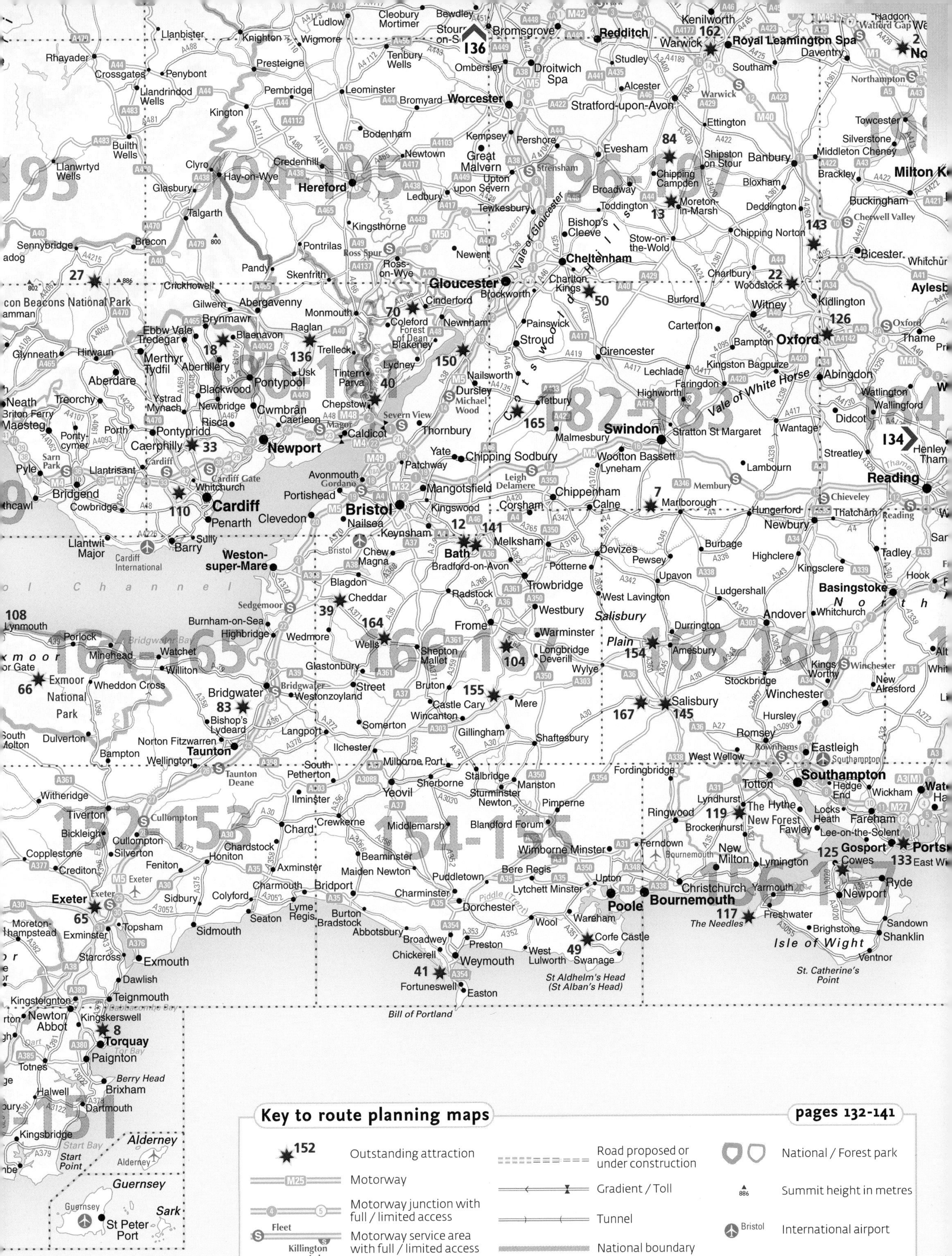

Key to route planning maps

pages 132-141

152	Outstanding attraction
M25	Motorway
4 5	Motorway junction with full / limited access
Fleet S / Killington Lake S	Motorway service area with full / limited access
A82	Primary route dual / single carriageway
A894	'A' road dual / single carriageway
	'B' road
	Road proposed or under construction
	Gradient / Toll
	Tunnel
	National boundary
	Channel Tunnel
	River
	Canal
	National / Forest park
886	Summit height in metres
Bristol	International airport
	Other airport
156	Main map page

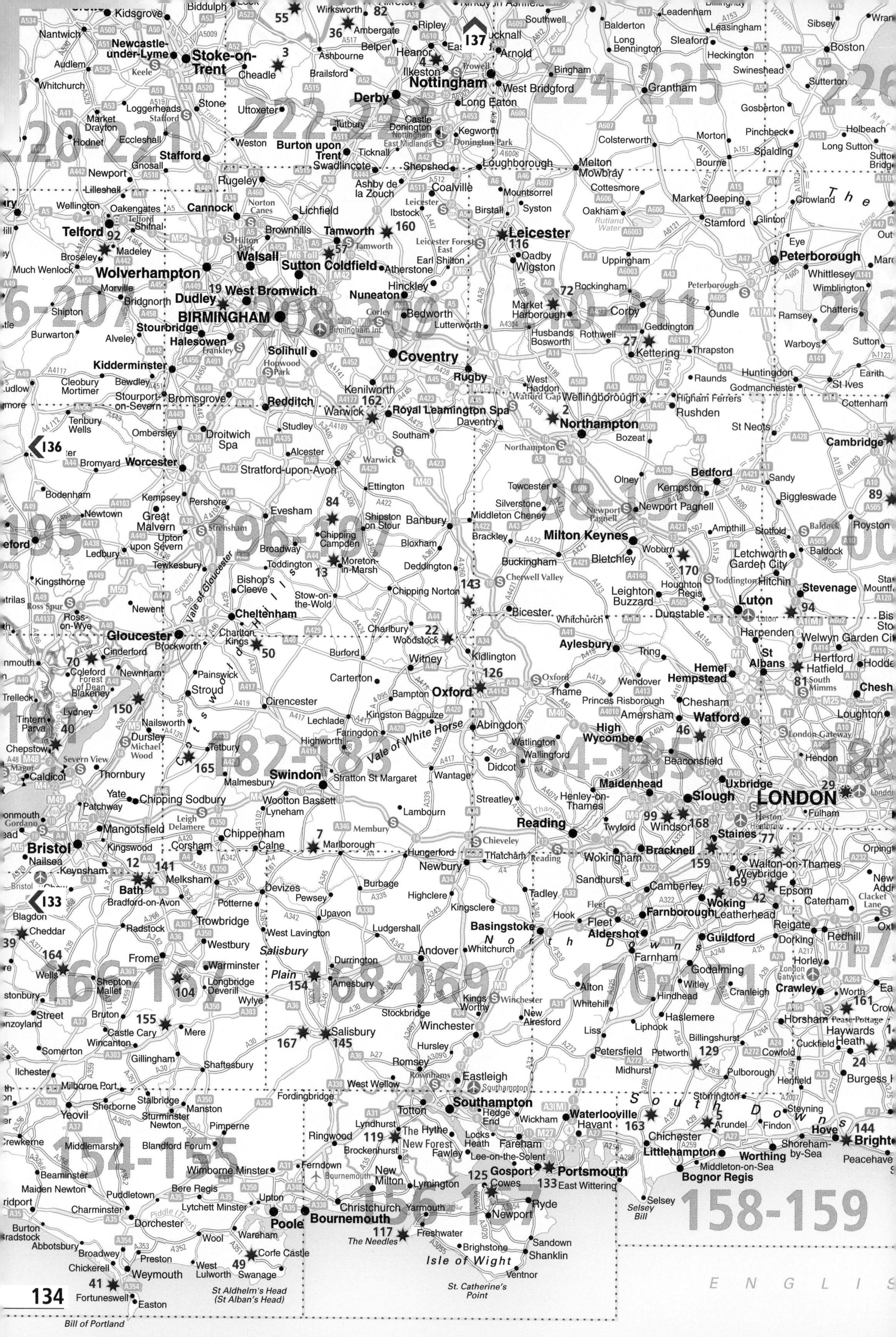

Kidsgrove
Biddulph
55
Wirksworth
82
Southwell
Leadenham
Balderton
Leasingham
Sibsey
Nantwich
Newcastle-under-Lyme
Stoke-on-Trent
3
36
Ambergate
Ripley
137
Hucknall
Arnold
Long Bennington
Sleaford
Boston
Audlem
Keele
Cheadle
Ashbourne
Belper
Heanor
Ilkeston
Bingham
Heckington
Swineshead
Whitchurch
Brailsford
4
Nottingham
West Bridgford
Grantham
Sutterton
Loggerheads
Stone
Uttoxeter
Derby
Long Eaton
224-225
Gosberton
Market Drayton
Stafford
Tutbury
222-223
Castle Donington
Kegworth
Donington Park
East Midlands
Holbeach
Hodnet
Eccleshall
Weston
Burton upon Trent
Colsterworth
Morton
Pinchbeck
Spalding
Long Sutton
Gnosall
Stafford
Ticknall
Loughborough
Melton Mowbray
Bourne
Newport
Swadlincote
Shepshed
220-221
Rugeley
Ashby de la Zouch
Coalville
Cottesmore
Market Deeping
Crowland
Lilleshall
Mountsorrel
Oakham
Rutland Water
Wellington
Oakengates
Cannock
Norton Canes
Lichfield
Leicester
Birstall
Syston
Stamford
Glinton
Telford
Shifnal
Ibstock
Telford
92
Brownhills
Tamworth
160
Leicester
116
Eye
Hilton Park
Walsall
57
Tamworth
Leicester Forest East
Broseley
Madeley
Earl Shilton
Oadby
Wigston
Peterborough
Much Wenlock
Wolverhampton
Sutton Coldfield
Atherstone
Uppingham
Whittlesey
Morville
19
West Bromwich
Hinckley
Rockingham
Peterborough
Wimblington
Bridgnorth
Dudley
Nuneaton
72
Market Harborough
Corby
Oundle
Chatteris
Shipton
BIRMINGHAM
208-209
Corley
Bedworth
210-211
Ramsey
Burwarton
Alveley
Stourbridge
Birmingham Int.
Lutterworth
Husbands Bosworth
Rothwell
Geddington
212
Halesowen
Frankley
27
Warboys
Sutton
Solihull
Coventry
Kettering
Thrapston
Kidderminster
Hopwood Park
Huntingdon
Earith
Cleobury Mortimer
Bewdley
Rugby
West Haddon
Raunds
Godmanchester
St Ives
Ludlow
Stourport-on-Severn
Bromsgrove
Kenilworth
Watford Gap
Wellingborough
Higham Ferrers
Redditch
162
Rushden
Cottenham
Tenbury Wells
Warwick
Royal Leamington Spa
Daventry
2
Northampton
Ombersley
Droitwich Spa
Studley
Southam
St Neots
Cambridge
136
Bromyard
Worcester
Alcester
Warwick
Northampton
Bozeat
Stratford-upon-Avon
Bedford
Sandy
Bodenham
Kempsey
Pershore
Ettington
Towcester
Olney
Kempston
Newtown
Great Malvern
Evesham
84
Shipston on Stour
Banbury
Silverstone
Newport Pagnell
Biggleswade
89
195
Strensham
196-197
Middleton Cheney
198-199
Newport Pagnell
Ampthill
Stotfold
Baldock
Royston
Upton upon Severn
Chipping Campden
Bloxham
Brackley
Milton Keynes
Woburn
200
Hereford
Ledbury
Broadway
Moreton-in-Marsh
Buckingham
Bletchley
Letchworth Garden City
Baldock
Tewkesbury
Toddington
13
Deddington
170
Kingsthorne
Bishop's Cleeve
Cherwell Valley
Toddington
Hitchin
Stevenage
Ross Spur
Newent
Cotswold Hills
Stow-on-the-Wold
Chipping Norton
143
Leighton Buzzard
Houghton Regis
Luton
94
Ross-on-Wye
Vale of Gloucester
Cheltenham
Bicester
Whitchurch
Dunstable
Luton
Gloucester
Charlton Kings
Brockworth
Charlbury
22
Woodstock
Harpenden
Welwyn Garden City
Cinderford
50
Burford
Kidlington
Aylesbury
Tring
St Albans
Hertford
Hatfield
Hoddesdon
70
Coleford
Forest of Dean
Newnham
Painswick
Witney
Carterton
126
Oxford
Oxford
Wendover
Hemel Hempstead
81
South Mimms
Blakeney
Stroud
Bampton
Thame
Princes Risborough
Chesham
Chelmsford
Lydney
150
Cirencester
Lechlade
Kingston Bagpuize
Abingdon
Amersham
Watford
Loughton
Tintern Parva
40
Nailsworth
Dursley
Faringdon
High Wycombe
46
London Gateway
Chepstow
Michael Wood
Tetbury
Highworth
182-183
Vale of White Horse
Watlington
Wallingford
184-185
Hendon
Severn View
Magor
Caldicot
Thornbury
165
Malmesbury
Swindon
Stratton St Margaret
Wantage
Didcot
Beaconsfield
Maidenhead
Uxbridge
29
Yate
Chipping Sodbury
Patchway
Wootton Bassett
Lyneham
Lambourn
Streatley
Henley-on-Thames
Slough
LONDON
Leigh Delamere
Reading
Windsor
168
Heston
Fulham
Mangotsfield
Chippenham
Membury
99
Twyford
Staines
77
Heathrow
Bristol
Kingswood
Corsham
Calne
7
Marlborough
Hungerford
Chieveley
Thatcham
Reading
Wokingham
Bracknell
159
Nailsea
12
141
Newbury
Walton-on-Thames
Weybridge
Keynsham
Melksham
Devizes
Burbage
Sandhurst
169
Epsom
Bristol
Bath
Pewsey
Highclere
Kingsclere
Tadley
Camberley
Woking
42
Caterham
133
Bradford-on-Avon
Potterne
Upavon
Fleet
Farnborough
Leatherhead
Blagdon
Radstock
Trowbridge
West Lavington
Ludgershall
Basingstoke
Hook
Fleet
Aldershot
Guildford
Reigate
Cheddar
Westbury
Salisbury Plain
Durrington
Andover
Whitchurch
North Downs
Farnham
Dorking
Redhill
164
Frome
Warminster
168-169
170-171
Godalming
Horley
London Gatwick
Wells
166-167
Shepton Mallet
Longbridge Deverill
104
154
Amesbury
Winchester
Alton
Witley
Cranleigh
Crawley
Worth
Wylye
Kings Worthy
Whitehill
Hindhead
161
Street
Bruton
155
Mere
Stockbridge
Winchester
New Alresford
Haslemere
Horsham
Pease Pottage
Castle Cary
167
Salisbury
145
Liss
Liphook
Billingshurst
Haywards Heath
Somerton
Wincanton
Gillingham
Hursley
Petersfield
Petworth
129
Cowfold
Cuckfield
Ilchester
Shaftesbury
Romsey
Midhurst
Pulborough
24
Milborne Port
West Wellow
Rownhams
Eastleigh
Southampton
Henfield
Burgess Hill
Yeovil
Sherborne
Stalbridge
Fordingbridge
Southampton
Hedge End
Wickham
Waterlooville
Storrington
Steyning
Sturminster Newton
Manston
Totton
Havant
163
South Downs
Crewkerne
Pimperne
Lyndhurst
The Hythe
Arundel
Findon
Hove
144
Brighton
Middlemarsh
Blandford Forum
119
Ringwood
Brockenhurst
New Forest
Locks Heath
Fareham
Chichester
Shoreham-by-Sea
154-155
Fawley
Lee-on-the-Solent
Littlehampton
Worthing
Peacehaven
Beaminster
Wimborne Minster
Ferndown
Bournemouth
New Milton
Lymington
125
Gosport
Cowes
133
Portsmouth
East Wittering
Middleton-on-Sea
Bognor Regis
Maiden Newton
Puddletown
Bere Regis
Upton
Selsey
Bridport
Charminster
Lytchett Minster
Christchurch
Yarmouth
Ryde
Selsey Bill
158-159
Dorchester
Poole
Bournemouth
156-157
Newport
Burton Bradstock
Abbotsbury
Wool
Wareham
117
The Needles
Freshwater
Sandown
Broadwey
Preston
49
Corfe Castle
Brighstone
Shanklin
Chickerell
West Lulworth
Swanage
Isle of Wight
Weymouth
Ventnor
ENGLISH
41
Fortuneswell
Easton
St Aldhelm's Head (St Alban's Head)
St. Catherine's Point
Bill of Portland

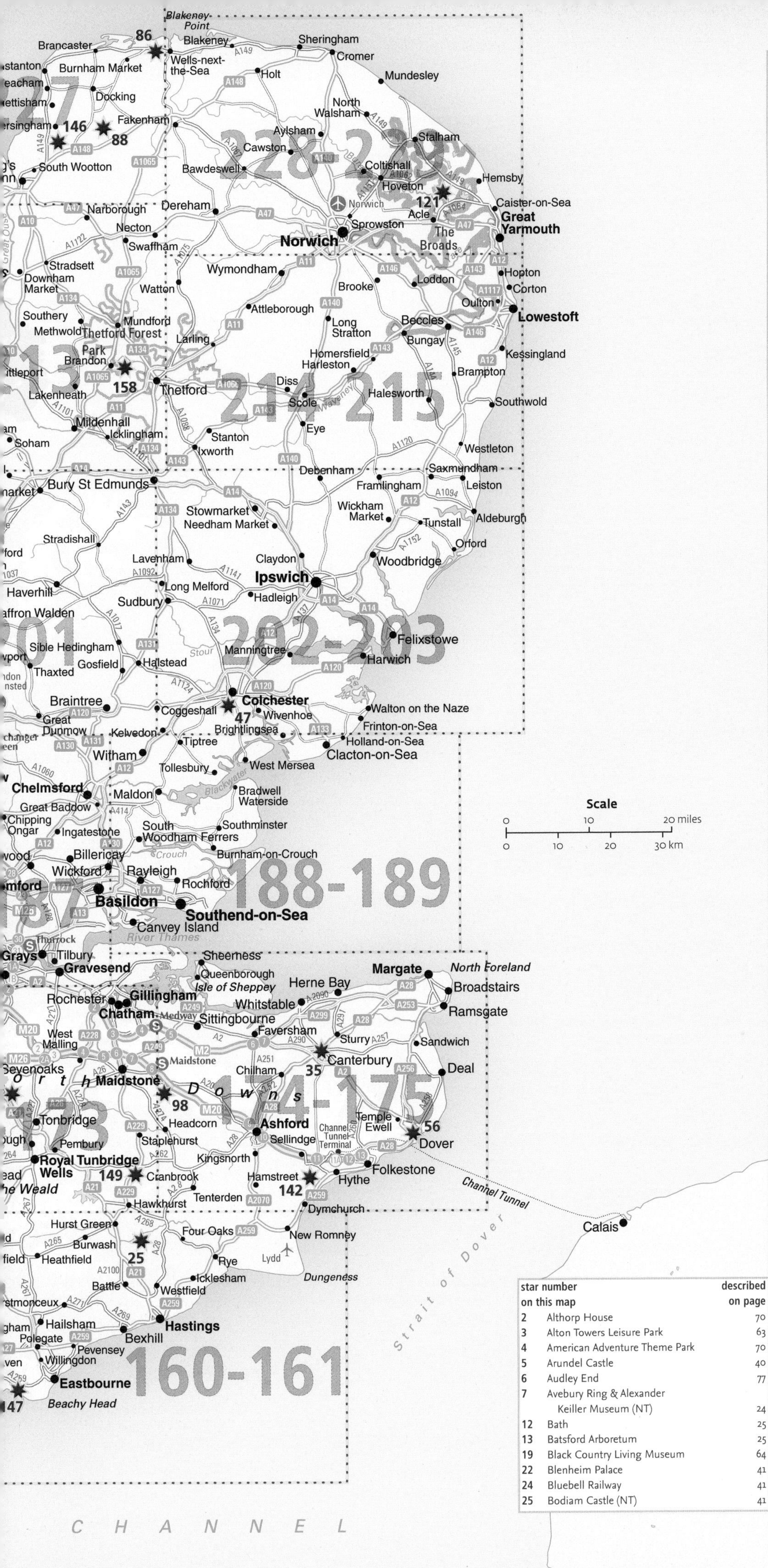

Outstanding attractions

star number on this map		described on page
2	Althorp House	70
3	Alton Towers Leisure Park	63
4	American Adventure Theme Park	70
5	Arundel Castle	40
6	Audley End	77
7	Avebury Ring & Alexander Keiller Museum (NT)	24
12	Bath	25
13	Batsford Arboretum	25
19	Black Country Living Museum	64
22	Blenheim Palace	41
24	Bluebell Railway	41
25	Bodiam Castle (NT)	41
27	Boughton House	70
29	LONDON: British Museum, Buckingham Palace, Greenwich, Houses of Parliament, Aquarium, Eye, Zoo, Madame Tussaud's & the Planetarium, National Gallery, National Portrait Gallery, Natural History Museum, Royal Academy of Arts, Royal Botanic Gardens Kew, St. Paul's Cathedral, Science Museum, Shakespeare's Globe Theatre, Tate Britain, Tate Modern, Tower of London, Victoria & Albert Museum, Westminster Abbey	
29	British Museum	55
29	Buckingham Palace	55
34	Cambridge	77
35	Canterbury Cathedral	42
36	Carsington Water	71
39	Cheddar Gorge & Caves	26
40	Chepstow Castle	55
41	Chesil Beach	26
42	Chessington World of Adventures	55
46	Chiltern Open Air Museum	43
47	Colchester Zoo	78
49	Corfe Castle (NT)	27
50	Cotswold Hills	28
55	Dove Dale	71
56	Dover Castle	44
57	Drayton Manor Park	65
70	Forest of Dean	29
72	Foxton Locks	72
29	Greenwich	56
77	Hampton Court Palace and Garden	56
81	Hatfield House	79
84	Hidcote Manor Gardens (NT)	30
86	Holkham Hall	80
88	Houghton Hall	80
29	Houses of Parliament	56
89	Imperial War Museum (Duxford)	80
92	Ironbridge Gorge	66
94	Knebworth House	81
95	Knole (NT)	46
98	Leeds Castle & Gardens	46
99	Legoland	46
29	London Aquarium	57
29	London Eye	57
29	London Zoo	57
104	Longleat House	32
29	Madame Tussaud's and the Planetarium	57
29	National Gallery	58
29	National Portrait Gallery	58
116	National Space Centre	73
29	Natural History Museum	59
117	Needles Pleasure Park	47
119	New Forest	47
121	Norfolk Broads	82
125	Osborne House	48
126	Oxford	48
129	Petworth House (NT)	49
133	Portsmouth Historic Dockyard	49
141	Roman Baths & Pump Room	35
142	Romney, Hythe & Dymchurch Railway	50
143	Rousham House	50
29	Royal Academy of Arts	59
29	Royal Botanic Gardens, Kew	59
144	Royal Pavilion	50
29	St. Paul's Cathedral	59
145	Salisbury Cathedral	35
146	Sandringham House	83
29	Science Museum	60
147	Seven Sisters Country Park	51
29	Shakespeare's Globe Theatre	60
148	Sheffield Park (NT)	51
149	Sissinghurst Castle (NT)	51
150	Slimbridge Wildfowl & Wetlands Trust	36
154	Stonehenge	36
155	Stourhead (NT)	36
29	Tate Britain	60
29	Tate Modern	60
158	Thetford Forest Park	83
159	Thorpe Park	52
29	Tower of London	61
160	Twycross Zoo	75
29	Victoria & Albert Museum	61
161	Wakehurst Place (NT)	52
162	Warwick Castle	68
163	Weald & Downland Open Air Museum	52
164	Wells Cathedral	38
29	Westminster Abbey	61
165	Westonbirt - The National Arboretum	38
167	Wilton House	38
168	Windsor Castle	53
169	Wisley R.H.S. Gardens	53
170	Woburn Abbey	84

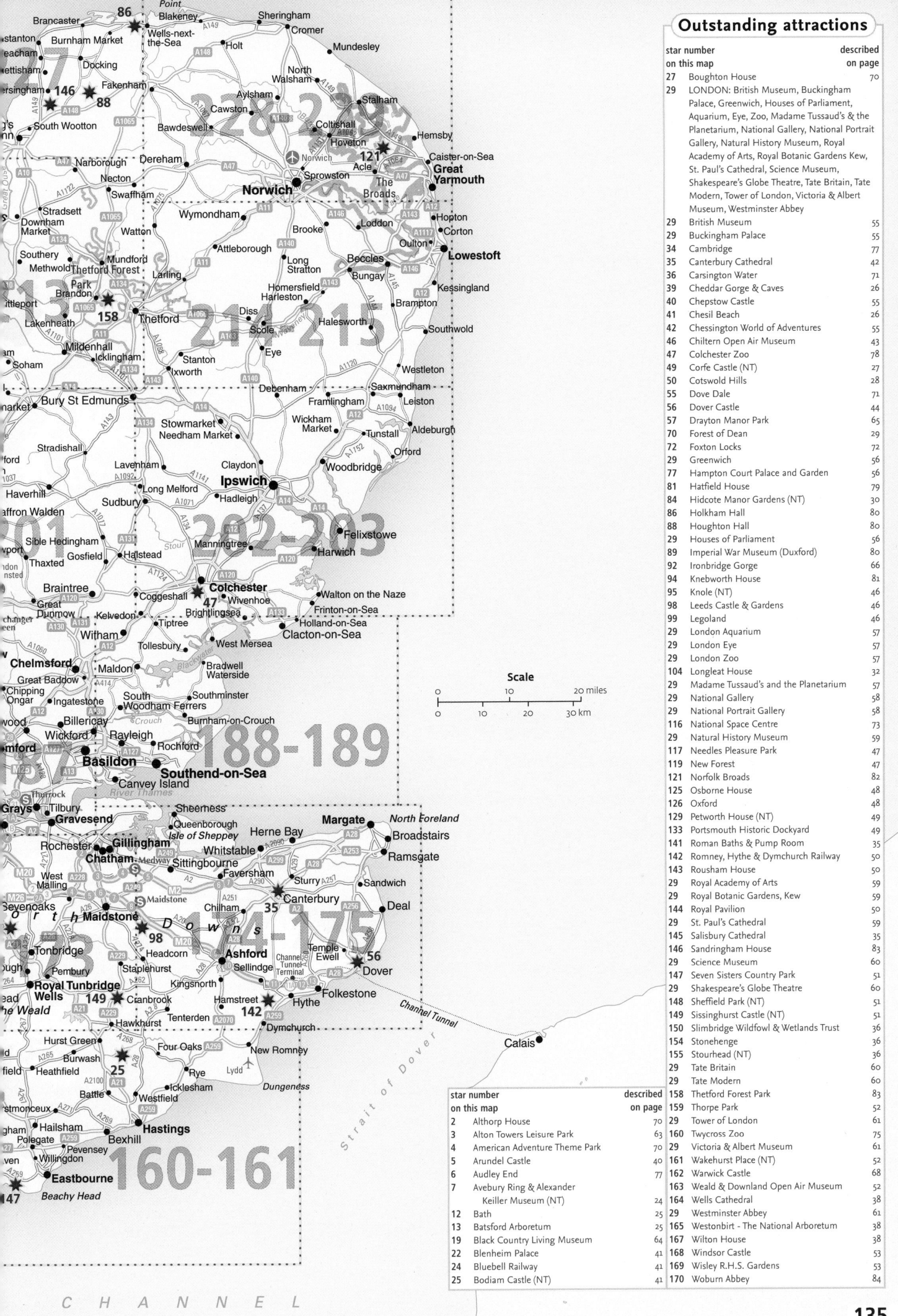

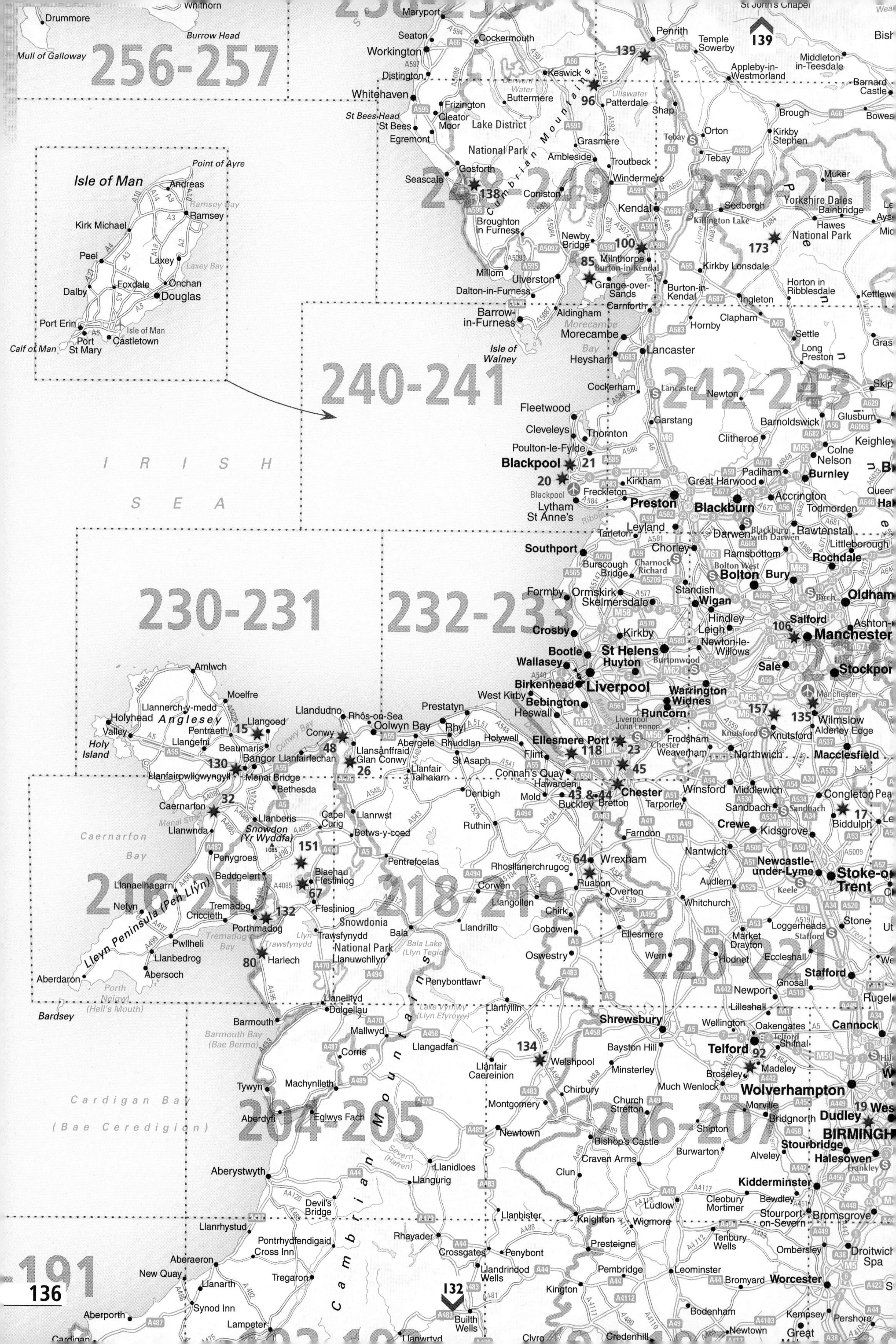

256-257
248-249
250-251
240-241
242-243
230-231
232-233
216-217
218-219
220-221
204-205
206-207
139
132
Drummore
Whithorn
Burrow Head
Mull of Galloway
Maryport
Seaton
Workington
Cockermouth
Distington
Whitehaven
St Bees Head
St Bees
Egremont
Frizington
Cleator Moor
Keswick
Buttermere
Lake District
National Park
Cumbrian Mountains
Penrith
Temple Sowerby
Appleby-in-Westmorland
Middleton-in-Teesdale
Barnard Castle
Bowes
Ullswater
Patterdale
Shap
Orton
Tebay
Brough
Kirkby Stephen
Grasmere
Ambleside
Troutbeck
Windermere
Gosforth
Seascale
Coniston
Kendal
Sedbergh
Killington Lake
Yorkshire Dales
National Park
Bainbridge
Hawes
Muker
Broughton in Furness
Newby Bridge
Milnthorpe
Burton-in-Kendal
Millom
Ulverston
Grange-over-Sands
Dalton-in-Furness
Kirkby Lonsdale
Burton-in-Kendal
Ingleton
Horton in Ribblesdale
Kettlewell
Barrow-in-Furness
Aldingham
Carnforth
Morecambe
Morecambe Bay
Isle of Walney
Heysham
Lancaster
Hornby
Clapham
Settle
Long Preston
Isle of Man
Point of Ayre
Andreas
Ramsey Bay
Ramsey
Kirk Michael
Peel
Laxey
Laxey Bay
Dalby
Foxdale
Onchan
Douglas
Port Erin
Port St Mary
Castletown
Isle of Man
Calf of Man
IRISH SEA
Cockerham
Fleetwood
Cleveleys
Thornton
Poulton-le-Fylde
Blackpool
Freckleton
Lytham St Anne's
Garstang
Newton
Barnoldswick
Clitheroe
Glusburn
Keighley
Colne
Nelson
Padiham
Burnley
Great Harwood
Kirkham
Preston
Blackburn
Accrington
Todmorden
Leyland
Tarleton
Darwen
Rawtenstall
Littleborough
Southport
Chorley
Burscough Bridge
Charnock Richard
Ramsbottom
Rochdale
Bolton
Bury
Formby
Ormskirk
Skelmersdale
Standish
Wigan
Oldham
Hindley
Crosby
Kirkby
Leigh
Salford
Manchester
Ashton-
Bootle
St Helens
Newton-le-Willows
Wallasey
Huyton
Burtonwood
Sale
Stockport
Birkenhead
Liverpool
Warrington
Widnes
Bebington
West Kirby
Heswall
Runcorn
Liverpool John Lennon
Wilmslow
Alderley Edge
Knutsford
Macclesfield
Ellesmere Port
Frodsham
Weaverham
Northwich
Chester
Connah's Quay
Hawarden
Mold
Buckley
Bretton
Tarporley
Winsford
Middlewich
Congleton
Sandbach
Biddulph
Crewe
Kidsgrove
Nantwich
Newcastle-under-Lyme
Stoke-on-Trent
Audlem
Keele
Whitchurch
Market Drayton
Loggerheads
Stone
Hodnet
Eccleshall
Stafford
Gnosall
Newport
Lilleshall
Rugeley
Wellington
Oakengates
Telford
Shifnal
Cannock
Madeley
Wolverhampton
Broseley
Much Wenlock
Bridgnorth
Dudley
Birmingham
Stourbridge
Halesowen
Alveley
Kidderminster
Bewdley
Stourport-on-Severn
Bromsgrove
Ombersley
Droitwich Spa
Worcester
Kempsey
Pershore
Great
Prestatyn
Rhyl
Rhuddlan
Abergele
Holywell
Flint
St Asaph
Denbigh
Ruthin
Rhosllanerchrugog
Wrexham
Ruabon
Overton
Farndon
Llangollen
Corwen
Chirk
Gobowen
Ellesmere
Wem
Oswestry
Llandrillo
Shrewsbury
Bayston Hill
Minsterley
Church Stretton
Shipton
Chirbury
Welshpool
Montgomery
Llanfair Caereinion
Newtown
Bishop's Castle
Craven Arms
Clun
Burwarton
Ludlow
Cleobury Mortimer
Knighton
Wigmore
Tenbury Wells
Llanbister
Presteigne
Penybont
Crossgates
Llandrindod Wells
Pembridge
Leominster
Bromyard
Kington
Bodenham
Builth Wells
Credenhill
Newtown
Rhayader
Llanidloes
Llangurig
Devil's Bridge
Aberystwyth
Pontrhydfendigaid
Cross Inn
Tregaron
Aberaeron
New Quay
Llanarth
Synod Inn
Lampeter
Aberporth
Llanrhystud
Cardigan Bay
(Bae Ceredigion)
Aberdyfi
Eglwys Fach
Machynlleth
Tywyn
Corris
Cambrian Mountains
Mallwyd
Llangadfan
Lake Vyrnwy (Llyn Efyrnwy)
Llanfyllin
Penybontfawr
Dolgellau
Llanelltyd
Barmouth
Barmouth Bay (Bae Bermo)
Harlech
Trawsfynydd
Llanuwchllyn
Bala
Bala Lake (Llyn Tegid)
Snowdonia National Park
Ffestiniog
Blaenau Ffestiniog
Porthmadog
Tremadog
Tremadog Bay
Criccieth
Pwllheli
Llanbedrog
Abersoch
Aberdaron
Porth Neigwl (Hell's Mouth)
Bardsey
Lleyn Peninsula (Pen Llŷn)
Llanaelhaearn
Nefyn
Beddgelert
Penygroes
Caernarfon Bay
Llanwnda
Caernarfon
Snowdon (Yr Wyddfa)
Llanberis
Capel Curig
Betws-y-coed
Pentrefoelas
Llanrwst
Bethesda
Menai Bridge
Bangor
Llanfairpwllgwyngyll
Llanfairfechan
Llansanffraid Glan Conwy
Llanfair Talhaiarn
Conwy
Conwy Bay
Llandudno
Rhôs-on-Sea
Colwyn Bay
Beaumaris
Llangoed
Llangefni
Pentraeth
Anglesey
Llannerch-y-medd
Moelfre
Amlwch
Holyhead
Valley
Holy Island

Outstanding attractions

star number on this map		described on page
2	Althorp House	70
3	Alton Towers Leisure Park	63
4	American Adventure Theme Park	70
6	Audley End	77
15	Beaumaris Castle	107
17	Biddulph Grange Garden (NT)	63
19	Black Country Living Museum	64
20	Blackpool Pleasure Beach	93
21	Blackpool Tower	93
23	Blue Planet Aquarium	94
26	Bodnant Gardens (NT)	107
27	Boughton House	70
32	Caernarfon Castle	108
34	Cambridge	77
36	Carsington Water	71
37	Castle Howard	86
38	Chatsworth House	71
43	Chester	94
44	Chester Cathedral	95
45	Chester Zoo	95
48	Conwy Castle	109
52	Dalby Forest Drive	87
55	Dove Dale	71
57	Drayton Manor Park	65
62	Eden Camp	87
64	Erddig (NT)	110
67	Ffestiniog Railway	110
68	Flamingo Land Theme Park	87
71	Fountains Abbey & Studley Royal Water Garden (NT)	87
72	Foxton Locks	72
75	Haddon Hall	72
78	Hardwick Hall (NT)	72
79	Harewood House	87
80	Harlech Castle	110
82	Heights of Abraham	73
84	Hidcote Manor Gardens (NT)	30
85	Holker Hall	96
89	Imperial War Museum (Duxford)	80
92	Ironbridge Gorge	66
93	Jorvik	88
96	Lake District	96
100	Levens Hall	97
101	Lightwater Valley Park	88
102	Lincoln Cathedral	73
106	Lowry, The	97
114	National Museum of Photography, Film & TV	89
115	National Railway Museum	89
116	National Space Centre	73
118	Ness Botanic Gardens	98
123	North York Moors	89
124	North Yorkshire Moors Railway	89
127	Peak District	74
130	Plas Newydd (NT), Anglesey	112
131	Poole's Cavern	74
132	Portmeirion Village	113
134	Powis Castle & Garden (NT)	113
135	Quarry Bank Mill & Styal Estate (NT)	98
138	Ravenglass & Eskdale Railway	99
139	Rheged-the Village in the Hill	99
140	Rievaulx Abbey	90
151	Snowdonia	114
157	Tatton Park (NT)	100
158	Thetford Forest Park	83
160	Twycross Zoo	75
162	Warwick Castle	68
166	Whitby Abbey	91
171	York	91
172	York Minster	91
173	Yorkshire Dales	91

140

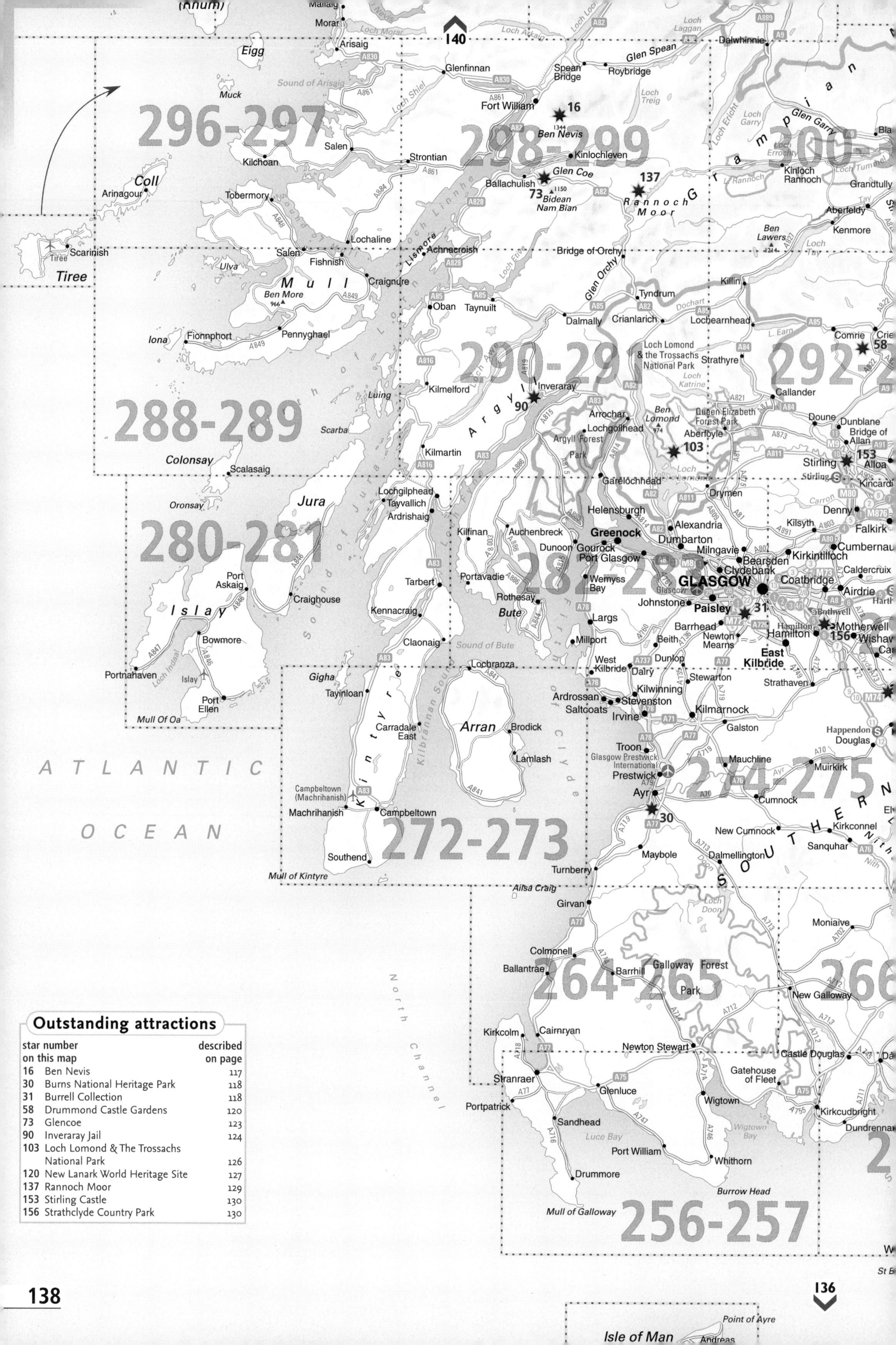

Outstanding attractions

star number on this map		described on page
16	Ben Nevis	117
30	Burns National Heritage Park	118
31	Burrell Collection	118
58	Drummond Castle Gardens	120
73	Glencoe	123
90	Inveraray Jail	124
103	Loch Lomond & The Trossachs National Park	126
120	New Lanark World Heritage Site	127
137	Rannoch Moor	129
153	Stirling Castle	130
156	Strathclyde Country Park	130

136

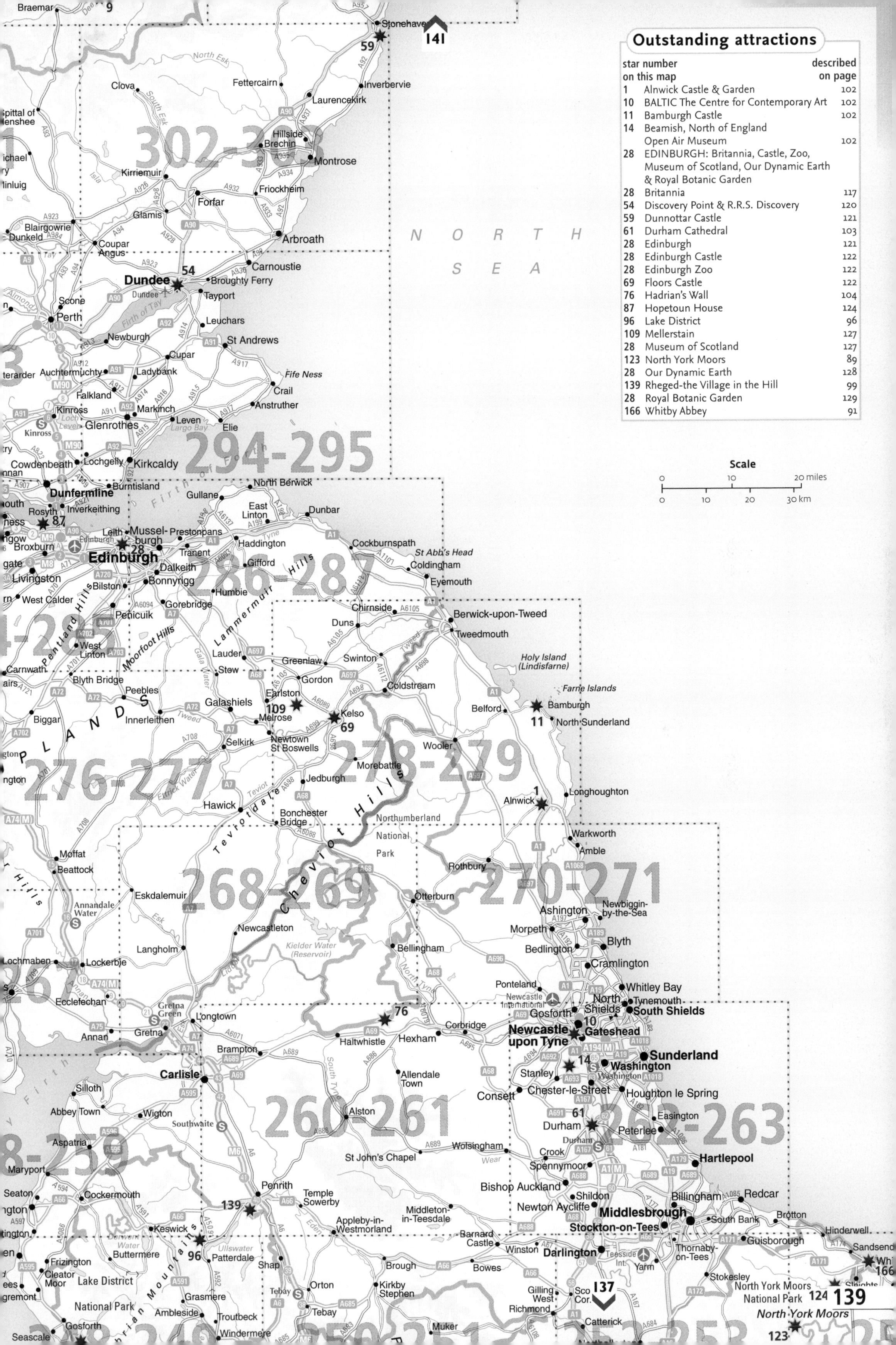

Outstanding attractions

star number on this map		described on page
1	Alnwick Castle & Garden	102
10	BALTIC The Centre for Contemporary Art	102
11	Bamburgh Castle	102
14	Beamish, North of England Open Air Museum	102
28	EDINBURGH: Britannia, Castle, Zoo, Museum of Scotland, Our Dynamic Earth & Royal Botanic Garden	
28	Britannia	117
54	Discovery Point & R.R.S. Discovery	120
59	Dunnottar Castle	121
61	Durham Cathedral	103
28	Edinburgh	121
28	Edinburgh Castle	122
28	Edinburgh Zoo	122
69	Floors Castle	122
76	Hadrian's Wall	104
87	Hopetoun House	124
96	Lake District	96
109	Mellerstain	127
28	Museum of Scotland	127
123	North York Moors	89
28	Our Dynamic Earth	128
139	Rheged-the Village in the Hill	99
28	Royal Botanic Garden	129
166	Whitby Abbey	91

Outstanding attractions

star number on this map		described on page
9	Balmoral Castle	116
51	Cuillin Hills	119
59	Dunnottar Castle	121
60	Dunrobin Castle	121
91	Inverewe Gardens (NTS)	125
122	North West Highlands	128

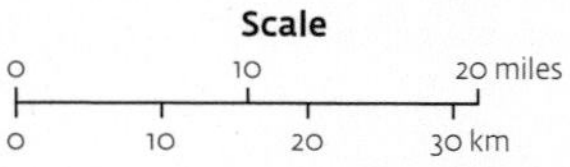

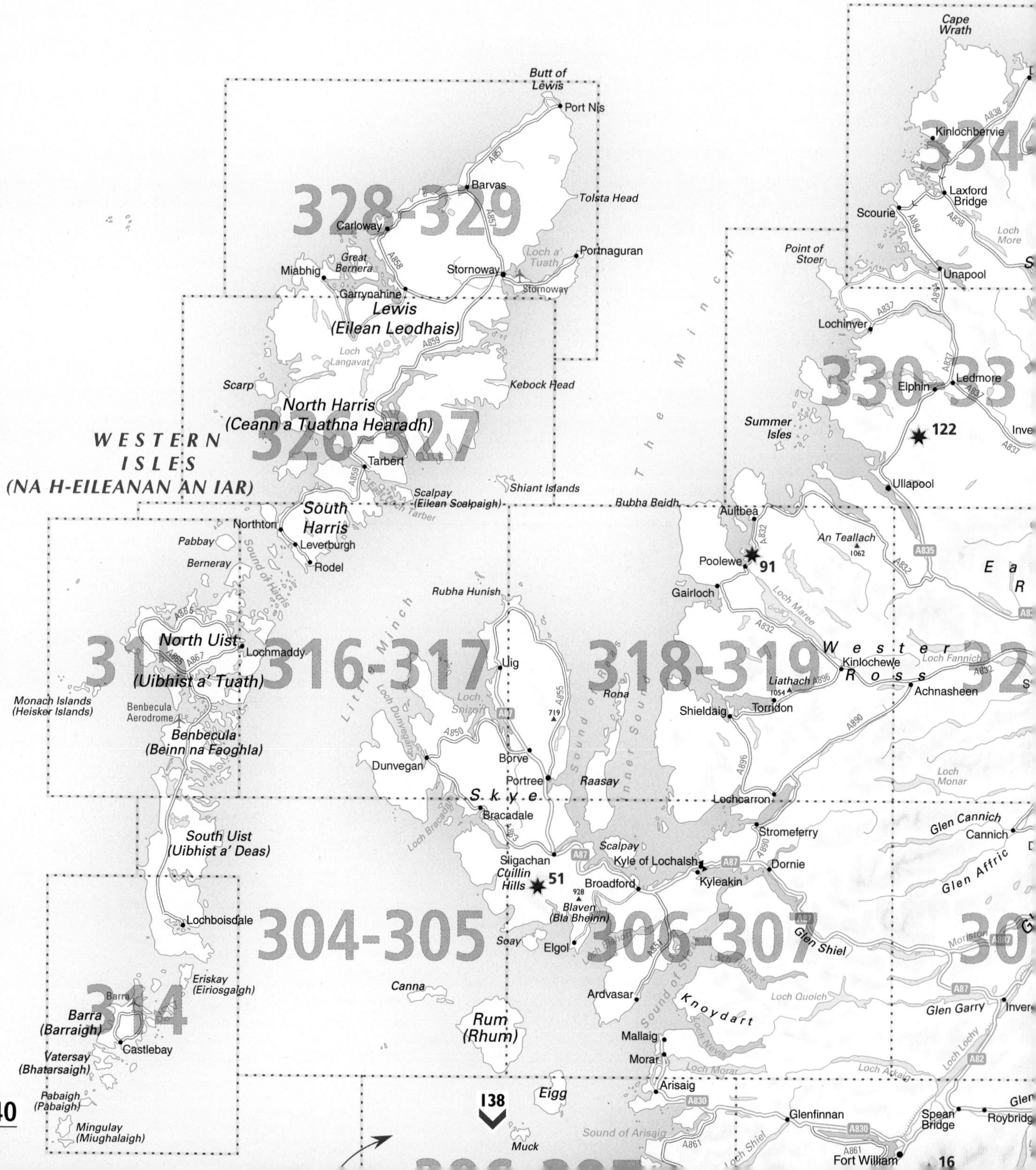

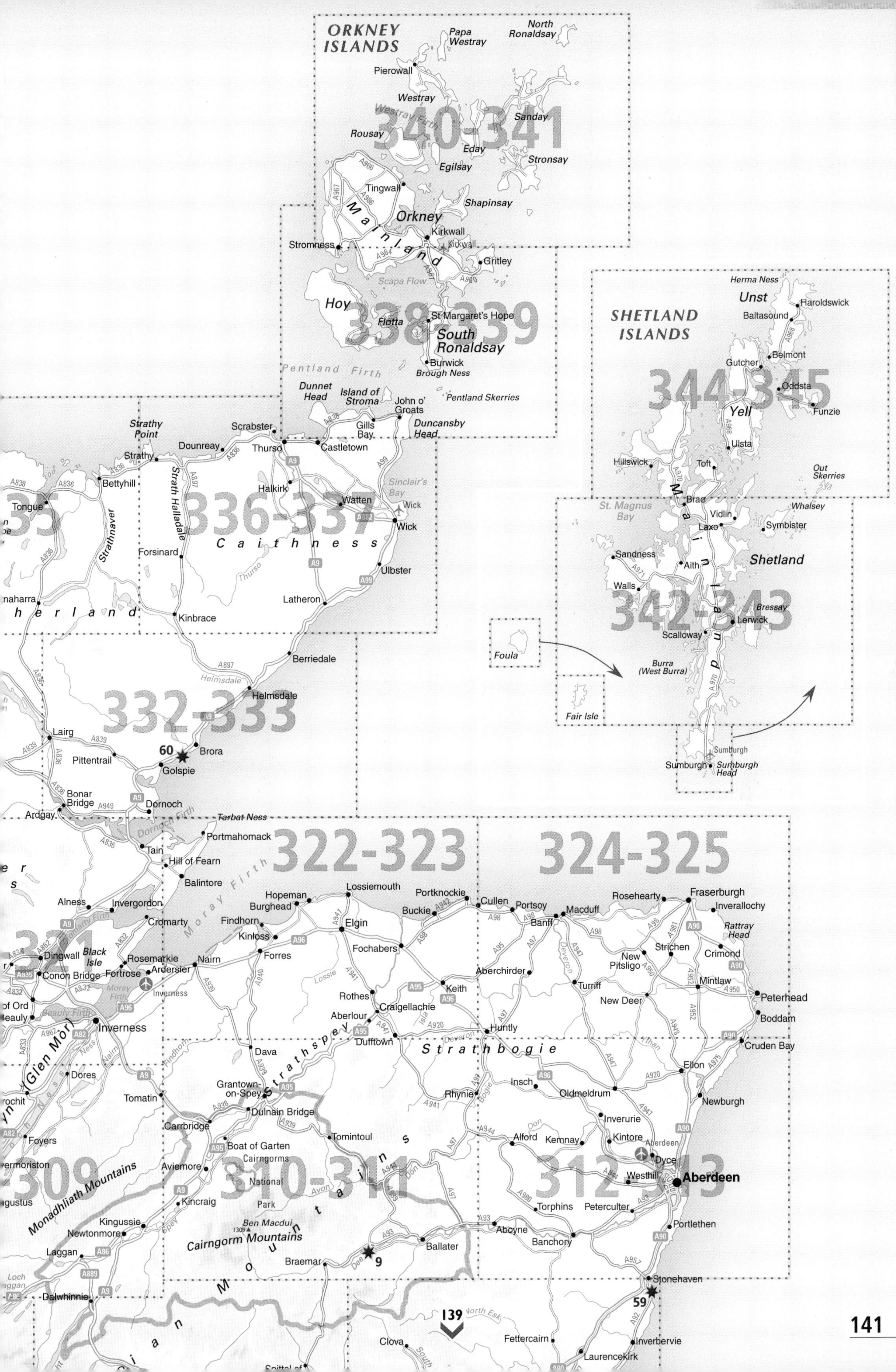
ORKNEY ISLANDS
340-341
Papa Westray
North Ronaldsay
Pierowall
Westray
Westray Firth
Sanday
Rousay
Eday
Stronsay
Egilsay
Tingwall
Shapinsay
Mainland
Orkney
Kirkwall
Stromness
Gritley
Scapa Flow
Hoy
338-339
Flotta
St Margaret's Hope
South Ronaldsay
Burwick
Brough Ness
Pentland Firth
Dunnet Head
Island of Stroma
John o' Groats
Pentland Skerries
Gills Bay
Duncansby Head
SHETLAND ISLANDS
Herma Ness
Unst
Haroldswick
Baltasound
Belmont
Gutcher
344-345
Oddsta
Yell
Funzie
Ulsta
Hillswick
Toft
Out Skerries
St. Magnus Bay
Brae
Whalsey
Vidlin
Laxo
Symbister
Sandness
Aith
Shetland
Walls
342-343
Bressay
Lerwick
Scalloway
Foula
Burra (West Burra)
Fair Isle
Sumburgh
Sumburgh Head
Strathy Point
Scrabster
Dounreay
Thurso
Castletown
Strathy
Bettyhill
Tongue
Strathnaver
Strath Halladale
Halkirk
Sinclair's Bay
Watten
Wick
336-337
Caithness
Forsinard
Ulbster
Latheron
Kinbrace
naharra
herland
Berriedale
Helmsdale
332-333
Lairg
Pittentrail
60
Brora
Golspie
Bonar Bridge
Dornoch
Ardgay
Dornoch Firth
Tarbat Ness
Portmahomack
Tain
322-323
324-325
Hill of Fearn
Balintore
Moray Firth
Alness
Invergordon
Cromarty
Hopeman
Burghead
Lossiemouth
Portknockie
Buckie
Cullen
Portsoy
Banff
Macduff
Rosehearty
Fraserburgh
Inverallochy
Rattray Head
Findhorn
Kinloss
Elgin
Forres
Fochabers
Strichen
Crimond
New Pitsligo
Dingwall
Black Isle
Rosemarkie
Nairn
Ardersier
Conon Bridge
Fortrose
Inverness
Aberchirder
Turriff
Mintlaw
Peterhead
Keith
Rothes
New Deer
Boddam
Craigellachie
Aberlour
Beauly Firth
Inverness
Dufftown
Huntly
Strathspey
Strathbogie
Cruden Bay
Dava
Ellon
Dores
Grantown-on-Spey
Rhynie
Insch
Oldmeldrum
Newburgh
Tomatin
Dulnain Bridge
Carrbridge
Inverurie
Tomintoul
Alford
Kemnay
Kintore
Foyers
Boat of Garten
Aberdeen
Dyce
Cairngorms National Park
310-311
309
312-313
Aviemore
Westhill
Aberdeen
Monadhliath Mountains
Kincraig
Torphins
Peterculter
Kingussie
Ben Macdui
Cairngorm Mountains
Aboyne
Portlethen
Newtonmore
Banchory
Ballater
Laggan
Braemar
9
Stonehaven
Dalwhinnie
59
139
North Esk
Fettercairn
Clova
Inverbervie
Laurencekirk

KEY TO MAP SYMBOLS

This map appears in the top corner of all road map pages. The regions covered by the mapping on each page are highlighted in the appropriate colour.

- South West England
- South East England
- London
- West Midlands
- East Midlands
- East of England
- Yorkshire
- North West England
- North East England
- Wales
- Scotland

The tourist features that are described on the preceding pages fall into two categories; Outstanding and Popular. These are highlighted on the mapping in the following colours:

British Museum	Outstanding attractions have a purple symbol and name which are highlighted in yellow.
Museum of London	Popular attractions have a purple symbol with a purple name.
Edinburgh Castle / Dean Gallery	On large scale mapping the tourist symbol may be replaced by a building shape. These are depicted in the same colours as the symbols.

For a full list of all the tourist symbols please see panel at the bottom of this page.
Within the attraction descriptions, any feature with an empty symbol can be found as a place or area name on the road mapping.

A51-TO CHESTER — Destination boxes surround the mapping to indicate the next key place along major routes.

158 — Page continuation arrow

Road mapping

pages 144-345

M5	Motorway
M6Toll	Toll motorway
8 9	Motorway junction with full / limited access
Maidstone, Birch, Sarn	Motorway service area with off road / full / limited access
A556	Primary route with dual / single carriageway
A30	'A' road dual / single carriageway
B1403	'B' road dual / single carriageway
	Minor road
	Road with restricted access
	Roads with passing places
	Road proposed or under construction
24	Multi-level junction (occasionally with junction number)
	Roundabout
4	Road distance in miles between markers
	Road tunnel
	Steep hill (arrows point downhill)
Toll	Level crossing / Toll
St. Malo 8hrs(10hrs)	Car ferry route with journey times; daytime and (night-time)
	Railway line / station / tunnel
South Downs Way	National Trail / Long Distance Route
	Airport with scheduled services
	Heliport
	Park and Ride site (operates at least 5 days a week)
	Built up area
	Town / Village / Other settlement
Hythe	Seaside destination
	National boundary
KENT	County / Unitary Authority boundary and name
	National Park
	Forest / Regional Park boundary
	Woodland
Danger Zone	Military range
468 941	Spot / Summit height (in metres)
	Lake / Dam / River / Waterfall
	Canal / Dry canal / Canal tunnel
	Lighthouse
	Beach
SEE PAGE 347	Area covered by urban area map

metres	feet
900	2950
700	2295
500	1640
300	985
150	490
0	0
water	water
land below sea level	land below sea level

Scale bar: 0, 2, 4, 6 miles; 0, 2, 4, 6, 8, 10 km

Map scale 1:200,000
3.2 miles to 1 inch / 2km to 1 cm

Tourist information

pages 144-375

A selection of tourist detail is shown on the mapping. It is advisable to check with the attraction or local tourist information centre regarding opening times and facilities available. Where a symbol appears purple on the map, its description can be found within pages 23–131.

- Tourist information centre (open all year)
- Tourist information centre (open seasonally)
- Ancient monument
- Battlefield (1643)
- Camp site / Caravan site
- Castle
- Country park
- Ecclesiastical building
- Football club (Major British club)
- Garden
- Golf course
- Historic house
- Major shopping centre / Outlet village
- Major sports venue
- Motor racing circuit
- Museum / Art gallery
- Nature reserve
- Preserved railway
- Racecourse
- Theme park
- University
- Wildlife park or Zoo
- Other interesting feature
- (NT) (NTS) National Trust / National Trust for Scotland property

Urban area maps

pages 346-375

- 12 13 Motorway junctions with full access
- 14 15 Motorway junctions with limited access
- LEICESTER SERVICES Motorway service area
- M6 Toll Toll motorway
- A316 Primary route dual / single carriageway
- A4054 'A' road dual / single carriageway
- B7078 'B' road dual / single carriageway
- Minor road dual / single carriageway
- Road proposed or under construction
- Road tunnel
- Roundabout
- T Toll
- One way street
- Level crossing
- Park and Ride site (operates at least 5 days a week)
- Dublin 8hrs Car ferry with destination
- Airport with scheduled services
- Railway line / Railway tunnel
- Railway station / Light rail station
- London underground / Glasgow Subway station
- Congestion charging zone
- Public building
- 362 ▲ Spot height in metres
- Built up area
- Woodland / Park
- BRISTOL County / Unitary Authority boundary and name
- SEE PAGE 389 Area covered by town plan

Central city maps

pages 376-387

- M8 Motorway
- A4 Primary route dual / single carriageway
- A40 'A' road dual / single carriageway
- B507 'B' road
- Other road
- One way street
- Access restriction
- Pedestrian street
- Street market
- Track/Footpath
- Main / other national rail station
- London Underground / Glasgow Subway station
- Manchester Metro / Birmingham Metro station
- Bus/Coach station
- Vehicle / Pedestrian ferry
- Car park
- Tourist information centre
- Theatre
- Major hotel
- Pol Police station
- PO Post office
- Lib Library
- JAPAN Embassy
- Cinema
- Church
- Mosque
- Synagogue
- Mormon Other place of worship
- Leisure & tourism
- Shopping
- Administration & law
- Health & welfare
- Education
- Industry & commerce
- Park / Garden / Sports ground
- Cemetery
- Built up area
- Central London congestion charging zone

Town plans

pages 388-415

- Motorway
- Primary route dual / single carriageway
- 'A' road dual / single carriageway
- 'B' road dual / single carriageway
- Through route dual / single carriageway
- Other road dual / single carriageway
- Restricted access street
- Pedestrian street
- Path / Footbridge
- One way street
- Car park
- Park and Ride site (operates at least 5 days a week)
- Railway line / station
- Underground station
- Metro station
- Light rail station
- Ecclesiastical building
- Tourist information centre (open all year / seasonally)
- Tourist building
- Important building
- Higher Education building
- Hospital
- Cemetery
- Recreational area / Open space

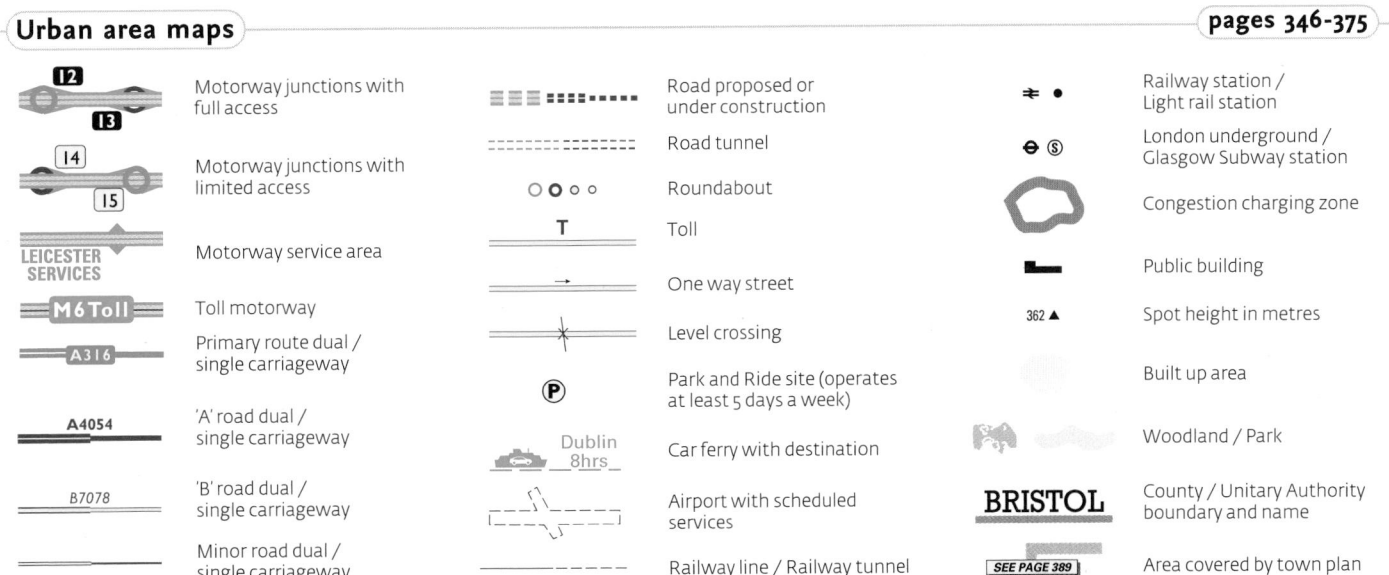

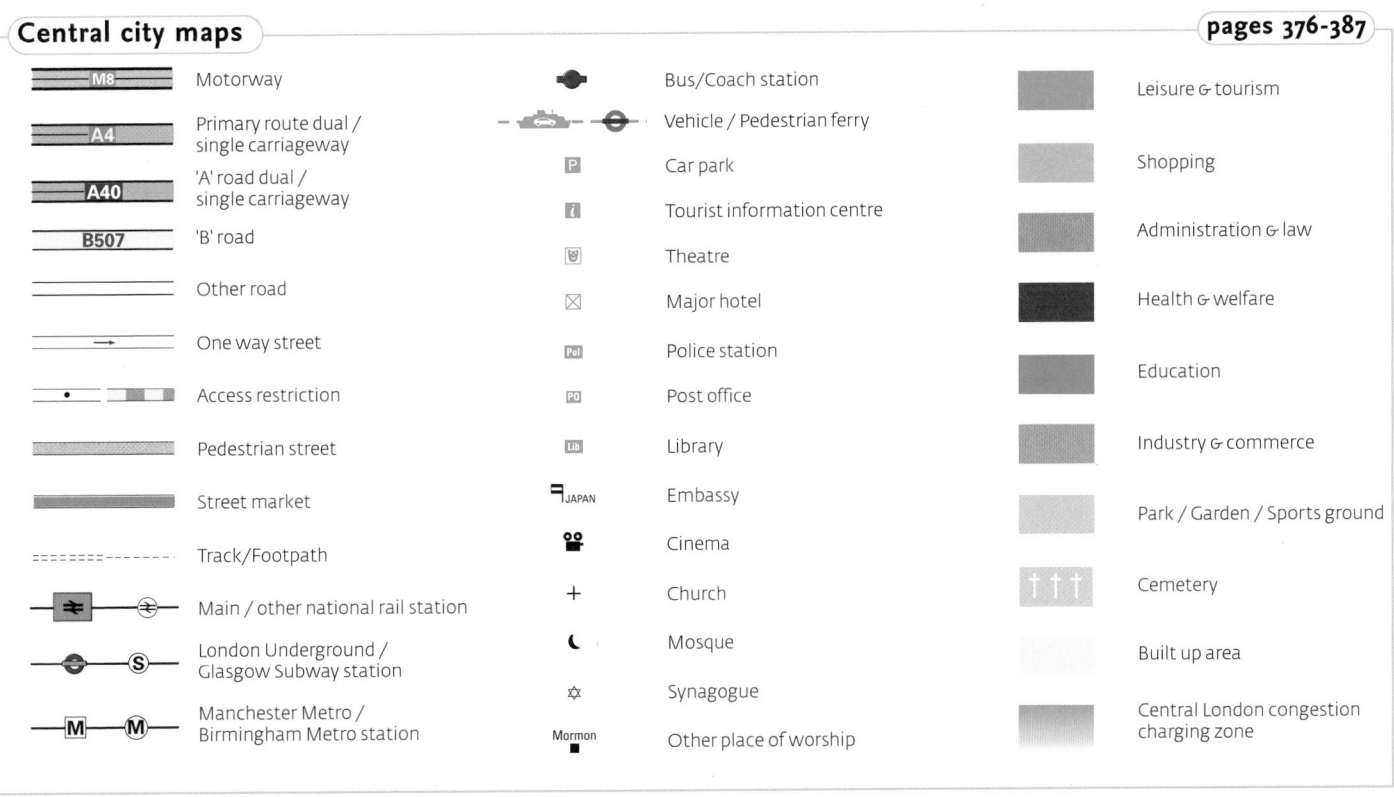

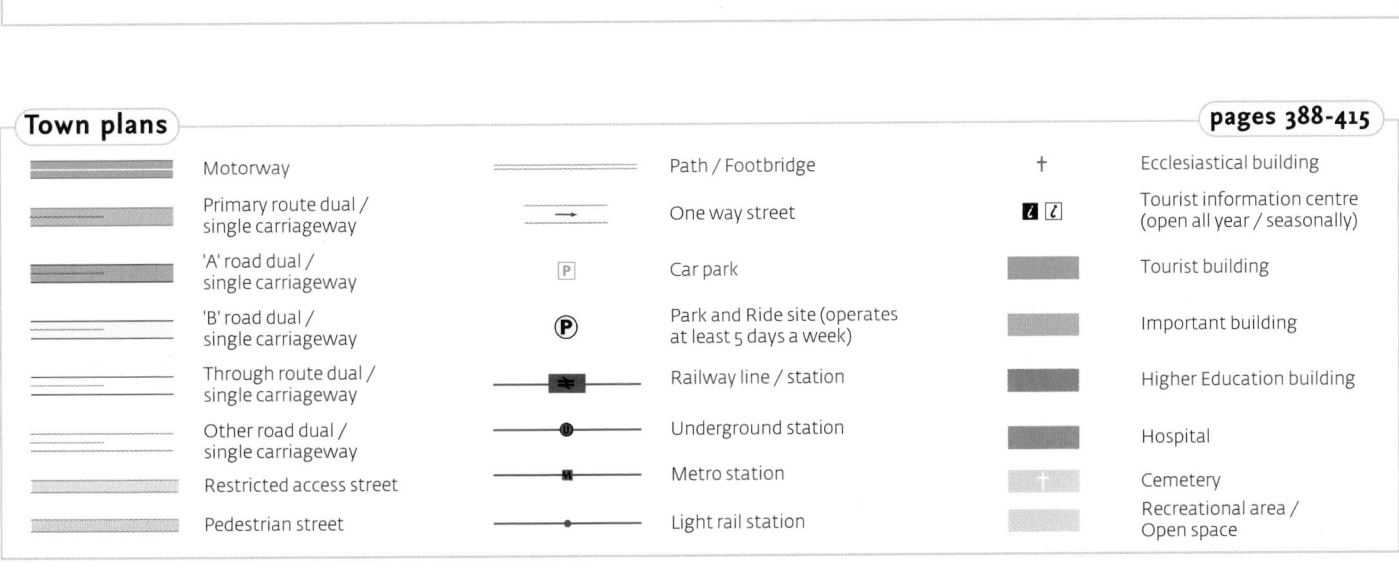

The sea level at **Newlyn** is the point from which all heights in Britain are measured. For example, Snowdon is calculated to be 3,560 feet (1,085m) above sea level, so it is 3,560 feet (1,085m) higher than the sea level at Newlyn.
Sea level at Newlyn was originally calculated from hourly readings, using an automatic tide gauge, taken between May 1915 and April 1921.
This tide gauge is located in the Ordnance Survey Tidal Observatory on the south pier at Newlyn. ***Map ref. B4***

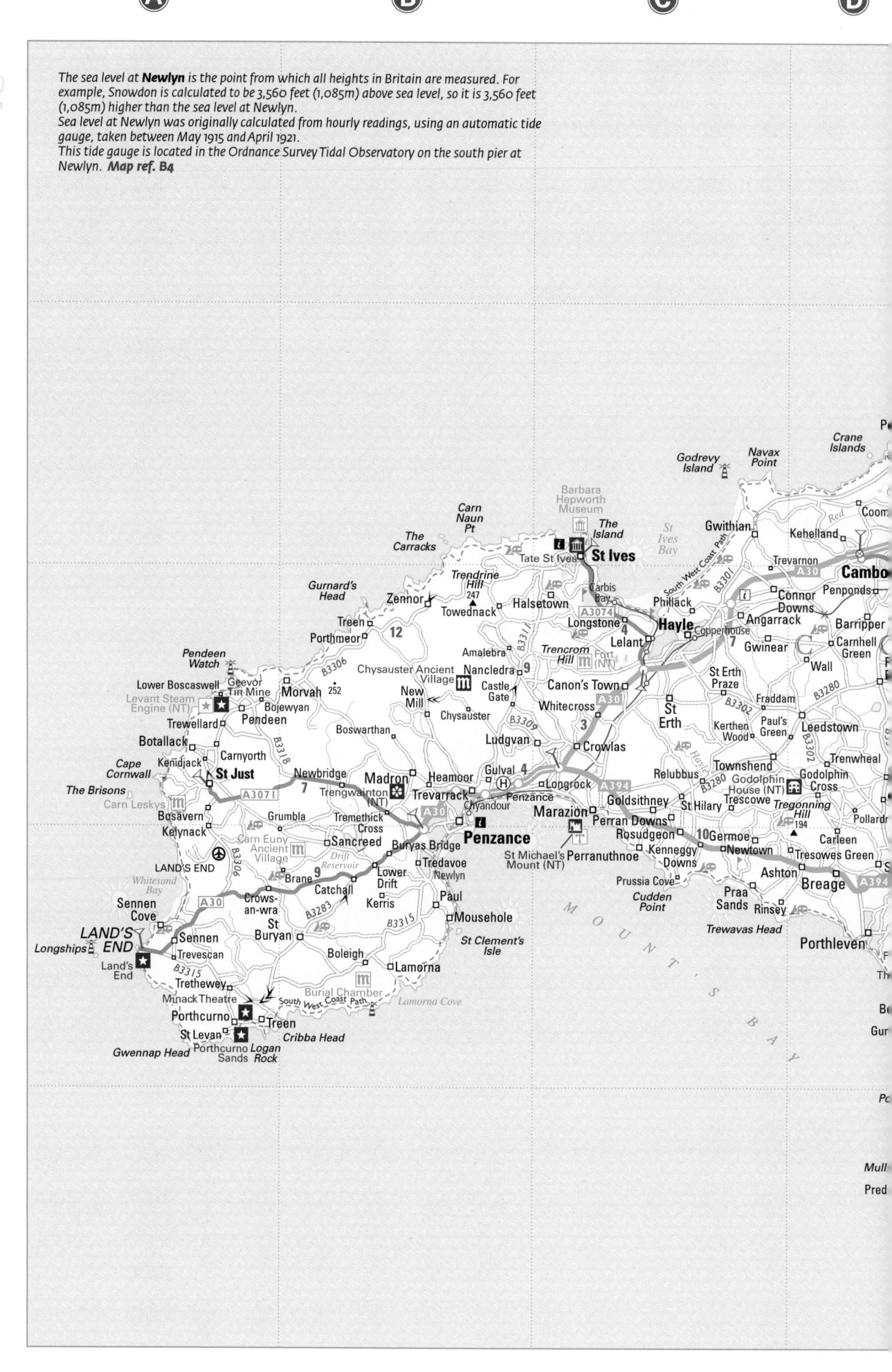

Lands End *is the most westerly point of mainland Britain and is 874 miles (1,407km) by road from John O' Groats. It is the closest point to North America, if you travel due west, for 2,500 miles (4,000km), from here, you will arrive in Newfoundland.* ***Map ref. A4*** ***Also on page 31***

Gwennap Head: *Hang on to your hat, at 118 mph (190 km/h) the highest ever gust of wind, on a low level site in Britain, was recorded here on the 15th December 1979.* ***Map ref. A4***

D E 146 F G

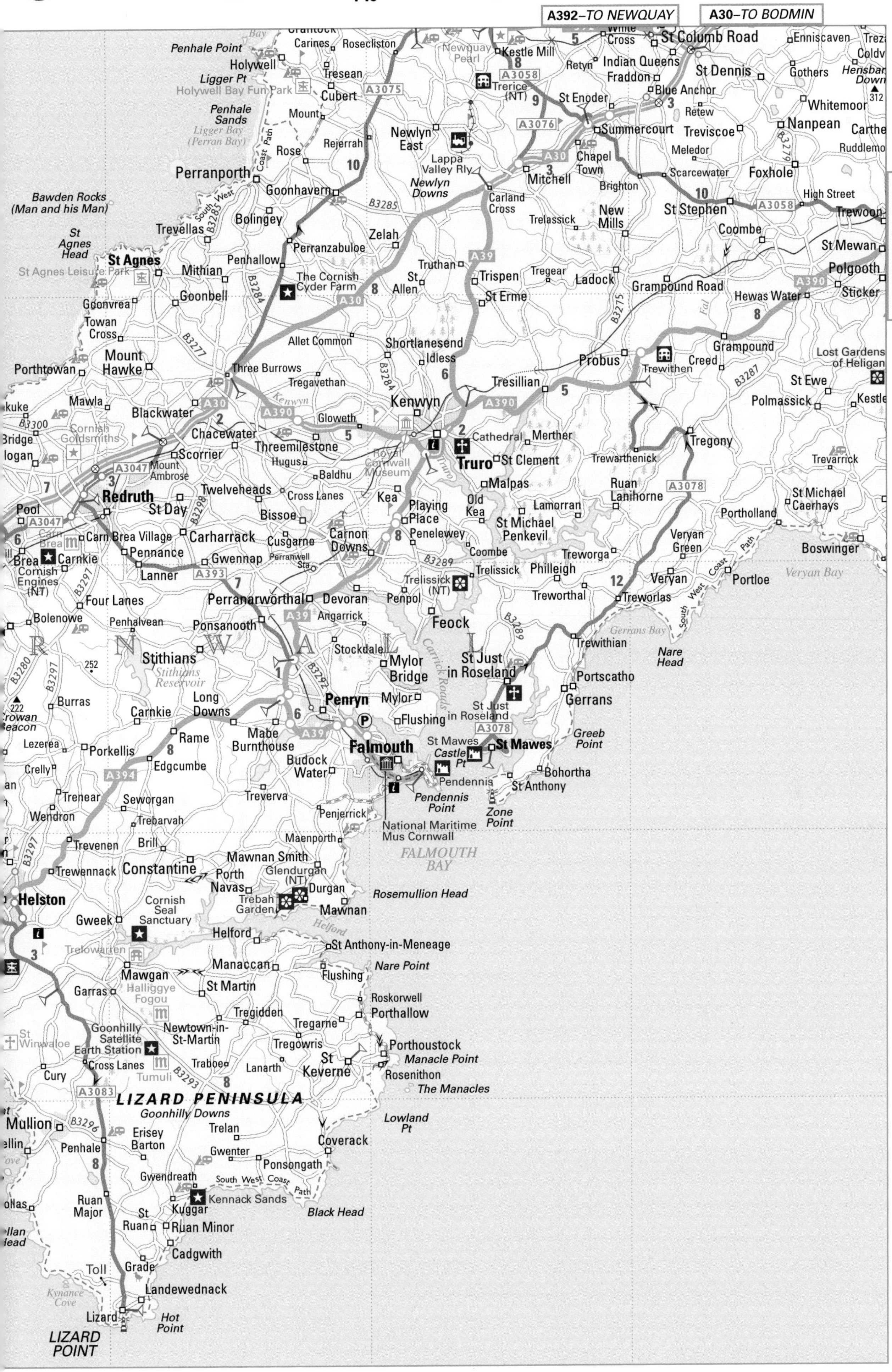
A392–TO NEWQUAY
A30–TO BODMIN
A390–TO LISKEARD
Penhale Point
Carines
Rosecliston
Holywell
Ligger Pt
Holywell Bay Fun Park
Tresean
Cubert
A3075
Newquay Pearl
Kestle Mill
A3058
Trerice (NT)
Retyn
Indian Queens
Fraddon
St Columb Road
St Dennis
Enniscaven
Gothers
Hensbarrow Down
Blue Anchor
St Enoder
Retew
Whitemoor
Penhale Sands
Ligger Bay (Perran Bay)
Mount
Newlyn East
A3076
Summercourt
Treviscoe
Nanpean
Carthew
Rose
Rejerrah
Lappa Valley Rly
Chapel Town
Meledor
Ruddlemoor
Perranporth
Goonhavern
Mitchell
Scarcewater
Foxhole
Newlyn Downs
Brighton
High Street
Bawden Rocks (Man and his Man)
Carland Cross
New Mills
St Stephen
A3058
Trewoon
Trevellas
Bolingey
B3285
Trelassick
Coombe
St Agnes Head
St Agnes
St Agnes Leisure Park
Zelah
Perranzabuloe
St Mewan
Penhallow
Mithian
Truthan
Polgooth
The Cornish Cyder Farm
St Allen
Trispen
Tregear
Ladock
Grampound Road
Hewas Water
Sticker
A390
Goonvrea
Goonbell
A30
St Erme
B3284
B3275
Fal
Towan Cross
B3277
Allet Common
Shortlanesend
Grampound
Porthtowan
Mount Hawke
Idless
Probus
Creed
Lost Gardens of Heligan
Three Burrows
Tregavethan
Trewithen
B3287
St Ewe
Tresillian
Kenwyn
Polmassick
Kestle
Mawla
Blackwater
A390
Gloweth
Cornish Goldsmiths
Chacewater
Cathedral
Merther
Threemilestone
Scorrier
Royal Cornwall Museum
Truro
St Clement
Tregony
Trewarthenick
Trevarrick
Mount Ambrose
Hugus
Baldhu
A3047
Malpas
Ruan Lanihorne
A3078
Redruth
Twelveheads
Cross Lanes
St Michael Caerhays
St Day
Kea
Old Kea
Lamorran
Pool
B3298
Bissoe
Playing Place
Portholland
A3047
Carn Brea Village
Carharrack
Cusgarne
Carnon Downs
Penelewey
St Michael Penkevil
Veryan Green
Pennance
Coombe
Treworga
Boswinger
Brea
Carnkie
Cornish Engines (NT)
Gwennap
Perranwell Sta
B3289
Trelissick
Philleigh
Lanner
A393
Trelissick (NT)
Veryan
Portloe
Veryan Bay
Four Lanes
Perranarworthal
Devoran
Penpol
Treworthal
Treworlas
Bolenowe
Penhalvean
Ponsanooth
A39
Angarrick
Feock
Gerrans Bay
Trewithian
Stithians
Stithians Reservoir
Stockdale
Mylor Bridge
St Just in Roseland
Nare Head
B3280
B3297
252
B3292
Carrick Roads
Portscatho
Burras
Long Downs
Penryn
Mylor
Gerrans
222
Crowan Beacon
Carnkie
St Just in Roseland
Flushing
A3078
Rame
Mabe Burnthouse
A39
Falmouth
St Mawes
St Mawes Castle
Greeb Point
Lezerea
Porkellis
Budock Water
Bohortha
Crelly
A394
Edgcumbe
Pendennis
St Anthony
Pendennis Point
Trenear
Seworgan
Treverva
Zone Point
Wendron
Penjerrick
Trebarvah
National Maritime Mus Cornwall
Trevenen
Brill
Maenporth
FALMOUTH BAY
B3297
Trewennack
Constantine
Mawnan Smith
Glendurgan (NT)
Porth Navas
Durgan
Helston
Cornish Seal Sanctuary
Trebah Garden
Rosemullion Head
Gweek
Mawnan
Helford
Helford
Trelowarren
St Anthony-in-Meneage
Manaccan
Nare Point
Mawgan
St Martin
Flushing
Garras
Halliggye Fogou
Roskorwell
Tregidden
Porthallow
St Winwaloe
Goonhilly Satellite Earth Station
Newtown-in-St-Martin
Tregarne
Tregowris
Porthoustock
Traboe
St Keverne
Manacle Point
Cross Lanes
Tumuli
B3293
Lanarth
Rosenithon
Cury
The Manacles
A3083
LIZARD PENINSULA
Goonhilly Downs
Lowland Pt
Mullion
B3296
Trelan
Erisey Barton
Penhale
Coverack
Gwenter
Ponsongath
Gwendreath
South West Coast Path
Kennack Sands
Ruan Major
St Ruan
Kuggar
Black Head
Ruan Minor
Cadgwith
Grade
Toll
Kynance Cove
Landewednack
Lizard
Hot Point
LIZARD POINT

1 147 2 3 4 5

*At 49° 57' 30" N **Lizard Point** is the most southerly point of mainland Britain. **Map ref. D5***

A B C D

1 2 3 4 5

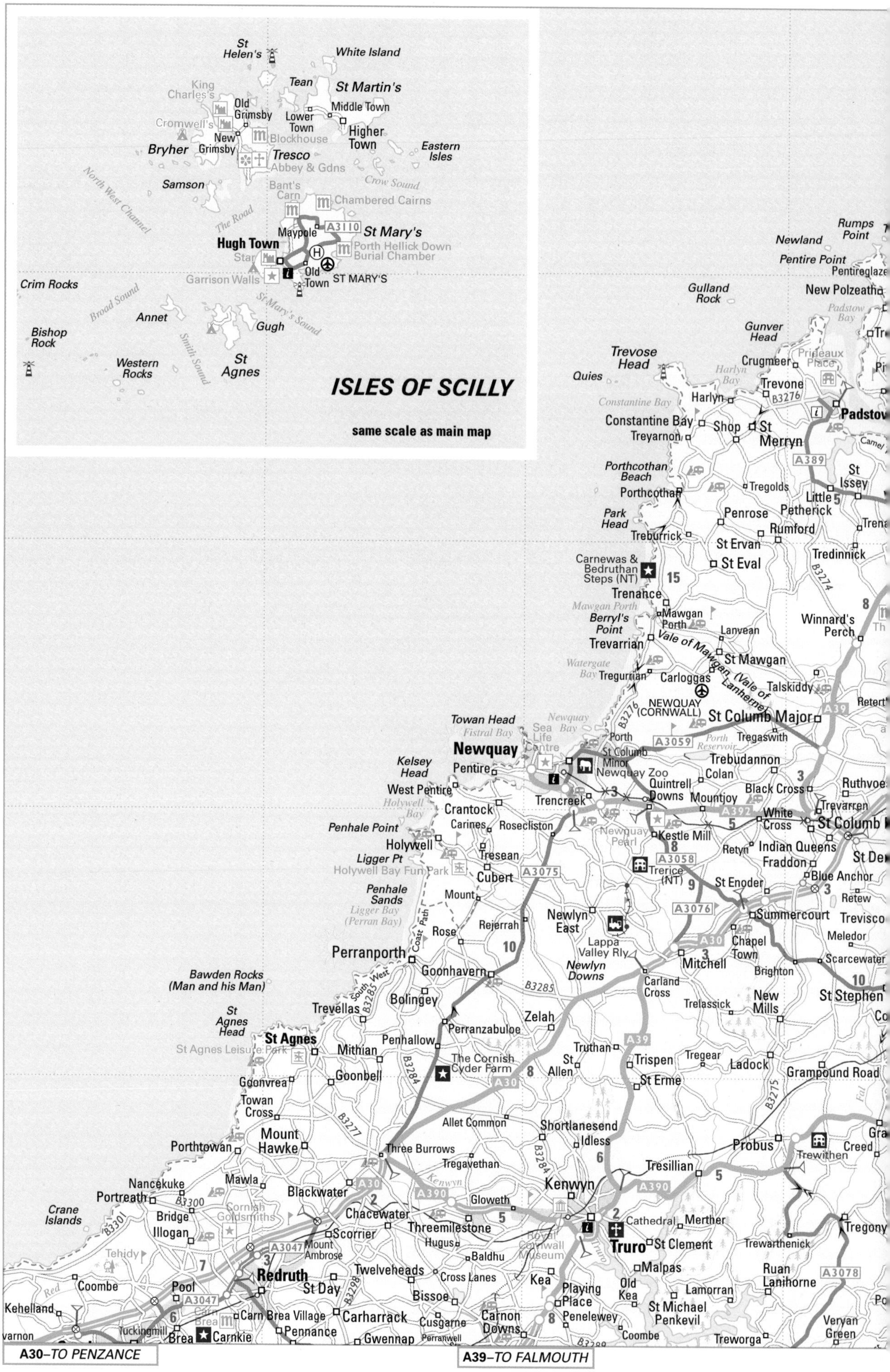

St Helen's
White Island
Tean
St Martin's
King Charles's
Old Grimsby
Lower Town
Middle Town
Higher Town
Cromwell's
New Grimsby
Blockhouse
Bryher
Tresco
Abbey & Gdns
Eastern Isles
Samson
North West Channel
Bant's Carn
Chambered Cairns
Crow Sound
The Road
Maypole
A3110
St Mary's
Hugh Town
Star
Porth Hellick Down Burial Chamber
Garrison Walls
Old Town
ST MARY'S
Crim Rocks
Broad Sound
St Mary's Sound
Annet
Gugh
Bishop Rock
Smith Sound
Western Rocks
St Agnes
ISLES OF SCILLY
same scale as main map
Rumps Point
Newland
Pentire Point
Pentireglaze
Gulland Rock
New Polzeath
Padstow Bay
Gunver Head
Trevose Head
Prideaux Place
Crugmeer
Quies
Harlyn Bay
Harlyn
Trevone
B3276
Constantine Bay
Padstow
Shop
St Merryn
Treyarnon
Camel
A389
Porthcothan Beach
St Issey
Tregolds
Porthcothan
Little Petherick
Penrose
Park Head
Rumford
Treburrick
St Ervan
Tredinnick
St Eval
Carnewas & Bedruthan Steps (NT)
B3274
Trenance
Mawgan Porth
Berryl's Point
Mawgan Porth
Lanvean
Winnard's Perch
Trevarrian
Vale of Mawgan (Vale of Lanherne)
St Mawgan
Watergate Bay
Tregurrian
Carloggas
Talskiddy
NEWQUAY (CORNWALL)
B3276
A39
Towan Head
Fistral Bay
Newquay Bay
Sea Life Centre
St Columb Major
Porth
A3059
Porth Reservoir
Tregaswith
Newquay
St Columb Minor
Trebudannon
Kelsey Head
Pentire
Newquay Zoo
Colan
Quintrell Downs
Black Cross
Ruthvoes
West Pentire
Trencreek
Mountjoy
Trevarren
Holywell Bay
A392
White Cross
St Columb Road
Crantock
Carines
Rosecliston
Penhale Point
Newquay Pearl
Kestle Mill
Retyn
Indian Queens
Holywell
Tresean
A3058
Fraddon
Ligger Pt
Holywell Bay Fun Park
Cubert
A3075
Trerice (NT)
St Enoder
Blue Anchor
Penhale Sands
Ligger Bay (Perran Bay)
Mount
Retew
A3076
Summercourt
Trevisco
Newlyn East
Coast Path
Rose
Rejerrah
Lappa Valley Rly
Chapel Town
Meledor
Perranporth
Mitchell
Scarcewater
Newlyn Downs
Brighton
Goonhavern
Bawden Rocks (Man and his Man)
South West
Carland Cross
B3285
St Stephen
Bolingey
New Mills
Trelassick
Trevellas
B3285
St Agnes Head
Zelah
Perranzabuloe
St Agnes
Penhallow
Truthan
A39
St Agnes Leisure Park
Mithian
The Cornish Cyder Farm
Trispen
Tregear
St Allen
Ladock
Grampound Road
B3284
St Erme
Goonbell
A30
Goonvrea
Towan Cross
B3275
B3277
Allet Common
Shortlanesend
Mount Hawke
Idless
Porthtowan
Three Burrows
Probus
Creed
B3284
Trewithen
Tregavethan
Tresillian
Nancekuke
Mawla
Kenwyn
Kenwyn
A390
Portreath
B3300
Blackwater
A30
A390
Gloweth
Crane Islands
Bridge
Cornish Goldsmiths
Chacewater
Cathedral
Merther
B3301
Tregony
Illogan
Scorrier
Threemilestone
Truro
St Clement
Trewarthenick
Tehidy
Hugus
Royal Cornwall Museum
A3047
Mount Ambrose
Baldhu
Malpas
Ruan Lanihorne
Redruth
Twelveheads
A3078
Coombe
Pool
St Day
Cross Lanes
Kea
Old Kea
Lamorran
Red
A3047
B3298
Playing Place
Kehelland
Carn Brea
Bissoe
Carnon Downs
Penelewey
St Michael Penkevil
Carn Brea Village
Carharrack
Cusgarne
Veryan Green
Tuckingmill
Pennance
Perranwell
Coombe
Treworga
Brea
Carnkie
Gwennap
A30–TO PENZANCE
A39–TO FALMOUTH

145

Newquay *is recognised as the 'Surf Capital' of the UK. The resort hosts world championship events at Fistral Bay.* ***Map ref. B3***

D
E
F
G
148
A39–TO BUDE
1
2
3
4
5
148
A30–TO OKEHAMPTON
A38–TO PLYMOUTH
Tintagel Head
Tintagel Old Post Office (NT)
Tintagel
Bossiney
Trewarmett
Treknow
Start Point
Trebarwith
Penpethy
Rockhead
Delabole
Treligga
Westdowns
Trewalder
Port Isaac Bay
Port Isaac
Port Gaverne
Tregeare Rounds
St Teath
Trelights
Long Cross Victorian Gdns
Pendoggett
St Endellion
St Minver
Trewethern
Chapel Amble
St Kew
Trelill
Trequite
St Kew Highway
St Tudy
Treworna
Kelly
Bodieve
Trevanson
Wadebridge
Egloshayle
St Breock
Sladesbridge
Burlawn
Inscribed Stone
Washaway
Pencarrow
Lane-end
Helland
Hellandbridge
Boscarne
Dunmere
Bodmin
Nanstallon
Rutherbridge
St Lawrence
Withielgoose
Bodmin & Wenford Rly
Withiel
Tremore
Tregullon
Lanivet
Victoria
Roche
Higher Town
Lockengate
Criggan
Bodwen
Roche Chapel
Enniscaven
Trezaise
Bilberry
Coldvreath
Bugle
Gothers
Hensbarrow Downs
Rosevean
Luxulyan
Whitemoor
Stenalees
Rescorla
Penwithick
Nanpean
Carthew
Trethurgy
Ruddlemoor
Eden Project
St Blazey
Tregrehan Mills
St Blazey Gate
High Street
Wheal Martyn
Mount Charles
Trewoon
Par
St Mewan
ST AUSTELL
Carlyon Bay
Charlestown
Polgooth
St Austell Bay
Porthpean
Sticker
London Apprentice
Trenarren
Black Head
Lost Gardens of Heligan
St Ewe
Pentewan
Tregiskey
Kestle
Penare Point
Mevagissey Bay
Mevagissey
Trevarrick
Portmellon
Chapel Point
St Michael Caerhays
Gorran Churchtown
Gorran Haven
Maenease Point
Boswinger
Camelford
Valley Truckle
Lanteglos
Helstone
Pencarrow
Tresinney
Treveighan
Michaelstow
St Breward
Row
Lank
Wenfordbridge
Bradford
St Mabyn
Blisland
CORNWALL
Cardinham Moor
Millpool
Maidenwell
Warleggan
Cardinham
Treslea
Mount
Fletchersbridge
Respryn
Bodmin Parkway Sta
Lanhydrock (NT)
Trebyan
Bokiddick
Sweetshouse
Restormel
Redmoor
Bridgend
Lostwithiel
Lanlivery
Milltown
Saint Winnow
Lerryn
Tywardreath Highway
Treesmill
Torfrey
Golant
Tywardreath
Polkerris
Lanteglos Highway
Penpoll
St Veep
Bodinnick
Fowey
St Catherine's
Menabilly
Polruan
Pencarrow Head
Gribbin Head
Hendraburnick
Trewassa
Davidstow
Tremail
Hallworthy
Cold Northcott
Trevivian
St Clether
Tregoodwell
Lower Moor
New Park
Bowithick
Rough Tor
Buttern Hill
Bray Down
Brown Willy
Watergate
Garrow Tor
Codda
BODMIN MOOR
Bolventor
Temple
Colliford Reservoir
Dozmary Pool
Brown Gelly
Smallacombe Downs
Kilmar Tor
Siblyback Reservoir
Hurlers Stone Circle
Minions
Common Moor
Caradon Hill
Draynes
King Doniert's Stone
Trethevy Quoit
St Neot
Dobwalls Family Adventure Park
Dobwalls
Ley
Middle Drift
Doublebois
West Taphouse
Middle Taphouse
East Taphouse
Trevelmond
St Pinnock
Braddock
Braddock Down 1643
Boconnoc
Herodsfoot
Couch's Mill
Bocaddon
Lanreath
Muchlarnick
Pelynt
Trenewan
Lansallos
Porthallow
Talland
Polperro
Lantivet Bay
South West Coast Path
Tremaine
Penrose
North Petherwin
Treneglos
Three Hammers
Tresmeer
Trebeath
Egloskerry
Langore
Badgall
Tregeare
Red Down
Launceston Steam
Downhead
Laneast
Pipers Pool
Tregadillett
Tregunnon
Trewen
Polyphant
Altarnun
Tredaule
Trewint
Fivelanes
Lewannick
Plusha
Trevadlock
Congdon's Shop
Trebartha
Coad's Green
North Hill
Berriowbridge
Bathpool
Henwood
Rilla Mill
Upton
Upton Cross
Caradon Town
Pensilva
Darite
Crow's Nest
Tremar
St Cleer
Merrymeet
Pengover Green
Liskeard
Lamellion
Menheniot
Bodrane
St Keyne
Horningtops
Trewidland
Bylane End
Duloe
Tredinnick
Tregarland
Widegates
Sandplace
Morval
No Man's Land
St Martin
Looe
West Looe
East Looe
Looe Bay
Portlooe
St George's Island (Looe Island)

In 1584 Sir Francis Drake was voted into the House of Commons as MP for **Bossiney**. ***Map ref. E1***

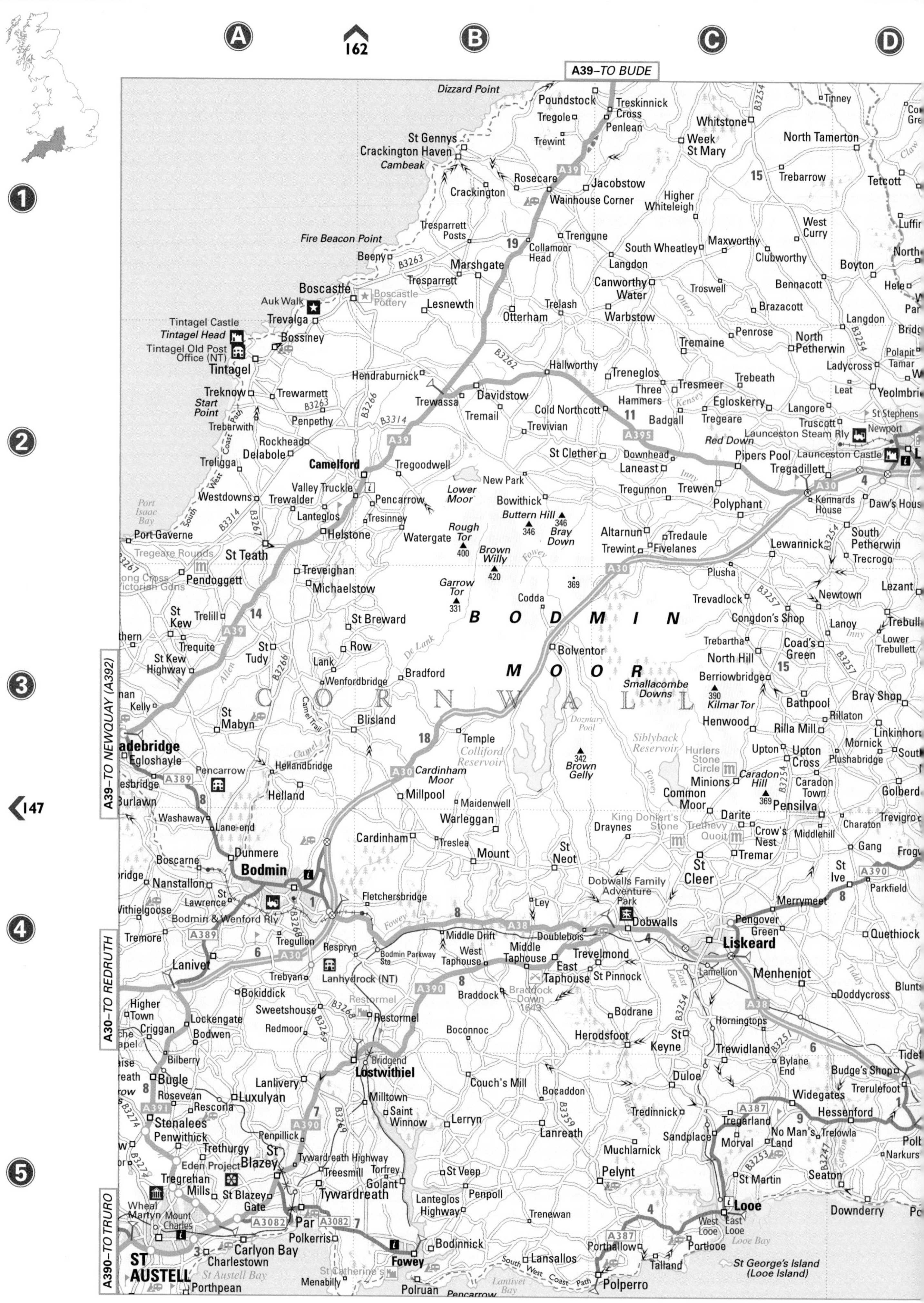

Bodmin Moor: *This is a sweeping expanse of rugged moorland covering over a hundred square miles of central Cornwall. The area is seeped in myth and legend, not least the tales of the 'Beast of Bodmin Moor'. Over the last twenty years there have been more than sixty recorded sighting of the 'Beast', generally thought to be a big cat, like a panther, which preys on other wild animals and farm livestock.* ***Map ref. B3 Also on page 25***

Tavistock: *Crowndale, just south of Tavistock is the birthplace of Sir Francis Drake. Drake is one of Britain's most famous sea captains. He was the first Englishman to sail around the World in 1580 and later became famous for routing the Spanish Armada.* ***Map ref. E3***

Dartmoor Prison, Princetown: *Built in 1809 to hold prisoners of war. Almost 1,500 French and American prisoners died here under a very brutal regime and were all buried just outside the prison walls. Dartmoor closed as a prisoner of war establishment in 1815 but was reopened in 1850 for civilian prisoners serving long sentences and those subject to hard labour. It was always regarded as 'the end of the line' for inmates and there have been numerous calls for it to close. However, as a listed building it cannot be demolished, so since 1980 it has been revamped and modernised and continues to be part of the prison system.* ***Map ref. F3***

149

149

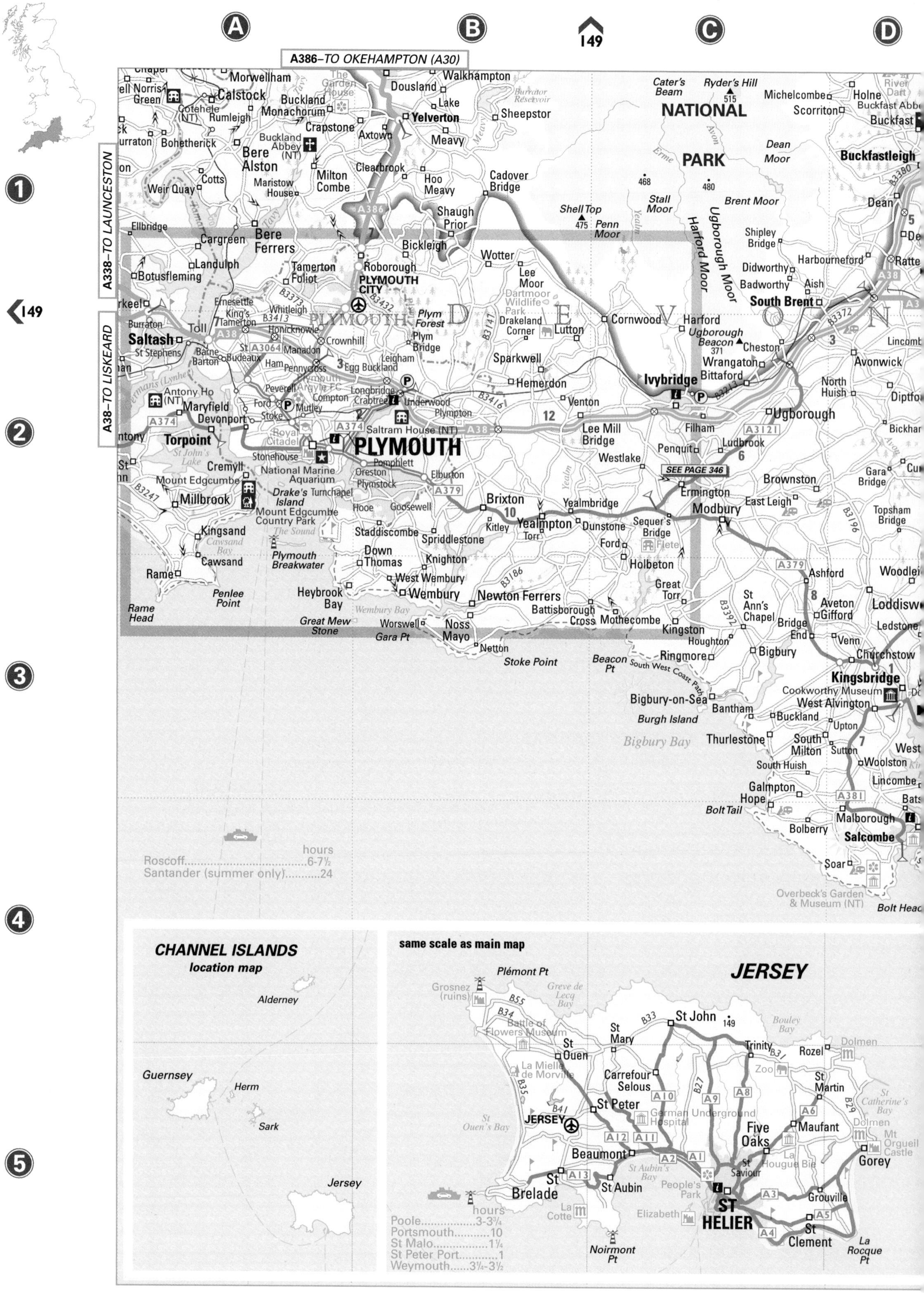

Plymouth: *On the 15th August 1620 the original group of 'Pilgrim Fathers' left Southampton in two ships, the Speedwell and the Mayflower. But the Speedwell became un-seaworthy before they reached Land's End and both ships returned to Plymouth. There, many of the Speedwell's passengers transferred to the Mayflower and on the 6th September 1620 they set off again in search of their new life in the New World. The Mayflower took 66 days to reach Cape Cod where eventually the settlers created a new settlement which they called Plymouth.* ***Map ref. A2***

Devonport: *Infamous double agent Guy Burgess was born here in 1910. He became a Soviet spy and fled to Russia in 1951. Burgess died in Moscow in 1963.* ***Map ref. A2***

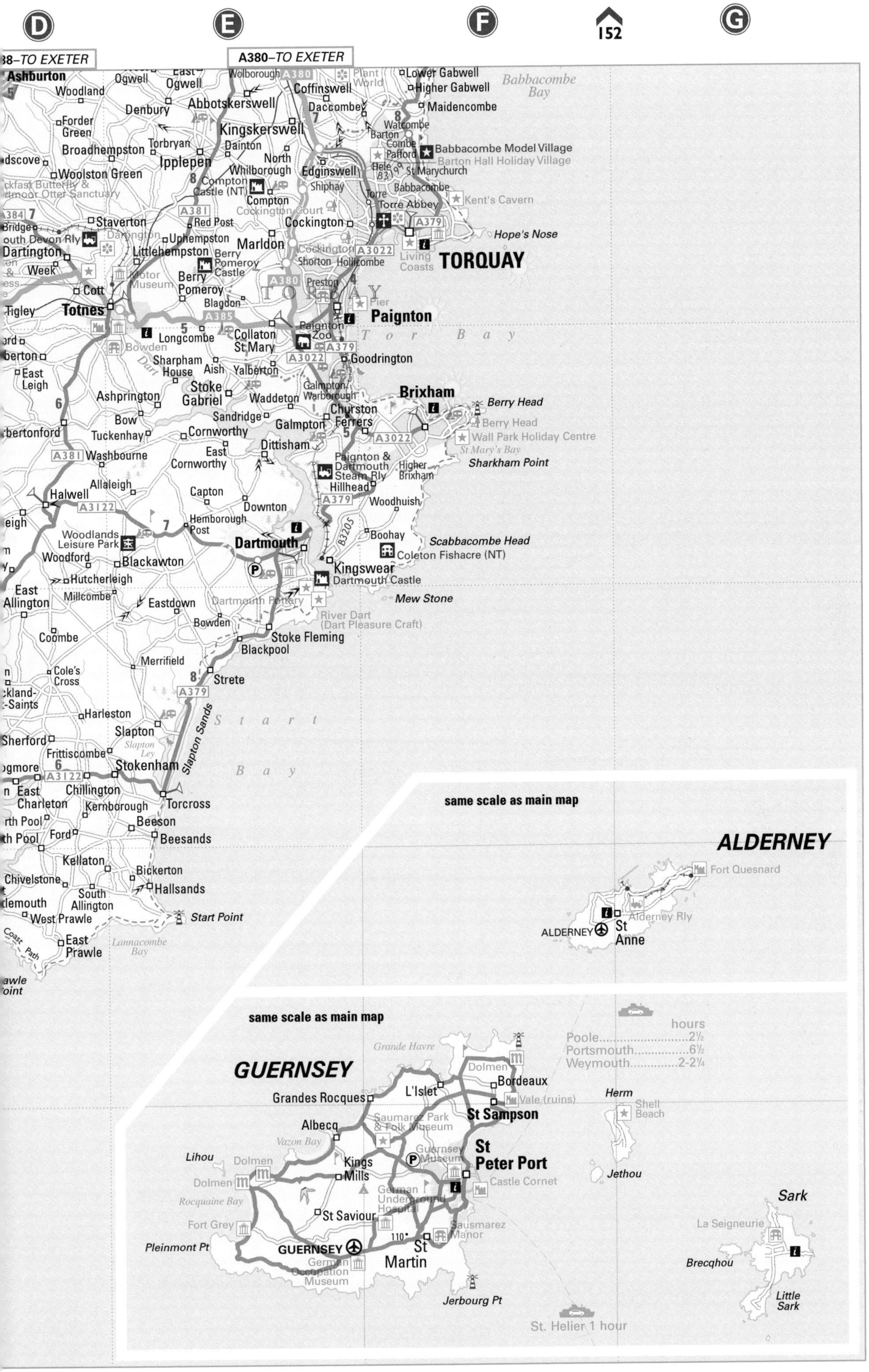

Slapton Sands: *During Exercise Tiger, a training exercise for D Day, German E-Boats intercepted and sank some of the small landing craft, killing over 700 American soldiers. A recovered Sherman Tank, on the beach, is a permanent memorial to this action.* ***Map ref. E3***

Torquay: *The Gleneagles Hotel in Asheldon Road, Wellswood was the original setting for Fawlty Towers the 1970s comedy series which starred John Cleese.* ***Map ref. F1***

Torquay: *Agatha Christie, Britain's greatest 'whodunnit' novelist, was born here in 1896. In all she wrote 78 crime stories and died aged 80 in 1976.* ***Map ref. F1***

A B C D
164
1 2 3 4 5
163
149

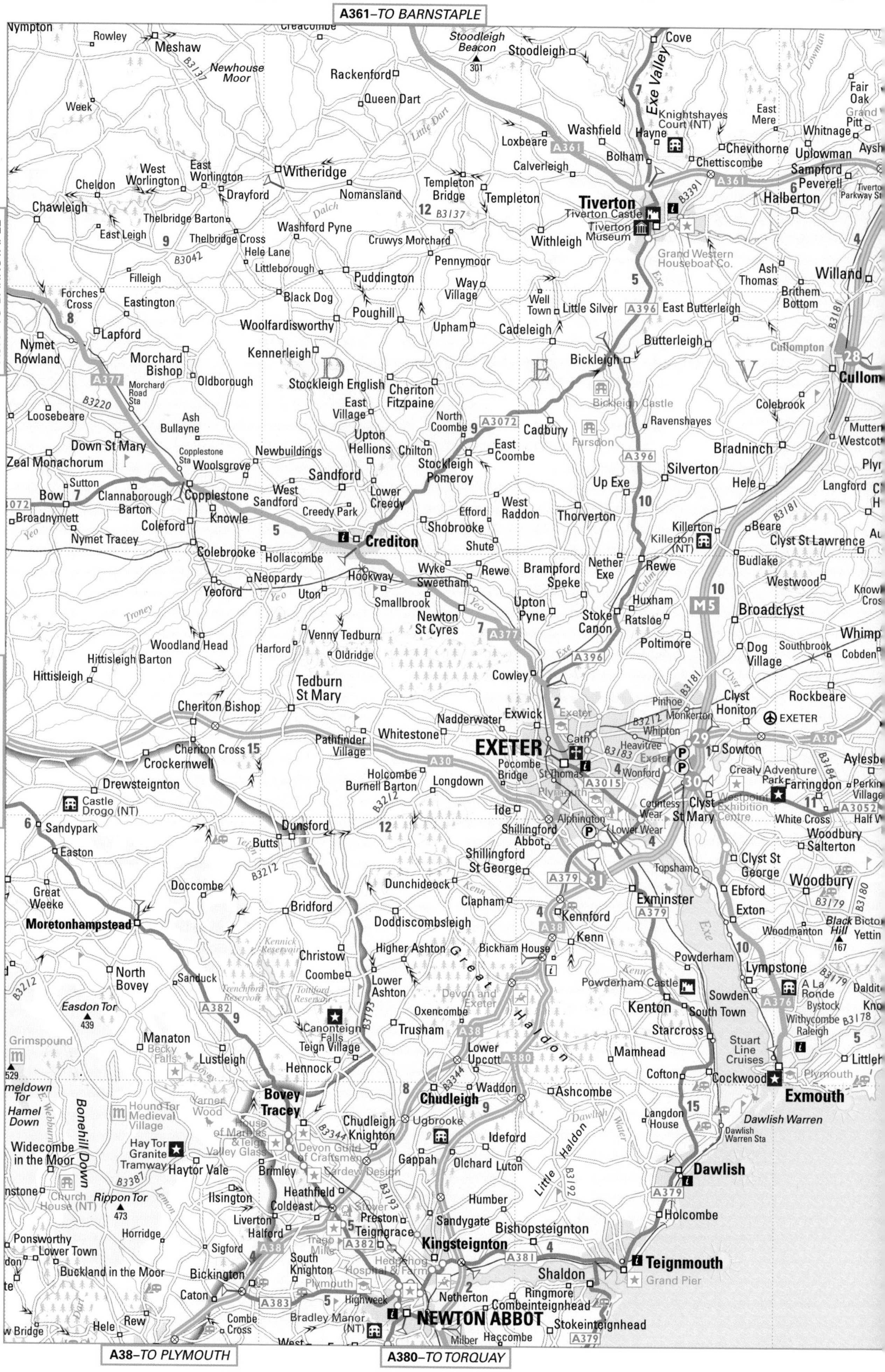

151

Widecombe in the Moor: Widecombe Fair, made famous in the song concerning the adventures of Old Uncle Tom Cobley and all, is held here. The fair dates back to around the 1850s. **Map ref. A5**

Exeter: The Exeter Ship Canal runs for 5.3 miles (8.5km) and is the oldest post-Roman canal in Britain, dating back to 1563. **Map ref. C3**

D E F G

165

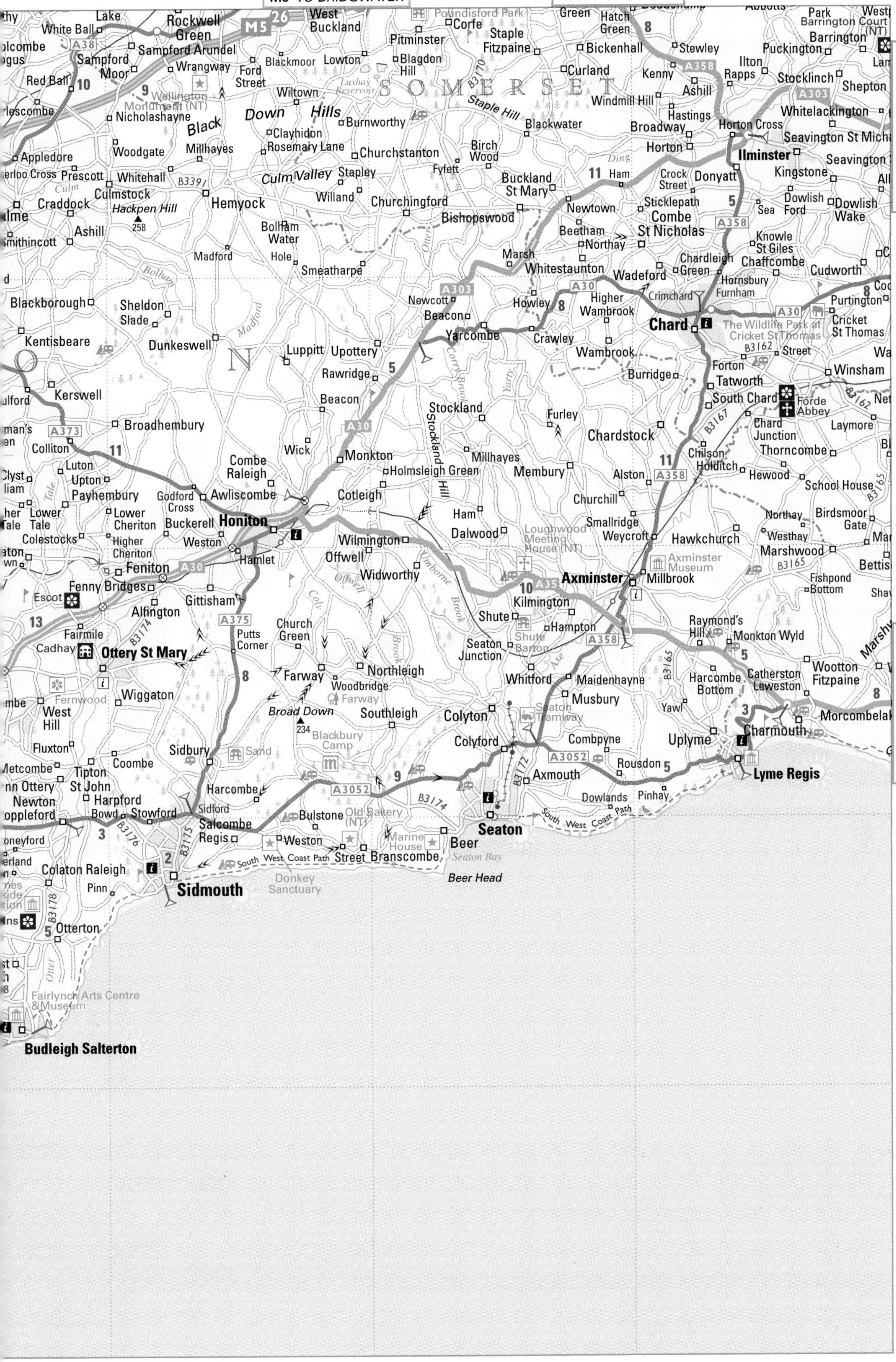

1 2 3 4 5

154

Axminster carpets were first produced here in 1755 and the company is still located here today. ***Map ref. F3***

Lyme Regis, and the beach along to Charmouth, is a haven for fossil hunters. Along with the more common ammonites, belemnites and gryphaea, finds also include dinosaur fossils, such as ichthyosaur, plesiosaur and pterosaur, in the Jurassic rocks. ***Map ref. G3***

1
2
153
3
4
5

*On the 18th July 1955, **Martinstown** recorded almost 11 inches (279mm) of rain in 24 hours. This is the highest to date of anywhere in Britain.*
Map ref. C4

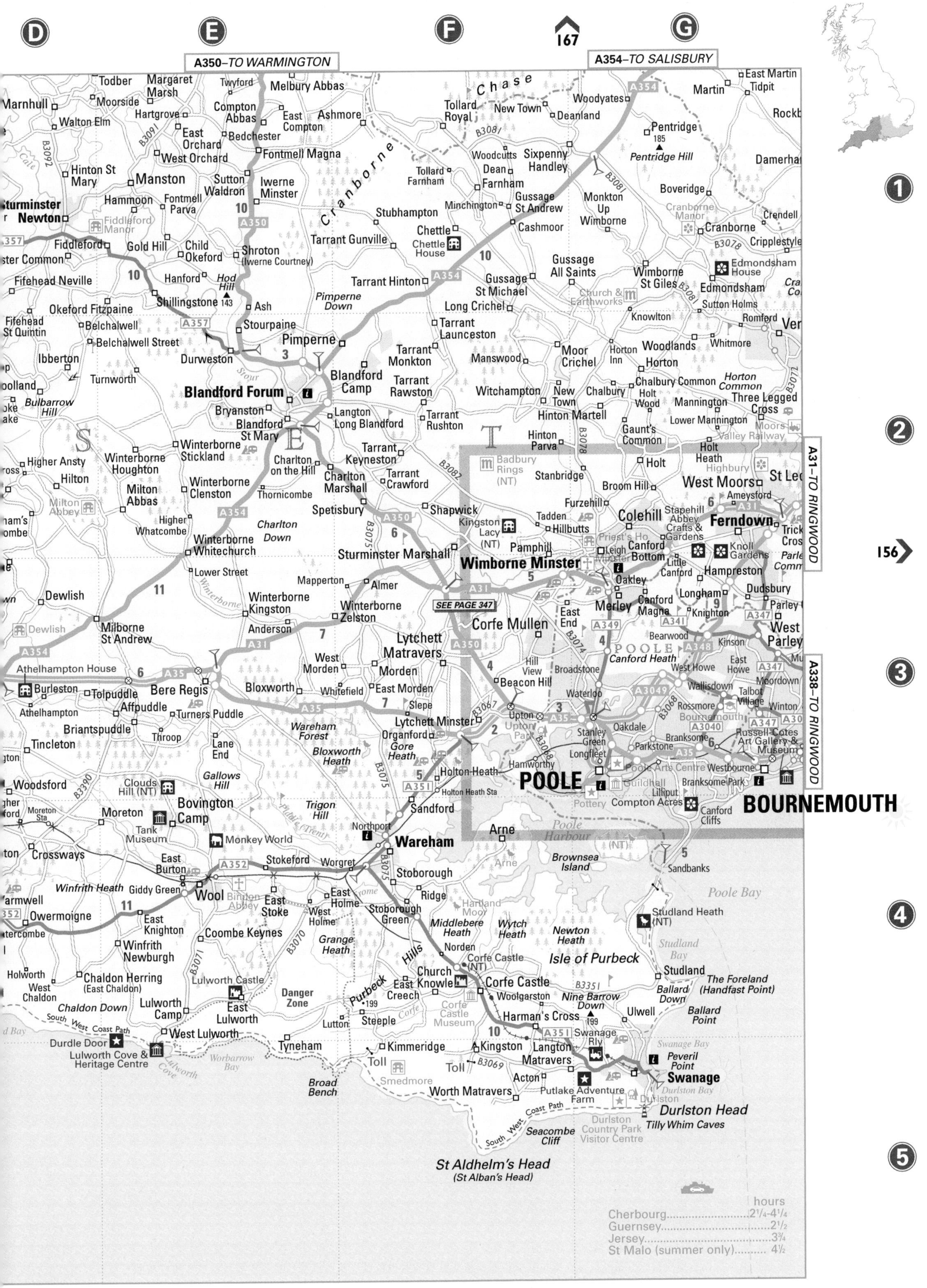

Tolpuddle: *Six farm labourers were arrested here in 1834 for trade union activity and sentenced to be transported to Australia. They became known as the Tolpuddle Martyrs. Following this a great working class struggle was organised demanding the freedom of the six and they were eventually returned to England.* ***Map ref. D3***

Clouds Hill: *This is the former home of T E Lawrence, commonly known as Lawrence of Arabia. He died in the nearby Bovington Camp Military Hospital on the 19th May 1935 following an accident on his Brough Superior Motorcycle.* ***Map ref. E3 Also on page 27***

A B 168 C D

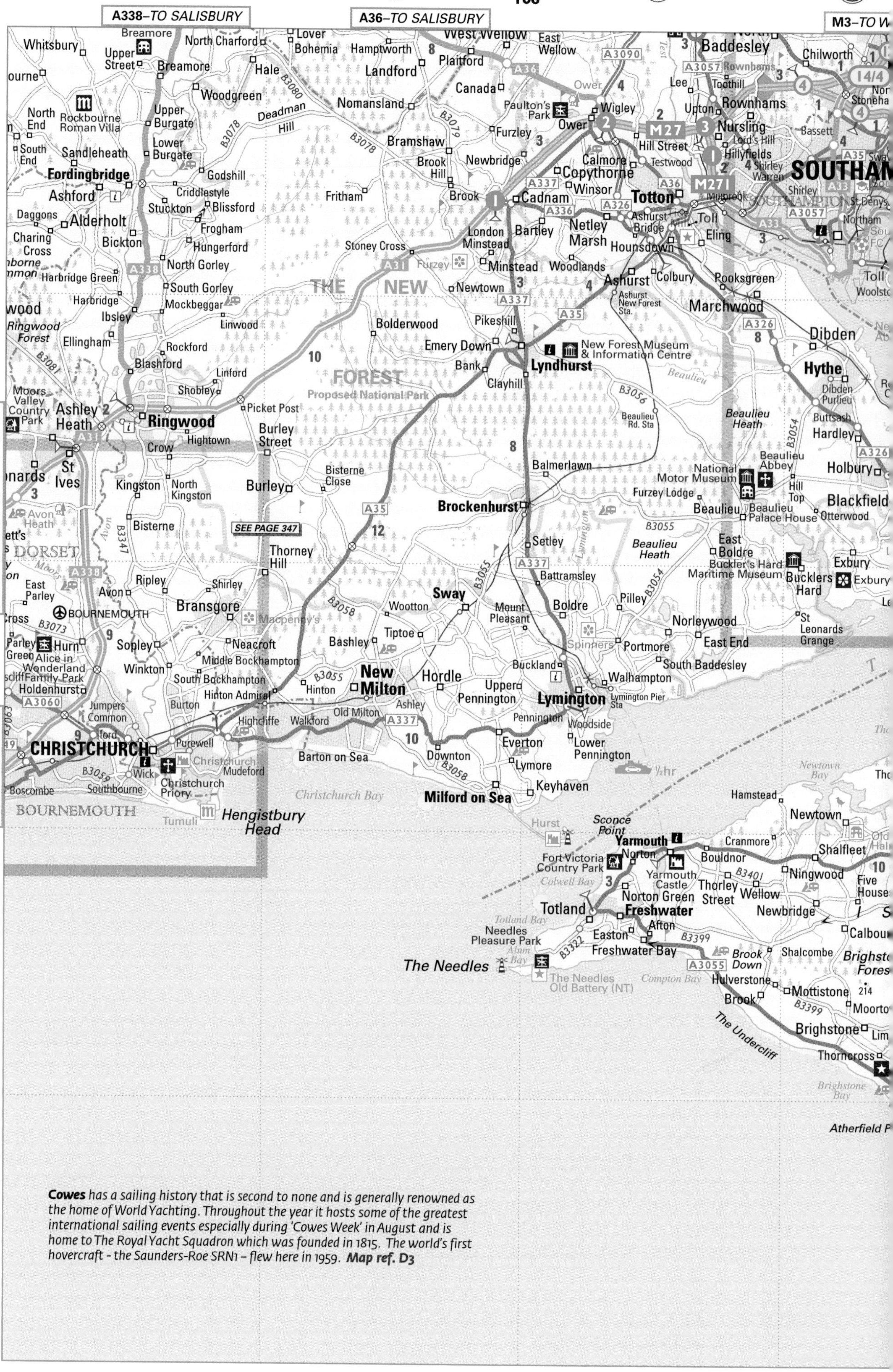

Cowes *has a sailing history that is second to none and is generally renowned as the home of World Yachting. Throughout the year it hosts some of the greatest international sailing events especially during 'Cowes Week' in August and is home to The Royal Yacht Squadron which was founded in 1815. The world's first hovercraft - the Saunders-Roe SRN1 – flew here in 1959.* ***Map ref. D3***

155

The ***New Forest*** *was created by William the Conqueror in 1079 mainly for the purpose of hunting deer and wild boars. 21 years later, his son, William II, was killed while hunting in the forest by a misdirected arrow near the spot now marked by the Rufus Stone. It is now an important recreational area which retains many original rural practices such as the pasturing of ponies and the rights of local inhabitants known as commoners. It is soon to become Britain's smallest National Park.* ***Map ref. B2 Also on page 47***

Parkhurst: *Nearby is Parkhurst Prison which has held some of the most dangerous and notorious prisoners in Britain, including the Great Train Robbers, the Kray twins and the Yorkshire Ripper. The prison was opened in 1838 and the location was chosen because it was close to a deep water anchorage that could be used by ships transporting the convicts to Australia.* ***Map ref. D3***

169

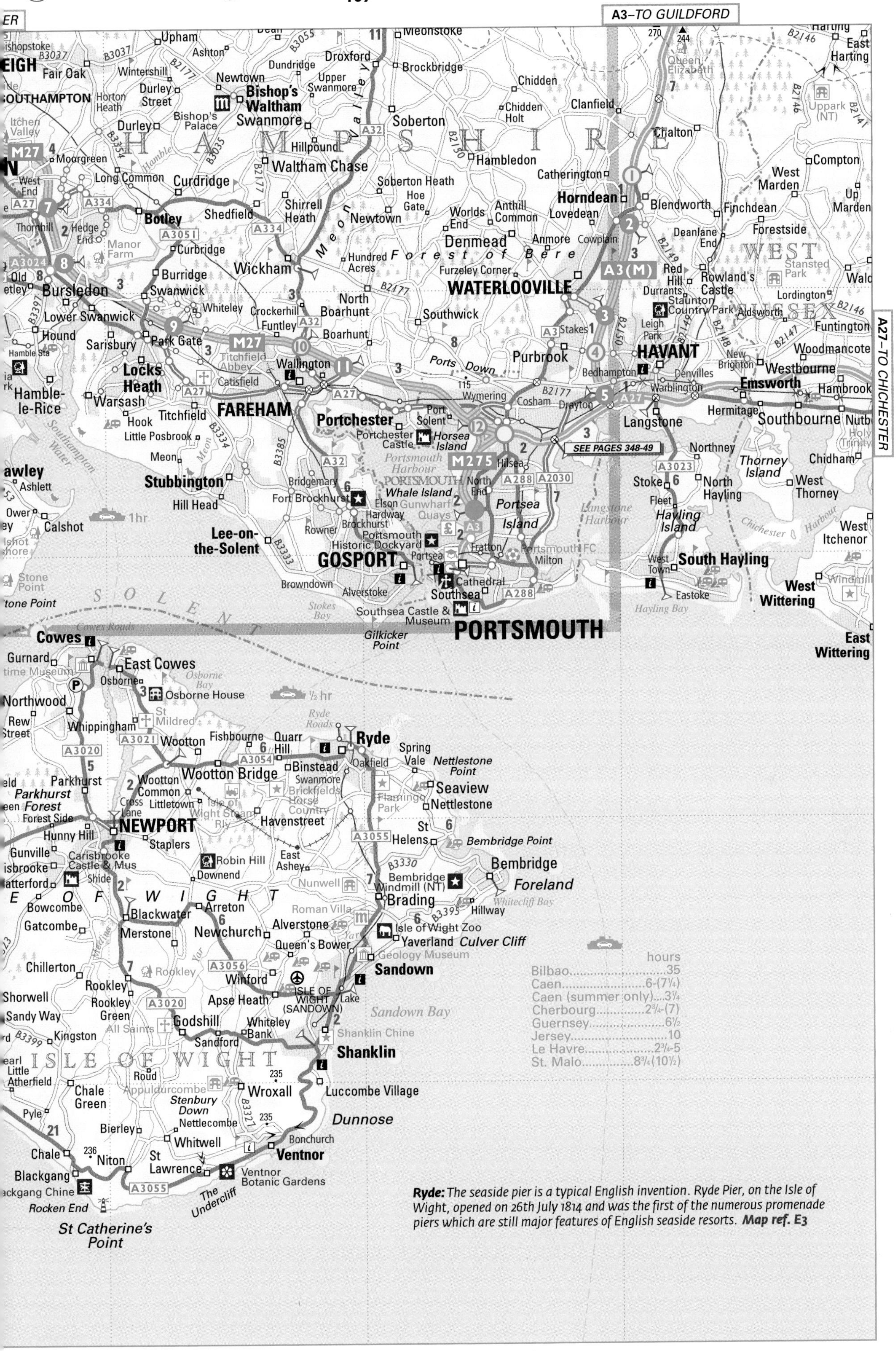

Ryde: *The seaside pier is a typical English invention. Ryde Pier, on the Isle of Wight, opened on 26th July 1814 and was the first of the numerous promenade piers which are still major features of English seaside resorts.* ***Map ref. E3***

158

The Needles: *These are a series of chalk stacks on the western most point of the Isle of Wight. The sea around The Needles is treacherous and the first lighthouse was built here in 1785. The current lighthouse, at the western edge of The Needles was built in 1850.* ***Map ref. B4 Also on page 47***
In all the Isle of Wight has 60 miles (97km) of coastline and there are over 4000 shipwrecks recorded on the Admiralty Charts of the area. ***Map ref. D4 Also on page 47***

Lee-on-the-Solent: *Location of the former Fleet Air Arm base H.M.S. Daedalus. From here in 1931 a Supermarine S6b designed by RJ Mitchell, creator of the Spitfire, set a new world air speed record of 407.5 mph (656km/h)* ***Map ref. E2***

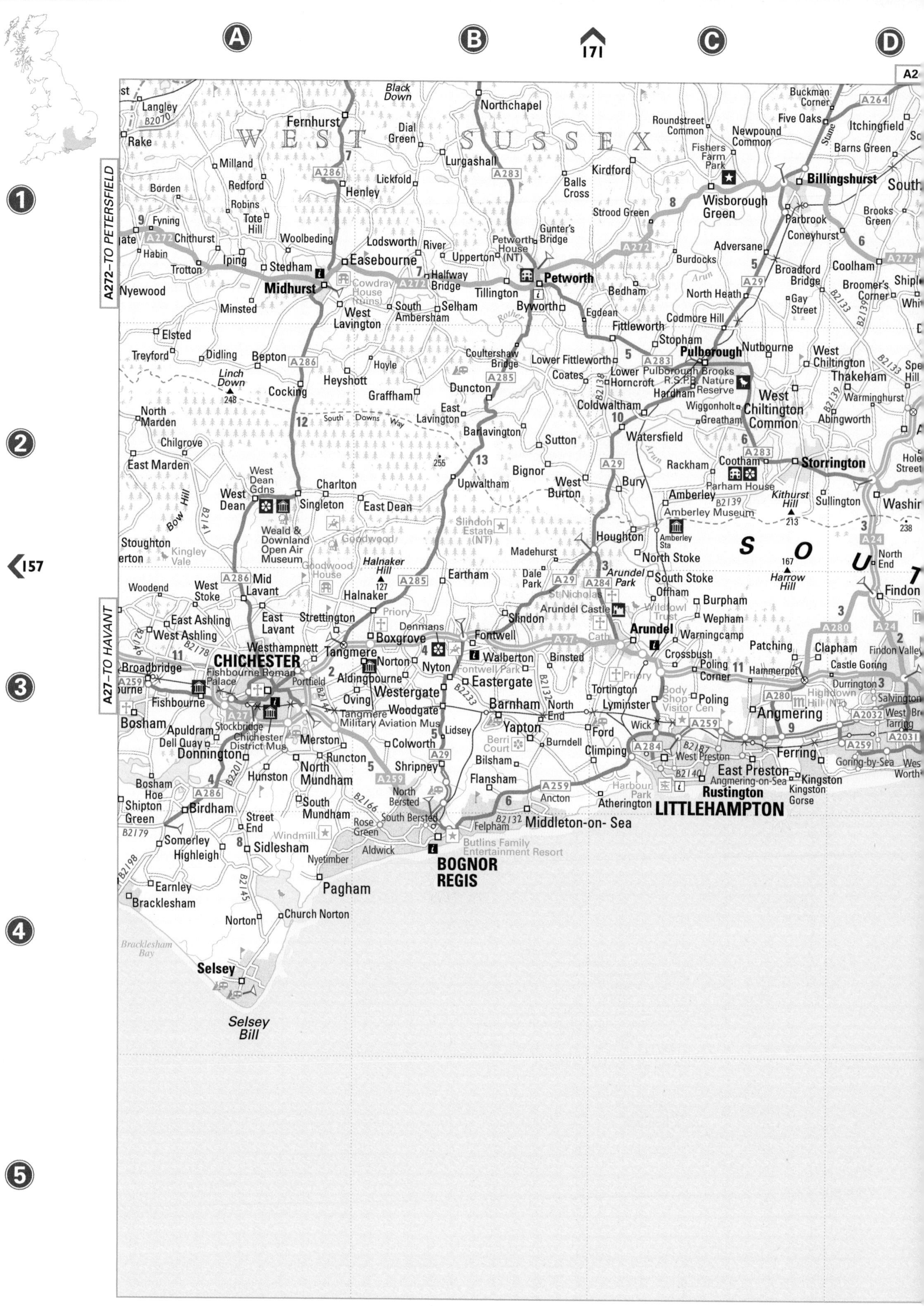

The airfield at **Tangmere** played a crucial role in the 1940 Battle of Britain. One of its most famous fighter pilots was Douglas Bader who was stationed there, first as CO of 242 Squadron, flying Hurricanes and later as leader of three Spitfire Squadrons.
On 9th August 1941 Bader shot down two German ME109s before colliding with a third. He was forced to bale out and was taken POW by the Germans. In all he was credited with destroying 23 enemy aircraft. His exciting association with Tangmere is marked by the nearby Bader Arms Public House. **Map ref. B3**

Brighton: The Aquarium roundabout near Brighton Pier is claimed to be Britain's oldest traffic roundabout, dating from 1925. **Map ref. F3**

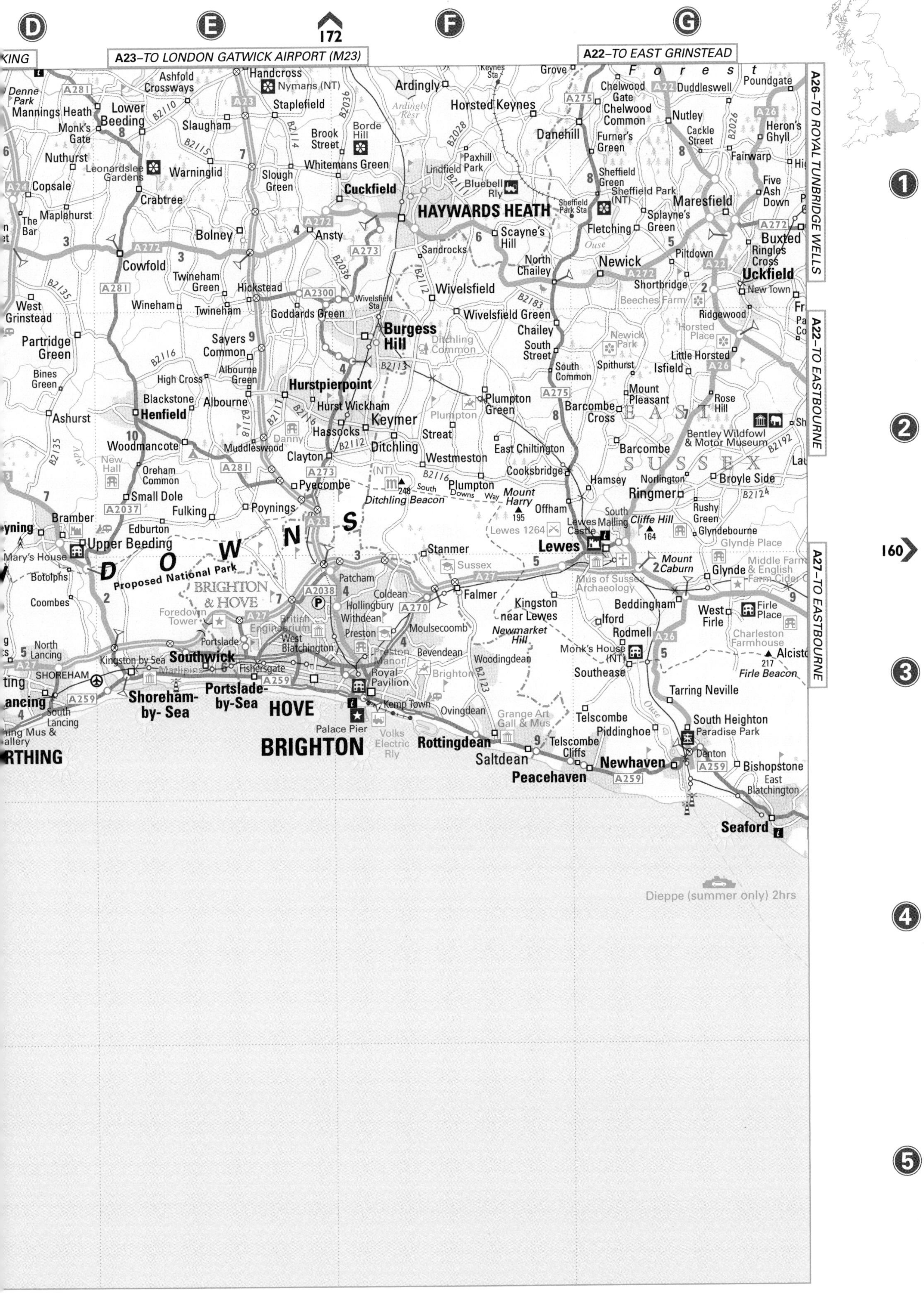

Bluebell Railway: *Following the swingeing cuts of the 1960s the Bluebell Railway became the first preserved standard gauge passenger railway in the world. It has now been in service for over 40 years. Today, whenever you see an old railway or railway station on a film or TV programme, chances are it is this one.* ***Map ref. F1 Also on page 41***

Battle of Lewes 1264: *Following the rebel barons' victory over King Henry III, Simon de Montfort established England's first parliament before he was killed in battle at Evesham in 1265.* ***Map ref. F2***

A B C D
173
1 2 3 4 5
159

John 'Mad Jack' Fuller was born in ***Brightling*** *in 1757 and inherited a thriving iron forge which made weapons for the British Navy. Mad Jack later became Squire of Brightling and an MP but is best remembered as a great English eccentric who was obsessed with building follies. The Sussex countryside is dotted with his creations which include towers, a temple, a needle and a pyramid. He gifted a lifeboat station and the first wooden lighthouse at Beachy Head. Mad Jack also bought Bodiam Castle in order to save it from a firm of builders who intended to demolish it. He died in 1834.* ***Map ref. B1***

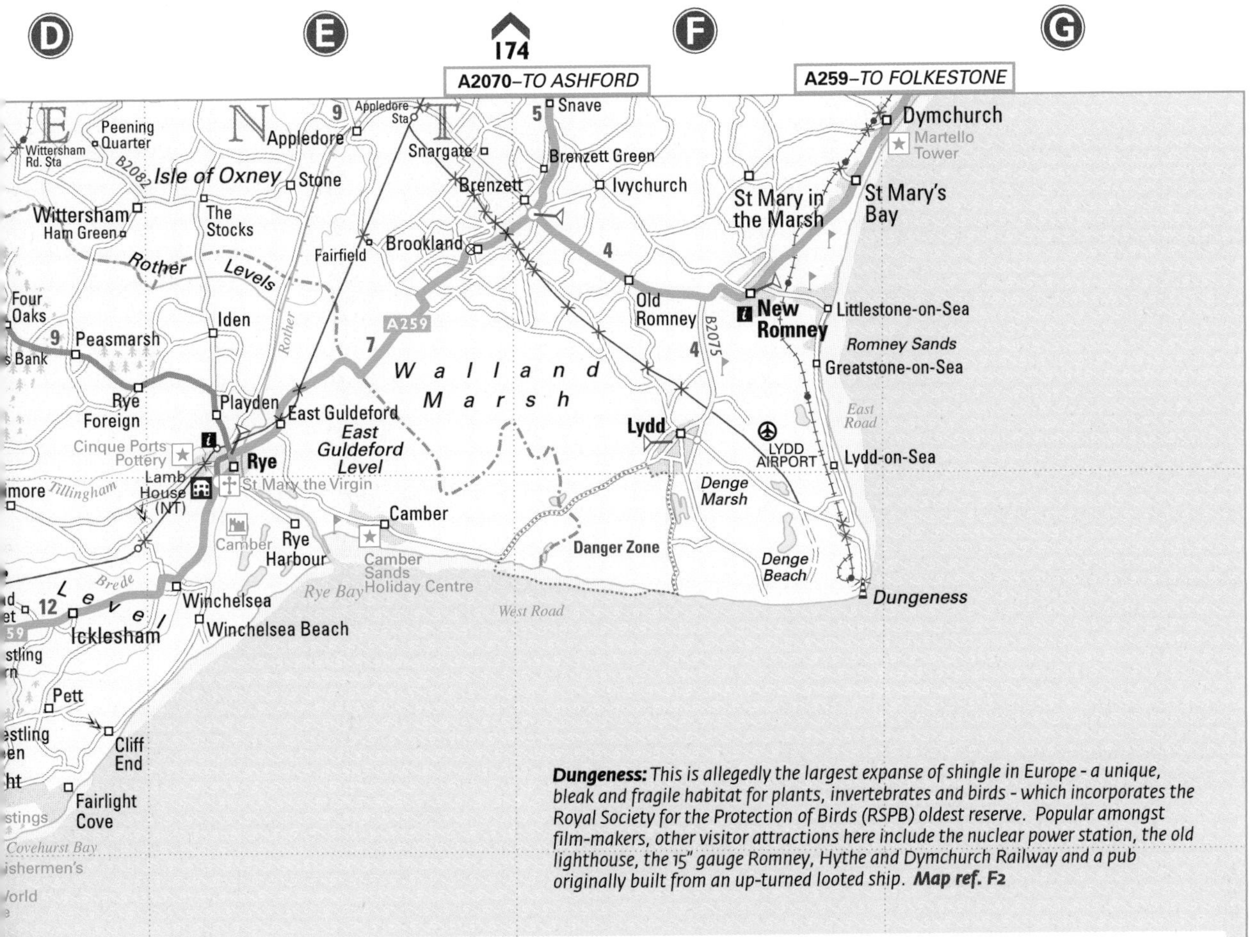

Dungeness: *This is allegedly the largest expanse of shingle in Europe - a unique, bleak and fragile habitat for plants, invertebrates and birds - which incorporates the Royal Society for the Protection of Birds (RSPB) oldest reserve. Popular amongst film-makers, other visitor attractions here include the nuclear power station, the old lighthouse, the 15" gauge Romney, Hythe and Dymchurch Railway and a pub originally built from an up-turned looted ship.* ***Map ref. F2***

CHANNEL TUNNEL TERMINAL MAPS

Eurotunnel: Access from the UK

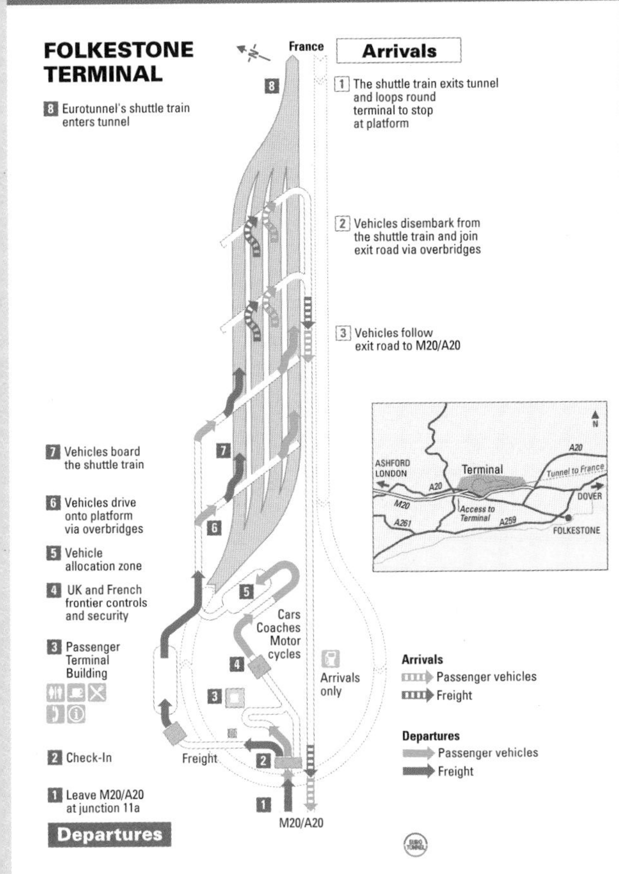

Eurotunnel: Access from France

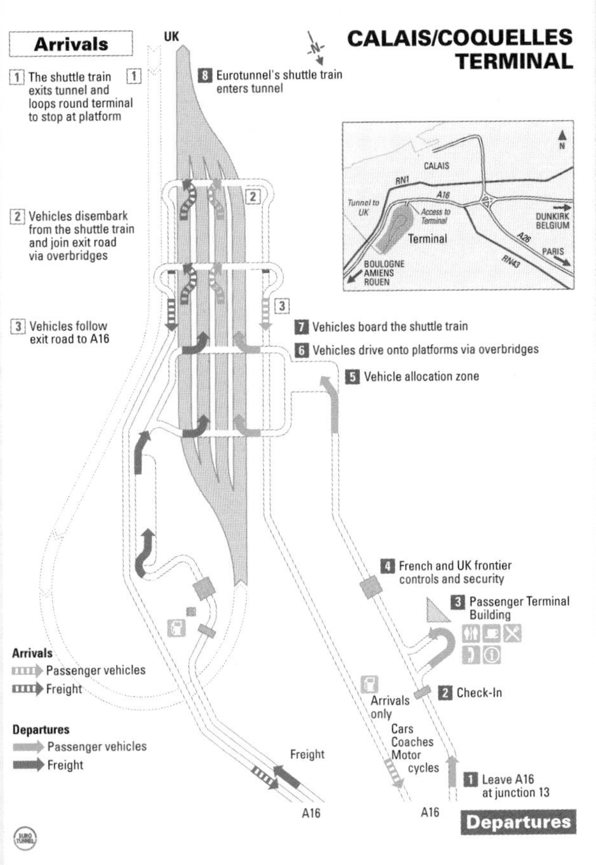

Norman's Bay: *The Norman Army sailed from St. Valery across the English Channel on the evening of the 27th September 1066 and landed in England, on the morning of 28th September, at what has since been called Norman's Bay. From there they proceeded inland and two weeks later defeated King Harold at the Battle of Hastings.* ***Map ref. B3***

Rye: *This picturesque Sussex town was one of the entry points for the 'Black Death' which plagued Britain from 1348 to 1353. The Cinque Ports of the south east, which traded with the rest of the world, and the smugglers who haunted the marshes, brought in the fleas which carried the deadly Tersina Pestis bacteria which eventually killed a third of Europe's people. Deadman's Lane, in Rye, is thought to be where they buried their plague victims.* ***Map ref. E1***

A B C D
1 2 3 4 5

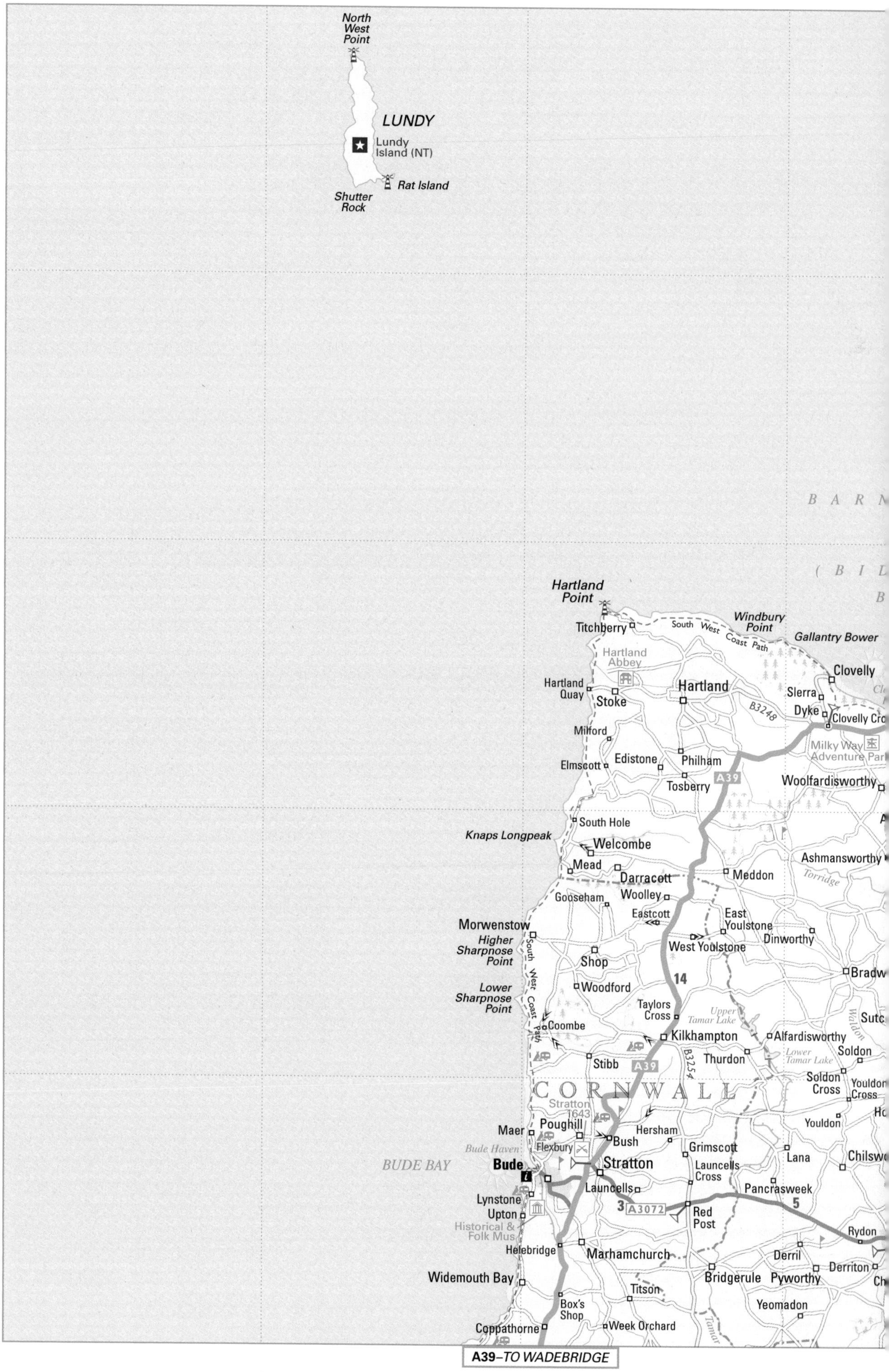

148

Lundy: *The island is 3 miles (4.8km) long and lies 14 miles (22.5km) off the North Devon coast. It boasts a castle, three lighthouses, an inn and a church and is the first designated Marine Nature Reserve in Britain. Lundy's rugged shores have proved to be a graveyard for over 130 ships which lie wrecked off its coast.*
Map ref. B1 Also on page 32

D E F G

Widmouth Head
Watermouth Castle
Mouth
Woody Bay
Trentishoe
Martinhoe
Toll
Ilfracombe
Hele
A399
Berrynarbor
South West Coast Path
Hunter's Inn
Heale
Kemacott
A39
Lee Bay
Bull Point
Rockham Bay
Morte Point
Mortehoe
Lee
Slade
Chambercombe Manor
Sterridge
Combe Martin
Killington
10
Combe Martin Wildlife & Dinosaur Park
Parracombe
Churchtown
A361
B3230
Mullacott Cross
Seymour Villas
Woolacombe
B3343
Once Upon A Time
Trimstone
Dean Cross
Cheglinch
A3123
Berry Down Cross
A399
Kentisbury
B3229
Blackmoor Gate
480
Challacombe Common
Morte Bay
Bradwell
West Down
13
Patchole
Kentisbury Ford
Swincombe
Resr
Bittadon
East Down
Clifton
Arlington Beccott
Challacombe
Baggy Point
Putsborough
Pickwell
North Buckland
B3230
Churchill
Arlington
Arlington Court (NT)
Knightacott
Barton Town
Croyde Bay
Croyde Bay
Georgeham
Croyde
Winsham
Halsinger
Middle Marwood
Milltown
Muddiford
Upcott
10
A39
Leworthy
Knowle
Lobb
B3231
Saunton
Boode
Marwood
Higher Muddiford
Loxhore
Fullaford
Bray
Pippacott
Lower Loxhore
Bratton Fleming
Saunton Sands
Braunton
Marwood Hill
Kingsheanton
Prixford
Shirwell Cross
Shirwell
Lydcott
Heanton Punchardon
Stoke Rivers
Benton
11
Braunton Burrows
Toll
Wrafton
West Ashford
A361
Ashford
Brayford
Chivenor
Goodleigh
Bradiford
Pilton
St Anne's Chapel Heritage Centre
High Bray
Gunn
West Coast Path
BARNSTAPLE
Lilly
Northleigh
Charles
South
Bickington
Newport
Willesleigh
Stoodleigh
A361
East Buckland
The Neck
B3233
9
Yelland
Fremington
Lake
P
Landkey
Swimbridge Newland
West Buckland
A P L E
Northam Burrows
Appledore
1
Yarnacott
Riverton
North Devon Maritime Mus
Instow
Bickleton
A39
Tawstock
Bishop's Tawton
A361–TO TIVERTON
Westward Ho!
St John's Chapel
Tapeley Park
Swimbridge
O R D
A386
Tapeley
9
Filleigh
A361
Northam
7
B3236
Westleigh
Horwood
A377
Cobbaton
Herner
Eastleigh
Stowford
Burton Art Gallery
Lower Lovacott
Harracott
Chapelton
East-the-Water
Woodtown
B3232
Newton Tracey
Hiscott
Ensis
7
Chittlehampton
Abbotsham
Bideford
The Big Sheep
4
A386
Gammaton
B3227
7
Bray
Alverdiscott
Fishleigh Barton
Hudscott
9
Fairy Cross
Ford
Gammaton Moor
Umberleigh
Horns Cross
10
Yeo Vale
Huntshaw Water
Yarnscombe
Atherington
Clapworthy
A39
Landcross
Eastacott
8
Alwington
Littleham
Langridgeford
Langridge
Warkleigh
Mole
Goldworthy
Huntshaw
Huntshaw Cross
8
Satterleigh
Saltrens
Weare Giffard
B3227
Chittlehamholt
Buckland Brewer
A388
B3226
Parkham
High Bullen
Taw
Parkham Ash
Monkleigh
4
Sherwood Green
High Bickington
Portsmouth Arms Sta
Kings
8
Great Torrington
Dodscott
Head Bridge
Melbury
Dartington Crystal
Frithelstock Stone
Frithelstock
St Giles in the Wood
Northcote Manor
A377
Taddiport
Powler's Piece
Rosemoor
Kingscott
Roborough
B3217
Cadbury Barton
Little Torrington
Burrington
King's Nympton Sta
East Putford
B3227
Torridge
Elstone
Langtree
Langtree Week
Villavin
Colleton Mills
West Putford
A386
Great Potheridge
Beaford
D
15
E
V
O
N
Chulmleigh
Stibb Cross
Berry Cross
Cottwood
5
Haytown
Little Potheridge
Copy Lake
B3096
Peters Marland
17
Riddlecombe
Ashreigney
Bulkworthy
Bridge Reeve
Winswell
Frendon
Woollaton
Merton
Dolton
Hollacombe Town
A377–TO EXETER
Abbots Bickington
13
Heanton Satchville
B3217
A3124
Ashley
Newton St Petrock
Little Marland
Huish
Hollocombe
Eggesford Barton
Venngreen
Dowland
Milton Damerel
Wembworthy
Taw
Buckland Filleigh
North Town
Petrockstowe
Shebbear
Winkleigh
Coldridge
Thornbury
Ash Barton
Meeth
Iddesleigh
Brushford
Woodacott
Bradford
B3220
Brendon
Lashbrook
Ingleigh Green
Taw Bridge
West Leigh
Sheepwash
Torridge
Hele Bridge
Okement
Cookbury
Middlecott
Broadwood Kelly
Cookbury Wick
Black Torrington
Monkokehampton
Bondleigh
East Leigh
Brandis Corner
9
B3217
Lowton
Anvil Corner
A3072
Highampton
Hatherleigh
A3072
4
Dunsland Cross
Graddon Moor
Lydacott
Bassett's Cross
B3216
North Tawton
Hollacombe
Chilla
Odham
Honeychurch
Halwill Forest
Jacobstowe
5
Exbourne
4
Lew
Shilstone
Sampford Courtenay
A386
A3072
Trecott
2
Halwill Junction
A386–TO TAVISTOCK

1
164
2
3
4
152
5
149

Braunton Burrows: *Almost 2450 acres (1000ha) of shifting sand dunes make this area so unusual that it has been designated by UNESCO as a 'Biosphere Reserve'. This recognises its status and affords it international protection.* ***Map ref. E2.***

1 2 3 4 5 ‹163

Lynmouth: *Scene of the disastrous floods of the East and West Lyn rivers during the night of 15 August 1952 which resulted in the destruction of much of the village. 34 people were killed and 165 buildings wholly or partially destroyed.* ***Map ref. A3.***

Porlock Hill: *Over the years this notorious stretch of road, with its 25% (1 in 4) incline and tight curves, has caused travellers countless problems. The main coast road was first negotiated by a motor car in 1900 as a bet. If required, the nearby scenic toll road avoids the need to travel along this road.* ***Map ref. B3***

152

Quantock Hills: *Covering an area of 48 square miles and reaching a height of 1260 feet (384m) the Quantock countryside is one of the most delightful areas of Britain. It was the first in England to get AONB (Area of Outstanding Natural Beauty) status back in 1956 and is also designated as a SSSI (Site of Special Scientific Interest) because it contains almost 10% of the world's maritime heathland.* ***Map ref. E3***

D E F G

180

M5–TO BRISTOL

A371–TO BRISTOL (A38)

A38–TO BRISTOL

A39–TO GLASTONBURY

M5–TO EXETER

A358–TO ILMINSTER

1 2 3 4 5

166

153

Hatch Beauchamp: *The nearby church is the final resting place of Col. John Rouse Merriot Chard VC Royal Engineers. As Lt. Chard be commanded a small garrison of 140 soldiers which heroically defended Rorke's Drift during the Zulu Wars.* ***Map ref. G5***

Weston-super-Mare: *Traditional seaside resort with two piers. The Grand Pier built in 1904 is still open and is listed by the Department of the Environment as a monument of historic importance. The other, Birnbeck Pier, which opened in 1867, is now closed, but is unusual because it is the only pier in the country that links the mainland to an island. This pier is a Grade II listed structure.* ***Map ref. G1***

181

M5–TO BRISTOL

A38, A37, A4–TO BRISTOL

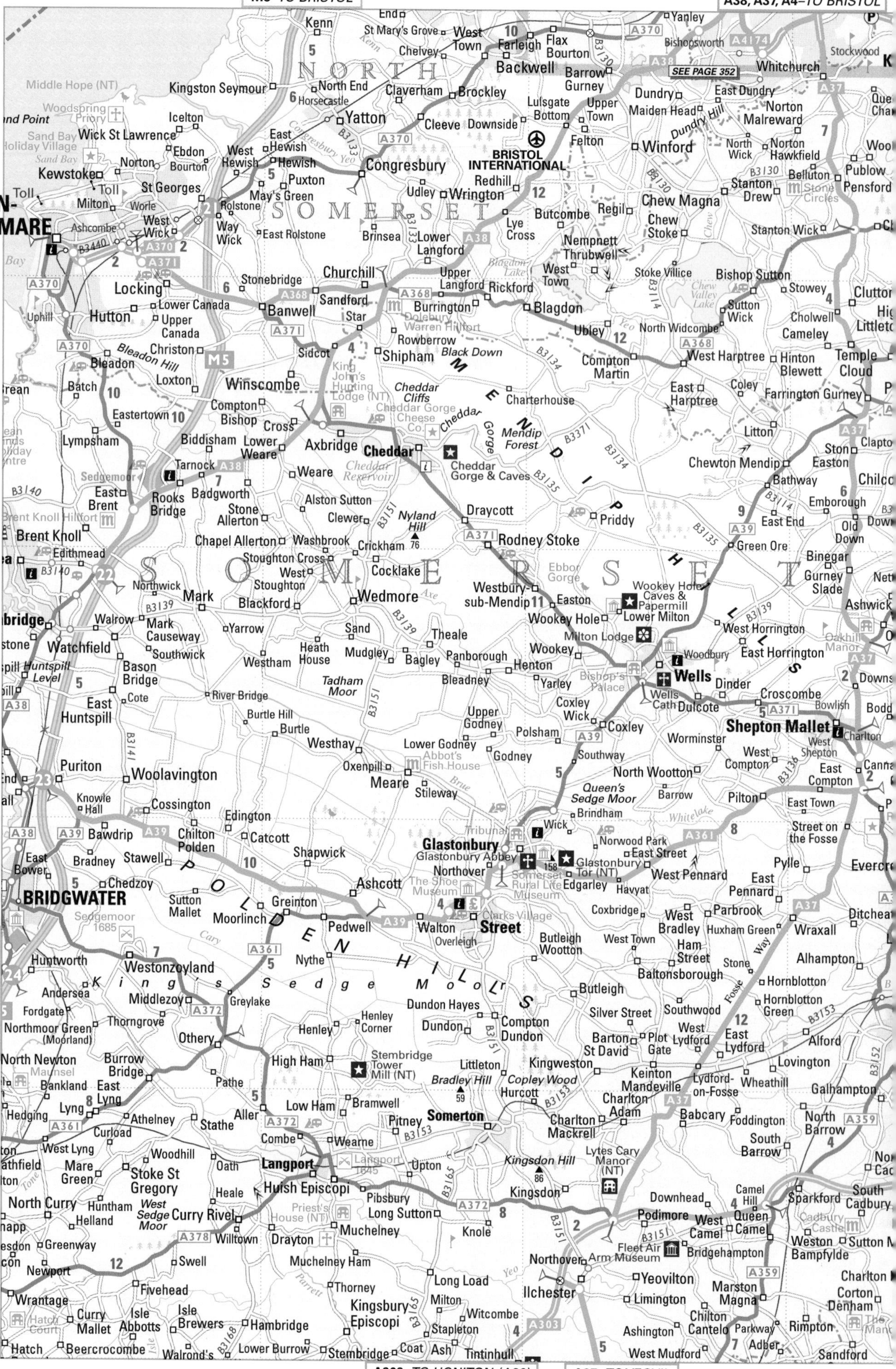

M5–TO TAUNTON

165

A303–TO HONITON (A30)

A37–TO YEOVIL

154

Cheddar: *The cathedral-like caves and Britain's biggest gorge were formed here by ice-age rivers over one million years ago. As well as being a major UK tourist attraction for over 200 years the area is also an SSSI (Site of Special Scientific Interest).* ***Map ref. B2***

East Knoyle: *Christopher Wren, one of Britain's greatest architects was born here in 1632. Following the Great Fire of London Wren designed and supervised the building of 51 London Churches including St Paul's Cathedral.* ***Map ref. F4***

D E 182 F G

1

2

168

3

4

5

Glastonbury is one of Britain's most mysterious and sacred places. Myths and legends abound, one being that it is the site of the first church in Britain founded by Joseph of Arimathea who landed here with the Holy Grail. Also, as the Isle of Avalon, it is associated with King Arthur. Even today the strangely terraced Tor, with its enigmatic tower, is a magnet for those into nature, mythology, folklore, legend, Christianity and paganism...... Not a bad music festival either. ***Map ref. B4***

155

182

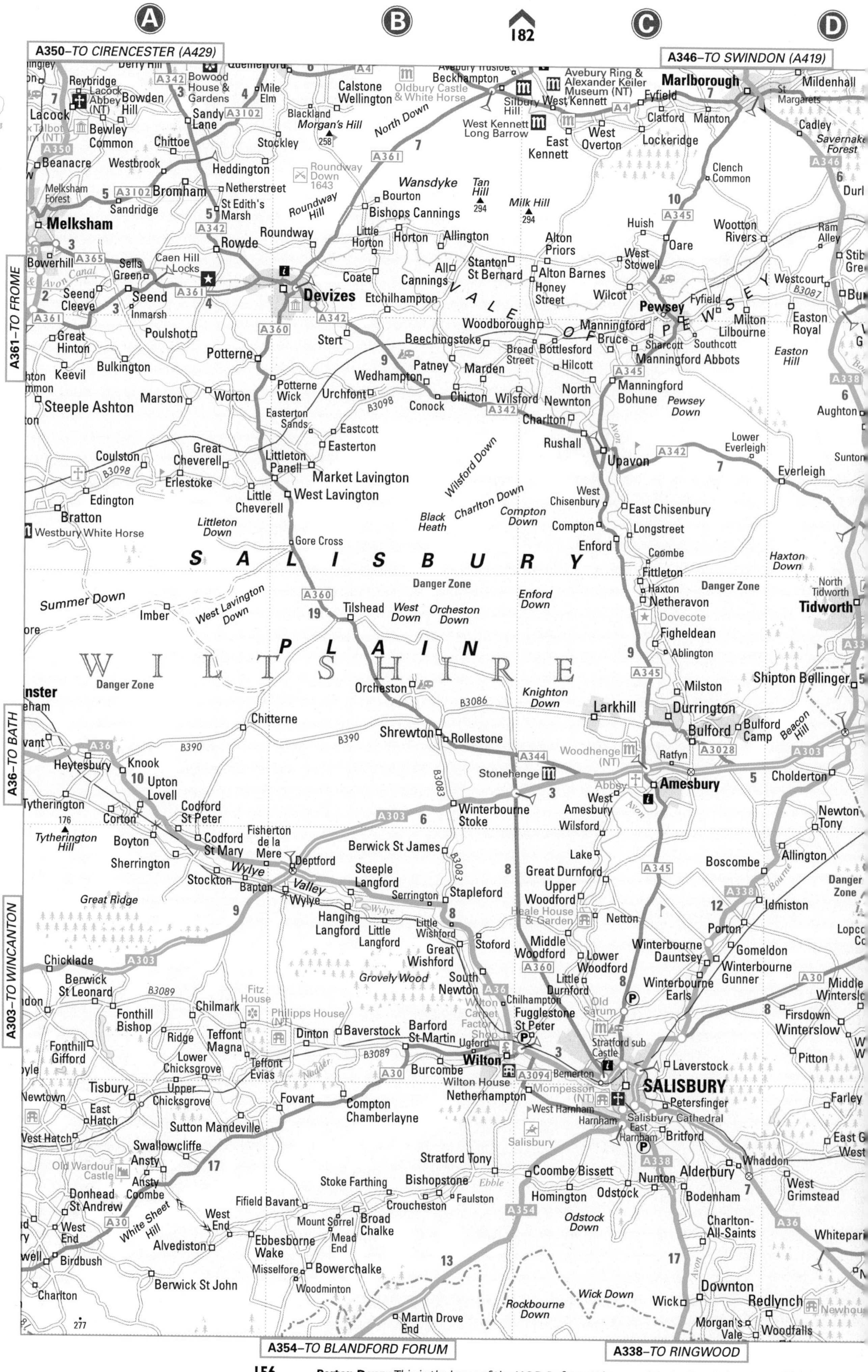

167

156

Porton Down: *This is the home of the MOD Defence Science and Technology Laboratory which houses one of the largest groups of scientists and engineers employed within Britain's public service.*
From 1939 up to the 1960s it is alleged that almost 20,000 so called human 'guinea pigs' volunteered to assist in tests carried out here which were supposedly aimed at finding a cure for the common cold.
Map ref. C4/D4

D E [183] F G

A34, A339–TO M4

A36–TO M27

M3–TO M27

1 2 3 4 5

[170]

157

Romsey: *Famous as 'Kingsmarkham' in the 1988–1993 TV adaptation of the Ruth Rendell Mysteries starring George Baker.* ***Map ref. E5***

184

A B C D

1 2 3 4 5

169

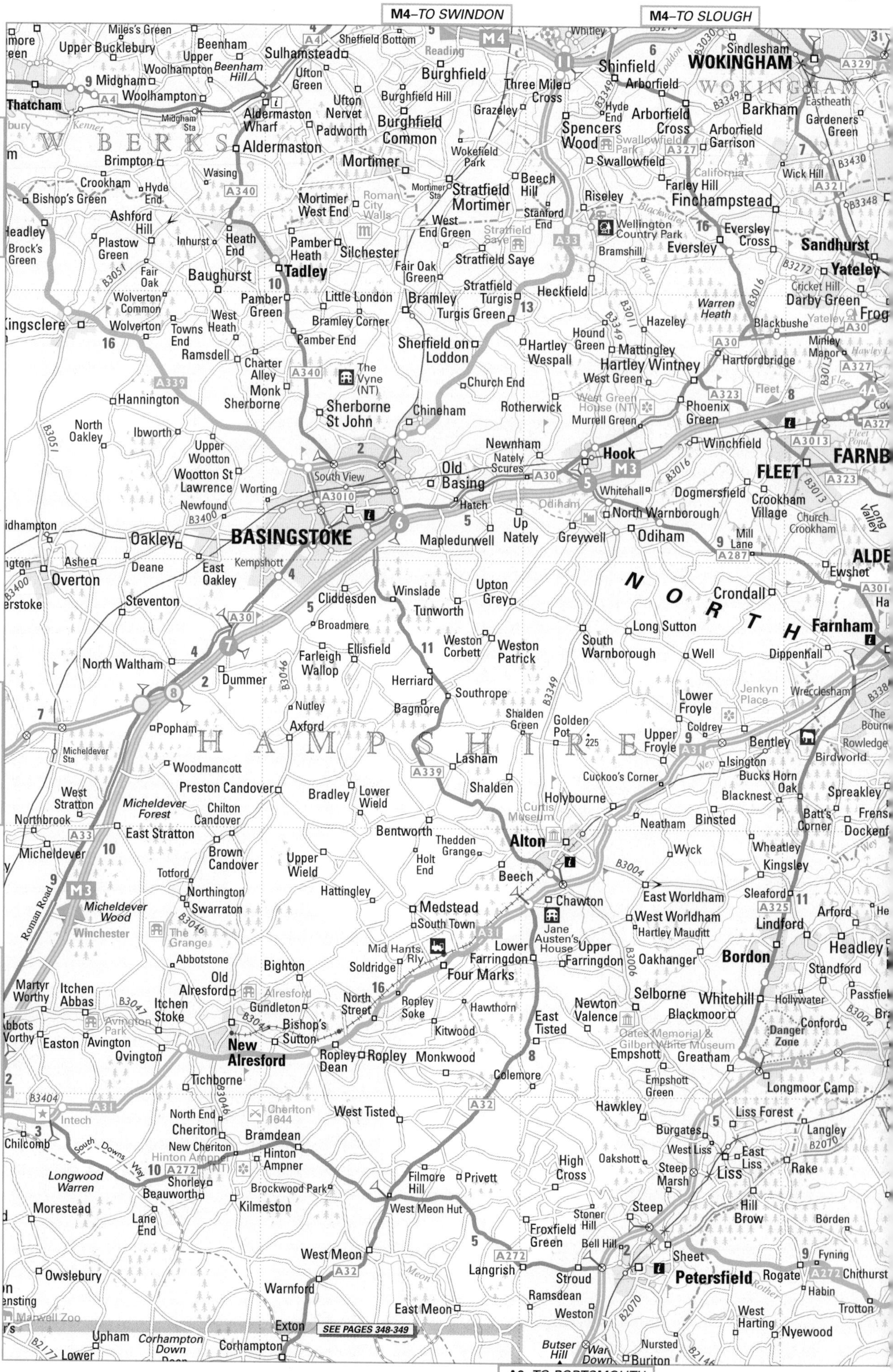

Basingstoke: *Designated an overspill town for London in 1961, Basingstoke was almost totally rebuilt with a new town centre, pedestrian precincts and multi-storey car parks. The population increased from 26,000 in 1960 to 60,000 in 1973 and is today over 100,000.* ***Map ref. B2***

157

Guildford: *Birthplace of the great English comedy writer P G Wodehouse (1881–1975). Pelham Grenville Wodehouse, 'Plum' to his friends, is best remembered for the creation of Bertie Wooster and his faithful and resourceful manservant Jeeves.* ***Map ref. E3***

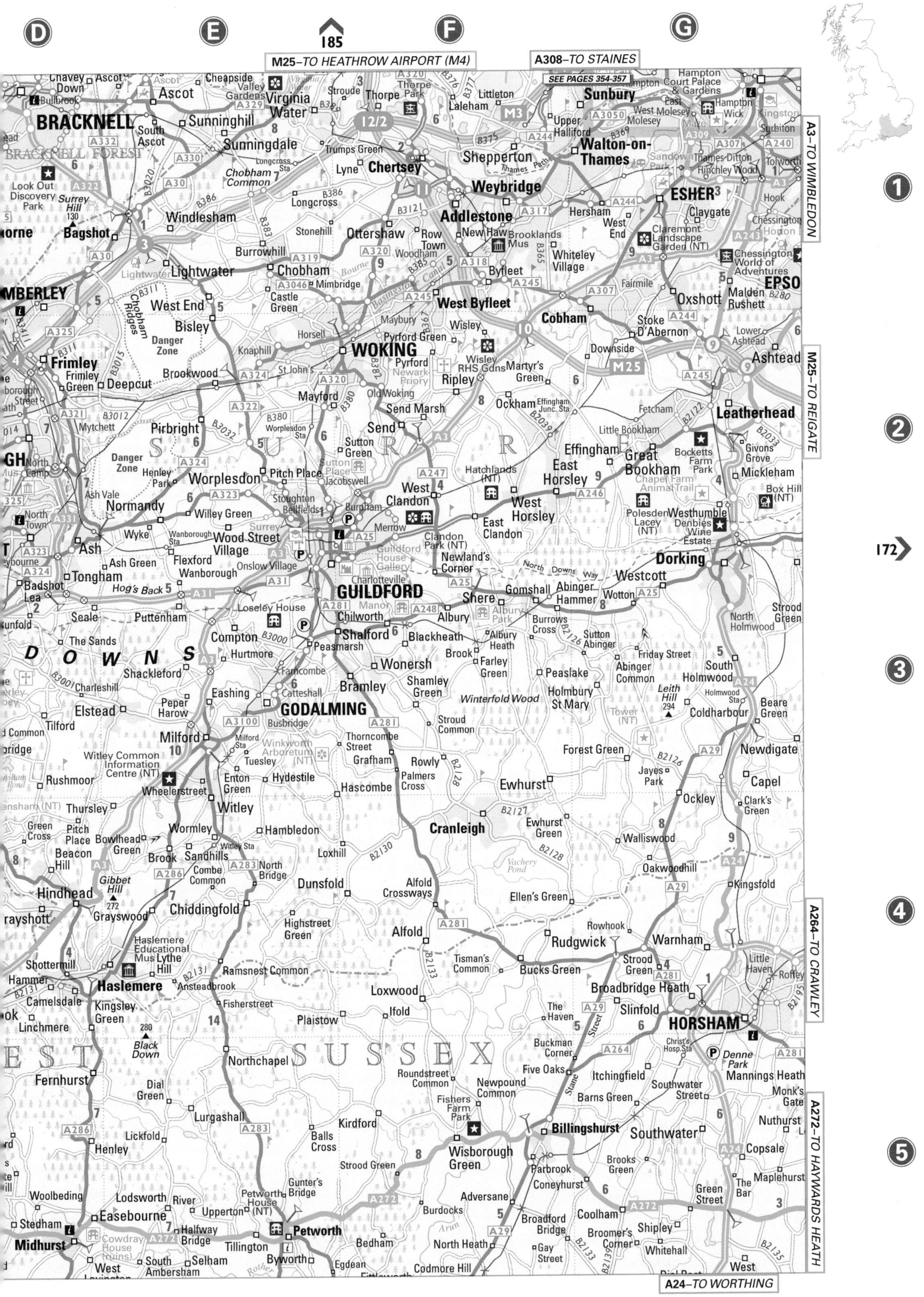

158

Horsham: *During a violent hailstorm on 5th September 1958 hailstones of 2–3 inches (70–80mm) diameter were measured. One single hailstone weighed in at 6.7 oz (190 grams) and is the largest recorded hailstone in Britain.* ***Map ref. G4***

Brookwood: *From the mid nineteenth century, the amount of bodies in London requiring burial was causing great concern, so 2,000 acres (800ha) of Woking's common land was purchased from Lord Onslow in 1852 in order to establish a single great metropolitan cemetery. By 1854 Brookwood was the largest cemetery in the world and even today it remains the largest in the UK. Since 1854 almost a quarter of a million bodies have been interred here. Since 1917 separate military cemeteries, administered by the Commonwealth War Graves Commission have also been located here.* ***Map ref. E2***

186

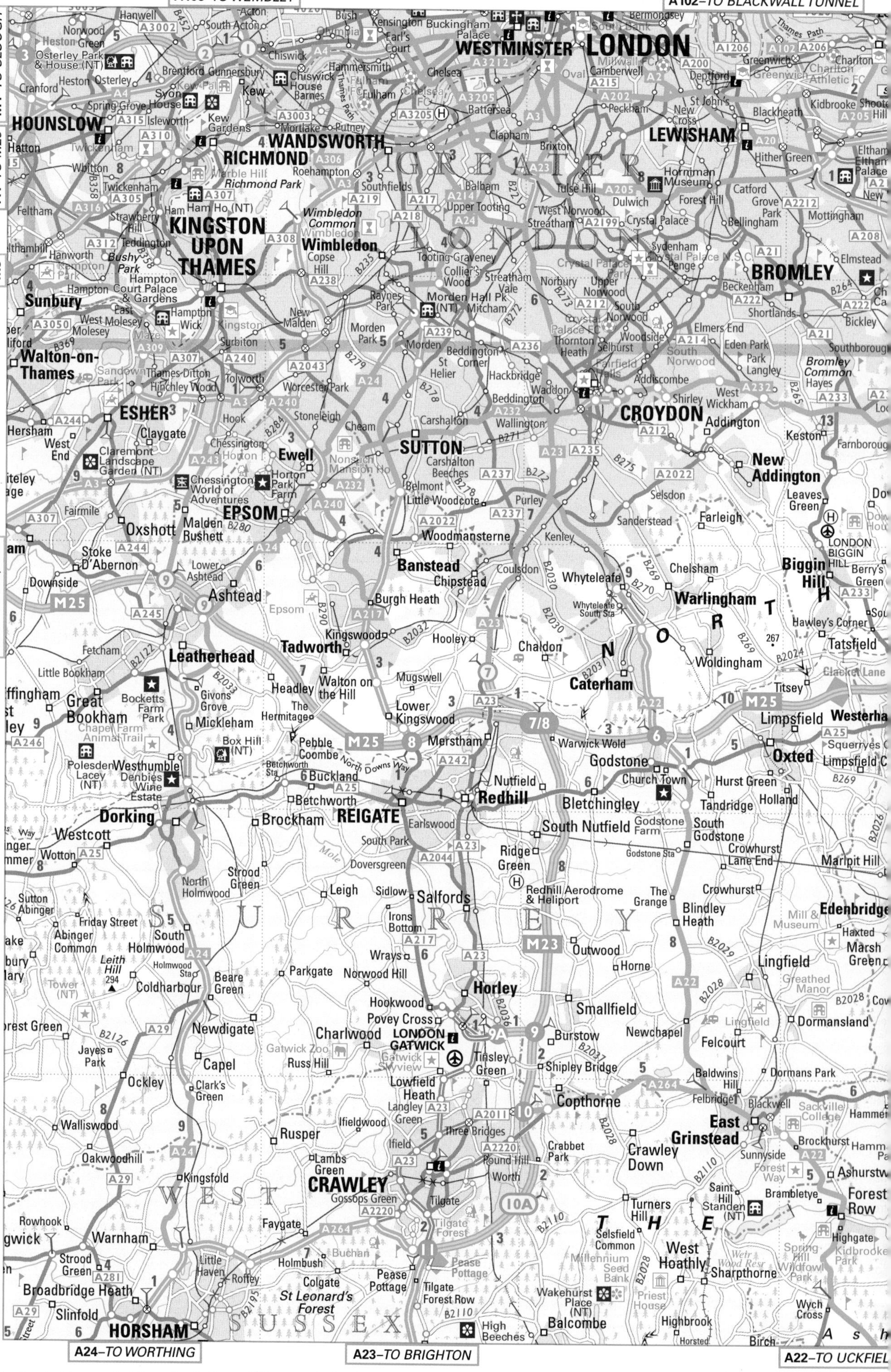

Purley: *In February 1898 Henry Lindfield became the first person ever to die in a car crash. He died from injuries he sustained when his car left the road at Purley Corner whilst driving to Brighton.* ***Map ref. C2***

159

Biggin Hill Airport *was first established as a Royal Flying Corps station in 1917, but it is best known as a World War II 'fighter station' from which the RAF fought the crucial 'Battle of Britain' in the summer of 1940.* ***Map ref. D2***

171

D E F G
187
M25–TO M11, M1
A1089–TO A13

M2–TO CANTERBURY (A2)
M20–TO ASHFORD
174
1 2 3 4 5
A26–TO UCKFIELD
A21, A229–TO HASTINGS
160

Dorking: *Sir Laurence Olivier (1907–1989) was born here. He won an Academy Award for his role as Hamlet in 1948 and went on to become one of Britain's best known actors.* ***Map ref. A4***

Hartfield: *In 1925 the Milne family moved into nearby Cotchford Farm where A A Milne wrote his Winnie the Pooh books, including his son Christopher Robin in the stories. Some of the locations from the stories are identifiable in the area, including the recently restored bridge where the Poohsticks game was invented.* ***Map ref. D5***

A B C D

188

1 2 3 4 5

173

Pluckley: *The original location for the 1991 filming of H E Bates' The Darling Buds of May which starred David Jason, Pam Ferris, Catherine Zeta Jones and Philip Franks.* ***Map ref. B4***

161

Faversham: *just off Junction 6 of the M2 has the highest ever recorded temperature in Britain. On the 10th August 2003 it peaked at 38.5°C (101.3°F).* ***Map ref. C2***

Canterbury: *King's School, founded between 597 and 600, is both Britain's oldest recorded school and its oldest recorded charity.* ***Map ref. D3***

Channel Tunnel: *The idea of a cross channel tunnel had been around for years before one eventually opened in 1994. An early scheme was discussed between Britain and France in 1802 but never got off the ground because of the Napoleonic Wars. Between 1880 and 1883 trial tunnels were dug on both sides of the Channel but were abandoned in 1883 amidst fears of a French invasion. In 1973, after Britain joined the Common Market, it was agreed to build a traditional rail tunnel, but construction was abandoned by Harold Wilson's government due to a financial crisis. Work on the current tunnel started in 1987 and it was eventually opened in 1994, two years late and millions of pounds over budget. The tunnel is 31 miles (50km) long and an average of 150 feet (45.5m) below the seabed. It was constructed by 13,000 engineers and workers. Interestingly the size of Britain increased by 90 acres (36.5ha) when spoil from the tunnel was deposited and landscaped at an area now known as Samphire Hoe.* ***Map ref. F4***

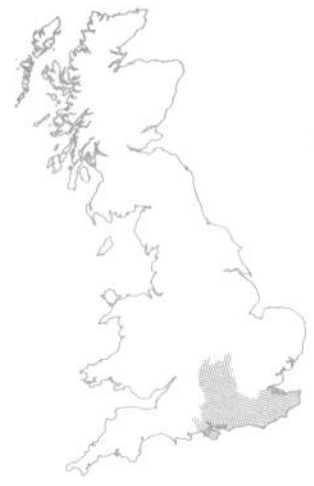

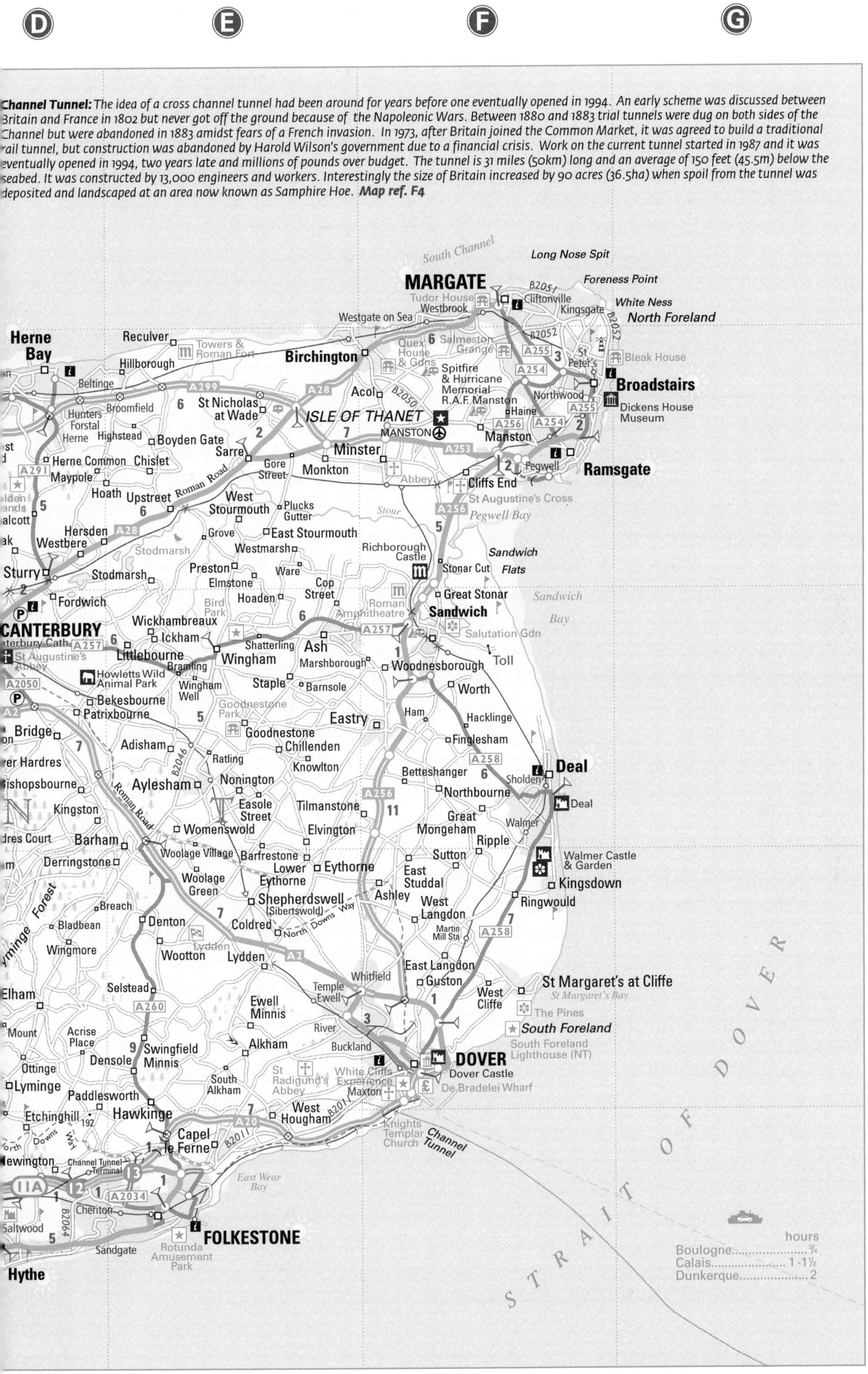

Folkestone: *William Harvey (1578–1657) was born here. Harvey studied medicine at Cambridge and is credited with discovering the circulation of the blood.* ***Map ref. E5***

Sandwich, Dover, Hythe, New Romney and Hastings: *Collectively these towns are the original 'Cinque Ports'. In medieval times, Royal Charters granted them special privileges such as freedom from tolls and customs duties, freedom of trade and their own judicial courts. This was in return for the use of their fishing and cargo vessels and crews for military service. This service, which lasted over three hundred years eventually formed into the first British Navy.*

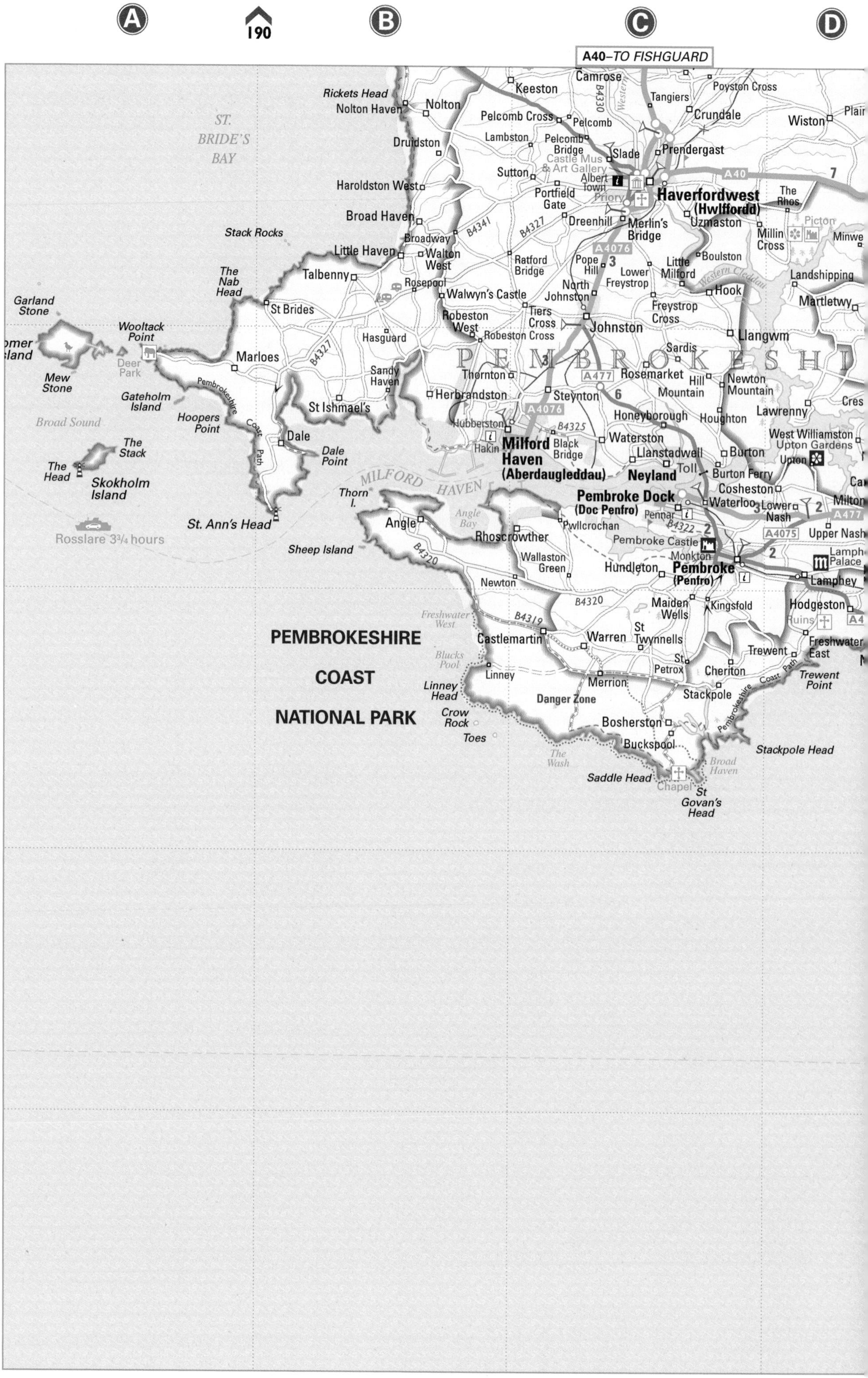

1

2

3

4

5

Milford Haven: *The largest port in Wales and the fifth largest port in the UK.* ***Map ref. B2***

Pendine Sands: *During the 1920s, this was the scene of 5 successful extensions of the world land speed record by the drivers Malcolm Campbell and J G Parry-Thomas. Parry-Thomas was tragically killed here trying to take the record back off Campbell in 1927 – the last attempt at the land speed record made on British 'soil'.* ***Map ref. F2***

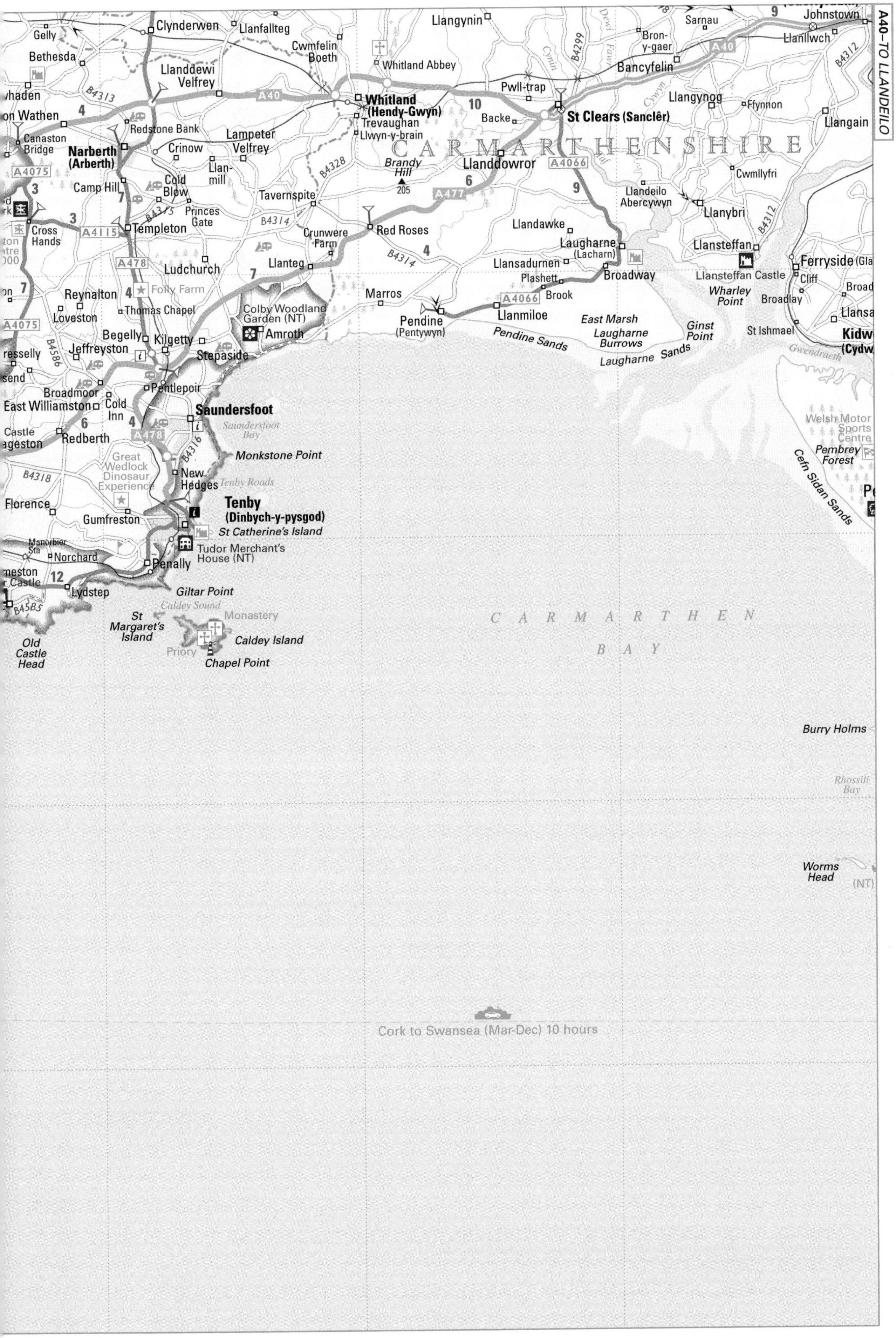

1 2 3 178 4 5

Laugharne: *This ancient town is best known for its association with poet and writer Dylan Thomas who lived in the Georgian Boathouse overlooking the River Taf for sixteen years. Dylan Marlais Thomas was born in Swansea on the 27th October 1914 and died in New York on the 9th November 1953. He is buried in Laugharne churchyard.* ***Map ref. G1***

A 192 B C D

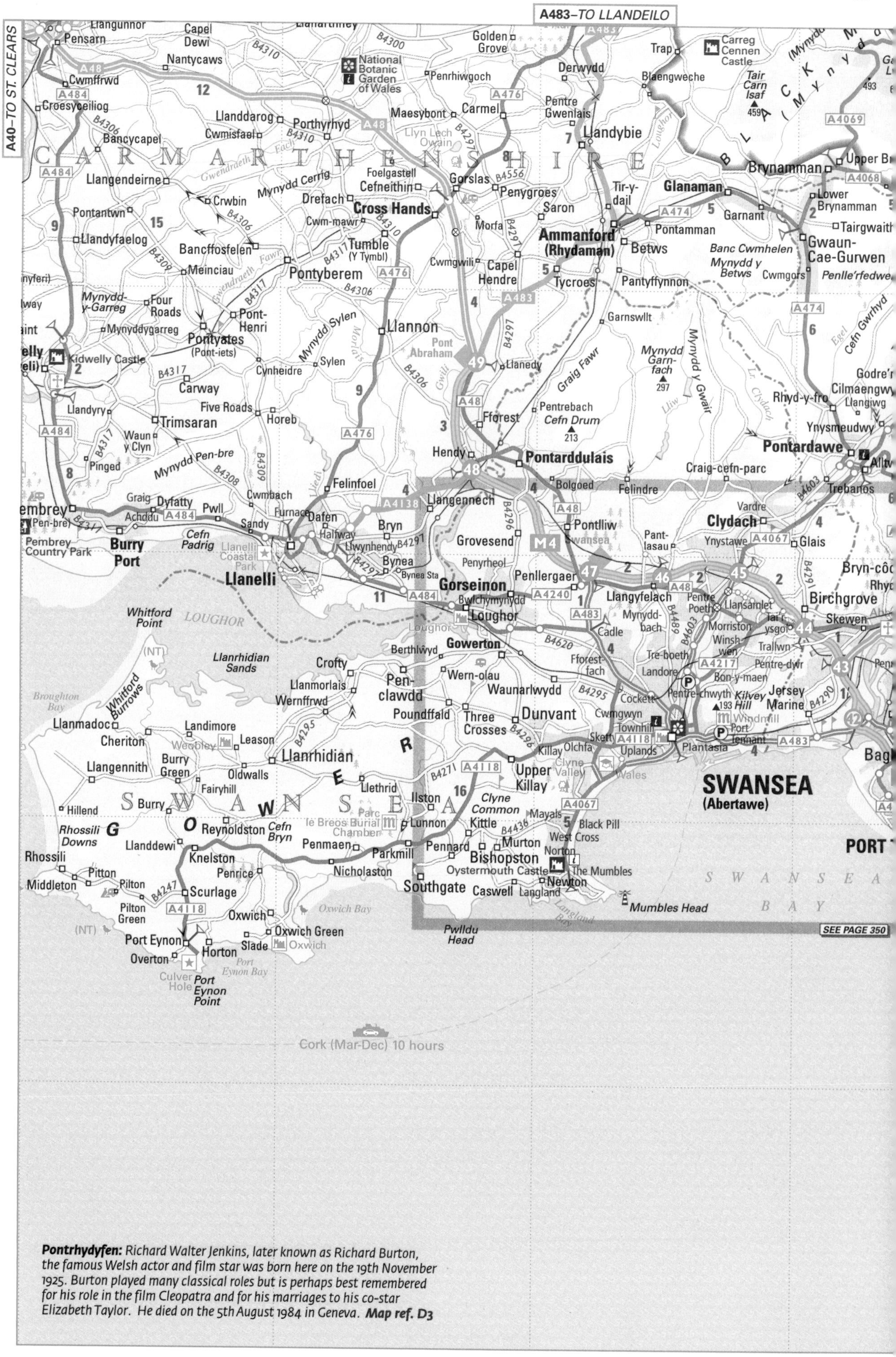

Pontrhydyfen: *Richard Walter Jenkins, later known as Richard Burton, the famous Welsh actor and film star was born here on the 19th November 1925. Burton played many classical roles but is perhaps best remembered for his role in the film Cleopatra and for his marriages to his co-star Elizabeth Taylor. He died on the 5th August 1984 in Geneva.* ***Map ref. D3***

1
2
177
3
4
5

The Mumbles: *On the 25th March 1807 the first ever passenger railway service in the world was opened between here and Swansea. Prior to the opening of The Swansea and Mumbles Railway, the only route between the two places was along the beach.* ***Map ref. C4***

Swansea: *Sir Harry Secombe, comedian, singer, film star and writer was born in the St Thomas area of Swansea on the 8th September 1921. Sir Harry is best remembered as Neddy Seagoon, a member of the 'Goon Show'. He died aged 79 on the 12th April 2001.* ***Map ref. C3***

Merthyr Tydfil: *On 21st February 1804 the world's first steam railway engine, built by Richard Trevithick, successfully hauled 70 passengers and 10 tons of iron on the 9 mile (14km) route from Merthyr to Abercynon.* ***Map ref. G2***

D E 193 F G

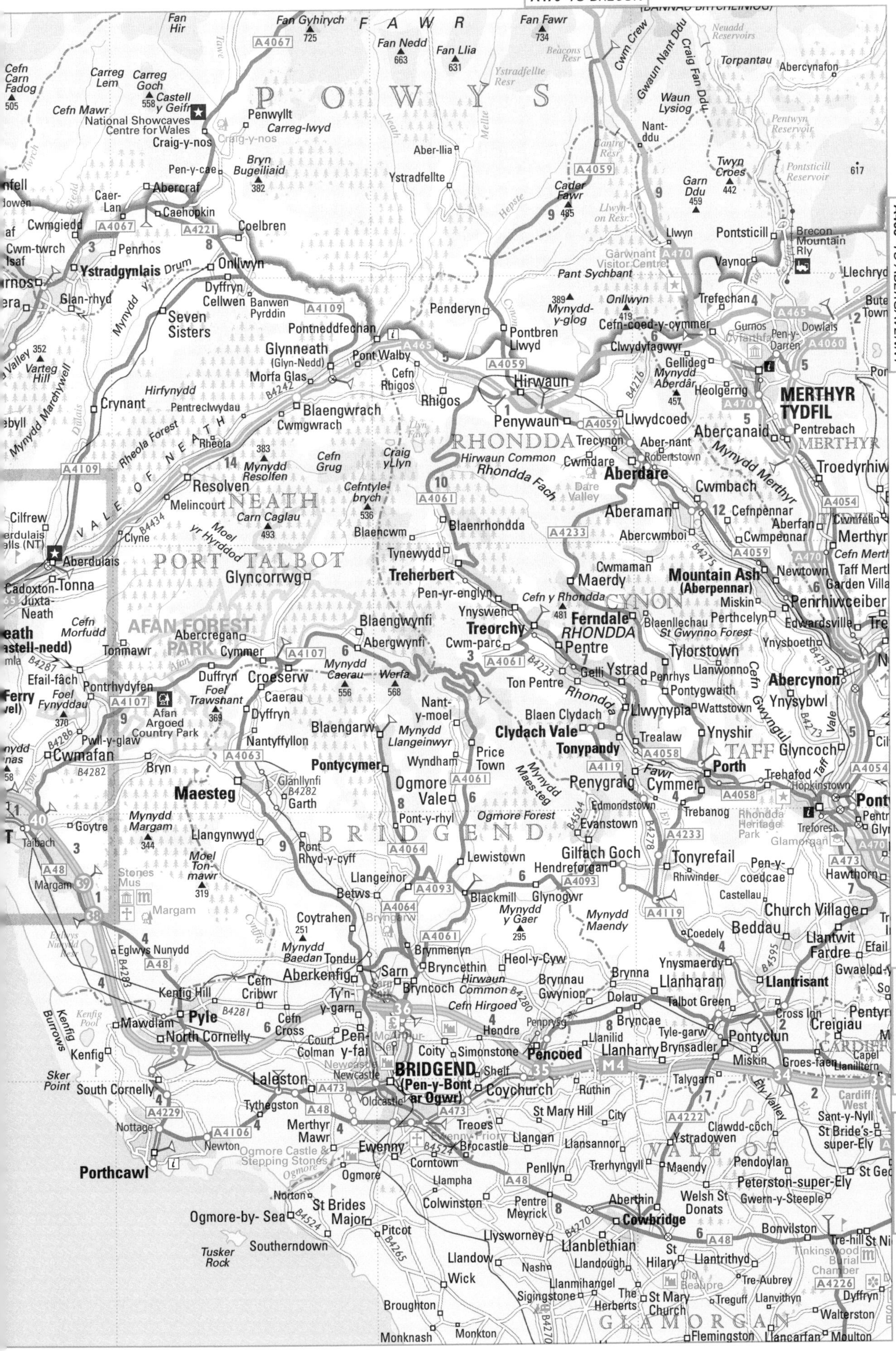

1 2 3 4 5 180

Aberfan: *At 9.15 am on Friday 21st October 1966 a coal waste tip, made unstable by heavy rain, slid down a Welsh mountainside engulfing the Pantglas Junior School and almost twenty houses in the small village of Aberfan. The disaster happened so quickly that nobody was rescued after 11am on that day and 116 school children, half of the entire school, and 5 of their teachers were amongst the dead. After a week of round the clock digging, the final death toll was confirmed as 144.* ***Map ref. G2***

164

Llantrisant: *Famous as the town which houses The Royal Mint. Here they produce all the currency for the UK. The Royal Mint is Britain's oldest surviving business, having been founded in London in 886.* ***Map ref. G4***

A B 194 C D

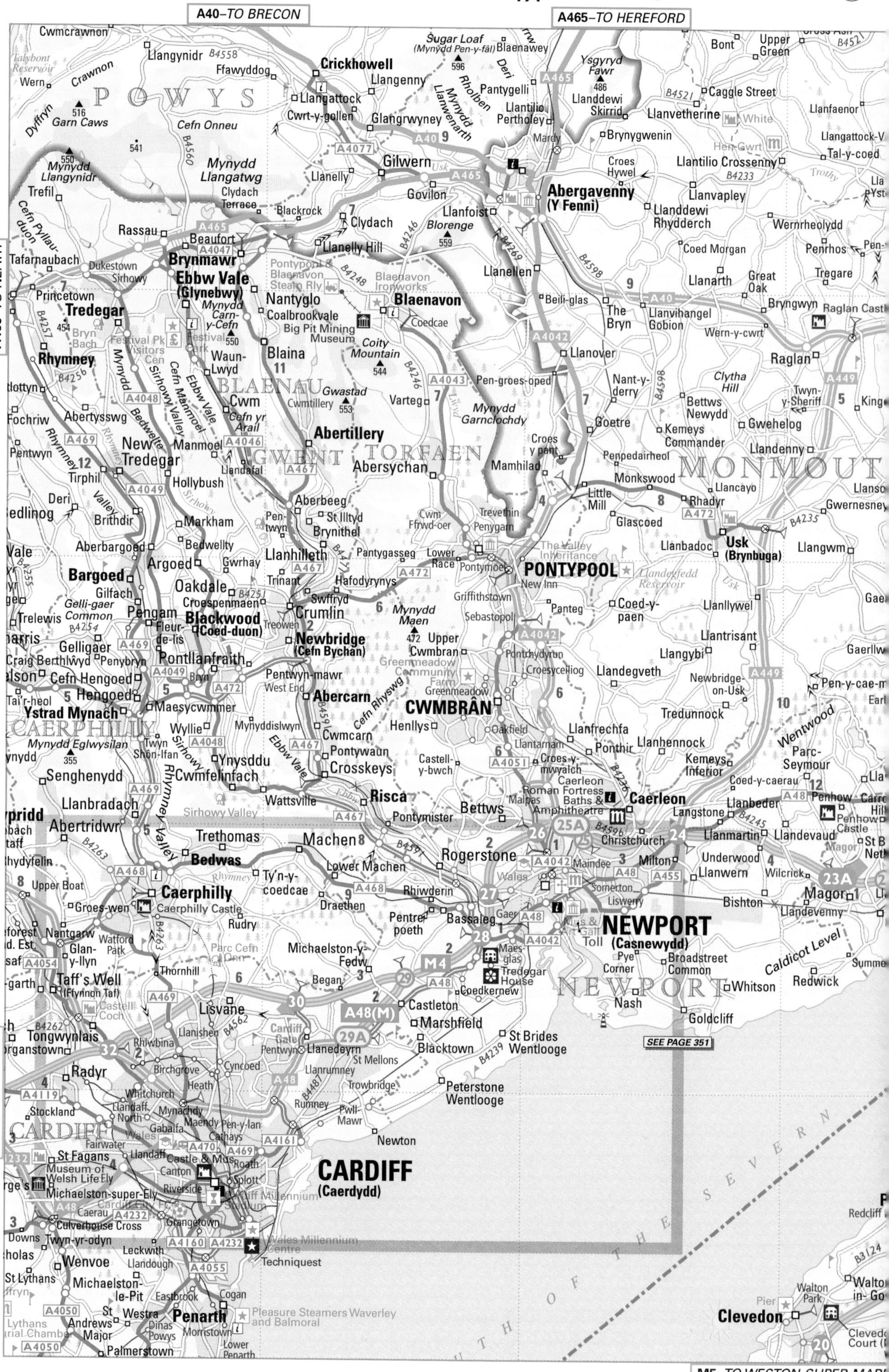

1
2
3
4
5
179
165

River Severn Road Bridges: *The first Severn Road Bridge, which linked the M4 motorway to South Wales, was opened by the Queen on the 8th September 1966. The bridge is in two parts, the first crosses the River Severn and replaced the old Beachley to Aust ferry. The second part spans the River Wye near Chepstow. The main span is 3,240 feet (987m), the tops of the towers reach 445 feet (135.5m) and the structure is built to withstand 100 mph (160km/h) winds. The second Severn Bridge joining England and Wales was opened on the 5th June 1996. It is almost 3.2 miles (5km) long and the pylon heights reach 449 feet (137m). This bridge is reputed to have cost over £300m.* ***Map ref. E4***

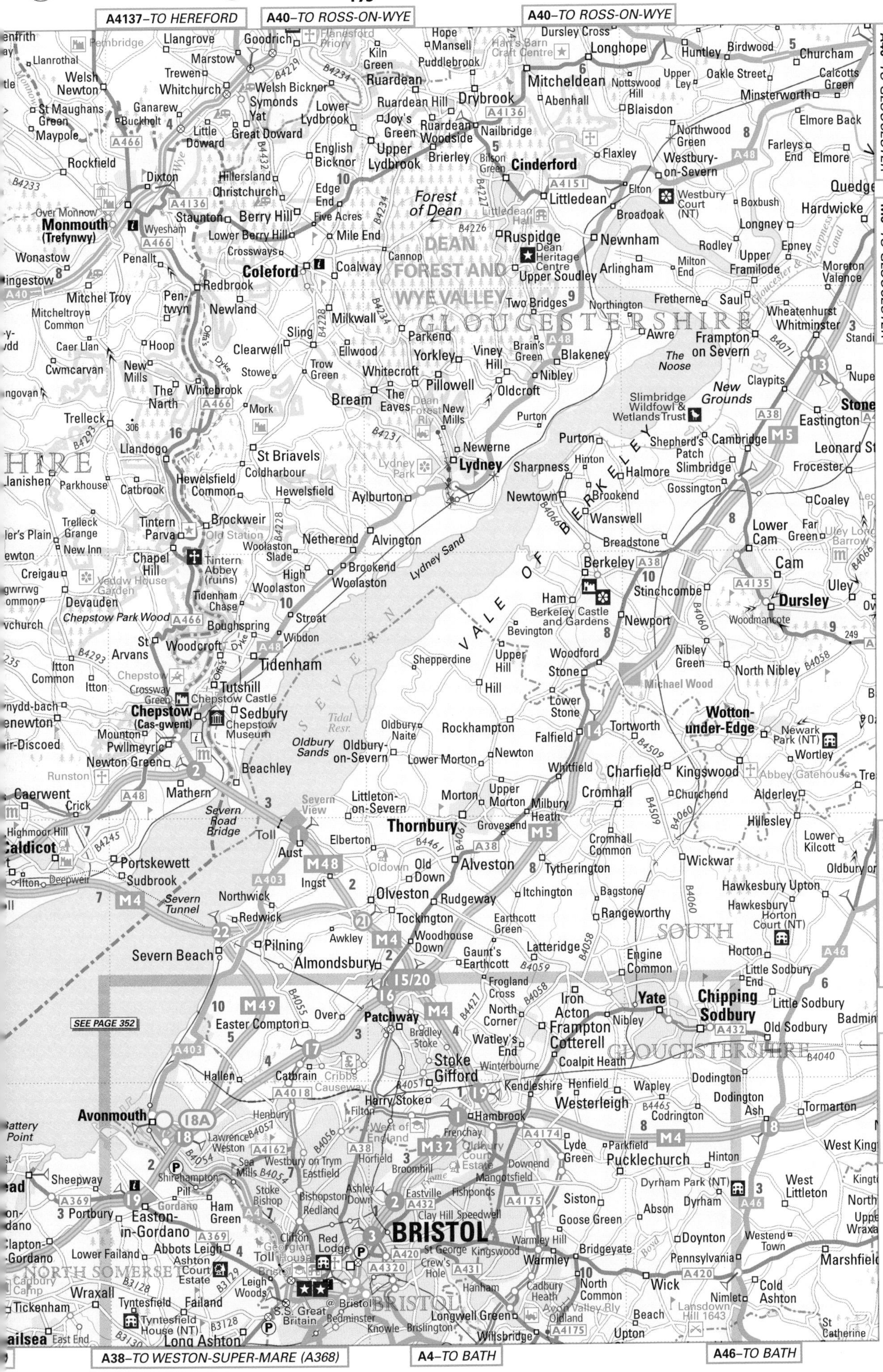

1 2 182 3 4 5

Crickhowell: *Sir George Everest, Surveyor General of India was born here in 1790. Everest spent over 25 years of his life mapping India and was the first person to survey the Himalayas. He was knighted in 1861 and the highest peak in the Himalayas was officially named after him in 1865.* ***Map ref. B1***

166

Severn Bore: *This is one of the most spectacular natural wonders in Britain. The Bore is a large 'surge wave' caused by the huge tidal range and shape of the river estuary. It can reach up to 10 feet (3m) in height and travel at up to 13 mph (21km/h). The best Bores usually occur ahead of the spring tide and travel up the river for over 20 miles (32km) between Awre and Gloucester. The Severn is also Britain's longest river at 220 miles (354km).* ***Map ref. G2***

196

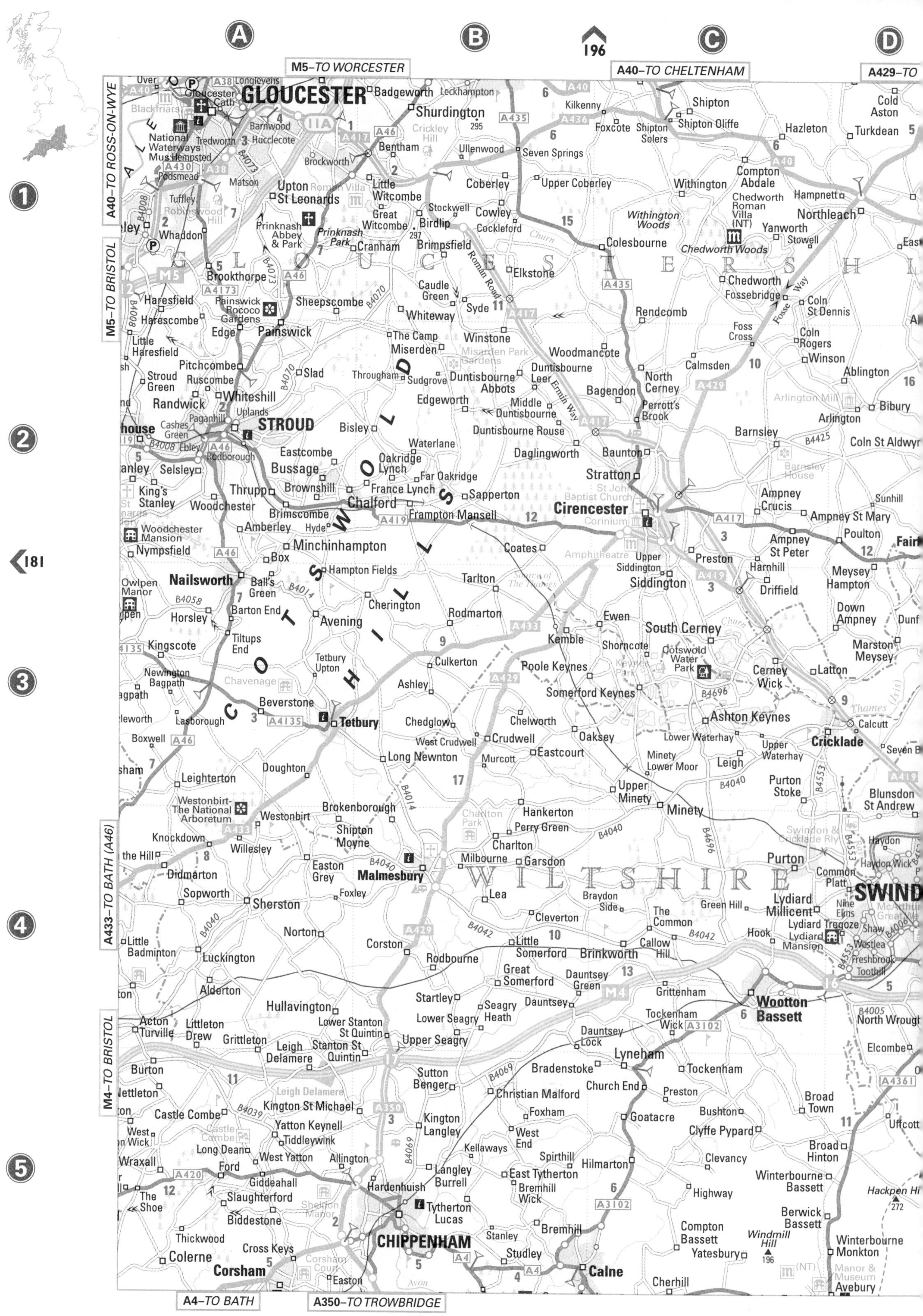

181

Slad: *The Woolpack here was the 'local' of the writer Laurie Lee. The pub features in his most famous book 'Cider with Rosie'. Laurie Lee died in 1997 and is buried in the churchyard just across the road.* ***Map ref. A2***

167

The River Thames: *The official source of the Thames is at Trewsbury Mead near Kemble. Although very little water is visible at this point, a stone marks the exact spot. From its source the River Thames journeys some 215 miles (346km) to the North Sea, making it England's longest river, with 191 miles (307km), from Lechlade, being navigable waterway. Below Teddington Lock the river is tidal although it remains as fresh water down as far as Battersea.* ***Map ref. B3***

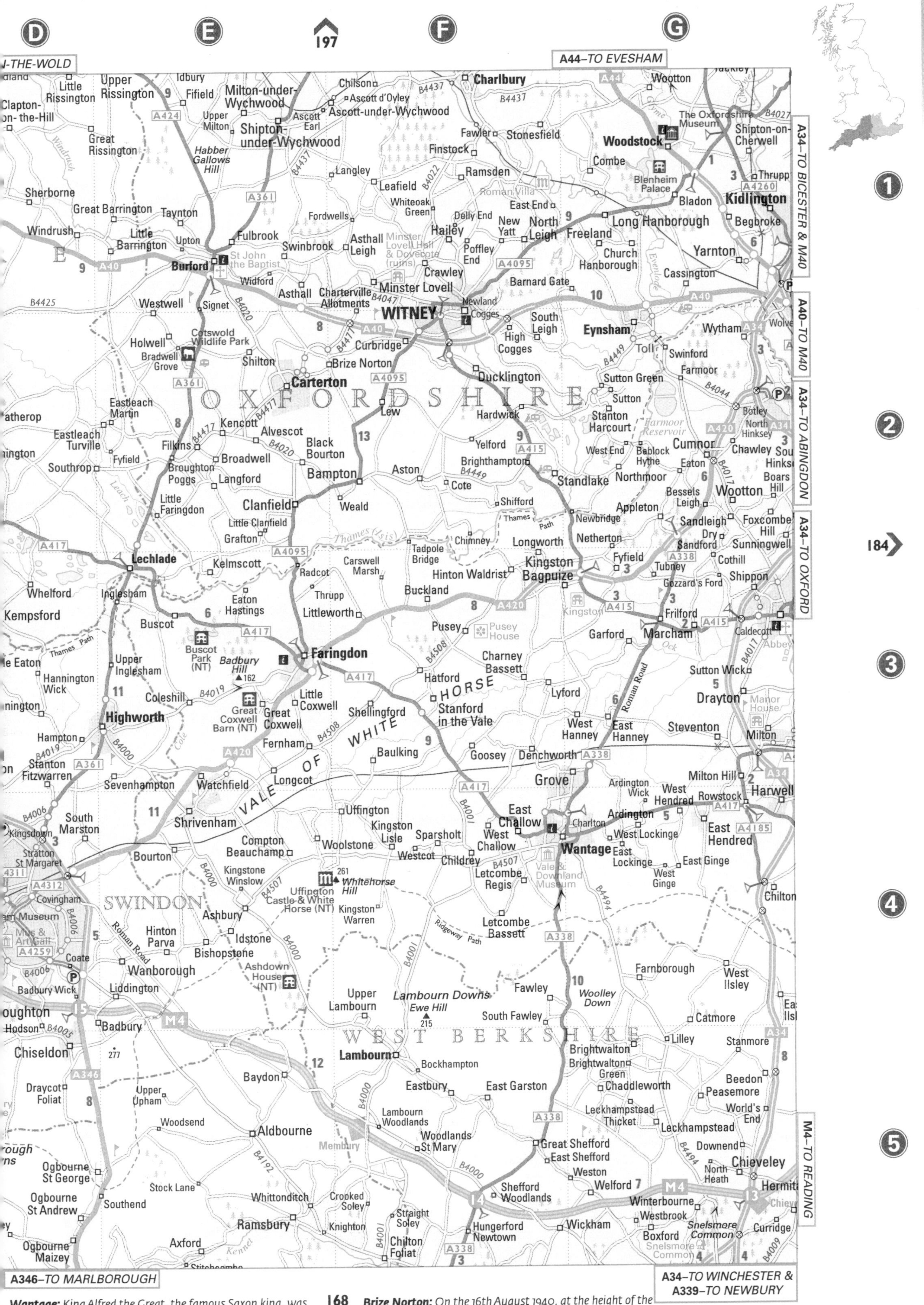

Wantage: *King Alfred the Great, the famous Saxon king, was born here in AD849. Renowned for defending his kingdom against the Vikings, and for burning the cakes, Alfred died in AD899 at the age of 50 and is buried in Winchester Cathedral.* ***Map ref. F4***

168

Brize Norton: *On the 16th August 1940, at the height of the Battle of Britain, two maraurdering German Junkers 88 bombers attacked the RAF station at Brize Norton destroying 46 British aircraft which were still in the hangers of the maintenance unit and training school.* ***Map ref. E2***

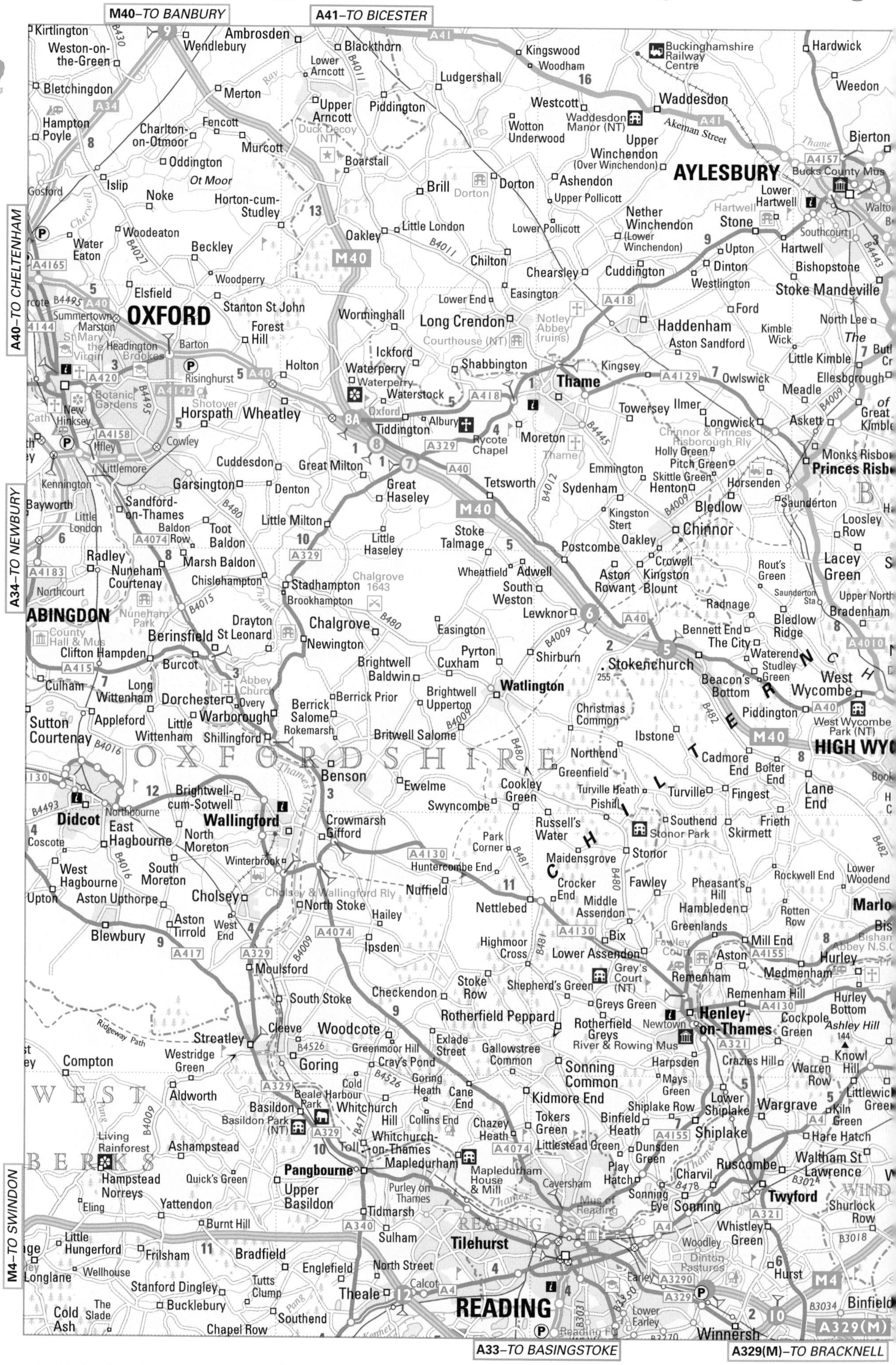

Oxford University *is the oldest English-speaking university in the world, having been founded over 900 years ago. During this time it has provided the world with 40 Nobel prize-winners and the country with 25 Prime Ministers.* ***Map ref. A2***

170

Beaconsfield: *Although born in East Dulwich on the 11th August 1897, Enid Blyton, creator of 'Noddy' and 'The Famous Five', lived here, in Penn Road, Beaconsfield from 1938 up to her death in 1968. During her lifetime she wrote over 700 books which were translated into 40 different languages and sold over 400 million copies worldwide.* ***Map ref. E3***

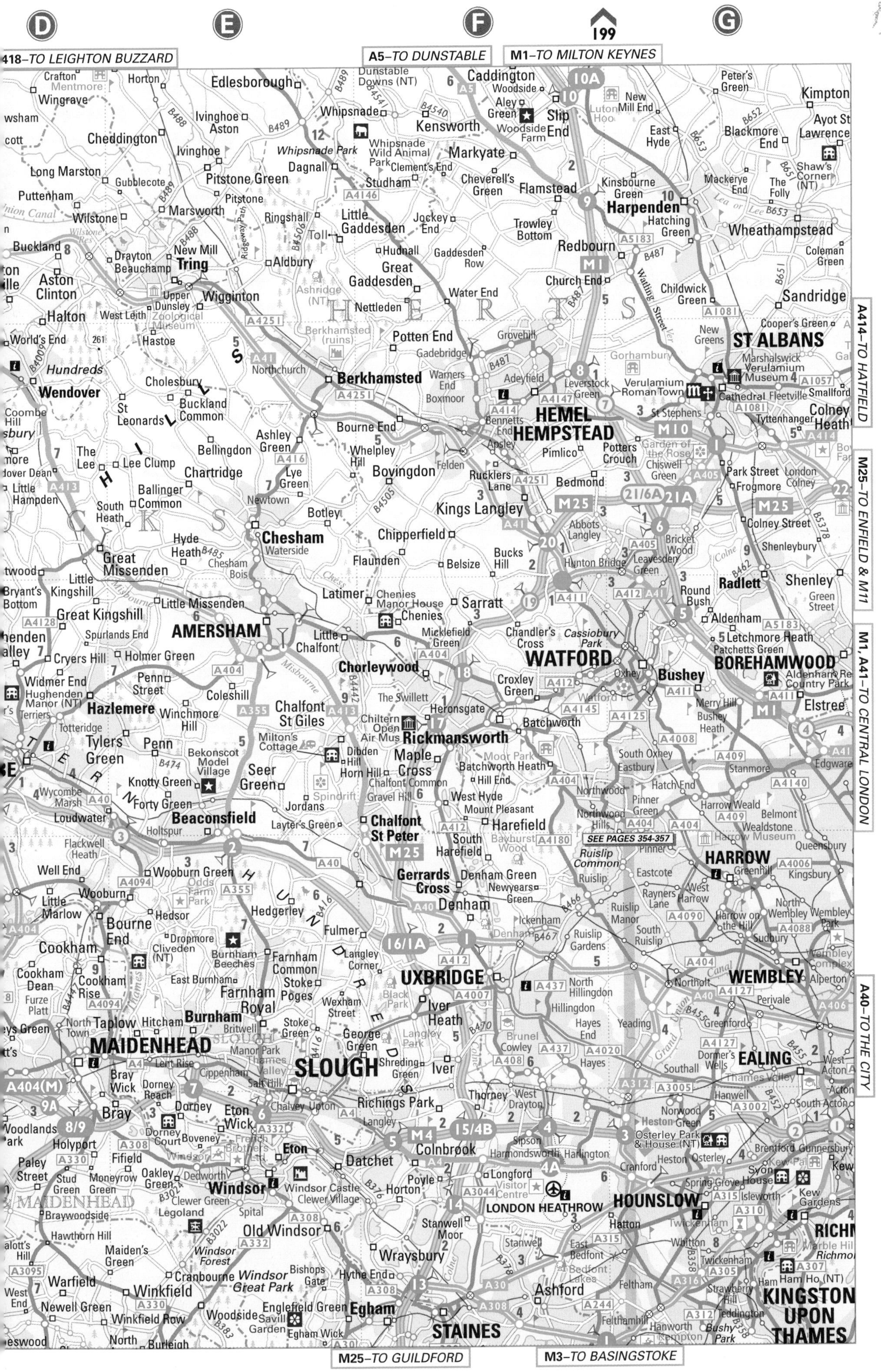

171

Iver Heath: *The Pinewood Studios located here, house the world's largest film stage, used in the production of the James Bond films.* ***Map ref. F4***

London Heathrow Airport: *The world's busiest international airport, handling around 63 million passengers per year. To the west of the airport, the section of the M25 between junctions 13 and 14 is Britain's busiest road.* ***Map ref. F5***

200

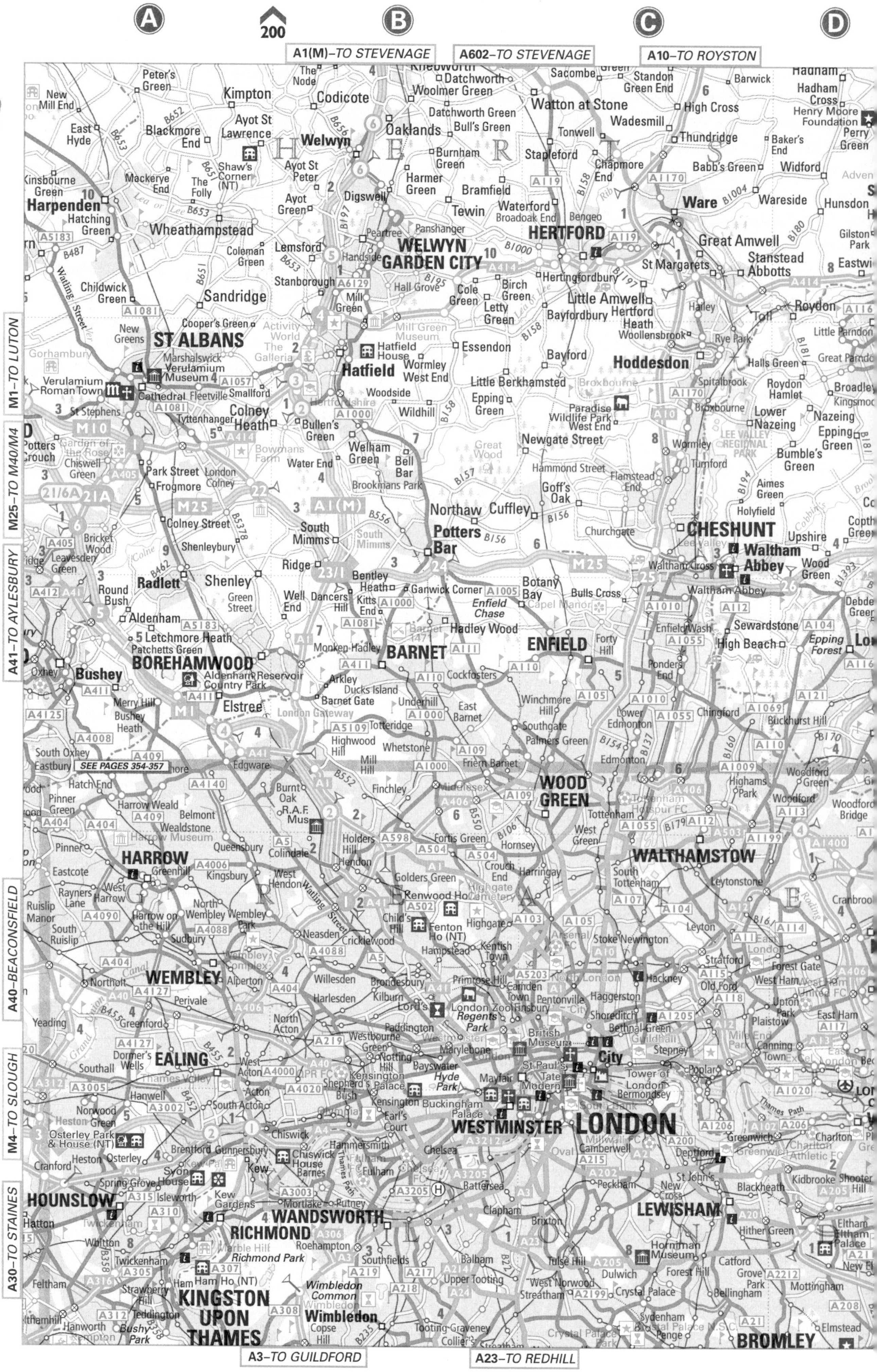

185

London: *The world's first Underground railway was opened by the Metropolitan Railway Company in 1863 between Paddington and Farringdon.* ***Map ref. B4***

172

Barking: *Bobby Moore, captain of the England football team that won the 1966 World Cup was born here on the 12th April 1941. He began his career at West Ham in 1956 and is acknowledged to be one of the best defenders ever to play in the English league. Bobby died of cancer on the 24th February 1993 at the age of 51.* ***Map ref. D4***

201

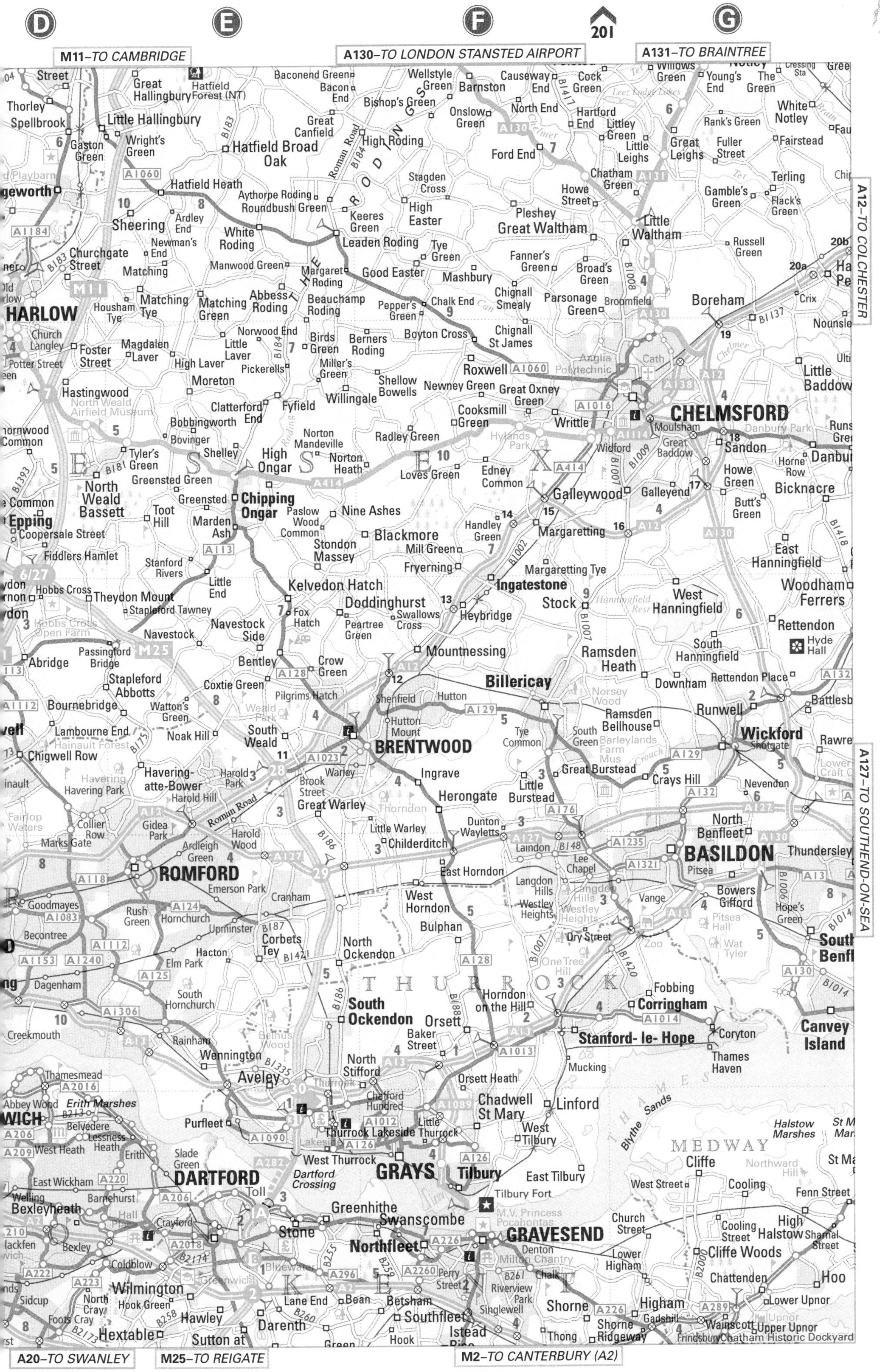

188

173

Greensted: *The Saxon church here is known as the oldest wooden church in the world.* ***Map ref. E2***

202

A B C D

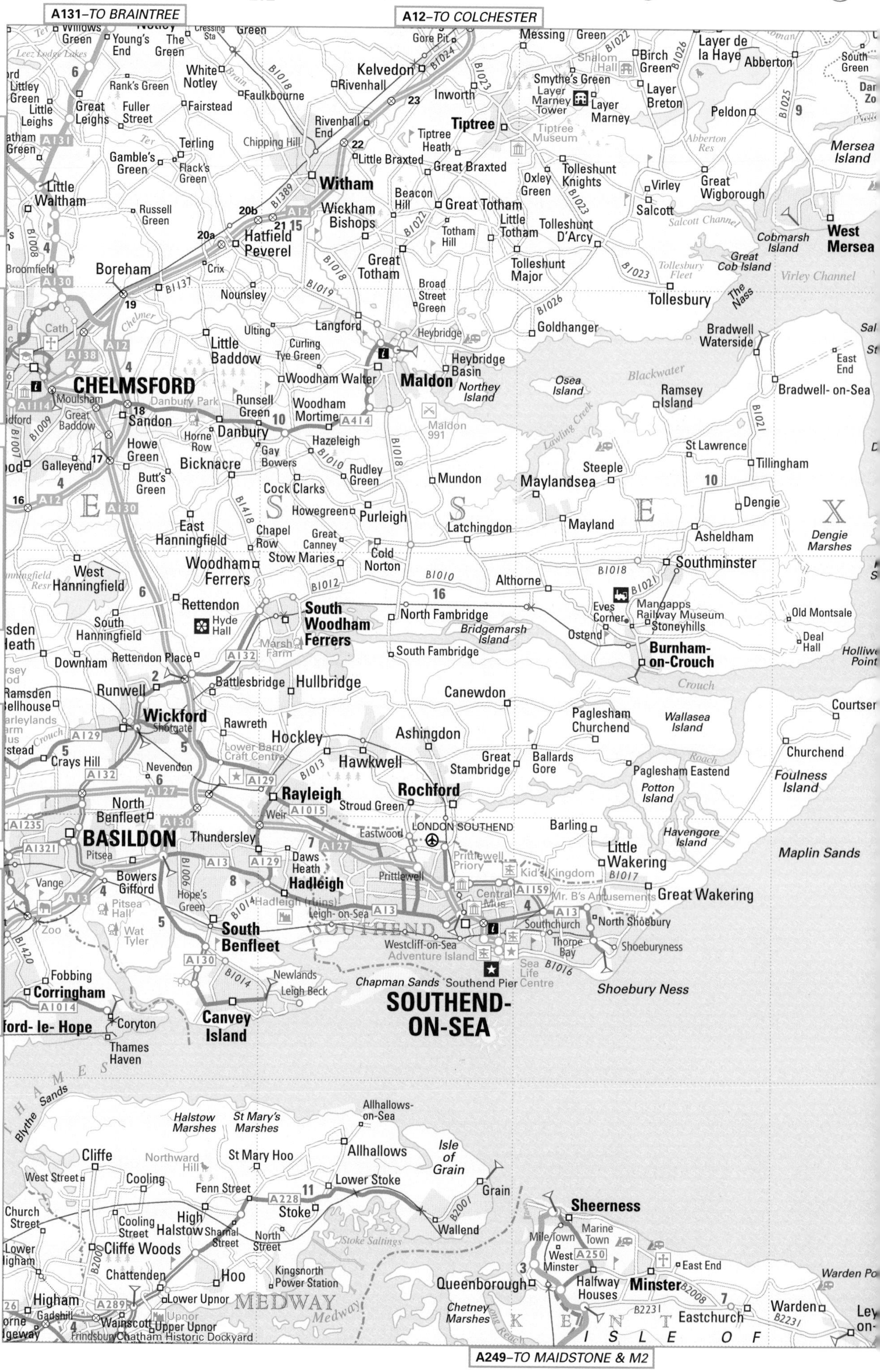

1 2 3 4 5

187

Great Wakering: *Considered to be the driest place in Britain with an average rainfall of less than 20 inches (500mm) per year.* ***Map ref. C4***

174

Messing: *This is the ancestral home of the Bush Family who have provided two American Presidents. The Bush family left Essex to settle in America during the 17th Century.* ***Map ref. C1***

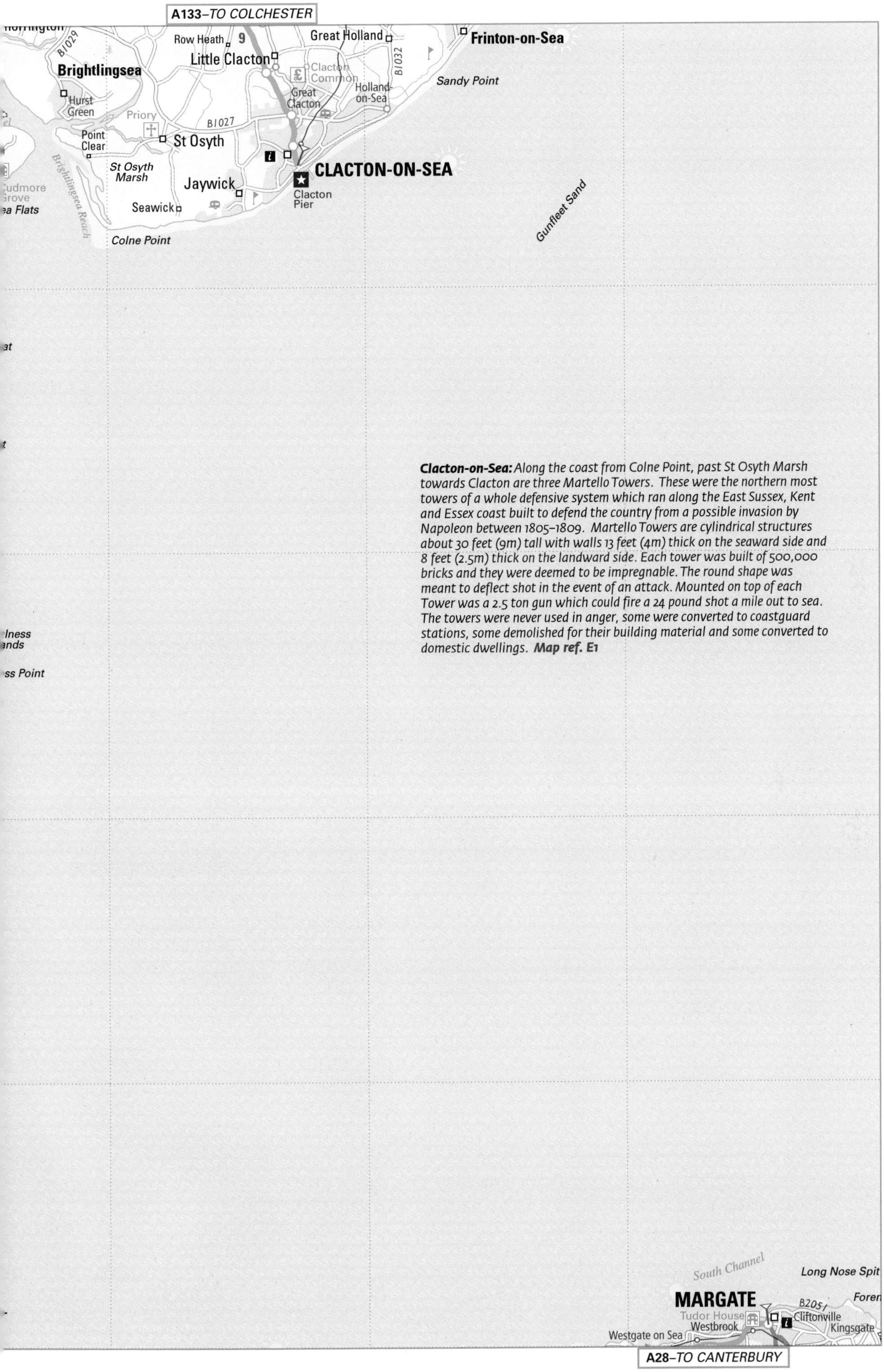

Clacton-on-Sea: *Along the coast from Colne Point, past St Osyth Marsh towards Clacton are three Martello Towers. These were the northern most towers of a whole defensive system which ran along the East Sussex, Kent and Essex coast built to defend the country from a possible invasion by Napoleon between 1805–1809. Martello Towers are cylindrical structures about 30 feet (9m) tall with walls 13 feet (4m) thick on the seaward side and 8 feet (2.5m) thick on the landward side. Each tower was built of 500,000 bricks and they were deemed to be impregnable. The round shape was meant to deflect shot in the event of an attack. Mounted on top of each Tower was a 2.5 ton gun which could fire a 24 pound shot a mile out to sea. The towers were never used in anger, some were converted to coastguard stations, some demolished for their building material and some converted to domestic dwellings.* ***Map ref. E1***

1 2 3 4 5

175

Canvey Island: *From 6pm on the 31st January 1953, exceptionally strong winds combined with a higher than average spring tide caused a 'storm surge' which led to devastating flooding all along the east coast of England. Hurricane force winds were recorded at 10pm at Felixstowe and the surge reached Canvey Island just after midnight on the 1st February causing absolute devastation. In all 307 people lost their lives in the flood, over 250,000 acres (100,000ha) of land were immersed and the cost in today's figures would be over five billion pounds. These floods are generally regarded as Britain's worst ever peacetime disaster.* ***Map ref. A4***

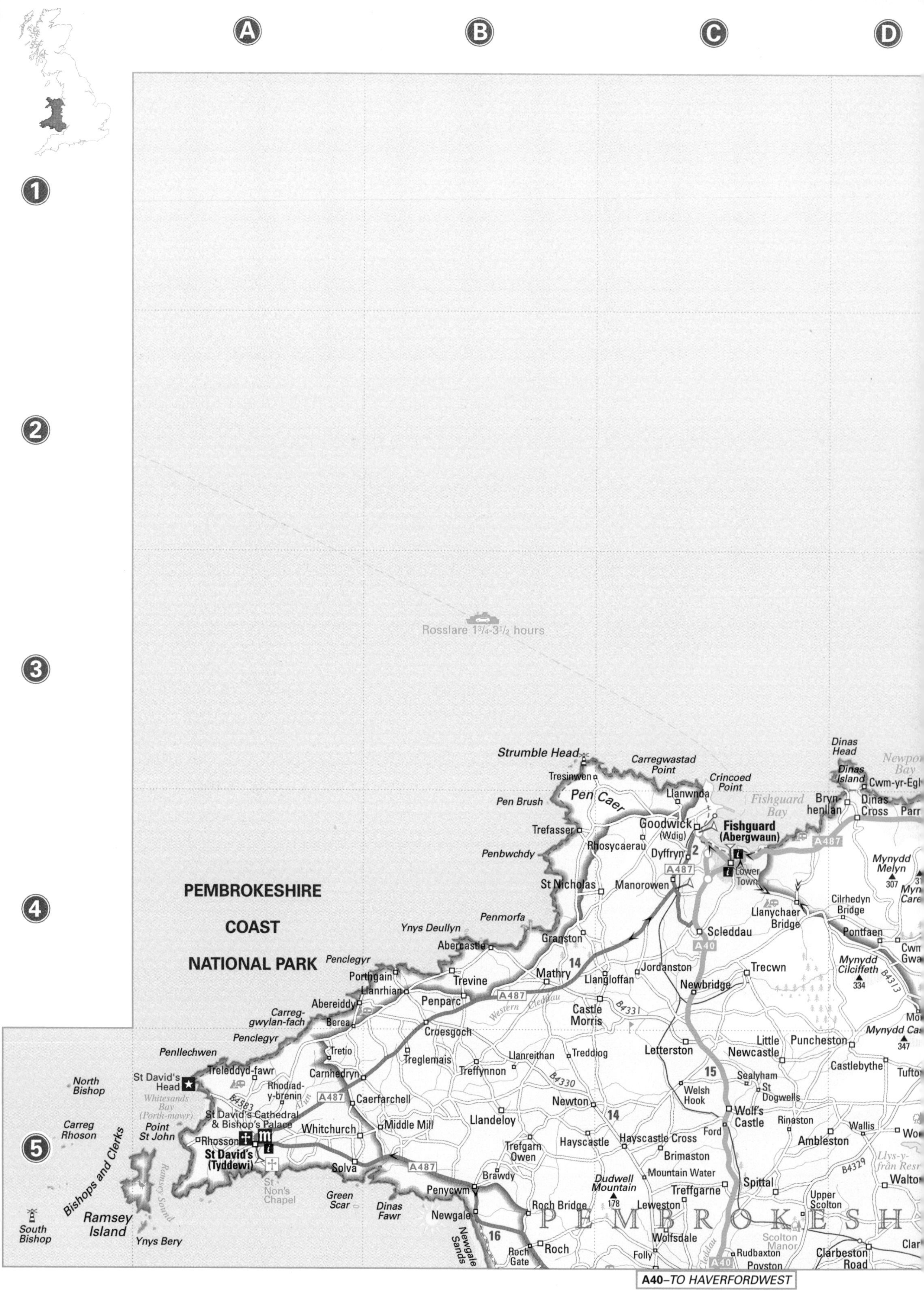

St David's: *Britain's smallest city, and an area steeped in ancient religion, both Christian and pagan. St David's Cathedral, built in AD1180 has been a place of pilgrimage for over 1200 years. It is a Celtic Cathedral and a focal point of Celtic heritage.* ***Map ref. A5***

176

Little Newcastle: *Birthplace in 1682 of Bartholomew Roberts (Black Bart) one of the most notorious Pirates ever. Roberts was the first sea captain to fly the 'Jolly Roger' (the skull and crossbones flag). He was killed by grapeshot aboard his flagship Royal Fortune, during a battle with HMS Swallow, off the coast of Gabon in 1722.* ***Map ref. C5***

Mynydd Preseli (Prescelly Mountains) : *Up to 80 4-ton 'blue stones' used in the building of Stonehenge in Wiltshire were quarried here. They were probably transported overland from the mountains down to Milford Haven and then taken by raft and finally overland again to their destination, a distance of 135 miles.* ***Map ref. D4***

192

177

204
A487–TO ABERYSTWYTH

A487–TO CARDIGAN
191
A40–TO ST. CLEARS
A483–TO AMMANFORD
178

Llanwrtyd Wells: *Claims to be the smallest town in Wales and is the home of the annual World Bog Snorkelling Championships.* ***Map ref. E3***

Lampeter *has the oldest University in Wales and with less than 2000 students can claim to be the smallest university in Europe. It was founded by Bishop Thomas Burgess in 1822 and admitted its first students on St David's Day 1827.* ***Map ref. B3***

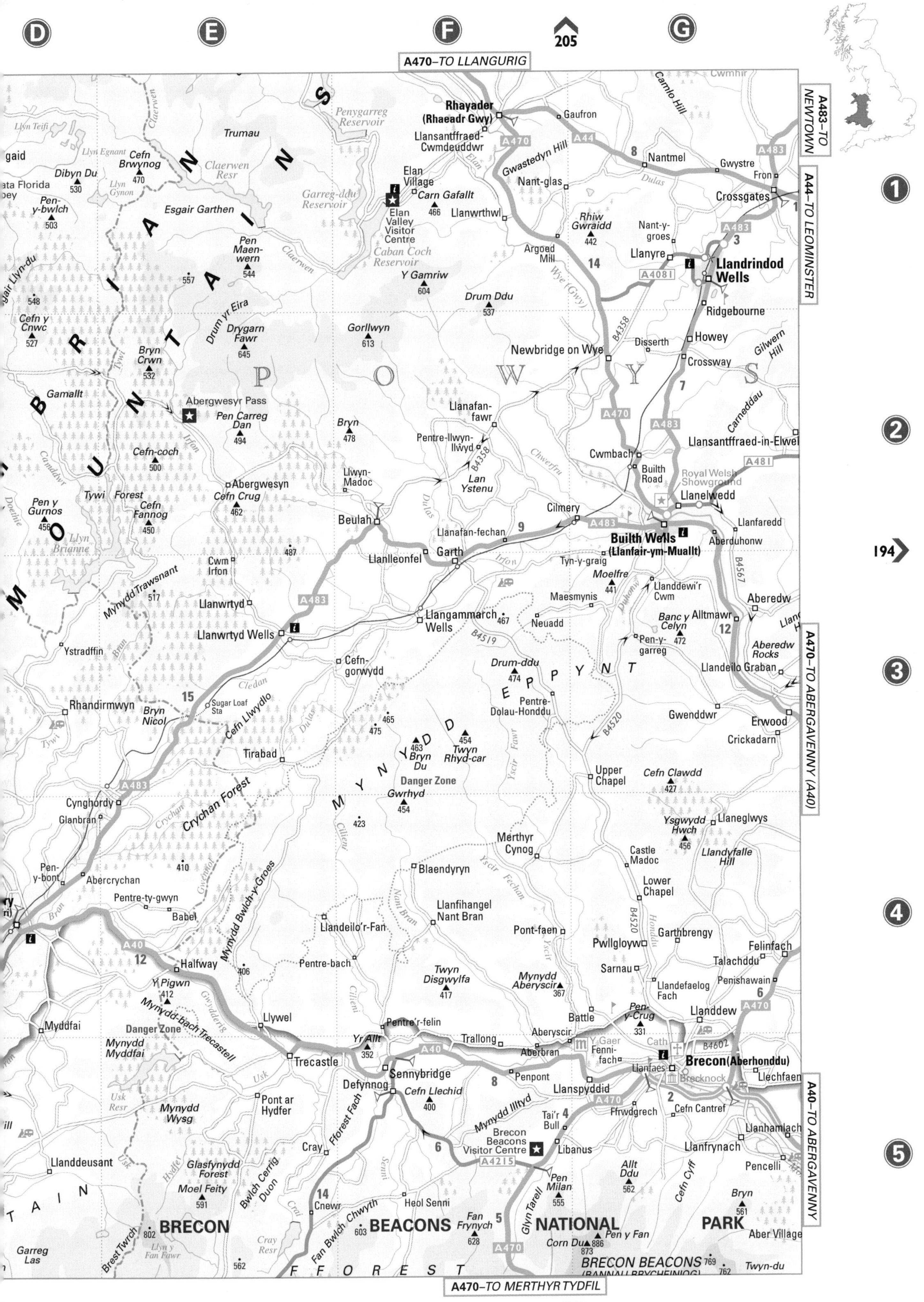

Tregaron: *A 19th century 'Drovers' town where welsh farmers gathered to walk their sheep and cattle all the way to London to sell at the markets. Famous as the birthplace of Twm Sion Cati, an outlaw described as the Welsh Robin Hood on whom the popular TV series Hawkmoor was based. To the north of the town, Tregaron Bog (Cors Caron) is the best remaining example of an active raised bog in Wales.* ***Map ref. C2***

206

A B C D

1 2 3 4 5

193

Hay-on-Wye: *Small market town on the banks of the River Wye famous for its large concentration of bookshops. With over 30 of these to choose from Hay-on-Wye is the most popular centre in Britain for booklovers.* ***Map ref. B3***

180

Hereford *Cathedral houses the famous Mappa Mundi. This is one of the first maps of the world created on a single sheet of vellum (calf skin) around AD1300. As well as being a map it also depicts the history of mankind and illustrates the marvels of the natural world, biblical events and mythology.* ***Map ref. E4***

207

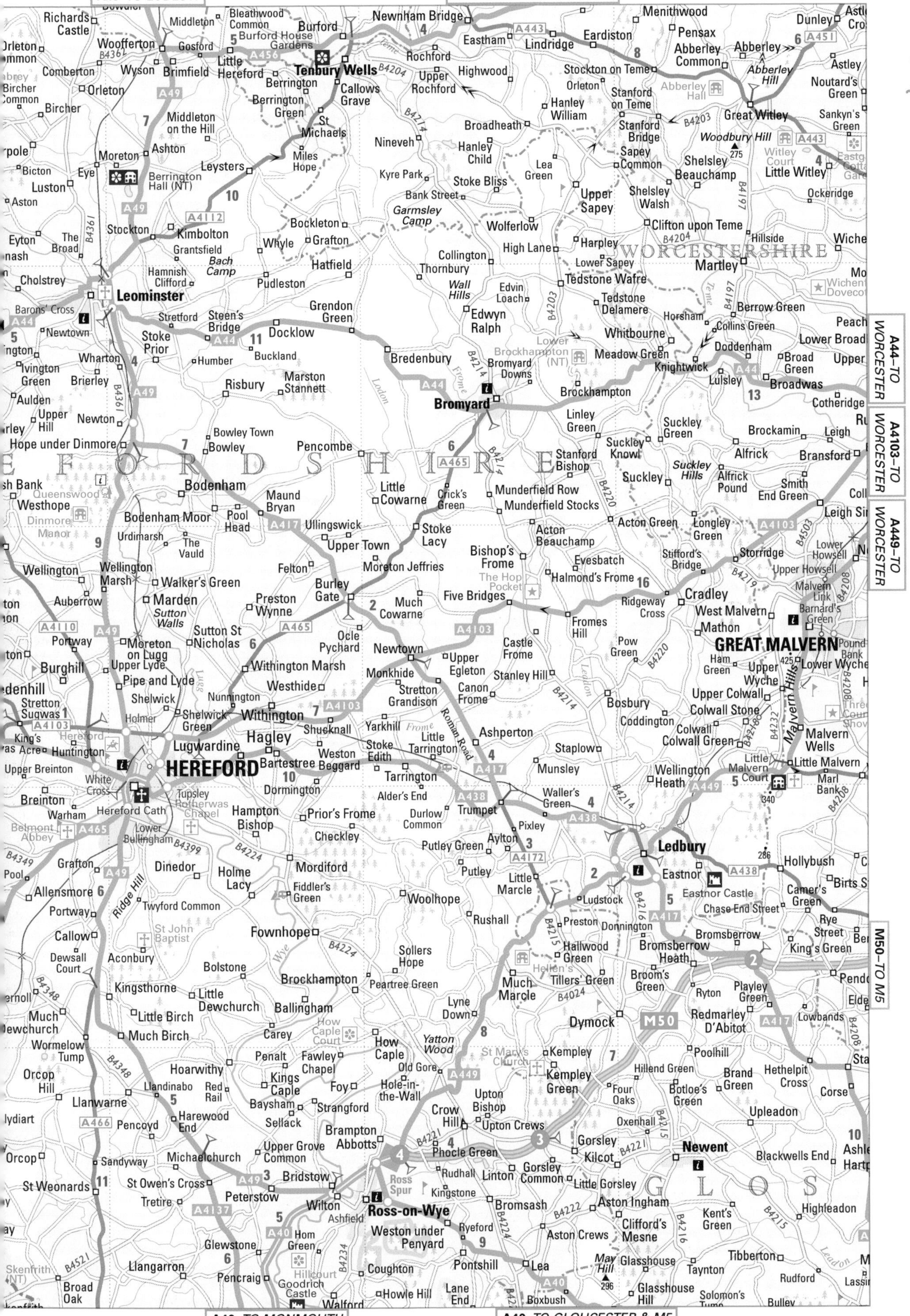

196

181

***Great Malvern:** Famous for its abundance of springs and wells. It is claimed that St Ann's Well was the source of the first bottled water to be sold in Britain in 1850.*
Map ref. G3

Little Malvern: *Basil Charles Godfrey Place, Royal Navy, was born here on the 19th July 1921. Lieutenant Place was awarded the Victoria Cross for a daring midget submarine attack on the German Battleship Tirpitz. The Tirpitz, sister ship of the Bismark, was 50,000 tons and had a crew of 2,340. The attack at Kaa Fjord, Norway on the 22nd September 1943 involved attaching magnetic mines to the hull which put the battleship out of action for several weeks. Lt. Place VC died in December 1994.* ***Map ref. G3***

208

195

182

Tewkesbury: *Scene of a bloody battle of the Wars of the Roses. Many of the defeated Lancastrians sought refuge in Tewkesbury Abbey only to be captured by the Yorkists and executed in the town square. The site of the battle is still known locally as 'Bloody Meadow'.* ***Map ref. A4.***

Droitwich: *Famous for its Brine Spa. The natural Droitwich brine contains 2.5 pounds of salt for each gallon of water, that's ten times more than normal sea water and on a par with the Dead Sea. It was possible to float weightless in the warm brine of the 1876 Brine Baths. These baths were replaced in 1985 with the first new Spa facility to be built in Britain in the twentieth century.* ***Map ref. A1.***

209

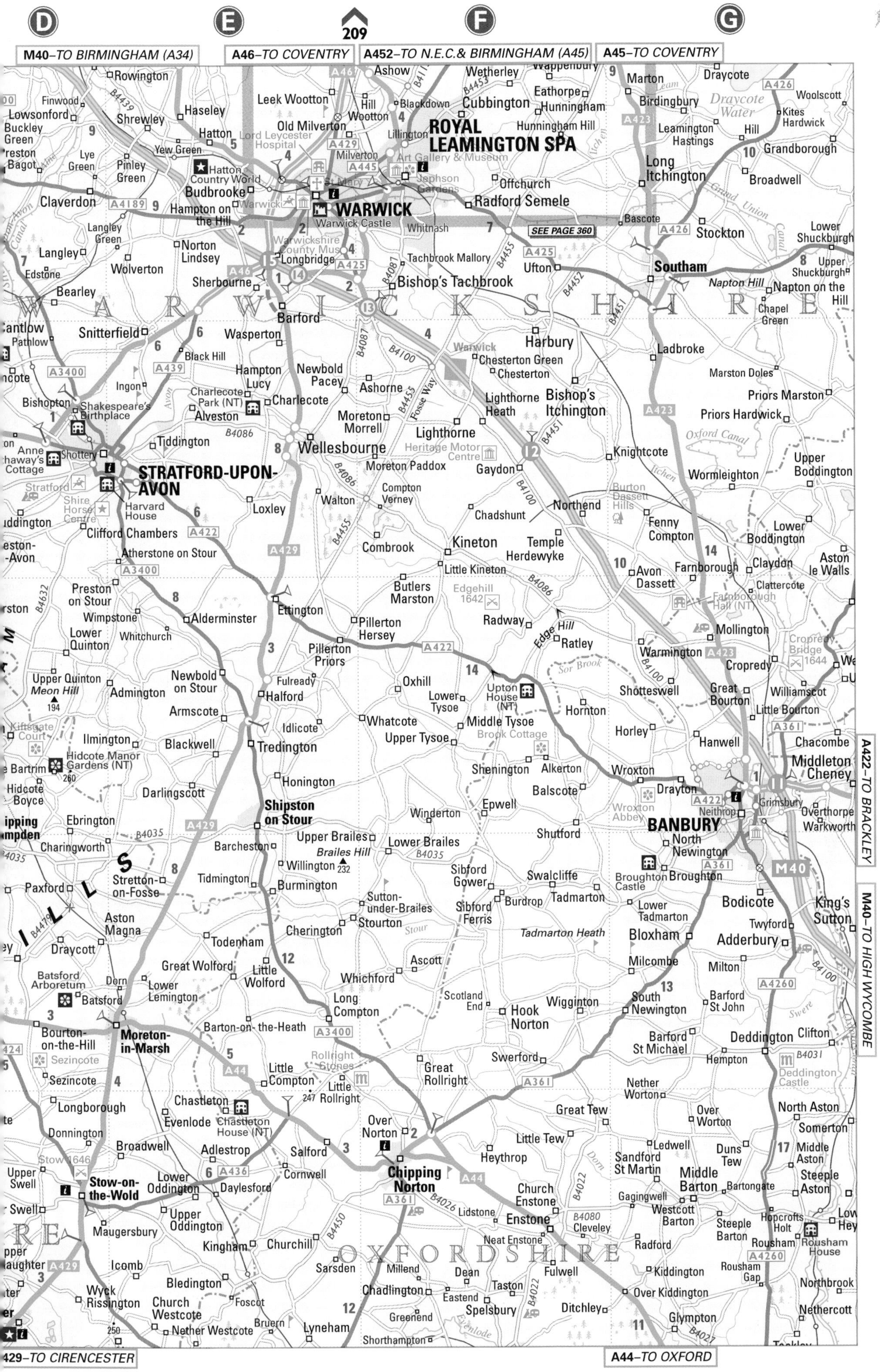

198

Stow-on-the-Wold: *The Royalist in Digbeth Street is probably the oldest pub building in Britain, containing beams carbon-dated to 947AD.* ***Map ref. D5.***

183

Banbury: *The place in the nursery rhyme 'Ride a Cock Horse to Banbury Cross'. In fact there have been several Banbury Crosses over the years but the surviving one stands at the junction of four major roads and was built in 1859 to commemorate the marriage of the then Princess Royal to Prince Frederick of Prussia.* ***Map ref. G3.***

A B C D

210

M1–TO LEICESTER & M6 | A508–TO MARKET HARBOROUGH | A43–TO KETTERING

A45–TO COVENTRY | A422–TO BANBURY & M40 | M40–TO WARWICK

1 2 3 4 5

185

A34–TO OXFORD | M40–TO HIGH WYCOMBE | A41–TO AYLESBURY

184

Stony Stratford: *The Cock and The Bull Inns sit side by side on the main street which was the old coach route from London. Coach drivers would stop over here and exchange gossip; this gave rise to the term Cock and Bull Story.* ***Map ref. C3***

Milton Ernest: *The famous wartime bandleader Glenn Miller flew from nearby Twinwood Airfield, in a single-engine Norseman aircraft on Friday 15th December 1944 and was never seen again. His band were due to play a concert to allied troops stationed in Paris and Miller was flying out ahead of the main band. At 6pm on Christmas Eve 1944 a Press Release announced that Glenn Miller was dead.* ***Map ref. F2***

D E 211 F G
09–TO KETTERING | A6–TO KETTERING | A45–TO PETERBOROUGH (A605) | A1–TO A1(M)

A428–TO CAMBRIDGE
A1–TO A1(M)
1
2
200
3
4
5
A418–TO AYLESBURY | A5–TO M1 | M1–TO ST. ALBANS
185

The M1 Motorway: *towards Birmingham was opened on the 2nd November 1959 by Ernest Marples the Minister of Transport. When it was first opened there was no speed limit. The first 72 miles was built in 19 months, employing a 5,000 labour force, at a cost of £17,000,000. One mile was constructed every 8 days. The motorway currently carries 88,000 vehicles per day compared to 13,000 when it was first opened. Traffic is heaviest between junctions 7 and 10, St Albans to Luton.*

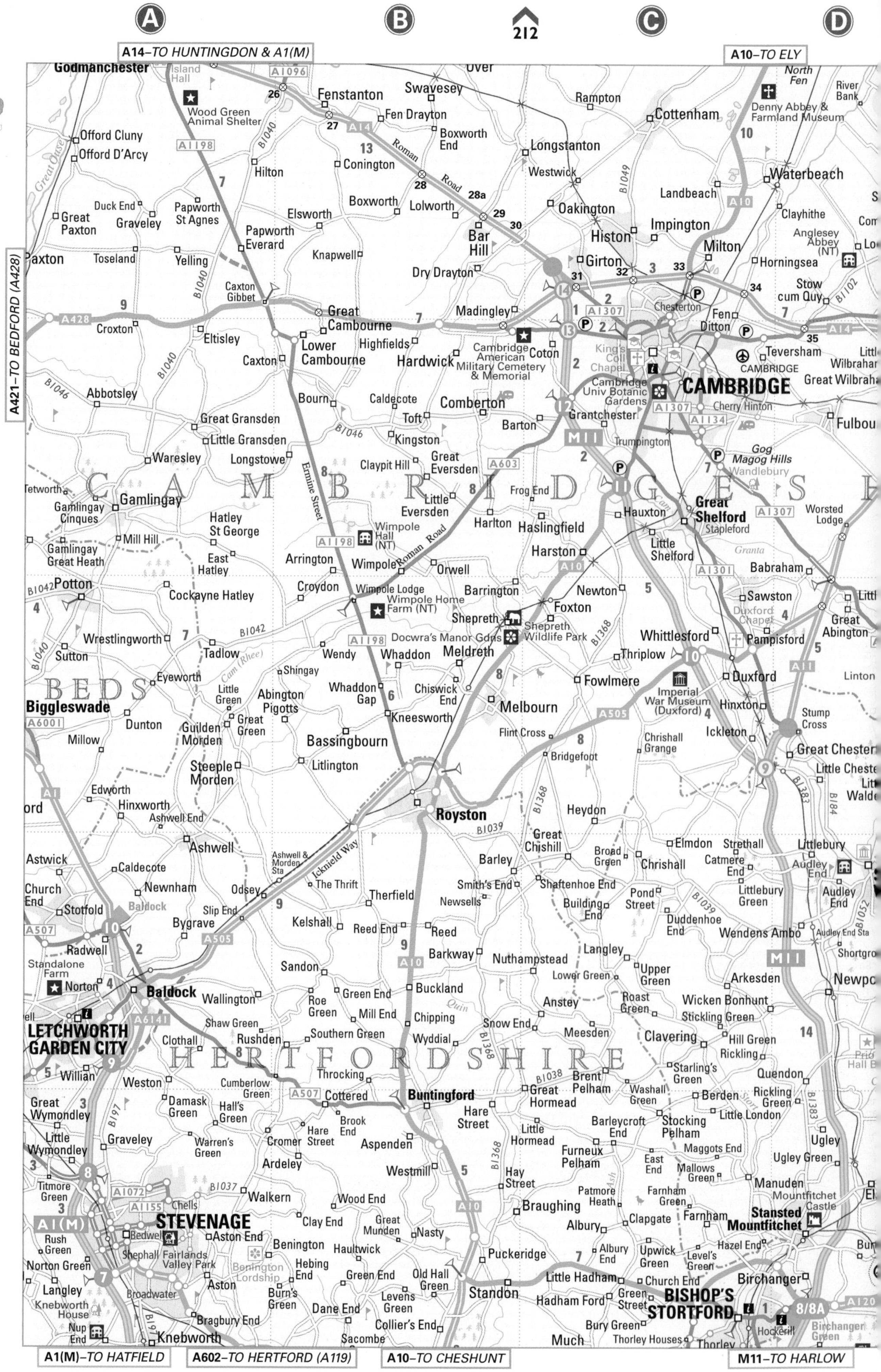

Letchworth Garden City: *This was the first Garden City to be built in Britain. Ebenezer Howard (1850–1928) was the driving force behind its development. He and others formed Garden City Ltd. in 1903 and issued shares to raise the capital needed. They purchased Letchworth Manor and the surrounding land and building work started in 1903.* ***Map ref. A4***

Newmarket: *Horse Racing started here with the first recorded race taking place in 1622. A horse belonging to Lord Salisbury beat one owned by the Marquess of Buckingham for a prize of £100.* ***Map ref. E1***

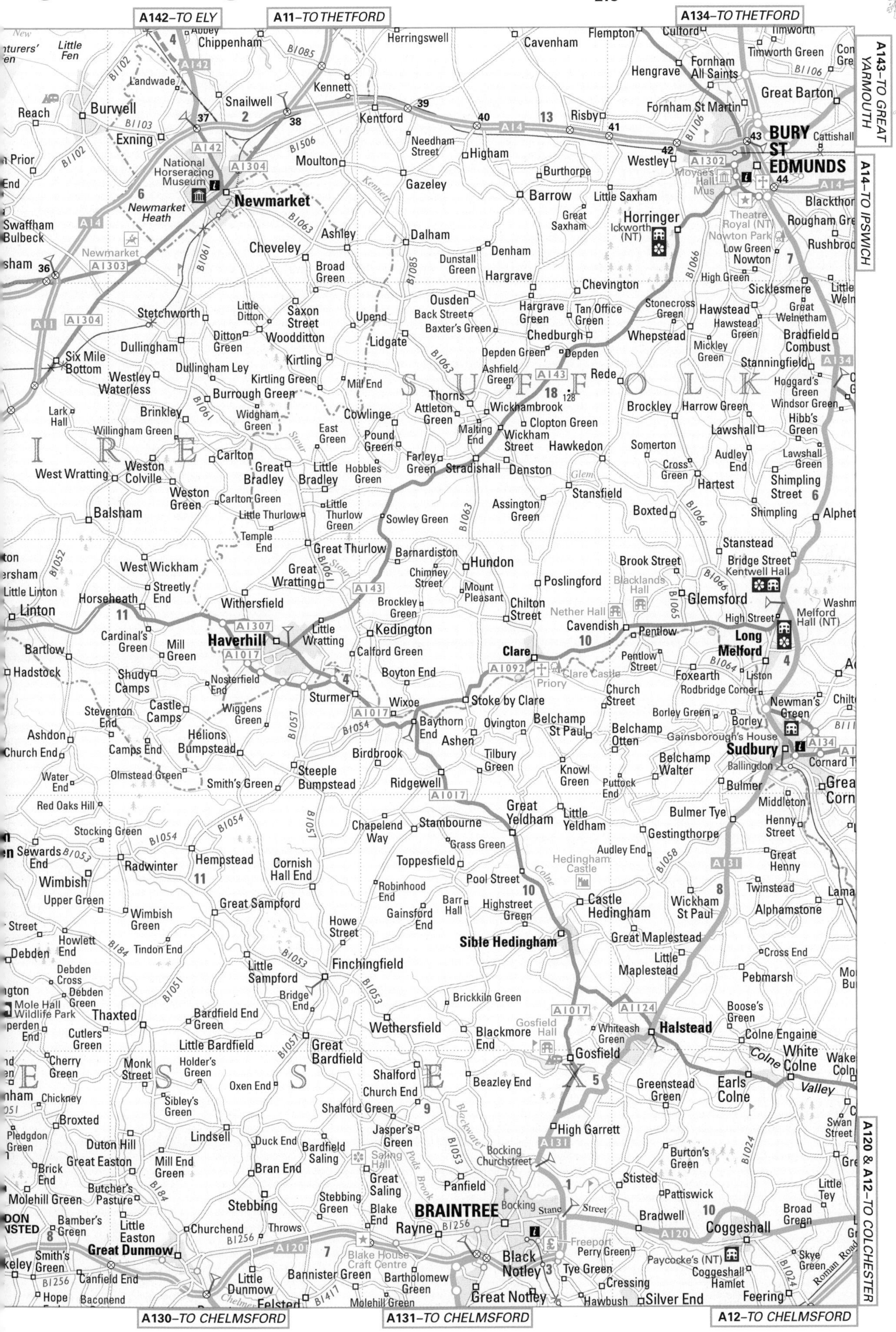

A142–TO ELY A11–TO THETFORD A134–TO THETFORD

A143–TO GREAT YARMOUTH

A14–TO IPSWICH

A120 & A12–TO COLCHESTER

1 2 202 3 4 5

4

5

New
Little
Fen
Chippenham
B1085
Herringswell
Cavenham
Flempton
Timworth
Timworth Green
Con
Gre
nturers'
Abbey
Landwade
B1102
Reach
Burwell
Exning
B1103
B1102
Prior
A142
Newmarket
4
A142
Snailwell
37
2
38
Kennett
Kentford
39
40
A14
13
Risby
41
Culford
Hengrave
Fornham
All Saints
B1106
Fornham St Martin
Great Barton
Fornham St Martin
42
43
BURY
ST
EDMUNDS
Cattishall
44
A1304
B1506
Moulton
Needham
Street
Higham
Burthorpe
Westley
A1304
B1063
A1303
36
B1061
National
Horseracing
Museum
6
Newmarket
Newmarket
Heath
A14
Gazeley
Barrow
Little Saxham
Great
Saxham
Horringer
Ickworth (NT)
Newton Park
Low Green
Nowton
Moyse's
Hall
Mus
Theatre
Royal (NT)
Blackthor
Rougham Gre
Rushbro
7
Swaffham
Bulbeck
sham
Ashley
Cheveley
Dalham
Denham
Chevington
Tan Office
Green
Hargrave
Green
High Green
Sicklesmere
Little
Weln
Stetchworth
Little
Ditton
Saxon
Street
Woodditton
Upend
Dunstall
Green
Hargrave
Back Street
Baxter's Green
Chedburgh
Depden
Depden Green
Whepstead
Stonecross
Green
Hawstead
Hawstead
Green
Mickley
Green
Great
Welnetham
Bradfield
Combust
A134
Dullingham
Ditton
Green
Kirtling
Lidgate
Ousden
Rede
Hoggard's
Green
Windsor Green
Hibb's
Green
Six Mile
Bottom
Westley
Waterless
Dullingham Ley
Kirtling Green
Mill End
SUFFOLK
18
128
Brockley
Harrow Green
Lawshall
Stanningfield
Stanningfield
Lark
Hall
Brinkley
Burrough Green
Widgham
Green
Cowlinge
Thorns
Attleton
Green
Wickhambrook
Malting
End
Clopton Green
Wickham
Street
Hawkedon
Somerton
Cross
Green
Audley
End
Lawshall
Green
Shimpling
Street
6
West Wratting
Weston
Colville
Carlton
Great
Bradley
Little
Bradley
East
Green
Pound
Green
Hobbles
Green
Farley
Green
Stradishall
Denston
Hartest
Weston
Green
Carlton Green
Little Thurlow
Temple
End
Little
Thurlow
Green
Sowley Green
Assington
Green
Stansfield
Boxted
Shimpling
Alphet
Balsham
West Wickham
Great
Wratting
Great Thurlow
Barnardiston
Hundon
Poslingford
Brook Street
Stanstead
Bridge Street
Kentwell Hall
Streetly
End
A143
Chimney
Street
Mount
Pleasant
Blacklands
Hall
B1066
Linton
Horseheath
11
Withersfield
A1307
Little
Wratting
Brockley
Green
Kedington
Chilton
Street
Cavendish
Nether Hall
Glemsford
High Street
Melford
Hall (NT)
Washm
Little Linton
ersham
B1052
Bartlow
Hadstock
Cardinal's
Green
Mill
Green
Haverhill
A1017
Calford Green
Boyton End
A1092
Clare
Clare Castle
Priory
10
Pentlow
Pentlow
Street
Foxearth
Rodbridge Corner
Liston
Long
Melford
B1064
4
Shudy
Camps
Nosterfield
End
Wiggens
Green
Sturmer
Wixoe
Stoke by Clare
Church
Street
Borley Green
Newman's
Green
Chilt
Steventon
End
Castle
Camps
Hélions
Bumpstead
A1017
Baythorn
End
Ovington
Ashen
Belchamp
St Paul
Belchamp
Otten
Gainsborough's House
Borley
Sudbury
A134
A1
Ashdon
Church End
Camps End
Olmstead Green
Smith's Green
Steeple
Bumpstead
Birdbrook
Tilbury
Green
Knowl
Green
Belchamp
Walter
Bulmer
Ballingdon
Cornard
Grea
Corn
Water
End
Red Oaks Hill
Ridgewell
A1017
Great
Yeldham
Little
Yeldham
Puttock
End
Bulmer Tye
Middleton
Henny
Street
Great
Henny
Stocking Green
B1054
Chapelend
Way
Stambourne
Grass Green
Toppesfield
Hedingham
Castle
Audley End
B1058
Twinstead
Alphamstone
Lama
Sewards
End
B1053
Radwinter
Hempstead
11
Cornish
Hall End
Pool Street
Colne
Castle
Hedingham
Wickham
St Paul
A131
Wimbish
Upper Green
Wimbish
Green
Great Sampford
Robinhood
End
Highstreet
Green
10
Castle
Hedingham
Great Maplestead
Cross End
Pebmarsh
Street
Howlett
End
Tindon End
Howe
Street
Barr
Hall
Gainsford
End
Sible Hedingham
Little
Maplestead
Boose's
Green
Mo
Bu
Debden
Debden
Cross
Mole Hall
Wildlife Park
Green
Debden
Thaxted
Little
Sampford
B1053
Finchingfield
Brickkiln Green
A1017
A1124
Halstead
Colne Engaine
White
Colne
White
Coln
erden
End
gton
Cutlers
Green
Cherry
Green
Monk
Street
Holder's
Green
B1057
Bridge
End
Little Bardfield
Great
Bardfield
Wethersfield
Blackmore
End
Gosfield
Hall
Whiteash
Green
Gosfield
Greenstead
Green
Earls
Colne
Valley
Molehill Green
Broxted
B1051
Sibley's
Green
Oxen End
Shalford
Church End
Shalford Green
Beazley End
9
High Garrett
A131
Stisted
Burton's
Green
Swan
Street
B1024
Grea
Pledgdon
Green
Duton Hill
Lindsell
Duck End
Bardfield
Saling
Jasper's
Green
B1053
Bocking
Churchstreet
A131
Pattiswick
Little
Tey
Brick
End
Great Easton
Mill End
Green
Bran End
Great
Saling
Saling
Hall
Panfield
Bradwell
Coggeshall
Broad
Green
Molehill Green
DON
STED
8
Bamber's
Green
Little
Easton
Stebbing
Stebbing
Green
Blake
End
BRAINTREE
Bocking
Stane
Street
1
Stisted
A120
Skye
Green
Roman Road
Keley
Green
Great Dunmow
B1256
Churchend
Throws
Rayne
B1256
A120
7
Bannister Green
Blake House
Craft Centre
Black
Notley
Perry Green
Freeport
Tye Green
Paycocke's (NT)
Coggeshall
Hamlet
Feering
Hope
Baconend
Canfield End
Little
Dunmow
Felsted
Chelmer
B1417
Bartholomew
Green
Great Notley
Black
Notley
3
Cressing
Hawbush
Silver End

A130–TO CHELMSFORD A131–TO CHELMSFORD A12–TO CHELMSFORD

Bury St Edmunds: *The Nutshell Pub here claims to be the smallest pub in Britain.* ***Map ref. G1***

Sudbury: *Thomas Gainsborough (1727–1788) the famous portrait painter was born here.* ***Map ref. G3***

187

Little Dunmow: *Lionel Lukin (1742–1834) the inventor of the lifeboat was born here.* ***Map ref. E5***

Borley: *Reputed to be the most haunted village in Britain. Lots of paranormal activity is associated with the old Rectory which was built in 1863, gutted by fire in 1939 and demolished in 1944.* ***Map ref. G3***

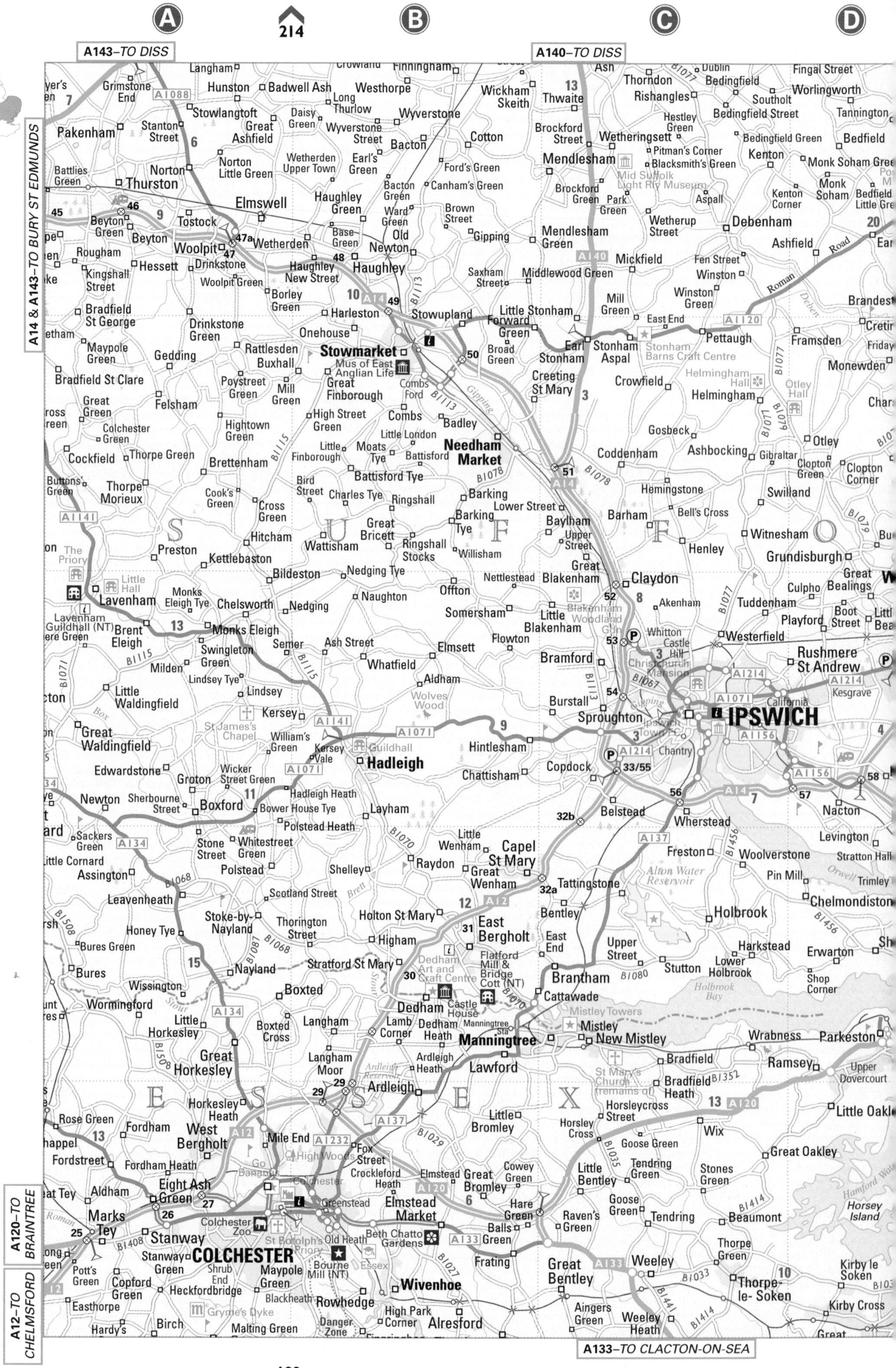

East Bergholt: *Birthplace of the famous painter John Constable (1176–1837) who went to school at nearby Dedham. So famous are his works that the surrounding area is known as Constable Country.* ***Map ref. B4***

Colchester: *Originally called Camulodunum and ruled by King Cunobelin, who was Old King Cole in the nursery rhyme. Colchester claims to be the oldest recorded town in Britain. It was a main centre of Roman Britain and its Norman Castle is the biggest in Europe.* ***Map ref. A5 Also on page 78***

Manningtree *claims to be England's smallest market town.* ***Map ref. C4***

1
2
3
4
5

Dunwich Heath: *Set within an Area of Outstanding Natural Beauty (AONB), this is a remnant of the original Sandlings Heaths. It is an important conservation area and very popular with birdwatchers as it is home to some rare species such as the Nightjar and Dartford Warbler.*
Map ref. F1 Also on page 78

189

Felixstowe: *This is the largest container port in the UK and one of the largest in Europe. Almost 50% of all British deep sea container trade now passes through Felixstowe. The port was first developed as 'The Felixstowe Railway and Pier Company', by Colonel George Tomline in 1875.*
Map ref. E4

217

A B C D

1

2

3

4

5

Aberystwyth: *Home of the National Library of Wales the University of Wales, Aberystwyth. The river Rheidol, which feeds into the old harbour is the steepest river in Britain and the Electric Cliff Railway, which climbs Constitution Hill, is the longest cliff railway in the country.* ***Map ref. B4***

192

Trannon: *The moor here is home to the Carno Wind Farm, which at the time of completion in 1996 was the largest in Europe. There are 56 turbines with a combined maximum generating capacity of 33.6MW.* ***Map ref. F3***

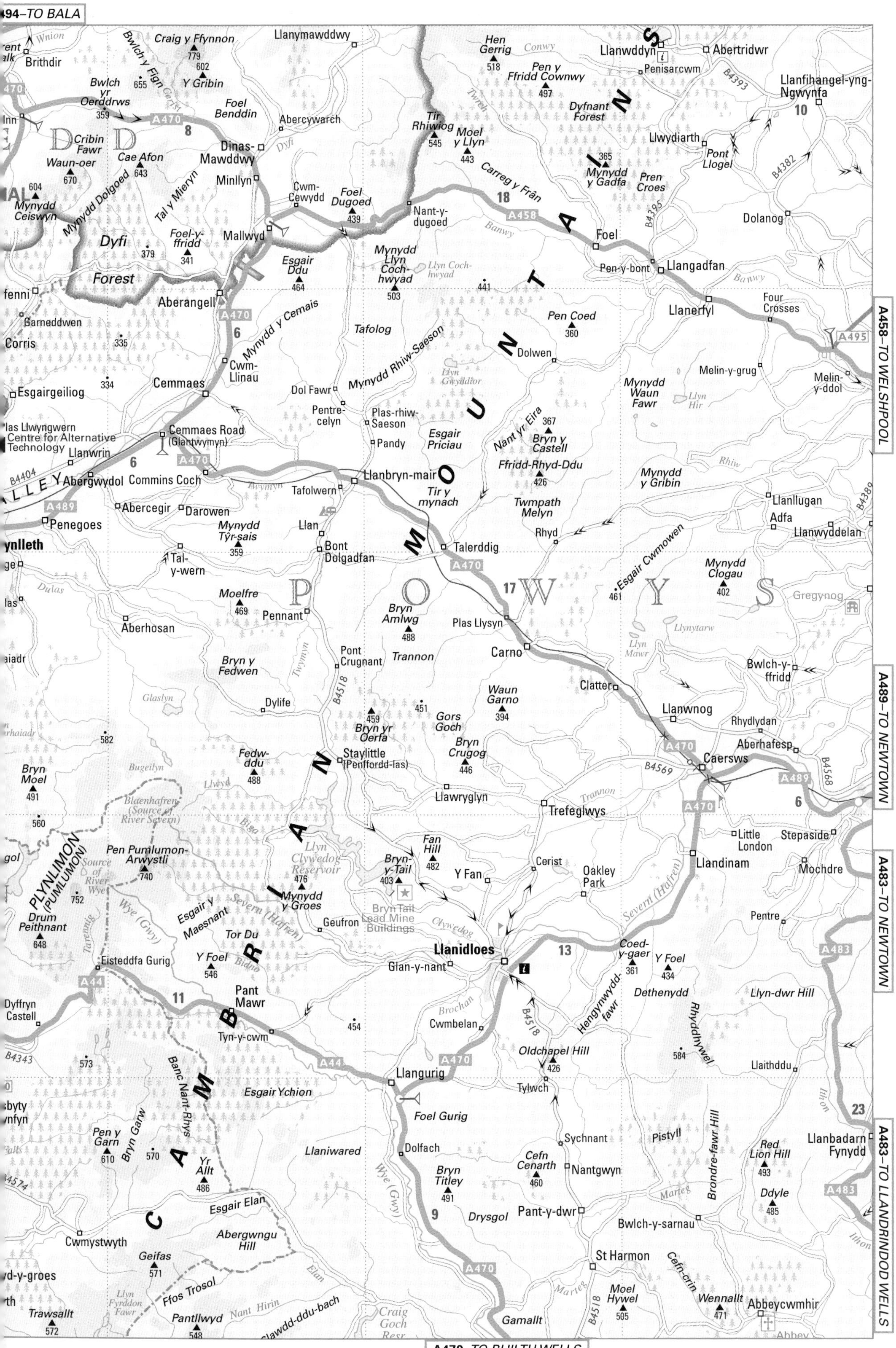

1
2
206
3
4
5

Llanfihangel yng Ngwynfa: *Anne Griffiths, the famous Welsh Methodist hymn writer was born here in 1776. Anne wrote 70 hymns in her short life. She died, aged 29 on the 12th August 1805 and is buried in the village.* ***Map ref. G1***

193

Llyn Clywedog: *The Dam, at the southern end of Llyn Clywedog Reservoir is the highest dam in Britain. It was constructed 1965–67 to regulate the flow of water into the River Severn. The dam is 236 feet (72m) high, 750 feet (229m) long and holds back 11,000,000 gallons (50,000 cubic metres) of water. The lake has a surface area of 615 acres (249ha), is 216 feet (66m) deep and 6 miles (9.5km) long.* ***Map ref. F4***

219
220
205
194

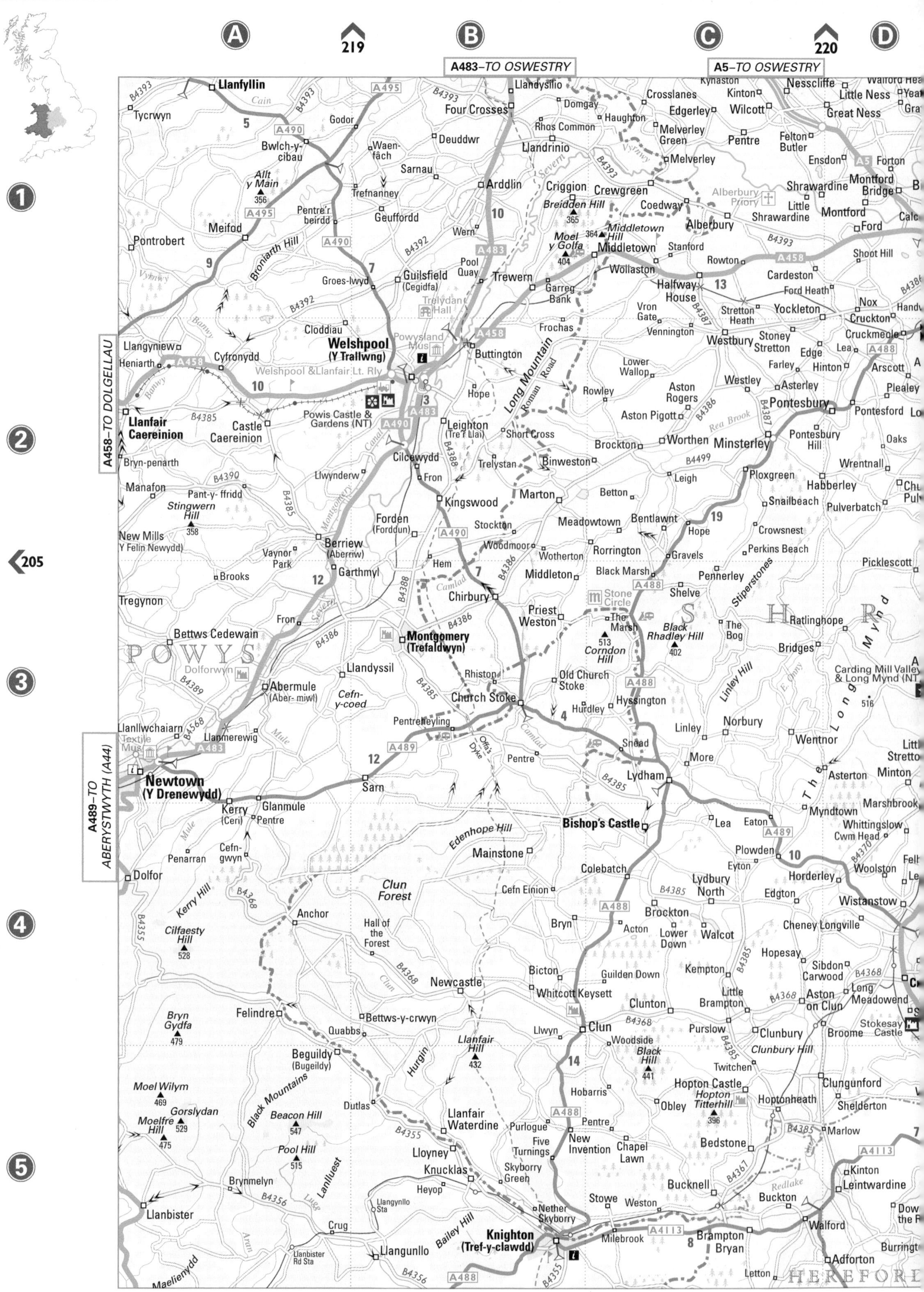

Welshpool: *The Welshpool and Llanfair Light Railway starts from here. The railway was opened in 1903 with an unusual gauge of 2 feet 6 inches to allow it to negotiate the tight curves and steep gradients. It officially closed in 1956 but was re-opened by a group of enthusiasts in 1963. It is remarkable for the miscellany of rolling stock which they have sourced from different countries around the world. These include a Taiwan Sugar Corporation Locomotive, Romanian ballast hopper wagons and other locomotives that have seen service in Antigua, Sierra Leone, Austria and Finland.* ***Map ref. B2***

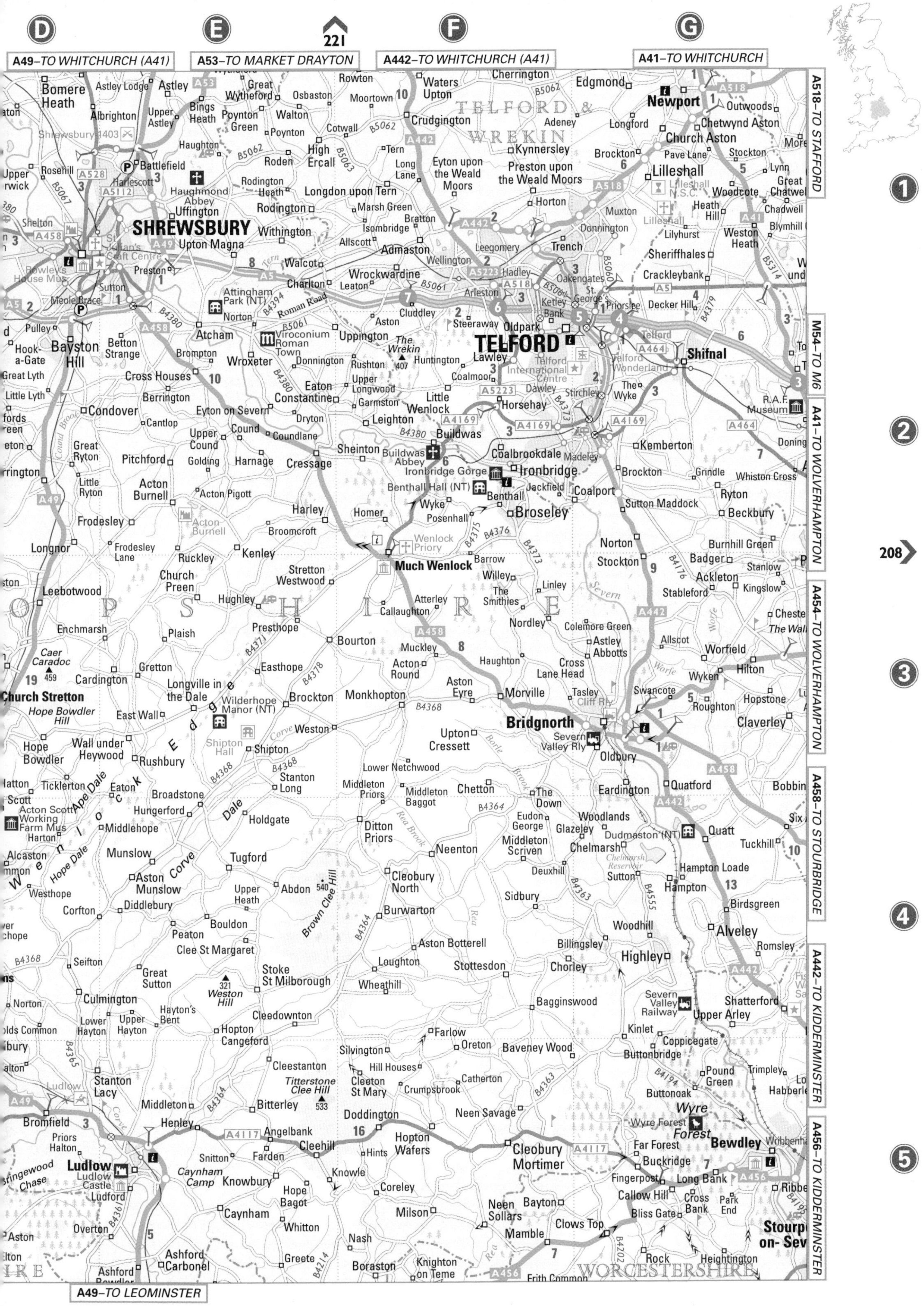

195

Much Wenlock: *Here in 1850 local doctor William Penny Brookes started the Wenlock Olympian Games, which inspired the modern revival of the Olympic Games. The games are still held annually.* ***Map ref. F2***

Dawley: *Captain Matthew Webb the first person to swim the English Channel was born here on the 19th January 1848. Webb swam from Dover to Cap Gris Nez on the 24/25th August 1875 in 21 hours 45 minutes. In total he swam 38 miles (61km) to cover the 20 mile (32km) straight line distance. Webb died on the 24th July 1883 in an attempt to swim across the bottom of Niagara Falls.* ***Map ref. F2***

222

207

Barwell: *The largest meteorite ever found in Britain, weighing almost 7 stone (44Kg), landed here on the 24th December 1965.* ***Map ref. G3***

196

Coventry: *Because of its concentration of vehicle manufacturing, during World War II, Coventry was a major target for German air raids. On the night of the 14th November 1940 500 German bombers dropped 500 tons of explosives and 900 incendiary bombs on the city in less than 10 hours. The city, including the Cathedral was almost totally destroyed and many people were killed. In 1948 during major rebuilding work, Coventry opened Europe's first ever traffic-free shopping precinct and in 1962 a new Cathedral was consecrated alongside the ruins of the old one.* ***Map ref. F5 Also on page 64***

D E 223 F G

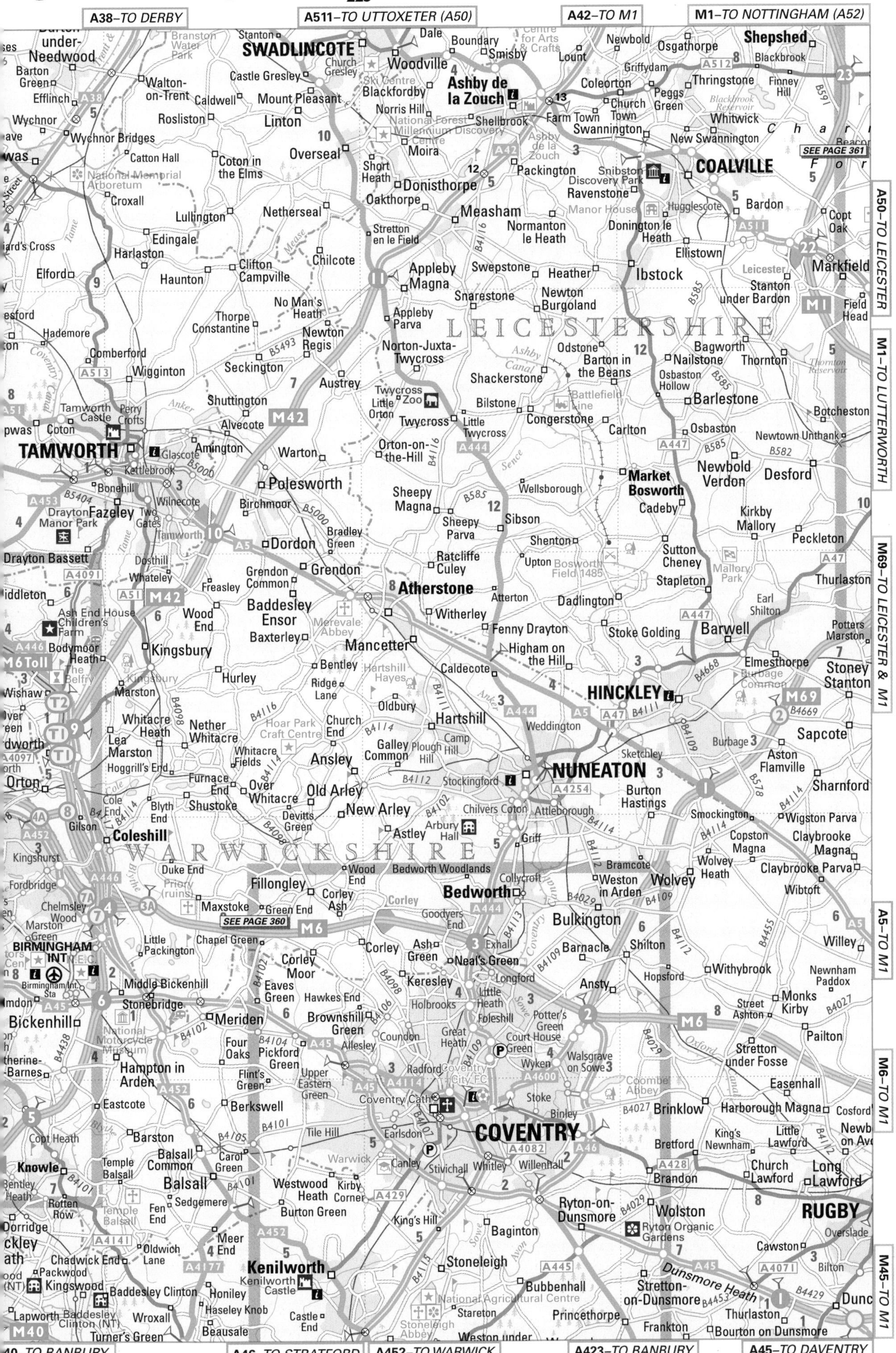

210

197

Earlsdon: *Sir Frank Whittle, inventor of the jet engine was born here in 1907. The first jet aircraft to fly in Britain, a Gloster E28/39, made its maiden flight on the 15th May 1941 piloted by Gerry Sayer the Gloster test pilot. Frank Whittle moved to the USA in 1976 and died at his home in Maryland on the 8th August 1996.* ***Map ref. F5***

Fenny Drayton: *The geographical centre of England is at Lindley Hall Farm, just 1.5km east of Fenny Drayton, OS Grid Reference SP 36373.66 96143.05. Traditionally however, the village of Meriden near Coventry (square E4) has always been considered the centre and an historic monument there marks the spot. The point furthest from the sea in the whole of Britain is actually near Coton in the Elms (square E1).* ***Map ref. F3***

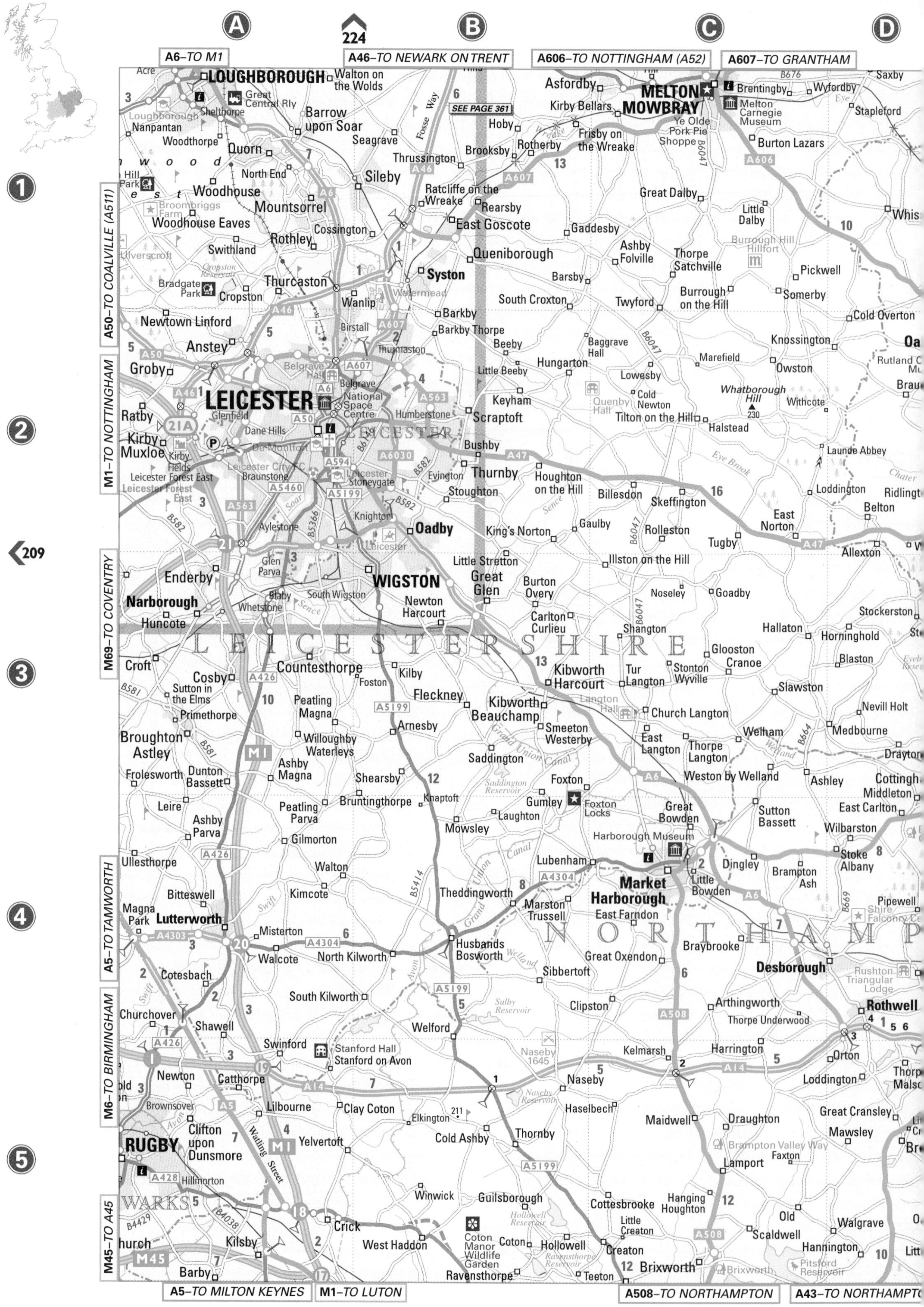

Rutland Water: *One of the largest man-made reservoirs in Europe covering 3,100 acre (1,225ha). Completed in 1977 to supply 65 million gallons (300,000 cubic metres) of water per day to cities in the east Midlands.* ***Map ref. D2***

198

Rugby: *The sport of Rugby originated at Rugby School in the 19th Century. It is reputed that during a football game in 1823, William Webb Ellis picked up the ball and ran with it. His name lives on through the Webb Ellis Trophy, that is presented to the winners of the Rugby World Cup.* ***Map ref. A5***

Essendine: *On 3rd July 1938, a train hauled by Class A4 locomotive 'Mallard' here achieved the world rail record speed for steam traction of 126 mph (201km/h).* ***Map ref. F1***

212

199

Stamford: *The film of George Eliot's classic novel Middlemarch, released in 1994, was made on location around Stamford.* ***Map ref. F2***

Seaton and Harringworth: *The largest brick-built railway viaduct in Britain crosses the River Welland between these two villages. Built in 1875, of 20 million bricks, it stands 69 feet (21m) high, is 3,750 feet (1,143m) long and has 82 arches. The viaduct is no longer used by mainline passenger trains.* ***Map ref. E3***

226

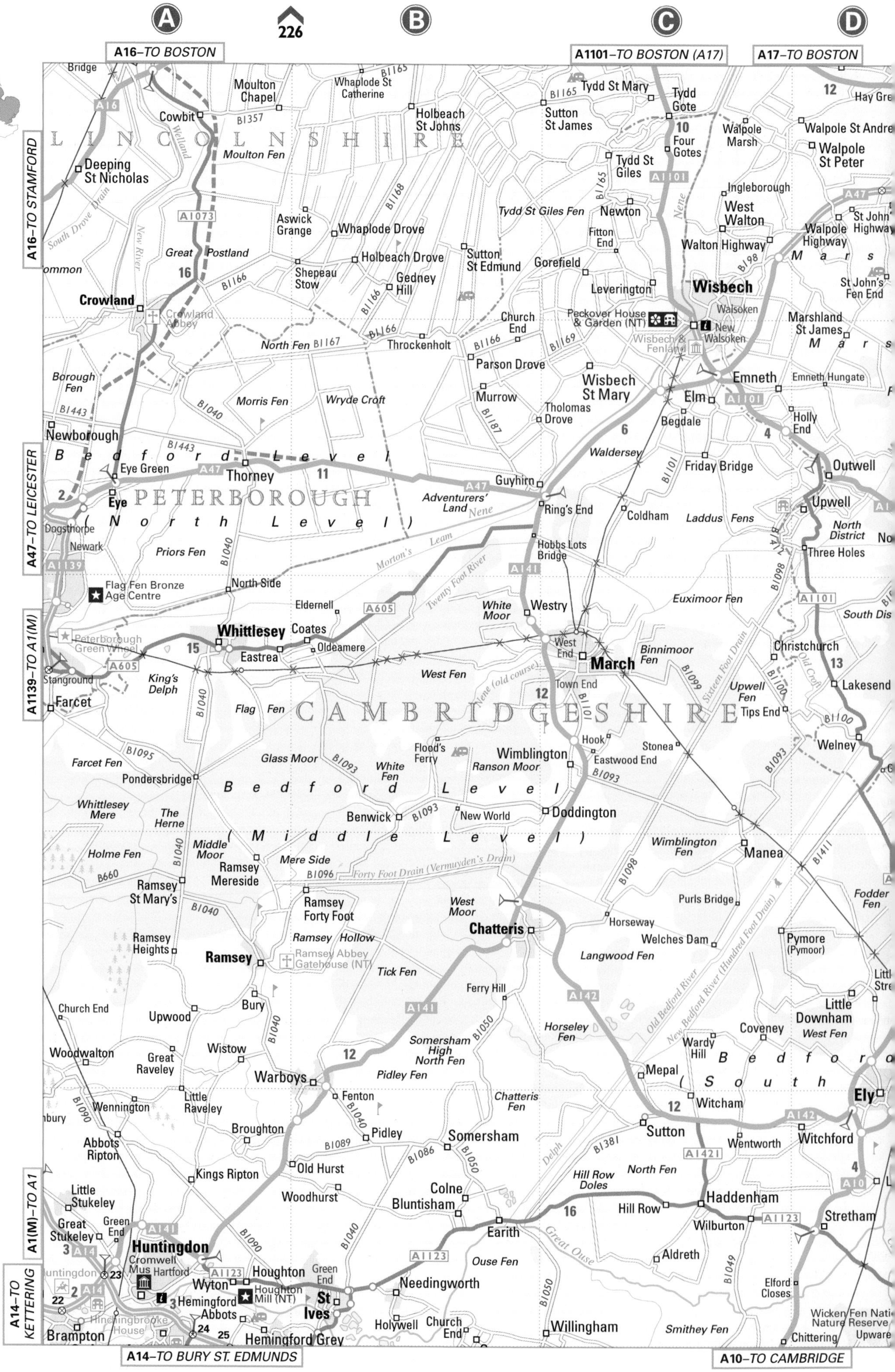

Holme Fen *is the lowest land area of Britain. It is 9 feet (2.75m) below sea level.* ***Map ref. A4***

200

Huntingdon: *Oliver Cromwell was born here on the 25th April 1599. Despite modest beginnings, Cromwell became Lord Protector when Great Britain became a Commonwealth following the execution of Charles I in 1649. In 1657 he was offered the crown of England but refused it. He died on the 3rd September 1658 and was granted a state funeral. With the restoration of Charles II to the throne in 1660 Cromwell was discredited and on the 30th January 1661 his body was exhumed and he was symbolically executed and reburied at Tyburn.* ***Map ref. A5*** ***See page 78 for Cromwell Museum***

D E F 227 G

A149–TO HUNSTANTON

A1065–TO FAKENHAM

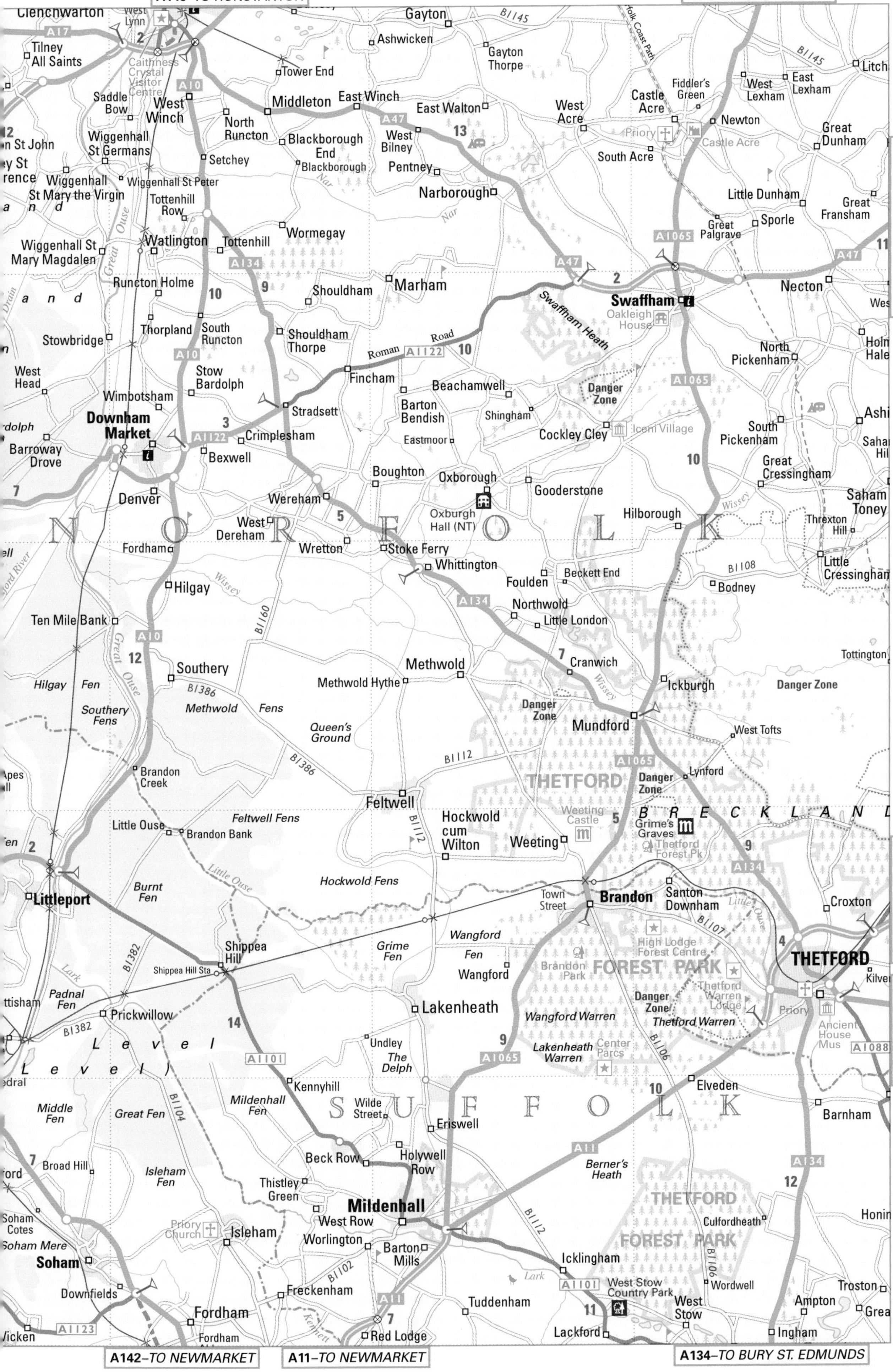

1 2 214 3 4 5

A142–TO NEWMARKET

A11–TO NEWMARKET

A134–TO BURY ST. EDMUNDS

201

Mildenhall : *RAF Mildenhall officially opened in 1934 and just days later became the starting point for what is still known as the 'greatest air race in the world'. 20 aircraft from 7 different countries competed in the Royal Aero Club race to Melbourne, Australia. The winners, Charles Scott and Thomas Black, flying a De Havilland DH88 Comet, completed the flight in 2 days 23 hours.* ***Map ref. F5***

228

A B C D

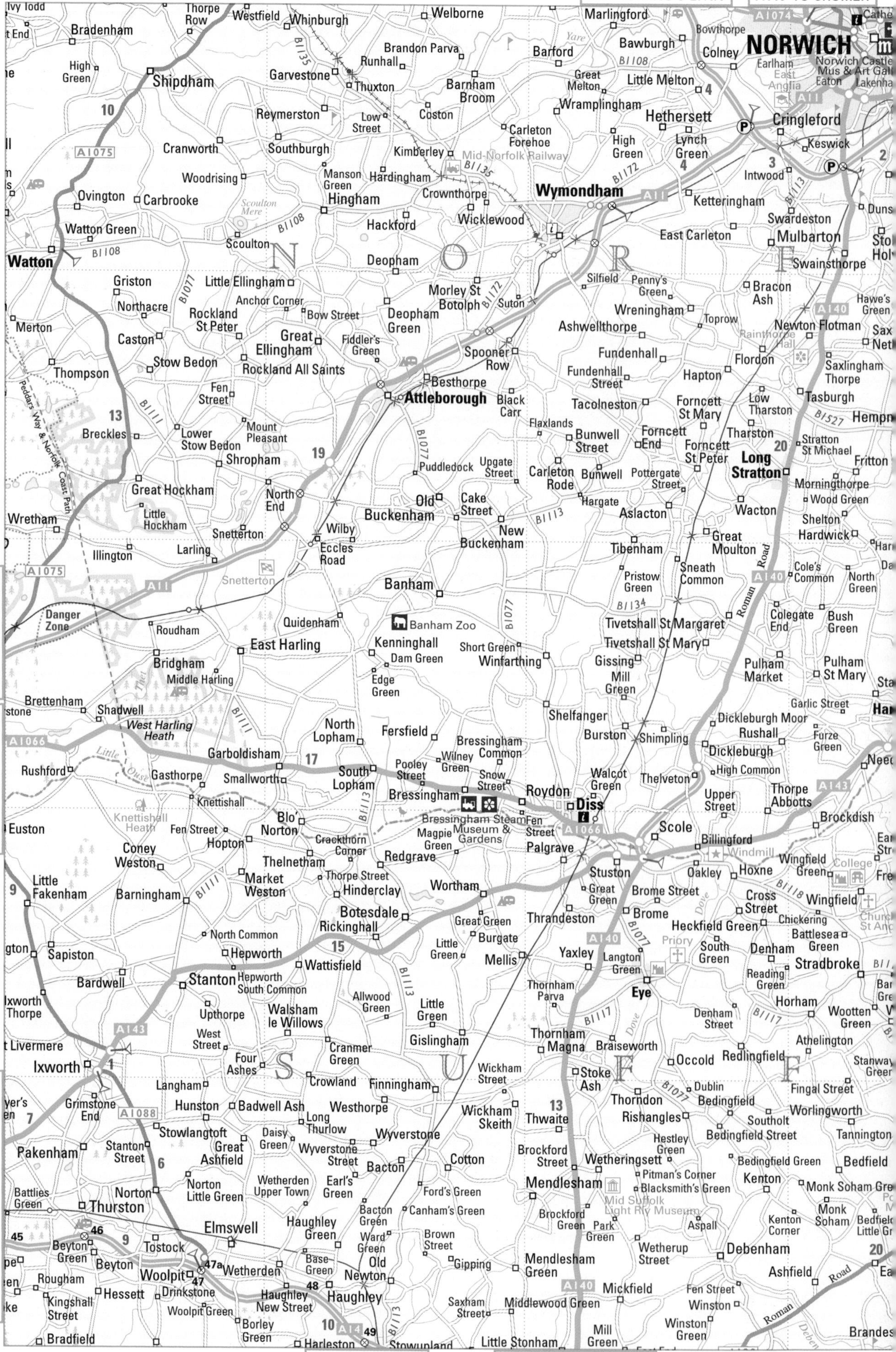

1 2 3 4 5

213

202

Norwich: *Elizabeth Fry, nee Gurney, was born here in 1780. She campaigned relentlessly for better conditions for prisoners, particularly women prisoners. In 1840 she founded the Institute of Nursing Sisters to train nurses to care for poor people in their own homes. Elizabeth Fry died in 1845.* ***Map ref. D1***

D E 229 F G

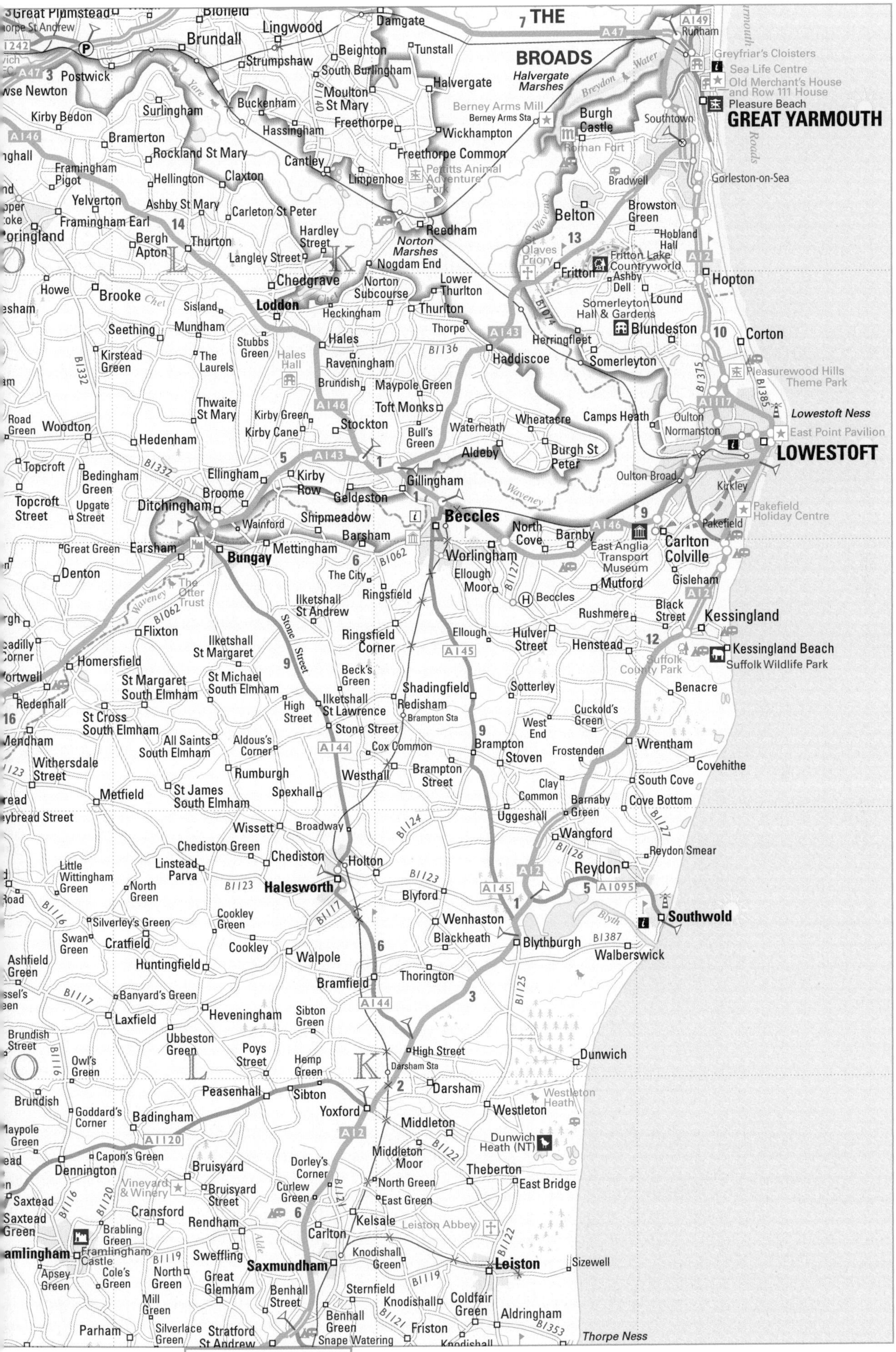

1
2
3
4
5

Lowestoft Ness: *This is the most easterly point in Britain.* ***Map ref. G2***

203

Sizewell: *Location of the Nuclear Power Station where, in August 2003, local residents were given anti-radiation pills aimed at reducing the risk of cancer in the thyroid.* ***Map ref. F5***

A B 230 C D

1 2 3 4 5

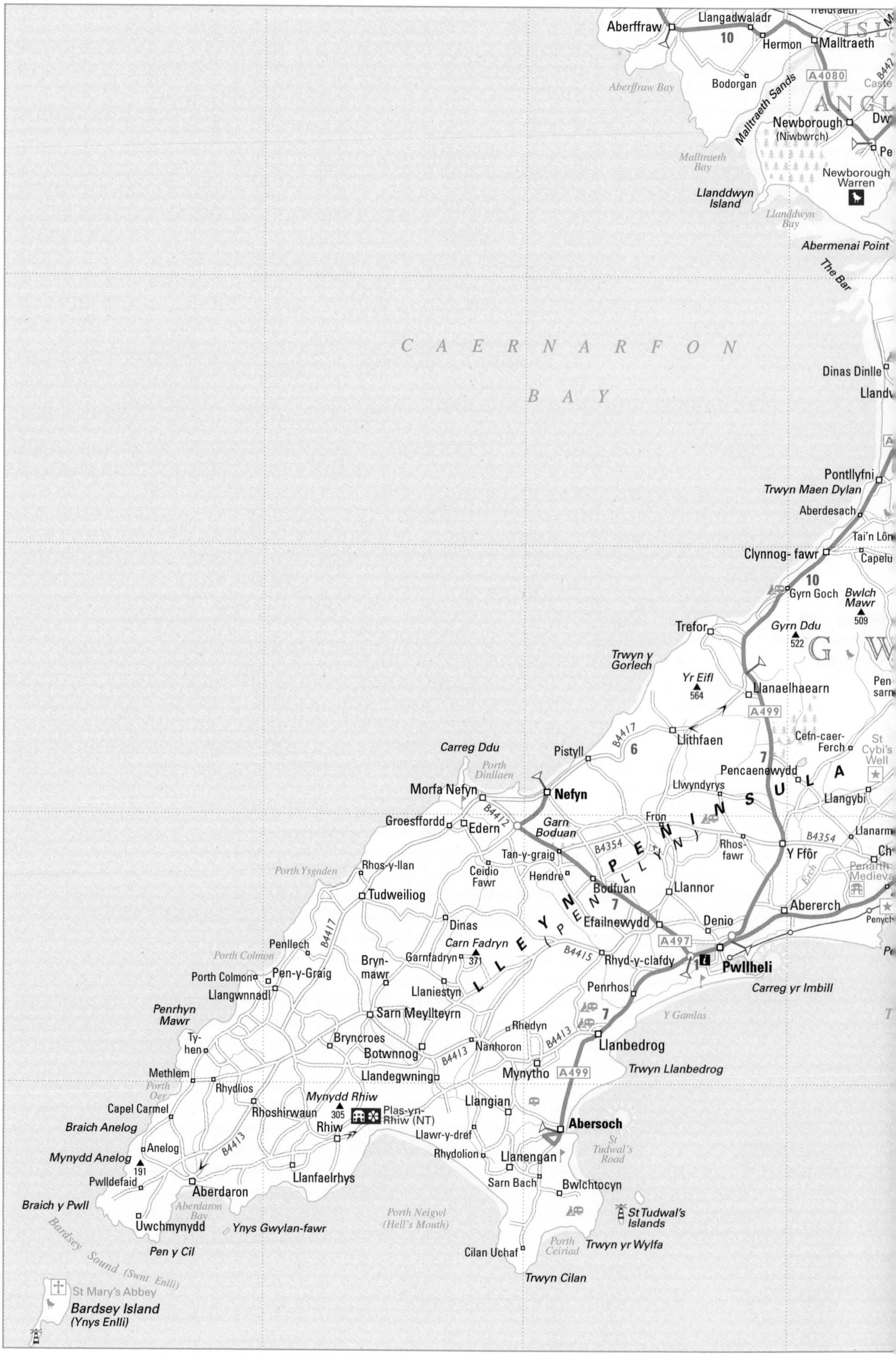

Bardsey Island (Ynys Enlli): *A place of pilgrimage and centre of the Celtic church from the 6th century where according to legend 20,000 saints are buried. Particularly noted for its wildlife, it is home to a large breeding colony of up to 16,000 Manx Shearwater.* ***Map ref. A5***

Llanystumdwy: *Although born in Manchester where his father was a schoolteacher, David Lloyd George was brought up here in Llanystumdwy. He served as Prime Minister from 1916–22 and has been credited with the introduction of the Welfare State.* ***Map ref. D4***

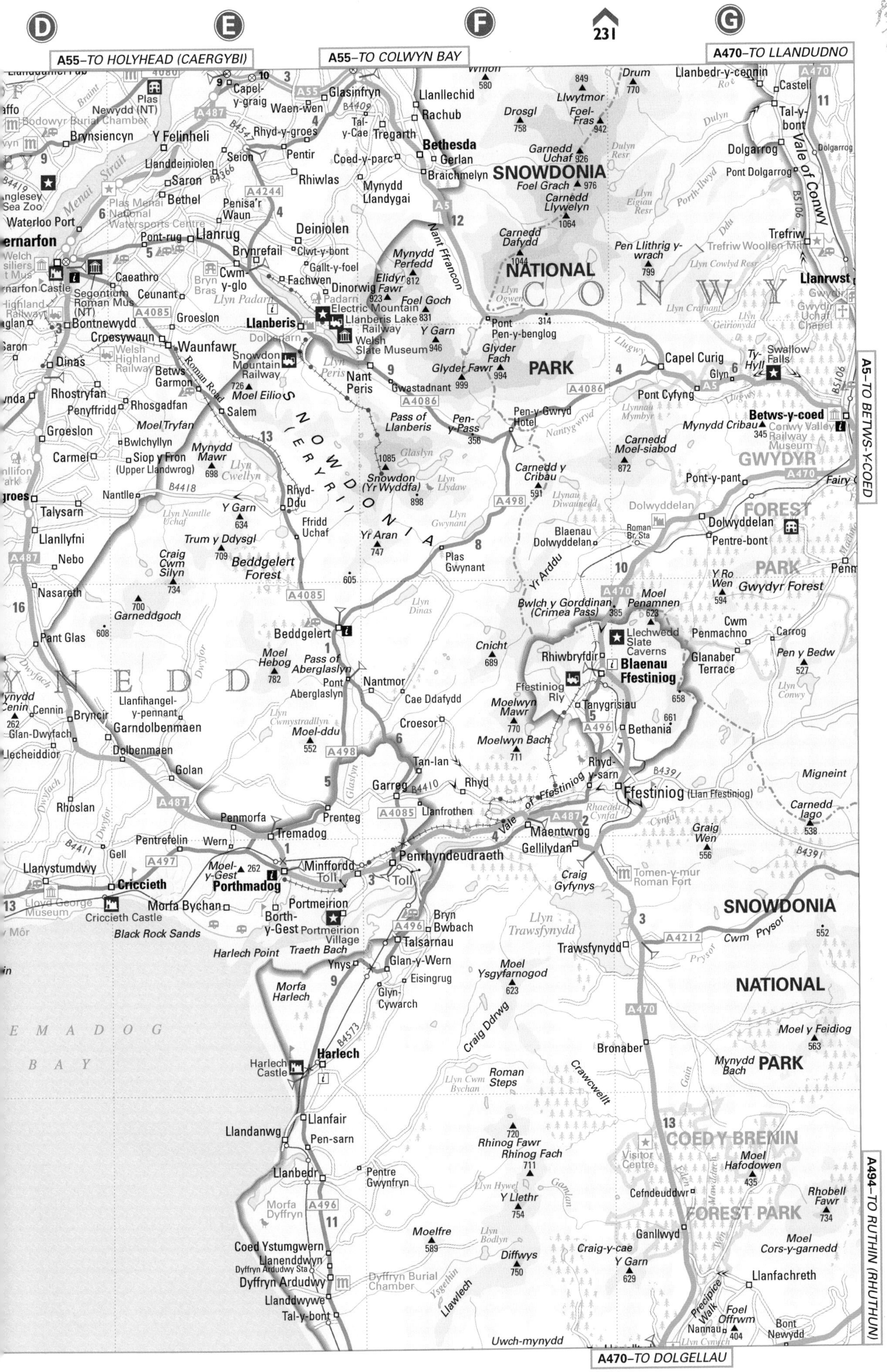

Snowdon: *At 3,560 feet (1085 metres) Snowdon is the highest mountain in England and Wales. It is possible to ascend the north-western side of Snowdon on the Snowdon Mountain Railway. This passenger railway opened on the 6th April 1896 but an accident on the first day led to its closure for the next year. The service reopened in April 1897 and has operated safely ever since.*
Map ref. F2 ***Also on page 14***

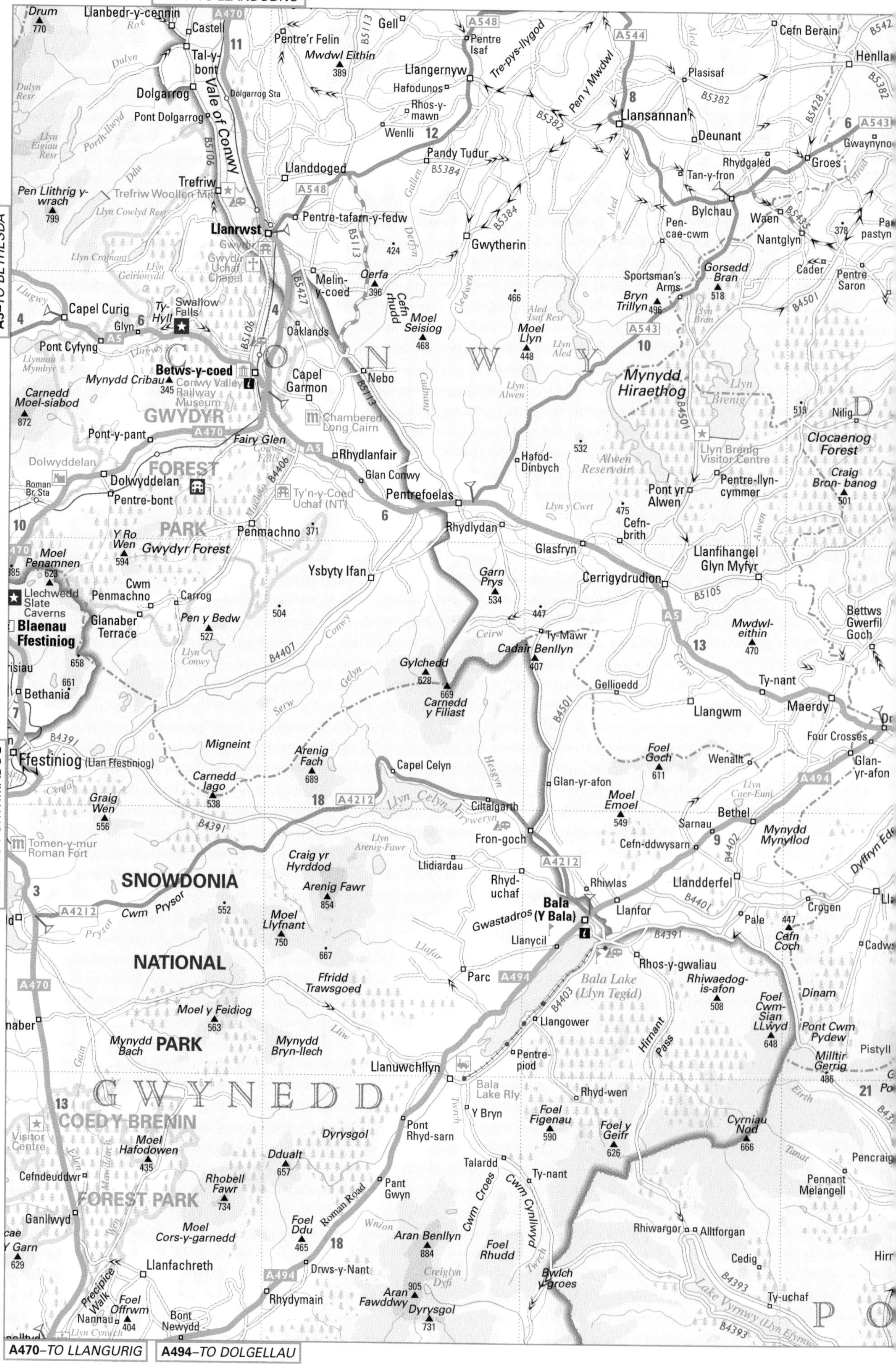

231

217

205

Bala: *A centre for watersports near to both Bala Lake (Llyn Tegid), the largest natural lake in Wales, and the National White Water Centre. The Bala Lake Railway runs along the south-eastern shoreline of the lake.* ***Map ref. C4***

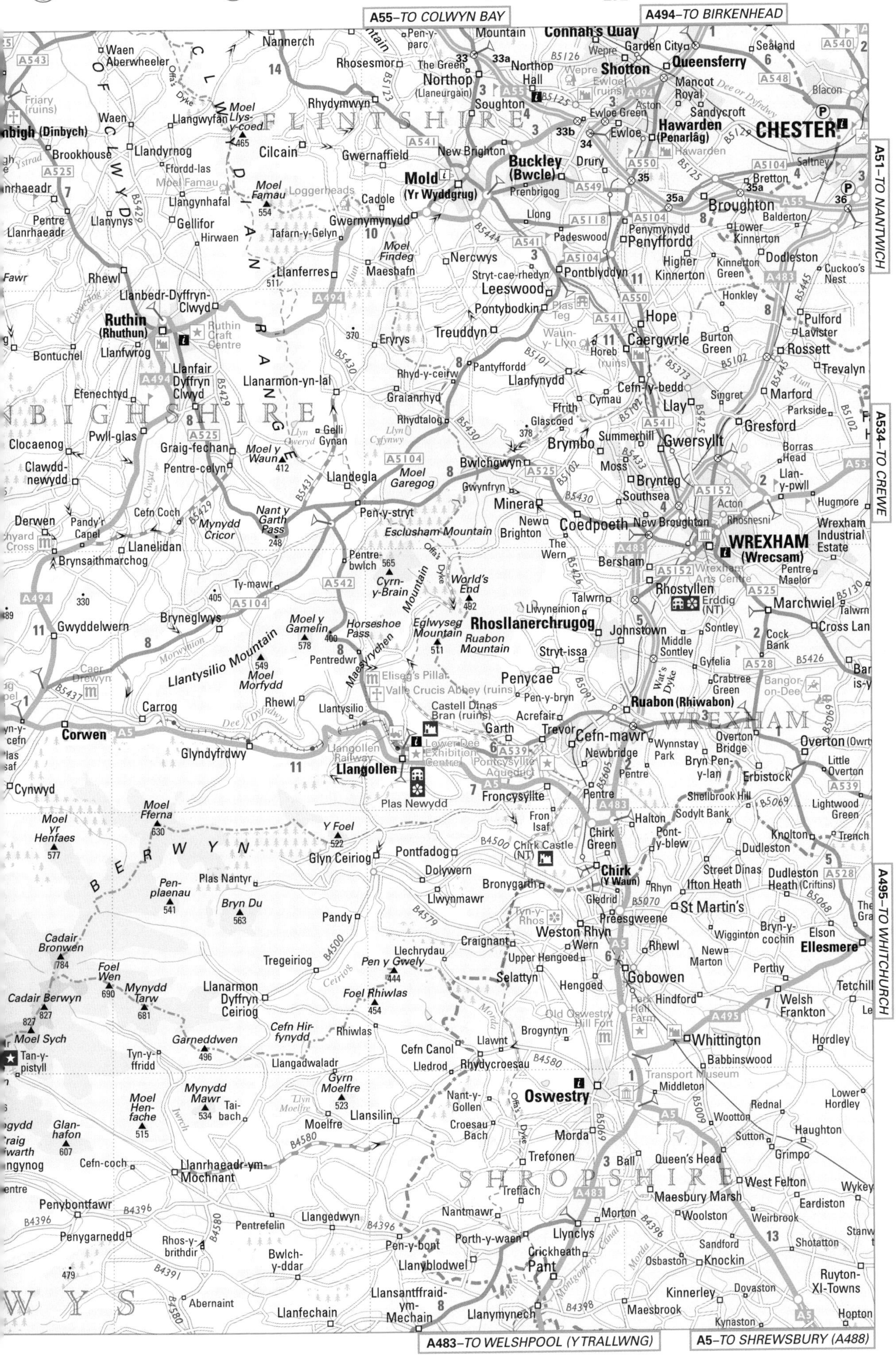

220
206

Llangollen: *Home every summer to the Eisteddfod Gerddorol Rygwladol Llangollen (International Musical Eisteddfod) a colourful festival of music, costume and dance famous the world over. The 14th century bridge here is one of the "Seven Wonders of Wales".* ***Map ref. F3***

233

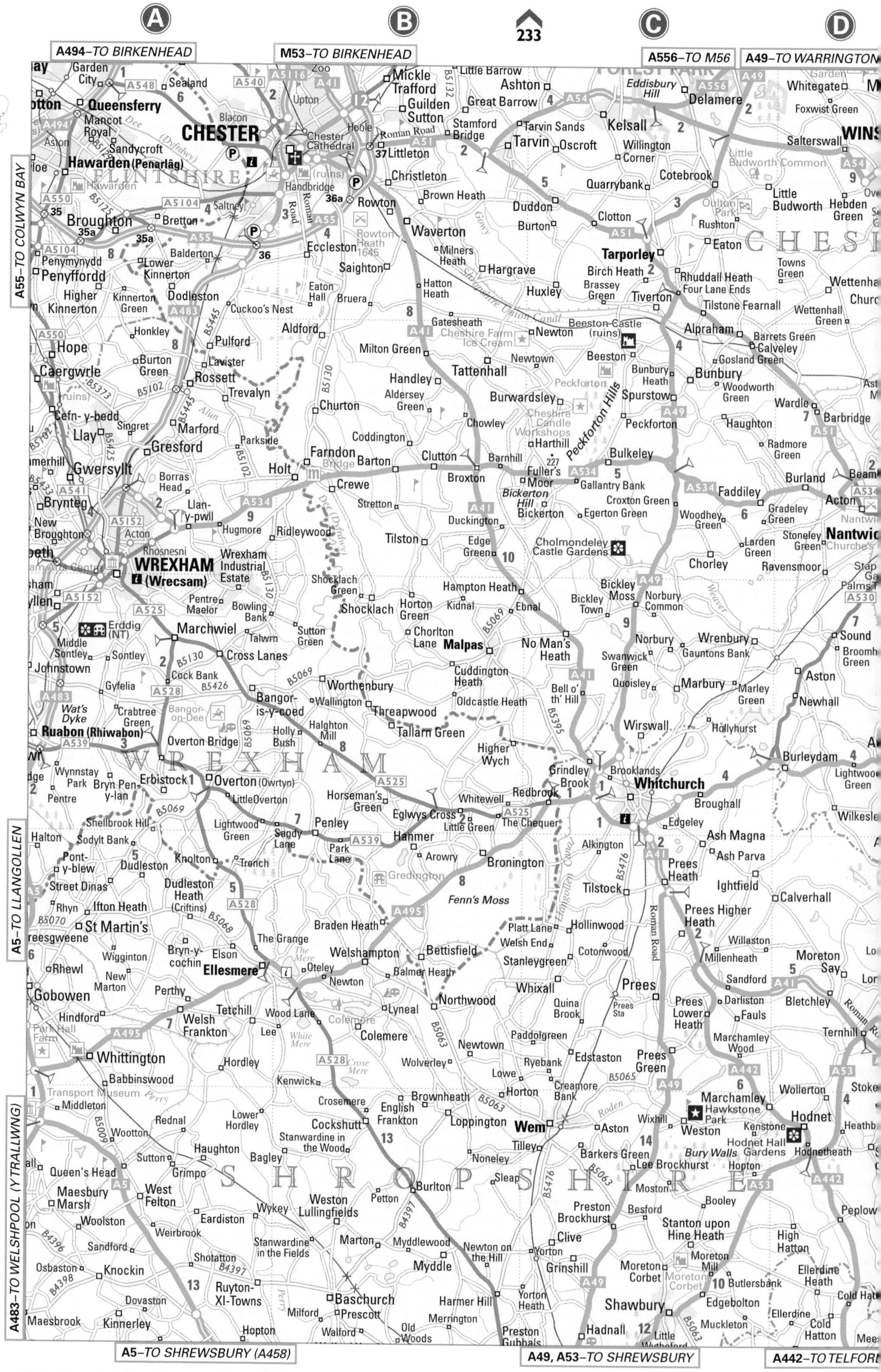

219

Wem: *Home of the Sweet Pea, created by Henry Eckford and now famous throughout the world. Each July there is a Sweet Pea Festival in the town.* ***Map ref. C5***

206

Ruyton XI Towns: *A village created from eleven small hamlets under a charter of 1310. Believed to be the only village in Britain with Roman Numerals in its name.* ***Map ref. A5***

1
2
222
3
4
5

207

Stoke-on-Trent: *The city of Stoke-on-Trent is unique in that it is made up of six separate towns; Tunstall, Burslem, Hanley, Stoke, Fenton and Longton. Together they are affectionately known as 'The Potteries' and are the home of Britain's ceramics industry. Some of the world's leading pottery manufacturers such as Wedgwood, Royal Doulton and Spode are based here.* ***Map ref. F3***

235

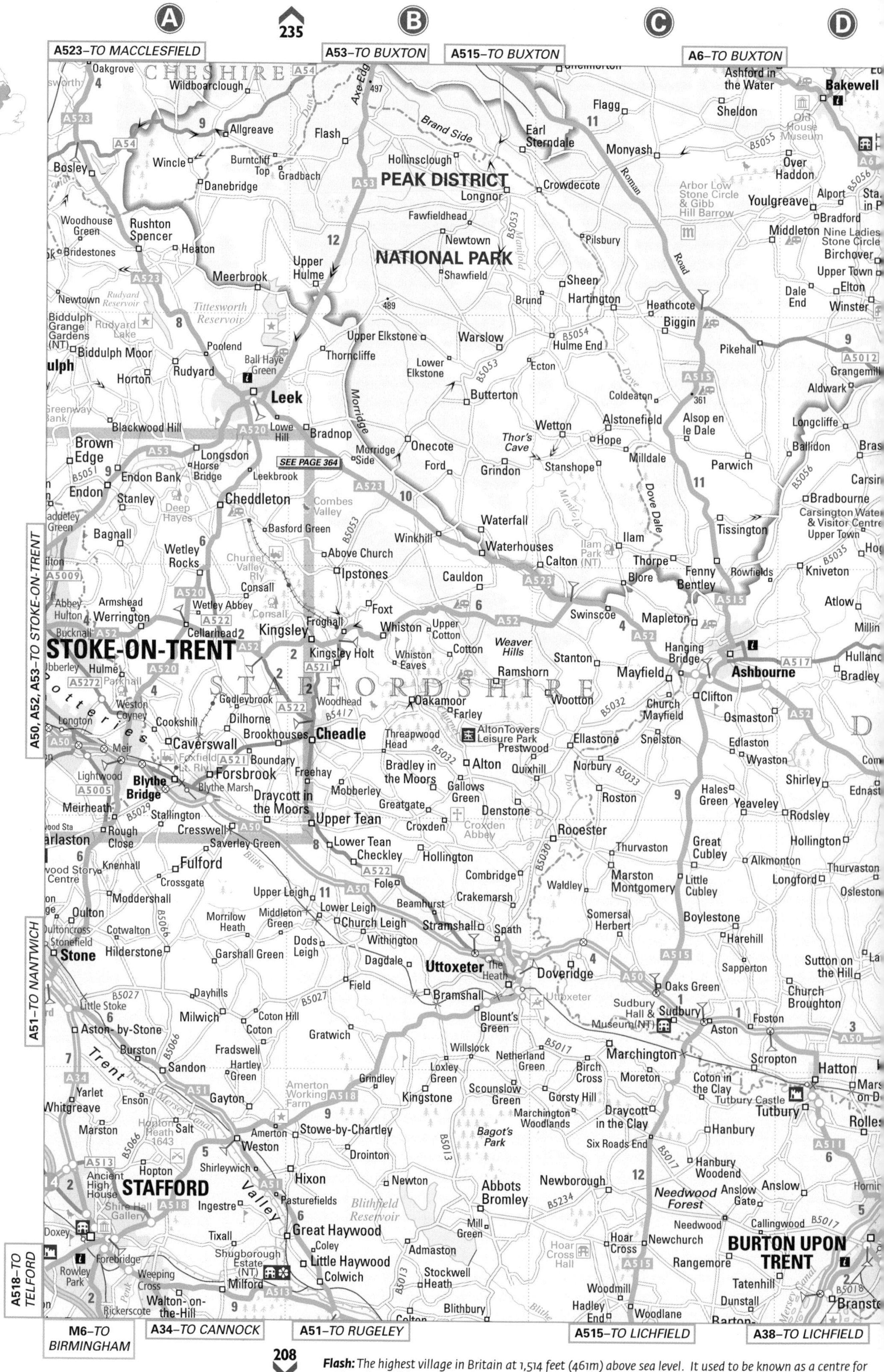

221

208

Flash: *The highest village in Britain at 1,514 feet (461m) above sea level. It used to be known as a centre for outlawed activities, such as the production of counterfeit money, which became known as 'flash' because of its origin. Its position near the junction of three counties helped the locals to evade police forces by moving out of their jurisdiction into the next county.* ***Map ref. B1***

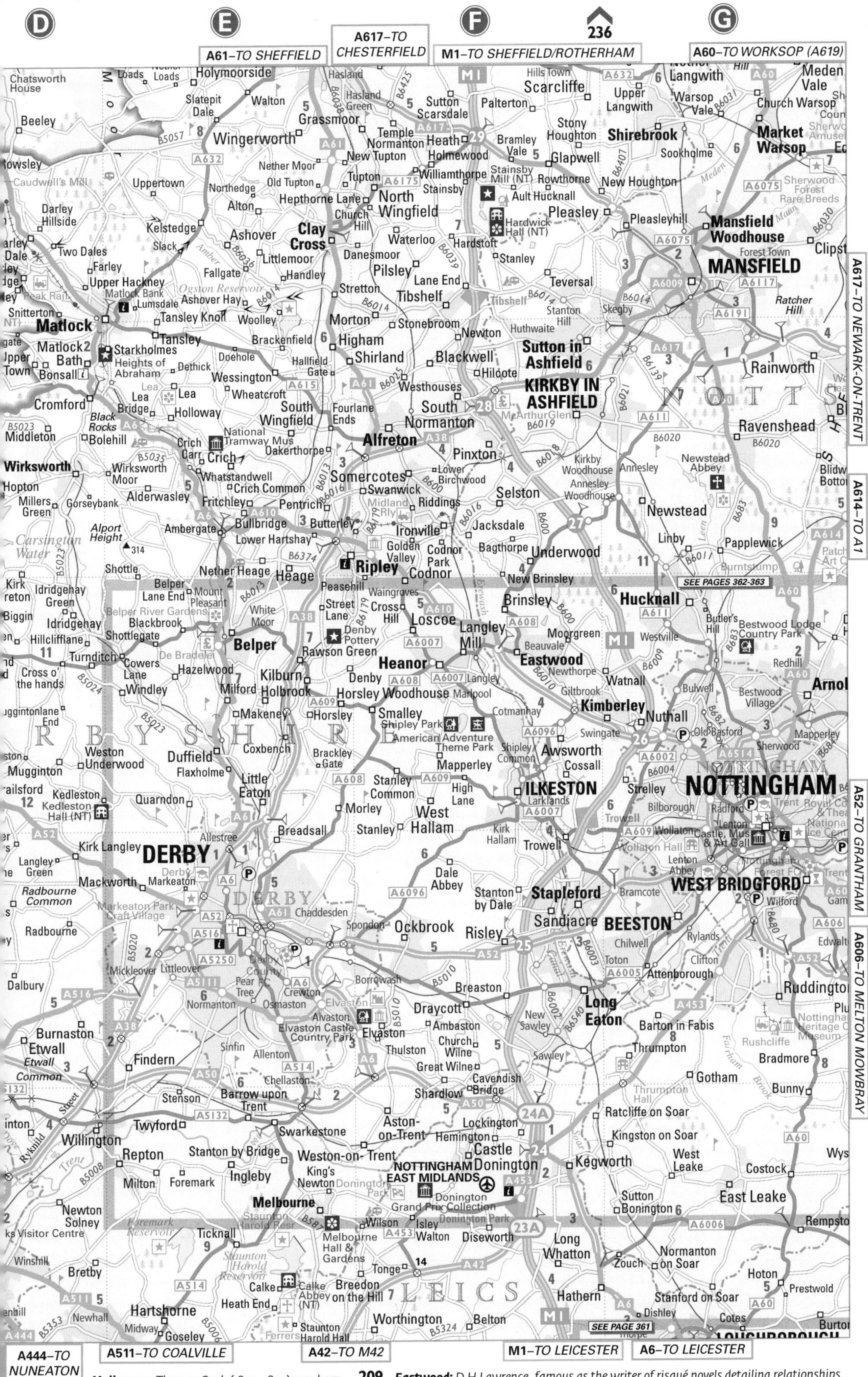

209

Melbourne: *Thomas Cook (1820–1892) was born here. Cook pioneered packaged holiday travel through the rail excursions he organised in 1841.* ***Map ref. E5***

Eastwood: *D H Lawrence, famous as the writer of risqué novels detailing relationships between men and women, was born here on the 11th September 1885. Lawrence left England in 1918 and settled in Italy. He eventually moved to France where he died on the 2nd March 1930. He is buried at Venice overlooking the Adriatic.* ***Map ref. F3***

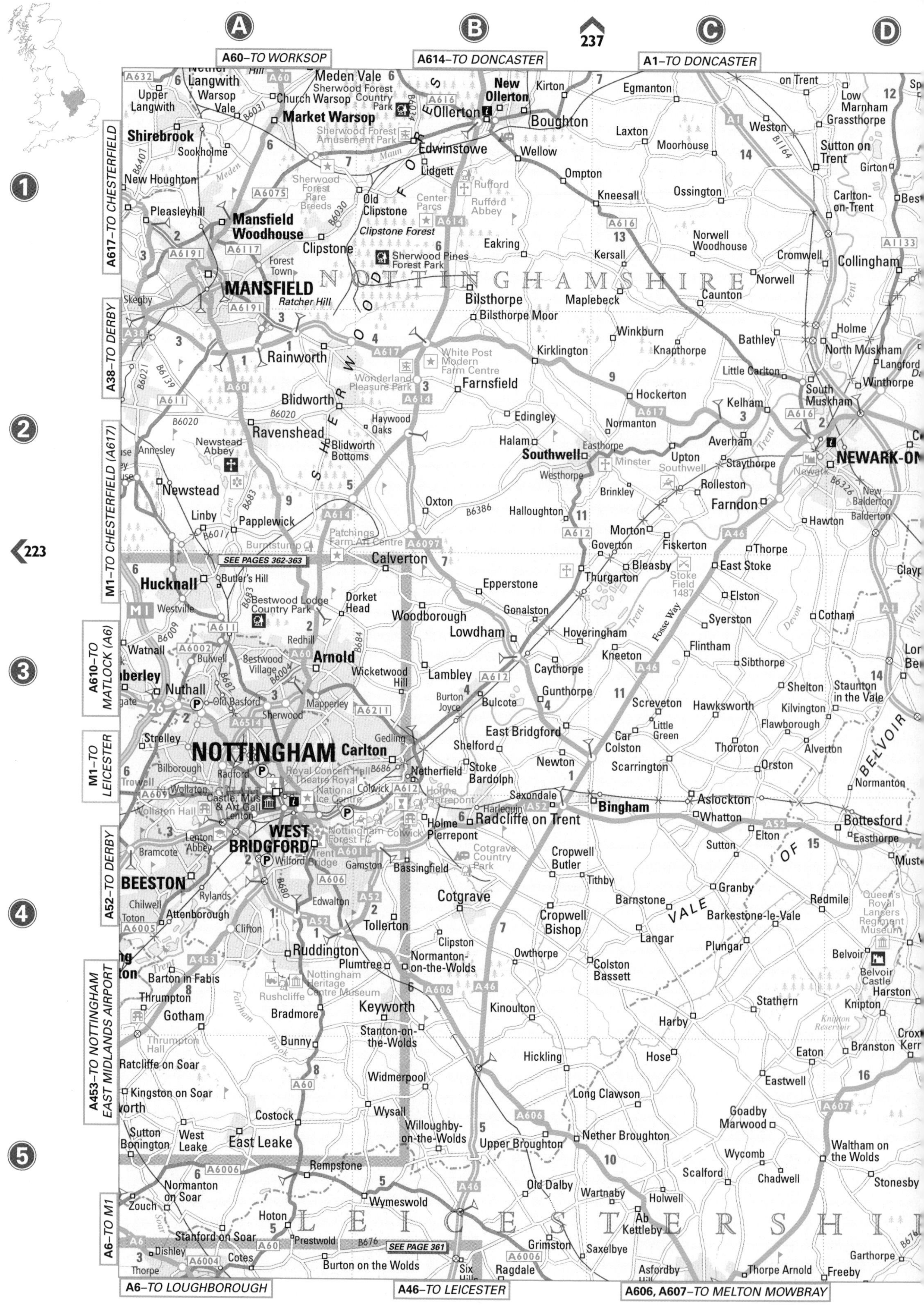

Sherwood Forest: Famous for tales of Robin Hood and his Merry Men. The forest contains the 'Major Oak', a tree reputed to be well over 800 years old. Its vital statistics are: spread over 90 feet (27.5m), girth 33 feet (10m) and weight estimated to be 23 tons (23.4 tonnes). It is so big that Robin is reputed to have hidden from his enemies inside its hollow trunk. In 1972 it was fenced off from the public after the 200,000 plus visitors it attracts every year were judged to be causing it damage. ***Map ref. B1 Also on page 75***

210

Nottingham claims the oldest pub in the country, perhaps even in the World. Ye Olde Trip to Jerusalem claims to date back to 1189 which was when King Richard I ascended the throne. It is said that the pub was a favourite resting place for soldiers on their way to the Crusades and in old English the word trip actually means rest or stop rather than journey as it does now. ***Map ref. A3***

238

D E F G

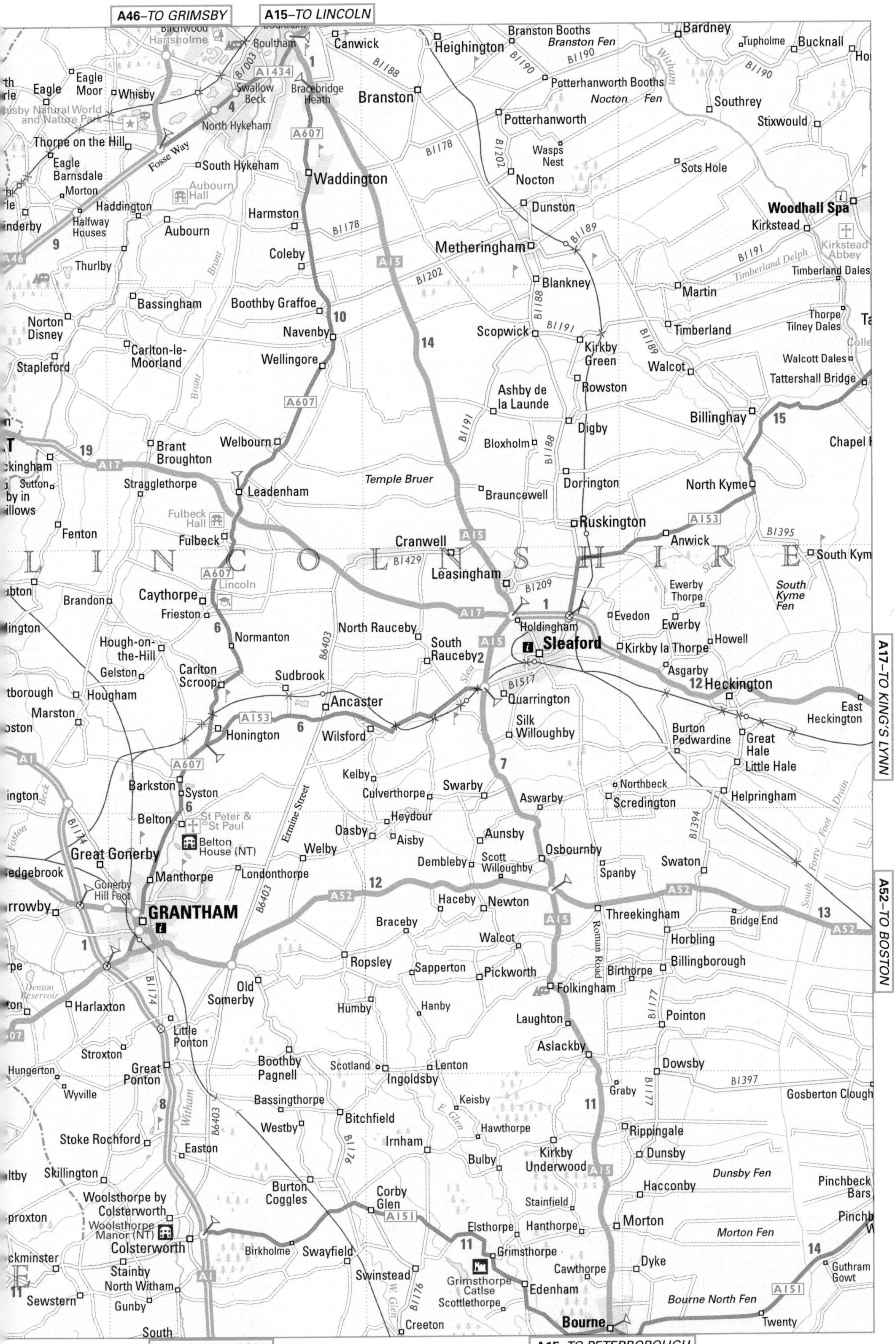

226

1 2 3 4 5

Fosse Way: *This was the first Roman Road in Britain built around AD47. It extended from Exeter to Lincoln, running through Bath, Cirencester and Leicester. Much of its alignment is followed by present-day roads such as the A46.* ***Map ref.*** ***C3***

211

Woolsthorpe: *Sir Isaac Newton (1642–1727) was born at nearby Woolsthorpe Manor. Newton devoted his life to science, researching and developing theories on colour, light and the laws of motion, but is best remembered for his theory of universal gravitation.* ***Map ref. A4 Also on page 75***

Grantham: *Margaret Thatcher, Britain's first female Prime Minister, was born here on the 13th October 1925. She was elected as MP for Finchley in 1959 and went on to serve as PM from 1979 until her resignation in 1990.* ***Map ref. E4***

238

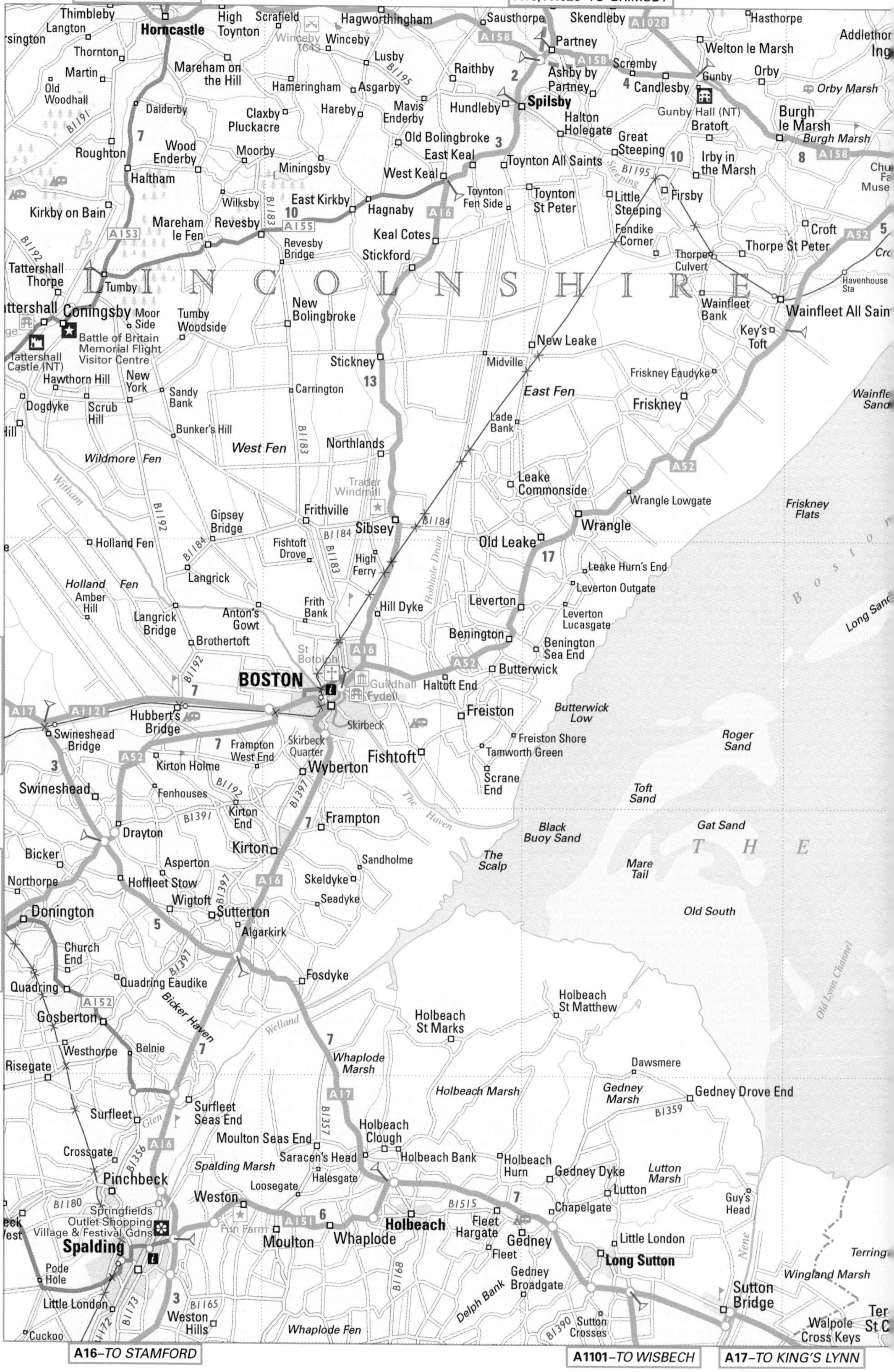

225

Sutton Bridge: *King John, travelling from Spalding to King's Lynn is reputed to have lost his crown jewels here in the 12th Century. The coastal track running by The Wash was swamped by the incoming tide and the King's baggage train was swept away, never to be seen again.* ***Map ref. C5***

212

Boston: *St. Botolph's Church, better known as Boston Stump, is the largest parish church in England. It measures 282 feet (86m) long stands 272 feet (83m) high and covers 20,070 square feet (1865 sq m) in area. The main church was begun in 1309 and the tower was completed in 1520. From the tower, on a clear day, it is possible to see Lincoln Cathedral 32 miles (50km) away.* ***Map ref. B3***

D 239 E F G

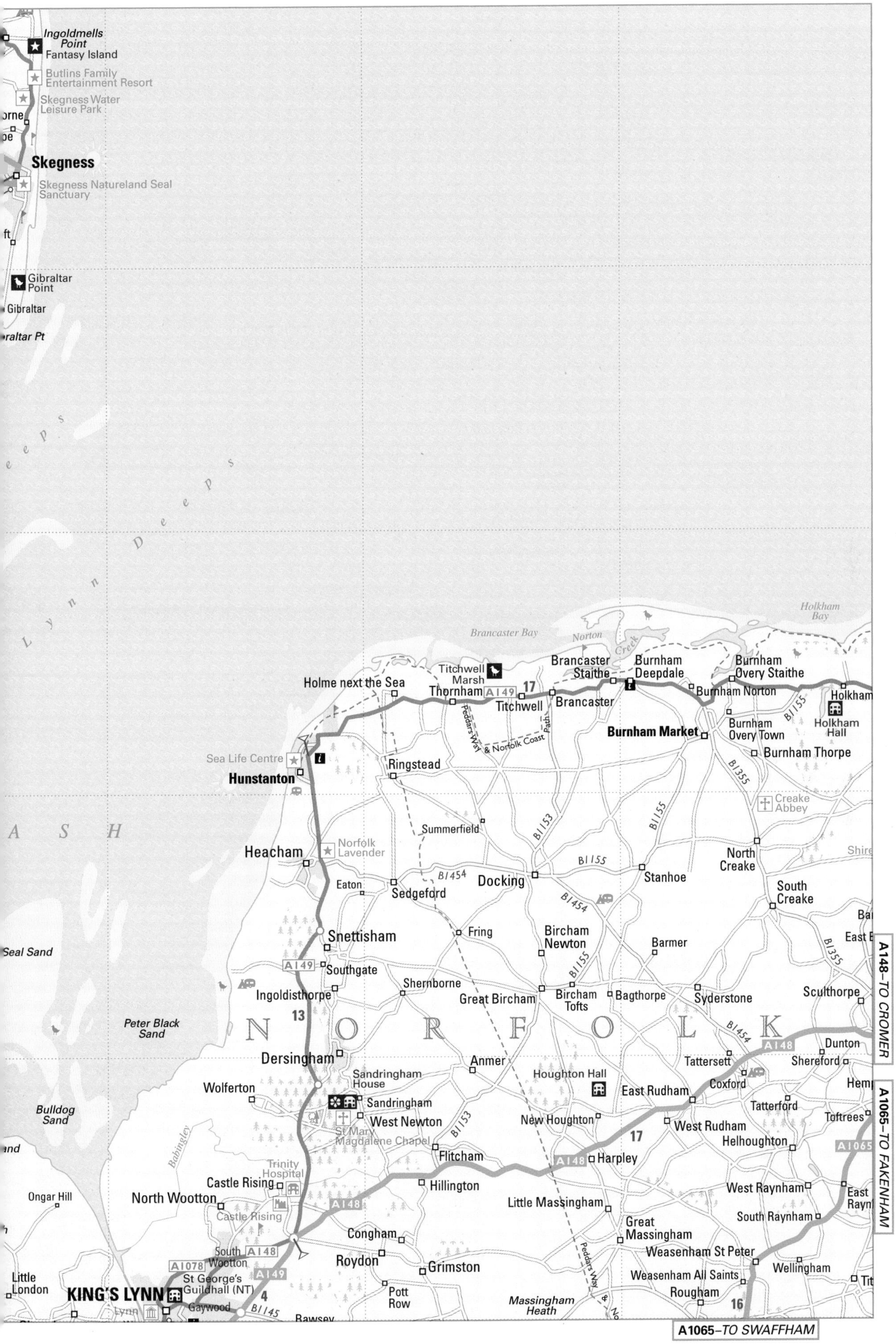

1
2
3
228
4
5

Skegness: *Billy Butlin opened his first ever holiday camp here in 1935. The camp was taken over by the Royal Navy for the duration of World War II and named HMS Royal Arthur. It was then returned to Butlins in 1946 and continued as Butlin's Holiday Camp until it was bought by the Rank Organisation in 1972.* ***Map ref. D1***

213

Burnham Thorpe: *Lord Nelson was born here in 1758. As Horatio Nelson he joined the Navy at the age of twelve and from then on spent almost his entire life at sea. He was dogged by ill health but from 1793 was almost always involved in a battle. He lost an eye at Calvi in Corsica, an arm at Santa Cruz in Tenerife and finally his life at the Battle of Trafalgar. As a monument to this inspirational leader Nelson's column was built in Trafalgar Square in London in 1840 and stands 170 feet (52m) high.* ***Map ref. G3***

A B C D

1 2 3 4 5

227

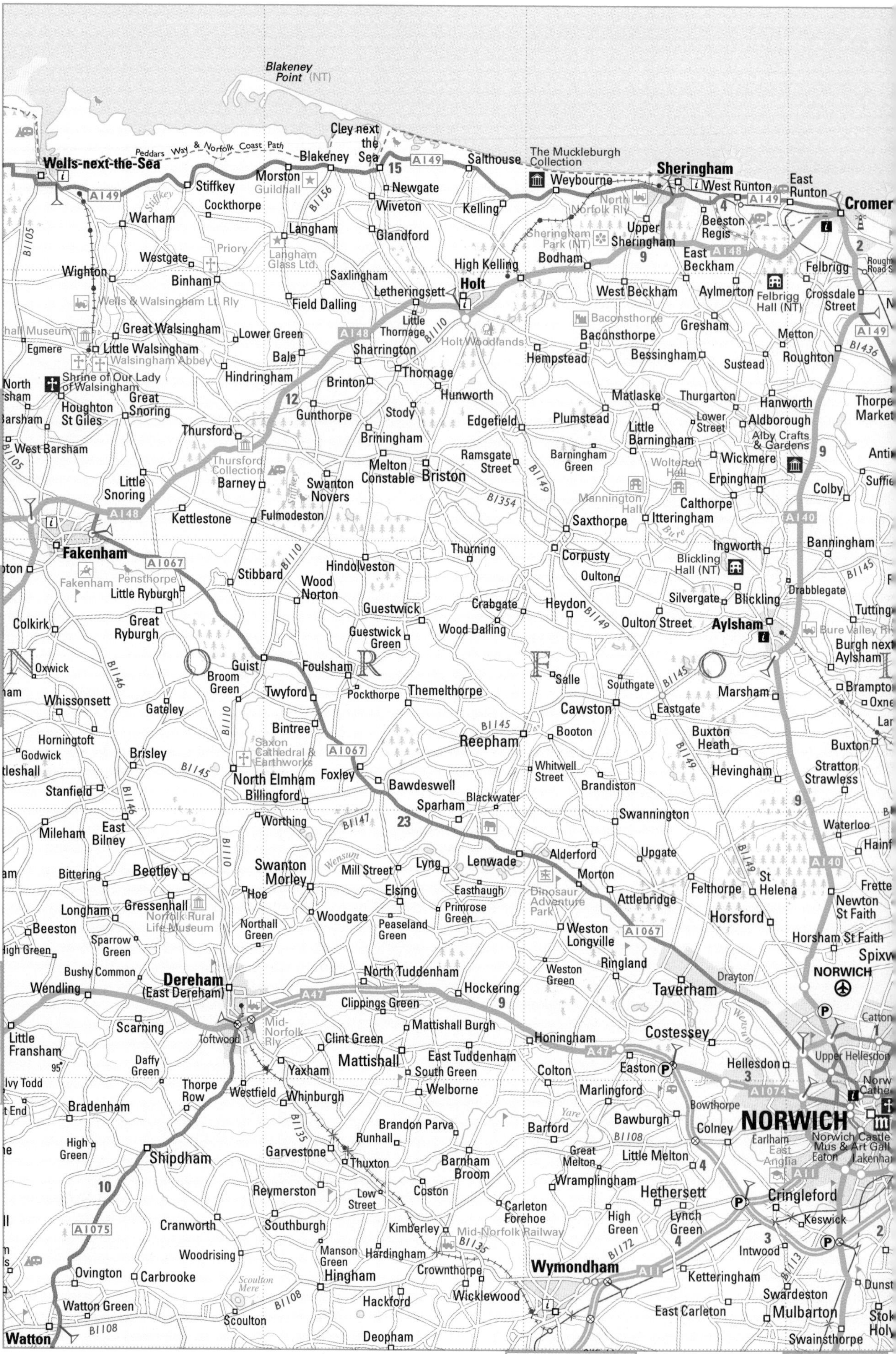

A148–TO KING'S LYNN
A1065–TO SWAFFHAM
A47–TO SWAFFHAM
A11–TO THETFORD
A140–TO DISS

Wells and Walsingham Light Railway: *With a line gauge of 10.25 inches (260mm), this is the narrowest public railway in the world.* ***Map ref. A2***

214

Swardeston: *Edith Cavell was born here in 1865. As a nurse working in Brussels during World War I, Edith helped over 200 French, Belgian and British soldiers to escape from the Germans. She was eventually arrested, convicted of treason and executed by firing squad on the 12th October 1915. After the war her body was exhumed and reburied in Norwich Cathedral.* ***Map ref. D5***

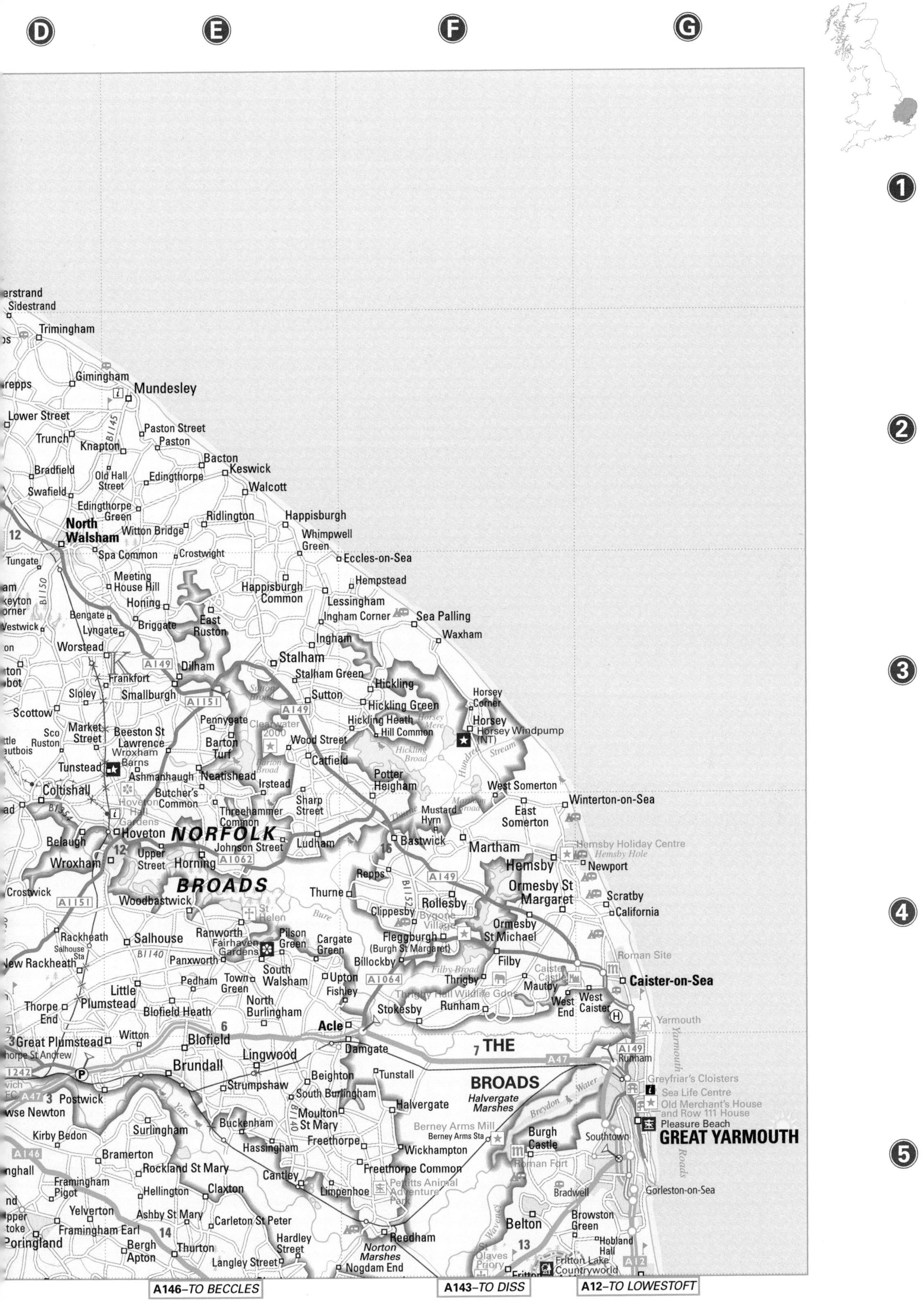

Sheringham:** Norfolk is best known for its flat fenland and Broads. The highest point in the entire county is Roman Camp near Sheringham at just 336 feet (103 metres) above sea level. **Map ref. C1

215

Great Yarmouth:** Anna Sewell, writer of the children's classic Black Beauty was born here on the 30th March 1820. Anna was crippled at an early age but constantly championed the better treatment and understanding of horses through her writing. She died on the 25th April 1878 and is buried at Lammas, near Buxton. **Map ref. G5

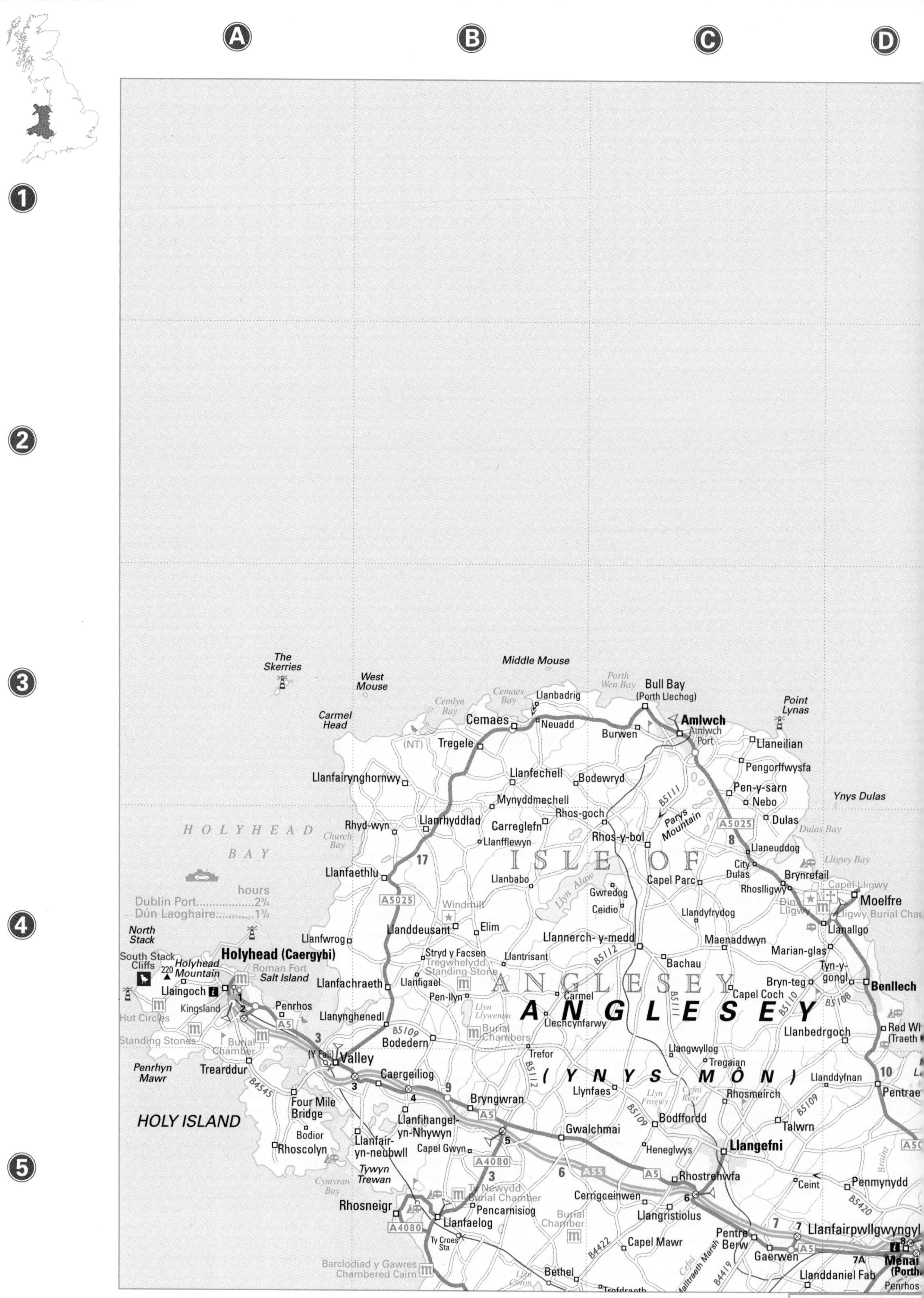

Llandudno: *Wales' largest seaside resort. The town has numerous attractions and is the only place in Britain to feature a redundant lighthouse as a B&B.* ***Map ref. F4***

216

Llanfairpwllgwyngyllgogerychwyrndrobwllllantysiliogogogoch: *This is the village with the longest name in Britain. The final 38 characters of the name were added on in the 19th Century to attract tourists. The name actually means 'The Church of St Mary in a hollow of white hazel near a rapid whirlpool and near St Tysilio's Church by the red cave....but now it's generally called Llanfair PG. Add the .com, and since 1999 it's also been the world's longest single-word internet domain name.* ***Map ref. D5***

D E F G

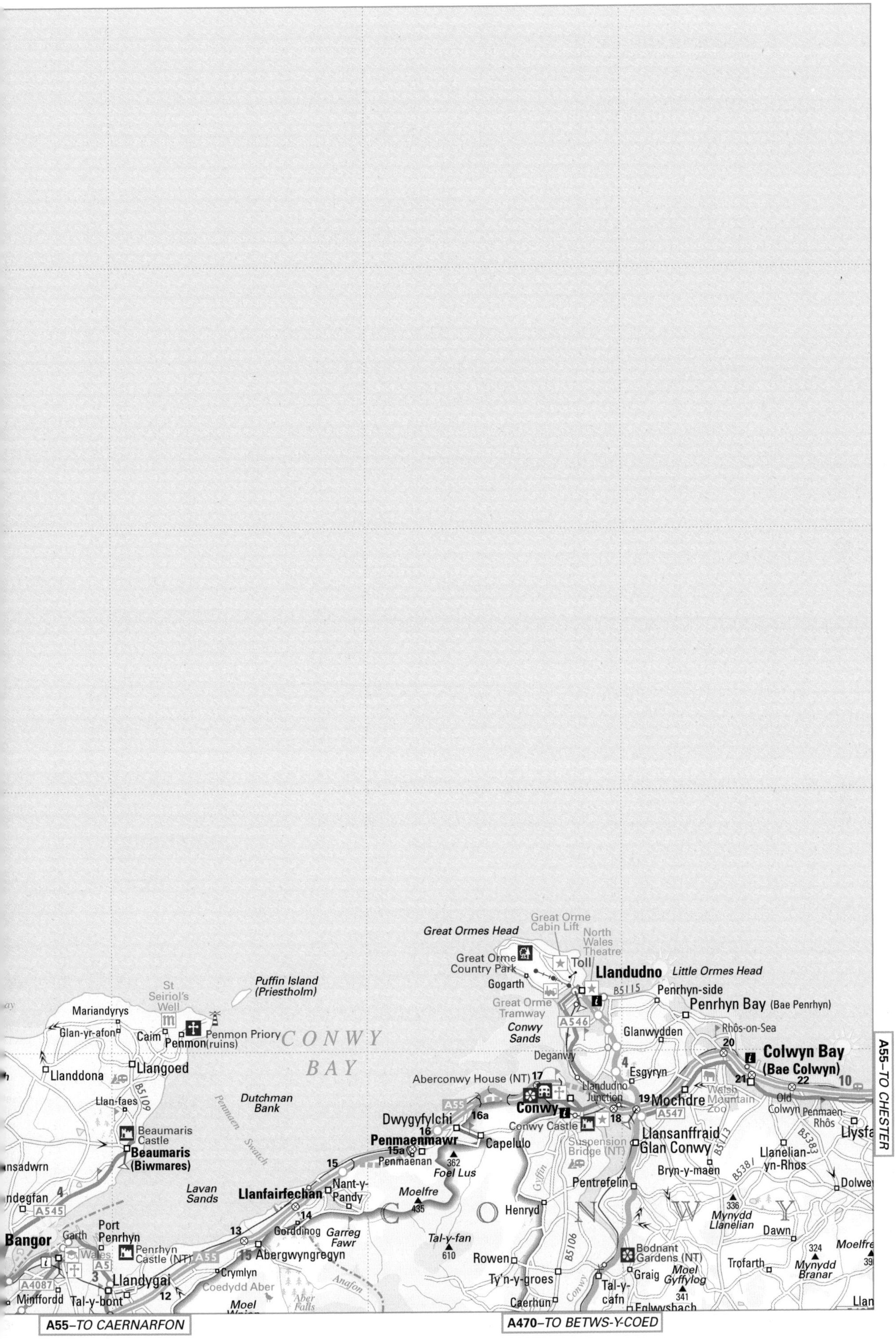

1 2 3 4 5
232
217

Conwy: *The Quay House here is officially the world's smallest house.* ***Map ref. F5***

Puffin Island (Priestholm): *Site of a monastic community founded by St Seiriol in the 6th Century. By 2000, the Puffin population had been so severely decimated by rats that the Royal Air Force were called in to airlift in 2.5 tons of poisoned wheat onto the island in an attempt to wipe out the rat population.* ***Map ref. E4***

Port Sunlight: *Village created by William Hesketh Lever who owned a soap factory making Sunlight Soap. This later became Lever Bros. The village was built to house his workforce. Work started on the 3rd March 1888 and by 1909 the village had 700 dwellings with all the facilities: school, theatre, library etc.* ***Map ref. E4***

231

Prestatyn: *Offa's Dyke was built by Offa, King of Mercia AD 757–796, to mark the boundary between England and Wales. It runs from Prestatyn in the north, to Sedbury, near Chepstow in the south, a distance of 182 miles (293km).* ***Map ref. B4***

219

Rhyl: *Ruth Ellis was born here in 1926. She was hanged on the 13th July 1955 at Holloway Prison for the murder of her lover. The execution so enraged the population that it opened the whole debate on capital punishment and she became the last woman in Britain to be hanged for murder. All executions were subsequently suspended from 1965 and capital punishment was abolished altogether in 1970.* ***Map ref. B4***

242

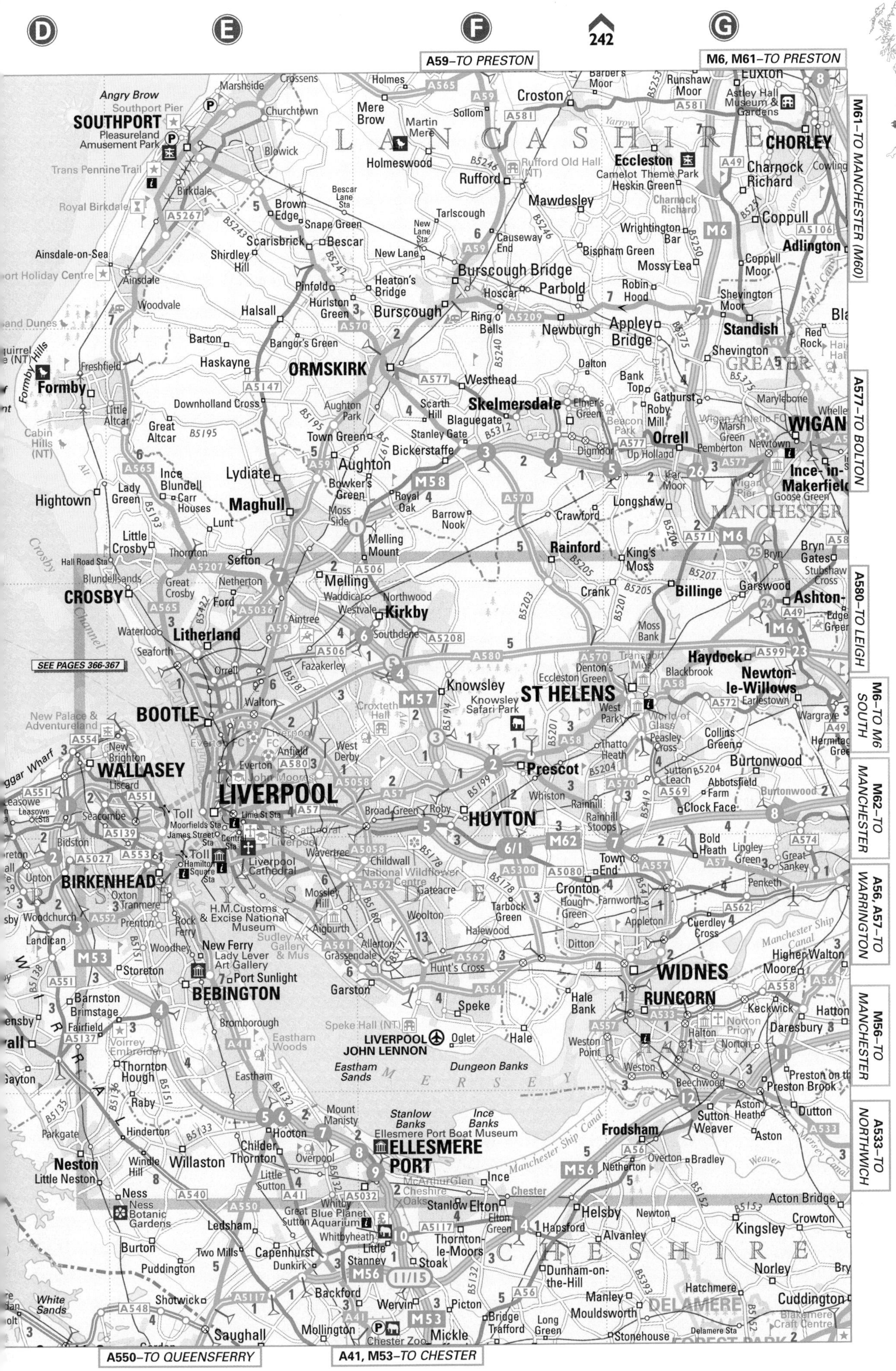

234

Southport: *The sands here were the scene of Henry Segrave's successful attempt on the world land speed record. On 16th March 1926, he took his Sunbeam to 152.3 mph (245km/h) to beat Malcolm Campbell's record.* ***Map ref. E1***

Eastham: *The Manchester Ship Canal starts here and runs for 35 miles (56km) to Salford. Construction on the canal started in 1887 and it was opened to the first ships on the 1st January 1894.* ***Map ref. E4***

220

St. Asaph (Llanelwy): *This tiny city boasts the smallest cathedral in Britain.* ***Map ref. B5***

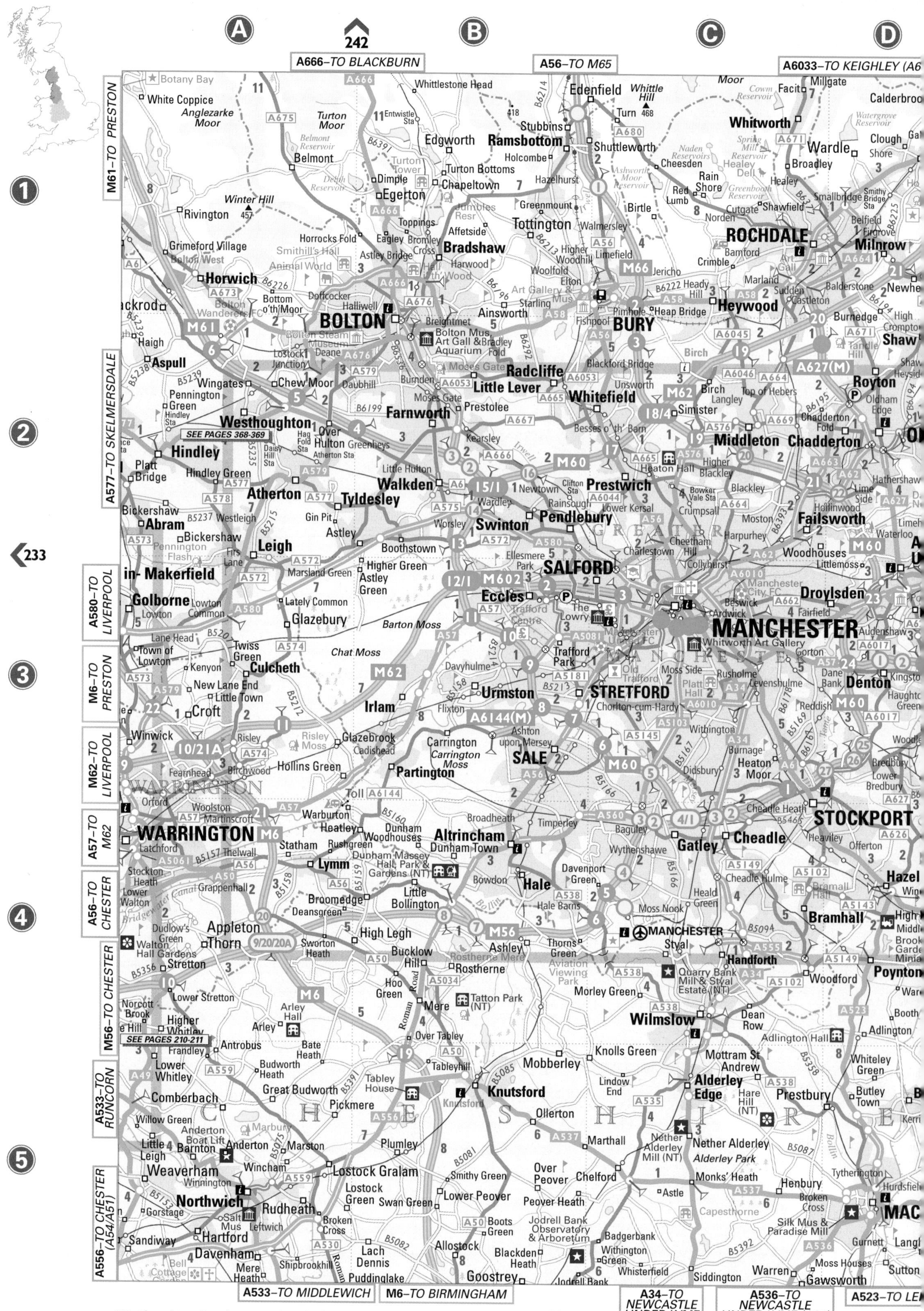

242

233

221

Westhoughton: *Despite repeated Coal Mining Acts passed in the nineteenth century, in the late 1800s and early 1900s, at least 1,500 miners were losing their lives every year down the pits. England's worst pit disaster occurred here, between Atherton and Westhoughton, on the 21st December 1910. An underground explosion at Hulton Colliery's Pretoria Pit, Number 3 Bank, killed 344 mine workers. It was later proved that over 300 of these had died from Carbon Monoxide poisoning.* ***Map ref. A2***

Hadfield: *The TV comedy series The League of Gentlemen which follows the bizarre exploits of the very peculiar locals, is filmed in Hadfield. In the programme the village is known as Royston Vasey.* ***Map ref. E3***

D 243 E F 244 G

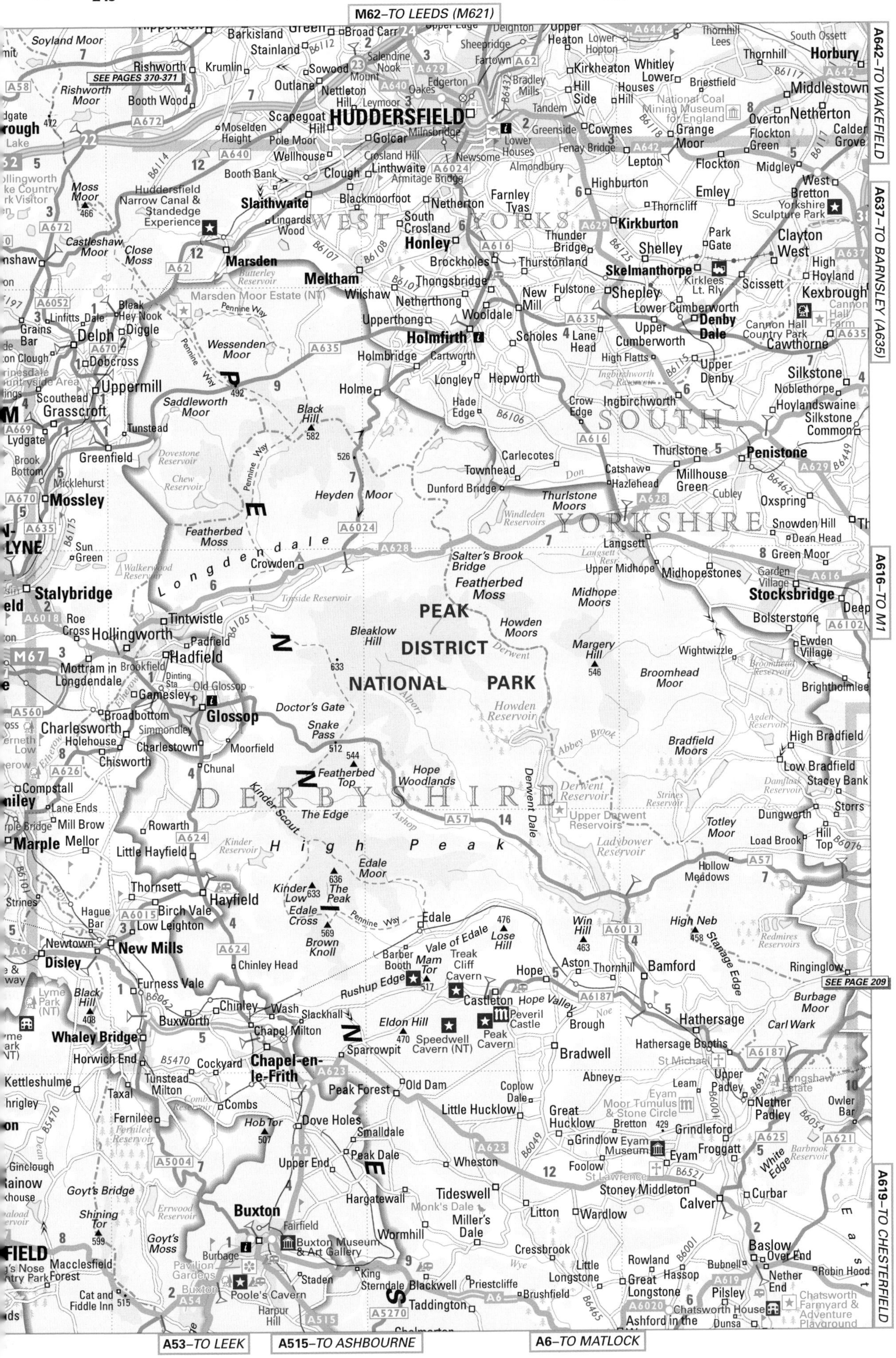

236

222

Kinder Scout: *Rising to 2,088 feet (636m), this is the highest point in the Peak District National Park. On the 24th April 1932 over 450 Ramblers set off from Bowden Bridge near Hayfield on an organised 'mass trespass' in order to gain access to Kinder Scout for members of the public. They eventually succeeded when, in 1951, it was designated as Britain's first National Park.* ***Map ref. E4***

Rochdale: *Gracie Fields was born Gracie Stansfield here in 1898. She went on to become a famous music hall star and recording artist . She eventually retired to the Isle of Capri and was created Dame of the British Empire in 1979. She died later the same year.* ***Map ref. C1***

Holmfirth: *Britain's longest running comedy series, Last of the Summer Wine has been filmed on location here since 1973.* ***Map ref. F2***

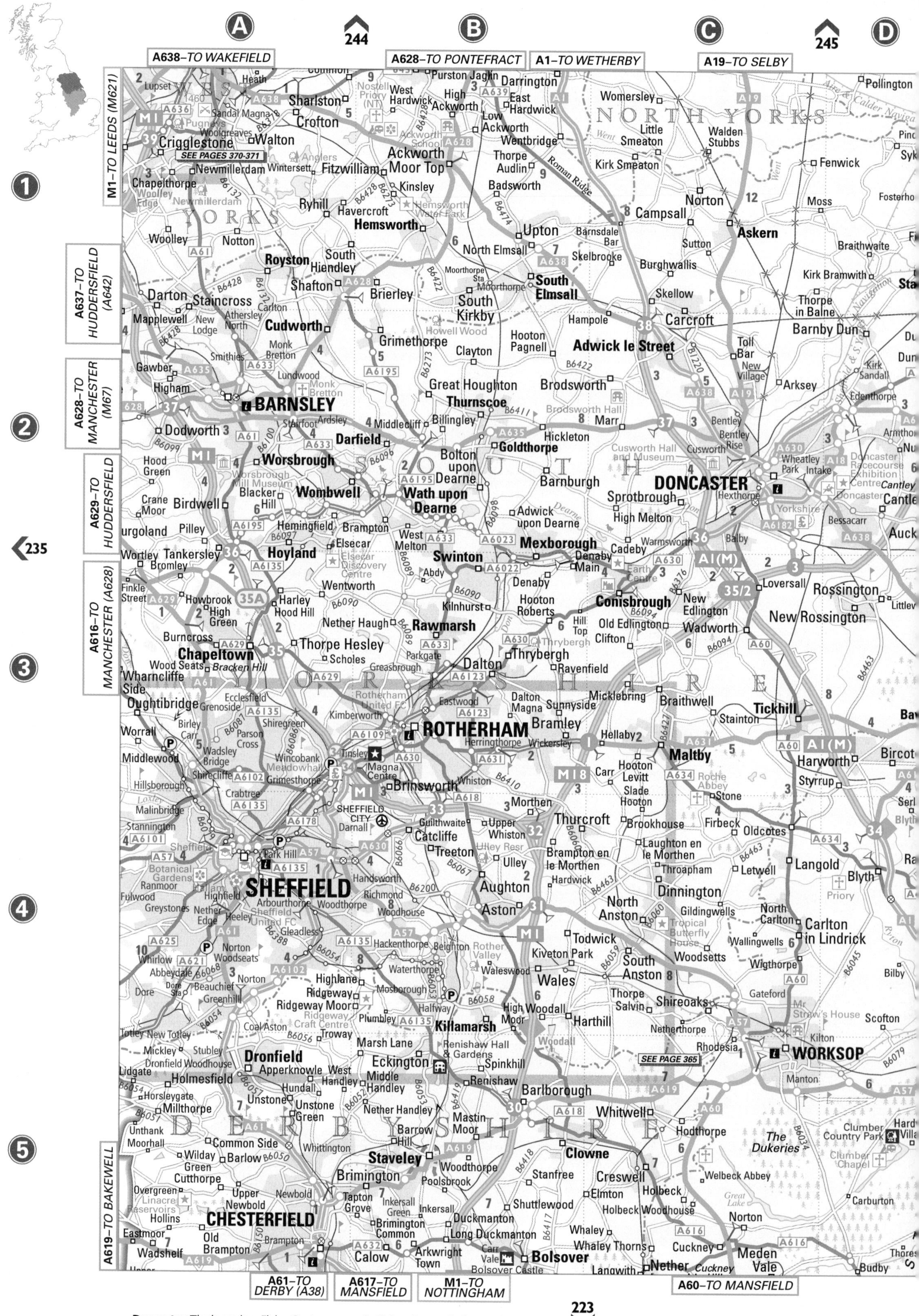

Doncaster: *The legendary Flying Scotsman was built here in 1923 for just under £8000. As a passenger express train on the East Coast main line between London and Edinburgh it regularly reached a speed of 100 mph (160km/h). During its working life, up to 1963, it covered 2.4 million miles (3.86 million km). The Flying Scotsman is now in the National Railway Museum, York.* ***Map ref. C2***

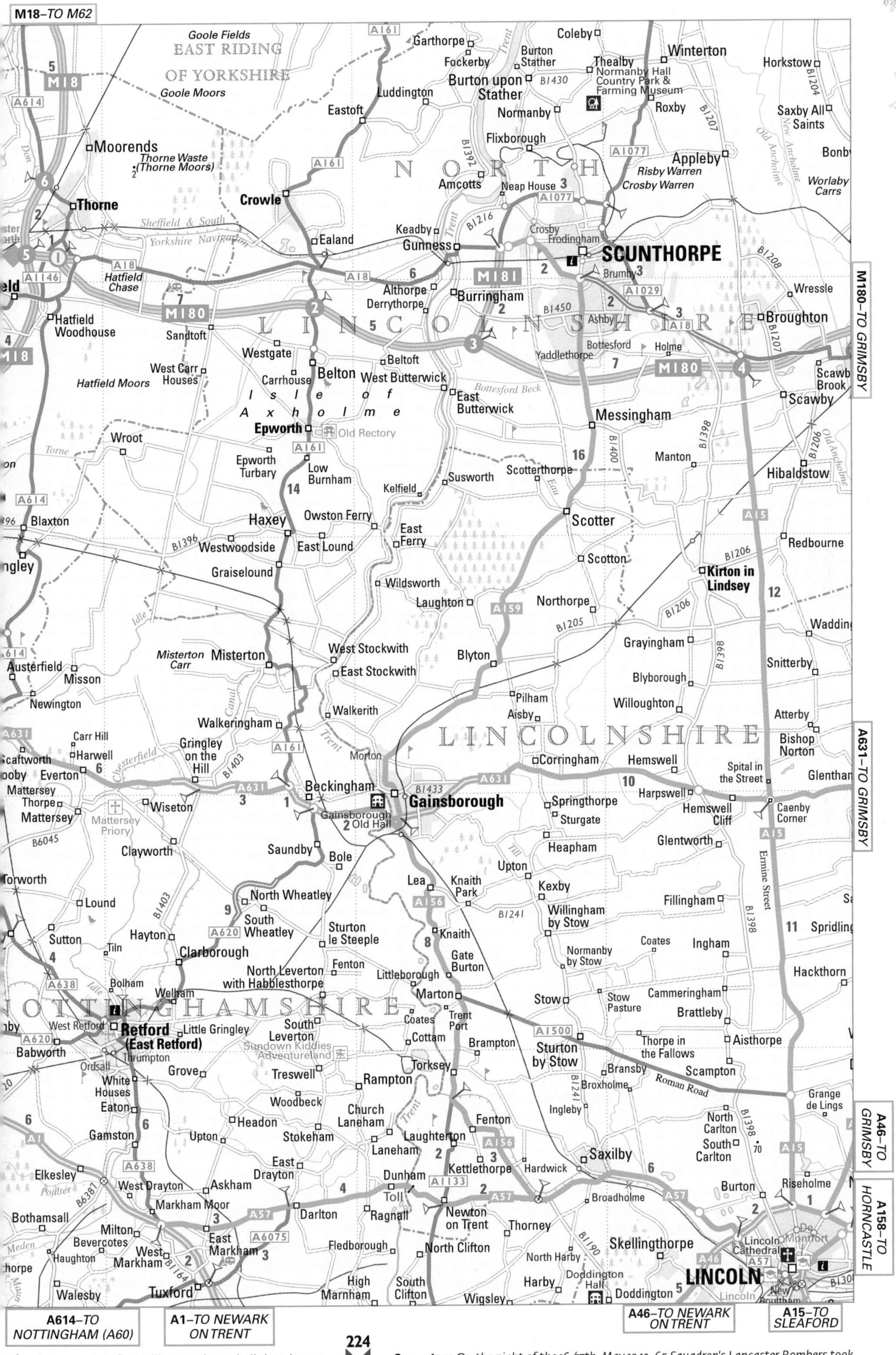

224

Lincoln: *The world's first military tank was built here in 1915. The tank was built by Fosters and, to protect its secrecy, it was designated as a water carrier, hence it became shortened to 'tank'.* ***Map ref. G5***

Scampton: *On the night of the 16/17th May 1943, 65 Squadron's Lancaster Bombers took off from their base at RAF Scampton to attack dams in the Ruhr area of Germany. This was the famous Dam Busters raid. Although the operation was hailed as a great success, it cost the lives of 53 airmen and over 1300 mainly Ukrainian prisoners of war who were being held at a camp close to one of the dams.* ***Map ref. G5***

246

A B C D

1 2 3 4 5

237

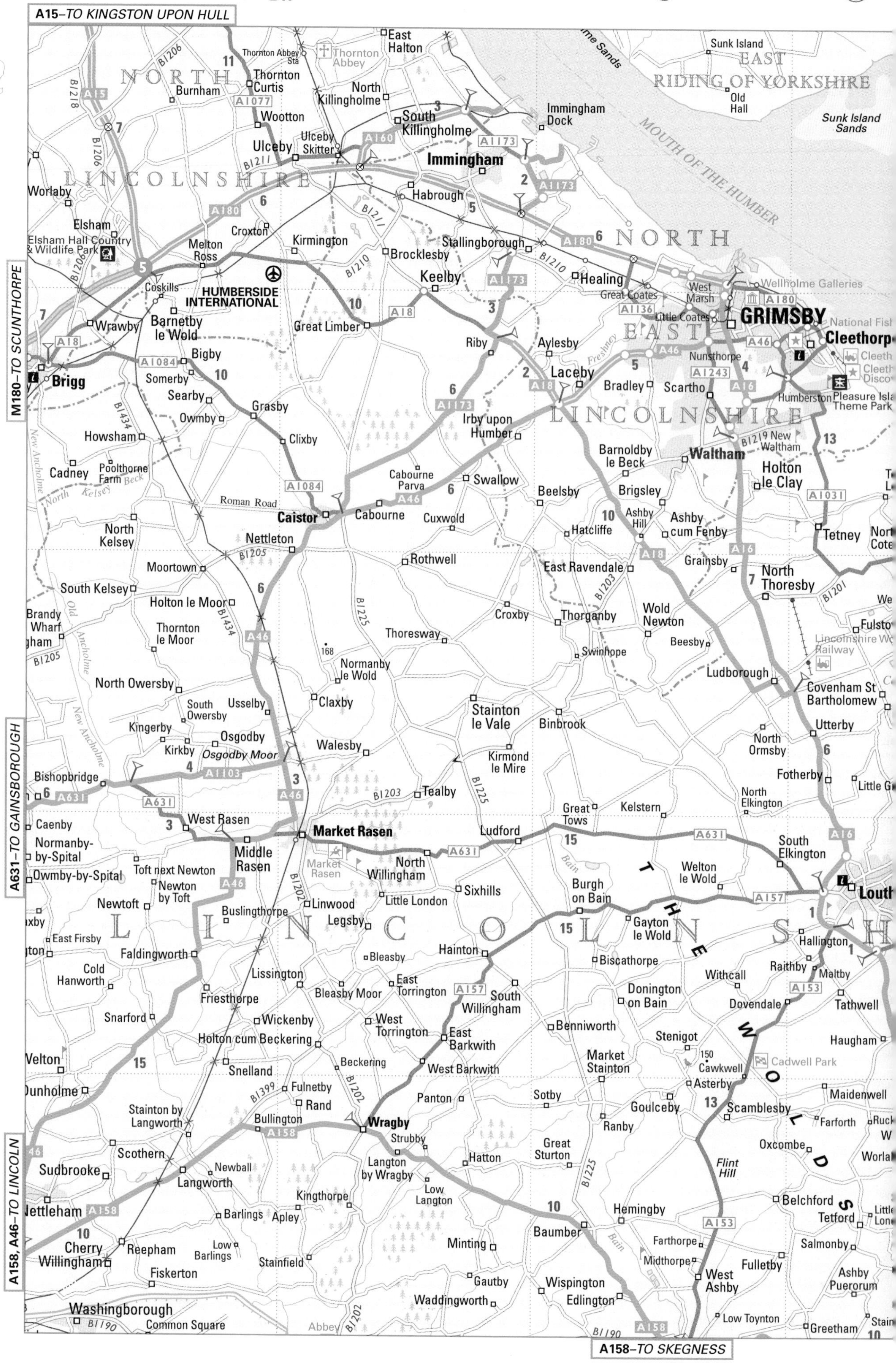

Louth *is a small market town which sits astride the Greenwich Meridian and is famous for its magnificent 15th Century church. The spire of St James at 295 feet (91 metres) high is the tallest parish church spire in England.* ***Map ref. D4***

226

Somersby: *The great poet Alfred Lord Tennyson was born here on the 5th August 1809. He was the fourth son of the Rev. George Tennyson, Rector of Somersby and Bag Enderby.* ***Map ref. D5***

Grimsby: *The game of darts was invented in the 1800s by the landlord of the Docker Arms Pub which stood in Freeman Street. The Spider's Web Pub, in Carr Lane, is so called because of the design of a dartboard* ***Map ref. C2***

247

227

Spurn Head: *Because of the rapid coastal erosion in this area, the road to the head is frequently eroded away and has to be relaid.* ***Map ref. E1***

Donna Nook: *An RAF Bombing Range which on the 18th July 2002 became the first national nature reserve to be established on MOD land. The reserve, which stretches for over 6 miles (10km) along the coast, is home to a range of flora and fauna including a colony of grey seals.* ***Map ref. E3***

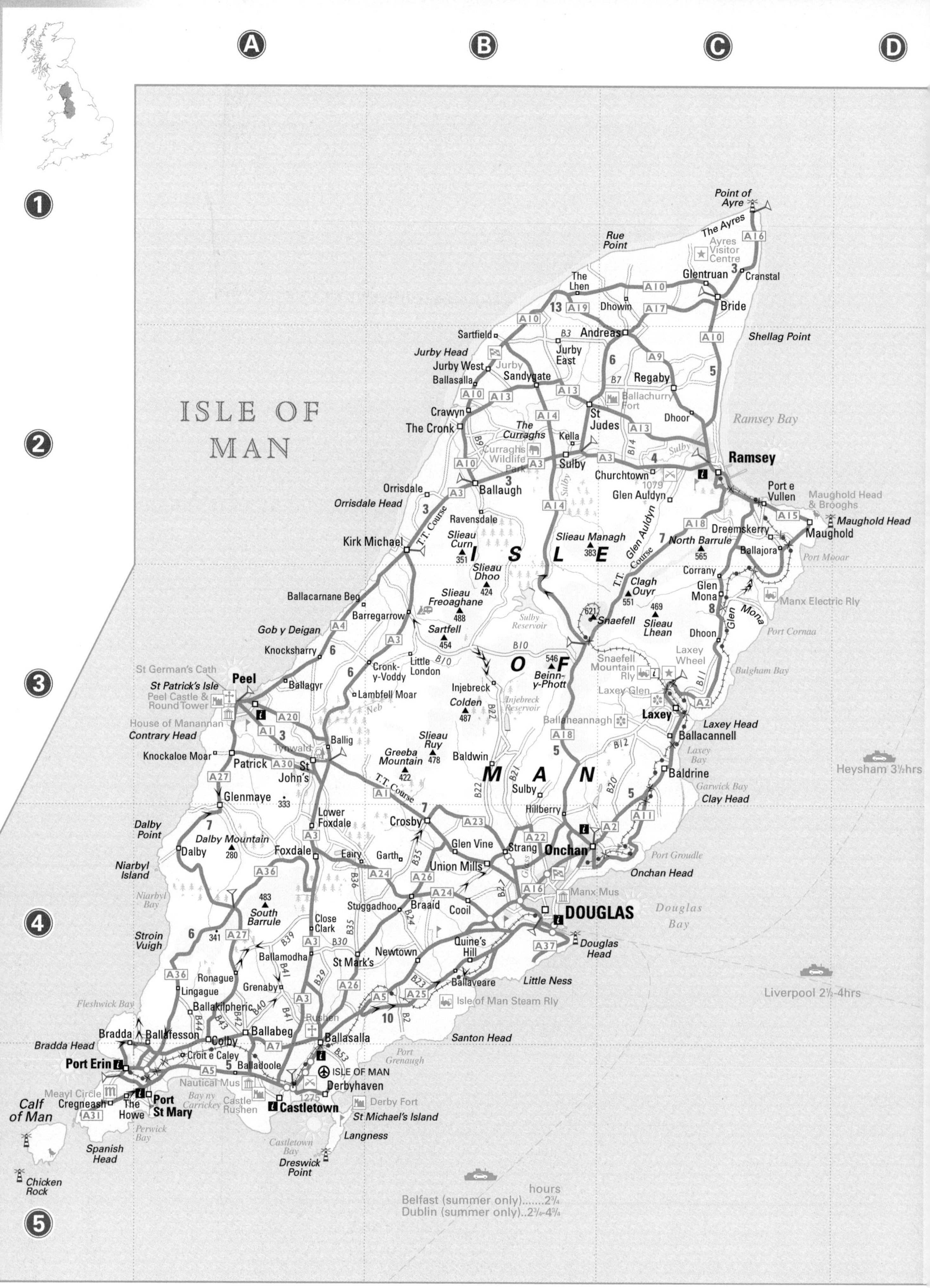

Laxey: *The Lady Isabella water wheel, built in 1854 to pump water from local mine workings, is allegedly the world's largest water wheel, with a diameter of over 72 feet (22 metres). It still turns, but no longer pumps.* ***Map ref. C3***

Isle of Man: *The Isle of Man is a self-governing Island. Although a Crown Dependency it doesn't belong to either the UK or the European Union. The Island is 33 miles (53km) long, 13 miles (21km) wide and covers 227 square miles (588 sq km). Over 40% of the island is uninhabited. Its strange three legged symbol means 'Quocunque Jeceris Stabit' (whichever way you throw me I stand).* ***Map ref. B3***

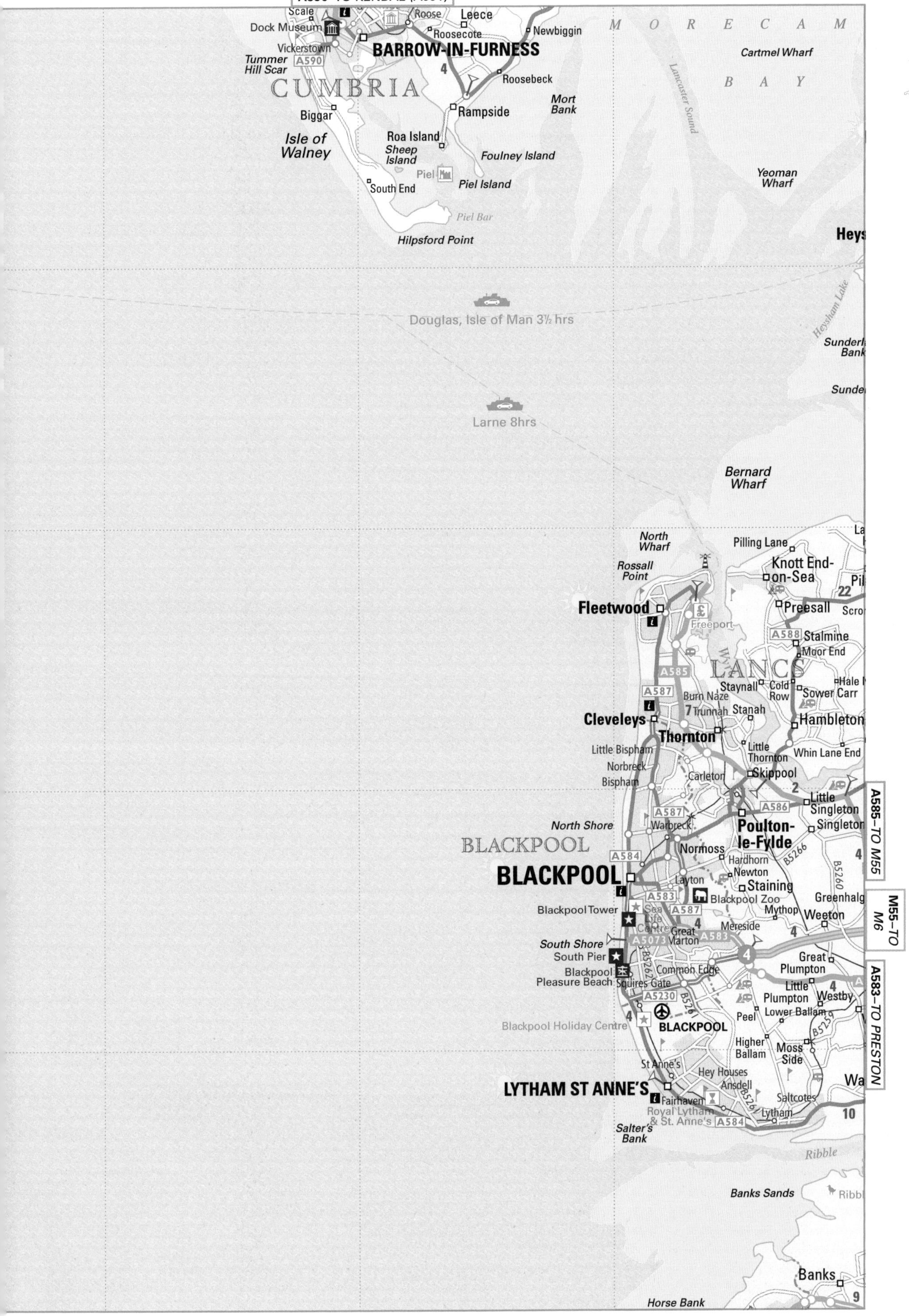

Manx Electric Railway: *Cars 1 and 2, dating from 1893, are the oldest trams still in service in the world, regularly running the 18 miles (29km) between Douglas and Ramsey.* ***Map ref. C3***

Barrow in Furness: *Famous for its steel and shipbuilding. In 1876 Barrow in Furness had the largest steelworks in the world. Today, it is England's busiest shipyard with the largest covered ship building hall in Europe.* ***Map ref. F1***

250

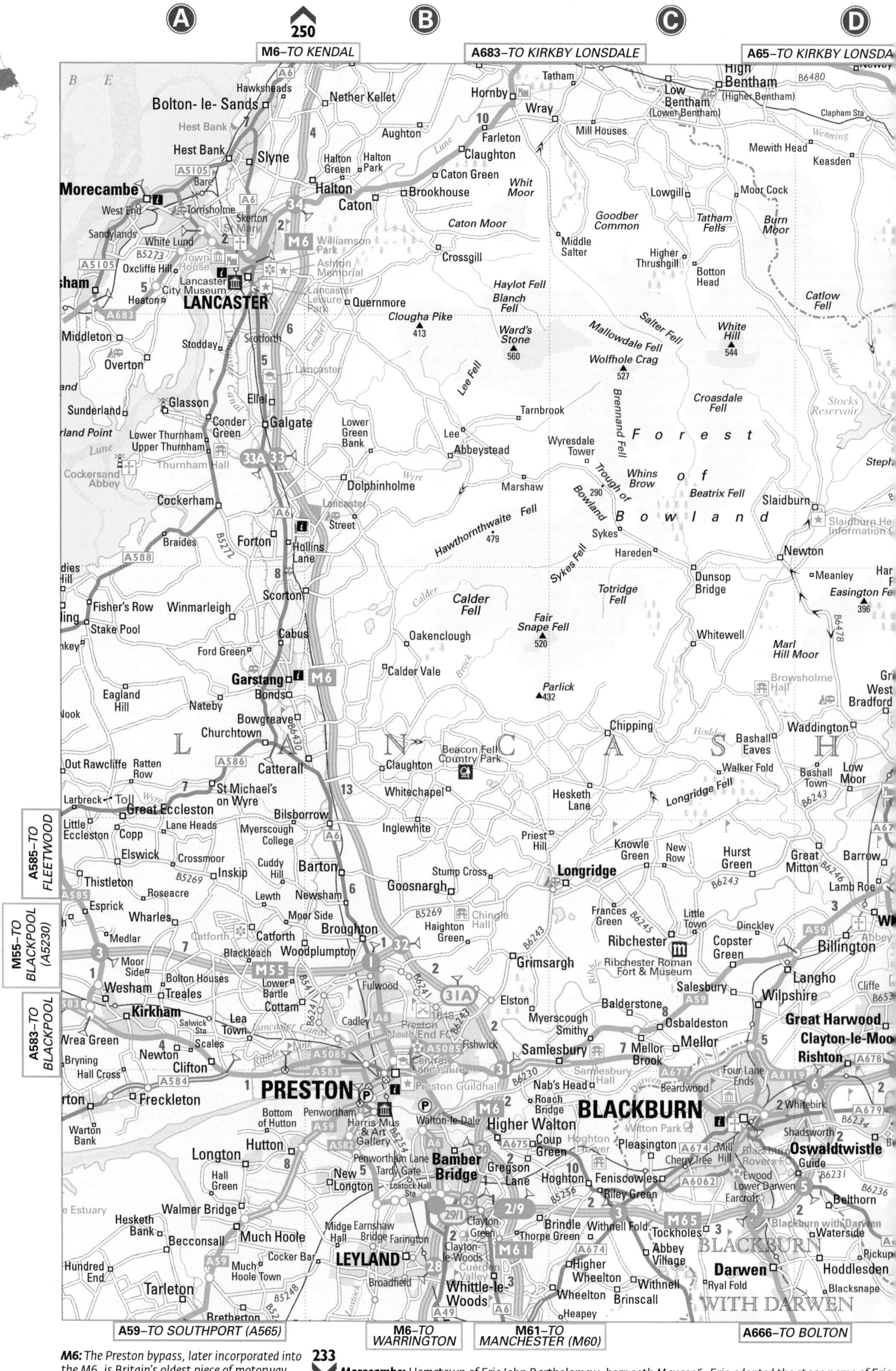

241

M6: *The Preston bypass, later incorporated into the M6, is Britain's oldest piece of motorway and was opened on 5th December 1958.* ***Map ref. B4***

233

Morecambe: *Hometown of Eric John Bartholomew, born 14th May 1926. Eric adopted the stage name of Eric Morecambe and, along with Ernie Wise, formed 'Morecambe and Wise'. They became one of Britain's most successful comedy double-acts. Eric died on the 28th May 1984.* ***Map ref. A1***

251

D E F G

244

1 2 3 4 5

234

Whalley: *A point to the west of the village, near Calderstones Hospital, can be calculated to be the 'centre of gravity' of mainland Britain.* ***Map ref. D4***

Oswaldtwistle: *James Hargreaves, inventor of the 'Spinning Jenny', was born here in 1720. The Spinning Jenny was the first machine to improve on the traditional spinning wheel and was capable of doing the work of 8 traditional spinners. The invention put Britain at the forefront of the textile industry.* ***Map ref. D5***

A
252
B
C
D
1
2
243
3
4
5

Ilkley Moor: *Vast expanse of moorland famous as the setting of the unofficial Yorkshire anthem recognised throughout the world 'On Ilkley Moor Bah t 'at'.* ***Map ref. A3***

235

York: *Guy Fawkes was born in York in 1570. Along with a group of conspirators he tried to blow up the Houses of Parliament on the 5th November 1605 but was arrested in the cellars before he could ignite the explosives. He is remembered every 5th November when we celebrate Bonfire Night.* ***Map ref. F2***

Wetherby: *The UK's longest lasting rainbow (6 hours) was recorded here on 14th March 1994.* ***Map ref. D3***

1
2
246
3
4
5

Knaresborough: *Haunt of Mother Shipton, England's most famous prophetess and witch. Although born in 1488 she allegedly foretold of the Civil War, the Black Death and the Great Fire of London and one of her best known rhymes is uncannily accurate:*
Carriages without horses shall go, and accidents fill the world with woe. Around the world thoughts shall fly, in the twinkling of an eye. Under water men shall walk, shall ride, shall sleep, shall talk. In the air men shall be seen, in white, in black and in green. Iron on the water shall float, as easy as a wooden boat. ***Map ref. C2***

236

254

A B C D

1
2
3
4
5

245

237

Humber Bridge: *Despite plans for a tunnel scheme in 1872 and numerous plans for a bridge, the first traffic didn't finally crossed the river until the 24th June 1981. Work on the present suspension bridge began in 1973 with, at times, over 1000 workers being employed on the construction. The bridge was finally opened by HM The Queen on the 17th July 1981. At this time it had the longest bridge span in the world of 4626 feet (1410m).* ***Map ref. C5***

255

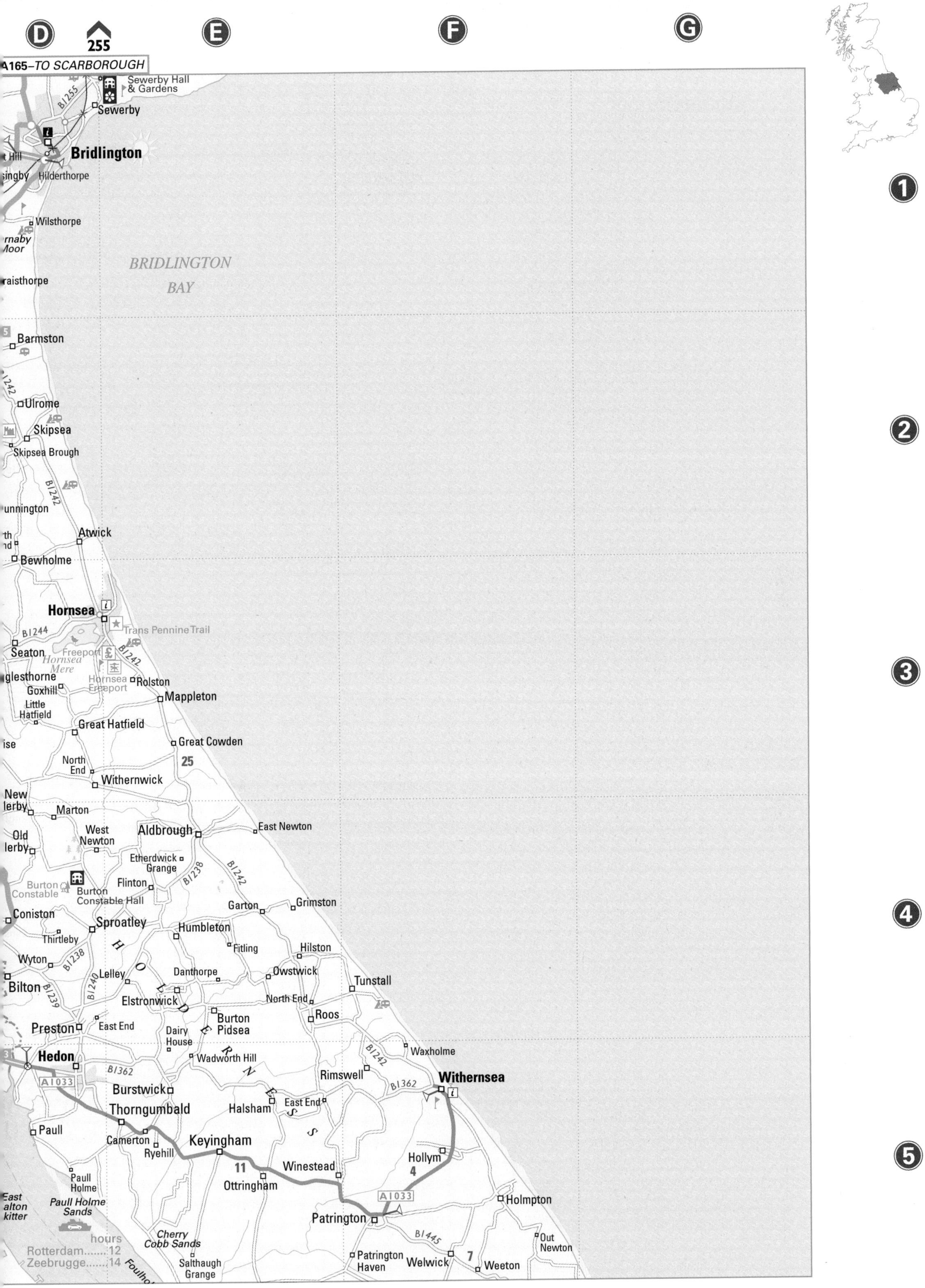

Kingston Upon Hull: *William Wilberforce, the most important figure in the abolition of slavery, was born here in 1759. After years of campaigning, Wilberforce died on the 29th July 1833 and just one month later Parliament passed the Slavery Abolition Act which gave all slaves in the British Empire their freedom.* ***Map ref. D5***

239

Holderness Coast: *The coastline here is reputed to have the fastest rate of coastal erosion in the world. The Boulder Clay cliffs along this shoreline offer little resistance to the full force of the sea and are constantly 'slumping' (sliding slowly into the sea). This part of the coast from Spurn Head to Bridlington has lost a mile of shore in the last hundred years and is currently losing a further 6.5 feet (2m) every year.* ***Map ref. E4***

259

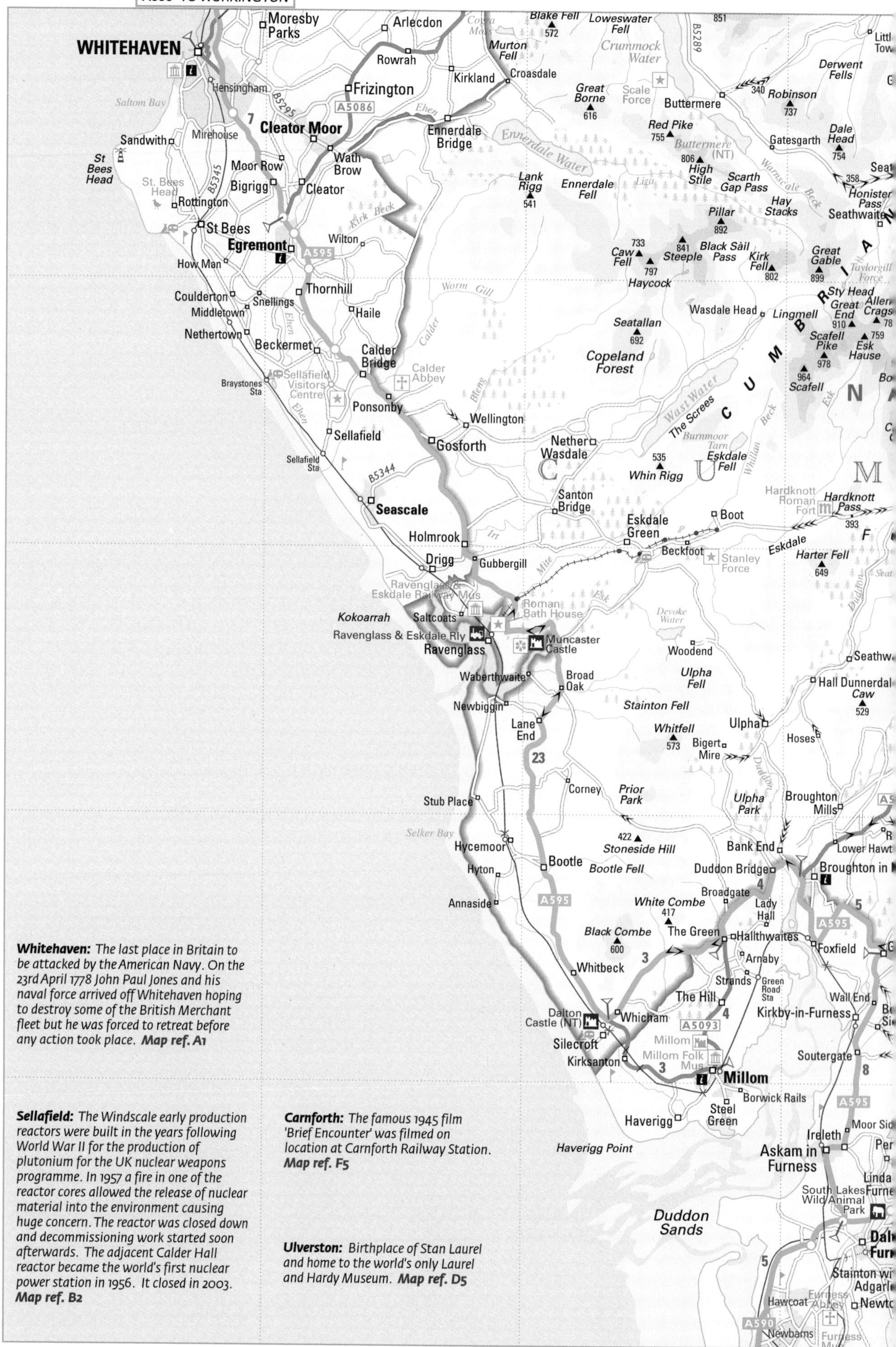

Whitehaven: *The last place in Britain to be attacked by the American Navy. On the 23rd April 1778 John Paul Jones and his naval force arrived off Whitehaven hoping to destroy some of the British Merchant fleet but he was forced to retreat before any action took place.* ***Map ref. A1***

Sellafield: *The Windscale early production reactors were built in the years following World War II for the production of plutonium for the UK nuclear weapons programme. In 1957 a fire in one of the reactor cores allowed the release of nuclear material into the environment causing huge concern. The reactor was closed down and decommissioning work started soon afterwards. The adjacent Calder Hall reactor became the world's first nuclear power station in 1956. It closed in 2003.* ***Map ref. B2***

Carnforth: *The famous 1945 film 'Brief Encounter' was filmed on location at Carnforth Railway Station.* ***Map ref. F5***

Ulverston: *Birthplace of Stan Laurel and home to the world's only Laurel and Hardy Museum.* ***Map ref. D5***

241

Coniston Water: *Scene of five successful world water speed record attempts by Malcolm Campbell and Donald Campbell between 1939 and 1959. Donald Campbell was killed here on the 4th January 1967 whilst trying to break his own record, when his boat Bluebird K7 bounced off the surface of the lake at about 300 mph (483 km/h), somersaulted several times and then sank. The wreck of Bluebird and Campbell's remains were eventually recovered from the lake in March 2001.* ***Map ref. E3***

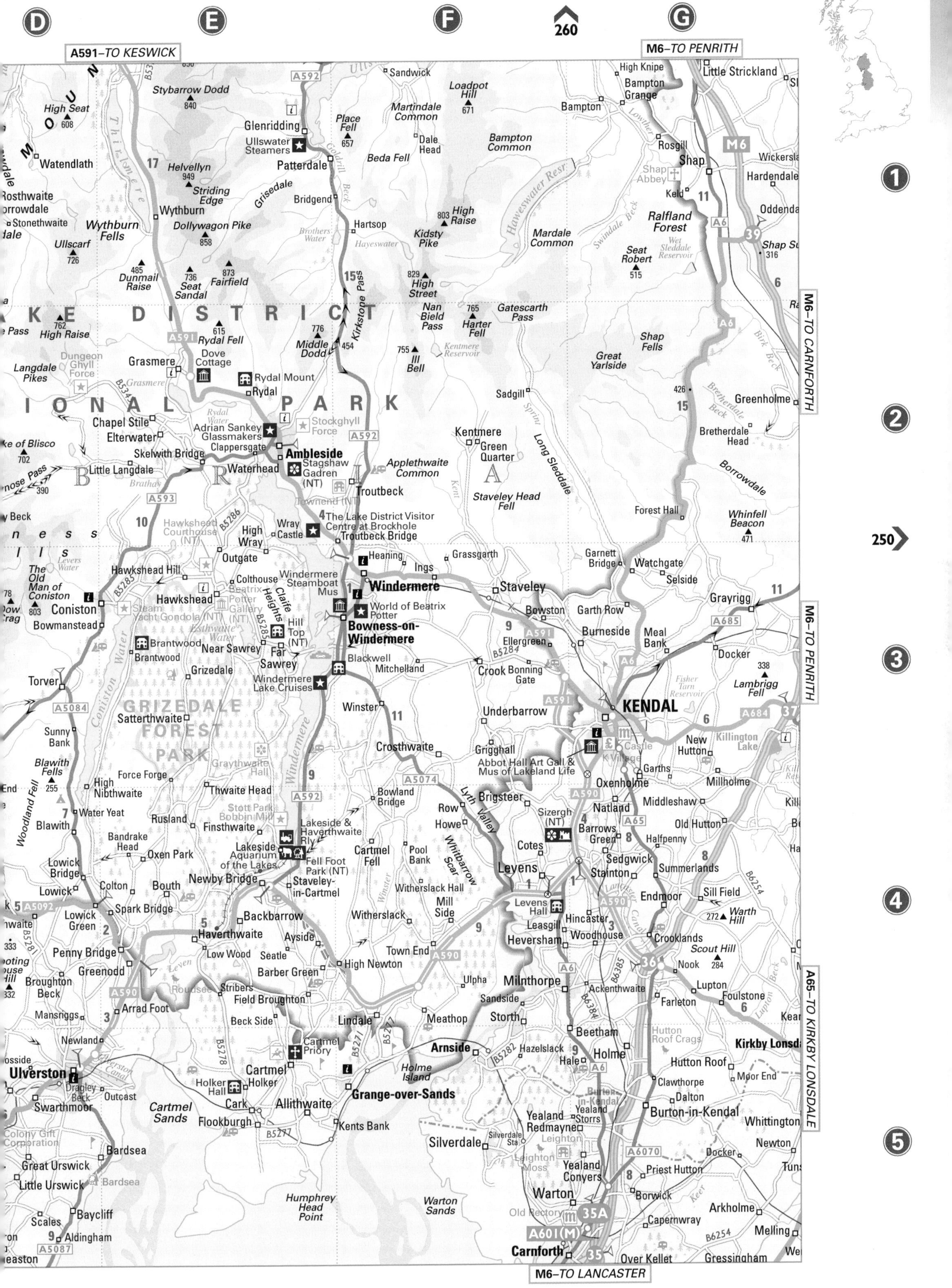

Grasmere: *William Wordsworth lived for a number of years at nearby Dove Cottage. He died in 1850 and is buried in the churchyard of St Oswald's Church. His simple tombstone has since become one of the most visited literary shrines in the world.* ***Map ref. E2***

Windermere: *Lake Windermere is the largest natural lake in England. It is 12 miles (19.3km) long, 1 mile (1.6km) wide and 220 feet (67m) deep. The lake is a major centre for water sports and there are over 10,000 boats registered on the lake. Henry Segrave was killed here in breaking the world water speed record in 1930.* ***Map ref. E3***

260

A B C D

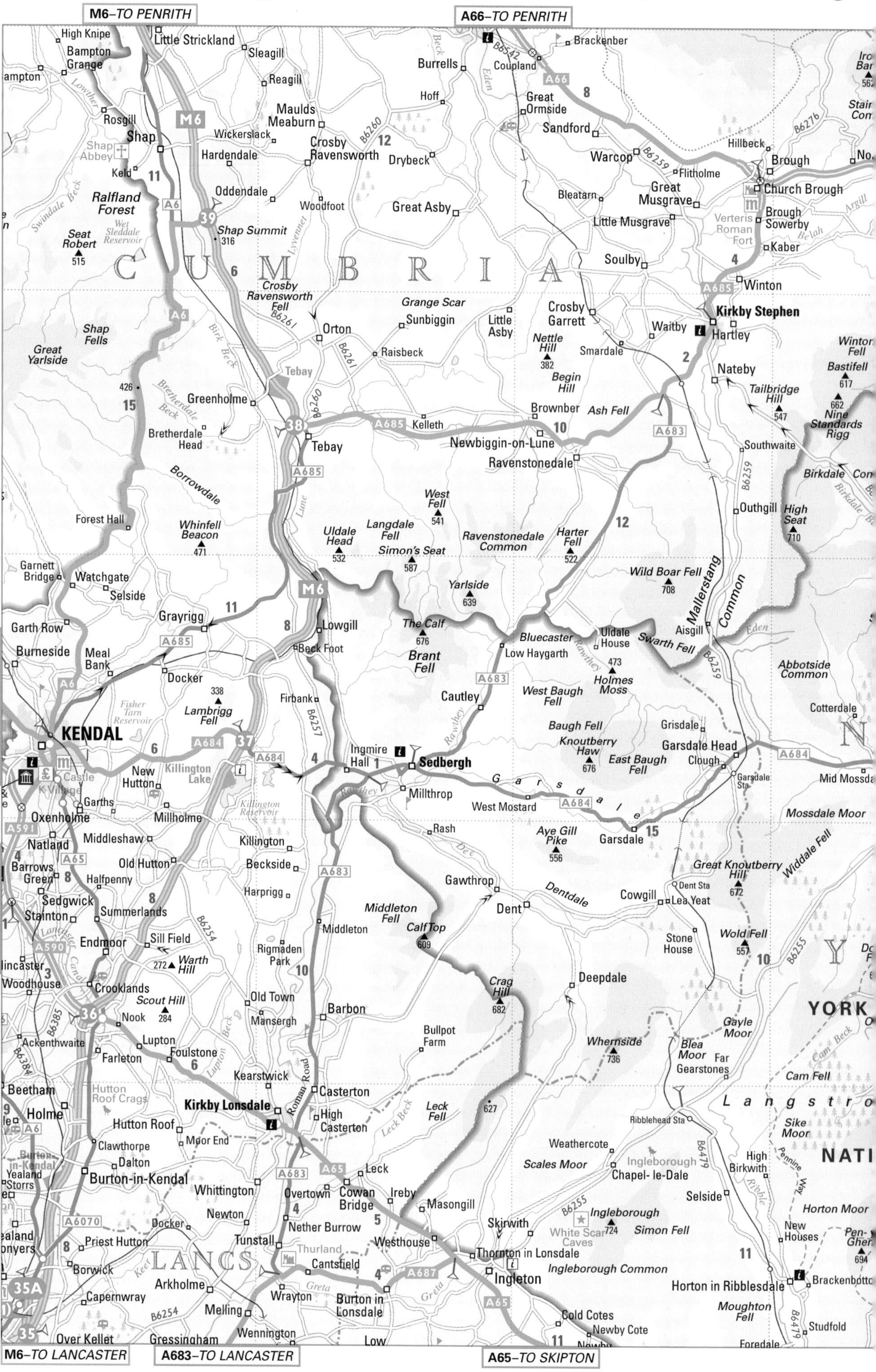

1 2 3 4 5

249

Orton: *Home of George Whitehead (1636–1723) one of the founders of the Quaker Movement. Like many Quakers at the time Whitehead was imprisoned for his beliefs.* ***Map ref. B2***

242

Kendal: *Home of the famous Kendal Mint Cake, popular as an energy boosting food and eaten by Shackleton on his 1914–1917 Transarctic Expedition and by the 1953 Everest Expedition. Reputedly made by accident when a local confectioner Joseph Wiper, at his tiny Ferney Green factory, was intending to make glacier mints. It is now famous the world over.* ***Map ref. A3***

261

D E F G

A688–TO BISHOP AUCKLAND

Hunderthwaite Moor
Blackton Reservoir
Balderhead Reservoir
Baldersdale
Hury Reservoir
Pennine Way
Clove Lodge
Cotherstone Moor
Deep Dale
Deepdale
Beldoo Hill
477
Stainmore Summit
13
A66
447
Greta
Bowes Moor
DURHAM
Stainmore Forest
Scargill High Moor
Sleightholme Moor
Kaber Fell
Taylor Rigg
Tan Hill
Cleasby Hill
Arkle Beck
Arkengarthdale Moor
Stonesdale Moor
Water Crag
668
Rogan's Seat
671
Whaw
Arkengarthdale
West Stonesdale
Melbecks Moor
Gunnerside Gill
Hard Level Gill
Great Pinseat
583
Langthwaite
Booze
Arkle Town
487
Calver Hill
Keld
Angram
Swale
Thwaite
Ivelet
Gunnerside
Feetham
Low Row
Muker
B6270
35
Satron
Crackpot
478
Butter Tubs Pass
Oxnop Ghyll
Summer Lodge
526
675
Askrigg Common
NORTH
High Shaw
Hardraw Force
Sedbusk
Askrigg
Newbiggin
Woodhall
Wensleydale
Bainbridge
Worton
A684
10
Hawes
Gayle
Ropemaker
Burtersett
Wensleydale Cheese Visitor Centre
Countersett
Thornton Rust
Widdale Fell
614
Marsett
Semer Water
Stake Fell
Stalling Busk
YORKSHIRE
Oughtershaw Moss
DALES
Cragdale Moor
Middle Tongue
643
Oughtershaw
Beckermonds
Deepdale
Kidstones
564
Walden Head
Langstrothdale Chase
Yockenthwaite
Buckden Pike
702
Cray
Cover Head Bents
Hubberholme
NATIONAL PARK
Buckden
B6160
Foxup
Halton Gill
Wharfe
Starbotton
19
Nether Heselden
Litton
Littondale
Darnbrook Fell
Fountains Fell
668
Arncliffe
Kettlewell
Wharfedale
Hawkswick
Arncliffe Cote
Stone Cross
Cotherstone
Lartington
Stainton
Barnard Castle
Bowes Museum
Startforth
5
A67
Boldron
B6277
Westwick
Egglestone
Bowes
Gilmonby
Tees
Greta Bridge
Brignall
Barningham
Scargill
Barningham Moor
Hope Moor
Holgate Moor
Kexwith Moor
Hurst Moor
Helwith
Hurst
Washfold
Marske Moor
Marrick Moor
Skelton
Kearton
B6270
Reeth
Fremington
Healaugh
Grinton
Harkerside Moor
Marrick
Swale
Ellerton Priory
Ellerton Abbey
Gibbon Hill
Stainton Moor
565
East Bolton Moor
Redmire Moor
Preston Moor
Bellerby Moor
Castle Bolton
Bolton Castle
Leyburn Moor
Redmire
Preston-under-Scar
Low Bolton
Carperby
Swinithwaite
Wensley
Aysgarth
Ure
Aysgarth Falls & National Park Centre
West Witton
6
Thoralby
West Burton
Penhill
546
Newbiggin
Bishopdale Beck
Agglethorpe
Coverham
Melmerby
Harland Hill
536
Carlton Moor
Carlton
Caldbergh
Cover
B6160
Walden
West Scrafton
Gammersgill
Coverdale
Swineside
Horsehouse
Hindlethwaite Moor
Braidley
Arkleside
Woodale
Great Haw
544
Masham Moor
Little Whernside
605
Brown Ridge
Angram Reservoir
Scar House Reservoir
Nidd
Nidderdale
429
Great Whernside
703
Middlesmoor
How Stean Beck
Stean
Lofthouse
Riggs Moor
Conistone Moor
Meugher
575
Stean Moor
Ramsgill
Humbleton
Broomielaw
Little Newsham
A688
Cleatlam
B6274
Langton
Headlam
Summerhouse
15
Winston
Gainford
A67
High Close
Piercebridge
Whorlton
Ovington
Wycliffe
Eppleby
Caldwell
Hutton Magna
Forcett
Lane Head
Aldbrough St John
B6274
West Layton
East Layton
Stanwick Camp
15
Newsham
Roman Road
Melsonby
Dalton
Ravensworth
Skeeby Beck
Gayles
Kirby Hill
Whashton
Hartforth
Gilling West
High Moor
Skeeby
Georgian Theatre Royal
Richmond
A6108
Richmond Castle
B6271
Marske
5
Hudswell
Brokes
A6136
Hipswell
Downholme
Catterick Garrison
Hipswell Moor
7
Stainton
Scotton
Barden
East Hauxwell
A6108
Garriston
Burton Hall
Bellerby
A684
Constable Burton
Leyburn
Finghall
Harmby
Spennithorne
Hutton Hang
Thornton Resr
Middleham
Abbey (rems of)
Thornton Steward
East Witton
Braithwaite Hall (NT)
Jervaulx Abbey
Ellingstring
High Ellington
20
Gollinglith Foot
Colsterdale
Colsterdale Moor
Fearby
Healey
Leighton
Ilton
Leighton Reservoir
Roundhill Reservoir
Kirkby Malzeard Moor
Hambleton Hill
406
Greygarth
Laver
Bouthwaite
Dallowgill Moor
Dallow

A66–TO SCOTCH CORNER

1 2 3 4 5

252

Askrigg: *The village scenes for 'All Creatures Great and Small' were filmed here. The TV series, based on books by James Herriot was about country vets located in the Yorkshire Dales. The series ran from 1978 to 1990.* ***Map ref. E3***

243

Tan Hill: *The highest pub in Britain is the Tan Hill Inn, which stands 1732 feet (528m) above sea level.* ***Map ref. E2***

A B C D

262

1

2

251

3

4

5

Ripon: Ripon is the oldest city in Britain with a charter dating back to AD886. *Map ref. C5*

244

263

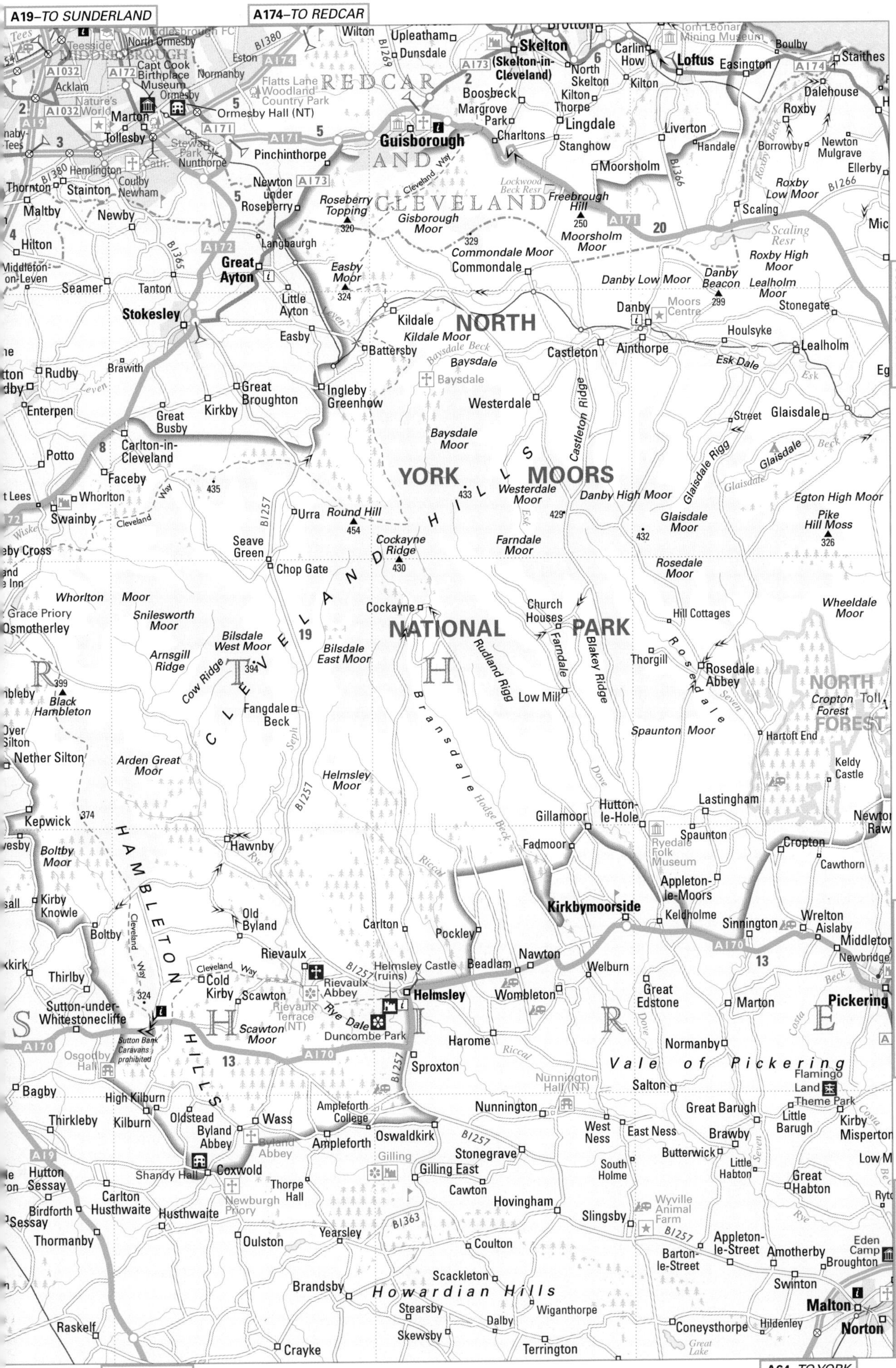

254

Boulby: *Boulby Cliff is the highest sea cliff on the east coast of Britain at 666 feet (203m).* ***Map ref. G1***

245

Marton: *Captain James Cook was born here on 27th October 1728. Cook enlisted in the Royal Navy and in 1768 began the first of three voyages to the Pacific where he spent over eight years charting previously unknown islands. He was stabbed to death by natives on the island of Hawaii in February 1779.* ***Map ref. G4***

263

A B C D

1 2 3 4 5

253

246

Goathland: *Since 1992 the popular drama series Heartbeat has been filmed here. In the series the village is called Aidensfield and frequent references are made to nearby Whitby* ***Map ref. B2.***
The spin-off hospital series 'The Royal' is located in Scarborough. ***Map ref. D4***

Filey: *The Royal Crescent, built by John Wilkes Unett in 1850, was for 100 years the most fashionable address in the whole of the north of England.* ***Map ref. E4***

247

Flamborough Head: *This rocky chalk headland juts out 6 miles into the North Sea and features picturesque coves and sea caves. Because of its chalk-loving flora it is designated a Special Area of Conservation (SAC).* ***Map ref. F5***

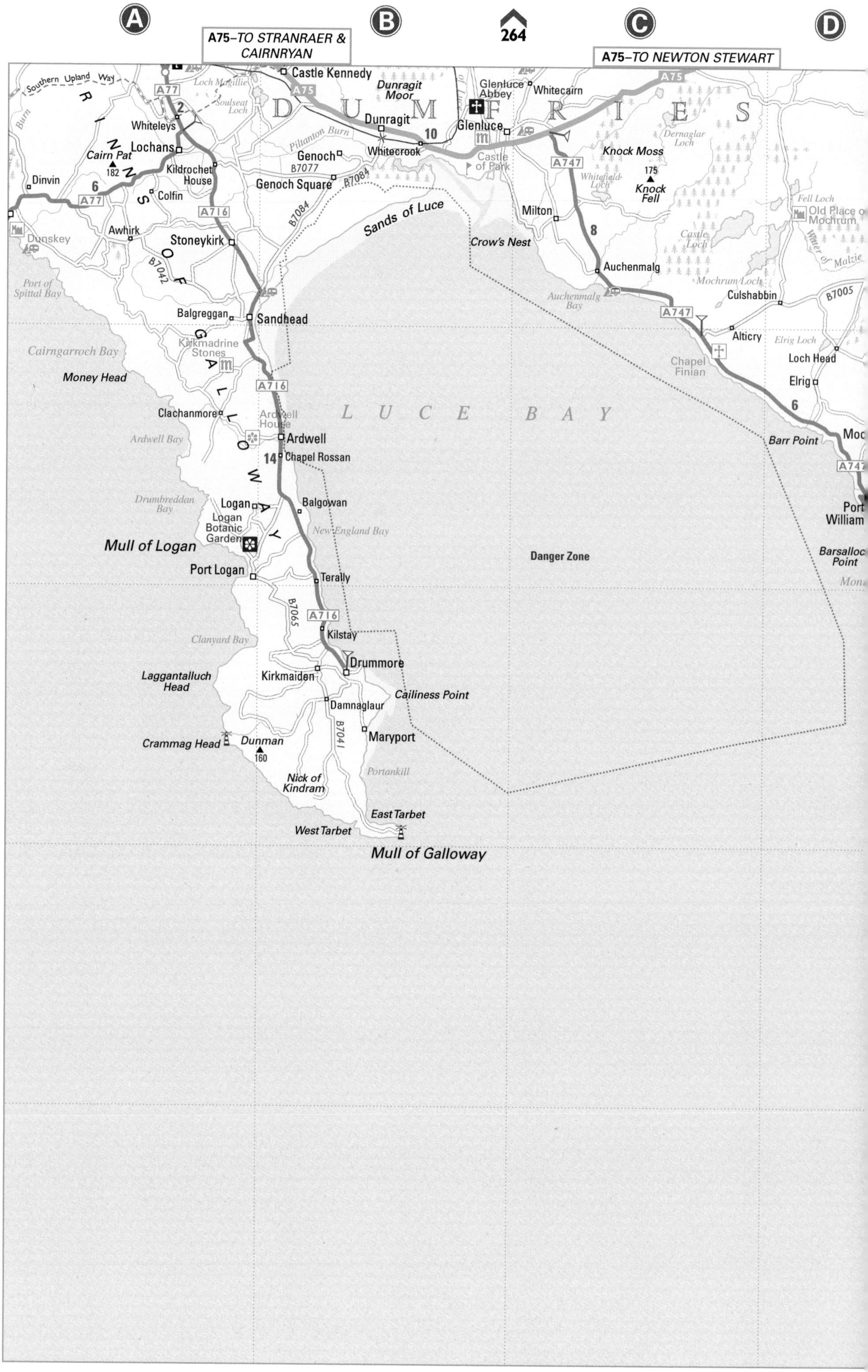

Port Logan: *Now famous as the setting for the BBC Television Series '2000 Acres of Sky', which starred Michelle Collins.*
Map ref. A2

Mull of Galloway: *A Mull is a high point of land on a rocky coast that juts out into the sea. Here, the Mull of Galloway is the most southerly point in Scotland.*
Map ref. B3

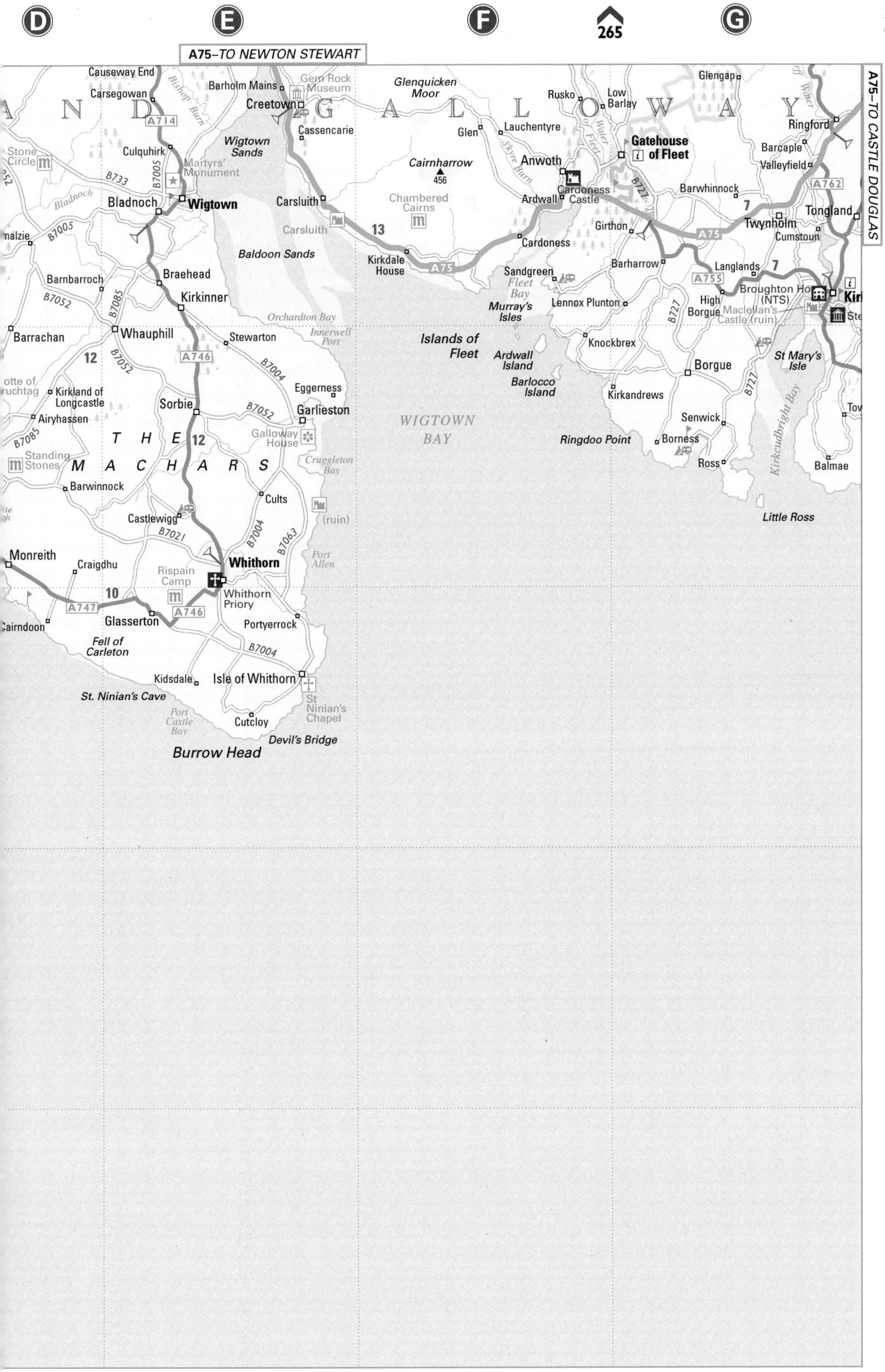

Wigtown: *The Martyrs Stake here marks the location of the execution by drowning of the 'Covenanters' Margaret Wilson and Margaret McLachlane in 1685. Their gravestones are in Wigtown churchyard.*
***Map ref.* E1**

A 266 B C 267 D

1

257

2

3

4

5

A595–TO BARROW-IN-FURNES

Cockermouth: *Fletcher Christian, ringleader of the Mutiny on the Bounty was born here in 1789. Following the mutiny Christian and eight other mutineers took refuge on Pitcairn Island where they founded a settlement.* ***Map ref. E3***

St Bees: *The nearby RSPB Nature Reserve is home to England's only colony of Black Guillemots.* ***Map ref. C5***

248

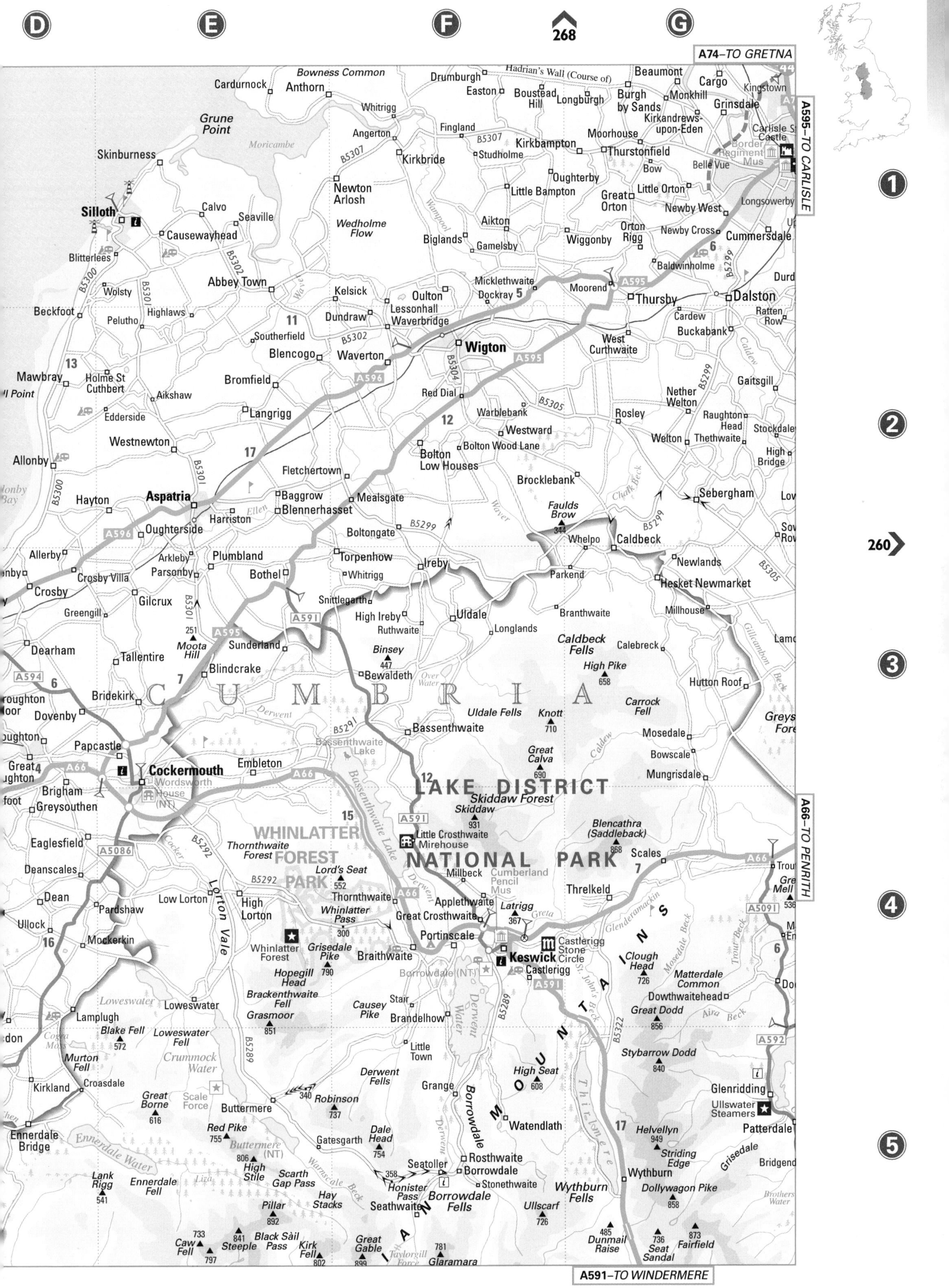

Seathwaite: *The small village of Seathwaite is northeast of Scafell Pike, at 3,210 feet (978m) the highest mountain in England. Seathwaite is thought to be the wettest settlement in Britain with about 130 inches (330 cm) average rainfall per year.* ***Map ref. F5***

A 268 B C D

1

2

259

3

4

5

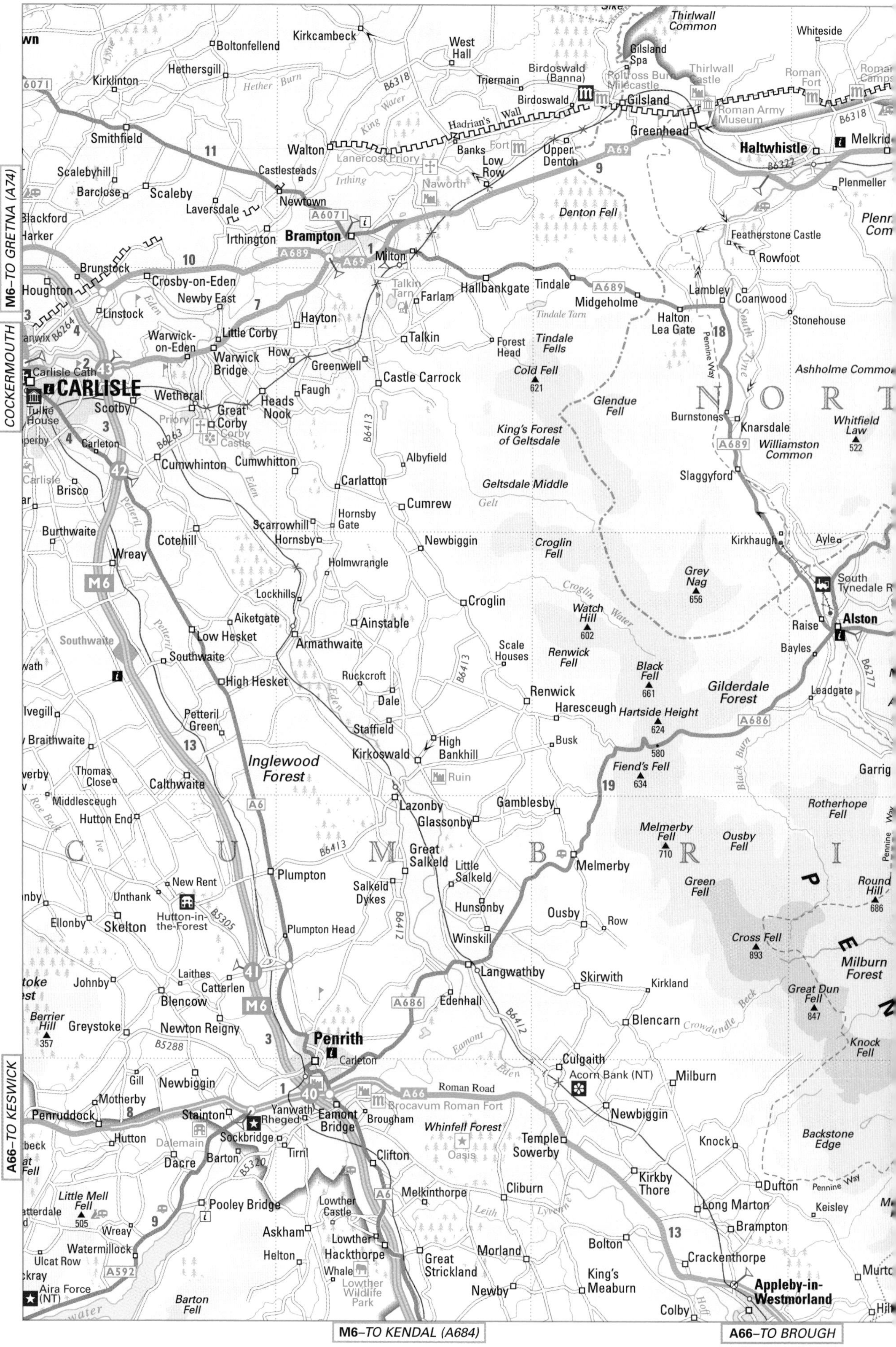

Kirkoswald: *St. Oswald's church has a unique feature in that the church bell tower is perched on a hill top 200 yards (180m) away from the actual church building. **Map ref. B3***

250

Allendale Town: *Since 1842 this town has claimed to be the geographical centre of Britain, on the grounds that it is halfway between Cape Wrath and Beachy Head. Latitude and longitude figures are displayed on the sundial on the church tower. However, nearby Haltwhistle (**Map ref. D1**) also makes this claim, as the mid-point of Britain's longest line of longitude which stretches from the Orkney Islands to Dorset. **Map ref. E2***

D 269 E 270 F G

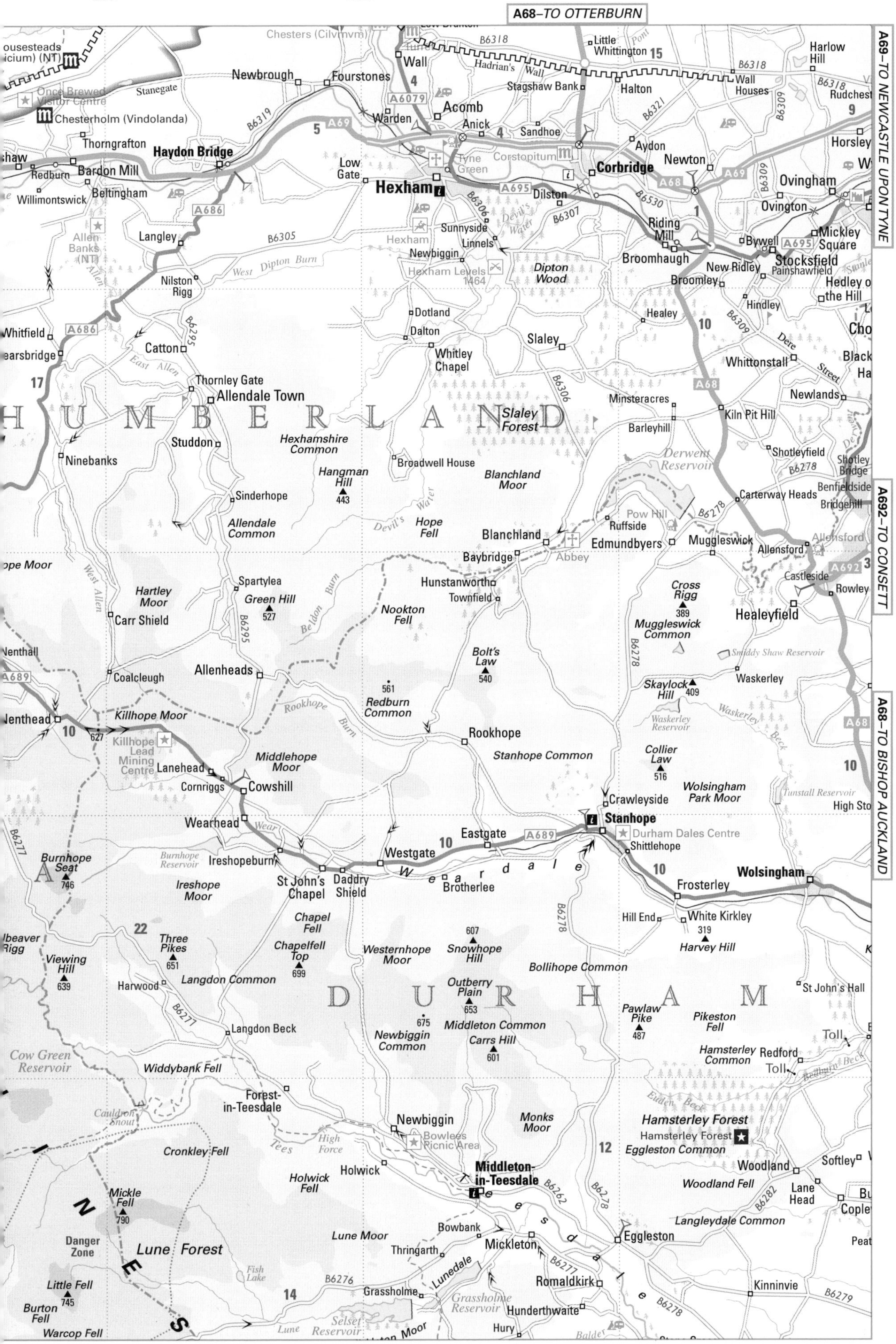

262

Hexham: *This is the administrative centre for Tynedale, the largest local authority district in England. With a land area of 856 square miles (2217 sq km) and only 57,400 residents, the authority has a population density of just 67 people per square mile (26 per sq km).* ***Map ref. F1***

251

Cauldron Snout: *This is now commonly cited as England's highest waterfall at 200 feet (61m), although it is more a cascade than a single unbroken fall.* ***Map ref. E5***

A B C D
270 271
A696–TO OTTERBURN
A1–TO MORPETH
A19–TO ASHINGTON (A189)
1 2 3 4 5
A69–TO CORBRIDGE
A692–TO CORBRIDGE (A68)
A68–TO CONSETT
261
SEE PAGE 372
A688–TO BARNARD CASTLE
252
A68–TO DARLINGTON
A1(M)–TO SCOTCH CORNER

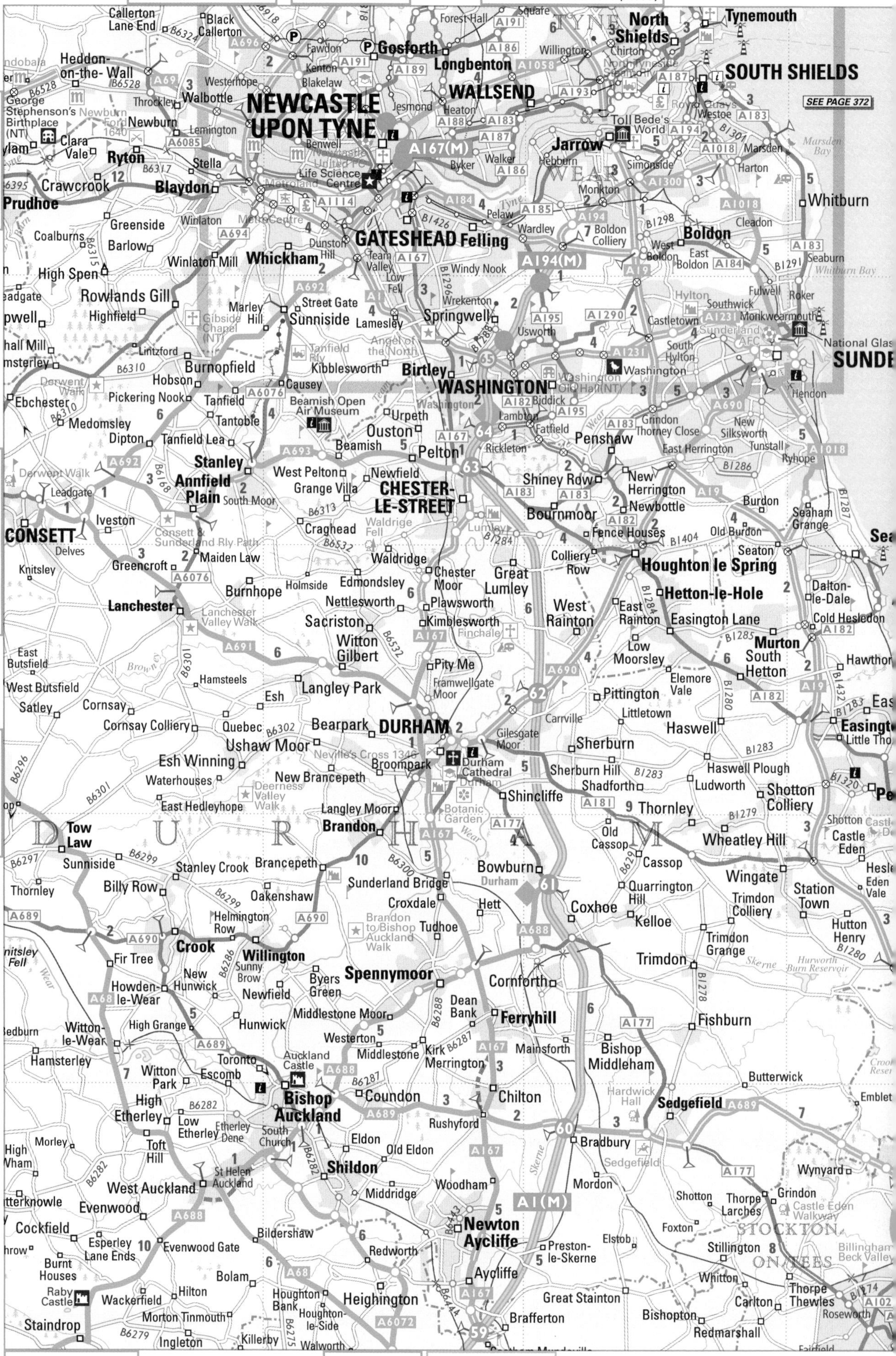

Angel of the North: *Britain's largest sculpture, the Angel, created by Anthony Gormley, stands 65 feet (20m) high, has a wingspan of 175 feet (54m) and weighs 197 tons (200 tonnes). The sculpture is made of weather resistant steel, can withstand 100 mph (160km/h) winds and has an estimated lifespan of 100 years.* ***Map ref. B2***

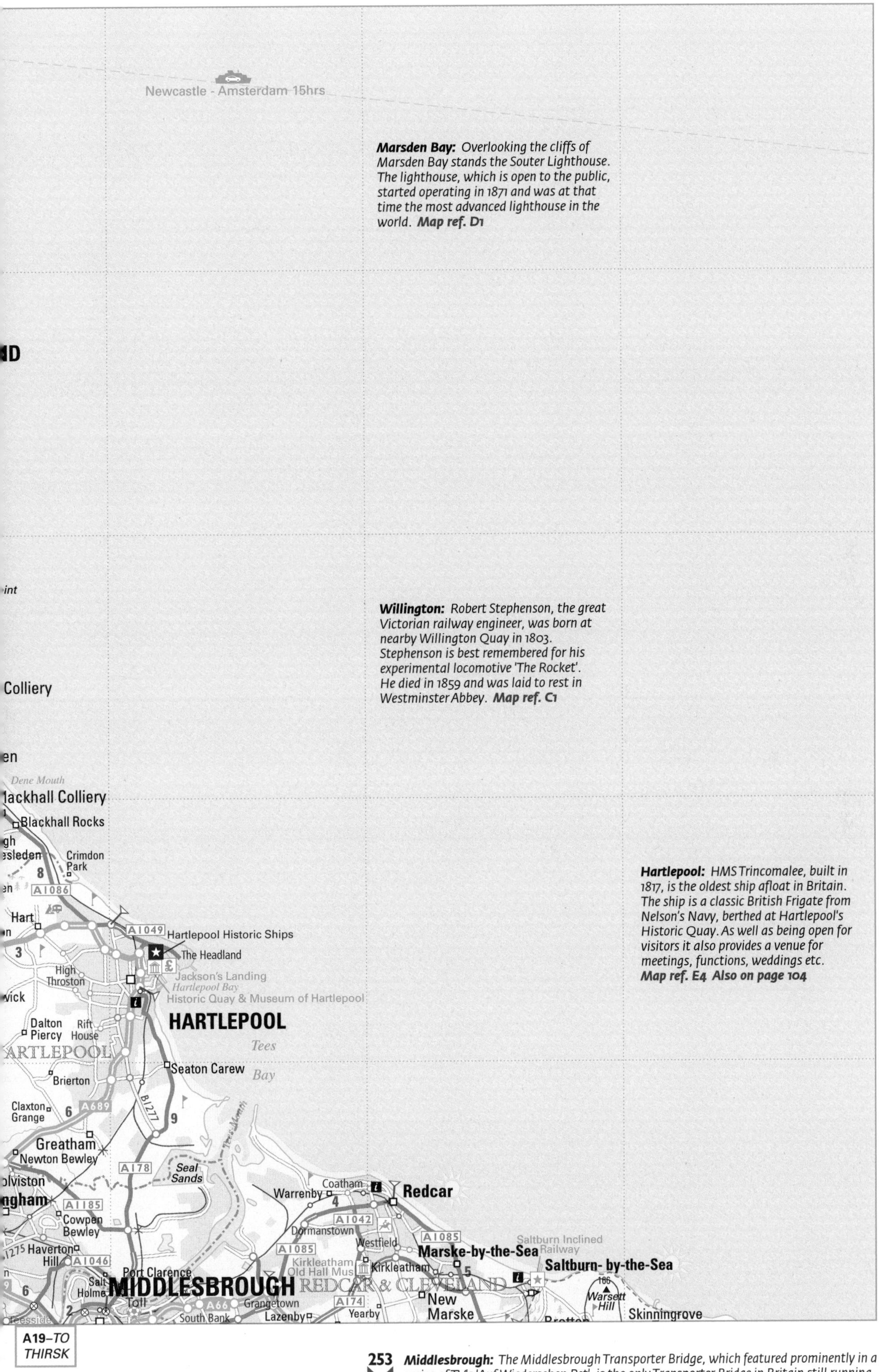

Marsden Bay: *Overlooking the cliffs of Marsden Bay stands the Souter Lighthouse. The lighthouse, which is open to the public, started operating in 1871 and was at that time the most advanced lighthouse in the world.* ***Map ref. D1***

Willington: *Robert Stephenson, the great Victorian railway engineer, was born at nearby Willington Quay in 1803. Stephenson is best remembered for his experimental locomotive 'The Rocket'. He died in 1859 and was laid to rest in Westminster Abbey.* ***Map ref. C1***

Hartlepool: *HMS Trincomalee, built in 1817, is the oldest ship afloat in Britain. The ship is a classic British Frigate from Nelson's Navy, berthed at Hartlepool's Historic Quay. As well as being open for visitors it also provides a venue for meetings, functions, weddings etc.* ***Map ref. E4 Also on page 104***

253

Middlesbrough: *The Middlesbrough Transporter Bridge, which featured prominently in a series of TV's 'Auf Wiedersehen Pet', is the only Transporter Bridge in Britain still running a daily service. It was built in 1911 and is over 850 feet (260m) long, 220 feet (67m) high and crosses the River Tees.* ***Map ref. D5***

273

Ailsa Craig: *Unpopulated Island but features a lighthouse on Foreland Point built by Thomas and David Stevenson in 1886. Until 1935 all contact between the lighthouse and the mainland was by carrier pigeon. It is now unmanned and powered by solar panels.* **Map ref.B1**

256

Stranraer: *The world's first high-speed ferry operates from Stranraer to Belfast and is known as Stena HSS. This is one of the largest ferries in the world, capable of carrying 1500 passengers plus their cars and coaches. It is powered by four jet engines which provide the same thrust as that required for a jumbo jet and give it a cruising speed of 40 knots.* **Map ref. B4**

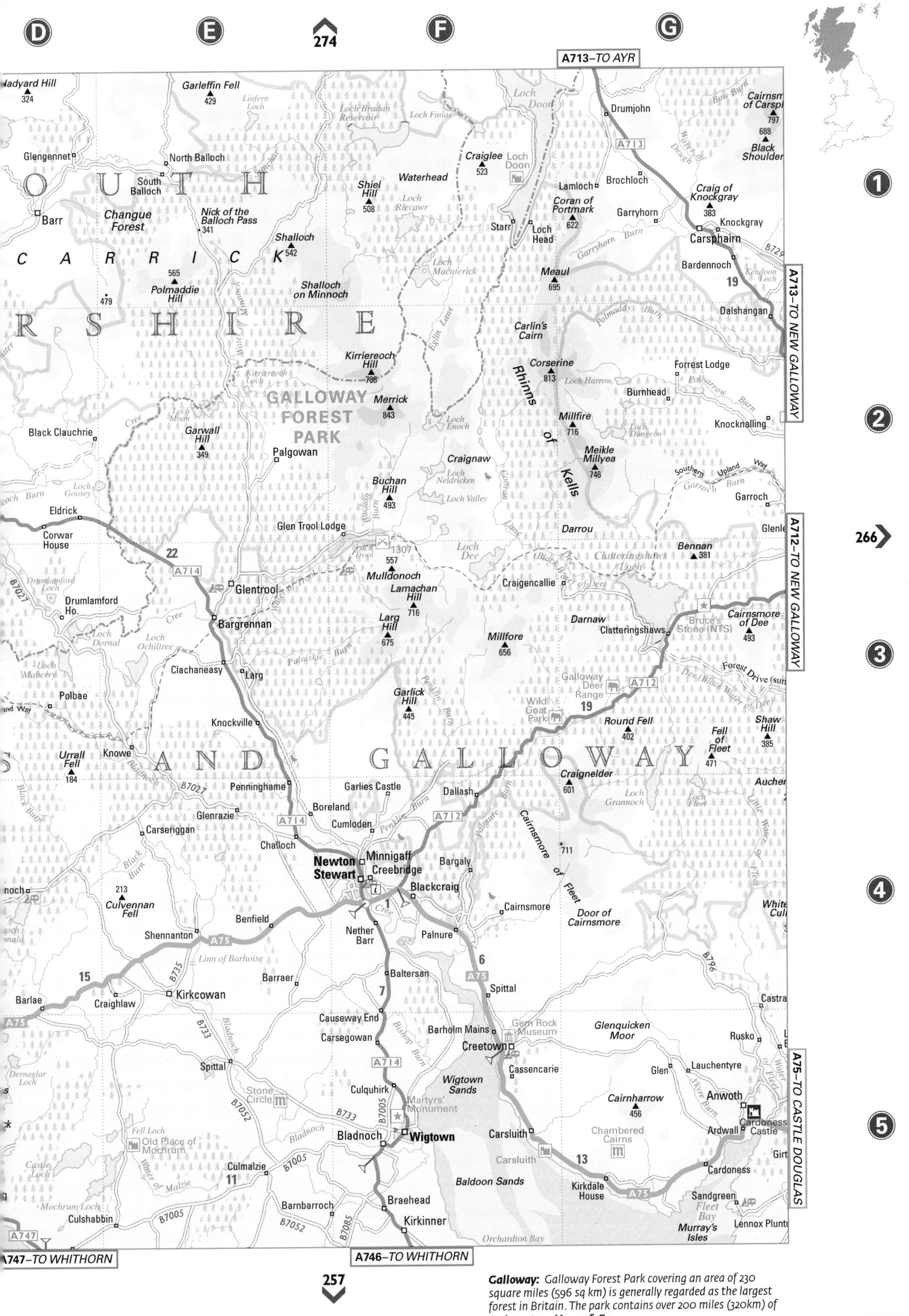
D
E
274
F
G
A713–TO AYR
1
2
3
4
5
266
A713–TO NEW GALLOWAY
A712–TO NEW GALLOWAY
A75–TO CASTLE DOUGLAS
A747–TO WHITHORN
A746–TO WHITHORN
257
SOUTH
CARRICK
AYRSHIRE
DUMFRIES AND GALLOWAY
GALLOWAY FOREST PARK
Garleffin Fell
429
Linfern Loch
Loch Bradan Reservoir
Loch Finlas
Loch Doon
Drumjohn
Bow Burn
Cairnsmore of Carsphairn
797
688
Black Shoulder
Water of Deugh
A713
Glengennet
North Balloch
South Balloch
Barr
Changue Forest
Nick of the Balloch Pass
341
Shiel Hill
508
Waterhead
Loch Riecawr
Craiglee
523
Lamloch
Brochloch
Coran of Portmark
622
Garryhorn
Craig of Knockgray
383
Knockgray
Carsphairn
Starr
Loch Head
Shalloch
542
Loch Macaterick
Meaul
695
Garryhorn Burn
B729
Bardennoch
Kendoon Loch
19
565
Polmaddie Hill
479
Shalloch on Minnoch
Water of Minnoch
Dalshangan
Polmaddy Burn
Carlin's Cairn
Eglin Lane
Kirriereoch Hill
786
Kirriereoch Loch
Corserine
813
Loch Harrow
Forrest Lodge
Polharrow Burn
Burnhead
Merrick
843
Rhinns of Kells
Millfire
716
Knocknalling
Loch Moan
Cree
Garwall Hill
349
Loch Enoch
Loch Dungeon
Black Clauchrie
Palgowan
Meikle Millyea
746
Craignaw
Loch Neldricken
Southern Upland Way
Garroch Burn
Garroch
Loch Goosey
Buchan Hill
493
Buchan Burn
Loch Valley
Cooran Lane
Eldrick
Corwar House
Glen Trool Lodge
Darrou
Glenlee
22
A714
Loch Trool
1307
557
Mulldonoch
Loch Dee
Black Water of Dee
Clatteringshaws Loch
Bennan
381
Drumlamford Loch
B7027
Drumlamford Ho.
Glentrool
Lamachan Hill
716
Craigencallie
Bargrennan
Loch Dornal
Loch Ochiltree
Larg Hill
675
Darnaw
Clatteringshaws
Bruce's Stone (NTS)
Cairnsmore of Dee
493
Millfore
656
Loch Maberry
Clachaneasy
Larg
Palnuskie Burn
Penkiln Burn
Forest Drive
Dee (Black Water of Dee)
Galloway Deer Range
A712
Polbae
Garlick Hill
445
Wild Goat Park
19
Round Fell
402
Shaw Hill
385
Knockville
Fell of Fleet
471
Urrall Fell
184
Knowe
Bladnoch
Craignelder
601
Aucher
Penninghame
Garlies Castle
Dallash
Loch Grannoch
Loch Fleet
Little Water of Fleet
Black Burn
Glenrazie
Boreland
Cumloden
Penkiln Burn
Palnure Burn
Carseriggan
Cairnsmore of Fleet
711
Challoch
Newton Stewart
Minnigaff
Creebridge
Bargaly
213
Culvennan Fell
Blackcraig
Cairnsmore
Door of Cairnsmore
White Cull
1
Cree
Benfield
Nether Barr
Palnure
Shennanton
A75
Linn of Barhoise
6
B796
15
B735
Barraer
Baltersan
Spittal
Barlae
Craighlaw
Kirkcowan
7
Castra
B733
Causeway End
Barholm Mains
Gem Rock Museum
Glenquicken Moor
Rusko
Carsegowan
Bishop Burn
Creetown
Cassencarie
Spittal
Dernaglar Loch
Wigtown Sands
Glen
Lauchentyre
Water of Fleet
Skyre Burn
Culquhirk
Stone Circle
B7052
B7005
Martyrs' Monument
Cairnharrow
456
Anwoth
Fell Loch
Old Place of Mochrum
Bladnoch
Wigtown
Carsluith
Chambered Cairns
Ardwall
Cardoness Castle
Castle Loch
Water of Malzie
Culmalzie
11
Carsluith
13
Girt
Cardoness
Baldoon Sands
Kirkdale House
Braehead
Sandgreen
Fleet Bay
Mochrum Loch
Barnbarroch
Culshabbin
B7085
Kirkinner
Murray's Isles
Lennox Plunt
A747
Orchardton Bay

Galloway: *Galloway Forest Park covering an area of 230 square miles (596 sq km) is generally regarded as the largest forest in Britain. The park contains over 200 miles (320km) of cycle routes.* ***Map ref. E2***

A
275
B
C
D
1
2
265
3
4
5

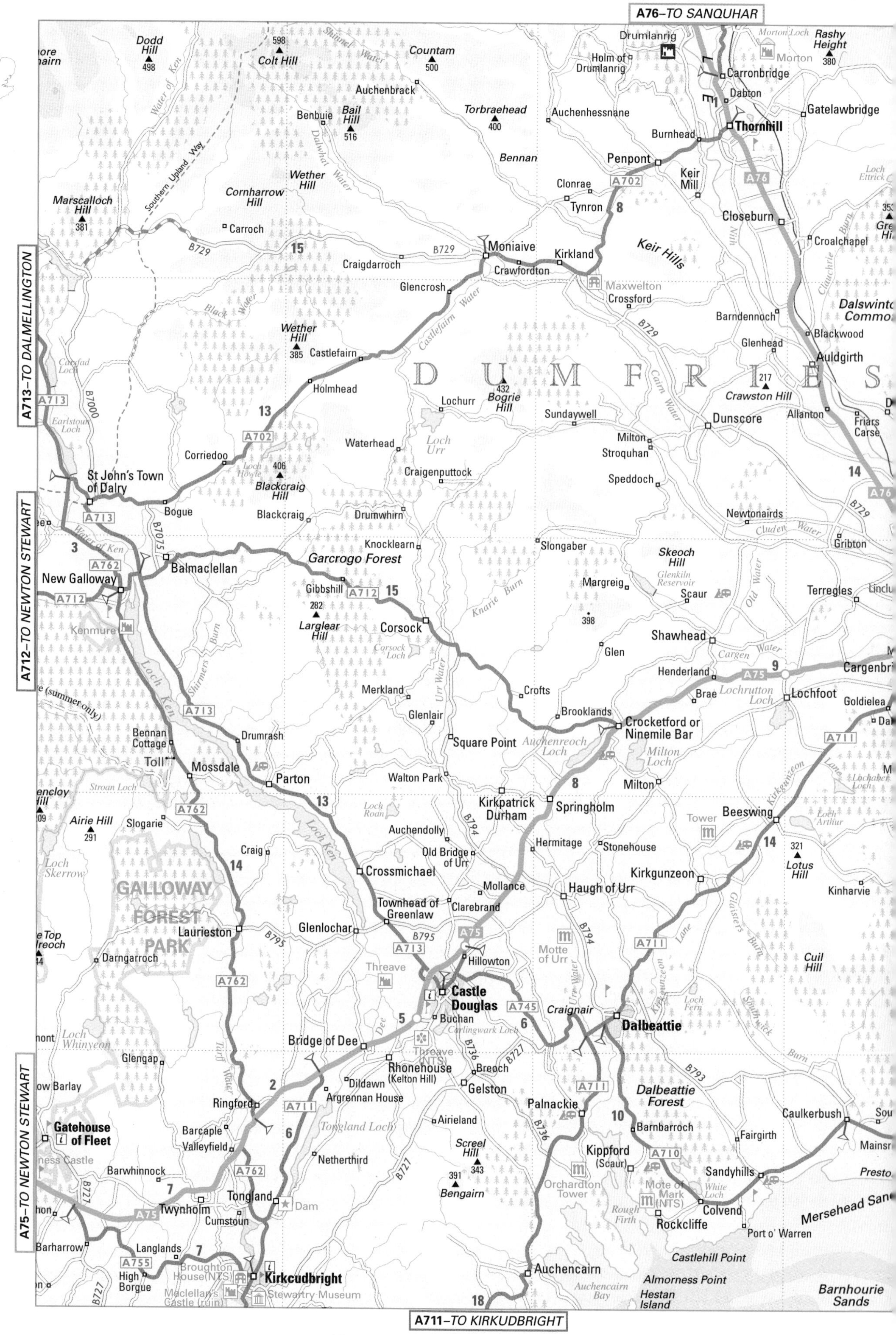

258

Loch Ken: *The ruins of Kenmure Castle at the head of the loch were made famous in Sir Walter Scott's ballad 'Young Lochinvar' and also in Robert Burns Jacobite song 'Kenmure's up and awa', Willie'*
Map ref. A3

Dalbeattie: *Birthplace on the 28th February 1873 of Lieutenant William McMaster Murdoch, First Officer of the RMS Titanic. Lieutenant Murdoch died aboard ship when the Titanic struck an iceberg and sank on the 15th April 1912.*
Map ref. C4

D E F G
276

A701–TO MOFFAT

A74(M)–TO GLASGOW (M74)

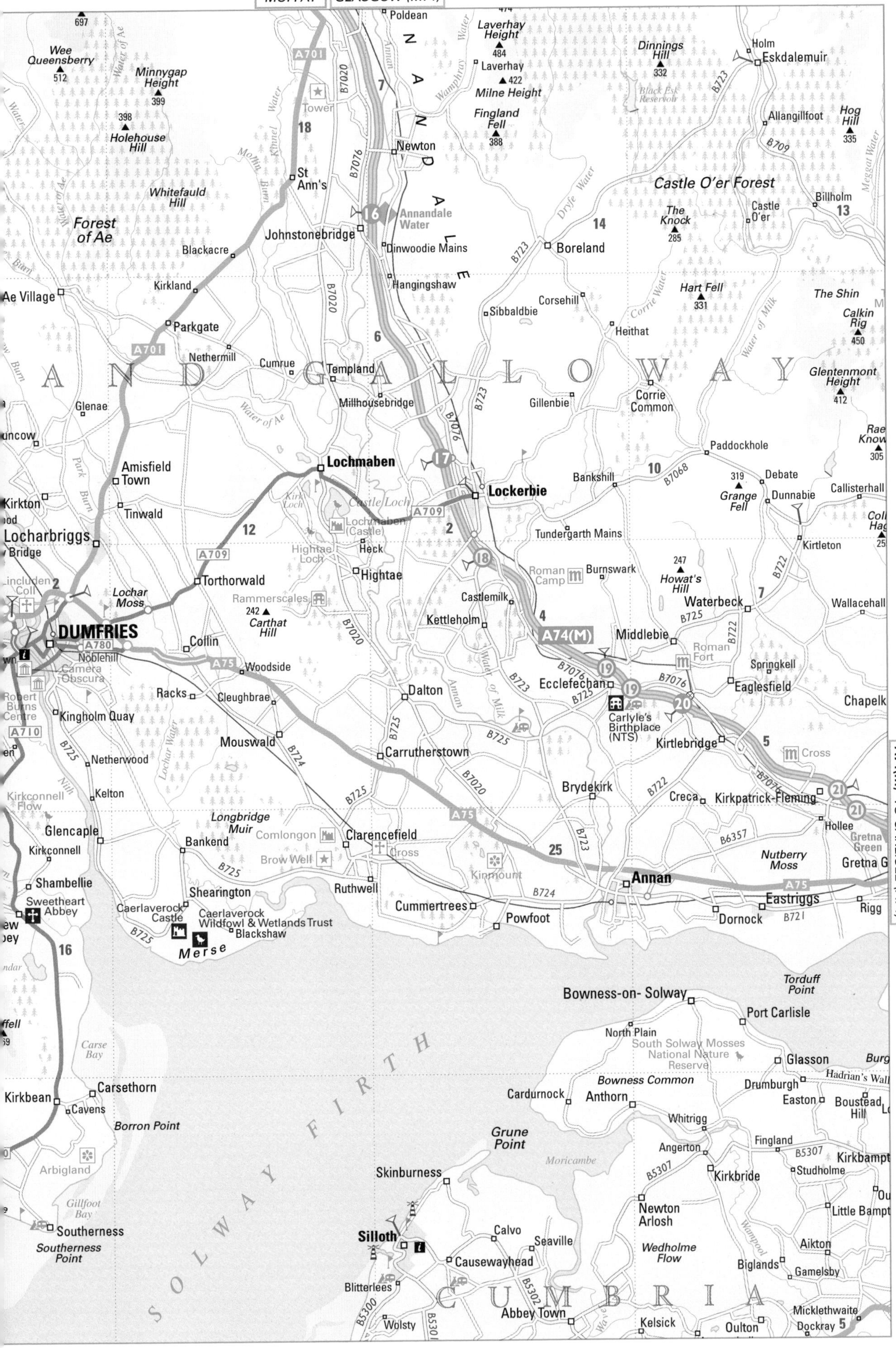

1
2
268
3
4
5
259

Ruthwell: *Dr Henry Duncan (1774–1846) opened the worlds first bank here when he was the minister of this parish. He is regarded as the founder of savings banks and is remembered in Henry Duncan House, the Edinburgh headquarters of a national banking group.* ***Map ref. E4***

Lockerbie: *On the evening of the 21st December 1988 terrorists placed a bomb on board Pan Am flight 103. The plane exploded 6 miles (9.65km) above this small Scottish town. All 259 people on board, plus 11 people on the ground lost their lives in what proved to be the biggest mass murder in British history.* ***Map ref. F2***

A
277
B
C
D
1
2
267
3
4
5

259

Newcastleton: *This village was planned and built specifically as a handloom weaving centre, in 1793, by the Duke of Buccleuch for his employees.* ***Map ref. C3***

Gretna: *Britain's worst ever rail disaster happened at Quintinshill, just north-east of Gretna on the 22nd May 1915. A troop train, towing wooden carriages, collided with a stationary passenger train and was then itself hit by an oncoming express train. 227 people, most of them soldiers, were killed in the crashes and subsequent fire.* ***Map ref. B5***

1
2
270
3
4
5

Kielder Forest: *This is the largest forest in England covering an area of 200 square miles (518 sq km) and planted with over 150 million trees. The forest is man-made and the first tree was planted at Smales Farm in 1926.* ***Map ref. E2***

260

Kielder Water: *With a shoreline of over 27 miles (44km), Kielder Water is the largest artificial lake in Northern Europe.* ***Map ref. E3***

A B C D
278

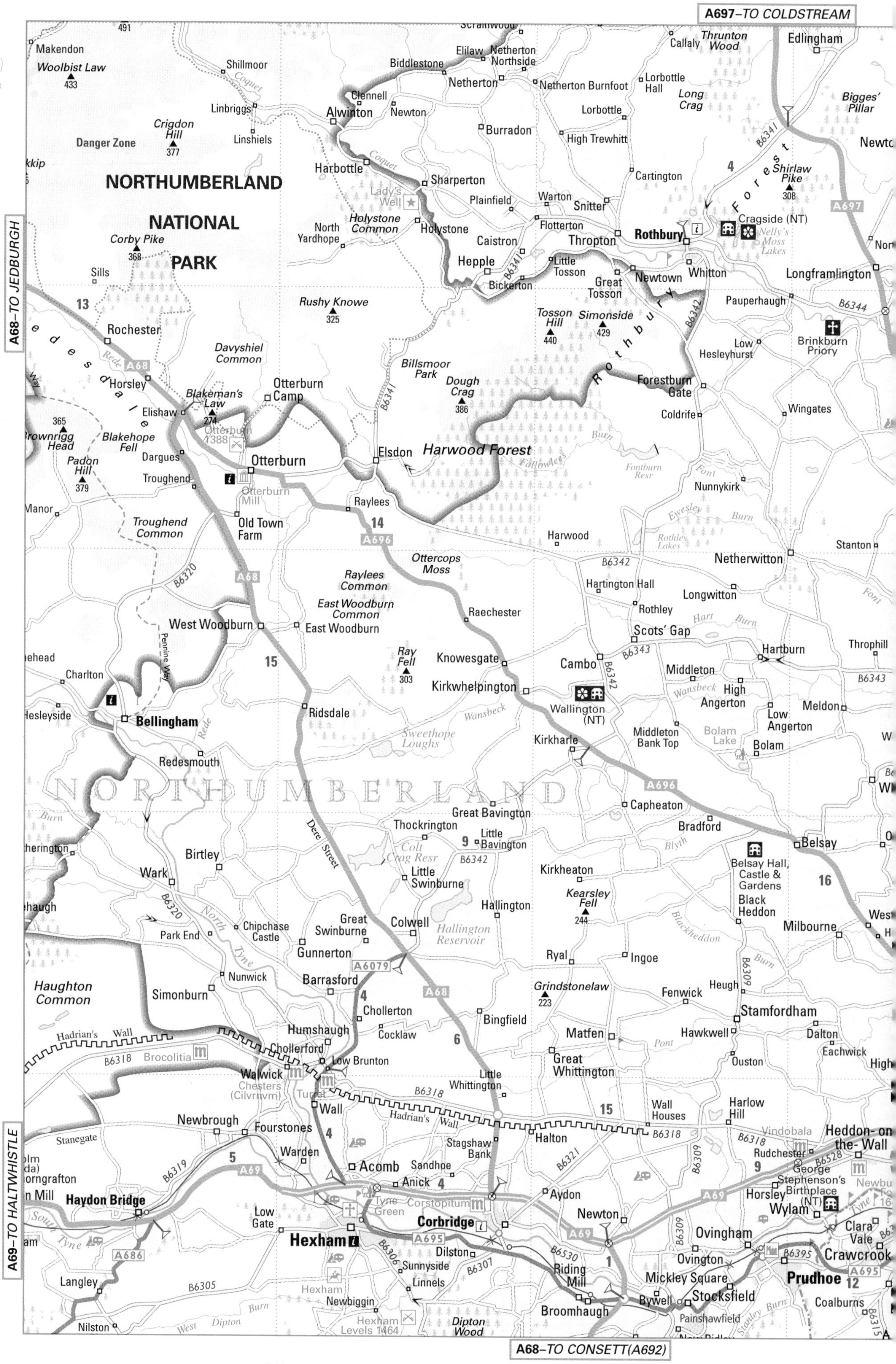

269
1
2
3
4
5
261

Kirkharle: *Lancelot 'Capability' Brown, one of Britain's greatest landscape gardeners, was born here in 1715. He designed gardens for many stately homes and became head gardener at Hampton Court Palace in 1761. 'Capability' Brown died on the 6th February 1783.* ***Map ref. C3***

BERWICK-UPON-TWEED
A1068–TO ALNWICK

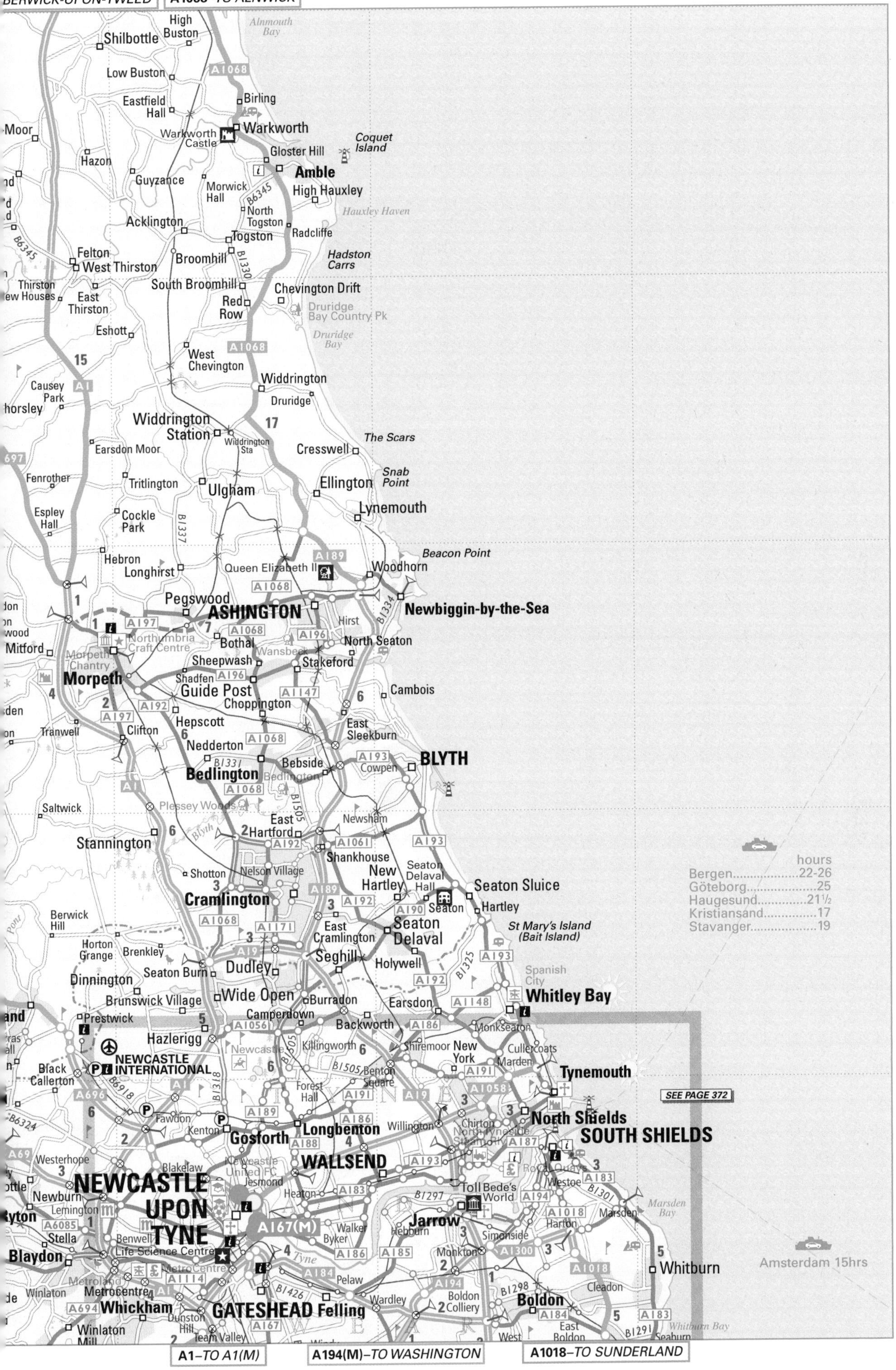

1

2

3

4

5

A1–TO A1(M)
A194(M)–TO WASHINGTON
A1018–TO SUNDERLAND
262
263

Jarrow: *Starting point on the 1st November 1936 of the protest march from Jarrow to London a distance of 300 miles (480km). 200 men marched in protest at the miseries of unemployment and the injustice of 'means testing'. The last surviving marcher Cornelius Whalen died in September 2003 aged 93.* ***Map ref. F5***

281

A B C D

1 2 3 4 5

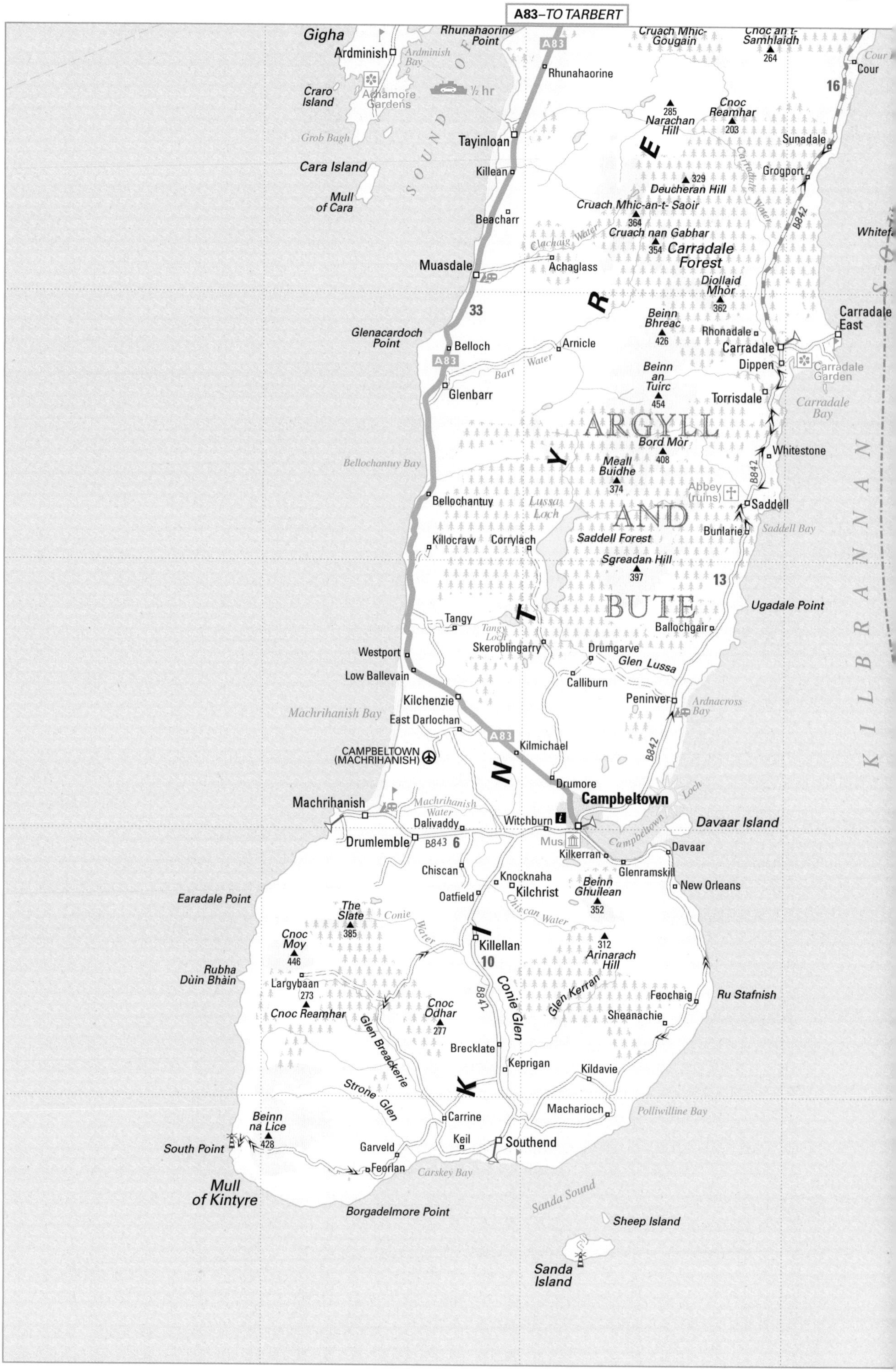

A83–TO TARBERT
Gigha
Ardminish
Ardminish Bay
Rhunahaorine Point
Rhunahaorine
Cruach Mhic-Gougain
Cnoc an t-Samhlaidh
264
Cour
Cour Bay
16
Craro Island
Achamore Gardens
½ hr
SOUND OF
Narachan Hill
285
Cnoc Reamhar
203
Sunadale
Grob Bagh
Tayinloan
Cara Island
Killean
Grogport
Carradale Water
B842
329
Deucheran Hill
Mull of Cara
Cruach Mhic-an-t- Saoir
364
Beacharr
Cruach nan Gabhar
Clachaig Water
354
Carradale Forest
Whitef
Muasdale
Achaglass
Diollaid Mhòr
362
33
Beinn Bhreac
426
Carradale East
Rhonadale
Glenacardoch Point
Belloch
Arnicle
Carradale
A83
Barr Water
Dippen
Carradale Garden
Glenbarr
Beinn an Tuirc
454
Torrisdale
Carradale Bay
ARGYLL
Bord Mòr
408
Whitestone
Bellochantuy Bay
Meall Buidhe
374
Abbey (ruins)
Saddell
Bellochantuy
Lussa Loch
AND
Bunlarie
Saddell Bay
Killocraw
Corrylach
Saddell Forest
Sgreadan Hill
397
13
BUTE
Ugadale Point
Tangy
Tangy Loch
Ballochgair
Skeroblingarry
Drumgarve
Glen Lussa
Westport
Low Ballevain
Calliburn
Kilchenzie
Peninver
Ardnacross Bay
Machrihanish Bay
East Darlochan
A83
Kilmichael
B842
KILBRANNAN SOUND
CAMPBELTOWN (MACHRIHANISH)
Drumore
Campbeltown
Campbeltown Loch
Machrihanish
Machrihanish Water
Davaar Island
Dalivaddy
Witchburn
Drumlemble
B843
6
Mus
Davaar
Kilkerran
Glenramskill
Chiscan
Knocknaha
New Orleans
Earadale Point
Oatfield
Kilchrist
Beinn Ghuilean
352
The Slate
385
Conie Water
Chiscan Water
Cnoc Moy
446
Killellan
10
312
Arinarach Hill
Rubha Dùin Bhàin
Largybaan
273
Conie Glen
B842
Glen Kerran
Feochaig
Ru Stafnish
Cnoc Reamhar
Glen Breackerie
Cnoc Odhar
277
Sheanachie
Brecklate
Keprigan
Kildavie
Strone Glen
KINTYRE
Machariooch
Polliwilline Bay
Beinn na Lice
428
Carrine
South Point
Keil
Southend
Garveld
Feorlan
Carskey Bay
Mull of Kintyre
Sanda Sound
Borgadelmore Point
Sheep Island
Sanda Island

Mull of Kintyre: *Made famous in the song 'Mull of Kintyre' by Paul McCartney and Wings in 1977.* ***Map ref. A5***

282

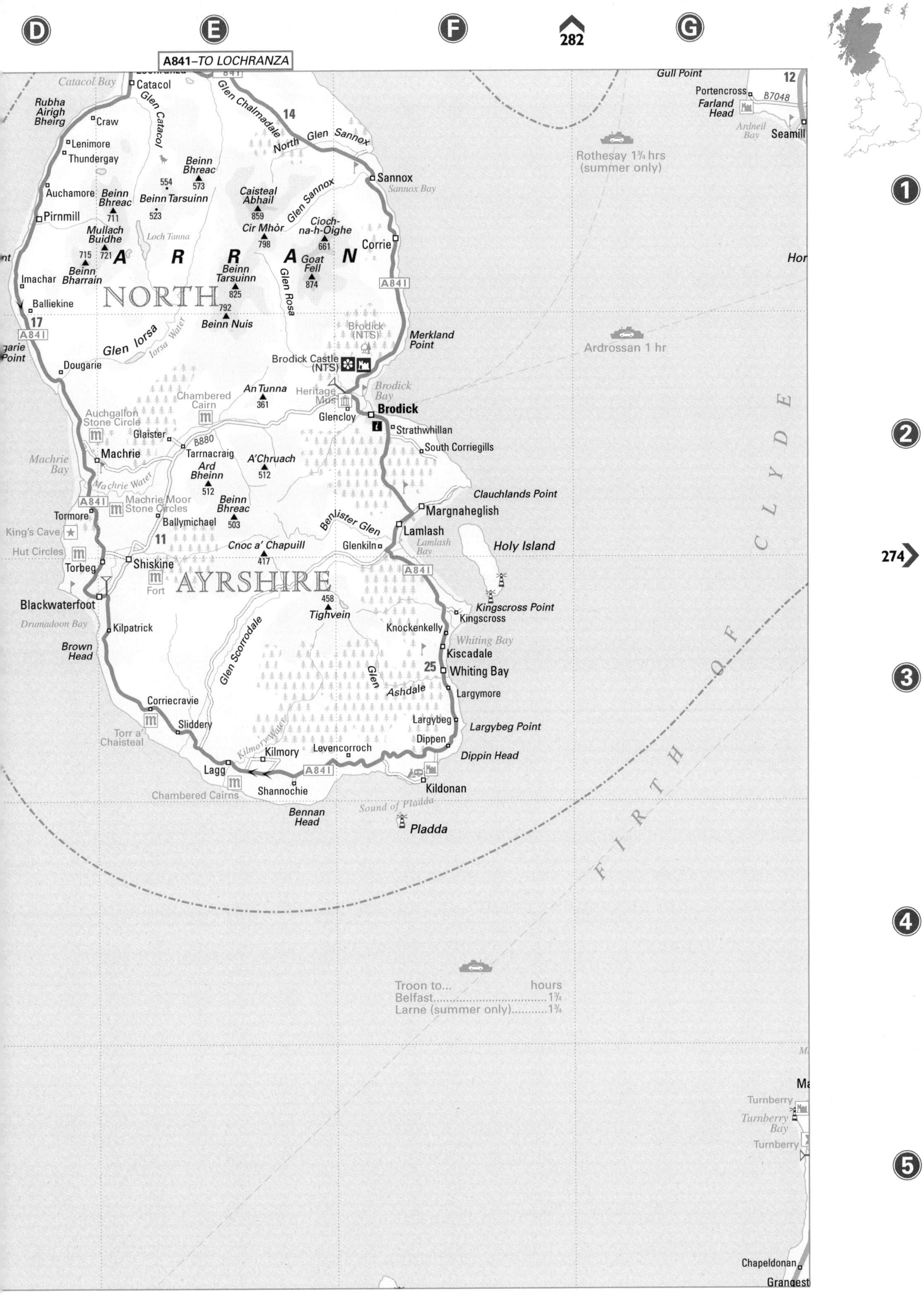

264

***Lamlash Bay** is where King Haakon of Norway sheltered his fleet on the way to the Battle of Largs in 1263. A cave on nearby Holy Island contains Viking inscriptions thought to have been made by his fighters.*
Map ref. F2

283

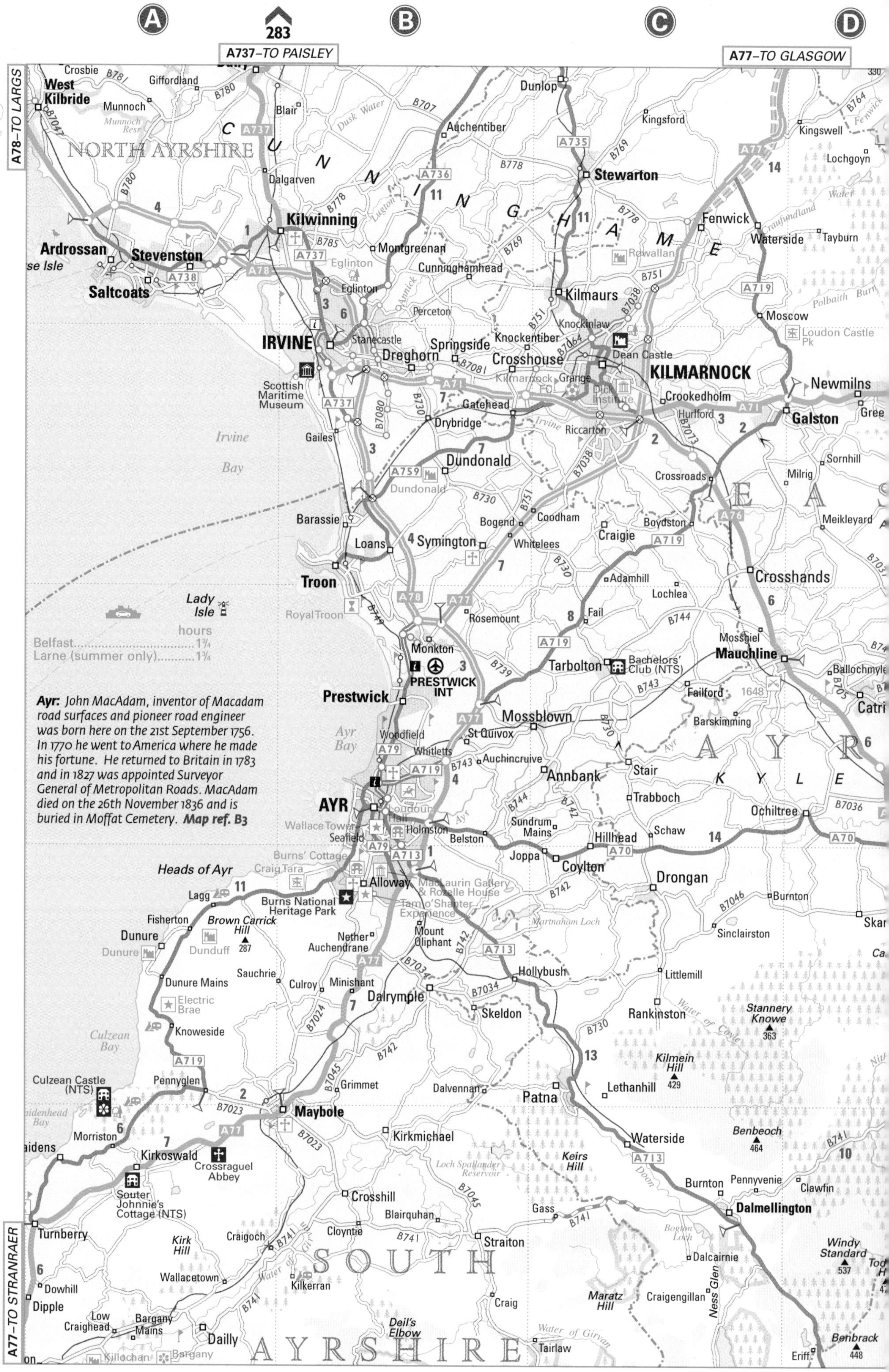

Ayr: *John MacAdam, inventor of Macadam road surfaces and pioneer road engineer was born here on the 21st September 1756. In 1770 he went to America where he made his fortune. He returned to Britain in 1783 and in 1827 was appointed Surveyor General of Metropolitan Roads. MacAdam died on the 26th November 1836 and is buried in Moffat Cemetery.* ***Map ref. B3***

273

Turnberry: *Robert Bruce (1274–1329) was born here. Bruce was proclaimed King of Scotland following the execution of William Wallace in 1306 and went on to defeat the English in several battles culminating at the Battle of Bannockburn on the 23–24th June 1314.* ***Map ref. A5***

265

Alloway: *Scotland's most famous poet, Robert Burns, was born here on the 25th January 1759. He died on the 21st July 1796 of heart disease at the age of 37, on the same day as his wife Jean gave birth to his last son. It is said that 10,000 people turned out for his funeral and, in his honour, Burns Nights are celebrated all around the world on his birthday. See Burns National Heritage Park.* ***Map ref. B4 Also on page 118***

D E F G

284

M74–TO GLASGOW

A76–TO DUMFRIES

M74–TO MOFFAT

1 2 3 4 5

276

266

Darvel: *Sir Alexander Fleming, medical scientist and discoverer of the world's first antibiotic drug Penicillin was born at nearby Lochfield Farm in 1881. He made his discovery in 1928 and was widely honoured with a knighthood in 1944 and the Nobel Prize for Medicine in 1945. Fleming died in 1955 and is buried in St Paul's Cathedral, London.* ***Map ref. D2***

Sanquhar *Home to the oldest post office in the world, established in 1712.* ***Map ref. F5***

285

A B C D

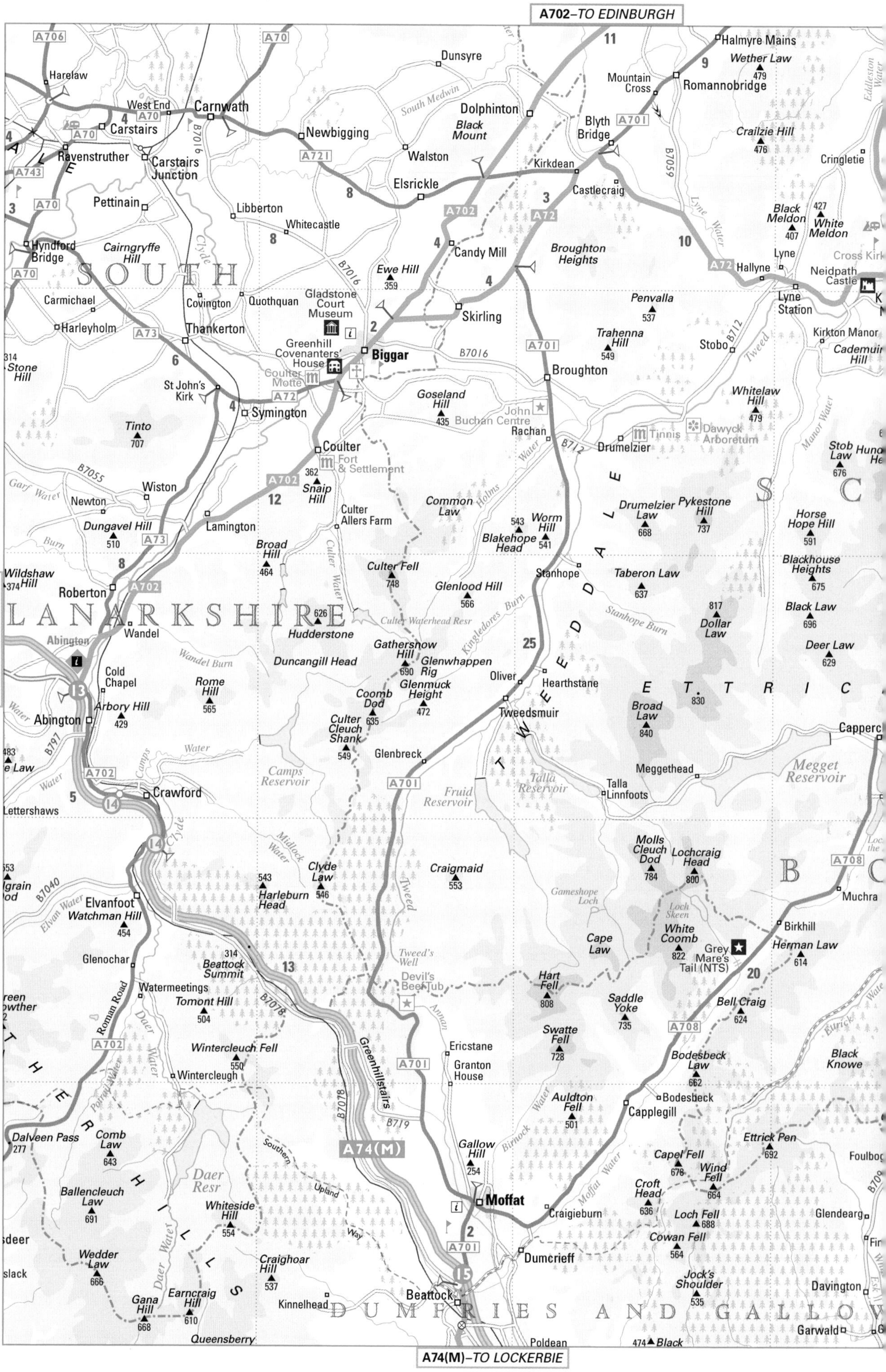

1 2 3 4 5

275

Tweeddale: *The area was the setting for some of the novels of John Buchan (1875-1940) – most famously The Thirty-Nine Steps.* ***Map ref. C3***

267

Biggar: *Biggar Gasworks was first opened in 1839. In 1973, when natural gas from the North Sea, came to the town, the gasworks closed. However, unlike most other towns, Biggar didn't demolish its gasworks, instead it made it into a Gasworks Museum. It is now preserved for future generations by Historic Buildings and Monuments and the Museums of Scotland.* ***Map ref. B2***

Blackhope Scar
651
Dewar
Dun Law
Ladyside Height
Eastside Heights
593
Totto Hill
Whitehope Law
621
Dunslair Heights
602
Black Law
Windlestraw Law
659
Glentress Forest
538
Black Knowe
521
Colquhar
Peebles
Priesthope Hill
549
Seathope Law
542
Glentress
Cardrona
Lee Pen
502
Kailzie
Kirkburn
Cardrona Forest
Wallace's Hill
469
Innerleithen
Walkerburn
Elibank and Traquair Forest
Traquair House
Traquair
Minch Moor
567
Blake Muir
467
Deuchar Law
542
Yarrow Kirk
Yarrow
Yarrow Feus
Mountbenger
Sundhope
FOREST
Sundhope Height
513
Black Knowe Head
550
St Mary's Loch
The Wiss
589
Gilmanscleuch
Newburgh
Mossbrae Height
466
Crosslee
RDERS
Cacrabank
Hopehouse
Home Law
412
Ettrick
Law Kneis
498
Buccleuch
Coutlair Knowe
418
Glenkerry
Sauchie Law
442
Redcleuch Edge
Craik Forest
423
Dalgliesh
The Pike
443
451
Crib Law
Craik
Black Knowe
Howpasley
Stell Hill
385
Craik Cross Hill
451
Pike Hill
417
Langshawburn
Lamblair Knowe
406
Stock Hill
477
Eweslees Knowe
448
Blaeberry Hill
419
Fountainhall
Torquhan
Inchkeith Hill
365
Lauder Common
Galabank
Killochyett
Stow
Torsonce
Yardstone Knowe
513
508
Great Law
Caddon Water
Knowes Hill
372
Blackhaugh
Thornylee
Clovenfords
Ashiestiel Hill
401
Ashiestiel
Yair Hill Forest
Broomy Law
463
Peat Law
426
Selkirk Glass
Yarrowford
Broadmeadows
Fastheugh Hill
501
Philiphaugh
1645
Bowhill House
Aikwood Tower
Kirkhope
Ettrickbridge
Shaw's Hill
393
Akermoor Loch
Shaws Under Loch
Langhope Burn
Hellmoor Loch
Alemoor Loch
Borthwickshiels
Roberton
Borthwickbrae
Burnfoot
Deanburnhaugh
High Seat
347
Dryden Fell
351
Harwood on Teviot
Hott Hill
312
Newmill
Broadhaugh
Northhouse
Teviothead
Castleweary
Skelfhill Pen
532
Comb Hill
514
Linhope
Millstone Edge
565
Cauldcleuch Head
608
Thirlestane Castle
Lauder
Thirlestane
Whiteburn
Nether Blainslie
Legerwood
Birkhill
East Mor
William Law
401
Langshaw
Torwoodlee
Buckholm
Galashiels
Glendearg
Earlston
Meigle Hill
423
Woollen Mill
Caddonfoot
Gala Hill
276
Abbotsford House
Heriot-Watt
Gattonside
Drygrange
Melrose Abbey
Leaderfoot
Redpath
Newstead
Melrose
Boleside
Darnick
Priorwood (NTS)
Eildon Hills
422
Eildon
Cauldshiels Loch
Cauldshiels Hill
328
Newtown St Boswells
Dryburgh Abbey
Bowden
Lindean
Charlesfield
Selkirk
Sir Walter Scott's Courtroom
Halliwell's House Mus
Longnewton
Midlem
New Belses
Old Belses
Lilliesleaf
Clerklands
Riddell
Woll
Ashkirk
Minto Hills
Minto
Hassendean
Drinkstone Hill
318
Groundistone Heights
Horsleyhill
Clarilaw
Knowetownhead
Bedrule
Denholm
Ashybank
Appletreehall
Burnfoot
Hawick
Cavers
Rubers Law
424
Wilton
Hawick Mus & Scott Gallery
Drumlanrigs Tower
Kirkton
Hallrule
Branxholm Bridgend
Branxholme
White Hill
301
Bonchester Bridge
Hobkirk
Cleuch Head
Wolfelee
393
Berryfell Hill
393
Hyndlee
Shankend
The Pike
462
Wyndburgh Hill
507
Note o' the Gate
376
Fanna Hill
514
Singdean
Maiden Paps
Sandy Edge
Greatmoor Hill
599
511
LAUDERDALE
TEVIOTDALE

A697–TO COLDSTREAM
A68–TO JEDBURGH
278
A7–TO LANGHOLM
268

1
2
3
4
5

Selkirk: *Stomping ground of William Wallace 'Braveheart' who was declared 'Guardian of Scotland' here in the 13th Century. For much of his life Wallace lived like an outlaw attacking anything English. He was finally caught and executed in 1305.* ***Map ref. F3***

A
287
B
C
D

1
286
2
3
4
277
5

A697–TO EDINBURGH (A68)
A68–TO GALASHIELS (A6091)

A68–TO OTTERBURN (A696)

269

Chesters: *Steve Hislop regarded by many as the fastest motorcycle racer of all time, was born here on the 11th January 1962. 'Hizzy' won 11 TT races on the Isle of Man and was British Superbike Champion in 1995 and 2002. He was tragically killed in a helicopter crash near Teviothead on the 30th July 2003.* ***Map ref. A4***

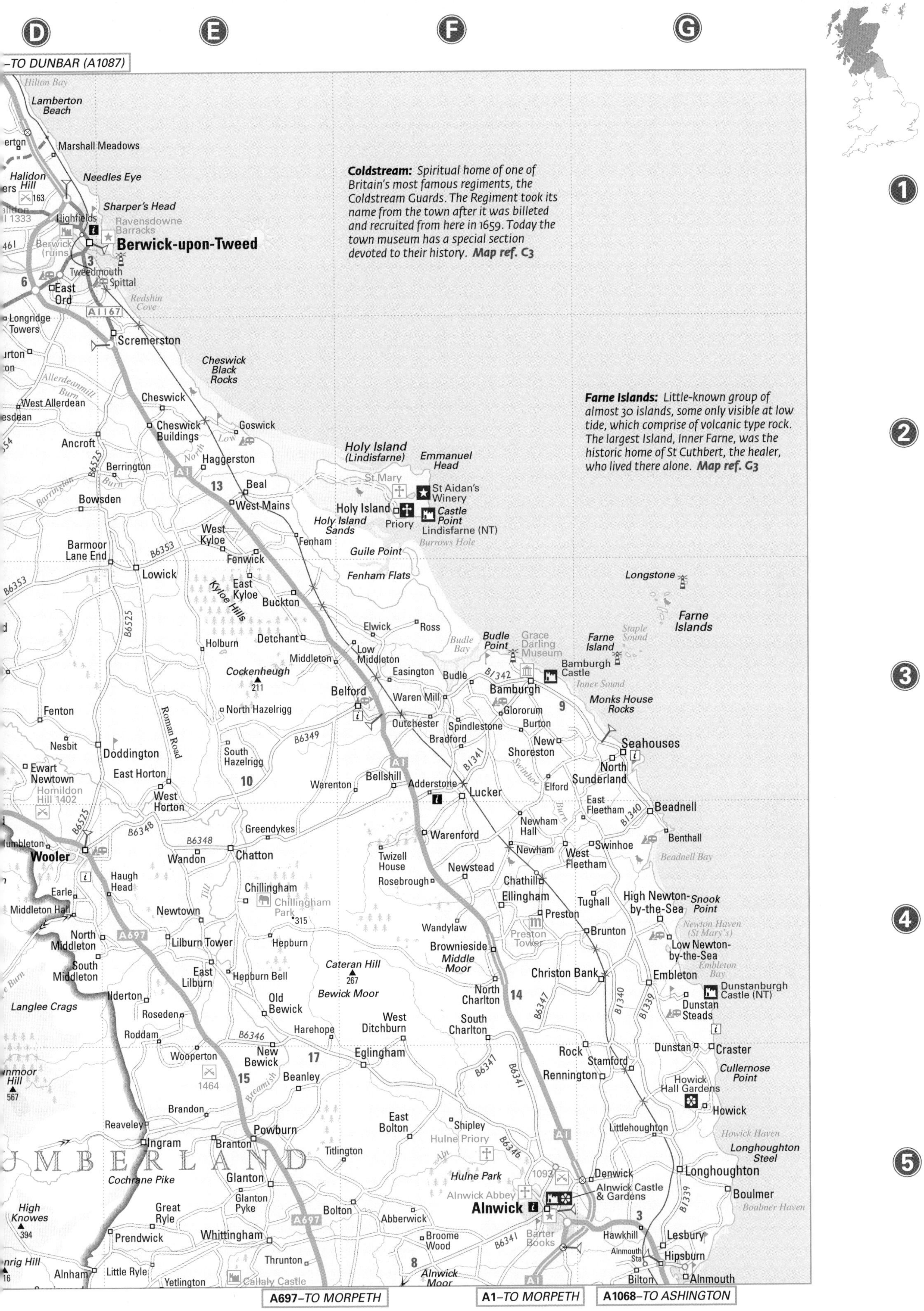

Bamburgh: *The great sandstone castle here was the first castle in Britain to be attacked by cannon fire when it was besieged by the artillery of Edward IV in 1464.* ***Map ref. F3 Also on page 102***

270

Bamburgh: *Grace Darling lived here with her father, a lighthouse keeper. She is famous for spotting a shipwreck during a dreadful storm and then assisting her father in the rescue of 5 survivors she had seen clinging to Big Harcar Rock. Grace died of flu in October 1842.* ***Map ref. F3***

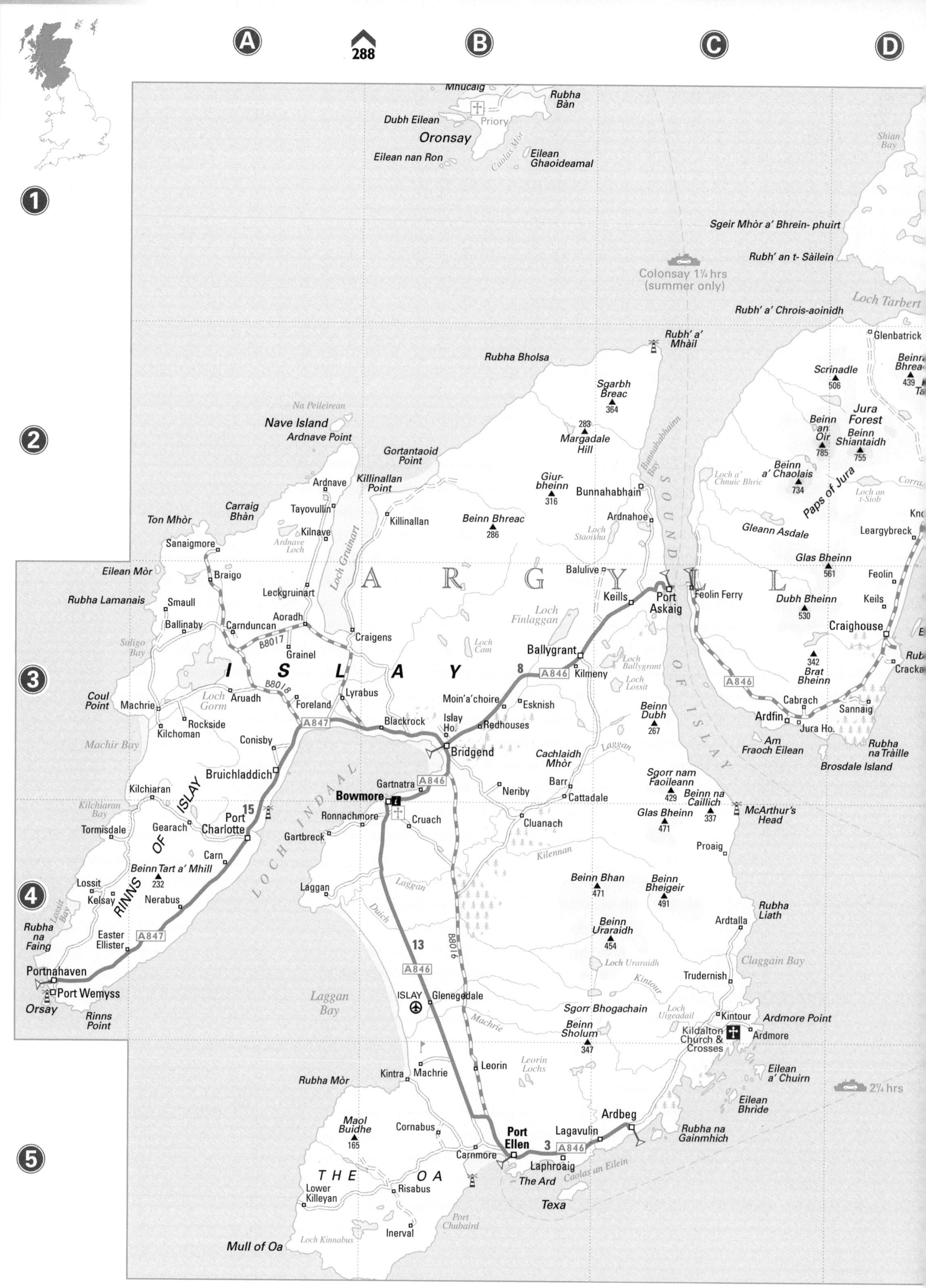

Islay: *Known as the 'Jewel of the Hebrides' this beautiful island is a major bird watching destination and is home to 8 different whisky distilleries. Islay enjoys a sort of micro-climate, warmed by the Gulf Stream: it has more hours of sunshine than most of mainland Britain and relatively mild winters as well.* ***Map ref. A3***

D E F G

289

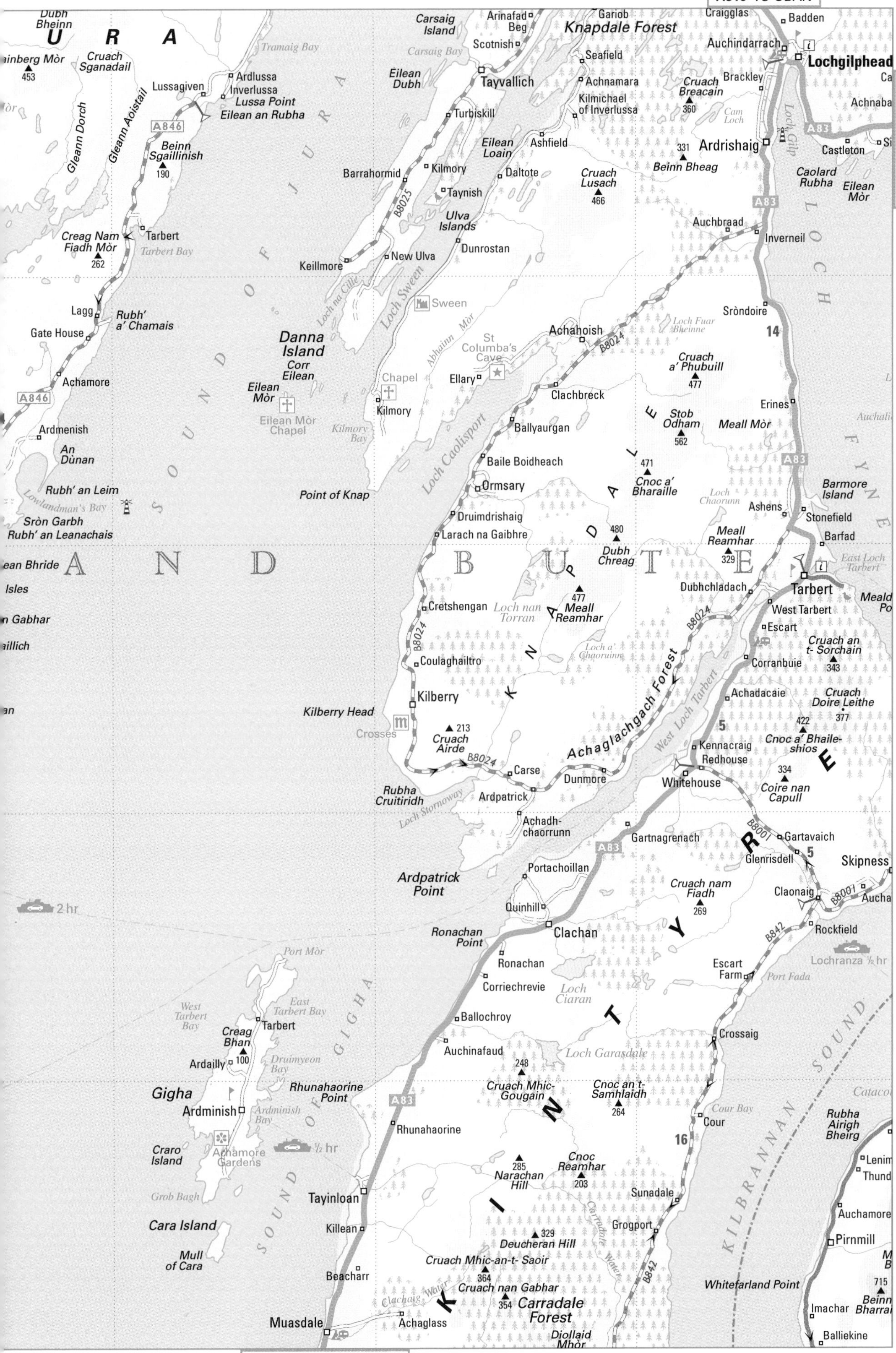
A816–TO OBAN
A83–TO INVERARY
A83–TO CAMPBELTOWN
Dubh Bheinn
U R A
ainberg Mòr
453
Cruach Sganadail
Tramaig Bay
Carsaig Island
Carsaig Bay
Arinafad Beg
Gariob
Knapdale Forest
Craigglas
Badden
Auchindarrach
Lochgilphead
Scotnish
Seafield
Eilean Dubh
Tayvallich
Achnamara
Kilmichael of Inverlussa
Cruach Breacain
360
Brackley
Ardlussa
Inverlussa
Lussagiven
Lussa Point
Eilean an Rubha
Gleann Dorch
Gleann Aoistail
A846
Beinn Sgaillinish
190
Turbiskill
Eilean Loain
Ashfield
Cam Loch
Loch Gilp
Ardrishaig
331
Beinn Bheag
A83
Castleton
Achnaba
Caolard Rubha
Eilean Mòr
Barrahormid
Kilmory
Daltote
Cruach Lusach
466
Taynish
B8025
Ulva Islands
Dunrostan
Auchbraad
Inverneil
Tarbert
Tarbert Bay
Creag Nam Fiadh Mòr
262
Keillmore
New Ulva
SOUND OF JURA
LOCH FYNE
Loch na Cille
Loch Sween
Sween
Lagg
Rubh' a' Chamais
Gate House
Sròndoire
14
Loch Fuar Bheinne
Danna Island
Corr Eilean
Abhainn Mòr
St Columba's Cave
Achahoish
B8024
Cruach a' Phubuill
477
Achamore
Eilean Mòr
Eilean Mòr Chapel
Chapel
Kilmory
Ellary
Clachbreck
Kilmory Bay
Erines
Stob Odham
562
Meall Mòr
Ardmenish
An Dùnan
Ballyaurgan
Loch Caolisport
Baile Boidheach
471
Cnoc a' Bharaille
Rubh' an Leim
Lowlandman's Bay
Point of Knap
Ormsary
Loch Chaorunn
Ashens
Barmore Island
Stonefield
Sròn Garbh
Rubh' an Leanachais
Druimdrishaig
Larach na Gaibhre
480
Dubh Chreag
Meall Reamhar
329
Barfad
ean Bhride
A N D B U T E
East Loch Tarbert
Isles
Dubhchladach
Tarbert
Meald
n Gabhar
Cretshengan
Loch nan Torran
477
Meall Reamhar
West Tarbert
Escart
ailllich
Loch a' Chaoruinn
Cruach an t- Sorchain
343
Coulaghailtro
Corranbuie
KNAPDALE
West Loch Tarbert
Achadacaie
Cruach Doire Leithe
377
Kilberry
Achaglachgach Forest
an
Kilberry Head
Crosses
213
Cruach Airde
422
5
Cnoc a' Bhaile-shios
Kennacraig
Redhouse
Carse
Dunmore
334
Whitehouse
Coire nan Capull
Rubha Cruitiridh
Loch Stornoway
Ardpatrick
Achadh-chaorrunn
B8001
Gartnagrenach
Gartavaich
5
Glenrisdell
Ardpatrick Point
Portachoillan
Skipness
Cruach nam Fiadh
269
Claonaig
Aucha
2 hr
Quinhill
Ronachan Point
Clachan
B842
Rockfield
Ronachan
Port Mòr
Lochranza ½ hr
Escart Farm
Port Fada
Corriechrevie
Loch Ciaran
West Tarbert Bay
East Tarbert Bay
Creag Bhan
Tarbert
Ballochroy
SOUND OF GIGHA
Crossaig
Ardailly
100
Druimyeon Bay
Auchinafaud
Loch Garasdale
248
Gigha
Rhunahaorine Point
Cruach Mhic-Gougain
Cnoc an t-Samhlaidh
264
Catacol
Ardminish
Ardminish Bay
A83
Rhunahaorine
Cour Bay
Cour
Rubha Airigh Bheirg
Craro Island
Achamore Gardens
½ hr
16
KILBRANNAN SOUND
Lenim
Thund
285
Narachan Hill
Cnoc Reamhar
203
Sunadale
Grob Bagh
Tayinloan
Carradale Water
Auchamore
Cara Island
Killean
Grogport
Pirnmill
329
Deucheran Hill
Mull of Cara
Beacharr
Cruach Mhic-an-t- Saoir
364
Cruach nan Gabhar
Whitefarland Point
715
Beinn Bharrai
Clachaig Water
354
Carradale Forest
Imachar
Muasdale
Achaglass
Diollaid Mhòr
Balliekine

1 2 3 4 5

282

272

Ardrishaig: *The 9 mile (14.5km) long Crinan Canal was started here in 1794 by John Ronnie. The canal links Loch Fyne with the Atlantic Ocean and cuts out a 120 mile (193km) voyage around the Mull of Kintyre.* ***Map ref. G1***

290

A B C D

1 2 3 4 5

281

A841–TO BRODICK

Holy Loch: *During the Cold War of the 1960s this was a controversial US Navy nuclear submarine base housing Polaris Missiles. Over 700 Americans lived in the area and when it closed in 1992 many feared that the local economy would collapse. However the Government allocated £12 million to recreate employment in the area and a crisis was averted.* ***Map ref. C1***

273

Largs: *Scene of a great Scottish victory over the Vikings in 1263. The Viking fleet, under King Haakon left their base in the Western Isles to sail down the Clyde to subdue the Scottish resistance to Viking rule. But the Scots army, under Alexander III, helped by bad weather, managed to repulse the assault and end the Viking threat to mainland Scotland. The battle is commemorated by a monument just south of the town.* ***Map ref. D4***

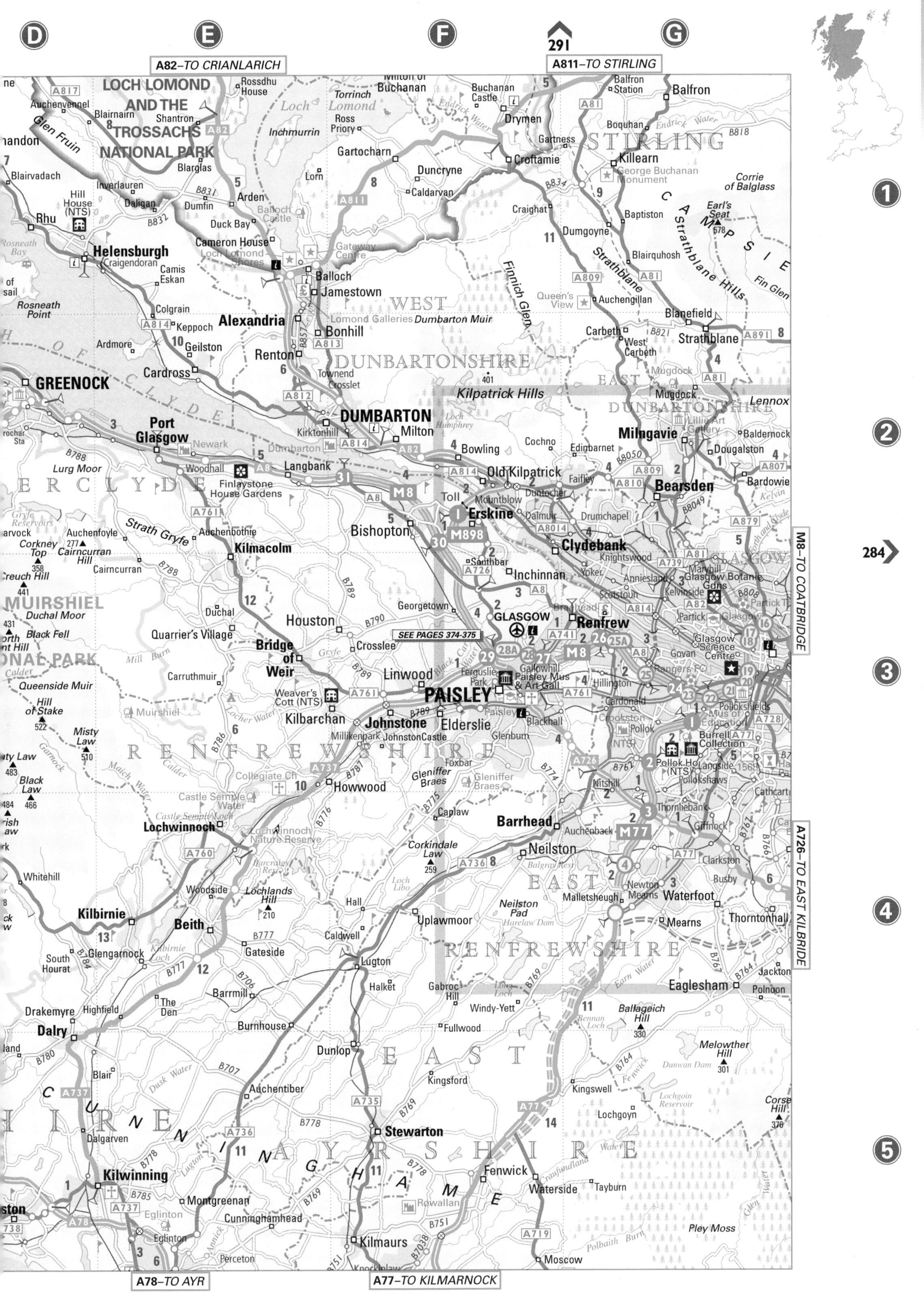

274

Helensburgh: *John Logie Baird, inventor of the television was born here on the 13th August 1888. He created the first televised pictures of an object in motion in 1925. He died on the 14th June 1946 at Bexhill, East Sussex.* ***Map ref. D1***

Clydebank: *The liner Queen Mary (81,235 tons/82,539 tonnes) was built here at the John Brown Shipyard. It is said that over one million people turned out to watch her leaving the Clyde on the 24th March 1936.* ***Map ref. F3***

Glasgow: *On the 17th April 1937 150,000 soccer supporters crammed into Hampden Park to watch Scotland play England. This is the European attendance record and stood as a world record until 1950.* ***Map ref. G3***

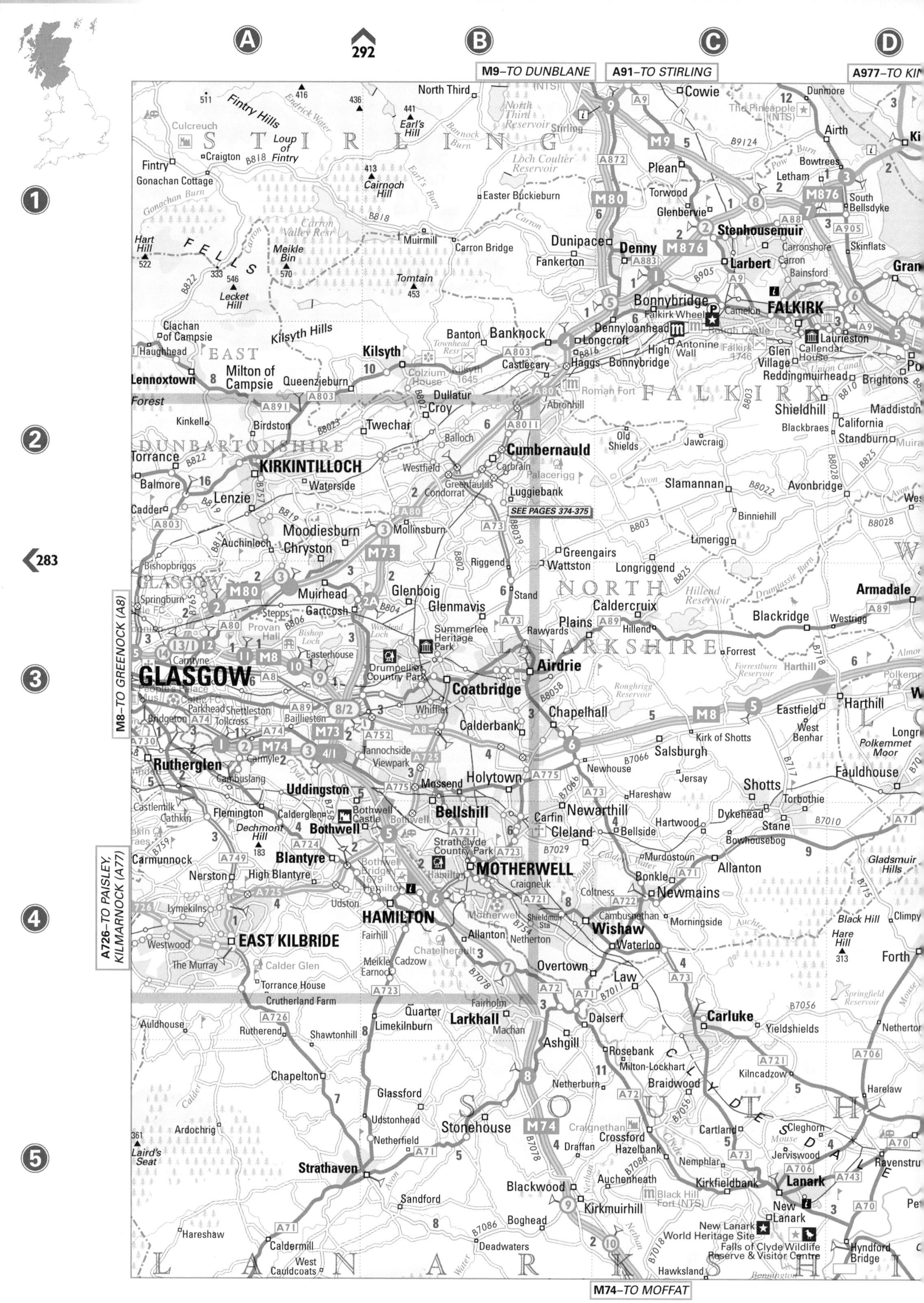

Holytown: *James Kier Hardie, radical socialist, member of parliament and the person central to the formation of the British Independent Labour Party was born at nearby Legbranock in 1856. Hardie died in Glasgow in 1915.* ***Map ref. B3***

275

Blantyre: *The great missionary and explorer David Livingstone was born here on the 19th March 1813. He spent time in Africa in 1841 and whilst mapping the Zambezi River discovered and named the Victoria Falls. Livingstone died of fever in Africa in 1873 and his embalmed body was brought back to England and buried in Westminster Abbey.* ***Map ref. A4***

Bellshill: *Sir Matt Busby, famous manager of Manchester United Football Club was born here in 190 He is credited with re-building the team following the Munich Air Disaster of 1958. He was knighted for his services to football in 1967, retired as manager in 1971 and died in 1994.* ***Map ref. B4***

D E 293 F G
M90–TO PERTH
A92–TO KIRKCALDY (A910)

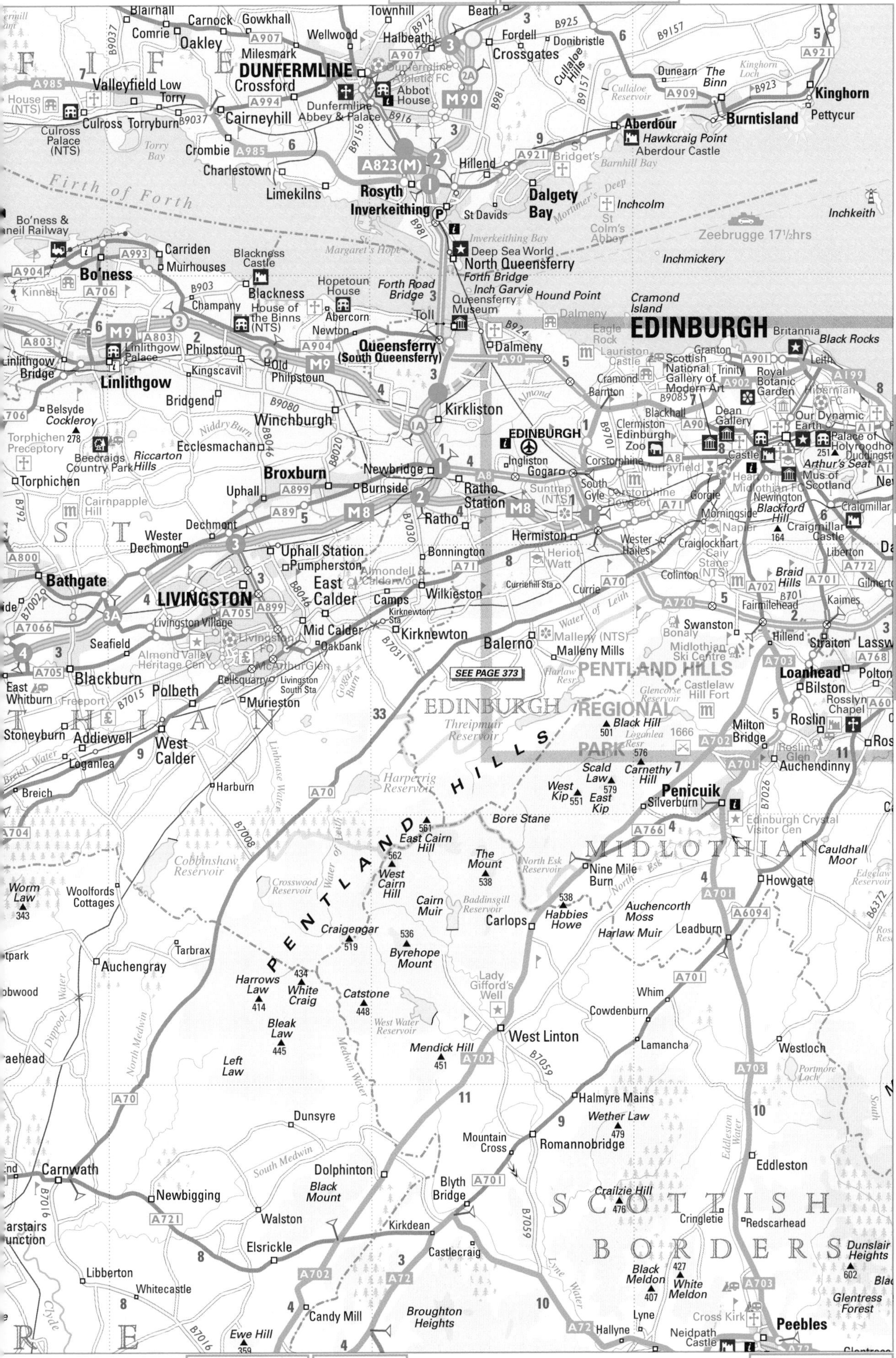

1
A1–TO NORTH BERWICK (A198)
2
286
A720–TO DALKEITH (A68)
3
4
5
A702–TO BIGGAR
A72–TO A702
A72–TO GALASHIELS
276

Forth Rail Bridge: *At 1.5 miles (2.4km) long and 150 feet (46m) high, this remarkable cantilever structure is universally recognised as an engineering marvel. Its span of 1,710 feet (521m) is the largest of any railway bridge in Britain. Construction began under Sir William Arrol in 1883 and it was opened by the Prince of Wales in 1890. In all it cost £3.2 million and used 54,000 tons (54,900 tonnes) of steel, 640,000 cubic feet (18,123 cubic metres) of granite and 6.5 million rivets. It also cost the lives of 57 construction workers. And, yes, for over 100 years it was continuously being painted.* ***Map ref. F2***

A B C D

294

1 2 3 4 5

285

A1–TO EDINBURGH

A720–TO M8 & M9

1

FIRTH OF FORTH

Rosyth to Zeebrugge 17½hrs

Fidra
Lamb
Yellowcraig
North Berwick
Craigleith
Scottish
Seabird Centre
Bass Rock

Muirfield
Gullane Bents
Dirleton
7
North Berwick Law
Tantallon Castle
St Baldred's Boat
Auldhame
Scoughall
Bal Cr

Gullane Bay
Gullane Point
Dirleton Castle & Gardens
Fenton Barns
Kingston
Whitekirk
8

Aberlady Bay
Gullane
187
A198
B1347
Tyninghame House

Luffness
Aberlady
Craigielaw
Luffness House (NTS)
Drem
East Fortune
B1345
Preston Mill & Phantassie Dovecot (NTS)
Tyninghame

Craigielaw Point
Friary
Mungoswells
Chesters Hill Fort
Museum of Flight
B1377
Preston
East Linton

Gosford Bay
Gosford House
Ballencrieff
Church of Plaque
B1343
Athelstaneford
Hailes
Traprain
Pitco

Longniddry Bents
A198
Spittal
B1377
Garleton Hills
B1341
9
Traprain Law Fort
Luggate
Church
Stento

2

SEE PAGE 373

Cockenzie and Port Seton
Seton Collegiate Church
7
B1348
Longniddry
St Mary's Church
A1
A6093
Haddington
Whitelaw Hill
Luggate Burn
B1370
Deuch Do

Preston Tower & Hamilton House (NTS)
Prestonpans 1745
Meadowmill
Elvingston
7
Gladsmuir
Papple
B6370
Press Lo

Prestonpans
Levenhall
Tranent
B6363
New Winton
Penston
Samuelston
Lennoxlove
B6368
B6369
Bolton
Whitelaw Hill
Garvald
Dunba

Musselburgh
A199
Wallyford
6
Elphinstone
New Winton
Market Cross
New Town
Winton House
Samuelston
Bolton
Gifford Church
Carfrae
Nunraw Abbey
Clints Dod
398

Inveresk
Whitecraig
5
Carberry Tower
Crossgatehall
Ormiston
Pencaitland
West Saltoun
East Saltoun
B6355
Gifford
Danskine
White
400
Rangely Kip
Dunn

Millerhill
A6064
Dalkeith
Cousland
A6093
5
Peastonbank
Gilchriston
B6355
Longyester
Newlands Hill
423

3

Dalkeith 4
Whitehill
A68
Oxenford
Peaston
B6371
Humbie
Lammer Law
528
Penshiel Hill

Newbattle
Easthouses
Edgehead
Ford
Pathhead
Fala Dam
Crib Law
509
Meikle Says Law
535
Seenes Law
513
467
Meikle Law

Bonnyrigg
Mayfield
B482
13
Fala
West Hill
451

Newtongrange
Amiston Engine
Newlandrig
Crichton
Soutra Hill
368
Dun Law
394
Hunt Law
495
Blythe Edge

MIDLOTHIAN
Gorebridge
Borthwick
Crichton Castle
B6367
Tynehead
Fala Moor
363
Turf Law
A68
Hogs Law
448

4

Temple
North Middleton
Middleton
6
A7
Gilston
Oxton
A697
Carfraemill

Torfichen Hill
460
Falahill
B7007
Heriot
B6368
Collie Law
381
Edgehope Wood
363
Scoured Rig
Westruther

Gladhouse Reservoir
MOORFOOT HILLS
A7
Inchkeith Hill
365
Thirlestane Castle
A6456

Heriot Water
B109
Torquhan
Thirlestane

Dewar
Dun Law
Fountainhall
Galabank
Lauder
Whiteburn
A697
Hour

Blackhope Scar
651
Ladyside Height
Lauder Common
11
Legerwood
Huntlywood

5

Totto Hill
15
Eastside Heights
593
Killochyett
Stow
B6362
Nether Blainslie
A68
Birkhill
East Morriston
A6089
Greenknowe Tower

Whitehope Law
621
Windlestraw Law
659
Torsonce
6
West Morriston
Fans

Black Knowe
521
Colquhar
Seathope Law
508
Yardstone Knowe
513
Great Law
William Law
A6105

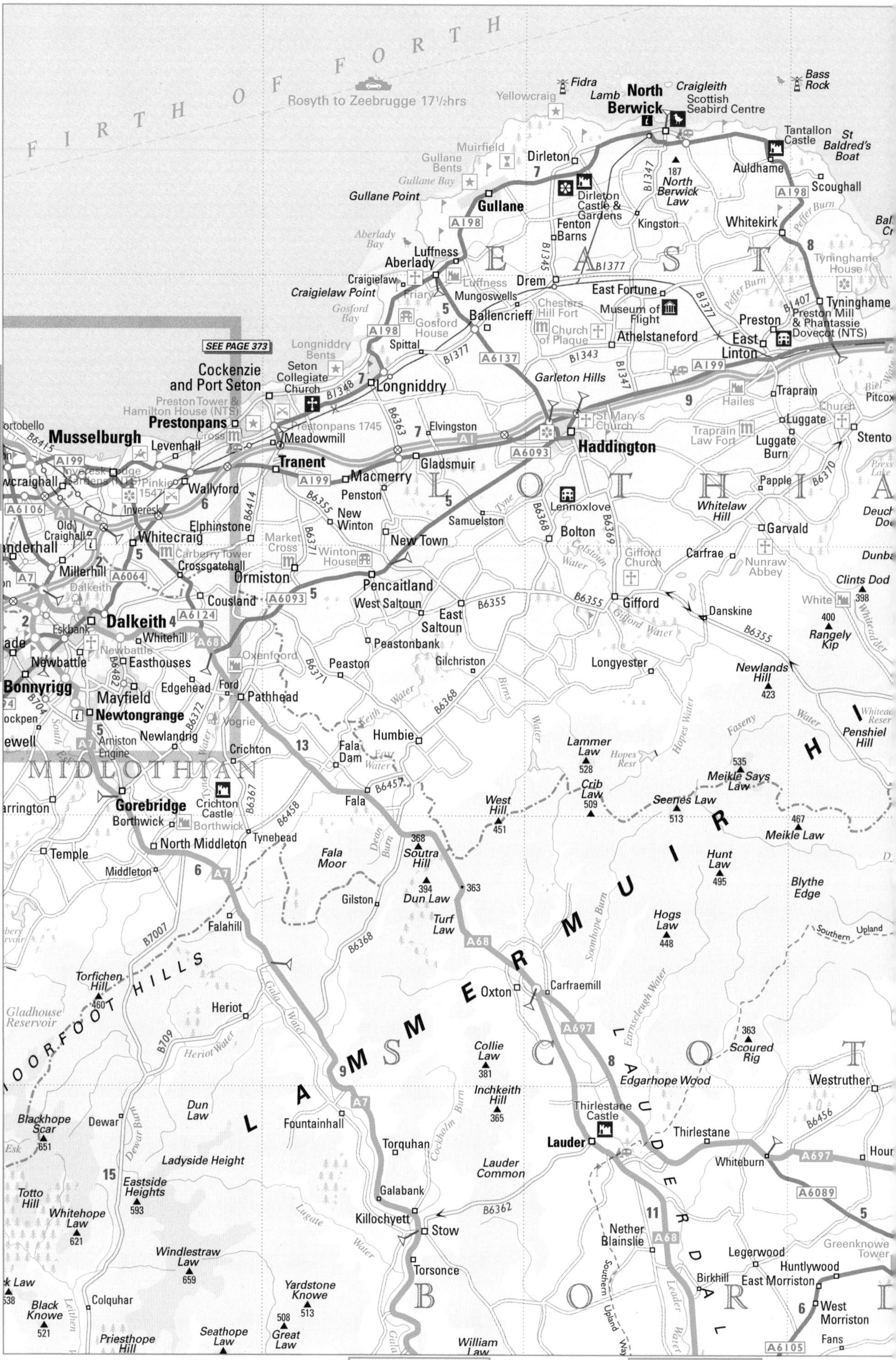

A7–TO GALASHIELS, MELROSE

A68–TO NEWTOWN ST BOSWELLS

Portobello: *The great singer and music hall entertainer Sir Harry Lauder was born here in 1870. Lauder died in 1950 and is buried in Bent Cemetery, Hamilton.*
Map ref. A2

277

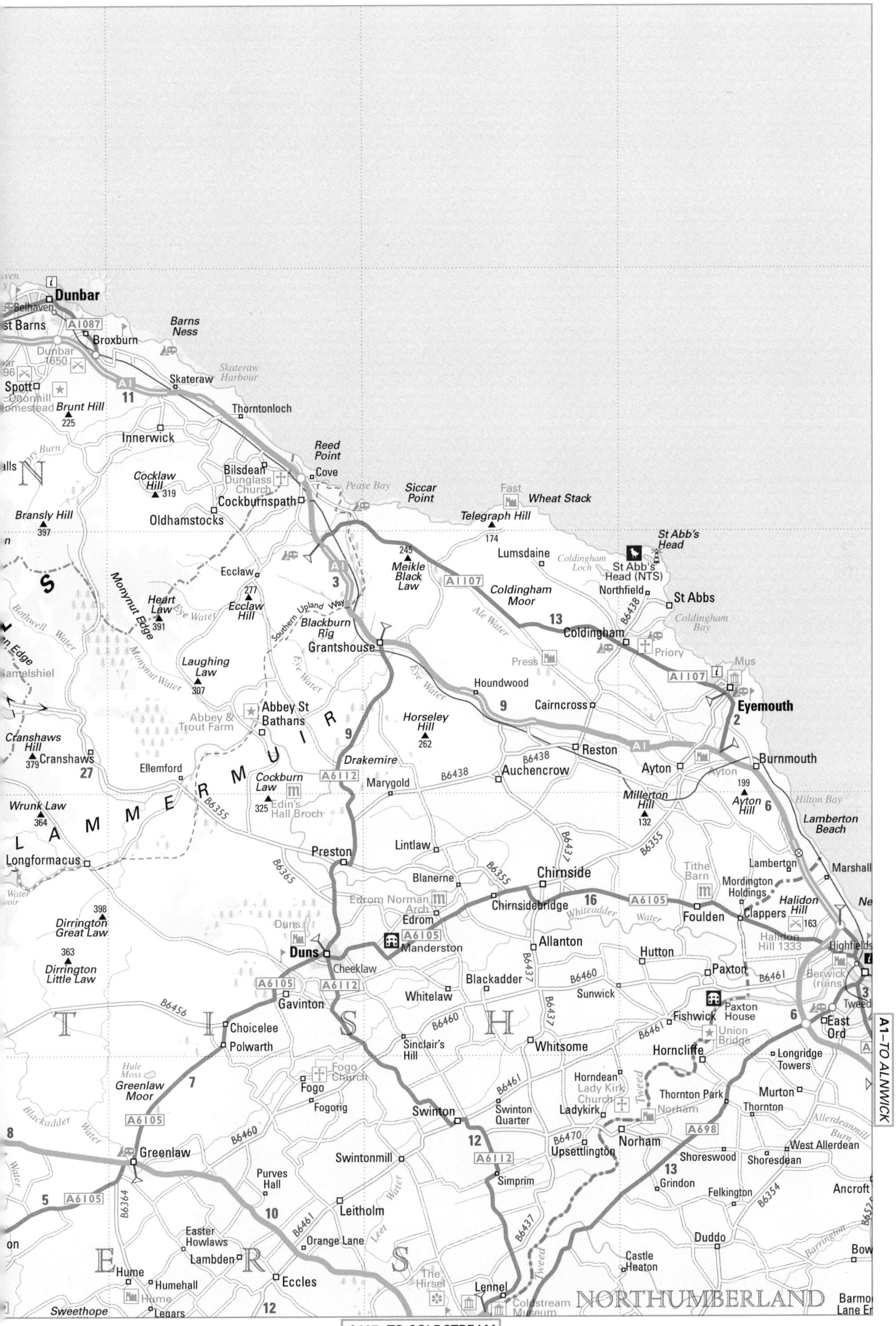

A1–TO ALNWICK

279

A697–TO COLDSTREAM & WOOLER

278

Soutra Hill: *Site of the first hospital in Scotland dating back to the 12th Century. Soutra Aisle was a medieval hospital and refuge for travellers on the 'Royal Road'; the main England to Scotland route. Now an archaeological site.* ***Map ref. B4***

296

A B C D

1 2 3 4 5

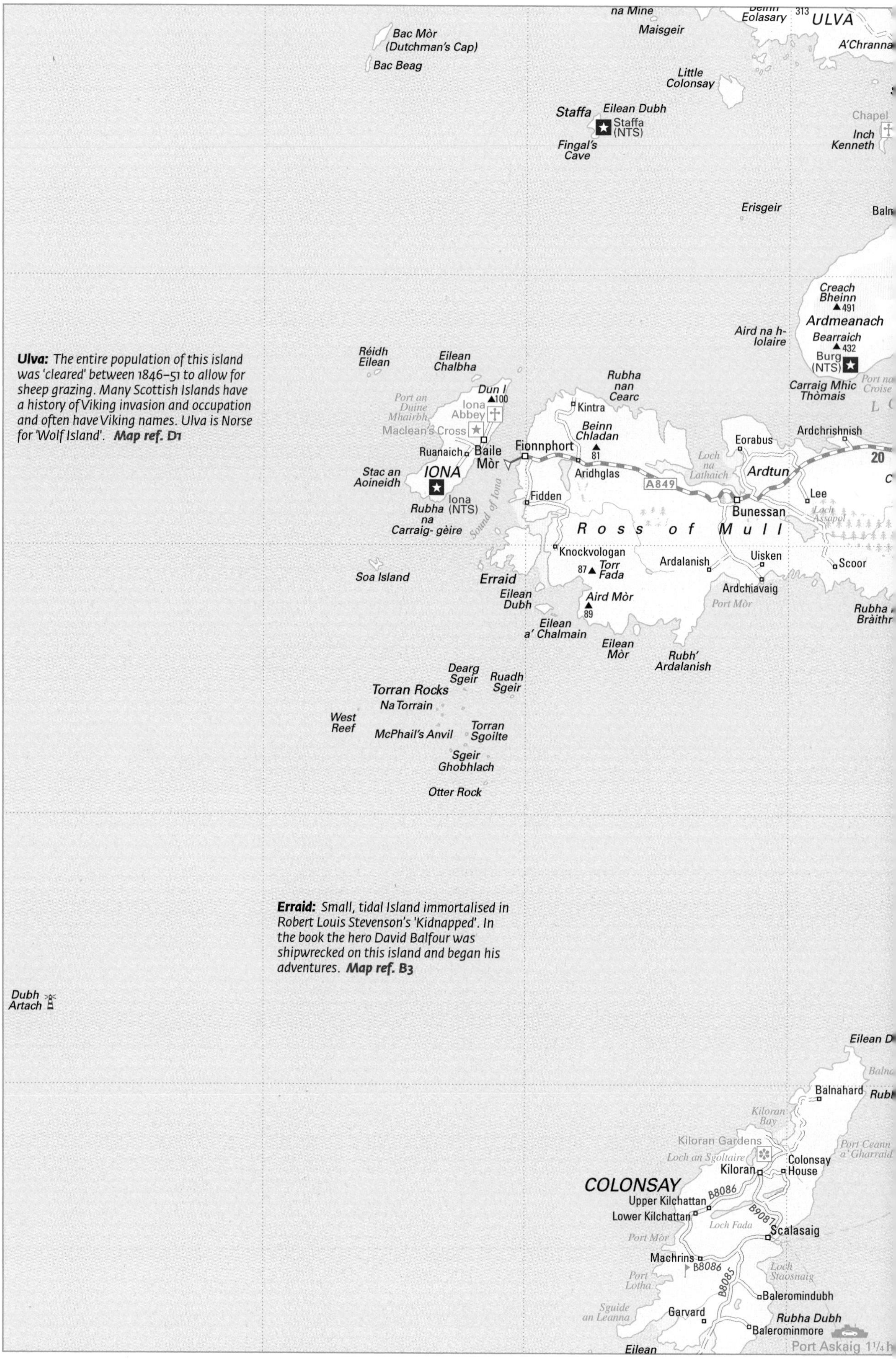

Ulva: The entire population of this island was 'cleared' between 1846–51 to allow for sheep grazing. Many Scottish Islands have a history of Viking invasion and occupation and often have Viking names. Ulva is Norse for 'Wolf Island'. **Map ref. D1**

Erraid: Small, tidal Island immortalised in Robert Louis Stevenson's 'Kidnapped'. In the book the hero David Balfour was shipwrecked on this island and began his adventures. **Map ref. B3**

Staffa: An island discovered in 1772 by Sir Joseph Banks. Its now famous Fingals Cave is said to have been the inspiration behind Mendelssohn's 'Hebrides Overture'. This natural phenomenon has been visited by many famous people including Queen Victoria, David Livingstone and Jules Verne. **Map ref. C1 Also on page 130**

280

297

290

Clachan-Seil: *A hump-backed stone bridge here links Seil Island to the mainland. It is known as 'The Bridge over the Atlantic' and was designed by Thomas Telford in 1792.* ***Map ref. G3***

281

Corryvreckan: *The swirling whirlpool here is one of the largest in the world and makes the Straits of Corryvreckan the most dangerous stretch of water around the British Isles. The sound of the raging water can often be heard 10 miles (16km) away.* ***Map ref. F4***

A B C D

298

A828–TO FORT WILLIAM

A816–TO LOCHGILPHEAD

A83–TO LOCHGILPHEAD

1 2 3 4 5

289

282

Loch Fyne: *The longest sea loch in Scotland stretching inland for 44 miles (71km).* ***Map ref. B5***

Ben Cruachan: *Known as the 'Hollow Mountain' because housed inside is Cruachan Power Station one of the most remarkable feats of engineering in Scotland. Deep in the mountain a huge man-made cavern houses the world's first 'high head reversible pumped storage hydro scheme'.* ***Map ref. C2 Also on page 119***

1
2
292
3
4
5

Loch Lomond: *In Scotland the word 'loch' refers to an inland body of water. Loch Lomond is the largest such feature in Scotland. It has an area of 27.5 square miles (71 sq km) and is 617 feet (190m) deep. Here on 16th July 1932 Kaye Don in Miss England 3 raised the world water speed record to 119.81 mph (193km/h).* ***Map ref. F4***
See Loch Lomond & The Trossachs National Park ***on page 126***

283

An area known as ***The Trossachs*** *which was immortalised in Sir Walter Scott's ballads 'The Lady of the Lake' (1810) and 'Rob Roy' (1817).*
So wondrous wild the whole might seem
The scenery of a fairy dream. ***Map ref. G4***
See Loch Lomond & The Trossachs National Park ***on page 126***

A B C D
1 2 3 4 5
300
291
284

A827–TO ABERFELDY
A85–TO CRIANLARICH
A811–TO DUMBARTON
M9–TO FALKIRK
Meall nan Tarmachan
1043
Lawers
Carie
Ardtalnaig
Creagan na Beinne
888
Garrow
Auchnaclo
Tullich
Duncroist
Milton Morenish
Kiltyrie
Tullich Hill
682
Gleann a' Chilleine
Meall nam Fuaran
805
Lochay
Falls of Lochay
Murlaganmore
Boreland
Finlarig
Morenish
Camusurich
Ardeonaig
Loch Tay
Auchnafree Craig
Creag Mhòr
719
Killin
Breadalbane Folklore Cen
Achmore
Kinnell
Cloichrich
Creag Gharbh
637
Dalriech
Auchnafree
Craignavie
Ruadh Mheall
682
Creag Uchdag
879
BREADALBANE
Bovain
Mid Lix
Lochan Breaclaich
Loch Lednock Resr
Ben Chonzie
931
Auchnafree Hill
789
Glen
Auchlyne
Ardchyle
Ledcharrie
Beinn Leabhain
705
Glen Beich
Glen Tarken
Meall nam Fiadh
Spout Rolla
Invergeldie
Loch Turret Reservoir
Carn Chois
786
Loch Lairig Eala
Glen Ogle
Meall a' Mhadaidh
Sròn Mòr
672
Loch Boltachan
Glen Lednock
Carroglen
Creag Each
302
Glen Turret
Meall an Fhiodhain
791
Glenbeich
Ardveich
Dalveich
St Fillans
499
Creag Liath
Dunira
Melville's Mon
Devil's Cauldron
Ochtertyre
Falls of Turret
Meall an t-Seallaidh
852
Lochearnhead
Edinchip
Auchraw
Loch Earn
Derry
Ardtrostan
Rob Roy's Grave
Edinample
Ardvorlich
Meall Reamhar
678
Strath Earn
Tullybannocher
Comrie
Lawers
Quoig
Balquhidder
Auchtubh
Kingshouse
Dalginross
Ross
Lochlane
Ben Halton
620
Mill of Fortune
Crieff
Stronvar
Loch Voil
Strathyre Forest
Glen Ample
Ben Vorlich
985
Forest of Glenartney
Cultybraggan Camp
Torlum
393
Stuc a' Chroin
972
Glen Artney
Water of Ruchill
Culloch
Torlum Wood
Ballimore
Immeroin
Strathyre
Craggan
Tighnablair
Kipp
Dalchruin
Dunruchan Hill
304
Ochtermuthill
Machany Water
Meall Odhar
646
Auchinner
Findhuglen
Knaik
Ben Clach
533
Runacraig
Ben Vane
820
Laggan
Ardchullarie More
Creag Beinn nan Eun
Findhu Glen
Langside
Meall Cala
674
Ardnandave Hill
715
Meall Leathan Dhail
484
Beinn Odhar
632
Coire Nochd Mòr
497
Greenscares
Glenlichorn
405
Cromlet
STIRLING
Uamh Bheag
665
Loch Lubnaig
Braeleny
Gleann Casaig
Ben Ledi
879
Anie
Pass of Leny
Slymaback
Bracklinn Falls
Kilmahog Woollen Mill
Kilmahog
Glen Finglas Reservoir
Ben An
461
Brig o'Turk
Falls of Leny
Bochastle
Callander
Cambushinnie Hill
Bullie Burn
Braco
Milton of Callander
Coilantogle
Rob Roy & Trossachs Visitor Centre
Loch Achray
Duncraggan
Lendrick Lodge
Loch Venachar
Drummond
Loch Mahaick
Easter Dullater
Braes of Doune
Mickle Burn
Strathallan
Forest Drive
West Dullater
Kinbuck
Balhaldie
Dukes Pass
243
Invertrossachs
Drumvaich
Burn of Cambus
Glassingall
Achray Forest
Toll
Loch Drunkie
Beinn Dearg
427
Menteith Hills
Loch Rusky
Ashfield
Sheriffmuir 1715
Argaty
Port of Menteith
Torrie Forest
Stockbridge
Milton
Aberfoyle
Blairhoyle
Easter Borland
Deanston
Doune
Dunblane
Balleich
Braeval
Malling
Inchmahome Priory
Ruskie
Thornhill
Inverardoch Mains
Pisgah
Gartincaber
Cauldham
Kippenross Ho
Blair Drummond
Lake of Menteith
Tamavoid
Goodie Water
Cobleland
Safari Park
Keir House
Sunnylaw
Cunninghame Graham Memorial (NTS)
Gartmore
Dykehead
Flanders Moss
Easter Poldar
Nyadd
Ochtertyre
Bridge of Allan
Drip Moss
Causewayhead
Blairlogie
National Wallace Mo
Dalmary
Forth
Gargunnock
Stirling Castle
Cambuskenneth
Arnprior
Arngomery
Garden
Cauldhame
Kippen
Leckie
Gargunnock House
Smith Art Gallery & Museum
Abbey
Arngibbon
Gartachoil
Buchlyvie
STIRLING
Argyll & Sutherland Highlanders Mus
Royal Burgh of Stirling Visitor Centre
Wrightpark
485
Touch Hills
Cambusbarron
St Ninians
Bannockburn 1314
Gargunnock Hills
Bannockburn Heritage Centre (NTS)
Balafark
Ling Hill
Bannockb

Stirling: *Stirling Castle houses the museum of The Argyll and Sutherland Highlanders. This famous regiment won 6 Victoria Crosses in a single day's action at the Battle of Lucknow (India) in 1857.* ***Map ref. C5 Also on page 130***

301

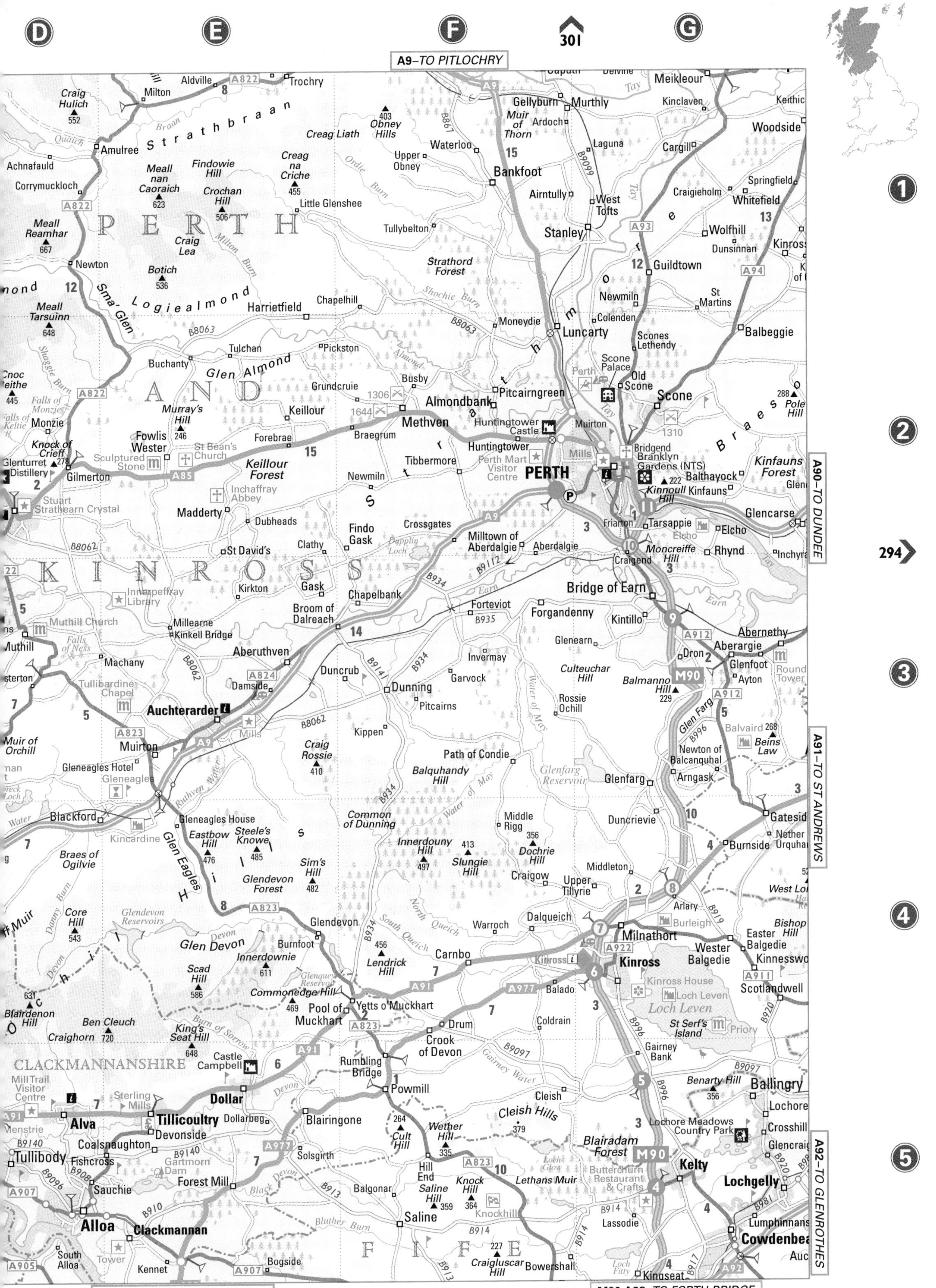

294

285

Crieff: *The Glenturret Distillery in Crieff is the oldest distillery in Britain. In the 18th century illegal stills were rife in this area and one operated here from 1717. It was legalised in 1775 and was a working still up to 1921 when it ceased production. It was re-born in 1957 and today is one of the Highland's established malts.* ***Map ref. D2***

Alloa: *Brewer and philanthropist William McEwan was born here in 1827. He went on to establish the Fountain Brewery in Edinburgh and to brew McEwans Export. He died in 1913 but both the brewery and beer survive.* ***Map ref. D5***

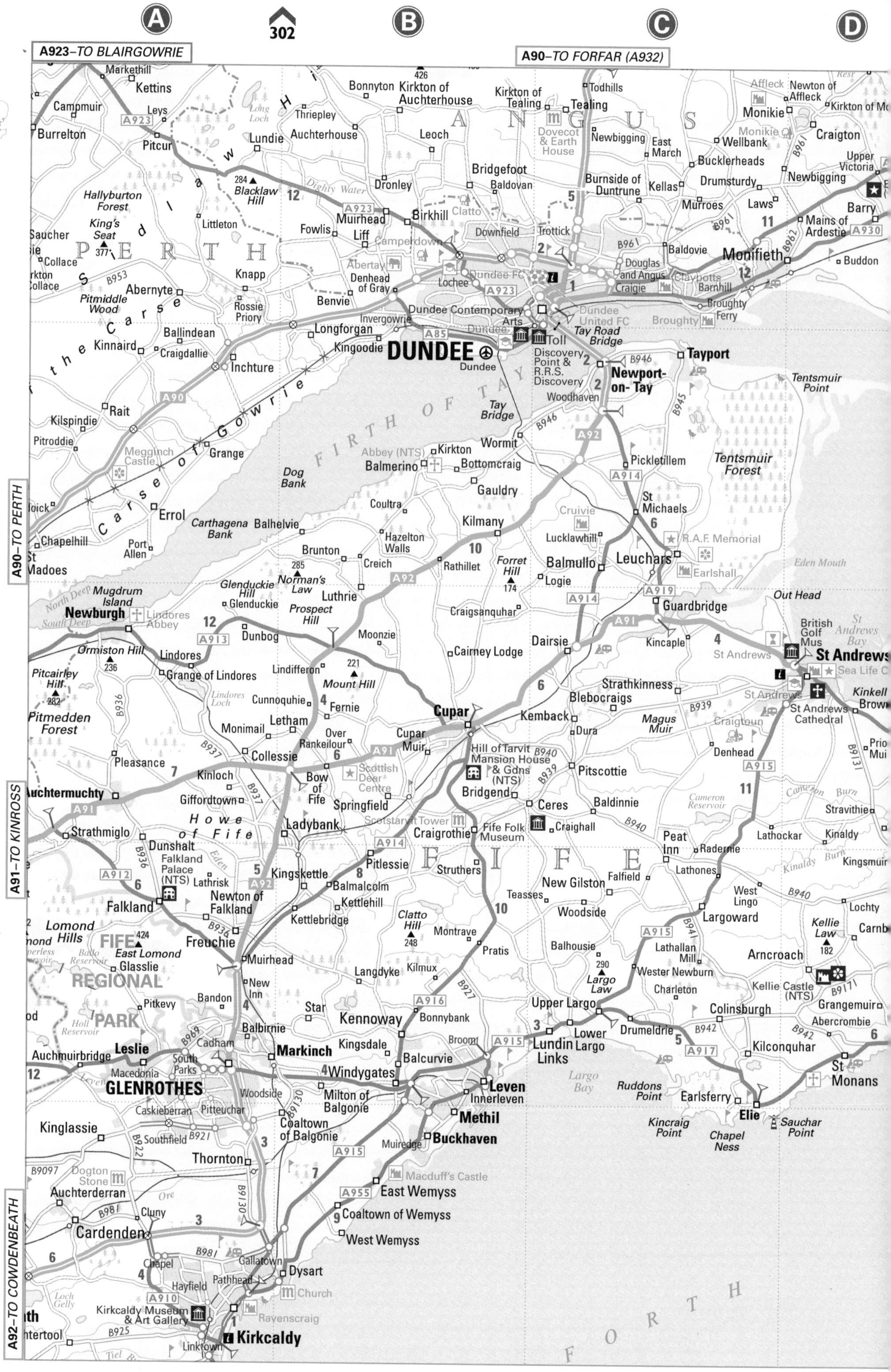

Lower Largo: *Alexander Selkirk, the sailor, was born here in 1676. He was marooned on the uninhabited Island of Juan Fenandez for 4 years and became the model for the book Robinson Crusoe written by Daniel Defoe.* ***Map ref. C4***

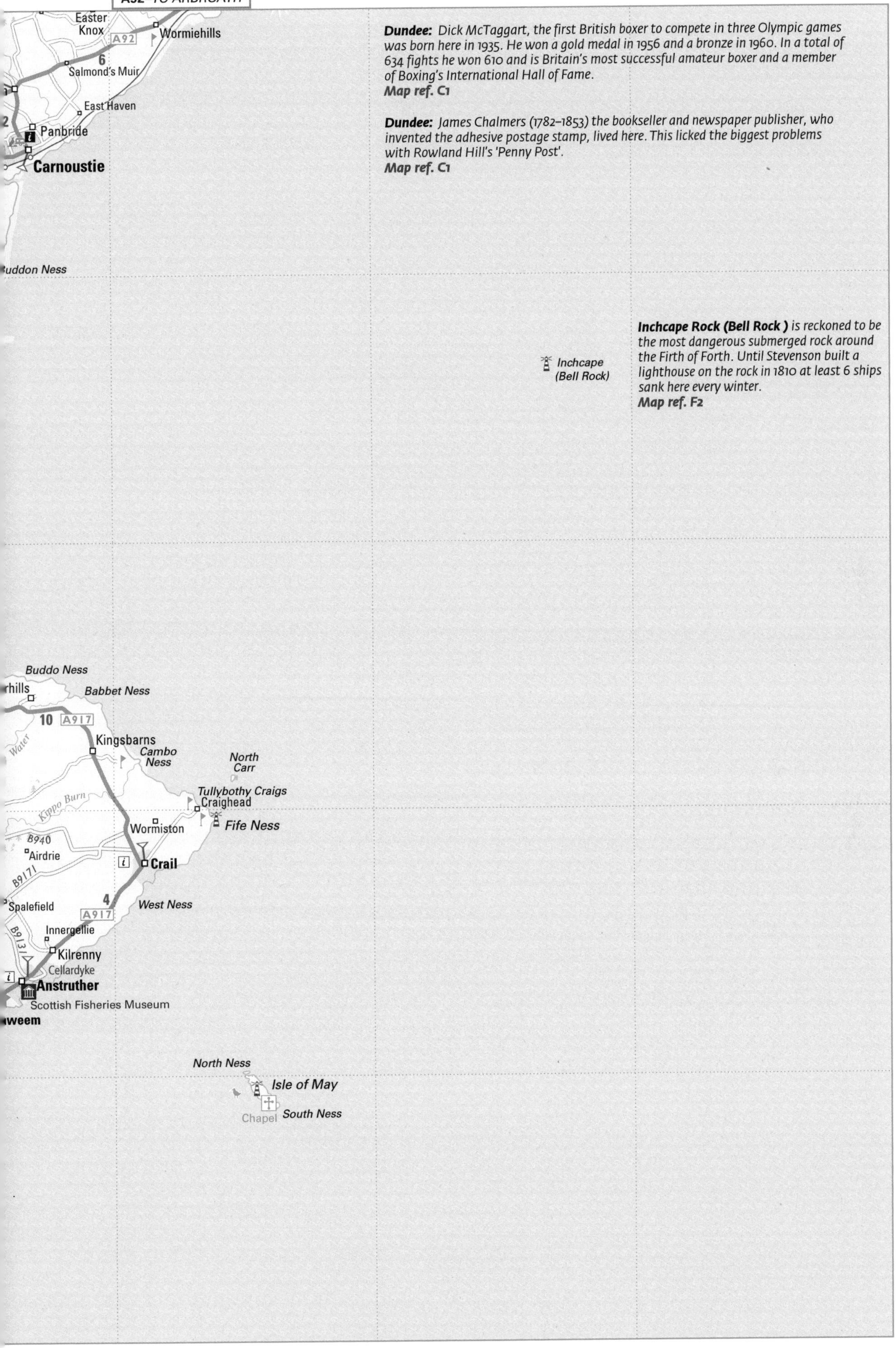

Dundee: *Dick McTaggart, the first British boxer to compete in three Olympic games was born here in 1935. He won a gold medal in 1956 and a bronze in 1960. In a total of 634 fights he won 610 and is Britain's most successful amateur boxer and a member of Boxing's International Hall of Fame.*
Map ref. C1

Dundee: *James Chalmers (1782–1853) the bookseller and newspaper publisher, who invented the adhesive postage stamp, lived here. This licked the biggest problems with Rowland Hill's 'Penny Post'.*
Map ref. C1

Inchcape Rock (Bell Rock) *is reckoned to be the most dangerous submerged rock around the Firth of Forth. Until Stevenson built a lighthouse on the rock in 1810 at least 6 ships sank here every winter.*
Map ref. F2

Tay Rail Bridge: *At about 7.15pm on the night of the 28th December 1879 the central spans of the Tay Rail Bridge collapsed during gale force winds. The bridge had only been open for 19 months. A passenger train from Edinburgh, which was crossing the bridge at the time, plunged into the water below. In all 75 people lost their lives in the disaster, there were no survivors and only 46 bodies were ever found. The engine itself, however, was recovered from the river bed and put back into service where it continued to haul carriages until 1908. Even today the supporting masonry piers of the old bridge in the river are still visible.* ***Map ref. B2***

Isle of May: *Largest island in the Firth of Forth and site of the first permanently manned lighthouse beacon in Scotland built by Alexander Cunningham in 1636.*
Map ref. E5

A 305 B C D

1 2 3 4 5

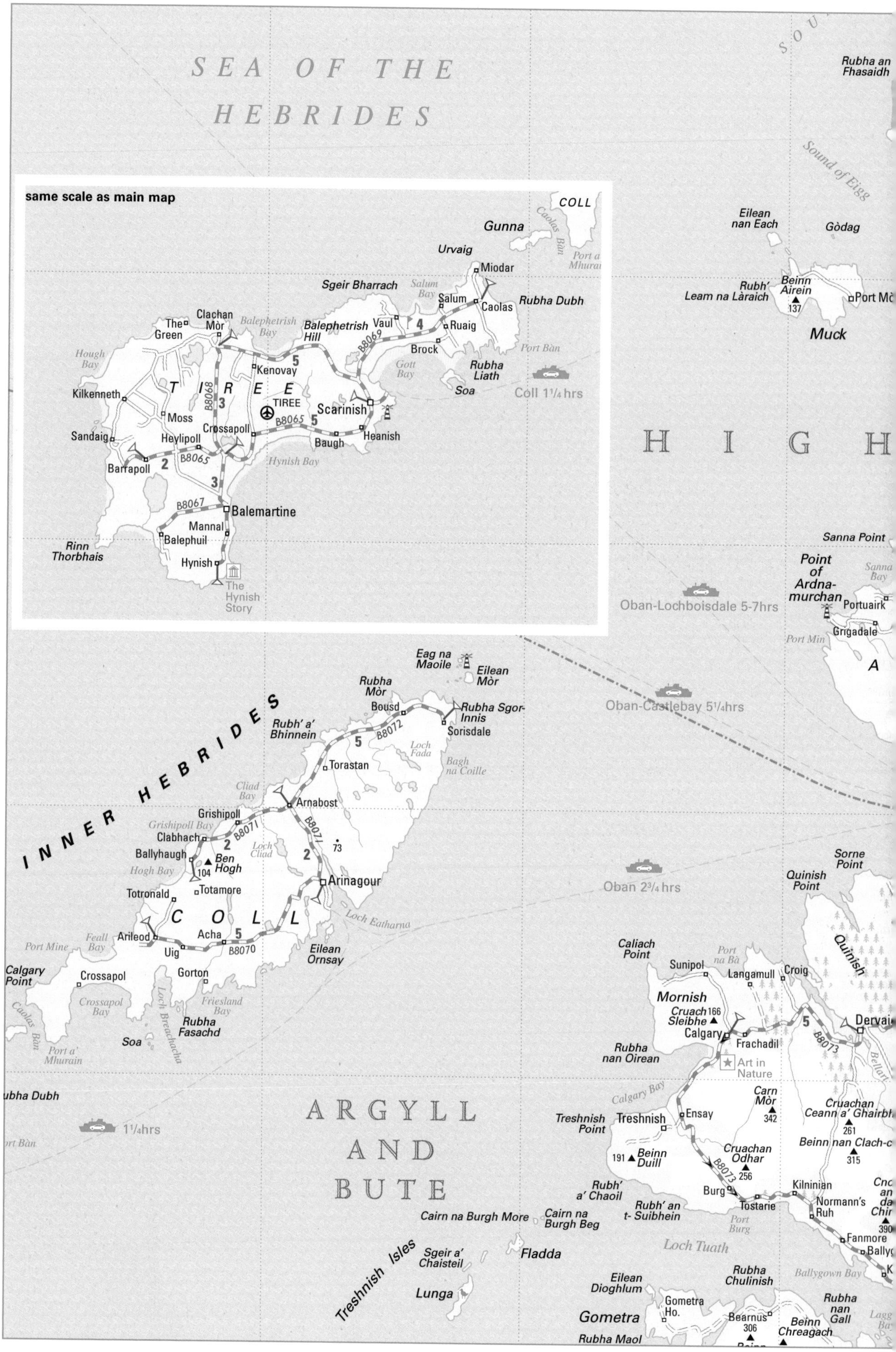

Eilean Ornsay: *Just a small uninhabited island. There are dozens like it called Eilean something or other. In this case Eilean simply means Island.* ***Map ref. B4***

288

The Hebrides: *Because of the lack of street lighting and pollution and because the sky is unusually clear, the Hebridean Islands are the best place in the UK for seeing the Aurora Borealis (The Northern Lights). This fantastic lightshow occurs naturally every autumn in the Arctic regions.*

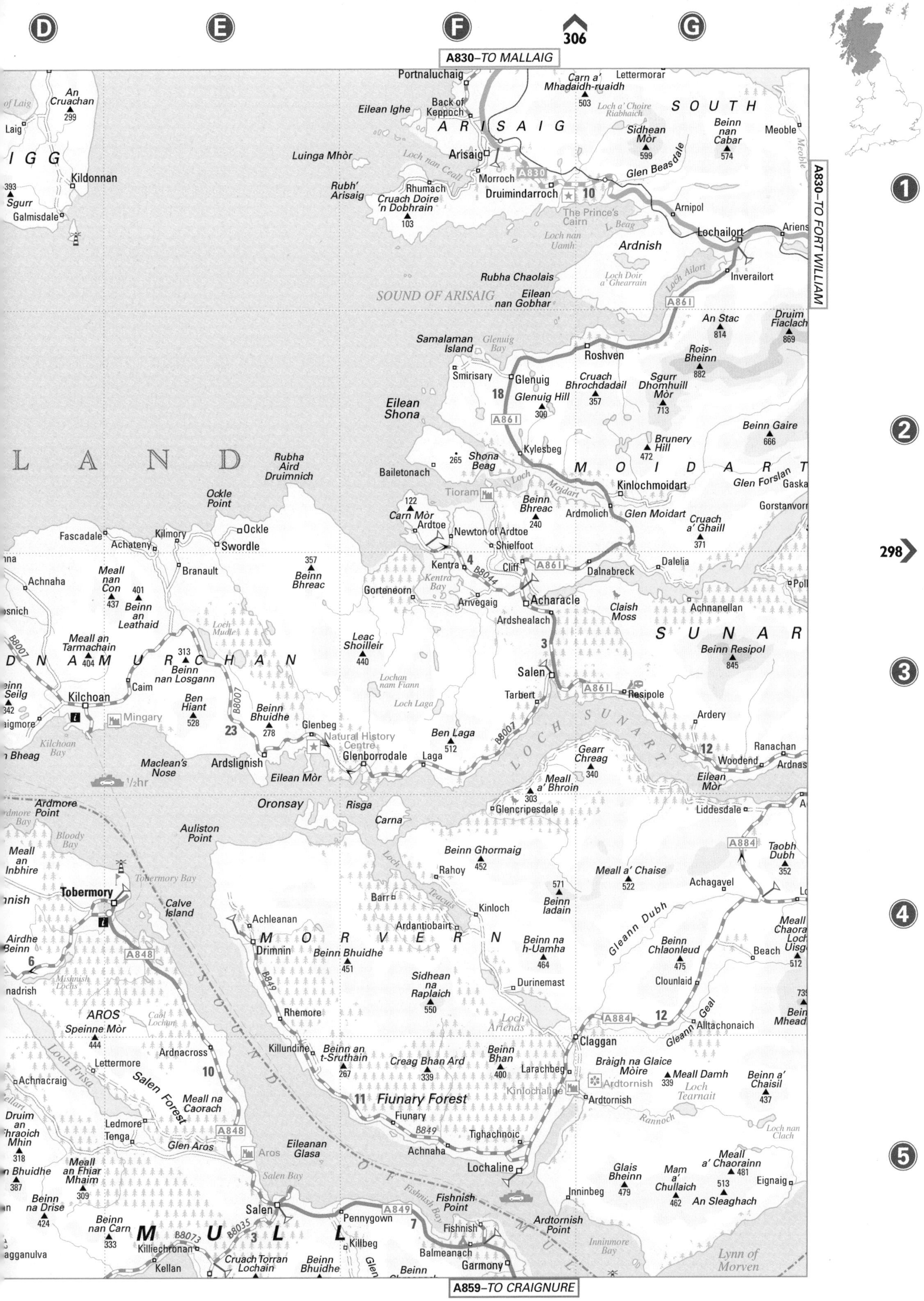

289

Eigg: *Feuding and fighting amongst the Scottish clans is legendary. Massacre Cave on the south side of Eigg is where 395 MacDonalds died in 1577. They were hiding in the cave when the MacLeods caught up with them. The MacLeods blocked the cave entrance and started a fire which suffocated the MacDonalds. After being owned by a succession of absentee landlords, the 60 islanders set up a trust which succeeded in buying Eigg for £1.5 million in 1997 and is dedicated to conserving the island and developing a sustainable economy.*
Map ref. D1

A B C D
307
1 2 3 4 5
297

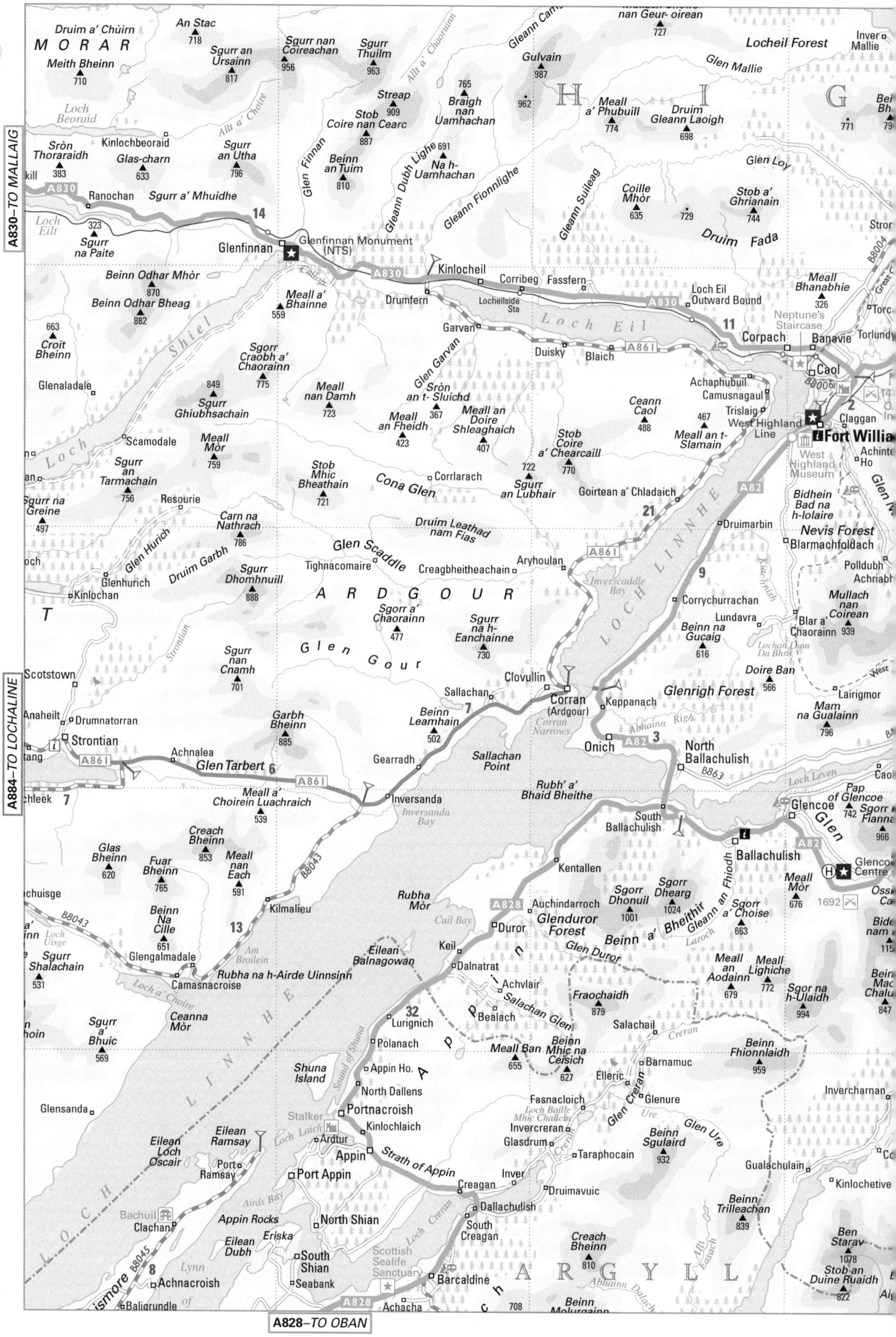

Corpach: *Starting point of the Caledonian Canal which is the longest canal in Scotland and connects Corpach, near Fort William to Clachnacarry, near Inverness, a distance of 60 miles (96.5km). Much of its length is made up of the lochs it passes through.* ***Map ref. D2***

290

Ballachulish: *James Stewart was hanged here in 1752 for the 'Appin' murder of the King's Factor, Colin Campbell of Glenure, as he rode through the woods of Lettermoor. Stewart's body was left on the gibbet for years afterwards with his bones wired.* ***Map ref. C4***

D E F G
308
1 2 3 4 5
300
291

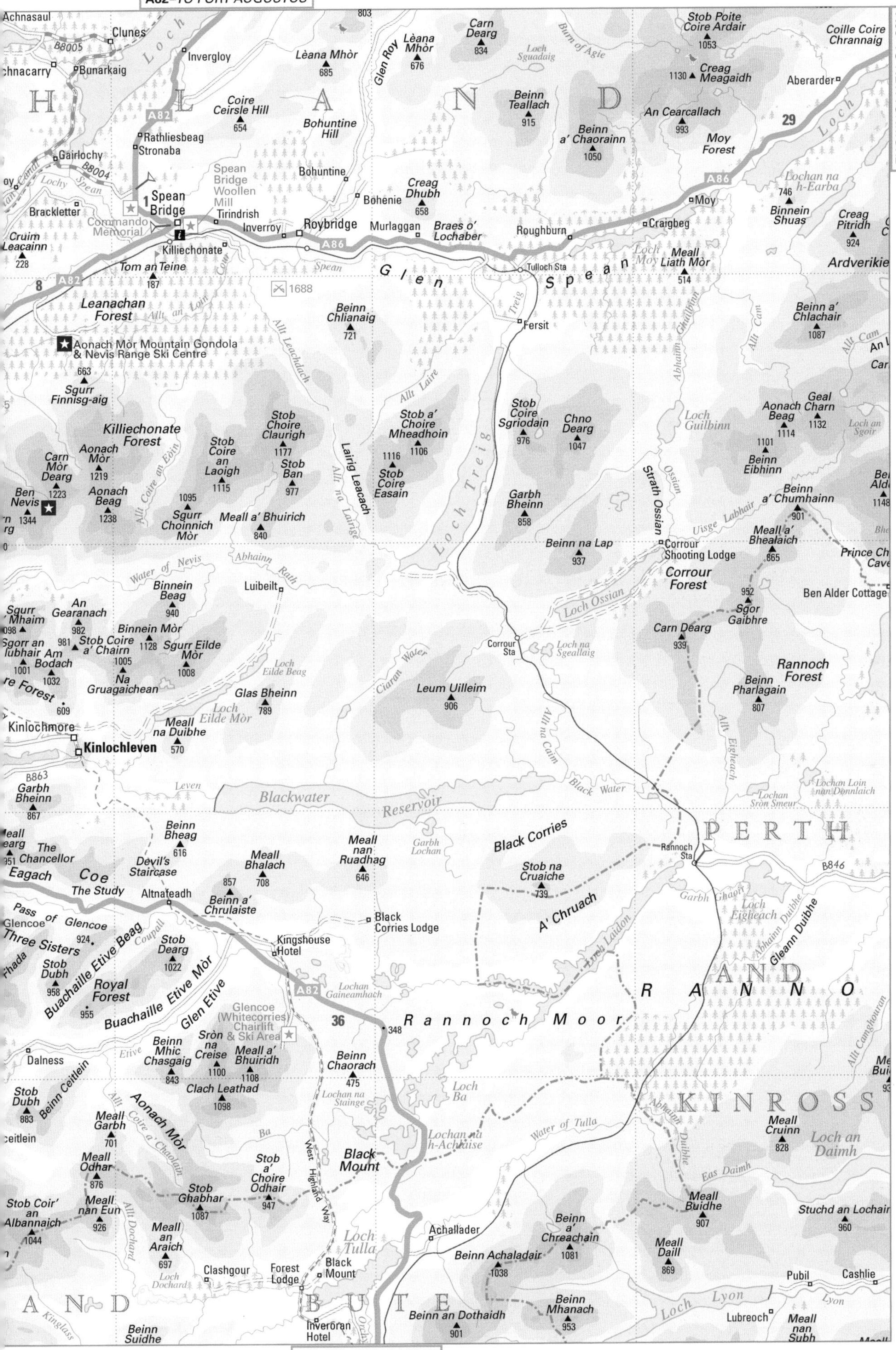

Ben Nevis: *At 4406 feet (1344m) Ben Nevis is the highest mountain in Britain. Scotland has 284 distinct mountains over 3000 feet (914.4m) which are collectively known as Munros, after Sir Hugh Munro who was the first man to catalogue them.* ***Map ref. D2***

Corrour Station: *This is Britain's most isolated railway station – there isn't even a road to it.* ***Map ref. F3***

Rannoch Moor: *Covering over 50 square miles and stretching from Bridge of Orchy to Loch Rannoch, this area is thought to be the largest uninhabited wilderness in Britain.* ***Map ref. F4 Also on page 129***

309

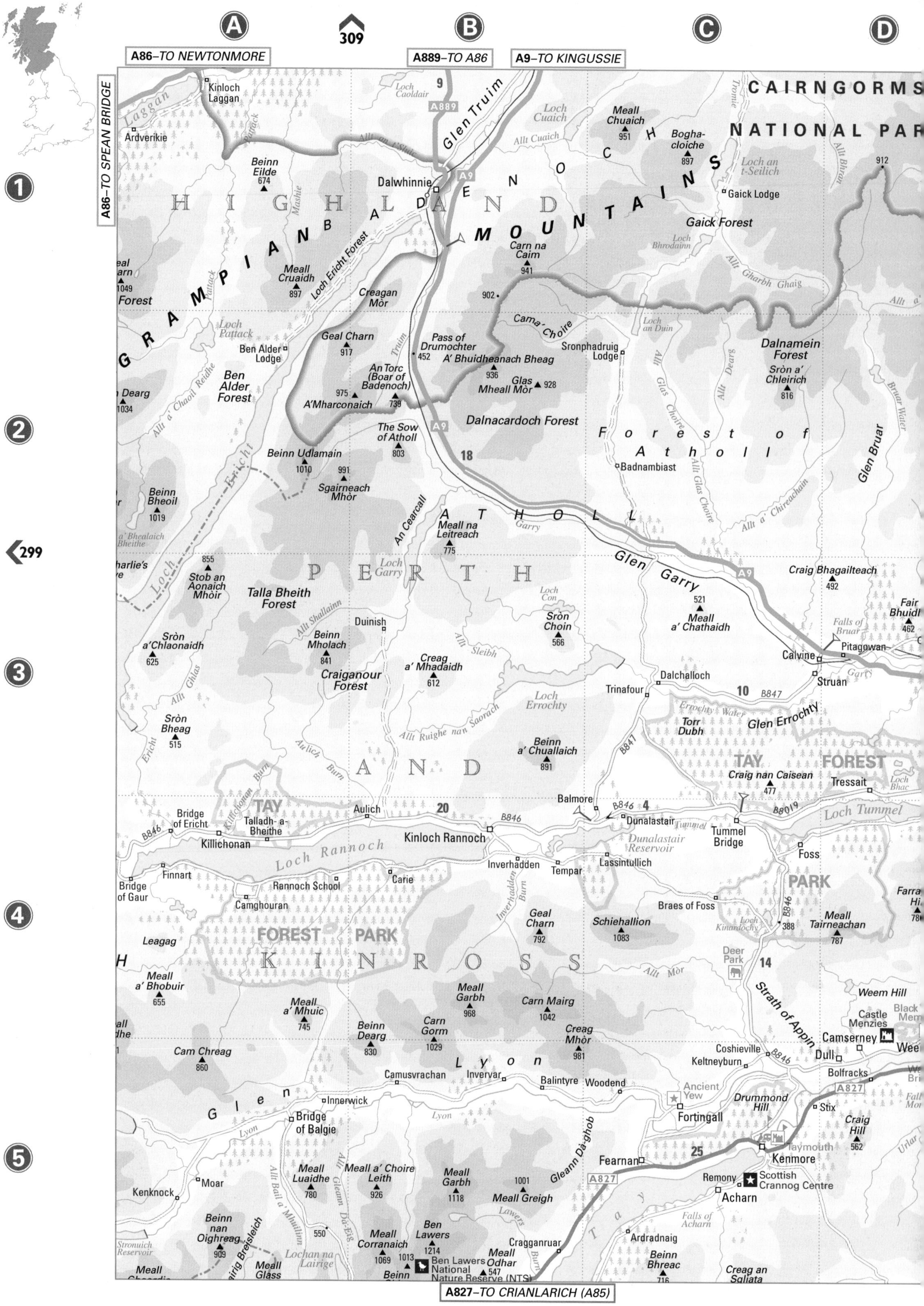

Pass of Drumochter: *At 1484 feet (452m) this is the highest point on the British railway network. Allegedly, trains used to be so slow coming up to the summit, that passengers used to get off and walk instead. Nearby Dalwhinnie (**Map ref. B1**) claims to be the highest village in the Scottish Highlands at 1160 feet (358 metres). **Map ref. B2***

299

292

D E F G

310

A93–TO BRAEMAR

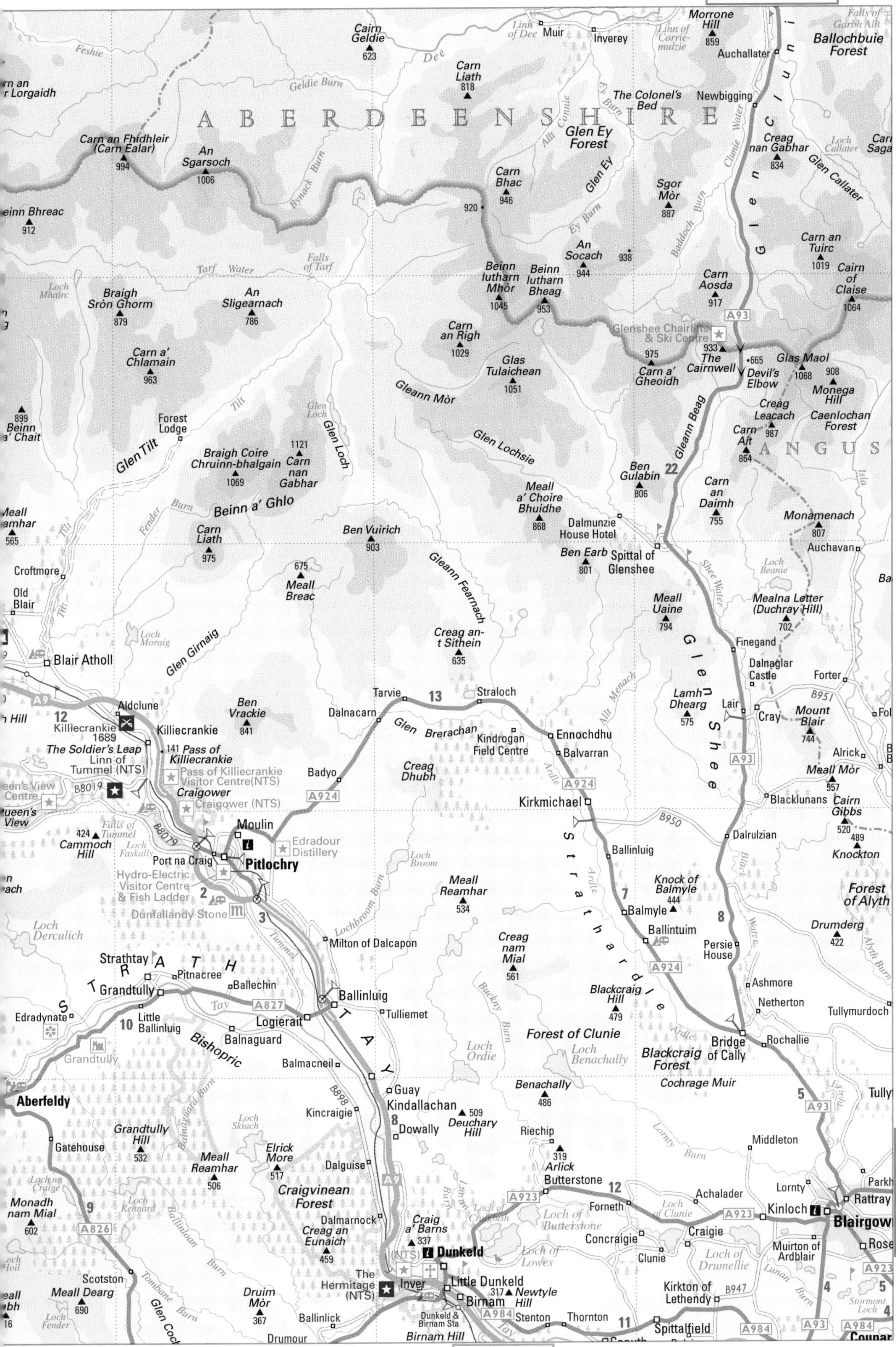

302

1 2 3 4 5

A9–TO PERTH

293

Fortingall: *Britain's oldest tree is thought to be the Fortingall Yew (Taxus baccata) in the churchyard, which is estimated to be 3000 years old and consequently the oldest living thing in Europe. There is a long oral tradition that Pontius Pilate was born in the village.* ***Map ref. C5***

Blair Atholl: *Queen Victoria loved the Highlands and was a keen 'rambler'. A cairn, close to here, marks the spot where she had a picnic in October 1861.* ***Map ref. D3***

1 2 3 4 5

301

Kirriemuir: *James Barrie, creator of Peter Pan, 'the boy who wouldn't grow up', was born here in 1860. The book was published in 1904. Barrie died on the 19th June 1937 and is buried next to his mother in Kirriemuir.* ***Map ref. B4***

294

Kirriemuir: *The famous Hollywood actor David Niven was born here in 1909. He starred in over 100 films including 'Separate Tables', for which he won an Academy Award in 1958. Although Scottish, David Niven was invariably cast as the archetypal Englishman.* ***Map ref. B4***

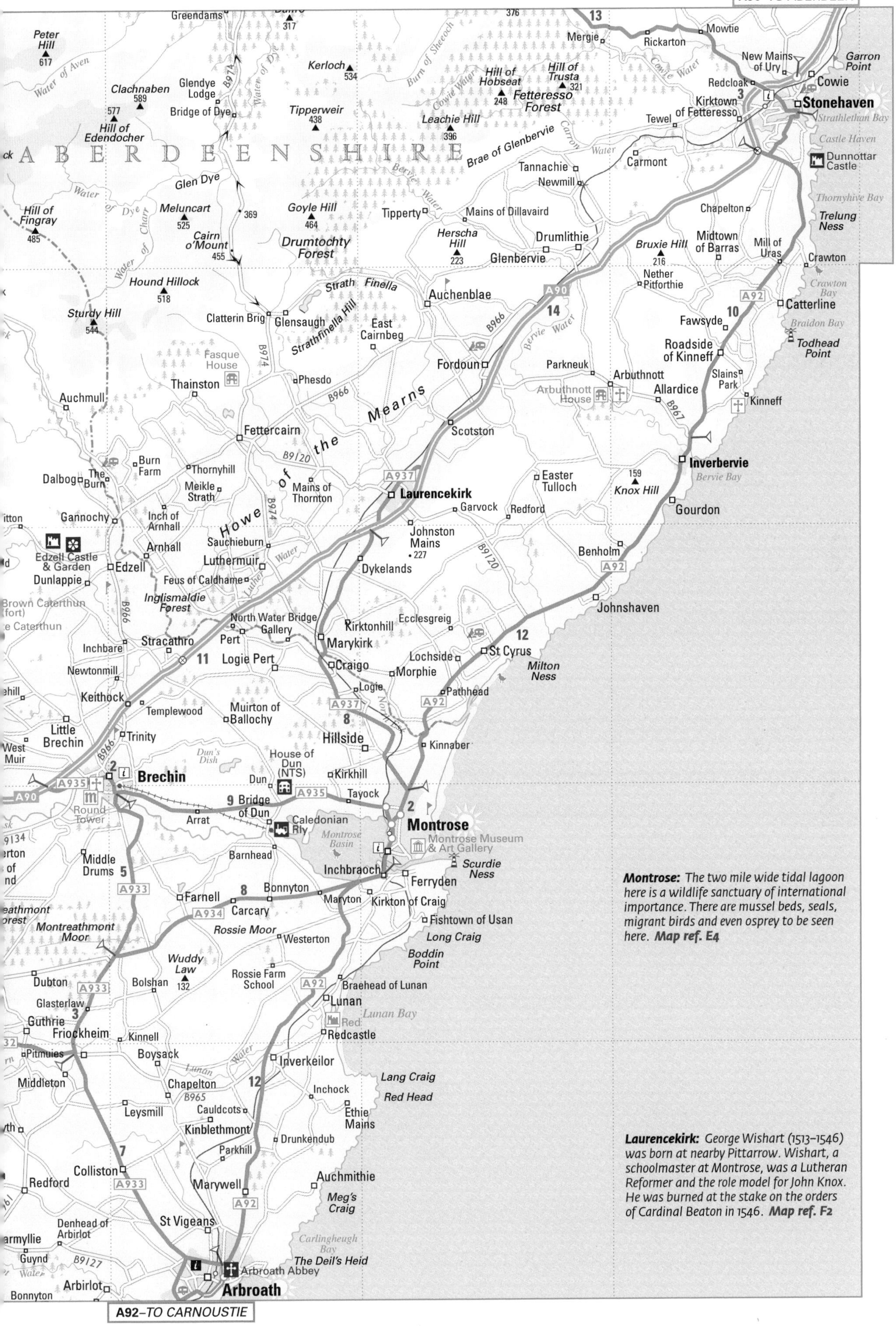

Montrose: *The two mile wide tidal lagoon here is a wildlife sanctuary of international importance. There are mussel beds, seals, migrant birds and even osprey to be seen here.* ***Map ref. E4***

Laurencekirk: *George Wishart (1513–1546) was born at nearby Pittarrow. Wishart, a schoolmaster at Montrose, was a Lutheran Reformer and the role model for John Knox. He was burned at the stake on the orders of Cardinal Beaton in 1546.* ***Map ref. F2***

Arbroath: *Home of the legendary Arbroath Smokie, pairs of haddock tied by their tails and smoked over hardwood chips. Arbroath Smokies are afforded the same protection under EU law as Champagne and Parma Ham if they don't come from Arbroath then they cannot be called Arbroath Smokies.* ***Map ref. E5***

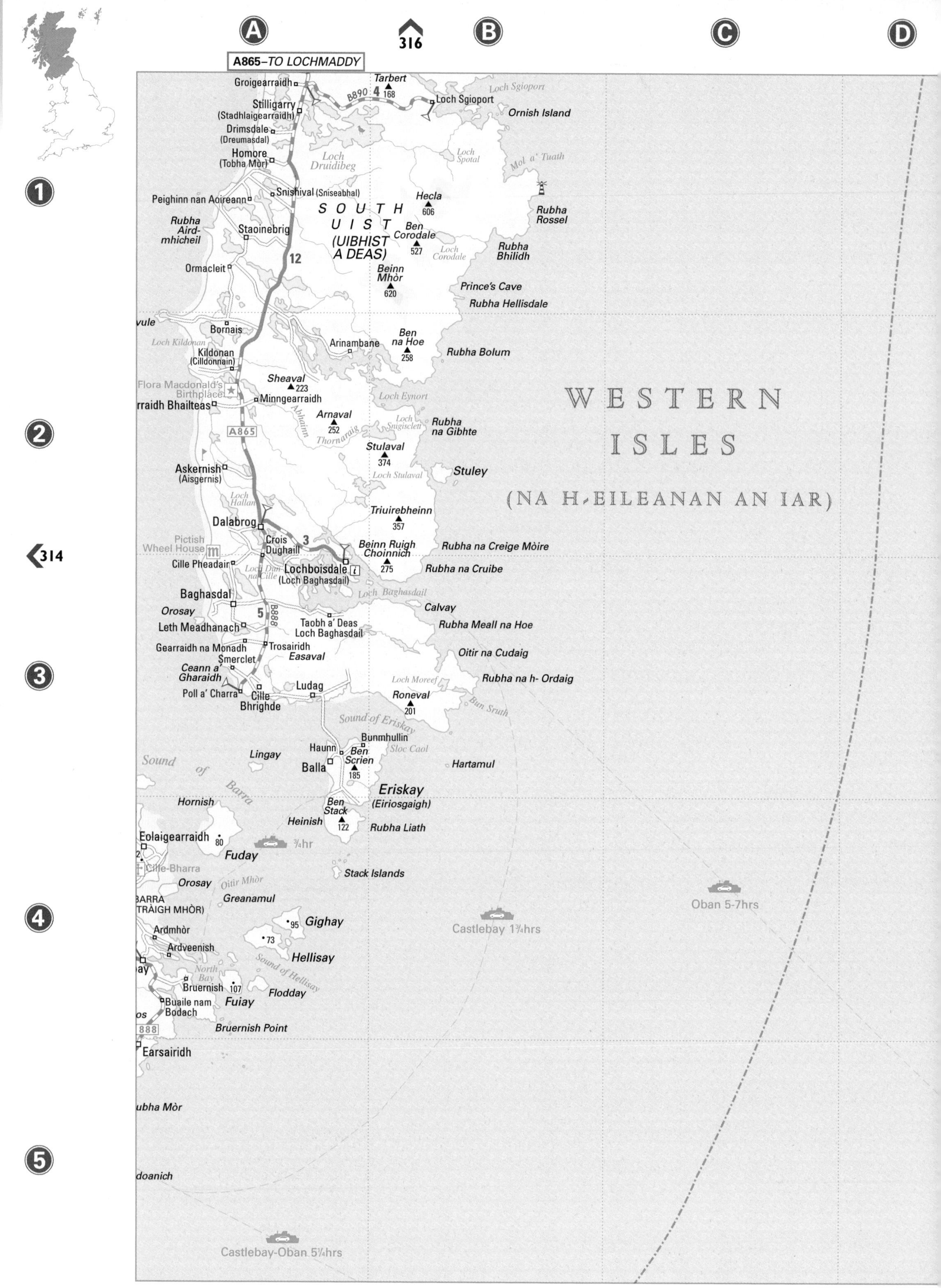

Flora Macdonald's Birthplace: *South Uist was the home of Flora MacDonald who helped Bonnie Prince Charlie escape from the English army after the defeat of his army at the battle of Culloden in April 1746. After narrowly evading the enemy several times she eventually got him to the Isle of Skye and then on to safety. Her home is now a ruin but a nearby memorial marks the site.* ***Map ref. A2***

D E F G

317

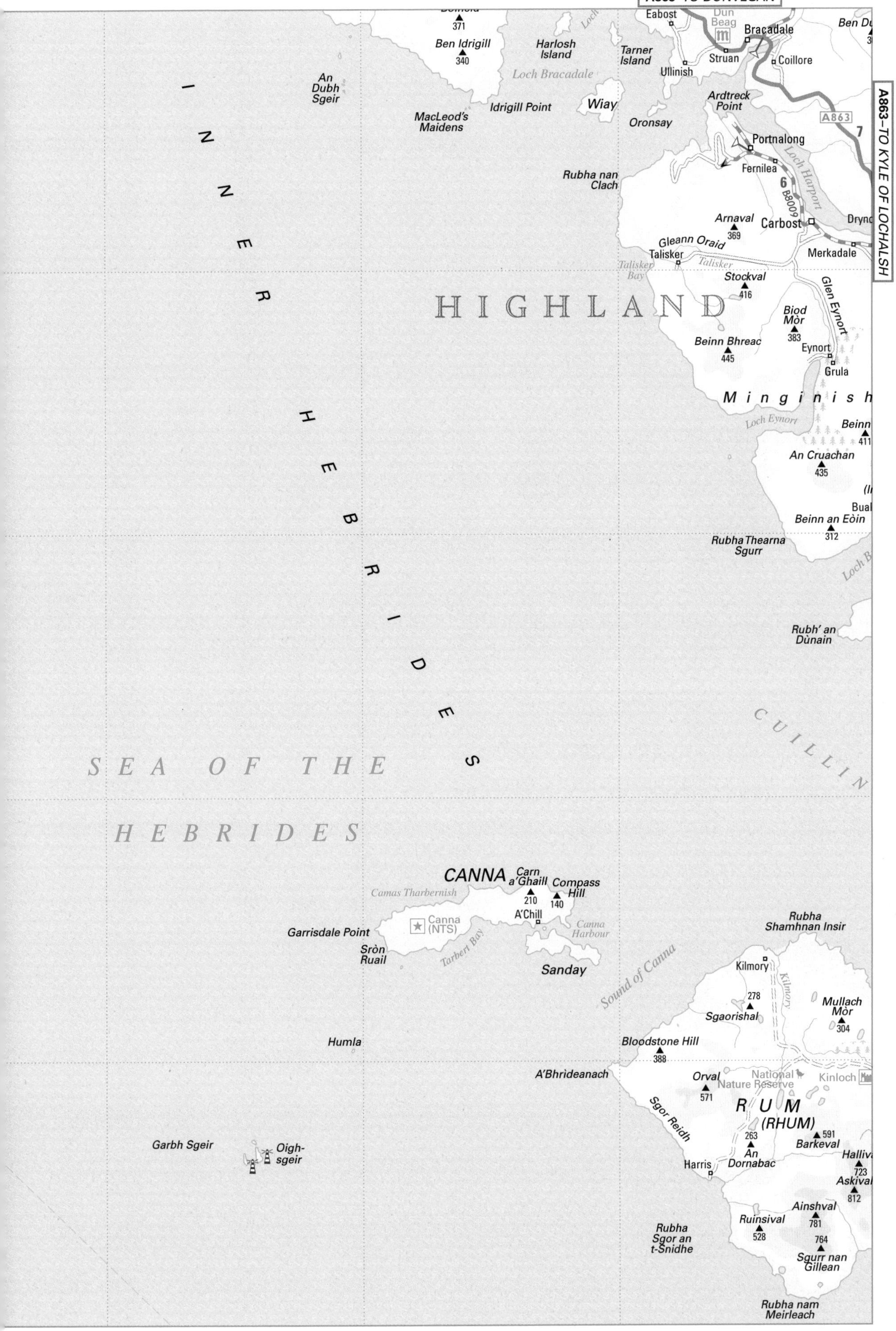

1 2 3 4 5

306

296

Rum: *Semi precious stones and rocks on this island are similar to those found on the moon. In the 19th Century the island was 'cleared' for sheep farming and the residents shipped off to Nova Scotia. It is now owned by the Nature Conservancy Council.* ***Map ref. G5***

A B C D

318

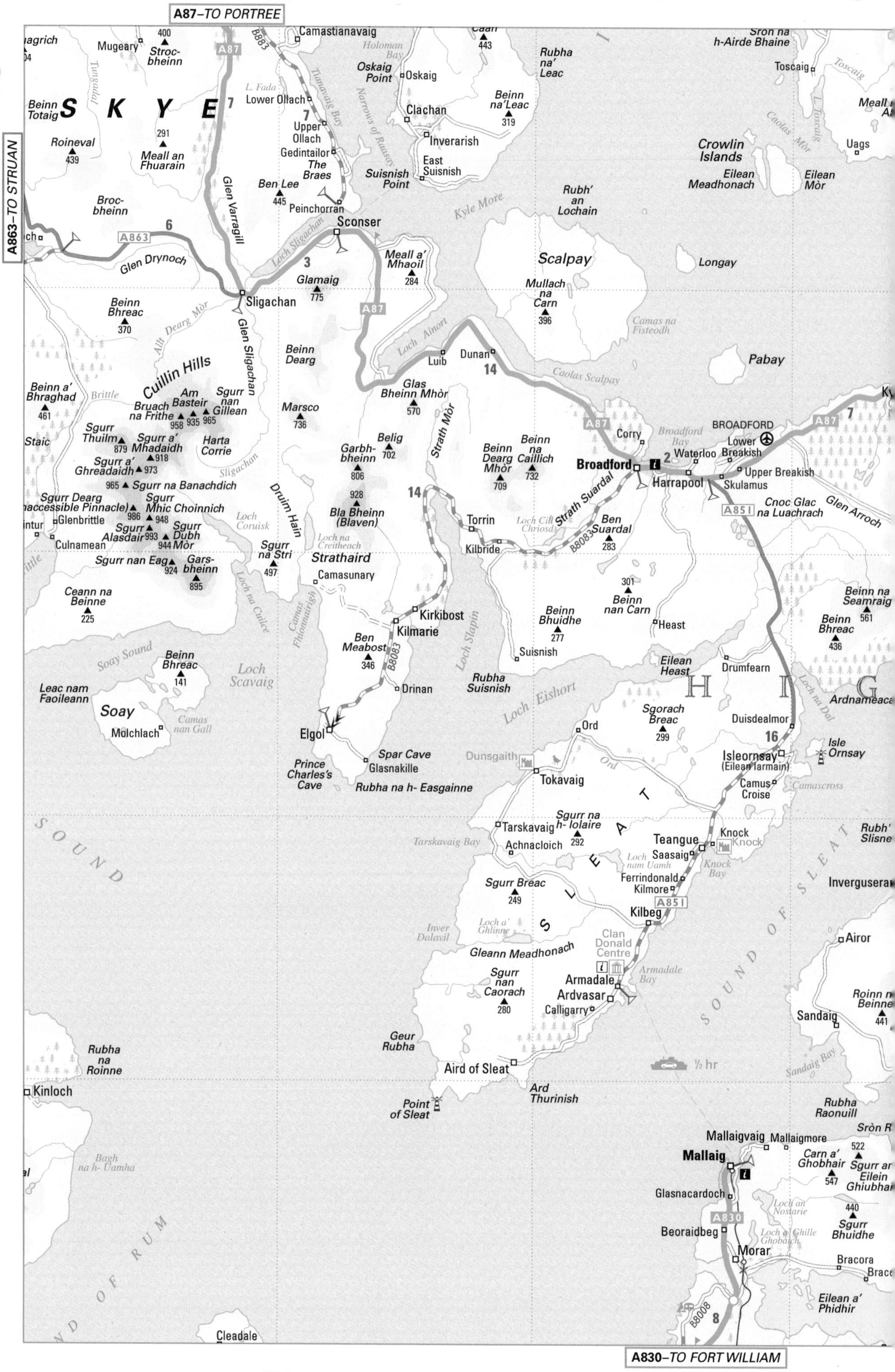

1 2 3 4 5

305

Loch Morar: *Known as the 'Loch without a bottom'. Loch Morar covers an area of over 10 square miles (28.6 sq km) and at 1077 feet (328m) is the deepest lake in Britain.* ***Map ref. D5***

297

The Cuillin Hills *Considered by many to be the most dramatic mountain range in Britain. Comprises the tall, jagged peaks of the main Cuillin Ridge, known as the Black Cuillin and the more rounded hills of the Red Cuillin. There are over 20 Munros in the Cuillin Hills which have a fascinating geological composition dating back 500 million years.* ***Map ref. A2 Also on page 119***

Elgol: *Just south of the village is a cave called Suidhe Biorach where Bonnie Prince Charlie is said to have hidden before makin his escape to Europe in 1746.* ***Map ref. B3***

D E F G
319
A890–TO ACHNASHEEN

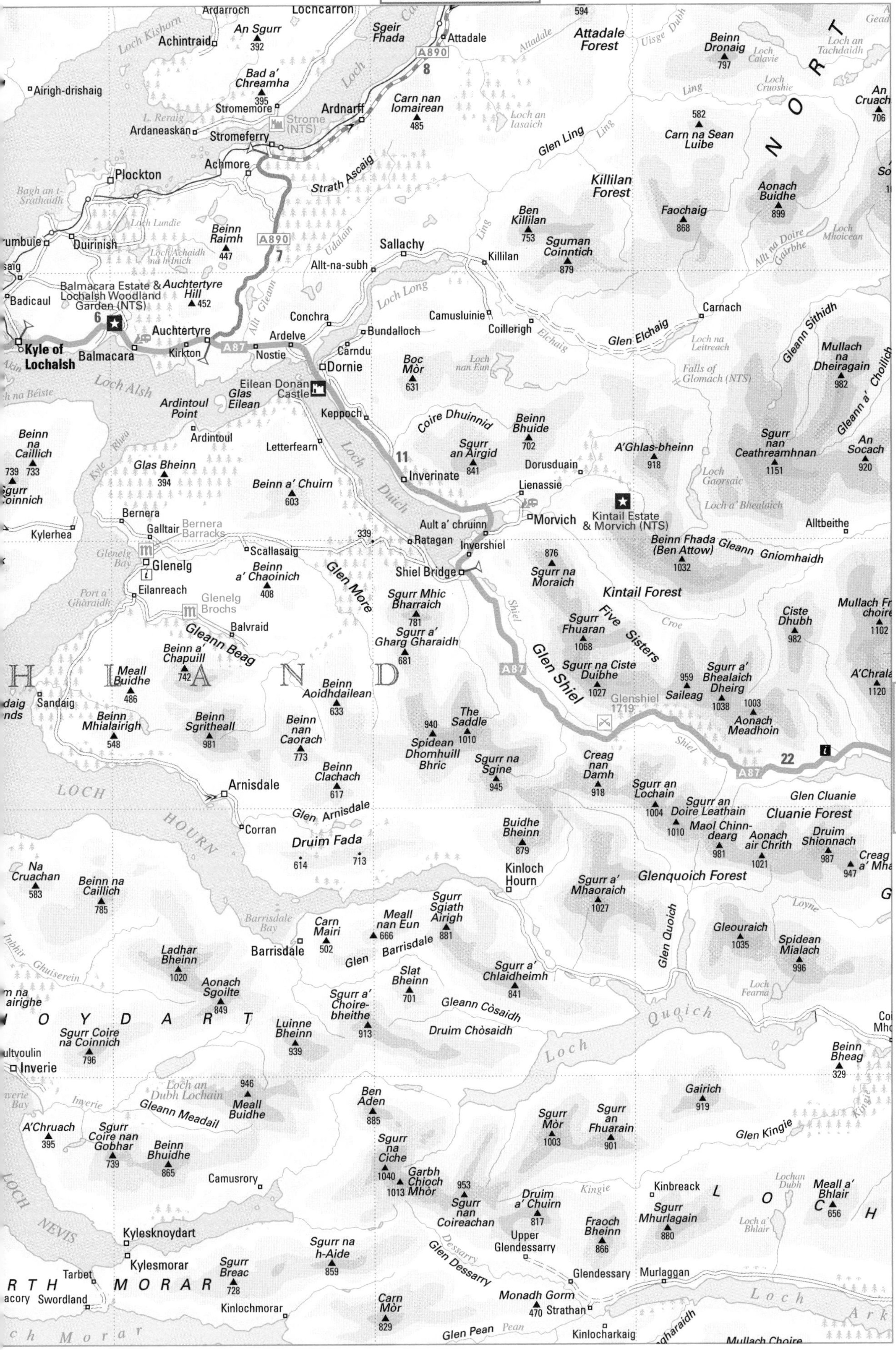

1
2
308
3
4
5

Sandaig: *Former home of the enigmatic writer Gavin Maxwell (1914-1969) which he described as Camusfearna in his autobiographical 'Ring of Bright Water'. His grave is on the site of his house which burned down in 1968.* ***Map ref. D3***

298

Eilean Donan Castle *is used as a location for several famous films, including 'Highlander', 'Entrapment' and 'The World is not Enough'. It was originally built in the 13th century as a defence against the Vikings and was destroyed by three English warships during the 1715 Jacobite uprising. It was rebuilt in the 1930s and is today one of Scotland's most picturesque castles.* ***Map ref. E2 Also on page 122***

320

307

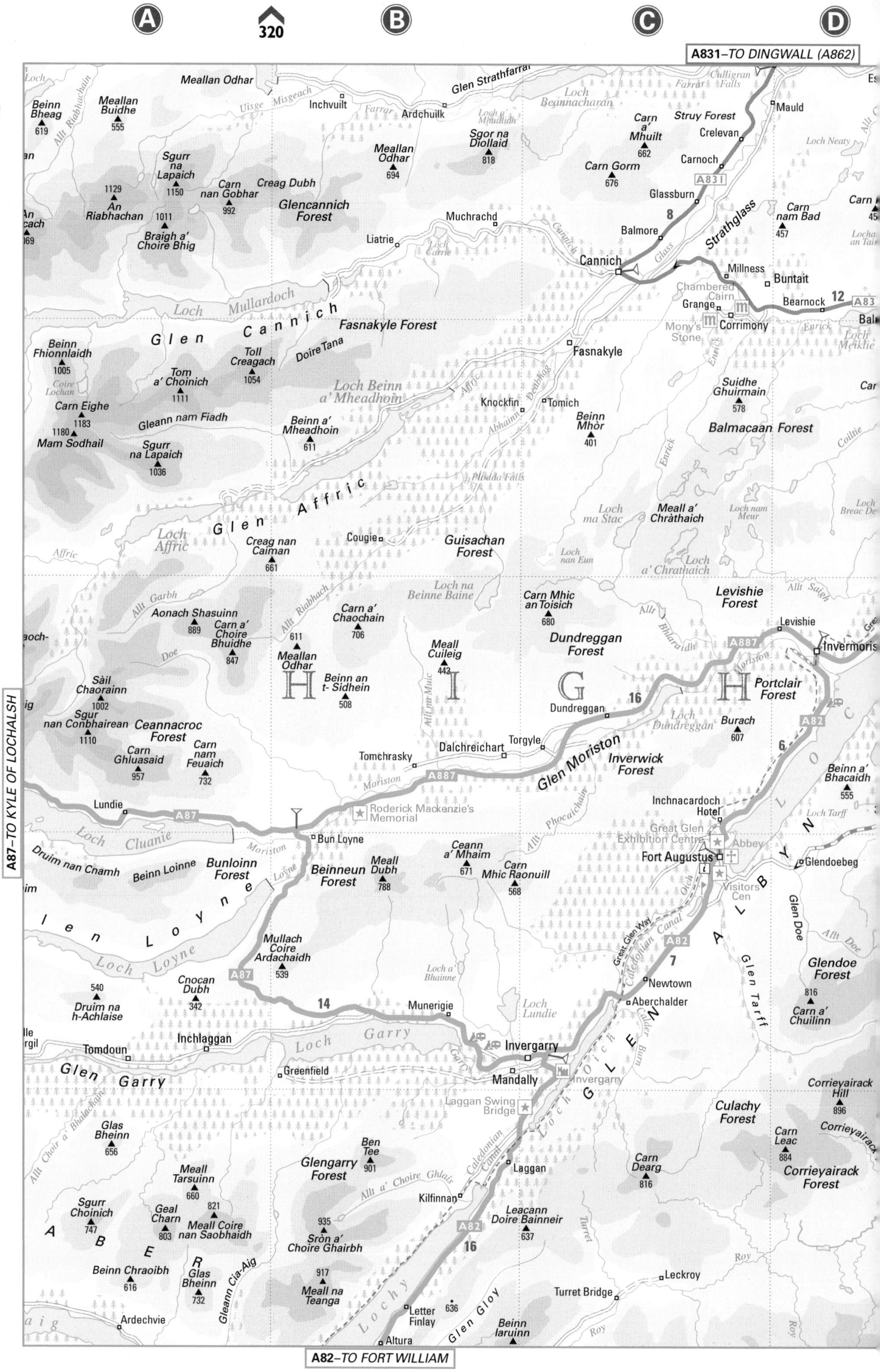

299

Invergarry: *Historic home of the MacDonells of Glen Garry whose nearby castle was repeatedly attacked and finally razed in 1746 by the Duke of Cumberland. It remains today as a ruin.* ***Map ref. C4***

Loch Ness: *John Cobb, the 'record breakers' record breaker', died here whilst attempting to beat the world water speed record on 29th September 1952. Cobb had dedicated his life to speed records as a racing driver at Brooklands, then as holder of the world land speed record. He was recovered from the water following the accident and carried up the hill to Achnahannet where he died. Fifty years later his speedboat Crusader was located in 650 feet (200m) of water on the bed of Loch Ness.* ***Map ref. E2***

D E F G
321

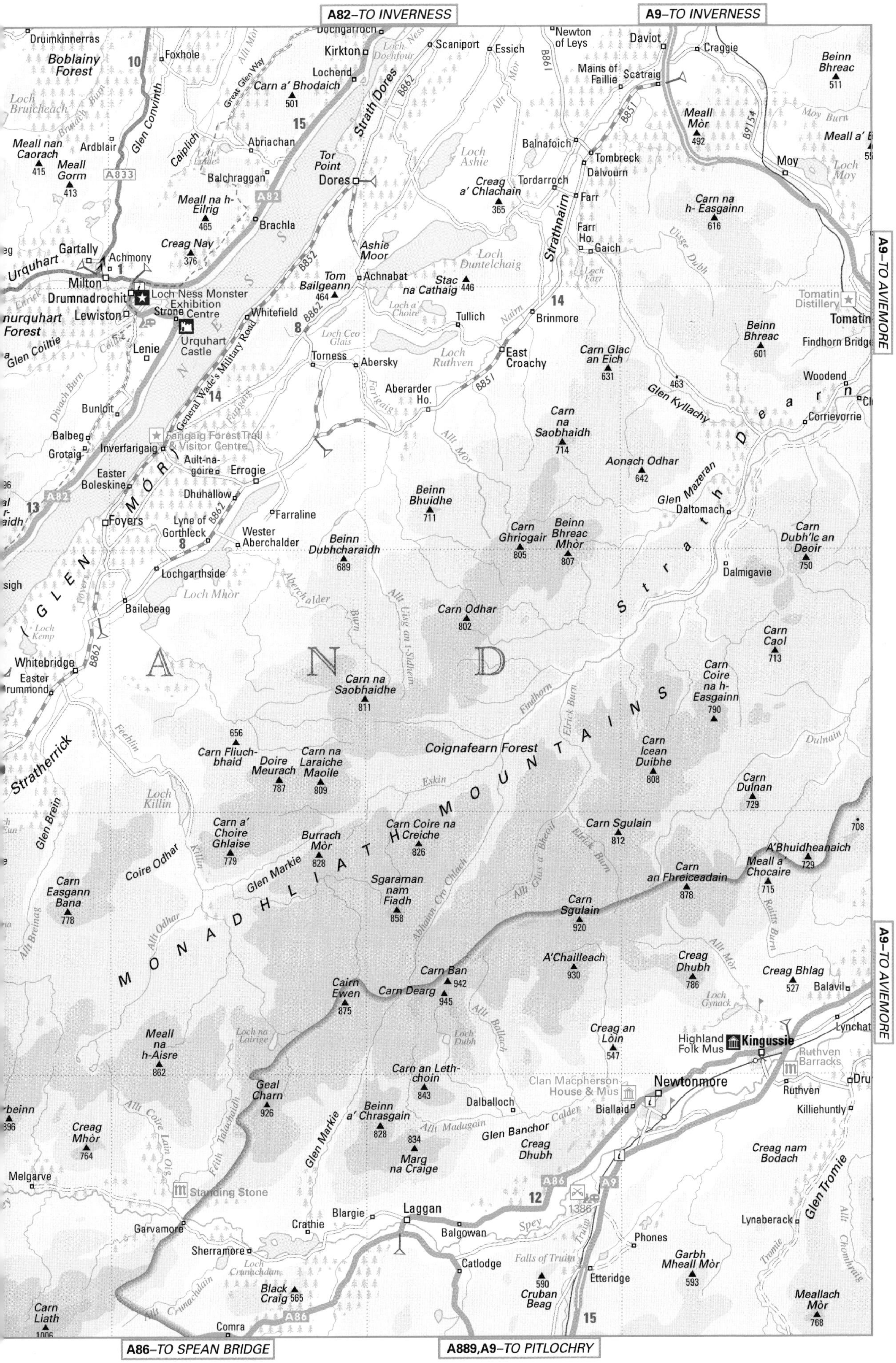

1
2
310
3
4
5
300

Newtonmore: *The Spey valley is the heartland of the sport of Shinty. The advantages of being double-handed in the sport have led to the area having allegedly the highest proportion of left-handed golfers in the country: about half of the members of Newtonmore Golf Club play left-handed, and it regularly hosts the Scottish left-handed golf championships.* ***Map ref. G5***

A B C D
322
1 2 3 4 5
309
301

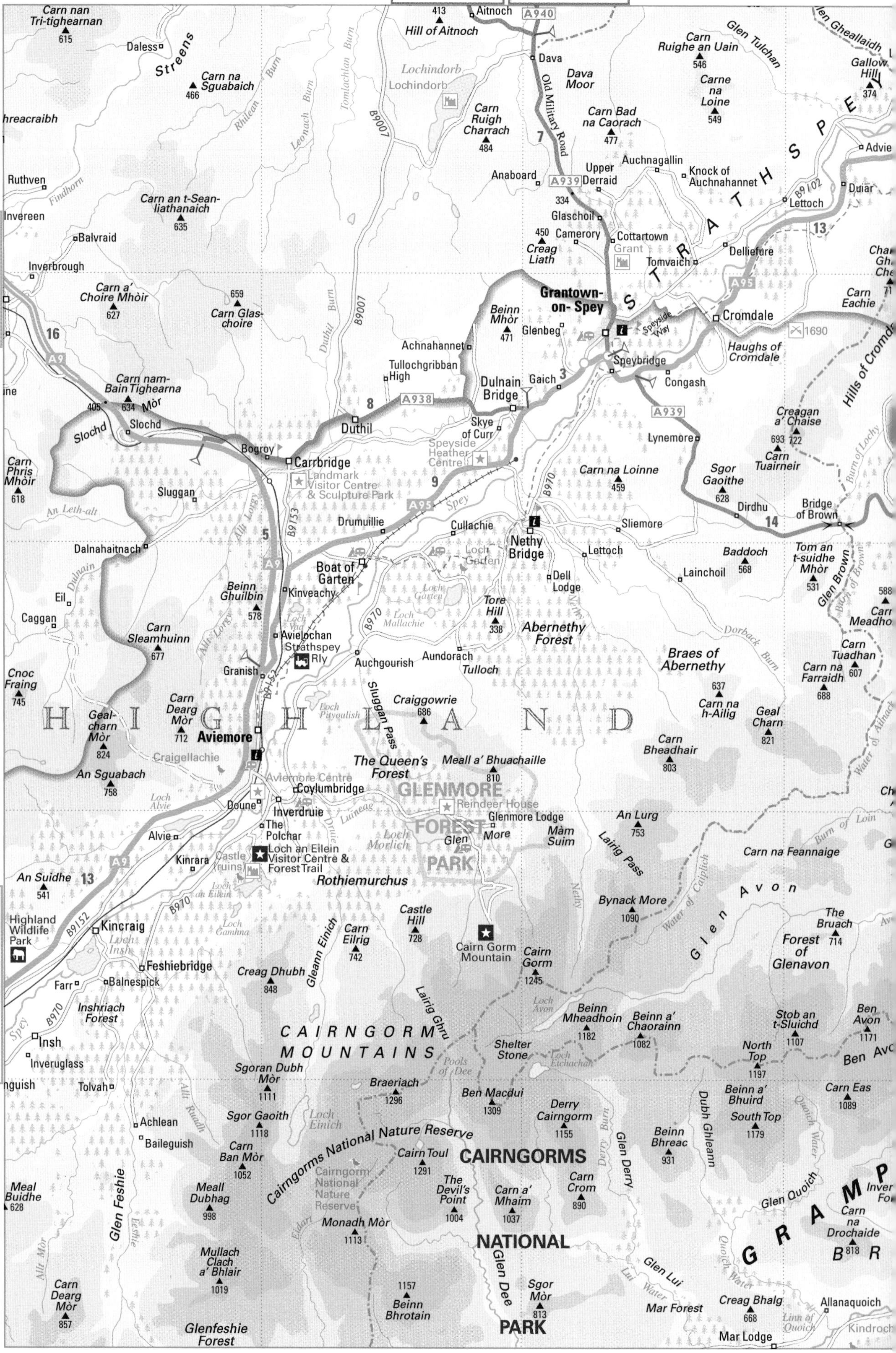
A939–TO NAIRN
A940–TO FORRES
A9–TO INVERNESS
A9–TO NEWTONMORE (A86)
Carn nan Tri-tighearnan 615
Daless
Streens
Carn na Sguabaich 466
Hill of Aitnoch
Aitnoch
413
Dava
Dava Moor
Old Military Road
Lochindorb
Carn Ruigh Charrach 484
Carn Bad na Caorach 477
Carn Ruighe an Uain 546
Glen Tulchan
Carne na Loine 549
Glen Gheallaidh
Gallow Hill 374
Advie
Duiar
Lettoch
hreacraibh
Ruthven
Findhorn
Inverreen
Balvraid
Inverbrough
Carn an t-Sean-liathanaich 635
Rhilean Burn
Leonach Burn
Tomlachlan Burn
B9007
Anaboard
Upper Derraid
Auchnagallin
Knock of Auchnahannet
STRATHSPEY
334
Glaschoil
450 Camerory
Creag Liath
Cottartown
Grant
Tomvaich
Dellefure
13
Grantown-on-Spey
Beinn Mhòr 471
Glenbeg
Speyside Way
Cromdale
Haughs of Cromdale
1690
Hills of Cromdale
Carn Eachie
Carn a' Choire Mhòir 627
659 Carn Glas-choire
Duthil Burn
16
A9
Achnahannet
Tullochgribban High
Dulnain Bridge
Gaich
3
Speybridge
Congash
Carn nam-Bain Tighearna 634
Mòr
405
Slochd
8
A938
Duthil
Skye of Curr
Speyside Heather Centre
A939
Lynemore
Creagan a' Chaise
693 722
Carn Tuairneir
Carn Phris Mhòir 618
Bogroy
Carrbridge
Landmark Visitor Centre & Sculpture Park
9
B970
Carn na Loinne 459
Sgor Gaoithe 628
Dirdhu
Bridge of Brown
14
Burn of Lochy
Sluggan
An Leth-allt
A95
Spey
Drumuillie
B9153
Allt Lorgy
5
Cullachie
Nethy Bridge
Sliemore
Dalnahaitnach
Loch Garten
Lettoch
Baddoch 568
Lainchoil
Tom an t-suidhe Mhòr 531
Glen Brown
Burn of Brown
Dulnain
Eil
Caggan
Boat of Garten
Beinn Ghuilbin 578
Kinveachy
Dell Lodge
Tore Hill 338
Loch Mallachie
Abernethy Forest
Carn Sleamhuinn 677
Avielochan
Strathspey Rly
Auchgourish
Aundorach
Tulloch
Braes of Abernethy
Dorback Burn
Carn Tuadhan 607
Carn na Farraidh 688
588
Carn Meadho
Cnoc Fraing 745
Granish
B9152
Sluggan Pass
Craiggowrie 686
637 Carn na h-Ailig
Geal Charn 821
HIGHLAND
Geal-charn Mòr 824
Carn Dearg Mòr 712
Aviemore
Loch Pityoulish
Craigellachie
The Queen's Forest
Meall a' Bhuachaille 810
Carn Bheadhair 803
Water of Ailnack
An Sguabach 758
Aviemore Centre
Coylumbridge
GLENMORE FOREST PARK
Reindeer House
Glenmore Lodge
Loch Alvie
Doune
Inverdruie
Luineag
An Lurg 753
Màm Suim
Glen More
Lairig Pass
Loch Morlich
Alvie
The Polchar
Carn na Feannaige
Kinrara
Castle (ruins)
Loch an Eilein Visitor Centre & Forest Trail
Rothiemurchus
An Suidhe 541
13
Loch an Eilein
Nethy
Bynack More 1090
Water of Caiplich
Glen Avon
Avon
The Bruach
Highland Wildlife Park
Kincraig
Loch Insh
Loch Gamhna
Gleann Einich
Carn Eilrig 742
Castle Hill 728
Cairn Gorm Mountain
Cairn Gorm 1245
Forest of Glenavon 714
Feshiebridge
Farr
Balnespick
Creag Dhubh 848
Lairig Ghru
Loch Avon
Beinn Mheadhoin 1182
Beinn a' Chaorainn 1082
Stob an t-Sluichd 1107
Ben Avon 1171
Inshriach Forest
B970
Spey
Insh
Inveruglass
CAIRNGORM MOUNTAINS
Shelter Stone
Loch Etchachan
North Top 1197
Ben Avon
nguish
Tolvah
Sgoran Dubh Mòr 1111
Braeriach 1296
Pools of Dee
Ben Macdui 1309
Derry Cairngorm 1155
Dubh Ghleann
Beinn a' Bhuird
South Top 1179
Carn Eas 1089
Quoich Water
Achlean
Baileguish
Allt Ruadh
Sgor Gaoith 1118
Loch Einich
Cairngorms National Nature Reserve
Cairn Toul 1291
CAIRNGORMS
Derry Burn
Glen Derry
Beinn Bhreac 931
Carn Ban Mòr 1052
Cairngorm National Nature Reserve
The Devil's Point 1004
Carn a' Mhaim 1037
Carn Crom 890
Glen Quoich
Inver Fo
Meal Buidhe 628
Glen Feshie
Eidart
Meall Dubhag 998
Monadh Mòr 1113
NATIONAL PARK
Glen Dee
Glen Lui
Lui Water
Carn na Drochaide 818
GRAMPIAN
Allt Mòr
Eidart
Mullach Clach a' Bhlair 1019
1157 Beinn Bhrotain
Sgor Mòr 813
Mar Forest
Creag Bhalg 668
Allanaquoich
Linn of Quoich
Kindroch
Carn Dearg Mòr 857
Glenfeshie Forest
Mar Lodge

Findhorn: *One of the best fishing rivers in Scotland, famous for its salmon and trout. It is said that 360 salmon were caught here in one day from a single pool.* ***Map ref. A1***

Cairngorms: *Home of Britain's biggest Ski Centre with 28 runs and over 22 miles (35km) of pistes* ***Map ref. B4***

D E 323 F G

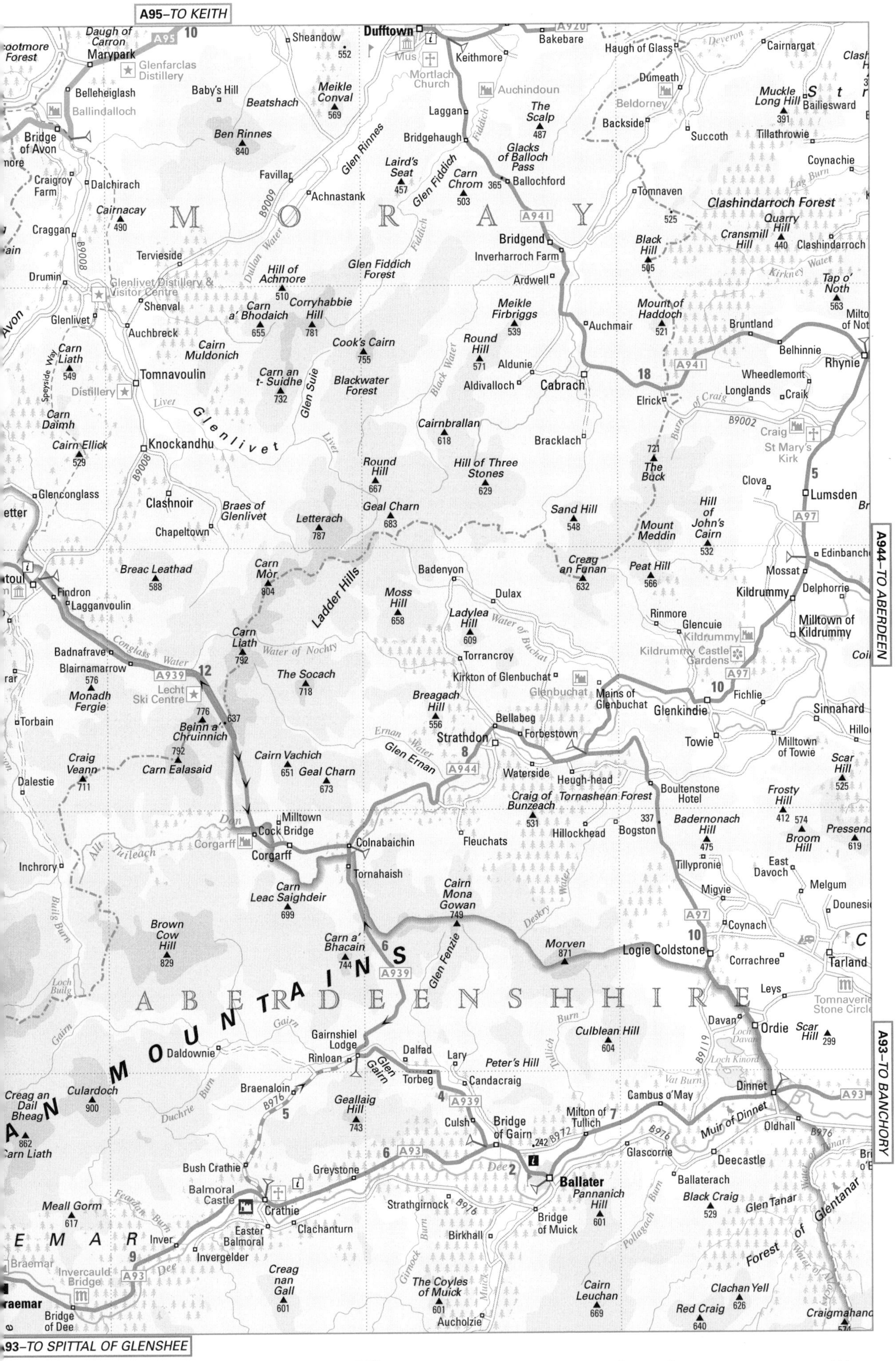

1 2 312 3 4 5

Tomintoul: *At a height of 1160 feet (354m) this claims to be the highest village in the Scottish Highlands. The A939 from here across the Lecht pass to Cock Bridge (**Map ref. E4**) is frequently closed in winter.* ***Map ref. D3***

302

Braemar: *Location of the most famous of the Highland Games. The Braemar Gathering has a history going back almost 1,000 years and is always held on the first Saturday in September.* ***Map ref. D5***

Dufftown: *With seven separate whisky distilleries, the earliest of which dates back to 1823, Dufftown is described as the Malt Whisky Capital of Scotland.* ***Map ref. F1***

A B C D
324
1 2 3 4 5
311

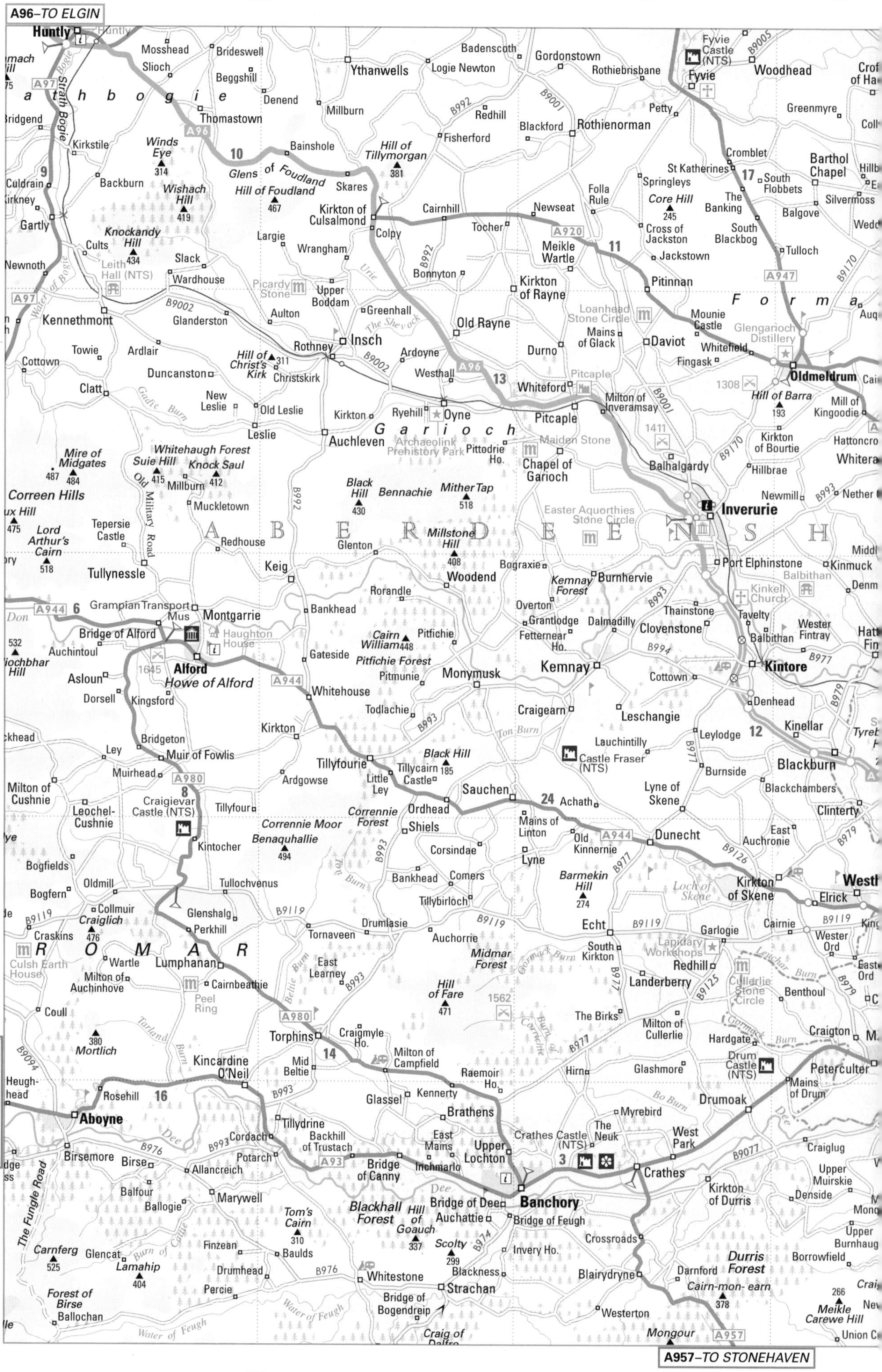

303

Huntly:** George MacDonald, novelist, poet and preacher was born here in 1824. His works of fantasy and fairy tales are said to have influenced the work of J R R Tolkien and C S Lewis. He died in Italy in 1905.* ***Map ref. A1

Tillyfour:** In the 1820s William McCombie and others in this area perfected the breeding of the 'Aberdeen Angus' which is acknowledged as one of the best cattle breeds in the world.* ***Map ref. A3

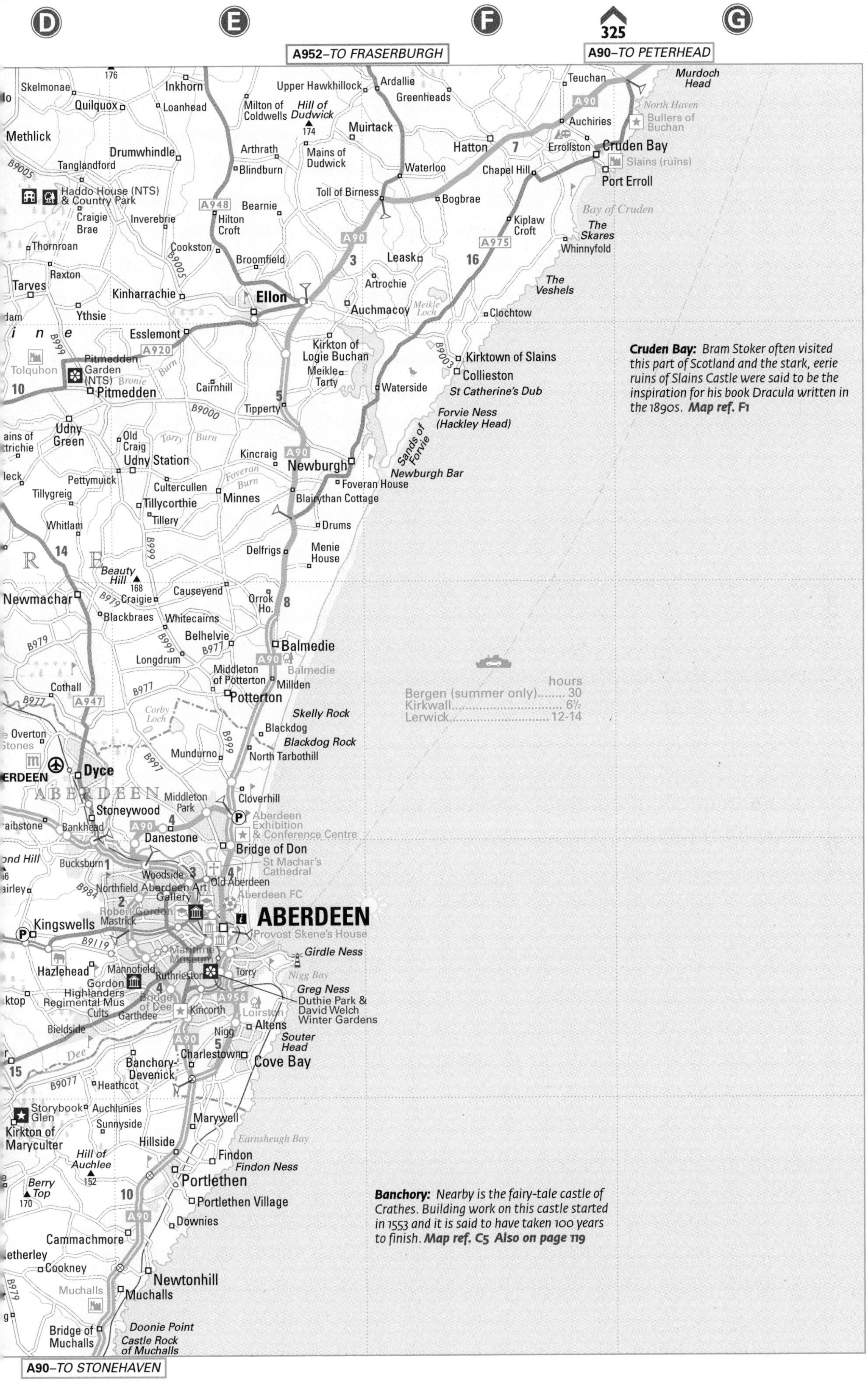

Cruden Bay: *Bram Stoker often visited this part of Scotland and the stark, eerie ruins of Slains Castle were said to be the inspiration for his book Dracula written in the 1890s.* ***Map ref. F1***

Banchory: *Nearby is the fairy-tale castle of Crathes. Building work on this castle started in 1553 and it is said to have taken 100 years to finish.* ***Map ref. C5 Also on page 119***

1

2

3

4

5

Kemnay: *Famous for its magnificent silver-grey granite which was quarried here for generations before the main quarry closed in 1960. Kemnay granite was used in building many of the bridges over the River Thames.* ***Map ref. C3***

304

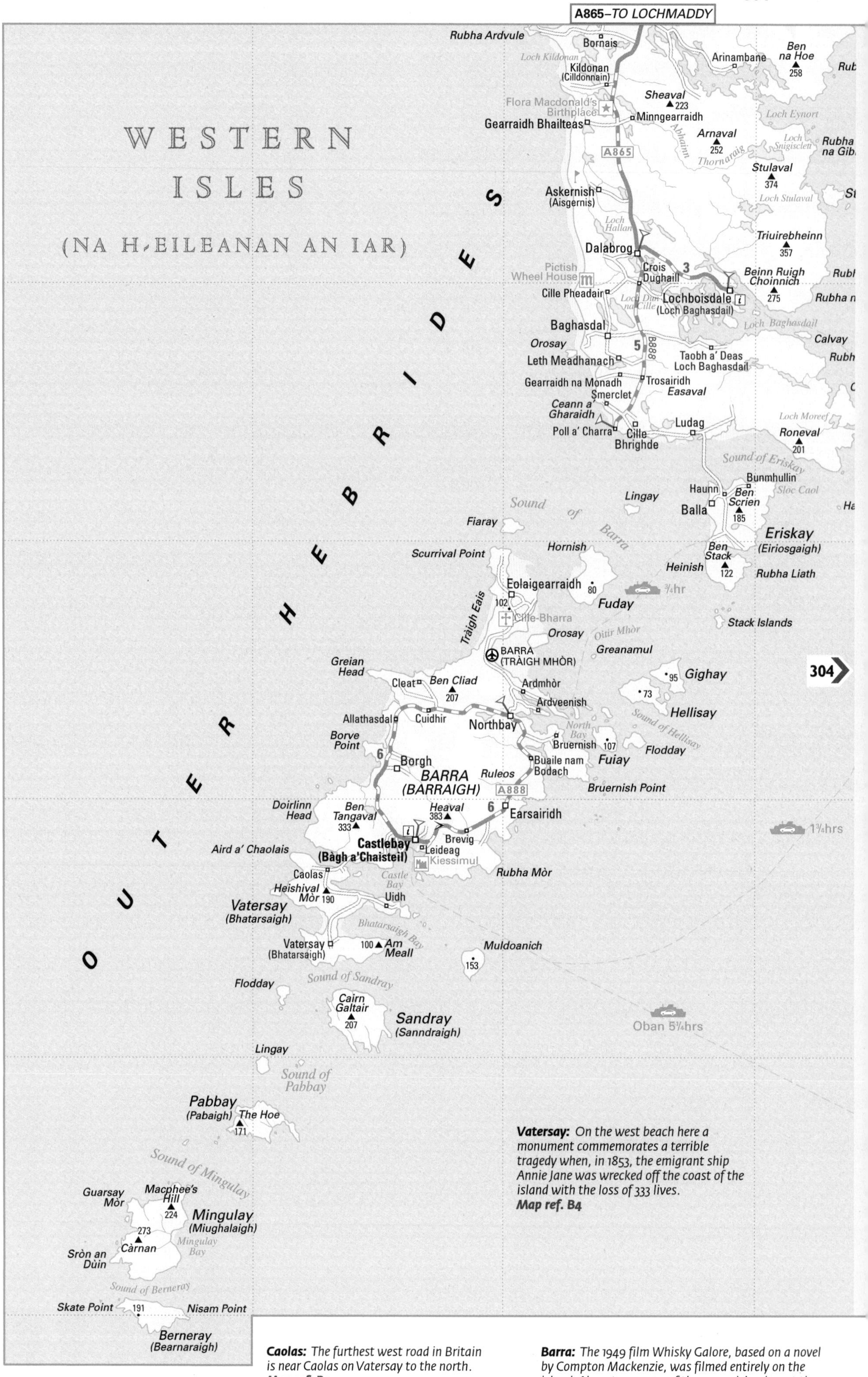

Vatersay: *On the west beach here a monument commemorates a terrible tragedy when, in 1853, the emigrant ship Annie Jane was wrecked off the coast of the island with the loss of 333 lives.*
Map ref. B4

Caolas: *The furthest west road in Britain is near Caolas on Vatersay to the north.*
Map ref. B4

Barra: *The 1949 film Whisky Galore, based on a novel by Compton Mackenzie, was filmed entirely on the island. Almost everyone of the 2,000 islanders at the time was involved in making it in some way or another.*
Map ref. B3

D E F G

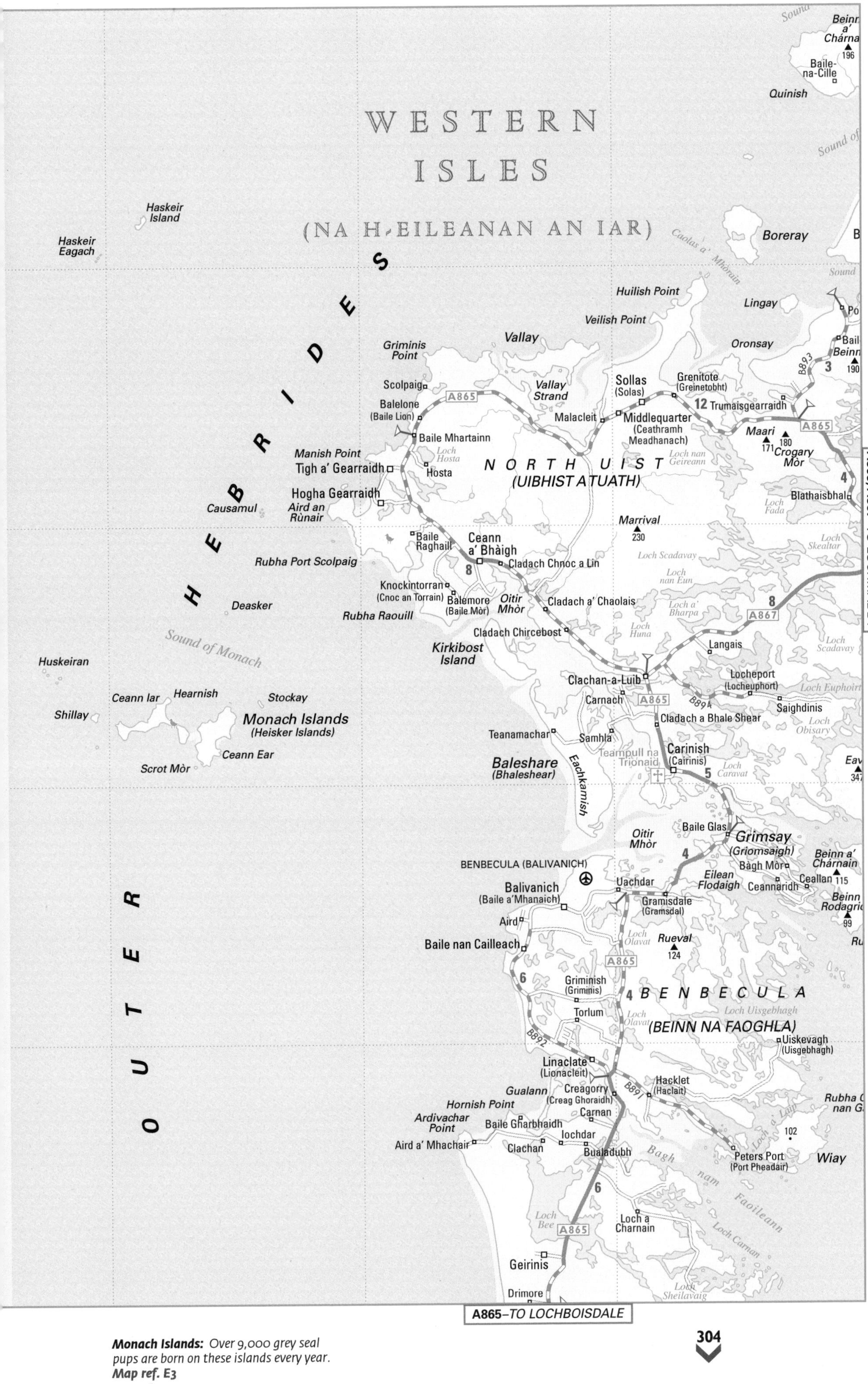
WESTERN ISLES
(NA H-EILEANAN AN IAR)
OUTER HEBRIDES
Sound
Beinn a' Chàrna
196
Baile-na-Cille
Quinish
Sound of
Haskeir Island
Haskeir Eagach
Caolas a' Mhòrain
Boreray
Sound
Huilish Point
Lingay
Veilish Point
Vallay
Griminis Point
Oronsay
B893
3
190
Scolpaig
A865
Vallay Strand
Sollas (Solas)
Grenitote (Greinetobht)
12 Trumaisgearraidh
Balelone (Baile Lìon)
Malacleit
Middlequarter (Ceathramh Meadhanach)
A865
Maari 171
180 Crogary Mòr
Baile Mhartainn
Manish Point
Loch Hosta
Tigh a' Gearraidh
Hosta
NORTH UIST
(UIBHIST A TUATH)
Loch nan Geireann
4
Hogha Gearraidh
Blathaisbhal
Causamul
Aird an Rùnair
Loch Fada
Marrival 230
Baile Raghaill
Ceann a' Bhàigh
Loch Scadavay
Loch Skealtar
Rubha Port Scolpaig
8
Cladach Chnoc a Lin
Loch nan Eun
Knockintorran (Cnoc an Torrain)
Balemore (Baile Mòr)
Oitir Mhòr
Cladach a' Chaolais
Loch a' Bharpa
8
A867
Deasker
Rubha Raouill
Loch Hùna
Sound of Monach
Cladach Chircebost
Kirkibost Island
Langais
Loch Scadavay
Huskeiran
Clachan-a-Luib
Locheport (Locheuphort)
Loch Euphort
Carnach
A865
B894
Hearnish
Stockay
Ceann Iar
Shillay
Saighdinis
Monach Islands (Heisker Islands)
Cladach a Bhale Shear
Loch Obisary
Teanamachar
Samhla
Ceann Ear
Teampull na Trionaid
Carinish (Cairinis)
Eaval 347
Scrot Mòr
Baleshare (Bhaleshear)
5
Loch Caravat
Eachkamish
Baile Glas
Grimsay (Griomsaigh)
Oitir Mhòr
4
Bàgh Mòr
Beinn a' Chàrnain
BENBECULA (BALIVANICH)
Eilean Flodaigh
Ceallan 115
Uachdar
Ceannaridh
Balivanich (Baile a'Mhanaich)
Gramisdale (Gramsdal)
Beinn Rodagrich 99
Aird
Loch Olavat
Rueval 124
Baile nan Cailleach
A865
6
Griminish (Griminis)
4 BENBECULA
Loch Uisgebhagh
Torlum
Loch Olavat
(BEINN NA FAOGHLA)
B892
Uiskevagh (Uisgebhagh)
Linaclate (Lionacleit)
Hacklet (Haclait)
B891
Gualann
Creagorry (Creag Ghoraidh)
Rubha Cnoc nan Gall
Hornish Point
Loch a' Laip
Ardivachar Point
Carnan
Baile Gharbhaidh
102
Iochdar
Aird a' Mhachair
Clachan
Bualadubh
Bagh nam Faoileann
Peters Port (Port Pheadair)
Wiay
6
Loch Bee
A865
Loch a Charnain
Loch Carnan
Geirinis
Loch Sheilavaig
Drimore

1 2 3 4 5

316

A865, A867–TO LOCHMADDY

A865–TO LOCHBOISDALE

304

Monach Islands: *Over 9,000 grey seal pups are born on these islands every year.*
Map ref. E3

326

A B C D

1 2 3 4 5

315

Lochmaddy: *The loch covers an area of just 9 square miles (23 sq km) but it has so many nooks, crannies, inlets, bays, projections etc. that the total length of the coastline is a remarkable 200 miles (320km).* ***Map ref. C3***

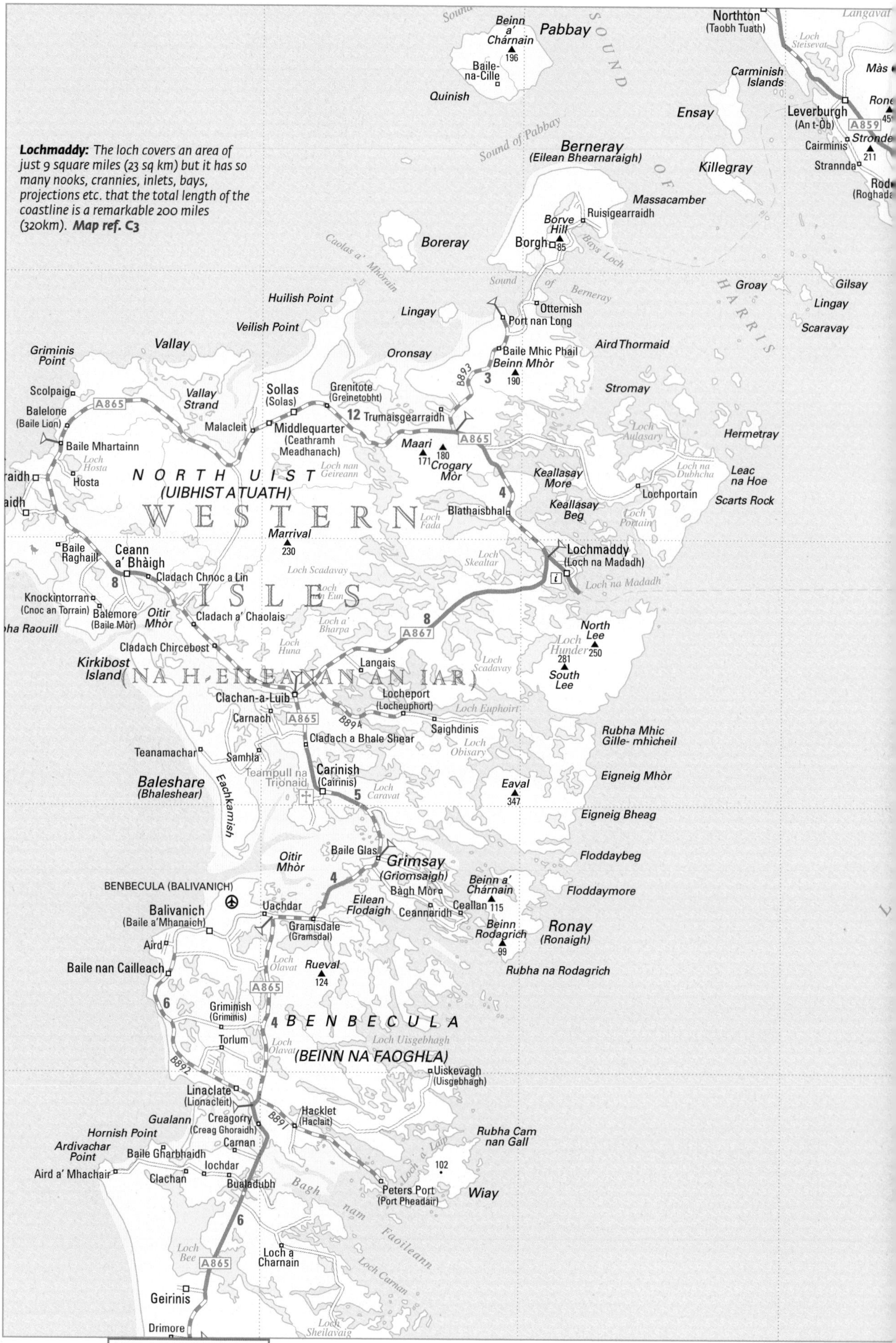

Pabbay
Beinn a' Chàrnain
196
Baile-na-Cille
Quinish
Sound of Harris
Northton
(Taobh Tuath)
Loch Steisevat
Langavat
Carminish Islands
Màs
Ensay
Leverburgh
(An t-Ob)
A859
Strond
Cairminis
211
Strannda
Rodel
(Roghadal)
Sound of Pabbay
Berneray
(Eilean Bhearnaraigh)
Killegray
Massacamber
Borve Hill
85
Ruisigearraidh
Borgh
Boreray
Bays Loch
Caolas a' Mhorain
Sound of Berneray
Groay
Gilsay
Lingay
Scaravay
Huilish Point
Veilish Point
Lingay
Otternish
Port nan Long
Oronsay
Aird Thormaid
Vallay
Griminis Point
Baile Mhic Phail
Beinn Mhòr
190
B893
3
Stromay
Scolpaig
Vallay Strand
Sollas
(Solas)
Grenitote
(Greinetobht)
12
Trumaisgearraidh
Balelone
(Baile Lion)
A865
Malacleit
Middlequarter
(Ceathramh Meadhanach)
Maari
171
180
Crogary Mòr
Loch Aulasary
Hermetray
Baile Mhartainn
Loch Hosta
Hosta
NORTH UIST
(UIBHIST A TUATH)
Loch nan Geireann
Keallasay More
Loch na Dubhcha
Leac na Hoe
Lochportain
Scarts Rock
Keallasay Beg
WESTERN ISLES
(NA H-EILEANAN AN IAR)
Blathaisbhal
4
Loch Fada
Loch Portain
Marrival
230
Baile Raghaill
Ceann a' Bhàigh
Loch Skealtar
Lochmaddy
(Loch na Madadh)
Loch Scadavay
Cladach Chnoc a Lin
Loch na Madadh
Loch an Eun
8
Knockintorran
(Cnoc an Torrain)
Balemore
(Baile Mòr)
Oitir Mhòr
Cladach a' Chaolais
Loch a' Bharpa
A867
North Lee
Loch Hunder
281
250
South Lee
Cladach Chircebost
Loch Huna
Langais
Loch Scadavay
Kirkibost Island
Clachan-a-Luib
Locheport
(Locheuphort)
Loch Euphoirt
Carnach
B894
Saighdinis
Rubha Mhic Gille-mhicheil
Cladach a Bhale Shear
Teanamachar
Samhla
Loch Obisary
Teampull na Trionaid
Carinish
(Cairinis)
Eigneig Mhòr
Baleshare
(Bhaleshear)
Eachkamish
5
Loch Caravat
Eaval
347
Eigneig Bheag
Baile Glas
Floddaybeg
Oitir Mhòr
Grimsay
(Griomsaigh)
BENBECULA (BALIVANICH)
Bàgh Mòr
Beinn a' Chàrnain
115
Floddaymore
Balivanich
(Baile a'Mhanaich)
Uachdar
Eilean Flodaigh
Ceannaridh
Ceallan
Gramisdale
(Gramsdal)
Beinn Rodagrich
99
Ronay
(Ronaigh)
Aird
Baile nan Cailleach
Loch Olavat
Rueval
124
Rubha na Rodagrich
6
Griminish
(Griminis)
BENBECULA
(BEINN NA FAOGHLA)
Torlum
Loch Olavat
Loch Uisgebhagh
B892
Uiskevagh
(Uisgebhagh)
Linaclate
(Lionacleit)
Hacklet
(Haclait)
B891
Gualann
Creagorry
(Creag Ghoraidh)
Hornish Point
Rubha Cam nan Gall
Ardivachar Point
Carnan
Baile Gharbhaidh
Loch a' Laip
102
Aird a' Mhachair
Iochdar
Clachan
Bualadubh
Bagh nam Faoileann
Peters Port
(Port Pheadair)
Wiay
Loch Bee
Loch a Charnain
Loch Carnan
Geirinis
Drimore
Loch Sheilavaig

A865–TO LOCHBOISDALE

304

327

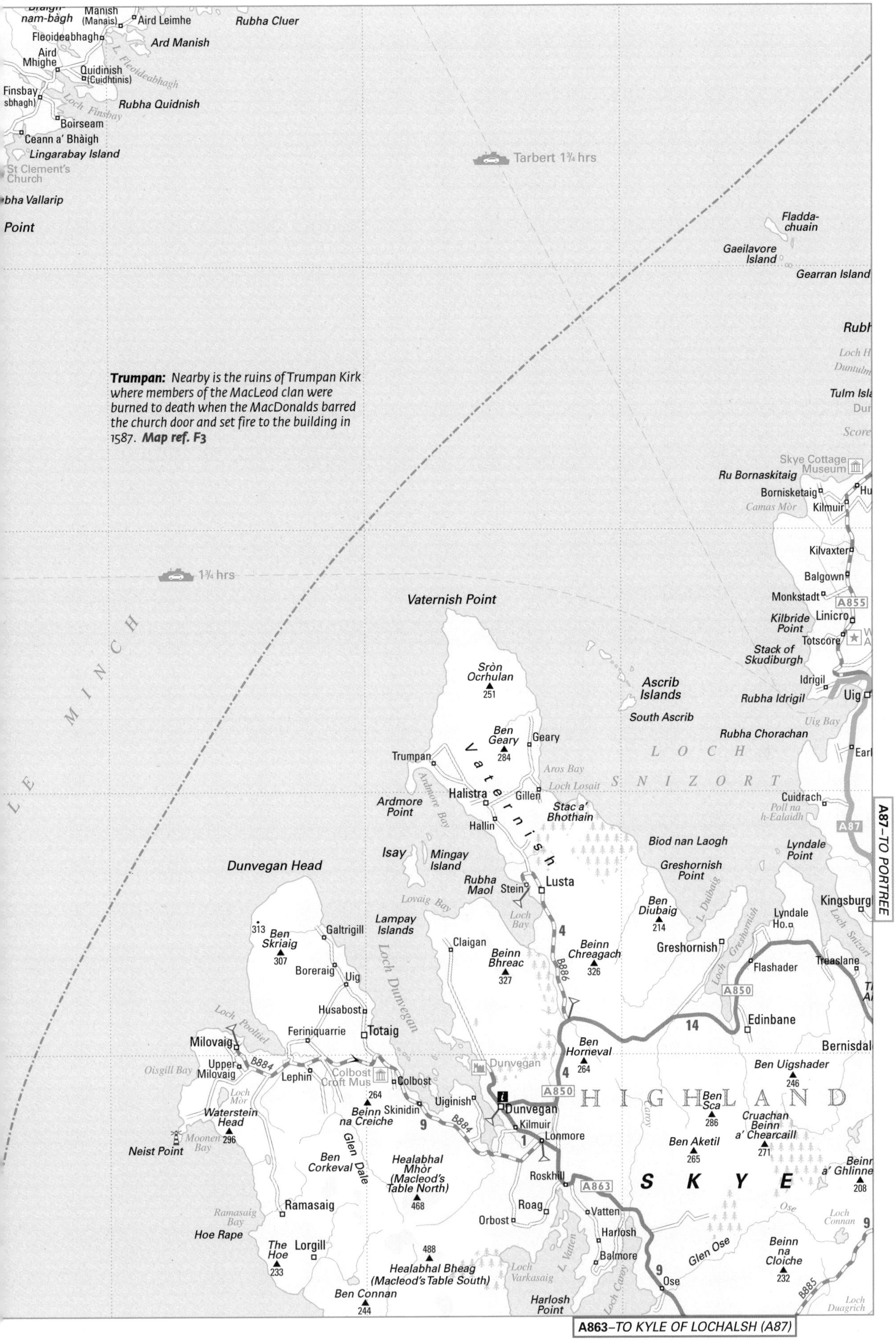
D
E
F
G
1
2
3
4
5
Manish (Manais)
Aird Leimhe
Rubha Cluer
Fleoideabhagh
Ard Manish
Aird Mhighe
Quidinish (Cuidhtinis)
L. Fleoideabhagh
Finsbay
Loch Finsbay
Rubha Quidnish
Boirseam
Ceann a' Bhàigh
Lingarabay Island
St Clement's Church
Point
Tarbert 1¾ hrs
1¾ hrs
Fladda-chuain
Gaeilavore Island
Gearran Island
Skye Cottage Museum
Ru Bornaskitaig
Bornisketaig
Camas Mòr
Kilmuir
Kilvaxter
Balgown
Monkstadt
A855
Kilbride Point
Linicro
Totscore
Stack of Skudiburgh
Idrigil
Rubha Idrigil
Uig
Uig Bay
Rubha Chorachan
LOCH SNIZORT
Cuidrach
Poll na h-Ealaidh
A87
A87–TO PORTREE
Lyndale Point
Kingsburgh
Lyndale Ho.
Treaslane
Flashader
A850
Edinbane
Bernisdale
THE MINCH
Vaternish Point
Sròn Ocrhulan
251
Ascrib Islands
South Ascrib
Ben Geary
284
Geary
Trumpan
Vaternish
Aros Bay
Loch Losait
Ardmore Point
Ardmore Bay
Halistra
Gillen
Stac a' Bhothain
Hallin
Biod nan Laogh
Greshornish Point
L. Diubaig
Isay
Mingay Island
Rubha Maol
Stein
Lusta
Ben Diubaig
214
Loch Greshornish
Dunvegan Head
Lovaig Bay
Loch Bay
Lampay Islands
313
Ben Skriaig
307
Galtrigill
Claigan
Beinn Bhreac
327
Beinn Chreagach
326
Greshornish
Boreraig
Uig
B886
Loch Dunvegan
Husabost
Loch Pooltiel
Feriniquarrie
Totaig
14
Milovaig
Upper Milovaig
B884
Lephin
Oisgill Bay
Colbost Croft Mus
Colbost
Dunvegan
Ben Horneval
264
A850
HIGHLAND
Ben Uigshader
246
Loch Mòr
Waterstein Head
296
Moonen Bay
Neist Point
264
Beinn na Creiche
Skinidin
Uiginish
Dunvegan
Kilmuir
Lonmore
Ben Sca
286
Cruachan Beinn a' Chearcaill
271
Ben Aketil
265
Beinn a' Ghlinne
208
Glen Dale
Ben Corkeval
Healabhal Mhòr (Macleod's Table North)
468
Roskhill
A863
SKYE
Ramasaig
Ramasaig Bay
Hoe Rape
Roag
Orbost
Vatten
Harlosh
Balmore
L. Vatten
Glen Ose
Ose
Loch Connan
Beinn na Cloiche
232
The Hoe
233
Lorgill
488
Healabhal Bheag (Macleod's Table South)
Loch Varkasaig
Loch Caroy
Ben Connan
244
Harlosh Point
B885
Loch Duagrich
A863–TO KYLE OF LOCHALSH (A87)

Trumpan: *Nearby is the ruins of Trumpan Kirk where members of the MacLeod clan were burned to death when the MacDonalds barred the church door and set fire to the building in 1587.* ***Map ref. F3***

318

305

A B C D

1 2 3 4 5

317

Flodigarry: *Flora MacDonald moved to a cottage in this village in 1751 and gave birth to five of her seven children here.*
Map ref. A2

Beinn Edra: *There is wreckage here of an American B-17 Flying Fortress which crashed into the mountain in the winter of 1944 when heading back to the USA.*
Map ref. A3

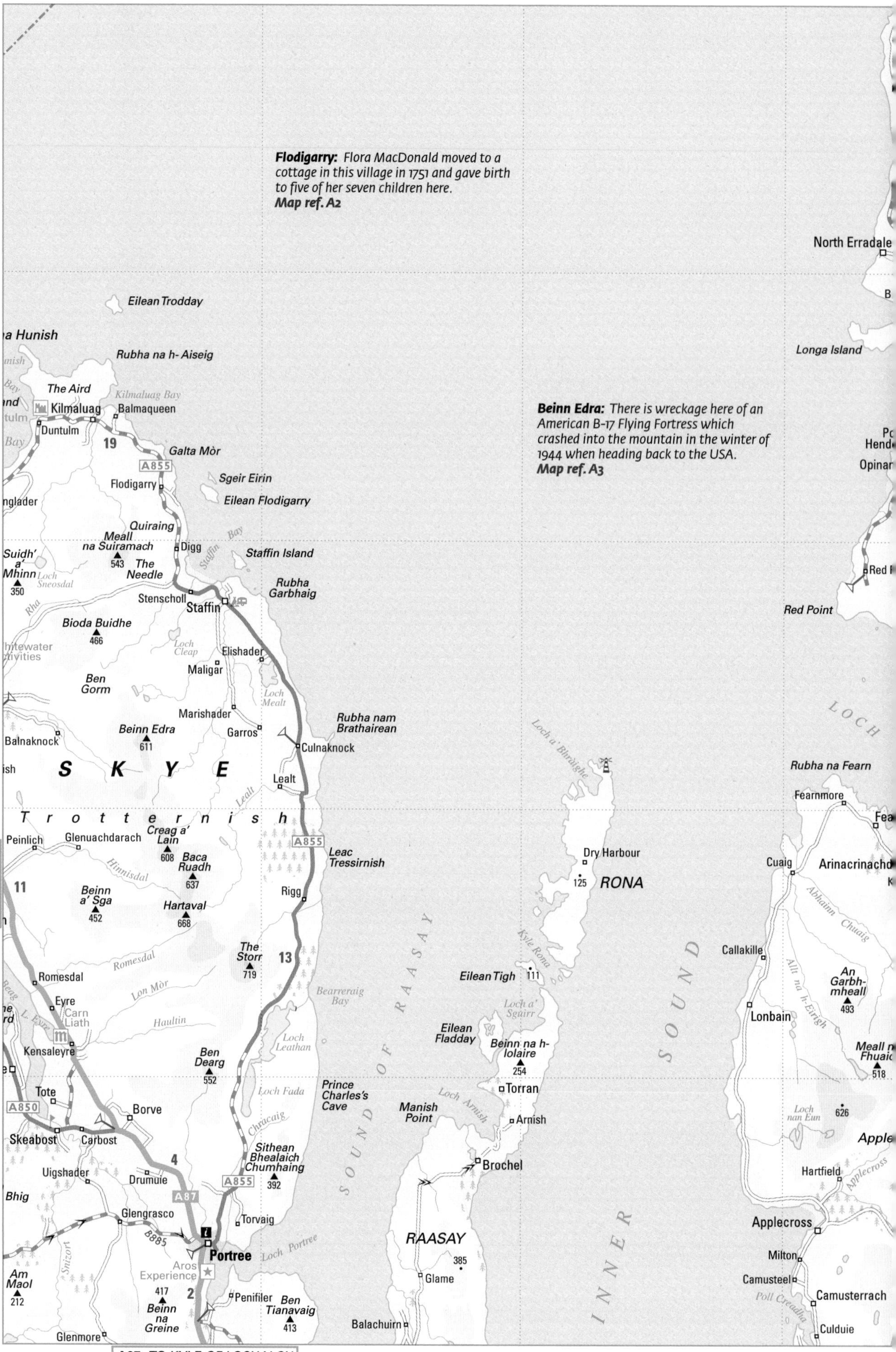

306

Beinn Eighe: *10,000 acres of mountains and moors were designated as Britain's first national nature reserve in 1951.*
Map ref. F3

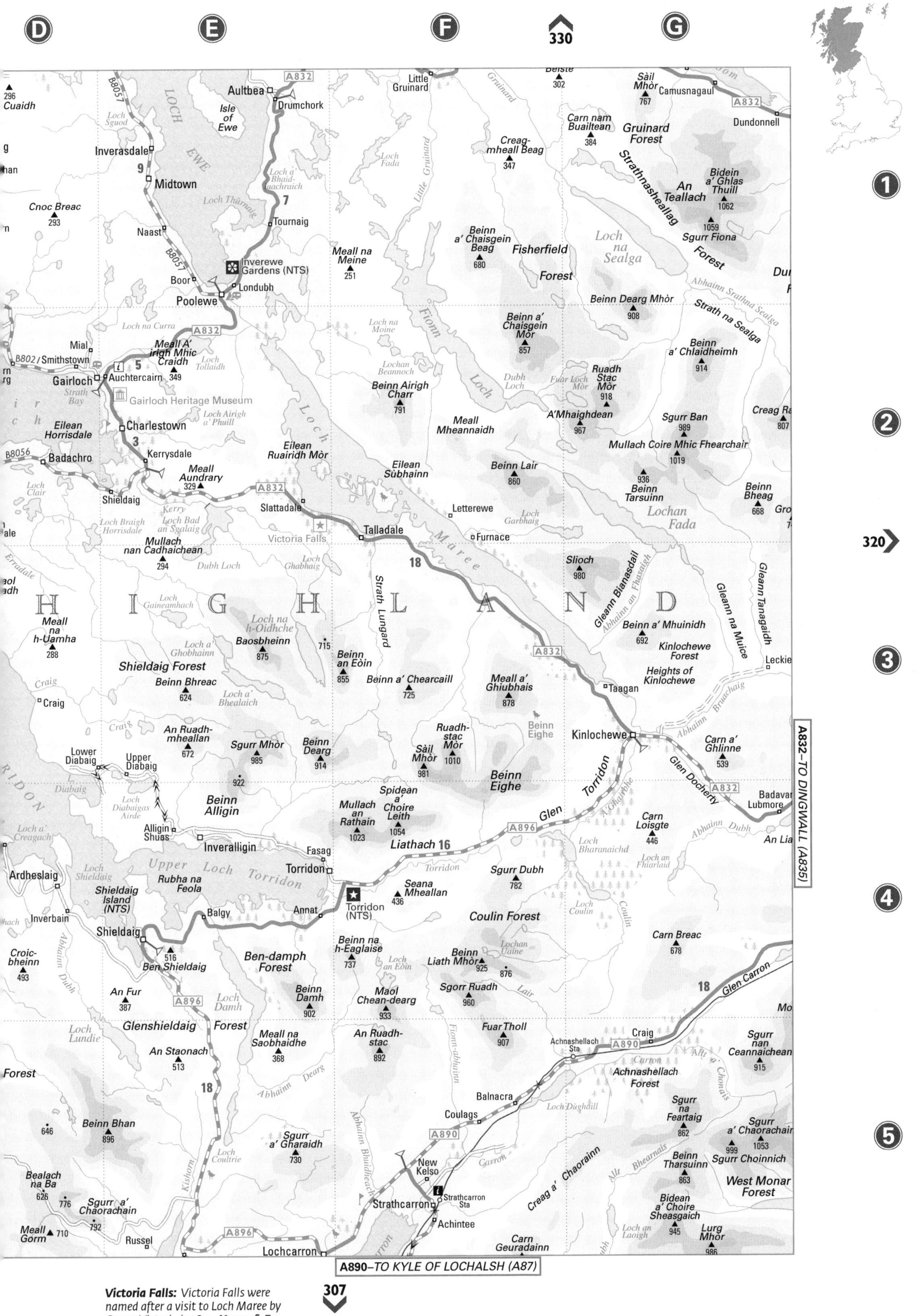

Victoria Falls: *Victoria Falls were named after a visit to Loch Maree by Queen Victoria in 1877.* ***Map ref. E2***

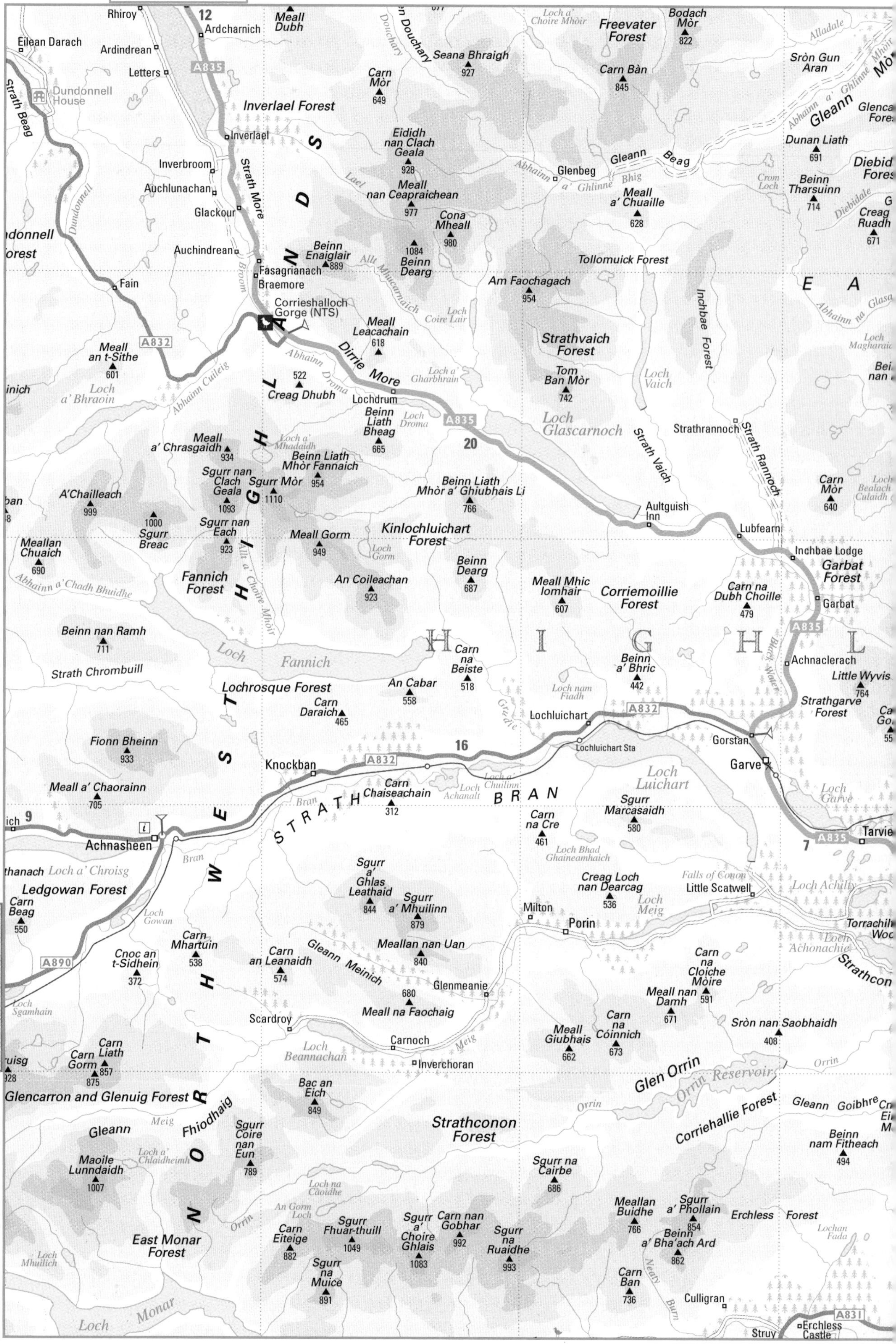

Loch a' Chroisg: *The landscape here features some spectacular reminders of the ice-age. Here the moving glaciers have left unusual flat-topped terraces on the south side of the Loch.* ***Map ref. A4***

308

Culloden: *The last battle to be fought on British soil took place here on the 16th April 1746 between the supporters of Bonnie Prince Charlie, known as Jacobites and the Government troops, known as Hanoverians. The engagement itself was over in less than an hour and resulted in a resounding defeat for the Jacobites, who lost over 1,200 men on the battlefield.* ***Map ref. G5 Also on page 119***

D E F G
332

1
2
322
3
4
5

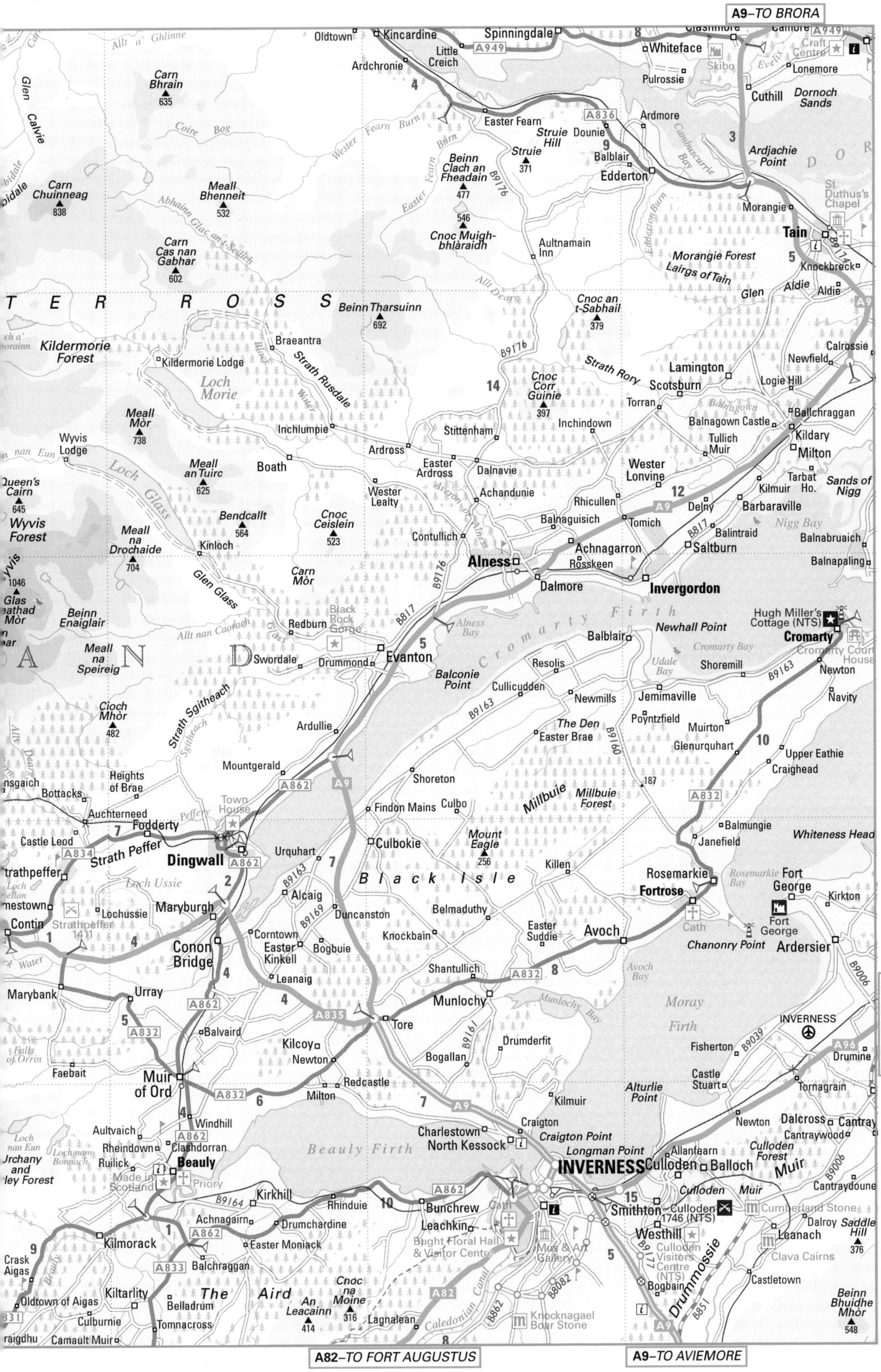

309

Cromarty Firth: *The navy cruiser Natal accidentally exploded here on the 30th December 1915. Although over 280 survivors were plucked from the water, over 370 officers and men lost their lives including many preparing to celebrate Hogmanay on board ship.* ***Map ref. F3***

Fort George: *This is the largest fort in the world, enclosing an area of 42 acres (17ha) and almost a mile (1.6km) around. The fort was built during the reign of George II as a defence against any further unrest by the Jacobite Army. Despite taking 21 years to build, Fort George never saw any military action.* ***Map ref. G4 Also on page 123***

A B C D

333

1 2 3 4 5

321

Burghead: *Site of the biggest 'Iron Age' fort in Britain built on the end of a promontory by the Picts between the 4th and 7th centuries AD. The Picts lived in northern Britain and though very little is known about them they are thought to be the original inhabitants of Scotland. From the 9th century however they seem to have vanished, perhaps swallowed up in battles with the Vikings, Romans and between their own tribes.* ***Map ref. D3.***

310

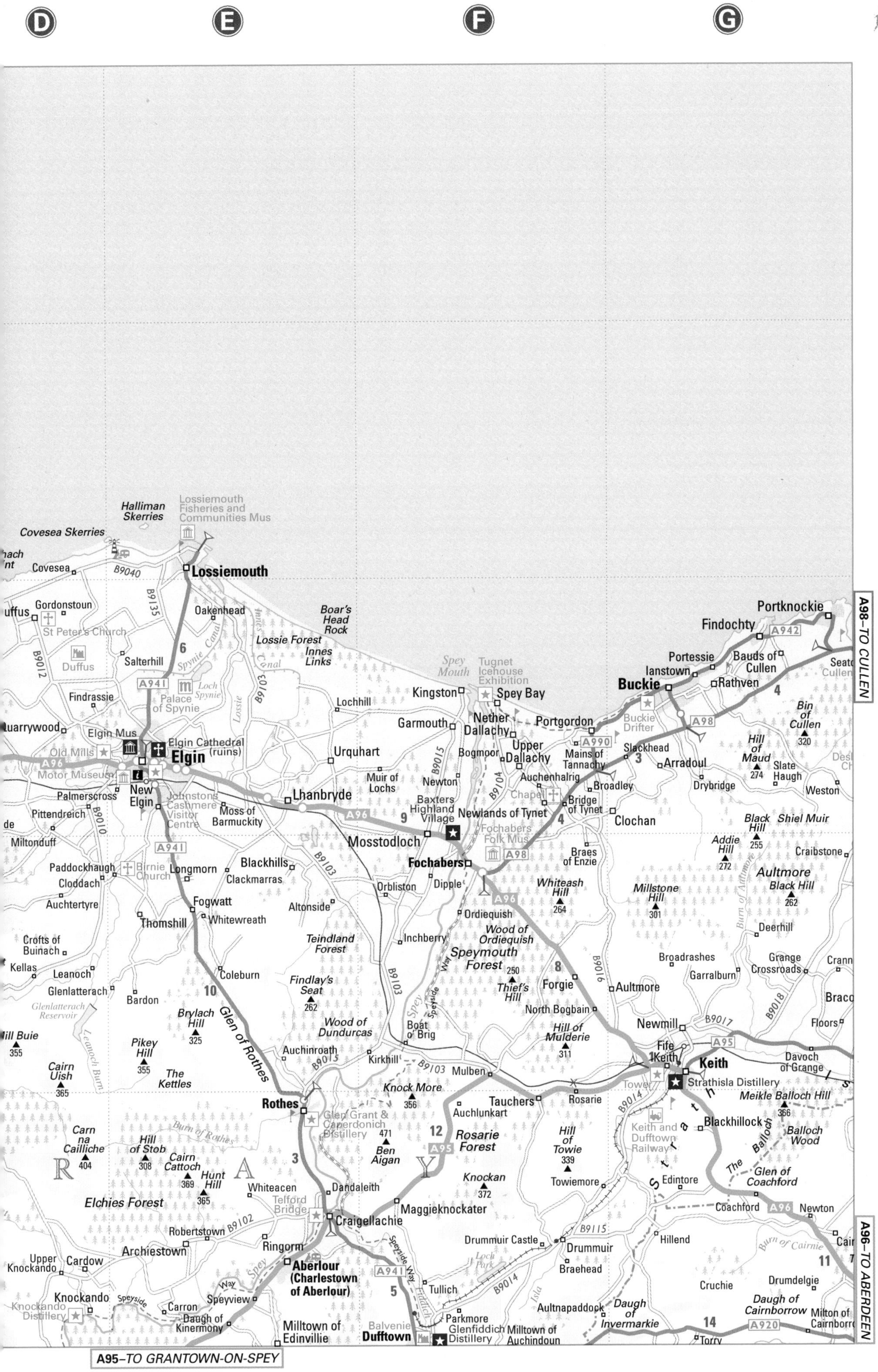

D
E
F
G
1
2
3
4
5
Halliman Skerries
Lossiemouth Fisheries and Communities Mus
Covesea Skerries
Covesea
B9040
Lossiemouth
Gordonstoun
St Peter's Church
B9135
Oakenhead
Boar's Head Rock
Lossie Forest
Innes Links
Innes Canal
Spynie Canal
B9012
Duffus
Salterhill
6
A941
Loch Spynie
Palace of Spynie
B9103
Lossie
Findrassie
Lochhill
Kingston
Spey Mouth
Tugnet Icehouse Exhibition
Spey Bay
Quarrywood
Elgin Mus
Old Mills
A96
Elgin Cathedral (ruins)
Elgin
Urquhart
Garmouth
Nether Dallachy
Portgordon
Buckie Drifter
Motor Museum
Upper Dallachy
Bogmoor
B9015
A990
Mains of Tannachy
Slackhead
Arradoul
Palmerscross
New Elgin
Johnstons Cashmere Visitor Centre
Lhanbryde
Muir of Lochs
Newton
B9104
Auchenhalrig
Chapel
Broadley
Bridge of Tynet
Pittendreich
B9010
Moss of Barmuckity
Baxters Highland Village
9
Newlands of Tynet
4
Clochan
Miltonduff
A941
Mosstodloch
Fochabers Folk Mus
A98
Braes of Enzie
Paddockhaugh
Birnie Church
Longmorn
Blackhills
Clackmarras
B9103
Fochabers
Cloddach
Orbliston
Dipple
A96
Whiteash Hill
264
Auchtertyre
Fogwatt
Altonside
Thomshill
Whitewreath
Ordiequish
Wood of Ordiequish
Crofts of Buinach
Teindland Forest
Inchberry
Speymouth Forest
250
Kellas
Leanoch
Coleburn
Findlay's Seat
262
B9103
Speyside Way
8
Forgie
Thief's Hill
Glenlatterach
Bardon
10
Glenlatterach Reservoir
Brylach Hill
325
Glen of Rothes
Wood of Dundurcas
Boat o' Brig
Spey
North Bogbain
Hill of Mulderie
311
Hill Buie
355
Pikey Hill
355
Auchinroath
B9015
Kirkhill
B9103
Mulben
Cairn Uish
365
The Kettles
Leanoch Burn
Knock More
356
Tauchers
Rosarie
Rothes
Glen Grant & Caperdonich Distillery
471
Auchlunkart
Carn na Cailliche
404
Hill of Stob
308
Burn of Rothes
Cairn Catthoch
369
Ben Aigan
12
Rosarie Forest
A95
Hill of Towie
339
R
A
Y
3
Hunt Hill
365
Whiteacen
Dandaleith
Knockan
372
Towiemore
Elchies Forest
Telford Bridge
Maggieknockater
Craigellachie
B9102
Robertstown
Drummuir Castle
B9115
Drummuir
Archiestown
Ringorm
Speyside Way
Loch Park
Braehead
Upper Knockando
Cardow
Aberlour (Charlestown of Aberlour)
A941
5
B9014
Knockando
Speyside Way
Tullich
Fiddich
Isla
Carron
Speyview
Aultnapaddock
Daugh of Invermarkie
Knockando Distillery
Daugh of Kinermony
Milltown of Edinvillie
Balvenie
Dufftown
Parkmore
Glenfiddich Distillery
Milltown of Auchindoun
Portknockie
Findochty
A942
A98–TO CULLEN
Portessie
Bauds of Cullen
Ianstown
Seatown Cullen
Buckie
Rathven
4
A98
Bin of Cullen
320
Hill of Maud
274
Slate Haugh
Drybridge
Weston
Black Hill
Shiel Muir
Addie Hill
272
255
Craibstone
Aultmore
Black Hill
262
Millstone Hill
301
Burn of Aultmore
Deerhill
B9016
Broadrashes
Garralburn
Grange Crossroads
Aultmore
B9018
Newmill
B9017
Floors
Fife Keith
A95
Davoch of Grange
Keith
Strathisla Distillery
Tower
B9014
Meikle Balloch Hill
366
Keith and Dufftown Railway
Blackhillock
Balloch Wood
The Balloch
Strath Isla
Edintore
Glen of Coachford
Coachford
A96
Newton
Hillend
Burn of Cairnie
11
A96–TO ABERDEEN
Cruchie
Drumdelgie
Daugh of Cairnborrow
Milton of Cairnborrow
14
A920
Torry
A95–TO GRANTOWN-ON-SPEY

324

311

Lossiemouth: *Birthplace in 1866 of James Ramsay MacDonald, Britain's first Labour Prime Minister. After a successful first term in 1924 he was re-elected in 1929 to form a 'National Government' during the Depression. He died at sea, en-route to South America, in 1937 and is buried near Lossiemouth in Old Spynie churchyard.* ***Map ref. E2.***

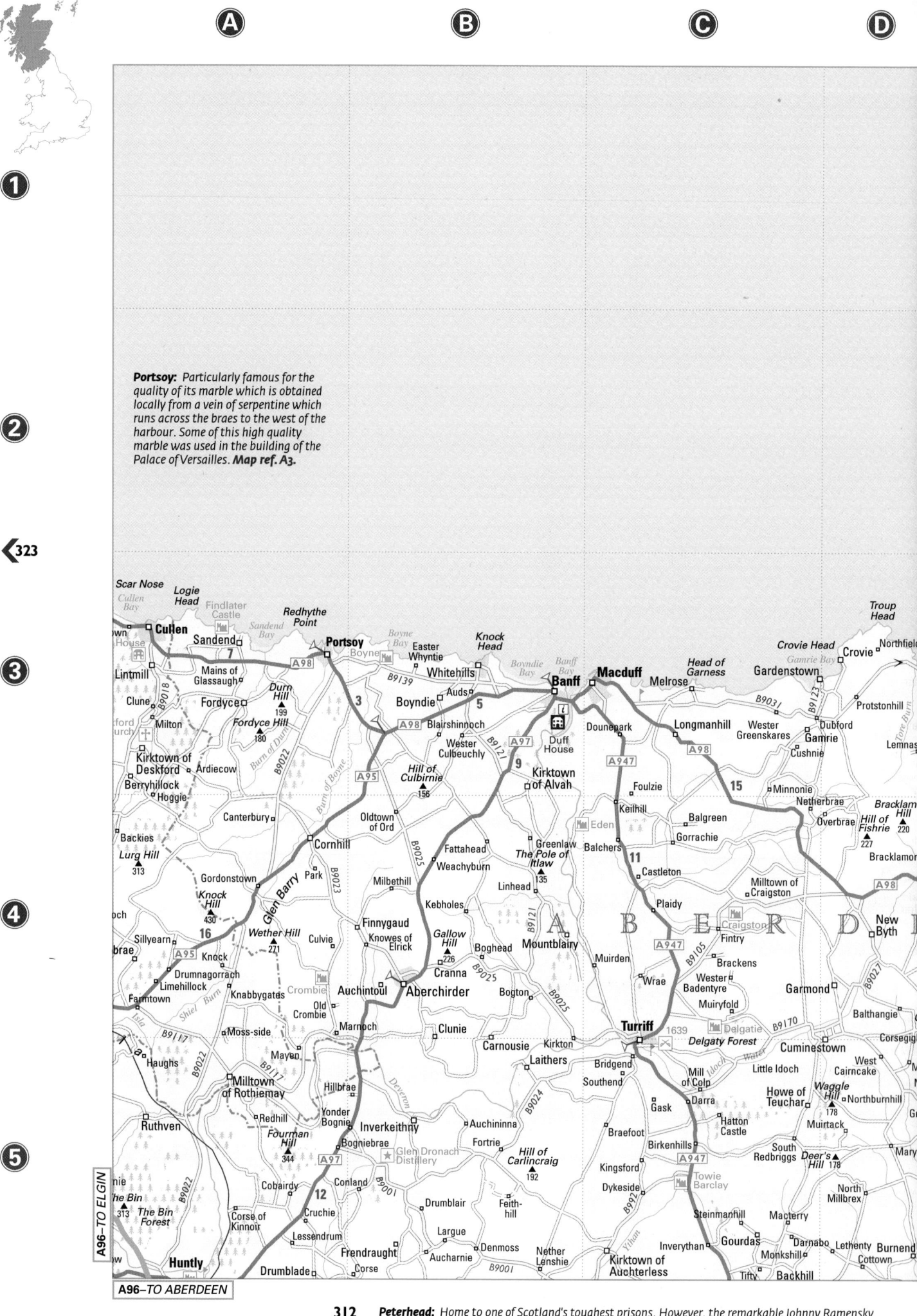

A B C D

1

2

Portsoy: *Particularly famous for the quality of its marble which is obtained locally from a vein of serpentine which runs across the braes to the west of the harbour. Some of this high quality marble was used in the building of the Palace of Versailles.* ***Map ref. A3.***

323

3

4

5

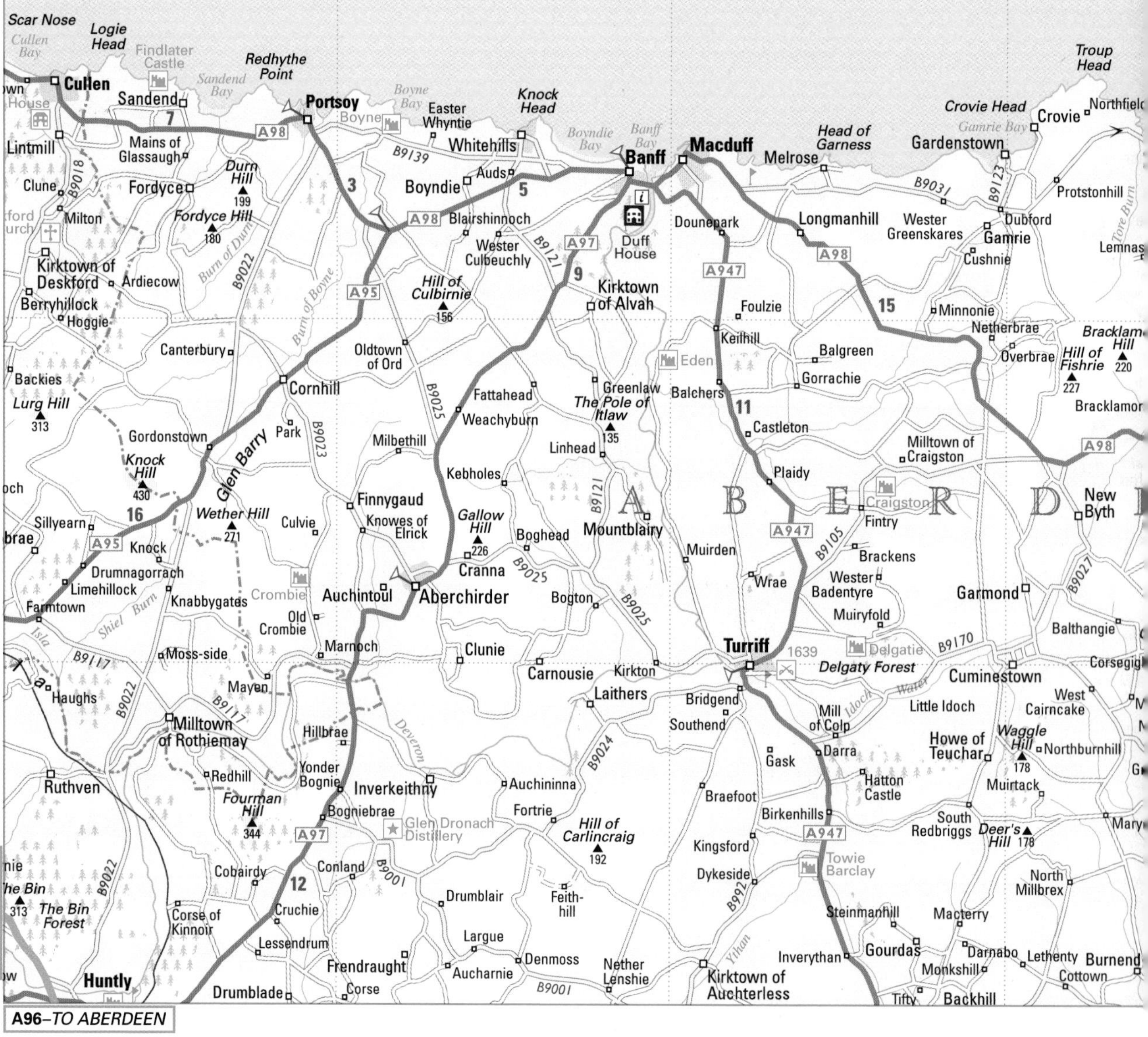

312

Peterhead: *Home to one of Scotland's toughest prisons. However, the remarkable Johnny Ramensky escaped from it five times (three times in a single year in 1958). Ramensky was a career burglar who was released from prison in 1942 and joined a crack commando unit which operated behind German lines. Using his explosives and burglary skills he stole important documents. His wartime exploits became legendary and he was awarded the Military Medal and granted a free pardon. Unfortunately he returned to a life of crime and died while serving time in Perth Prison, in 1972 at the age of 67.* ***Map ref. G5.***

Fraserburgh: *Both the oldest, and the newest lighthouses in Scotland are situated here. The old Kinnaird Head Lighthouse was built in 1787 into the 16th Century Fraser Castle. This was replaced by a new unmanned lighthouse in 1991. The old Lighthouse is now the Museum of Scottish Lighthouses.* ***Map ref. E3.***

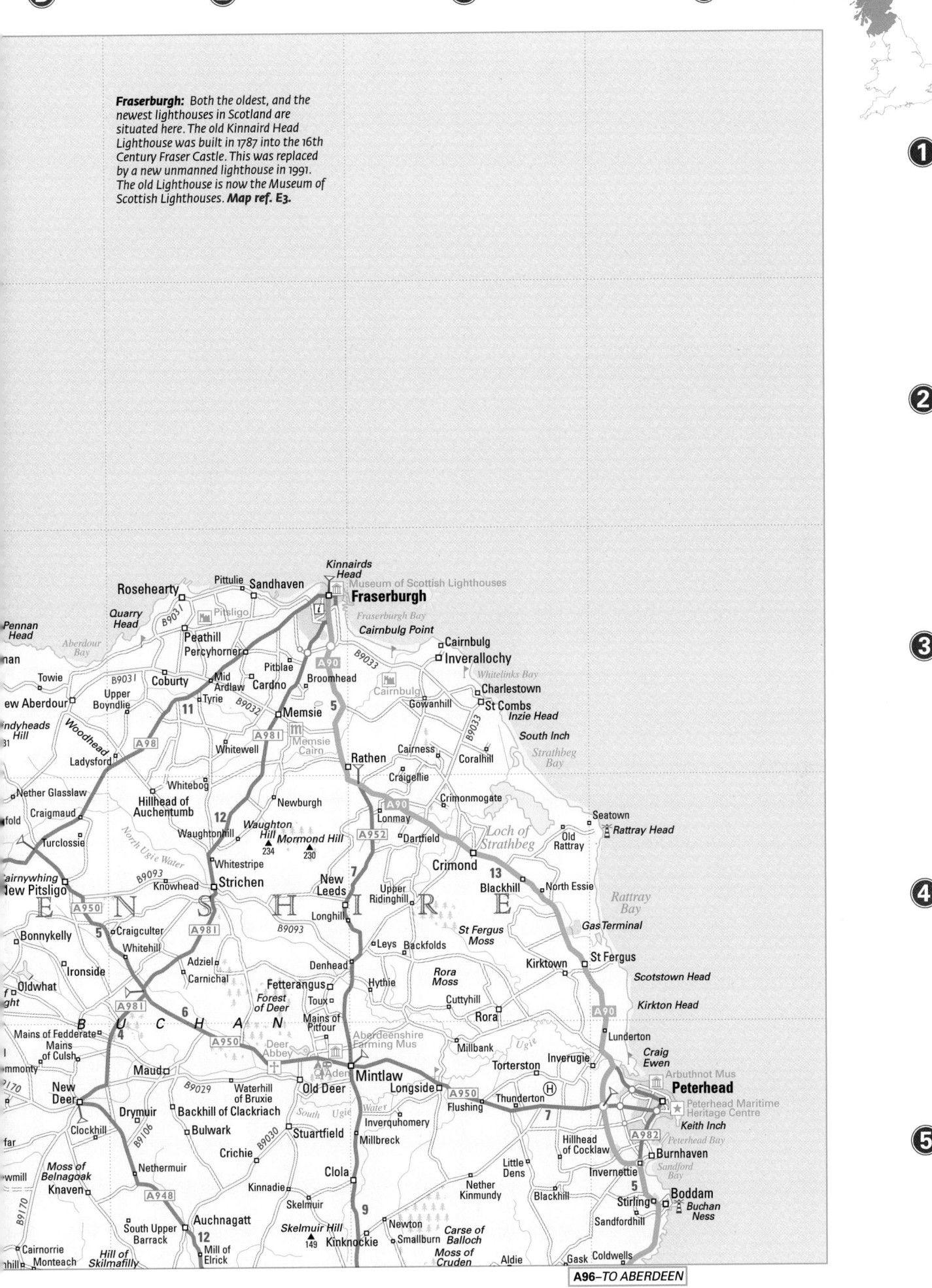

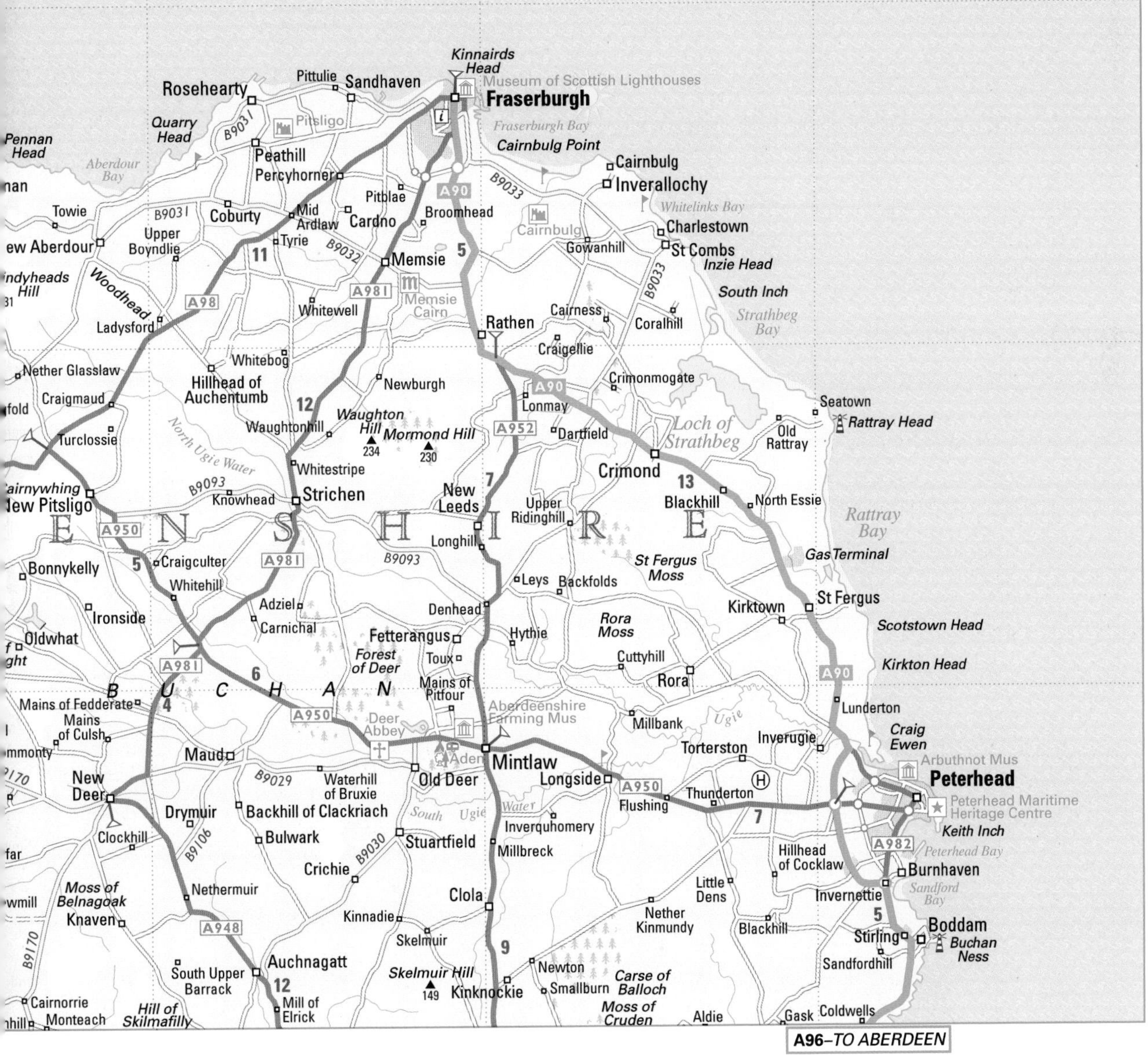

313

A B C D

328

1 2 3 4 5

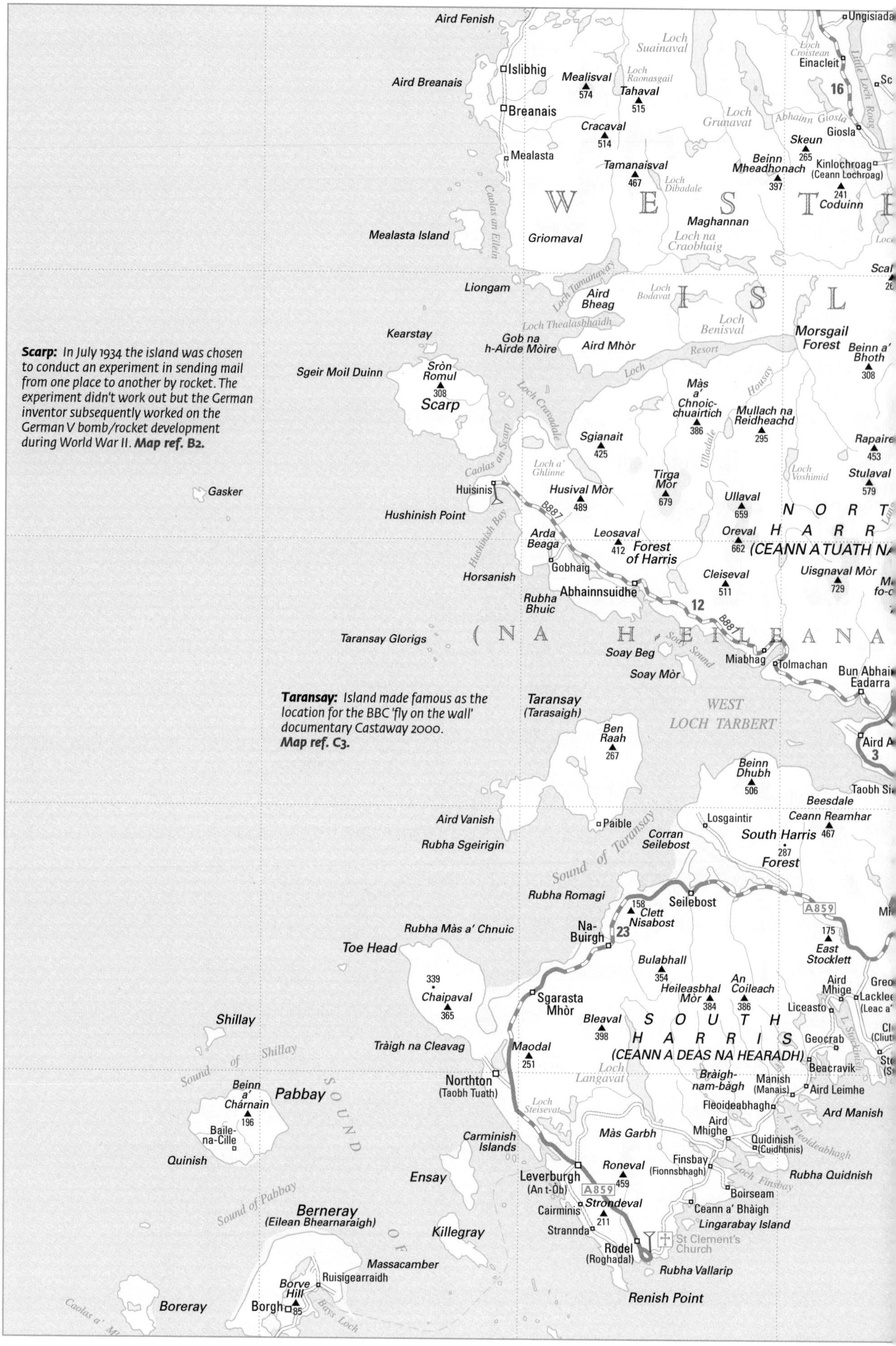

Scarp: In July 1934 the island was chosen to conduct an experiment in sending mail from one place to another by rocket. The experiment didn't work out but the German inventor subsequently worked on the German V bomb/rocket development during World War II. **Map ref. B2.**

Taransay: Island made famous as the location for the BBC 'fly on the wall' documentary Castaway 2000. **Map ref. C3.**

316

D E F G

329

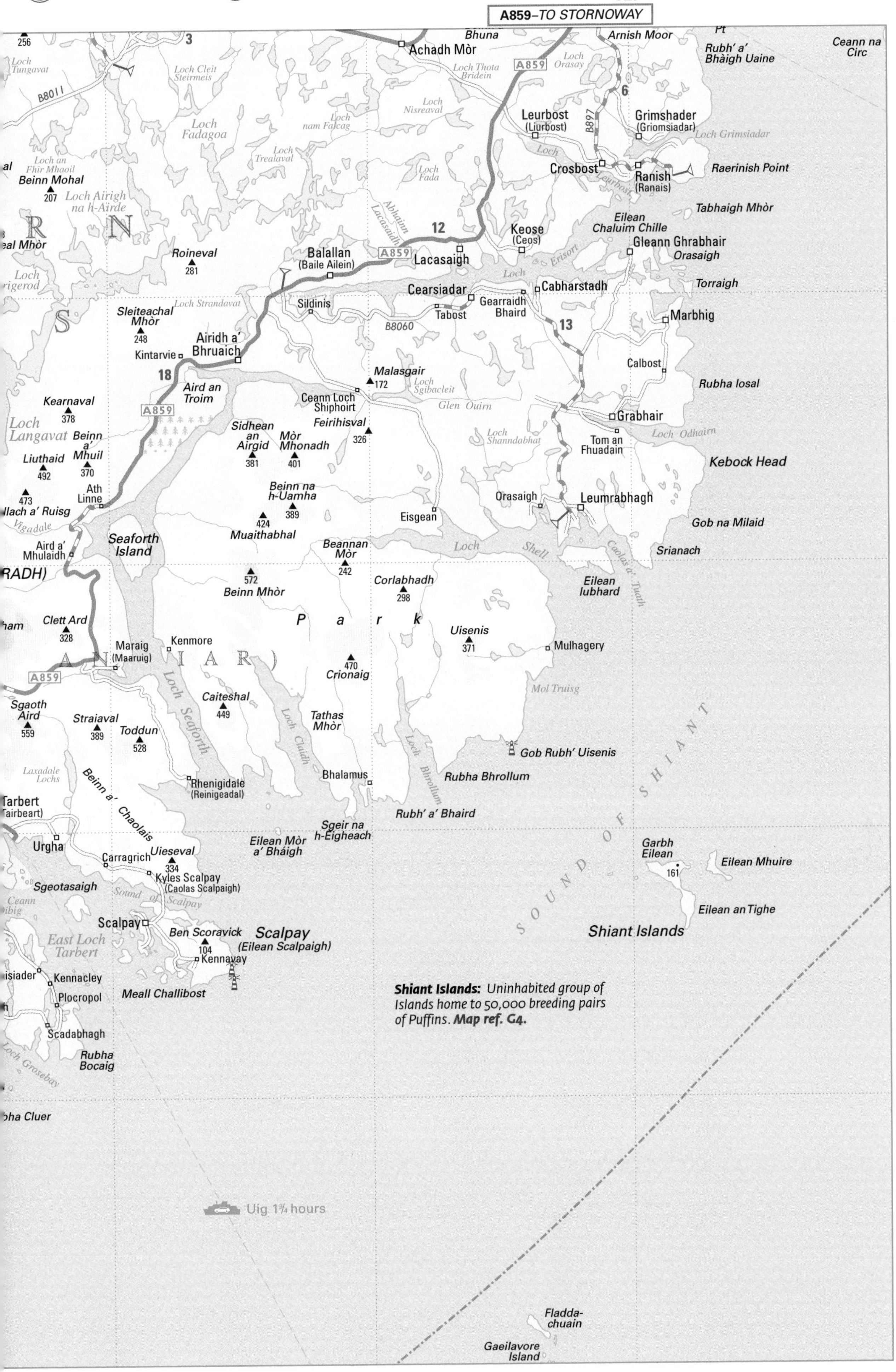
A859–TO STORNOWAY
Bhuna
Arnish Moor
Pt
Ceann na Circ
Rubh' a' Bhàigh Uaine
256
3
Loch Tungavat
Loch Cleit Steirmeis
Achadh Mòr
Loch Thota Bridein
A859
Loch Orasay
B8011
6
Loch Nisreaval
Loch nam Falcag
Leurbost (Liurbost)
B897
Grimshader (Griomsiadar)
Loch Grimsiadar
Loch Fadagoa
Loch Trealaval
Loch Fada
Loch
Crosbost
Ranish (Ranais)
Raerinish Point
Loch an Fhir Mhaoil
Beinn Mohal
207
Loch Airigh na h-Airde
Leurbost
Tabhaigh Mhòr
Abhainn Lacasaidh
12
Keose (Ceos)
Eilean Chaluim Chille
Gleann Ghrabhair
Orasaigh
Erisort
R
N
eal Mhòr
Roineval
281
Balallan (Baile Ailein)
A859
Lacasaigh
Loch
Torraigh
Loch
rigerod
Loch Strandavat
Cearsiadar
Cabharstadh
S
Sleiteachal Mhòr
248
Sildinis
Tabost
Gearraidh Bhaird
B8060
13
Marbhig
Airidh a' Bhruaich
Kintarvie
18
Calbost
Malasgair
172
Loch Sgibacleit
Rubha Iosal
Aird an Troim
Kearnaval
378
A859
Ceann Loch Shiphoirt
Glen Ouirn
Grabhair
Feirihisval
326
Loch Langavat
Beinn a' Mhuil
370
Sidhean an Airgid
381
Mòr Mhonadh
401
Loch Shanndabhat
Tom an Fhuadain
Loch Odhairn
Liuthaid
492
Kebock Head
Ath Linne
473
llach a' Ruisg
Beinn na h-Uamha
389
424
Orasaigh
Leumrabhagh
Muaithabhal
Eisgean
Gob na Milaid
Vigadale
Seaforth Island
Aird a' Mhulaidh
Beannan Mòr
242
Loch
Shell
Srianach
Caolas a' Tuath
RADH)
572
Beinn Mhòr
Corlabhadh
298
Eilean Iubhard
Clett Ard
328
P a r k
Uisenis
371
ham
Maraig (Maaruig)
Kenmore
Mulhagery
A859
I A R)
470
Crionaig
Mol Truisg
Sgaoth Aird
559
Loch Seaforth
Caiteshal
449
Straiaval
389
Toddun
528
Loch Claidh
Tathas Mhòr
Laxadale Lochs
Beinn a' Chaolais
Gob Rubh' Uisenis
SOUND OF SHIANT
Loch Bhrollum
Rhenigidale (Reinigeadal)
Bhalamus
Rubha Bhrollum
Tarbert (Tairbeart)
Rubh' a' Bhaird
Ургha
Sgeir na h-Eigheach
Eilean Mòr a' Bhàigh
Garbh Eilean
Uieseval
Carragrich
334
161
Eilean Mhuire
Kyles Scalpay (Caolas Scalpaigh)
Sgeotasaigh
Sound of Scalpay
Ceann Dibig
Eilean an Tighe
Scalpay
Ben Scoravick
104
Scalpay (Eilean Scalpaigh)
Shiant Islands
East Loch Tarbert
Kennavay
isiader
Kennacley
Plocropol
Meall Challibost
Scadabhagh
Rubha Bocaig
Loch Grosebay
bha Cluer
Uig 1¾ hours
Fladda-chuain
Gaeilavore Island

Shiant Islands: Uninhabited group of Islands home to 50,000 breeding pairs of Puffins. **Map ref. G4.**

1
2
3
4
5

317

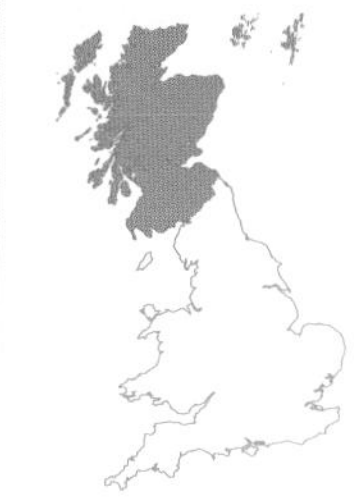

The Western Isles: *Consisting of the Outer and Inner Hebrides these are a 150 mile (240km) chain of islands on the very north-western edge of Europe. The earliest reference to these islands is contained in Norse folklore and the influence of the Norse invaders and settlers is still evident in the names of the places and islands. The Islands became part of Scotland in the 13th century.*

WESTERN ISLES

(NA H-EILEANAN AN IAR)

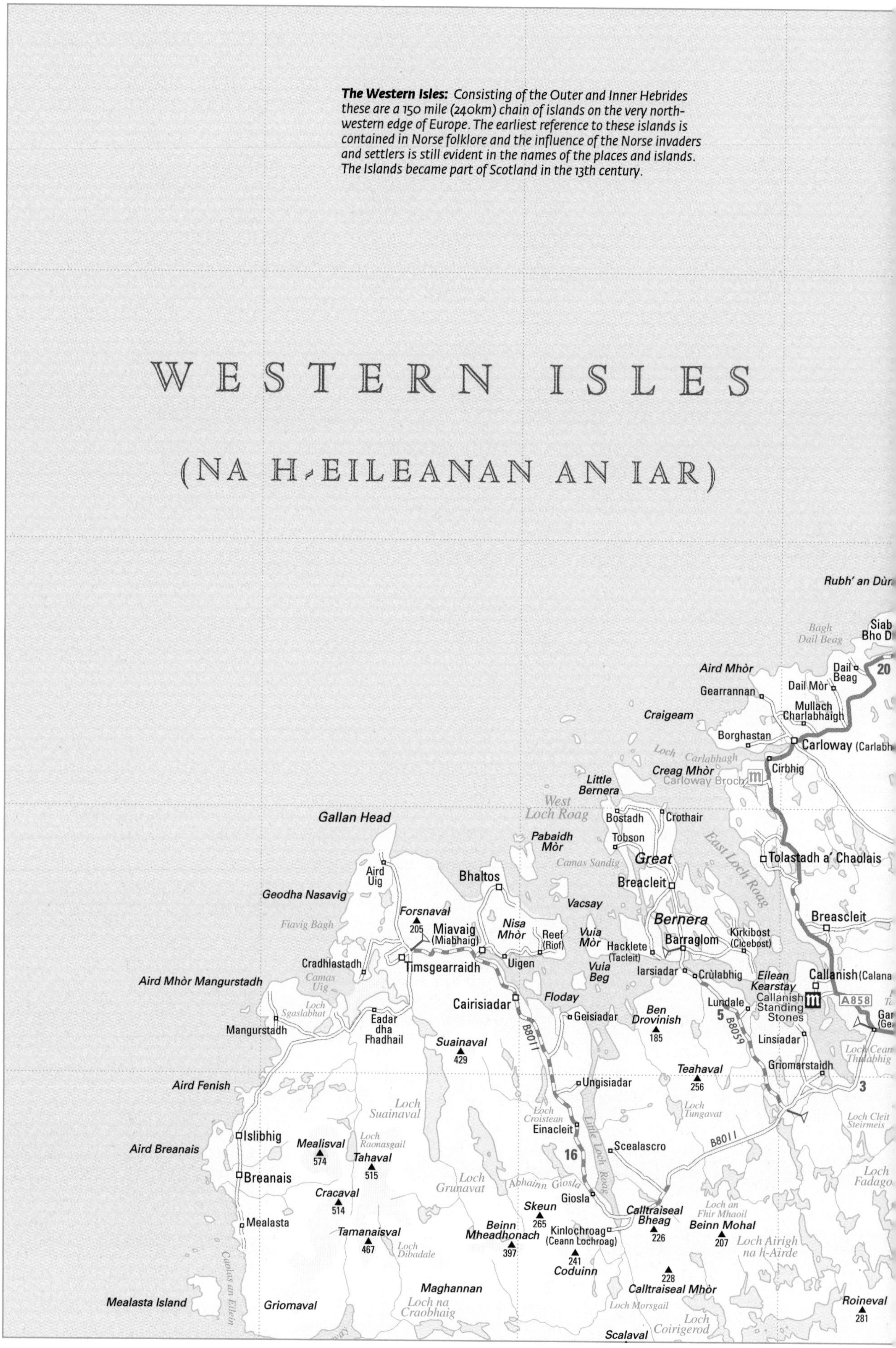

326

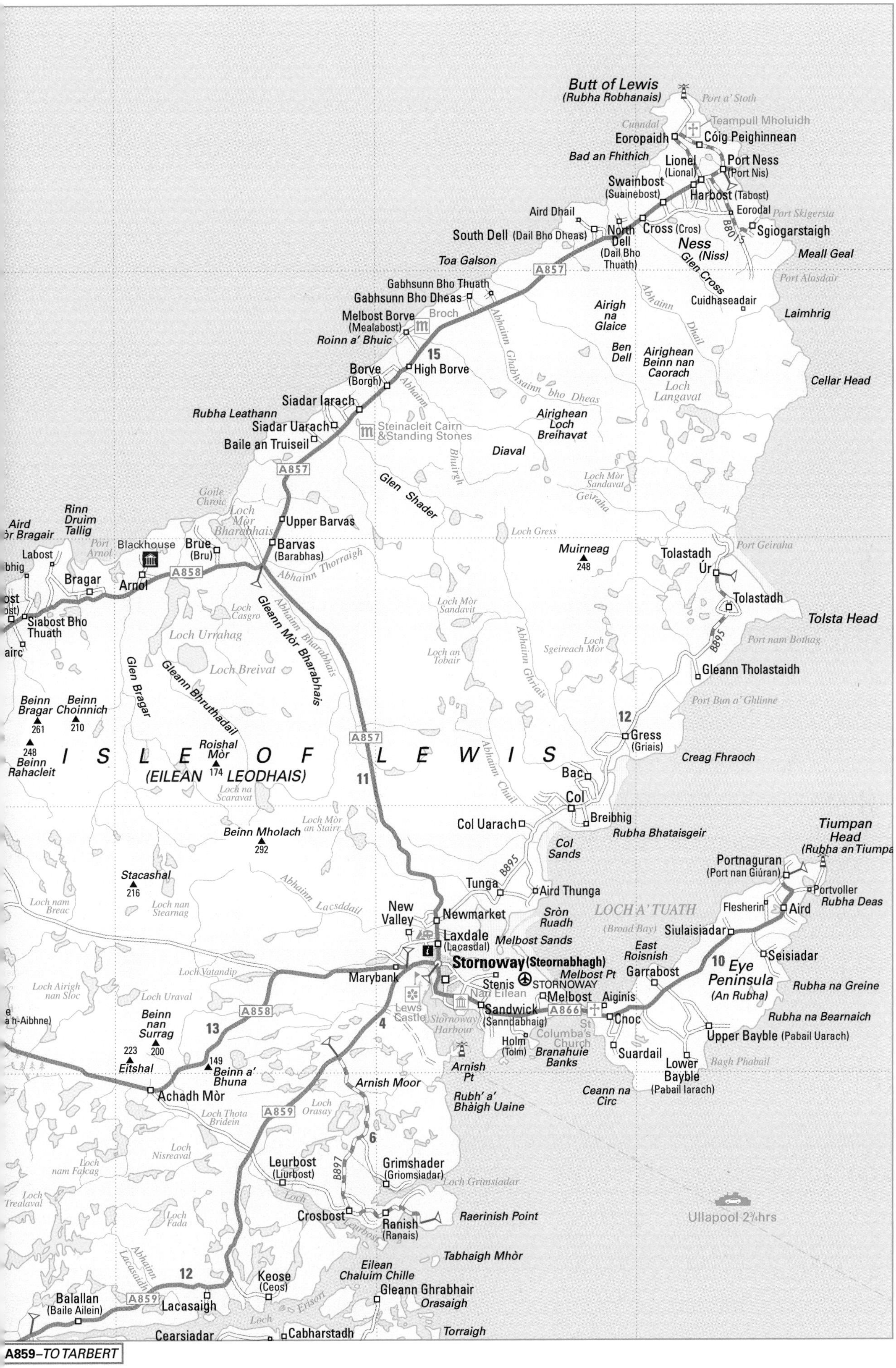

327

Stornoway: *One of Stornoway's most famous sons is Sir Alexander Mackenzie who, in 1793, became the first European to cross the North American continent as far as the Arctic Ocean. The river that he followed was subsequently called the Mackenzie River.* ***Map ref. F4.***

A B C D

1 2 3 4 5

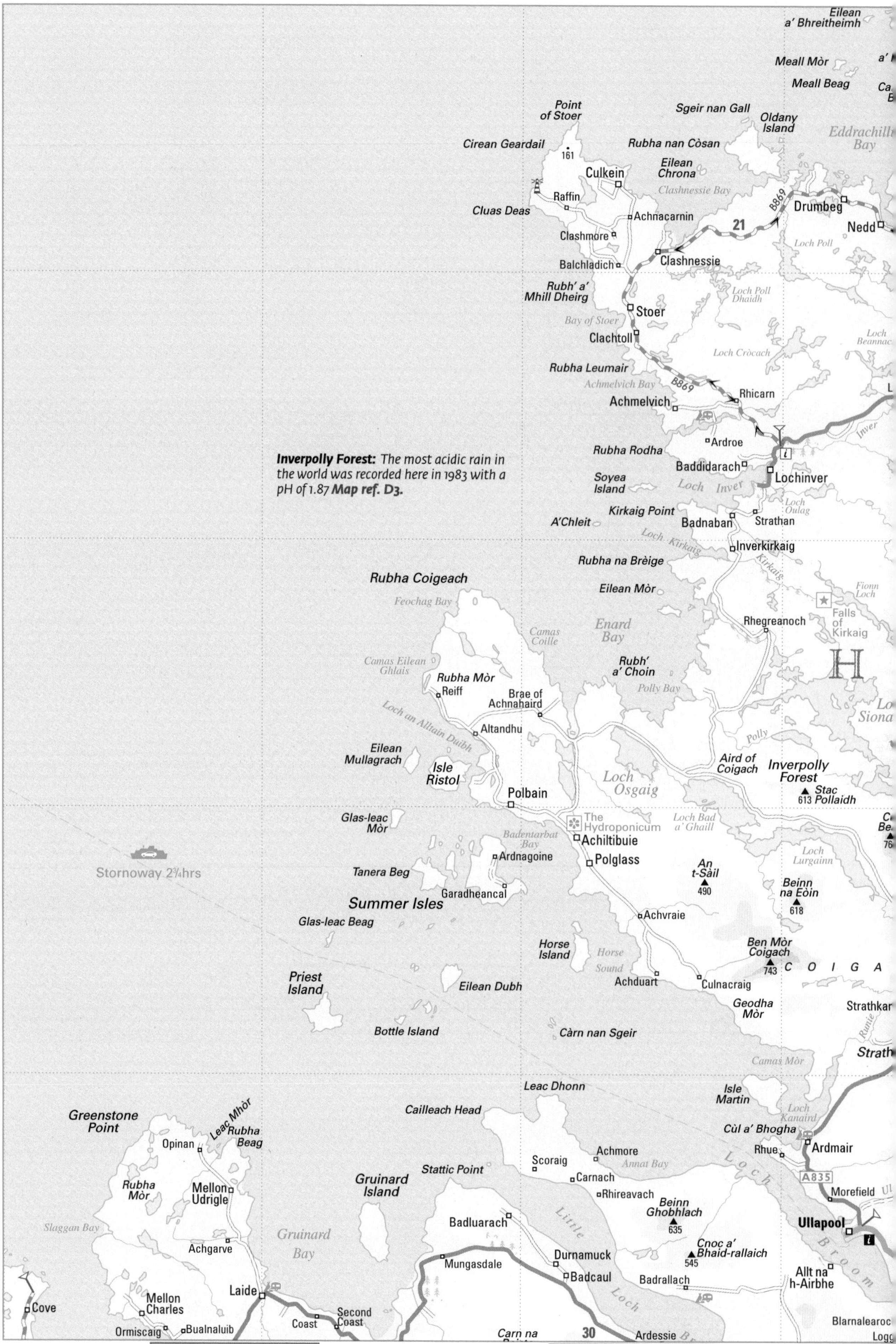

Inverpolly Forest: *The most acidic rain in the world was recorded here in 1983 with a pH of 1.87* ***Map ref. D3.***

A832–TO AUCHTERCAIRN

A832–TO ACHNASHEEN

319

Gruinard Island: *Known as 'Anthrax Island' because of 1942 biological warfare experiments. Anthrax spores were released on this 520 acre (210ha), uninhabited island to test its killing power on a flock of sheep. The island was so contaminated that it remained out of bounds for 50 years. In 1986 a company was paid £500,000 to decontaminate it by soaking the ground in 276 tons (280 tonnes) of formaldehyde diluted in 1,968 tons (2,000 tonnes) of sea water. Also much of the topsoil was removed in sealed containers. A flock of sheep have since grazed there without harm…still not the place to go for a picnic!* ***Map ref. B5***

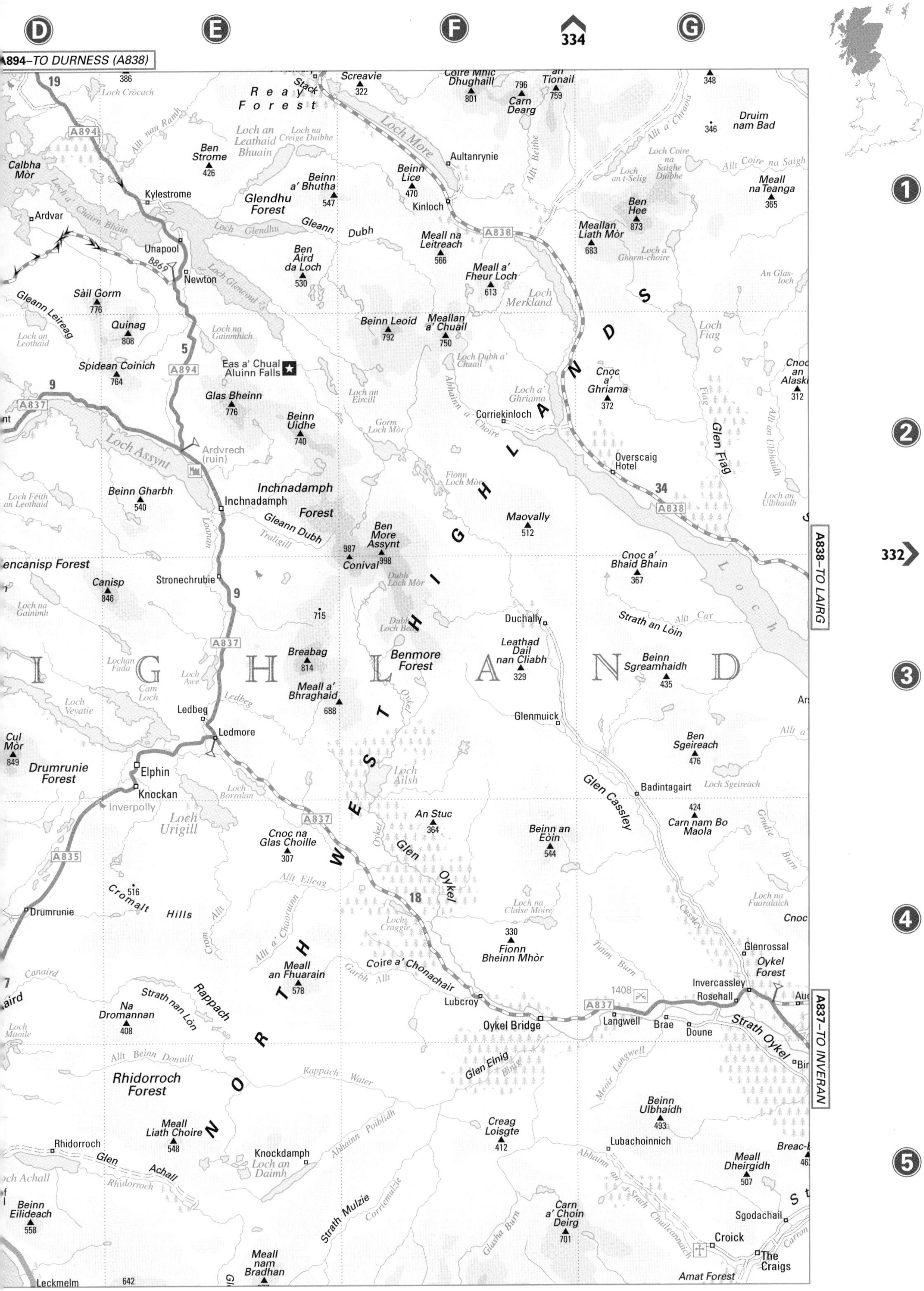

Achmelvich: *Could almost be in the tropics, a stunning little bay with fantastic white sand and clear turquoise water. Go on, check it out.* ***Map ref. C2.***

The Hydroponicum: *This demonstrates how to cultivate plants by growing them in gravel or similar material and pumping water containing dissolved nutrient salts through them.* ***Map ref. C4.***

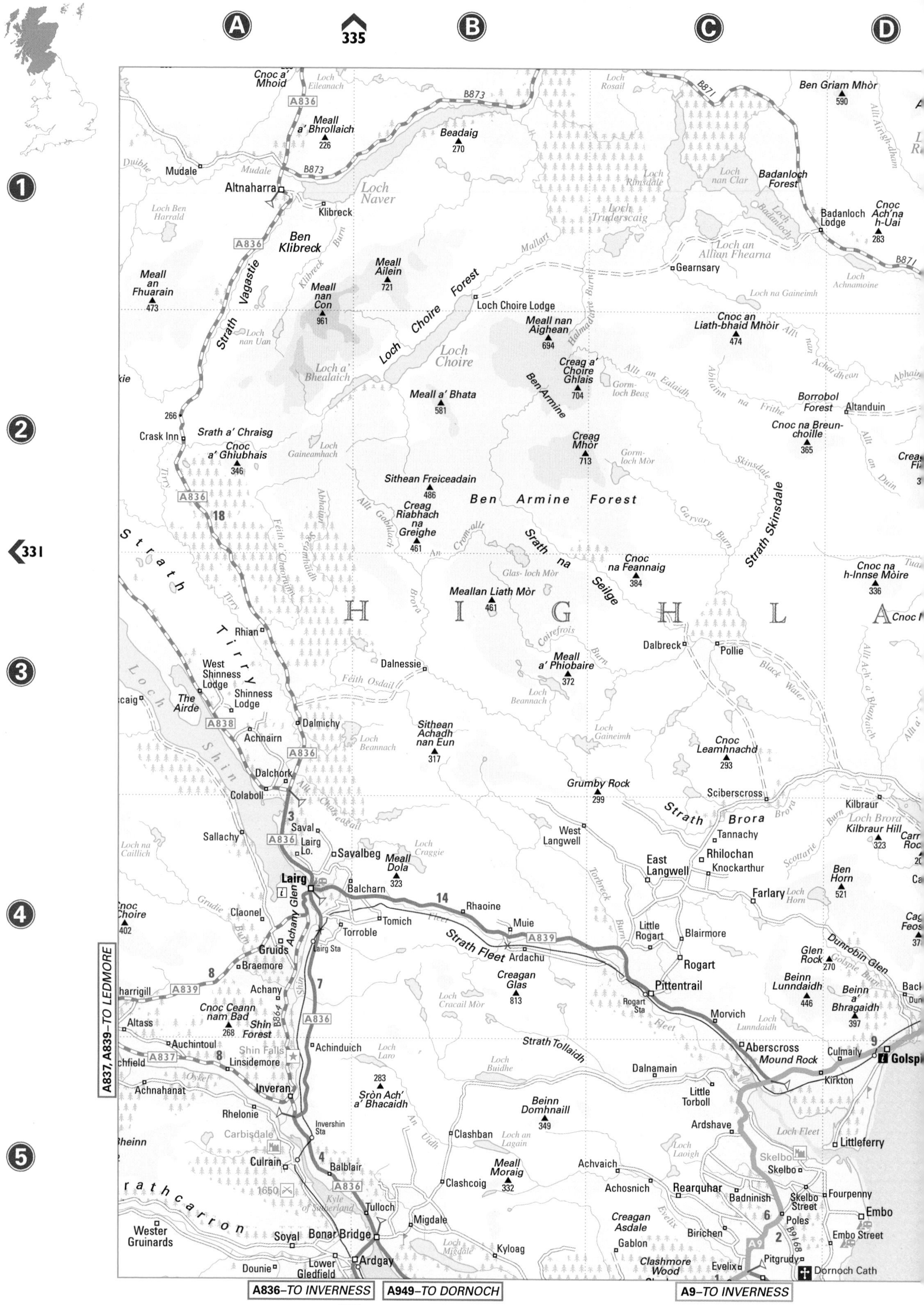
A
B
C
D
335
1
2
3
4
5
331
321
Cnoc a' Mhoid
Loch Eileanach
A836
B873
Loch Rosail
B871
Ben Griam Mhòr
590
Meall a' Bhrollaich
226
Beadaig
270
Duibhe
Mudale
B873
Altnaharra
Loch Naver
Klibreck
Loch Rimsdale
Loch nan Clar
Badanloch Forest
Loch Badanloch
Badanloch Lodge
Cnoc Ach'na h-Uai
283
Loch Ben Harrald
Ben Klibreck
A836
Loch Truderscaig
Loch an Allian Fhearna
Gearnsary
B871
Mallart
Loch Achnamoine
Meall an Fhuarain
473
Strath Vagastie
Meall Ailein
721
Meall nan Con
961
Loch Choire Forest
Loch Choire Lodge
Loch na Gaineimh
Meall nan Aighean
694
Cnoc an Liath-bhaid Mhòir
474
Loch nan Uan
Loch Choire
Loch a' Bhealaich
Creag a' Choire Ghlais
704
Ben Armine
Allt an Ealaidh
Gorm-loch Beag
Abhainn na Frithe
Achar dhean
Abhainn
Meall a' Bhata
581
Borrobol Forest
Altanduin
266
Crask Inn
Strath a' Chraisg
Cnoc a' Ghiubhais
346
Loch Gaineamhach
Creag Mhòr
713
Gorm-loch Mòr
Cnoc na Breun-choille
365
Skinsdale
Sithean Freiceadain
486
Ben Armine Forest
A836
18
Creag Riabhach na Greighe
461
Garvary Burn
Strath Skinsdale
Strath Tirry
Strath na Seilge
Cnoc na Feannaig
384
Cnoc na h-Innse Mòire
336
Glas-loch Mòr
Meallan Liath Mòr
461
HIGHLA
Cnoc
Rhian
Dalbreck
Pollie
Meall a' Phiobaire
372
Black Water
Dalnessie
Fèith Osdail
West Shinness Lodge
Shinness Lodge
The Airde
Loch Shin
Loch Beannach
A838
Dalmichy
Achnairn
Sithean Achadh nan Eun
317
Loch Gaineimh
Cnoc Leamhnachd
293
A836
Dalchork
Colaboll
Grumby Rock
299
Sciberscross
Kilbraur
Strath Brora
Loch Brora
Kilbraur Hill
323
3
Saval
Sallachy
A836
Lairg Lo.
Savalbeg
Meall Dola
323
Loch Craggie
West Langwell
Tannachy
Rhilochan
Knockarthur
Loch na Caillich
East Langwell
Ben Horn
521
Lairg
Balcharn
Farlary
Loch Horn
14
Rhaoine
Claonel
Achany Glen
Tomich
Torroble
Muie
A839
Strath Fleet
Ardachu
Little Rogart
Blairmore
Lairg Sta
Gruids
Rogart
Glen Rock
270
Dunrobin Glen
8
Braemore
Creagan Glas
813
Pittentrail
Beinn Lunndaidh
446
Beinn a' Bhragaidh
397
A839
Achany
7
Loch Cracail Mòr
Rogart Sta
Morvich
Loch Lunndaidh
Cnoc Ceann nam Bad
268
Shin Forest
A836
Altass
Auchintoul
Shin Falls
Achinduich
Loch Laro
Strath Tollaidh
Aberscross
Mound Rock
Culmaily
9
Golspie
A837
Linsidemore
Loch Buidhe
Dalnamain
Kirkton
Achnahanat
Inveran
283
Spòn Ach' a' Bhacaidh
Little Torboll
Rhelonie
Invershin Sta
Beinn Domhnaill
349
Ardshave
Loch Fleet
Carbisdale
Clashban
Loch an Lagain
Littleferry
Culrain
4
Balblair
Meall Moraig
332
Achvaich
Skelbo
Strathcarron
1650
A836
Clashcoig
Achosnich
Rearquhar
Badninish
Skelbo Street
Fourpenny
Kyle of Sutherland
Tulloch
Creagan Asdale
6
Poles
Embo
Wester Gruinards
Soyal
Bonar Bridge
Migdale
Birichen
2
B9168
Embo Street
Loch Migdale
Kyloag
Gablon
A9
Pitgrudy
Dounie
Lower Gledfield
Ardgay
Clashmore Wood
Evelix
Dornoch Cath
A837, A839–TO LEDMORE
A836–TO INVERNESS
A949–TO DORNOCH
A9–TO INVERNESS

Loch Shin: *The largest freshwater lake in Sutherland. The Lairg Dam, at the southern end of the loch is 1,400 feet (427m) long and 40 feet (12m) high. It raised the water level of the loch by 36 feet (11m) and is used to create hydro-electricity. It is the most northern hydro-electric scheme in mainland Britain.* ***Map ref. A3.***

Helmsdale: *The practise of deer stalking in the Highlands dates back to the 19th Century and was made popular by Queen Victoria and Prince Albert who took out a lease on Balmoral in 1848. Deer stalking is regarded as a skilful way of hunting deer by getting within 100 yards (91m) of the quarry before making the kill. There are now over 300,000 Red Deer in the Highlands and deer stalking remains a popular sport with hunters and photographers from both Britain and abroad. The area around Helmsdale is regarded as particularly good 'deer stalking' country.* ***Map ref. F3.***

337
322

Dunbeath: *Purpose built village created in the early 1800s to take advantage of the Herring boom. Dunbeath is also the birthplace of Neil Miller Gunn the celebrated Scottish novelist (1891–1973).* ***Map ref. G1.***

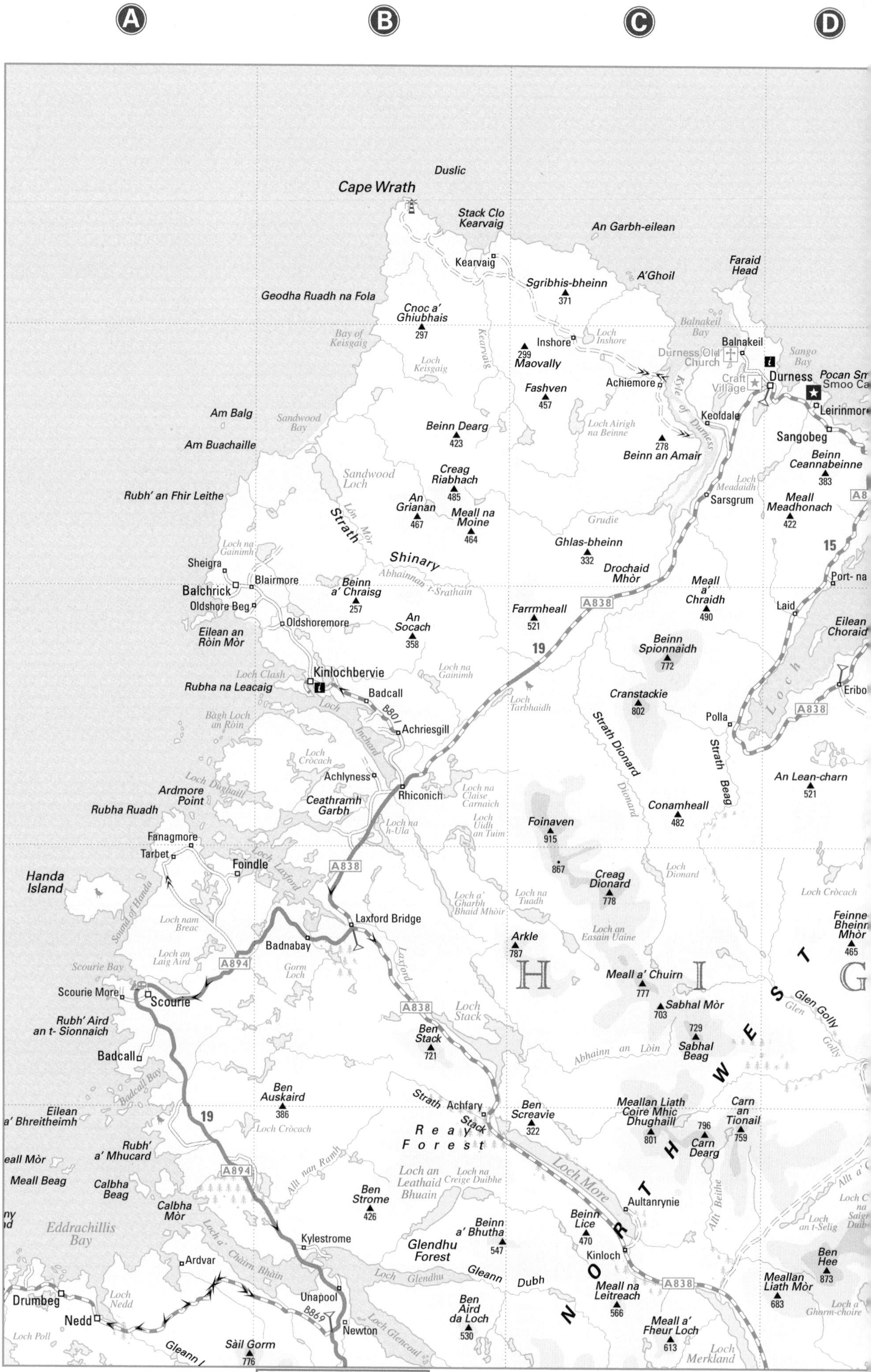

A894–TO ULLAPOOL (A835)

331

Laid: *Between 1785 and 1850 the Highlands and Islands were subjected to 'The Clearances'. Under this system tens of thousands of clansmen were removed from their homes and holdings to make way for large-scale sheep farming by the wealthy landowners. Though generally acrimonious, son resettlement took place often involving re-location to poorer land along the coast where fishing and kelping were supposed to compensate for the previous existence. Some however were more fortunate and new villages were built to house them. Such a place is Laid which was created in 1832 t house those cleared from Eriboll on the other side of the loch.* ***Map ref. D3.***

D E F G

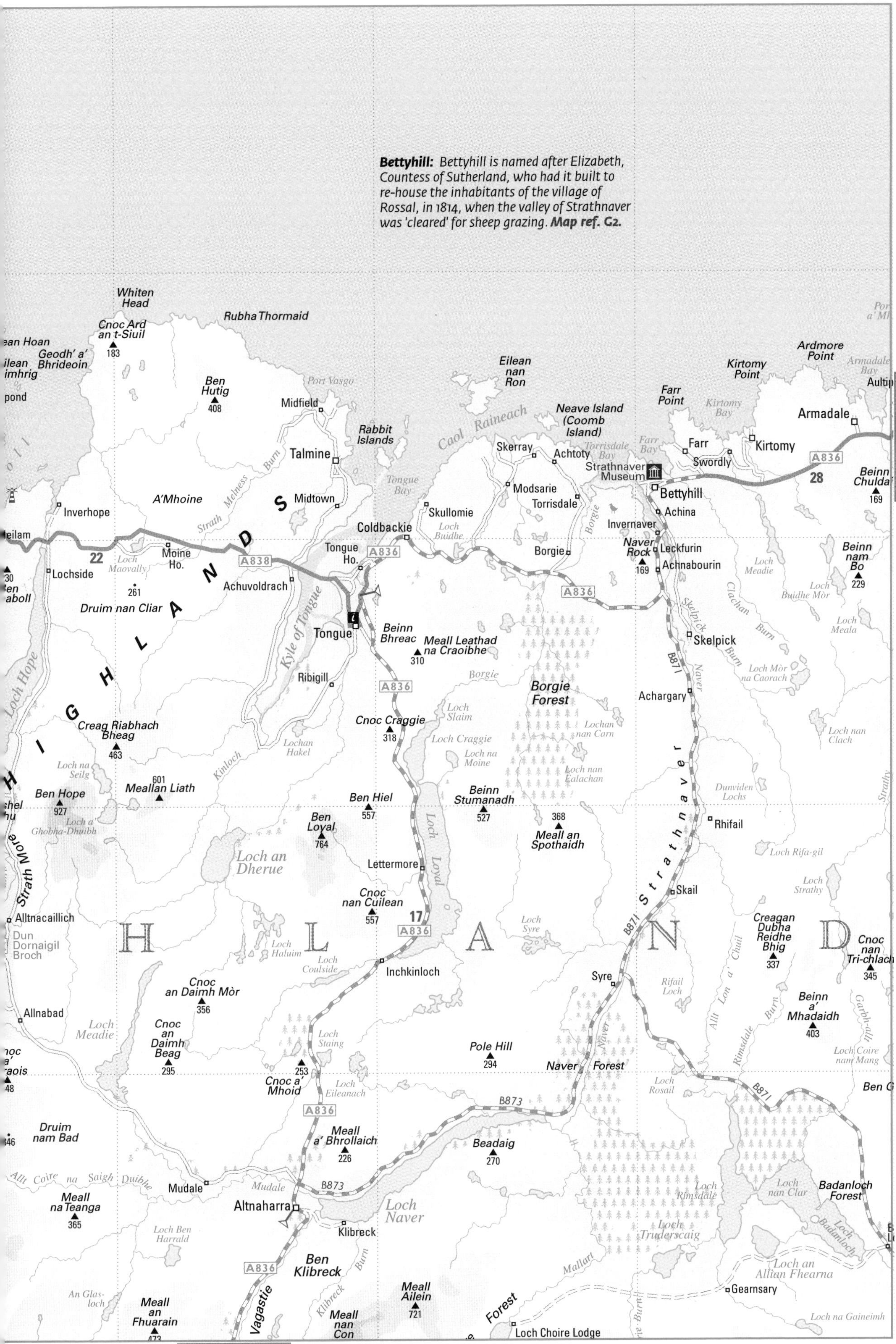

Bettyhill: *Bettyhill is named after Elizabeth, Countess of Sutherland, who had it built to re-house the inhabitants of the village of Rossal, in 1814, when the valley of Strathnaver was 'cleared' for sheep grazing.* ***Map ref. G2.***

1 2 3 4 5

336

332

Altnaharra: *Altnaharra recorded the lowest ever temperature in Britain (-27.2°C) on the 30th December 1955.*
Map ref. E5.

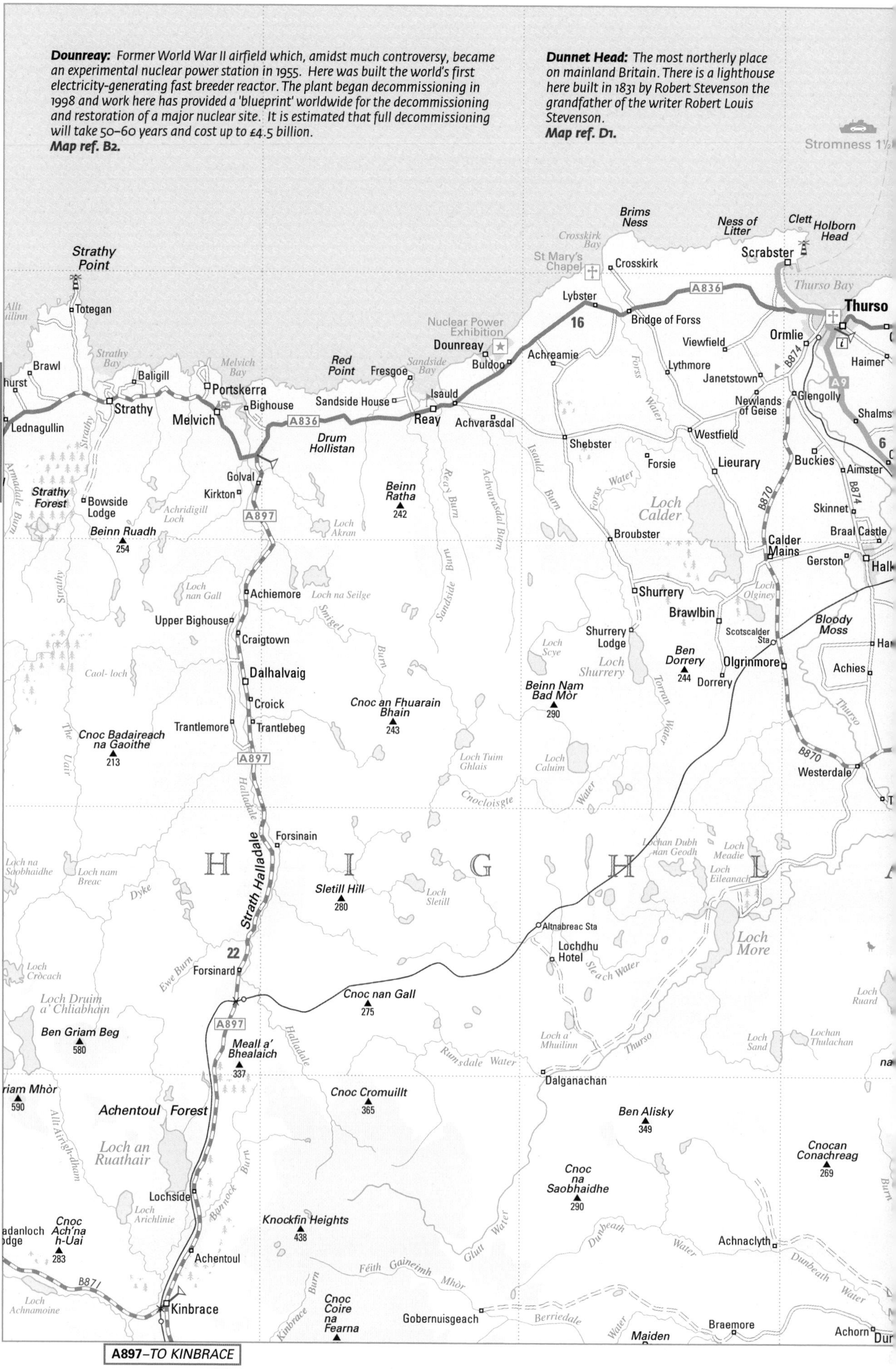

A836–TO BETTYHILL

335

Dounreay: *Former World War II airfield which, amidst much controversy, became an experimental nuclear power station in 1955. Here was built the world's first electricity-generating fast breeder reactor. The plant began decommissioning in 1998 and work here has provided a 'blueprint' worldwide for the decommissioning and restoration of a major nuclear site. It is estimated that full decommissioning will take 50–60 years and cost up to £4.5 billion.* ***Map ref. B2.***

Dunnet Head: *The most northerly place on mainland Britain. There is a lighthouse here built in 1831 by Robert Stevenson the grandfather of the writer Robert Louis Stevenson.* ***Map ref. D1.***

A897–TO KINBRACE

333

Olrig: *The old 'kirkyard' at Olrig contains the grave of the unfortunate 'Selkie Woman'. She was found as a baby wrapped in a sealskin and grew up around the settlement. She was later accused of Devil Worship and banished from the kirk and later died in childbirth. It is said that the stone which covers her grave fills with tears and never dries out.* ***Map ref. D2.***

D E F 338 G

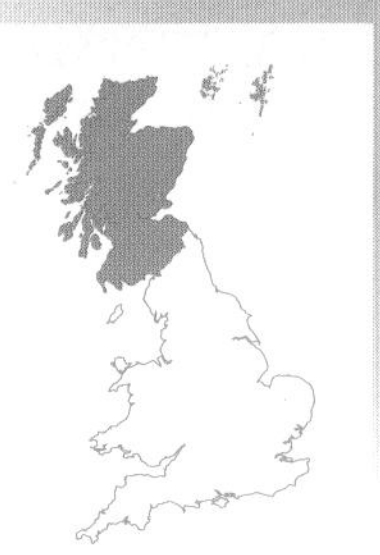

John O' Groats: *Though Dunnet Head is slightly further north and Duncansby Head further east, John O' Groats is generally regarded as the most north-easterly settlement of mainland Britain. It therefore features as the start or finish point for all sorts of games and charity events. From here a sign says it is 874 miles to Land's End.* ***Map ref. F1.***

1 2 3 4 5

Island of Stroma: *This is the only island in Caithness and has been uninhabited since 1962. Once the home of the notorious Sweyn the Pirate who raided and plundered along the northern coast of Scotland in the 12th Century.* ***Map ref. F1.***

A
B
C
D
1
2
3
4
5
340
337
A966–TO TINGWALL
A836–TO THURSO
A99–TO WICK
Skara Brae
Skaill
Stromness
Finstown
Ring of Brogar
Maes Howe
Stones of Stenness
Orphir
Graemsay
Hoy Sound
Old Man of Hoy
HOY
ORKNEY
MAINLAND
SCAPA FLOW
Flotta
Fara
Cava
South Walls
Swona
Island of Stroma
PENTLAND FIRTH
Dunnet Head
Mey
John o' Groats
Duncansby Head
HIGHLAND

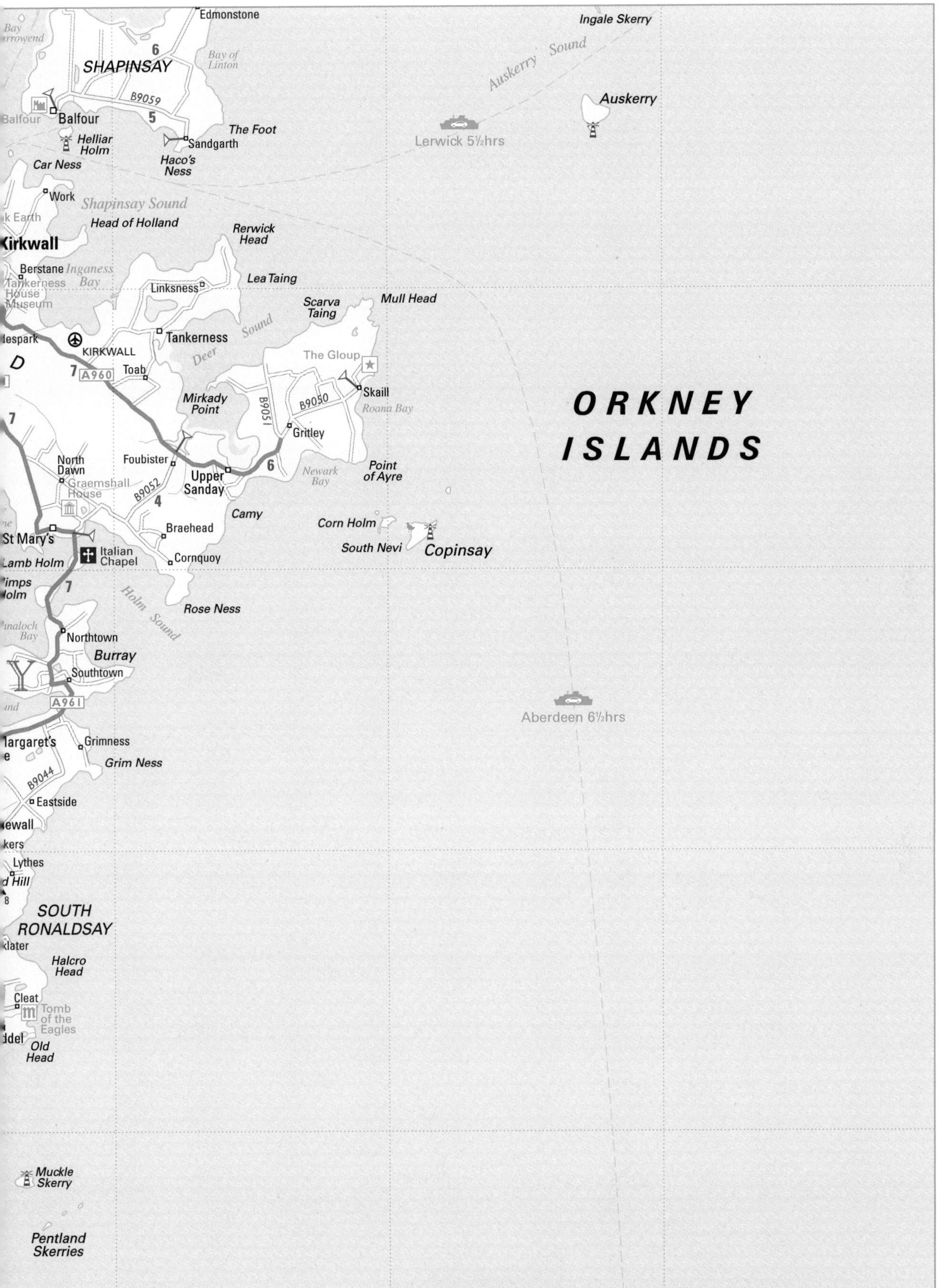

1
2
3
4
5

Scapa Flow: *This huge natural harbour was the scene of much wartime naval activity. At the end of World War I, Admiral von Reuter scuttled most of the 74 ships of the German High Seas Fleet here, though most were later salvaged.*
At the start of World War II the area was blocked with old ships to keep out the German U-Boats. One however got through and sunk HMS Royal Oak which still lies at the bottom of Scapa Flow. ***Map ref. C2***

Lamb Holm: *After the sinking of HMS Royal Oak in World War II Churchill ordered the entrance to Scapa Flow to be filled in. This work was carried out by Italian Prisoners of War and became known as the Churchill Barrier. During their stay the Italians converted two Nissen huts into a Roman Catholic Chapel which still stands today.* ***Also on page 125****. The barrier now forms part of the A961 road.*
Map ref. D2

A B C D

1 2 3 4 5

‹ ???

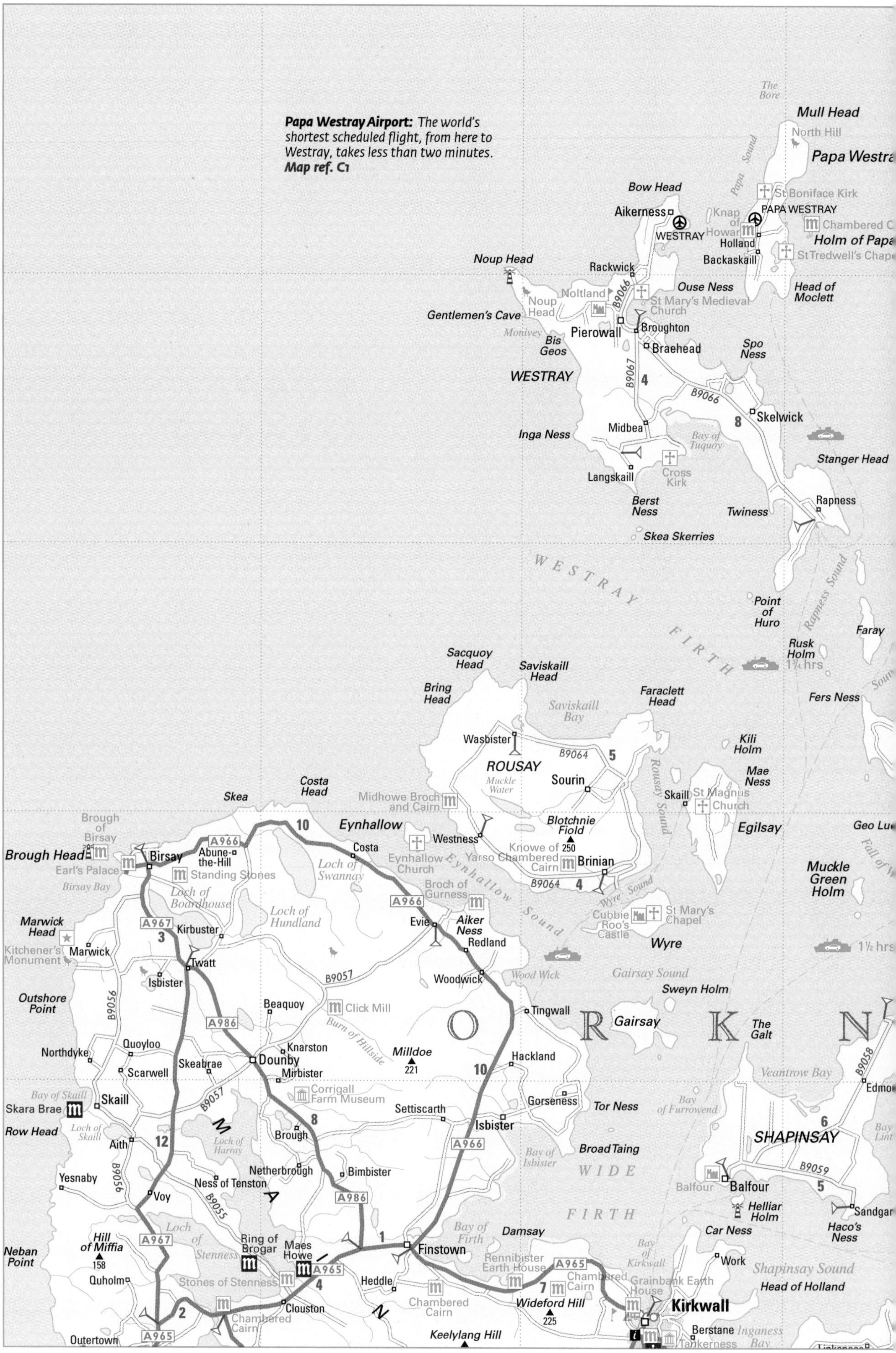

Papa Westray Airport: *The world's shortest scheduled flight, from here to Westray, takes less than two minutes.* ***Map ref. C1***

338

Birsay: *Sir Thomas Clouston (1840–1915) who pioneered the humane treatment of the mentally ill was born here. In 1883 his book on mental diseases established his international reputation as a leading figure in the diagnosis and treatment of such illnesses.* ***Map ref. A4***

339

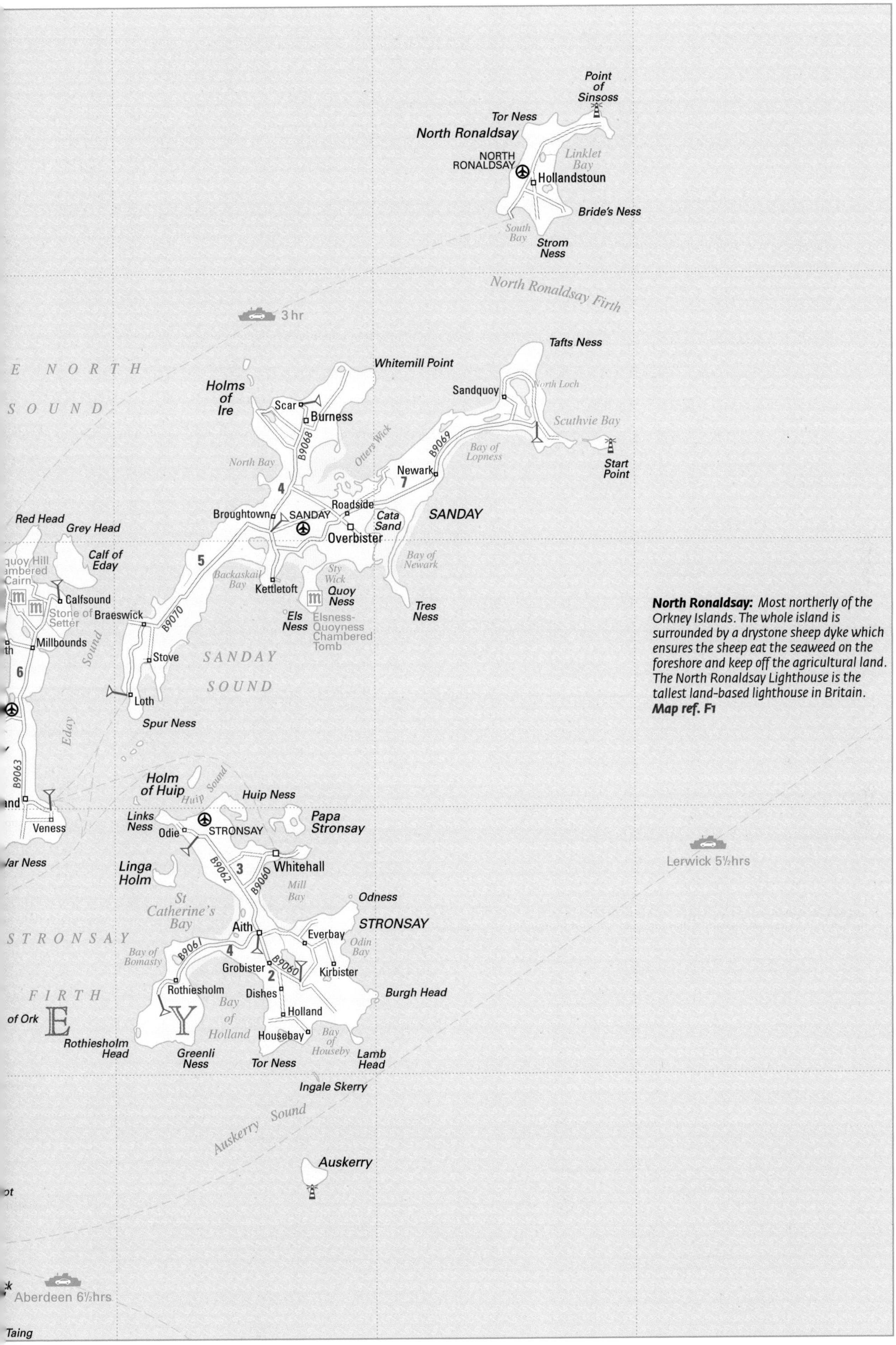

North Ronaldsay: *Most northerly of the Orkney Islands. The whole island is surrounded by a drystone sheep dyke which ensures the sheep eat the seaweed on the foreshore and keep off the agricultural land. The North Ronaldsay Lighthouse is the tallest land-based lighthouse in Britain.* ***Map ref. F1***

Orkney Islands: *There are more than 70 islands in the Orkneys but only 17 are inhabited. Orkney summers feature almost continual daylight with the sun above the horizon for over 18 hours a day....by contrast, in winter, the sun rises after 9am and sets around 3.30pm so there are barely 7 hours of daylight.*

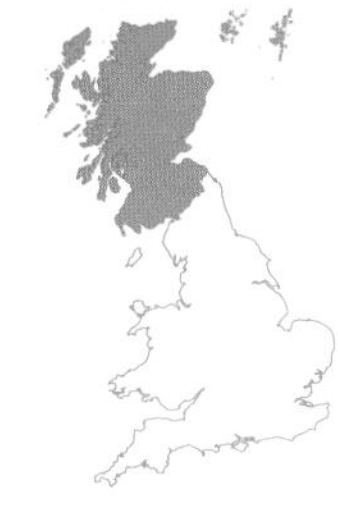

A B C D
1 2 3 4 5
344

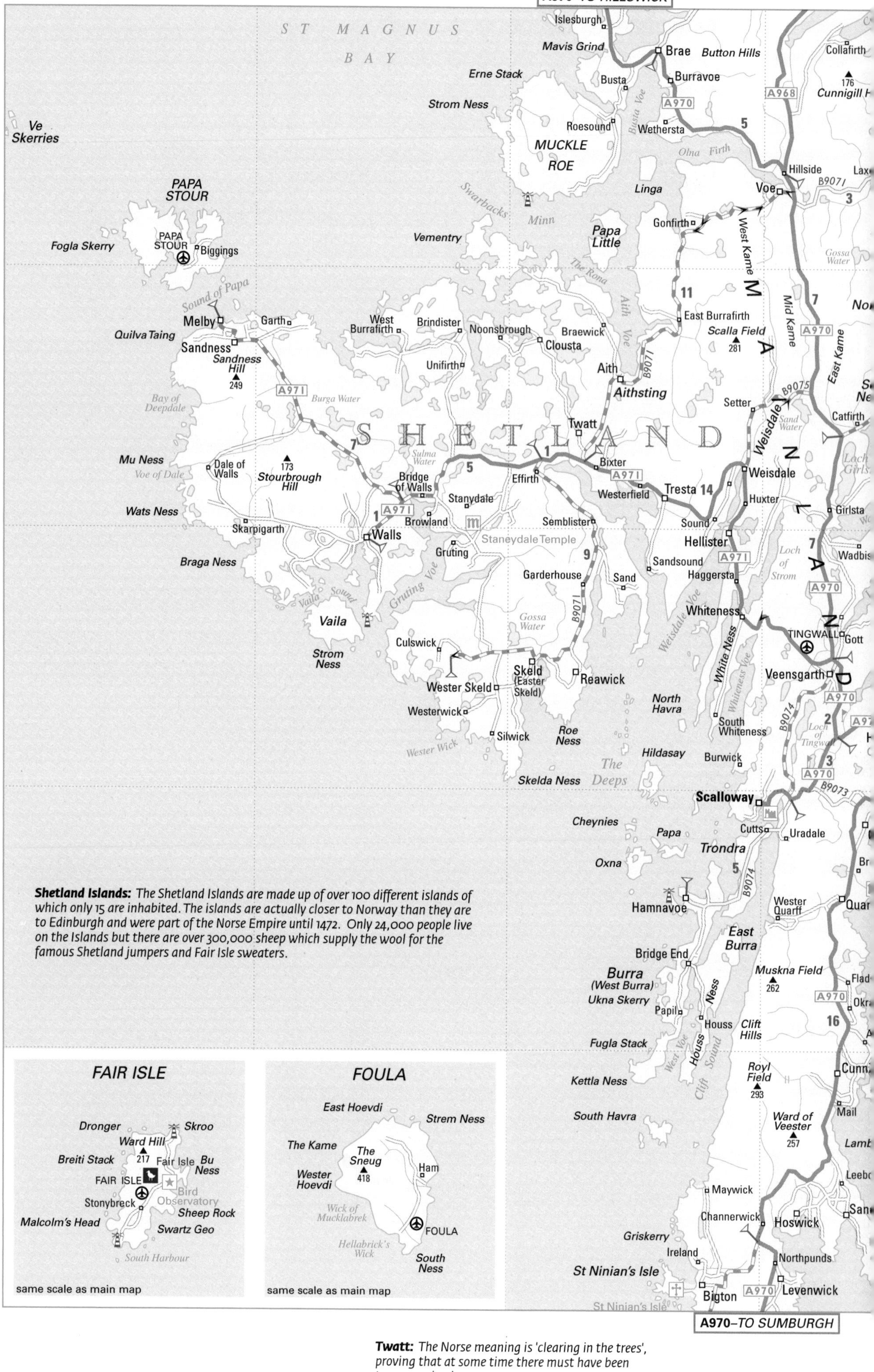

Shetland Islands: *The Shetland Islands are made up of over 100 different islands of which only 15 are inhabited. The islands are actually closer to Norway than they are to Edinburgh and were part of the Norse Empire until 1472. Only 24,000 people live on the Islands but there are over 300,000 sheep which supply the wool for the famous Shetland jumpers and Fair Isle sweaters.*

Twatt: *The Norse meaning is 'clearing in the trees', proving that at some time there must have been trees growing here.*
Map ref. C2

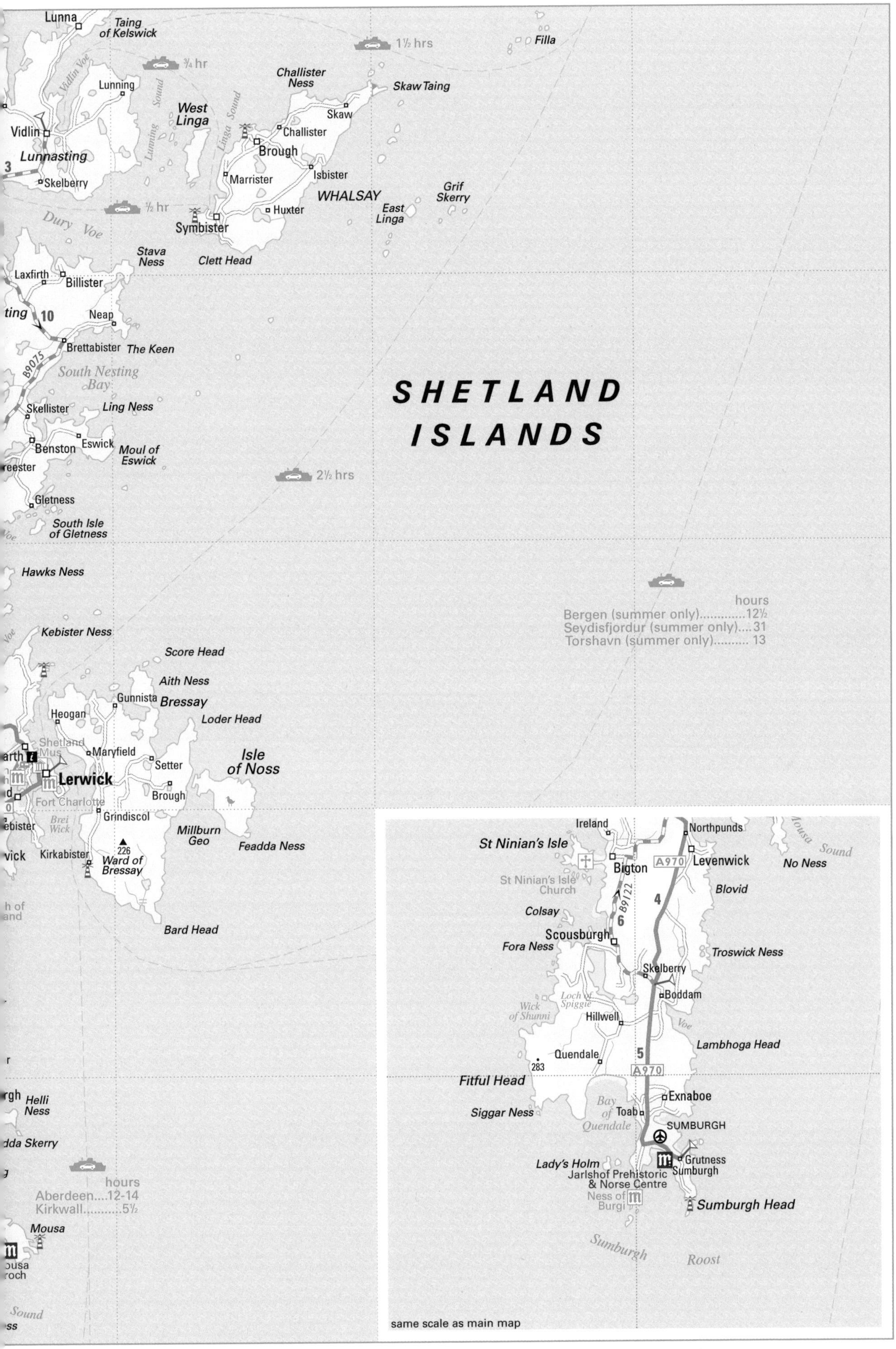

Lerwick: *Arthur Anderson (1792–1868) was born here. Anderson formed the Union Steam Ship Company in 1853 which later became the great Union-Castle Line.*
Map ref. D3

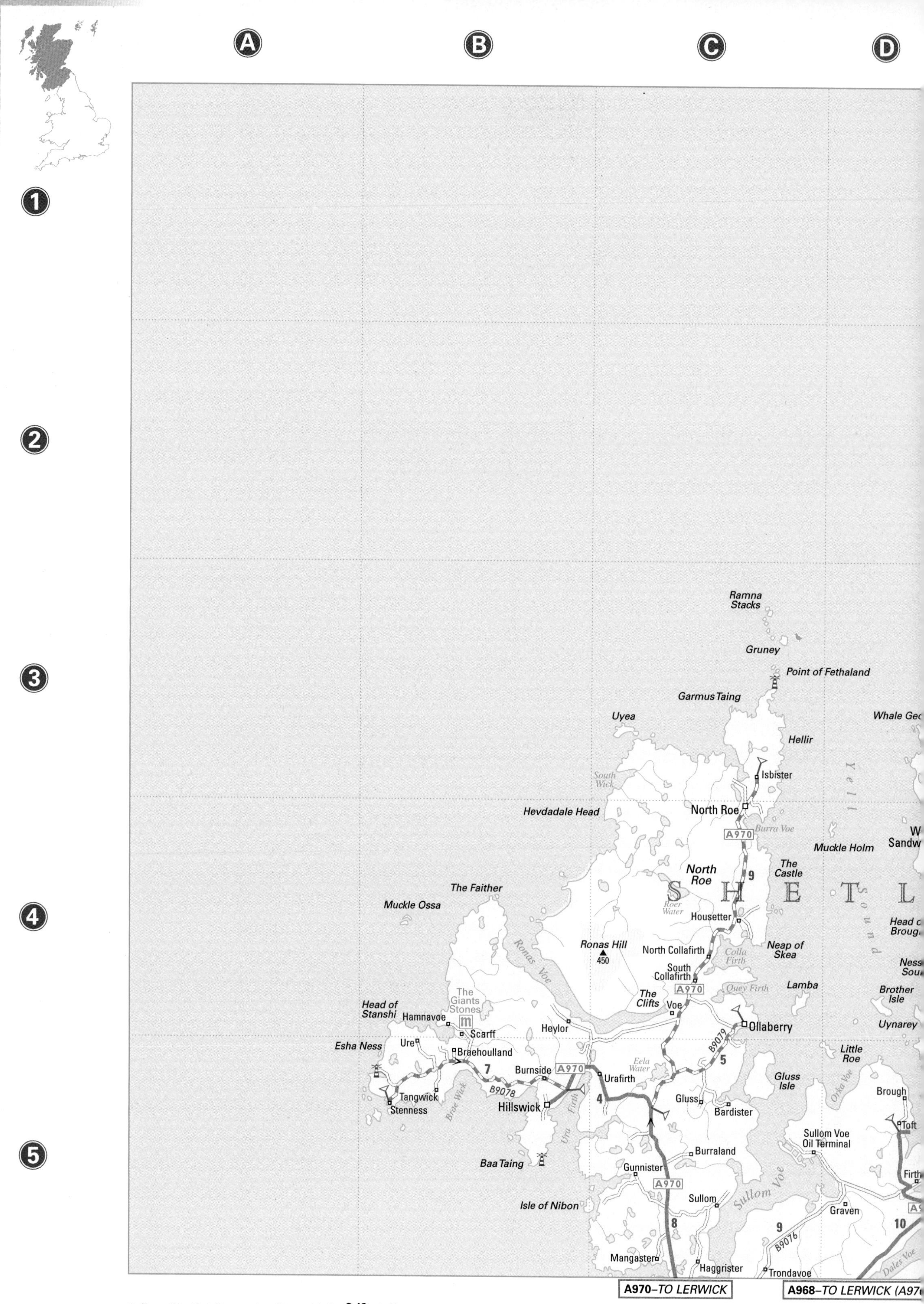

Sullom: *The first German bombing raid of World War II took place here on the 13th November 1939 and the first casualty of a German bomb on British soil was a rabbit.* ***Map ref. C5***

342

Sullom Voe: *Between 1973 and 1982 this was one of the biggest construction sites in Europe with over 6,000 people employed building the oil terminal.* ***Map ref. C5***

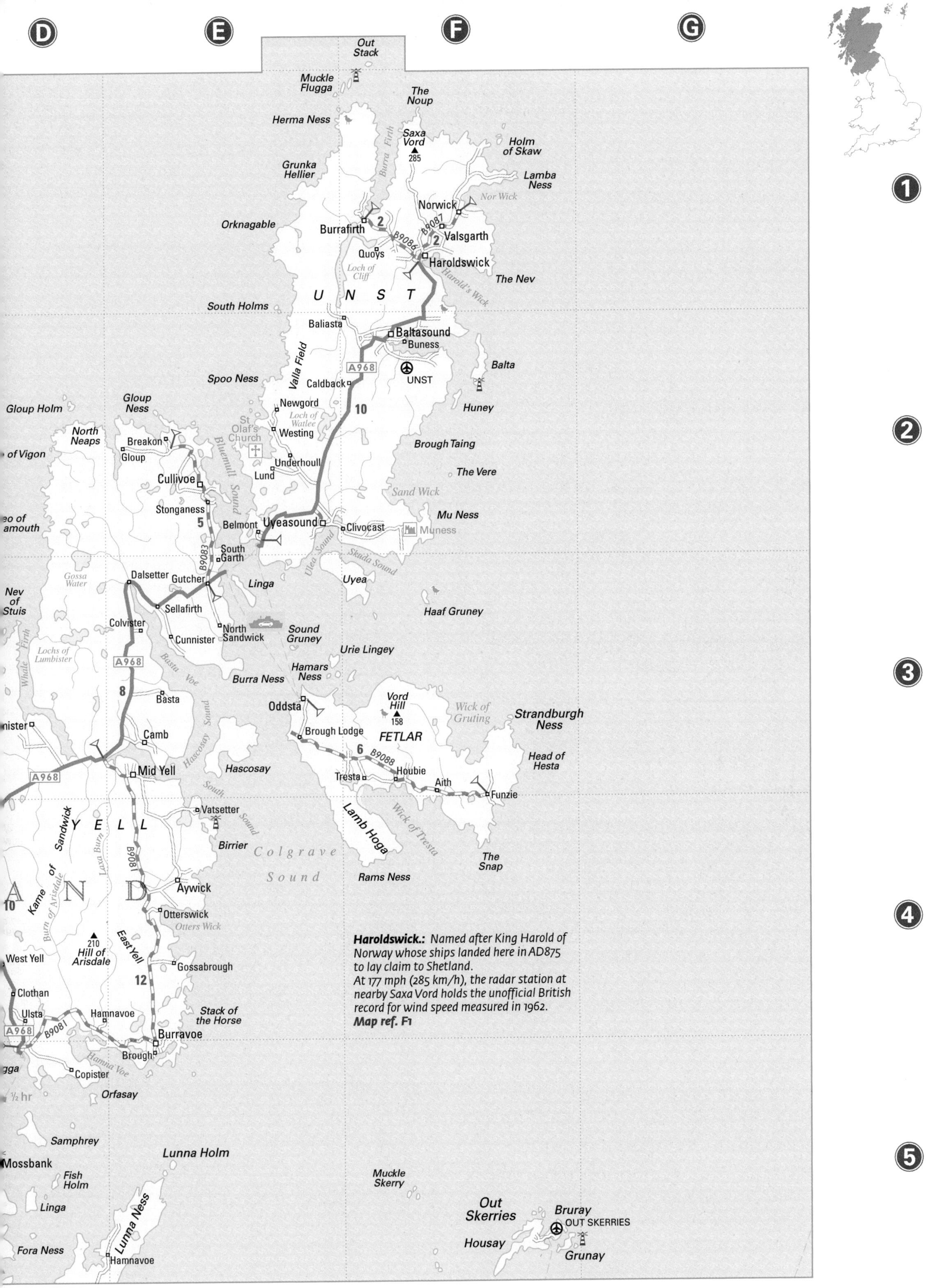

Haroldswick.: *Named after King Harold of Norway whose ships landed here in AD875 to lay claim to Shetland.*
At 177 mph (285 km/h), the radar station at nearby Saxa Vord holds the unofficial British record for wind speed measured in 1962. **Map ref. F1**

Graven: *During the war this was an air base from which the RAF flying boats patrolled the North Atlantic in search of German U Boats.* **Map ref. D5**

343

Muckle Flugga: *When the lighthouse keeper was at home this was once the most northerly inhabited island in Britain. The next rock along, the uninhabited 'Out Stack' is the most northern bit of the whole of Britain.* **Map ref. F1**

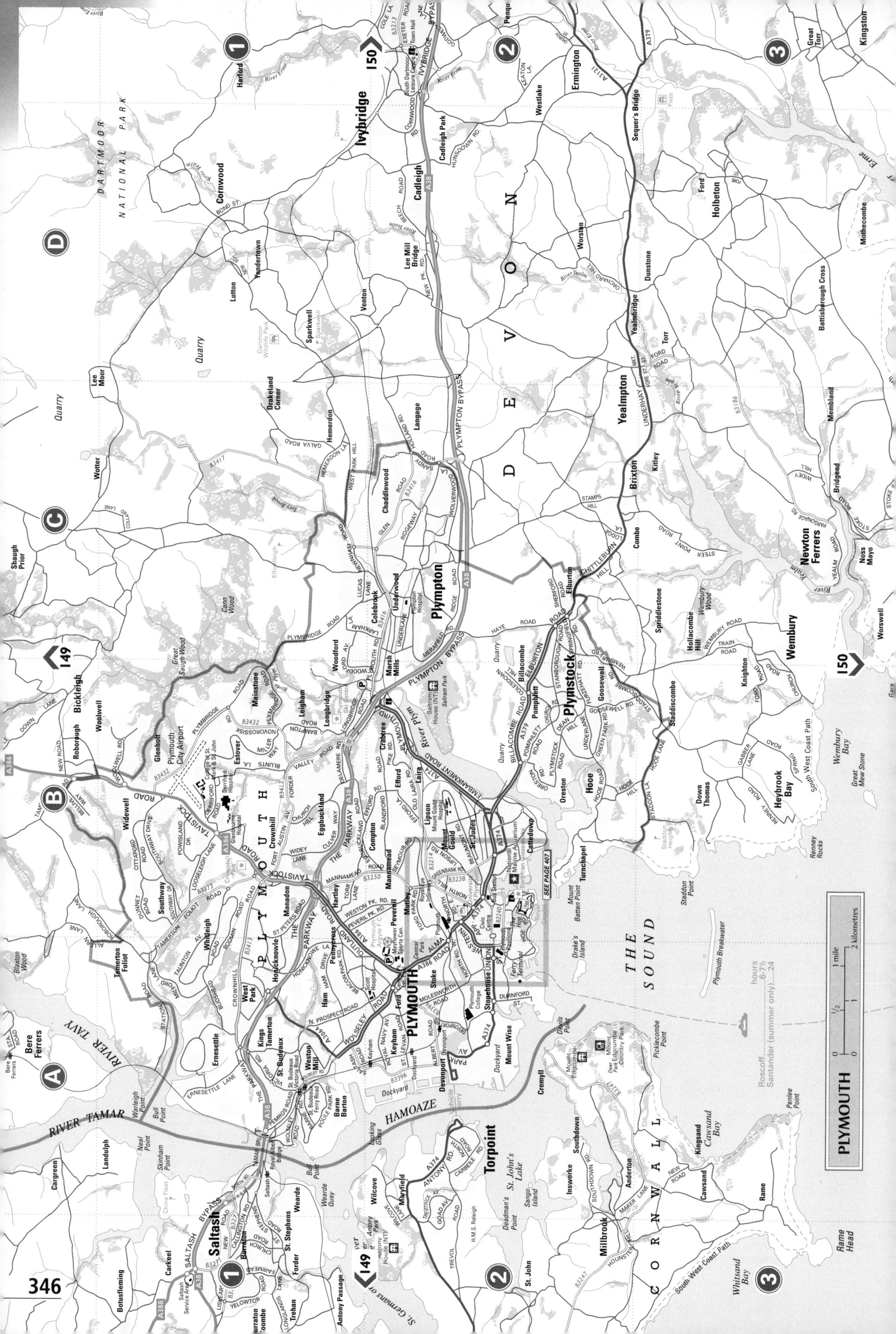
PLYMOUTH
THE SOUND
DARTMOOR NATIONAL PARK
DEVON
CORNWALL
RIVER TAMAR
RIVER TAVY
HAMOAZE
SEE PAGE 407
Saltash
Torpoint
Plymouth
Plympton
Plymstock
Ivybridge
Yealmpton
Wembury
Newton Ferrers
Noss Mayo
Cornwood
Bickleigh
Roborough
Tamerton Foliot
Crownhill
Estover
Glenholt
Plymouth City Airport
Hooe
Elburton
Brixton
Millbrook
Cawsand
Kingsand
Rame
Rame Head
Whitsand Bay
Cremyll
Mount Edgcumbe
Drake's Island
Plymouth Breakwater
Wembury Bay
Great Mew Stone
Staddon Point
Renney Rocks
Shaugh Prior
Lee Moor
Sparkwell
Lutton
Wotter
Hemerdon
Lee Mill Bridge
Cadleigh
Ermington
Holbeton
Mothecombe
Membland
Sequer's Bridge
Roscoff, Santander (summer only)
1 mile
2 kilometres
A
B
C
D
1
2
3
149
150

BOURNEMOUTH
0 1/2 1 mile
0 1 2 kilometres
THE NEW FOREST
HAMPSHIRE
DORSET
POOLE BAY
POOLE
BOURNEMOUTH
Christchurch
Christchurch Bay
Christchurch Harbour
Hengistbury Head
Poole Harbour
Brownsea Island
Wareham Channel
Holes Bay
Wimborne Minster
Ferndown
West Moors
St. Leonards
West Parley
Bournemouth Airport
Kinson
Broadstone
Corfe Mullen
Upton
Hamworthy
Parkstone
Branksome
Westbourne
Boscombe
Southbourne
Sandbanks
Canford Heath
Merley
Colehill
Hurn
Throop
Moordown
Winton
Charminster
Littledown
Iford
Mudeford
Somerford
Burton
Sopley
Ripley
Bransgore
SEE PAGE 389
Cherbourg hours 2¼-4¼
Guernsey 2½
Jersey 3¾
St. Malo (summer only) 4½
155
156

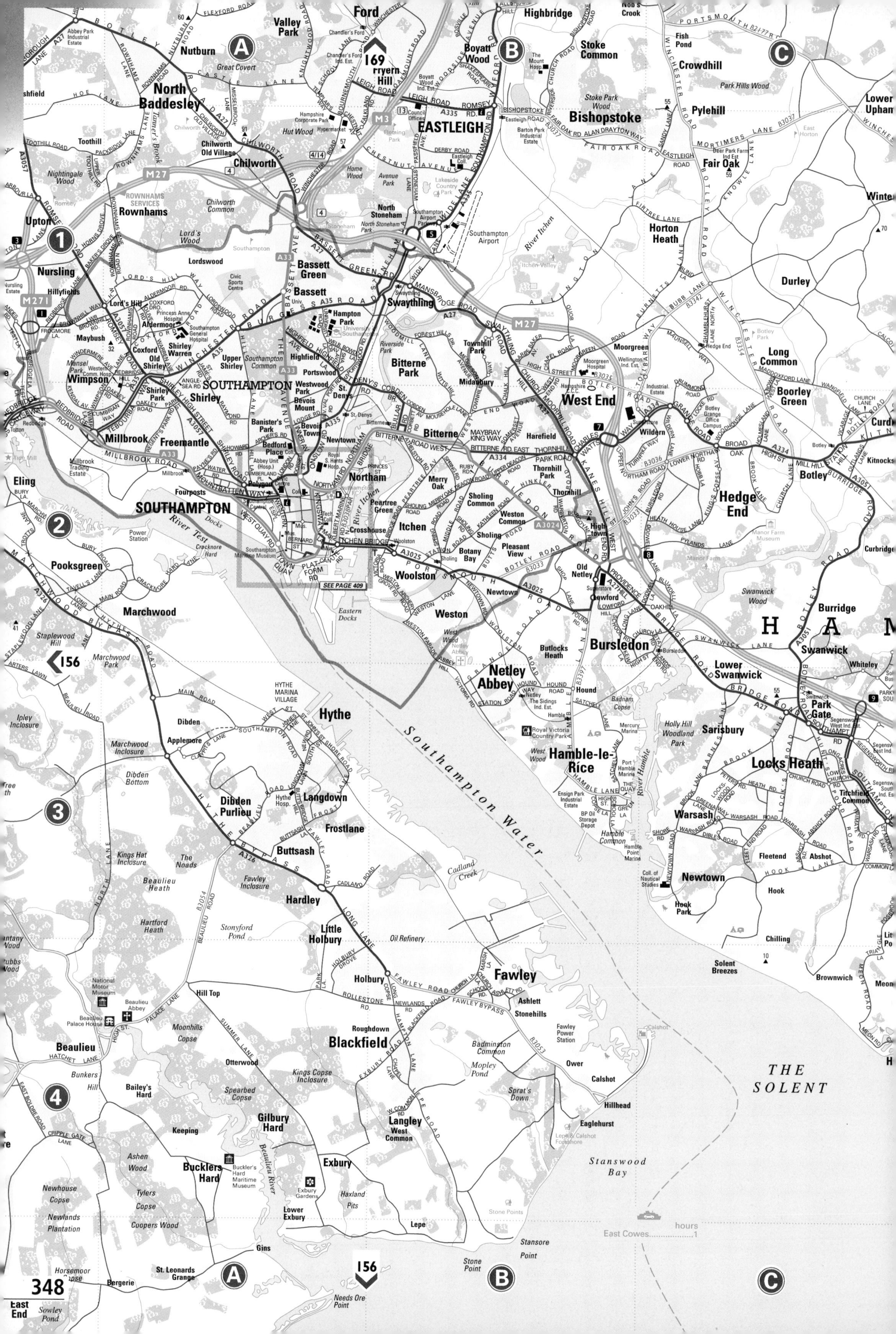
Ford
Valley Park
Nutburn
Highbridge
Nob's Crook
Fish Pond
Crowdhill
169
Boyatt Wood
Stoke Common
North Baddesley
Chilworth
Chilworth Old Village
Toothill
EASTLEIGH
Bishopstoke
Pylehill
Fair Oak
Lower Upham
Nightingale Wood
Rownhams
Chilworth Common
North Stoneham
Southampton Airport
Horton Heath
Durley
Upton
Nursling
Hillyfields
Lord's Wood
Lordswood
Bassett Green
Bassett
Swaythling
Lord's Hill
Aldermoor
Maybush
Coxford
Shirley Warren
Hampton Park
Highfield
Bitterne Park
Townhill Park
Midanbury
Moorgreen
Long Common
Boorley Green
Wimpson
Old Shirley
Upper Shirley
SOUTHAMPTON
Shirley
Portswood
St. Denys
Bevois Mount
Bevois Town
West End
Wildern
Curdridge
Millbrook
Freemantle
Banister's Park
Bedford Place
Newtown
Bitterne
Harefield
Thornhill Park
Thornhill
Botley
Kitnocks
Northam
Merry Oak
Sholing Common
Weston Common
Sholing
Hedge End
Eling
Fourposts
Polygon
Itchen
Pleasant View
Botany Bay
High town
Old Netley
Woolston
Newtown
Crosshouse
Power Station
Cracknore Hard
Pooksgreen
SEE PAGE 409
Eastern Docks
Marchwood
Weston
Swanwick Wood
Burridge
Bursledon
Butlocks Heath
Swanwick
Staplewood Hill
156
Marchwood Park
Netley Abbey
Lower Swanwick
Whiteley
Hythe Marina Village
Hythe
Dibden
Applemore
Hound
Sarisbury
Park Gate
Ipley Inclosure
Marchwood Inclosure
Dibden Bottom
Hamble-le-Rice
Holly Hill Woodland Park
Locks Heath
Dibden Purlieu
Langdown
Frostlane
Warsash
Titchfield Common
Buttsash
Fleetend
Abshot
Kings Hat Inclosure
The Noads
Beaulieu Heath
Fawley Inclosure
Cadland Creek
Newtown
Hardley
Hook
Hook Park
Hartford Heath
Stonyford Pond
Little Holbury
Oil Refinery
Chilling
Solent Breezes
Brownwich
Holbury
Fawley
National Motor Museum
Hill Top
Ashlett
Beaulieu Abbey
Stonehills
Beaulieu Palace House
Moonhills Copse
Roughdown
Fawley Power Station
Beaulieu
Blackfield
Badminston Common
Ower
Calshot
Bunkers Hill
Otterwood
Kings Copse Inclosure
Mopley Pond
THE SOLENT
Bailey's Hard
Spearbed Copse
Sprat's Down
Hillhead
Gilbury Hard
Langley
West Common
Eaglehurst
Keeping
Exbury
Stanswood Bay
Ashen Wood
Bucklers Hard
Buckler's Hard Maritime Museum
Exbury Gardens
Haxland Pits
Newhouse Copse
Tylers Copse
Lower Exbury
Newlands Plantation
Coopers Wood
Lepe
Stone Points
East Cowes
Gins
Stansore Point
Horsemoor Copse
St. Leonards Grange
Stone Point
Bergerie
Needs Ore Point
East End
Sowley Pond
Southampton Water
River Test
River Itchen
River Hamble
Beaulieu River
M27
M3
M271
A27
A35
A33
A326
A3025
A3024
A334
A3051
A3057
B3054
B3053
B3033
B3035
B3036
B3037
B3342
B3354
B3397

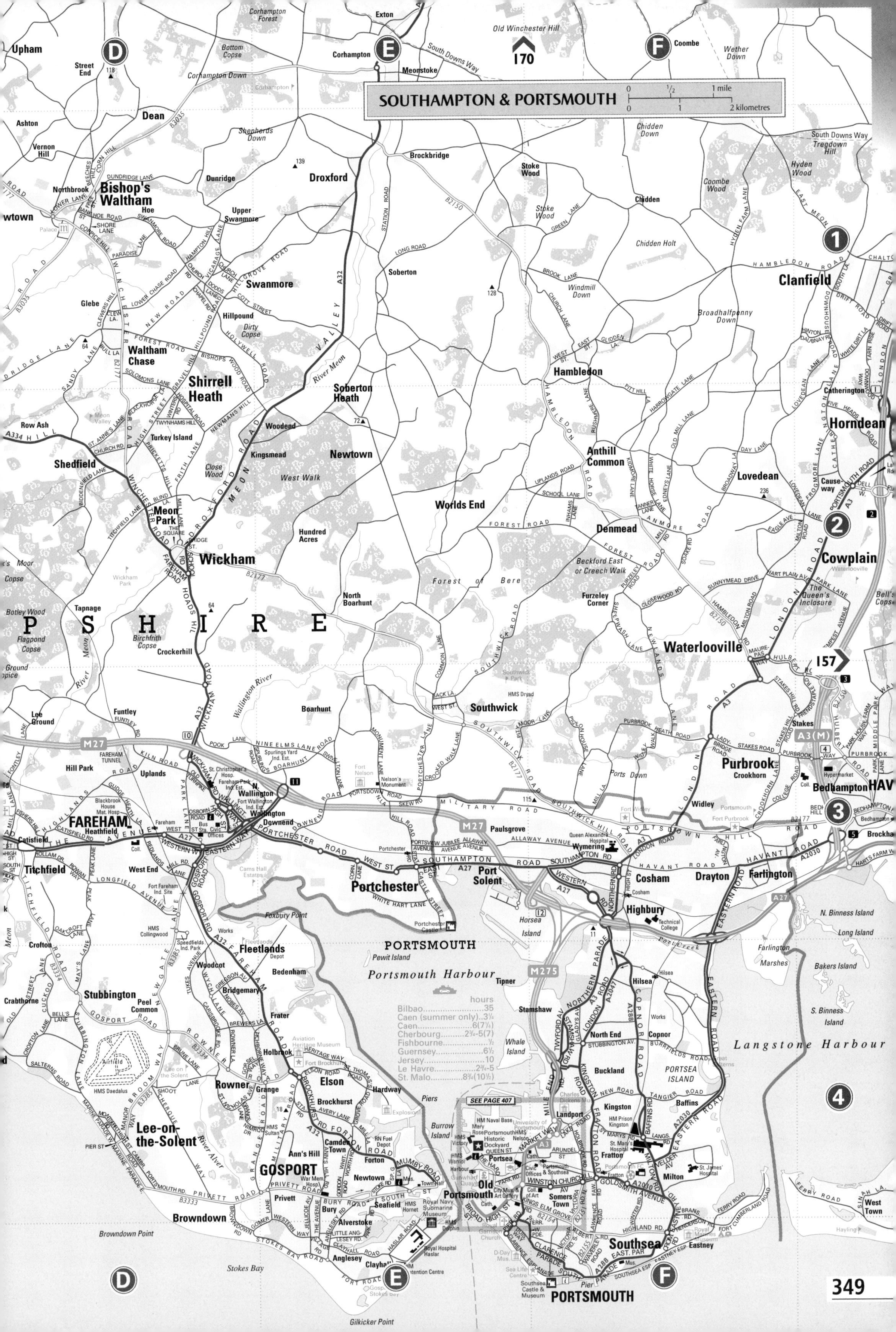
SOUTHAMPTON & PORTSMOUTH
0 1/2 1 mile
0 1 2 kilometres
Old Winchester Hill
170
157
SEE PAGE 407
Upham
Street End
Bottom Copse
Corhampton Forest
Exton
Corhampton
Meonstoke
Corhampton Down
South Downs Way
Coombe
Wether Down
Dean
Ashton
Vernon Hill
Shepherds Down
Brockbridge
Droxford
Dunridge
Northbrook
Bishop's Waltham
Hoe
Upper Swanmore
Stoke Wood
Chidden Down
Chidden
Chidden Holt
Hyden Wood
Coombe Wood
Tregown Hill
Soberton
Swanmore
Hillpound
Dirty Copse
Glebe
Windmill Down
Clanfield
Broadhalfpenny Down
Waltham Chase
Shirrell Heath
Hambledon
Soberton Heath
Catherington
Horndean
Row Ash
Turkey Island
Woodend
Kingsmead
Newtown
West Walk
Anthill Common
Lovedean
Shedfield
Close Wood
Meon Park
Worlds End
Causeway
Denmead
Hundred Acres
Wickham
Beckford East or Creech Walk
Cowplain
Forest of Bere
Furzeley Corner
The Queen's Inclosure
North Boarhunt
Tapnage
Botley Wood
Flagpond Copse
Birchfrith Copse
Crockerhill
Waterlooville
P S H I R E
River Meon
Wallington River
Southwick
HMS Dryad
Boarhunt
Funtley
Lee Ground
Stakes
Purbrook
Crookhorn
Bedhampton
Hill Park
Uplands
Fareham Tunnel
Nelson's Monument
Ports Down
Widley
Fort Nelson
FAREHAM
Heathfield
Paulsgrove
Wymering
Catisfield
Titchfield
West End
Portchester
Port Solent
Cosham
Drayton
Farlington
Portchester Castle
Highbury
Horsea Island
N. Binness Island
Long Island
Foxbury Point
PORTSMOUTH
Pewit Island
Portsmouth Harbour
Tipner
Fleetlands
Bedenham
Crofton
Stubbington
Peel Common
Bridgemary
Frater
Farlington Marshes
Bakers Island
Hilsea
Stamshaw
S. Binness Island
Crabthorne
North End
Copnor
Langstone Harbour
Whale Island
Holbrook
Rowner
Elson
Buckland
PORTSEA ISLAND
Lee-on-the-Solent
HMS Daedalus
Grange
Brockhurst
Hardway
Kingston
Baffins
Ann's Hill
Camden Town
Burrow Island
Landport
GOSPORT
Newtown
Portsea
Fratton
Milton
Old Portsmouth
Somers Town
Browndown
Privett
Bury
Seafield
Alverstoke
Southsea
Eastney
Browndown Point
Anglesey
Clayhall
Stokes Bay
Gilkicker Point
West Town
hours
Bilbao...........35
Caen (summer only)..3 1/4
Caen...............6 (7 1/4)
Cherbourg..........2 3/4-5 (7)
Fishbourne.........1/2
Guernsey...........6 1/2
Jersey.............10
Le Havre...........2 3/4-5
St. Malo...........8 3/4 (10 1/2)
M27
M275
A3(M)
A27
A32
A3
A2030
B2177
B2150
D
E
F
1
2
3
4

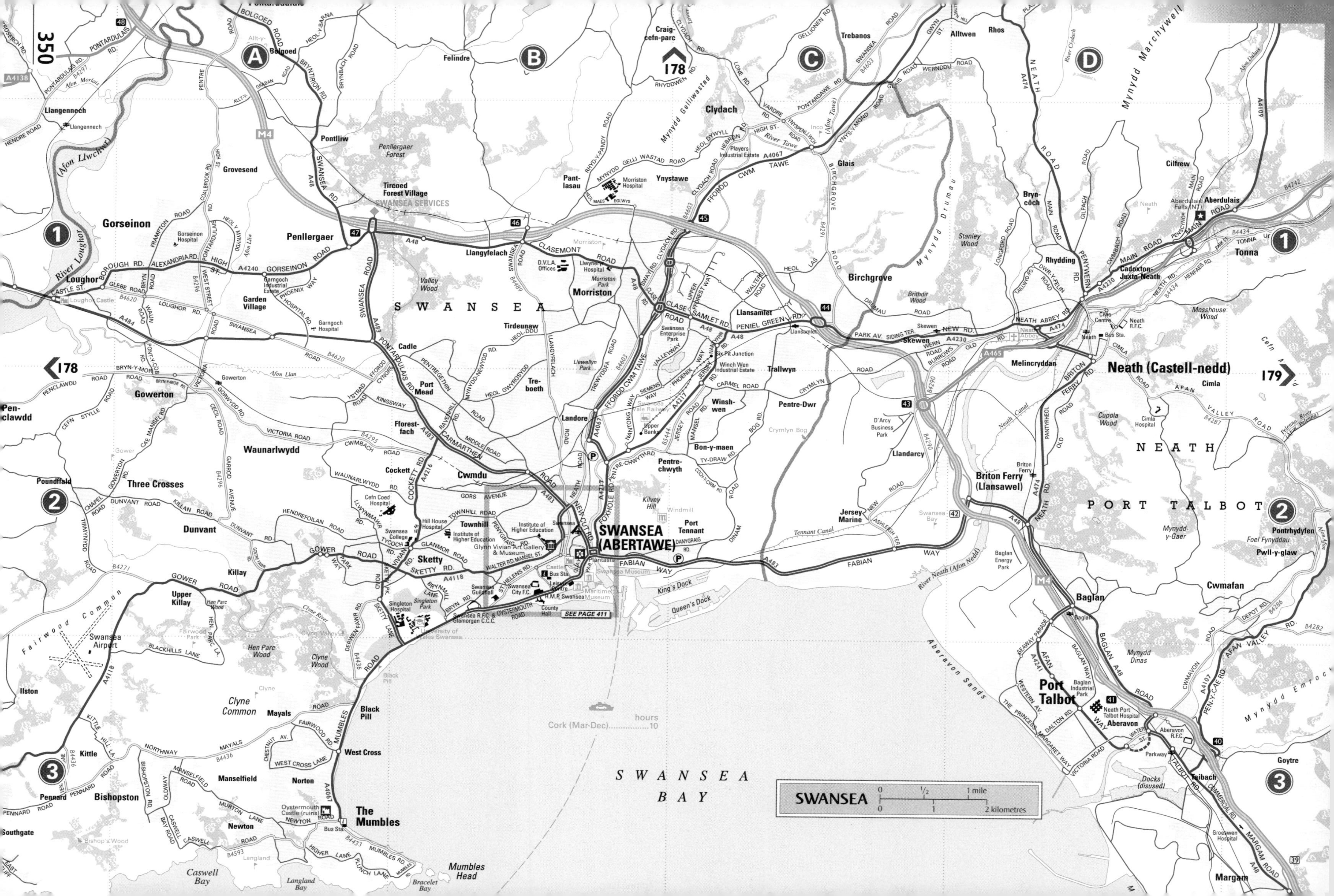

SWANSEA
0 1/2 1 mile
0 1 2 kilometres
SWANSEA BAY
SWANSEA (ABERTAWE)
SEE PAGE 411
Neath (Castell-nedd)
NEATH PORT TALBOT
SWANSEA
178
179
Port Talbot
Briton Ferry (Llansawel)
Gorseinon
Loughor
Penllergaer
Pontlliw
Gowerton
Waunarlwydd
Three Crosses
Dunvant
Killay
Upper Killay
Sketty
Cwmdu
Cockett
Fforest-fach
Port Mead
Cadle
Tirdeunaw
Tre-boeth
Landore
Morriston
Llangyfelach
Clydach
Ynystawe
Glais
Birchgrove
Llansamlet
Trallwyn
Pentre-Dwr
Winsh-wen
Bon-y-maen
Pentre-chwyth
Port Tennant
Jersey Marine
Llandarcy
Skewen
Melincryddan
Cimla
Baglan
Aberavon
Cwmafan
Taibach
Margam
Goytre
Tonna
Aberdulais
Cadoxton-Juxta-Neath
Rhydding
Bryn-côch
Alltwen
Rhos
Trebanos
Craig-cefn-parc
Felindre
Pant-lasau
Cilfrew
Penyrheol
Garden Village
Grovesend
Llangennech
Pen-clawdd
Poundffald
Ilston
Kittle
Pennard
Bishopston
Southgate
Manselfield
Newton
Norton
Mayals
West Cross
Black Pill
The Mumbles
Mumbles Head
Caswell Bay
Langland Bay
Bracelet Bay
Clyne Common
Fairwood Common
Swansea Airport
Tircoed Forest Village
SWANSEA SERVICES
Penllergaer Forest
Mynydd Gelliwastad
Mynydd Drumau
Mynydd Marchywell
Aberavon Sands
King's Dock
Queen's Dock
Cork (Mar-Dec) hours 10
River Loughor
River Tawe
River Neath (Afon Nedd)
Tennant Canal
Neath Canal
Crymlyn Bog

CARDIFF & NEWPORT
0 1/2 1 mile
0 1 2 kilometres
BRISTOL CHANNEL
CAERPHILLY
CARDIFF
NEWPORT
RHONDDA CYNON TAFF
VALE OF GLAMORGAN
Caerphilly
Bedwas
Machen
Rogerstone
Bettws
Pontymister
Michaelston-y-Fedw
Castleton
Marshfield
St. Brides Wentlooge
Peterstone Wentlooge
St.Mellons
Llanrumney
Rumney
Trowbridge
Newton
Wentloog
Whitchurch
Llandaff
Riverside
Butetown
Grangetown
Splott
Roath
Cathays
Heath
Llanishen
Lisvane
Cyncoed
Pentwyn
Pontprennau
Tongwynlais
Radyr
Fairwater
St. Fagans
Duffryn
Maes-glas
Pillgwenlly
Nash
Uskmouth
Broadstreet Common
Pye Corner
Bristol Channel
SEE PAGE 392
180
179
180
180

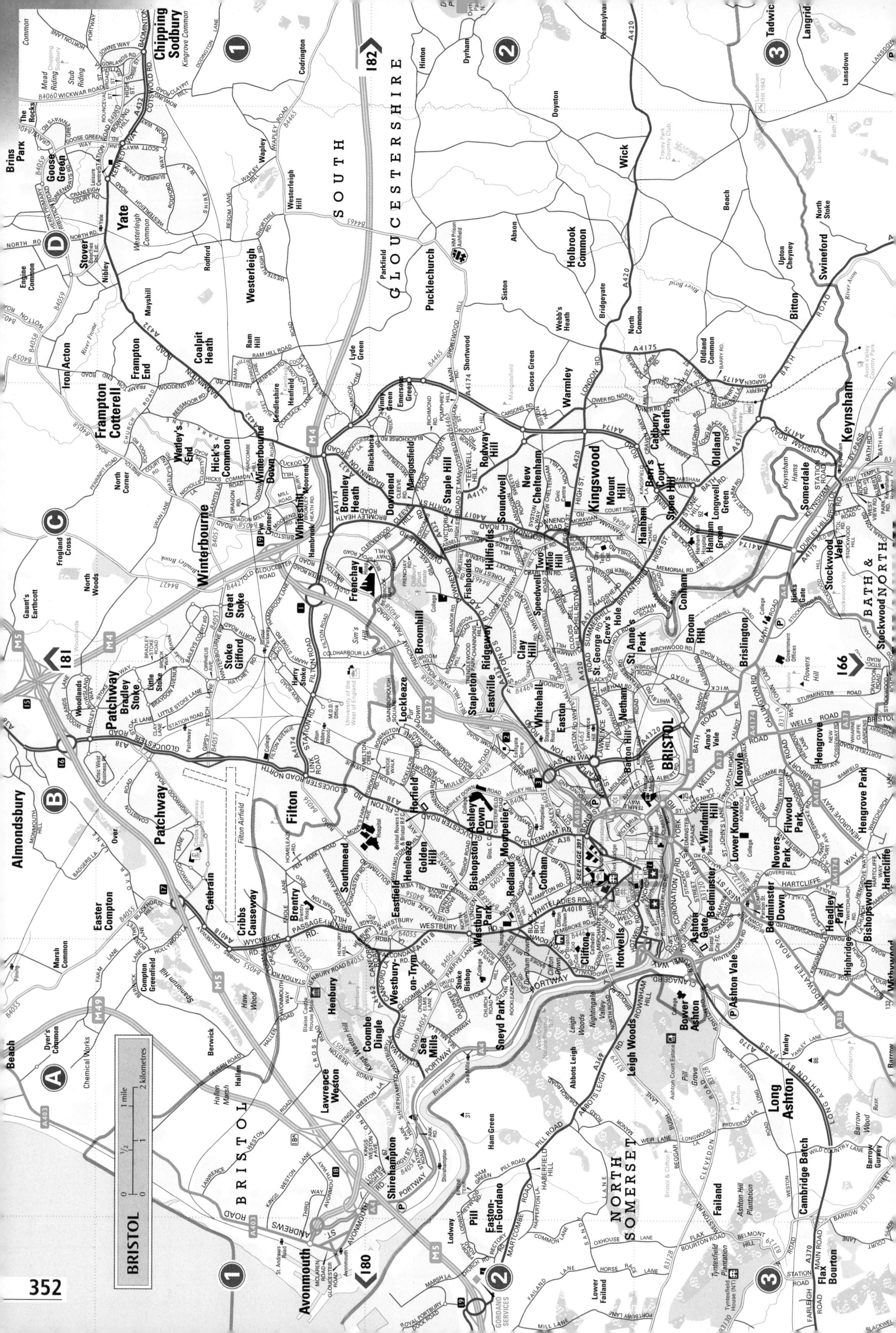

BRISTOL
0 1/2 1 mile
0 1 2 kilometres
SOUTH GLOUCESTERSHIRE
NORTH SOMERSET
BRISTOL
Chipping Sodbury
Yate
Frampton Cotterell
Winterbourne
Almondsbury
Patchway
Bradley Stoke
Stoke Gifford
Filton
Avonmouth
Shirehampton
Lawrence Weston
Henbury
Coombe Dingle
Sea Mills
Westbury-on-Trym
Southmead
Horfield
Henleaze
Redland
Clifton
Hotwells
Cotham
Montpelier
Easton
Eastville
Fishponds
Stapleton
Frenchay
Downend
Mangotsfield
Staple Hill
Kingswood
Hanham
Keynsham
Brislington
Knowle
Bedminster
Ashton Vale
Long Ashton
Leigh Woods
Pill
Easton-in-Gordano
Failand
Flax Bourton
Hengrove Park
Hartcliffe
Whitchurch
Bishopsworth
Warmley
Pucklechurch
Wick
Emersons Green
Oldland
Bitton
Swineford
Saltford
Westerleigh
Coalpit Heath
Hambrook
Whiteshill
Cribbs Causeway
Compton Greenfield
Easter Compton
Pilning
Hallen
Berwick
Filton Airfield
River Avon
180
181
182
166

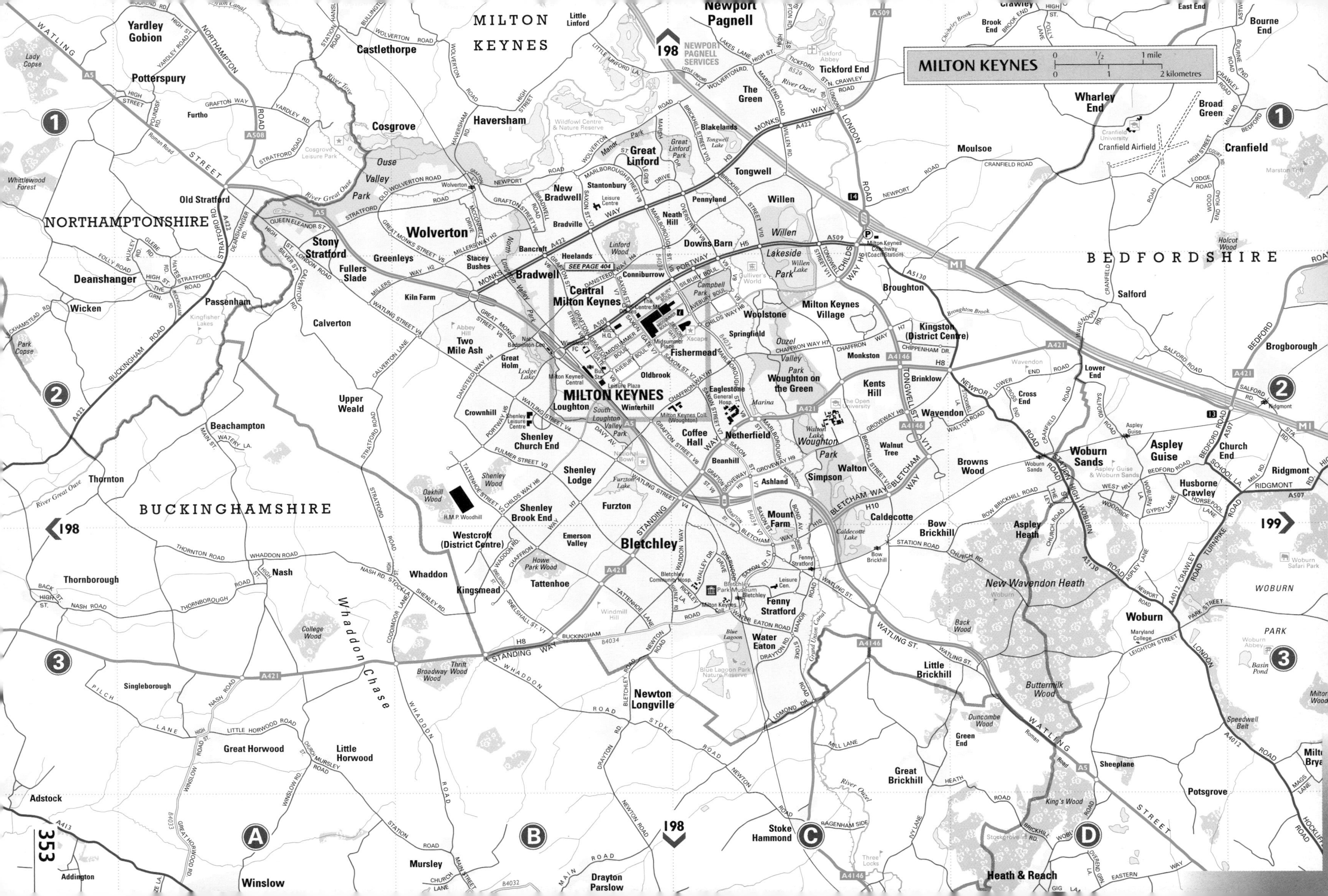
MILTON KEYNES
0 1/2 1 mile
0 1 2 kilometres
MILTON KEYNES
BEDFORDSHIRE
BUCKINGHAMSHIRE
NORTHAMPTONSHIRE
Newport Pagnell
NEWPORT PAGNELL SERVICES
Central Milton Keynes
SEE PAGE 404
Wolverton
Bletchley
Stony Stratford
Bradwell
Fenny Stratford
Woburn
Woburn Sands
Aspley Guise
Cranfield
Wavendon
Newton Longville
Great Horwood
Winslow
Deanshanger
Yardley Gobion
Potterspury
Old Stratford
Cosgrove
Castlethorpe
Haversham
Heath & Reach
Great Brickhill
Little Brickhill
Woburn Sands
Ridgmont
Salford
Moulsoe
Broughton
Kingston (District Centre)
Westcroft (District Centre)
New Wavendon Heath
Whaddon Chase
198
199
M1
A5
A421
A422
A509
A4146
A5130
A507
A4012
14
13

LONDON - WEST
0
1/2
1 mile
1
2 kilometres
HENDON
WEMBLEY
HARROW
EALING
ACTON
HAMPSTEAD
FINCHLEY
MARYLEBONE
PADDINGTON
EDGWARE
STANMORE
PINNER
NORTHOLT
GREENFORD
WILLESDEN
KILBURN
CAMDEN
BRENT
356
185

CHELSEA
BATTERSEA
FULHAM
HAMMERSMITH
WANDSWORTH
PUTNEY
BARNES
CHISWICK
KEW
RICHMOND
TWICKENHAM
ISLEWORTH
HOUNSLOW
HESTON
WIMBLEDON
MERTON
MORDEN
MITCHAM
KINGSTON upon THAMES
Richmond Park
Wimbledon Common
Hampton Court Park
Bushy Park
River Thames
357
171

LONDON - EAST
0 ½ 1 mile
0 1 2 kilometres
186
354
SEE PAGES 376-377

WOOLWICH
Thamesmead West
Plumstead
Shooters Hill
Avery Hill
New Eltham
Chislehurst
Chislehurst West
Petts Wood
New Charlton
Charlton
Eltham
Mottingham
Elmstead
Sundridge
Bickley
Southborough
BROMLEY
Widmore
GREENWICH
Kidbrooke
Blackheath Park
Lee
Grove Park
Plaistow
Cubitt Town
Millwall
Blackheath
Hither Green
Downham
Shortlands
Park Langley
Deptford
Lewisham
Catford
Southend
Bellingham
St. John's
Ladywell
Brockley
New Cross
New Cross Gate
Honor Oak Park
Bell Green
Lower Sydenham
Forest Hill
Beckenham
New Beckenham
Elmers End
Upper Elmers End
Monks Orchard
BERMONDSEY
Nunhead
Honor Oak
SYDENHAM
Penge
Peckham
East Dulwich
Upper Sydenham
Anerley
CAMBERWELL
DULWICH
Upper Norwood
South Norwood
Woodside
Selhurst
Walworth
Herne Hill
West Dulwich
Tulse Hill
West Norwood
Norwood
Thornton Heath
Brixton
Norwood New Town
LAMBETH
Kennington
Stockwell
Streatham Hill
STREATHAM
Norbury
Streatham Vale
Vauxhall
South Lambeth
Clapham
Clapham Park
Pimlico
BATTERSEA
Balham
Streatham Park
Furzedown
Tooting Graveney
Collier's Wood
MITCHAM
Brompton
LONDON

WEST MIDLANDS
0 1/2 1 mile
0 1 2 kilometres
STAFFORDSHIRE
WORCESTERSHIRE
WOLVERHAMPTON
DUDLEY
SANDWELL
STOURBRIDGE
HALESOWEN
WALSALL
208
A
B
C
1
2
3
4
Castlecroft
Bradmore
Merry Hill
Blakenhall
Goldthorn Park
Penn
Colton Hills
Lower Penn
Spring Hill
Orton
Wombourne
Himley
Blakeley
Sedgley
Gospel End
Gornalwood
Redhall
Upper Gornal
Lower Gornal
Ruiton
Wall Heath
Kingswinford
Ashwood
Summer Hill
Mount Pleasant
Wordsley
Buckpool
Hawbush
Audnam
Amblecote
Wollaston
High Park
Gigmill
Brockmoor
Bromley
Pensnett
Woodside
Brierley Hill
Withymoor Village
Quarry Bank
Lye
Stambermill
The Hayes
Wollescote
Netherton
Baptist End
Primrose Hill
Dudley Wood
Cradley Heath
Cradley
Overend
Belle Vale
Hawne
Hasbury
Spring Hill
Old Hill
Haden Cross
Cockshot
Coombeswood
Blackheath
Rowley Regis
Ross
Hurst Green
Quinton
Lapal
Moor Street
Woodgate
Bartley Green
California
Ridgacre
Harborne
Warley
Bearwood
Smethwick
Langley Green
Causeway Green
Bristnall Fields
Langley
Rood End
Oldbury
Portway
The Knowle
Darby End
Bowling Green
Tividale
Brades Village
Rounds Green
Oakham
Darby's Hill
Dixon's Green
Kate's Hill
Russell's Hall
London Fields
Eve Hill
Burnt Tree
Dudley Port
Tipton
Tipton Green
Horseley Heath
Ocker Hill
Toll End
Princes End
Summer Hill
Bloomfield
Wednesbury Oak
Great Bridge
Swan Village
Guns Village
West Bromwich
Hill Top
Golds Green
Black Lake
Harvills Hawthorn
Hateley Heath
Charlemont
Churchfield
Stone Cross
Friar Park
Mesty Croft
The Woods
The Delves
Yew Tree
Wednesbury
Kings Hill
Fallings Heath
Wood Green
Church Hill
Moxley
Darlaston
Darlaston Green
Woods Bank
Bescot
Pleck
Caldmore
Palfrey
The Chuckery
Bentley
Willenhall
Moseley
Portobello
Stow Lawn
Monmore Green
Priestfield
Parkfield
Ettingshall
Bilston
Spring Vale
Lanesfield
Ettingshall Park
Cinder Hill
Coseley
Hurst Hill
Roseville
Bramford
Wallbrook
Bradley
Lower Bradley
Hagley
West Hagley
Blakedown
Churchill
Broome
Holy Cross
Clent
Romsley
Romsley Hill
Dayhouse Bank
Hunnington
Illey
Frankley
Rubery
Rednal
Longbridge
Northfield
Turves Green
West Heath
Shenley Fields
Weoley Castle
Lodge Hill
Belbroughton
Bell End
Drayton
Fairfield
Cofton Hackett
M5
M6
FRANKLEY SERVICES

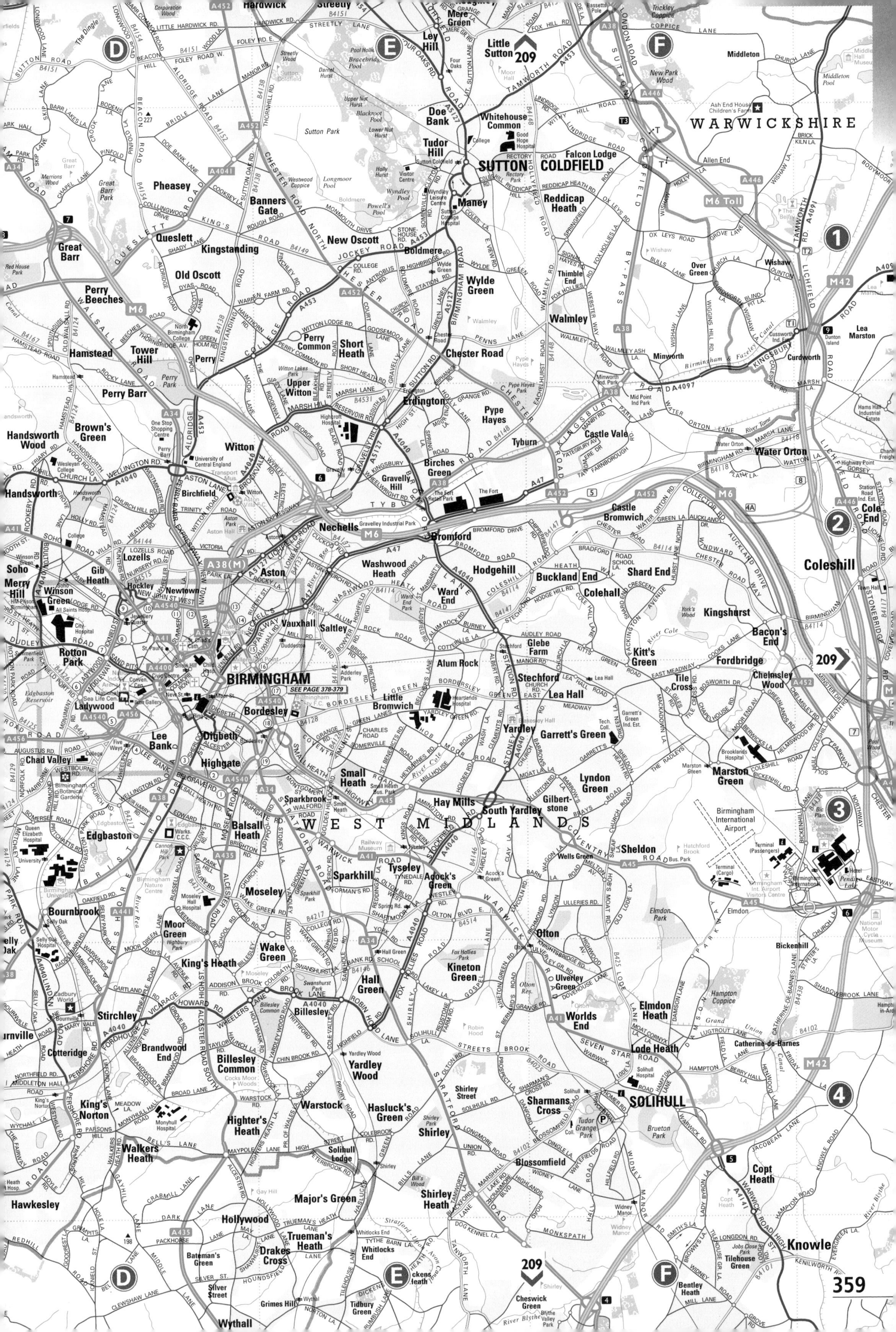
WARWICKSHIRE
WEST MIDLANDS
BIRMINGHAM
SEE PAGE 378-379
SUTTON COLDFIELD
SOLIHULL
Little Sutton
209
Mere Green
Ley Hill
Four Oaks
Middleton
Doe Bank
Whitehouse Common
Tudor Hill
Falcon Lodge
Reddicap Heath
Maney
Sutton Park
Pheasey
Banners Gate
New Oscott
Boldmere
Wylde Green
Great Barr
Queslett
Kingstanding
Old Oscott
Perry Beeches
Hamstead
Tower Hill
Perry
Perry Common
Short Heath
Chester Road
Walmley
Minworth
Curdworth
Lea Marston
Perry Barr
Upper Witton
Erdington
Pype Hayes
Handsworth Wood
Brown's Green
Witton
Tyburn
Castle Vale
Water Orton
Birches Green
Gravelly Hill
Handsworth
Birchfield
Nechells
Bromford
Castle Bromwich
Coleshill
Cole End
Lozells
Aston
Washwood Heath
Hodgehill
Buckland End
Shard End
Soho
Gib Heath
Newtown
Ward End
Colehall
Kingshurst
Merry Hill
Winson Green
Hockley
Vauxhall
Saltley
Bacon's End
Rotton Park
Alum Rock
Glebe Farm
Kitt's Green
Fordbridge
Chelmsley Wood
Stechford
Lea Hall
Tile Cross
Ladywood
Little Bromwich
Bordesley
Yardley
Garrett's Green
Lee Bank
Digbeth
Chad Valley
Highgate
Small Heath
Lyndon Green
Marston Green
Sparkbrook
Hay Mills
South Yardley
Gilbertstone
Balsall Heath
Edgbaston
Birmingham International Airport
Sheldon
Sparkhill
Tyseley
Acock's Green
Moseley
Bournbrook
Elmdon
Moor Green
Wake Green
King's Heath
Olton
Kineton Green
Ulverley Green
Bickenhill
Hall Green
Stirchley
Billesley
Elmdon Heath
Worlds End
Brandwood End
Cotteridge
Lode Heath
Catherine-de-Barnes
Billesley Common
Yardley Wood
King's Norton
Highter's Heath
Warstock
Hasluck's Green
Shirley
Shirley Street
Sharmans Cross
Walkers Heath
Solihull Lodge
Blossomfield
Copt Heath
Hawkesley
Major's Green
Shirley Heath
Hollywood
Trueman's Heath
Drakes Cross
Whitlocks End
Knowle
Bateman's Green
Silver Street
Grimes Hill
Tidbury Green
Cheswick Green
Bentley Heath
Wythall
M6
M6 Toll
M42
A38(M)
A34
A38
A45
A41
A435
A452
A453
A4040
A4540

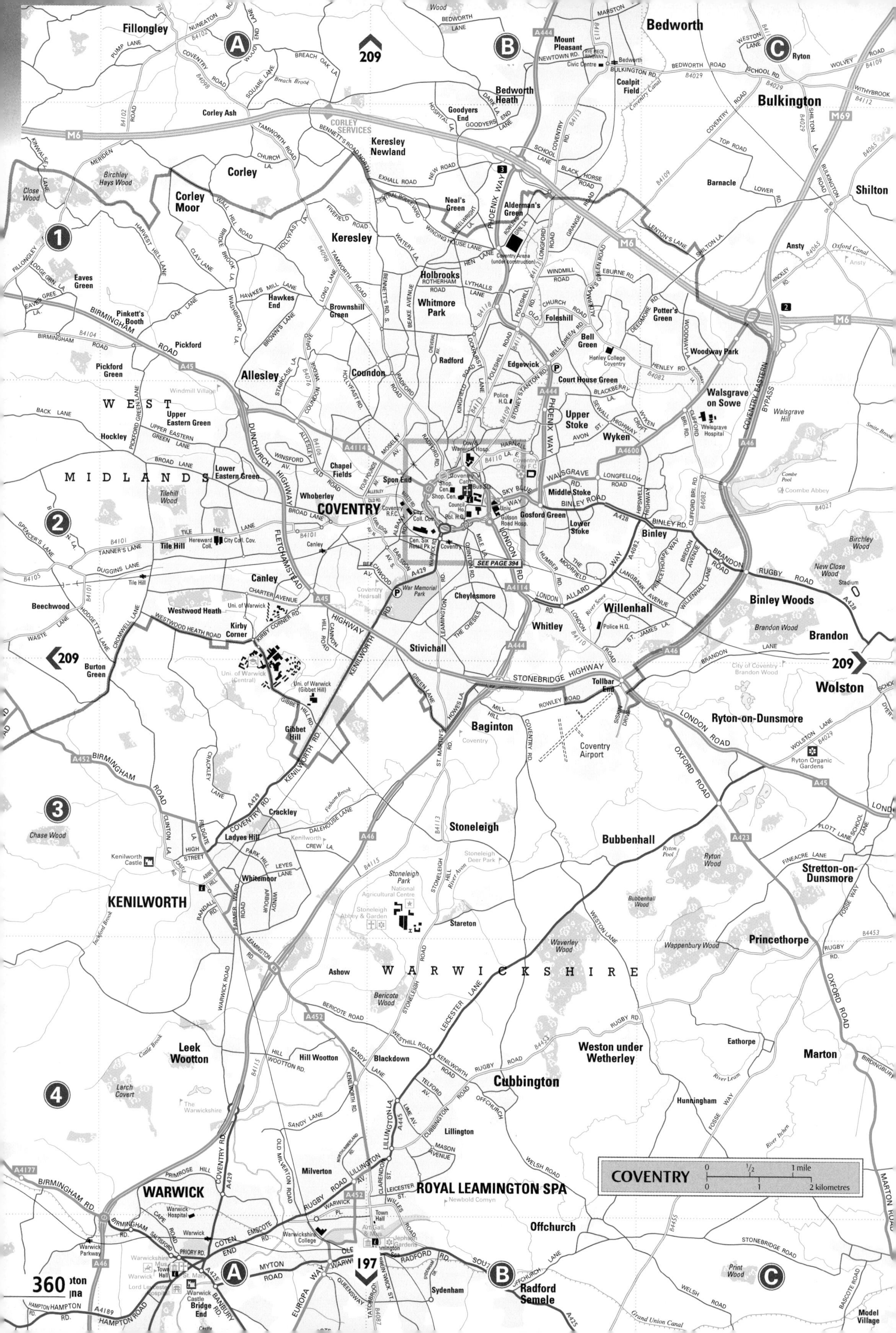
COVENTRY
SEE PAGE 394
209
197
COVENTRY 0 1/2 1 mile 0 1 2 kilometres
WEST MIDLANDS
WARWICKSHIRE
Fillongley
Bedworth
Bedworth Heath
Bulkington
Ryton
Shilton
Barnacle
Ansty
Corley Ash
Corley
Corley Moor
Corley Services
Keresley Newland
Keresley
Neal's Green
Alderman's Green
Holbrooks
Whitmore Park
Brownshill Green
Hawkes End
Eaves Green
Pinkett's Booth
Pickford
Pickford Green
Allesley
Coundon
Radford
Edgewick
Foleshill
Bell Green
Potter's Green
Woodway Park
Court House Green
Walsgrave on Sowe
Upper Stoke
Wyken
Hockley
Upper Eastern Green
Lower Eastern Green
Chapel Fields
Spon End
Whoberley
Middle Stoke
Gosford Green
Lower Stoke
Binley
Tile Hill
Canley
Beechwood
Westwood Heath
Kirby Corner
Cheylesmore
Willenhall
Whitley
Stivichall
Binley Woods
Brandon
Burton Green
Wolston
Tollbar End
Baginton
Coventry Airport
Ryton-on-Dunsmore
Gibbet Hill
Crackley
Ladyes Hill
Whitemoor
Stoneleigh
Bubbenhall
KENILWORTH
Stretton-on-Dunsmore
Stareton
Princethorpe
Ashow
Leek Wootton
Hill Wootton
Blackdown
Weston under Wetherley
Cubbington
Eathorpe
Marton
Hunningham
Lillington
Milverton
ROYAL LEAMINGTON SPA
WARWICK
Offchurch
Sydenham
Radford Semele
Bridge End
Model Village
M6
M69
A45
A46
A444
A452
A423
A429
A428
A425
A4114
A4600
A4177
A4189

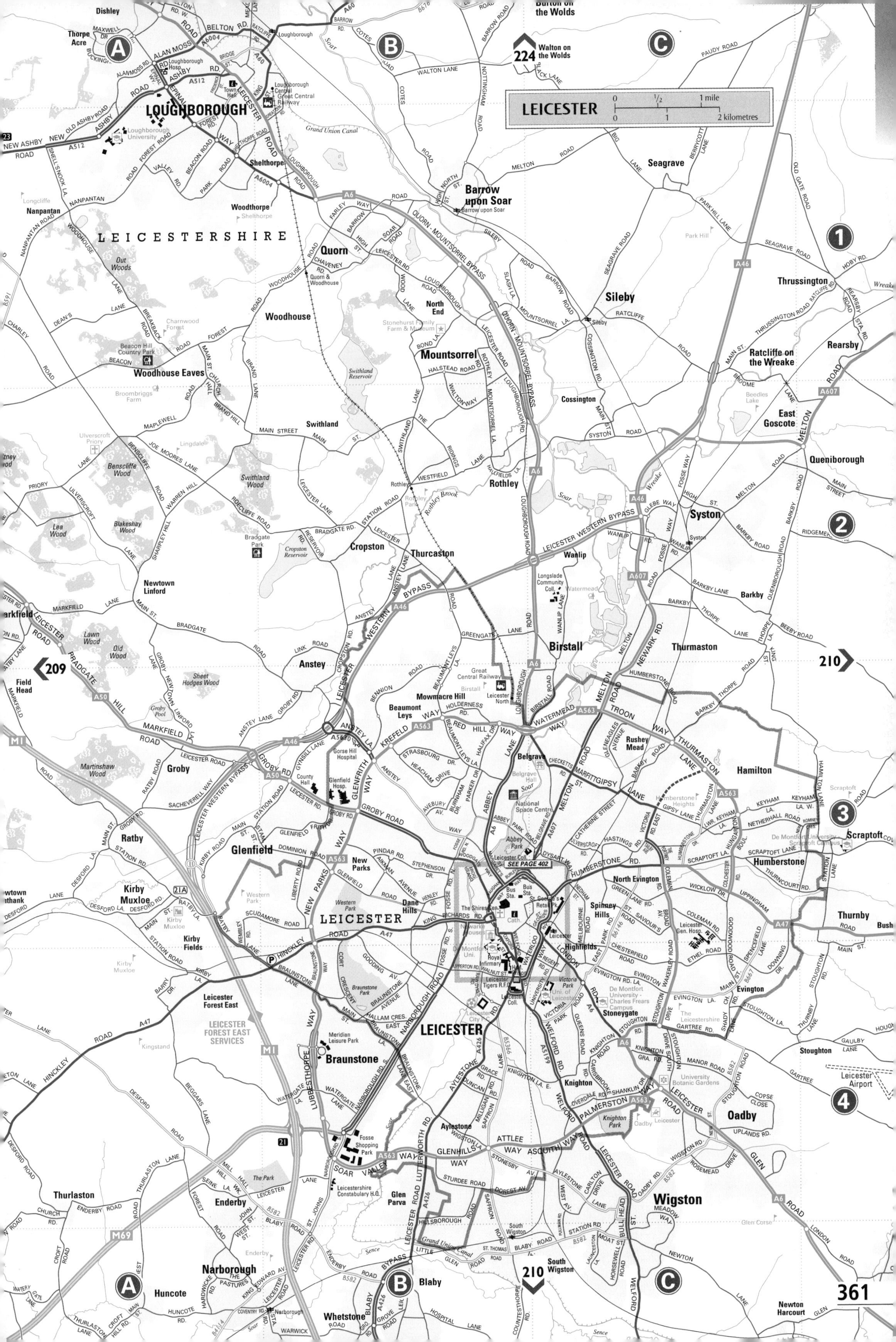
LEICESTER
0 1/2 1 mile
0 1 2 kilometres
A
B
C
1
2
3
4
224
Walton on the Wolds
209
210
LEICESTERSHIRE
Dishley
Thorpe Acre
LOUGHBOROUGH
Loughborough
Loughborough Hosp.
Loughborough University
Town Hall
Loughborough Central Great Central Railway
Grand Union Canal
Shelthorpe
Nanpantan
Longcliffe
Woodthorpe
Shelthorpe
Barrow upon Soar
Seagrave
Park Hill
Thrussington
Rearsby
Ratcliffe on the Wreake
East Goscote
Queniborough
Quorn
Quorn & Woodhouse
Woodhouse
Out Woods
Charnwood Forest
Beacon Hill Country Park
Woodhouse Eaves
Broombriggs Farm
North End
Stonehurst Family Farm & Museum
Mountsorrel
Swithland Reservoir
Swithland
Sileby
Cossington
Rothley
Ulverscroft Priory
Lingdale
Bencliffe Wood
Swithland Wood
Lea Wood
Blakeshay Wood
Bradgate Park
Cropston Reservoir
Cropston
Thurcaston
Syston
Wanlip
Longslade Community Coll.
Watermead
Birstall
Barkby
Thurmaston
Newtown Linford
Markfield
Lawn Wood
Old Wood
Field Head
Sheet Hedges Wood
Groby Pool
Anstey
Great Central Railway
Leicester North
Mowmacre Hill
Beaumont Leys
Rushey Mead
Belgrave
Belgrave Hall
National Space Centre
Hamilton
Humberstone Heights
Scraptoft
De Montfort University Scraptoft Campus
Martinshaw Wood
Groby
Gorse Hill Hospital
County Hall
Glenfield Hosp.
Ratby
Glenfield
New Parks
Abbey Park
Leicester Coll.
SEE PAGE 402
Western Park
LEICESTER
Kirby Muxloe
Kirby Fields
Dane Hills
The Shires
Bus Sta.
Cath.
St George's Retail Pk.
North Evington
Spinney Hills
Leicester Gen. Hosp.
Humberstone
Thurnby
Highfields
Newarke Houses
De Montfort Uni.
Royal Infirmary
Leicester Tigers R.F.C.
Victoria Park
Uni. of Leicester
De Montfort University - Charles Frears Campus
Stoneygate
Evington
The Leicestershire
Leicester City F.C.
Braunstone Park
Leicester Forest East
LEICESTER FOREST EAST SERVICES
Kingstand
Meridian Leisure Park
Braunstone
LEICESTER
Aylestone
Knighton
University Botanic Gardens
Oadby
Stoughton
Leicester Airport
Knighton Park
Fosse Shopping Park
The Park
Thurlaston
Enderby
Leicestershire Constabulary H.Q.
Glen Parva
South Wigston
Wigston
Glen Corse
Narborough
Huncote
Whetstone
Blaby
South Wigston
Newton Harcourt
M1
M69
A6
A46
A47
A50
A60
A426
A512
A563
A607
A6004
B5366
B582
Grand Union Canal
Soar
Sence
Wreake
Rothley Brook
LEICESTER WESTERN BYPASS
QUORN - MOUNTSORREL BYPASS
HINCKLEY ROAD
MELTON ROAD
NARBOROUGH ROAD
AYLESTONE
WELFORD RD.
LONDON RD.
UPPINGHAM
GROBY ROAD
ABBEY LANE
FOSSE WAY
NEWARK RD.
SOAR VALLEY WAY
GLENHILLS WAY
PALMERSTON WAY

A
B
C
1
2
3
4
223
SEE PAGE 395
DERBY
DERBYSHIRE
LEICESTERSH
Mount Pleasant
Blackbrook
Illcliffane
Turnditch
Cowers Lane
Shottlegate
Farnah Green
Hazelwood
Windley
Belper
Belper River Gardens
Derwent Valley Visitor Centre
Babington Hospital
Open Woodgate
Bargate
Milford
Holbrook Moor
Holbrook
Makeney
Duffield
Duffieldbank
Flaxholme
Weston Underwood
Kedlestone
Kedleston Park
Kedleston Hall
Quarndon
Little Eaton
Allestree
Allestree Park
Darley Abbey
Darley Abbey Park
Markeaton
Markeaton Park
Markeaton Park Craft Village
Mackworth
University of Derby (Kedleston Road)
University of Derby (Britannia Mill)
Little Chester
Tomlinson Ind. Est.
Meteor Centre
Racecourse Park
Derbyshire Constabulary HQ
Queen's Leisure Centre
Derbyshire County Cricket Club
The Council House
Bus Station
Derby Museum and Art Gallery
The Eagle Shopping Centre
Derbyshire Royal Infirmary
Royal Crown Derby Visitor Centre
Pride Park
Derby County FC
Wyvern Retail Park
Derby College (Pride Parkway Campus)
New Zealand
Derby College
Kingsway Retail Park
Derby City General Hospital
University of Derby (Mickleover Campus)
Mickleover
Littleover
Normanton
Rose Hill
Pear Tree
Osmaston
Osmaston Park Ind. Est.
Crewton
Alvaston
Boulton
Moorways Sports Complex
Rolls-Royce Works
Sunny Hill
Sinfin
Allenton
Shelton Lock
Chellaston
Mickleemeadow
Pastures
Findern
Stenson
Twyford
Willington
Barrow upon Trent
Swarkestone
Stanton by Bridge
Ingleby
Repton
Milton
Foremark
King's Newton
Melbourne
Melbourne Hall
Street Lane
Denby Pottery
Smithy Houses
Denby
Denby Bottles
Rawson Green
Kilburn
Lower Kilburn
Horsley
Horsley Woodhouse
Coxbench
Woodside
Brackley Gate
Morley Hayes
Breadsall Priory
Morley
Derby College (Broomfield Hall Campus)
Breadsall
Chaddesden Common
Breadsall Hilltop
Oakwood
Springwood Leisure Centre
Chaddesden
Cherrytree Hill
Locko Park
Spondon
Ockbrook
Borrowash
Dale Moor
Dale Abbey
Cross Hill
Loscoe
Loscoe Dam
Aldercar
Heanor
Langley Mill
Newlands
Langley
Common Side
Heanor Memorial Hospital
Heanor Gate
Heanor Gate Ind. Est.
Marlpool
Smalley
Shipley Lake
Shipley Park
American Adventure Theme Park
Ilkeston Community Hospital
Mapperley Reservoir
Mapperley
Shipley Common
Stanley Common
West Hallam
High Lane
Mannners Ind. Est.
Stanley
Kirk Hallam
Shacklecross
Draycott
Elvaston Castle Country Park
Elvaston
Ambaston
Thulston
Church Wilne
Great Wilne
Shardlow
Shardlow Service Area
The Grove Hospital
Cavendish Bridge
Aston-on-Trent
Weston-on-Trent
Castle Donington
Hemington
Donington Park
Donington Grand Prix Collection
Nottingham East Midlands
River Derwent
River Trent
River Ecclesbourne
Trent and Mersey Canal
A6
A38
A52
A50
A61
A111
A514
A516
A517
A608
A609
A610
A6005
A6096
A6007
A5132
A5111
A453
B5023
B5024
B6179
B5010
B5008
B5020
B587
B6013

DERBY & NOTTINGHAM
0 1/2 1 mile
0 1 2 kilometres
NOTTINGHAMSHIRE
NOTTINGHAM
Beauvale
Ruffs
Hucknall
Hazelgrove
Westville
Broomhill
Bestwood Village
Calverton
Moorgreen
Greasley
Beauvale
Newthorpe
Eastwood
Giltbrook
Newthorpe Common
Kimberley
Watnall
Nuthall
Awsworth
Swingate
Cossall Marsh
Cossall
Strelley
Trowell
Stanton Gate
Sandiacre
Stapleford
Toton
Long Eaton
Wilsthorpe
New Sawley
Sawley
Trentlock
Thrumpton
Ratcliffe on Soar
Kingston on Soar
Kegworth
Sutton Bonington
West Leake
East Leake
Rise Park
Top Valley
Bestwood
Bulwell
Hempshill Vale
Highbury Vale
Cinderhill
Old Basford
Broxtowe
Aspley
Whitemoor
Bilborough
Wollaton
Bramcote Hills
Bramcote
Lenton Abbey
Lenton
Radford
New Basford
Carrington
Sherwood
Mapperley
Mapperley Park
Daybrook
Redhill
Arnold
Woodthorpe
Porchester
Gedling
Lambley
Carlton
Thorneywood
St. Ann's
Sneinton
Colwick
Netherfield
Lace Market
Meadows
Dunkirk
Beeston
Chilwell
Rylands
Attenborough
Barton in Fabis
Clifton
Wilford
West Bridgford
Adbolton
Holme Pierrepont
Gamston
Edwalton
Tollerton
Mickleborough Hill
Brook Hill
Manor Park
Ruddington
Plumtree
Plumtree Park
Normanton-on-the-Wolds
Bradmore
Keyworth
Gotham
Bunny
Bunny Hill
Wysall
Sharpley Hill
Costock
Ruddington Moor
TROWELL SERVICES
SEE PAGE 405
224

STOKE-ON-TRENT
1 mile
2 kilometres
STAFFORDSHIRE
CHESHIRE
222
221
Cheddleton
Cheadle
Consall
Wetley Rocks
Cellarhead
Werrington
Bagnall
Stanley
Endon
Brown Edge
Milton
Abbey Hulton
Bucknall
Hanley
Burslem
Tunstall
Kidsgrove
Newchapel
Talke
Talke Pits
Red Street
Chesterton
Wolstanton
Etruria
Shelton
Stoke
Fenton
Longton
Meir
Blythe Bridge
Caverswall
Weston Coyney
Hulme
Ash Bank
Adderley Green
Ubberley
Berry Hill
Trentham
Hanford
Blurton
Newstead
Wedgwood
Clayton
Westlands
Newcastle-under-Lyme
Silverdale
Knutton
Keele
Madeley
Madeley Heath
Audley
Alsager
Church Lawton
Butt Lane
Hardings Wood
Radway Green
Barthomley
Betley
Balterley
Whitmore
Baldwin's Gate
Hanchurch
Acton
Butterton
Draycott in the Moors
Stonehouses
Dilhorne
Meir Heath
Longsdon
Denford
Dunwood
Birchall
Barnfields
Biddulph Road
Packmoor
Goldenhill
Sandyford
Smallthorne
Norton Green
Norton-in-the-Moors
Baddeley Edge
Baddeley Green
Light Oaks
Carmountside
Northwood
Cobridge
Middleport
Longport
Porthill
Bradwell
Cross Heath
May Bank
Springfields
Trent Vale
Oak Hill
Boothen
Mount Pleasant
Hollybush
Dresden
Lightwood
Normacot
Keele Services
SEE PAGE 410
M6
A50
A34
A500
A53
A52
A520
A522

SHEFFIELD
1 mile
2 kilometres
SOUTH YORKSHIRE
DERBYSHIRE
SEE PAGE 409
ROTHERHAM
SHEFFIELD
Grenoside
Oughtibridge
Worrall
Birley Edge
Birley Carr
Wadsley Bridge
Wadsley
Loxley
Hillsborough
Malin Bridge
Knowle Top
Stannington
Den Bank
Hallam Head
Carsick
Sandygate
Crookes
Crookesmoor
Walkley
Owlerton
Shirecliffe
Norwood
Parson Cross
Sheffield Lane Top
Southey Green
Longley
Shiregreen
Pismire Hill
Wincobank
Brightside
Grimesthorpe
Crabtree
Pitsmoor
Parkwood Springs
Burngreave
Attercliffe
Darnall
Greenland
Blackburn
Meadow Hall
Hill Top
Kimberworth Park
Kimberworth
Richmond Park
Masbrough
Bradgate
Tinsley
Ickles
Canklow
Broom
Moorgate
Clifton
Eastwood
East Dene
Herringthorpe
Dalton
Dalton Parva
Dalton Magna
Listerdale
Wickersley
Bramley
Hellaby
Maltby
Hooton Levitt
Whiston
Brinsworth
Catcliffe
Treeton
Upper Whiston
Morthen
Thurcroft
Brookhouse
Slade Hooton
Brampton en le Morthen
Laughton en le Morthen
Laughton Common
Dinnington
North Anston
South Anston
Todwick
Ulley
Aughton
Swallownest
Aston
Orgreave
Handsworth
Handsworth Hill
Park Hill
Manor Park
Manor Estate
Woodthorpe
Richmond
Stradbroke
Woodhouse
Woodhouse Mill
Normanton Spring
Intake
Hollins End
Gleadless Townend
Frecheville
Hackenthorpe
Beighton
Wales
Kiveton Park
Harthill
Thorpe Salvin
Norwood
Killamarsh
Halfway
Holbrook
Mosborough
Eckington
Renishaw
Spinkhill
Ridgeway
Marsh Lane
Middle Handley
Troway
Apperknowle
Dronfield
Dronfield Woodhouse
Holmesfield
Coal Aston
Batemoor
Jordanthorpe
Lowedges
Bradway
Greenhill
Norton
Meadow Head
Norton Woodseats
Hemsworth
Charnock Hall
Gleadless
Meersbrook Bank
Heeley
Arbourthorne
Lowfield
Highfield
Sharrow
Brincliffe
Nether Edge
Ecclesall
Carter Knowle
Beauchief
Abbeydale
Millhouses
Whirlow
Parkhead
Bents Green
Fulwood
Greystones
Ranmoor
Broomhill
Lydgate
Dore
Abbeydale Park
Totley Rise
Totley Brook
Totley
New Totley
Townhead
Causeway Head
Woodall Services
235
236

MERSEYSIDE
0 ½ 1 mile
0 1 2 kilometres
LIVERPOOL BAY
Crosby Channel
hours
Belfast 7½
Douglas 2½-4
Dublin 4-8
River Mersey
233
232
SEE PAGE 380-381
CROSBY
Great Crosby
Waterloo
Waterloo Park
Seaforth
Litherland
Aintree
Orrell
Northwood
Westvale
Kirkby
Southdene
Gillmoss
Croxteth
Knowsley
Fazakerley
BOOTLE
Walton
Dog and Gun
Norris Green
Kirkdale
Anfield
Clubmoor
Tuebrook
Stoneycroft
Fairfield
Everton
LIVERPOOL
Old Swan
Knotty Ash
Dovecot
Swanside
Page Moss
Roby
Huyton with Roby
Huyton Park
Court Hey
Bowring Park
Fincham
Woolfall Heath
Edge Hill
Princes Park
Childwall
Toxteth
Dingle
St Michael's
Hamlet
Mossley Hill
Calderstones
Aigburth
Otterspool
Grassendale
Allerton
Belle Vale
Netherley
Gateacre
Woolton
Halewood
Hunts Cross
Garston
Speke
Liverpool John Lennon Airport
New Brighton
WALLASEY
Liscard
Egremont
Poulton
Seacombe
Bidston
BIRKENHEAD
Claughton
Oxton
Tranmere
Prenton
Rock Ferry
Woodhey
Higher Bebington
Storeton
BEBINGTON
Lower Bebington
Port Sunlight
New Ferry
Bromborough Pool
MERSEYSIDE
Barnston
Brimstage
Poulton
Bromborough
Thornton Hough
Brookhurst
Eastham
Raby
Willaston
Hooton
Childer Thornton
ELLESMERE PORT
Overpool
Little Sutton
Greater Sutton
Whitby
Stanlow
Little Neston
Ness
Stanlow Banks
CHE
MERS

Rainford
Billinge
Garswood
Ashton in Makerfield
Golborne
GREATER MANCHESTER
Lowton
Moss Bank
Haydock
Blackbrook
Denton's Green
Newtown
Eccleston
ST. HELENS
West Park
Parr
Broad Oak
Derbyshire Hill
Newton-le-Willows
Wargrave
Vulcan Village
Town of Lowton
Ravenhead
Toll Bar
Grange Park
Portico
Thatto Heath
Peasley Cross
Sutton Oak
Collins Green
Prescot
Eccleston Park
Nutgrove
Sutton Heath
Marshall's Cross
Sutton Leach
Burtonwood
Winwick
Holt
Whiston Cross
Whiston
Rainhill
Clock Face
Sutton Manor
Rainhill Stoops
Windy Arbor
Hulme
Cinnamon Brow
Longford
Orford
Callands
Dallam
Bewsey
Old Hall
Lingley Green
WARRINGTON
Great Sankey
Bold Heath
Town End
Cronton
Lunts Heath
Farnworth
Penketh
Sankey Bridges
Howley
Latchford
Tarbock Green
Hough Green
Crow Wood
Cuerdley Cross
Appleton
Halton
Moss Bank
Stockton Heath
Lower Walton
Ditton
Ball o' Ditton
Kingsway
Lugs Dale
Hillcliffe
Cobbs
Woodend
WIDNES
Higher Walton
West Bank
Hale Bank
Moore
Appleton Park
HALTON
Astmoor
Keckwick
Castlefields
Norton
Hatton
Daresbury
Stretton
Hale
Halton Brook
RUNCORN
Halton
Grange
Halton Lea
Weston Point
Weston
Beechwood
Preston on the Hill
Preston Brook
Higher Whitley
Dutton
Lower Whitley
Sutton Weaver
Aston
Frodsham Bridge
Frodsham
Bradley
Marsh Green
Overton
Netherton
Acton Bridge
Helsby
Woodhouses
M6
M62
M56
M57
233
368

GREATER MANCHESTER
0 1/2 1 mile
0 1 2 kilometres
GREATER
CHESHIRE
WARRINGTON
234
367
234
A
B
C
1
2
3
4
Deane
Furnhill
Burnden
Darcy Lever
Little Lever
Radcliffe
Chew Moor
Hunger Hill
Wingates
Water's Nook
Lever Edge
Great Lever
Moses Gate
Harper Green
Nob End
Farnworth
New Bury
Highfield
Kearsley
Stoneclough
Prestolee
Cinder Hill
Ringley
Outwood
Chapel Field
Stand
Park Lane
Daisy Hill
Atherton
Dangerous Corner
Greenheys
Little Hulton
Hill Top
Kearsley Moss
Clifton
Clifton Junction
Clifton Green
Shakerley
Linnyshaw
Walkden
Wardley
Newtown
Pendlebury
Howe Bridge
Hindsford
Tyldesley
Tamer Lane End
Westleigh
Gin Pit
Parr Brow
Mosley Common
Roe Green
Swinton
Moorside
Hazelhurst
Worsley
Swinton Park
Irlams o' th' Height
LEIGH
Higher Folds
Blackmoor
Astley
Boothstown
Firs Lane
Bedford
Lark Hill
Higher Green
Alder Forest
Dales Brow
Pennington
Town Lane
Astley Green
Ellesmere Park
Monton
Seedley
Winton
Patricroft
Little Bolton
ECCLES
Moss Side
Botany Bay Wood
Lately Common
Aspull Common
Pocket Nook
Worsley Moss
Astley Moss
Peel Green
Barton upon Irwell
Dumplington
Glazebury
Barton Moss
Trafford Park
Chat Moss
Fowley Common
Twiss Green
Crofts Bank
Davyhulme
Culcheth
Larkhill
Higher Irlam
URMSTON
STRETFORD
Little Town
Irlam
Little Woolden Moss
Flixton
Cadishead Moss
Lower Irlam
Holcroft Moss
Glazebrook
Risley
Risley Moss
Cadishead
Carrington
Ashton upon Mersey
Sale Ees
SALE
Birchwood
Hollins Green
Partington
Carrington Moss
Woolston Moss
Pixton Moss
Woodhouses
Brooklands
Sinderland Green
Warburton
Broadheath
Mossbrow
Timperley
Oldfield Brow
Heatley
Carr Green
Dunham Woodhouses
Dunham Town
ALTRINCHAM
Statham
Rushgreen
Lymm
Little Bollington
Bowdon
Hale
Well Green
Rosehill
Bowgreen
Ashley Heath
Broomedge
Arthill
Booth Bank
Halebarns
Warburton Green
Sworton Heath
Ashley
Appleton Thorn
High Legh
Dunham Massey Hall, Park & Gardens (NT)
Manchester Ship Canal
Bridgewater Canal
Leeds & Liverpool Canal
M61
M60
M62
M6
M56
A6144(M)
EAST LANCASHIRE ROAD
LIVERPOOL ROAD
MANCHESTER ROAD

MANCHESTER
STOCKPORT
OLDHAM
ASHTON-UNDER-LYNE
CHESHIRE
Middleton
Rhodes
Chadderton
Royton
Shaw
Higginshaw
Heyside
Moorside
Watersheddings
Derker
Oldham Edge
Mumps
Greenacres
Austerlands
Scouthead
Grotton
Lees
Springhead
Moorhey
Glodwick
Werneth
Coppice
Hathershaw
Hollinwood
Failsworth
Woodhouses
Limehurst
Waterloo
Smallshaw
Hurst
Hazelhurst
Heyrod
Ridge Hill
Mossley
Quick Edge
Copley
Stalybridge
Dukinfield
Yew Tree
Audenshaw
Guide Bridge
Droylsden
Fairfield
Openshaw
Clayton
Newton Heath
Miles Platting
Collyhurst
Cheetham Hill
Cheetham
Crumpsall
Blackley
Higher Blackley
Charlestown
Moston
Harpurhey
Broughton Park
Higher Broughton
Lower Broughton
Kersal
Lower Kersal
Pendleton
Salford
Ordsall
Hulme
Old Trafford
Moss Side
Rusholme
Whalley Range
Chorlton-cum-Hardy
Fallowfield
Withington
Didsbury
West Didsbury
East Didsbury
Burnage
Ladybarn
Levenshulme
Longsight
Gorton
Debdale
Abbey Hey
Denton
Dane Bank
Haughton Green
Hyde
Kingston
Godley
Newton
Flowery Field
Gee Cross
Backbower
Woodley
Bredbury
Romiley
Compstall
Marple
Marple Bridge
Marpleridge
Hazel Grove
Torkington
Bramhall
Cheadle
Cheadle Hulme
Heaton Moor
Heaton Chapel
Heaton Norris
Heaton Mersey
Reddish
North Reddish
South Reddish
Brinnington
Portwood
Edgeley
Cheadle Heath
Shaw Heath
Heaviley
Great Moor
Offerton
Stepping Hill
Woods Moor
Davenport
Adswood
Gatley
Sharston
Northenden
Benchill
Wythenshawe
Peel Hall
Woodhouse Park
Heald Green
Moss Nook
Heyhead
Manchester Airport
Norbury Moor
Windlehurst
Middlewood
Poynton
Kitt's Moss
Smithy Green
Baguley
Newall Green
Prestwich
Heaton Park
Whitefield
Unsworth
Langley
Alkrington
Nimble Nook
White Gate
Chain Bar
Failsworth
Ancoats
Bradford
Beswick
Ardwick
Brunswick
West Gorton
Strangeways
Cheetwood
Barlow Moor
Heaton Mersey
Lane End
Green End
Norris Bank
Bunkers Hill
Foggbrook
Offerton Green
Ley Hey Park
Greave
Cherry Tree
M60
M62
M56
M67
234
235
D
E
F
1
2
3
4

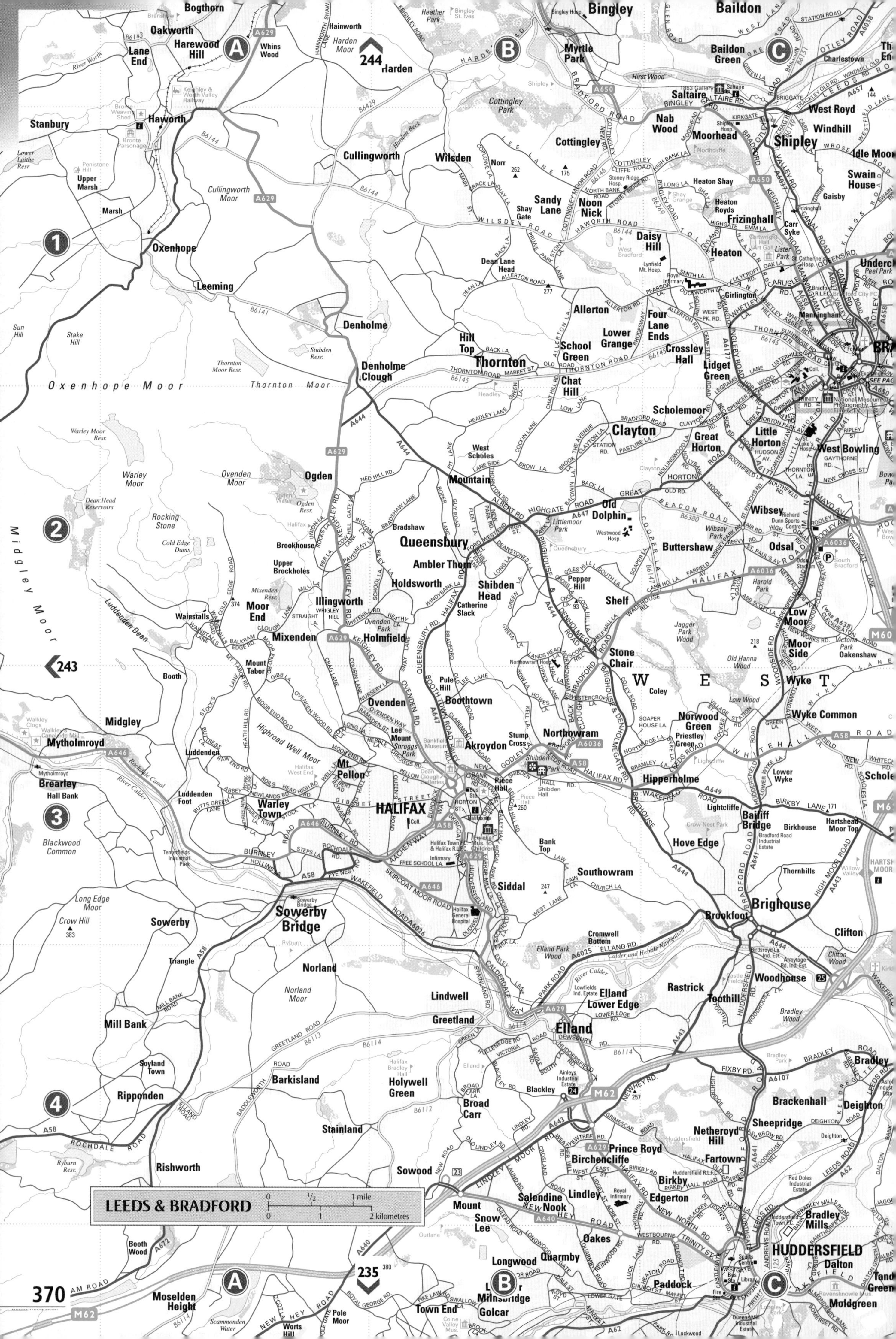
LEEDS & BRADFORD
0 1/2 1 mile
0 1 2 kilometres
A
B
C
1
2
3
4
244
243
235
Bogthorn
Oakworth
Harewood Hill
Lane End
Whins Wood
Hainworth
Harden Moor
Harden
Heather Park
Bingley
Myrtle Park
Baildon
Baildon Green
Charlestown
Hirst Wood
Saltaire
Nab Wood
Moorhead
Shipley
West Royd
Windhill
Idle Moor
Swain House
Gaisby
Haworth
Stanbury
Lower Laithe Resr
Upper Marsh
Marsh
Cullingworth
Cullingworth Moor
Cottingley Park
Wilsden
Norr
Cottingley
Sandy Lane
Shay Gate
Noon Nick
Heaton Shay
Heaton Royds
Frizinghall
Carr Syke
Daisy Hill
Heaton
Oxenhope
Leeming
Dean Lane Head
Allerton
Girlington
Manningham
Sun Hill
Stake Hill
Denholme
Stubden Resr.
Thornton Moor Resr.
Hill Top
Thornton
School Green
Four Lane Ends
Lower Grange
Crossley Hall
Lidget Green
Oxenhope Moor
Thornton Moor
Denholme Clough
Chat Hill
Scholemoor
Clayton
Great Horton
Little Horton
West Bowling
Warley Moor Resr.
Warley Moor
Ovenden Moor
Ogden
Ogden Resr.
Mountain
West Scholes
Dean Head Reservoirs
Rocking Stone
Cold Edge Dams
Bradshaw
Queensbury
Ambler Thorn
Old Dolphin
Littlemoor Park
Wibsey
Buttershaw
Odsal
Brookhouse
Upper Brockholes
Holdsworth
Shibden Head
Catherine Slack
Shelf
Pepper Hill
Harold Park
Low Moor
Midgley Moor
Mixenden Resr.
Moor End
Illingworth
Wainstalls
Luddenden Dean
Mixenden
Holmfield
Ovenden Park
Mount Tabor
Jagger Park Wood
Old Hanna Wood
Moor Side
Oakenshaw
Booth
Pule Hill
Boothtown
Stone Chair
W E S T
Coley
Wyke
Low Wood
Ovenden
Norwood Green
Wyke Common
Midgley
Mytholmroyd
Brearley
Hall Bank
Luddenden
Lee Mount
Shroggs Park
Akroydon
Stump Cross
Northowram
Priestley Green
Mt Pellon
Highroad Well Moor
Shibden Hall
Hipperholme
Lower Wyke
Luddenden Foot
Warley Town
HALIFAX
Piece Hall
Lightcliffe
Bailiff Bridge
Birkhouse
Hartshead Moor Top
Blackwood Common
Bank Top
Hove Edge
Thornhills
Southowram
Siddal
Brighouse
Long Edge Moor
Crow Hill
Sowerby
Sowerby Bridge
Brookfoot
Clifton
Ryburn
Norland
Norland Moor
Triangle
Cromwell Bottom
Elland Park Wood
Rastrick
Woodhouse
Clifton Wood
Lindwell
Elland
Lower Edge
Toothill
Greetland
Bradley Wood
Mill Bank
Soyland Town
Barkisland
Holywell Green
Blackley
Bradley
Brackenhall
Deighton
Ripponden
Broad Carr
Sheepridge
Netherloyd Hill
Stainland
Prince Royd
Birchencliffe
Fartown
Ryburn Resr.
Rishworth
Sowood
Birkby
Lindley
Salendine Nook
Edgerton
Mount
Snow Lee
Bradley Mills
Oakes
Quarmby
HUDDERSFIELD
Dalton
Booth Wood
Longwood
Paddock
Milnsbridge
Golcar
Moselden Height
Scammonden Water
Worts Hill
Pole Moor
Town End
Moldgreen
Lockwood
M62
A629
A644
A646
A58
A641
A643
A6036
A647
A650
A640
A62
A672
A6107
A6025
A6026
A649
A6177
A6145
B6144
B6141
B6145
B6113
B6114
B6112
B6380
Rochdale Canal
River Calder
Calder and Hebble Navigation
River Worth

Rawdon
Tinshill
Lawnswood
Moor Allerton
Moortown
Roundhay Park
Horsforth
Horsforth Woodside
West Park
Meanwood
Weetwood
Chapel Allerton
Roundhay
Monkswood
Calverley
Apperley Bridge
Newlay Wood
Hawksworth
Gledhow
Beech-wood
Greengates
Wellroyd
Potternewton
Oakwood
Headingley
Ravenscliffe
Rodley
Whitecote
Bagley
Moorside
Kirkstall
Brooklands
Farsley
Fagley
Woodhouse
Gipton
Harehills
Bramley
Burley
Stanningley
Upper Armley
Thornbury
Swinnow Moor
LEEDS
Burmantofts
Hillfoot
Chapeltown
Armley
Gamble Hill
Osmondthorpe
Halton Moor
Laisterdyke
Pudsey
Upper Moor
Tyresal
Wortley
Holbeck
Farnley
Cross Green
Fulneck
Hunslet
Far Royds
Beeston Hill
Dudley Hill
Holme Shay
Beeston
New Farnley
Mill Shaw
Stourton
Tong Street
Beeston Park Side
Cockersdale
Moor Head
East Bierley
Churwell
Gildersome
Belle Isle
Drighlington
Daisy Hill
Bantam Grove
Rothwell
Gildersome Street
New Brighton
Middleton
Robin Hood
Birkenshaw
Moorside
Bruntcliffe
Birkenshaw Bottoms
Morley
YORKS
Oakwell
Topcliffe
Thorpe on the Hill
Carlton
Merchant Fields
Gomersal
Copley Hill
Tingley
Lofthouse
Birstall
East Ardsley
Cleckheaton
Spen
Popeley Fields
Upper Green
Carlinghow
Batley
Haigh Moor
Stanley Lane Ends
Littletown
Westfield
Healey
Carr Gate
Hightown
Heckmondwike
Clerk Green
Mount Pleasant
Stanley
Liversedge
Staincliffe
Hanging Heaton
Outwood
Norristhorpe
Batley Carr
Chidswell
Kirkhamgate
Wrenthorpe
Newton Hill
Robertown
DEWSBURY
Dewsbury Moor
Boothroyd
Gawthorpe
WAKEFIELD
Crossley
Mirfield Moor
Chickenley
Alverthorpe
Earlsheaton
East-moor
Northorpe
Flushdyke
Ossett
Flanshaw
Battyeford
Mirfield
Savile Town
Ravensthorpe
Lower Hopton
Thornhill Lees
Ossett Spa
Lupset
South Ossett
Healey
Combs
Thornes
Thornhill
Kirkheaton
Overthorpe
Horbury
Portobello
Upper Hopton
Thornhill Edge
Horbury Bridge
Middlestown
Hill Side
Overton
Calder Grove
Durkar
Woolgreaves
Netherton
Crigglestone
Cowmes
Fenay Bridge
Lepton
Grange Moor
Chapelthorne
SEE PAGE 384-385
244
245
236

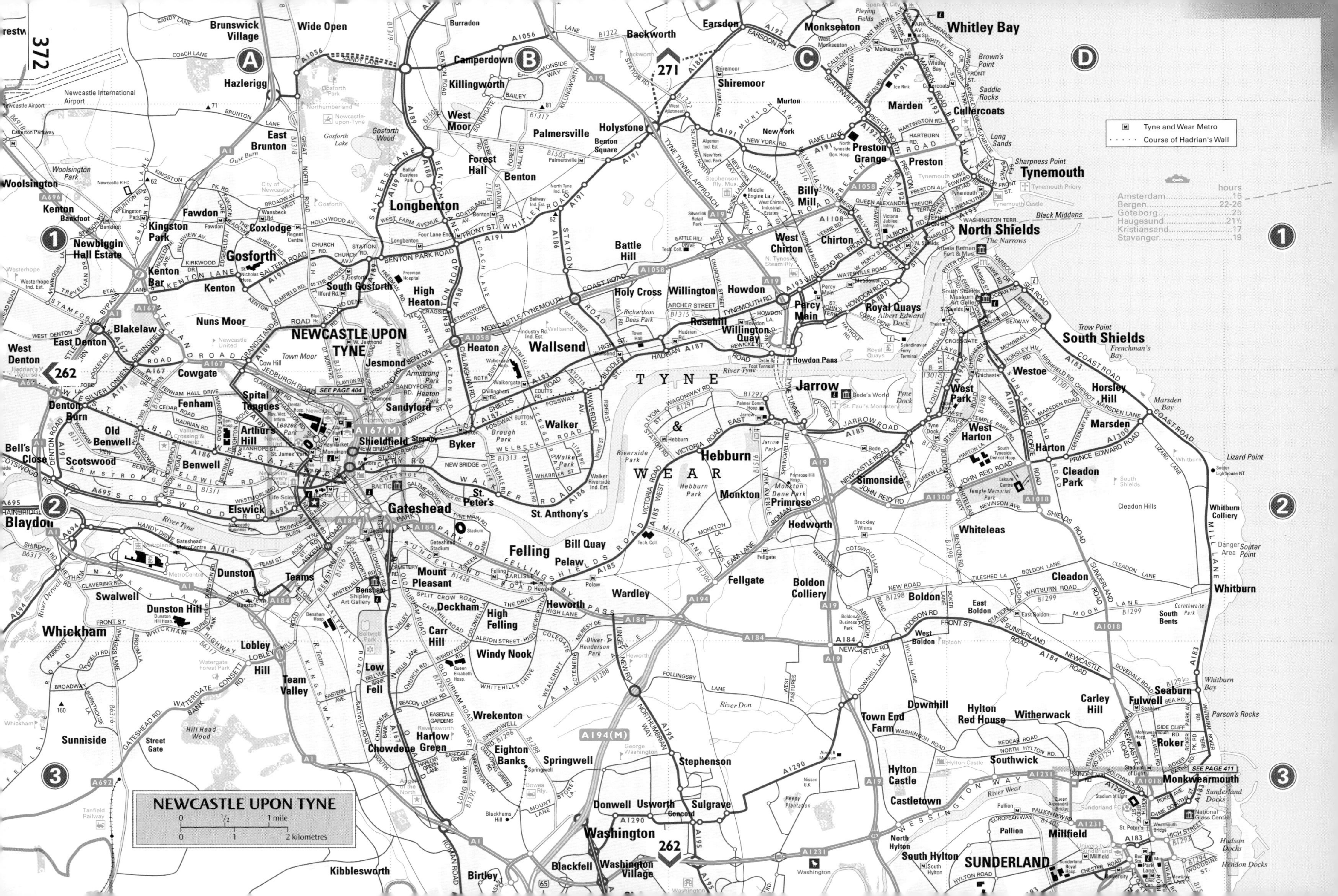
NEWCASTLE UPON TYNE
0 1/2 1 mile
0 1 2 kilometres
Tyne and Wear Metro
Course of Hadrian's Wall
hours
Amsterdam 15
Bergen 22-26
Göteborg 25
Haugesund 21½
Kristiansand 17
Stavanger 19
SEE PAGE 404
SEE PAGE 411
262
271
Whitley Bay
Tynemouth
North Shields
South Shields
Cullercoats
Monkseaton
Earsdon
Backworth
Shiremoor
Holystone
Wide Open
Brunswick Village
Hazlerigg
Camperdown
Killingworth
West Moor
Palmersville
Forest Hall
Benton
Longbenton
Gosforth
Kenton
Fawdon
Kingston Park
Woolsington
Newcastle International Airport
Newbiggin Hall Estate
Blakelaw
Cowgate
West Denton
East Denton
Denton Burn
Fenham
Spital Tongues
Arthur's Hill
Benwell
Scotswood
Elswick
Blaydon
Whickham
Swalwell
Dunston
Dunston Hill
Teams
Lobley Hill
Team Valley
Sunniside
Kibblesworth
Low Fell
Gateshead
Felling
Wallsend
Walker
Byker
Heaton
High Heaton
Jesmond
Sandyford
Shieldfield
NEWCASTLE UPON TYNE
Nuns Moor
Town Moor
Howdon
Willington Quay
Rosehill
Percy Main
Royal Quays
Jarrow
Hebburn
Monkton
Primrose
Hedworth
Fellgate
Boldon Colliery
Boldon
West Boldon
East Boldon
Cleadon
Whitburn
Marsden
Westoe
Harton
Simonside
Whiteleas
Washington
Sunderland
SUNDERLAND
Monkwearmouth
Roker
Fulwell
Seaburn
Southwick
Millfield
Pallion
South Hylton
Castletown
Hylton Castle
Downhill
Town End Farm
Witherwack
Carley Hill
Hylton Red House
Usworth
Sulgrave
Stephenson
Donwell
Springwell
Wrekenton
Eighton Banks
Harlow Green
Chowdene
Windy Nook
Carr Hill
Deckham
Mount Pleasant
High Felling
Heworth
Wardley
Pelaw
Bill Quay
St. Anthony's
St. Peter's
Birtley
Blackfell
Washington Village
River Tyne
River Wear
River Don
TYNE & WEAR

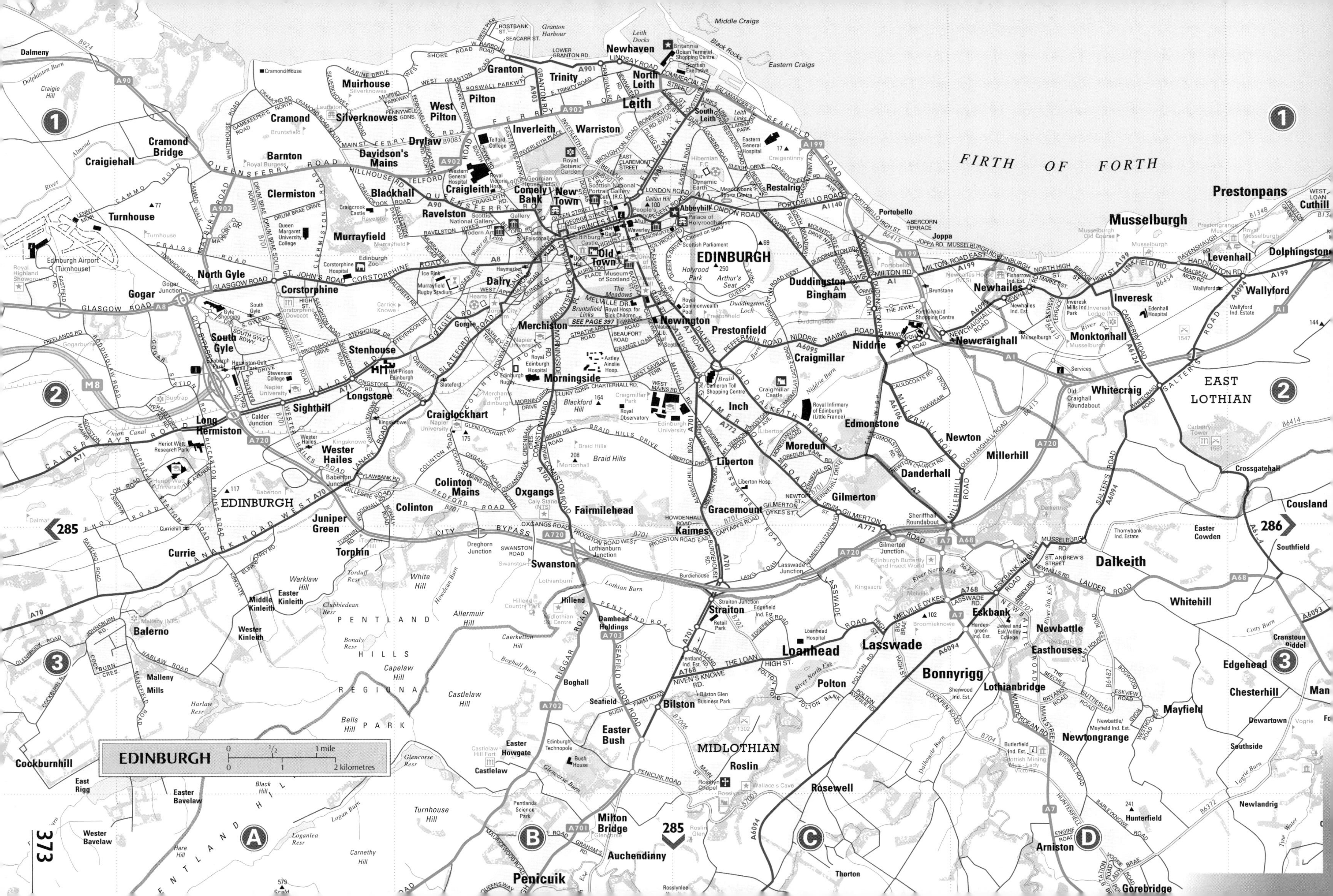
EDINBURGH
FIRTH OF FORTH
EAST LOTHIAN
MIDLOTHIAN
PENTLAND HILLS REGIONAL PARK
SEE PAGE 397
285
286
Dalmeny
Craigiehall
Cramond Bridge
Cramond
Barnton
Turnhouse
Edinburgh Airport (Turnhouse)
Gogar
North Gyle
South Gyle
Corstorphine
Clermiston
Davidson's Mains
Silverknowes
Muirhouse
Pilton
West Pilton
Drylaw
Granton
Trinity
Newhaven
North Leith
Leith
South Leith
Inverleith
Warriston
Blackhall
Craigleith
Comely Bank
New Town
Old Town
Ravelston
Murrayfield
Dalry
Gorgie
Stenhouse
Sighthill
Longstone
Craiglockhart
Merchiston
Morningside
Newington
Prestonfield
Duddingston
Bingham
Craigmillar
Niddrie
Inch
Liberton
Edmonstone
Moredun
Gilmerton
Gracemount
Kaimes
Fairmilehead
Oxgangs
Colinton Mains
Colinton
Juniper Green
Wester Hailes
Long Hermiston
Currie
Balerno
Torphin
Swanston
Restalrig
Abbeyhill
Portobello
Joppa
Newhailes
Newcraighall
Musselburgh
Inveresk
Monktonhall
Whitecraig
Levenhall
Prestonpans
Cuthill
Dolphingstone
Wallyford
Crossgatehall
Cousland
Danderhall
Newton
Millerhill
Dalkeith
Eskbank
Newbattle
Easthouses
Whitehill
Lasswade
Loanhead
Straiton
Bonnyrigg
Lothianbridge
Newtongrange
Mayfield
Edgehead
Chesterhill
Polton
Bilston
Roslin
Rosewell
Arniston
Gorebridge
Easter Bush
Penicuik
Milton Bridge
Auchendinny
Castlelaw
Cockburnhill
Middle Kinleith
Wester Kinleith
Malleny Mills
EDINBURGH 0 1/2 1 mile 0 1 2 kilometres

GLASGOW
0 1/2 1 mile
0 1 2 kilometres
A
B
C
1
2
3
4
283
283
WEST DUNBARTONSHIRE
EAST DUNBARTONSHIRE
RENFREWSHIRE
EAST RENFREWSHIRE
SEE PAGE 386-387
Milngavie
Bearsden
Mugdock
Baldernock
Bardowie
Balmore
Torrance
Cadder
Buckhey
Old Kilpatrick
Duntocher
Faifley
Hardgate
Mountblow
Parkhall
Radnor Park
Kilbowie
Dalmuir
Drumry
Drumchapel
Clydebank
Whitecrook
Erskine
Bargarran
North Barr
Linburn
Park Mains
Southbar
Freeland
Inchinnan
Knightswood
Yoker
Scotstounhill
Scotstoun
Anniesland
Temple
Kelvindale
Kelvinside
Maryhill
Gilshochill
Lambhill
Summerston
Bishopbriggs
Kenmure
Milton
Crowhill
Springburn
Possilpark
Dowanhill
Partick
Whiteinch
Shieldhall
Renfrew
Dean Park
Moorpark
Shortroods
Gallowhill
Hillington
Cardonald
Govan
Ibrox
Craigton
Finnieston
Dennistoun
Bridgeton
GLASGOW
Pollokshields
Oatlands
Rutherglen
Polmadie
Govanhill
Crossmyloof
Mount Florida
King's Park
Langside
Shawlands
Battlefield
Cathcart
Pollokshaws
Newlands
Croftfoot
Castlemilk
Mansewood
Muirend
Merrylee
Netherlee
Giffnock
Thornliebank
Stamperland
Carmunnock
Williamwood
Sheddens
Clarkston
Busby
Whitecraigs
Broom
Crookfur
Newton Mearns
Mearns
Waterfoot
Braehead
Thorntonhall
Lawmuir
Jackton
Eaglesham
Netherplace
Neilston
Barrhead
Darnley
Arden
Carnwadric
Priesthill
Nitshill
Hurlet
Pollok
Mosspark
Dumbreck
Crookston
Ralston
Oldhall
Hawkhead
Blackhall
Charleston
Thornly Park
Glenburn
Foxbar
PAISLEY
Castlehead
Millarston
Ferguslie Park
M8
M77
M898
GLASGOW SOUTHERN ORBITAL ROUTE

Milton of Campsie
Croy
Carrickstone
Twechar
284
Craigmarloch
Dullatur
Westerwood
Abronhill
Kildrum
Seafar
Eastfield
Cumbernauld
Carbrain
Balloch
Birdston
Harestanes
Kirkintilloch
Broadwood
Westfield
Greenfaults
Lenziemill
Condorrat
Gallowhill
Oxgang
Waterside
Blairlinn
Luggiebank
Lenzie
HM Prison Low Moss
Mollinsburn
Greengairs
Gadloch
Auchinloch
Bridgend
Moodiesburn
Annathill
Riggend
Wattston
Woodhill
Chryston
NORTH
LANARKSHIRE
Greenfoot
Rigghead
Stand
Marnock
Muirhead
Garnkirk
Stepps
Glenboig
Gartcosh
Craigendmuir
Millerston
Glenmavis
Airdriehill
Provanmill
Riddrie
Ruchazie
Garthamlock
Hogganfield Loch
Bishop Loch
Woodend Loch
Gartgill
Townhead
Holehills
Thrashbush
Rawyards
Plains
Lochwood
Easterhouse
Gartsherrie
Monklands Hospital
Drumgelloch
Airdrie
Craigneuk
Carntyne
Springboig
Barlanark
Swinton
Coatbridge
Coatdyke
Gartlea
Gartness
Whifflet
Greenend
Barrachnie
Baillieston
Garrowhill
Shettleston
Crosshill
Bargeddie
Kirkwood
Old Monkland
Kirkshaws
Rosehall
Shawhead
Carnbroe
Calderbank
Muirhead
Woodlands
Braidfauld
Mount Vernon
Broomhouse
Chapelhall
Carmyle
Birkenshaw
Thorniewood
Tannochside
Viewpark
Newhouse
West
Eastfield
Newton
Kylepark
Uddingston
Fallside
Mossend
Holytown
New Stevenston
Hallside
Bellshill
Yett
Cambuslang
Flemington
Kirkfield
Forgewood
Carfin
Dalton
Low Blantyre
Bothwell
North Motherwell
SOUTH
LANARKSHIRE
Barnhill
Motherwell
Cleekhimin
Blantyre
Springwells
Whitehill
Craigneuk
Nerston
High Blantyre
Burnbank
Rogerton
Hamilton
Shieldmuir
Stewartfield
Calderwood
East Mains
Hillhouse
Muirhouse
Auchentibber
West Mains
EAST KILBRIDE
Earnock
Laighstonehall
Low Waters
Ferniegair
Allanton
Netherton
Gowkthrapple
Westwood
St. Leonards
Woodhead
Fairhill
Silvertonhill
Cadzow
The Murray
Birniehill
Meikle Earnock
Bellewood
Greenhills
Blantyre Moor
M8
M73
M74
M80
A8
A73
A80
A725
A721
A723
A724
A749
A726
A752
River Clyde
Monkland Canal
North Calder Water
1
2
3
4
D
E
F

CENTRAL LONDON
0 1/4 mile
0 0.25 0.5 kilometres
A B C D E F G H J
1 2 3 4 5 6 7 8 9 10 11 12 13
356
357
MAYFAIR
SOHO
ST. JAMES'S
BELGRAVIA
WESTMINSTER
BLOOMSBURY
GREEN PARK
ST. JAMES'S PARK
BUCKINGHAM PALACE GARDENS
BUCKINGHAM PALACE
THE BRITISH MUSEUM
NATIONAL GALLERY
TRAFALGAR SQ
WESTMINSTER ABBEY
OXFORD STREET
PICCADILLY
PICCADILLY CIRCUS
OXFORD CIRCUS
MARBLE ARCH
HYDE PARK CORNER
VICTORIA
REGENT'S PARK
BAKER STREET
TOTTENHAM COURT RD
LEICESTER SQ
PARK LANE
WHITEHALL
PALL MALL
THE MALL
GROSVENOR SQUARE

London Population 6,679,332 capital of England and Europe's largest city. Consists of 32 boroughs together with City of London, totalling over 620 square miles, centred on River Thames. Legislative capital of UK. Financial, commercial, distribution and communications centre. London developed from Roman settlement of Londinium, dating from AD 43. Despite successful attack by Queen Boudicca (AD 61), London became national capital by end of 1st century. Major expansion during Norman era after William the Conqueror became first king crowned at Westminster Abbey. The Great Fire of 1666 destroyed over 13,000 buildings and was followed by period of rebuilding and rapid expansion, giving London many enduring landmarks such as Saint Paul's Cathedral. Home to vast array of galleries and museums including Victoria and Albert and British Museums, National and Tate Galleries. Theatres and shopping in West End. Other attractions include Tower of London and Trafalgar Square. Many universities.

TOURIST INFORMATION CENTRE ☎ 09068 663344
(60p per minute)
1 REGENT STREET, PICCADILLY CIRCUS
LONDON, SW1Y 4XT

www.visitlondon.com

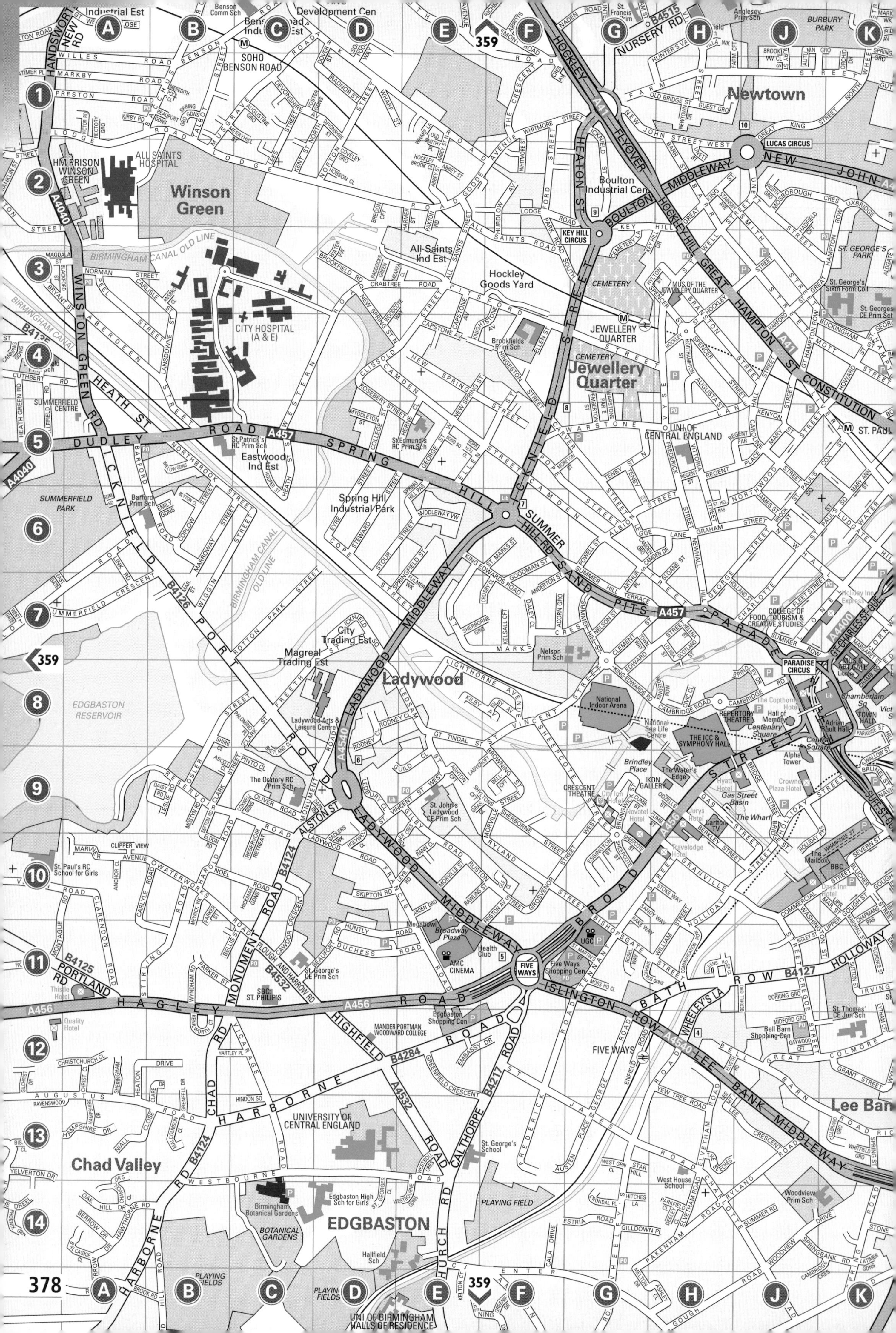
359
Winson Green
HM PRISON WINSON GREEN
ALL SAINTS HOSPITAL
CITY HOSPITAL (A & E)
BIRMINGHAM CANAL OLD LINE
Newtown
LUCAS CIRCUS
Boulton Industrial Cen
KEY HILL CIRCUS
Jewellery Quarter
JEWELLERY QUARTER
CEMETERY
All Saints Ind Est
Hockley Goods Yard
Eastwood Ind Est
Spring Hill Industrial Park
SUMMERFIELD PARK
EDGBASTON RESERVOIR
City Trading Est
Magreal Trading Est
Ladywood
Ladywood Arts & Leisure Centre
National Indoor Arena
THE ICC & SYMPHONY HALL
PARADISE CIRCUS
UNI OF CENTRAL ENGLAND
COLLEGE OF FOOD, TOURISM & CREATIVE STUDIES
Brindley Place
IKON GALLERY
Gas Street Basin
The Wharf
CRESCENT THEATRE
FIVE WAYS
Five Ways Shopping Cen
Broadway Plaza
AMC CINEMA
Edgbaston Shopping Cen
MANDER PORTMAN WOODWARD COLLEGE
UNIVERSITY OF CENTRAL ENGLAND
Chad Valley
EDGBASTON
BOTANICAL GARDENS
PLAYING FIELD
Lee Bank
UNI OF BIRMINGHAM HALLS OF RESIDENCE
HAGLEY ROAD
DUDLEY ROAD
SPRING HILL
LADYWOOD MIDDLEWAY
BROAD STREET
HARBORNE ROAD
ISLINGTON ROW
LEE BANK MIDDLEWAY
HOCKLEY FLYOVER
GREAT HAMPTON ST
CONSTITUTION HILL
NEW JOHN STREET WEST
SUMMER HILL RD
SAND PITS PARADE

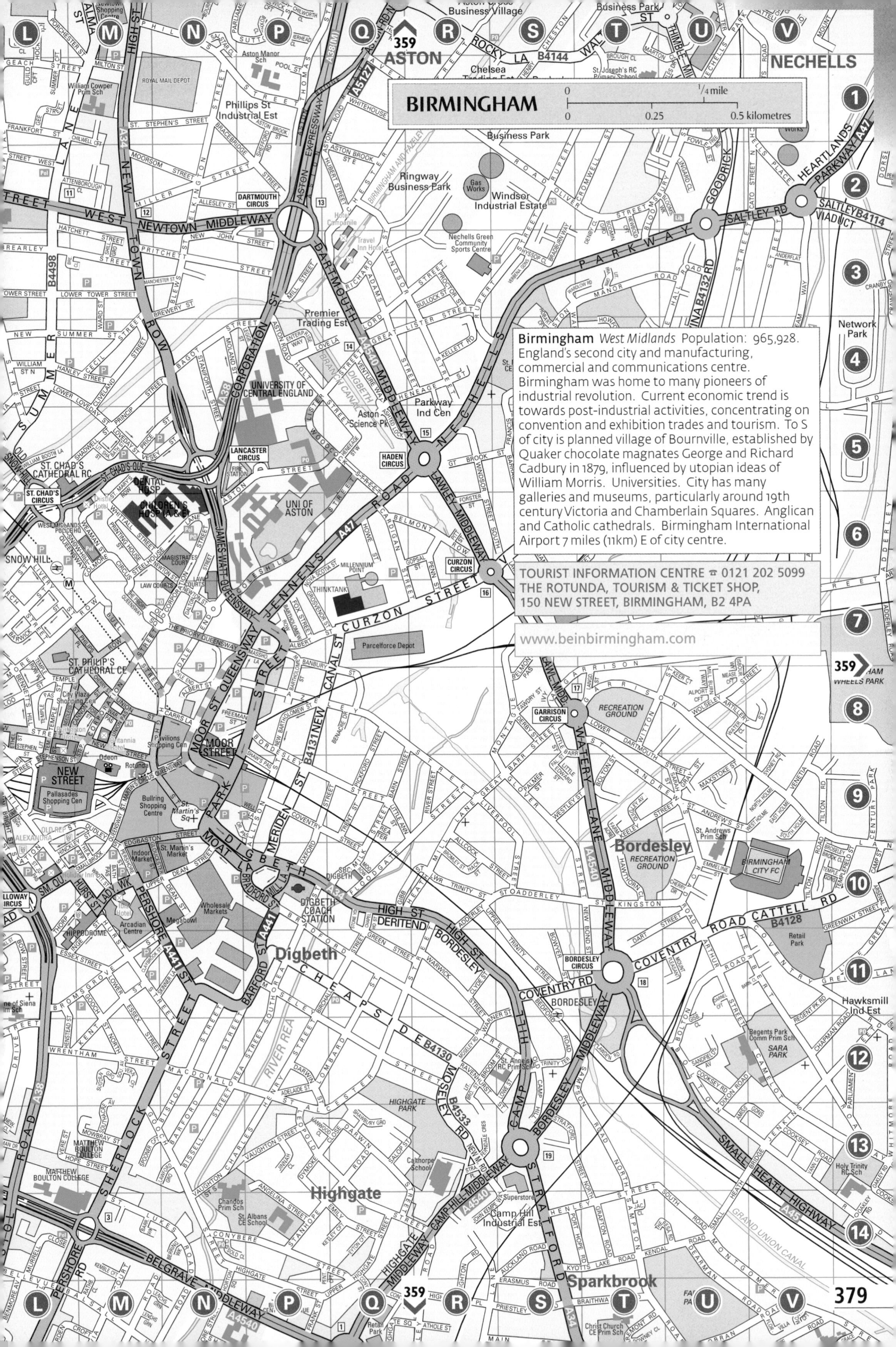

BIRMINGHAM

0 — 1/4 mile
0 — 0.25 — 0.5 kilometres

Birmingham *West Midlands* Population: 965,928. England's second city and manufacturing, commercial and communications centre. Birmingham was home to many pioneers of industrial revolution. Current economic trend is towards post-industrial activities, concentrating on convention and exhibition trades and tourism. To S of city is planned village of Bournville, established by Quaker chocolate magnates George and Richard Cadbury in 1879, influenced by utopian ideas of William Morris. Universities. City has many galleries and museums, particularly around 19th century Victoria and Chamberlain Squares. Anglican and Catholic cathedrals. Birmingham International Airport 7 miles (11km) E of city centre.

TOURIST INFORMATION CENTRE ☎ 0121 202 5099
THE ROTUNDA, TOURISM & TICKET SHOP,
150 NEW STREET, BIRMINGHAM, B2 4PA

www.beinbirmingham.com

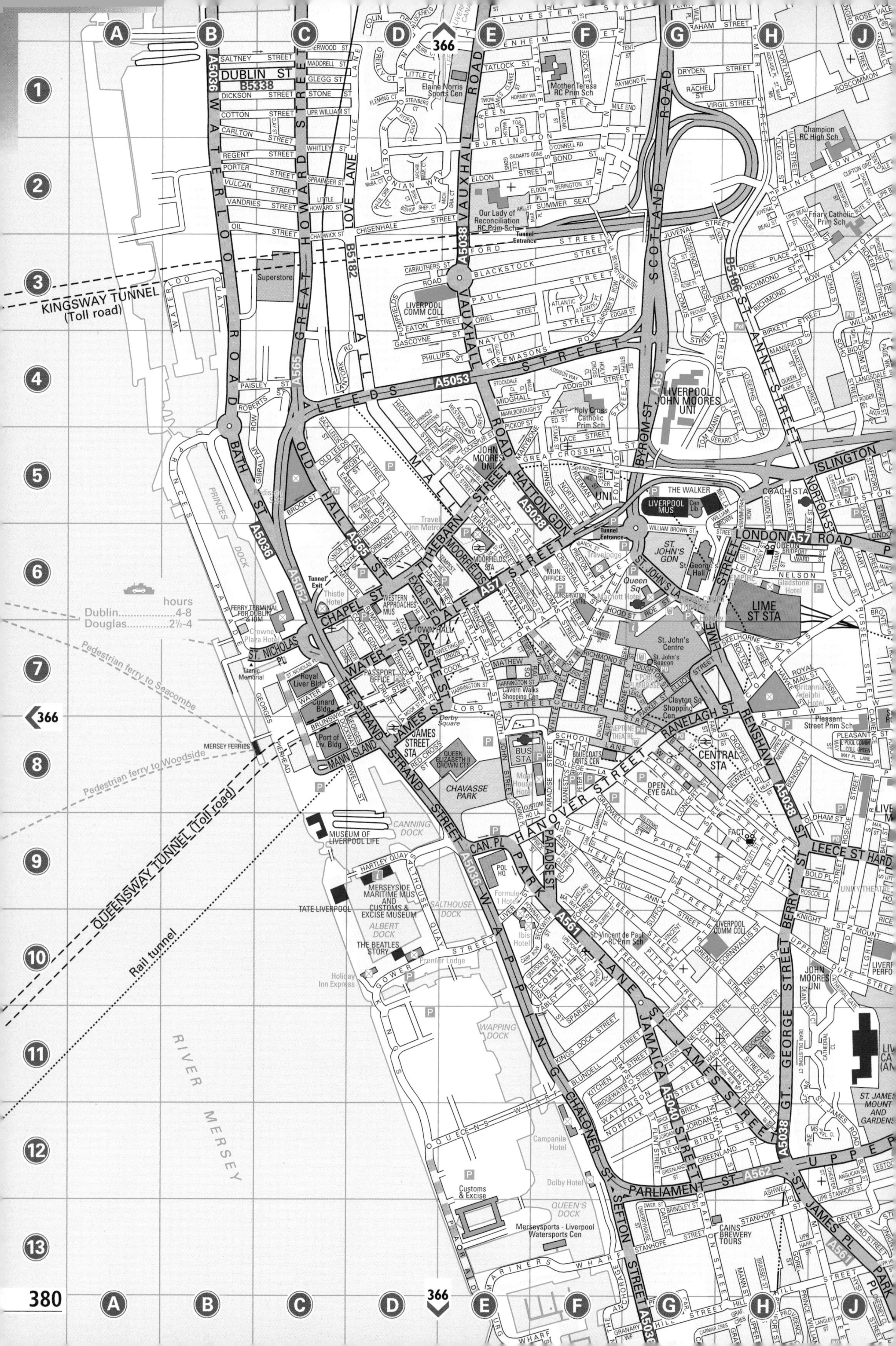
A B C D E F G H J
1 2 3 4 5 6 7 8 9 10 11 12 13
366
KINGSWAY TUNNEL (Toll road)
QUEENSWAY TUNNEL (Toll road)
Rail tunnel
RIVER MERSEY
hours
Dublin.................4-8
Douglas...............2½-4
Pedestrian ferry to Seacombe
Pedestrian ferry to Woodside
MERSEY FERRIES
FERRY TERMINAL FOR DUBLIN & IOM
Titanic Memorial
Royal Liver Bldg
Cunard Bldg
Port of Liv. Bldg
PIERHEAD
MANN ISLAND
MUSEUM OF LIVERPOOL LIFE
CANNING DOCK
MERSEYSIDE MARITIME MUS AND CUSTOMS & EXCISE MUSEUM
TATE LIVERPOOL
ALBERT DOCK
SALTHOUSE DOCK
THE BEATLES STORY
Premier Lodge
Holiday Inn Express
WAPPING DOCK
Campanile Hotel
Dolby Hotel
Customs & Excise
QUEEN'S DOCK
Merseysports - Liverpool Watersports Cen
PRINCES DOCK
Crowne Plaza Hotel
Radisson SAS
Superstore
WATERLOO ROAD
A5036
BATH ST
PRINCES PARADE
ST. NICHOLAS PL
GREAT HOWARD STREET
A565
LEEDS STREET
A5053
OLD HALL ST
TITHEBARN STREET
MOORFIELDS
MOORFIELDS STA
CHAPEL ST
WATER ST
DALE STREET
A57
CASTLE ST
TOWN HALL
JAMES ST
JAMES STREET STA
Derby Square
QUEEN ELIZABETH II CROWN CTS
CHAVASSE PARK
THE STRAND
STRAND STREET
WAPPING
A5036
Thistle Hotel
WESTERN APPROACHES MUS
PASSPORT OFFICE
Cavern Walks Shopping Cen
BUS STA
LORD ST
CHURCH ST
SCHOOL LANE
BLUECOATS ARTS CEN
HANOVER STREET
PARADISE ST
CENTRAL STA
Clayton Sq Shopping Cen
St. John's Centre
St. John's Beacon
L'POOL PLAYHOUSE
Queen Sq
Marriott Hotel
ROYAL COURT THEATRE
LIME ST STA
LIME STREET
ST. JOHN'S GDN
St. George's Hall
LIVERPOOL MUS
THE WALKER
Cen Lib
WILLIAM BROWN ST
ISLINGTON
LONDON ROAD
A57
ODEON
EMPIRE THEATRE
Gladstone Hotel
Britannia Adelphi Hotel
RENSHAW ST
RANELAGH ST
BOLD ST
OPEN EYE GALL
FACT
POL HQ
Formule 1 Hotel
Ibis Hotel
St. Vincent de Paul RC Prim Sch
LIVERPOOL COMM COLL
A561
ST. JAMES STREET
JAMAICA STREET
A5040
PARLIAMENT ST
A562
UPPER PARLIAMENT
CHALONER ST
SEFTON STREET
CAINS BREWERY TOURS
BERRY ST
GT. GEORGE STREET
A5038
LEECE ST
HARDMAN ST
UNITY THEATRE
RODNEY STREET
JOHN MOORES UNI
ST. JAMES MOUNT AND GARDENS
Pleasant Street Prim Sch
VAUXHALL ROAD
A5038
SCOTLAND ROAD
A59
BYROM ST
HATTON GDN
LIVERPOOL JOHN MOORES UNI
Holy Cross Catholic Prim Sch
ST. ANNE STREET
B5186
Champion RC High Sch
Friary Catholic Prim Sch
Mother Teresa RC Prim Sch
Elaine Norris Sports Cen
Our Lady of Reconciliation RC Prim Sch
LIVERPOOL COMM COLL
Tunnel Entrance
Tunnel Exit
LOVE LANE
PALL MALL
B5182
DUBLIN ST
B5338
Travelodge
MUN. OFFICES
NEPTUNE THEATRE

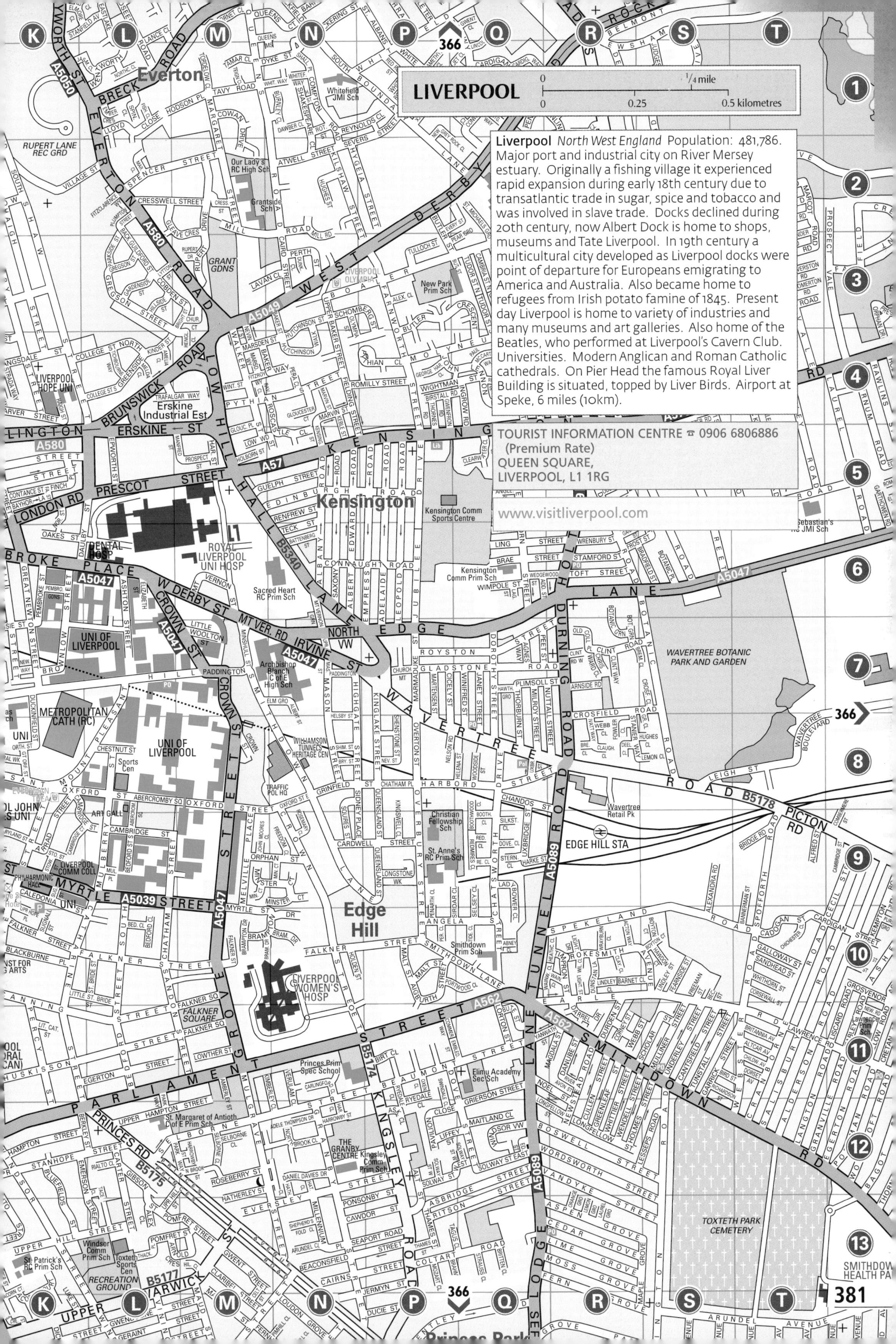
LIVERPOOL
0 1/4 mile
0 0.25 0.5 kilometres
Liverpool North West England Population: 481,786. Major port and industrial city on River Mersey estuary. Originally a fishing village it experienced rapid expansion during early 18th century due to transatlantic trade in sugar, spice and tobacco and was involved in slave trade. Docks declined during 20th century, now Albert Dock is home to shops, museums and Tate Liverpool. In 19th century a multicultural city developed as Liverpool docks were point of departure for Europeans emigrating to America and Australia. Also became home to refugees from Irish potato famine of 1845. Present day Liverpool is home to variety of industries and many museums and art galleries. Also home of the Beatles, who performed at Liverpool's Cavern Club. Universities. Modern Anglican and Roman Catholic cathedrals. On Pier Head the famous Royal Liver Building is situated, topped by Liver Birds. Airport at Speke, 6 miles (10km).
TOURIST INFORMATION CENTRE ☎ 0906 6806886 (Premium Rate)
QUEEN SQUARE, LIVERPOOL, L1 1RG
www.visitliverpool.com
366
Everton
Kensington
Edge Hill
Erskine Industrial Est
ROYAL LIVERPOOL UNI HOSP
UNI OF LIVERPOOL
METROPOLITAN CATH (RC)
LIVERPOOL WOMEN'S HOSP
WAVERTREE BOTANIC PARK AND GARDEN
TOXTETH PARK CEMETERY
EDGE HILL STA
Wavertree Retail Pk
RUPERT LANE REC GRD
GRANT GDNS
FALKNER SQUARE
RECREATION GROUND
LIVERPOOL HOPE UNI
WEST DERBY ROAD
PRESCOT STREET
LONDON RD
ERSKINE ST
PARLIAMENT STREET
SMITHDOWN ROAD
LODGE LANE
TUNNEL ROAD
DURNING ROAD
WAVERTREE ROAD
EDGE LANE
PICTON RD
UPPER PARLIAMENT STREET
GROVE STREET
CROWN ST
MYRTLE STREET
KINGSLEY ROAD
PRINCES RD
A5050 A580 A5049 A57 B5340 A5047 A5039 A562 A5089 B5174 B5175 B5177 B5178
K L M N P Q R S T
1 2 3 4 5 6 7 8 9 10 11 12 13

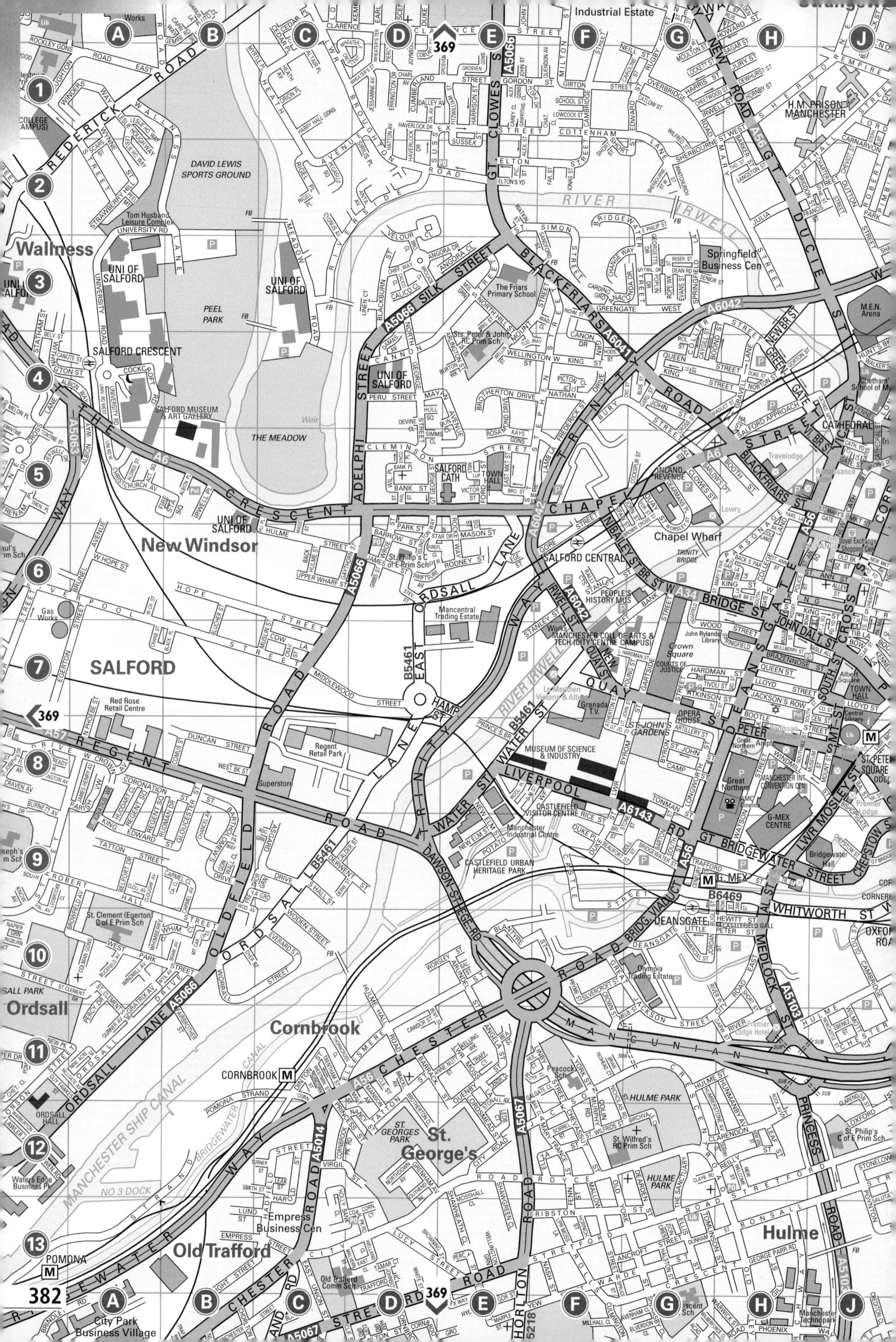
A
B
C
D
E
F
G
H
J
369
Industrial Estate
Wallness
DAVID LEWIS SPORTS GROUND
Tom Husband Leisure Complex
UNI OF SALFORD
PEEL PARK
SALFORD CRESCENT
SALFORD MUSEUM & ART GALLERY
THE MEADOW
RIVER IRWELL
Springfield Business Cen
The Friars Primary School
Sts. Peter & John RC Prim Sch
H.M. PRISON MANCHESTER
M.E.N. Arena
Chetham's School of Music
CATHEDRAL
Travelodge
INLAND REVENUE
Lowry
Chapel Wharf
SALFORD CENTRAL
PEOPLE'S HISTORY MUS
Mancentral Trading Estate
MANCHESTER COLL OF ARTS & TECH (CITY CENTRE CAMPUS)
John Rylands Library
Crown Square
COURTS OF JUSTICE
Granada T.V.
OPERA HOUSE
ST. JOHN'S GARDENS
MUSEUM OF SCIENCE & INDUSTRY
Great Northern
MANCHESTER INT CONVENTION CEN
G-MEX CENTRE
Bridgewater Hall
Albert Square
TOWN HALL
Central Library
ST. PETER'S SQUARE
Royal Exchange Shopping Cen
New Windsor
SALFORD
St. Philip's C of E Prim Sch
Red Rose Retail Centre
Regent Retail Park
Superstore
CASTLEFIELD VISITOR CENTRE
Manchester Industrial Centre
CASTLEFIELD URBAN HERITAGE PARK
DEANSGATE
G.MEX
Olympia Trading Estate
Premier Lodge Hotel
St. Clement (Egerton) C of E Prim Sch
Ordsall
ORDSALL HALL
Cornbrook
CORNBROOK
MANCHESTER SHIP CANAL
BRIDGEWATER CANAL
NO 3 DOCK
Waters Edge Business Pk
POMONA
St. George's
ST. GEORGES PARK
Peacock Sch
HULME PARK
St. Wilfred's RC Prim Sch
Hulme
St. Philip's C of E Prim Sch
Empress Business Cen
Old Trafford
Old Trafford Comm Sch
City Park Business Village
Manchester Technopark
REGENT ROAD
CHESTER ROAD
MANCUNIAN WAY
TRINITY WAY
PRINCESS ROAD
DEANSGATE
GT. DUCIE ST
A6
A56
A57
A5066
A6042
A6041
A6143
A5067
A5014
A5103
B5461
B6469
WHITWORTH ST W
GT BRIDGEWATER STREET
LIVERPOOL RD
QUAY ST
PETER ST
JOHN DALTON ST
BRIDGE ST
CHAPEL STREET
THE CRESCENT
OLDFIELD ROAD
ORDSALL LANE
TRAFFORD ROAD
BRIDGEWATER WAY
STRETFORD RD
CITY ROAD
GREENGATE WEST

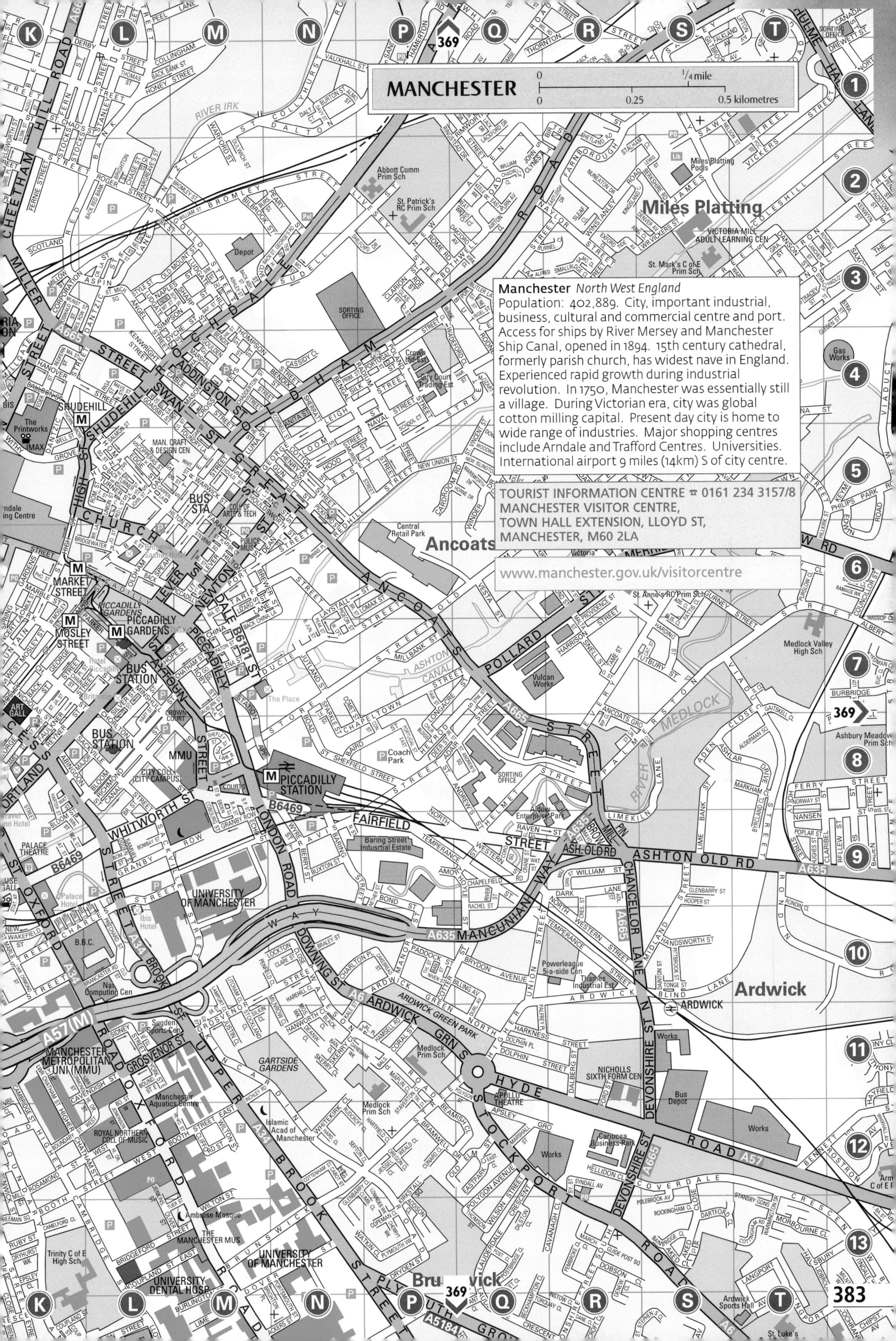
MANCHESTER
0
1/4 mile
0
0.25
0.5 kilometres
Manchester North West England
Population: 402,889. City, important industrial, business, cultural and commercial centre and port. Access for ships by River Mersey and Manchester Ship Canal, opened in 1894. 15th century cathedral, formerly parish church, has widest nave in England. Experienced rapid growth during industrial revolution. In 1750, Manchester was essentially still a village. During Victorian era, city was global cotton milling capital. Present day city is home to wide range of industries. Major shopping centres include Arndale and Trafford Centres. Universities. International airport 9 miles (14km) S of city centre.
TOURIST INFORMATION CENTRE ☎ 0161 234 3157/8
MANCHESTER VISITOR CENTRE,
TOWN HALL EXTENSION, LLOYD ST,
MANCHESTER, M60 2LA
www.manchester.gov.uk/visitorcentre
369
Miles Platting
Ancoats
Ardwick
PICCADILLY STATION
UNIVERSITY OF MANCHESTER
MANCHESTER METROPOLITAN UNI (MMU)
PICCADILLY GARDENS
SHUDEHILL
MARKET STREET
MOSLEY STREET
ARDWICK
A665
A635
A6
A34
A57(M)
A57
B6469
B6181
K
L
M
N
P
Q
R
S
T
1
2
3
4
5
6
7
8
9
10
11
12
13

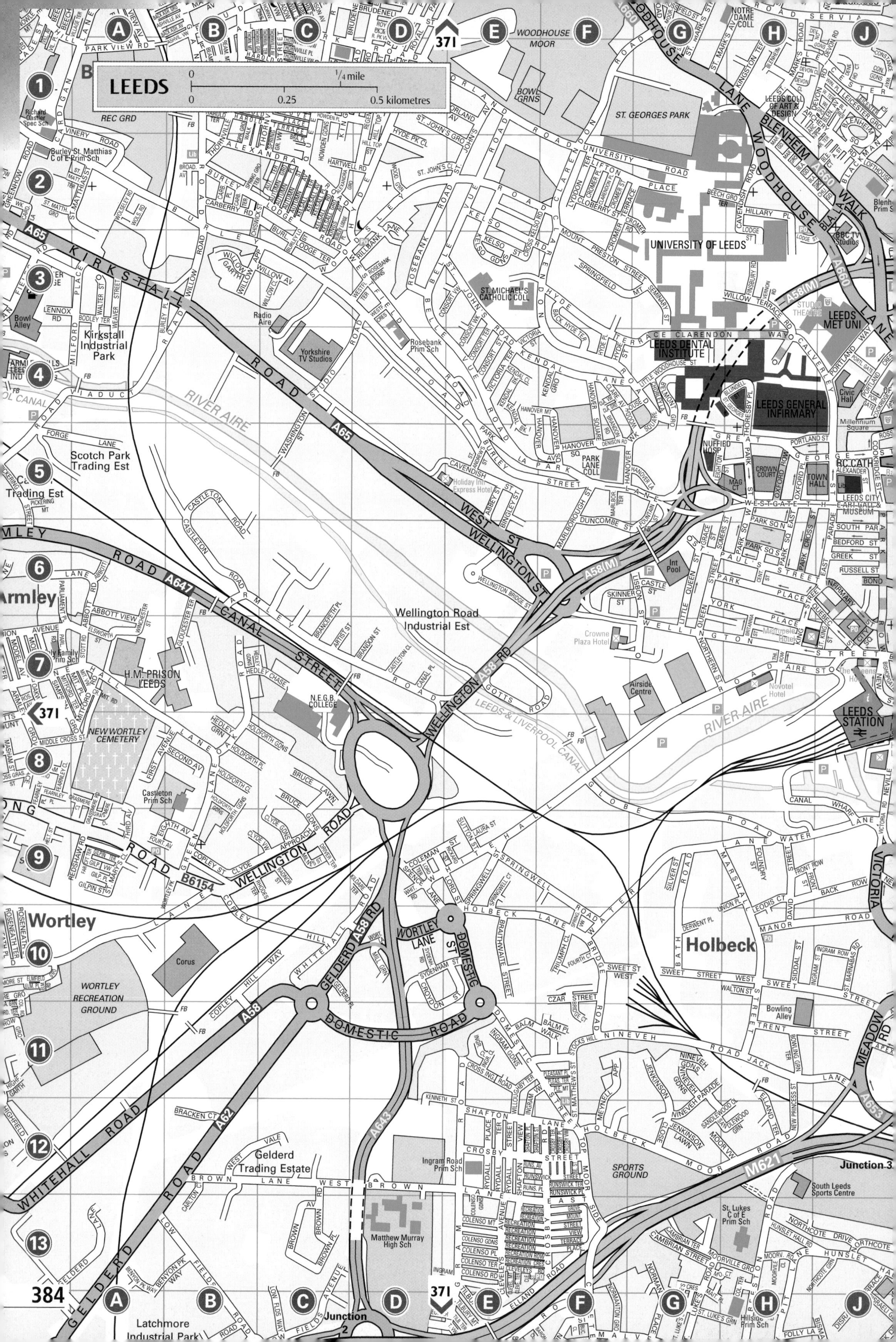

LEEDS
0 1/4 mile
0 0.25 0.5 kilometres
A B C D E F G H J
1 2 3 4 5 6 7 8 9 10 11 12 13
371
WOODHOUSE MOOR
ST. GEORGES PARK
UNIVERSITY OF LEEDS
LEEDS DENTAL INSTITUTE
LEEDS GENERAL INFIRMARY
LEEDS MET UNI
LEEDS COLL OF ART & DESIGN
Civic Hall
Millennium Square
TOWN HALL
CROWN COURT
LEEDS CITY ART GALL & MUSEUM
LEEDS STATION
RIVER AIRE
LEEDS & LIVERPOOL CANAL
Kirkstall Industrial Park
Scotch Park Trading Est
Yorkshire TV Studios
Radio Aire
Wellington Road Industrial Est
H.M. PRISON LEEDS
NEW WORTLEY CEMETERY
N.E.G.B. COLLEGE
Armley
Wortley
Holbeck
WORTLEY RECREATION GROUND
Corus
Gelderd Trading Estate
Ingram Road Prim Sch
Matthew Murray High Sch
SPORTS GROUND
South Leeds Sports Centre
St. Lukes C of E Prim Sch
Latchmore Industrial Park
Junction 2
Junction 3
KIRKSTALL ROAD
WELLINGTON ROAD
CANAL STREET
WHITEHALL ROAD
GELDERD ROAD
DOMESTIC ROAD
ELLAND ROAD
WOODHOUSE LANE
BLENHEIM WALK
A65 A647 A58(M) A58 A62 A643 A660 A653 M621 B6154

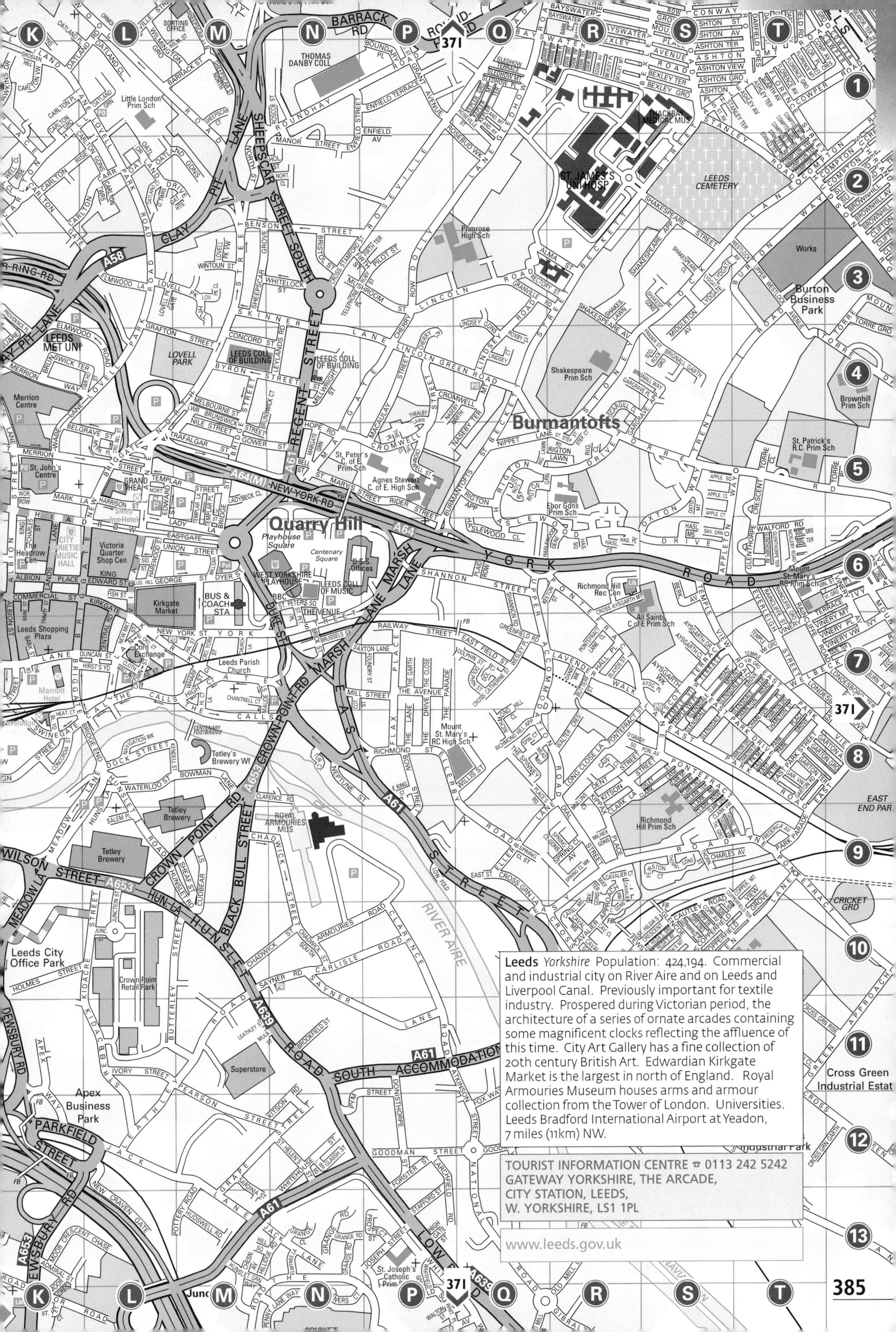

Leeds *Yorkshire* Population: 424,194. Commercial and industrial city on River Aire and on Leeds and Liverpool Canal. Previously important for textile industry. Prospered during Victorian period, the architecture of a series of ornate arcades containing some magnificent clocks reflecting the affluence of this time. City Art Gallery has a fine collection of 20th century British Art. Edwardian Kirkgate Market is the largest in north of England. Royal Armouries Museum houses arms and armour collection from the Tower of London. Universities. Leeds Bradford International Airport at Yeadon, 7 miles (11km) NW.

TOURIST INFORMATION CENTRE ☎ 0113 242 5242
GATEWAY YORKSHIRE, THE ARCADE,
CITY STATION, LEEDS,
W. YORKSHIRE, LS1 1PL

www.leeds.gov.uk

Kelvingrove
Yorkhill
Kelvinhaugh
Finnieston
Cranston Hill
Garnethill
Blythswood
Anderston
Broomielaw
Cessnock
Kinning Park
Kingston
Tradeston
Port Eglington
KELVINGROVE PARK
RIVER KELVIN
RIVER CLYDE
KINGSTON BRIDGE
PRINCE'S DOCK
FESTIVAL PARK
WESTERN INFIRMARY
UNI OF GLASGOW
HUNTERIAN MUS
HUNTERIAN ART GALLERY
VISITOR CENTRE
TRANSPORT MUS
KELVIN HALL
KELVINGROVE ARTGALL & MUS (RE-OPENS MARCH 2006)
GLASGOW CALEDONIAN UNI PARK CAMPUS
QUEEN MOTHER'S MATERNITY HOSP
ROYAL HOSP FOR SICK CHILDREN
SCOTTISH EXHIB & CONFERENCE CEN
CLYDE AUDITORIUM
EXHIBITION CENTRE STA
GLASGOW SCIENCE CEN
IMAX CINEMA
Glasgow Tower
FINNIESTON CRANE
P.S. WAVERLEY (PADDLE STEAMER)
CHARING CROSS STA
ANDERSTON STA
ST. GEORGES CROSS
KELVINBRIDGE
KINNING PARK
CESSNOCK
SHIELDS ROAD
WEST STREET
SCOTLAND STREET SCHOOL: MUS OF EDUCATION
Parcelforce Depot
Junction 18
Junction 19
Junction 20
Junction 21
Junction 22
CLYDESIDE EXPRESSWAY
STOBCROSS ST A814
LANCEFIELD QUAY A814
ANDERSTON QUAY
ARGYLE STREET
PAISLEY ROAD WEST A8
MORRISON ST A8
WESTERN RD A82
ST. GEORGES RD
M8
A804
374

GLASGOW

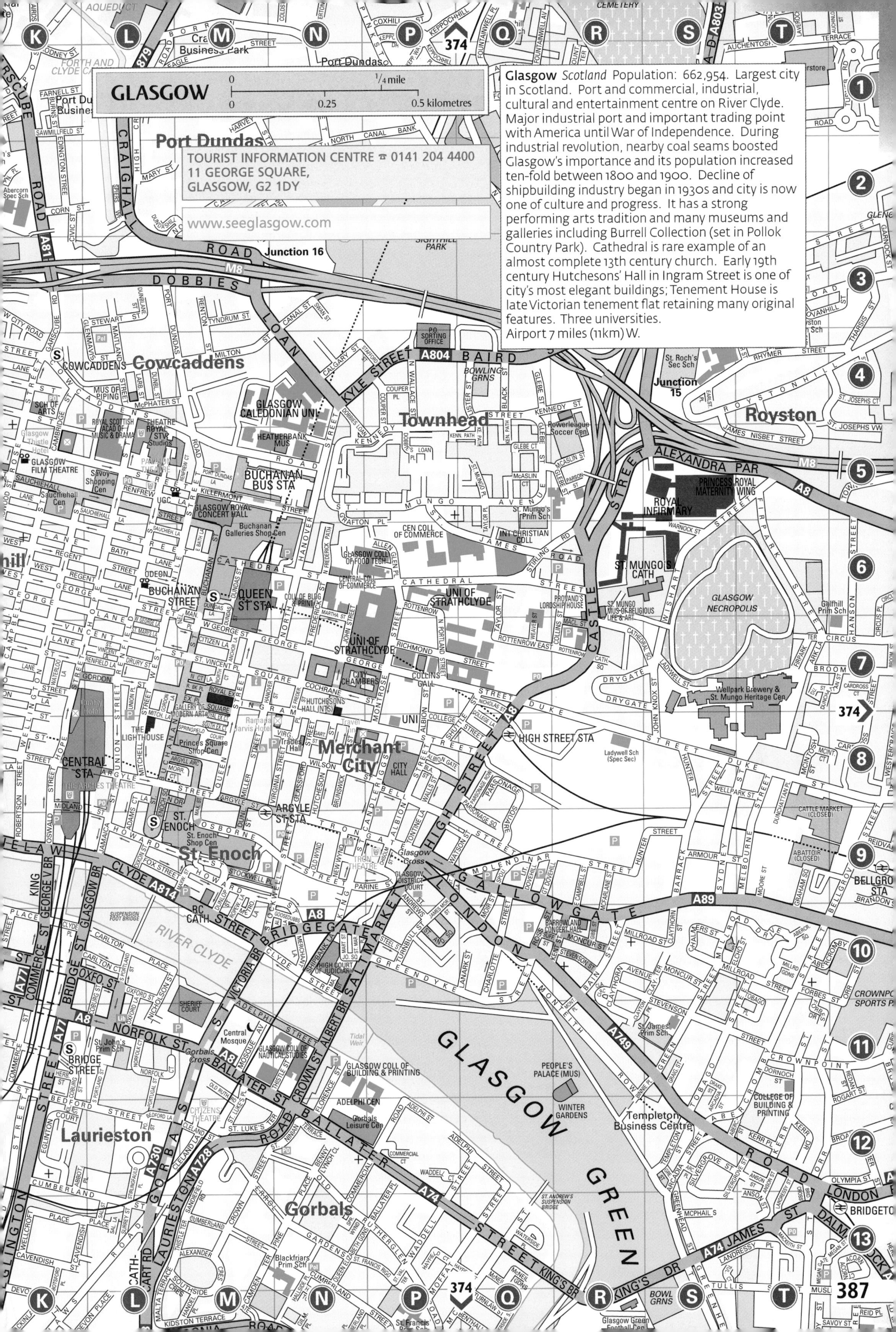

TOURIST INFORMATION CENTRE ☎ 0141 204 4400
11 GEORGE SQUARE,
GLASGOW, G2 1DY

www.seeglasgow.com

Glasgow *Scotland* Population: 662,954. Largest city in Scotland. Port and commercial, industrial, cultural and entertainment centre on River Clyde. Major industrial port and important trading point with America until War of Independence. During industrial revolution, nearby coal seams boosted Glasgow's importance and its population increased ten-fold between 1800 and 1900. Decline of shipbuilding industry began in 1930s and city is now one of culture and progress. It has a strong performing arts tradition and many museums and galleries including Burrell Collection (set in Pollok Country Park). Cathedral is rare example of an almost complete 13th century church. Early 19th century Hutchesons' Hall in Ingram Street is one of city's most elegant buildings; Tenement House is late Victorian tenement flat retaining many original features. Three universities.
Airport 7 miles (11km) W.

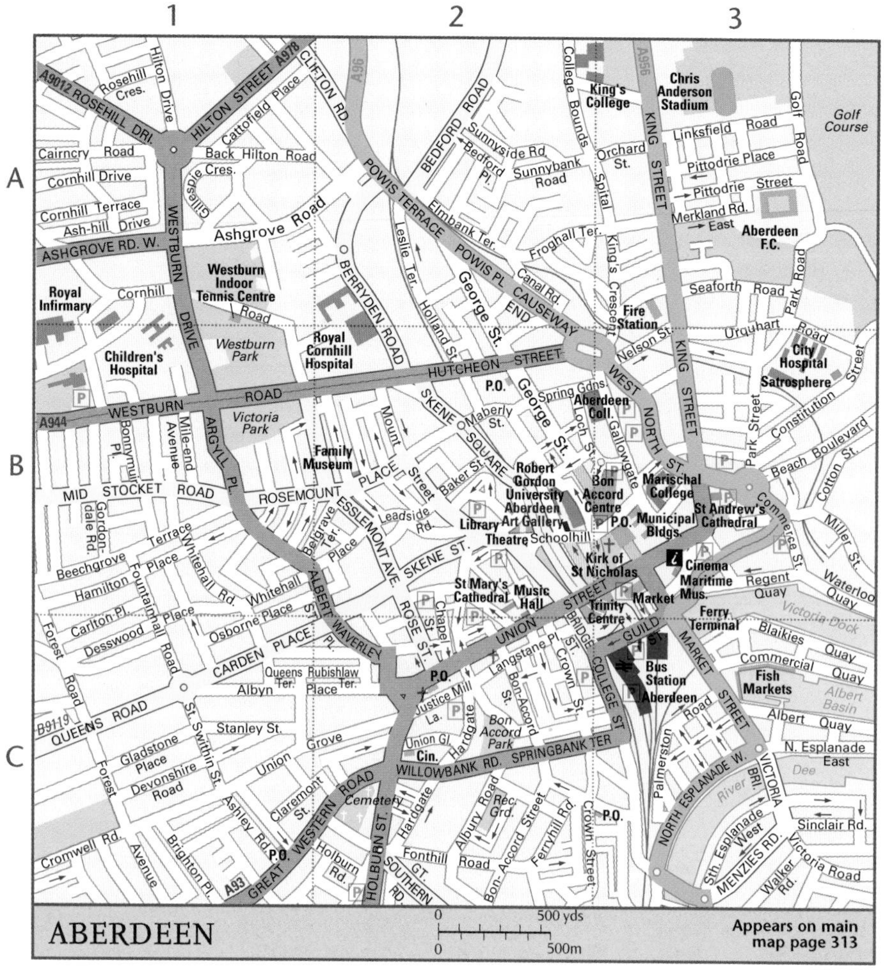

TOURIST INFORMATION CENTRE ☎ 01224 288828
23 UNION STREET,
ABERDEEN, AB11 5BP

HOSPITAL A & E ☎ 01224 681818
ABERDEEN ROYAL INFIRMARY,
FORESTERHILL, ABERDEEN, AB25 2ZN

COUNCIL OFFICE ☎ 01224 522000
ST. NICHOLAS HOUSE, BROAD STREET,
ABERDEEN, AB10 1AR

Aberdeen *Scotland* Population: 189,707. Cathedral and university city and commercial centre on E coast. Known as 'The Granite City', local stone having been used in many of its buildings. By 13th century, Aberdeen had become an important centre for trade and fishing and remains a major port and commercial base. In 19th century shipbuilding brought great prosperity to the city. These industries had receded by mid 20th century but the city's prospects were transformed when North Sea oil was discovered in 1970, turning it into a city of great wealth. St. Machar's Cathedral at Old Aberdeen. Many museums and art galleries. Extensive flower gardens. Airport at Dyce, 6 miles (9km) NW of Aberdeen.

LOCAL RADIO:
BBC RADIO SCOTLAND 585, 810, 990 AM / 92.6-94.7 FM;
NORTHSOUND ONE 96.9, 97.6, 103 FM;
NORTHSOUND TWO 1035 AM

www.agtb.org

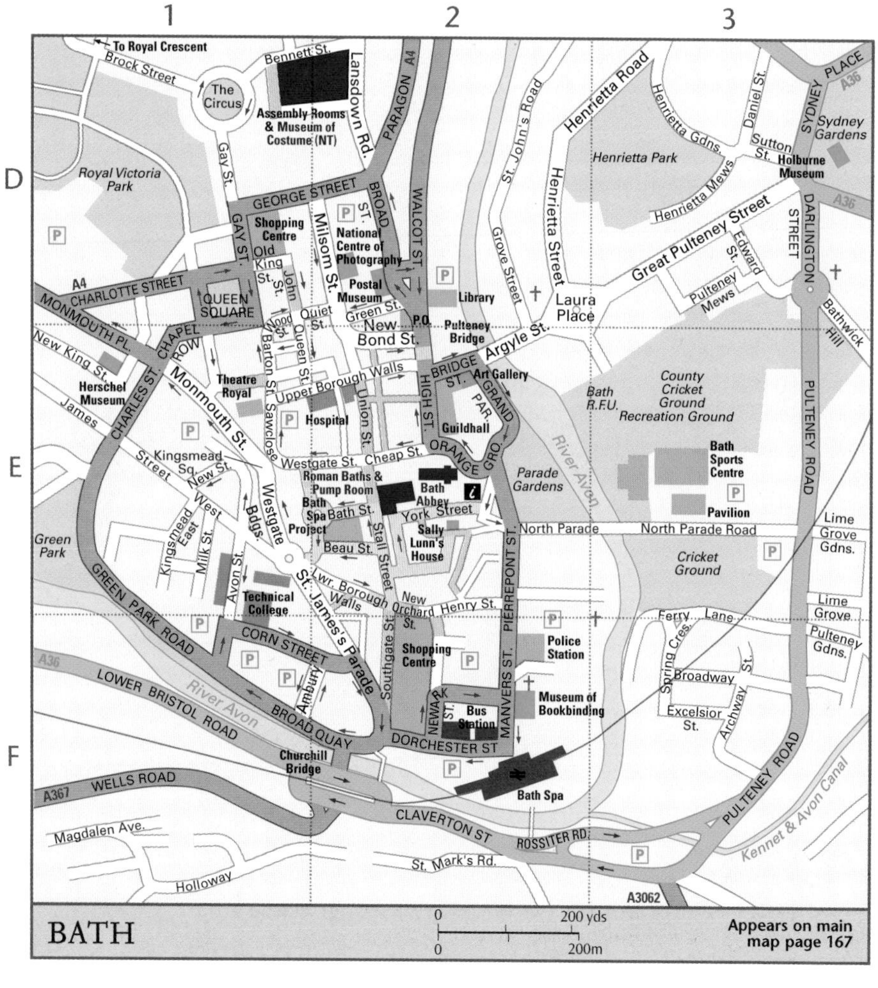

TOURIST INFORMATION CENTRE ☎ 0906 7112000
(Premium Rate)
ABBEY CHAMBERS, ABBEY CHURCHYARD,
BATH, BA1 1LY

HOSPITAL A & E ☎ 01225 428331
ROYAL UNITED HOSPITAL, COMBE PARK,
BATH, BA1 3NG

COUNCIL OFFICE ☎ 01225 477000
THE GUILDHALL, HIGH STREET,
BATH, BA1 5AW

Bath *South West England* Population: 85,202. City, spa on River Avon. Abbey church rebuilt 1501. Natural hot springs unique in Britain drew Romans to Bath, which they named 'Aquae Sulis'. Roman baths and 18th century Pump Room are open to visitors. In 18th century, it was most fashionable resort in country. Many Georgian buildings and elegant crescents remain, including The Circus and Royal Crescent. Museum of Costume in restored Assembly Rooms. Holds annual summer music festival. University 3 miles (4km) SE.

LOCAL RADIO:
BBC RADIO BRISTOL 1548 AM / 104.6 FM; BATH FM 107.9 FM;
CLASSIC GOLD 1260 AM; GWR (BATH) FM 103 FM

www.visitbath.co.uk

TOURIST INFORMATION CENTRE ☎ 01253 478222
1 CLIFTON STREET,
BLACKPOOL, FY1 1LY

HOSPITAL A & E ☎ 01253 300000
VICTORIA HOSPITAL, WHINNEY HEYS ROAD,
BLACKPOOL, FY3 8NR

COUNCIL OFFICE ☎ 01253 477477
TOWN HALL, TALBOT SQUARE,
BLACKPOOL, FY1 1AD

Blackpool *North West England* Population: 146,262. Town, large coastal resort and conference centre on Irish Sea. 19th century fashionable resort, still very popular today. 7 miles (11km) long 'Golden Mile' of tram route, beach, piers and amusement arcades. Blackpool Pleasure Beach, 518 ft (158m) high Tower entertainment complex, annual autumn Illuminations along 5 miles (8km) of Promenade, Zoo, Sea Life Centre, The Sandcastle indoor pool complex and Winter Gardens. Airport 3 miles (5km) S.

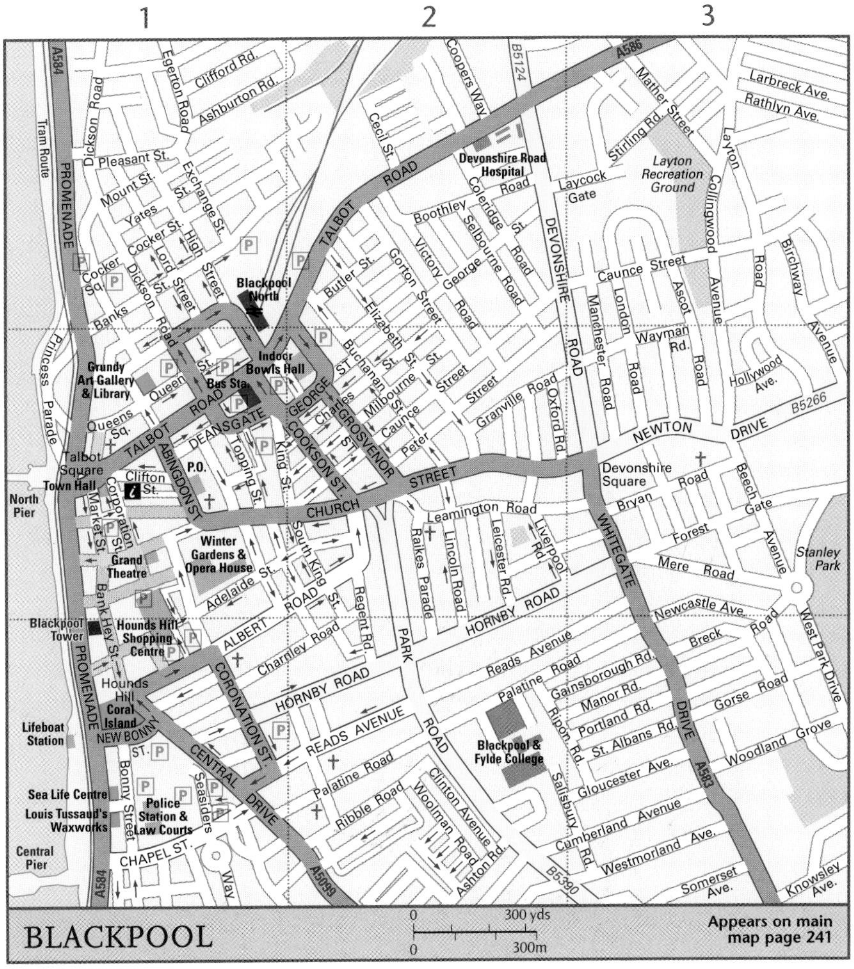

LOCAL RADIO:
BBC RADIO LANCASHIRE 104.5 FM
MAGIC 999 AM; WAVE 96.5 FM; ROCK FM 97.4 FM

www.visitblackpool.com

TOURIST INFORMATION CENTRE ☎ 0906 802 0234
(Premium Rate)
WESTOVER ROAD, BOURNEMOUTH, BH1 2BU

HOSPITAL A & E ☎ 01202 303626
ROYAL BOURNEMOUTH HOSPITAL,
CASTLE LANE EAST, BOURNEMOUTH, BH7 7DW

COUNCIL OFFICE ☎ 01202 451451
TOWN HALL, BOURNE AVENUE,
BOURNEMOUTH, BH2 6DY

Bournemouth *South West* Population: 155,488. Town, large seaside resort with mild climate. Town developed from a few cottages in 1810 to present conurbation. Sandy beach and pier. Extensive parks and gardens including Compton Acres, a display of international garden styles. Russell-Cotes Art Gallery and Museum houses Victorian and oriental collection. University. Conference, business and shopping centre. Bournemouth International Airport, 5 miles (8km) NE of town centre.

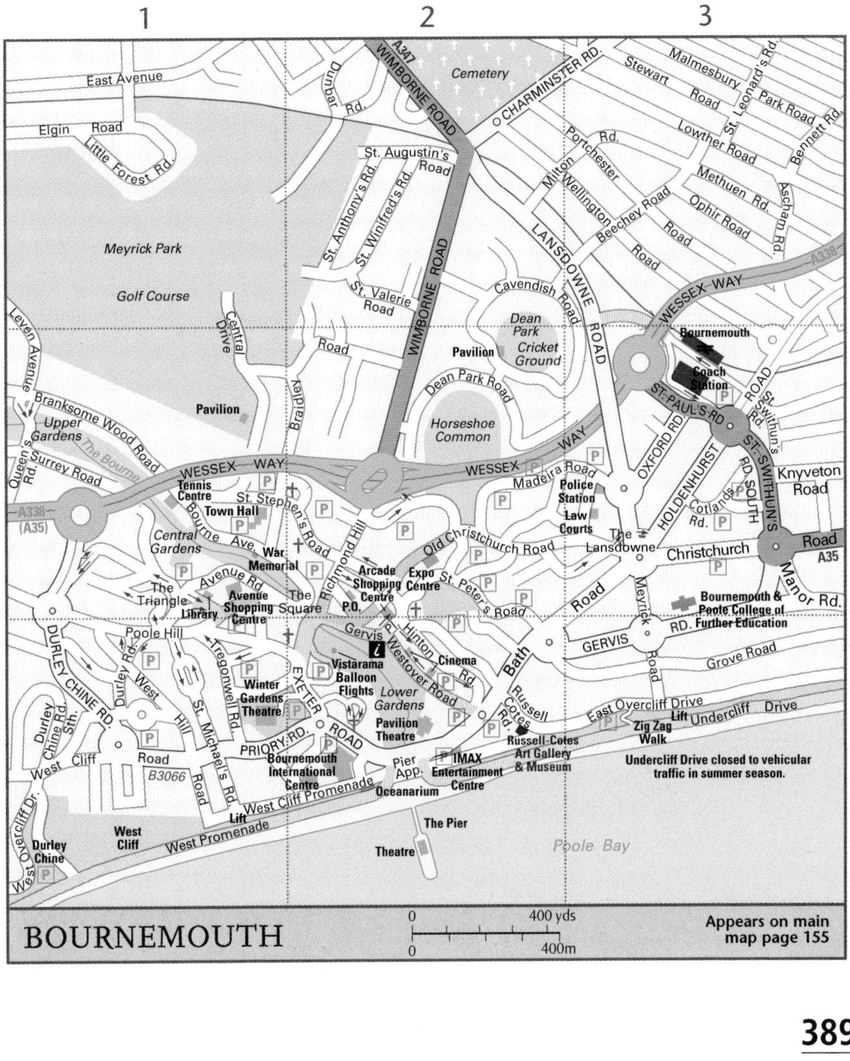

LOCAL RADIO:
BBC RADIO SOLENT (DORSET) 1359 AM / 103.8 FM;
2CR FM 102.3 FM; CLASSIC GOLD 828 AM; FIRE 107.6 FM;
WAVE 105 105.2 FM

www.bournemouth.co.uk

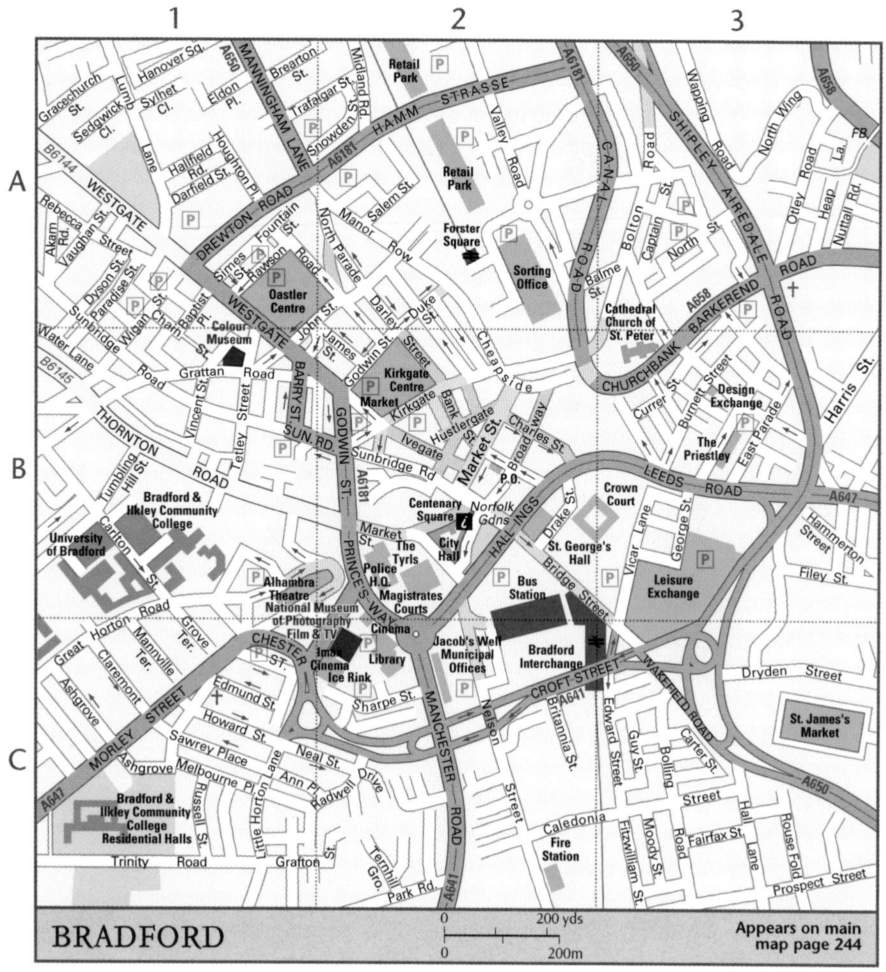

TOURIST INFORMATION CENTRE ☎ 01274 753678 CITY HALL, CENTENARY SQUARE, BRADFORD, BD1 1HY

HOSPITAL A & E ☎ 01274 542200 BRADFORD ROYAL INFIRMARY, DUCKWORTH LANE, BRADFORD, BD9 6RJ

COUNCIL OFFICE ☎ 01274 752111 CITY HALL, CENTENARY SQUARE, BRADFORD, BD1 1HY

Bradford *Yorkshire* Population: 289,376. Industrial city. Cathedral is former parish church. Previously known as wool capital of the world, Bradford is now less dependent upon the textile industry. Colour Museum documents history of dyeing and textile printing. University. Home to National Museum of Photography, Film and Television with IMAX cinema screen. Titus Salt built Saltaire 3 miles (5km) N, which is now considered a model industrial village. Salt's Mill, originally for textiles, now houses David Hockney art in the 1853 gallery. Leeds Bradford International Airport at Yeadon, 6 miles (10km) NE.

LOCAL RADIO: BBC RADIO LEEDS 774 AM / 92.4, 95.3 FM; WEST YORKS CLASSIC GOLD 1278 AM; THE PULSE 97.5 FM; SUNRISE RADIO 103.2 FM

www.visitbradford.com

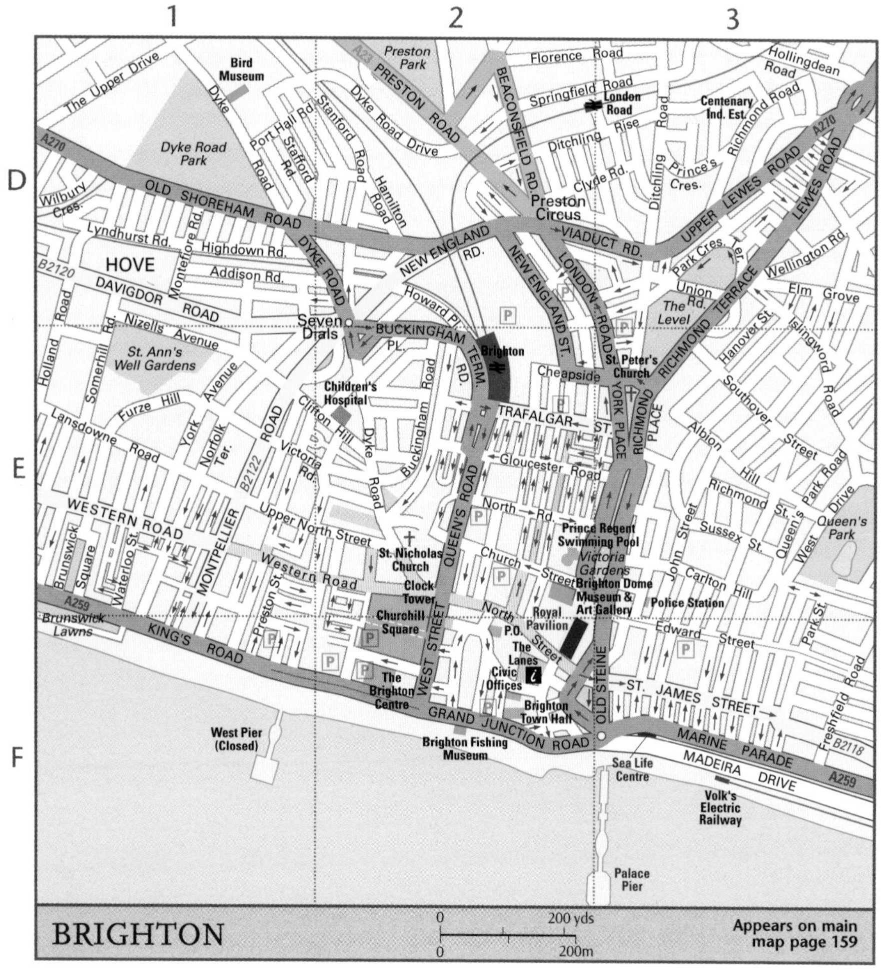

TOURIST INFORMATION CENTRE ☎ 0906 711 2255 (Premium Rate) 10 BARTHOLOMEW SQUARE, BRIGHTON, BN1 1JS

HOSPITAL A & E ☎ 01273 696955 ROYAL SUSSEX COUNTY HOSPITAL, EASTERN ROAD, BRIGHTON, BN2 5BE

COUNCIL OFFICE ☎ 01273 290000 TOWN HALL, BARTHOLOMEW SQUARE BRIGHTON, BN1 1JA

Brighton *South East England* Population: 124,851. Town, seaside resort, sailing and conference centre. Previously a fishing village known as Brighthelmstone, centred on current Lanes area. Brighton became fashionable as a sea-bathing resort in the 18th century. Patronized by the Prince Regent in 1780s who built the Royal Pavilion in Oriental style as a summer palace. Regency squares at Kemp Town. Amusement arcades on 1899 Palace Pier. Annual festivals. Language schools. Universities.

LOCAL RADIO: BBC SOUTHERN COUNTIES RADIO 1485 AM / 95.3 FM; CAPITAL GOLD 1323 AM; SOUTHERN FM 103.5; JUICE 107.2 FM

www.visitbrighton.com

TOURIST INFORMATION CENTRE ☎ 0906 711 2191 (Premium Rate)
THE ANNEXE, WILDSCREEN WALK, HARBOURSIDE, BRISTOL, BS1 5DB

HOSPITAL A & E ☎ 0117 923 0000
BRISTOL ROYAL INFIRMARY, MARLBOROUGH STREET, BRISTOL, BS2 8HW

COUNCIL OFFICE ☎ 0117 922 2000
THE COUNCIL HOUSE, COLLEGE GREEN, BRISTOL, BS1 5TR

Bristol *South West England* Population: 407,992. City. Port on River Avon dates from medieval times. Bristol grew from transatlantic trade in rum, tobacco and slaves. In Georgian times, Bristol's population was second only to London and many Georgian buildings still stand, including the Theatre Royal, the oldest working theatre in the country. Bristol is now a commercial and industrial centre. Cathedral dates from 12th century and was originally an abbey. 15th century Temple Church tower and walls (English Heritage). Restored iron ship SS Great Britain and Industrial Museum in city docks area. Universities. 245 ft (75m) high Clifton Suspension Bridge completed in 1864 across the Avon Gorge NW of the city. Bristol International Airport at Lulsgate 7 miles (11km) SW.

LOCAL RADIO:
BBC RADIO BRISTOL 1548 AM / 94.9 FM; CLASSIC GOLD 1260 AM; GWR FM 96.3 FM; VIBE 101 97.2 FM; STAR 107.2 FM

www.visitbristol.co.uk

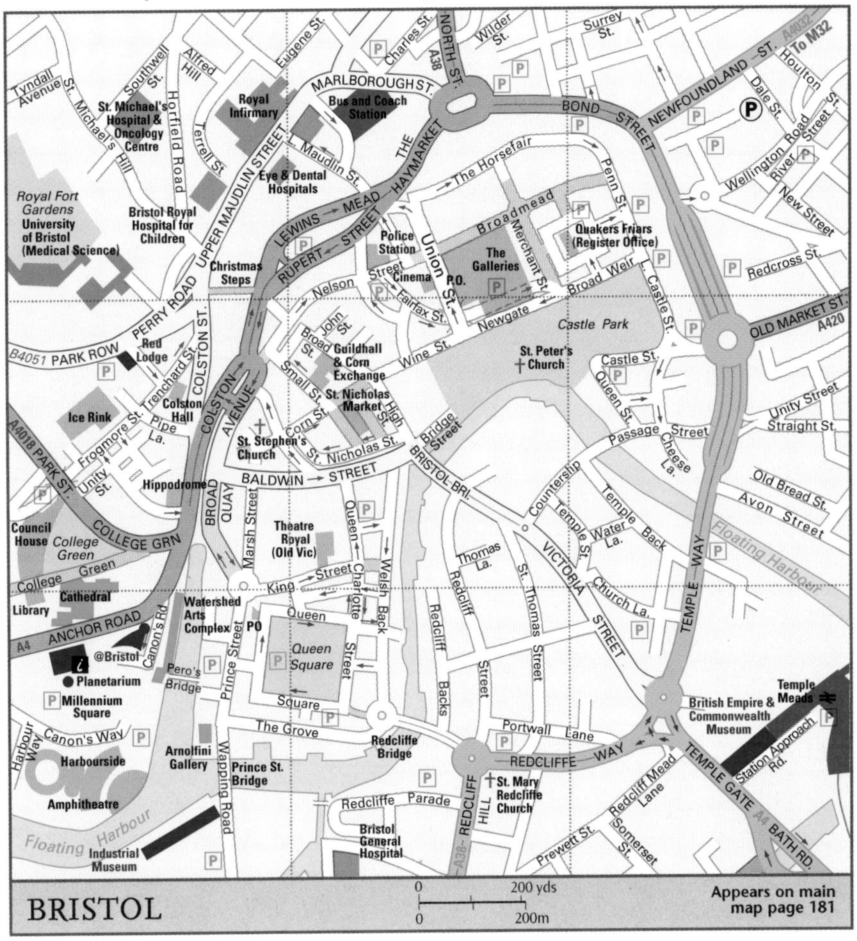

TOURIST INFORMATION CENTRE ☎ 0870 225 4900
WHEELER STREET, CAMBRIDGE, CAMBRIDGESHIRE, CB2 3QB

HOSPITAL A & E ☎ 01223 245151
ADDENBROOKE'S HOSPITAL, HILLS ROAD, CAMBRIDGE, CB2 2QQ

COUNCIL OFFICE ☎ 01223 457000
THE GUILDHALL, MARKET SQUARE, CAMBRIDGE, CB2 3QJ

Cambridge *East of England* Population: 95,682. University city on River Cam. First college founded here in 1284. Historic tensions existed between students and townspeople since 14th century, and came to a head during Peasants' Revolt of 1381 in which five townsfolk were hanged. Oliver Cromwell was a graduate of Sidney Sussex College and local MP at a time when the University was chiefly Royalist. 1870's saw foundation of first women's colleges, but women were not awarded degrees until after 1947. University's notable graduates include prime ministers, foreign heads of state, literary giants, philosophers and spies. Cambridge Footlights regularly provide a platform for future stars of stage, screen and television. Cambridge boasts many fine museums, art galleries and buildings of interest, including King's College Chapel and Fitzwilliam Museum. Airport at Teversham 3 miles (4km) E.

LOCAL RADIO:
BBC RADIO CAMBRIDGESHIRE 96 FM; Q 103 FM; STAR 107.9 FM

www.visitcambridge.org

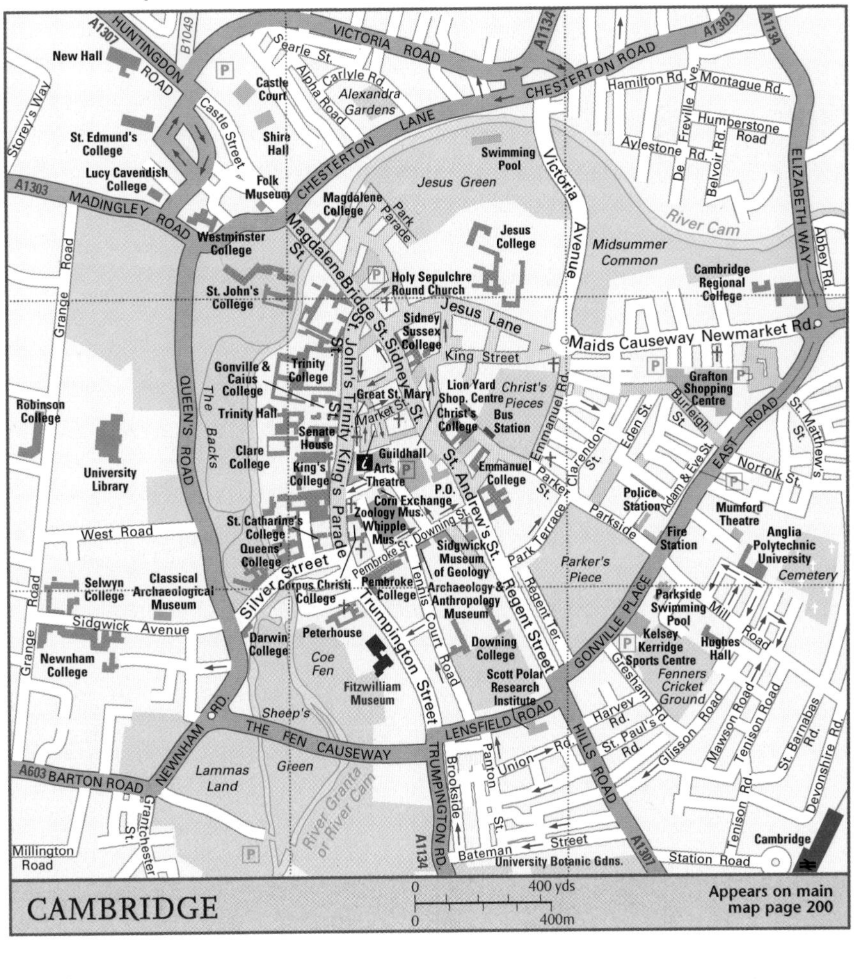

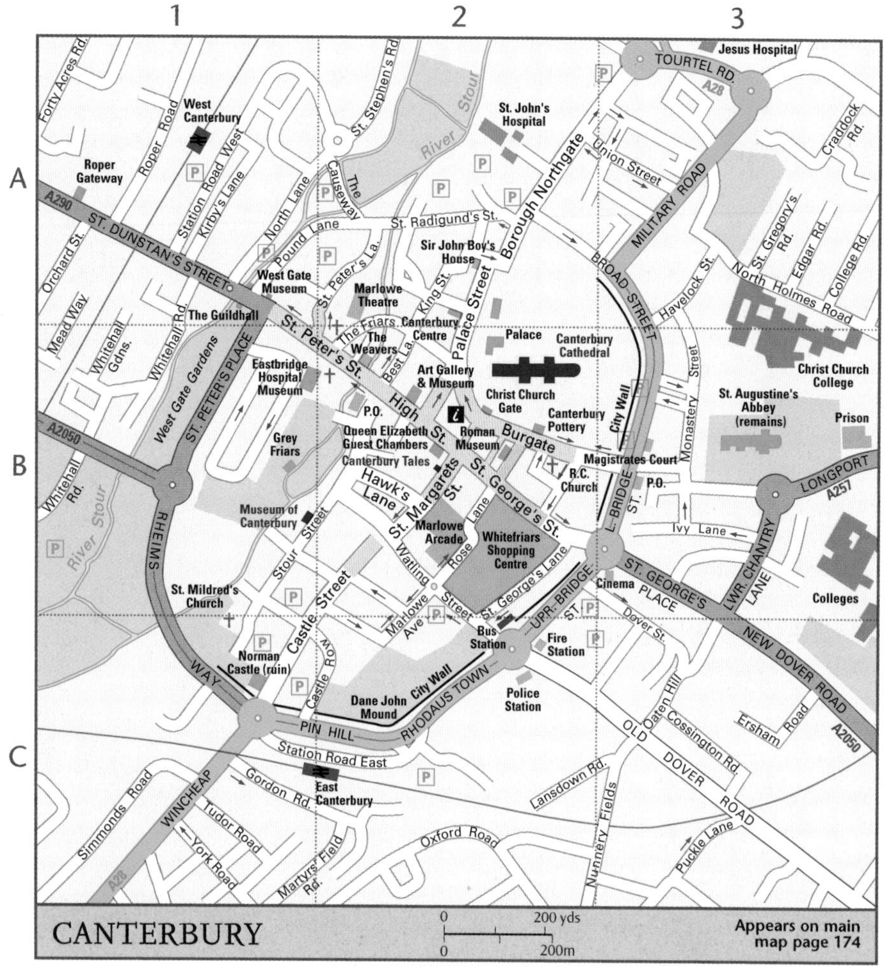

TOURIST INFORMATION CENTRE ☎ 01227 378100
12/13 SUN STREET, THE BUTTERMARKET,
CANTERBURY, CT1 2HX

HOSPITAL A & E ☎ 01227 766877
KENT & CANTERBURY HOSPITAL,
ETHELBERT ROAD, CANTERBURY, CT1 3NG

COUNCIL OFFICE ☎ 01227 862000
COUNCIL OFFICES, MILITARY ROAD,
CANTERBURY, CT1 1YW

Canterbury *South East England* Population: 36,464. Premier cathedral city and seat of Primate of Church of England on Great Stour River. Site of Roman settlement Durovernum. After Romans left, Saxons renamed town Cantwarabyrig. First cathedral in England built on site of current Christ Church Cathedral in AD 602. Thomas à Becket assassinated in Canterbury in 1170, turning Cathedral into great Christian shrine and destination of many pilgrimages, such as those detailed in Geoffrey Chaucer's Canterbury Tales. Becket's tomb destroyed on orders of Henry VIII. Cathedral was backdrop for premiere of T.S. Eliot's play 'Murder in the Cathedral' in 1935. City suffered extensive damage during World War II. Many museums and galleries explaining city's rich heritage. Roman and medieval remains, including city walls. Modern shopping centre; industrial development on outskirts. University of Kent on hill to N.

LOCAL RADIO:
BBC RADIO KENT 774 AM / 97.6 FM;
INVICTA FM 103.1 FM; KM-fm 106 FM

www.canterbury.co.uk

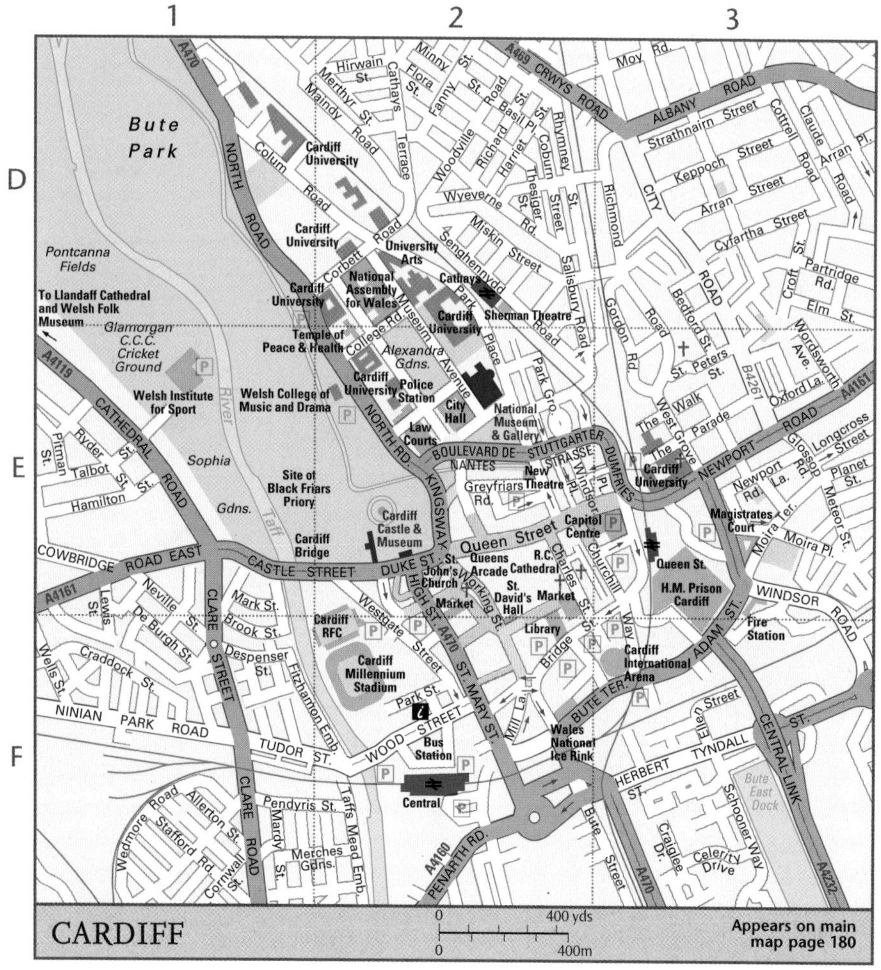

TOURIST INFORMATION CENTRE ☎ 029 2022 7281
CARDIFF VISITOR CENTRE, 16 WOOD STREET,
CARDIFF, CF10 1ES

HOSPITAL A & E ☎ 029 2074 7747
UNIVERSITY HOSPITAL OF WALES, HEATH PARK,
CARDIFF, CF14 4XW

COUNCIL OFFICE ☎ 029 2087 2087
THE HELP CENTRE, MARLAND HOUSE,
CENTRAL SQUARE, CARDIFF, CF10 1EP

Cardiff (Caerdydd) *Wales* Population: 272,129. City, capital of Wales since 1955, since when, many governmental, administrative and media organisations have moved to city. Romans founded military fort and small settlement on site of present day Cardiff. Uninhabited between departure of Romans and Norman conquest centuries later. Fishing village until development of coal mining in 19th century. Population rose from 1000 in 1801 to 170,000 a century later, becoming one of busiest ports in the world. Dock trade collapsed in 1930's. Major development programme still under way. Cardiff Bay area now major tourist centre and includes Techniquest, a science discovery centre, and the location of the new Welsh Assembly building. Millennium Stadium Cardiff Arms Park is the home of the Welsh Rugby Union and also hosts other sporting and entertainment events. Many museums including National Museum of Wales. Universities.

LOCAL RADIO:
BBC RADIO WALES 657, 882 AM / 103.9 FM; CAPITAL GOLD 1305, 1359 AM; RED DRAGON FM 103.2 FM; REAL 105-106 FM

www.visitcardiff.info

TOURIST INFORMATION CENTRE ☎ 01228 625600
CARDIFF VISITOR CENTRE, OLD TOWN HALL,
GREEN MARKET, CARLISLE, CA3 8JH

HOSPITAL A & E ☎ 01228 523444
CUMBERLAND INFIRMARY, NEWTOWN ROAD,
CARLISLE, CA2 7HY

COUNCIL OFFICE ☎ 01228 817000
CARLISLE CITY COUNCIL, THE CIVIC CENTRE,
CARLISLE, CA3 8QG

Carlisle *North West England* Population: 72,439. Cathedral city at confluence of River Eden and River Caldew. Once a Roman military base and later fought over by Scots and English, line of Hadrian's wall runs through the northern suburbs. Castle above the River Eden, completed in 12th century, houses a military museum. Cathedral partially destroyed by fire in 17th century has two surviving bays of 12th century and a magnificent East window. Tullie House Museum imaginatively tells of the city's turbulent past. University of Northumbria. Racecourse . Airport 6 miles (9km) NE.

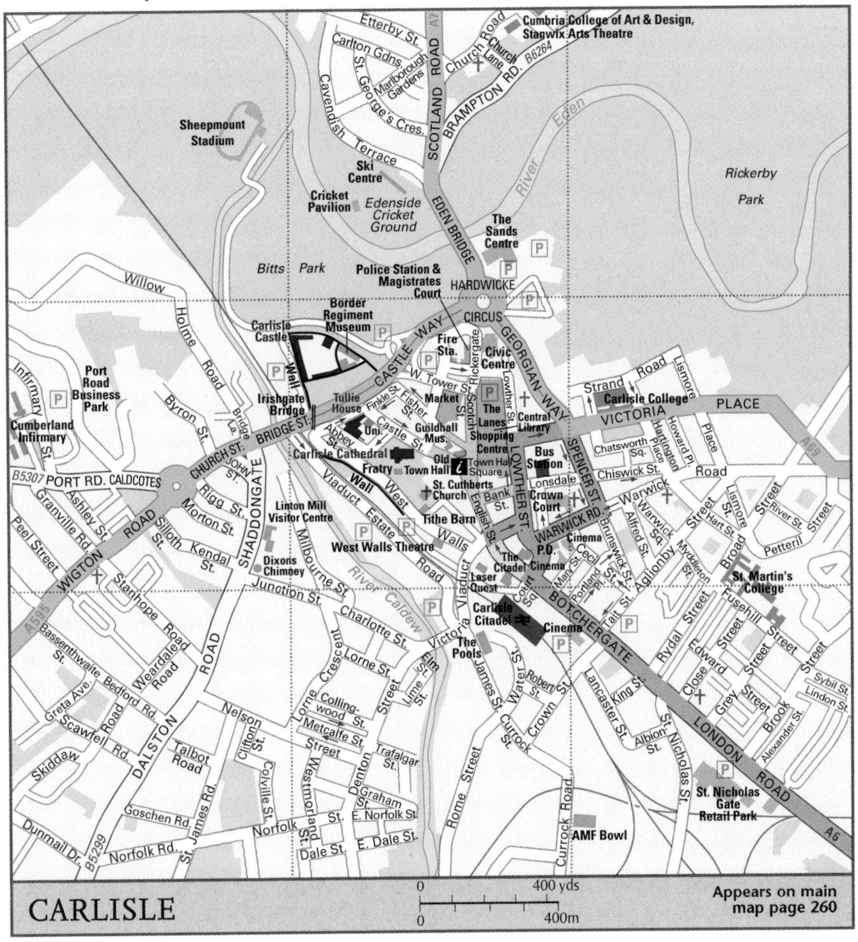

LOCAL RADIO:
BBC RADIO CUMBRIA 95.6, 96.1 & 104.1 FM;
CFM RADIO 96.4 FM

www.historic-carlisle.org.uk

TOURIST INFORMATION CENTRE ☎ 01242 522878
77 THE PROMENADE, CHELTENHAM,
GLOUCESTERSHIRE, GL50 1PJ

HOSPITAL A & E ☎ 08454 222222
CHELTENHAM GENERAL HOSPITAL,
SANDFORD ROAD, CHELTENHAM, GL53 7AN

COUNCIL OFFICE ☎ 01242 262626
MUNICIPAL OFFICES, THE PROMENADE,
CHELTENHAM, GL50 1PP

Cheltenham *South West England* Population: 91,301. Largest town in The Cotswolds. Shopping and tourist centre, with some light industry. Mainly residential, with many Regency and Victorian buildings and public gardens. Formerly a spa town, Pittville Pump Room built between 1825 and 1830 overlooks Pittville Park and is now used for concerts. Art Gallery and Museum. Ladies' College founded 1853. Racecourse to the N hosts Cheltenham Gold Cup race meeting, Cheltenham International Music Festival and Festival of Literature, among other events. Birthplace of composer Gustav Holst. University of Gloucestershire.

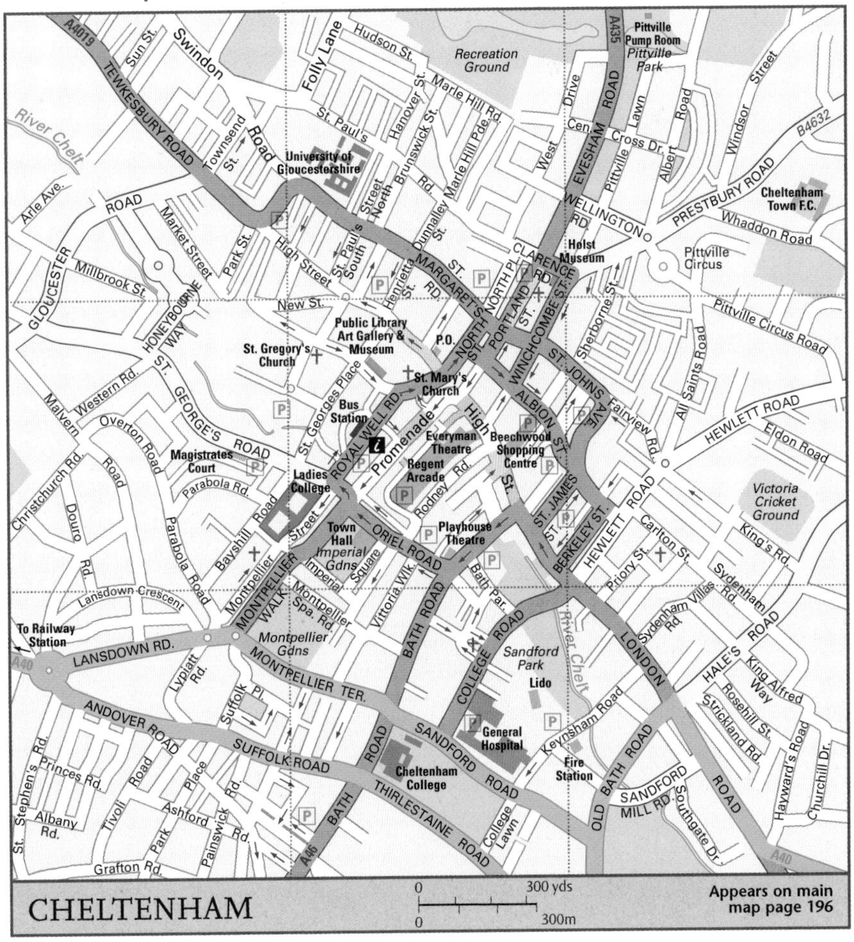

LOCAL RADIO:
BBC RADIO GLOUCESTERSHIRE 1413 AM / 104.7 FM;
CLASSIC GOLD 774 AM; SEVERN SOUND FM 102.4 FM;
STAR 107.5 FM

www.visitcheltenham.info

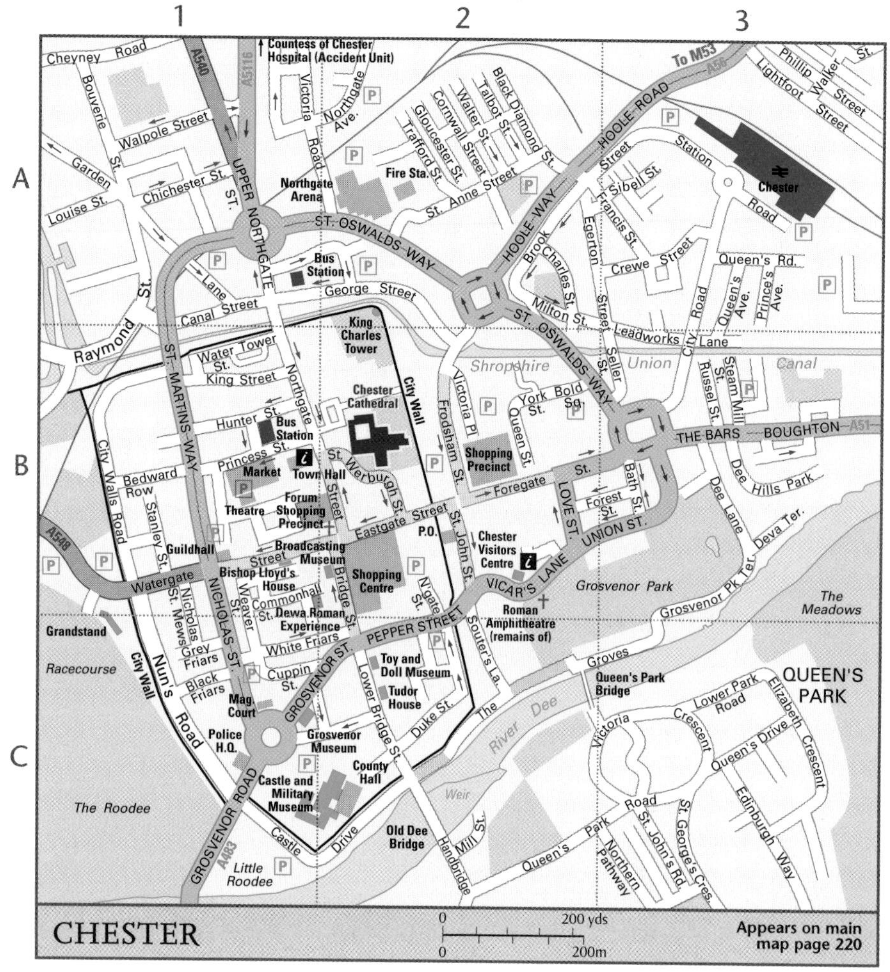

TOURIST INFORMATION CENTRE ☎ 01244 402111
TOWN HALL, NORTHGATE STREET,
CHESTER, CHESHIRE, CH1 2HJ

HOSPITAL A & E ☎ 01244 365000
COUNTESS OF CHESTER HOSPITAL, HEALTH PK,
LIVERPOOL ROAD, CHESTER, CH2 1UL

COUNCIL OFFICE ☎ 01244 324324
THE FORUM,
CHESTER, CH1 2HS

Chester *North West England* Population: 80110. County town and cathedral city on River Dee. Commercial, financial and tourist centre built on Roman town of Deva. Includes biggest Roman amphitheatre in Britain and well preserved medieval walls. Castle, now county hall, includes 12th century Agricola Tower. Cathedral with remains of original Norman abbey. Famed for Tudor timber-framed buildings which include Chester Rows, two-tier galleried shops and Bishop Lloyd's House, with ornate 16th century carved façade. Eastgate clock built to commemorate Queen Victoria's diamond jubilee in 1897. Racecourse and zoo.

LOCAL RADIO:
BBC RADIO MERSEYSIDE 95.8 FM;
MAGIC 1548 AM; MFM 103.4 FM; RADIO CITY 96.7 FM

www.chestercc.gov.uk/tourism

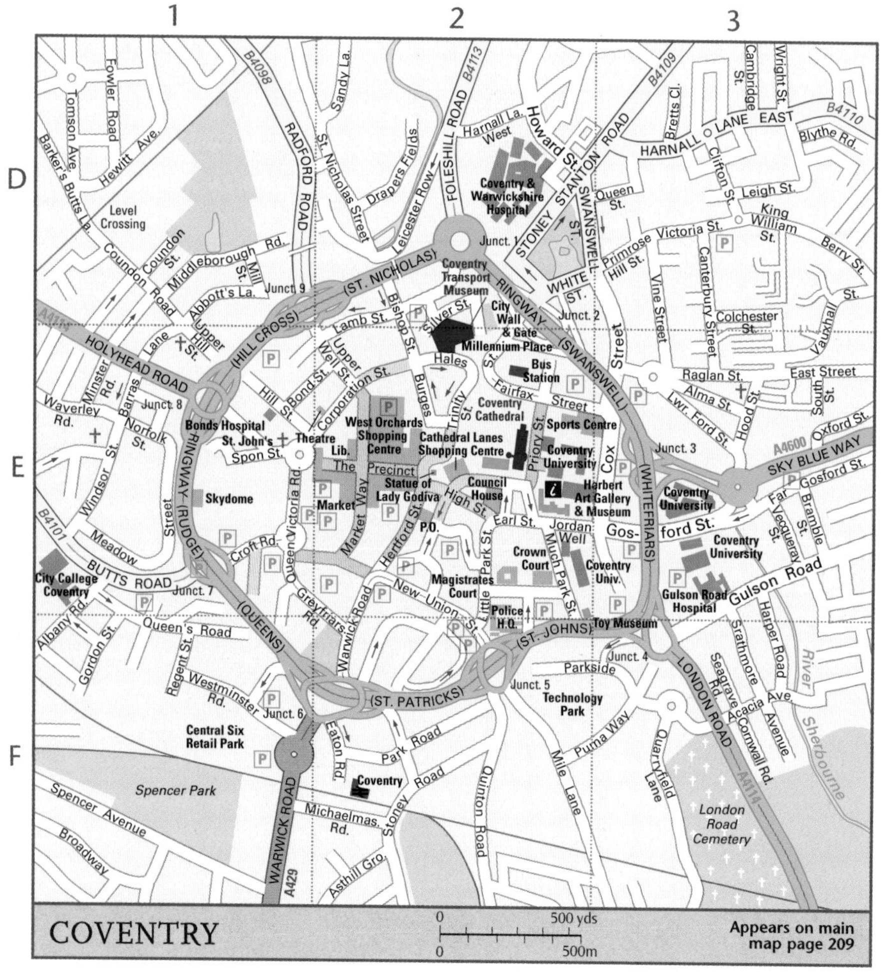

TOURIST INFORMATION CENTRE ☎ 024 7622 7264
BAYLEY LANE, COVENTRY,
WEST MIDLANDS, CV1 5RN

HOSPITAL A & E ☎ 024 7622 4055
COVENTRY & WARWICKSHIRE HOSPITAL,
STONEY STANTON ROAD, COVENTRY, CV1 4FH

COUNCIL OFFICE ☎ 024 7683 3333
COUNCIL HOUSE, EARL STREET,
COVENTRY, CV1 5RR

Coventry *West Midlands* Population: 299,316. City. St. Michael's cathedral built 1954-62 beside ruins of medieval cathedral destroyed in air raid in 1940. The centre of the city was rebuilt in the 1950s and 1960s following WW II bombing, but some old buildings remain, including Bonds Hospital and the medieval Guildhall. A town rich from textile industry in middle ages, Coventry is now known for its motor car industry; other important industries are manufacturing and engineering. Coventry Transport Museum. Herbert Art Gallery and Museum. Universities. Civil airport at Baginton to S. Coventry Canal runs N to Trent and Mersey Canal at Fradley Junction near Lichfield.

LOCAL RADIO:
BBC RADIO WM 103.7 FM; CLASSIC GOLD 1359 AM; KIX 96.2 FM;
MERCIA FM 97 FM; HEART FM 100.7 FM

www.visitcoventry.co.uk

TOURIST INFORMATION CENTRE ☎ 01332 255802
ASSEMBLY ROOMS, MARKET PLACE,
DERBY, DE1 3AH

HOSPITAL A & E ☎ 01332 347141
DERBYSHIRE ROYAL INFIRMARY,
LONDON ROAD, DERBY, DE1 2QY

COUNCIL OFFICE ☎ 01332 293111
THE COUNCIL HOUSE, CORPORATION STREET,
DERBY, DE1 2FS

Derby *East Midlands* Population: 223,836. Industrial city and county town on River Derwent. Shopping and entertainment centre. Cathedral mainly by James Gibbs, 1725. Both manufacturing and engineering are important to local economy. Derby Industrial Museum charts city's industrial history with emphasis on Rolls Royce aircraft engineering. Tours at Royal Crown Derby porcelain factory. University.

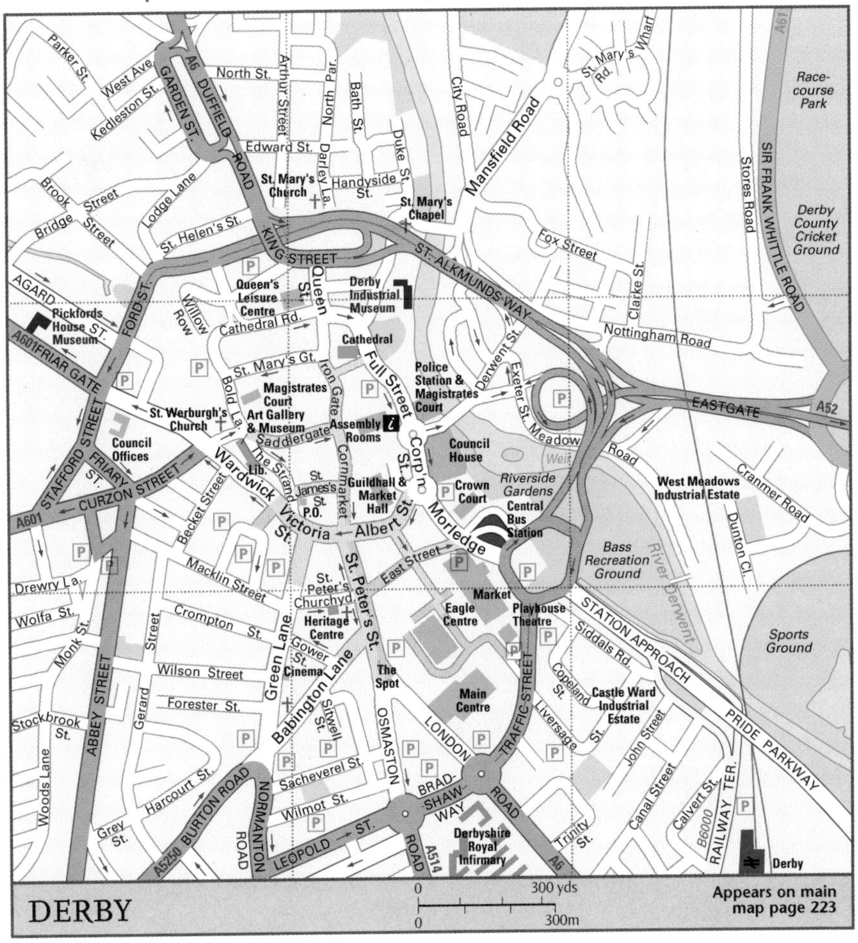

LOCAL RADIO:
BBC RADIO DERBY 1116 AM / 104.5 FM;
CLASSIC GOLD GEM 945 AM; RAM FM 102.8 FM;
96 TRENT FM 96.2 FM

www.visitderby.co.uk

TOURIST INFORMATION CENTRE ☎ 01304 205108
THE OLD TOWN GAOL, BIGGIN STREET,
DOVER, CT16 1DL

HOSPITAL A & E ☎ 01227 766877
KENT & CANTERBURY HOSPITAL,
ETHELBERT ROAD, CANTERBURY, CT1 3NG

COUNCIL OFFICE ☎ 01304 821199
WHITE CLIFFS BUSINESS PARK,
DOVER, CT16 3PJ

Dover *South East England* Population: 34,179. Town, cinque port, resort and Channel port on Strait of Dover, with large modern docks for freight and passengers. Dominated by high white cliffs and medieval castle enclosing the Pharos, AD50 remains of Roman lighthouse. Remains of 12th century Knights Templar Church across valley from castle. Sections of moat of 19th century fort at Western Heights, above town on W side of harbour.

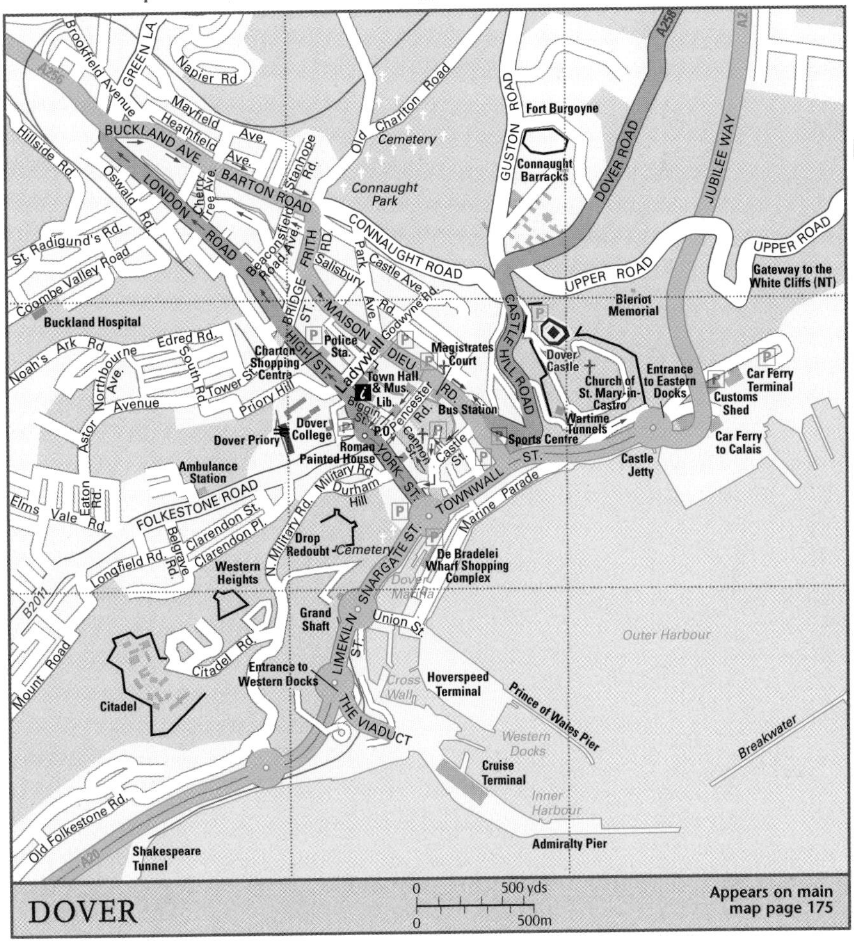

LOCAL RADIO:
BBC RADIO KENT 774 AM / 104.2 FM;
KM-fm 106.8 FM; INVICTA FM 97 FM

www.whitecliffscountry.org.uk

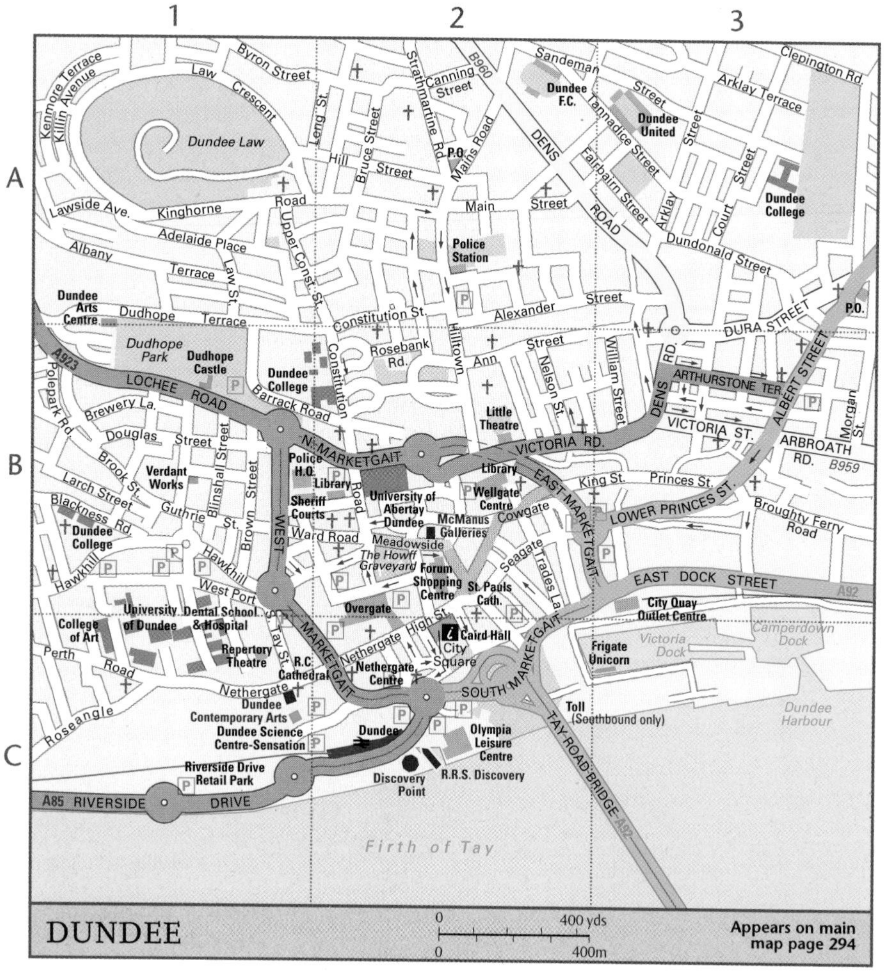

TOURIST INFORMATION CENTRE ☎ 01382 527527
21 CASTLE STREET,
DUNDEE, DD1 3AA

HOSPITAL A & E ☎ 01382 660111
NINEWELLS HOSPITAL, NINEWELLS ROAD,
DUNDEE, DD1 9SY

COUNCIL OFFICE ☎ 01382 434000
CITY CHAMBERS, 21 CITY SQUARE,
DUNDEE, DD1 3BY

Dundee *Scotland* Population: 158,981. Scotland's fourth largest city, commercial and industrial centre and port. Robert the Bruce declared King of the Scots in Dundee in 1309. Sustained severe damage during Civil War and again prior to Jacobite uprising. City recovered in early 19th century and became Britain's main processor of jute. One of largest employers in Dundee today is D.C. Thomson, publisher of The Beano and The Dandy. Many museums and art galleries. Cultural centre, occasionally playing host to overflow from Edinburgh Festival. Episcopal cathedral on site of former castle. Universities. Ship 'Discovery' in which Captain Scott travelled to Antarctic has returned to Victoria dock, where she was built.

LOCAL RADIO:
BBC RADIO SCOTLAND 585, 810, 990 AM / 92.6-94.7 FM;
TAY AM 1161 AM; TAY FM 102.8 FM; WAVE 102 FM

www.angusanddundee.co.uk

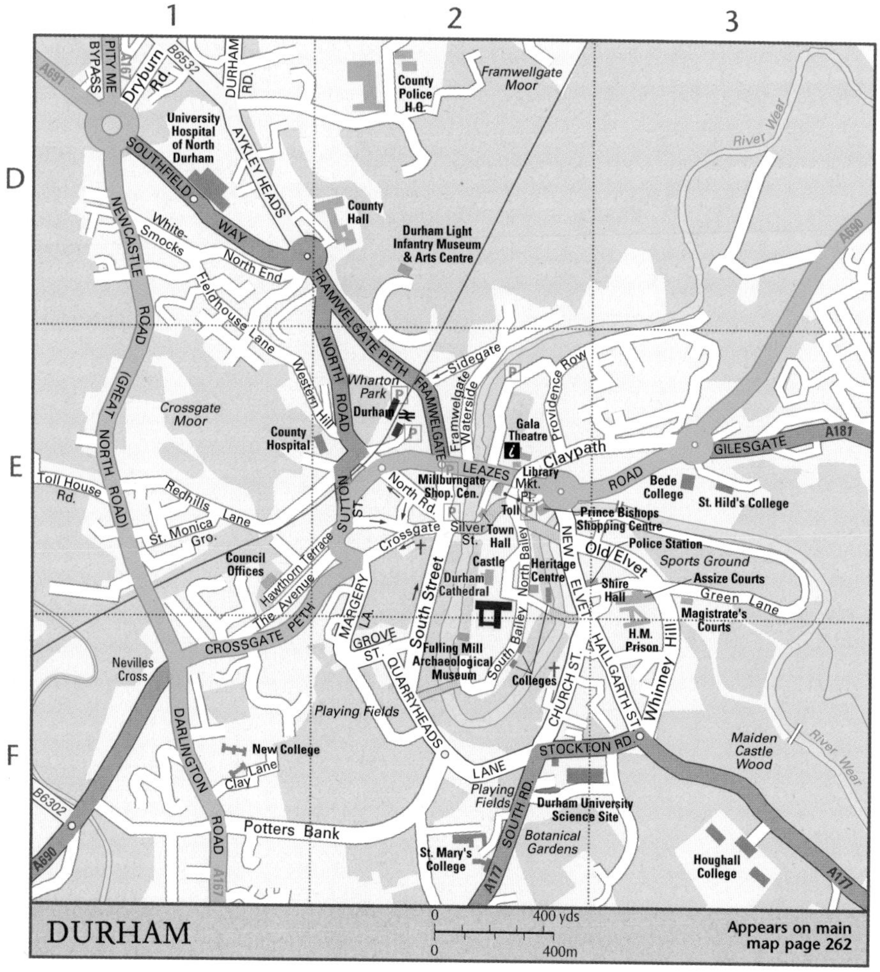

TOURIST INFORMATION CENTRE ☎ 0191 384 3720
2 MILLENNIUM PLACE, DURHAM,
COUNTY DURHAM, DH1 1WA

HOSPITAL A & E ☎ 0191 333 2333
UNIVERSITY HOSPITAL OF NORTH DURHAM,
NORTH ROAD, DURHAM, DH1 5TW

COUNCIL OFFICE ☎ 0191 386 4411
COUNTY HALL,
DURHAM, DH1 5UB

Durham *North East England* Population: 36,937. Cathedral city on narrow bend in River Wear. Norman-Romanesque cathedral founded in 1093 on site of shrine of St. Cuthbert is World Heritage Site. England's third oldest University founded in 1832. Motte-and-bailey castle dating from 1072 now part of the University. Collection in Fulling Mill Museum of Archaelogy illustrates history of city. Museum of Oriental Art. Light Infantry Museum. Art Gallery. University Botanic Garden S of city.

LOCAL RADIO:
BBC RADIO NEWCASTLE 95.4 FM;
SUN FM 103.4 FM; GALAXY 105-106 105.3, 105.6, 105.8 & 106.4 FM

www.durhamtourism.co.uk

TOURIST INFORMATION CENTRE ☎ 01323 411400
3 CORNFIELD ROAD,
EASTBOURNE, BN21 4QL

HOSPITAL A & E ☎ 01323 417400
EASTBOURNE DISTRICT GENERAL HOSPITAL,
KING'S DRIVE, EASTBOURNE, BN21 2UD

COUNCIL OFFICE ☎ 01323 410000
EASTBOURNE BOROUGH COUNCIL, TOWN HALL,
GROVE ROAD, EASTBOURNE BN21 4UG,

Eastbourne *South East England* Population: 94,793. Town, coastal resort and conference centre. Towner Art Gallery in 18th century manor house shows a contemporary collection of work. South Downs Way begins at Beachy Head, the 536 ft (163m) chalk cliff on the outskirts of the town. Eastbourne hosts an International Folk Festival and international tennis at Devonshire Park.

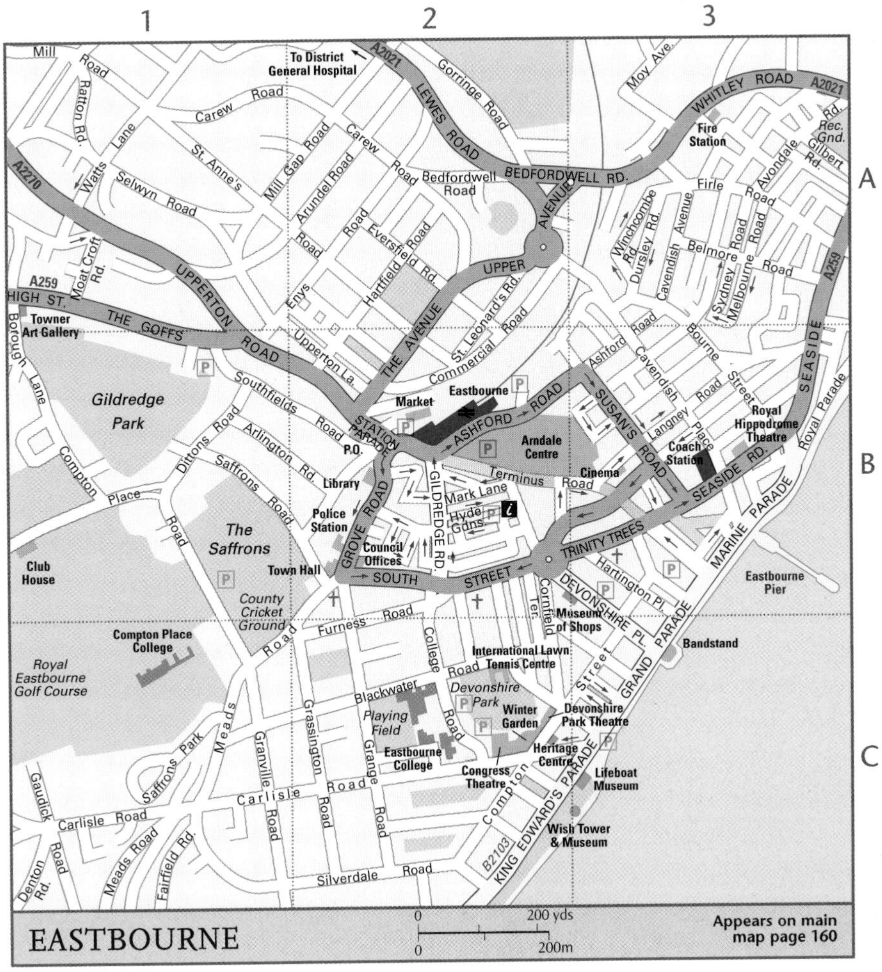

LOCAL RADIO:
BBC SOUTHERN COUNTIES RADIO 1161 AM / 104.5 FM;
SOVEREIGN RADIO 107.5 FM

www.eastbourne.org

TOURIST INFORMATION CENTRE ☎ 0131 473 3800
EDINBURGH & SCOTLAND INFORMATION CENTRE,
3 PRINCES STREET, EDINBURGH, EH2 2QP

HOSPITAL A & E ☎ 0131 536 1000
ROYAL INFIRMARY OF EDINBURGH
(LITTLE FRANCE), 51 LITTLE FRANCE CRESCENT,
EDINBURGH, EH16 4SA

COUNCIL OFFICE ☎ 0131 200 2000
COUNCIL HEADQUARTERS, 10 WATERLOO PLACE,
EDINBURGH, EH1 3EG

Edinburgh *Scotland* Population: 401,910. City, capital of Scotland, built on a range of rocky crags and extinct volcanoes, on S side of Firth of Forth. Administrative, financial and legal centre of Scotland. Medieval castle overlooks centre and was one of main seats of Royal court, while Arthur's Seat (largest of the volcanoes) guards eastern approaches. Three universities. Royal Yacht Britannia docked at Leith and is open to public. Important industries include brewing, distilling, food and electronics. Palace of Holyroodhouse is chief royal residence of Scotland. Old Town typified by Gladstone's Land, 17th century six-storey tenement with arcaded front, outside stair and stepped gables. Birthplace of Sir Arthur Conan Doyle. Many galleries and museums including National Gallery of Scotland. Largest arts festival in the world attracting over a million visitors each year.

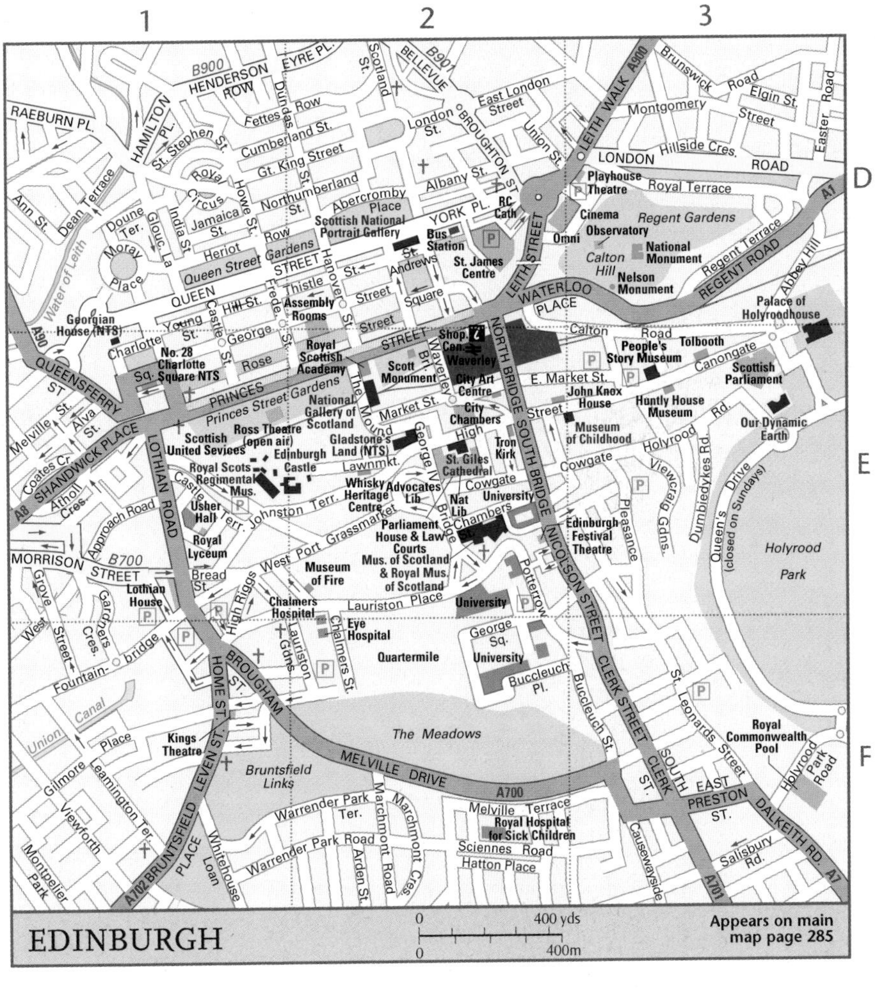

LOCAL RADIO:
BBC RADIO SCOTLAND 585, 810, 990 AM / 92.6-94.7 FM;
BEAT 106 105.7 FM; FORTH ONE 97.3, 97.6, 102.2 FM;
FORTH 2 1548 AM; REAL RADIO 101.1, 100.3 FM

www.edinburgh.org

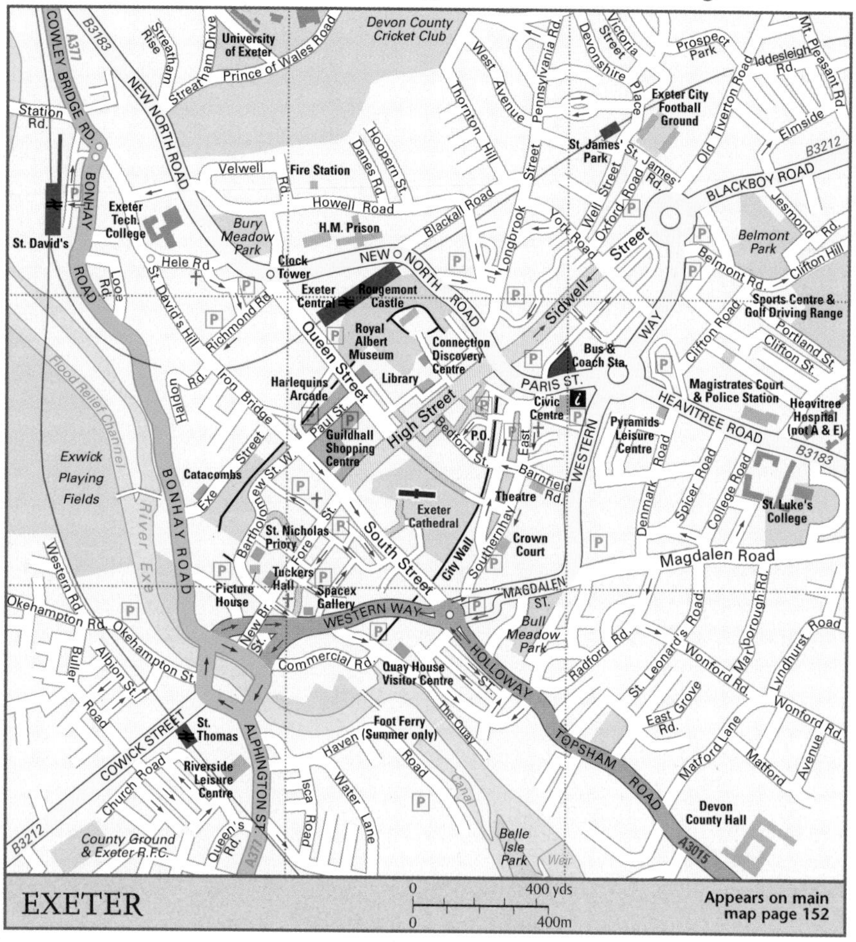

TOURIST INFORMATION CENTRE ☎ 01392 265700
CIVIC CENTRE, PARIS STREET, EXETER,
DEVON, EX1 1JJ

HOSPITAL A & E ☎ 01392 411611
ROYAL DEVON & EXETER HOSPITAL (WONFORD),
BARRACK ROAD, EXETER, EX2 5DW

COUNCIL OFFICE ☎ 01392 277888
CIVIC CENTRE, PARIS STREET,
EXETER, EX1 1JN

Exeter *South West England* Population: 94,717. City, county capital on River Exe. Major administrative, business and financial centre on site of Roman town Isca Dumnoniorum. Cathedral is decorated, with Norman towers and façade with hundreds of stone statues. 15th century guildhall. Modern buildings in centre built after extensive damage from World War II. Beneath the city lie remains of medieval water-supply system built in 14th century to supply fresh water to city centre. Royal Albert Memorial Museum and Art Gallery. Early 16th century mansion of Bowhill, with preserved Great Hall, 2 miles (3km) SW. University. Airport 5 miles (8km) E at Clyst Honiton.

LOCAL RADIO:
BBC RADIO DEVON 990 AM / 95.8 FM;
CLASSIC GOLD 666 AM; GEMINI FM 97 & 103 FM

www.exeter.gov.uk/visiting

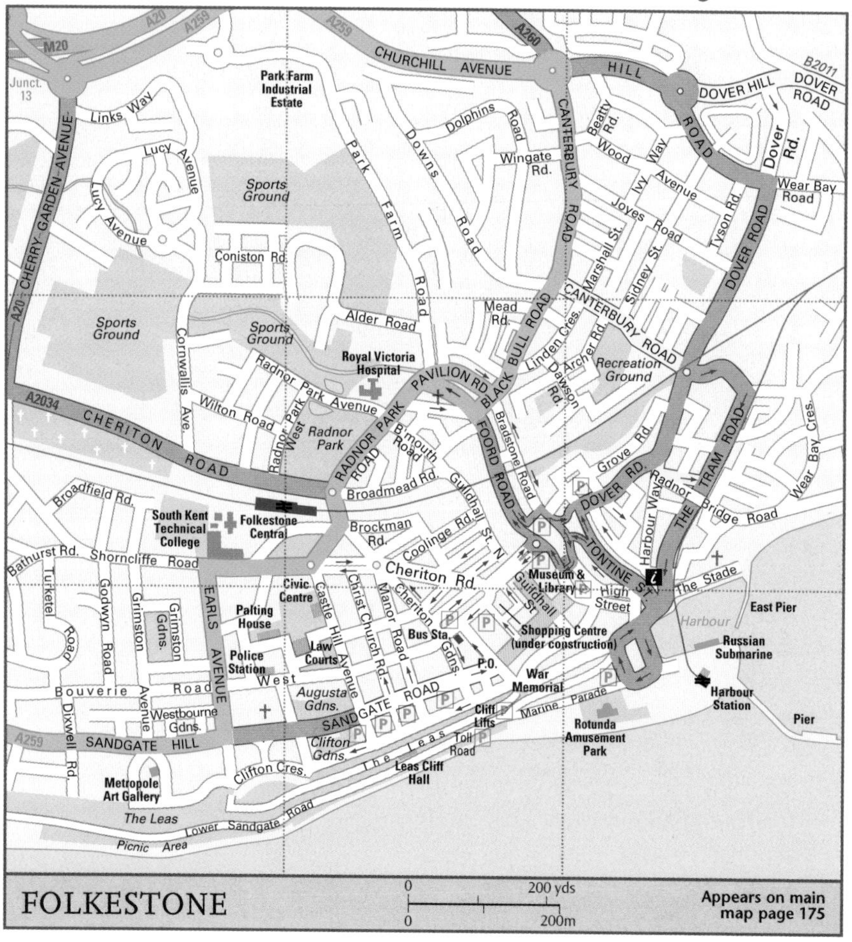

TOURIST INFORMATION CENTRE ☎ 01303 258594
HARBOUR STREET, FOLKESTONE,
KENT, CT20 1QN

HOSPITAL A & E ☎ 01233 633331
WILLIAM HARVEY HOSPITAL, KENNINGTON RD,
WILLESBOROUGH, ASHFORD, TN24 0LZ

COUNCIL OFFICE ☎ 01303 850388
CIVIC CENTRE, CASTLE HILL AVENUE,
FOLKESTONE, CT20 2QY

Folkestone *South East England* Population: 45,587. Town, Channel port and resort. Russian submarine docked in harbour is open to the public. The Lear marine promenade accessed by Victorian cliff lift. Ornate Victorian hotels. Martello tower on East Cliff. Kent Battle of Britain Museum at Hawkinge airfield 3 miles (5km) N. Channel Tunnel terminal on N side.

LOCAL RADIO:
BBC RADIO KENT 97.6 FM;
INVICTA FM 97 FM

www.discoverfolkestone.co.uk

TOURIST INFORMATION CENTRE ☎ 01452 421188
28 SOUTHGATE STREET, GLOUCESTER,
GLOUCESTERSHIRE, GL1 2DP

HOSPITAL A & E ☎ 08454 222222
GLOUCESTERSHIRE ROYAL HOSPITAL
GREAT WESTERN RD, GLOUCESTER, GL1 3NN

COUNCIL OFFICE ☎ 01452 522232
COUNCIL OFFICES, NORTH WAREHOUSE,
THE DOCKS, GLOUCESTER, GL1 2EP

Gloucester *South West England* Population: 114,003. Industrial city on River Severn, on site of Roman town of Glevum. Norman era saw Gloucester grow in political importance, from here William the Conqueror ordered survey of his Kingdom which resulted in Domesday Book of 1086. City became a religious centre during middle ages. Cathedral built in mixture of Norman and Perpendicular styles, has cloisters and England's largest stained glass window, dating from 14th century. Remains of 15th century - 16th century Franciscan friary, Greyfriars. Historic docks, now largely redeveloped, on Gloucester and Sharpness Canal. Three Choirs Festival held every third year.

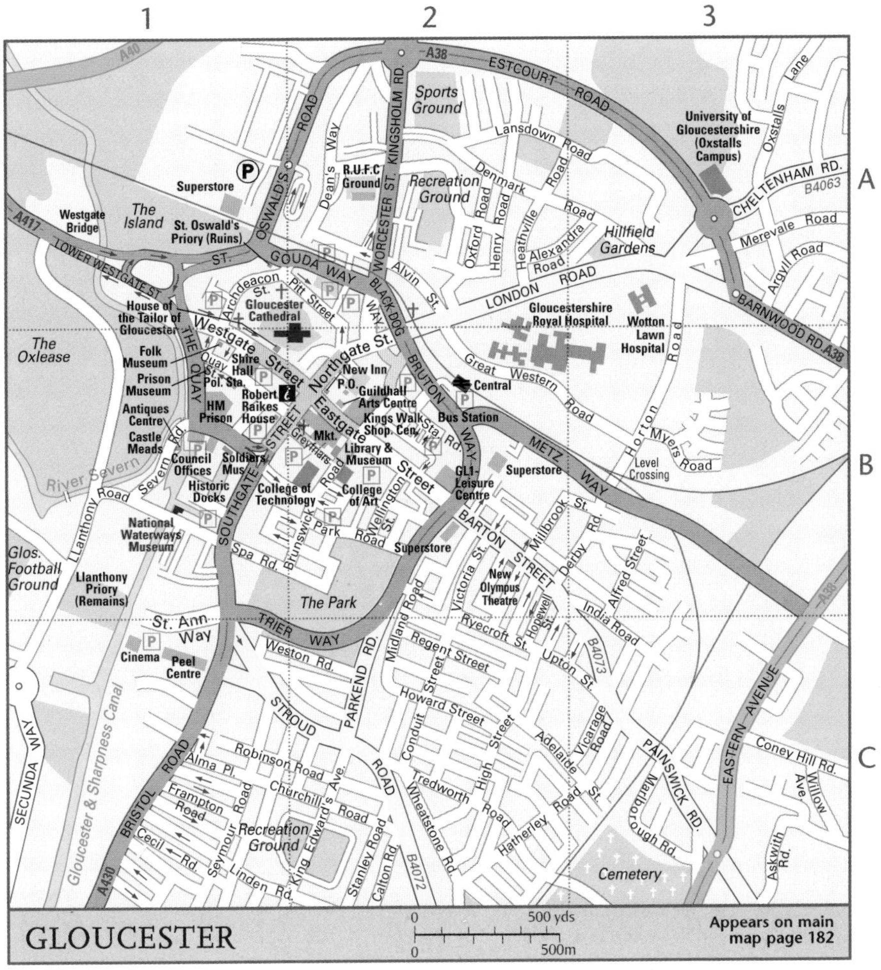

LOCAL RADIO:
BBC RADIO GLOUCESTERSHIRE 1413 AM / 104.7 FM;
CLASSIC GOLD 774 AM, SEVERN SOUND FM 102.4 & 103 FM

www.gloucester.gov.uk/tourism

TOURIST INFORMATION CENTRE ☎ 01483 444333
14 TUNSGATE,
GUILDFORD, GU1 3QT

HOSPITAL A & E ☎ 01483 571122
ROYAL SURREY COUNTY HOSPITAL,
EGERTON ROAD, GUILDFORD, GU2 5XX

COUNCIL OFFICE ☎ 01483 505050
GUILDFORD BOROUGH COUNCIL,
MILLMEAD HOUSE, MILLMEAD,
GUILDFORD, GU2 4BB

Guildford *South East England* Population: 65,998. County town and former weaving centre on River Wey. High Street lined with Tudor buildings, the Guildhall the most impressive. Remains of Norman castle keep built c.1173, on an 11th century motte, used as county gaol for 400 years. Cathedral consecrated in 1961 and built of red brick, the interior is designed in a modern gothic style. University of Surrey. Royal Grammar School noted for its chained library

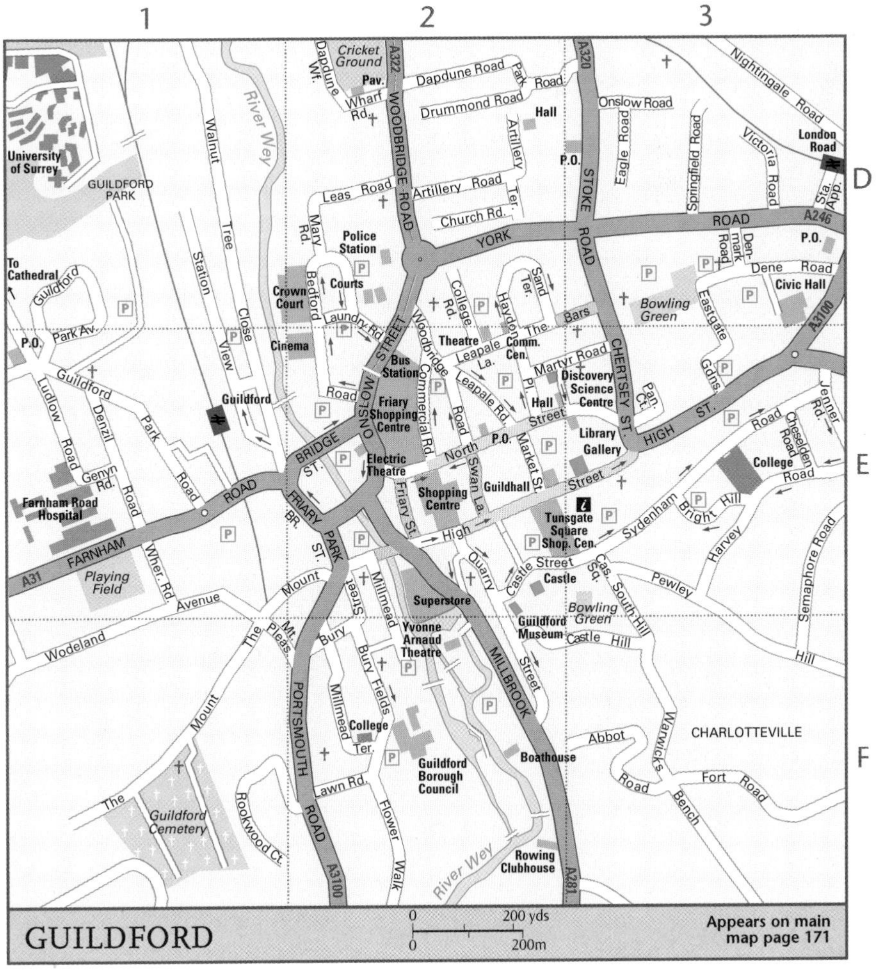

LOCAL RADIO:
BBC SOUTHERN COUNTIES RADIO 104.6 FM;
THE EAGLE 96.4 FM; COUNTY SOUND 1566 AM

www.guildfordborough.co.uk

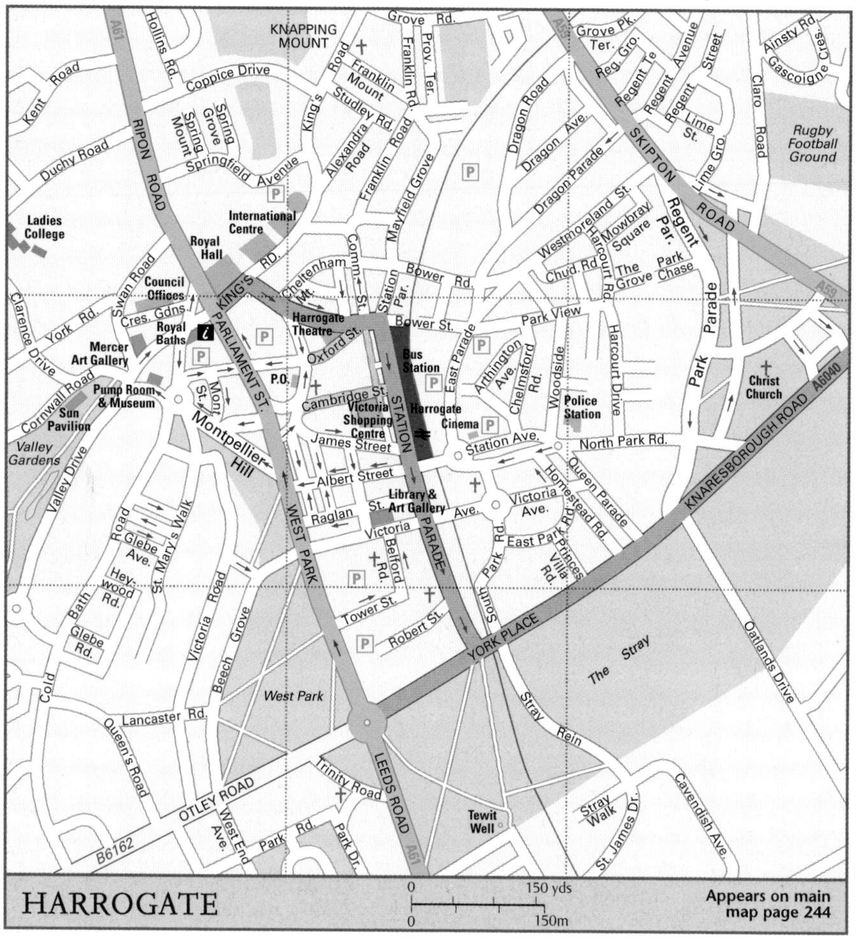

TOURIST INFORMATION CENTRE ☎ 01423 537300 ROYAL BATHS ASSEMBLY ROOMS, CRESCENT RD, HARROGATE, NORTH YORKSHIRE, HG1 2RR
HOSPITAL A & E ☎ 01423 885959 HARROGATE DISTRICT HOSPITAL, LANCASTER PARK ROAD, HARROGATE, HG2 7SX
COUNCIL OFFICE ☎ 01423 500600 COUNCIL OFFICES, CRESCENT GARDENS HARROGATE, HG1 2SG

Harrogate *Yorkshire* Population: 66,178. Spa town and conference centre. Fashionable spa town of 19th century with many distinguished Victorian buildings, extensive gardens and pleasant tree-lined streets. Royal Baths Assembly Rooms (1897) open for Turkish baths. Royal Pump Room (1842) now a museum. The Stray park and gardens are S of town centre. The Valley Gardens to the SW are the venue for band concerts and flower shows. Harlow Carr Botanical Gardens and Museum of Gardening 2 miles (3km) SW. Mother Shipton's cave, reputed home to the 16th century prophetess, near Knaresborough, 4 miles (6km) NW.

LOCAL RADIO:
BBC RADIO YORK 103.7 FM;
STRAY FM 97.2 FM

www.harrogate.gov.uk/tourism

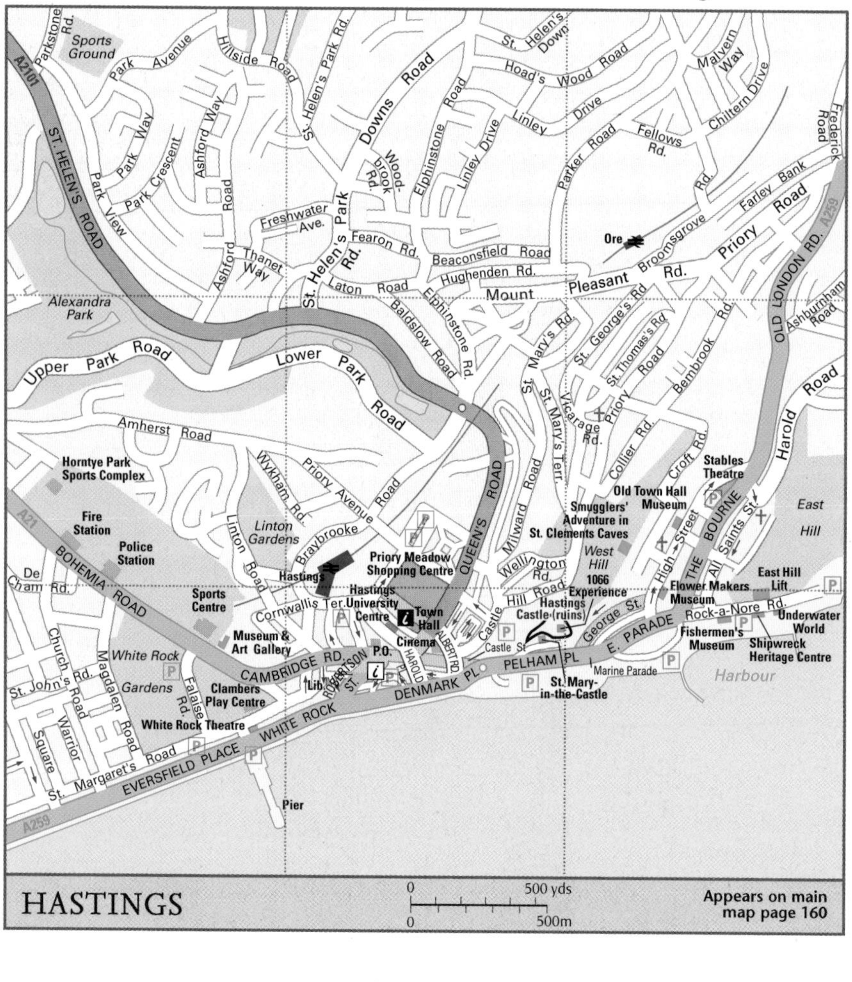

TOURIST INFORMATION CENTRE ☎ 01424 781111 QUEENS SQUARE, PRIORY MEADOW, HASTINGS,TN34 1TL
HOSPITAL A & E ☎ 01424 755255 CONQUEST HOSPITAL, THE RIDGE, ST. LEONARDS-ON-SEA, TN37 7RD
COUNCIL OFFICE ☎ 01424 781066 HASTINGS BOROUGH COUNCIL, TOWN HALL, QUEENS ROAD, HASTINGS, TN34 1QR

Hastings *South East England* Population: 84,139. Town, Cinque port and seaside resort. Remains of Norman castle built 1068-1080 on hill in town centre, houses the 1066 exhibition which relates the history of castle and Norman invasion. Battle of 1066 fought at Battle, 6 miles (9km) NW. Former smugglers caves have a display on smuggling, once a vital part of the towns economy.

LOCAL RADIO:
BBC SOUTHERN COUNTIES RADIO 1161 AM / 104.5 FM;
ARROW FM 107.8 FM

www.visithastings.com

TOURIST INFORMATION CENTRE ☎ 01432 268430
1 KING STREET,
HEREFORD, HR4 9BW

HOSPITAL A & E ☎ 01432 355444
COUNTY HOSPITAL,
STONEBOW ROAD, HEREFORD, HR1 2ER

COUNCIL OFFICE ☎ 01432 260456
COUNCIL OFFICES, THE TOWN HALL,
ST. OWEN STREET, HEREFORD, HR1 2PJ

Hereford *West Midlands* Population: 54,326. County town and cathedral city on River Wye. Many old buildings and museums, including Waterworks museum and City Museum and Art Gallery. 1621 Old House is a museum of local history. Medieval Wye Bridge. Cathedral includes richly ornamented Early English style Lady chapel. New building houses Chained Library of 1500 volumes and 1289 Mappa Mundi Map of the world. Three Choirs Festival every third year. Cider Museum and King Offa Distillery W of city centre depicts history of cider making.

LOCAL RADIO:
BBC RADIO HEREFORD & WORCESTER 1584 AM / 94.7 FM
WYVERN FM 97.6 FM; CLASSIC HITS 954 AM

www.visitherefordshire.co.uk

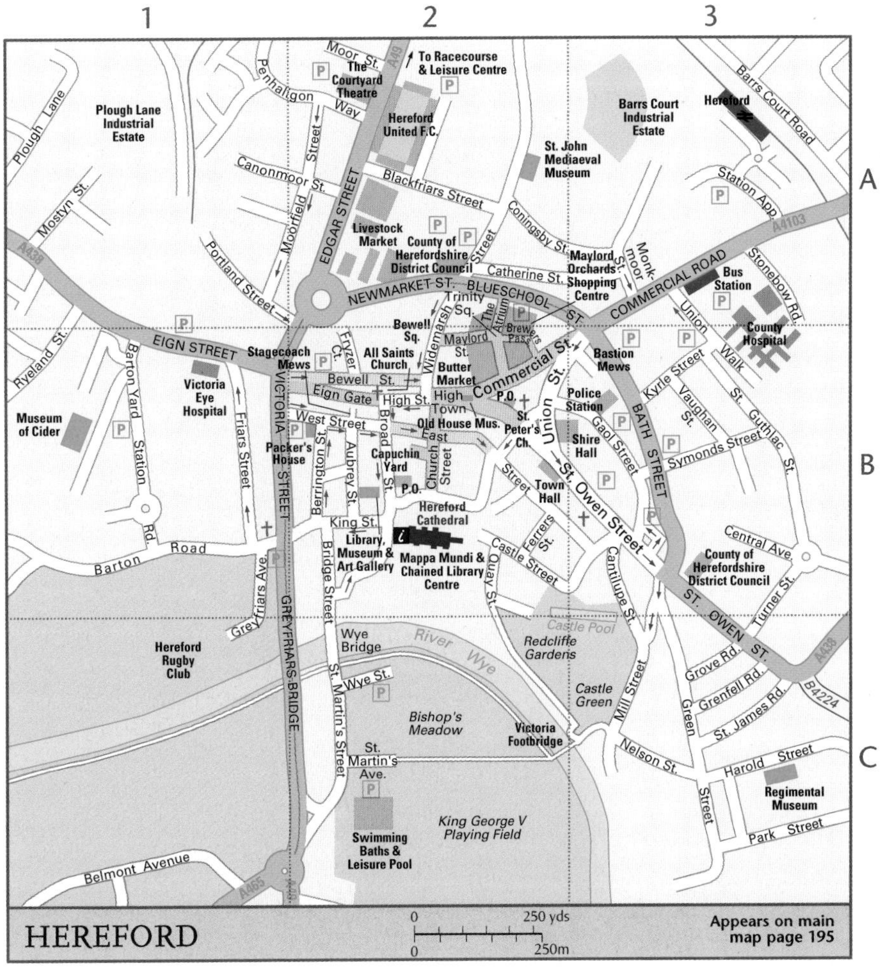

TOURIST INFORMATION CENTRE ☎ 0845 2255121
CASTLE WYND,
INVERNESS, HIGHLAND, IV2 3BJ

HOSPITAL A & E ☎ 01463 704000
RAIGMORE HOSPITAL, OLD PERTH ROAD,
INVERNESS, IV2 3UJ

COUNCIL OFFICE ☎ 01463 702000
COUNCIL OFFICES, GLENURQUHART ROAD,
INVERNESS, IV3 5NX

Inverness *Scotland* Population: 41,234. Town, at mouth of River Ness at entrance to Beauly Firth. Administrative, commercial and tourist centre. Caledonian Canal passes to W of town. Victorian castle in town centre used as law courts. Inverness Museum and Art Gallery depicts history of Highlands. Balnain House is a museum of Highland music and musical instruments. University of the Highlands and Islands. 1746 Culloden battle site 5 miles (8km) E. Airport at locality of Dalcross, 7 miles (11km) NE of town.

LOCAL RADIO:
BBC RADIO SCOTLAND 585, 810, 990 AM / 92.6-94.7 FM
MORAY FIRTH RADIO (MFR) 1107 AM / 96.6, 96.7, 97.4, 102.5, 102.8 FM

www.visithighlands.com/inverness-loch-ness

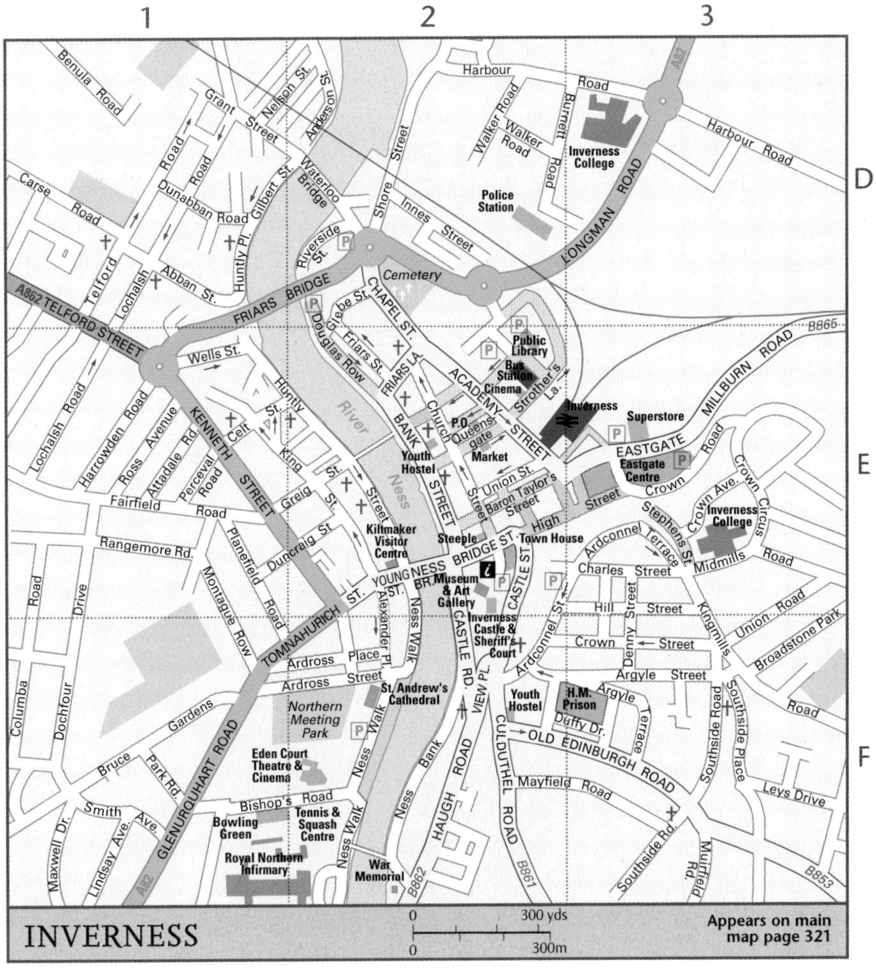

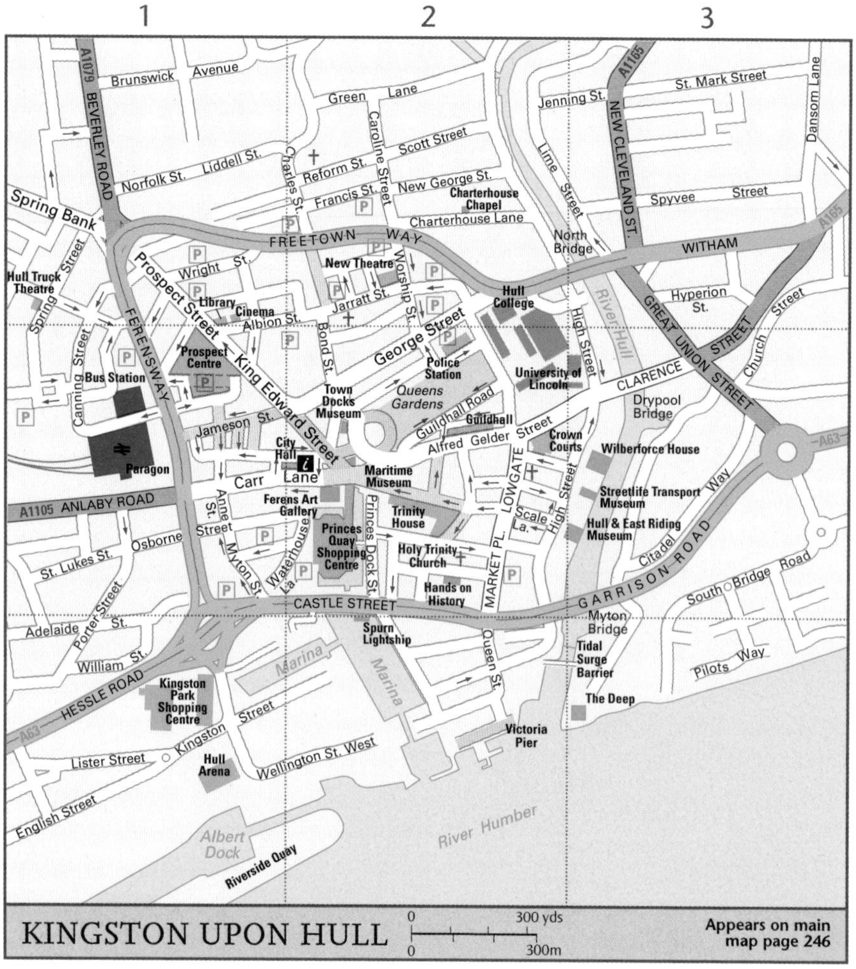

TOURIST INFORMATION CENTRE ☎ 01482 223559
1 PARAGON STREET,
KINGSTON UPON HULL, HU1 3NA

HOSPITAL A & E ☎ 01482 328541
HULL ROYAL INFIRMARY, ANLABY ROAD,
KINGSTON UPON HULL, HU3 2JZ

COUNCIL OFFICE ☎ 01482 300300
GUILDHALL, ALFRED GELDER STREET,
KINGSTON UPON HULL, HU1 2AA

Kingston upon Hull (Commonly known as Hull.) *Yorkshire* Population: 310,636. City, port at confluence of Rivers Humber and Hull. Much of town destroyed during bombing of World War II; town centre has been rebuilt. Formerly had a thriving fishing industry. Major industry nowadays is frozen food processing. Restored docks, cobble streeted Old Town and modern marina. Universities. Birthplace of William Wilberforce, slavery abolitionist, 1759. Wilberforce Museum covers history of slavery. Streetlife Transport Museum. Town Docks Museum explores city's maritime history. Famous for associations with poets Andrew Marvell, Stevie Smith and Philip Larkin.

LOCAL RADIO:
BBC RADIO HUMBERSIDE 1485 AM / 95.9 FM;
MAGIC 1161 AM; VIKING FM 96.9 FM

www.hullcc.gov.uk/visithull

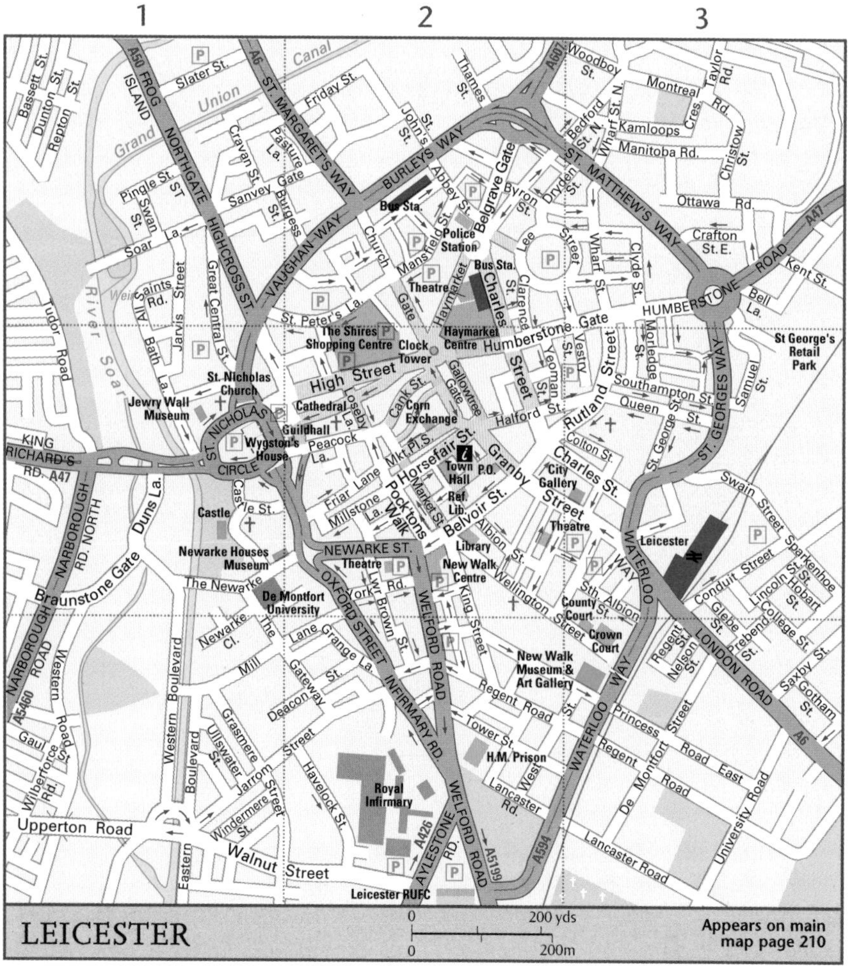

TOURIST INFORMATION CENTRE ☎ 0906 294 1113
(Premium Rate)
7-9 EVERY STREET, TOWN HALL SQUARE,
LEICESTER, LE1 6AG

HOSPITAL A & E ☎ 0116 254 1414
LEICESTER ROYAL INFIRMARY,
INFIRMARY SQUARE, LEICESTER, LE1 5WW

COUNCIL OFFICE ☎ 0116 252 6480
COUNCIL OFFICES, NEW WALK CENTRE,
WELFORD PLACE, LEICESTER, LE1 6ZG

Leicester *East Midlands* Population: 318,518. City, county town and commercial and industrial centre on River Soar, on site of Roman town of Ratae Coritanorum. Industries include hosiery and footwear, alongside more modern industries. Universities. Many historic remains including Jewry Wall , one of largest surviving sections of Roman wall in the country, Roman baths and a medieval guildhall. Saxon Church of St. Nicholas. 11th century St. Martin's Cathedral. Victorian clock tower. Newarke Houses Museum explores the city's social history. Home to England's second biggest street festival after Notting Hill Carnival. Joseph Merrick, the 'Elephant Man' born and lived here.

LOCAL RADIO:
BBC RADIO LEICESTER 104.9 FM
SABRAS 1260 AM; LEICESTER SOUND 105.4 FM

www.discoverleicester.co.uk

TOURIST INFORMATION CENTRE ☎ 01522 873213
9 CASTLE HILL, LINCOLN,
LINCOLNSHIRE, LN1 3AA

HOSPITAL A & E ☎ 01522 512512
LINCOLN COUNTY HOSPITAL,
GREETWELL ROAD, LINCOLN, LN2 5QY

COUNCIL OFFICE ☎ 01522 881188
CITY HALL, BEAUMONT FEE,
LINCOLN, LN1 1DD

Lincoln *East Midlands* Population: 80,281. County town and cathedral city on River Witham, on site of Roman town of Lindum. City grew as a result of strategic importance in the wool trade. Many ancient monuments and archaeological features. Castle built by William I. 13th century cathedral, is the third largest in Britain with its three towers on hilltop dominating the skyline. Carvings in the Angel Choir include the stone figure of the Lincoln Imp which is the city's emblem. Lincoln Bishop's Old Palace is medieval building on S side of cathedral. 12th century Jew's House. Museum of Lincolnshire Life. Universities.

LOCAL RADIO:
BBC RADIO LINCOLNSHIRE 1368 AM / 94.9 FM;
LINCS FM 102.2 FM

www.lincoln.gov.uk

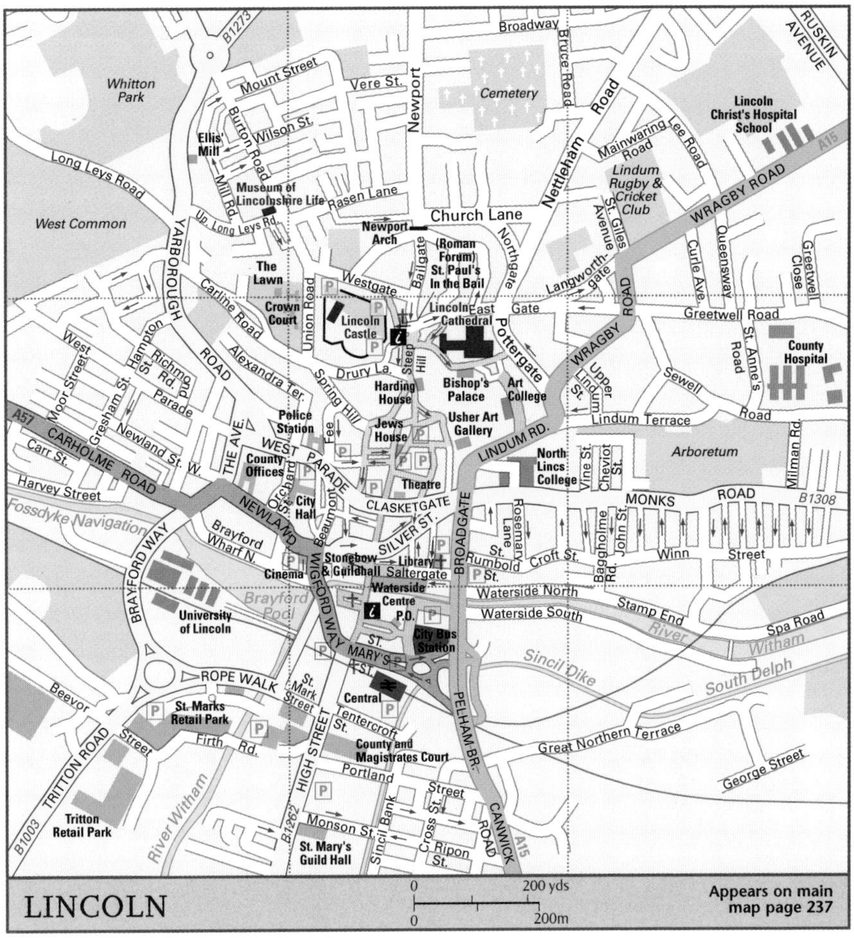

TOURIST INFORMATION CENTRE ☎ 01642 358086
99-101 ALBERT ROAD,
MIDDLESBROUGH, TS1 2PA

HOSPITAL A & E ☎ 01642 850850
JAMES COOK UNIVERSITY HOSPITAL,
MARTON ROAD, MIDDLESBROUGH, TS4 3BW

COUNCIL OFFICE ☎ 01642 245432
MUNICIPAL BUILDINGS, PO BOX 99A,
RUSSELL STREET, MIDDLESBROUGH, TS1 2QQ

Middlesbrough *North East England* Population: 147,430. Town, port, with extensive dock area, on S bank of River Tees, forming part of Teesside urban complex. A former iron and steel town, its chief industries now involve oil and petrochemicals. Unusual 1911 transporter bridge over River Tees. University of Teesside. Captian Cook Birthplace Museum in Stewart Park at Marton.

LOCAL RADIO:
BBC RADIO CLEVELAND 95 FM;
MAGIC 1170 AM; TFM 96.6 FM; CENTURY FM 100.7 FM

www.destinationteesvalley.co.uk

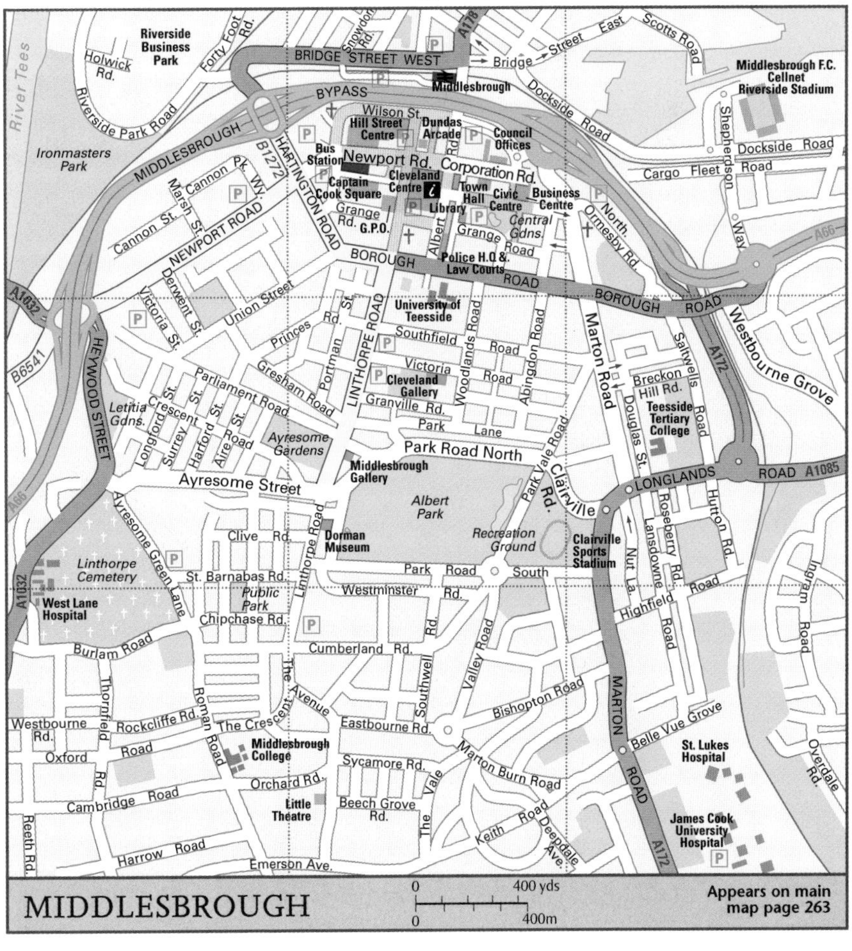

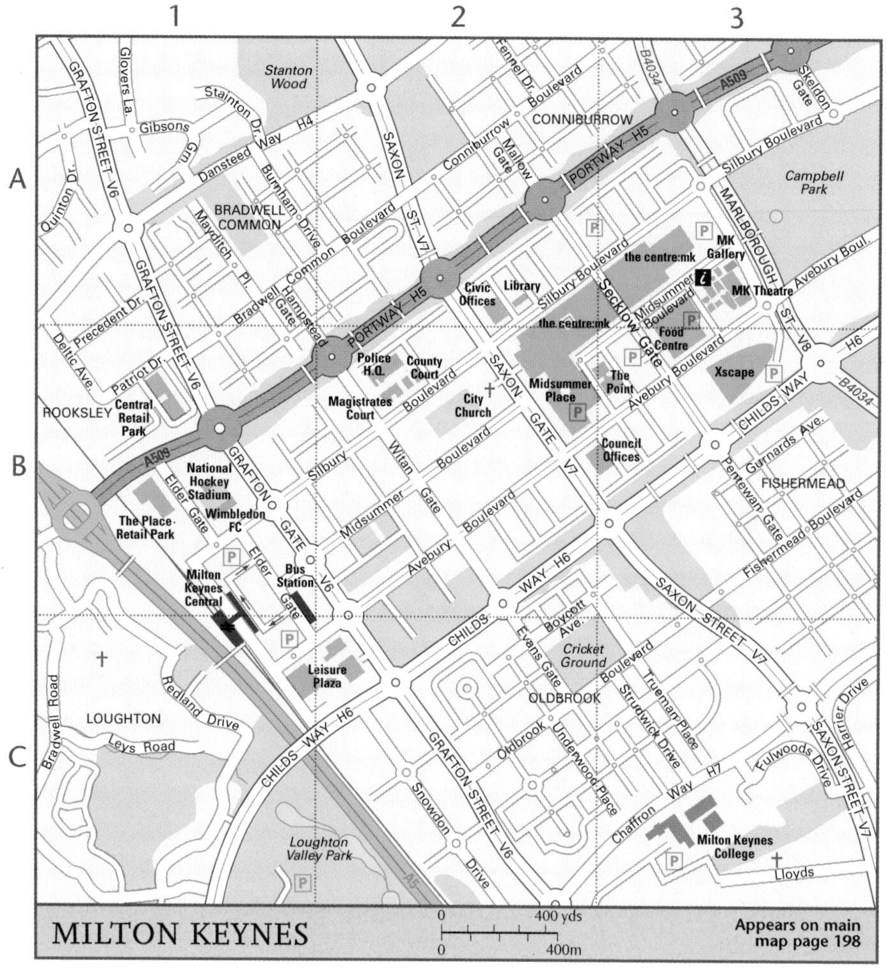

TOURIST INFORMATION CENTRE ☎ 01908 558300
MARGARET POWELL SQUARE,
890 MIDSUMMER BOULEVARD,
MILTON KEYNES, MK9 3QA

HOSPITAL A & E ☎ 01908 660033
MILTON KEYNES GENERAL HOSPITAL,
STANDING WAY, EAGLESTONE,
MILTON KEYNES, MK6 5LD

COUNCIL OFFICE ☎ 01908 691691
CIVIC OFFICES, 1 SAXON GATE EAST,
MILTON KEYNES, MK9 3HQ

Milton Keynes *South East England*
Population: 156,148. New town designated in 1967. Includes Bletchley, Stony Stratford, Wolverton and original village of Milton Keynes. Regional commercial centre and location for many international companies. The centre:mk is one of the longest under-cover shopping areas in Europe. Major open-air concert venue at the National Bowl. MK Theatre and art gallery. Cinema, bowling, climbing wall and Europe's largest indoor snow ski slope at Xscape. The Open University at Walton Hall. Woburn Safari Park 8 miles (13km) SE.

LOCAL RADIO:
BBC THREE COUNTIES RADIO 1161 AM / 104.5 FM;
FM 103 HORIZON 103.3 FM

www.mkweb.co.uk/visitorinfo

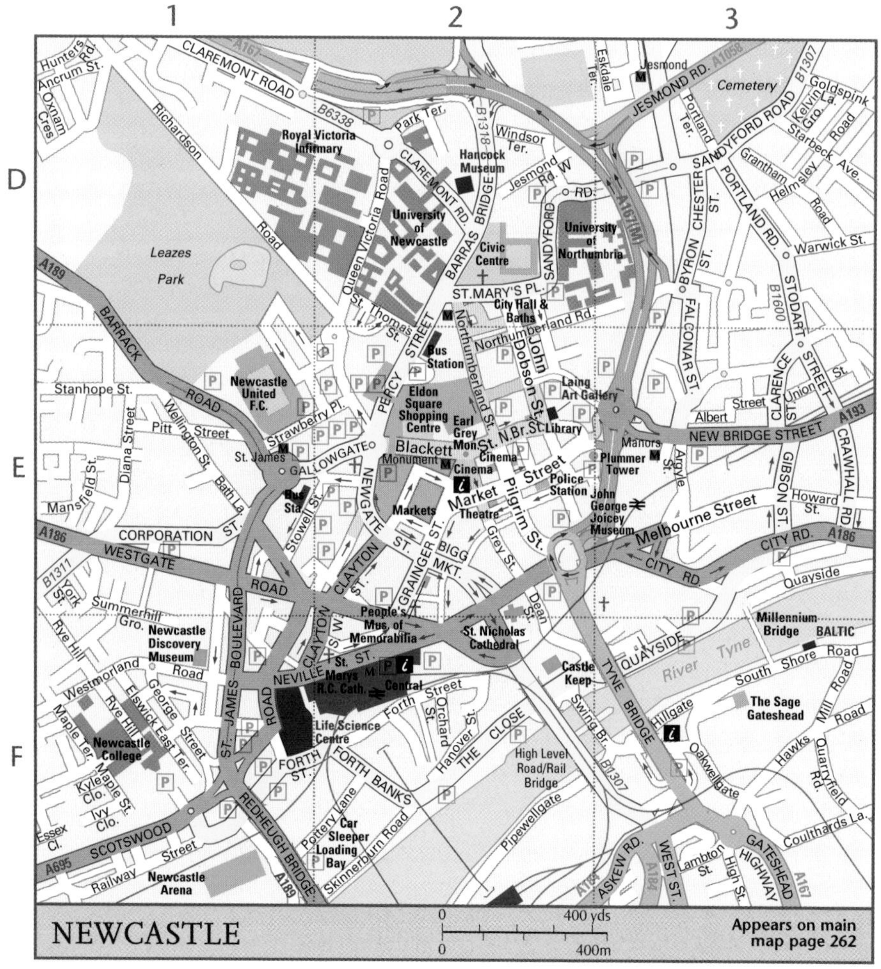

TOURIST INFORMATION CENTRE ☎ 0191 277 8000
132 GRAINGER STREET, NEWCASTLE
UPON TYNE, TYNE & WEAR, NE1 5AF

HOSPITAL A & E ☎ 0191 273 8811
NEWCASTLE GENERAL HOSPITAL, WESTGATE
ROAD, NEWCASTLE UPON TYNE, NE4 6BE

COUNCIL OFFICE ☎ 0191 232 8520
CIVIC CENTRE, BARRAS BRIDGE,
NEWCASTLE UPON TYNE, NE99 1RD

Newcastle upon Tyne *North East England*
Population: 189,150. City, port on River Tyne about 11 miles (17km) upstream from river mouth. The 'new castle' of city's name started in 1080 by Robert Curthose, eldest son of William the Conqueror. 13th century castle gatehouse known as 'Black Gate'. Commercial and industrial centre, previously dependent upon coalmining and shipbuilding. In its heyday, 25 percent of world's shipping built here. Cathedral dates from 14th to 15th century. Bessie Surtees House comprises 16th and 17th century merchants' houses. Tyne Bridge, opened in 1928 and longest of its type at the time. Venerable Bede (AD 672-735) born near Jarrow. Catherine Cookson, writer, also born in Jarrow, Universities. Newcastle International Airport 5m/8km NW.

LOCAL RADIO:
BBC RADIO NEWCASTLE 95.4 FM;
MAGIC 1152 AM; METRO RADIO 97.1 FM; CENTURY FM 101.8 FM

www.visitnewcastlegateshead.com

TOURIST INFORMATION CENTRE ☎ 0870 225 4830
THE FORUM, MILLENNIUM PLAIN,
NORWICH, NR2 1TF

HOSPITAL A & E ☎ 01603 286286
NORFOLK & NORWICH UNIVERSITY HOSPITAL,
COLNEY LANE, NORWICH, NR4 7UZ

COUNCIL OFFICE ☎ 01603 622233
CITY HALL, ST. PETER'S STREET,
NORWICH, NR2 1NH

Norwich *East of England* Population: 171,304. County town and cathedral city at confluence of River Wensum and River Yare. Middle ages saw Norwich become second richest city in country through exporting textiles. Medieval streets and buildings are well preserved. Sections of 14th century flint city wall defences still exist, including Cow Tower. Current chief industries are high technology and computer based. Notable buildings include partly Norman cathedral with second highest spire in Britain, Norman castle with keep (now museum and art gallery), 15th century guildhall, modern city hall, numerous medieval churches. University of East Anglia. Airport 3 miles (5km) N.

LOCAL RADIO:
BBC RADIO NORFOLK 95.1, 104.4 FM;
CLASSIC GOLD AMBER 1152 AM; BROADLAND 102 102.4 FM

www.visitnorwich.co.uk

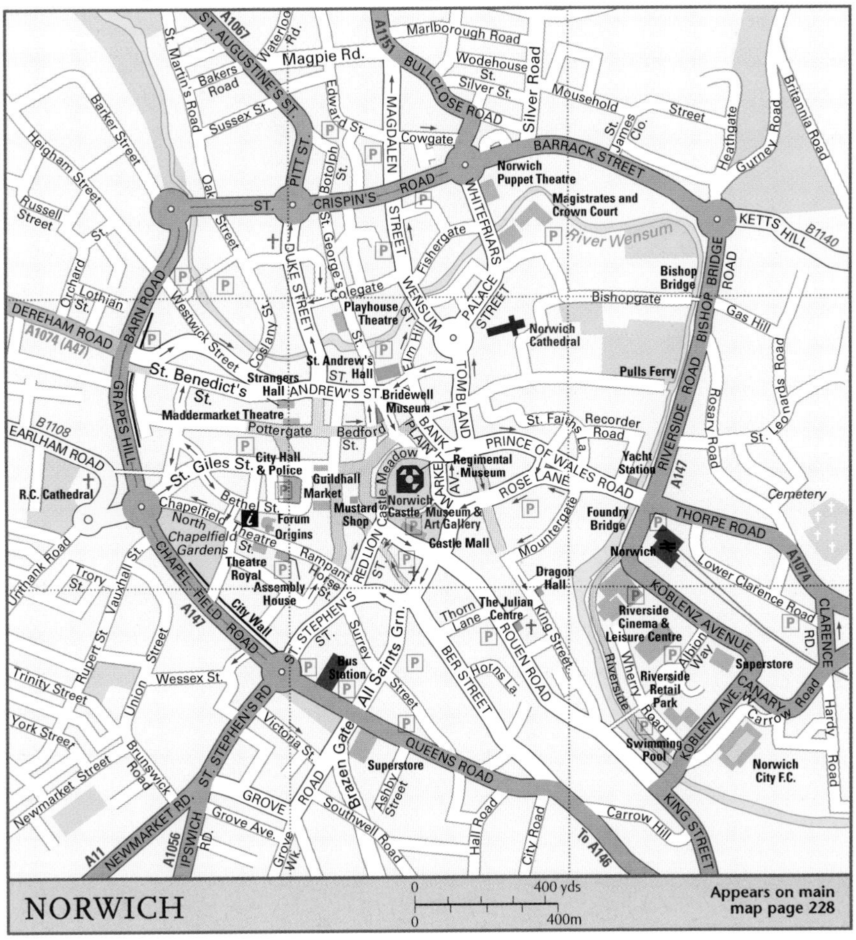

TOURIST INFORMATION CENTRE ☎ 0115 915 5330
1-4 SMITHY ROW,
NOTTINGHAM, NG1 2BY

HOSPITAL A & E ☎ 0115 924 9924
QUEENS MEDICAL CENTRE, UNIVERSITY HOSP,
DERBY ROAD, NOTTINGHAM, NG7 2UH

COUNCIL OFFICE ☎ 0115 915 5555
THE GUILDHALL, SOUTH SHERWOOD STREET,
NOTTINGHAM, NG1 4BT

Nottingham *East Midlands* Population: 270,222. City, on River Trent. Originally Saxon town built on one of a pair of hills. In 1068, Normans built castle on other hill and both communities traded in valley between. Important commercial, industrial, entertainment and sports centre. Key industries include manufacture of lace, mechanical products, tobacco and pharmaceuticals. 17th century castle, restored 19th century, houses museum and art gallery. Two universities. Repertory theatre.

LOCAL RADIO:
BBC RADIO NOTTINGHAM 103.8 FM; CENTURY FM 106 FM;
CLASSIC GOLD GEM 999 AM; SAGA 101.4, 106.6 FM;
TRENT FM 96.2 FM

www.nottinghamcity.gov.uk/visitors

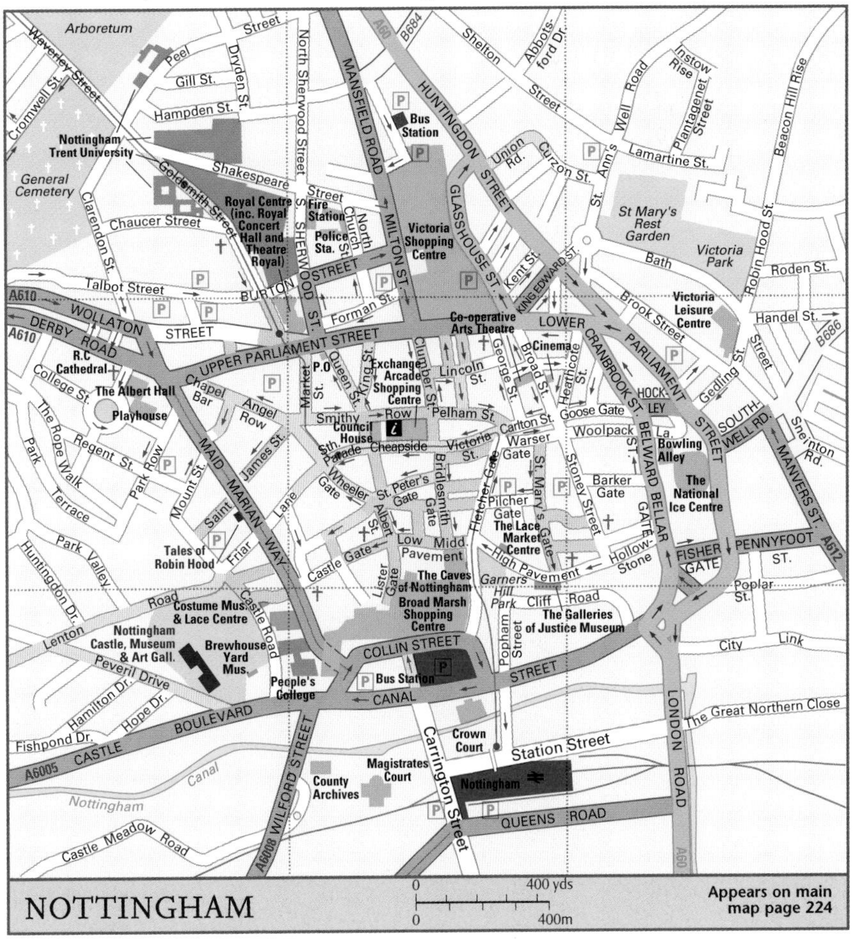

OXFORD PERTH

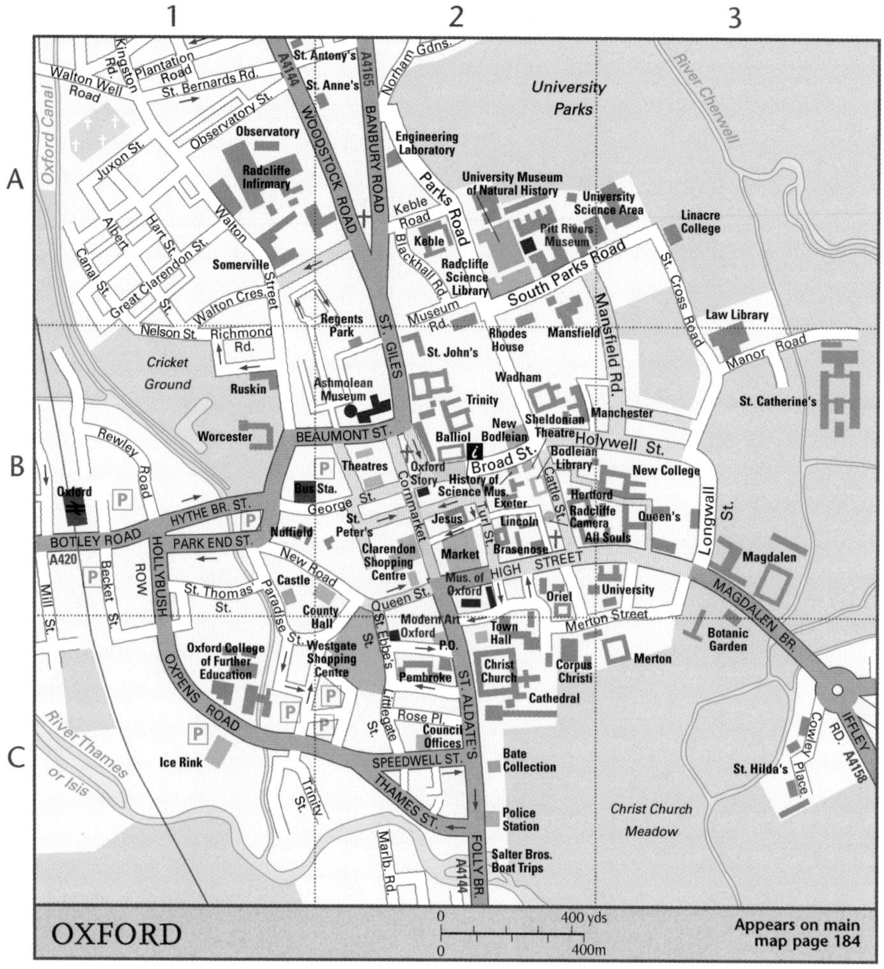

TOURIST INFORMATION CENTRE ☎ 01865 726871
15-16 BROAD STREET,
OXFORD, OX1 3AS

HOSPITAL A & E ☎ 01865 741166
JOHN RADCLIFFE HOSPITAL, HEADLEY WAY,
HEADINGTON, OXFORD, OX3 9DU

COUNCIL OFFICE ☎ 01865 249811
PO BOX 10,
OXFORD, OX1 1EN

Oxford *South East England* Population: 118,795. City, at confluence of Rivers Thames and Cherwell. Began as Saxon settlement, flourished under Normans when it was chosen as royal residence. University dating from 13th century, recognised as being among best in the world. Many notable buildings create spectacular skyline. Cathedral. Bodleian Library, second largest in UK. Ashmolean museum, oldest public museum in country. Tourist and commercial centre. Ancient St. Giles Fair held every September. Oxford Brookes University at Headington. Airport at Kidlington.

LOCAL RADIO:
BBC RADIO OXFORD 95.2 FM;
FOX FM 102.6 FM; FUSION 107.3 FM

www.visitoxford.org

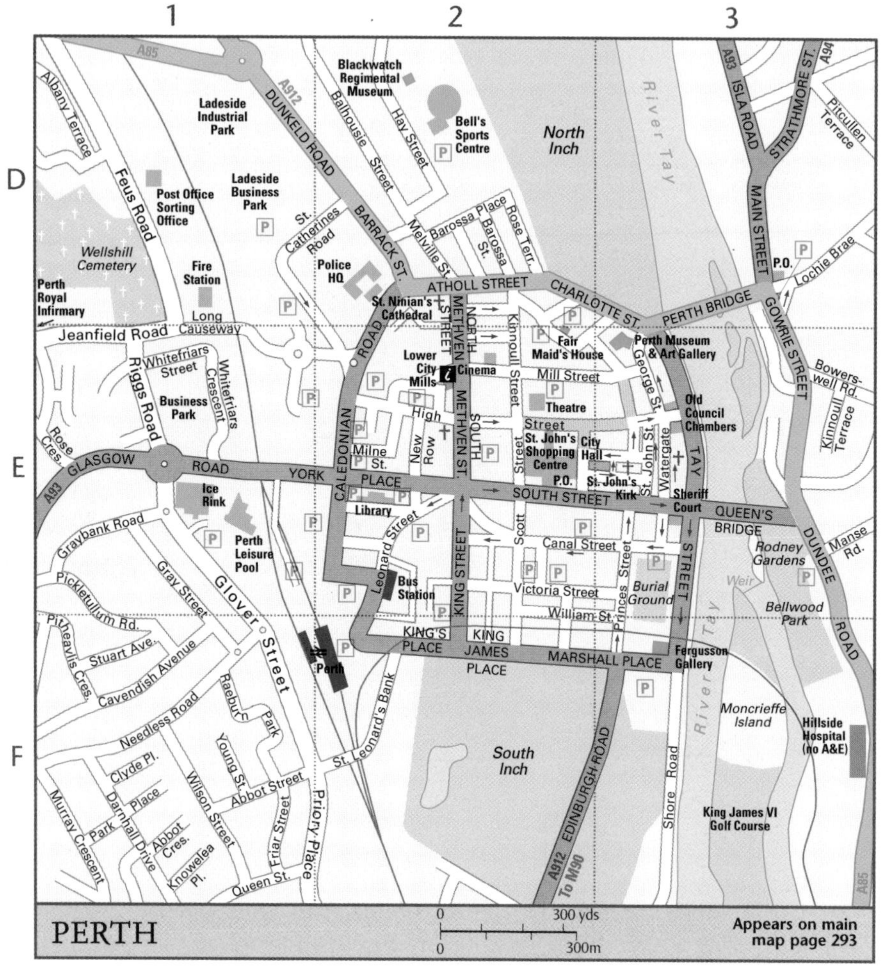

TOURIST INFORMATION CENTRE ☎ 01738 450600
LOWER CITY MILLS, WEST MILL STREET,
PERTH, PH1 5QP

HOSPITAL A & E ☎ 01738 623311
PERTH ROYAL INFIRMARY,
TAYMOUNT TERRACE, PERTH, PH1 1NX

COUNCIL OFFICE ☎ 01738 475000
PERTH & KINROSS COUNCIL,
2 HIGH STREET, PERTH, PH1 5PH

Perth *Scotland* Population: 41,453. Ancient cathedral city (Royal Charter granted 1210) on River Tay. Once capital of Medieval Scotland. Centre of livestock trade. Previously cotton manufacturing centre; now important industries include whisky distilling. St. John's Kirk founded 1126. 15th century Balhousie Castle houses regimental headquarters and Museum of the Black Watch. Art Gallery and Museum. 16th century Fair Maid's House. Gothic mansion Scone Palace 2 miles (3km) N contains collections of furniture, needlework and porcelain with site of Coronation Stone of Destiny in its grounds. Airfield (Scone) to NE.

LOCAL RADIO:
BBC RADIO SCOTLAND 810 AM / 92.4-94.7 FM;
TAY AM1584, TAY FM 96.4 FM

www.perthshire.co.uk

TOURIST INFORMATION CENTRE ☎ 01752 264849
ISLAND HOUSE, 9 THE BARBICAN,
PLYMOUTH, DEVON, PL1 2LS

HOSPITAL A & E ☎ 01752 777111
DERRIFORD HOSPITAL, DERRIFORD ROAD,
CROWNHILL, PLYMOUTH, PL6 8DH

COUNCIL OFFICE ☎ 01752 668000
CIVIC CENTRE, ARMADA WAY,
PLYMOUTH, PL1 2EW

Plymouth *South West England* Population: 245,295. Largest city in SW England. Port and naval base. Regional shopping centre. City centre rebuilt after bombing in World War II. Has strong commercial and naval tradition. In 1588 Sir Francis Drake sailed from Plymouth to defeat Spanish Armada. Captain Cook's voyages to Australia, South Seas and Antarctica all departed from here. University. Plymouth City Airport to N of city.

LOCAL RADIO:
BBC RADIO DEVON 103.4 FM;
CLASSIC GOLD 1152 AM; PLYMOUTH SOUND 97 FM

www.visitplymouth.co.uk

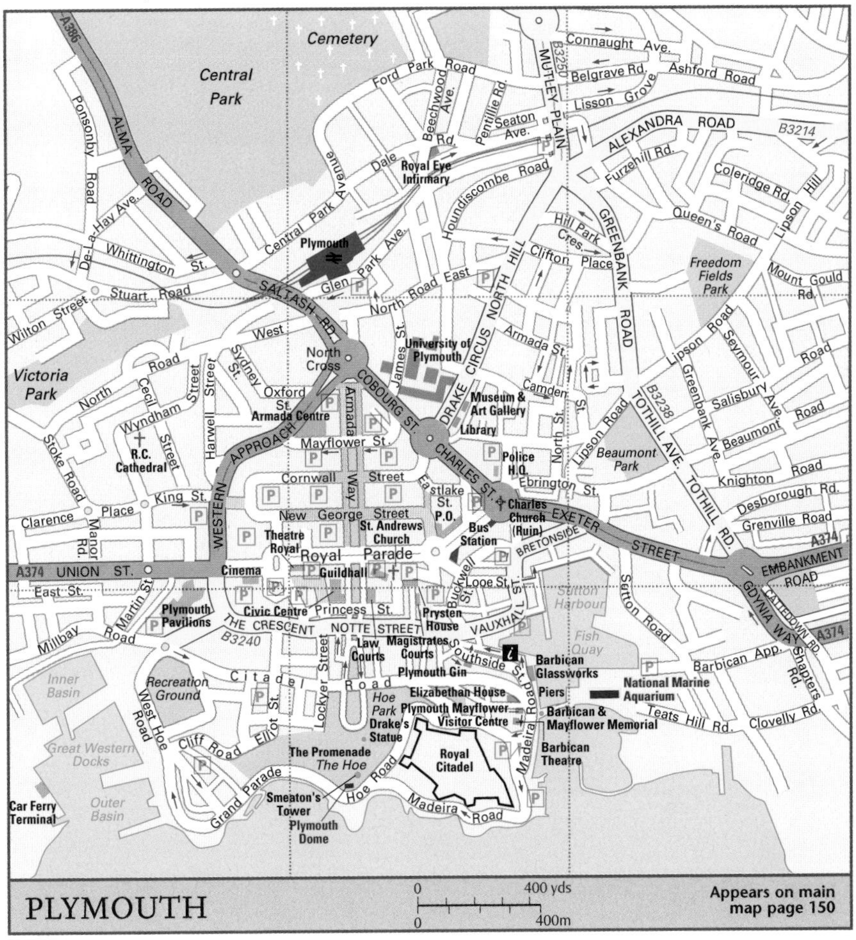

TOURIST INFORMATION CENTRE ☎ 023 9282 6722
THE HARD,
PORTSMOUTH, PO1 3QJ

HOSPITAL A & E ☎ 023 9228 6000
QUEEN ALEXANDRA HOSPITAL, SOUTHWICK
HILL ROAD, COSHAM, PORTSMOUTH, PO6 3LY

COUNCIL OFFICE ☎ 023 9283 4092
CIVIC OFFICES, GUILDHALL SQUARE,
PORTSMOUTH, PO1 2AL

Portsmouth *South East England* Population: 174,690. City, port and naval base (Portsmouth Harbour, on W side of city), extending from S end of Portsea Island to S slopes of Ports Down. Various industries, including tourism, financial services and manufacturing. Partly bombed in World War II and now rebuilt; however, some 18th century buildings remain. Boat and hovercraft ferries to Isle of Wight. University. Two cathedrals. Nelson's ship, HMS Victory, in harbour, alongside which are remains of Henry VIII's flagship, Mary Rose, which sank in 1545. King James's Gate and Landport Gate were part of 17th century defences, and Fort Cumberland is 18th century coastal defence at Eastney. Royal Garrison Church was 16th century chapel prior to Dissolution. Museums, many with nautical theme.

LOCAL RADIO:
BBC RADIO SOLENT 96.1 FM;
CAPITAL GOLD 1170 AM; OCEAN FM 97.5 FM; THE QUAY 107.4 FM;
WAVE 105.2 FM

www.visitportsmouth.co.uk

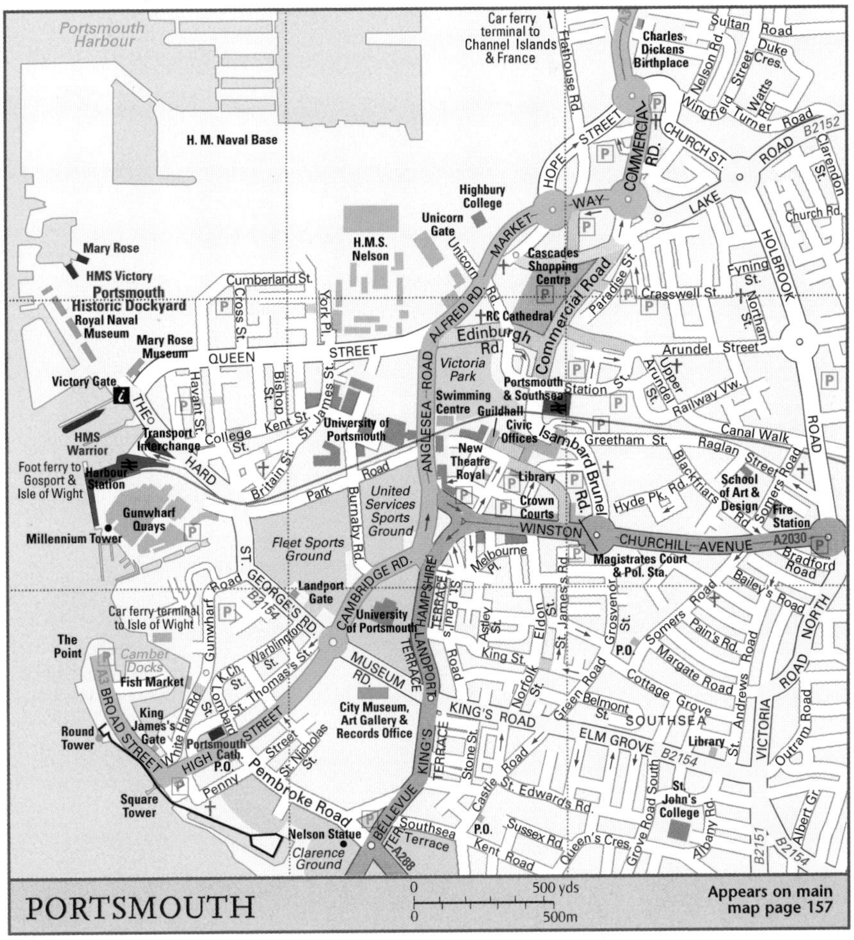

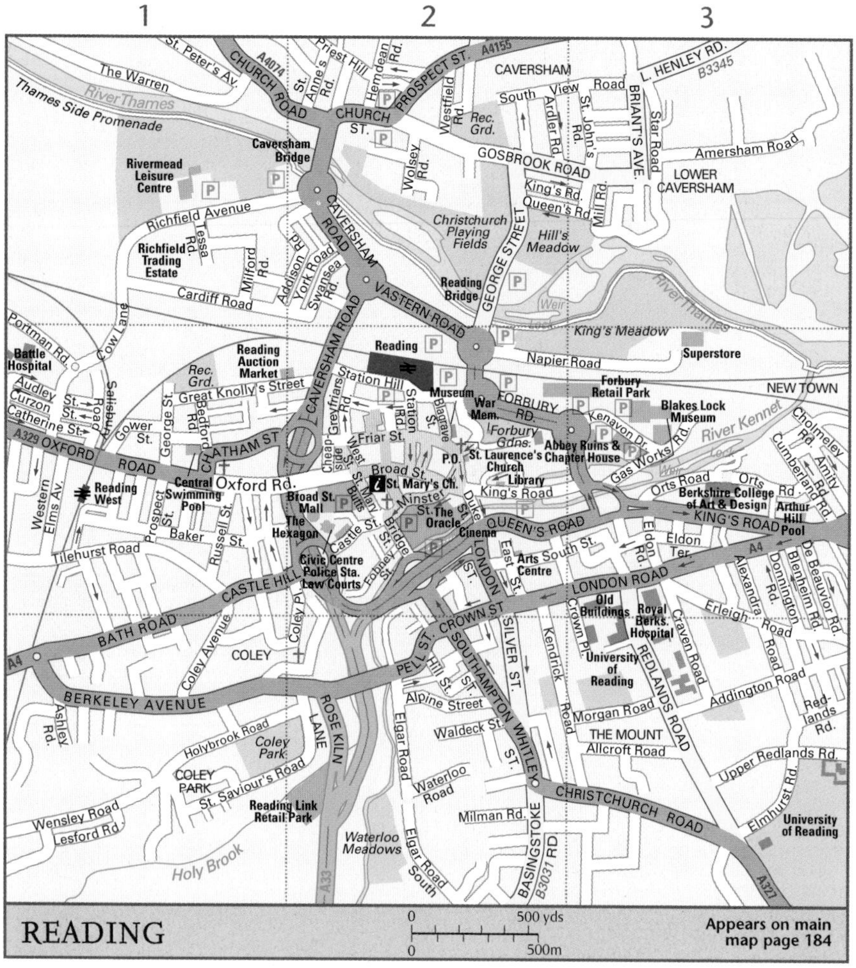

TOURIST INFORMATION CENTRE ☎ 0118 956 6226
CHURCH HOUSE, CHAIN STREET,
READING, RG1 2HX

HOSPITAL A & E ☎ 0118 987 5111
ROYAL BERKSHIRE HOSPITAL, LONDON ROAD,
READING, RG1 5AN

COUNCIL OFFICE ☎ 0118 939 0900
CIVIC CENTRE,
READING, RG1 7TD

Reading *South East England* Population: 213,474. County and industrial town and railway centre on River Thames. During Victorian times Reading was an important manufacturing town, particularly for biscuit-making and brewing. University. Remains of Norman abbey, founded by Henry I who lies buried there. Currently major centre for information technology.

LOCAL RADIO:
BBC RADIO BERKSHIRE 104.4 FM;
CLASSIC GOLD 1431/1485 AM; 2-TEN FM 97 FM; READING 107 FM

www.readingtourism.org.uk

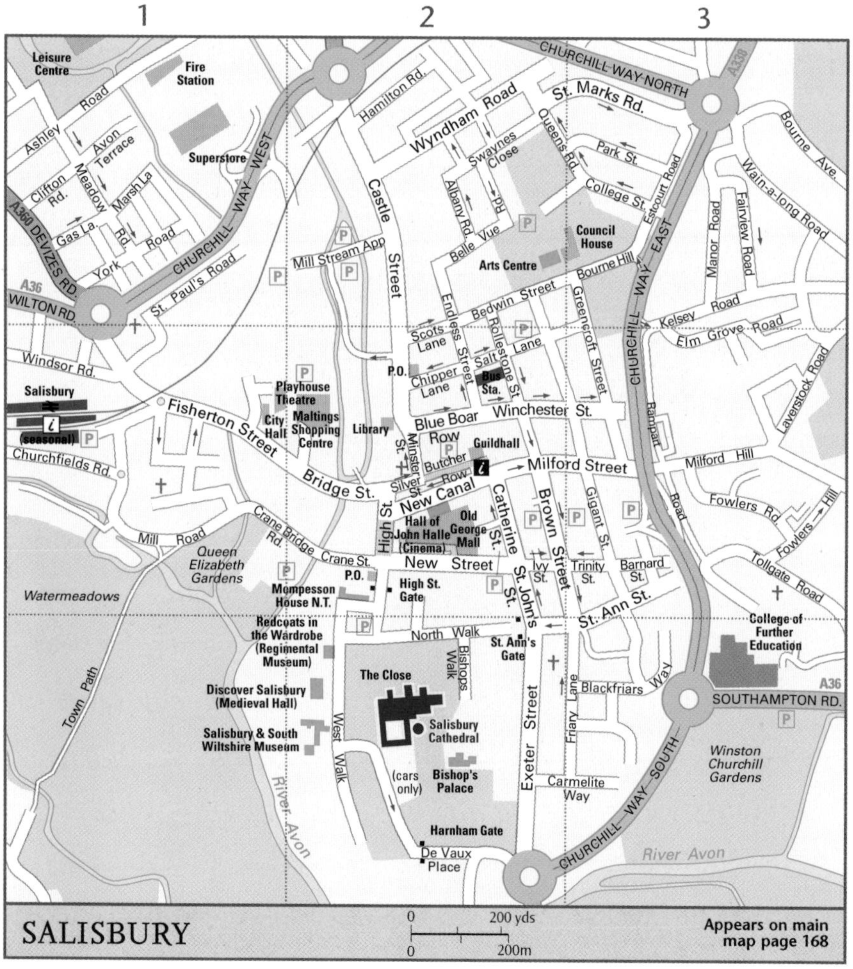

TOURIST INFORMATION CENTRE ☎ 01722 334956
FISH ROW,
SALISBURY, SP1 1EJ

HOSPITAL A & E ☎ 01722 336262
SALISBURY DISTRICT HOSPITAL, ODSTOCK ROAD,
SALISBURY, SP2 8BJ

COUNCIL OFFICE ☎ 01722 336272
THE COUNCIL HOUSE, BOURNE HILL,
SALISBURY, SP1 3UZ

Salisbury (Former and official name New Sarum) *South East England* Population: 39,268. Cathedral city at confluence of Rivers Avon and Nadder. Shopping centre and market town, with buildings ranging from medieval to Victorian; several medieval churches. Cathedral, in Early English style, built between 1220 and 1260, has the tallest spire in England at 123 metres (404ft).

LOCAL RADIO:
BBC WILTSHIRE SOUND 1368 AM / 103.5 FM;
SPIRE FM 102 FM

www.visitsalisbury.com

TOURIST INFORMATION CENTRE ☎ 0114 221 1900
1 TUDOR SQUARE,
SHEFFIELD, S1 2LH

HOSPITAL A & E ☎ 0114 243 4343
NORTHERN GENERAL HOSPITAL, HERRIES ROAD,
SHEFFIELD, S5 7AU

COUNCIL OFFICE ☎ 0114 272 6444
FIRST POINT, 1 UNION STREET,
SHEFFIELD, S1 2SH

Sheffield *Yorkshire* Population: 431,607. City, on River Don. Former centre of heavy steel industry, now largely precision steel and cutlery industries. University of Sheffield and Sheffield Hallam University. Various museums dedicated to Sheffield's industrial past. Meadowhall shopping centre and Sheffield City Airport, 3 miles (5km) NE of city centre.

LOCAL RADIO:
BBC RADIO SHEFFIELD 88.6 FM; GALAXY 105 105.6 FM;
HALLAM FM 97.4 FM; MAGIC AM 1548 AM; REAL RADIO 107.7 FM

www.sheffield.gov.uk/out--about

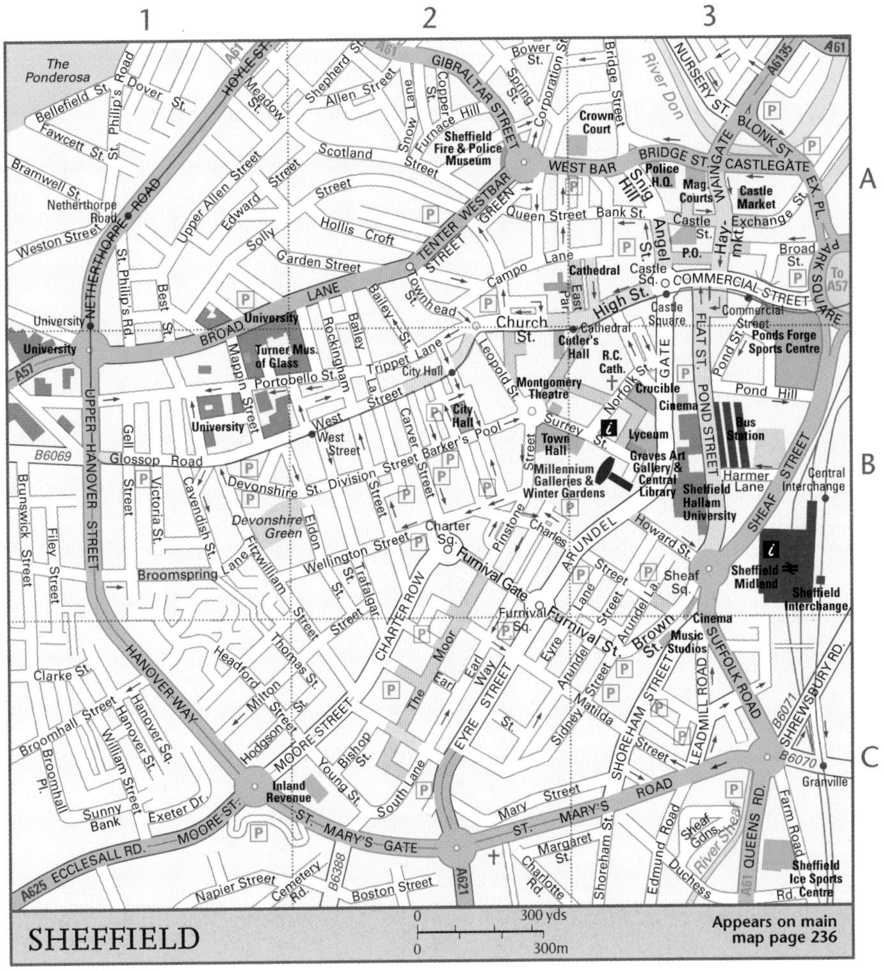

TOURIST INFORMATION CENTRE ☎ 023 8083 3333
9 CIVIC CENTRE ROAD,
SOUTHAMPTON, SO14 7FJ

HOSPITAL A & E ☎ 023 8077 7222
SOUTHAMPTON GENERAL HOSP, TREMONA RD,
SHIRLEY, SOUTHAMPTON, SO16 6YD

COUNCIL OFFICE ☎ 023 8083 3333
CIVIC CENTRE, CIVIC CENTRE ROAD,
SOUTHAMPTON, SO14 7LY

Southampton *South East England* Population: 210,138. City, at confluence of Rivers Itchen and Test at head of Southampton Water. Southern centre for business, culture and recreation. Container and transatlantic passenger port, dealing with 7 percent of UK's seaborne trade. Site of many famous departures: Henry V's army bound for Agincourt; the Pilgrim Fathers sailed to America on the Mayflower in 1620; maiden voyage of Queen Mary and only voyage of Titanic. Remains of medieval town walls. Medieval Merchant's House has authentically recreated furnishings. Boat and helicopter ferries to Isle of Wight. Host to many international boating events including Southampton International Boat Show, Whitbread Round the World, and BT Global Challenge. University. Southampton International Airport 1 mile (2km) S of Eastleigh.

LOCAL RADIO:
BBC RADIO SOLENT 999 AM / 96.1 FM;
CAPITAL GOLD 1557 AM; POWER FM 103.2 FM;
SOUTHCITY 107.8 FM; WAVE 105.2 FM

www.southampton.co.uk/leisure/tourism

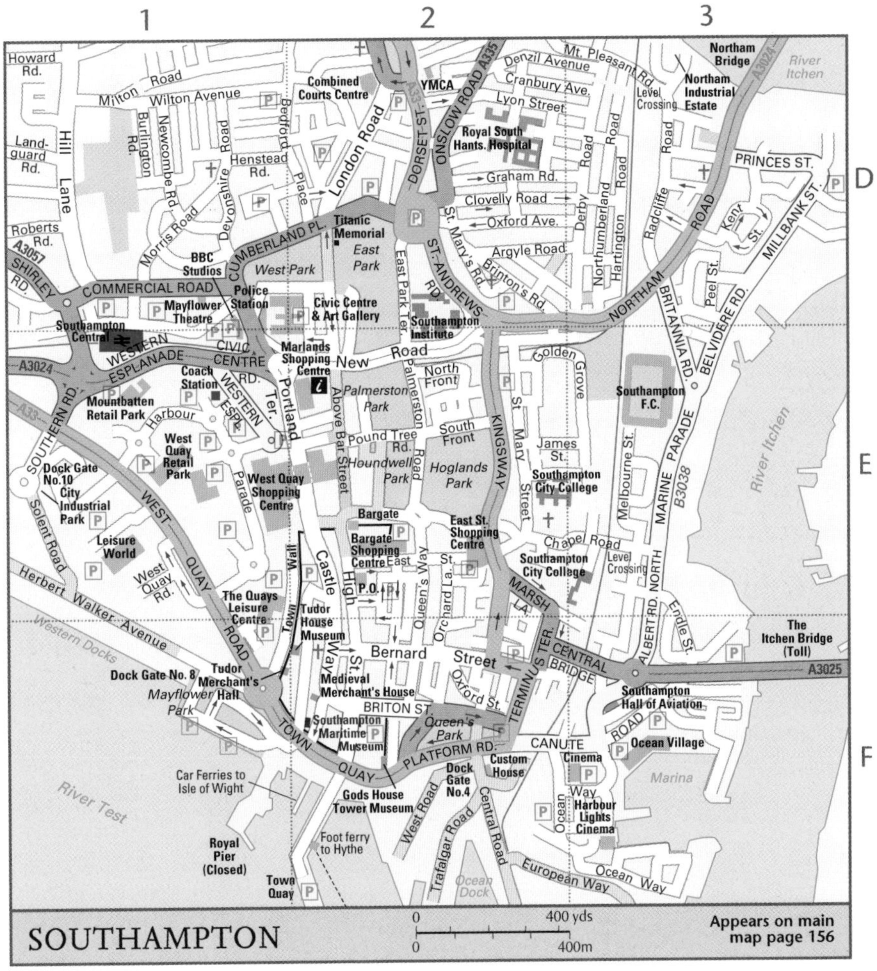

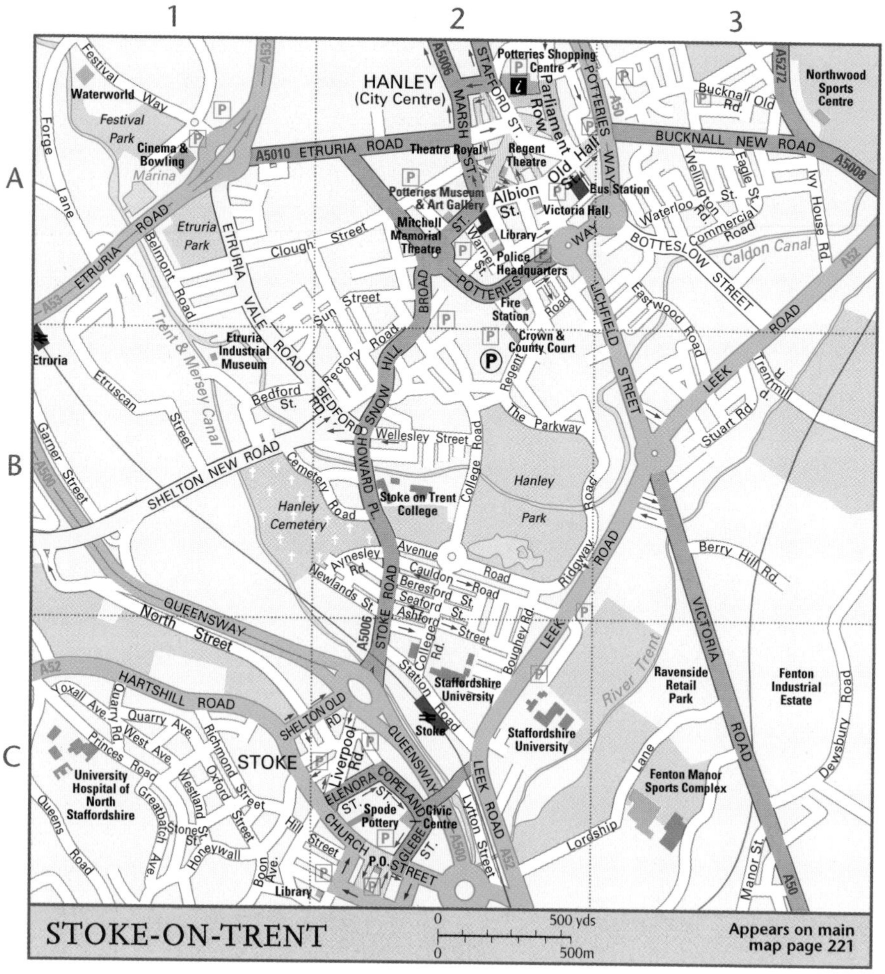

TOURIST INFORMATION CENTRE ☎ 01782 236000
POTTERIES SHOPPING CENTRE, QUADRANT ROAD, HANLEY, STOKE-ON-TRENT, ST1 1RZ

HOSPITAL A & E ☎ 01782 715444
UNIVERSITY HOSP. OF NORTH STAFFORDSHIRE, PRINCE'S ROAD, STOKE-ON-TRENT, ST4 7LN

COUNCIL OFFICE ☎ 01782 234567
TOWN HALL, CIVIC CENTRE, GLEBE STREET, STOKE-ON-TRENT, ST4 1RN

Stoke-on-Trent *West Midlands* Population: 266,543. City, on River Trent. Centre for employment, shopping and leisure. Created by an amalgamation of former Stoke-upon-Trent and the towns of Burslem, Fenton, Hanley, Longton and Tunstall in 1910. Capital of The Potteries (largest claywear producer in the world), now largely a finishing centre for imported pottery. Many pottery factories open to public including Wedgwood, Royal Doulton and Spode. Potteries Museum in Hanley charts history of the potteries. Gladstone Pottery Museum in Longton is centred around large bottle-kiln and demonstrates traditional skills of pottery production. Staffordshire University.

LOCAL RADIO:
BBC RADIO STOKE 94.6 FM
SIGNAL TWO 1170 AM; SIGNAL 1 102.6 FM

www.visitstoke.co.uk

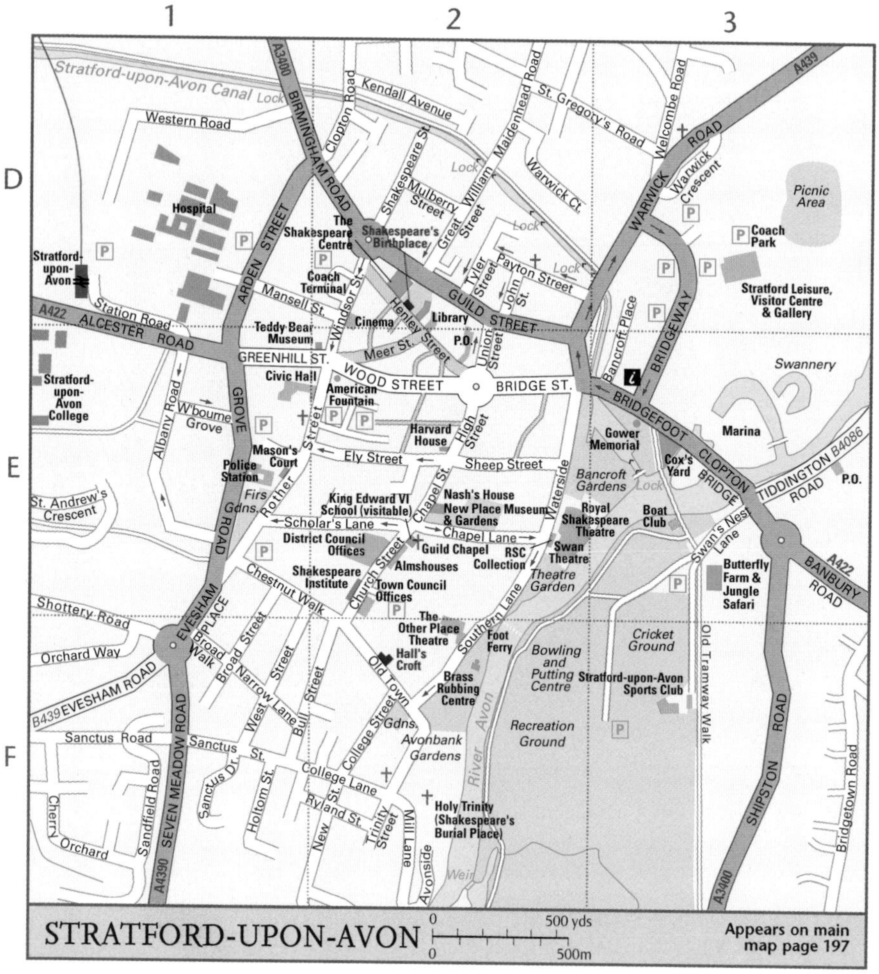

TOURIST INFORMATION CENTRE ☎ 0870 160 7930
BRIDGEFOOT, STRATFORD-UPON-AVON, WARWICKSHIRE, CV37 6GW

HOSPITAL A & E ☎ 01926 495321
WARWICK HOSPITAL, LAKIN ROAD, WARWICK, CV34 5BW

COUNCIL OFFICE ☎ 01789 267575
COUNCIL OFFICES, ELIZABETH HOUSE, CHURCH ST, STRATFORD-UPON-AVON, CV37 6HX

Stratford-upon-Avon (Also called Stratford-on-Avon.) *West Midlands* Population: 22,231. Town, on River Avon. Tourist centre. Many attractive 16th century buildings. Reconstructed Shakespeare's Birthplace. Elizabethan garden at New Place. Hall's Croft Elizabethan town house and doctor's dispensary. Royal Shakespeare Theatre. Shakespeare's grave at Holy Trinity Church. Anne Hathaway's Cottage to W, at Shottery.

LOCAL RADIO:
BBC RADIO COVENTRY & WARWICKSHIRE 94.8 & 103.7 FM
FM 102 - THE BEAR 102 FM

www.shakespeare-country.co.uk

TOURIST INFORMATION CENTRE ☎ 0191 553 2000
50 FAWCETT STREET,
SUNDERLAND, SR1 1RF

HOSPITAL A & E ☎ 0191 565 6256
SUNDERLAND ROYAL HOSPITAL,
KAYLL ROAD, SUNDERLAND, SR4 7TP

COUNCIL OFFICE ☎ 0191 553 1000
SUNDERLAND CITY COUNCIL, CIVIC CENTRE,
BURDON ROAD, SUNDERLAND, SR2 7DN

Sunderland *North East England* Population 183,310. Industrial city and seaport at mouth of River Wear. Previously largest ship-building town in the world; coal mining was also important. Several museums celebrate city's industrial past. Service sector and manufacturing account for largest contribution to local economy. National Glass Centre commemorates importance of stained glass to area. University.

LOCAL RADIO:
BBC RADIO NEWCASTLE 1458 AM / 95.4 FM;
CENTURY RADIO 100.7 FM; GALAXY 105.3 FM;
METRO RADIO 97.1, 103 FM; SUN FM 103.4 FM

www.sunderland.gov.uk/visitors

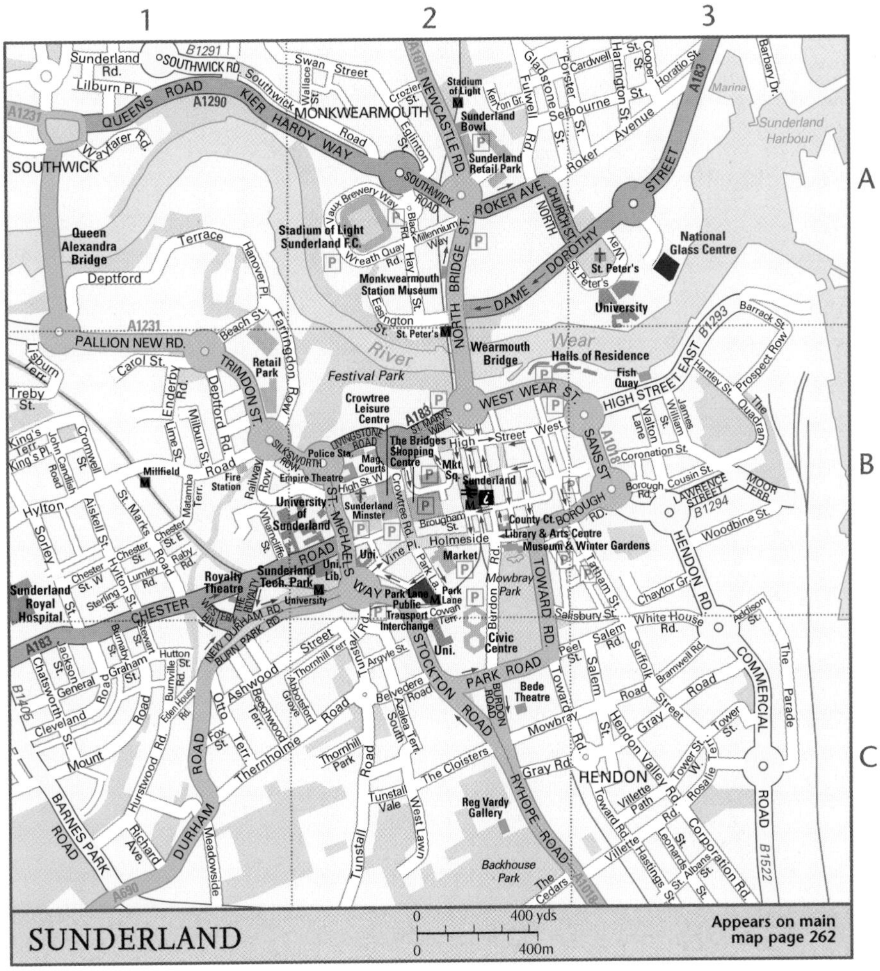

TOURIST INFORMATION CENTRE ☎ 01792 468321
WESTWAY,
SWANSEA, SA1 3QG

HOSPITAL A & E ☎ 01792 702222
MORRISTON HOSPITAL, MORRISTON,
SWANSEA, SA6 6NL

COUNCIL OFFICE ☎ 01792 636000
COUNTY HALL, OYSTERMOUTH ROAD,
SWANSEA, SA1 3SN

Swansea (Abertawe) *Wales* Population: 171,038. City, port on Swansea Bay at mouth of River Tawe, and Wales' second city. Settlement developed next to Norman castle built in 1099, but claims made that a Viking settlement existed before this date. Previously a port for local metal smelting industries. Bombed in World War II, and city centre rebuilt. Birthplace of Dylan Thomas, who described it as 'an ugly, lovely town'. Remains of 14th century castle or fortified manor house. University of Wales. Tropical plant and wildlife leisure centre, Plantasia. Airport 5 miles (9km) W at Fairwood Common.

LOCAL RADIO:
BBC RADIO WALES 657, 882 AM / 93.9 FM;
REAL RADIO 106 FM; SWANSEA SOUND 1170 AM

www1.swansea.gov.uk/tourism

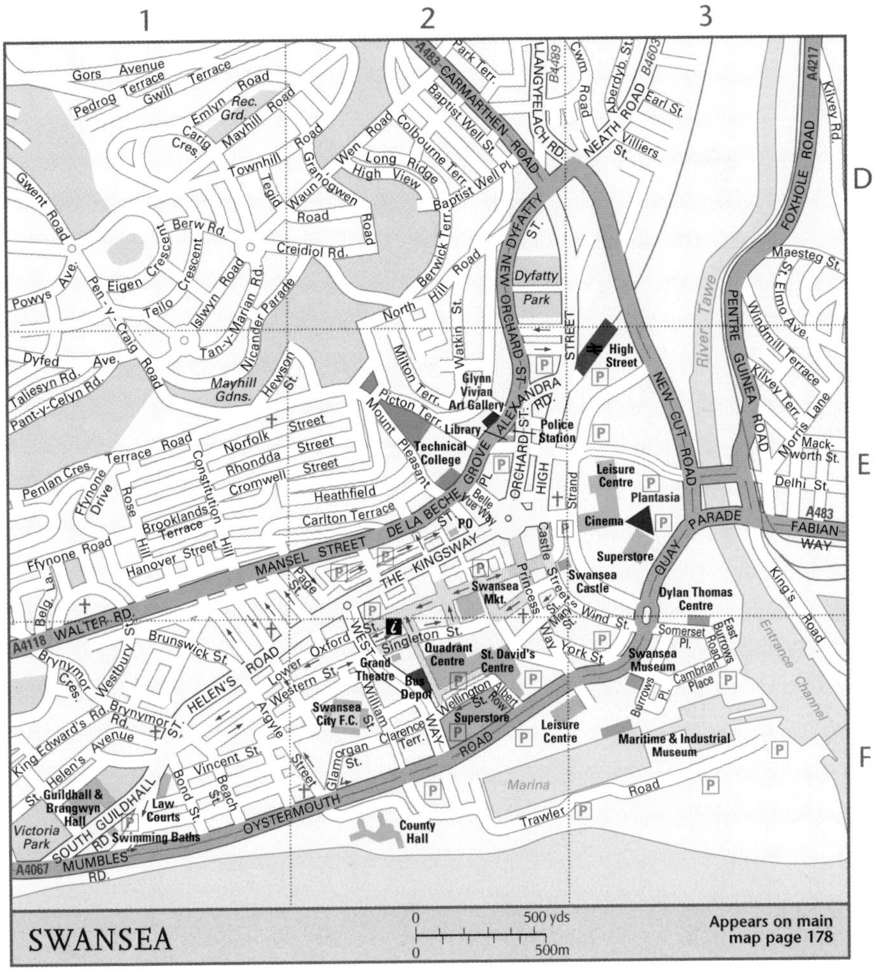

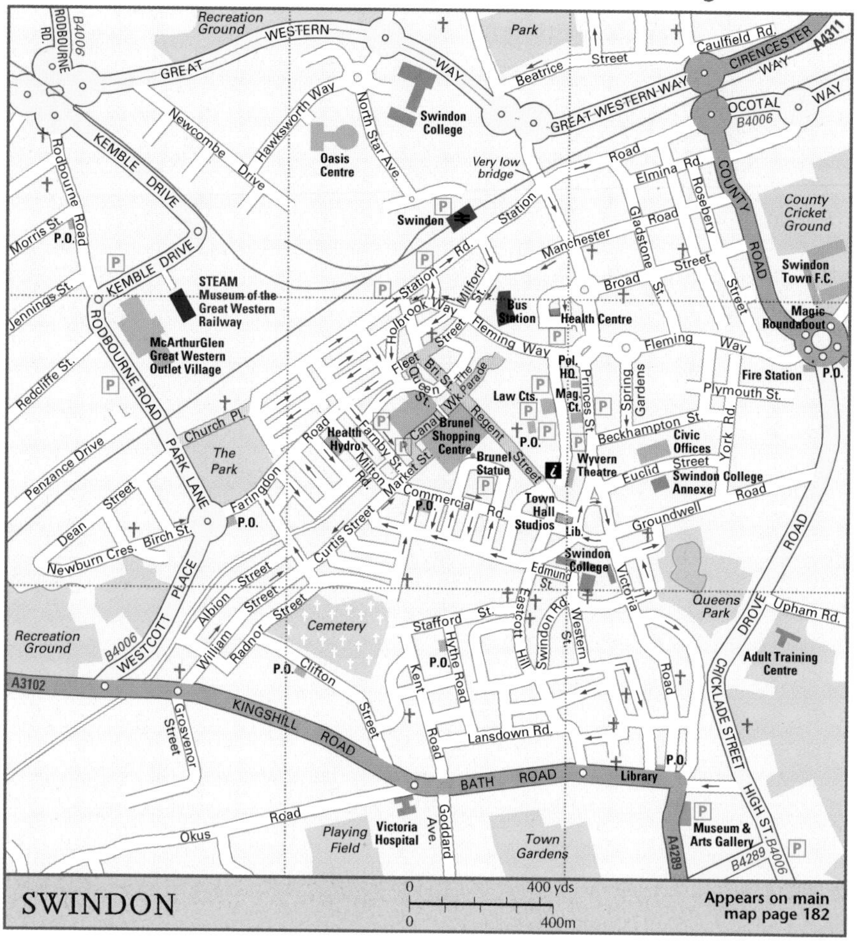

TOURIST INFORMATION CENTRE ☎ 01793 530328
37 REGENT STREET,
SWINDON, SN1 1JL

HOSPITAL A & E ☎ 01793 604020
GREAT WESTERN HOSPITAL, MARLBOROUGH RD,
SWINDON, SN3 6BB

COUNCIL OFFICE ☎ 01793 463000
CIVIC OFFICES, EUCLID STREET,
SWINDON, SN1 2JH

Swindon *South West England* Population: 145,236. Town, industrial and commercial centre. Large, modern shopping centre. Town expanded considerably in 19th century with arrival of the railway. The Museum of the Great Western Railway exhibits Swindon built locomotives and documents the history of the railway works.

LOCAL RADIO:
BBC WILTSHIRE SOUND 103.6 FM / 1368 MW;
CLASSIC GOLD 1161 AM; GWR FM 97.2 FM

www.swindon.gov.uk/tourism

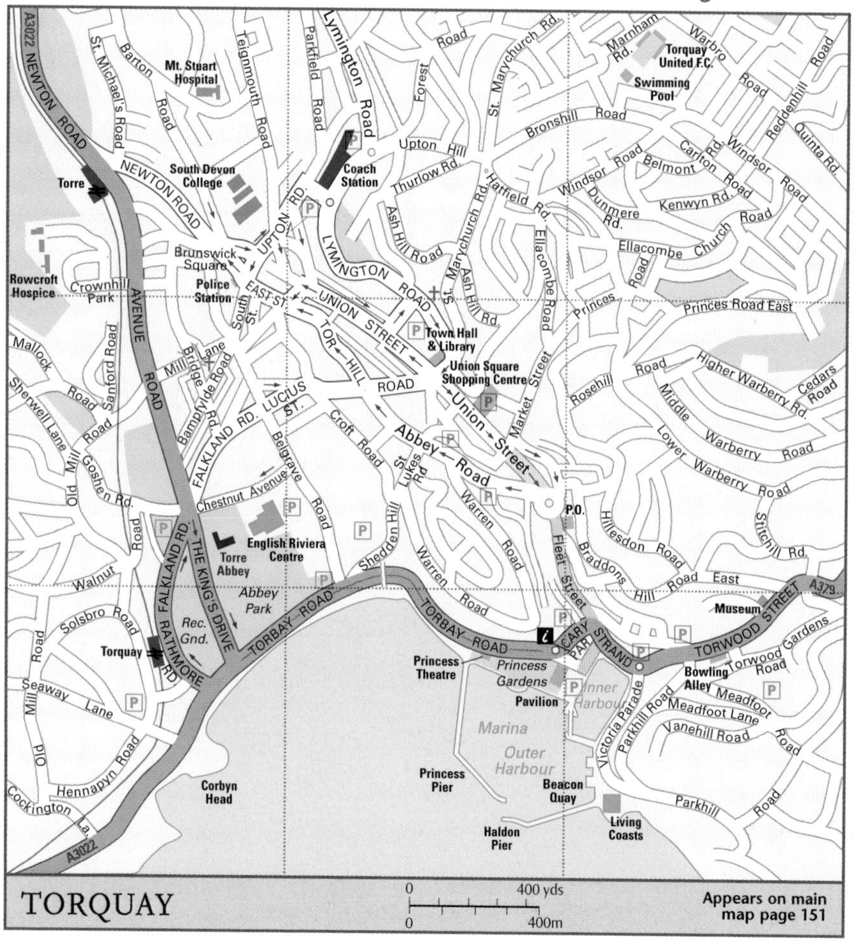

TOURIST INFORMATION CENTRE ☎ 01803 297428
VAUGHAN PARADE,
TORQUAY, TQ2 5JG

HOSPITAL A & E ☎ 01803 614567
TORBAY DISTRICT GENERAL HOSPITAL,
NEWTON ROAD, TORQUAY, TQ2 7AA

COUNCIL OFFICE ☎ 01803 201201
TOWN HALL, CASTLE CIRCUS,
TORQUAY, TQ1 3DR

Torquay *South West England* Population: 59,587. Chief town and resort of Torbay English Riviera district, with harbour and several beaches. Noted for mild climate. Torre Abbey with 15th century gatehouse, is a converted monastery housing a collecion of furniture and glassware. Torquay Museum has display on crimewriter Agatha Christie born in Torquay. Kent's Cavern showcaves are an important prehistoric site. Babbacombe Model village 2 miles (3km) N.

LOCAL RADIO:
BBC RADIO DEVON 104.3 FM;
CLASSIC GOLD 954 AM; GEMINI FM 96.4 FM;
SOUTH HAMS RADIO 100.8 FM

www.theenglishriviera.co.uk

TOURIST INFORMATION CENTRE ☎ 01727 864511
TOWN HALL, MARKET PLACE,
ST ALBANS, AL3 5DJ

HOSPITAL A & E ☎ 01923 244366
WATFORD GENERAL HOSPITAL, VICARAGE ROAD,
WATFORD, WD1 8HB

COUNCIL OFFICE ☎ 01923 226400
WATFORD COUNCIL, TOWN HALL,
WATFORD, WD17 3EX

Watford *East of England* Population: 113,080. Old market town on River Colne. Printing and brewing developed as the main industries; now the industrial base is more diverse. Shopping and leisure centre with modern sculptures in redeveloped central area. Parish church of Saint Mary's has 16th century chapel. Local history museum housed in Georgian house. Edwardian Palace Theatre originally opened as a music hall in 1908.

LOCAL RADIO:
BBC THREE COUNTIES RADIO 1161 AM / 103.8 FM;
MERCURY 96.6 FM

www.watford.gov.uk/tourism

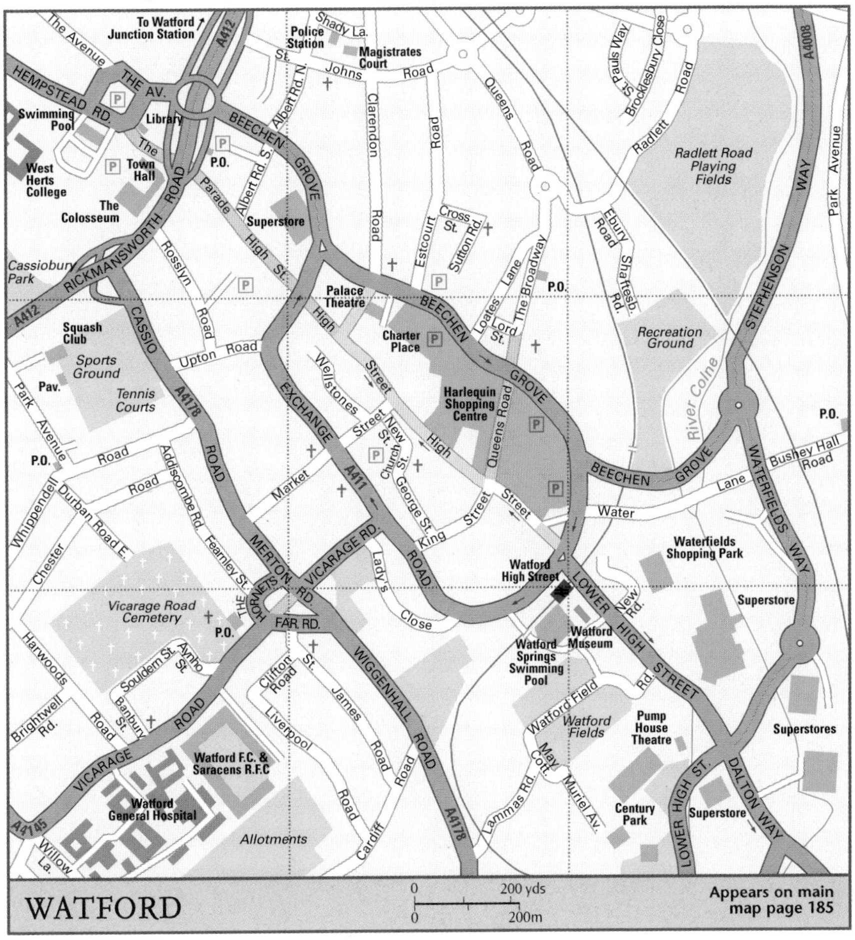

TOURIST INFORMATION CENTRE ☎ 01934 888800
BEACH LAWNS,
WESTON-SUPER-MARE, BS23 1AT

HOSPITAL A & E ☎ 01934 636363
WESTON GENERAL HOSPITAL, GRANGE ROAD,
UPHILL, WESTON-SUPER-MARE, BS23 3NT

COUNCIL OFFICE ☎ 01934 888888
NORTH SOMERSET COUNCIL, TOWN HALL,
WESTON-SUPER-MARE, BS23 1UJ

Weston-super-Mare *South West England* Population: 69,372. Town and popular resort on the Bristol Channel, situated on Weston Bay and first developed in the 19th century. Over 1 mile (2km) of sands with traditional beach donkeys; promenade, marine lake, miniature steam railway and Winter Gardens. Amusement park located on the central Grand Pier, built in 1904. The Aquarium houses ocean and coastal waters display tanks. Local history and heritage museums give an insight into the town as a Victorian seaside resort. Annual motorbike beach race, Enduro, is held in October. International Helicopter Museum at Locking 2 miles (3km) E.

LOCAL RADIO:
BBC SOMERSET SOUND 94.9, 104.6 FM
STAR 107.7 FM

www.somersetcoast.com

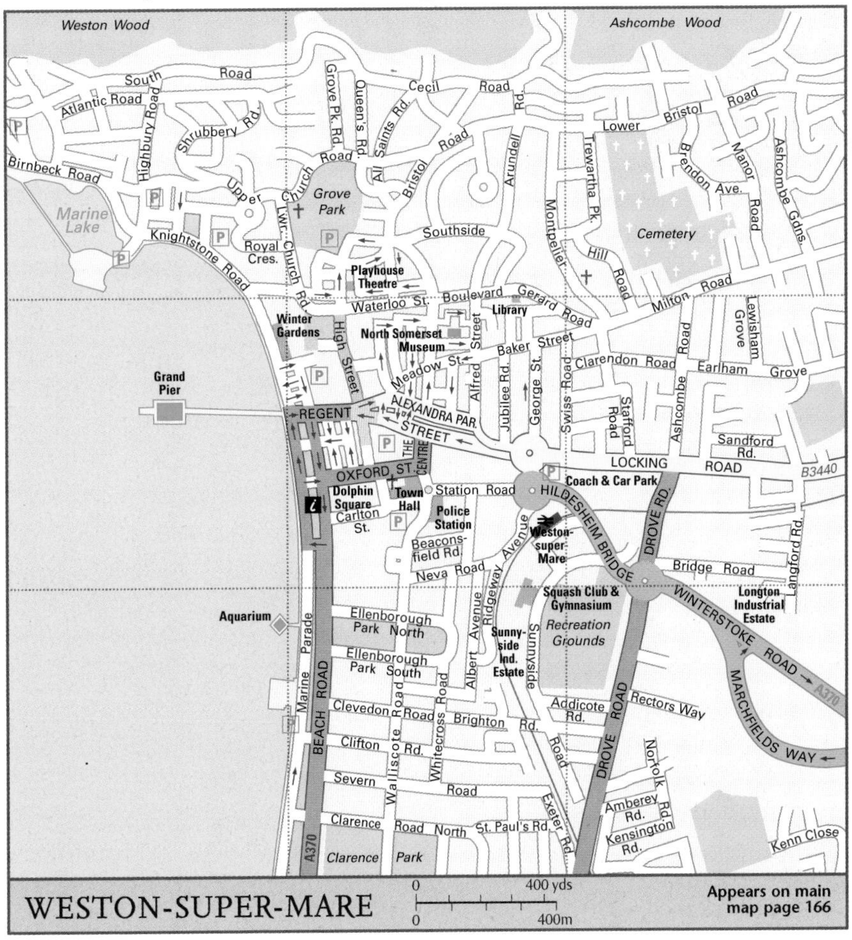

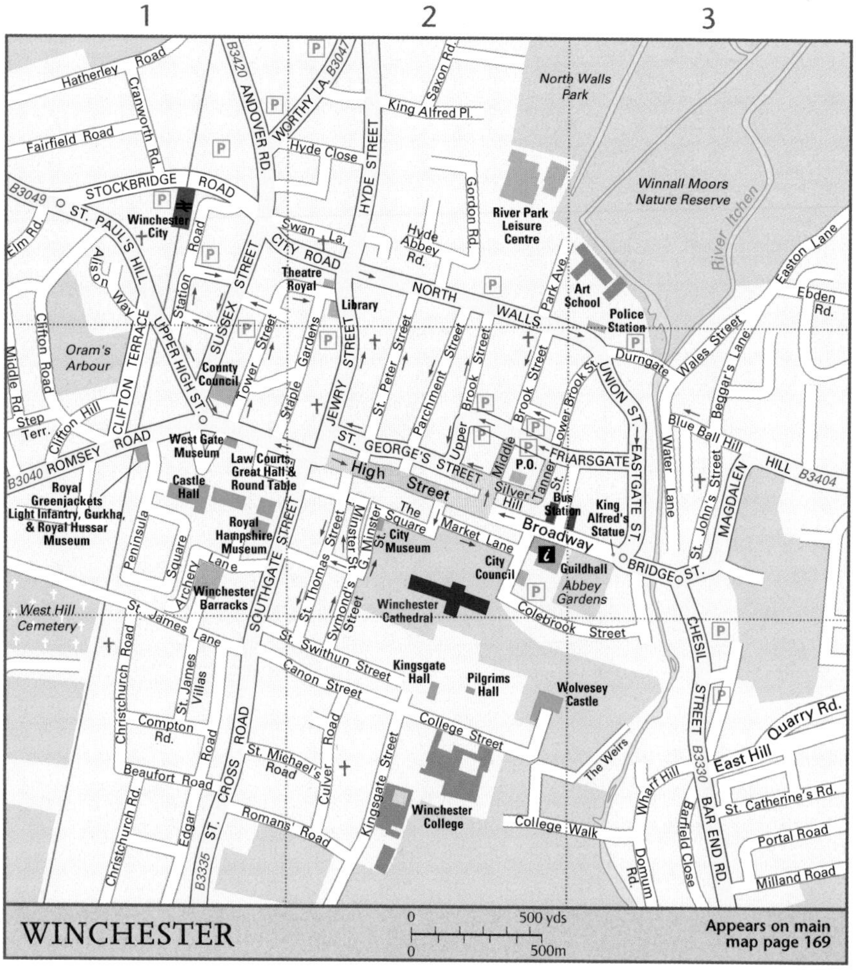

TOURIST INFORMATION CENTRE ☎ 01962 840500
GUILDHALL, THE BROADWAY, WINCHESTER
HAMPSHIRE, SO23 9LJ

HOSPITAL A & E ☎ 01962 863535
ROYAL HAMPSHIRE COUNTY HOSPITAL,
ROMSEY ROAD, WINCHESTER, SO22 5DG

COUNCIL OFFICE ☎ 01962 840222
CITY OFFICES, COLEBROOK STREET,
WINCHESTER, SO23 9LJ

Winchester *South East England* Population: 36,121. City, county town on River Itchen on site of Roman town of Venta Belgarum. Ancient capital of Wessex and of Anglo-Saxon England. 11th century cathedral, longest in Europe with carved Norman font and England's oldest complete choir-stalls. Winchester College, boys' public school founded 1382. 13th century Great Hall is only remaining part of Winchester Castle. Westgate Museum is in 12th century gatehouse in medieval city wall, once a debtors' prison. 12th century hospital of St. Cross. City Mill, built over river in 18th century. To S across river, St. Catherine's Hill, Iron Age fort. Extensive ruins of medieval Wolvesey Castle, also known as Old Bishop's Palace, 1 mile (2km) SE.

LOCAL RADIO:
BBC RADIO SOLENT 999 AM / 96.1 FM;
OCEAN FM 96.7 FM; WIN 107.2 FM

www.visitwinchester.co.uk

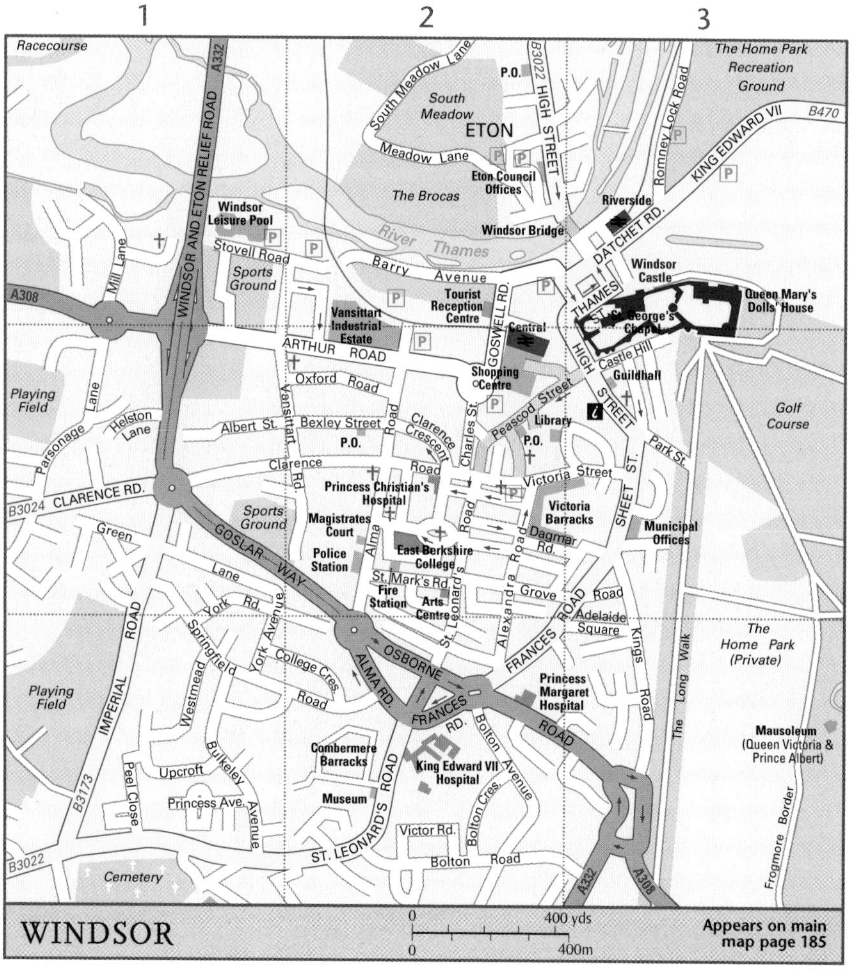

TOURIST INFORMATION CENTRE ☎ 01753 743900
24 HIGH STREET,
WINDSOR, SL4 1LH

HOSPITAL A & E ☎ 01753 633000
WEXHAM PARK HOSPITAL, WEXHAM STREET,
SLOUGH, SL2 4HL

COUNCIL OFFICE ☎ 01753 810525
COUNCIL OFFICES, YORK HOUSE, SHEET STREET,
WINDSOR, SL4 1DD

Windsor *South East England* Population: 26,369. Town, attractive market town on S bank of River Thames. Castle is royal residence. Great Park to S of town is open to public; Home Park bordering river is private. St. George's Chapel is impressive. Many Georgian houses, and guildhall designed by Sir Christopher Wren.

LOCAL RADIO:
BBC RADIO BERKSHIRE 95.4 FM;
STAR FM 106.6 FM

www.windsor.gov.uk

TOURIST INFORMATION CENTRE ☎ 01905 726311
THE GUILDHALL, HIGH STREET,
WORCESTER, WR1 2EY

HOSPITAL A & E ☎ 01905 763333
WORCESTERSHIRE ROYAL HOSPITAL,
CHARLES HASTINGS WAY,
WORCESTER, WR5 1DD

COUNCIL OFFICE ☎ 01905 723471
THE GUILDHALL, HIGH STREET,
WORCESTER, WR1 2EY

Worcester *West Midlands* Population: 82,661. City, on River Severn. Shopping, cultural, sports and industrial centre; industries include porcelain and sauces and condiments. 18th century Guildhall. Cathedral mainly Early English includes England's largest Norman crypt, 13th century choir and Lady Chapel and tomb of King John. Three Choirs Festival held here every third year. Civil War Centre at the Commandery, headquarters for Charles II during Battle of Worcester. Factory tours and museum at Royal Worcester Porcelain. Elgar's Birthplace, home of composer Sir Edward Elgar, in Broadheath, 3 miles (5km) W.

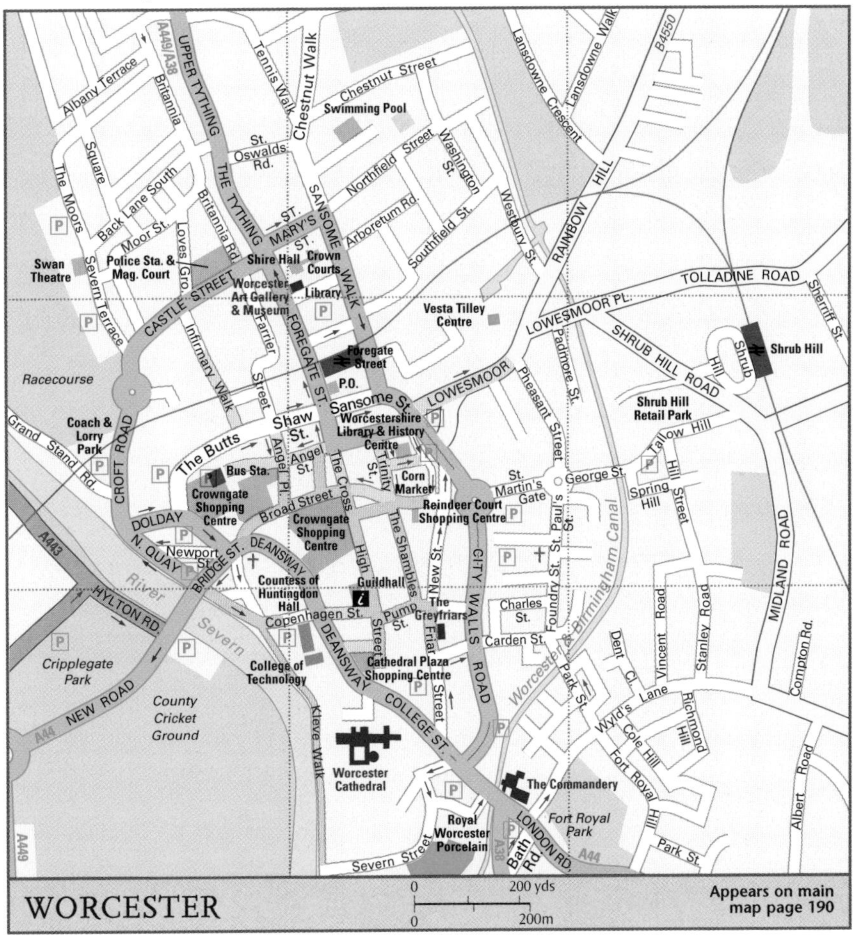

LOCAL RADIO:
BBC RADIO HEREFORD & WORCESTER 738 AM / 104 FM;
CLASSIC HITS 1530 AM; WYVERN FM 102.8 FM

www.visitworcester.com

TOURIST INFORMATION CENTRE ☎ 01904 621756
DE GREY ROOMS, EXHIBITION SQUARE,
YORK, YO1 2HB

HOSPITAL A & E ☎ 01904 631313
YORK DISTRICT HOSPITAL, WIGGINTON ROAD,
YORK, YO31 8HE

COUNCIL OFFICE ☎ 01904 613161
THE GUILDHALL,
YORK, YO1 9QN

York *Yorkshire* Population: 124,609. Ancient city and archiepiscopal see on River Ouse. On site of Roman Eboracum. Constantine the Great proclaimed Roman Emperor in York in AD 306; only emperor to be enthroned in Britain. City fell to Danes in AD 867 and became known as Jorvik. Medieval wall largely intact, other fortifications including Clifford's Tower. York Minster has largest Medieval stained glass window in country. Previously a wool trading, craft and railway centre. Home to National Railway Museum. Jorvik Viking Centre in Coppergate. Merchant Adventurers' Hall in Fossgate is finest remaining guildhall in Europe. University of York at Heslington. Racecourse at Knavesmire.

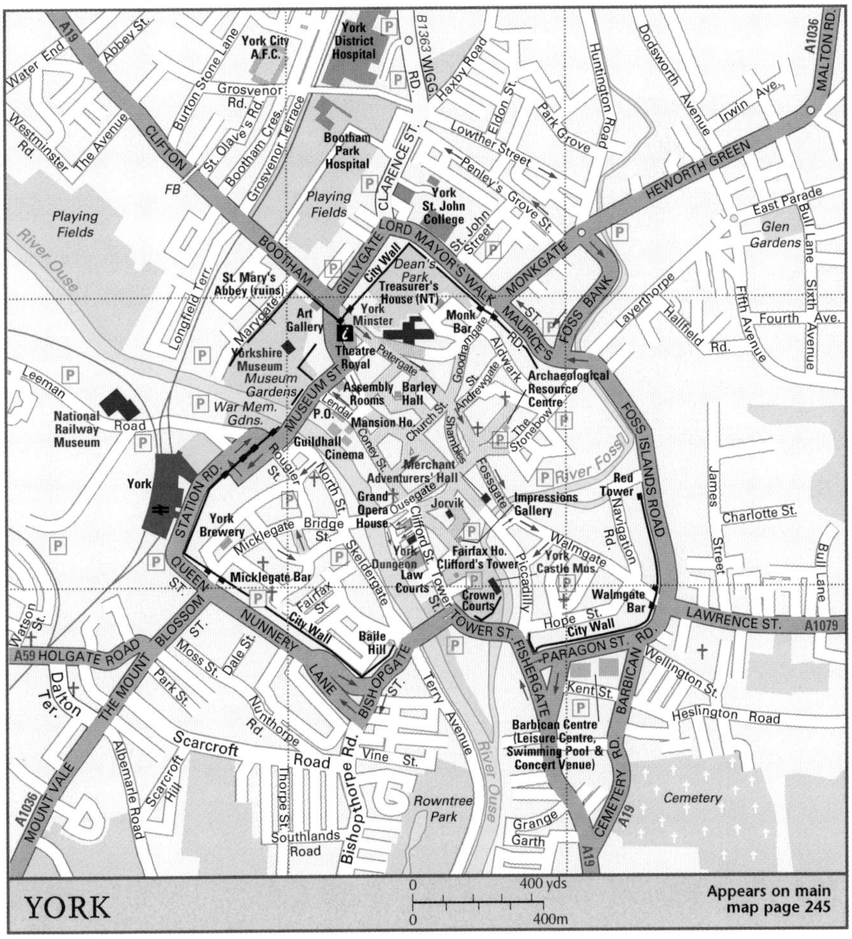

LOCAL RADIO:
BBC RADIO YORK 666, 1260 AM / 103.7 FM;
MINSTER FM 104.7 FM; GALAXY 105 105.1 FM

www.visityork.org

INDEX

Abbreviations

Aber.	Aberdeenshire	E.Ayr.	East Ayrshire	Lancs.	Lancashire	P. & K.	Perth & Kinross	Surr.	Surrey
Arg. & B.	Argyll & Bute	E.Dun.	East Dunbartonshire	Leic.	Leicester	Pembs.	Pembrokeshire	Swan.	Swansea
B'burn.	Blackburn with Darwen	E.Loth.	East Lothian	Leics.	Leicestershire	Peter.	Peterborough	Swin.	Swindon
B'pool	Blackpool	E.Renf.	East Renfrewshire	Lincs.	Lincolnshire	Plym.	Plymouth	T. & W.	Tyne & Wear
B. & H.	Brighton & Hove	E.Riding	East Riding of Yorkshire	M.K.	Milton Keynes	Ports.	Portsmouth	Tel. & W.	Telford & Wrekin
B. & N.E.Som.	Bath & North East Somerset	E.Suss.	East Sussex	M.Tyd.	Merthyr Tydfil	R. & C.	Redcar & Cleveland	Thur.	Thurrock
B.Gwent	Blaenau Gwent	Edin.	Edinburgh	Med.	Medway	R.C.T.	Rhondda Cynon Taff	V. of Glam.	Vale of Glamorgan
Beds.	Bedfordshire	Falk.	Falkirk	Mersey.	Merseyside	Read.	Reading	W'ham	Wokingham
Bourne.	Bournemouth	Flints.	Flintshire	Middbro.	Middlesbrough	Renf.	Renfrewshire	W. & M.	Windsor & Maidenhead
Brack.F.	Bracknell Forest	Glas.	Glasgow	Midloth.	Midlothian	Rut.	Rutland	W.Berks.	West Berkshire
Bucks.	Buckinghamshire	Glos.	Gloucestershire	Mon.	Monmouthshire	S'end	Southend	W.Dun.	West Dunbartonshire
Caerp.	Caerphilly	Gt.Lon.	Greater London	N.Ayr.	North Ayrshire	S'ham.	Southampton	W.Isles	Western Isles (Na h-Eileanan an Iar)
Cambs.	Cambridgeshire	Gt.Man.	Greater Manchester	N.E.Lincs.	North East Lincolnshire	S.Ayr.	South Ayrshire	W.Loth.	West Lothian
Carmar.	Carmarthenshire	Gwyn.	Gwynedd	N.Lan.	North Lanarkshire	S.Glos.	South Gloucestershire	W.Mid.	West Midlands
Cere.	Ceredigion	Hants.	Hampshire	N.Lincs.	North Lincolnshire	S.Lan.	South Lanarkshire	W.Suss.	West Sussex
Chan.I.	Channel Islands	Hart.	Hartlepool	N.P.T.	Neath Port Talbot	S.Yorks.	South Yorkshire	W.Yorks.	West Yorkshire
Ches.	Cheshire	Here.	Herefordshire	N.Som.	North Somerset	Sc.Bord.	Scottish Borders	Warks.	Warwickshire
Cornw.	Cornwall	Herts.	Hertfordshire	N.Yorks.	North Yorkshire	Shet.	Shetland	Warr.	Warrington
Cumb.	Cumbria	High.	Highland	Norf.	Norfolk	Shrop.	Shropshire	Wilts.	Wiltshire
D. & G.	Dumfries & Galloway	Hull	Kingston upon Hull	Northants.	Northamptonshire	Slo.	Slough	Worcs.	Worcestershire
Darl.	Darlington	I.o.A.	Isle of Anglesey	Northumb.	Northumberland	Som.	Somerset	Wrex.	Wrexham
Denb.	Denbighshire	I.o.M.	Isle of Man	Nott.	Nottingham	Staffs.	Staffordshire		
Derbys.	Derbyshire	I.o.S.	Isles of Scilly	Notts.	Nottinghamshire	Stir.	Stirling		
Dur.	Durham	I.o.W.	Isle of Wight	Ork.	Orkney	Stock.	Stockton-on-Tees		
		Inclyde	Inverclyde	Oxon.	Oxfordshire	Stoke	Stoke-on-Trent		
						Suff.	Suffolk		

Places of interest are shown in the index in **purple** type.

Alperton 186 A4
Alphamstone 201 G4
Alpheton 201 G2
Alphington 152 C3
Alport 222 D1
Alpraham 220 C2
Alresford 202 B5
Alrewas 209 D1
Alrick 301 G3
Alsager 221 E2
Alsagers Bank 221 F3
Alsop en le Dale 222 C2
Alston *Cumb.* 260 D3
Alston *Devon* 153 G2
Alston Sutton 166 B2
Alstone *Glos.* 196 B4
Alstone *Som.* 166 A3
Alstone *Staffs.* 208 A1
Alstonefield 222 C2
Alswear 164 A5
Alt 234 D2
Altandhu 330 B3
Altanduin 332 D2
Altarnun 147 G1
Altass 332 A4
Altens 313 E4
Alterwall 337 E2
Altham 243 D4
Althorne 188 C3
Althorp House 70
Althorpe 237 F2
Alticry 265 D5
Altnafeadh 299 E4
Altnaharra 335 E5
Altofts 244 C5
Alton *Derbys.* 223 E1
Alton *Hants.* 170 C4
Alton *Staffs.* 222 B3
Alton Barnes 168 C1
Alton Pancras 154 D2
Alton Priors 168 C1
Alton Towers Leisure Park 63
Altonside 323 E4
Altrincham 234 B4
Altura 308 B5
Alva 293 D5
Alvanley 233 F5
Alvaston 223 E4
Alvechurch 208 C5
Alvecote 209 E2
Alvediston 168 A5
Alveley 207 G4
Alverdiscott 163 F3
Alverstoke 157 F3
Alverstone 157 E4
Alverthorpe 244 C5
Alverton 224 C3
Alves 322 D3
Alvescot 183 E2
Alveston *S.Glos.* 181 F4
Alveston *Warks.* 197 E2
Alvie 310 A4
Alvingham 239 D3
Alvington 181 F2
Alwalton 211 G3
Alweston 154 C1
Alwington 163 E3
Alwinton 270 B1
Alwoodley 244 C3
Alwoodley Gates 244 C3
Alyth 302 A5
Amalebra 144 B3
Ambaston 223 F4
Amber Hill 226 A3
Ambergate 223 E2
Amberley *Glos.* 182 A2
Amberley *W.Suss.* 158 C2
Amberley Museum 40
Amble 271 E1
Amblecote 208 A4
Ambleside 249 E2
Ambleston 190 D5
Ambrismore 282 B4
Ambrosden 184 B1
Amcotts 237 F1
American Adventure Theme Park 70
American Museum 24
Amersham 185 E3
Amerton 221 G5
Amesbury 168 C3
Ameysford 155 G2
Amington 209 E2
Amisfield Town 267 E2
Amlwch 230 C3
Amlwch Port 230 C3
Ammanford (Rhydaman) 178 C1
Amotherby 253 G5
Ampfield 169 E5
Ampleforth 253 E5
Ampleforth College 253 E5
Ampney Crucis 182 C2
Ampney St. Mary 182 C2
Ampney St. Peter 182 C2
Amport 169 E3
Ampthill 199 F4
Ampton 213 G5
Amroth 177 E2
Amulree 293 D1
An Tairbeart (Tarbert) 327 D3
An T-òb (Leverburgh) 326 C5
Anaboard 310 C1
Anaheilt 298 A3
Ancaster 225 E3
Anchor 206 A4
Anchor Corner 214 B2
Ancient High House 63
Ancroft 279 G5
Ancrum 278 A4
Ancton 158 B3
Anderby 239 F5
Anderby Creek 239 F5
Andersea 166 A4
Andersfield 165 F4
Anderson 155 E3
Anderton 234 A5
Anderton Boat Lift 93
Andover 169 E3
Andover Down 169 E3
Andoversford 182 C1
Andreas 240 C2
Anelog 216 A5
Anfield 233 E3
Angarrack 144 C3
Angarrick 145 E3
Angelbank 207 E5
Angerton 259 F1
Angle 176 B2
Angler's Retreat 204 D3
Anglesey (Ynys Môn) 230 B4
Anglesey Abbey 77
Anglesey Sea Zoo 107
Angmering 158 C3
Angmering-on-Sea 158 C3
Angram *N.Yorks.* 245 E3
Angram *N.Yorks.* 251 D3
Angus Folk Museum 116
Anick 261 F1
Anie 292 A3
Ankerville 322 A2
Anlaby 246 C5
Anmer 227 F5
Anmore 157 F1
Anna Valley 169 E3
Annan 267 F4
Annaside 248 B4
Annat *Arg. & B.* 290 C2
Annat *High.* 319 E4
Annbank 274 C3
Anne Hathaway's Cottage 63
Annesley 223 G2
Annesley Woodhouse 223 F2
Annfield Plain 262 A2
Anniesland 283 G3
Annscroft 207 D2
Ansdell 241 G5
Ansford 166 D4
Ansley 209 E3
Anslow 222 D5
Anslow Gate 222 C5
Ansteadbrook 171 E4
Anstey *Herts.* 200 C4
Anstey *Leics.* 210 A2
Anstruther 295 D4
Ansty *W.Suss.* 159 E1
Ansty *Warks.* 209 F4
Ansty *Wilts.* 168 A5
Ansty Coombe 168 A5
Ansty Cross 155 D2
Anthill Common 157 F1
Anthorn 259 E1
Antingham 229 D2
Antonine Wall 116
Anton's Gowt 226 A3
Antony 149 D5
Antony House 24
Antrobus 234 A5
Anvil Corner 163 D5
Anvil Green 174 D4
Anwick 225 G2
Anwoth 265 G5
Aonach Mòr Mountain Gondola & Nevis Range Ski Centre 116
Aoradh 280 A3
Apes Hall, The 213 D3
Apethorpe 211 F3
Apeton 208 A1
Apley 238 B5
Apperknowle 236 A5
Apperley 196 A5
Apperley Bridge 244 A4
Appersett 251 D3
Appin 298 B5
Appin House 298 B5
Appleby 237 G1
Appleby Magna 209 F1
Appleby Parva 209 F2
Appleby-in-Westmorland 260 C5
Applecross 318 D5
Appledore *Devon* 163 E2
Appledore *Devon* 153 D1
Appledore *Kent* 161 E1
Appledore Heath 174 B5
Appleford 184 A3
Appleshaw 169 E3
Applethwaite 259 F4
Appleton *Halton* 233 G4
Appleton *Oxon.* 183 G2
Appleton Roebuck 245 E3
Appleton Thorn 234 A4
Appleton Wiske 252 C2
Appleton-le-Moors 253 G4
Appleton-le-Street 253 G5
Appletreehall 277 G4
Appletreewick 243 G1
Appley 165 D5
Appley Bridge 233 G2
Apse Heath 157 E4
Apsey Green 203 D1
Apsley 185 F2
Apsley End 199 G4
Apuldram 158 A3
Aquarium of the Lakes 93
Arbeia Roman Fort & Museum 102
Arberth (Narberth) 177 E1
Arbirlot 303 D5
Arborfield 170 C1
Arborfield Cross 170 C1
Arborfield Garrison 170 C1
Arbourthorne 236 A4
Arbroath 303 E5
Arbroath Abbey 116
Arbury Hall 63
Arbuthnott 303 F2
Archdeacon Newton 252 B1
Archiestown 323 E5
Arclid 221 E1
Ard a' Chapuill 282 B1
Ardachearanbeg 282 B1
Ardacheranmor 282 B1
Ardachoil 289 G1
Ardachu 332 B4
Ardailly 281 E4
Ardalanish 288 C3
Ardallie 313 F1
Ardanaiseig 290 C2
Ardaneaskan 307 E1
Ardanstur 290 A3
Ardantiobairt 297 F4
Ardantrive 290 A2
Ardarroch 319 E5
Ardbeg *Arg. & B.* 282 B3
Ardbeg *Arg. & B.* 280 C5
Ardbeg *Arg. & B.* 282 C1
Ardblair 309 E1
Ardbrecknish 290 C2
Ardcharnich 320 A1
Ardchiavaig 288 C3
Ardchonnel 290 B1
Ardchonnell 290 B3
Ardchrishnish 288 D2
Ardchronie 321 F1
Ardchuilk 308 B1
Ardchullarie More 292 A3
Ardchyle 292 A2
Arddlin 206 B1
Ardechvie 308 A5
Ardeley 200 B5
Ardelve 307 E2
Arden 283 E1
Ardencaple House 289 G3
Ardens Grafton 196 D2
Ardentallan 290 A2
Ardentinny 282 C1
Ardeonaig 292 B1
Ardersier 321 G4
Ardery 297 G3
Ardessie 319 G1
Ardfad 289 G3
Ardfern 290 A4
Ardfin 280 C3
Ardgartan 291 E4
Ardgay 332 B5
Ardgenavan 291 D3
Ardgowan 282 D2
Ardgowse 312 B3
Ardgye 322 D3
Ardhallow 282 C2
Ardheslaig 319 D4
Ardiecow 324 A3
Ardinamar 289 G3
Ardindrean 320 A1
Ardingly 159 F1
Ardington 183 G4
Ardington Wick 183 G4
Ardintoul 307 E2
Ardkinglas House 291 D3
Ardkinglas Woodland Garden 116
Ardlair 312 A2
Ardlamont 282 A3
Ardleigh 202 B5
Ardleigh Green 187 E4
Ardleigh Heath 202 B4
Ardleish 291 F3
Ardler 302 A5
Ardley 198 A5
Ardley End 187 E1
Ardlui 291 F3
Ardlussa 281 E1
Ardmaddy 290 C1
Ardmair 330 D5
Ardmaleish 282 B3
Ardmay 291 E4
Ardmenish 281 D2
Ardmhór 314 C3
Ardminish 281 E5
Ardmolich 297 G2
Ardmore *Arg. & B.* 280 C4
Ardmore *Arg. & B.* 289 G2
Ardmore *Arg. & B.* 283 E2
Ardmore *High.* 321 G1
Ardnackaig 289 G5
Ardnacross 297 E5
Ardnadam 282 C1
Ardnadrochit 289 G1
Ardnagoine 330 B4
Ardnagowan 290 D4
Ardnahein 291 D5
Ardnahoe 280 C2
Ardnarff 307 E1
Ardnastang 298 A3
Ardnave 280 A2
Ardno 291 D4
Ardo 313 D1
Ardoch *D. & G.* 275 G5
Ardoch *Moray* 322 D4
Ardoch *P. & K.* 293 F1
Ardochrig 284 A5
Ardoyne 312 B2
Ardpatrick 281 F3
Ardpeaton 282 D1
Ardradnaig 300 C5
Ardrishaig 281 G1
Ardroe 330 C2
Ardross 321 F2
Ardrossan 282 D5
Ardscalpsie 282 B4
Ardshave 332 C5
Ardshealach 297 F3
Ardshellach 289 G3
Ardsley 236 A2
Ardslignish 297 E3
Ardtalla 280 C4
Ardtalnaig 292 C1
Ardtaraig 282 B1
Ardteatle 290 D2
Ardtoe 297 F2
Ardtornish 297 G5
Ardtrostan 292 B2
Ardtur 298 B5
Arduaine 290 A3
Arduaine Gardens 116
Ardullie 321 E3
Ardura 289 F1
Ardvar 334 A5
Ardvasar 306 C4
Ardveenish 314 C3
Ardveich 292 B2
Ardverikie 300 A1
Ardvorlich *Arg. & B.* 291 F3
Ardvorlich *P. & K.* 292 B2
Ardwall 265 G5
Ardwell *D. & G.* 256 B2
Ardwell *Moray* 311 F1
Ardwell *S.Ayr.* 264 C1
Ardwick 234 C3
Areley Kings 208 A5
Arford 170 D4
Argaty 292 C4
Argoed 180 A3
Argoed Mill 193 F1
Argos Hill 160 A1
Argrennan House 266 B5
Arichamish 290 B4
Arichastlich 291 E1
Arichonan 289 G5
Aridhglas 288 C2
Arienskill 297 G1
Arileod 296 A4
Arinacrinachd 318 D4
Arinafad Beg 281 F1
Arinagour 296 B4
Arinambane 314 C1
Arisaig 297 F1
Arivegaig 297 F3
Arkendale 244 C1
Arkesden 200 C4
Arkholme 249 G5
Arkle Town 251 F2
Arkleby 259 E3
Arkleside 251 F4
Arkleton 268 B2
Arkley 186 B3
Arksey 236 C2
Arkwright Town 236 B5
Arlary 293 G4
Arle 196 B5
Arlecdon 258 D5
Arlesey 199 G4
Arleston 207 F1
Arley 234 A4
Arley Hall 93
Arlingham 181 G1
Arlington *Devon* 163 G1
Arlington *E.Suss.* 160 A3
Arlington *Glos.* 182 D2
Arlington Beccott 163 G1
Arlington Court 24
Armadale *High.* 335 G2
Armadale *High.* 306 C4
Armadale *W.Loth.* 284 D3
Armathwaite 260 B3
Arminghall 229 D5
Armitage 208 C1
Armitage Bridge 235 F1
Armley 244 B4
Armscote 197 E3
Armshead 221 G3
Armston 211 F4
Armthorpe 236 D2
Arnabost 296 B3
Arnaby 248 C4
Arncliffe 251 E5
Arncliffe Cote 251 E5
Arncroach 294 D4
Arne 155 F4
Arnesby 210 B3
Arngask 293 G3
Arngibbon 292 B5
Arngomery 292 B5
Arnhall 303 E3
Arnicle 272 C2
Arnipol 297 G1
Arnisdale 307 E3
Arnish 318 B5
Arniston Engine 286 A3
Arnol 329 E3
Arnold *E.Riding* 246 D3
Arnold *Notts.* 223 G3
Arnprior 292 B5
Arnside 249 F5
Arowry 220 B4
Arrad Foot 249 E4
Arradoul 323 G3
Arram 246 C3
Arran 273 E2
Arras 246 B3
Arrat 303 E4
Arrathorne 252 B3
Arreton 157 E4
Arrington 200 B2
Arrivain 291 E1
Arrochar 291 F4
Arrow 196 C2
Arscaig 332 A3
Arscott 206 D2
Arthington 244 B3
Arthingworth 210 C4
Arthog 204 C1
Arthrath 313 E1
Arthurstone 302 A5
Artrochie 313 F1
Aruadh 280 A3
Arundel 158 C3
Arundel Castle 40
Aryhoulan 298 C3
Asby 259 D4
Ascog 282 C3
Ascot 171 E1
Ascott *Bucks.* 40
Ascott *Warks.* 197 F4
Ascott d'Oyley 183 F1
Ascott Earl 183 E1
Ascott-under-Wychwood 183 F1
Ascreavie 302 B4
Asenby 252 D5
Asfordby 210 C1
Asfordby Hill 210 C1
Asgarby *Lincs.* 226 B1
Asgarby *Lincs.* 225 G3
Ash *Dorset* 155 E1
Ash *Kent* 175 E3
Ash *Kent* 173 F2
Ash *Som.* 166 B5
Ash *Surr.* 171 D2
Ash Barton 163 F5
Ash Bullayne 152 A2
Ash End House Children's Farm 63
Ash Green *Surr.* 171 E3
Ash Green *Warks.* 209 F4
Ash Magna 220 C4
Ash Mill 164 A5
Ash Parva 220 C4
Ash Priors 165 E5
Ash Street 202 B3
Ash Thomas 152 D1
Ash Vale 171 D2
Ashampstead 184 A5
Ashbocking 202 C2
Ashbourne 222 C3
Ashbrittle 165 D5
Ashburnham Place 160 B2
Ashburton 151 D1
Ashbury *Devon* 149 F1
Ashbury *Oxon.* 183 E4
Ashby 237 F2
Ashby by Partney 226 C1
Ashby cum Fenby 238 C2
Ashby de la Launde 225 F2
Ashby de la Zouch 209 F1
Ashby Dell 215 F2
Ashby Folville 210 C1
Ashby Hill 238 C2
Ashby Magna 210 A3
Ashby Parva 210 A4
Ashby Puerorum 238 D5
Ashby St. Ledgers 198 A1
Ashby St. Mary 229 E5
Ashchurch 196 B4
Ashcombe *Devon* 152 C5
Ashcombe *N.Som.* 166 A1
Ashcott 166 B4
Ashdon 201 D3
Ashdown House 40
Ashe 169 G3
Asheldham 188 C2
Ashen 201 F3
Ashenden 174 A5
Ashendon 184 C1
Ashens 281 G2
Ashfield *Arg. & B.* 281 F1
Ashfield *Here.* 195 E5
Ashfield *Stir.* 292 C4
Ashfield *Suff.* 202 D1
Ashfield Green *Suff.* 215 D4
Ashfield Green *Suff.* 201 F2
Ashfold Crossways 159 E1
Ashford *Devon* 150 C3
Ashford *Devon* 163 F2
Ashford *Hants.* 156 A1
Ashford *Kent* 174 C4
Ashford *Surr.* 185 F5
Ashford Bowdler 207 E5
Ashford Carbonel 207 E5
Ashford Hill 169 G1
Ashford in the Water 235 F5
Ashgill 284 B4
Ashiestiel 277 F2
Ashill *Devon* 153 D1
Ashill *Norf.* 213 G2
Ashill *Som.* 153 G1
Ashingdon 188 B3
Ashington *Northumb.* 271 E3
Ashington *Som.* 166 C5
Ashington *W.Suss.* 158 D2
Ashkirk 277 F3
Ashlett 157 D2
Ashleworth 196 A5
Ashleworth Quay 196 A5
Ashley *Cambs.* 201 E1
Ashley *Ches.* 234 B4
Ashley *Devon* 163 G4
Ashley *Glos.* 182 B3
Ashley *Hants.* 169 E4
Ashley *Hants.* 156 B3
Ashley *Kent* 175 F4
Ashley *Northants.* 210 C3
Ashley *Staffs.* 221 E4
Ashley *Wilts.* 167 F1
Ashley Down 181 E5
Ashley Green 185 E2
Ashley Heath *Dorset* 156 A2
Ashley Heath *Staffs.* 221 E4
Ashmanhaugh 229 E3
Ashmansworth 169 F2
Ashmansworthy 162 D4
Ashmolean Museum 40
Ashmore *Dorset* 155 F1
Ashmore *P. & K.* 301 G4
Ashmore Green 169 G1
Ashorne 197 F2
Ashover 223 E1
Ashover Hay 223 E1
Ashow 209 F5
Ashperton 195 F3
Ashprington 151 E2
Ashreigney 163 G4
Ashtead 171 G2
Ashton *Ches.* 220 C1
Ashton *Cornw.* 144 D4
Ashton *Cornw.* 149 D4
Ashton *Hants.* 157 E1
Ashton *Here.* 195 E1
Ashton *Inclyde* 282 D2
Ashton *Northants.* 211 F4
Ashton *Northants.* 198 C3
Ashton *Peter.* 211 G2
Ashton Common 167 F2
Ashton Court Estate 24
Ashton Keynes 182 C3
Ashton under Hill 196 B4
Ashton upon Mersey 234 B3
Ashton-in-Makerfield 233 G3
Ashton-under-Lyne 234 D3
Ashurst *Hants.* 156 C1
Ashurst *Kent* 173 E5
Ashurst *W.Suss.* 159 D2
Ashurst Bridge 156 C1
Ashurstwood 172 D5
Ashwater 149 D1
Ashwell *Herts.* 200 A4
Ashwell *Rut.* 211 D1
Ashwell End 200 A3
Ashwellthorpe 214 C2
Ashwick 166 D3
Ashwicken 213 F1
Ashybank 277 G4
Askam in Furness 248 D5
Askern 236 C1
Askernish (Aisgernis) 314 C1
Askerswell 154 B3
Askett 184 D2
Askham *Cumb.* 260 B5
Askham *Notts.* 237 E5
Askham Bryan 245 E3
Askham Richard 245 E3
Asknish 290 B5
Askrigg 251 E3
Askwith 244 A3
Aslackby 225 F4
Aslacton 214 C2
Aslockton 224 C3
Asloun 312 A3
Aspall 202 C1
Aspatria 259 E2
Aspenden 200 B5
Asperton 226 A4
Aspley Guise 199 E4
Aspley Heath 199 E4
Aspull 234 A2
Asselby 245 G5
Asserby 239 E5
Assington 202 A4
Assington Green 201 F2
Astbury 221 F1
Astcote 198 B2
Asterby 238 C5
Asterley 206 C2
Asterton 206 D3
Asthall 183 E1
Asthall Leigh 183 F1
Astle 234 C5
Astley *Gt.Man.* 234 B2
Astley *Shrop.* 207 E1
Astley *Warks.* 209 F4
Astley *Worcs.* 195 G1
Astley Abbotts 207 G3
Astley Bridge 234 B1
Astley Cross 196 A1
Astley Green 234 B3
Astley Hall Museum & Gardens 93
Astley Lodge 207 E1
Aston *Ches.* 220 D3
Aston *Ches.* 233 G5
Aston *Derbys.* 235 F4
Aston *Derbys.* 222 C4
Aston *Flints.* 220 A1
Aston *Here.* 207 D5
Aston *Here.* 195 D1
Aston *Herts.* 200 A5
Aston *Oxon.* 183 F2
Aston *S.Yorks.* 236 B4
Aston *Shrop.* 220 C5
Aston *Shrop.* 208 A3
Aston *Staffs.* 221 E3
Aston *Tel. & W.* 207 F2
Aston *W'ham* 184 C4
Aston *W.Mid.* 208 C4
Aston Abbotts 198 D5
Aston Botterell 207 F4
Aston Cantlow 196 D2
Aston Clinton 185 D1
Aston Crews 195 F5
Aston Cross 196 B4
Aston End 200 A5
Aston Eyre 207 F3
Aston Fields 196 B1
Aston Flamville 209 G3
Aston Heath 233 G5
Aston Ingham 195 F5
Aston juxta Mondrum 221 D2
Aston le Walls 197 G2
Aston Magna 197 D4
Aston Munslow 207 E4
Aston on Carrant 196 B4
Aston on Clun 206 C4
Aston Pigott 206 C2
Aston Rogers 206 C2
Aston Rowant 184 C3
Aston Sandford 184 C2
Aston Somerville 196 C4
Aston Subedge 196 D3
Aston Tirrold 184 A4
Aston Upthorpe 184 A4
Aston-by-Stone 221 G4
Aston-on-Trent 223 F5
Astwick 200 A4
Astwood 199 E3
Astwood Bank 196 C1
Aswarby 225 F3
Aswardby 239 D5
Aswick Grange 212 B1
At-Bristol 24
Atch Lench 196 C2
Atcham 207 E2
Ath Linne 327 D2
Athelhampton *Dorset* 155 D3
Athelhampton *Dorset* 24
Athelington 214 D4
Athelney 166 A5
Athelstaneford 286 C2
Atherington *Devon* 163 F3
Atherington *W.Suss.* 158 C3
Athersley North 236 A2
Atherstone 209 F3
Atherstone on Stour 197 E2
Atherton 234 A2
Atlow 222 D3
Attadale 307 F1
Attenborough 223 G4
Atterby 237 G3
Attercliffe 236 A4
Atterley 207 F3
Atterton 209 F3
Attingham Park 63
Attleborough *Norf.* 214 B2
Attleborough *Warks.* 209 F3
Attlebridge 228 C4
Attleton Green 201 F2
Atwick 247 D2
Atworth 167 F1
Auberrow 195 D3
Aubourn 225 E1
Auch 291 F1
Auchairne 264 C2
Auchallater 301 G1
Auchameanach 281 G4
Auchamore 281 G5
Aucharnie 324 B5
Aucharrigill 331 G4
Auchattie 312 B5
Auchavan 301 G3
Auchbraad 281 G1
Auchbreck 311 E2
Auchenback 283 G4
Auchenblae 303 F2
Auchenbothie 283 E2
Auchenbrack 266 B1
Auchenbreck 282 B1
Auchencairn 266 B5
Auchencrow 287 F3
Auchendinny 285 G3
Auchendolly 266 B4
Auchenfoyle 283 E2
Auchengillan 283 G1
Auchengray 285 D4
Auchenhalrig 323 F3
Auchenheath 284 C5
Auchenhessnane 266 C1
Auchenlochan 282 A2
Auchenmalg 264 D5
Auchenrivock 268 B3
Auchentiber 283 E5
Auchenvennel 283 D1
Auchessan 291 G2
Auchgourish 310 B3
Auchinafaud 281 F4
Auchincruive 274 B3
Auchindarrach 281 G1
Auchindarroch 298 C4
Auchindrain 290 C4
Auchindrain Township Open Air Museum 116
Auchindrean 320 A1
Auchininna 324 B5
Auchinleck 274 D3
Auchinloch 284 A2
Auchinner 292 B3
Auchinroath 323 E4
Auchintoul *Aber.* 312 A3
Auchintoul *Aber.* 324 B4
Auchintoul *High.* 332 A5
Auchiries 313 F1
Auchleven 312 B2
Auchlochan 275 G2
Auchlunachan 320 A1
Auchlunies 313 D5
Auchlunkart 323 F5
Auchlyne 292 A2
Auchmacoy 313 E1
Auchmair 311 F2
Auchmantle 264 C4
Auchmithie 303 E5
Auchmuirbridge 294 A4
Auchmull 303 D2
Auchnabony 258 A2
Auchnabreac 290 C4
Auchnacloich 292 D1
Auchnacraig 289 G1
Auchnacree 302 C3
Auchnafree 292 D1
Auchnagallin 310 C1
Auchnagatt 325 E5
Auchnaha 282 A1
Auchnangoul 290 C4
Aucholzie 311 F5
Auchorrie 312 B4
Auchrannie 302 A4
Auchraw 292 A2
Auchreoch 291 F2
Auchronie 302 C1
Auchterarder 293 E3
Auchtercairn 319 E2
Auchterderran 294 A5
Auchterhouse 294 B1
Auchtermuchty 294 A3
Auchterneed 321 D4
Auchtertool 294 A5
Auchtertyre *Angus* 302 A5
Auchtertyre *High.* 307 E2
Auchtertyre *Moray* 323 D4
Auchtertyre *Stir.* 291 F2
Auchtubh 292 A2
Auckengill 337 F2
Auckland Castle 102
Auckley 236 D2
Audenshaw 234 D3
Audlem 221 D3
Audley 221 E2
Audley End *Essex* 200 D4
Audley End *Essex* 201 G4
Audley End *Essex* 77
Audley End *Suff.* 201 G2
Audmore 221 F5
Auds 324 B3
Aughton *E.Riding* 245 G4
Aughton *Lancs.* 233 E2
Aughton *Lancs.* 242 B1
Aughton *S.Yorks.* 236 B4
Aughton *Wilts.* 168 D2
Aughton Park 233 F2
Auk Walk 24
Auldearn 322 B4
Aulden 195 D2
Auldgirth 266 D2
Auldhame 286 C1
Auldhouse 284 A4
Aulich 300 B4

B

Brampton *Suff.* 215 F3
Brampton Abbotts 195 F5
Brampton Ash 210 C4
Brampton Bryan 206 C5
Brampton en le Morthen 236 B4
Brampton Street 215 F3
Bramshall 222 B4
Bramshaw 156 B1
Bramshill 170 C1
Bramshott 170 D4
Bramwell 166 B5
Bran End 201 E5
Branault 297 E3
Brancaster 227 F3
Brancaster Staithe 227 F3
Brancepeth 262 B4
Branchill 322 C4
Brand Green 195 G5
Brandelhow 259 F4
Branderburgh 323 E2
Brandesburton 246 D3
Brandeston 202 D1
Brandis Corner 163 E5
Brandiston 228 C3
Brandon *Dur.* 262 B4
Brandon *Lincs.* 225 E3
Brandon *Northumb.* 279 E5
Brandon *Suff.* 213 F4
Brandon *Warks.* 209 G5
Brandon Bank 213 E4
Brandon Creek 213 E3
Brandon Parva 228 B5
Brandsby 253 E5
Brandy Wharf 238 A3
Brane 144 B4
Branklyn Gardens 117
Branksome 155 G3
Branksome Park 155 G3
Bransbury 169 F3
Bransby 237 F5
Branscombe 153 E4
Bransford 195 G2
Bransford Bridge 196 A2
Bransgore 156 A3
Bransholme 246 D4
Branson's Cross 208 C5
Branston *Leics.* 224 D5
Branston *Lincs.* 225 F1
Branston *Staffs.* 222 D5
Branston Booths 225 F1
Brant Broughton 225 E2
Brantham 202 C4
Branthwaite *Cumb.* 259 F3
Branthwaite *Cumb.* 259 D4
Brantingham 246 B5
Branton *Northumb.* 279 E5
Branton *S.Yorks.* 236 D2
Brantwood *Cumb.* 249 E3
Brantwood *Cumb.* 94
Branxholm Bridgend 277 F4
Branxholme 277 F4
Branxton 278 C3
Brassey Green 220 C1
Brassington 222 D2
Brasted 173 D3
Brasted Chart 173 D3
Bratch, The 208 A3
Brathens 312 B5
Bratoft 226 C1
Brattleby 237 G4
Bratton *Som.* 164 C3
Bratton *Tel. & W.* 207 F1
Bratton *Wilts.* 168 A2
Bratton Clovelly 149 E1
Bratton Fleming 163 G2
Bratton Seymour 167 D5
Braughing 200 B5
Brauncewell 225 F2
Braunston *Northants.* 198 A1
Braunston *Rut.* 210 D2
Braunstone 210 A2
Braunton 163 E2
Brawby 253 G5
Brawdy 190 B5
Brawith 253 E2
Brawl 336 A2
Brawlbin 336 C3
Bray 185 E5
Bray Shop 148 D3
Bray Wick 185 D5
Braybrooke 210 C4
Braydon Side 182 C4
Brayford 163 G2
Brayshaw 243 D2
Braythorn 244 B3
Brayton 245 F4
Braywoodside 185 D5
Brazacott 148 C1
Brea 146 A5
Breach *Kent* 175 D4
Breach *Kent* 174 A2
Breachwood Green 199 G5
Breacleit 328 C4
Breadsall 223 E4
Breadstone 181 G2
Breage 144 D4
Breakon 345 E2
Bream 181 F2
Breamore *Hants.* 156 A1
Breamore *Hants.* 42
Brean 165 F2
Breanais 328 A5
Brearton 244 C1
Breascleit 328 D4
Breaston 223 F4
Brechfa 192 B4
Brechin 303 E3
Brecklate 272 B4
Breckles 214 A2
Brecon (Aberhonddu) 193 G5
Brecon Beacons 107
Brecon Beacons Visitor Centre 108
Brecon Mountain Railway 108
Breconside 275 G5
Bredbury 234 D3
Brede 160 D2
Bredenbury 195 F2
Bredfield 203 D2
Bredgar 174 A2
Bredhurst 173 G2
Bredon 196 B4
Bredon Tithe Barn 64
Bredon's Hardwick 196 B4
Bredon's Norton 196 B4
Bredwardine 194 C3
Breedon on the Hill 223 F5
Breibhig 329 F4
Breich 285 D3
Breightmet 234 B2
Breighton 245 G4
Breinton 195 D4
Breinton Common 195 D4
Bremhill 182 B5
Bremhill Wick 182 B5
Brenachoille 290 C4
Brenchley 173 F4
Brendon *Devon* 164 A3
Brendon *Devon* 163 D4
Brendon *Devon* 163 D5
Brenkley 271 E4
Brent Eleigh 202 A3
Brent Knoll 166 A2
Brent Pelham 200 C4
Brentford 186 A5
Brentingby 210 C1
Brentwood 187 E3
Brenzett 161 F1
Brenzett Green 161 F1
Breoch 266 B5
Brereton 208 C1
Brereton Green 221 E1
Brereton Heath 221 F1
Breretonhill 208 C1
Bressay 343 E3
Bressingham 214 B3
Bressingham Common 214 B3
Bressingham Steam Museum & Gardens 77
Bretby 223 D5
Bretford 209 G5
Bretforton 196 C3
Bretherdale Head 249 G2
Bretherton 242 A5
Brettabister 343 D2
Brettenham *Norf.* 214 A3
Brettenham *Suff.* 202 A2
Bretton *Derbys.* 235 F5
Bretton *Flints.* 220 A1
Brevig 314 B4
Brewers Quay 25
Brewood 208 A2
Briach 322 C4
Briantspuddle 155 E3
Brick End 201 D5
Bricket Wood 186 A2
Brickkiln Green 201 F4
Bricklehampton 196 B3
Bride 240 C1
Bridekirk 259 E3
Bridell 191 E3
Bridestones 221 G1
Bridestowe 149 F2
Brideswell 312 A1
Bridford 152 B4
Bridge *Cornw.* 146 A5
Bridge *Kent* 175 D3
Bridge End *Cumb.* 248 D4
Bridge End *Devon* 150 C3
Bridge End *Essex* 201 E4
Bridge End *Lincs.* 225 G4
Bridge End *Shet.* 342 C4
Bridge Hewick 252 C5
Bridge o' Ess 312 A5
Bridge of Alford 312 A3
Bridge of Allan 292 C5
Bridge of Avon 311 D1
Bridge of Balgie 300 A5
Bridge of Bogendreip 312 B5
Bridge of Brewlands 301 G3
Bridge of Brown 310 D2
Bridge of Cally 301 G4
Bridge of Canny 312 B5
Bridge of Craigisla 302 A4
Bridge of Dee *Aber.* 311 D5
Bridge of Dee *Aber.* 312 B5
Bridge of Dee *D. & G.* 266 B4
Bridge of Don 313 E4
Bridge of Dun 303 E4
Bridge of Dye 303 E1
Bridge of Earn 293 G3
Bridge of Ericht 300 A4
Bridge of Feugh 312 B5
Bridge of Forss 336 C2
Bridge of Gairn 311 F5
Bridge of Gaur 300 A4
Bridge of Muchalls 313 D5
Bridge of Muick 311 F5
Bridge of Orchy 291 E1
Bridge of Tynet 323 F3
Bridge of Walls 342 B2
Bridge of Weir 283 E3
Bridge Reeve 163 G4
Bridge Sollers 194 D3
Bridge Street 201 G3
Bridge Trafford 233 F5
Bridgefoot *Angus* 294 B1
Bridgefoot *Cambs.* 200 C3
Bridgefoot *Cumb.* 259 D4
Bridgehampton 166 C5
Bridgehaugh 311 F1
Bridgehill 261 G2
Bridgemary 157 E2
Bridgemere 221 E3
Bridgemere Garden World 94
Bridgend *Aber.* 312 A1
Bridgend *Aber.* 324 C5
Bridgend *Angus* 302 D3
Bridgend *Arg. & B.* 280 B3
Bridgend *Arg. & B.* 290 A5
Bridgend (Pen-y-bont ar Ogwr) *Bridgend* 179 F5
Bridgend *Cornw.* 147 F4
Bridgend *Cumb.* 249 F1
Bridgend *Fife* 294 B3
Bridgend *Moray* 311 F1
Bridgend *P. & K.* 293 G2
Bridgend *W.Loth.* 285 E2
Bridgend of Lintrathen 302 A4
Bridgerule 162 C5
Bridges 206 C3
Bridgeton *Aber.* 312 A3
Bridgeton *Glas.* 284 A3
Bridgetown *Cornw.* 148 D2
Bridgetown *Som.* 164 C4
Bridgeyate 181 F5
Bridgham 214 A3
Bridgnorth 207 G3
Bridgtown 208 B2
Bridgwater 165 F4
Bridlington 247 D1
Bridport 154 A3
Bridstow 195 E5
Brierfield 243 E4
Brierley *Glos.* 181 F1
Brierley *Here.* 195 D2
Brierley *S.Yorks.* 236 B1
Brierley Hill 208 B4
Brierton 263 D5
Briestfield 235 G1
Brig o'Turk 292 A4
Brigg 238 A2
Briggate 229 E3
Briggswath 254 B2
Brigham *Cumb.* 259 D3
Brigham *E.Riding* 246 C2
Brighouse 244 A5
Brighstone 156 D4
Brightgate 223 D2
Brighthampton 183 F2
Brightholmlee 235 G3
Brightling 160 B1
Brightlingsea 189 D1
Brighton *B. & H.* 159 F3
Brighton *Cornw.* 146 D4
Brighton Pavilion (see Royal Pavilion) 50
Brightons 284 D2
Brightwalton 183 G5
Brightwalton Green 183 G5
Brightwell 202 D3
Brightwell Baldwin 184 B3
Brightwell Upperton 184 B3
Brightwell-cum-Sotwell 184 A3
Brignall 251 F1
Brigsley 238 C2
Brigsteer 249 F4
Brigstock 211 E4
Brill *Bucks.* 184 B1
Brill *Cornw.* 145 E4
Brilley 194 B3
Brilley Mountain 194 B2
Brimaston 190 C5
Brimfield 195 E1
Brimington 236 B5
Brimington Common 236 B5
Brimley 152 B5
Brimpsfield 182 B1
Brimpton 169 G1
Brims 338 B4
Brimscombe 182 A2
Brimstage 233 E4
Brinacory 307 D5
Brindham 166 C3
Brindister *Shet.* 342 D4
Brindister *Shet.* 342 B2
Brindle 242 B5
Brindley Ford 221 F2
Brineton 208 A1
Bringhurst 210 D3
Brington 211 F5
Brinian 340 C4
Briningham 228 B2
Brinkburn Priory 103
Brinkhill 239 D5
Brinkley *Cambs.* 201 E2
Brinkley *Notts.* 224 C2
Brinklow 209 G5
Brinkworth 182 C4
Brinmore 309 F2
Brinscall 242 C5
Brinsea 166 B1
Brinsley 223 F3
Brinsop 194 D3
Brinsworth 236 B3
Brinton 228 B2
Brisco 260 A2
Brisley 228 A3
Brislington 181 F5
Brissenden Green 174 B5
Bristol 181 E5
Bristol City Museum & Art Gallery 25
Bristol Industrial Museum 25
Bristol International Airport 166 C1
Bristol Zoo 26
Briston 228 B2
Britain At War 55
Britannia *Edin.* 117
Britannia *Lancs.* 243 E5
Britford 168 C5
Brithdir *Caerp.* 180 A2
Brithdir *Gwyn.* 205 D1
Brithem Bottom 152 D1
British Empire & Commonwealth Museum 26
British Golf Museum 117
British Museum 55
Briton Ferry (Llansawel) 178 D3
Britwell 185 E4
Britwell Salome 184 B3
Brixham 151 F2
Brixton *Devon* 150 B2
Brixton *Gt.Lon.* 186 C5
Brixton Deverill 167 F4
Brixworth 210 C5
Brize Norton 183 E2
Broad Alley 196 A1
Broad Blunsdon 183 D3
Broad Campden 197 D4
Broad Carr 235 E1
Broad Chalke 168 B5
Broad Ford 173 G5
Broad Green *Beds.* 199 E3
Broad Green *Cambs.* 201 E2
Broad Green *Essex* 201 G5
Broad Green *Essex* 200 C4
Broad Green *Mersey.* 233 F3
Broad Green *Suff.* 202 B2
Broad Green *Worcs.* 195 G2
Broad Haven 176 B1
Broad Hill 213 D5
Broad Hinton 182 D5
Broad Laying 169 F1
Broad Marston 196 D3
Broad Oak *Carmar.* 192 B5
Broad Oak *Cumb.* 248 C3
Broad Oak *E.Suss.* 160 D2
Broad Oak *E.Suss.* 160 B1
Broad Oak *Here.* 195 D5
Broad Road 215 D4
Broad Street *E.Suss.* 161 D2
Broad Street *Kent* 174 A3
Broad Street *Kent* 174 D5
Broad Street *Wilts.* 168 C2
Broad Street Green 188 B2
Broad, The 195 D1
Broad Town 182 C5
Broadbottom 235 D3
Broadbridge 158 A3
Broadbridge Heath 171 G4
Broadclyst 152 C3
Broadfield *Lancs.* 242 D5
Broadfield *Lancs.* 242 B5
Broadford 306 C2
Broadford Bridge 171 F5
Broadgate 248 C4
Broadhaugh 277 F5
Broadhaven 337 F3
Broadheath *Gt.Man.* 234 B4
Broadheath *Worcs.* 195 F1
Broadhembury 153 E2
Broadhempston 151 E1
Broadholme 237 F5
Broadland Row 160 D2
Broadlands 42
Broadlay 177 G2
Broadley *Lancs.* 234 C1
Broadley *Moray* 323 F3
Broadley Common 186 D2
Broadmayne 154 D4
Broadmeadows 277 F2
Broadmere 170 B3
Broadmoor 177 D2
Broadnymett 152 A2
Broadoak *Dorset* 154 A3
Broadoak *Glos.* 181 F1
Broadoak *Kent* 175 D2
Broadoak End 186 C1
Broadrashes 323 G4
Broad's Green 187 F1
Broadsea 325 E3
Broadstairs 175 F2
Broadstone *Poole* 155 G3
Broadstone *Shrop.* 207 E4
Broadstreet Common 180 C4
Broadwas 195 G2
Broadwater *Herts.* 200 A5
Broadwater *W.Suss.* 158 D3
Broadwater Down 173 E5
Broadwaters 208 A5
Broadway *Carmar.* 177 G2
Broadway *Carmar.* 177 F1
Broadway *Pembs.* 176 B1
Broadway *Som.* 153 G1
Broadway *Suff.* 215 E4
Broadway *Worcs.* 196 D4
Broadwell *Glos.* 197 E5
Broadwell *Oxon.* 183 E2
Broadwell *Warks.* 197 G1
Broadwell House 261 F2
Broadwey 154 C4
Broadwindsor 154 A2
Broadwood Kelly 163 G5
Broadwoodwidger 149 E2
Brobury 194 C3
Brocastle 179 F5
Brochel 318 B5
Brochloch 265 G1
Brock 296 B2
Brockamin 195 G2
Brockbridge 157 F1
Brockdish 214 D4
Brockenhurst 156 B2
Brockford Green 202 C1
Brockford Street 202 C1
Brockhall 198 B1
Brockham 171 G3
Brockhampton *Glos.* 196 C5
Brockhampton *Glos.* 196 B5
Brockhampton *Here.* 195 E4
Brockhampton *Here.* 195 F2
Brockhampton Green 154 D2
Brockholes 235 F1
Brockhurst *Hants.* 157 E2
Brockhurst *W.Suss.* 172 D5
Brocklebank 259 G2
Brocklesby 238 B1
Brockley *N.Som.* 166 B1
Brockley *Suff.* 201 G2
Brockley Green 201 F3
Brock's Green 169 F1
Brockton *Shrop.* 207 E3
Brockton *Shrop.* 207 G2
Brockton *Shrop.* 206 C2
Brockton *Shrop.* 206 C4
Brockton *Tel. & W.* 207 G1
Brockweir 181 E2
Brockwood Park 170 B5
Brockworth 182 A1
Brocton 208 B1
Brodick 273 F2
Brodick Castle 117
Brodie Castle 117
Brodsworth 236 C2
Brogborough 199 E4
Brogden 243 E3
Brogyntyn 219 F4
Broken Cross *Ches.* 234 C5
Broken Cross *Ches.* 234 A5
Brokenborough 182 B4
Brokes 252 A3
Bromborough 233 E4
Brome 214 C4
Brome Street 214 C4
Bromeswell 203 E2
Bromfield *Cumb.* 259 E2
Bromfield *Shrop.* 207 D5
Bromham *Beds.* 199 F2
Bromham *Wilts.* 168 A1
Bromley *Gt.Lon.* 172 D2
Bromley *S.Yorks.* 236 A3
Bromley Cross 234 B1
Bromley Green 174 B5
Brompton *Med.* 173 G2
Brompton *N.Yorks.* 252 C3
Brompton *N.Yorks.* 254 C4
Brompton *Shrop.* 207 E2
Brompton on Swale 252 B3
Brompton Ralph 165 D4
Brompton Regis 164 C4
Bromsash 195 F5
Bromsberrow 195 G4
Bromsberrow Heath 195 G4
Bromsgrove 208 B5
Bromstead Heath 208 A1
Bromyard 195 F2
Bromyard Downs 195 F2
Bronaber 218 A4
Brondesbury 186 B4
Brongest 191 G3
Bronington 220 B4
Bronllys 194 A4
Bronnant 192 C1
Brontë Parsonage Museum 86
Bronwydd Arms 192 A5
Bronydd 194 B3
Bron-y-gaer 177 G1
Bronygarth 219 F4
Brook *Carmar.* 177 F2
Brook *Hants.* 156 B1
Brook *Hants.* 169 E5
Brook *I.o.W.* 156 C4
Brook *Kent* 174 C4
Brook *Surr.* 171 E4
Brook *Surr.* 171 F3
Brook Bottom 235 D2
Brook End *Beds.* 199 F1
Brook End *Herts.* 200 B5
Brook End *M.K.* 199 E3
Brook End *Worcs.* 196 A3
Brook Hill 156 B1
Brook Street *Essex* 187 E3
Brook Street *Kent* 174 B5
Brook Street *Suff.* 201 G3
Brook Street *W.Suss.* 159 F1
Brooke *Norf.* 215 D2
Brooke *Rut.* 210 D2
Brookend *Glos.* 181 E3
Brookend *Glos.* 181 F2
Brookfield 235 E3
Brookhampton 184 B3
Brookhouse *Ches.* 234 D5
Brookhouse *Denb.* 219 D1
Brookhouse *Lancs.* 242 B1
Brookhouse *S.Yorks.* 236 C4
Brookhouse Green 221 F1
Brookhouses 221 G3
Brookland 161 E1
Brooklands *D. & G.* 266 C3
Brooklands *Shrop.* 220 C3
Brooklands Museum 42
Brookmans Park 186 B2
Brooks 206 A3
Brooks Green 171 G5
Brooksby 210 B1
Brookside Garden Centre & Miniature Railway 94
Brookthorpe 182 A1
Brookwood 171 E2
Broom *Beds.* 199 G3
Broom *Fife* 294 B4
Broom *Warks.* 196 C2
Broom Green 228 A3
Broom Hill *Dorset* 155 G2
Broom Hill *Worcs.* 208 B5
Broom of Dalreach 293 F3
Broomcroft 207 E2
Broome *Norf.* 215 E2
Broome *Shrop.* 206 D4
Broome *Worcs.* 208 B5
Broome Wood 279 F5
Broomedge 234 B4
Broomer's Corner 171 G5
Broomfield *Aber.* 313 E1
Broomfield *Essex* 187 G1
Broomfield *Kent* 175 D2
Broomfield *Kent* 174 A3
Broomfield *Som.* 165 F4
Broomfleet 246 A5
Broomhall Green 220 D3
Broomhaugh 261 G1
Broomhead 325 E3
Broomhill *Bristol* 181 F5
Broomhill *Northumb.* 271 E1
Broomielaw 251 F1
Broomley 261 G1
Broompark 262 B3
Broom's Green 195 G4
Brora 333 E4
Broseley 207 F2
Brotherlee 261 F4
Brothertoft 226 A3
Brotherton 245 D5
Brotton 253 F1
Broubster 336 C2
Brough *Cumb.* 250 C1
Brough *Derbys.* 235 F4
Brough *E.Riding* 246 B5
Brough *High.* 337 E1
Brough *Notts.* 224 D2
Brough *Ork.* 340 B5
Brough *Shet.* 343 E3
Brough *Shet.* 344 D5
Brough *Shet.* 343 E1
Brough *Shet.* 345 E5
Brough Lodge 345 E3
Brough Sowerby 250 C1
Broughall 220 C3
Brougham 260 B5
Broughton *Bucks.* 184 D1
Broughton *Cambs.* 212 A5
Broughton *Flints.* 220 A1
Broughton *Hants.* 169 E4
Broughton *Lancs.* 242 B4
Broughton *M.K.* 199 D3
Broughton *N.Lincs.* 237 G2
Broughton *N.Yorks.* 253 G5
Broughton *N.Yorks.* 243 F2
Broughton *Northants.* 210 D5
Broughton *Ork.* 340 C2
Broughton *Oxon.* 197 G4
Broughton *Sc.Bord.* 276 C2
Broughton *V. of Glam.* 179 F5
Broughton Astley 210 A3
Broughton Beck 249 D4
Broughton Castle 42
Broughton Gifford 167 F1
Broughton Green 196 B1
Broughton Hackett 196 B2
Broughton House 118
Broughton in Furness 248 D4
Broughton Mills 248 D3
Broughton Moor 259 D3
Broughton Poggs 183 E2
Broughtown 341 E2
Broughty Ferry 294 C1
Browland 342 B2
Brown Candover 169 G4
Brown Edge *Lancs.* 233 E1
Brown Edge *Staffs.* 221 G2
Brown Heath 220 B1
Brown Lees 221 F2
Brown Street 202 B1
Brownber 250 C2
Browndown 157 E3
Brownheath 220 B5
Brownhill 325 D5
Brownhills *Fife* 294 D3
Brownhills *W.Mid.* 208 C2
Brownieside 279 F4
Brownlow 221 F1
Brownlow Heath 221 F1
Brown's Bank 220 D3
Brownsea Island 26
Brownshill 182 A2
Brownshill Green 209 F4
Brownsover 210 A5
Brownston 150 C2
Browston Green 229 F5
Broxa 254 C3
Broxbourne 186 C2
Broxburn *E.Loth.* 287 D2
Broxburn *W.Loth.* 285 E2
Broxholme 237 G5
Broxted 201 D5
Broxton 220 B2
Broxwood 194 C2
Broyle Side 159 G2
Bru (Brue) 329 E3
Bruachmary 322 A5
Bruan 337 F5
Brue (Bru) 329 E3
Bruera 220 B1
Bruern 197 E5
Bruernish 314 C3
Bruichladdich 280 A3
Bruisyard 203 E1
Bruisyard Street 203 E1
Brumby 237 G1
Brund 222 C1
Brundall 229 E5
Brundish *Norf.* 215 E2
Brundish *Suff.* 203 D1
Brundish Street 215 D4
Brunstock 260 A2
Brunswick Village 271 E4
Bruntingthorpe 210 B3
Bruntland 311 G2
Brunton *Fife* 294 B2
Brunton *Northumb.* 279 G4
Brunton *Wilts.* 168 D2
Brushfield 235 F5
Brushford *Devon* 163 G5
Brushford *Som.* 164 C5
Bruton 167 D4
Bryanston 155 E2
Bryant's Bottom 185 D3
Brydekirk 267 F3
Brymbo 219 F2
Brympton 154 B1
Bryn *Caerp.* 180 A3
Bryn *Carmar.* 178 B2
Bryn *Ches.* 234 A5
Bryn *Gt.Man.* 233 G2
Bryn *N.P.T.* 179 E3
Bryn *Shrop.* 206 B4
Bryn Bwbach 217 F4
Bryn Gates 233 G2
Bryn Pen-y-lan 220 A3
Bryn, The 180 C2
Brynamman 178 D1
Brynberian 191 E4
Bryncae 179 F4
Bryncethin 179 F4
Bryncir 217 D3
Bryncoch *Bridgend* 179 F4
Bryn-côch *N.P.T.* 178 D3
Bryncroes 216 B4
Bryncrug 204 C2
Bryneglwys 219 E3
Brynford 232 C5
Bryngwran 230 B5
Bryngwyn *Mon.* 180 C2
Bryngwyn *Powys* 194 A3
Bryn-henllan 190 D4
Brynhoffnant 191 G2
Bryning 242 A4
Brynithel 180 B2
Brynmawr *B.Gwent* 180 A1
Bryn-mawr *Gwyn.* 216 B4
Brynmelyn 206 A5
Brynmenyn 179 F4
Brynna 179 F4
Brynnau Gwynion 179 F4
Brynog 192 B2
Bryn-penarth 206 A2
Brynrefail *Gwyn.* 217 E1
Brynrefail *I.o.A.* 230 C4
Brynsadler 179 G4
Brynsaithmarchog 219 D2
Brynsiencyn 217 D1
Bryn-teg *I.o.A.* 230 C4
Brynteg *Wrex.* 220 A2
Bryn-y-cochin 220 A4
Brynygwenin 180 C1
Bryn-y-maen 231 G5
Buaile nam Bodach 314 C3
Bualadubh 315 F5
Bualintur 306 A2
Bualnaluib 330 A5
Bubbenhall 209 F5
Bubnell 235 G5
Bubwith 245 G4
Buccleuch 277 E4
Buchan 266 B4
Buchanan Castle 283 F1
Buchanhaven 325 G5
Buchanty 293 E2
Buchlyvie 292 A5
Buckabank 259 G2
Buckby Wharf 198 B1
Buckden *Cambs.* 199 G1
Buckden *N.Yorks.* 251 E5
Buckenham 229 E5
Buckerell 153 E2
Buckfast 150 D1
Buckfast Abbey 26
Buckfastleigh 150 D1
Buckhaven 294 B5
Buckholm 277 F2
Buckholt 181 E1
Buckhorn Weston 167 E5
Buckhurst Hill 186 D3
Buckie 323 G3
Buckies 336 D2
Buckingham 198 B4
Buckingham Palace 55
Buckinghamshire County Museum 42
Buckinghamshire Railway Centre 42
Buckland *Bucks.* 185 D1
Buckland *Devon* 150 C3
Buckland *Glos.* 196 C4
Buckland *Hants.* 156 C3
Buckland *Here.* 195 E2
Buckland *Herts.* 200 B4
Buckland *Kent* 175 F4
Buckland *Oxon.* 183 F3
Buckland *Surr.* 172 B3
Buckland Abbey 26
Buckland Brewer 163 E3
Buckland Common 185 E2
Buckland Dinham 167 E2
Buckland Filleigh 163 E5
Buckland in the Moor 152 A5
Buckland Monachorum 150 A1
Buckland Newton 154 C2
Buckland Ripers 154 C4
Buckland St. Mary 153 F1
Buckland-tout-Saints 151 D3
Bucklebury 184 A5
Bucklerheads 294 C1
Bucklers Hard 156 D3
Buckler's Hard Maritime Museum 42
Bucklesham 202 D3
Buckley (Bwcle) 219 F1
Buckley Green 197 D1
Bucklow Hill 234 B4
Buckman Corner 171 G5
Buckminster 225 D5
Bucknall *Lincs.* 225 G1
Bucknall *Stoke* 221 G3
Bucknell *Oxon.* 198 A5
Bucknell *Shrop.* 206 C5
Buckridge 207 G5
Buck's Cross 162 D3
Bucks Green 171 F4
Bucks Hill 185 F2
Bucks Horn Oak 170 D3
Buck's Mills 163 D3
Bucksburn 313 D4

Combe *Here.* 194 C1
Combe *Oxon.* 183 G1
Combe *Som.* 166 B5
Combe *W.Berks.* 169 E1
Combe Common 171 E4
Combe Cross 152 A5
Combe Down 167 E1
Combe Florey 165 E4
Combe Hay 167 E2
Combe Martin 163 F1
Combe Martin Wildlife & Dinosaur Park 27
Combe Pafford 151 F1
Combe Raleigh 153 E2
Combe St. Nicholas 153 G1
Combeinteignhead 152 B5
Comberbach 234 A5
Comberford 209 D2
Comberton *Cambs.* 200 B2
Comberton *Here.* 195 D1
Combpyne 153 F3
Combridge 222 B4
Combrook 197 F2
Combs *Derbys.* 235 E5
Combs *Suff.* 202 B2
Combs Ford 202 B2
Combwich 165 F3
Comer 291 F4
Comers 312 B4
Comhampton 196 A1
Comins Coch 204 C4
Commandery, The 64
Commercial End 201 D1
Commins Coch 205 E2
Common Edge 241 G4
Common Moor 147 G2
Common Platt 182 D4
Common Side 236 A5
Common Square 238 A5
Common, The *Wilts.* 168 D4
Common, The *Wilts.* 182 C4
Commondale 253 F1
Commonside 222 D3
Compstall 235 D3
Compton *Devon* 151 E1
Compton *Hants.* 169 F5
Compton *Plym.* 150 A2
Compton *Staffs.* 208 A4
Compton *Surr.* 171 E3
Compton *W.Berks.* 184 A5
Compton *W.Suss.* 157 G1
Compton *W.Yorks.* 244 D3
Compton *Wilts.* 168 C2
Compton Abbas 155 E1
Compton Abdale 182 C1
Compton Acres 27
Compton Bassett 182 C5
Compton Beauchamp 183 E4
Compton Bishop 166 A2
Compton Castle 27
Compton Chamberlayne 168 B5
Compton Dando 166 D1
Compton Dundon 166 B4
Compton Martin 166 C2
Compton Pauncefoot 166 D5
Compton Valence 154 B3
Compton Verney 197 F2
Comra 309 E5
Comrie *Fife* 285 E1
Comrie *P. & K.* 292 C2
Conchra *Arg. & B.* 282 B1
Conchra *High.* 307 E2
Concraigie 301 G5
Conder Green 242 A2
Conderton 196 B4
Condicote 196 D5
Condorrat 284 B2
Condover 207 D2
Coney Weston 214 A4
Coneyhurst 171 G5
Coneysthorpe 253 G5
Coneythorpe 244 C2
Conford 170 D4
Congash 310 C2
Congdon's Shop 147 G2
Congerstone 209 F2
Congham 227 F5
Congleton 221 F1
Congresbury 166 B1
Congreve 208 B1
Conicavel 322 B4
Coningsby 226 A2
Conington *Cambs.* 211 G4
Conington *Cambs.* 200 B1
Conisbrough 236 C3
Conisby 280 A3
Conisholme 239 E3
Coniston *Cumb.* 249 E3
Coniston *E.Riding* 247 D4
Coniston Cold 243 F2
Conistone 243 F1
Conland 324 B5
Connah's Quay 219 F1
Connel 290 B1
Connel Park 275 E4
Connor Downs 144 C3
Conock 168 B2
Conon Bridge 321 E4
Cononish 291 F2
Cononley 243 F3
Cononsyth 303 D5
Consall 221 G3
Consett 262 A2
Constable Burton 252 A3
Constantine 145 E4
Constantine Bay 146 C2
Contin 321 D4
Contlaw 312 D4
Contullich 321 F2
Conwy 231 F5
Conwy Castle 109
Conyer 174 B2
Conyer's Green 201 G1
Cooden 160 C3
Coodham 274 C2
Cooil 240 B4
Cookbury 163 E5
Cookbury Wick 163 D5
Cookham 185 D4
Cookham Dean 185 D4
Cookham Rise 185 D4
Cookhill 196 C2
Cookley *Suff.* 215 E4
Cookley *Worcs.* 208 A4
Cookley Green *Oxon.* 184 B3
Cookley Green *Suff.* 215 E4
Cookney 313 D5
Cook's Green 202 A2
Cooksbridge 159 F2
Cooksey Green 196 B1
Cookshill 221 G3
Cooksmill Green 187 F2
Cookston 313 E1
Cookworthy Museum 27
Coolham 171 G5
Cooling 187 G5
Cooling Street 187 G5
Coombe *Cornw.* 147 D4
Coombe *Cornw.* 162 C4
Coombe *Cornw.* 146 A5
Coombe *Cornw.* 146 C5
Coombe *Devon* 151 D3
Coombe *Devon* 152 B4
Coombe *Devon* 153 E3
Coombe *Som.* 165 F5
Coombe *Som.* 154 A2
Coombe *Wilts.* 168 C2
Coombe Bissett 168 C5
Coombe End 164 D5
Coombe Hill *Bucks.* 43
Coombe Hill *Glos.* 196 A5
Coombe Keynes 155 E4
Coombes 159 D3
Coombes Moor 194 C1
Cooper's Corner *E.Suss.* 160 C1
Cooper's Corner *Kent* 173 D4
Cooper's Green 186 A2
Coopersale Common 187 D2
Coopersale Street 187 D2
Coors Visitor Centre 64
Cootham 158 C2
Cop Street 175 E3
Copdock 202 C3
Copford Green 202 A5
Copgrove 244 C1
Copister 345 D5
Cople 199 G3
Copley *Dur.* 261 G5
Copley *W.Yorks.* 243 G5
Coplow Dale 235 F5
Copmanthorpe 245 E3
Copmere End 221 F5
Copp 242 A4
Coppathorne 162 C5
Coppenhall 208 B1
Coppenhall Moss 221 E2
Copperhouse 144 C3
Coppicegate 207 G4
Coppingford 211 G4
Coppleridge 167 F5
Copplestone 152 A2
Coppull 233 G1
Coppull Moor 233 G1
Copsale 171 G5
Copse Hill 172 B2
Copster Green 242 C4
Copston Magna 209 G4
Copt Heath 209 D5
Copt Hewick 252 C5
Copt Oak 209 G1
Copthall Green 186 D2
Copthorne 172 C5
Copy Lake 163 G4
Copythorne 156 C1
Coralhill 325 F3
Corbets Tey 187 E4
Corbiegoe 337 F4
Corbridge 261 F1
Corby 211 D4
Corby Glen 225 F5
Cordach 312 B5
Coreley 207 F5
Corfcott Green 148 D1
Corfe 153 F1
Corfe Castle *Dorset* 155 F4
Corfe Castle *Dorset* 27
Corfe Mullen 155 F3
Corfton 207 D4
Corgarff 311 E4
Corhampton 170 B5
Corley 209 E4
Corley Ash 209 E4
Corley Moor 209 E4
Cornabus 280 B5
Cornard Tye 202 A3
Corndon 149 G2
Corney 248 C3
Cornforth 262 C4
Cornhill 324 A4
Cornhill on Tweed 278 C3
Cornholme 243 F5
Cornish Cyder Farm, The 27
Cornish Engines 27
Cornish Hall End 201 E4
Cornish Seal Sanctuary 27
Cornquoy 339 E2
Cornriggs 261 E3
Cornsay 262 A3
Cornsay Colliery 262 A3
Corntown *High.* 321 E4
Corntown *V. of Glam.* 179 F5
Cornwell 197 E5
Cornwood 150 C2
Cornworthy 151 E2
Corpach 298 D2
Corpusty 228 C3
Corrachree 311 G4
Corran *Arg. & B.* 291 E5
Corran *High.* 307 E4
Corran *High.* 298 C3
Corranbuie 281 G3
Corranmore 289 G4
Corrany 240 C3
Corribeg 298 B2
Corrie 282 B5
Corrie Common 268 A3
Corriechrevie 281 F4
Corriecravie 273 E3
Corriedoo 266 A2
Corriekinloch 331 F2
Corrielorne 290 A3
Corrieshalloch Gorge 119
Corrievorrie 309 G2
Corrimony 308 C1
Corringham *Lincs.* 237 F3
Corringham *Thur.* 187 G4
Corris 205 D2
Corris Uchaf 204 D2
Corrlarach 298 B2
Corrour Shooting Lodge 299 G3
Corrow 291 D4
Corry 306 C2
Corrychurrachan 298 C3
Corrylach 272 C2
Corrymuckloch 293 D1
Corsback 337 E2
Corscombe 154 B2
Corse *Aber.* 324 B5
Corse *Glos.* 195 G5
Corse Lawn 196 A4
Corse of Kinnoir 324 A5
Corsebank 275 G4
Corsegight 324 D4
Corsehill 267 F2
Corsewall 264 B4
Corsham 182 A5
Corsindae 312 B4
Corsley 167 F3
Corsley Heath 167 F3
Corsock 266 B3
Corston *B. & N.E.Som.* 167 D1
Corston *Wilts.* 182 B4
Corstorphine 285 F2
Cortachy 302 B4
Corton *Suff.* 215 G2
Corton *Wilts.* 168 A3
Corton Denham 166 D5
Corwar House 265 D2
Corwen 219 D3
Coryton *Devon* 149 E2
Coryton *Thur.* 187 G4
Cosby 210 A3
Coscote 184 A4
Coseley 208 B3
Cosford *Shrop.* 207 G2
Cosford *Warks.* 210 A5
Cosgrove 198 C3
Cosham 157 F2
Cosheston 176 D2
Coshieville 300 C5
Coskills 238 A2
Cosmeston 165 E1
Cosmeston Country Park 109
Cossall 223 F3
Cossington *Leics.* 210 B1
Cossington *Som.* 166 A3
Costa 340 B4
Costessey 228 C4
Costock 223 G5
Coston *Leics.* 224 D5
Coston *Norf.* 228 B5
Cote *Oxon.* 183 F2
Cote *Som.* 166 A3
Cotebrook 220 C1
Cotehele 27
Cotehill 260 A2
Cotes *Cumb.* 249 F4
Cotes *Leics.* 223 G5
Cotes *Staffs.* 221 F4
Cotesbach 210 A4
Cotgrave 224 B4
Cothall 313 D3
Cotham 224 C3
Cothelstone 165 E4
Cotheridge 195 G2
Cotherstone 251 F1
Cothill 183 G3
Cotleigh 153 F2
Cotmanhay 223 F3
Coton *Cambs.* 200 C2
Coton *Northants.* 210 B5
Coton *Staffs.* 221 G4
Coton *Staffs.* 209 D2
Coton *Staffs.* 221 F5
Coton Clanford 221 F5
Coton Hill 221 G4
Coton in the Clay 222 C5
Coton in the Elms 209 E1
Coton Manor Wildlife Garden 71
Cotonwood *Shrop.* 220 C4
Cotonwood *Staffs.* 221 F5
Cotswold Farm Park 27
Cotswold Hills 28
Cotswold Water Park 28
Cotswold Wildlife Park 43
Cott 151 D1
Cottam *Lancs.* 242 A4
Cottam *Notts.* 237 F4
Cottartown 310 C1
Cottenham 200 C1
Cotterdale 250 D3
Cottered 200 B5
Cotteridge 208 C5
Cotterstock 211 F3
Cottesbrooke 210 C5
Cottesmore 211 E1
Cottingham *E.Riding* 246 C4
Cottingham *Northants.* 210 D3
Cottingley 244 A4
Cottisford 198 A4
Cotton *Staffs.* 222 B3
Cotton *Suff.* 202 B1
Cotton End 199 F3
Cottonworth 169 E4
Cottown *Aber.* 312 A2
Cottown *Aber.* 324 D5
Cottown *Aber.* 312 C3
Cotts 150 A1
Cottwood 163 G4
Cotwall 207 F1
Cotwalton 221 G4
Couch's Mill 147 F4
Coughton *Here.* 195 E5
Coughton *Warks.* 196 C1
Coughton Court 64
Cougie 308 B2
Coulaghailtro 281 F3
Coulags 319 F5
Coulby Newham 253 E1
Coulderton 248 A2
Coull 312 A4
Coulport 282 D1
Coulsdon 172 B3
Coulston 168 A2
Coulter 276 B2
Coultershaw Bridge 158 B2
Coultings 165 F3
Coulton 253 F5
Coultra 294 B2
Cound 207 E2
Coundlane 207 E2
Coundon *Dur.* 262 B5
Coundon *W.Mid.* 209 F4
Countersett 251 E4
Countess Wear 152 C3
Countesthorpe 210 A3
Countisbury 164 A3
Coup Green 242 B5
Coupar Angus 302 A5
Coupland *Cumb.* 250 C1
Coupland *Northumb.* 278 D3
Cour 281 G5
Court Colman 179 E4
Court Henry 192 B5
Court House Green 209 F4
Court-at-Street 174 C5
Courteenhall 198 C2
Courtsend 188 D3
Courtway 165 F4
Cousland 286 A3
Cousley Wood 173 F5
Coustonn 282 B2
Cove *Arg. & B.* 282 D1
Cove *Devon* 152 C1
Cove *Hants.* 170 D2
Cove *High.* 330 A5
Cove *Sc.Bord.* 287 E2
Cove Bay 313 E4
Cove Bottom 215 F3
Covehithe 215 G3
Coven 208 B2
Coveney 212 C4
Covenham St. Bartholomew 238 D3
Covenham St. Mary 238 D3
Covent Garden 55
Coventry 209 F5
Coventry Cathedral 64
Coventry Transport Museum 64
Coverack 145 E5
Coverham 252 A4
Covesea 323 D2
Covington 183 D4
Covington *Cambs.* 211 F5
Covington *S.Lan.* 276 A2
Cowan Bridge 250 B5
Cowbeech 160 B2
Cowbit 212 A1
Cowbridge *Som.* 164 C3
Cowbridge *V. of Glam.* 179 F5
Cowden 173 D4
Cowden Pound 173 D4
Cowdenbeath 293 G5
Cowdenburn 285 G4
Cowers Lane 223 E3
Cowes 157 D3
Cowesby 253 D4
Cowesfield Green 169 D5
Cowey Green 202 B5
Cowfold 159 E1
Cowgill 250 C4
Cowie *Aber.* 303 G1
Cowie *Stir.* 284 C1
Cowlam Manor 246 B1
Cowley *Devon* 152 C3
Cowley *Glos.* 182 B1
Cowley *Gt.Lon.* 185 F4
Cowley *Oxon.* 184 A2
Cowling *Lancs.* 233 G1
Cowling *N.Yorks.* 243 F3
Cowling *N.Yorks.* 252 B4
Cowlinge 201 F2
Cowmes 235 F1
Cowpe 243 E5
Cowpen 271 E3
Cowpen Bewley 263 D5
Cowper & Newton Museum 43
Cowplain 157 F1
Cowsden 196 B2
Cowshill 261 E3
Cowthorpe 244 D2
Cox Common 215 E3
Coxbank 221 D3
Coxbench 223 E3
Coxbridge 166 C4
Coxford 227 G5
Coxheath 173 G3
Coxhoe 262 C4
Coxley 166 C3
Coxley Wick 166 C3
Coxpark 149 E3
Coxtie Green 187 E3
Coxwold 253 E5
Coychurch 179 F5
Coylet 282 C1
Coylton 274 C4
Coylumbridge 310 B3
Coynach 311 G4
Coynachie 311 G1
Coytrahen 179 E4
Crabbet Park 172 C5
Crabgate 228 B3
Crabtree *Plym.* 150 B2
Crabtree *S.Yorks.* 236 A4
Crabtree *W.Suss.* 159 E1
Crabtree Green 220 A3
Crackaig 280 D3
Crackenthorpe 260 C5
Crackington 148 B1
Crackington Haven 148 B1
Crackley 221 F3
Crackleybank 207 G1
Crackpot 251 E3
Crackthorn Corner 214 B4
Cracoe 243 F1
Craddock 153 D1
Cradhlastadh 328 B4
Cradley *Here.* 195 G3
Cradley *W.Mid.* 208 B4
Cradley Heath 208 B4
Crafthole 149 D5
Crafton 185 D1
Cragg 243 G5
Cragg Hill 244 B4
Craggan *Moray* 311 D1
Craggan *P. & K.* 292 D3
Cragganruar 300 B5
Craggie *High.* 309 G1
Craggie *High.* 333 D3
Craghead 262 B2
Cragside 103
Craibstone *Aberdeen* 313 D3
Craibstone *Moray* 323 G4
Craichie 302 D5
Craig *Arg. & B.* 290 C1
Craig *Arg. & B.* 289 E1
Craig *D. & G.* 266 A4
Craig *High.* 319 D3
Craig *High.* 319 G5
Craig *S.Ayr.* 274 B5
Craig Berthlŵyd 179 G3
Craigans 290 A5
Craigbeg 299 G1
Craig-cefn-parc 178 C2
Craigcleuch 268 B3
Craigculter 325 E4
Craigdallie 294 A2
Craigdam 312 D1
Craigdarroch *D. & G.* 266 B1
Craigdarroch *E.Ayr.* 275 E5
Craigdhu *D. & G.* 257 D2
Craigdhu *High.* 321 D5
Craigearn 312 C3
Craigellachie 323 E5
Craigellie 325 F3
Craigencallie 265 G3
Craigend *Moray* 322 D4
Craigend *P. & K.* 293 G2
Craigendive 282 B1
Craigendoran 283 E1
Craigengillan 274 C5
Craigenputtock 266 B2
Craigens 280 A3
Craigglas 290 A5
Craighall 294 C3
Craighat 283 F1
Craighead *Fife* 295 E3
Craighead *High.* 321 G3
Craighlaw 265 E4
Craighouse 280 D3
Craigie *Aber.* 313 E3
Craigie *Dundee* 294 C1
Craigie *P. & K.* 301 G5
Craigie *S.Ayr.* 274 C2
Craigie Brae 313 D1
Craigieburn 276 C5
Craigieholm 293 G1
Craigielaw 286 B2
Craigievar Castle 119
Craiglockhart 285 G2
Craiglug 312 D5
Craigmaud 325 D4
Craigmillar 285 G2
Craigmillar Castle 119
Craigmore 282 C3
Craigmyle House 312 B4
Craignafeoch 282 A2
Craignant 219 F4
Craignavie 292 A1
Craigneil 264 C2
Craigneuk 284 B4
Craignure 289 G1
Craigo 303 E3
Craigoch 274 A5
Craigow 293 F4
Craigrothie 294 B3
Craigroy 322 D4
Craigroy Farm 311 D1
Craigruie 291 G2
Craigs, The 331 G5
Craigsanquhar 294 B3
Craigton *Aberdeen* 312 D4
Craigton *Angus* 294 D1
Craigton *Angus* 302 B4
Craigton *High.* 321 F5
Craigton *Stir.* 284 A1
Craigtown 336 A3
Craig-y-nos 179 E1
Craik *Aber.* 311 G2
Craik *Sc.Bord.* 277 E5
Crail 295 E4
Crailing 278 A4
Crailinghall 278 A4
Crakehill 252 D5
Crakemarsh 222 B4
Crambe 245 G1
Cramlington 271 E4
Cramond 285 F2
Cranage 221 E1
Cranberry 221 F4
Cranborne 155 G1
Cranbourne 185 E5
Cranbrook *Gt.Lon.* 186 D4
Cranbrook *Kent* 173 G5
Cranbrook Common 173 G5
Crane Moor 236 A2
Cranfield 199 E3
Cranford *Devon* 162 D3
Cranford *Gt.Lon.* 186 A5
Cranford St. Andrew 211 E5
Cranford St. John 211 E5
Cranham *Glos.* 182 A1
Cranham *Gt.Lon.* 187 E4
Crank 233 G3
Cranleigh 171 F4
Cranmer Green 214 B4
Cranmore *I.o.W.* 156 C4
Cranmore *Som.* 167 D3
Cranna 324 B4
Crannoch 323 G4
Cranoe 210 C3
Cransford 203 E1
Cranshaws 287 D3
Cranstal 240 C1
Crantock 146 B3
Cranwell 225 F3
Cranwich 213 F3
Cranworth 228 A5
Craobh Haven 289 G4
Crapstone 150 B1
Crarae 290 B5
Crask Inn 332 A2
Crask of Aigas 321 D5
Craskins 312 A4
Craster 279 G5
Craswall 194 B4
Crateford 208 B2
Cratfield 215 E4
Crathes 312 C5
Crathes Castle 119
Crathie *Aber.* 311 E5
Crathie *High.* 309 E5
Crathorne 252 D2
Craven Arms 206 D4
Craw 281 G5
Crawcrook 262 A1
Crawford *Lancs.* 233 F2
Crawford *S.Lan.* 276 A3
Crawfordjohn 275 G3
Crawfordton 266 B1
Crawick 275 F4
Crawley *Devon* 153 F2
Crawley *Hants.* 169 F4
Crawley *Oxon.* 183 F1
Crawley *W.Suss.* 172 B5
Crawley Down 172 C5
Crawleyside 261 F3
Crawshawbooth 243 E5
Crawton 303 G2
Crawyn 240 B2
Cray *N.Yorks.* 251 E5
Cray *P. & K.* 301 G3
Cray *Powys* 193 E5
Crayford 187 E5
Crayke 253 E5
Crays Hill 187 G3
Cray's Pond 184 B4
Crazies Hill 184 C4
Creacombe 152 B1
Creag Ghoraidh (Creagorry) 315 F5
Creagan 298 B5
Creagbheitheachain 298 B3
Creagorry (Creag Ghoraidh) 315 F5
Crealy Adventure Park 28
Creamore Bank 220 C4
Creaton 210 C5
Creca 268 A4
Credenhill 195 D3
Crediton 152 B2
Creebridge 265 F4
Creech Heathfield 165 F5
Creech St. Michael 165 F5
Creed 146 D5
Creedy Park 152 B2
Creekmouth 187 D4
Creeting St. Mary 202 B2
Creeton 225 F5
Creetown 265 F5
Creggans 290 C4
Cregneash 240 A5
Cregrina 194 A2
Creich 294 B2
Creigau 181 D3
Creigiau 179 G4
Crelevan 308 C1
Crelly 145 D3
Cremyll 150 A2
Crendell 155 G1
Cressage 207 E2
Cressbrook 235 F5
Cresselly 177 D2
Cressing 201 F5
Cressing Temple Barns 78
Cresswell *Northumb.* 271 E2
Cresswell *Staffs.* 221 G4
Cresswell Quay 177 D2
Creswell 236 C5
Cretingham 202 D2
Cretshengan 281 F3
Crewe *Ches.* 221 E2
Crewe *Ches.* 220 B2
Crewe Green 221 E2
Crewgreen 206 C1
Crewkerne 154 A2
Crew's Hole 181 F5
Crewton 223 E4
Crianlarich 291 F2
Cribbs Causeway 181 E4
Cribyn 192 B2
Criccieth 217 D4
Criccieth Castle 110
Crich 223 E2
Crich Carr 223 E2
Crich Common 223 E2
Crichie 325 E5
Crichton 286 A3
Crichton Castle 119
Crick *Mon.* 181 D3
Crick *Northants.* 210 A5
Crickadarn 193 G3
Cricket Hill 170 D1
Cricket St. Thomas 153 G2
Crickham 166 B3
Crickheath 219 F5
Crickhowell 180 B1
Cricklade 182 D3
Cricklewood 186 B4
Crick's Green 195 F2
Criddlestyle 156 A1
Cridling Stubbs 245 E5
Crieff 293 D2
Criggan 147 E3
Criggion 206 B1
Crigglestone 236 A1
Crimble 234 C1
Crimchard 153 G2
Crimdon Park 263 D4
Crimond 325 F4
Crimonmogate 325 F4
Crimplesham 213 E2
Crinan 289 G5
Crinan Ferry 289 G5
Cringleford 228 C5
Cringletie 285 G5
Crinow 177 E1
Cripplestyle 155 G1
Cripp's Corner 160 C1
Crix 187 G1
Crizeley 194 D4
Croalchapel 266 D1
Croasdale 259 D5
Crock Street 153 G1
Crockenhill 173 E2
Crocker End 184 C4
Crockerhill 157 E2
Crockernwell 152 A3
Crockerton 167 F3
Crockerton Green 167 F3
Crocketford (Ninemile Bar) 266 C3
Crockey Hill 245 F3
Crockham Hill 172 D3
Crockhurst Street 173 F4
Crockleford Heath 202 B5
Croes Hywel 180 C1
Croes y pant 180 C2
Croesau Bach 219 F5
Croeserw 179 E3
Croesgoch 190 B4
Croes-lan 191 G3
Croesor 217 F3
Croespenmaen 180 A3
Croesyceiliog *Carmar.* 178 A1
Croesyceiliog *Torfaen* 180 C3
Croes-y-mwyalch 180 C3
Croesywaun 217 E2
Croford 165 E5
Croft *Here.* 195 D1
Croft *Leics.* 210 A3
Croft *Lincs.* 226 D1
Croft *Warr.* 234 A3
Croft Castle 64
Croftamie 283 F1
Crofthead 268 B4
Croftmore 301 D3
Crofton *W.Yorks.* 236 A1
Crofton *Wilts.* 169 D1
Croft-on-Tees 252 B2
Crofts 266 B3
Crofts of Benachielt 337 D5
Crofts of Buinach 323 D4
Crofts of Haddo 312 D1
Crofty 178 B3
Crogen 218 D4
Croggan 289 G2
Croglin 260 B3
Croick *High.* 331 G5
Croick *High.* 336 A3
Croig 296 D4
Crois Dughaill 314 C2
Croit e Caley 240 A5
Cromarty 321 G3
Crombie 285 E1
Crombie Mill 294 D1
Cromblet 312 C1
Cromdale 310 C2
Cromer *Herts.* 200 A5
Cromer *Norf.* 228 D1
Cromford 223 D2
Cromhall 181 F3
Cromhall Common 181 F4
Crompton Fold 235 D1
Cromwell 224 C1
Cromwell Museum 78
Cronberry 275 E3
Crondall 170 C3
Cronk, The 240 B2
Cronk-y-Voddy 240 B3
Cronton 233 F4
Crook *Cumb.* 249 F3
Crook *Dur.* 262 A4
Crook of Devon 293 F4
Crooked Soley 183 F5
Crookedholm 274 C2
Crookham *Northumb.* 278 D3
Crookham *W.Berks.* 169 G1
Crookham Eastfield 278 D3
Crookham Village 170 C2
Crooklands 249 G4
Cropredy 197 G3
Cropston 210 A1
Cropthorne 196 B3
Cropton 253 G4
Cropwell Bishop 224 B4
Cropwell Butler 224 B4
Cros (Cross) 329 G1
Crosbie 282 D5
Crosbost 329 E5
Crosby *Cumb.* 259 D3
Crosby *I.o.M.* 240 B4

D

E

East Cowick 245 F5
East Cowton 252 C2
East Cramlington 271 E4
East Cranmore 167 D3
East Creech 155 F4
East Croachy 309 F2
East Darlochan 272 B3
East Davoch 311 G4
East Dean *E.Suss.* 160 A4
East Dean *Hants.* 169 D5
East Dean *W.Suss.* 158 B2
East Dereham (Dereham) 228 A4
East Down 163 F1
East Drayton 237 E5
East Dundry 166 C1
East Ella 246 C5
East End *E.Riding* 247 D4
East End *E.Riding* 247 E5
East End *Essex* 188 D2
East End *Hants.* 169 F1
East End *Hants.* 156 C3
East End *Herts.* 200 C5
East End *Kent* 174 A5
East End *Kent* 174 B1
East End *M.K.* 199 E3
East End *N.Som.* 181 D5
East End *Oxon.* 183 F1
East End *Poole* 155 F3
East End *Som.* 166 C2
East End *Suff.* 202 C4
East End *Suff.* 202 C2
East Farleigh 173 G3
East Farndon 210 C4
East Ferry 237 F3
East Firsby 238 A4
East Fleetham 279 G4
East Fortune 286 C2
East Garston 183 F5
East Ginge 183 G4
East Goscote 210 B1
East Grafton 169 D1
East Green *Suff.* 203 F1
East Green *Suff.* 201 E2
East Grimstead 168 D5
East Grinstead 172 C5
East Guldeford 161 E1
East Haddon 198 B1
East Hagbourne 184 A4
East Halton 238 B1
East Ham 186 D4
East Hanney 183 G3
East Hanningfield 187 G2
East Hardwick 236 B1
East Harling 214 A3
East Harlsey 252 D3
East Harnham 168 C5
East Harptree 166 C2
East Hartford 271 E4
East Harting 157 G1
East Hatch 168 A5
East Hatley 200 A2
East Hauxwell 252 A3
East Haven 295 D1
East Heckington 225 G3
East Hedleyhope 262 A3
East Helmsdale 333 F3
East Hendred 183 G4
East Herrington 262 C2
East Heslerton 254 C5
East Hewish 166 B1
East Hoathly 160 A2
East Holme 155 E4
East Horndon 187 F4
East Horrington 166 C3
East Horsley 171 F2
East Horton 279 E3
East Howe 155 G3
East Huntspill 166 A3
East Hyde 186 A1
East Ilsley 183 G4
East Keal 226 B1
East Kennett 168 C1
East Keswick 244 C3
East Kilbride 284 A4
East Kimber 149 E1
East Kirkby 226 B1
East Knapton 254 B5
East Knighton 155 E4
East Knowstone 164 B5
East Knoyle 167 F4
East Kyloe 279 E3
East Lambrook 154 A1
East Lambrook Manor 28
East Langdon 175 F4
East Langton 210 C3
East Langwell 332 C4
East Lavant 158 A3
East Lavington 158 B2
East Layton 252 A1
East Leake 223 G5
East Learmouth 278 C3
East Learney 312 B4
East Leigh *Devon* 152 A2
East Leigh *Devon* 152 A1
East Leigh *Devon* 151 D2
East Leigh *Devon* 150 C2
East Lexham 213 G1
East Lilburn 279 E4
East Linton 286 C2
East Liss 170 C5
East Lockinge 183 G4
East Looe 147 G4
East Lound 237 E2
East Lulworth 155 E4
East Lutton 246 B1
East Lydford 166 C4
East Lyn 164 A3
East Lyng 166 A5
East Mains 312 B5
East Malling 173 G3
East Malling Heath 173 F3
East March 294 C1
East Marden 158 A2
East Markham 237 E5
East Martin 155 G1
East Marton 243 F2
East Meon 170 B5
East Mere 152 C1
East Mersea 189 D1
East Mey 337 F1
East Molesey 171 G1
East Moor 244 C5
East Morden 155 F3
East Morriston 286 D5
East Morton 244 A3
East Ness 253 F5
East Newton 247 E4
East Norton 210 C2
East Oakley 169 G2
East Ogwell 152 B5
East Orchard 155 E1
East Ord 287 G4
East Panson 149 D1
East Parley 156 A3
East Peckham 173 F4
East Pennard 166 C4
East Portlemouth 150 D4
East Prawle 151 D4
East Preston 158 C3
East Pulham 154 D2
East Putford 163 D4
East Quantoxhead 165 E3
East Rainton 262 C3
East Ravendale 238 C3
East Raynham 227 G5
East Rigton 244 C3
East Rolstone 166 A1
East Rounton 252 D2
East Row 254 B1
East Rudham 227 G5
East Runton 228 D1
East Ruston 229 E3
East Saltoun 286 B3
East Shefford 183 F5
East Sleekburn 271 E3
East Somerset Railway 29
East Somerton 229 F4
East Stockwith 237 E3
East Stoke *Dorset* 155 E4
East Stoke *Notts.* 224 C3
East Stour 167 F5
East Stourmouth 175 E2
East Stratton 169 G3
East Street 166 C4
East Studdal 175 F4
East Suisnish 306 B1
East Taphouse 147 F3
East Thirston 271 D2
East Tilbury 187 F5
East Tisted 170 C4
East Torrington 238 B4
East Town 166 D3
East Tuddenham 228 B4
East Tytherley 169 D5
East Tytherton 182 B5
East Village 152 B2
East Wall 207 E3
East Walton 213 F1
East Wellow 169 E5
East Wemyss 294 B5
East Whitburn 285 D3
East Wickham 187 D5
East Williamston 177 D2
East Winch 213 E1
East Winterslow 168 D4
East Wittering 157 G3
East Witton 252 A4
East Woodburn 270 B3
East Woodhay 169 F1
East Woodlands 167 E3
East Worldham 170 C4
East Worlington 152 A1
East Youlstone 162 C4
Eastacott 163 G3
Eastbourne 160 B4
Eastbourne Pier 44
Eastbrook 180 A5
Eastburn *E.Riding* 246 B2
Eastburn *W.Yorks.* 243 G3
Eastbury *Herts.* 186 A3
Eastbury *W.Berks.* 183 F5
Eastby 243 G2
Eastchurch 174 B1
Eastcombe *Glos.* 182 A2
Eastcombe *Som.* 165 E4
Eastcote *Gt.Lon.* 186 A4
Eastcote *Northants.* 198 B2
Eastcote *W.Mid.* 209 D5
Eastcott *Cornw.* 162 C4
Eastcott *Wilts.* 168 B2
Eastcourt 182 B3
Eastdown 151 E3
Eastend 197 F5
Easter Ardross 321 F2
Easter Balgedie 293 G4
Easter Balmoral 311 E5
Easter Boleskine 309 E2
Easter Borland 292 B4
Easter Brae 321 F3
Easter Buckieburn 284 B1
Easter Compton 181 E4
Easter Drummond 309 D3
Easter Dullater 292 A4
Easter Ellister 280 A4
Easter Fearn 321 F1
Easter Galcantray 322 A5
Easter Howlaws 287 E5
Easter Kinkell 321 E4
Easter Knox 303 D5
Easter Lednathie 302 B3
Easter Moniack 321 E5
Easter Ord 312 D4
Easter Poldar 292 B5
Easter Skeld (Skeld) 342 C3
Easter Suddie 321 F4
Easter Tulloch 303 F2
Easter Whyntie 324 B3
Eastergate 158 B3
Easterhouse 284 A3
Easterton 168 B2
Easterton Sands 168 B2
Eastertown 166 A2
Eastfield *Bristol* 181 E5
Eastfield *N.Lan.* 284 C3
Eastfield *N.Yorks.* 254 D4
Eastfield Hall 271 E1
Eastgate *Dur.* 261 F4
Eastgate *Lincs.* 211 G1
Eastgate *Norf.* 228 C3
Easthall 200 A5
Eastham *Mersey.* 233 E4
Eastham *Worcs.* 195 F1
Easthampstead 171 D1
Easthampton 194 D1
Easthaugh 228 B4
Eastheath 170 D1
Easthope 207 E3
Easthorpe *Essex* 202 A5
Easthorpe *Leics.* 224 D4
Easthorpe *Notts.* 224 C2
Easthouses 286 A3
Eastington *Devon* 152 A2
Eastington *Glos.* 182 D1
Eastington *Glos.* 181 G2
Eastleach Martin 183 E2
Eastleach Turville 183 E2
Eastleigh *Devon* 163 E3
Eastleigh *Hants.* 156 D1
Eastling 174 B3
Eastmoor *Derbys.* 236 A5
Eastmoor *Norf.* 213 F2
Eastnor 195 G4
Eastnor Castle 65
Eastoft 237 F1
Eastoke 157 G3
Easton *Cambs.* 211 G5
Easton *Cumb.* 268 C4
Easton *Cumb.* 259 F1
Easton *Devon* 152 A4
Easton *Dorset* 154 C5
Easton *Hants.* 169 G4
Easton *I.o.W.* 156 C4
Easton *Lincs.* 225 E5
Easton *Norf.* 228 C4
Easton *Som.* 166 C3
Easton *Suff.* 203 D2
Easton *Wilts.* 182 A5
Easton Farm Park 79
Easton Grey 182 A4
Easton Maudit 199 D2
Easton on the Hill 211 F2
Easton Royal 168 D1
Easton-in-Gordano 181 E5
Eastrea 212 A3
Eastriggs 268 A5
Eastrington 245 G4
Eastry 175 F3
Eastside 339 D3
East-the-Water 163 E3
Eastville 181 F5
Eastwell 224 C5
Eastwick 186 D1
Eastwood *Notts.* 223 F3
Eastwood *S'end* 188 B4
Eastwood *S.Yorks.* 236 B3
Eastwood *W.Yorks.* 243 F5
Eastwood End 212 C3
Eathorpe 197 F1
Eaton *Ches.* 221 F1
Eaton *Ches.* 220 C1
Eaton *Leics.* 224 C5
Eaton *Norf.* 228 D5
Eaton *Norf.* 227 E4
Eaton *Notts.* 237 E5
Eaton *Oxon.* 183 G2
Eaton *Shrop.* 207 E3
Eaton *Shrop.* 206 C4
Eaton Bishop 194 D4
Eaton Bray 199 E5
Eaton Constantine 207 F2
Eaton Ford 199 G2
Eaton Hall 220 B1
Eaton Hastings 183 E3
Eaton Socon 199 G2
Eaton upon Tern 221 D5
Eaves Green 209 E4
Eaves, The 181 F2
Eavestone 244 B1
Ebberston 254 B4
Ebbesborne Wake 168 A5
Ebbw Vale 180 A2
Ebchester 262 A2
Ebdon 166 A1
Ebford 152 C4
Ebley 182 A2
Ebnal 220 B3
Ebrington 197 D3
Ebsworthy Town 149 F1
Ecchinswell 169 F2
Ecclaw 287 E3
Ecclefechan 267 F3
Eccles *Gt.Man.* 234 B3
Eccles *Kent* 173 G2
Eccles *Sc.Bord.* 287 E5
Eccles Green 194 C3
Eccles Road 214 B2
Ecclesfield 236 A3
Ecclesgreig 303 F3
Eccleshall 221 F5
Eccleshill 244 A4
Ecclesmachan 285 E2
Eccles-on-Sea 229 F3
Eccleston *Ches.* 220 B1
Eccleston *Lancs.* 233 G1
Eccleston *Mersey.* 233 F3
Eccup 244 B3
Echt 312 C4
Eckford 278 B4
Eckington *Derbys.* 236 B5
Eckington *Worcs.* 196 B3
Ecton *Northants.* 198 D1
Ecton *Staffs.* 222 B2
Edale 235 F4
Eday 340 D3
Edburton 159 E2
Edderside 259 E2
Edderton 321 G1
Eddington 169 E1
Eddleston 285 G5
Eden Camp 87
Eden Park 172 C2
Eden Project 29
Eden Vale 262 D4
Edenbridge 172 D4
Edendonich 291 D2
Edenfield 234 B1
Edenhall 260 B4
Edenham 225 F5
Edensor 235 G5
Edentaggart 291 F5
Edenthorpe 236 D2
Edern 216 B4
Edgarley 166 C4
Edgbaston 208 C4
Edgcote 198 A3
Edgcott *Bucks.* 198 B5
Edgcott *Som.* 164 B4
Edgcumbe 145 E3
Edge *Glos.* 182 A2
Edge *Shrop.* 206 C2
Edge End 181 E1
Edge Green *Ches.* 220 B2
Edge Green *Gt.Man.* 233 G3
Edge Green *Norf.* 214 B3
Edgebolton 220 C5
Edgefield 228 B2
Edgehead 286 A3
Edgeley 220 C3
Edgerley 206 C1
Edgerton 235 F1
Edgeworth 182 B2
Edginswell 151 E1
Edgmond 207 G1
Edgmond Marsh 221 E5
Edgton 206 C4
Edgware 186 B3
Edgworth 234 B1
Edinample 292 B2
Edinbanchory 311 G3
Edinbane 317 G4
Edinbarnet 283 G2
Edinburgh 121
Edinburgh Airport 285 F2
Edinburgh Castle 122
Edinburgh Zoo 122
Edinchip 292 A2
Edingale 209 E1
Edingley 224 B2
Edingthorpe 229 E2
Edingthorpe Green 229 E2
Edington *Som.* 166 A4
Edington *Wilts.* 168 A2
Edintore 323 G5
Edinvale 322 D4
Edistone 162 C3
Edith Weston 211 E2
Edithmead 166 A3
Edlaston 222 C3
Edlesborough 185 E1
Edlingham 270 D1
Edlington 238 C5
Edmondsham 155 G1
Edmondsham House 29
Edmondsley 262 B3
Edmondstown 179 G3
Edmondthorpe 211 D1
Edmonstone 340 D4
Edmonton *Cornw.* 147 D2
Edmonton *Gt.Lon.* 186 C3
Edmundbyers 261 G2
Ednam 278 B3
Ednaston 222 D3
Edney Common 187 F2
Edra 291 G3
Edradynate 301 D4
Edrom 287 F4
Edstaston 220 C4
Edstone 197 D1
Edvin Loach 195 F2
Edwalton 223 G4
Edwardstone 202 A3
Edwardsville 179 G3
Edwinsford 192 C4
Edwinstowe 224 B1
Edworth 200 A3
Edwyn Ralph 195 F2
Edzell 303 E3
Edzell Castle & Garden 122
Efail Isaf 179 G4
Efail-fâch 179 D3
Efailnewydd 216 C4
Efailwen 191 E5
Efenechtyd 219 E2
Effingham 171 G2
Effirth 342 C2
Efflinch 209 D1
Efford 152 B2
Egbury 169 F2
Egdean 171 E5
Egdon 196 B2
Egerton *Gt.Man.* 234 B1
Egerton *Kent* 174 B4
Egerton Forstal 174 A4
Egerton Green 220 C2
Egg Buckland 150 A2
Eggborough 245 E5
Eggerness 257 E2
Eggesford Barton 163 G4
Eggington 199 E5
Egginton 223 D5
Egglescliffe 252 D1
Eggleston 261 F5
Egham 185 F5
Egham Wick 185 E5
Egilsay 340 C4
Egleton 211 D2
Eglingham 279 F5
Eglinton 283 E5
Egloshayle 147 E2
Egloskerry 147 G1
Eglwys Cross 220 B3
Eglwys Fach 204 C3
Eglwys Nunydd 179 D4
Eglwysbach 231 G5
Eglwys-Brewis 164 D1
Eglwyswrw 191 E4
Egmanton 224 C1
Egmere 228 A2
Egremont 258 D5
Egton 254 B2
Egton Bridge 254 B2
Egypt 169 F3
Eigg 297 D1
Eight Ash Green 202 A5
Eignaig 297 G5
Eil 310 A3
Eilanreach 307 E3
Eildon 277 G2
Eilean Bhearnaraigh (Berneray) 326 B5
Eilean Darach 320 A1
Eilean Donan Castle 122
Eilean Iarmain (Isleornsay) 306 C3
Eilean Leodhais (Isle of Lewis) 329 E3
Eilean Scalpaigh (Scalpay) 327 E4
Eilean Shona 297 F2
Einacleit 328 C5
Eiriosgaigh (Eriskay) 314 C2
Eisgean 327 F2
Eisingrug 217 F4
Eisteddfa Gurig 205 D4
Elan Valley Visitor Centre 110
Elan Village 193 F1
Elberton 181 F4
Elburton 150 B2
Elcho 293 G2
Elcombe 182 D4
Elder Street 201 D4
Eldernell 212 B3
Eldersfield 195 G4
Elderslie 283 F3
Eldon 262 B5
Eldrick 265 D2
Eldroth 243 D1
Eldwick 244 A3
Electric Mountain 110
Elemore Vale 262 C3
Elerch (Bont-goch) 204 C4
Elford *Northumb.* 279 F3
Elford *Staffs.* 209 D1
Elford Closes 212 D5
Elgin 323 E3
Elgin Cathedral 122
Elgin Museum 122
Elgol 306 B3
Elham 175 D4
Elie 294 C4
Elilaw 270 B1
Elim 230 B4
Eling *Hants.* 156 C1
Eling *W.Berks.* 184 A5
Eliock 275 G5
Elishader 318 A3
Elishaw 270 A2
Elkesley 237 D5
Elkington 210 B5
Elkstone 182 B1
Elland 244 A5
Elland Upper Edge 244 A5
Ellary 281 F2
Ellastone 222 C3
Ellbridge 150 A1
Ellel 242 A2
Ellemford 287 E3
Ellenborough 258 D3
Ellenhall 221 F5
Ellen's Green 171 F4
Ellerbeck 252 D3
Ellerby 253 G1
Ellerdine 220 D5
Ellerdine Heath 220 D5
Ellergreen 249 F3
Elleric 298 C5
Ellerker 246 B5
Ellerton *E.Riding* 245 G3
Ellerton *N.Yorks.* 252 B3
Ellerton *Shrop.* 221 E5
Ellerton Abbey 251 F3
Ellesborough 184 D2
Ellesmere 220 A4
Ellesmere Park 234 B3
Ellesmere Port 233 F5
Ellesmere Port Boat Museum 95
Ellingham *Hants.* 156 A2
Ellingham *Norf.* 215 E2
Ellingham *Northumb.* 279 F4
Ellingstring 252 A4
Ellington *Cambs.* 211 G5
Ellington *Northumb.* 271 E2
Ellington Thorpe 211 G5
Elliot's Green 167 E3
Ellisfield 170 B3
Ellistown 209 G1
Ellon 313 E1
Ellonby 260 A4
Ellough 215 F3
Ellough Moor 215 F3
Elloughton 246 B5
Ellwood 181 E2
Elm 212 C2
Elm Park 187 E4
Elmbridge 196 B1
Elmdon *Essex* 200 C4
Elmdon *W.Mid.* 209 D4
Elmdon Heath 209 D4
Elmers End 172 C2
Elmer's Green 233 F2
Elmesthorpe 209 G3
Elmhurst 208 D1
Elmley Castle 196 B3
Elmley Lovett 196 A1
Elmore 181 G1
Elmore Back 181 G1
Elmscott 162 C3
Elmsett 202 B3
Elmstead *Essex* 202 B5
Elmstead *Gt.Lon.* 186 D5
Elmstead Market 202 B5
Elmstone 175 E2
Elmstone Hardwicke 196 B5
Elmswell *E.Riding* 246 B2
Elmswell *Suff.* 202 A1
Elmton 236 C5
Elphin 331 E3
Elphinstone 286 A2
Elrick *Aber.* 312 D4
Elrick *Moray* 311 G2
Elrig 256 D2
Elrigbeag 290 D3
Elsdon 270 B2
Elsecar 236 A2
Elsenham 200 D5
Elsfield 184 A1
Elsham 238 A1
Elsham Hall Country & Wildlife Park 87
Elsing 228 B4
Elslack 243 F3
Elson *Hants.* 157 F2
Elson *Shrop.* 220 A4
Elsrickle 285 E5
Elstead 171 E3
Elsted 158 A2
Elsthorpe 225 F5
Elstob 262 C5
Elston *Lancs.* 242 B4
Elston *Notts.* 224 C3
Elstone 163 G4
Elstow 199 F3
Elstree 186 A3
Elstronwick 247 E4
Elswick 242 A4
Elsworth 200 B1
Elterwater 249 E2
Eltham 186 D5
Eltham Palace 55
Eltisley 200 A2
Elton *Cambs.* 211 F3
Elton *Ches.* 233 F5
Elton *Derbys.* 222 D1
Elton *Glos.* 181 G1
Elton *Gt.Man.* 234 B1
Elton *Here.* 207 D5
Elton *Notts.* 224 C4
Elton *Stock.* 252 D1
Elton Green 233 F5
Elton Hall 79
Elvanfoot 276 A4
Elvaston 223 F4
Elvaston Castle Country Park 72
Elveden 213 G5
Elvingston 286 B2
Elvington *Kent* 175 E3
Elvington *York* 245 G3
Elwick *Hart.* 263 D4
Elwick *Northumb.* 279 F3
Elworth 221 E1
Elworthy 165 D4
Ely *Cambs.* 212 D5
Ely *Cardiff* 180 A5
Ely Cathedral 79
Emberton 199 D3
Embleton *Cumb.* 259 E3
Embleton *Hart.* 262 D5
Embleton *Northumb.* 279 G4
Embo 332 D5
Embo Street 332 D5
Emborough 166 D2
Embsay 243 G2
Emerson Park 187 E4
Emery Down 156 B2
Emley 235 G1
Emmetts 44
Emmington 184 C2
Emneth 212 C2
Emneth Hungate 212 D2
Empingham 211 E2
Empshott 170 C4
Empshott Green 170 C4
Emsworth 157 G2
Enborne 169 F1
Enborne Row 169 F1
Enchmarsh 207 E3
Enderby 210 A3
Endmoor 249 G4
Endon 221 G2
Endon Bank 221 G2
Enfield 186 C3
Enfield Wash 186 C3
Enford 168 C2
Engine Common 181 F4
Englefield 184 B5
Englefield Green 185 E5
Englesea-brook 221 E2
English Bicknor 181 E1
English Frankton 220 B5
Englishcombe 167 E1
Enham Alamein 169 E3
Enmore 165 F4
Ennerdale Bridge 259 D5
Enniscaven 147 D4
Ennochdhu 301 F3
Ensay 296 C5
Ensdon 206 D1
Ensis 163 F3
Enson 221 G5
Enstone 197 F5
Enterkinfoot 275 G5
Enterpen 253 D2
Enton Green 171 E3
Enville 208 A4
Eolaigearraidh 314 C3
Eorabus 288 C2
Eorodal 329 G1
Eoropaidh 329 G1
Epney 181 G1
Epperstone 224 B3
Epping 187 D2
Epping Forest 79
Epping Green *Essex* 186 D2
Epping Green *Herts.* 186 B2
Epping Upland 186 D2
Eppleby 252 A1
Eppleworth 246 C4
Epsom 172 B2
Epwell 197 F3
Epworth 237 E2
Epworth Turbary 237 E2
Erbistock 220 A3
Erbusaig 307 D2
Erchless Castle 320 D5
Erddig 110
Erdington 208 D3
Eredine 290 B4
Eriboll 334 D3
Ericstane 276 B4
Eridge Green 173 E5
Eriff 274 D5
Erines 281 G2
Erisey Barton 145 E5
Eriskay (Eiriosgaigh) 314 C2
Eriswell 213 F5
Erith 187 E5
Erlestoke 168 A2
Ermington 150 C2
Ernesettle 150 A1
Erpingham 228 C2
Erringden Grange 243 F5
Errogie 309 E2
Errol 294 A2
Errollston 313 F1
Erskine 283 F2
Ervie 264 A4
Erwarton 202 D4
Erwood 193 G3
Eryholme 252 C2
Eryrys 219 F2
Escart 281 G3
Escart Farm 281 G4
Escomb 262 A5
Escot 29
Escrick 245 F3
Esgair 191 G5
Esgairgeiliog 205 D2
Esgyryn 231 G5
Esh 262 A3
Esh Winning 262 A3
Esher 171 G1
Eshott 271 E2
Eshton 243 F2
Eskadale 309 D1
Eskbank 286 A3
Eskdale Green 248 C2
Eskdalemuir 268 A2
Eskham 239 D3
Esknish 280 B3
Esperley Lane Ends 262 A5
Espley Hall 271 D2
Esprick 242 A4
Essendine 211 F1
Essendon 186 B2
Essich 309 F1
Essington 208 B2
Esslemont 313 E2
Eston 253 E1
Eswick 343 D2
Etal 278 D3
Etchilhampton 168 B1
Etchingham 160 C1
Etchinghill *Kent* 175 D5
Etchinghill *Staffs.* 208 C1
Etherdwick Grange 247 E4
Etherley Dene 262 A5
Ethie Mains 303 E5
Eton 185 E5
Eton Wick 185 E5
Etteridge 309 F5
Ettiley Heath 221 E1
Ettington 197 E3
Etton *E.Riding* 246 B3
Etton *Peter.* 211 G2
Ettrick 277 D4
Ettrickbridge 277 E3
Ettrickhill 277 D4
Etwall 223 D4
Eudon George 207 F4
Eurach 290 A4
Eureka! Museum for Children 87
Euston 213 G5
Euxton 233 G1
Evanstown 179 F4
Evanton 321 F3
Evedon 225 F3
Evelix 332 C5
Evenjobb 194 B1
Evenley 198 A4
Evenlode 197 E5
Evenwood 262 A5
Evenwood Gate 262 A5
Everbay 341 E4
Evercreech 166 D4
Everdon 198 A2
Everingham 246 A3
Everleigh 168 D2
Everley *High.* 337 F2
Everley *N.Yorks.* 254 C4
Eversholt 199 E4
Evershot 154 B2
Eversley 170 C1
Eversley Cross 170 C1
Everthorpe 246 B4
Everton *Beds.* 200 A2
Everton *Hants.* 156 B3
Everton *Mersey.* 233 E3
Everton *Notts.* 237 D3
Evertown 268 B4
Eves Corner 188 C3
Evesbatch 195 F3
Evesham 196 C3
Evie 340 B4
Evington 210 B2
Ewart Newtown 279 D3
Ewden Village 235 G3
Ewell 172 B2
Ewell Minnis 175 E4
Ewelme 184 B3
Ewen 182 C3
Ewenny 179 F5
Ewerby 225 G3
Ewerby Thorpe 225 G3
Ewhurst *E.Suss.* 160 C1
Ewhurst *Surr.* 171 F3
Ewhurst Green 171 F4
Ewloe 220 A1
Ewloe Green 219 F1
Ewood 242 C5
Ewood Bridge 243 D5
Eworthy 149 E1
Ewshot 170 D3
Ewyas Harold 194 C5
Exbourne 163 G5
Exbury 156 D2
Exbury Gardens 44
Exceat 160 A4

Exebridge 164 C5
Exelby 252 B4
Exeter 152 C3
Exeter Airport 152 C3
Exeter Cathedral 29
Exford 164 B4
Exfords Green 207 D2
Exhall *Warks.* 196 D2
Exhall *Warks.* 209 F4
Exlade Street 184 B4
Exminster 152 C4
Exmoor 29
Exmouth 152 D4
Exnaboe 343 G5
Exning 201 E1
Exton *Devon* 152 C4
Exton *Hants.* 170 B5
Exton *Rut.* 211 E1
Exton *Som.* 164 C4
Exwick 152 C3
Eyam 235 G5
Eyam Museum 72
Eydon 198 A3
Eye *Here.* 195 D1
Eye *Peter.* 212 A2
Eye *Suff.* 214 C4
Eye Green 212 A2
Eyemouth 287 G3
Eyeworth 200 A3
Eyhorne Street 174 A3
Eyke 203 E2
Eynesbury 199 G2
Eynort 305 G2
Eynsford 173 E2
Eynsham 183 G2
Eype 154 A3
Eyre 318 A4
Eythorne 175 E4
Eyton *Here.* 195 D1
Eyton *Shrop.* 206 C4
Eyton on Severn 207 E2
Eyton upon the Weald Moors 207 F1
Eywood 194 C2

F

Faccombe 169 E2
Faceby 253 D2
Fachwen 217 E1
Facit 234 C1
Faddiley 220 C2
Fadmoor 253 F4
Faebait 321 D4
Faifley 283 G2
Fail 274 C3
Failand 181 E5
Failford 274 C3
Failsworth 234 C2
Fain 320 A2
Fair Isle 122
Fair Oak *Devon* 152 D1
Fair Oak *Hants.* 157 D1
Fair Oak *Hants.* 169 G1
Fair Oak Green 170 B1
Fairbourne 204 C1
Fairburn 245 D5
Fairfield *Derbys.* 235 E5
Fairfield *Gt.Man.* 234 D3
Fairfield *Kent* 161 E1
Fairfield *Mersey.* 233 D4
Fairfield *Stock.* 252 D1
Fairfield *Worcs.* 208 B5
Fairford 182 D2
Fairgirth 266 C5
Fairhaven 241 G5
Fairhaven Gardens 79
Fairhill 284 B4
Fairholm 284 B4
Fairlands Valley Park 79
Fairley 313 D4
Fairlie 282 D4
Fairlight 161 D2
Fairlight Cove 161 D2
Fairmile *Devon* 153 D3
Fairmile *Surr.* 171 G1
Fairmilehead 285 G3
Fairnington 278 A4
Fairoak 221 E4
Fairseat 173 F2
Fairstead 187 G1
Fairwarp 159 G1
Fairwater 180 A5
Fairy Cross 163 E3
Fairyhill 178 A3
Fakenham 228 A3
Fala 286 B3
Fala Dam 286 B3
Falahill 286 A4
Faldingworth 238 A4
Falfield *Fife* 294 C4
Falfield *S.Glos.* 181 F3
Falin-Wnda 191 G3
Falkenham 203 D4
Falkirk 284 C2
Falkirk Wheel 122
Falkland 294 A4
Falkland Palace 122
Falla 278 B5
Fallgate 223 E1
Fallin 292 D5
Falls of Clyde Wildlife Reserve & Visitor Centre 122
Falmer 159 F3
Falmouth 145 F3
Falsgrave 254 D4
Falstone 269 F3
Fanagmore 334 A4
Fanans 290 C2
Fancott 199 F5
Fangdale Beck 253 E3
Fangfoss 245 G2
Fankerton 284 B1
Fanmore 296 D5
Fanner's Green 187 F1
Fans 286 D5
Fantasy Island 72
Far Cotton 198 C2
Far Forest 207 G5
Far Gearstones 250 C4
Far Green 181 G2
Far Moor 233 G2
Far Oakridge 182 B2
Far Royds 244 B4
Far Sawrey 249 E3
Farcet 212 A3
Farden 207 E5
Fareham 157 E2
Farewell 208 C1
Farforth 238 D5
Faringdon 183 E3
Farington 242 B5
Farlam 260 B2
Farlary 332 C4
Farleigh *N.Som.* 166 C1
Farleigh *Surr.* 172 C2
Farleigh Hungerford 167 F2
Farleigh Hungerford Castle 29
Farleigh Wallop 170 B3
Farlesthorpe 239 E5
Farleton *Cumb.* 249 G4
Farleton *Lancs.* 242 B1
Farley *Derbys.* 223 D1
Farley *Shrop.* 206 C2
Farley *Staffs.* 222 B3
Farley *Wilts.* 168 D5
Farley Green *Suff.* 201 F2
Farley Green *Surr.* 171 F3
Farley Hill 170 C1
Farleys End 181 G1
Farlington 245 F1
Farlow 207 F4
Farm Town 209 F1
Farmborough 167 D1
Farmcote 196 C5
Farmington 182 D1
Farmoor 183 G2
Farmtown 324 A4
Farnborough *Gt.Lon.* 172 D2
Farnborough *Hants.* 171 D2
Farnborough *W.Berks.* 183 G4
Farnborough *Warks.* 197 G3
Farnborough Street 171 D2
Farncombe 171 E3
Farndish 199 E1
Farndon *Ches.* 220 B2
Farndon *Notts.* 224 C2
Farne Islands 279 G3
Farnell 303 E4
Farnham *Dorset* 155 F1
Farnham *Essex* 200 C5
Farnham *N.Yorks.* 244 C1
Farnham *Suff.* 203 E1
Farnham *Surr.* 170 D3
Farnham Common 185 E4
Farnham Green 200 C5
Farnham Royal 185 E4
Farningham 173 E2
Farnley *N.Yorks.* 244 B3
Farnley *W.Yorks.* 244 B4
Farnley Tyas 235 F1
Farnsfield 224 B2
Farnworth *Gt.Man.* 234 B2
Farnworth *Halton* 233 G4
Farr *High.* 335 G2
Farr *High.* 309 F1
Farr *High.* 310 A4
Farr House 309 F1
Farraline 309 E2
Farringdon 152 D3
Farrington Gurney 166 D2
Farsley 244 B4
Farthing Corner 174 A2
Farthing Green 174 A4
Farthinghoe 198 A4
Farthingstone 198 B2
Farthorpe 238 C5
Fartown 235 F1
Farway 153 E3
Fasag 319 E4
Fasagrianach 320 A1
Fascadale 297 E2
Faslane 282 D1
Fasnacloich 298 C5
Fasnakyle 308 C2
Fassfern 298 C2
Fatfield 262 C2
Fattahead 324 B4
Faugh 260 B2
Fauldhouse 284 D3
Faulkbourne 187 G1
Faulkland 167 E2
Fauls 220 C4
Faulston 168 B5
Faversham 174 C2
Favillar 311 E1
Fawdington 252 D5
Fawdon 262 B1
Fawfieldhead 222 B1
Fawkham Green 173 E2
Fawler 183 F1
Fawley *Bucks.* 184 C4
Fawley *Hants.* 157 D2
Fawley *W.Berks.* 183 F4
Fawley Chapel 195 E5
Fawsyde 303 G2
Faxfleet 246 A5
Faxton 210 C5
Faygate 172 B5
Fazakerley 233 E3
Fazeley 209 E2
Fearby 252 A4
Fearn 322 A2
Fearnan 300 C5
Fearnbeg 318 D4
Fearnhead 234 A3
Fearnmore 318 D3
Fearnoch *Arg. & B.* 282 B2
Fearnoch *Arg. & B.* 282 A1
Featherstone *Staffs.* 208 B2
Featherstone *W.Yorks.* 244 D5
Featherstone Castle 260 C1
Feckenham 196 C1
Feering 201 G5
Feetham 251 E3
Feith-hill 324 B5
Feizor 243 D1
Felbridge 172 C5
Felbrigg 228 D2
Felbrigg Hall 79
Felcourt 172 C4
Felden 185 F2
Felhampton 206 D4
Felindre *Carmar.* 192 D5
Felindre *Carmar.* 192 B5
Felindre *Carmar.* 191 G4
Felindre *Carmar.* 192 C4
Felindre *Cere.* 192 B2
Felindre *Powys* 206 A4
Felindre *Powys* 194 A5
Felindre *Swan.* 178 C2
Felinfach *Cere.* 192 B2
Felinfach *Powys* 193 G4
Felinfoel 178 B2
Felingwmisaf 192 B5
Felingwmuchaf 192 B5
Felixkirk 253 D4
Felixstowe 203 E4
Felixstowe Ferry 203 E4
Felkington 287 G5
Fell Foot Park 95
Felldownhead 149 D2
Felling 262 B1
Fellonmore 289 F2
Felmersham 199 E2
Felmingham 229 D3
Felpham 158 B4
Felsham 202 A2
Felsted 201 E5
Feltham 186 A5
Felthamhill 186 A5
Felthorpe 228 C4
Felton *Here.* 195 E3
Felton *N.Som.* 166 C1
Felton *Northumb.* 271 D1
Felton Butler 206 C1
Feltwell 213 F3
Fen Ditton 200 C1
Fen Drayton 200 B1
Fen End 209 E5
Fen Street *Norf.* 214 A2
Fen Street *Norf.* 214 B4
Fen Street *Suff.* 214 A4
Fen Street *Suff.* 202 C1
Fenay Bridge 235 F1
Fence 243 E4
Fence Houses 262 C2
Fencott 184 A1
Fendike Corner 226 C1
Fenham 279 E2
Fenhouses 226 A3
Feniscowles 242 C5
Feniton 153 E3
Fenn Street 187 G5
Fenni-fach 193 G5
Fenny Bentley 222 C2
Fenny Bridges 153 E3
Fenny Compton 197 G2
Fenny Drayton 209 F3
Fenny Stratford 199 D4
Fenrother 271 D2
Fenstanton 200 B1
Fenton *Cambs.* 212 B5
Fenton *Lincs.* 237 F5
Fenton *Lincs.* 225 D2
Fenton *Northumb.* 279 D3
Fenton *Notts.* 237 E4
Fenton *Stoke* 221 F3
Fenton Barns 286 C1
Fenton House 56
Fenwick *E.Ayr.* 283 F5
Fenwick *Northumb.* 270 C4
Fenwick *Northumb.* 279 E2
Fenwick *S.Yorks.* 236 C1
Feochaig 272 C4
Feock 145 F3
Feolin 280 D3
Feolin Ferry 280 C3
Feorlan 272 B5
Feorlin 290 B5
Ferguslie Park 283 F3
Feriniquarrie 317 E4
Fern 302 C3
Ferndale 179 F3
Ferndown 155 G2
Ferness 322 B5
Fernham 183 E3
Fernhill Heath 196 A2
Fernhurst 171 D5
Fernie 294 B3
Fernilea 305 G1
Fernilee 235 E5
Fernybank 302 D2
Ferrensby 244 C1
Ferrindonald 306 C4
Ferring 158 C3
Ferry Hill 212 B4
Ferrybridge 245 D5
Ferryden 303 F4
Ferryhill 262 B4
Ferryside (Glanyferi) 177 G1
Fersfield 214 B3
Fersit 299 F2
Ferwig 191 E3
Feshiebridge 310 A4
Fetcham 171 G2
Fetlar 345 F3
Fetterangus 325 E4
Fettercairn 303 E2
Fetternear House 312 C3
Feus of Caldhame 303 E3
Fewcott 198 A5
Fewston 244 A2
Ffairfach 192 C5
Ffair-Rhos 192 D1
Ffaldybrenin 192 C3
Ffarmers 192 C3
Ffawyddog 180 B1
Ffestiniog (Llan Ffestiniog) 218 A3
Ffestiniog Railway 110
Ffordd-las *Denb.* 219 E1
Ffordd-las *Powys* 194 B4
Fforest 178 B2
Fforest-fach 178 C3
Ffostrasol 191 G3
Ffos-y-ffin 192 A1
Ffridd Uchaf 217 E2
Ffrith *Denb.* 232 B4
Ffrith *Flints.* 219 F2
Ffrwdgrech 193 G5
Ffynnon 177 G1
Ffynnon Taf (Taff's Well) 180 A4
Ffynnongroyw 232 C4
Fibhig 329 D3
Fichlie 311 G3
Fidden 288 C2
Fiddington *Glos.* 196 B4
Fiddington *Som.* 165 F3
Fiddleford 155 E1
Fiddler's Green *Glos.* 196 B5
Fiddler's Green *Here.* 195 E4
Fiddler's Green *Norf.* 213 G1
Fiddler's Green *Norf.* 214 B2
Fiddlers Hamlet 187 D2
Field 222 B4
Field Broughton 249 E4
Field Dalling 228 B2
Field Head 209 G2
Fife Folk Museum 122
Fife Keith 323 G4
Fifehead Magdalen 167 E5
Fifehead Neville 155 D1
Fifehead St. Quintin 155 D1
Fifield *Oxon.* 183 E1
Fifield *W. & M.* 185 E5
Fifield Bavant 168 B5
Figheldean 168 C3
Filby 229 F4
Filey 255 E4
Filgrave 199 D3
Filham 150 C2
Filkins 183 E2
Filleigh *Devon* 163 G3
Filleigh *Devon* 152 A1
Fillingham 237 G4
Fillongley 209 E4
Filmore Hill 170 B5
Filton 181 F5
Fimber 246 A1
Finavon 302 C4
Finch Foundry 29
Fincham 213 E2
Finchampstead 170 C1
Finchdean 157 G1
Finchingfield 201 E4
Finchley 186 B3
Findern 223 E4
Findhorn 322 C3
Findhorn Bridge 310 A2
Findhuglen 292 C3
Findo Gask 293 F2
Findochty 323 G3
Findon *Aber.* 313 E5
Findon *W.Suss.* 158 D3
Findon Mains 321 F3
Findon Valley 158 D3
Findrassie 323 D3
Findron 311 D3
Finedon 211 E5
Finegand 301 G3
Fingal Street 214 D4
Fingal's Cave (see Staffa) 130
Fingask 312 C2
Fingerpost 207 G5
Fingest 184 C3
Finghall 252 A4
Fingland *Cumb.* 259 F1
Fingland *D. & G.* 276 D5
Fingland *D. & G.* 275 F4
Finglesham 175 F3
Fingringhoe 202 B5
Finkle Street 236 A3
Finkley Down Farm Park 44
Finlarig 292 A1
Finlaystone House Gardens 122
Finmere 198 B4
Finnart *Arg. & B.* 291 E5
Finnart *P. & K.* 300 A4
Finney Hill 209 G1
Finningham 202 B1
Finningley 237 D3
Finnygaud 324 B4
Finsbay (Fionnsbhagh) 326 C5
Finsbury 186 C4
Finstall 208 B5
Finsthwaite 249 E4
Finstock 183 F1
Finstown 340 B5
Fintry *Aber.* 324 C4
Fintry *Stir.* 284 A1
Finwood 197 D1
Finzean 312 A5
Fionnphort 288 B2
Fionnsbhagh (Finsbay) 326 C5
Fir Tree 262 A4
Firbank 250 B3
Firbeck 236 C4
Firby *N.Yorks.* 252 B4
Firby *N.Yorks.* 245 G1
Firgrove 234 D1
Firle Place 44
Firs Lane 234 A2
Firsby 226 C1
Firsdown 168 D4
Firth 344 D5
Fishbourne *I.o.W.* 157 E3
Fishbourne *W.Suss.* 158 A3
Fishbourne Roman Palace 44
Fishburn 262 C4
Fishcross 293 E5
Fisherford 312 B1
Fisher's Farm Park 44
Fisher's Pond 169 F5
Fisher's Row 242 A3
Fishersgate 159 E3
Fisherstreet 171 E4
Fisherton *High.* 321 G4
Fisherton *S.Ayr.* 274 A4
Fisherton de la Mere 168 A4
Fishguard (Abergwaun) 190 C4
Fishlake 237 D1
Fishleigh Barton 163 F3
Fishley 229 F4
Fishnish 297 F5
Fishpond Bottom 153 G3
Fishponds 181 F5
Fishpool 234 C2
Fishtoft 226 B3
Fishtoft Drove 226 B3
Fishtown of Usan 303 F4
Fishwick *Lancs.* 242 B4
Fishwick *Sc.Bord.* 287 G4
Fiskerton *Lincs.* 238 A5
Fiskerton *Notts.* 224 C2
Fitling 247 E4
Fittleton 168 C3
Fittleworth 158 C2
Fitton End 212 C1
Fitz 206 D1
Fitzhead 165 E5
Fitzroy 165 E5
Fitzwilliam 236 B1
Fitzwilliam Museum 79
Fiunary 297 F5
Five Acres 181 E1
Five Ash Down 159 G1
Five Ashes 160 A1
Five Bridges 195 F3
Five Houses 156 D4
Five Lanes 180 D3
Five Oak Green 173 F4
Five Oaks *Chan.I.* 150 C5
Five Oaks *W.Suss.* 171 F5
Five Roads 178 A2
Five Turnings 206 B5
Five Wents 174 A3
Fivehead 166 A5
Fivelanes 147 G1
Flack's Green 187 G1
Flackwell Heath 185 D4
Fladbury 196 B3
Fladdabister 342 D4
Flag Fen Bronze Age Centre 79
Flagg 222 C1
Flambards Village Theme Park 29
Flamborough 255 F5
Flamingo Land Theme Park 87
Flamstead 185 F1
Flamstead End 186 C2
Flansham 158 B3
Flanshaw 244 C5
Flasby 243 F2
Flash 222 B1
Flashader 317 G4
Flask Inn 254 C2
Flatford Mill & Bridge Cottage 79
Flatt, The 269 D4
Flaunden 185 F2
Flawborough 224 C3
Flawith 245 D1
Flax Bourton 166 C1
Flax Moss 243 D5
Flaxby 244 C2
Flaxholme 223 E3
Flaxlands 214 C2
Flaxley 181 F1
Flaxpool 165 E4
Flaxton 245 F1
Fleckney 210 B3
Flecknoe 198 A1
Fledborough 237 F5
Fleece Inn, The 65
Fleet *Hants.* 170 D2
Fleet *Hants.* 157 G2
Fleet *Lincs.* 226 B5
Fleet Air Arm Museum 29
Fleet Hargate 226 B5
Fleetville 186 A2
Fleetwood 241 G3
Fleggburgh (Burgh Saint Margaret) 229 F4
Flemingston 179 G5
Flemington 284 A4
Flempton 201 G1
Fleoideabhagh 326 C5
Flesherin 329 G4
Fletchersbridge 147 F3
Fletchertown 259 F2
Fletching 159 G1
Flete 150 C2
Fleuchats 311 F4
Fleur-de-lis 180 A3
Flexbury 162 C5
Flexford 171 E2
Flimby 258 D3
Flimwell 173 G5
Flint (Y Fflint) 232 D5
Flint Cross 200 C3
Flint Mountain 232 D5
Flintham 224 C3
Flinton 247 E4
Flint's Green 209 E5
Flishinghurst 173 G5
Flitcham 227 F5
Flitholme 250 C1
Flitton 199 F4
Flitwick 199 F4
Flixborough 237 F1
Flixton *Gt.Man.* 234 B3
Flixton *N.Yorks.* 254 D5
Flixton *Suff.* 215 E3
Flockton 235 G1
Flockton Green 235 G1
Flodden 278 D3
Flodigarry 318 A2
Flood's Ferry 212 B3
Flookburgh 249 E5
Floors 323 G4
Floors Castle 122
Flordon 214 C2
Flore 198 B1
Flotta 338 C3
Flotterton 270 C1
Flowton 202 B3
Flushdyke 244 B5
Flushing *Aber.* 325 F5
Flushing *Cornw.* 145 F3
Flushing *Cornw.* 145 E4
Fluxton 153 D3
Flyford Flavell 196 B2
Foals Green 215 D4
Fobbing 187 G4
Fochabers 323 F4
Fochriw 180 A2
Fockerby 237 F1
Fodderletter 310 D2
Fodderty 321 E4
Foddington 166 C5
Foel 205 F1
Foelgastell 178 B1
Foggathorpe 245 G4
Fogo 287 E5
Fogorig 287 E5
Fogwatt 323 E4
Foindle 334 A4
Folda 301 G3
Fole 222 B4
Foleshill 209 F4
Folke 154 C1
Folkestone 175 E5
Folkingham 225 F4
Folkington 160 A3
Folksworth 211 G4
Folkton 255 D5
Folla Rule 312 C1
Follifoot 244 C2
Folly *Dorset* 154 D2
Folly *Pembs.* 190 C5
Folly Gate 149 F1
Folly, The 186 A1
Fonmon 165 D1
Fonthill Bishop 168 A4
Fonthill Gifford 168 A4
Fontmell Magna 155 E1
Fontmell Parva 155 E1
Fontwell 158 B3
Font-y-gary 165 D1
Foolow 235 F5
Footherley 208 D2
Foots Cray 187 D5
Forbestown 311 F3
Force Forge 249 E3
Force Green 172 D3
Forcett 252 A1
Forches Cross 152 A2
Ford *Arg. & B.* 290 A4
Ford *Bucks.* 184 C2
Ford *Devon* 150 C2
Ford *Devon* 163 E3
Ford *Devon* 151 D3
Ford *Glos.* 196 C5
Ford *Mersey.* 233 E3
Ford *Midloth.* 286 A3
Ford *Northumb.* 279 D3
Ford *Pembs.* 190 C5
Ford *Plym.* 150 A2
Ford *Shrop.* 206 D1
Ford *Som.* 165 D5
Ford *Staffs.* 222 B2
Ford *W.Suss.* 158 B3
Ford *Wilts.* 182 A5
Ford End 187 F1
Ford Green 242 A3
Ford Heath 206 D1
Ford Street 153 E1
Forda 149 F1
Fordbridge 209 D4
Fordcombe 173 E4
Forde Abbey 29
Fordell 285 F1
Forden 206 B2
Forder Green 151 D1
Fordgate 166 A4
Fordham *Cambs.* 213 E5
Fordham *Essex* 202 A5
Fordham *Norf.* 213 E3
Fordham Abbey 201 E1
Fordham Heath 202 A5
Fordhouses 208 B2
Fordingbridge 156 A1
Fordon 255 D5
Fordoun 303 F2
Ford's Green 202 B1
Fordstreet 202 A5
Fordwells 183 F1
Fordwich 175 D3
Fordyce 324 A3
Forebrae 293 E2
Forebridge 221 G5
Foredale 243 E1
Foreland 280 A3
Foremark 223 E5
Forest 252 B2
Forest Coal Pit 194 B5
Forest Gate 186 D4
Forest Green 171 G3
Forest Hall *Cumb.* 249 G2
Forest Hall *T. & W.* 262 B1
Forest Head 260 B2
Forest Hill *Gt.Lon.* 186 C5
Forest Hill *Oxon.* 184 A2
Forest Lane Head 244 C2
Forest Lodge *Arg. & B.* 299 E5
Forest Lodge *P. & K.* 301 E2
Forest Mill 293 E5
Forest of Dean 29
Forest Row 172 D5
Forest Side 157 D4
Forest Town 223 G1
Forestburn Gate 270 C2
Forest-in-Teesdale 261 E5
Forestside 157 G1
Forfar 302 C4
Forgandenny 293 F3
Forge 205 D3
Forge, The 194 C2
Forgie 323 F4
Forhill 208 C5
Formby 233 D2
Formby Red Squirrel Reserve 95
Forncett End 214 C2
Forncett St. Mary 214 C2
Forncett St. Peter 214 C2
Forneth 301 F5
Fornham All Saints 201 G1
Fornham St. Martin 201 G1
Fornighty 322 B4
Forres 322 C4
Forrest 284 C3
Forrest Lodge 265 G2
Forsbrook 221 G3
Forse 337 E5
Forsie 336 C2
Forsinain 336 B4
Forsinard 336 A4
Forstal, The *E.Suss.* 173 E5
Forstal, The *Kent* 174 C5
Forston 154 C3
Fort Augustus 308 C4
Fort Brockhurst 44
Fort George *High.* 321 G4
Fort George *High.* 123
Fort Victoria Country Park 44
Fort William 298 D2
Forter 301 G3
Forteviot 293 F3
Forth 284 D4
Forthampton 196 A4
Fortingall 300 C5
Fortis Green 186 B4
Forton *Hants.* 169 F3
Forton *Lancs.* 242 A2
Forton *Shrop.* 206 D1
Forton *Som.* 153 G2
Forton *Staffs.* 221 E5
Fortrie 324 B5
Fortrose 321 G4
Fortuneswell 154 C5
Forty Green 185 E3
Forty Hill 186 C3
Forward Green 202 B2
Fosbury 169 E2
Foscot 197 E5
Fosdyke 226 B4
Foss 300 C4
Foss Cross 182 C2
Fossdale 251 D3
Fossebridge 182 C1
Foster Street 187 D2
Fosterhouses 236 D1
Foster's Booth 198 B2
Foston *Derbys.* 222 C4
Foston *Leics.* 210 B3
Foston *Lincs.* 225 D3
Foston *N.Yorks.* 245 F1
Foston on the Wolds 246 D2
Fotherby 238 D3
Fotheringhay 211 F3
Foubister 339 E2
Foul Mile 160 B2
Foula 342 B5
Foulbog 276 D5
Foulden *Norf.* 213 F3
Foulden *Sc.Bord.* 287 G4
Foulness Island 188 D3
Foulridge 243 E3
Foulsham 228 B3
Foulstone 249 G4
Foulzie 324 C3
Fountainhall 286 B5
Fountains Abbey & Studley Royal Water Garden 87
Four Ashes *Staffs.* 208 B2
Four Ashes *Staffs.* 208 A4
Four Ashes *Suff.* 214 A4
Four Crosses *Denb.* 218 D3
Four Crosses *Powys* 206 B1
Four Crosses *Powys* 205 G2
Four Crosses *Staffs.* 208 B2
Four Elms 173 D4
Four Forks 165 F4
Four Gotes 212 C1
Four Lane Ends *B'burn.* 242 C5
Four Lane Ends *Ches.* 220 C1
Four Lane Ends *York* 245 F2
Four Lanes 145 D3
Four Marks 170 B4
Four Mile Bridge 230 A5
Four Oaks *E.Suss.* 161 D1
Four Oaks *Glos.* 195 F5
Four Oaks *W.Mid.* 209 E4
Four Oaks *W.Mid.* 208 D3
Four Oaks Park 208 D3
Four Roads 178 A2
Four Throws 160 C1
Fourlane Ends 223 E2
Fourlanes End 221 F2
Fourpenny 332 D5
Fourstones 261 E1
Fovant 168 B5
Foveran House 313 E2
Fowey 147 F4
Fowlis 294 B1
Fowlis Wester 293 E2
Fowlmere 200 C3
Fownhope 195 E4
Fox Hatch 187 E3
Fox Lane 171 D2
Fox Street 202 B3
Foxbar 283 F3

Foxcombe Hill 183 G2
Foxcote Glos. 182 C1
Foxcote Som. 167 E2
Foxdale 240 A4
Foxearth 201 G3
Foxfield 248 D4
Foxham 182 B5
Foxhole Cornw. 147 D4
Foxhole High. 309 E1
Foxholes 254 D5
Foxhunt Green 160 A2
Foxley Here. 194 D3
Foxley Norf. 228 B3
Foxley Northants. 198 B2
Foxley Wilts. 182 A4
Foxt 222 B3
Foxton Cambs. 200 C3
Foxton Dur. 262 C5
Foxton Leics. 210 B3
Foxton Locks 72
Foxup 251 D5
Foxwist Green 220 D1
Foy 195 E5
Foyers 309 D2
Frachadil 296 C4
Fraddam 144 C3
Fraddon 146 D4
Fradley 209 D1
Fradswell 221 G4
Fraisthorpe 247 D1
Framfield 159 G1
Framingham Earl 229 D5
Framingham Pigot 229 D5
Framlingham 203 D1
Framlingham Castle 79
Frampton Dorset 154 C3
Frampton Lincs. 226 B4
Frampton Cotterell 181 F4
Frampton Mansell 182 B2
Frampton on Severn 181 G2
Frampton West End 226 A3
Framsden 202 D2
Framwellgate Moor 262 B3
France Lynch 182 B2
Frances Green 242 C4
Franche 208 A5
Frandley 234 A5
Frankby 232 D4
Frankfort 229 E3
Frankley 208 C4
Franksbridge 194 A2
Frankton 209 G5
Frant 173 E5
Fraserburgh 325 E3
Frating 202 B5
Fratton 157 F2
Freasley 209 E3
Freathy 149 D5
Freckenham 213 E5
Freckleton 242 A5
Freeby 224 D5
Freefolk 169 F3
Freehay 222 B3
Freeland 183 G1
Freester 343 D2
Freethorpe 229 F5
Freethorpe Common 229 F5
Freiston 226 B3
Freiston Shore 226 B3
Fremington Devon 163 F2
Fremington N.Yorks. 251 F3
Frenchay 181 F5
Frenchbeer 149 G2
Frendraught 324 B5
Frenich 291 G4
Frensham 170 D3
Fresgoe 336 B2
Freshbrook 182 D4
Freshfield 233 D2
Freshford 167 E2
Freshwater 156 C4
Freshwater Bay 156 C4
Freshwater East 176 D3
Fressingfield 215 D4
Freston 202 C4
Freswick 337 F2
Fretherne 181 G2
Frettenham 228 D4
Freuchie 294 A4
Freystrop Cross 176 C1
Friars Carse 266 D2
Friar's Gate 173 D5
Friarton 293 G2
Friday Bridge 212 C2
Friday Street E.Suss. 160 B3
Friday Street Suff. 202 D2
Friday Street Suff. 203 E2
Friday Street Surr. 171 G3
Fridaythorpe 246 A2
Friern Barnet 186 B3
Friesthorpe 238 A4
Frieston 225 E3
Frieth 184 C3
Frilford 183 G3
Frilsham 184 A5
Frimley 171 D2
Frimley Green 171 D2
Frindsbury 173 G2
Fring 227 F4
Fringford 198 B5
Friningham 174 A3
Frinsted 174 A3
Frinton-on-Sea 189 F1
Friockheim 303 D4
Friog 204 C1
Frisby on the Wreake 210 B1
Friskney 226 C2
Friskney Eaudyke 226 C2
Friston E.Suss. 160 A4
Friston Suff. 203 F1
Fritchley 223 E2
Frith 174 B3
Frith Bank 226 B3
Frith Common 195 F1
Fritham 156 B1
Frithelstock 163 E4
Frithelstock Stone 163 E4
Frithville 226 B2
Frittenden 174 A4
Frittiscombe 151 E3
Fritton Norf. 214 D2
Fritton Norf. 229 F5
Fritton Lake Countryworld 79
Fritwell 198 A5
Frizinghall 244 A4
Frizington 258 D5
Frocester 181 G2
Frochas 206 B2
Frodesley 207 E2
Frodesley Lane 207 E2
Frodingham 237 F1
Frodsham 233 G5
Frog End 200 C2
Frog Pool 195 G1
Frogden 278 B4
Froggatt 235 G5
Froghall 222 B3
Frogham 156 A1
Frogland Cross 181 F4
Frogmore Devon 151 D3
Frogmore Hants. 170 D2
Frogmore Herts. 186 A2
Frogwell 148 D4
Frolesworth 210 A3
Frome 167 E3
Frome Market 167 F2
Frome St. Quintin 154 B2
Frome Whitfield 154 C3
Fromes Hill 195 F3
Fron Gwyn. 216 C4
Fron Powys 206 B2
Fron Powys 193 G1
Fron Powys 206 A3
Fron Isaf 219 F4
Froncysyllte 219 F3
Fron-goch 218 C4
Frostenden 215 F3
Frosterley 261 G4
Froxfield 169 E1
Froxfield Green 170 C5
Fryerning 187 F2
Fugglestone St. Peter 168 C4
Fulbeck 225 E2
Fulbourn 200 D2
Fulbrook 183 E1
Fulflood 169 F5
Fulford Som. 165 F5
Fulford Staffs. 221 G4
Fulford York 245 F3
Fulham 186 B5
Fulking 159 E2
Full Sutton 245 G2
Fullaford 163 G2
Fuller Street 187 G1
Fuller's Moor 220 B2
Fullerton 169 E4
Fulletby 238 C5
Fullwood 283 F4
Fulmer 185 F4
Fulmodeston 228 A2
Fulnetby 238 B5
Fulready 197 E3
Fulstone 235 F2
Fulstow 238 D3
Fulwell Oxon. 197 F5
Fulwell T. & W. 262 C2
Fulwood Lancs. 242 B4
Fulwood S.Yorks. 236 A4
Fundenhall 214 C2
Fundenhall Street 214 C2
Funtington 158 A3
Funtley 157 E2
Funzie 345 F3
Furley 153 F2
Furnace Arg. & B. 290 C4
Furnace Carmar. 178 B2
Furnace Cere. 204 C3
Furnace High. 319 F2
Furnace End 209 E3
Furner's Green 159 G1
Furness Abbey 95
Furness Vale 235 E4
Furneux Pelham 200 C5
Furnham 153 G2
Further Quarter 174 A5
Furtho 198 C3
Furze Green 214 D3
Furze Platt 185 D4
Furzehill Devon 164 A3
Furzehill Dorset 155 G2
Furzeley Corner 157 F1
Furzey Lodge 156 C2
Furzley 156 B1
Fyfett 153 F1
Fyfield Essex 187 E2
Fyfield Glos. 183 E2
Fyfield Hants. 169 D3
Fyfield Oxon. 183 G3
Fyfield Wilts. 168 C1
Fyfield Wilts. 168 C1
Fylingthorpe 254 C2
Fyning 170 D5
Fyvie 312 C1
Fyvie Castle 123

G

Gabalfa 180 A5
Gabhsunn Bho Dheas 329 F2
Gabhsunn Bho Thuath 329 F2
Gablon 332 C5
Gabroc Hill 283 F4
Gaddesby 210 B1
Gaddesden Row 185 F1
Gadebridge 185 F2
Gadshill 187 G5
Gaer Newport 180 B4
Gaer Powys 194 A5
Gaer-fawr 180 D3
Gaerllwyd 180 D3
Gaerwen 230 C5
Gagingwell 197 G5
Gaich High. 310 C2
Gaich High. 309 F1
Gaick Lodge 300 C1
Gailes 274 B2
Gailey 208 B1
Gainford 252 A1
Gainsborough 237 F3
Gainsborough Old Hall 72
Gainsborough's House 79
Gainsford End 201 F4
Gairloch 319 D2
Gairlochy 299 D1
Gairney Bank 293 G5
Gairnshiel Lodge 311 E4
Gaitsgill 259 G2
Galabank 286 B5
Galashiels 277 F2
Galdenoch 264 C4
Gale 234 D1
Galgate 242 A2
Galhampton 166 D5
Gallanach 290 A2
Gallantry Bank 220 C2
Gallatown 294 A5
Gallchoille 289 G5
Gallery 303 E3
Gallery of Modern Art 123
Galley Common 209 F3
Galleyend 187 G2
Galleywood 187 G2
Gallowfauld 302 C5
Gallowhill 283 F3
Gallows Green 222 B3
Gallowstree Common 184 B4
Gallowstree Elm 208 A4
Gallt Melyd (Meliden) 232 B4
Galltair 307 E2
Gallt-y-foel 217 E1
Gallypot Street 173 D5
Galmington 165 F5
Galmisdale 297 D1
Galmpton Devon 150 C3
Galmpton Torbay 151 E2
Galmpton Warborough 151 E2
Galphay 252 B5
Galston 274 C2
Galtrigill 317 E4
Gamble's Green 187 G1
Gamblesby 260 C4
Gamelsby 259 F1
Gamesley 235 E3
Gamlingay 200 A2
Gamlingay Cinques 200 A2
Gamlingay Great Heath 200 A2
Gammaton 163 E3
Gammaton Moor 163 E3
Gammersgill 251 F4
Gamrie 324 C3
Gamston Notts. 237 E5
Gamston Notts. 224 B4
Ganarew 181 E1
Gang 148 D4
Ganllwyd 218 A5
Gannochy 303 E2
Ganstead 247 D4
Ganthorpe 253 F5
Ganton 254 C5
Ganwick Corner 186 B3
Gaodhail 289 F1
Gappah 152 B5
Gara Bridge 150 D2
Garabal 291 F3
Garadheancal 330 B4
Garbat 320 D3
Garbhallt 290 C5
Garboldisham 214 B3
Garden 292 A5
Garden City 220 A1
Garden Village 235 G3
Gardeners Green 170 D1
Gardenstown 324 C3
Garderhouse 342 C3
Gardham 246 B3
Gare Hill 167 E3
Garelochhead 291 E5
Garford 183 G3
Garforth 244 D4
Gargrave 243 F2
Gargunnock 292 C5
Gariob 281 F1
Garlic Street 214 D3
Garlies Castle 265 F4
Garlieston 257 E2
Garlinge Green 174 D3
Garlogie 312 C4
Garmelow 221 F5
Garmond 324 D4
Garmony 297 F5
Garmouth 323 F3
Garmston 207 F2
Garnant 178 C1
Garndolbenmaen 217 D3
Garneddwen 205 D2
Garnett Bridge 249 G3
Garnfadryn 216 B4
Garnswllt 178 C2
Garrabost 329 G4
Garrachra 282 B1
Garralburn 323 G4
Garras 145 E4
Garreg 217 F3
Garreg Bank 206 B1
Garrett's Green 209 D4
Garrick 292 D3
Garrigill 260 D3
Garriston 252 A3
Garroch 265 G2
Garrochty 282 B4
Garros 318 A3
Garrow 292 D1
Garryhorn 265 G1
Garrynahine (Gearraidh na h-Aibhne) 328 D4
Garsdale 250 C4
Garsdale Head 250 C3
Garsdon 182 B4
Garshall Green 221 G4
Garsington 184 A2
Garstang 242 A3
Garston 233 F4
Garswood 233 G3
Gartachoil 292 A5
Gartally 309 D1
Gartavaich 281 G4
Gartbreck 280 A4
Gartcosh 284 A3
Garth Bridgend 179 E3
Garth Cere. 204 C4
Garth Gwyn. 231 D5
Garth I.o.M. 240 B4
Garth Powys 193 F3
Garth Shet. 342 B2
Garth Wrex. 219 F3
Garth Row 249 G3
Garthbrengy 193 G4
Garthdee 313 E4
Gartheli 192 B2
Garthmyl 206 A3
Garthorpe Leics. 224 D5
Garthorpe N.Lincs. 237 F1
Garths 249 G3
Garthynty 192 D3
Gartincaber 292 B4
Gartly 312 A1
Gartmore 292 A5
Gartnagrenach 281 F4
Gartnatra 280 B3
Gartness 283 G1
Gartocharn 283 F1
Garton 247 E4
Garton-on-the-Wolds 246 B1
Gartymore 333 F3
Garvald 286 C2
Garvamore 309 E5
Garvan 298 B2
Garvard 288 C5
Garve 320 C3
Garveld 272 B5
Garvestone 228 B5
Garvie 282 B1
Garvock Aber. 303 F2
Garvock Inclyde 283 D2
Garvock P. & K. 293 F3
Garwald 276 D5
Garwaldwaterfoot 276 D5
Garway 195 D5
Garway Hill 194 D5
Gask Aber. 325 F5
Gask Aber. 324 C5
Gask P. & K. 293 E3
Gaskan 298 A2
Gass 274 C5
Gastard 167 F1
Gasthorpe 214 A3
Gaston Green 187 E1
Gatcombe 157 D4
Gate Burton 237 F4
Gate Helmsley 245 F2
Gate House 281 D2
Gateacre 233 F4
Gateford 236 C4
Gateforth 245 E5
Gatehead 274 B2
Gatehouse 301 D5
Gatehouse of Fleet 266 A5
Gatelawbridge 266 D1
Gateley 228 A3
Gatenby 252 C4
Gatesgarth 259 E5
Gateshaw 278 B4
Gateshead 262 B1
Gatesheath 220 B1
Gateside Aber. 312 B3
Gateside Angus 302 C5
Gateside Fife 293 G4
Gateside N.Ayr. 283 E4
Gateslack 275 G5
Gathurst 233 G2
Gatley 234 C4
Gattonside 277 G2
Gatwick Airport (London Gatwick Airport) 172 B4
Gaufron 193 F1
Gaulby 210 B2
Gauldry 294 B2
Gauntons Bank 220 C3
Gaunt's Common 155 G2
Gaunt's Earthcott 181 F4
Gautby 238 B5
Gavinton 287 E4
Gawber 236 A2
Gawcott 198 B4
Gawsworth 234 C5
Gawthorpe Hall 95
Gawthrop 250 B4
Gawthwaite 249 D4
Gay Bowers 187 G2
Gay Street 171 F5
Gaydon 197 F2
Gayhurst 198 D3
Gayle 251 D4
Gayles 252 A2
Gayton Mersey. 233 D4
Gayton Norf. 213 F1
Gayton Northants. 198 C2
Gayton Staffs. 221 G5
Gayton le Marsh 239 E4
Gayton le Wold 238 C4
Gayton Thorpe 213 F1
Gaywood 227 E5
Gazeley 201 F1
Geanies House 322 A2
Gearach 280 A4
Gearnsary 335 G5
Gearradh 298 B3
Gearraidh Bhailteas 314 C1
Gearraidh Bhaird 329 E5
Gearraidh na h-Aibhne (Garrynahine) 328 D4
Gearraidh na Monadh 314 C2
Gearrannan 328 C3
Geary 317 F3
Gedding 202 A2
Geddington 211 D4
Gedgrave Hall 203 F3
Gedintailor 306 B1
Gedling 224 B3
Gedney 226 C5
Gedney Broadgate 226 C5
Gedney Drove End 226 C5
Gedney Dyke 226 C5
Gedney Hill 212 B1
Gee Cross 235 D3
Geevor Tin Mine 30
Geffrye Museum 56
Geilston 283 E2
Geirinis 315 F5
Geisiadar 328 C4
Geldeston 215 E2
Gell Conwy 218 B1
Gell Gwyn. 217 D4
Gelli 179 F3
Gelli Gynan 219 E2
Gellideg 179 G2
Gellifor 219 E1
Gelligaer 180 A3
Gellilydan 217 F4
Gellioedd 218 C3
Gelly 177 D1
Gellyburn 293 F1
Gellywen 191 F5
Gelston D. & G. 266 B5
Gelston Lincs. 225 E3
Gembling 246 D2
Gemmil 289 G4
Genoch 264 C5
Genoch Square 264 C5
Gentleshaw 208 C1
Geocrab 326 D4
George Green 185 F4
George Nympton 164 A5
George Stephenson's Birthplace 103
Georgeham 163 E2
Georgetown 283 F3
Georgian House 123
Gerlan 217 F1
Germansweek 149 E1
Germoe 144 C4
Gerrans 145 F3
Gerrards Cross 185 F4
Gerston 336 D3
Gestingthorpe 201 G4
Geuffordd 206 B1
Geufron 205 E4
Gibbet Hill 167 E3
Gibbshill 266 B3
Gibraltar Lincs. 227 D2
Gibraltar Suff. 202 C2
Gibraltar Point 72
Giddeahall 182 A5
Giddy Green 155 E4
Gidea Park 187 E4
Gidleigh 149 G2
Giffnock 283 G4
Gifford 286 C3
Giffordland 283 D5
Giffordtown 294 A3
Giggleswick 243 E1
Gigha 281 E5
Gilberdyke 246 A5
Gilbert's End 196 A3
Gilchriston 286 B3
Gilcrux 259 E3
Gildersome 244 B5
Gildingwells 236 C4
Gilesgate Moor 262 B3
Gileston 164 D1
Gilfach 180 A3
Gilfach Goch 179 F4
Gilfachrheda 192 A2
Gilgarran 258 D4
Gill 260 A5
Gillamoor 253 F4
Gillen 317 F3
Gillenbie 267 F2
Gillfoot 267 D3
Gilling East 253 F5
Gilling West 252 A2
Gillingham Dorset 167 F5
Gillingham Med. 173 G2
Gillingham Norf. 215 F2
Gillivoan 337 D5
Gillock 337 E3
Gillow Heath 221 F2
Gills 337 F1
Gill's Green 173 G5
Gilmanscleuch 277 E3
Gilmerton Edin. 285 G3
Gilmerton P. & K. 293 D2
Gilmilnscroft 275 D3
Gilmonby 251 E1
Gilmorton 210 A4
Gilsland 260 C1
Gilsland Spa 260 C1
Gilson 209 D4
Gilstead 244 A4
Gilston 286 B4
Gilston Park 186 D1
Giltbrook 223 F3
Gilwern 180 B1
Gimingham 229 D2
Gin Pit 234 A2
Ginclough 235 D5
Ginger's Green 160 B2
Giosla 328 C5
Gipping 202 B1
Gipsey Bridge 226 A3
Girlsta 342 D2
Girsby 252 C2
Girtford 199 G3
Girthon 266 A5
Girton Cambs. 200 C1
Girton Notts. 224 D1
Girvan 264 C1
Gisburn 243 E3
Gisburn Cotes 243 E3
Gisleham 215 G3
Gislingham 214 B4
Gissing 214 C3
Gittisham 153 E3
Givons Grove 171 G2
Glackour 320 A1
Gladestry 194 B2
Gladsmuir 286 B2
Gladstone Court Museum 123
Gladstones Land 123
Glaic 282 B2
Glais 178 D2
Glaisdale 253 G2
Glaister 273 E2
Glame 318 B5
Glamis 302 B5
Glamis Castle 123
Glan Conwy 218 B2
Glanaber Terrace 218 A3
Glanaman 178 C1
Glanbran 193 E4
Glan-Denys 192 B2
Glanderston 312 A2
Glandford 228 B1
Glan-Duar 192 B3
Glandwr 191 E5
Glan-Dwyfach 217 D3
Glangrwyney 180 B1
Glanllynfi 179 E3
Glanmule 206 A3
Glan-rhyd N.P.T. 179 D2
Glanrhyd Pembs. 191 E3
Glanton 279 E5
Glanton Pyke 279 E5
Glantwymyn (Cemmaes Road) 205 E2
Glanvilles Wootton 154 C2
Glanwern 204 C4
Glanwydden 231 G4
Glan-y-don 232 C5
Glanyferi (Ferryside) 177 G1
Glan-y-llyn 180 A4
Glan-y-nant 205 F4
Glan-yr-afon Gwyn. 218 C3
Glan-yr-afon Gwyn. 218 D3
Glan-yr-afon I.o.A. 231 E4
Glan-y-Wern 217 F4
Glapthorn 211 F3
Glapwell 223 F1
Glasahoile 291 G4
Glasbury 194 A4
Glaschoil 310 C1
Glascoed Mon. 180 C2
Glascoed Wrex. 219 F2
Glascorrie 311 G5
Glascote 209 E2
Glascwm 194 A2
Glasdrum 298 C5
Glasfryn 218 C2
Glasgow 283 G3
Glasgow Airport 283 F3
Glasgow Botanic Garden 123
Glasgow Prestwick International Airport (Prestwick International Airport) 274 B3
Glasgow School of Art 123
Glasgow Science Centre 123
Glashmore 312 C4
Glasinfryn 217 E1
Glasnacardoch 306 C5
Glasnakille 306 B3
Glaspant 191 F4
Glaspwll 204 D3
Glassburn 308 C1
Glassel 312 B5
Glassenbury 173 G5
Glasserton 257 E3
Glassford 284 B5
Glasshouse 195 G5
Glasshouse Hill 195 G5
Glasshouses 244 A1
Glassingall 292 C4
Glasslie 294 A4
Glasson Cumb. 268 A5
Glasson Lancs. 242 A2
Glassonby 260 B4
Glasterlaw 303 D4
Glaston 211 D2
Glastonbury 166 B4
Glastonbury Abbey 30
Glastonbury Tor 30
Glatton 211 G4
Glazebrook 234 A3
Glazebury 234 A3
Glazeley 207 G4
Gleadless 236 A4
Gleadsmoss 221 F1
Gleann Ghrabhair 329 F5
Gleann Tholastaidh 329 G3
Gleaston 249 D5
Glecknabae 282 B3
Gledhow 244 C4
Gledrid 219 F4
Glemsford 201 G3
Glen D. & G. 266 C3
Glen D. & G. 265 G5
Glen Auldyn 240 C2
Glen Mona 240 C3
Glen Parva 210 A3
Glen Trool Lodge 265 F2
Glen Village 284 C2
Glen Vine 240 B4
Glenae 267 D2
Glenaladale 298 A2
Glenald 291 E5
Glenamachrie 290 B2
Glenapp Castle 264 B2
Glenarm 302 B3
Glenbarr 272 B2
Glenbatrick 280 D2
Glenbeg High. 320 C1
Glenbeg High. 310 C2
Glenbeg High. 297 E3
Glenbeich 292 B2
Glenbervie Aber. 303 F1
Glenbervie Falk. 284 C1
Glenboig 284 B3
Glenborrodale 297 F3
Glenbranter 290 D5
Glenbreck 276 B3
Glenbrittle 306 A2
Glenbuck 275 F3
Glenburn 283 F3
Glenbyre 289 E2
Glencaple 267 D4
Glencarse 293 G2
Glencat 312 A5
Glenceitlein 298 D5
Glencloy 273 F2
Glencoe High. 298 D4
Glencoe High. 123
Glencoe Visitor Centre 123
Glenconglass 311 D2
Glencraig 293 G5
Glencripesdale 297 F4
Glencrosh 266 B2
Glencruittein 290 A2
Glencuie 311 G3
Glendearg D. & G. 276 D5
Glendearg Sc.Bord. 277 G2
Glendessary 307 F5
Glendevon 293 E4
Glendoebeg 308 D4
Glendoick 294 A2
Glendoll Lodge 302 A2
Glendoune 264 C1
Glendrissaig 264 C1
Glenduckie 294 A3
Glenduisk 264 D2
Glendurgan 30
Glendye Lodge 303 E1
Gleneagles Hotel 293 E3
Gleneagles House 293 E4
Glenearn 293 G3
Glenegedale 280 B4
Glenelg 307 E3
Glenfarg 293 G3
Glenfeochan 290 A2
Glenfiddich Distillery 123
Glenfield 210 A2
Glenfinnan 298 B1
Glenfinnan Monument 123
Glenfoot 293 G3
Glengalmadale 298 A4
Glengap 266 A5
Glengarnock 283 E4
Glengarrisdale 289 F5
Glengennet 265 D1
Glengolly 336 D2
Glengrasco 318 A5
Glengyle 291 F3
Glenhead 266 C2
Glenhead Farm 302 A3
Glenhurich 298 A3
Glenkerry 277 D4
Glenkiln 273 F2
Glenkin 282 C1
Glenkindie 311 G3
Glenlair 266 B3
Glenlatterach 323 E4
Glenlean 282 B1
Glenlee Angus 302 C2
Glenlee D. & G. 266 A2
Glenlichorn 292 C3
Glenlivet 311 D2
Glenlochar 266 B4
Glenluce 264 C5
Glenluce Abbey 123
Glenmallan 291 E5
Glenmanna 275 F5
Glenmavis 284 B3
Glenmaye 240 A4
Glenmeanie 320 B4
Glenmore Arg. & B. 282 B3
Glenmore High. 318 A5
Glenmore Lodge 310 B4
Glenmoy 302 C3
Glenmuick 331 F3
Glennoe 290 C1
Glenochar 276 A4
Glenogil 302 C3
Glenprosen Village 302 B3
Glenquiech 302 C3
Glenramskill 272 C4
Glenrazie 265 E4
Glenridding 259 G5
Glenrisdell 281 G4
Glenrossal 331 G4
Glenrothes 294 A4
Glensanda 298 A5
Glensaugh 303 E2
Glensgaich 321 D3
Glenshalg 312 A4
Glenshellish 290 D5
Glensluain 290 C5
Glentaggart 275 G3
Glentham 238 A3
Glenton 312 B2
Glentress 277 D2
Glentrool 265 E3
Glentruan 240 C1
Glenturret Distillery 123
Glentworth 237 G4
Glenuachdarach 318 A4
Glenuig 297 F2
Glenure 298 C5
Glenurquhart 321 G3
Glenwhilly 264 C3
Glespin 275 G3
Gletness 343 D2
Glewstone 195 E5
Glinton 211 G2
Globe Theatre (see Shakespeare's Globe Theatre) 60
Glooston 210 C3

Glororum 279 F3
Glossop 235 E3
Gloster Hill 271 E1
Gloucester 182 A1
Gloucester Cathedral 30
Gloucestershire & Warwickshire Railway 30
Gloup 345 E2
Gloweth 146 B5
Glusburn 243 G3
Gluss 344 C5
Glympton 197 G5
Glyn 218 A2
Glyn Ceiriog 219 F4
Glynarthen 191 G3
Glyncoch 179 G3
Glyncorrwg 179 E3
Glyn-Cywarch 217 F4
Glynde 159 G3
Glyndebourne 159 G2
Glyndyfrdwy 219 E3
Glynn Vivian Art Gallery & Museum 110
Glynneath 179 E2
Glynogwr 179 F4
Glyntaff 179 G4
Gnosall 221 F5
Gnosall Heath 221 F5
Goadby 210 C3
Goadby Marwood 224 C5
Goatacre 182 C5
Goatfield 290 C4
Goathill 154 C1
Goathland 254 B2
Goathurst 165 F4
Gobernuisgeach 336 B5
Gobhaig 326 C3
Gobowen 220 A4
Godalming 171 E3
Goddard's Corner 203 D1
Goddards Green 159 E1
Godden Green 173 E3
Goddington 173 D2
Godford Cross 153 E2
Godington 198 B5
Godleybrook 221 G3
Godmanchester 212 A5
Godmanstone 154 C3
Godmersham 174 C3
Godney 166 B3
Godolphin Cross 144 D3
Godolphin House 30
Godor 206 B1
Godre'r-graig 179 D2
Godshill *Hants.* 156 A1
Godshill *I.o.W.* 157 E4
Godstone 172 C3
Godstone Farm 44
Godwick 228 A3
Goetre 180 C2
Goff's Oak 186 C2
Gogar 285 F2
Gogarth 231 F4
Goginan 204 C4
Goirtean a' Chladaich 298 C2
Goirtein 282 A1
Golan 217 E3
Golant 147 F4
Golberdon 148 D3
Golborne 234 A3
Golcar 235 F1
Gold Hill *Cambs.* 212 D3
Gold Hill *Dorset* 155 E1
Goldcliff 180 C4
Golden Cap 30
Golden Cross 160 A2
Golden Green 173 F4
Golden Grove 178 B1
Golden Pot 170 C3
Golden Valley *Derbys.* 223 F2
Golden Valley *Glos.* 196 B5
Goldenhill 221 F2
Golders Green 186 B4
Goldhanger 188 C2
Goldielea 266 D3
Golding 207 E2
Goldington 199 F2
Goldsborough *N.Yorks.* 254 B1
Goldsborough *N.Yorks.* 244 C2
Goldsithney 144 C3
Goldstone 221 E5
Goldthorn Park 208 B3
Goldthorpe 236 B2
Goldworthy 163 D3
Golford 173 G5
Gollanfield 322 A4
Gollinglith Foot 252 A4
Golspie 332 D5
Golval 336 A2
Gomeldon 168 C4
Gomersal 244 B5
Gometra 296 C5
Gometra House 296 C5
Gomshall 171 F3
Gonachan Cottage 284 A1
Gonalston 224 B3
Gonerby Hill Foot 225 E4
Gonfirth 342 C1
Good Easter 187 F1
Gooderstone 213 F2
Goodleigh 163 G2
Goodmanham 246 A3
Goodmayes 187 D4
Goodnestone *Kent* 175 E3
Goodnestone *Kent* 174 C2
Goodrich 181 E1
Goodrich Castle 65
Goodrington 151 E2
Goodshaw 243 E5
Goodshaw Fold 243 E5
Goodwick (Wdig) 190 C4
Goodworth Clatford 169 E3
Goodyers End 209 F4
Goole 245 G5
Goom's Hill 196 C2
Goonbell 146 B5
Goonhavern 146 B4
Goonhilly Satellite Earth Station 30
Goonvrea 146 B5
Goose Green *Essex* 202 C5
Goose Green *Essex* 202 C5
Goose Green *Gt.Man.* 233 G2
Goose Green *Kent* 173 F3
Goose Green *S.Glos.* 181 F5
Goose Pool 195 D4
Gooseham 162 C4
Goosehill Green 196 B1
Goosewell 150 B2
Goosey 183 F3
Goosnargh 242 B4
Goostrey 234 B5
Gorcott Hill 196 C1
Gorddinog 231 E5
Gordon 286 D5
Gordon Highlanders Regimental Museum 124
Gordonbush 332 D4
Gordonstoun 323 D3
Gordonstown *Aber.* 324 A4
Gordonstown *Aber.* 312 C1
Gore Cross 168 B2
Gore End 169 F1
Gore Pit 188 B1
Gore Street 175 E2
Gorebridge 286 A3
Gorefield 212 C1
Gorey 150 D5
Gorgie 285 G2
Goring 184 B4
Goring Heath 184 B5
Goring-by-Sea 158 D3
Gorleston-on-Sea 229 G5
Gorllwyn 191 G4
Gornalwood 208 B3
Gorrachie 324 C4
Gorran Churchtown 147 D5
Gorran Haven 147 E5
Gors 204 C5
Gorsedd 232 C5
Gorseinon 178 B3
Gorseness 340 C5
Gorseybank 223 D2
Gorsgoch 192 A2
Gorslas 178 B1
Gorsley 195 F5
Gorsley Common 195 F5
Gorstage 234 A5
Gorstan 320 C3
Gorstanvorran 298 A2
Gorsty Hill 222 C5
Gorten 289 G1
Gortenbuie 289 E1
Gorteneorn 297 F3
Gorton *Arg. & B.* 296 A4
Gorton *Gt.Man.* 234 C3
Gosbeck 202 C2
Gosberton 226 A4
Gosberton Clough 225 G5
Goseley Dale 223 E5
Gosfield 201 F5
Gosford *Here.* 195 E1
Gosford *Oxon.* 184 A1
Gosforth *Cumb.* 248 B2
Gosforth *T. & W.* 262 B1
Gosland Green 220 C2
Gosmore 199 G5
Gospel End 208 B3
Gosport 157 F3
Gossabrough 345 E4
Gossington 181 G2
Gossops Green 172 B5
Goswick 279 E2
Gotham 223 G4
Gotherington 196 B5
Gothers 147 D4
Gott 342 D3
Gotton 165 F5
Goudhurst 173 G5
Goulceby 238 C5
Gourdas 324 C5
Gourdon 303 G2
Gourock 282 D2
Govan 283 G3
Goverton 224 C2
Goveton 151 D3
Govilon 180 B1
Gowanhill 325 F3
Gowdall 245 F5
Gower 110
Gowerton 178 B3
Gowkhall 285 E1
Gowthorpe 245 G2
Goxhill *E.Riding* 247 D3
Goxhill *N.Lincs.* 246 D5
Goytre 179 D4
Gozzard's Ford 183 G3
Grabhair 327 F2
Graby 225 F5
Gradbach 221 G1
Grade 145 E5
Gradeley Green 220 C2
Graffham 158 B2
Grafham *Cambs.* 199 G1
Grafham *Surr.* 171 F3
Grafham Water 79
Grafton *Here.* 195 D4
Grafton *N.Yorks.* 244 D1
Grafton *Oxon.* 183 E2
Grafton *Shrop.* 206 D1
Grafton *Worcs.* 195 E1
Grafton *Worcs.* 196 B4
Grafton Flyford 196 B2
Grafton Regis 198 C3
Grafton Underwood 211 E4
Grafty Green 174 A4
Graianrhyd 219 F2
Graig *Carmar.* 178 A2
Graig *Conwy* 231 G5
Graig *Denb.* 232 B5
Graig-fechan 219 E2
Grain 174 A1
Grainel 280 A3
Grainhow 325 D5
Grains Bar 235 D2
Grainsby 238 C3
Grainthorpe 239 D3
Graiselound 237 E3
Gramisdale (Gramsdal) 315 G4
Grampian Transport Museum 124
Grampound 146 D5
Grampound Road 146 D4
Gramsdal (Gramisdale) 315 G4
Granborough 198 C5
Granby 224 C4
Grandborough 197 G1
Grandes Rocques 151 F4
Grandtully 301 E4
Grange *Cumb.* 259 F5
Grange *E.Ayr.* 274 C2
Grange *High.* 308 C1
Grange *Med.* 173 G2
Grange *Mersey.* 232 D4
Grange *P. & K.* 294 A2
Grange Crossroads 323 G4
Grange de Lings 237 G5
Grange Hall 322 C3
Grange Hill 186 D3
Grange Moor 235 G1
Grange of Lindores 294 A3
Grange, The *Lincs.* 239 F5
Grange, The *Shrop.* 220 A4
Grange, The *Surr.* 172 C4
Grange Villa 262 B2
Grangemill 222 D2
Grangemouth 284 D1
Grangemuir 294 D4
Grange-over-Sands 249 F5
Grangeston 264 D1
Grangetown *Cardiff* 180 A5
Grangetown *R. & C.* 263 E5
Granish 310 B3
Gransmoor 246 D2
Granston 190 B4
Grantchester 200 C2
Grantham 225 E4
Grantley 252 B5
Grantlodge 312 C3
Granton 285 G2
Granton House 276 B5
Grantown-on-Spey 310 C2
Grantsfield 195 E1
Grantshouse 287 F3
Grappenhall 234 A4
Grasby 238 A2
Grasmere 249 E2
Grass Green 201 F4
Grasscroft 235 D2
Grassendale 233 E4
Grassgarth 249 F3
Grassholme 261 F5
Grassington 243 G1
Grassmoor 223 F1
Grassthorpe 224 C1
Grateley 169 D3
Gratwich 222 B4
Gravel Hill 185 F3
Graveley *Cambs.* 200 A1
Graveley *Herts.* 200 A5
Gravelly Hill 208 D3
Gravels 206 C2
Graven 344 D5
Graveney 174 C2
Gravesend 187 F5
Grayingham 237 G3
Grayrigg 249 G3
Grays 187 F5
Grayshott 171 D4
Grayswood 171 E4
Grazeley 170 B1
Greasbrough 236 B3
Greasby 233 D4
Great Aberystwyth Camera Obscura 110
Great Abington 200 D3
Great Addington 211 E5
Great Alne 196 D2
Great Altcar 233 E2
Great Amwell 186 C1
Great Asby 250 B1
Great Ashfield 202 A1
Great Ayton 253 E1
Great Baddow 187 G2
Great Bardfield 201 E4
Great Barford 199 G2
Great Barr 208 C3
Great Barrington 183 E1
Great Barrow 220 B1
Great Barton 201 G1
Great Barugh 253 G5
Great Bavington 270 B3
Great Bealings 202 D3
Great Bedwyn 169 D1
Great Bentley 202 C5
Great Bernera 328 C4
Great Billing 198 D1
Great Bircham 227 F4
Great Blakenham 202 C2
Great Bolas 220 D5
Great Bookham 171 G2
Great Bourton 197 G3
Great Bowden 210 C4
Great Bradley 201 E2
Great Braxted 188 B1
Great Bricett 202 B2
Great Brickhill 199 E4
Great Bridgeford 221 F5
Great Brington 198 B1
Great Bromley 202 B5
Great Broughton *Cumb.* 259 D3
Great Broughton *N.Yorks.* 253 E2
Great Buckland 173 F2
Great Budworth 234 A5
Great Burdon 252 C1
Great Burstead 187 F3
Great Busby 253 E2
Great Cambourne 200 B2
Great Canfield 187 E1
Great Canney 188 B2
Great Carlton 239 E4
Great Casterton 211 F2
Great Central Railway 72
Great Chalfield 167 F1
Great Chalfield Manor 30
Great Chart 174 B4
Great Chatwell 207 G1
Great Chell 221 F2
Great Chesterford 200 D3
Great Cheverell 168 A2
Great Chishill 200 C4
Great Clacton 189 E1
Great Clifton 258 D4
Great Coates 238 C2
Great Comberton 196 B3
Great Corby 260 A2
Great Cornard 201 G3
Great Cowden 247 E3
Great Coxwell 183 E3
Great Coxwell Barn 44
Great Crakehall 252 B4
Great Cransley 210 D5
Great Cressingham 213 G2
Great Crosby 233 E2
Great Crosthwaite 259 F4
Great Cubley 222 C4
Great Cumbrae 282 C4
Great Dalby 210 C1
Great Dixter 44
Great Doddington 199 D1
Great Doward 181 E1
Great Dunham 213 G1
Great Dunmow 201 E5
Great Durnford 168 C4
Great Easton *Essex* 201 E5
Great Easton *Leics.* 210 D3
Great Eccleston 242 A3
Great Edstone 253 G4
Great Ellingham 214 B2
Great Elm 167 E3
Great Eversden 200 B2
Great Fencote 252 B3
Great Finborough 202 B2
Great Fransham 213 G1
Great Gaddesden 185 F1
Great Gidding 211 G4
Great Givendale 246 A2
Great Glemham 203 E1
Great Glen 210 B3
Great Gonerby 225 D4
Great Gransden 200 A2
Great Green *Cambs.* 200 A3
Great Green *Norf.* 215 D3
Great Green *Suff.* 202 A2
Great Green *Suff.* 214 C4
Great Green *Suff.* 214 B4
Great Habton 253 G5
Great Hale 225 G3
Great Hallingbury 187 E1
Great Hampden 184 D2
Great Harrowden 211 D5
Great Harwood 242 D4
Great Haseley 184 B2
Great Hatfield 247 D3
Great Haywood 222 B5
Great Heath 209 F4
Great Heck 245 E5
Great Henny 201 G4
Great Hinton 168 A2
Great Hockham 214 A2
Great Holland 189 F1
Great Horkesley 202 A4
Great Hormead 200 C4
Great Horton 244 A4
Great Horwood 198 C4
Great Houghton *Northants.* 198 C2
Great Houghton *S.Yorks.* 236 B2
Great Hucklow 235 F5
Great Kelk 246 D2
Great Kimble 184 D2
Great Kingshill 185 D3
Great Langton 252 B3
Great Leighs 187 G1
Great Limber 238 B2
Great Linford 198 D3
Great Livermere 213 G5
Great Longstone 235 G5
Great Lumley 262 B3
Great Lyth 207 D2
Great Malvern 195 G3
Great Maplestead 201 G4
Great Marton 241 G4
Great Massingham 227 F5
Great Melton 228 C5
Great Milton 184 B2
Great Missenden 185 D2
Great Mitton 242 D4
Great Mongeham 175 F3
Great Moulton 214 C2
Great Munden 200 B5
Great Musgrave 250 C1
Great Ness 206 D1
Great Notley 201 F5
Great Nurcot 164 C4
Great Oak 180 C2
Great Oakley *Essex* 202 C5
Great Oakley *Northants.* 211 D4
Great Offley 199 G5
Great Orme Country Park 110
Great Ormside 250 C1
Great Orton 259 G1
Great Ouseburn 244 D1
Great Oxendon 210 C4
Great Oxney Green 187 F2
Great Palgrave 213 G1
Great Parndon 186 D2
Great Paxton 200 A1
Great Plumpton 241 G4
Great Plumstead 229 E5
Great Ponton 225 E4
Great Potheridge 163 F4
Great Preston 244 C5
Great Purston 198 A4
Great Raveley 212 A4
Great Rissington 183 D1
Great Rollright 197 F4
Great Ryburgh 228 A3
Great Ryle 279 E5
Great Ryton 207 D2
Great Saling 201 F5
Great Salkeld 260 B4
Great Sampford 201 E4
Great Sankey 233 G4
Great Saredon 208 B2
Great Saxham 201 F1
Great Shefford 183 F5
Great Shelford 200 C2
Great Smeaton 252 C2
Great Snoring 228 A2
Great Somerford 182 B4
Great Stainton 262 C5
Great Stambridge 188 C3
Great Staughton 199 G1
Great Steeping 226 C1
Great Stonar 175 F3
Great Strickland 260 B5
Great Stukeley 212 A5
Great Sturton 238 C5
Great Sutton *Ches.* 233 E5
Great Sutton *Shrop.* 207 E4
Great Swinburne 270 B4
Great Tew 44
Great Tey 201 G5
Great Thorness 157 D3
Great Thurlow 201 E3
Great Torr 150 C3
Great Torrington 163 E4
Great Tosson 270 C1
Great Totham *Essex* 188 B1
Great Totham *Essex* 188 B1
Great Tows 238 C3
Great Urswick 249 D5
Great Wakering 188 C4
Great Waldingfield 202 A3
Great Walsingham 228 A2
Great Waltham 187 F1
Great Warley 187 E3
Great Washbourne 196 B4
Great Weeke 152 A4
Great Welnetham 201 G2
Great Wenham 202 B4
Great Whittington 270 C4
Great Wigborough 188 C1
Great Wigsell 160 C1
Great Wilbraham 200 D2
Great Wilne 223 F4
Great Wishford 168 B4
Great Witcombe 182 B1
Great Witley 195 G1
Great Wolford 197 E4
Great Wratting 201 E3
Great Wymondley 200 A5
Great Wyrley 208 B2
Great Wytheford 207 E1
Great Yarmouth 229 G5
Great Yeldham 201 F4
Greatford 211 F1
Greatgate 222 B3
Greatham *Hants.* 170 C4
Greatham *Hart.* 263 D5
Greatham *W.Suss.* 158 C2
Greatness 173 E3
Greatstone-on-Sea 161 F1
Greatworth 198 A3
Green 219 D1
Green Cross 171 D4
Green End *Beds.* 199 G2
Green End *Bucks.* 199 E4
Green End *Cambs.* 212 A5
Green End *Cambs.* 212 B5
Green End *Herts.* 200 B5
Green End *Herts.* 200 B4
Green End *Warks.* 209 E4
Green Hammerton 245 D2
Green Hill 182 C4
Green Lane 196 C1
Green Moor 235 G3
Green Ore 166 C2
Green Quarter 249 F2
Green Street *E.Suss.* 160 C2
Green Street *Herts.* 186 A3
Green Street *Herts.* 200 C5
Green Street *W.Suss.* 171 G5
Green Street *Worcs.* 196 A3
Green Street Green *Gt.Lon.* 173 D2
Green Street Green *Kent* 187 E5
Green, The *Arg. & B.* 296 A2
Green, The *Cumb.* 248 C4
Green, The *Essex* 187 G1
Green, The *Flints.* 219 F1
Green, The *Wilts.* 167 F4
Green Tye 186 D1
Greenburn 302 C5
Greencroft 262 A3
Greendams 303 E1
Greendykes 279 E4
Greenend 197 F5
Greenfaulds 284 B2
Greenfield *Beds.* 199 F4
Greenfield (Maes-Glas) *Flints.* 232 C5
Greenfield *Gt.Man.* 235 E2
Greenfield *High.* 308 B4
Greenfield *Lincs.* 239 E5
Greenfield *Oxon.* 184 C3
Greenford 186 A4
Greengairs 284 B2
Greengates 244 A4
Greengill 259 E3
Greenhalgh 242 A4
Greenhall 312 B2
Greenham 169 F1
Greenhaugh 269 F3
Greenhead 260 C1
Greenheads 313 F1
Greenheys 234 B2
Greenhill *Gt.Lon.* 186 A4
Greenhill *High.* 333 E4
Greenhill *S.Yorks.* 236 A4
Greenhill Covenanters' House 124
Greenhithe 187 E5
Greenholm 274 D2
Greenholme 249 G2
Greenhow Hill 244 A1
Greenigo 338 D2
Greenland 337 E2
Greenlands 184 C4
Greenlaw *Aber.* 324 B4
Greenlaw *Sc.Bord.* 287 E5
Greenloaning 292 D4
Greenmeadow 180 B3
Greenmoor Hill 184 B4
Greenmount 234 B1
Greenmyre 312 D1
Greenock 283 D2
Greenodd 249 E4
Greens Norton 198 B3
Greenscares 292 C3
Greenside *T. & W.* 262 A1
Greenside *W.Yorks.* 235 F1
Greenstead 202 B5
Greenstead Green 201 G5
Greensted 187 E2
Greensted Green 187 E2
Greenway *Pembs.* 191 D4
Greenway *Som.* 166 A5
Greenwell 260 B2
Greenwich 56
Greet 196 C4
Greete 207 E5
Greetham *Lincs.* 238 D5
Greetham *Rut.* 211 E1
Greetland 243 G5
Gregson Lane 242 B5
Greinetobht (Grenitote) 315 G2
Greinton 166 B4
Grenaby 240 A4
Grendon *Northants.* 199 D1
Grendon *Warks.* 209 E3
Grendon Common 209 E3
Grendon Green 195 E2
Grendon Underwood 198 B5
Grenitote (Greinetobht) 315 G2
Grenofen 149 E3
Grenoside 236 A3
Greosabhagh 327 D4
Gresford 220 A2
Gresham 228 C2
Greshornish 317 G4
Gress (Griais) 329 F3
Gressenhall 228 A4
Gressingham 242 B1
Greta Bridge 251 F1
Gretna 268 B5
Gretna Green 268 B5
Gretton *Glos.* 196 C4
Gretton *Northants.* 211 E3
Gretton *Shrop.* 207 E3
Grewelthorpe 252 B5
Grey Mare's Tail 124
Greyfriars, The 65
Greygarth 252 A5
Greylake 166 A4
Grey's Court 45
Greys Green 184 C4
Greysouthen 259 D4
Greystead 269 F3
Greystoke 260 A4
Greystone *Aber.* 311 E5
Greystone *Angus* 302 D5
Greystone *Lancs.* 243 E3
Greystones 236 A4
Greywell 170 C2
Griais (Gress) 329 F3
Gribthorpe 245 G4
Gribton 266 D2
Griff 209 F4
Griffithstown 180 B3
Grigadale 296 D3
Grigghall 249 F3
Grimeford Village 234 A1
Grime's Graves 79
Grimesthorpe 236 A3
Grimethorpe 236 B2
Griminis (Griminish) 315 F4
Griminish (Griminis) 315 F4
Grimister 345 D3
Grimley 196 A1
Grimmet 274 B4
Grimness 339 D3
Grimoldby 239 D4
Grimpo 220 A5
Grimsargh 242 B4
Grimsay (Griomsaigh) 315 G4
Grimsbury 197 G3
Grimsby 238 C2
Grimscote 198 B2
Grimscott 162 C5
Grimshader (Griomsiadar) 329 F5
Grimsthorpe 225 F5
Grimsthorpe Castle 72
Grimston *E.Riding* 247 E4
Grimston *Leics.* 224 B5
Grimston *Norf.* 227 F5
Grimstone 154 C3
Grimstone End 202 A1
Grindale 255 E5
Grindiscol 343 D4
Grindle 207 G2
Grindleford 235 G5
Grindleton 243 D3
Grindley 222 B5
Grindley Brook 220 C3
Grindlow 235 F5
Grindon *Northumb.* 287 G5
Grindon *Staffs.* 222 B2
Grindon *Stock.* 262 C5
Grindon *T. & W.* 262 C2
Gringley on the Hill 237 E3
Grinsdale 259 G1
Grinshill 220 C5
Grinton 251 F3
Griomarstaidh 328 D4
Griomsaigh (Grimsay) 315 G4
Griomsiadar (Grimshader) 329 F5
Grisdale 250 C3
Grishipoll 296 A4
Gristhorpe 255 D4
Griston 214 A2
Gritley 339 E2
Grittenham 182 C4
Grittleton 182 A5
Grizebeck 248 D4
Grizedale 249 E3
Grizedale Forest Park 96
Grobister 341 E4
Groby 210 A2
Groes 218 D1
Groes-faen 179 G4
Groesffordd 216 B4
Groesffordd Marli 232 B5
Groeslon *Gwyn.* 217 D2
Groeslon *Gwyn.* 217 E1
Groes-lwyd 206 B1
Groes-wen 180 A4
Grogport 281 G5
Groigearraidh 304 A1
Gromford 203 E2
Gronant 232 B4
Groombridge 173 E5
Groombridge Place Gardens 45
Grosmont *Mon.* 194 D5
Grosmont *N.Yorks.* 254 B2
Grotaig 309 D2
Groton 202 A3
Groundistone Heights 277 F4
Grouville 150 C5
Grove *Bucks.* 199 E5
Grove *Dorset* 154 C5
Grove *Kent* 175 E2
Grove *Notts.* 237 E5
Grove *Oxon.* 183 G3
Grove End 174 A2
Grove Green 173 G3
Grove Park 186 D5
Grove, The 196 A3
Grove Town 245 D5
Grovehill 185 F2
Grovesend *S.Glos.* 181 F4
Grovesend *Swan.* 178 B2
Gruids 332 A4
Grula 305 G2
Gruline 297 E5
Grumbla 144 B4
Grundcruie 293 F2
Grundisburgh 202 D2
Gruting 342 B3
Grutness 343 G5
Gualachulain 298 D5
Guardbridge 294 C3
Guarlford 196 A3
Guay 301 F5
Gubbergill 248 B3
Gubblecote 185 E1
Guernsey 151 F5
Guernsey Airport 151 E5
Guestling Green 161 D2
Guestling Thorn 161 D2
Guestwick 228 B3
Guestwick Green 228 B3
Guide 242 D5
Guide Post 271 E3
Guilden Down 206 C4
Guilden Morden 200 A3
Guilden Sutton 220 B1
Guildford 171 E3
Guildtown 293 G1
Guilsborough 210 B5
Guilsfield (Cegidfa) 206 B1
Guilthwaite 236 B4
Guisborough 253 F1
Guiseley 244 A3
Guist 228 B3
Guith 341 D3
Guiting Power 196 C5
Gulberwick 342 D4
Gullane 286 B1
Gulval 144 B3
Gulworthy 149 E3
Gumfreston 177 E2
Gumley 210 B3
Gunby *Lincs.* 225 E5
Gunby *Lincs.* 226 C1
Gunby Hall 72
Gundleton 170 B4
Gunn 163 G2
Gunnersbury 186 A5
Gunnerside 251 E3
Gunnerton 270 B4
Gunness 237 F1
Gunnislake 149 E3
Gunnista 343 E3
Gunnister 344 C5
Gunstone 208 A2
Gunter's Bridge 171 E5
Gunthorpe *Norf.* 228 B2
Gunthorpe *Notts.* 224 B3
Gunthorpe *Rut.* 211 D2
Gunville 157 D4
Gunwalloe 145 D4
Gupworthy 164 C4

Gur - Hea

Gurnard 157 D3
Gurnett 234 D5
Gurney Slade 166 D3
Gurnos *M.Tyd.* 179 G2
Gurnos *Powys* 179 D2
Gushmere 174 C3
Gussage All Saints 155 G1
Gussage St. Andrew 155 F1
Gussage St. Michael 155 F1
Guston 175 F4
Gutcher 345 E3
Guthram Gowt 225 G5
Guthrie 303 D4
Guyhirn 212 B2
Guynd 303 D5
Guy's Head 226 C5
Guy's Marsh 167 F5
Guyzance 271 E1
Gwaelod-y-garth 180 A4
Gwaenysgor 232 B4
Gwaithla 194 B2
Gwalchmai 230 B5
Gwastad 190 D5
Gwastadnant 217 F2
Gwaun-Cae-Gurwen 178 D1
Gwaynynog 218 D1
Gwbert 191 E3
Gweek 145 E4
Gwehelog 180 C2
Gwenddwr 193 G3
Gwendreath 145 E5
Gwennap 146 B5
Gwenter 145 E5
Gwernaffield 219 F1
Gwernesney 180 D2
Gwernogle 192 B4
Gwernymynydd 219 F1
Gwern-y-Steeple 179 G5
Gwersyllt 220 A2
Gwespyr 232 C4
Gwinear 144 C3
Gwithian 144 C2
Gwredog 230 C4
Gwrhay 180 A3
Gwyddelwern 219 D3
Gwyddgrug 192 A4
Gwynfryn 219 F2
Gwystre 193 G1
Gwytherin 218 B1
Gyfelia 220 A3
Gyre 338 C2
Gyrn Goch 216 C3

H

Habberley 206 C2
Habin 170 D5
Habrough 238 B1
Haccombe 152 B5
Hacconby 225 G5
Haceby 225 F4
Hacheston 203 E2
Hackbridge 172 B2
Hackenthorpe 236 B4
Hackford 228 B5
Hackforth 252 B3
Hackland 340 B4
Hacklet (Haclait) 315 G5
Hacklete (Tacleit) 328 C4
Hackleton 198 D2
Hacklinge 175 F3
Hackness *N.Yorks.* 254 C3
Hackness *Ork.* 338 C3
Hackney 186 C4
Hackthorn 237 G4
Hackthorpe 260 B5
Haclait (Hacklet) 315 G5
Hacton 187 E4
Hadden 278 B3
Haddenham *Bucks.* 184 C2
Haddenham *Cambs.* 212 C5
Haddington *E.Loth.* 286 C2
Haddington *Lincs.* 225 E1
Haddiscoe 215 F2
Haddo House & Country Park 124
Haddon 211 G3
Haddon Hall 72
Hade Edge 235 F2
Hademore 209 D2
Hadfield 235 E3
Hadham Cross 186 D1
Hadham Ford 200 C5
Hadleigh *Essex* 188 B4
Hadleigh *Suff.* 202 B3
Hadleigh Heath 202 A3
Hadley *Tel. & W.* 207 F1
Hadley *Worcs.* 196 A1
Hadley End 222 C5
Hadley Wood 186 B3
Hadlow 173 F4
Hadlow Down 160 A1
Hadnall 220 C5
Hadrian's Wall 104
Hadspen 167 D4
Hadstock 201 D3
Hadzor 196 B1
Haffenden Quarter 174 A4
Hafod Bridge 192 C4
Hafod-Dinbych 218 B2
Hafodunos 218 B1
Hafodyrynys 180 B3
Haggate 243 E4
Haggbeck 268 C4
Haggersta 342 C3
Haggerston *Gt.Lon.* 186 C4
Haggerston *Northumb.* 279 E2
Haggrister 344 C5
Haggs 284 B2
Hagley *Here.* 195 E3
Hagley *Worcs.* 208 B4
Hagley Hall 65
Hagnaby *Lincs.* 226 B1
Hagnaby *Lincs.* 239 E5
Hague Bar 235 D4
Hagworthingham 226 B1
Haigh 234 A2
Haighton Green 242 B4
Hail Weston 199 G1
Haile 248 B2
Hailes 196 C4
Hailes Abbey 30
Hailey *Herts.* 186 C1
Hailey *Oxon.* 184 B4
Hailey *Oxon.* 183 F1
Hailsham 160 A3
Haimer 336 D2
Hainault 187 D3
Haine 175 F2
Hainford 228 D4
Hainton 238 B4
Haisthorpe 246 D1
Hakin 176 B2
Halam 224 B2
Halbeath 285 F1
Halberton 152 D1
Halcro 337 E2
Hale *Cumb.* 249 G5
Hale *Gt.Man.* 234 B4
Hale *Halton* 233 F4
Hale *Hants.* 156 A1
Hale *Surr.* 170 D3
Hale Bank 233 F4
Hale Barns 234 B4
Hale Nook 241 G3
Hale Street 173 F4
Hales *Norf.* 215 E2
Hales *Staffs.* 221 E4
Hales Green 222 C3
Hales Place 174 D3
Halesgate 226 B5
Halesowen 208 B4
Halesworth 215 E4
Halewood 233 F4
Half Way Inn 152 D4
Halford *Devon* 152 B5
Halford *Shrop.* 206 D4
Halford *Warks.* 197 E3
Halfpenny 249 G4
Halfpenny Green 208 A3
Halfway *Carmar.* 192 C4
Halfway *Carmar.* 178 B2
Halfway *Powys* 193 E4
Halfway *S.Yorks.* 236 B4
Halfway *W.Berks.* 169 F1
Halfway Bridge 171 E5
Halfway House 206 C1
Halfway Houses *Kent* 174 B1
Halfway Houses *Lincs.* 225 D1
Halghton Mill 220 B3
Halifax 243 G5
Halistra 317 F4
Halket 283 F4
Halkirk 336 D3
Halkyn 232 D5
Hall 283 F4
Hall Cross 242 A5
Hall Dunnerdale 248 D3
Hall Green *Ches.* 221 F2
Hall Green *Lancs.* 242 A5
Hall Green *W.Mid.* 208 D4
Hall Grove 186 B1
Hall of the Forest 206 B4
Halland 160 A2
Hallaton 210 C3
Hallatrow 166 D2
Hallbankgate 260 B2
Hallen 181 E4
Hallfield Gate 223 E2
Hallin 317 F4
Halling 173 G2
Hallington *Lincs.* 238 D4
Hallington *Northumb.* 270 B4
Halliwell 234 A1
Halloughton 224 B2
Hallow 196 A2
Hallow Heath 196 A2
Hallrule 277 G4
Halls 287 D2
Hall's Croft 65
Halls Green *Essex* 186 D2
Hall's Green *Herts.* 200 A5
Hallsands 151 E4
Hallthwaites 248 C4
Hallwood Green 195 F4
Hallworthy 147 F1
Hallyne 285 F5
Halmer End 221 E3
Halmond's Frome 195 F3
Halmore 181 F2
Halmyre Mains 285 F5
Halnaker 158 B3
Halsall 233 E1
Halse *Northants.* 198 A3
Halse *Som.* 165 E5
Halsetown 144 C3
Halsham 247 E5
Halsinger 163 F2
Halstead *Essex* 201 G4
Halstead *Kent* 173 D2
Halstead *Leics.* 210 C2
Halstock 154 B2
Halsway 165 E4
Haltemprice Farm 246 C4
Haltham 226 A1
Haltoft End 226 B3
Halton *Bucks.* 185 D1
Halton *Halton* 233 G4
Halton *Lancs.* 242 B1
Halton *Northumb.* 261 F1
Halton *Wrex.* 220 A4
Halton East 243 G2
Halton Gill 251 D5
Halton Green 242 B1
Halton Holegate 226 C1
Halton Lea Gate 260 C2
Halton Park 242 B1
Halton West 243 E2
Haltwhistle 260 D1
Halvergate 229 F5
Halwell 151 D2
Halwill 149 E1
Halwill Junction 149 E1
Ham *Devon* 153 F2
Ham *Glos.* 181 F3
Ham *Glos.* 196 B5
Ham *Gt.Lon.* 186 A5
Ham *High.* 337 E1
Ham *Kent* 175 F3
Ham *Plym.* 150 A2
Ham *Shet.* 342 B5
Ham *Som.* 165 F5
Ham *Som.* 153 F1
Ham *Wilts.* 169 E1
Ham Common 167 F5
Ham Green *Here.* 195 G3
Ham Green *Kent* 174 A2
Ham Green *Kent* 161 D1
Ham Green *N.Som.* 181 E5
Ham Green *Worcs.* 196 C1
Ham Hill 173 F2
Ham House 56
Ham Street 166 C4
Hambleden 184 C4
Hambledon *Hants.* 157 F1
Hambledon *Surr.* 171 E4
Hamble-le-Rice 157 D2
Hambleton *Lancs.* 241 G3
Hambleton *N.Yorks.* 245 E4
Hambridge 166 A5
Hambrook *S.Glos.* 181 F5
Hambrook *W.Suss.* 157 G2
Hameringham 226 B1
Hamerton 211 G5
Hamerton Zoo Park 79
Hamilton 284 B4
Hamlet *Devon* 153 E3
Hamlet *Dorset* 154 B2
Hammer 171 D4
Hammerpot 158 C3
Hammersmith 186 B5
Hammerwich 208 C2
Hammerwood 172 D5
Hammerwood Park 45
Hammond Street 186 C2
Hammoon 155 E1
Hamnavoe *Shet.* 342 C4
Hamnavoe *Shet.* 345 D4
Hamnavoe *Shet.* 344 B4
Hamnavoe *Shet.* 345 D5
Hamnish Clifford 195 E2
Hamp 165 F4
Hampden Park 160 B3
Hamperden End 201 D4
Hampnett 182 D1
Hampole 236 C2
Hampreston 155 G3
Hampstead 186 B4
Hampstead Norreys 184 A5
Hampsthwaite 244 B2
Hampton *Devon* 153 F3
Hampton *Gt.Lon.* 171 G1
Hampton *Kent* 175 D2
Hampton *Peter.* 211 G3
Hampton *Shrop.* 207 G4
Hampton *Swin.* 183 D3
Hampton *Worcs.* 196 C3
Hampton Bishop 195 E4
Hampton Court Palace and Garden 56
Hampton Fields 182 A3
Hampton Heath 220 B3
Hampton in Arden 209 E4
Hampton Loade 207 G4
Hampton Lovett 196 A1
Hampton Lucy 197 E2
Hampton on the Hill 197 E1
Hampton Poyle 184 A1
Hampton Wick 171 G1
Hamptworth 156 B1
Hamsey 159 G2
Hamstall Ridware 208 D1
Hamstead 156 C3
Hamstead Marshall 169 F1
Hamsteels 262 A3
Hamsterley *Dur.* 262 A4
Hamsterley *Dur.* 262 A2
Hamsterley Forest 104
Hamstreet 174 C5
Hamworthy 155 F3
Hanbury *Staffs.* 222 C5
Hanbury *Worcs.* 196 B1
Hanbury Hall 65
Hanbury Woodend 222 C5
Hanby 225 F4
Hanchurch 221 F3
Hancock Museum 104
Handa Island 334 A4
Handale 253 G1
Handbridge 220 B1
Handcross 172 B5
Handforth 234 C4
Handley *Ches.* 220 B2
Handley *Derbys.* 223 E1
Handley Green 187 F2
Handsacre 208 C1
Handside 186 B1
Handsworth *S.Yorks.* 236 B4
Handsworth *W.Mid.* 208 C3
Handwoodbank 206 D1
Handy Cross 185 D3
Hanford *Dorset* 155 E1
Hanford *Stoke* 221 F3
Hanging Bridge 222 C3
Hanging Houghton 210 C5
Hanging Langford 168 B4
Hangingshaw 267 F2
Hanham 181 F5
Hankelow 221 D3
Hankerton 182 B3
Hankham 160 B3
Hanley 221 F3
Hanley Castle 196 A3
Hanley Child 195 F1
Hanley Swan 196 A3
Hanley William 195 F1
Hanlith 243 F1
Hanmer 220 B4
Hannah 239 E5
Hannington *Hants.* 169 G2
Hannington *Northants.* 210 D5
Hannington *Swin.* 183 D3
Hannington Wick 183 D3
Hanslope 198 D3
Hanthorpe 225 F5
Hanwell *Gt.Lon.* 186 A4
Hanwell *Oxon.* 197 G3
Hanwood 206 D2
Hanworth *Gt.Lon.* 186 A5
Hanworth *Norf.* 228 C2
Happisburgh 229 E2
Happisburgh Common 229 E3
Hapsford 233 F5
Hapton *Lancs.* 243 D4
Hapton *Norf.* 214 C2
Harberton 151 D2
Harbertonford 151 D2
Harbledown 174 D3
Harborne 208 C4
Harborough Magna 209 G5
Harborough Museum 72
Harbost (Tarbost) 329 G1
Harbottle 270 B1
Harbourneford 150 D1
Harbridge 156 A1
Harbridge Green 156 A1
Harburn 285 E3
Harbury 197 F2
Harby *Leics.* 224 C4
Harby *Notts.* 237 F5
Harcombe 153 E3
Harcombe Bottom 153 G3
Harden *W.Mid.* 208 C2
Harden *W.Yorks.* 243 G4
Hardendale 249 G1
Hardenhuish 182 B5
Hardgate *Aber.* 312 C4
Hardgate *N.Yorks.* 244 B1
Hardham 158 C2
Hardhorn 241 G4
Hardingham 228 B5
Hardingstone 198 C2
Hardington 167 E2
Hardington Mandeville 154 B1
Hardington Marsh 154 B2
Hardington Moor 154 B1
Hardley 156 D2
Hardley Street 229 E5
Hardmead 199 E3
Hardraw 251 D3
Hardstoft 223 F1
Hardway *Hants.* 157 F2
Hardway *Som.* 167 E4
Hardwick *Bucks.* 184 D1
Hardwick *Cambs.* 200 B2
Hardwick *Lincs.* 237 F5
Hardwick *Norf.* 214 D2
Hardwick *Northants.* 199 D1
Hardwick *Oxon.* 183 F2
Hardwick *Oxon.* 198 A5
Hardwick *S.Yorks.* 236 B4
Hardwick *W.Mid.* 208 C3
Hardwick Hall 72
Hardwick Village 236 D5
Hardwicke *Glos.* 196 B5
Hardwicke *Glos.* 181 G1
Hardwicke *Here.* 194 B3
Hardy Monument 30
Hardy's Cottage 30
Hardy's Green 202 A5
Hare Green 202 B5
Hare Hatch 184 D5
Hare Hill 96
Hare Street *Herts.* 200 B5
Hare Street *Herts.* 200 B5
Hareby 226 B1
Harecroft 243 G4
Hareden 242 C2
Harefield 185 F3
Harehill 222 C4
Harehills 244 C4
Harehope 279 E4
Harelaw 284 D5
Hareplain 174 A5
Haresceugh 260 C3
Harescombe 182 A1
Haresfield 182 A1
Hareshaw *N.Lan.* 284 C3
Hareshaw *S.Lan.* 284 A5
Harestock 169 F4
Harewood 244 C3
Harewood End 195 E5
Harewood House 87
Harford *Devon* 150 C2
Harford *Devon* 152 B3
Hargate 214 C2
Hargatewall 235 F5
Hargrave *Ches.* 220 B1
Hargrave *Northants.* 211 F5
Hargrave *Suff.* 201 F2
Hargrave Green 201 F2
Harker 268 B5
Harkstead 202 C4
Harlaston 209 E1
Harlaxton 225 D4
Harle Syke 243 E4
Harlech 217 E4
Harlech Castle 110
Harlequin 224 B4
Harlescott 207 E1
Harlesden 186 B4
Harleston *Devon* 151 D3
Harleston *Norf.* 214 D3
Harleston *Suff.* 202 B1
Harlestone 198 C1
Harley *S.Yorks.* 236 A3
Harley *Shrop.* 207 E2
Harleyholm 276 A2
Harlington *Beds.* 199 F4
Harlington *Gt.Lon.* 185 F5
Harlosh 317 F5
Harlow 186 D1
Harlow Carr 87
Harlow Hill 261 G1
Harlthorpe 245 G4
Harlton 200 B2
Harlyn 146 C2
Harman's Cross 155 F4
Harmby 252 A4
Harmer Green 186 B1
Harmer Hill 220 B5
Harmondsworth 185 F5
Harmston 225 E1
Harnage 207 E2
Harnham 168 C5
Harnhill 182 C2
Harold Hill 187 E3
Harold Park 187 E3
Harold Wood 187 E3
Haroldston West 176 B1
Haroldswick 345 F1
Harome 253 F4
Harpenden 186 A1
Harpford 153 D3
Harpham 246 C1
Harpley *Norf.* 227 F5
Harpley *Worcs.* 195 F1
Harpole 198 B1
Harprigg 250 B4
Harpsdale 336 D3
Harpsden 184 C4
Harpswell 237 G4
Harpur Hill 235 E5
Harpurhey 234 C2
Harracott 163 F3
Harrapool 306 C2
Harrietfield 293 E1
Harrietsham 174 A3
Harringay 186 C4
Harrington *Cumb.* 258 C4
Harrington *Lincs.* 239 D5
Harrington *Northants.* 210 C5
Harringworth 211 E3
Harris 305 G5
Harris Green 214 D2
Harris Museum & Art Gallery 96
Harriseahead 221 F2
Harriston 259 E2
Harrogate 244 C2
Harrold 199 E2
Harrold-Odell Country Park 79
Harrop Fold 242 D3
Harrow *Gt.Lon.* 186 A4
Harrow *High.* 337 E1
Harrow Green 201 G2
Harrow on the Hill 186 A4
Harrow Weald 186 A3
Harrowbarrow 149 E3
Harrowden 199 F3
Harrowgate Hill 252 B1
Harry Stoke 181 F5
Harston *Cambs.* 200 C2
Harston *Leics.* 224 D4
Harswell 246 A3
Hart 263 D4
Hartburn 270 C3
Hartest 201 G2
Hartfield *E.Suss.* 173 D5
Hartfield *High.* 318 D5
Hartford *Cambs.* 212 A5
Hartford *Ches.* 234 A5
Hartford *Som.* 164 C5
Hartford End 187 F1
Hartfordbridge 170 C2
Hartforth 252 A2
Hartgrove 155 E1
Harthill *Ches.* 220 C2
Harthill *N.Lan.* 284 D3
Harthill *S.Yorks.* 236 B4
Hartington 222 C1
Hartington Hall 270 C3
Hartland 162 C3
Hartland Quay 30
Hartlebury 208 A5
Hartlepool 263 E4
Hartlepool Historic Ships 104
Hartley *Cumb.* 250 C2
Hartley *Kent* 173 F2
Hartley *Kent* 173 G5
Hartley *Northumb.* 271 F4
Hartley Green 221 G5
Hartley Mauditt 170 C4
Hartley Wespall 170 B2
Hartley Wintney 170 C2
Hartlington 243 G1
Hartlip 174 A2
Hartoft End 253 G3
Harton *N.Yorks.* 245 G1
Harton *Shrop.* 207 D4
Harton *T. & W.* 262 C1
Hartpury 196 A5
Hartrigge 278 A4
Hartshead 244 A5
Hartshill 209 F3
Hartshorne 223 E5
Hartsop 249 F1
Hartwell *Bucks.* 184 C1
Hartwell *E.Suss.* 173 D5
Hartwell *Northants.* 198 C2
Hartwith 244 B1
Hartwood 284 C4
Harvard House 65
Harvel 173 F2
Harvington *Worcs.* 196 C3
Harvington *Worcs.* 208 A5
Harvington Hall 66
Harwell *Notts.* 237 D3
Harwell *Oxon.* 183 G4
Harwich 202 D4
Harwood *Dur.* 261 E4
Harwood *Gt.Man.* 234 B1
Harwood *Northumb.* 270 C2
Harwood Dale 254 C3
Harwood on Teviot 277 F5
Harworth 236 D3
Hasbury 208 B4
Hascombe 171 F3
Haselbech 210 C5
Haselbury Plucknett 154 A1
Haseley 197 E1
Haseley Knob 209 E5
Haselor 196 D2
Hasfield 196 A5
Hasguard 176 B2
Haskayne 233 E2
Hasketon 203 D2
Hasland 223 E1
Hasland Green 223 E1
Haslemere 171 E4
Haslemere Educational Museum 45
Haslingden 243 D5
Haslingden Grane 243 D5
Haslingfield 200 C2
Haslington 221 E2
Hassall 221 E2
Hassall Green 221 E2
Hassell Street 174 C4
Hassendean 277 G3
Hassingham 229 E5
Hassocks 159 F2
Hassop 235 G5
Haster 337 F3
Hasthorpe 226 C1
Hastigrow 337 E2
Hastingleigh 174 C4
Hastings *E.Suss.* 160 D3
Hastings *Som.* 153 G1
Hastings Castle 45
Hastingwood 187 D2
Hastoe 185 E2
Haswell 262 C3
Haswell Plough 262 C3
Hatch *Beds.* 199 G3
Hatch *Hants.* 170 B2
Hatch Beauchamp 166 A5
Hatch End 186 A3
Hatch Green 153 G1
Hatching Green 186 A1
Hatchlands 45
Hatchmere 233 G5
Hatcliffe 238 C2
Hatfield *Here.* 195 E2
Hatfield *Herts.* 186 B2
Hatfield *S.Yorks.* 237 D2
Hatfield Broad Oak 187 E1
Hatfield Forest 79
Hatfield Heath 187 E1
Hatfield House 79
Hatfield Peverel 187 G1
Hatfield Woodhouse 237 D2
Hatford 183 F3
Hatherden 169 E2
Hatherleigh 163 F5
Hathern 223 F5
Hatherop 183 D2
Hathersage 235 G4
Hathersage Booths 235 G4
Hathershaw 234 D2
Hatherton *Ches.* 221 D3
Hatherton *Staffs.* 208 B1
Hatley St. George 200 A2
Hatt 149 D4
Hattingley 170 B4
Hatton *Aber.* 313 F1
Hatton *Derbys.* 222 D5
Hatton *Gt.Lon.* 186 A5
Hatton *Lincs.* 238 B5
Hatton *Shrop.* 207 D3
Hatton *Warks.* 197 E1
Hatton *Warr.* 233 G4
Hatton Castle 324 C5
Hatton Country World 66
Hatton Heath 220 B1
Hatton of Fintray 312 D3
Hattoncrook 312 D2
Haugh 239 E5
Haugh Head 279 E4
Haugh of Glass 311 G1
Haugh of Urr 266 C4
Haugham 238 D4
Haughhead 284 A2
Haughley 202 B1
Haughley Green 202 B1
Haughley New Street 202 B1
Haughmond Abbey 66
Haughs 324 A5
Haughton *Ches.* 220 C2
Haughton *Notts.* 237 D5
Haughton *Powys* 206 C1
Haughton *Shrop.* 207 F3
Haughton *Shrop.* 207 E1
Haughton *Shrop.* 220 A5
Haughton *Staffs.* 221 F5
Haughton Green 234 D3
Haughton Le Skerne 252 C1
Haultwick 200 B5
Haunn 314 C2
Haunton 209 E1
Hauxton 200 C2
Havannah 221 F1
Havant 157 G2
Haven 194 D2
Haven, The 171 F4
Havenstreet 157 E3
Havercroft 236 A1
Haverfordwest (Hwlffordd) 176 C1
Haverhill 201 E3
Haverigg 248 C5
Havering Park 187 D3
Havering-atte-Bower 187 E3
Haversham 198 D3
Haverthwaite 249 E4
Haverton Hill 263 D5
Haviker Street 173 G4
Havyat 166 C4
Hawarden 220 A1
Hawbridge 196 B3
Hawbush Green 201 F5
Hawcoat 248 D5
Hawes 251 D4
Hawe's Green 214 D2
Hawick 277 G4
Hawkchurch 153 G2
Hawkedon 201 F2
Hawkenbury *Kent* 173 E5
Hawkenbury *Kent* 174 A4
Hawkeridge 167 F2
Hawkerland 153 D4
Hawkes End 209 E4
Hawkesbury 181 G4
Hawkesbury Upton 181 G4
Hawkhill 279 G5
Hawkhurst 173 G5
Hawkinge 175 E4
Hawkley 170 C5
Hawkridge 164 B4
Hawkshead 249 E3
Hawkshead Hill 249 E3
Hawksheads 242 A1
Hawksland 284 C5
Hawkstone Park 66
Hawkswick 251 E5
Hawksworth *Notts.* 224 C3
Hawksworth *W.Yorks.* 244 A3
Hawksworth *W.Yorks.* 244 B4
Hawkwell *Essex* 188 B3
Hawkwell *Northumb.* 270 C4
Hawley *Hants.* 171 D2
Hawley *Kent* 187 E5
Hawley's Corner 172 D3
Hawling 196 C5
Hawnby 253 E4
Haworth 243 G4
Hawstead 201 G2
Hawstead Green 201 G2
Hawthorn *Dur.* 262 D3
Hawthorn *Hants.* 170 B4
Hawthorn *R.C.T.* 179 G4
Hawthorn *Wilts.* 167 F1
Hawthorn Hill *Brack.F.* 185 D5
Hawthorn Hill *Lincs.* 226 A2
Hawthorpe 225 F5
Hawton 224 C2
Haxby 245 F2
Haxey 237 E2
Haxted 172 D4
Haxton 168 C3
Hay Green 212 D1
Hay Mills 208 D4
Hay Street 200 B5
Hay Tor Granite Tramway 30
Haydock 233 G3
Haydon *Dorset* 154 C1
Haydon *Swin.* 182 D4
Haydon Bridge 261 E1
Haydon Wick 182 D4
Hayes *Gt.Lon.* 185 F4
Hayes *Gt.Lon.* 172 D2
Hayes End 185 F4
Hayfield *Arg. & B.* 290 C2
Hayfield *Derbys.* 235 E4
Hayfield *Fife* 294 A5
Hayfield *High.* 337 D2
Haygrove 165 F4
Hayhillock 302 D5
Hayle 144 C3
Hayling Island 157 G2
Haymoor Green 221 D2
Hayne 152 C1
Haynes 199 G3
Haynes Church End 199 F3
Haynes West End 199 F3
Hay-on-Wye 194 B3
Hayscastle 190 B5
Hayscastle Cross 190 C5
Hayton *Cumb.* 260 B2
Hayton *Cumb.* 259 E2
Hayton *E.Riding* 246 A3
Hayton *Notts.* 237 E4
Hayton's Bent 207 E4
Haytor Vale 152 A5
Haytown 163 D4
Haywards Heath 159 F1
Haywood Oaks 224 B2
Hazel End 200 C5
Hazel Grove 234 D4
Hazel Street 173 F5
Hazelbank *Arg. & B.* 290 C4
Hazelbank *S.Lan.* 284 C5
Hazelbury Bryan 154 D2
Hazeleigh 188 B2
Hazeley 170 C2
Hazelhurst 234 B1
Hazelside 275 G3
Hazelslack 249 F5
Hazelslade 208 C1
Hazelton Walls 294 B2
Hazelwood *Derbys.* 223 E3
Hazelwood *Gt.Lon.* 172 D2
Hazlefield 258 A2
Hazlehead *Aberdeen* 313 D4
Hazlehead *S.Yorks.* 235 F2
Hazlemere 185 D3
Hazlerigg 271 E4
Hazleton 182 C1
Hazon 271 D1
Heacham 227 E4
Head Bridge 163 G4
Headbourne Worthy 169 F4
Headcorn 174 A4
Headingley 244 B4
Headington 184 A2
Headlam 252 A1
Headland, The 263 E4
Headless Cross 196 C1
Headley *Hants.* 170 D4
Headley *Hants.* 169 G1
Headley *Surr.* 172 B3
Headley Down 170 D4
Headley Heath 208 C5
Headon 237 E5

Heads Nook 260 A2
Heady Hill 234 C1
Heage 223 E2
Healaugh *N.Yorks.* 251 F3
Healaugh *N.Yorks.* 245 E3
Heald Green 234 C4
Heale *Devon* 163 G1
Heale *Som.* 166 A5
Healey *Lancs.* 234 C1
Healey *N.Yorks.* 252 A4
Healey *Northumb.* 261 G2
Healey *W.Yorks.* 244 B5
Healeyfield 261 G3
Healing 238 C1
Heamoor 144 B3
Heaning 249 F3
Heanish 296 B2
Heanor 223 F3
Heanton Punchardon 163 F2
Heanton Satchville 163 F4
Heap Bridge 234 C1
Heapey 242 C5
Heapham 237 F4
Hearn 170 D4
Hearthstane 276 C3
Heasley Mill 164 A4
Heast 306 C3
Heath *Cardiff* 180 A4
Heath *Derbys.* 223 F1
Heath *W.Yorks.* 236 A1
Heath and Reach 199 E5
Heath End *Derbys.* 223 E5
Heath End *Hants.* 169 G1
Heath End *Hants.* 169 F1
Heath End *Surr.* 170 D3
Heath Hayes 208 C1
Heath Hill 207 G1
Heath House 166 B3
Heath, The 222 B4
Heath Town 208 B3
Heathbrook 220 D5
Heathcot 313 D4
Heathcote *Derbys.* 222 C1
Heathcote *Shrop.* 221 D5
Heathencote 198 C3
Heather 209 F1
Heathfield *Devon* 152 B5
Heathfield *E.Suss.* 160 A1
Heathfield *N.Yorks.* 244 A1
Heathfield *Som.* 165 E5
Heathrow Airport 185 F5
Heathton 208 A3
Heatley 234 B4
Heaton *Lancs.* 242 A1
Heaton *Staffs.* 221 G1
Heaton *T. & W.* 262 B1
Heaton *W.Yorks.* 244 A4
Heaton Hall 96
Heaton Moor 234 C3
Heaton's Bridge 233 F1
Heaverham 173 E3
Heaviley 234 D4
Heavitree 152 C3
Hebburn 262 C1
Hebden 243 G1
Hebden Bridge 243 F5
Hebden Green 220 D1
Hebing End 200 B5
Hebron *Carmar.* 191 E5
Hebron *Northumb.* 271 D3
Heck 267 E2
Heckfield 170 C1
Heckfield Green 214 C4
Heckfordbridge 202 A5
Heckingham 215 E2
Heckington 225 G3
Heckmondwike 244 B5
Heddington 168 A1
Heddle 340 B5
Heddon-on-the-Wall 262 A1
Hedenham 215 E2
Hedge End 157 D1
Hedgerley 185 E4
Hedging 166 A5
Hedley on the Hill 261 G2
Hednesford 208 C1
Hedon 247 D5
Hedsor 185 E4
Heeley 236 A4
Heglibister 342 C2
Heighington *Darl.* 262 B5
Heighington *Lincs.* 225 F1
Heightington 207 G5
Heights of Abraham 73
Heights of Brae 321 E3
Heilam 335 D3
Heisker Islands (Monach Islands) 315 E3
Heithat 267 F2
Heiton 278 B3
Hele *Devon* 163 F1
Hele *Devon* 152 C2
Hele *Devon* 148 D1
Hele *Devon* 152 A5
Hele *Som.* 165 E5
Hele *Torbay* 151 F1
Hele Bridge 163 F5
Hele Lane 152 A1
Helebridge 162 C5
Helensburgh 283 D1
Helford 145 E4
Helhoughton 227 G5
Helions Bumpstead 201 E3
Hell Corner 169 E1
Hellaby 236 C3
Helland *Cornw.* 147 E2
Helland *Som.* 166 A5
Hellandbridge 147 E2
Hellesdon 228 D4
Hellidon 198 A2
Hellifield 243 E2
Hellingly 160 A2
Hellington 229 E5
Hellister 342 C3
Helmdon 198 A3
Helmingham 202 C2
Helmington Row 262 A4
Helmsdale 333 F3
Helmshore 243 D5
Helmsley 253 F4
Helmsley Castle 88
Helperby 244 D1
Helperthorpe 254 C5
Helpringham 225 G3
Helpston 211 G2
Helsby 233 F5
Helsey 239 F5
Helston 145 D4
Helstone 147 E1
Helton 260 B5
Helwith 251 F2
Helwith Bridge 243 E1
Hem 206 B2
Hemborough Post 151 E2
Hemel Hempstead 185 F2
Hemerdon 150 B2
Hemingbrough 245 F4
Hemingby 238 C5
Hemingfield 236 A2
Hemingford Abbots 212 A5
Hemingford Grey 212 A5
Hemingstone 202 C2
Hemington *Leics.* 223 F5
Hemington *Northants.* 211 F4
Hemington *Som.* 167 E2
Hemley 203 D3
Hemlington 253 D1
Hemp Green 203 E1
Hempholme 246 C2
Hempnall 214 D2
Hempnall Green 214 D2
Hempriggs 322 D3
Hempriggs House 337 F4
Hempstead *Essex* 201 E4
Hempstead *Med.* 173 G2
Hempstead *Norf.* 229 F3
Hempstead *Norf.* 228 C2
Hempsted 182 A1
Hempton *Norf.* 228 A3
Hempton *Oxon.* 197 G4
Hemsby 229 F4
Hemswell 237 G3
Hemswell Cliff 237 G4
Hemsworth 236 B1
Hemyock 153 E1
Henbury *Bristol* 181 E5
Henbury *Ches.* 234 C5
Henderland 266 C3
Hendersyde Park 278 B3
Hendham 150 D2
Hendon *Gt.Lon.* 186 B4
Hendon *T. & W.* 262 C2
Hendraburnick 147 F1
Hendre *Bridgend* 179 F4
Hendre *Gwyn.* 216 C4
Hendreforgan 179 F4
Hendy 178 B2
Heneglwys 230 C5
Henfield *S.Glos.* 181 F5
Henfield *W.Suss.* 159 E2
Henford 149 D1
Henghurst 174 B5
Hengoed *Caerp.* 180 A3
Hengoed *Powys* 194 B2
Hengoed *Shrop.* 219 F4
Hengrave 201 G1
Henham 200 D5
Heniarth 206 A2
Henlade 165 F5
Henley *Dorset* 154 C2
Henley *Shrop.* 207 E5
Henley *Som.* 166 B4
Henley *Som.* 154 A2
Henley *Suff.* 202 C2
Henley *W.Suss.* 171 D5
Henley Corner 166 B4
Henley Park 171 E2
Henley-in-Arden 197 D1
Henley-on-Thames 184 C4
Henley's Down 160 C2
Henllan *Carmar.* 191 G3
Henllan *Denb.* 218 D1
Henllan Amgoed 191 E5
Henllys 180 B3
Henlow 199 G4
Hennock 152 B4
Henny Street 201 G4
Henry Moore Foundation 80
Henryd 231 F5
Henry's Moat 190 D5
Hensall 245 E5
Henshaw 261 D1
Hensingham 258 C5
Henstead 215 F3
Hensting 169 F5
Henstridge 154 D1
Henstridge Ash 154 D1
Henstridge Bowden 167 D5
Henstridge Marsh 167 E5
Henton *Oxon.* 184 C2
Henton *Som.* 166 B3
Henwood 147 G2
Heogan 343 D3
Heol Senni 193 F5
Heolgerrig 179 G2
Heol-y-Cyw 179 F4
Hepburn 279 E4
Hepburn Bell 279 E4
Hepple 270 B1
Hepscott 271 E3
Hepthorne Lane 223 F1
Heptonstall 243 F5
Hepworth *Suff.* 214 A4
Hepworth *W.Yorks.* 235 F2
Hepworth South Common 214 A4
Herberts, The 179 F5
Herbrandston 176 B2
Hereford 195 E3
Hereford Cathedral 66
Hergest Croft Gardens 66
Heriot 286 A4
Herm 151 F5
Hermiston 285 F2
Hermitage *D. & G.* 266 B4
Hermitage *Dorset* 154 C2
Hermitage *Sc.Bord.* 268 D2
Hermitage *W.Berks.* 184 A5
Hermitage *W.Suss.* 157 G2
Hermitage Castle 124
Hermitage Green 234 A3
Hermitage, The NTS) 124
Hermitage, The 172 B3
Hermon *Carmar.* 191 G4
Hermon *I.o.A.* 216 C1
Hermon *Pembs.* 191 F4
Herne 175 D2
Herne Bay 175 D2
Herne Common 175 D2
Herne Pound 173 F3
Herner 163 F3
Hernhill 174 C2
Herodsfoot 147 G3
Herongate 187 F3
Heron's Ghyll 159 G1
Heronsgate 185 F3
Herriard 170 B3
Herringfleet 215 F2
Herring's Green 199 F3
Herringswell 201 F1
Herringthorpe 236 B3
Hersden 175 D2
Hersham *Cornw.* 162 C5
Hersham *Surr.* 171 G1
Herstmonceux 160 B2
Herstmonceux Castle 45
Herston 338 D3
Hertford 186 C1
Hertford Heath 186 C1
Hertingfordbury 186 C1
Hesket Newmarket 259 G3
Hesketh Bank 242 A5
Hesketh Lane 242 C3
Heskin Green 233 G1
Hesleden 262 D4
Hesleyside 270 A3
Heslington 245 F2
Hessay 245 E2
Hessenford 148 D5
Hessett 202 A1
Hessle 246 C5
Hest Bank 242 A1
Hestercombe 30
Hester's Way 196 B5
Hestley Green 202 C1
Heston 186 A5
Heswall 233 D4
Hethe 198 A5
Hethelpit Cross 195 G5
Hetherington 270 A4
Hethersett 228 C5
Hethersgill 260 A1
Hethpool 278 C4
Hett 262 B4
Hetton 243 F2
Hetton-le-Hole 262 C3
Heugh 270 C4
Heugh-head *Aber.* 311 F3
Heugh-head *Aber.* 312 A5
Heveningham 215 E4
Hever 173 D4
Hever Castle 45
Heversham 249 F4
Hevingham 228 C3
Hewas Water 147 D5
Hewell Grange 196 C1
Hewell Lane 196 C1
Hewelsfield 181 E2
Hewelsfield Common 181 E2
Hewish *N.Som.* 166 B1
Hewish *Som.* 154 A2
Hewood 153 G2
Heworth 245 F2
Hewton 149 F1
Hexham 261 F1
Hextable 187 E5
Hexthorpe 236 C2
Hexton 199 G4
Hexworthy 149 G3
Hey 243 E3
Hey Houses 241 G5
Heybridge *Essex* 187 F3
Heybridge *Essex* 188 B2
Heybridge Basin 188 B2
Heybrook Bay 150 A3
Heydon *Cambs.* 200 C3
Heydon *Norf.* 228 C3
Heydour 225 F4
Heylipoll 296 A2
Heylor 344 B4
Heyop 206 B5
Heysham 242 A1
Heyshaw 244 A1
Heyshott 158 A2
Heyside 234 D2
Heytesbury 168 A3
Heythrop 197 F5
Heywood *Gt.Man.* 234 C1
Heywood *Wilts.* 167 F2
Hibaldstow 237 G2
Hibb's Green 201 G2
Hickleton 236 B2
Hickling *Norf.* 229 F3
Hickling *Notts.* 224 B5
Hickling Green 229 F3
Hickling Heath 229 F3
Hickstead 159 E1
Hidcote Bartrim 197 D3
Hidcote Boyce 197 D3
Hidcote Manor Gardens 30
High Ackworth 236 B1
High Angerton 270 C3
High Balantyre 290 C3
High Bankhill 260 B3
High Beach 186 D3
High Beeches 45
High Bentham 242 C1
High Bickington 163 F3
High Birkwith 250 C5
High Blantyre 284 A4
High Bonnybridge 284 C2
High Borgue 266 A5
High Borve 329 F2
High Bradfield 235 G3
High Bradley 243 G3
High Bransholme 246 D4
High Bray 163 G2
High Bridge 259 G2
High Brooms 173 E4
High Bullen 163 F3
High Burton 252 B4
High Buston 271 E1
High Callerton 271 D4
High Casterton 250 B5
High Catton 245 G2
High Close 252 A1
High Cogges 183 F2
High Common 214 C3
High Coniscliffe 252 B1
High Crompton 234 D2
High Cross *Hants.* 170 C5
High Cross *Herts.* 186 C1
High Cross *W.Suss.* 159 E2
High Cup Nick 96
High Easter 187 F1
High Ellington 252 A4
High Entercommon 252 C2
High Ercall 207 E1
High Etherley 262 A5
High Ferry 226 B3
High Flatts 235 G2
High Force 104
High Garrett 201 F5
High Gate 243 F5
High Grange 262 A4
High Green *Norf.* 228 C5
High Green *Norf.* 228 A4
High Green *Norf.* 228 A5
High Green *S.Yorks.* 236 A3
High Green *Suff.* 201 G1
High Green *Worcs.* 196 A3
High Halden 174 A5
High Halstow 187 G5
High Ham 166 B4
High Harrington 258 D4
High Harrogate 244 C2
High Hatton 220 D5
High Hauxley 271 E1
High Hawsker 254 C2
High Heath *Shrop.* 221 D5
High Heath *W.Mid.* 208 C2
High Hesket 260 A3
High Hesleden 263 D4
High Hoyland 235 G1
High Hunsley 246 B4
High Hurstwood 159 G1
High Hutton 245 G1
High Ireby 259 F3
High Kelling 228 B2
High Kilburn 253 E5
High Kingthorpe 254 B4
High Knipe 249 G1
High Lane *Derbys.* 223 F3
High Lane *Gt.Man.* 235 D4
High Lane *Worcs.* 195 F1
High Laver 187 E2
High Legh 234 B4
High Leven 252 D1
High Littleton 166 D2
High Lorton 259 E4
High Marishes 254 B5
High Marnham 237 F5
High Melton 236 C2
High Moor 236 B4
High Newton 249 F4
High Newton-by-the-Sea 279 G4
High Nibthwaite 249 D3
High Offley 221 E5
High Ongar 187 E2
High Onn 208 A1
High Park Corner 202 B5
High Roding 187 F1
High Shaw 251 D3
High Spen 262 A1
High Stoop 262 A3
High Street *Cornw.* 147 D4
High Street *Kent* 173 G5
High Street *Suff.* 203 F2
High Street *Suff.* 215 E3
High Street *Suff.* 215 F4
High Street *Suff.* 201 G3
High Street Green 202 B2
High Throston 263 D4
High Town 208 B1
High Toynton 226 A1
High Trewhitt 270 C1
High Wham 262 A5
High Wigsell 160 C1
High Woolaston 181 E3
High Worsall 252 C2
High Wray 249 E3
High Wych 187 D1
High Wycombe 185 D3
Higham *Derbys.* 223 E2
Higham *Kent* 187 G5
Higham *Lancs.* 243 E4
Higham *S.Yorks.* 236 A2
Higham *Suff.* 201 F1
Higham *Suff.* 202 B4
Higham Dykes 270 D4
Higham Ferrers 199 E1
Higham Gobion 199 G4
Higham on the Hill 209 F3
Higham Wood 173 F4
Highampton 163 E5
Highams Park 186 C3
Highbridge *Hants.* 169 F5
Highbridge *Som.* 166 A3
Highbrook 172 C5
Highburton 235 F1
Highbury 167 D3
Highclere 169 F1
Highclere Castle 45
Highcliffe 156 B3
Higher Alham 167 D3
Higher Ansty 155 D2
Higher Ashton 152 B4
Higher Ballam 241 G4
Higher Blackley 234 C2
Higher Brixham 151 F2
Higher Cheriton 153 E2
Higher Combe 164 C4
Higher Gabwell 151 F1
Higher Green 234 B3
Higher Halstock Leigh 154 B2
Higher Kingcombe 154 B3
Higher Kinnerton 220 A1
Higher Muddiford 163 F2
Higher Nyland 167 E5
Higher Prestacott 149 D1
Higher Standen 243 D3
Higher Tale 153 D2
Higher Thrushgill 242 C1
Higher Town *Cornw.* 147 E3
Higher Town *I.o.S.* 146 B1
Higher Walreddon 149 E3
Higher Walton *Lancs.* 242 B5
Higher Walton *Warr.* 233 G4
Higher Wambrook 153 F2
Higher Whatcombe 155 E2
Higher Wheelton 242 C5
Higher Whiteleigh 148 C1
Higher Whitley 234 A4
Higher Woodhill 234 B1
Higher Woodsford 155 D4
Higher Wraxall 154 B2
Higher Wych 220 B3
Highfield *E.Riding* 245 G4
Highfield *N.Ayr.* 283 E4
Highfield *Oxon.* 198 A5
Highfield *S.Yorks.* 236 A4
Highfield *T. & W.* 262 A2
Highfields *Cambs.* 200 B2
Highfields *Northumb.* 287 G4
Highgate *E.Suss.* 172 D5
Highgate *Gt.Lon.* 186 B4
Highgreen Manor 270 A2
Highland Folk Museum 124
Highland Wildlife Park 124
Highlane *Ches.* 221 F1
Highlane *Derbys.* 236 B4
Highlaws 259 E2
Highleadon 195 G5
Highleigh *Devon* 164 C5
Highleigh *W.Suss.* 158 A4
Highley 207 G4
Highmead 192 B3
Highmoor Cross 184 B4
Highmoor Hill 181 D4
Highnam 181 G1
Highstead 175 E2
Highsted 174 B2
Highstreet 174 C2
Highstreet Green *Essex* 201 F4
Highstreet Green *Surr.* 171 E4
Hightae 267 E3
Highter's Heath 208 C5
Hightown *Hants.* 156 A2
Hightown *Mersey.* 233 D2
Hightown Green 202 A2
Highway 182 C5
Highweek 152 B5
Highwood 195 F1
Highwood Hill 186 B3
Highworth 183 E3
Hilborough 213 G2
Hilcote 223 F2
Hilcott 168 C2
Hilden Park 173 E4
Hildenborough 173 E4
Hildenley 253 G5
Hildersham 200 D3
Hilderstone 221 G4
Hilderthorpe 247 D1
Hilfield 154 C2
Hilgay 213 E3
Hill *S.Glos.* 181 F3
Hill *Warks.* 197 G1
Hill *Worcs.* 196 B3
Hill Brow 170 C5
Hill Chorlton 221 E4
Hill Common 229 F3
Hill Cottages 253 G3
Hill Croome 196 A3
Hill Deverill 167 F3
Hill Dyke 226 B3
Hill End *Dur.* 261 G4
Hill End *Fife* 293 F5
Hill End *Glos.* 196 A4
Hill End *Gt.Lon.* 185 F3
Hill End *N.Yorks.* 243 G2
Hill Green 200 C4
Hill Head 157 E2
Hill House 124
Hill Houses 207 F5
Hill Mountain 176 C2
Hill of Beath 285 F1
Hill of Fearn 322 A2
Hill of Tarvit Mansion House & Garden 124
Hill Ridware 208 C1
Hill Row 212 C5
Hill Side 235 F1
Hill Street 156 C1
Hill, The 248 C4
Hill Top ***Cumb.*** 96
Hill Top *Hants.* 156 D2
Hill Top *S.Yorks.* 236 B3
Hill Top *S.Yorks.* 235 G4
Hill View 155 F3
Hill Wootton 197 F1
Hillam 245 E5
Hillbeck 250 C1
Hillberry 240 B4
Hillborough 175 E2
Hillbrae *Aber.* 324 B5
Hillbrae *Aber.* 312 C2
Hillbrae *Aber.* 312 D1
Hillbutts 155 F2
Hillclifflane 223 D3
Hillend *Aber.* 323 G5
Hillend *Fife* 285 F1
Hillend *Midloth.* 285 G3
Hillend *N.Lan.* 284 C3
Hillend *Swan.* 178 A3
Hillend Green 195 G5
Hillersland 181 E1
Hillesden 198 B5
Hillesley 181 G4
Hillfarrance 165 E5
Hillfoot End 199 G4
Hillhead *Devon* 151 F2
Hillhead *S.Ayr.* 274 C3
Hillhead of Auchentumb 325 E4
Hillhead of Cocklaw 325 F5
Hilliard's Cross 209 D1
Hilliclay 337 D2
Hillingdon 185 F4
Hillington *Glas.* 283 G3
Hillington *Norf.* 227 F5
Hillmorton 210 A5
Hillockhead *Aber.* 311 F4
Hillockhead *Aber.* 311 G3
Hillowton 266 B4
Hillpound 157 E1
Hill's End 199 E4
Hills Town 223 F1
Hillsborough 236 A3
Hillsford Bridge 164 A3
Hillside *Aber.* 313 E5
Hillside *Angus* 303 F3
Hillside *Moray* 323 D3
Hillside *Shet.* 342 D1
Hillside *Worcs.* 195 G1
Hillswick 344 B5
Hillway 157 F4
Hillwell 343 F4
Hillyfields 156 C1
Hilmarton 182 C5
Hilperton 167 F2
Hilsea 157 F2
Hilston 247 E4
Hilton *Cambs.* 200 A1
Hilton *Cumb.* 260 D5
Hilton *Derbys.* 222 D4
Hilton *Dorset* 155 D2
Hilton *Dur.* 262 A5
Hilton *High.* 322 B1
Hilton *Shrop.* 207 G3
Hilton *Staffs.* 208 C2
Hilton *Stock.* 253 D1
Hilton Croft 313 E1
Hilton of Cadboll 322 A2
Hilton of Delnies 322 A4
Himbleton 196 B2
Himley 208 A3
Hincaster 249 G4
Hinchley Wood 171 G1
Hinckley 209 G3
Hinderclay 214 B4
Hinderton 233 E5
Hinderwell 253 G1
Hindford 220 A4
Hindhead 171 D4
Hindley *Gt.Man.* 234 A2
Hindley *Northumb.* 261 G2
Hindley Green 234 A2
Hindlip 196 A2
Hindolveston 228 B3
Hindon *Som.* 164 C3
Hindon *Wilts.* 168 A4
Hindringham 228 A2
Hingham 228 B5
Hinksford 208 A4
Hinstock 221 D5
Hintlesham 202 B3
Hinton *Glos.* 181 F2
Hinton *Hants.* 156 B3
Hinton *Here.* 194 C4
Hinton *Northants.* 198 A2
Hinton *S.Glos.* 181 G5
Hinton *Shrop.* 206 D2
Hinton Admiral 156 B3
Hinton Ampner *Hants.* 169 G5
Hinton Ampner ***Hants.*** 45
Hinton Blewett 166 C2
Hinton Charterhouse 167 E2
Hinton Martell 155 G2
Hinton on the Green 196 C3
Hinton Parva *Dorset* 155 F2
Hinton Parva *Swin.* 183 E4
Hinton St. George 154 A1
Hinton St. Mary 155 D1
Hinton Waldrist 183 F3
Hinton-in-the-Hedges 198 A4
Hints *Shrop.* 207 F5
Hints *Staffs.* 209 D2
Hinwick 199 E1
Hinxhill 174 C4
Hinxton 200 C3
Hinxworth 200 A3
Hipperholme 244 A5
Hipsburn 279 G5
Hipswell 252 A3
Hirn 312 C4
Hirnant 219 D5
Hirst 271 E3
Hirst Courtney 245 F5
Hirwaen 219 E1
Hirwaun 179 F2
Hiscott 163 F3
Histon 200 C1
Hitcham *Bucks.* 185 E4
Hitcham *Suff.* 202 A2
Hitchin 199 G5
Hither Green 186 C5
Hittisleigh 152 A3
Hittisleigh Barton 152 A3
Hive 246 A4
Hixon 222 B5
H.M. Customs and Excise National Museum 96
H.M.S. Belfast 56
H.M.S. Victory 45
H.M.S. Warrior 45
Hoaden 175 E3
Hoaldalbert 194 C5
Hoar Cross 222 C5
Hoarwithy 195 E5
Hoath 175 E2
Hobarris 206 C5
Hobbister 338 C2
Hobbles Green 201 F2
Hobbs Cross 187 D3
Hobbs Lots Bridge 212 B2
Hobkirk 277 G4
Hobland Hall 229 G5
Hobson 262 A2
Hoby 210 B1
Hockerill 200 C5
Hockering 228 B4
Hockerton 224 C2
Hockley 188 B3
Hockley Heath 209 D5
Hockliffe 199 E5
Hockwold cum Wilton 213 F4
Hockworthy 152 D1
Hoddesdon 186 C2
Hoddlesden 242 D5
Hodgehill 221 F1
Hodgeston 176 D3
Hodnet 220 D5
Hodnet Hall Gardens 66
Hodnetheath 220 D5
Hodsoll Street 173 F2
Hodson 183 D4
Hodthorpe 236 C5
Hoe 228 A4
Hoe Gate 157 F1
Hoff 250 B1
Hoffleet Stow 226 A4
Hoggard's Green 201 G2
Hoggeston 198 D5
Hoggie 324 A4
Hoggrill's End 209 E3
Hogha Gearraidh 315 F2
Hoghton 242 C5
Hognaston 222 D2
Hogsthorpe 239 F5
Holbeach 226 B5
Holbeach Bank 226 B5
Holbeach Clough 226 B5
Holbeach Drove 212 B1
Holbeach Hurn 226 B5
Holbeach St. Johns 212 B1
Holbeach St. Marks 226 B4
Holbeach St. Matthew 226 C4
Holbeck 236 C5
Holbeck Woodhouse 236 C5
Holberrow Green 196 C2
Holbeton 150 C2
Holborough 173 G2
Holbrook *Derbys.* 223 E3
Holbrook *Suff.* 202 C4
Holbrooks 209 F4
Holburn 279 E3
Holbury 156 D2
Holcombe *Devon* 152 C5
Holcombe *Gt.Man.* 234 B1
Holcombe *Som.* 167 D3
Holcombe Burnell Barton 152 B3
Holcombe Rogus 153 D1
Holcot 198 C1
Holden 243 D3
Holden Gate 243 E5
Holdenby 198 B1
Holdenhurst 156 A3
Holder's Green 201 E5
Holders Hill 186 B4
Holdgate 207 E4
Holdingham 225 F3
Holditch 153 G2
Hole 153 E1
Hole Park 174 A5
Hole Street 158 D2
Holehouse 235 E3
Hole-in-the-Wall 195 F5
Holford 165 E3
Holgate 245 E2
Holker 249 E5
Holker Hall 96
Holkham 227 G3
Holkham Hall 80
Hollacombe *Devon* 163 D5
Hollacombe *Devon* 152 B2
Hollacombe Town 163 G4
Holland *Ork.* 340 C1
Holland *Ork.* 341 E4
Holland *Surr.* 172 D3
Holland Fen 226 A3
Holland-on-Sea 189 E1
Hollandstoun 341 F1
Hollee 268 A5
Hollesley 203 E3
Hollicombe 151 F1
Hollingbourne 174 A3
Hollingbury 159 F3
Hollingrove 160 B1
Hollington *Derbys.* 222 D4
Hollington *E.Suss.* 160 C2
Hollington *Staffs.* 222 B4
Hollingworth 235 E3
Hollins 236 A5
Hollins Green 234 A3
Hollins Lane 242 A2
Hollinsclough 222 B1
Hollinwood *Gt.Man.* 234 D2
Hollinwood *Shrop.* 220 C4
Hollocombe 163 G4
Hollow Meadows 235 G4
Holloway 223 E2
Hollowell 210 B5
Holly Bush 220 B3
Holly End 212 C2
Holly Green 184 C2
Hollybush *Caerp.* 180 A2
Hollybush *E.Ayr.* 274 B4
Hollybush *Worcs.* 195 G4

Inversanda 298 B4
Invershiel 307 F3
Invershore 337 E5
Inversnaid Hotel 291 F4
Invertrossachs 292 A4
Inverugie 325 G5
Inveruglas 291 F4
Inveruglass 310 A4
Inverurie 312 C2
Invervar 300 B5
Invervegain 282 B2
Invery House 312 B5
Inverythan 324 C5
Inwardleigh 149 F1
Inworth 188 B1
Iochdar 315 F5
Iona 288 B2
Iping 171 D5
Ipplepen 151 E1
Ipsden 184 B4
Ipstones 222 B3
Ipswich 202 C3
Irby 233 D4
Irby Hill 233 D4
Irby in the Marsh 226 C1
Irby upon Humber 238 B2
Irchester 199 E1
Ireby *Cumb.* 259 F3
Ireby *Lancs.* 250 B5
Ireland *Ork.* 338 C2
Ireland *Shet.* 342 C5
Ireland's Cross 221 E3
Ireleth 248 D5
Ireshopeburn 261 E4
Irlam 234 B3
Irnham 225 F5
Iron Acton 181 F4
Iron Cross 196 C2
Ironbridge 207 F2
Ironbridge Gorge 66
Irons Bottom 172 B4
Ironside 325 D4
Ironville 223 F2
Irstead 229 E3
Irthington 260 A1
Irthlingborough 211 E5
Irton 254 D4
Irvine 274 B2
Isauld 336 B2
Isbister *Ork.* 340 B5
Isbister *Ork.* 340 A4
Isbister *Shet.* 343 E1
Isbister *Shet.* 344 C3
Isfield 159 G2
Isham 211 D5
Ishriff 289 F1
Isington 170 C3
Island of Stroma 337 F1
Islay 280 A3
Islay Airport 280 B4
Islay House 280 B3
Isle Abbotts 166 A5
Isle Brewers 166 A5
Isle of Lewis (Eilean Leodhais) 329 E3
Isle of Man 240 B3
Isle of Man Airport 240 A5
Isle of May 295 E5
Isle of Noss 343 E3
Isle of Sheppey 174 B1
Isle of Walney 241 E1
Isle of Whithorn 257 E3
Isle of Wight 157 D4
Isle of Wight Pearl 45
Isle of Wight Zoo 45
Isle, The 207 D1
Isleham 213 E5
Isleornsay (Eilean Iarmain) 306 C3
Isles of Scilly (Scilly Isles) 146 B1
Islesburgh 342 C1
Isleworth 186 A5
Isley Walton 223 F5
Islibhig 328 A5
Islip *Northants.* 211 E5
Islip *Oxon.* 184 A1
Isombridge 207 F1
Istead Rise 173 F2
Italian Chapel 125
Itchen 156 D1
Itchen Abbas 169 G4
Itchen Stoke 169 G4
Itchingfield 171 G5
Itchington 181 F4
Itteringham 228 C2
Itton *Devon* 149 G1
Itton *Mon.* 181 D3
Itton Common 181 D3
Ivegill 260 A3
Ivelet 251 E3
Iver 185 F4
Iver Heath 185 F4
Iveston 262 A2
Ivetsey Bank 208 A1
Ivinghoe 185 E1
Ivinghoe Aston 185 E1
Ivington 195 D2
Ivington Green 195 D2
Ivy Hatch 173 E3
Ivy Todd 213 G2
Ivybridge 150 C2
Ivychurch 161 F1
Iwade 174 B2
Iwerne Courtney (Shroton) 155 E1
Iwerne Minster 155 E1
Ixworth 214 A4
Ixworth Thorpe 214 A4

J

Jack Hill 244 A2
Jackfield 207 F2
Jacksdale 223 F2
Jackstown 312 C1
Jackton 283 G4
Jacobstow 148 B1
Jacobstowe 163 F5
Jacobswell 171 E2
Jameston 177 D3
Jamestown *D. & G.* 268 B2
Jamestown *High.* 321 D4
Jamestown *W.Dun.* 283 E1
Jane Austen's House 46
Janefield 321 G4
Janetstown *High.* 336 C2
Janetstown *High.* 337 F3
Jarlshof Prehistoric & Norse Settlement 125
Jarrow 262 C1
Jarvis Brook 173 E5
Jasper's Green 201 F5
Jawcraig 284 C2
Jayes Park 171 G3
Jaywick 189 E1
Jealott's Hill 185 D5
Jeater Houses 252 D3
Jedburgh 278 A4
Jedburgh Abbey 125
Jeffreyston 177 D2
Jemimaville 321 G3
Jericho 234 C1
Jersay 284 C3
Jersey 150 C5
Jersey Airport 150 B5
Jersey Marine 178 D3
Jerviswood 284 C5
Jesmond 262 B1
Jevington 160 A3
J.M. Barrie's Birthplace & Camera Obscura 125
Jockey End 185 F1
Jodrell Bank 234 B5
Jodrell Bank Observatory & Arboretum 96
John o' Groats 337 F1
Johnby 260 A4
John's Cross 160 C1
Johnshaven 303 F3
Johnson Street 229 E4
Johnston 176 C1
Johnston Mains 303 F2
Johnstone 283 F3
Johnstone Castle 283 F3
Johnstonebridge 267 E1
Johnstown *Carmar.* 177 G1
Johnstown *Wrex.* 220 A3
Joppa 274 C4
Jordans 185 E3
Jordanston 190 C4
Jordanstone 302 A5
Jorvik 88
Jorvik Glass 88
Joy's Green 181 F1
Jumpers Common 156 A3
Juniper Hill 198 A4
Jura 281 D1
Jura House 280 C3
Jurassic Coast 31
Jurby East 240 B2
Jurby West 240 B2

K

Kaber 250 C1
Kaimes 285 G3
Kames *Arg. & B.* 282 A2
Kames *Arg. & B.* 290 A3
Kames *E.Ayr.* 275 E3
Kea 146 C5
Keadby 237 F1
Keal Cotes 226 B1
Kearsley 234 B2
Kearstwick 250 B5
Kearton 251 F3
Kearvaig 334 B1
Keasden 242 D1
Kebholes 324 B4
Keckwick 233 G4
Keddington 238 D4
Keddington Corner 239 D4
Kedington 201 F3
Kedleston 223 D3
Kedleston Hall 73
Keelby 238 B1
Keele 221 F3
Keeley Green 199 F3
Keelham 243 G4
Keeres Green 187 E1
Keeston 176 B1
Keevil 168 A2
Kegworth 223 F5
Kehelland 146 A5
Keig 312 B3
Keighley 243 G3
Keil *Arg. & B.* 272 B5
Keil *High.* 298 B4
Keilhill 324 C4
Keillmore 281 E1
Keillor 302 A5
Keillour 293 E2
Keills 280 C3
Keils 280 D3
Keinton Mandeville 166 C4
Keir House 292 C5
Keir Mill 266 C1
Keisby 225 F5
Keisley 260 D5
Keiss 337 F2
Keith 323 G4
Keithick 294 A1
Keithmore 311 F1
Keithock 303 E3
Kelbrook 243 F3
Kelburn Castle & Country Centre 125
Kelby 225 F3
Keld *Cumb.* 249 G1
Keld *N.Yorks.* 251 D2
Keldholme 253 G4
Keldy Castle 253 G3
Kelfield *N.Lincs.* 237 F2
Kelfield *N.Yorks.* 245 E4
Kelham 224 C2
Kella 240 B2
Kellacott 149 E2
Kellan 297 E5
Kellas *Angus* 294 C1
Kellas *Moray* 323 D4
Kellaton 151 D4
Kellaways 182 B5
Kelleth 250 B2
Kelleythorpe 246 C2
Kellie Castle 125
Kelling 228 B1
Kellington 245 E5
Kelloe 262 C4
Kelloholm 275 F4
Kelly *Cornw.* 147 E2
Kelly *Devon* 149 D2
Kelly Bray 149 D3
Kelmarsh 210 C5
Kelmscott 183 E3
Kelsale 203 E1
Kelsall 220 C1
Kelsay 280 A4
Kelshall 200 B4
Kelsick 259 F1
Kelso 278 B3
Kelso Abbey 125
Kelstedge 223 E1
Kelstern 238 C3
Kelston 167 E1
Keltneyburn 300 C5
Kelton 267 D3
Kelton Hill (Rhonehouse) 266 B5
Kelty 293 G5
Kelvedon 188 B1
Kelvedon Hatch 187 E3
Kelvinside 283 G3
Kelynack 144 A4
Kemacott 163 G1
Kemback 294 C3
Kemberton 207 G2
Kemble 182 B3
Kemerton 196 B4
Kemeys Commander 180 C2
Kemeys Inferior 180 C3
Kemnay 312 C3
Kemp Town 159 F3
Kempe's Corner 174 C4
Kempley 195 F5
Kempley Green 195 F5
Kemps Green 208 D5
Kempsey 196 A3
Kempsford 183 D3
Kempshott 169 G3
Kempston 199 F3
Kempston Hardwick 199 F3
Kempston West End 199 E3
Kempton 206 C4
Kemsing 173 E3
Kemsley 174 B2
Kenardington 174 B5
Kenchester 194 D3
Kencott 183 E2
Kendal 249 G3
Kenderchurch 194 D5
Kendleshire 181 F5
Kenfig 179 D4
Kenfig Hill 179 E4
Kenidjack 144 A3
Kenilworth 209 E5
Kenilworth Castle 66
Kenknock *P. & K.* 300 A5
Kenknock *Stir.* 291 G1
Kenley *Gt.Lon.* 172 C2
Kenley *Shrop.* 207 E2
Kenmore *Arg. & B.* 290 C4
Kenmore *High.* 319 D4
Kenmore *P. & K.* 300 C5
Kenmore *W.Isles* 327 E3
Kenn *Devon* 152 C4
Kenn *N.Som.* 166 B1
Kennack Sands 31
Kennacley 327 D4
Kennacraig 281 G3
Kennards House 147 G1
Kennavay 327 E4
Kenneggy Downs 144 C4
Kennerleigh 152 B2
Kennerty 312 B5
Kennet 293 E5
Kennethmont 312 A2
Kennett 201 E1
Kennford 152 C4
Kenninghall 214 B3
Kennington *Kent* 174 C4
Kennington *Oxon.* 184 A2
Kennoway 294 B4
Kenny 153 G1
Kennyhill 213 E5
Kennythorpe 245 G1
Kenovay 296 A2
Kensaleyre 318 A4
Kensington 186 B4
Kensington Palace 57
Kenstone 220 C5
Kensworth 185 F1
Kent & East Sussex Railway 46
Kent Street *E.Suss.* 160 C2
Kent Street *Kent* 173 F3
Kentallen 298 C4
Kentchurch 194 D5
Kentford 201 F1
Kentisbeare 153 D2
Kentisbury 163 G1
Kentisbury Ford 163 G1
Kentish Town 186 B4
Kentmere 249 F2
Kenton *Devon* 152 C4
Kenton *Suff.* 202 C1
Kenton *T. & W.* 262 B1
Kenton Corner 202 D1
Kentra 297 F3
Kents Bank 249 E5
Kent's Green 195 G5
Kent's Oak 169 E5
Kentwell Hall 81
Kenwick 220 B4
Kenwood House 57
Kenwyn 146 C5
Kenyon 234 A3
Keoldale 334 C2
Keose (Ceos) 329 E5
Keppanach 298 C3
Keppoch *Arg. & B.* 283 E2
Keppoch *High.* 307 E2
Keprigan 272 B4
Kepwick 253 D3
Keresley 209 F4
Kernborough 151 D3
Kerrera 290 A2
Kerridge 234 D5
Kerris 144 B4
Kerry 206 A3
Kerrycroy 282 C3
Kerry's Gate 194 C4
Kerrysdale 319 E2
Kersall 224 C1
Kersey 202 B3
Kersey Vale 202 B3
Kershopefoot 268 C3
Kerswell 153 D2
Kerswell Green 196 A3
Kerthen Wood 144 C3
Kesgrave 202 D3
Kessingland 215 G3
Kessingland Beach 215 G3
Kestle 147 D5
Kestle Mill 146 C4
Keston 172 D2
Keswick *Cumb.* 259 F4
Keswick *Norf.* 228 D5
Keswick *Norf.* 229 E2
Ketley Bank 207 F1
Ketsby 239 D5
Kettering 211 D5
Ketteringham 228 C5
Kettins 294 A1
Kettle Corner 173 G3
Kettlebaston 202 A2
Kettlebridge 294 B4
Kettlebrook 209 E2
Kettleburgh 203 D1
Kettlehill 294 B4
Kettleholm 267 F3
Kettleness 254 B1
Kettleshulme 235 D5
Kettlesing 244 B2
Kettlesing Bottom 244 B2
Kettlesing Head 244 B2
Kettlestone 228 A2
Kettlethorpe 237 F5
Kettletoft 341 E3
Kettlewell 251 E5
Ketton 211 E2
Kevingtown 173 D2
Kew 186 A5
Kew Gardens (see Royal Botanic Gardens, Kew) 59
Kewstoke 166 A1
Kexbrough 236 A2
Kexby *Lincs.* 237 F4
Kexby *York* 245 G2
Key Green 221 F1
Keyham 210 B2
Keyhaven 156 C3
Keyingham 247 E5
Keymer 159 F2
Keynsham 167 D1
Key's Toft 226 C2
Keysoe 199 F1
Keysoe Row 199 F1
Keyston 211 F5
Keyworth 224 B4
Kibblesworth 262 B2
Kibworth Beauchamp 210 B3
Kibworth Harcourt 210 B3
Kidbrooke 186 D5
Kiddemore Green 208 A2
Kidderminster 208 A5
Kiddington 197 G5
Kidlington 183 G1
Kidmore End 184 B5
Kidnal 220 B3
Kidsdale 257 E3
Kidsgrove 221 F2
Kidstones 251 E4
Kidwelly (Cydweli) 178 A2
Kidwelly Castle 111
Kiel Crofts 290 A1
Kielder 269 E2
Kielder Forest 105
Kilbarchan 283 F3
Kilbeg 306 C4
Kilberry 281 F3
Kilbirnie 283 E4
Kilblaan 290 D3
Kilbraur 332 D3
Kilbrennan 296 D5
Kilbride *Arg. & B.* 290 A2
Kilbride *Arg. & B.* 282 B3
Kilbride *High.* 306 B2
Kilbride Farm 282 A3
Kilbridemore 290 C5
Kilburn *Derbys.* 223 E3
Kilburn *Gt.Lon.* 186 B4
Kilburn *N.Yorks.* 253 E5
Kilby 210 B3
Kilchattan Bay 282 C4
Kilchenzie 272 B3
Kilcheran 290 A1
Kilchiaran 280 A3
Kilchoan *Arg. & B.* 289 G3
Kilchoan *High.* 297 D3
Kilchoman 280 A3
Kilchrenan 290 C2
Kilchrist 272 B4
Kilchurn Castle 125
Kilconquhar 294 C4
Kilcot 195 F5
Kilcoy 321 E4
Kilcreggan 282 D1
Kildale 253 F2
Kildalton Church & Crosses 125
Kildary 321 G2
Kildavie 272 C4
Kildermorie Lodge 321 E2
Kildonan *N.Ayr.* 273 F3
Kildonan (Cilldonnain) *W.Isles* 314 C1
Kildonan Lodge 333 E2
Kildonnan 297 D1
Kildrochet House 264 B5
Kildrummy 311 G3
Kildwick 243 G3
Kilfinan 282 A2
Kilfinnan 308 B5
Kilgetty 177 E2
Kilgwrrwg Common 181 D3
Kilham *E.Riding* 246 C1
Kilham *Northumb.* 278 C3
Kilkenneth 296 A2
Kilkenny 182 C1
Kilkerran *Arg. & B.* 272 C4
Kilkerran *S.Ayr.* 274 B5
Kilkhampton 162 C4
Killamarsh 236 B4
Killay 178 C3
Killbeg 297 F5
Killean *Arg. & B.* 281 E5
Killean *Arg. & B.* 290 C4
Killearn 283 G1
Killellan 272 B4
Killen 321 F4
Killerby 262 A5
Killerton *Devon* 152 C2
Killerton *Devon* 31
Killichonan 300 A4
Killiechonate 299 E1
Killiechronan 297 E5
Killiecrankie 301 E3
Killiecrankie 125
Killiehuntly 309 G5
Killiemor 289 D1
Killilan 307 F1
Killimster 337 F3
Killin *High.* 333 D4
Killin *Stir.* 292 A1
Killinallan 280 B2
Killinghall 244 B2
Killington *Cumb.* 250 B4
Killington *Devon* 163 G1
Killingworth 271 E4
Killochyett 286 B5
Killocraw 272 B2
Killunaig 289 D2
Killundine 297 E5
Kilmacolm 283 E3
Kilmaha 290 B4
Kilmahog 292 B4
Kilmalieu 298 A4
Kilmaluag 318 A2
Kilmany 294 B2
Kilmarie 306 B3
Kilmarnock 274 C2
Kilmartin 290 A5
Kilmartin House Museum 125
Kilmaurs 283 F5
Kilmelford 290 A3
Kilmeny 280 B3
Kilmersdon 167 D2
Kilmeston 169 G5
Kilmichael 272 B3
Kilmichael Glassary 290 A5
Kilmichael of Inverlussa 281 F1
Kilmington *Devon* 153 F3
Kilmington *Wilts.* 167 E4
Kilmington Common 167 E4
Kilmorack 321 D5
Kilmore *Arg. & B.* 290 A2
Kilmore *High.* 306 C4
Kilmory *Arg. & B.* 281 F1
Kilmory *Arg. & B.* 281 F2
Kilmory *High.* 305 G4
Kilmory *High.* 297 E2
Kilmory *N.Ayr.* 273 E3
Kilmote 333 E3
Kilmuir *High.* 317 F5
Kilmuir *High.* 321 F5
Kilmuir *High.* 321 G2
Kilmuir *High.* 317 G2
Kilmun 282 C1
Kilmux 294 B4
Kiln Green *Here.* 181 F1
Kiln Green *W'ham* 184 D5
Kiln Pit Hill 261 G2
Kilnave 280 A2
Kilncadzow 284 C5
Kilndown 173 G5
Kilnhurst 236 B3
Kilninian 296 D5
Kilninver 290 A2
Kilnsea 239 E1
Kilnsey 243 F1
Kilnwick 246 B3
Kilnwick Percy 246 A2
Kiloran 288 C5
Kilpatrick 273 E3
Kilpeck 194 D4
Kilphedir 333 E3
Kilpin 245 G5
Kilpin Pike 245 G5
Kilrenny 295 D4
Kilsby 210 A5
Kilspindie 294 A2
Kilstay 256 B3
Kilsyth 284 B2
Kiltarlity 321 E5
Kilton *Notts.* 236 C5
Kilton *R. & C.* 253 F1
Kilton *Som.* 165 E3
Kilton Thorpe 253 F1
Kiltyrie 292 B1
Kilvaxter 317 G3
Kilve 165 E3
Kilverstone 213 G4
Kilvington 224 D3
Kilwinning 283 E5
Kimberley *Norf.* 228 B5
Kimberley *Notts.* 223 G3
Kimberworth 236 B3
Kimble Wick 184 D2
Kimblesworth 262 B3
Kimbolton *Cambs.* 199 F1
Kimbolton *Here.* 195 E1
Kimbridge 169 E5
Kimcote 210 A4
Kimmeridge 155 F5
Kimmerston 279 D3
Kimpton *Hants.* 169 D3
Kimpton *Herts.* 186 A1
Kinaldy 294 D3
Kinblethmont 303 E5
Kinbrace 336 A5
Kinbreack 307 G5
Kinbuck 292 C4
Kincaldrum 302 C5
Kincaple 294 C3
Kincardine *Fife* 284 D1
Kincardine *High.* 321 F1
Kincardine O'Neil 312 A5
Kinclaven 293 G1
Kincorth 313 E4
Kincraig *Aber.* 313 E2
Kincraig *High.* 310 A4
Kincraigie 301 E5
Kindallachan 301 E4
Kindrogan Field Centre 301 F3
Kinellar 312 D3
Kineton *Glos.* 196 C5
Kineton *Warks.* 197 F2
Kineton Green 208 D4
Kinfauns 293 G2
King Sterndale 235 E5
Kingarth 282 B4
Kingcoed 180 D2
Kingerby 238 A3
Kingham 197 E5
Kingholm Quay 267 D3
Kinghorn 285 G1
Kinglassie 294 A5
Kingoodie 294 B2
King's Acre 195 D3
King's Bank 161 D1
King's Bromley 208 D1
Kings Caple 195 E5
King's Cliffe 211 F3
King's Coughton 196 C2
King's Green 195 G4
King's Heath 208 C4
Kings Hill *Kent* 173 F3
King's Hill *W.Mid.* 208 B3
King's Hill *Warks.* 209 F5
Kings Langley 185 F2
King's Lynn 227 E5
King's Meaburn 260 C5
Kings Mills 151 E5
King's Moss 233 G2
Kings Muir 277 D2
King's Newnham 209 G5
King's Newton 223 E5
King's Norton *Leics.* 210 B2
King's Norton *W.Mid.* 208 C5
Kings Nympton 163 G4
King's Pyon 194 D2
Kings Ripton 212 A5
King's Somborne 169 E4
King's Stag 154 D1
King's Stanley 182 A2
King's Sutton 197 G4
King's Tamerton 150 A2
King's Walden 199 G5
Kings Worthy 169 F4
Kingsand 150 A2
Kingsbarns 295 D3
Kingsbridge *Devon* 150 D3
Kingsbridge *Som.* 164 C4
Kingsburgh 317 G4
Kingsbury *Gt.Lon.* 186 A4
Kingsbury *Warks.* 209 E3
Kingsbury Episcopi 166 B5
Kingscavil 285 E2
Kingsclere 169 G2
Kingscote 182 A3
Kingscott 163 F4
Kingscross 273 F3
Kingsdale 294 B4
Kingsdon 166 C5
Kingsdown *Kent* 175 F4
Kingsdown *Swin.* 183 D4
Kingsdown *Wilts.* 167 F1
Kingseat 293 G5
Kingsey 184 C2
Kingsfold *Pembs.* 176 C3
Kingsfold *W.Suss.* 171 G4
Kingsford *Aber.* 324 C5
Kingsford *Aber.* 312 A3
Kingsford *Aberdeen* 313 D4
Kingsford *E.Ayr.* 283 F5
Kingsford *Worcs.* 208 A4
Kingsgate 175 F1
Kingshall Street 202 A1
Kingsheanton 163 F2
Kingshouse 292 A2
Kingshouse Hotel 299 E4
Kingshurst 209 D4
Kingskerswell 151 E1
Kingskettle 294 B4
Kingsland *Here.* 194 D1
Kingsland *I.o.A.* 230 A4
Kingsley *Ches.* 233 G5
Kingsley *Hants.* 170 C4
Kingsley *Staffs.* 222 B3
Kingsley Green 171 D4
Kingsley Holt 222 B3
Kingslow 207 G3
Kingsmoor 186 D2
Kingsmuir *Angus* 302 C5
Kingsmuir *Fife* 294 D4
Kingsnorth 174 C5
Kingsnorth Power Station 174 A1
Kingstanding 208 C3
Kingsteignton 152 B5
Kingsteps 322 B4
Kingsthorne 195 D4
Kingsthorpe 198 C1
Kingston *Cambs.* 200 B2
Kingston *Cornw.* 149 D3
Kingston *Devon* 150 C3
Kingston *Devon* 153 D4
Kingston *Dorset* 154 D2
Kingston *Dorset* 155 F5
Kingston *E.Loth.* 286 C1
Kingston *Gt.Man.* 234 D3
Kingston *Hants.* 156 A2
Kingston *I.o.W.* 157 D4
Kingston *Kent* 175 D3
Kingston *Moray* 323 F3
Kingston *W.Suss.* 158 C3
Kingston Bagpuize 183 F3
Kingston Blount 184 C3
Kingston by Sea 159 E3
Kingston Deverill 167 F4
Kingston Gorse 158 C3
Kingston Lacy 31
Kingston Lisle 183 F4
Kingston Maurward 154 D3
Kingston Maurward Park 31
Kingston near Lewes 159 F3
Kingston on Soar 223 G5
Kingston Russell 154 B3
Kingston St. Mary 165 F5
Kingston Seymour 166 B1
Kingston Stert 184 C2
Kingston Upon Hull 246 D5
Kingston upon Thames 171 G1
Kingston Warren 183 F4
Kingstone *Here.* 194 D4
Kingstone *Here.* 195 F5
Kingstone *Som.* 153 G1
Kingstone *Staffs.* 222 B5
Kingstone Winslow 183 E4
Kingstown 259 G1
Kingswear 151 E2
Kingswell 283 G5
Kingswells 313 D4
Kingswinford 208 A4
Kingswood *Bucks.* 184 B1
Kingswood *Glos.* 181 G3
Kingswood *Here.* 194 B2
Kingswood *Kent* 174 A3
Kingswood *Powys* 206 B2
Kingswood *S.Glos.* 181 F5
Kingswood *Som.* 165 E4
Kingswood *Surr.* 172 B3
Kingswood *Warks.* 209 D5
Kingthorpe 238 B5
Kington *Here.* 194 B2
Kington *Worcs.* 196 B2
Kington Langley 182 B5
Kington Magna 167 E5
Kington St. Michael 182 B5
Kingussie 309 G4
Kingweston 166 C4
Kinharrachie 313 E1
Kinharvie 266 D4
Kinkell 284 A2
Kinkell Bridge 293 E3
Kinknockie 325 F5
Kinlet 207 G4
Kinloch *Fife* 294 A3
Kinloch *High.* 334 C5
Kinloch *High.* 297 F4
Kinloch *High.* 306 A5
Kinloch *High.* 321 E2
Kinloch *P. & K.* 302 A5
Kinloch *P. & K.* 301 G5
Kinloch Hourn 307 F4
Kinloch Laggan 300 A1
Kinloch Rannoch 300 B4
Kinlochaline 298 A3
Kinlochard 291 G4
Kinlocharkaig 307 F5
Kinlochbeoraid 298 A1
Kinlochbervie 334 B3
Kinlocheil 298 B2
Kinlochetive 298 D5
Kinlochewe 319 G3
Kinlochlaich 298 B5
Kinlochleven 299 D3
Kinlochmoidart 297 G2
Kinlochmorar 307 E5
Kinlochmore 299 D3
Kinlochroag (Ceann Lochroag) 328 C5
Kinlochspelve 289 F2
Kinloss 322 C3
Kinmel Bay (Bae Cinmel) 232 A4
Kinmuck 312 D3
Kinnaber 303 F3
Kinnadie 325 E5
Kinnaird 294 A2
Kinneff 303 G2
Kinnelhead 276 B5
Kinnell *Angus* 303 E4
Kinnell *Stir.* 292 A1
Kinnerley 220 A5
Kinnersley *Here.* 194 C3
Kinnersley *Worcs.* 196 A3
Kinnerton 194 B1
Kinnerton Green 220 A1
Kinnesswood 293 G4
Kinnettles 302 C5
Kinninvie 261 G5
Kinnordy 302 B4
Kinoulton 224 B4
Kinrara 310 A4
Kinross 293 G4
Kinrossie 293 G1
Kinsbourne Green 186 A1
Kinsham *Here.* 194 C1
Kinsham *Worcs.* 196 B4
Kinsley 236 B1
Kinson 155 G3
Kintail Estate & Morvich 125
Kintarvie 327 E2
Kintbury 169 E1
Kintessack 322 B3
Kintillo 293 G3
Kintocher 312 A4
Kinton *Here.* 206 D5
Kinton *Shrop.* 206 C1
Kintore 312 C3
Kintour 280 C4
Kintra *Arg. & B.* 280 B5
Kintra *Arg. & B.* 288 C2

Kin - Lee

M

Portchester 157 F2
Portchester Castle 49
Portencross 282 C5
Portesham 154 C4
Portessie 323 G3
Portfield *Arg. & B.* 289 G2
Portfield *W.Suss.* 158 A3
Portfield Gate 176 C1
Portgate 149 E2
Portgordon 323 F3
Portgower 333 F3
Porth *Cornw.* 146 C3
Porth *R.C.T.* 179 G3
Porth Colmon 216 A4
Porth Mellin 145 D5
Porth Navas 145 E4
Porthaethwy (Menai Bridge) 231 D5
Porthallow *Cornw.* 145 E4
Porthallow *Cornw.* 147 G4
Porthcawl 179 E5
Porthcothan 146 C2
Porthcurno 144 A4
Porthcurno Sands 34
Porthgain 190 B4
Porthill 221 F3
Porthkerry 165 D1
Porthleven 144 D4
Porthmadog 217 E4
Porthmeor 144 B3
Portholland 147 D5
Porthoustock 145 F4
Porthpean 147 E4
Porthtowan 146 A5
Porthyrhyd *Carmar.* 192 D4
Porthyrhyd *Carmar.* 178 B1
Porth-y-waen 219 F5
Portincaple 291 E5
Portington 245 G4
Portinnisherrich 290 B3
Portinscale 259 F4
Portishead 181 D5
Portknockie 323 G3
Portland Castle 34
Portlethen 313 E5
Portlethen Village 313 E5
Portloe 145 G3
Portlooe 147 G4
Portmahomack 322 B1
Portmeirion 217 E4
Portmeirion Village 113
Portmellon 147 E5
Portmore 156 C3
Port-na-Con 334 D2
Portnacroish 298 B5
Portnaguran (Port nan Giùran) 329 G4
Portnahaven 280 A4
Portnalong 305 G1
Portnaluchaig 297 F1
Portobello 286 A2
Porton 168 C4
Portpatrick 264 B5
Portreath 146 A5
Portree 318 A5
Portscatho 145 F3
Portsea 157 F2
Portskerra 336 A2
Portskewett 181 E4
Portslade 159 E3
Portslade-by-Sea 159 E3
Portslogan 264 A5
Portsmouth 157 F3
Portsmouth Cathedral 49
Portsmouth Historic Dockyard 49
Portsonachan 290 C2
Portsoy 324 A3
Portuairk 296 D3
Portvoller 329 G4
Portway *Here.* 194 C3
Portway *Here.* 195 D3
Portway *Here.* 195 D4
Portway *Worcs.* 208 C5
Portwrinkle 149 D5
Portyerrock 257 E3
Posenhall 207 F2
Poslingford 201 F3
Postbridge 149 G3
Postcombe 184 C3
Postling 174 D5
Post-mawr (Synod Inn) 192 A2
Postwick 229 D5
Potarch 312 B5
Potsgrove 199 E5
Pott Row 227 F5
Pott Shrigley 234 D5
Potten End 185 F2
Potter Brompton 254 C5
Potter Heigham 229 F4
Potter Street 187 D2
Pottergate Street 214 C2
Potterhanworth 225 F1
Potterhanworth Booths 225 F1
Potteries Museum & Art Gallery 67
Potterne 168 A2
Potterne Wick 168 B2
Potternewton 244 C4
Potters Bar 186 B2
Potters Crouch 186 A2
Potter's Green 209 F4
Potters Marston 209 G3
Potterspury 198 C3
Potterton *Aber.* 313 E3
Potterton *W.Yorks.* 244 D4
Pottle Street 167 F3
Potto 253 D2
Potton 200 A3
Pott's Green 202 A5
Poughill *Cornw.* 162 C5
Poughill *Devon* 152 B2
Poulshot 168 A2
Poulton 182 D2
Poulton-le-Fylde 241 G4
Pound Bank 195 G3
Pound Green *E.Suss.* 160 A1
Pound Green *Suff.* 201 F2
Pound Green *Worcs.* 207 G5
Pound Hill 172 B5
Pound Street 169 F1
Poundbury 154 C3
Poundffald 178 B3
Poundfield 173 E5
Poundgate 159 G1
Poundland 264 C2
Poundon 198 B5
Poundsbridge 173 E4
Poundsgate 152 A5
Poundstock 148 C1
Povey Cross 172 B4
Pow Green 195 G3
Powburn 279 E5
Powderham 152 C4
Powderham Castle 34
Powerstock 154 B3
Powfoot 267 F4
Powick 196 A2
Powis Castle & Garden 113
Powler's Piece 163 D4
Powmill 293 F5
Poxwell 154 D4
Poyle 185 F5
Poynings 159 E2
Poyntington 167 D5
Poynton *Ches.* 234 D4
Poynton *Tel. & W.* 207 E1
Poynton Green 207 E1
Poyntzfield 321 G3
Poys Street 215 E4
Poyston 176 C1
Poyston Cross 176 C1
Poystreet Green 202 A2
Praa Sands 144 C4
Pratis 294 B4
Pratt's Bottom 173 D2
Praze-an-Beeble 144 D3
Predannack Wollas 145 D5
Prees 220 C4
Prees Green 220 C4
Prees Heath 220 C4
Prees Higher Heath 220 C4
Prees Lower Heath 220 C4
Preesall 241 G3
Preesgweene 219 F4
Prenbrigog 219 F1
Prendergast 176 C1
Prendwick 279 E5
Pren-gwyn 192 A3
Prenteg 217 E3
Prenton 233 E4
Prescot 233 F3
Prescott *Devon* 153 D1
Prescott *Shrop.* 220 B5
Presley 322 C4
Pressen 278 C3
Prestatyn 232 B4
Prestbury *Ches.* 234 D5
Prestbury *Glos.* 196 B5
Presteigne 194 C1
Presthope 207 E3
Prestleigh 166 D3
Prestolee 234 B2
Preston *B. & H.* 159 F3
Preston *Devon* 152 B5
Preston *Dorset* 154 D4
Preston *E.Loth.* 286 C2
Preston *E.Riding* 247 D4
Preston *Glos.* 195 F4
Preston *Glos.* 182 C2
Preston *Herts.* 199 G5
Preston *Kent* 174 C2
Preston *Kent* 175 E2
Preston *Lancs.* 242 B5
Preston *Northumb.* 279 F4
Preston *Rut.* 211 D2
Preston *Sc.Bord.* 287 E4
Preston *Shrop.* 207 E1
Preston *Som.* 165 D4
Preston *Suff.* 202 A2
Preston *Torbay* 151 E1
Preston *Wilts.* 182 C5
Preston Bagot 197 D1
Preston Bissett 198 B4
Preston Bowyer 165 E5
Preston Brockhurst 220 C5
Preston Brook 233 G4
Preston Candover 170 B3
Preston Capes 198 A2
Preston Deanery 198 C2
Preston Gubbals 207 D1
Preston Mill & Phantassie Dovecot 128
Preston on Stour 197 E3
Preston on the Hill 233 G4
Preston on Wye 194 C3
Preston Plucknett 154 B1
Preston upon the Weald Moors 207 F1
Preston Wynne 195 E3
Preston-le-Skerne 262 C5
Prestonpans 286 A2
Preston-under-Scar 251 F3
Prestwich 234 C2
Prestwick *Northumb.* 271 D4
Prestwick *S.Ayr.* 274 B3
Prestwick International Airport (Glasgow Prestwick International Airport) 274 B3
Prestwold 223 G5
Prestwood *Bucks.* 185 D2
Prestwood *Staffs.* 222 C3
Price Town 179 F3
Prickwillow 213 D4
Priddy 166 C2
Priest Hill 242 C4
Priest Hutton 249 G5
Priest Weston 206 B3
Priestcliffe 235 F5
Priestland 275 D2
Priestwood 173 F2
Primethorpe 210 A3
Primrose Green 228 B4
Primrose Hill 186 B4
Princes End 208 B3
Princes Gate 177 E1
Princes Risborough 184 D2
Princethorpe 209 G5
Princetown *Caerp.* 180 A1
Princetown *Devon* 149 F3
Prinknash Abbey & Park 34
Prior Muir 294 D3
Prior Park 34
Prior's Frome 195 E4
Priors Halton 207 D5
Priors Hardwick 197 G2
Priors Marston 197 G2
Prior's Norton 196 A5
Priors Park 196 A4
Priorslee 207 G1
Priorwood 128
Priory Wood 194 B3
Priston 167 D1
Pristow Green 214 C3
Prittlewell 188 B4
Privett 170 B5
Prixford 163 F2
Proaig 280 C4
Probus 146 C5
Protstonhill 324 D3
Prudhoe 261 G1
Prussia Cove 144 C4
Pubil 299 G5
Publow 166 D1
Puckeridge 200 B5
Puckington 153 G1
Pucklechurch 181 F5
Pucknall 169 E5
Puckrup 196 A4
Puddinglake 221 E1
Puddington *Ches.* 233 E5
Puddington *Devon* 152 B1
Puddlebrook 181 F1
Puddledock 214 B2
Puddletown 155 D3
Pudleston 195 E2
Pudsey 244 B4
Pugneys Country Park 90
Pulborough 158 C2
Pulborough Brooks R.S.P.B. Nature Reserve 49
Puldagon 337 F4
Puleston 221 E5
Pulford 220 A2
Pulham 154 D2
Pulham Market 214 C3
Pulham St. Mary 214 D3
Pulley 207 D2
Pulloxhill 199 F4
Pulrossie 321 G1
Pulverbatch 206 D2
Pumpherston 285 E3
Pumsaint 192 C3
Puncheston 190 D5
Puncknowle 154 B4
Punnett's Town 160 B1
Purbrook 157 F2
Purewell 156 A3
Purfleet 187 E5
Puriton 166 A3
Purleigh 188 B2
Purley 172 C2
Purley on Thames 184 B5
Purlogue 206 B5
Purlpit 167 F1
Purls Bridge 212 C4
Purse Caundle 154 C1
Purslow 206 C4
Purston Jaglin 236 B1
Purtington 153 G2
Purton *Glos.* 181 F2
Purton *Glos.* 181 F2
Purton *Wilts.* 182 C4
Purton Stoke 182 C3
Purves Hall 287 E5
Pury End 198 C3
Pusey 183 F3
Putlake Adventure Farm 34
Putley 195 F4
Putley Green 195 F4
Putney 186 B5
Putsborough 163 E1
Puttenham *Herts.* 185 D1
Puttenham *Surr.* 171 E3
Puttock End 201 G3
Putts Corner 153 E3
Puxton 166 B1
Pwll 178 A2
Pwllcrochan 176 C2
Pwlldefaid 216 A5
Pwll-glas 219 E2
Pwllgloyw 193 G4
Pwllheli 216 C4
Pwll-Mawr 180 B5
Pwllmeyric 181 E3
Pwll-trap 177 F1
Pwll-y-glaw 179 D3
Pye Corner *Herts.* 187 D1
Pye Corner *Kent* 174 A4
Pye Corner *Newport* 180 C4
Pye Green 208 B1
Pyecombe 159 E2
Pyle *Bridgend* 179 E4
Pyle *I.o.W.* 157 D5
Pyleigh 165 E4
Pylle 166 D4
Pymore *Cambs.* 212 C4
Pymore *Dorset* 154 A3
Pyrford 171 F2
Pyrford Green 171 F2
Pyrton 184 B3
Pytchley 211 D5
Pyworthy 162 D5

Q

Quabbs 206 B4
Quadring 226 A4
Quadring Eaudike 226 A4
Quainton 198 C5
Quarff 342 D4
Quarley 169 D3
Quarndon 223 E3
Quarr Hill 157 E3
Quarrier's Village 283 E3
Quarrington 225 F3
Quarrington Hill 262 C4
Quarry Bank 208 B4
Quarry Bank Mill & Styal Estate 98
Quarrybank 220 C1
Quarrywood 323 D3
Quarter 284 B4
Quarter, The 174 A4
Quatford 207 G3
Quatt 207 G4
Quebec 262 A3
Quebec House 49
Quedgeley 182 A1
Queen Adelaide 213 D4
Queen Camel 166 C5
Queen Charlton 166 D1
Queen Dart 152 B1
Queen Elizabeth II Country Park 105
Queen Oak 167 E4
Queen Street 173 F4
Queenborough 174 B1
Queen's Bower 157 E4
Queen's Head 220 A5
Queensbury *Gt.Lon.* 186 A4
Queensbury *W.Yorks.* 244 A4
Queensferry (South Queensferry) *Edin.* 285 F2
Queensferry *Flints.* 220 A1
Queensferry Museum 129
Queenzieburn 284 A2
Quemerford 168 B1
Quendale 343 F4
Quendon 200 D4
Queniborough 210 B1
Quenington 182 D2
Quernmore 242 B1
Queslett 208 C3
Quethiock 148 D4
Quholm 340 A5
Quick's Green 184 A5
Quidenham 214 B3
Quidhampton 169 G2
Quidinish (Cuidhtinis) 326 C5
Quilquox 313 E1
Quina Brook 220 C4
Quince Honey Farm 34
Quindry 338 D3
Quine's Hill 240 B4
Quinhill 281 F4
Quinton *Northants.* 198 C2
Quinton *W.Mid.* 208 B4
Quinton Green 198 C2
Quintrell Downs 146 C3
Quixhill 222 C3
Quoditch 149 E1
Quoig 292 D2
Quoiggs House 292 D4
Quoisley 220 C3
Quorn 210 A1
Quothquan 276 A2
Quoyloo 340 A4
Quoys 345 F1
Quoys of Reiss 337 F3

R

Raasay 318 B5
Raby 233 E5
Raby Castle 105
Rachan 276 C2
Rachub 217 F1
Rackenford 152 B1
Rackham 158 C2
Rackheath 229 D4
Racks 267 E3
Rackwick *Ork.* 338 B3
Rackwick *Ork.* 340 C2
Radbourne 223 D4
Radcliffe *Gt.Man.* 234 B2
Radcliffe *Northumb.* 271 E1
Radcliffe on Trent 224 B4
Radclive 198 B4
Radcot 183 E3
Raddington 164 D5
Radernie 294 C4
Radford *B. & N.E.Som.* 167 D2
Radford *Nott.* 223 G3
Radford *Oxon.* 197 G5
Radford *W.Mid.* 209 F4
Radford Semele 197 F1
Radipole 154 C4
Radlett 186 A2
Radley 184 A3
Radley Green 187 F2
Radmore Green 220 C2
Radnage 184 C3
Radstock 167 D2
Radstone 198 A3
Radway 197 F3
Radway Green 221 E2
Radwell *Beds.* 199 F2
Radwell *Herts.* 200 A4
Radwinter 201 E4
Radyr 180 A4
Raechester 270 B3
Raemoir House 312 B5
RAF Museum 67
Raffin 330 C1
Rafford 322 C4
Ragdale 224 B5
Ragged Appleshaw 169 E3
Raglan 180 D2
Raglan Castle 113
Ragley Hall 67
Ragnall 237 F5
Rahoy 297 F4
Railway Age, The 99
Rain Shore 234 C1
Rainford 233 F2
Rainham *Gt.Lon.* 187 E4
Rainham *Med.* 174 A2
Rainhill 233 F3
Rainhill Stoops 233 G3
Rainow 235 D5
Rainsough 234 B2
Rainton 252 C5
Rainworth 223 G2
Raisbeck 250 B2
Raise 260 D3
Rait 294 A2
Raithby *Lincs.* 226 B1
Raithby *Lincs.* 238 D4
Rake 170 D5
Raleigh's Cross 164 D4
Ram 192 B3
Ram Alley 168 D1
Ram Lane 174 B4
Ramasaig 317 E5
Rame *Cornw.* 145 E3
Rame *Cornw.* 150 A3
Rampisham 154 B2
Rampside 241 F1
Rampton *Cambs.* 200 C1
Rampton *Notts.* 237 F5
Ramsbottom 234 B1
Ramsbury 183 E5
Ramscraigs 333 G2
Ramsdean 170 C5
Ramsdell 169 G2
Ramsden 183 F1
Ramsden Bellhouse 187 G3
Ramsden Heath 187 G3
Ramsey *Cambs.* 212 A4
Ramsey *Essex* 202 D4
Ramsey *I.o.M.* 240 C2
Ramsey Forty Foot 212 B4
Ramsey Heights 212 A4
Ramsey Island *Essex* 188 C2
Ramsey Island *Pembs.* 190 A5
Ramsey Mereside 212 A4
Ramsey St. Mary's 212 A4
Ramsgate 175 F2
Ramsgate Street 228 B2
Ramsgill 252 A5
Ramsholt 203 E3
Ramshorn 222 B3
Ramsnest Common 171 E4
Ranachan 297 G3
Ranais (Ranish) 329 F5
Ranby *Lincs.* 238 C5
Ranby *Notts.* 237 D4
Rand 238 B5
Randwick 182 A2
Rangemore 222 C5
Rangeworthy 181 F4
Ranish (Ranais) 329 F5
Rankinston 274 C4
Rank's Green 187 G1
Ranmoor 236 A4
Rannoch Moor 129
Rannoch School 300 A4
Ranochan 298 A1
Ranscombe 164 C3
Ranskill 237 D4
Ranton 221 F5
Ranton Green 221 F5
Ranworth 229 E4
Rapness 340 D2
Rapps 153 G1
Rascarrel 258 A2
Rash 250 B4
Rashwood 196 B1
Raskelf 253 D5
Rassau 180 A1
Rastrick 244 A5
Ratagan 307 F3
Ratby 210 A2
Ratcliffe Culey 209 F3
Ratcliffe on Soar 223 F5
Ratcliffe on the Wreake 210 B1
Ratford Bridge 176 B1
Ratfyn 168 C3
Rathen 325 E3
Rathillet 294 B2
Rathliesbeag 299 E1
Rathmell 243 E1
Ratho 285 F2
Ratho Station 285 F2
Rathven 323 G3
Ratley 197 F3
Ratling 175 E3
Ratlinghope 206 D3
Ratsloe 152 C3
Rattar 337 E1
Ratten Row *Cumb.* 259 G2
Ratten Row *Lancs.* 242 A3
Rattery 150 D1
Rattlesden 202 A2
Rattray 301 G5
Raughton Head 259 G2
Raunds 211 E5
Ravenfield 236 B3
Ravenglass 248 B3
Ravenglass & Eskdale Railway 99
Raveningham 215 E2
Raven's Green 202 C5
Ravenscar 254 C2
Ravensdale 240 B2
Ravensden 199 F2
Ravenshaw 243 F3
Ravenshayes 152 C2
Ravenshead 223 G2
Ravensmoor 220 D2
Ravensthorpe *Northants.* 210 B5
Ravensthorpe *W.Yorks.* 244 B5
Ravenstone *Leics.* 209 G1
Ravenstone *M.K.* 199 D2
Ravenstonedale 250 C2
Ravenstruther 284 D5
Ravensworth 252 A2
Raw 254 C2
Rawcliffe *E.Riding* 245 F5
Rawcliffe *York* 245 E2
Rawcliffe Bridge 245 F5
Rawdon 244 B4
Rawmarsh 236 B3
Rawnsley 208 C1
Rawreth 187 G3
Rawridge 153 F2
Rawson Green 223 E3
Rawtenstall 243 E5
Rawyards 284 B3
Raxton 313 D1
Raydon 202 B4
Raylees 270 B2
Rayleigh 188 B3
Raymond's Hill 153 G3
Rayne 201 F5
Rayners Lane 186 A4
Raynes Park 172 B2
Reach 201 D1
Read 243 D4
Reading 184 C5
Reading Green 214 C4
Reading Street 174 B5
Reagill 250 B1
Rearquhar 332 C5
Rearsby 210 B1
Rease Heath 220 D2
Reaster 337 E2
Reaveley 279 E5
Reawick 342 C3
Reay 336 B2
Reculver 175 E2
Red Ball 153 D1
Red Bull 221 F2
Red Dial 259 F2
Red Hill *Hants.* 157 G1
Red Hill *Warks.* 196 D2
Red Lodge *Bristol* 34
Red Lodge *Suff.* 213 E5
Red Lumb 234 C1
Red Oaks Hill 201 D4
Red Point 318 D3
Red Post *Cornw.* 162 C5
Red Post *Devon* 151 E1
Red Rail 195 E5
Red Rock 233 G2
Red Roses 177 F1
Red Row 271 E2
Red Street 221 F2
Red Wharf Bay (Traeth Coch) 230 D4
Redberth 177 D2
Redbourn 186 A1
Redbourne 237 G3
Redbrook *Glos.* 181 E1
Redbrook *Wrex.* 220 C3
Redbrook Street 174 B5
Redburn *High.* 321 E3
Redburn *High.* 322 B5
Redburn *Northumb.* 261 D1
Redcar 263 F5
Redcastle *Angus* 303 E4
Redcastle *High.* 321 E5
Redcliff Bay 180 D5
Redcloak 303 G1
Reddingmuirhead 284 D2
Reddings, The 196 B5
Reddish 234 C3
Redditch 196 C1
Rede 201 G2
Redenhall 215 D3
Redesmouth 270 A3
Redford *Aber.* 303 F2
Redford *Angus* 303 D5
Redford *Dur.* 261 G4
Redford *W.Suss.* 171 D5
Redgrave 214 B4
Redheugh 302 C3
Redhill *Aber.* 312 B1
Redhill *Aber.* 312 C4
Redhill *Moray* 324 A5
Redhill *N.Som.* 166 B1
Redhill *Notts.* 223 G3
Redhill *Surr.* 172 B3
Redhill Aerodrome & Heliport 172 B4
Redhouse *Aber.* 312 A2
Redhouse *Arg. & B.* 281 G3
Redhouses 280 B3
Redisham 215 F3
Redland *Bristol* 181 E5
Redland *Ork.* 340 B4
Redlingfield 214 C4
Redlynch *Som.* 167 E4
Redlynch *Wilts.* 168 D5
Redmarley D'Abitot 195 G4
Redmarshall 262 C5
Redmile 224 C4
Redmire 251 F3
Redmoor 147 E3
Rednal 220 A5
Redpath 277 G2
Redruth 146 A5
Redscarhead 285 G5
Redshaw 275 G3
Redstone Bank 177 E1
Redwick *Newport* 180 D4
Redwick *S.Glos.* 181 E4
Redworth 262 B5
Reed 200 B4
Reed End 200 B4
Reedham 229 F5
Reedley 243 E4
Reedness 245 G5
Reef (Riof) 328 C4
Reepham *Lincs.* 238 A5
Reepham *Norf.* 228 B3
Reeth 251 F3
Regaby 240 C2
Regil 166 C1
Regoul 322 A4
Reiff 330 B3
Reigate 172 B3
Reighton 255 E5
Reinigeadal (Rhenigidale) 327 E3
Reisgill 337 E5
Reiss 337 F3
Rejerrah 146 B4
Releath 145 D3
Relubbus 144 C3
Relugas 322 B5
Remenham 184 C4
Remenham Hill 184 C4
Remony 300 C5
Rempstone 223 G5
Rendcomb 182 C1
Rendham 203 E1
Rendlesham 203 E2
Renfrew 283 G3
Renhold 199 F2
Renishaw 236 B5
Renishaw Hall & Gardens 74
Rennington 279 G5
Renton 283 E2
Renwick 260 B3
Repps 229 F4
Repton 223 E5
Rescobie 302 D4
Rescorla 147 E4
Resipole 297 G3
Resolis 321 F3
Resolven 179 E2
Resourie 298 A2
Respryn 147 F3
Reston 287 F3
Restormel 147 F3
Reswallie 302 D4
Reterth 146 D3
Retew 146 D4
Retford 237 E4
Rettendon 187 G3
Rettendon Place 187 G3
Retyn 146 C4
Revesby 226 A1
Revesby Bridge 226 B1
Rew 152 A5
Rew Street 157 D3
Rewe *Devon* 152 C3
Rewe *Devon* 152 B3
Reybridge 168 A1
Reydon 215 F4
Reydon Smear 215 G4
Reymerston 228 B5
Reynalton 177 D2
Reynoldston 178 A4
Rezare 149 D3
Rhadyr 180 C2
Rhandirmwyn 193 D3
Rhaoine 332 B4
Rhayader 193 F1
Rhedyn 216 B4
Rheged-the Village in the Hill 99
Rhegreanoch 330 C3
Rheindown 321 E5
Rhelonie 332 A5
Rhemore 297 E4
Rhenigidale (Reinigeadal) 327 E3
Rheola 179 E2
Rhes-y-cae 219 E1
Rhewl *Denb.* 219 E3
Rhewl *Denb.* 219 E1
Rhewl *Shrop.* 220 A4
Rhian 332 A3
Rhicarn 330 C2
Rhiconich 334 B3
Rhicullen 321 F2
Rhidorroch 331 D5
Rhifail 335 G4
Rhigos 179 F2
Rhilochan 332 C4
Rhinduie 321 E5
Rhireavach 330 C5
Rhiroy 320 A1
Rhiston 206 B3
Rhiw 216 B5
Rhiwargor 218 C5
Rhiwbina 180 A4
Rhiwbryfdir 217 F3
Rhiwderin 180 B4
Rhiwinder 179 G4
Rhiwlas *Gwyn.* 217 E1
Rhiwlas *Gwyn.* 218 C4
Rhiwlas *Powys* 219 F4
Rhode 165 F4
Rhodes Minnis 174 D4
Rhodesia 236 C5
Rhodiad-y-brenin 190 A5
Rhodmad 204 B5
Rhonadale 272 C2
Rhonehouse (Kelton Hill) 266 B5
Rhoose 165 D1
Rhos *Carmar.* 191 G4
Rhos *N.P.T.* 178 D2
Rhos Common 206 B1
Rhôs Lligwy 230 C4
Rhos, The 176 D1
Rhosaman 178 D1
Rhoscolyn 230 A5
Rhoscrowther 176 C2
Rhosesmor 219 F1
Rhos-fawr 216 C4
Rhosgadfan 217 E2
Rhos-goch *I.o.A.* 230 C4
Rhosgoch *Powys* 194 A3
Rhos-hill 191 E3
Rhoshirwaun 216 A5
Rhoslan 217 D3
Rhoslefain 204 B2
Rhosllanerchrugog 219 F3
Rhosmaen 192 C5
Rhosmeirch 230 C5
Rhosneigr 230 B5
Rhosnesni 220 A2
Rhôs-on-Sea 231 G4
Rhossili 178 A4
Rhosson 190 A5
Rhostrehwfa 230 C5
Rhostryfan 217 D2
Rhostyllen 220 A3

Shennanton 265 E4
Shenstone *Staffs.* 208 D2
Shenstone *Worcs.* 208 A5
Shenstone Woodend 208 D2
Shenton 209 F2
Shenval 311 E2
Shepeau Stow 212 B1
Shephall 200 A5
Shepherd's Bush 186 B5
Shepherd's Green 184 C4
Shepherd's Patch 181 G2
Shepherdswell (Sibertswold) 175 E4
Shepley 235 F2
Sheppardstown 337 E5
Shepperdine 181 F3
Shepperton 171 F1
Shepreth 200 B3
Shepreth Wildlife Park 83
Shepshed 209 G1
Shepton Beauchamp 154 A1
Shepton Mallet 166 D3
Shepton Montague 167 D4
Shepway 173 G3
Sheraton 262 D4
Sherborne *Dorset* 154 C1
Sherborne *Glos.* 183 D1
Sherborne Castle 35
Sherborne St. John 170 B2
Sherbourne 197 E1
Sherbourne Street 202 A3
Sherburn *Dur.* 262 C3
Sherburn *N.Yorks.* 254 C5
Sherburn Hill 262 C3
Sherburn in Elmet 245 D4
Shere 171 F3
Shereford 227 G5
Sherfield English 169 D5
Sherfield on Loddon 170 B2
Sherford *Devon* 151 D3
Sherford *Som.* 165 F5
Sheriff Hutton 245 F1
Sheriffhales 207 G1
Sheringham 228 C1
Sherington 199 D3
Shernal Green 196 B1
Shernborne 227 F4
Sherramore 309 E5
Sherrington 168 A4
Sherston 182 A4
Sherwood 223 G3
Sherwood Forest Country Park 75
Sherwood Green 163 F3
Sherwood Pines Forest Park 75
Shettleston 284 A3
Shevington 233 G2
Shevington Moor 233 G1
Sheviock 149 D5
Shibden Hall 90
Shide 157 E4
Shiel Bridge 307 F3
Shieldaig *High.* 319 E4
Shieldaig *High.* 319 E2
Shieldhill 284 C2
Shielfoot 297 F2
Shielhill 302 C4
Shiels 312 B4
Shifford 183 F2
Shifnal 207 G2
Shilbottle 271 D1
Shildon 262 B5
Shillingford *Devon* 164 C5
Shillingford *Oxon.* 184 A3
Shillingford Abbot 152 C4
Shillingford St. George 152 C4
Shillingstone 155 E1
Shillington 199 G4
Shillmoor 270 A1
Shilstone 163 F5
Shilton *Oxon.* 183 E2
Shilton *Warks.* 209 G4
Shimpling *Norf.* 214 C3
Shimpling *Suff.* 201 G2
Shimpling Street 201 G2
Shincliffe 262 B3
Shiney Row 262 C2
Shinfield 170 C1
Shingay 200 B3
Shingham 213 F2
Shingle Street 203 E3
Shinness Lodge 332 A3
Shipbourne 173 E3
Shipbrookhill 234 A5
Shipdham 228 A5
Shipham 166 B2
Shiphay 151 E1
Shiplake 184 C5
Shiplake Row 184 C5
Shipley *Northumb.* 279 F5
Shipley *Shrop.* 208 A3
Shipley *W.Suss.* 171 G5
Shipley *W.Yorks.* 244 A4
Shipley Art Gallery 105
Shipley Bridge *Devon* 150 C1
Shipley Bridge *Surr.* 172 C4
Shipley Common 223 F3
Shipley Country Park 75
Shipmeadow 215 E2
Shippea Hill 213 E4
Shippon 183 G3
Shipston on Stour 197 E3
Shipton *Glos.* 182 C1
Shipton *N.Yorks.* 245 E2
Shipton *Shrop.* 207 E3
Shipton Bellinger 168 D3
Shipton Gorge 154 A3
Shipton Green 158 A3
Shipton Moyne 182 A4
Shipton Oliffe 182 C1
Shipton Solers 182 C1
Shipton-on-Cherwell 183 G1
Shiptonthorpe 246 A3
Shipton-under-Wychwood 183 E1
Shira 291 D3
Shirburn 184 B3
Shirdley Hill 233 E1
Shire Oak 208 C2
Shirebrook 223 G1
Shirecliffe 236 A3
Shiregreen 236 A3
Shirehampton 181 E5
Shiremoor 271 F4
Shirenewton 181 D3
Shireoaks 236 C4
Shirl Heath 194 D2
Shirland 223 E2
Shirley *Derbys.* 222 D3
Shirley *Gt.Lon.* 172 C2
Shirley *Hants.* 156 A3
Shirley *S'ham.* 156 D1
Shirley *W.Mid.* 208 D5
Shirley Heath 208 D5
Shirley Warren 156 C1
Shirleywich 221 G5
Shirrell Heath 157 E1
Shirwell 163 F2
Shirwell Cross 163 F2
Shiskine 273 E3
Shittlehope 261 G4
Shobdon 194 C1
Shobley 156 A2
Shobrooke 152 B2
Shocklach 220 B3
Shocklach Green 220 B3
Shoe, The 182 A5
Shoeburyness 188 C4
Sholden 175 F3
Sholing 157 D1
Shoot Hill 206 D1
Shooter's Hill 186 D5
Shop *Cornw.* 146 C2
Shop *Cornw.* 162 C4
Shop Corner 202 D4
Shopnoller 165 E4
Shore 234 D1
Shoreditch 186 C4
Shoreham 173 E2
Shoreham-by-Sea 159 E3
Shoremill 321 G3
Shoresdean 287 G5
Shoreswood 287 G5
Shoreton 321 F3
Shorley 169 G5
Shorncote 182 C3
Shorne 187 F5
Shorne Ridgeway 187 F5
Short Cross 206 B2
Short Green 214 B3
Short Heath *Derbys.* 209 F1
Short Heath *W.Mid.* 208 C3
Shortacombe 149 F2
Shortbridge 159 G1
Shortfield Common 170 D3
Shortgate 159 G2
Shortgrove 200 D4
Shorthampton 197 F5
Shortlands 172 C2
Shortlanesend 146 C5
Shorton 151 E1
Shorwell 157 D4
Shoscombe 167 E2
Shotatton 220 A5
Shotesham 214 D2
Shotgate 187 G3
Shotley *Northants.* 211 E3
Shotley *Suff.* 202 D4
Shotley Bridge 261 G2
Shotley Gate 202 D4
Shotleyfield 261 G2
Shottenden 174 C3
Shottermill 171 D4
Shottery 197 D2
Shotteswell 197 G3
Shottisham 203 E3
Shottle 223 E3
Shottlegate 223 E3
Shotton *Dur.* 262 D4
Shotton *Dur.* 262 C5
Shotton *Flints.* 220 A1
Shotton *Northumb.* 271 E4
Shotton Colliery 262 C3
Shotts 284 C3
Shotwick 233 E5
Shouldham 213 E2
Shouldham Thorpe 213 E2
Shoulton 196 A2
Shover's Green 173 F5
Shrawardine 206 C1
Shrawley 196 A1
Shreding Green 185 F4
Shrewley 197 E1
Shrewsbury 207 D1
Shrewton 168 B3
Shrine of Our Lady of Walsingham 83
Shripney 158 B3
Shrivenham 183 E4
Shropham 214 A2
Shroton (Iwerne Courtney) 155 E1
Shrub End 202 A5
Shucknall 195 E3
Shudy Camps 201 E3
Shugborough Estate 67
Shurdington 182 B1
Shurlock Row 184 D5
Shurnock 196 C1
Shurrery 336 C3
Shurrery Lodge 336 C3
Shurton 165 F3
Shustoke 209 E3
Shut Heath 221 F5
Shute *Devon* 153 F3
Shute *Devon* 152 B2
Shutford 197 F3
Shuthonger 196 A4
Shutlanger 198 C3
Shutt Green 208 A2
Shuttington 209 E2
Shuttlewood 236 B5
Shuttleworth 234 B1
Siabost (Shawbost) 329 D3
Siabost Bho Dheas 329 D3
Siabost Bho Thuath 329 D3
Siadar Iarach 329 E2
Siadar Uarach 329 E2
Sibbaldbie 267 F2
Sibbertoft 210 B4
Sibdon Carwood 206 D4
Sibertswold (Shepherdswell) 175 E4
Sibford Ferris 197 F4
Sibford Gower 197 F4
Sible Hedingham 201 F4
Sibley's Green 201 E5
Sibsey 226 B2
Sibson *Cambs.* 211 F3
Sibson *Leics.* 209 F2
Sibster 337 F3
Sibthorpe 224 C3
Sibton 203 E1
Sibton Green 215 E4
Sicklesmere 201 G1
Sicklinghall 244 C3
Sidbury *Devon* 153 E3
Sidbury *Shrop.* 207 F4
Sidcot 166 B2
Sidcup 187 D5
Siddal 244 A5
Siddington *Ches.* 234 C5
Siddington *Glos.* 182 C3
Sidemoor 208 B5
Sidestrand 229 D2
Sidford 153 E3
Sidlesham 158 A4
Sidley 160 C3
Sidlow 172 B4
Sidmouth 153 E4
Sigford 152 A5
Sigglesthorne 247 D3
Sigingstone 179 F5
Signet 183 E1
Silbury Hill 36
Silchester 170 B1
Sildinis 327 E2
Sileby 210 B1
Silecroft 248 C4
Silfield 214 C2
Silian 192 B2
Silk Museum & Paradise Mill 99
Silk Willoughby 225 F3
Silkstead 169 F5
Silkstone 235 G2
Silkstone Common 235 G2
Sill Field 249 G4
Silloth 259 E1
Sills 270 A1
Sillyearn 324 A4
Silpho 254 C3
Silsden 243 G3
Silsoe 199 F4
Silver End *Beds.* 199 G3
Silver End *Essex* 201 G5
Silver Green 215 D2
Silver Street *Kent* 174 A2
Silver Street *Som.* 166 C4
Silverburn 285 G3
Silvercraigs 281 G1
Silverdale *Lancs.* 249 F5
Silverdale *Staffs.* 221 F3
Silvergate 228 C3
Silverhill 160 C2
Silverlace Green 203 E2
Silverley's Green 215 D4
Silvermoss 312 D1
Silverstone 198 B3
Silverton 152 C2
Silvington 207 F5
Silwick 342 B3
Simister 234 C2
Simmondley 235 E3
Simonburn 270 A4
Simonsbath 164 A4
Simonside 262 C1
Simonstone *Bridgend* 179 F4
Simonstone *Lancs.* 243 D4
Simprim 287 F5
Simpson 199 D4
Sinclair's Hill 287 F4
Sinclairston 274 C4
Sinderby 252 C4
Sinderhope 261 F2
Sindlesham 170 C1
Sinfin 223 E4
Singdean 277 G5
Singleton *Lancs.* 241 G4
Singleton *W.Suss.* 158 A2
Singlewell (Ifield) 187 F5
Singret 220 A2
Sinkhurst Green 174 A4
Sinnahard 311 G3
Sinnington 253 G4
Sinton Green 196 A1
Siop y Fron (Upper Llandwrog) 217 E2
Sipson 185 F5
Sir Alfred Munnings Art Museum (see Castle House) 78
Sir Harold Hillier Gardens & Arboretum 51
Sirhowy 180 A1
Sisland 215 E2
Sissinghurst 173 G5
Sissinghurst Castle 35
Siston 181 F5
Sithney 144 D4
Sittingbourne 174 B2
Siulaisiadar 329 G4
Six Ashes 207 G4
Six Hills 224 B5
Six Mile Bottom 201 D2
Six Roads End 222 C5
Sixhills 238 B4
Sixmile 174 D4
Sixpenny Handley 155 G1
Sizergh Castle & Gardens 99
Sizewell 203 F1
Skail 335 G4
Skaill *Ork.* 340 A5
Skaill *Ork.* 339 E2
Skaill *Ork.* 340 C3
Skara Brae 130
Skares *Aber.* 312 B1
Skares *E.Ayr.* 274 D4
Skarpigarth 342 A2
Skateraw 287 E2
Skaw 343 E1
Skeabost 318 A5
Skeabrae 340 A4
Skeeby 252 B2
Skeffington 210 C2
Skeffling 239 D1
Skegby 223 G1
Skegness 227 D1
Skelberry *Shet.* 343 G4
Skelberry *Shet.* 343 D1
Skelbo 332 C5
Skelbo Street 332 C5
Skelbrooke 236 C1
Skeld (Easter Skeld) 342 C3
Skeldon 274 B4
Skeldyke 226 B4
Skellingthorpe 237 G5
Skellister 343 D2
Skellow 236 C1
Skelmanthorpe 235 G1
Skelmersdale 233 F2
Skelmonae 313 D1
Skelmorlie 282 C3
Skelmuir 325 E5
Skelpick 335 G3
Skelton *Cumb.* 260 A4
Skelton *E.Riding* 245 G5
Skelton *N.Yorks.* 251 F2
Skelton *R. & C.* 253 F1
Skelton *York* 245 E2
Skelton-on-Ure 244 C1
Skelwick 340 C2
Skelwith Bridge 249 E2
Skendleby 226 C1
Skendleby Psalter 239 E5
Skenfrith 195 D5
Skerne 246 C2
Skeroblingarry 272 C3
Skerray 335 F2
Skerton 242 A1
Sketchley 209 G3
Sketty 178 C3
Skewen 178 D3
Skewsby 253 F5
Skeyton 228 D3
Skeyton Corner 229 D3
Skidbrooke 239 E3
Skidbrooke North End 239 E3
Skidby 246 C4
Skilgate 164 C5
Skillington 225 D5
Skinburness 259 E1
Skinflats 284 D1
Skinidin 317 F5
Skinnet 336 D2
Skinningrove 253 G1
Skipness 281 G4
Skippool 241 G3
Skipsea 247 D2
Skipsea Brough 247 D2
Skipton 243 F2
Skipton Castle 90
Skipton-on-Swale 252 C5
Skipwith 245 F4
Skirbeck 226 B3
Skirbeck Quarter 226 B3
Skirethorns 243 F1
Skirlaugh 246 D4
Skirling 276 B2
Skirmett 184 C4
Skirpenbeck 245 G2
Skirwith *Cumb.* 260 C4
Skirwith *N.Yorks.* 250 C5
Skirza 337 F2
Skittle Green 184 C2
Skomer Island 176 A2
Skulamus 306 C2
Skullomie 335 F2
Skyborry Green 206 B5
Skye 306 A1
Skye Green 201 G5
Skye of Curr 310 B2
Skyreholme 243 G1
Slack *Aber.* 312 A1
Slack *Derbys.* 223 E1
Slack *W.Yorks.* 243 F5
Slackhall 235 E4
Slackhead 323 G3
Slad 182 A2
Slade *Devon* 163 F1
Slade *Devon* 153 E2
Slade *Pembs.* 176 C1
Slade *Swan.* 178 A4
Slade Green 187 E5
Slade Hooton 236 C4
Slade, The 184 A5
Sladesbridge 147 E2
Slaggyford 260 C2
Slaidburn 242 D2
Slains Park 303 G2
Slaithwaite 235 E1
Slaley 261 F2
Slamannan 284 C2
Slapton *Bucks.* 199 E5
Slapton *Devon* 151 E3
Slapton *Northants.* 198 B3
Slate Haugh 323 G3
Slatepit Dale 223 E1
Slattadale 319 E2
Slaugham 159 E1
Slaughden 203 F2
Slaughterford 182 A5
Slawston 210 C3
Sleaford *Hants.* 170 D4
Sleaford *Lincs.* 225 F3
Sleagill 249 G1
Sleap 220 B5
Sledge Green 196 A4
Sledmere 246 B1
Sleights 254 B2
Slepe 155 F3
Slerra 162 D3
Slickly 337 E2
Sliddery 273 E3
Sliemore 310 C2
Sligachan 306 A2
Slimbridge 181 G2
Slimbridge Wildfowl & Wetlands Trust 36
Slindon *Staffs.* 221 F4
Slindon *W.Suss.* 158 B3
Slinfold 171 G4
Sling 181 E2
Slingsby 253 F5
Slioch 312 A1
Slip End *Beds.* 185 F1
Slip End *Herts.* 200 A4
Slipton 211 E5
Slitting Mill 208 C1
Slochd 310 A2
Slockavullin 290 A5
Slogarie 266 A4
Sloley 229 D3
Slongaber 266 C3
Sloothby 239 E5
Slough 185 E4
Slough Green *Som.* 165 F5
Slough Green *W.Suss.* 159 E1
Sluggan 310 A2
Slyne 242 A1
Smailholm 278 A3
Small Dole 159 E2
Small Hythe 174 A5
Smallbridge 234 D1
Smallbrook 152 B3
Smallburgh 229 E3
Smallburn *Aber.* 325 F5
Smallburn *E.Ayr.* 275 E3
Smalldale 235 E5
Smalley 223 F3
Smallfield 172 C4
Smallford 186 A2
Smallhythe Place 51
Smallridge 153 F2
Smallthorne 221 F2
Smallworth 214 B3
Smannell 169 E3
Smardale 250 C2
Smarden 174 A4
Smaull 280 A3
Smeatharpe 153 E1
Smeeth 174 C5
Smeeton Westerby 210 B3
Smerclet 314 C2
Smerral 337 D5
Smestow 208 A3
Smethwick 208 C4
Smethwick Green 221 F1
Smirisary 297 F2
Smisby 209 F1
Smith Art Gallery & Museum 130
Smith End Green 195 G2
Smithfield 260 A1
Smithies 236 A2
Smithies, The 207 F3
Smithincott 153 D1
Smith's End 200 B4
Smith's Green *Essex* 201 D5
Smith's Green *Essex* 201 E3
Smithstown 319 D2
Smithton 321 G5
Smithy Green 234 B5
Smockington 209 G4
Smoo Cave 130
Smyrton 264 C2
Smythe's Green 188 C1
Snailbeach 206 C2
Snailwell 201 E1
Snainton 254 C4
Snaith 245 F5
Snape *N.Yorks.* 252 B4
Snape *Suff.* 203 E2
Snape Green 233 E1
Snape Watering 203 E2
Snarestone 209 F2
Snarford 238 A4
Snargate 161 E1
Snave 161 F1
Sneachill 196 B2
Snead 206 C3
Snead's Green 196 A1
Sneath Common 214 C3
Sneaton 254 B2
Sneatonthorpe 254 C2
Snelland 238 A4
Snellings 248 A2
Snelston 222 C3
Snetterton 214 A2
Snettisham 227 E4
Snibston Discovery Park 75
Snipeshill 174 B2
Snishival 304 A1
Snitter 270 C1
Snitterby 237 G3
Snitterfield 197 E2
Snitterton 223 D1
Snittlegarth 259 F3
Snitton 207 E5
Snodhill 194 C3
Snodland 173 G2
Snow End 200 C4
Snow Street 214 B3
Snowden Hill 235 G2
Snowdon Mountain Railway 114
Snowdonia National Park 114
Snowshill 196 C4
Snowshill Manor 36
Soar *Cardiff* 179 G4
Soar *Carmar.* 192 C5
Soar *Devon* 150 D4
Soay 306 A3
Soberton 157 F1
Soberton Heath 157 F1
Sockbridge 260 B5
Sockburn 252 C2
Sodom 232 B5
Sodylt Bank 220 A4
Softley 261 G5
Soham 213 D5
Soham Cotes 213 D5
Solas (Sollas) 315 G2
Soldon 162 D4
Soldon Cross 162 D4
Soldridge 170 B4
Sole Street *Kent* 174 C4
Sole Street *Kent* 173 F2
Soleburn 264 B4
Solihull 209 D5
Solihull Lodge 208 C5
Sollas (Solas) 315 G2
Sollers Dilwyn 194 D2
Sollers Hope 195 F4
Sollom 233 F1
Solomon's Tump 181 G1
Solsgirth 293 E5
Solva 190 A5
Solwaybank 268 B4
Somerby *Leics.* 210 C1
Somerby *Lincs.* 238 A2
Somercotes 223 F2
Somerford 208 B2
Somerford Keynes 182 C3
Somerley 158 A4
Somerleyton 215 F2
Somerleyton Hall & Gardens 83
Somersal Herbert 222 C4
Somersby 238 D5
Somerset House 60
Somersham *Cambs.* 212 B5
Somersham *Suff.* 202 B3
Somerton *Newport* 180 C4
Somerton *Oxon.* 197 G5
Somerton *Som.* 166 B5
Somerton *Suff.* 201 G2
Sompting 159 D3
Sompting Abbotts 159 D3
Sonning 184 C5
Sonning Common 184 C4
Sonning Eye 184 C5
Sontley 220 A3
Sookholme 223 G1
Sopley 156 A3
Sopworth 182 A4
Sorbie 257 E2
Sordale 336 D2
Sorisdale 296 B3
Sorn 275 D3
Sornhill 274 D2
Soroba 290 A2
Sortat 337 E2
Sotby 238 C5
Sots Hole 225 G1
Sotterley 215 F3
Soudley 221 E5
Soughton 219 F1
Soulbury 199 D5
Soulby 250 C1
Souldern 198 A4
Souldrop 199 E1
Sound *Ches.* 220 D3
Sound *Shet.* 343 D3
Sound *Shet.* 342 C2
Sourhope 278 C4
Sourin 340 C3
Sourton 149 F1
Souter Johnnie's Cottage 130
Soutergate 248 D4
South Acre 213 G1
South Acton 186 A5
South Alkham 175 E4
South Allington 151 D4
South Alloa 293 D5
South Ambersham 171 E5
South Anston 236 C4
South Ascot 171 E1
South Baddesley 156 C3
South Ballachulish 298 C4
South Balloch 265 E1
South Bank 263 E5
South Barrow 166 D5
South Bellsdyke 284 D1
South Benfleet 187 G4
South Bersted 158 B3
South Blackbog 312 C1
South Bockhampton 156 A3
South Bowood 154 A3
South Brent 150 C1
South Brentor 149 E2
South Brewham 167 E4
South Broomhill 271 E2
South Burlingham 229 E5
South Cadbury 166 D5
South Cairn 264 A4
South Carlton 237 G5
South Cave 246 B4
South Cerney 182 C3
South Chard 153 G2
South Charlton 279 F4
South Cheriton 167 D5
South Church 262 B5
South Cliffe 246 A4
South Clifton 237 F5
South Cockerington 239 D4
South Collafirth 344 C4
South Common 159 F2
South Cornelly 179 E4
South Corriegills 273 F2
South Cove 215 F3
South Creagan 298 B5
South Creake 227 G4
South Crosland 235 F1
South Croxton 210 B1
South Dalton 246 B3
South Darenth 187 E5
South Dell (Dail Bho Dheas) 329 F1
South Devon Railway 36
South Duffield 245 F4
South Elkington 238 C4
South Elmsall 236 B1
South End *Bucks.* 199 D5
South End *Cumb.* 241 F1
South End *Hants.* 156 A1
South End *N.Lincs.* 246 D5
South Erradale 318 D2
South Fambridge 188 B3
South Fawley 183 F4
South Ferriby 246 B5
South Field 246 C5
South Flobbets 312 C1
South Garth 345 E3
South Godstone 172 C4
South Gorley 156 A1
South Green *Essex* 187 F3
South Green *Essex* 188 D1
South Green *Norf.* 228 B4
South Green *Suff.* 214 C4
South Gyle 285 F2
South Hall 282 B2
South Hanningfield 187 G3
South Harefield 185 F4
South Harting 157 G1
South Hayling 157 G3
South Hazelrigg 279 E3
South Heath 185 E2
South Heighton 159 G3
South Hetton 262 C3
South Hiendley 236 A1
South Hill 148 D3
South Hinksey 184 A2
South Hole 162 C4
South Holme 253 F5
South Holmwood 171 G3
South Hornchurch 187 E4
South Hourat 283 D4
South Huish 150 C3
South Hykeham 225 E1
South Hylton 262 C2
South Kelsey 238 A3
South Kessock 321 F5
South Killingholme 238 B1
South Kilvington 252 D4
South Kilworth 210 B4
South Kirkby 236 B1
South Kirkton 312 C4
South Knighton 152 B5
South Kyme 225 G3
South Lakes Wild Animal Park 99
South Lancing 159 D3
South Ledaig 290 B1
South Leigh 183 F2
South Leverton 237 E4
South Littleton 196 C3
South Lopham 214 B3
South Luffenham 211 E2
South Malling 159 G2
South Marston 183 D4
South Middleton 279 D4
South Milford 245 D4
South Milton 150 C3
South Mimms 186 B2
South Molton 164 A5
South Moor 262 A2
South Moreton 184 A4
South Mundham 158 A3
South Muskham 224 C2
South Newbald 246 B4
South Newington 197 G4
South Newton 168 B4
South Normanton 223 F2
South Norwood 172 C2
South Nutfield 172 C4
South Ockendon 187 E4
South Ormsby 239 D5
South Ossett 235 G1
South Otterington 252 C4
South Owersby 238 A3
South Oxhey 186 A3
South Park 172 B4
South Parks 294 A4
South Perrott 154 A2
South Petherton 154 A1
South Petherwin 148 D2
South Pickenham 213 G2
South Pool 151 D3
South Queensferry (Queensferry) 285 F2
South Radworthy 164 A4
South Rauceby 225 F3
South Raynham 227 G5
South Redbriggs 324 C5
South Reston 239 E4
South Ronaldsay 339 D4
South Ruislip 186 A4
South Runcton 213 E2
South Scarle 224 D1
South Shian 298 B5
South Shields 262 C1
South Shields Museum & Art Gallery 105
South Somercotes 239 E3
South Somercotes Fen Houses 239 E3
South Stack Cliffs 114
South Stainley 244 C1
South Stoke *Oxon.* 184 B4
South Stoke *W.Suss.* 158 C3
South Street *E.Suss.* 159 F2
South Street *Gt.Lon.* 172 D3
South Street *Kent* 173 F2
South Street *Kent* 174 D2
South Street *Kent* 174 A2
South Tawton 149 G1
South Thoresby 239 E5
South Tidworth 168 D3
South Tottenham 186 C4
South Town *Devon* 152 C4
South Town *Hants.* 170 B4
South Tynedale Railway 99

Sou - Sto

South Uist (Uibhist a Deas) 304 A1
South Upper Barrack 325 E5
South View 170 B2
South Walsham 229 E4
South Warnborough 170 C3
South Weald 187 E3
South Weston 184 C3
South Wheatley Cornw. 148 C1
South Wheatley Notts. 237 E4
South Whiteness 342 C3
South Wigston 210 A3
South Willingham 238 B4
South Wingfield 223 E2
South Witham 211 E1
South Wonston 169 F4
South Woodham Ferrers 188 B3
South Wootton 227 E5
South Wraxall 167 F1
South Yardley 208 D4
South Zeal 149 G1
Southall 186 A4
Southam Glos. 196 B5
Southam Warks. 197 G1
Southampton 156 D1
Southampton Airport 157 D1
Southampton Maritime Museum 51
Southbar 283 F3
Southborough Gt.Lon. 172 D2
Southborough Kent 173 E4
Southbourne Bourne. 156 A3
Southbourne W.Suss. 157 G2
Southbrook 152 D3
Southburgh 228 B5
Southburn 246 B2
Southchurch 188 C4
Southcott Devon 149 F1
Southcott Wilts. 168 C2
Southcourt 184 D1
Southdean 269 E1
Southdene 233 F3
Southease 159 G3
Southend Aber. 324 C5
Southend Arg. & B. 272 B5
Southend Bucks. 184 C4
Southend W.Berks. 184 A5
Southend Wilts. 183 D5
Southend Pier 83
Southend-on-Sea 188 B4
Southerfield 259 E2
Southerly 149 F2
Southern Green 200 B4
Southerndown 179 E5
Southerness 267 D5
Southery 213 E3
Southfield 294 A5
Southfields 186 B5
Southfleet 187 F5
Southgate Cere. 204 B4
Southgate Gt.Lon. 186 C3
Southgate Norf. 228 C3
Southgate Norf. 227 E4
Southgate Swan. 178 B4
Southill 199 G3
Southington 169 G3
Southleigh 153 F3
Southmarsh 167 E4
Southminster 188 C3
Southmuir 302 B4
Southoe 199 G1
Southolt 202 C1
Southorpe 211 F2
Southowram 244 A5
Southport 233 E1
Southrepps 229 D2
Southrey 225 G1
Southrop 183 D2
Southrope 170 B3
Southsea Ports. 157 F3
Southsea Wrex. 219 F2
Southsea Castle & Museum 51
Southstoke 167 E1
Southtown Norf. 229 G5
Southtown Ork. 339 D3
Southwaite Cumb. 250 C2
Southwaite Cumb. 260 A3
Southwater 171 G5
Southwater Street 171 G5
Southway 166 C3
Southwell Dorset 154 C5
Southwell Notts. 224 B2
Southwick D. & G. 266 D5
Southwick Hants. 157 F2
Southwick Northants. 211 F3
Southwick Som. 166 A3
Southwick T. & W. 262 C2
Southwick W.Suss. 159 E3
Southwick Wilts. 167 F2
Southwold 215 G4
Southwood 166 C4
Sowden 152 C4
Sower Carr 241 G3
Sowerby N.Yorks. 252 D4
Sowerby W.Yorks. 243 G5
Sowerby Bridge 243 G5
Sowerby Row 259 G2
Sowerhill 164 B5
Sowley Green 201 F2
Sowood 235 E1
Sowton 152 C3
Soyal 332 A5
Spa Common 229 D2
Spadeadam 269 D4
Spalding 226 A5
Spaldington 245 G4
Spaldwick 211 G5
Spalefield 295 D4
Spalford 224 D1
Spanby 225 F4
Sparham 228 B4
Spark Bridge 249 E4
Sparkford 166 D5
Sparkhill 208 C4
Sparkwell 150 B2
Sparrow Green 228 A4
Sparrowpit 235 E4
Sparrow's Green 173 F5
Sparsholt Hants. 169 F4
Sparsholt Oxon. 183 F4
Spartylea 261 E3
Spath 222 B4
Spaunton 253 G4
Spaxton 165 F4
Spean Bridge 299 E1
Spear Hill 158 D2
Speddoch 266 C2
Speedwell 181 F5
Speedwell Cavern 75
Speen Bucks. 184 D2
Speen W.Berks. 169 F1
Speeton 255 E5
Speke 233 F4
Speldhurst 173 E4
Spellbrook 187 D1
Spelsbury 197 F5
Spen Green 221 F1
Spencers Wood 170 C1
Spennithorne 252 A4
Spennymoor 262 B4
Spernall 196 C1
Spetchley 196 A2
Spetchley Park 67
Spetisbury 155 F2
Spexhall 215 E3
Spey Bay 323 F3
Speybridge 310 C2
Speyview 323 E5
Spilsby 226 B1
Spindlestone 279 F3
Spinkhill 236 B5
Spinningdale 321 F1
Spirthill 182 B5
Spital High. 337 D3
Spital W. & M. 185 E5
Spital in the Street 237 G3
Spitalbrook 186 C2
Spitfire & Hurricane Memorial, R.A.F. Manston 51
Spithurst 159 G2
Spittal D. & G. 265 F4
Spittal D. & G. 265 E5
Spittal E.Loth. 286 B2
Spittal Northumb. 279 E1
Spittal Pembs. 190 C5
Spittal of Glenmuick 302 B1
Spittal of Glenshee 301 G3
Spittalfield 301 G5
Spixworth 228 D4
Splayne's Green 159 G1
Splott 180 B5
Spofforth 244 C2
Spondon 223 F4
Spooner Row 214 B2
Spoonley 221 D4
Sporle 213 G1
Sportsman's Arms 218 C2
Spott 287 D2
Spratton 210 C5
Spreakley 170 D3
Spreyton 149 G1
Spriddlestone 150 B2
Spridlington 238 A4
Spring Grove 186 A5
Spring Vale 157 F3
Springburn 284 A3
Springfield Arg. & B. 282 B2
Springfield D. & G. 268 B5
Springfield Fife 294 B3
Springfield Moray 322 C4
Springfield P. & K. 293 G1
Springfield W.Mid. 208 C4
Springfields Outlet Shopping Village & Festival Gardens 75
Springfields Outlet Village 226 A5
Springhill Staffs. 208 C2
Springhill Staffs. 208 B2
Springholm 266 C4
Springkell 268 A4
Springleys 312 C1
Springside 274 B2
Springthorpe 237 F4
Springwell 262 B2
Sproatley 247 D4
Sproston Green 221 E1
Sprotbrough 236 C2
Sproughton 202 C3
Sprouston 278 B3
Sprowston 228 D4
Sproxton Leics. 225 D5
Sproxton N.Yorks. 253 F4
Sprytown 149 E2
Spurlands End 185 D3
Spurn Head 90
Spurstow 220 C2
Spyway 154 B3
Square Point 266 B3
Squerryes Court 51
Squires Gate 241 G4
Sròndoire 281 G2
Sronphadruig Lodge 300 C2
S.S. Great Britain 35
Stableford Shrop. 207 G3
Stableford Staffs. 221 F4
Stacey Bank 235 G3
Stackhouse 243 E1
Stackpole 176 C3
Stacksteads 243 E5
Staddiscombe 150 B2
Staddlethorpe 246 A5
Staden 235 E5
Stadhampton 184 B3
Stadhlaigearraidh (Stilligarry) 304 A1
Staffa (Fingal's Cave) 130
Staffield 260 B3
Staffin 318 A3
Stafford 221 G5
Stafford Castle 67
Stagden Cross 187 F1
Stagsden 199 E3
Stagshaw Bank 261 F1
Stagshaw Garden 99
Stain 337 F2
Stainburn Cumb. 258 D4
Stainburn N.Yorks. 244 B3
Stainby 225 E5
Staincross 236 A1
Staindrop 262 A5
Staines 185 F5
Stainfield Lincs. 225 F5
Stainfield Lincs. 238 B5
Stainforth N.Yorks. 243 E1
Stainforth S.Yorks. 236 D1
Staining 241 G4
Stainland 235 E1
Stainsacre 254 C2
Stainsby Derbys. 223 F1
Stainsby Lincs. 238 D5
Stainsby Mill 75
Stainton Cumb. 249 G4
Stainton Cumb. 260 A5
Stainton Dur. 251 F1
Stainton Middbro. 253 D1
Stainton N.Yorks. 252 A3
Stainton S.Yorks. 236 C3
Stainton by Langworth 238 A5
Stainton le Vale 238 B3
Stainton with Adgarley 248 D5
Staintondale 254 C3
Stair Cumb. 259 F4
Stair E.Ayr. 274 C3
Stairfoot 236 A2
Staithes 253 G1
Stake Pool 242 A3
Stakeford 271 E3
Stakes 157 F2
Stalbridge 154 D1
Stalbridge Weston 154 D1
Stalham 229 E3
Stalham Green 229 E3
Stalisfield Green 174 B3
Stalling Busk 251 E4
Stallingborough 238 B1
Stallington 221 G4
Stalmine 241 G3
Stalybridge 235 D3
Stambourne 201 F4
Stamford Lincs. 211 F2
Stamford Northumb. 279 G5
Stamford Bridge Ches. 220 B1
Stamford Bridge E.Riding 245 G2
Stamfordham 270 C4
Stanah 241 G3
Stanborough 186 B1
Stanbridge Beds. 199 E5
Stanbridge Dorset 155 G2
Stanbridge Earls 169 E5
Stanbury 243 G4
Stand 284 B3
Standalone Farm 83
Standburn 284 D2
Standedge Experience (see Huddersfield Narrow Canal) 88
Standeford 208 B2
Standen Kent 174 A5
Standen W.Suss. 51
Standen Street 174 A5
Standerwick 167 F2
Standford 170 D4
Standford Bridge 221 E5
Standish Glos. 182 A2
Standish Gt.Man. 233 G1
Standlake 183 F2
Standon Hants. 169 F5
Standon Herts. 200 B5
Standon Staffs. 221 F4
Standon Green End 186 C1
Stane 284 C4
Stanecastle 274 B2
Stanfield 228 A3
Stanford Beds. 199 G3
Stanford Kent 174 D5
Stanford Shrop. 206 C1
Stanford Bishop 195 F2
Stanford Bridge 195 G1
Stanford Dingley 184 A5
Stanford End 170 C1
Stanford Hall 75
Stanford in the Vale 183 F3
Stanford on Avon 210 A5
Stanford on Soar 223 G5
Stanford on Teme 195 G1
Stanford Rivers 187 E2
Stanford-le-Hope 187 F4
Stanfree 236 B5
Stanghow 253 F1
Stanground 212 A3
Stanhoe 227 G4
Stanhope Dur. 261 F4
Stanhope Sc.Bord. 276 C3
Stanion 211 E4
Stanklyn 208 A5
Stanley Derbys. 223 F3
Stanley Dur. 262 A2
Stanley Notts. 223 F1
Stanley P. & K. 293 G1
Stanley Staffs. 221 G2
Stanley W.Yorks. 244 C5
Stanley Wilts. 182 B5
Stanley Common 223 F3
Stanley Crook 262 A4
Stanley Gate 233 F2
Stanley Green 155 G3
Stanley Hill 195 F3
Stanleygreen 220 C4
Stanlow Ches. 233 F5
Stanlow Shrop. 207 G3
Stanmer 159 F2
Stanmore Gt.Lon. 186 A3
Stanmore W.Berks. 183 G5
Stannersburn 269 F3
Stanningfield 201 G2
Stanningley 244 B4
Stannington Northumb. 271 E4
Stannington S.Yorks. 236 A4
Stansbatch 194 C1
Stansfield 201 F2
Stanshope 222 C2
Stanstead 201 G3
Stanstead Abbotts 186 C1
Stansted 173 F2
Stansted Airport (London Stansted Airport) 200 D5
Stansted Mountfitchet 200 D5
Stanton Derbys. 209 E1
Stanton Glos. 196 C4
Stanton Northumb. 270 D2
Stanton Staffs. 222 C3
Stanton Suff. 214 A4
Stanton by Bridge 223 E5
Stanton by Dale 223 F4
Stanton Drew 166 C1
Stanton Fitzwarren 183 D3
Stanton Harcourt 183 G2
Stanton Hill 223 F1
Stanton in Peak 222 D1
Stanton Lacy 207 D5
Stanton Lees 223 D1
Stanton Long 207 E3
Stanton Prior 167 D1
Stanton St. Bernard 168 B1
Stanton St. John 184 A2
Stanton St. Quintin 182 B5
Stanton Street 202 A1
Stanton under Bardon 209 G1
Stanton upon Hine Heath 220 C5
Stanton Wick 166 D1
Stanton-on-the-Wolds 224 B4
Stanwardine in the Fields 220 B5
Stanwardine in the Wood 220 B5
Stanway Essex 202 A5
Stanway Glos. 196 C4
Stanway Green Essex 202 A5
Stanway Green Suff. 214 D4
Stanwell 185 F5
Stanwell Moor 185 F5
Stanwick 211 E5
Stanwix 260 A2
Stanydale 342 B2
Staoinebrig 304 A1
Stapehill Abbey Crafts & Garden 36
Stapeley 221 D3
Stapeley Water Gardens & Palms Tropical Oasis 99
Stapenhill 223 D5
Staple Kent 175 E3
Staple Som. 165 E3
Staple Cross 164 D5
Staple Fitzpaine 153 F1
Staplecross 160 C1
Staplefield 159 E1
Stapleford Cambs. 200 C2
Stapleford Herts. 186 C1
Stapleford Leics. 210 D1
Stapleford Lincs. 225 D2
Stapleford Notts. 223 F4
Stapleford Wilts. 168 B4
Stapleford Abbotts 187 D3
Stapleford Tawney 187 E3
Staplegrove 165 F5
Staplehay 165 F5
Staplehurst 173 G4
Staplers 157 E4
Staplestreet 174 C2
Stapleton Cumb. 268 D4
Stapleton Here. 194 C1
Stapleton Leics. 209 G3
Stapleton N.Yorks. 252 B1
Stapleton Shrop. 207 D2
Stapleton Som. 166 B5
Stapley 153 E1
Staploe 199 G1
Staplow 195 F3
Star Fife 294 B4
Star Pembs. 191 F4
Star Som. 166 B2
Starbotton 251 E5
Starcross 152 C4
Stareton 209 F5
Starkholmes 223 E2
Starling 234 B1
Starling's Green 200 C4
Starr 265 F1
Starston 214 D3
Startforth 251 F1
Startley 182 B4
Statham 234 A4
Stathe 166 A5
Stathern 224 C4
Station Town 262 D4
Staughton Green 199 G1
Staughton Highway 199 G1
Staunton Glos. 181 E1
Staunton Glos. 195 G5
Staunton Country Park 51
Staunton Harold Hall 223 E5
Staunton in the Vale 224 D3
Staunton on Arrow 194 C1
Staunton on Wye 194 C3
Staveley Cumb. 249 F3
Staveley Derbys. 236 B5
Staveley N.Yorks. 244 C1
Staveley-in-Cartmel 249 E4
Staverton Devon 151 D1
Staverton Glos. 196 A5
Staverton Northants. 198 A1
Staverton Wilts. 167 F1
Staverton Bridge 196 A5
Stawell 166 A4
Stawley 165 D5
Staxigoe 337 F3
Staxton 254 D5
Staylittle (Penffordd-las) 205 E3
Staynall 241 G3
Staythorpe 224 C2
STEAM Museum of the Great Western Railway 36
Stean 251 F5
Steane 198 A4
Stearsby 253 F5
Steart 165 F3
Stebbing 201 E5
Stebbing Green 201 E5
Stechford 208 D4
Stedham 171 D5
Steel Cross 173 E5
Steel Green 248 C5
Steele Road 268 D2
Steen's Bridge 195 E2
Steep 170 C5
Steep Marsh 170 C5
Steeple Dorset 155 F4
Steeple Essex 188 C2
Steeple Ashton 168 A2
Steeple Aston 197 G5
Steeple Barton 197 G5
Steeple Bumpstead 201 E3
Steeple Claydon 198 B5
Steeple Gidding 211 G4
Steeple Langford 168 B4
Steeple Morden 200 A3
Steeraway 207 F2
Steeton 243 G3
Stein 317 F4
Steinmanhill 324 C5
Stella 262 A1
Stelling Minnis 174 D4
Stembridge 166 B5
Stembridge Tower Mill 36
Stemster High. 337 D2
Stemster High. 337 D4
Stemster House 337 D2
Stenalees 147 E4
Stenhill 153 D1
Stenhousemuir 284 C1
Stenigot 238 C4
Stenis 329 F4
Stenness 344 B5
Stenscholl 318 A3
Stenson 223 E5
Stenton E.Loth. 286 D2
Stenton P. & K. 301 F5
Steornabhagh (Stornoway) 329 F4
Stepaside Pembs. 177 E2
Stepaside Powys 205 G4
Stepney 186 C4
Steppingley 199 F4
Stepps 284 A3
Sternfield 203 E1
Sterridge 163 F1
Stert 168 B2
Stetchworth 201 E2
Stevenage 200 A5
Stevenston 283 D5
Steventon Hants. 169 G3
Steventon Oxon. 183 G3
Steventon End 201 E3
Stevington 199 E2
Stewartby 199 F3
Stewarton D. & G. 257 E2
Stewarton E.Ayr. 283 F5
Stewartry Museum 130
Stewkley 199 D5
Stewley 153 G1
Stewton 239 D4
Steyning 159 D2
Steynton 176 C2
Stibb 162 C4
Stibb Cross 163 E4
Stibb Green 168 D1
Stibbard 228 A3
Stibbington 211 F3
Stichill 278 B3
Sticker 147 D4
Stickford 226 B1
Sticklepath Devon 149 G1
Sticklepath Som. 153 G1
Stickling Green 200 C4
Stickney 226 B2
Stiff Street 174 A2
Stiffkey 228 A1
Stifford's Bridge 195 G3
Stileway 166 B3
Stilligarry (Stadhlaigearraidh) 304 A1
Stillingfleet 245 E3
Stillington N.Yorks. 245 E1
Stillington Stock. 262 C5
Stilton 211 G4
Stinchcombe 181 G3
Stinsford 154 D3
Stirchley Tel. & W. 207 G2
Stirchley W.Mid. 208 C4
Stirkoke House 337 F3
Stirling Aber. 325 G5
Stirling Stir. 292 C5
Stirling Castle 130
Stirton 243 F2
Stisted 201 G5
Stitchcombe 183 E5
Stithians 145 E3
Stittenham 321 F2
Stivichall 209 F5
Stix 300 C5
Stixwould 225 G1
Stoak 233 F5
Stobo 276 C2
Stoborough 155 F4
Stoborough Green 155 F4
Stobwood 285 D4
Stocinis (Stockinish) 326 D4
Stock 187 F3
Stock Green 196 B2
Stock Lane 183 E5
Stock Wood 196 C2
Stockbridge Hants. 169 E4
Stockbridge Stir. 292 C4
Stockbridge W.Suss. 158 A3
Stockbury 174 A2
Stockcross 169 F1
Stockdale 145 E3
Stockdalewath 259 G2
Stockerston 210 D3
Stocking Green Essex 201 D4
Stocking Green M.K. 198 D3
Stocking Pelham 200 C5
Stockingford 209 F3
Stockinish (Stocinis) 326 D4
Stockland Cardiff 180 A5
Stockland Devon 153 F2
Stockland Bristol 165 F3
Stockleigh English 152 B2
Stockleigh Pomeroy 152 B2
Stockley 168 B1
Stocklinch 153 G1
Stockport 234 C3
Stocks, The 161 E1
Stocksbridge 235 G3
Stocksfield 261 G1
Stockton Here. 195 E1
Stockton Norf. 215 E2
Stockton Shrop. 207 G3
Stockton Shrop. 206 B2
Stockton Tel. & W. 207 G1
Stockton Warks. 197 G1
Stockton Wilts. 168 A4
Stockton Heath 234 A4
Stockton on Teme 195 G1
Stockton on the Forest 245 F2
Stockton-on-Tees 252 D1
Stockwell 182 B1
Stockwell Heath 222 B5
Stockwood Bristol 166 D1
Stockwood Dorset 154 B2
Stodday 242 A2
Stodmarsh 175 E2
Stody 228 B2
Stoer 330 C2
Stoford Som. 154 B1
Stoford Wilts. 168 B4
Stogumber 165 D4
Stogursey 165 F3
Stoke Devon 162 C3
Stoke Hants. 169 F2
Stoke Hants. 157 G2
Stoke Med. 174 A1
Stoke Plym. 150 A2
Stoke W.Mid. 209 F5
Stoke Abbott 154 A2
Stoke Albany 210 D4
Stoke Ash 214 C4
Stoke Bardolph 224 B3
Stoke Bishop 181 E5
Stoke Bliss 195 F1
Stoke Bruerne 198 C2
Stoke Bruerne Waterways Museum 75
Stoke by Clare 201 F3
Stoke Canon 152 C3
Stoke Charity 169 F4
Stoke Climsland 149 D3
Stoke D'Abernon 171 G2
Stoke Doyle 211 F4
Stoke Dry 211 D3
Stoke Edith 195 F3
Stoke Farthing 168 B5
Stoke Ferry 213 F3
Stoke Fleming 151 E3
Stoke Gabriel 151 E2
Stoke Gifford 181 F5
Stoke Golding 209 F3
Stoke Goldington 198 D3
Stoke Green 185 E4
Stoke Hammond 199 D5
Stoke Heath Shrop. 221 D5
Stoke Heath Worcs. 196 B1
Stoke Holy Cross 228 D5
Stoke Lacy 195 F3
Stoke Lyne 198 A5
Stoke Mandeville 184 D1
Stoke Newington 186 C4
Stoke on Tern 220 D5
Stoke Orchard 196 B5
Stoke Pero 164 B3
Stoke Poges 185 E4
Stoke Pound 196 B1
Stoke Prior Here. 195 E2
Stoke Prior Worcs. 196 B1
Stoke Rivers 163 G2
Stoke Rochford 225 E5
Stoke Row 184 B4
Stoke St. Gregory 166 A5
Stoke St. Mary 165 F5
Stoke St. Michael 167 D3
Stoke St. Milborough 207 E4
Stoke sub Hamdon 154 A1
Stoke sub Hamdon Priory 36
Stoke Talmage 184 B3
Stoke Trister 167 E5
Stoke Villice 166 C1
Stoke Wake 155 D2
Stoke-by-Nayland 202 A4
Stokeford 155 E4
Stokeham 237 E5
Stokeinteignhead 152 C5
Stokenchurch 184 C3
Stokenham 151 E3
Stoke-on-Trent 221 F3
Stokesay 206 D4
Stokesay Castle 67
Stokesby 229 F4
Stokesley 253 E2
Stolford 165 F3
Ston Easton 166 D2
Stonar Cut 175 F2
Stondon Massey 187 E2
Stone Bucks. 184 C1
Stone Glos. 181 F3
Stone Kent 187 E5
Stone Kent 161 E1
Stone S.Yorks. 236 C4
Stone Som. 166 C4
Stone Staffs. 221 G4
Stone Worcs. 208 A5
Stone Allerton 166 B2
Stone Cross Dur. 251 F1
Stone Cross E.Suss. 160 B3
Stone Cross E.Suss. 160 A1
Stone Cross Kent 174 C5
Stone Cross Kent 173 E5
Stone House 250 C4
Stone Street Kent 173 E3
Stone Street Suff. 215 E3
Stone Street Suff. 202 A4
Stonea 212 C3
Stoneacre 51
Stonebridge E.Suss. 160 A1
Stonebridge N.Som. 166 A2
Stonebridge Warks. 209 E4
Stonebroom 223 F2
Stonecross Green 201 G2
Stonefield Arg. & B. 281 G2
Stonefield Staffs. 221 G4
Stonegate E.Suss. 160 B1
Stonegate N.Yorks. 253 G2
Stonegrave 253 F5
Stonehaugh 269 F4
Stonehaven 303 G1
Stonehenge 36
Stonehill 171 E1
Stonehouse Ches. 233 G5
Stonehouse D. & G. 266 C4
Stonehouse Glos. 182 A2
Stonehouse Northumb. 260 C2
Stonehouse Plym. 150 A2
Stonehouse S.Lan. 284 B5
Stoneleigh Surr. 172 B2
Stoneleigh Warks. 209 F5
Stoneley Green 220 D2
Stonely 199 G1
Stoner Hill 170 C5
Stones 243 F5
Stones Green 202 C5
Stonesby 224 D5
Stonesfield 183 F1
Stonestreet Green 174 C5
Stonethwaite 259 F5
Stoney Cross 156 B1
Stoney Middleton 235 G5
Stoney Stanton 209 G3
Stoney Stoke 167 E4
Stoney Stratton 167 D4
Stoney Stretton 206 C2
Stoneyburn 285 D3
Stoneyford 153 D4
Stoneygate 210 B2
Stoneyhills 188 C3
Stoneykirk 264 B5
Stoneywood 313 D3
Stonganess 345 E2
Stonham Aspal 202 C2
Stonnall 208 C2
Stonor 184 C4
Stonor Park 51
Stonton Wyville 210 C3
Stony Houghton 223 F1
Stony Stratford 198 C3
Stonybreck 342 A5
Stoodleigh Devon 152 C1
Stoodleigh Devon 163 G2
Stopham 158 C2
Stopsley 199 G5
Stoptide 146 D2
Storeton 233 E4
Stornoway (Steornabhagh) 329 F4
Stornoway Airport 329 F4
Storridge 195 G3
Storrington 158 C2
Storrs 235 G4
Storth 249 F4
Storwood 245 G3
Storybook Glen 130
Stotfield 323 E2
Stotfold 200 A4
Stottesdon 207 F4
Stoughton Leics. 210 B2
Stoughton Surr. 171 E2
Stoughton W.Suss. 157 G1
Stoughton Cross 166 B3
Stoul 307 D5
Stoulton 196 B3
Stour Provost 167 E5
Stour Row 167 F5
Stourbridge 208 A4
Stourhead 36
Stourpaine 155 E2
Stourport-on-Severn 208 A5
Stourton Staffs. 208 A4
Stourton Warks. 197 E4
Stourton Wilts. 167 E4
Stourton Caundle 154 D1
Stove 341 E3
Stoven 215 F3
Stow Lincs. 237 F4
Stow Sc.Bord. 286 B5

T

Tre - Uss

Wyc - Zou

Published by Collins
An imprint of HarperCollins*Publishers*
77-85 Fulham Palace Road, Hammersmith, London W6 8JB

www.collins.co.uk

Mapping generated from Collins Bartholomew digital databases

The grid used on the main mapping in this atlas is the National Grid taken from the Ordnance Survey map with the permission of the Controller of Her Majesty's Stationery Office.

Printed in Italy

ISBN 0 007181957 QD11623 BDB

e-mail: roadcheck@harpercollins.co.uk

CREDITS

Contributors

Published by Mike Cottingham. Pages 5 to 22 researched and written by Karen Lloyd. Consultant geologist Duncan Friend Ph.D. Regional introductions written by Ellen Webster and Mike Cottingham. Attraction descriptions written by Amanda Berry, Andy Slater, Ellen Webster, Gill Coombs, Karen Lloyd, Rebekah Hart, Richard Knight and Rosemary MacLeod. All regional descriptions were edited by Juliet Lawler and Graham Gill. Infosnips compiled by Graham Gill and Mike Cottingham.

Picture credits

Aberdeen & Grampian Tourist Board: Red deer p16; Bottle nosed dolphin p19; Balmoral Castle p116

Althorp House: Althorp House p70

Ben BARDEN, Cumbria Tourist Board: Jetty on Derwent Water p92; Levens Hall p97; Hadrian's Wall p101

Beamish: Beamish p103

Ted BENTON, Frank Lane Picture Agency: Holly blue p15; Mountain ringlet p16; Marsh fritillary p18

Amanda BERRY: Babbacombe Model Village p24; London Aquarium p57; National Portrait Gallery p58; National Botanic Garden of Wales p111

Black Country Living Museum: Black Country Living Museum p64

Blue Planet Aquarium: Blue Planet Aquarium p94

John BRAINE: Arundel Castle p40

Helen BROWN: Lincoln Cathedral p69; Lincoln Cathedral p73

Burrell Collection: Burrell Collection p118

Chatsworth House: Chatsworth House p71

Chiltern Open Air Museum: Chiltern Open Air Museum p43

Clogau Welsh Gold mine: Welsh Gold p6

Colchester Zoo: Colchester Zoo p78

Colin Raw/Stone/Getty Images: View of hillside p85

Huw DAVIES: Ebley Mill p21

Dave DAWKINS: Poole's Cavern p74

Sonia DAWKINS: Roof tiles p8; Veteran tree p10; Cambrian Mountains p12; Tawny owl p15; Butterfly bush p17; Sculpture Trail p21; Severn Bore p22; Dartmoor p28; Forest of Dean p29; Goonhilly Satellite Earth Station p30; Lydford Gorge p33; Blenheim Palace p41; Oxford p48; Natural History Museum p59; American Adventure Theme Park p70; Carsington Water p71; Haddon Hall p72; Heights of Abraham p73; Twycross Zoo p75; Brecon Beacons p108; Chepstow Castle p109; Raglan Castle p113; Edinburgh p121; Our Dynamic Earth p128; Endpapers

Drayton Manor Park: Drayton Manor Park p65

Drummond Castle: Drummond Castle Gardens p120

Edinburgh & Lothians Tourist Board: The Royal Mile p13

English Heritage Photo Library: Grimes Graves p8; Dover Castle p44; Osborne House p48; Hardwick Hall p72; Audley End p77

Neil FORREST: Blue John p6; River Teifi p12; Royal Pavilion p50; St. Paul's Cathedral p59

Graham GILL: Dove Dale p71; Peak District p74; Loch Lomond p126

Helen GORDON: Gairloch sunset p1; Wast Water p4; Holker Hall Great Lime p10; Caledonian pines p10; background pp10 & 11; Wast Water p11; background p17; Dunsfold church p22; Batsford Arboretum p25; Chesil Beach p26; Bodiam Castle p39; Bodiam Castle p41; Knole p46; Wisley R.H.S. Gardens p53; Tower of London p61; Warwick Castle p68; Holker Hall p96; Lake District p97

John GORDON: Suilven p13; Callanish Stones p22; Seven Sisters Country Park p51; North West Highlands p128

Grampian Tourist Board: Dunnottar Castle p121

Sylvia GRAY: Leeds Castle & Gardens p46; Legoland p46; Imperial War Museum p81; National Railway Museum p89

Greater Glasgow & the Clyde Valley Tourist Board: New Lanark World Heritage Site p127

H.M. The Queen: Sandringham House p83 (photograph by gracious permission of H.M. The Queen)

Geoff HASSALL: New Forest p48

Hatfield House: Hatfield House p80

Hestercombe: Hestercombe p30

Highlands of Scotland Tourist Board - www.visithighlands.com: Cairngorms & Loch Morlich p14; Red squirrel p17; Ben Nevis p117; Cuillin Hills p119; Dunrobin Castle p121; Glencoe p123

His Grace The Duke of Buccleuch K.T.: Boughton House p70 (photograph by kind permission of His Grace The Duke of Buccleuch K.T.)

Paul HOBSON: Stag beetle p10; Silver-washed fritillary p15; Glow worm p15; Orange tip p16; Swallowtail p18; Banded demoiselle p18; Common toad p18

Holkham Hall: Holkham Hall p80

Hopetoun House: Hopetoun House p124

Houghton Hall: Houghton Hall p80

David HUNT: Pollarded tree p10; Hatfield Forest p10

G.E. HYDE, Frank Lane Picture Agency: Clouded buff moth p16

Ed JAMES: Alnwick Castle & Garden p102; Bamburgh Castle p102

Ele JAMES: Llywernog wind farm p20

Ian JENKINS: Loch Ness p13

Lou JOHNSON - www.walkingbritain.co.uk: Norber Stones p11

Sarah KIRK: Staffa, Fingal's Cave p14

Dave KJAER: Common newt p18

Knebworth House: Knebworth House p81

Richard KNIGHT: London Zoo p57; Westminster Abbey p61

Lancashire Tourism: Blackpool Tower p93

Mike LANE: Common dormouse p15; Ptarmigan p15; Hobby p16; Stoat p16; Exmoor pony p16; Harvest mouse p17; Grey partridge p17; Capercaillie p17; Wild cat p17; Pine marten p17; House cricket p17; Marsh harrier p18; Daubenton's bat p18; Bittern p18; Common lizard p19

Andrew LAWSON: Rousham House p50

Lightwater Valley Park: Lightwater Valley Park p88

Karen LLOYD: Fields - ridge & furrow p9; Field margin p9; Maiden Castle p9; Coppiced woodland p10; Winchelsea beach p10; Charmouth p10; Malham Cove p11; Gwaun Valley p12; Rhossili Beach p12; background p15; Hazlenut p15; Adder p16; Raft spider p18; Brown hare p17; Giant wood wasp p17; Mason bee p17; Hedgehog p17; Pinewood mushroom p17; Otter spraint p18; Atlantic salmon p18; Green tiger beetle p19; Sea gooseberry p19; Gem anemone p19; Green shore crab p19; Puffin p19; Common brittlestar p19; Common seal p19; Thornback ray p19; Field of short rotation willow coppice p20; Open ride in modern woodland p21; Nevern churchyard p22; Cowslip p22

Stephen LLOYD: Glastonbury Tor p9; Mortehoe coastline p10; Sand dunes p10; Pembrokeshire coastal path p10; Pillow Lava p12; Brampton Valley Way p20; The Sockburn Worm p22; Foxton Locks p72; Pembrokeshire Coast p112

Loch Lomond & Trossachs Tourist Boards: Inveraray Jail p125

Lynton & Lynmouth Cliff Railway: Lynton & Lynmouth Cliff Railway p32

Alan McDONNELL: Isolated sea eroded arch p14

Jackie McGEOUGH: Westonbirt p38; Chester Zoo p95; The Lowry p97

Rosemary MacLEOD: Edinburgh Castle p13; Fox p17; Britannia p117; Edinburgh Castle p122; Edinburgh Zoo p122; Museum of Scotland p127; Royal Botanic Garden p129

Madame Tussaud's: Madame Tussaud's and the Planetarium p57

Mellerstain Trust: Mellerstain p127

Derek MIDDLETON: Common shrew p15

National Marine Aquarium: National Marine Aquarium p33

National Trust: Avebury standing stone p8; Avebury Ring p24; Corfe Castle p27; Hidcote Manor Gardens p31; Petworth House p49; Sissinghurst Castle p51; Biddulph Grange Garden p63; Quarry Bank Mill & Styal Estate p98; Plas Newydd p112; Powis Castle & Garden p113

Needles Pleasure Park: Needles Pleasure Park p47

Mark NEWTON: Tree creeper p15; Blue tit p15; Song thrush p15; Golden eagle p15; Stonechat p16; Common blue p16; Barn owl p17; Peacock butterfly p17; Curlew p19; Shelduck p19

Norfolk Tourism: Norfolk Broads p82

Mike PAGE: Norfolk Broads p8

Perthshire Tourist Board: R.R.S. Discovery p120

Portsmouth Historic Dockyard: H.M.S. Victory p49

Leigh PRESTON: Flint building detail p8; North Pennines p11; Blea Tarn p11; High Force p11; Holy Island p11; Brecon Beacons p12; Rannoch Moor p13; Regular basalt columns p14; Raised beach p14; Railway track p20; Weavers Triangle p20; Colliery p20; Derelict mill p21; Block conifer plantation p21; Cranes in disused docks p21; Wicken Fen National Nature Reserve p76; Cambridge p77; Rannoch Moor p129

RAC: Stonehenge p36; Harlech Castle p110

Ravenglass & Eskdale Railway Co. Ltd: Ravenglass & Eskdale Railway p99

Richard REVELS: Cinnabar moth p16; Common field grasshopper p16; Emperor dragonfly p18

Science Museum: Science Museum p60

Scottish Borders Tourist Board: Floors Castle p122

Sheena SHANKS: Dunvegan Castle p22

Andy SLATER: Rackwick Bay p14

Jenny SLATER: Inverewe Gardens p125

Slimbridge Wildfowl & Wetlands Trust: Slimbridge p36

South West Tourism: Bowerman's Nose p9; Cerne Abbas giant p22; Bath p25; Lanhydrock p31; Longleat House p32; Roman Baths & Pump Room p35; Salisbury Cathedral p35

Robert TALBOT: Mevagissey harbour p23; National Maritime Museum Cornwall p34

Thetford Forest Park: Thetford Forest Park p83

Thorpe Park: Thorpe Park p52

Tourism South East: Canterbury Cathedral p42; Wakehurst Place p53

Visit London: Houses of Parliament p54; British Museum p55; Buckingham Palace p55; Houses of Parliament p56; London Eye p57; National Gallery p58; Royal Botanic Gardens, Kew p59; Tate Britain p60; Tate Modern p60; Victoria & Albert Museum p61

Joe WAINWRIGHT, Cheshire County Council: Chester p94; Chester Cathedral p95; Ness Botanic Gardens p98; Tatton Park p100

Alex WALLACE: BALTIC p102; Durham Cathedral p103

Norma WALLACE: Whitby Jet p6

Bill WATT: Marlborough Downs p8; Cotswold Water Park p8; background p18; Bibury p28; New Place Garden p62; Burns National Heritage Park p118; Stirling Castle p130; Strathclyde Country Park p131

Ellen WEBSTER: Hadrian's Wall p11; Llanberis Pass p12; Snowdonia p12; Loch Lomond p13; Eden Project p29; Lost Gardens of Heligan p32; Wells Cathedral p38; Jorvik p88; Hadrian's Wall p104; Bodnant Gardens p107; Erddig p110; Ffestiniog Railway p110; Portmeirion Village p113; Snowdonia p114

Welsh Tourist Board: Cardiff Bay p21; Llynnau Mymbyr & Snowdon p106; Beaumaris Castle p107; Big Pit Mining Museum p107; Caernarfon Castle p108; Caerphilly Castle p108; Conwy Castle p109

West Midlands Tourist Board: Shropshire Union Canal p20; Alton Towers Leisure Park p63; Ironbridge Gorge p66

Roger WILMSHURST: Badger p15; Mountain hare p15; Otter p18; Water vole p18

Woburn Abbey: Woburn Safari Park p84

Yorkshire Tourist Board: Ingleborough p11; Limestone pavement p11; background p16; Castle Howard p86; Eden Camp p87; Flamingo Land Theme Park p87; Fountains Abbey & Studley Royal Water Garden p87; National Museum of Photography, Film & TV p88; North York Moors p89; North Yorkshire Moors Railway p89; Rievaulx Abbey p90; Whitby Abbey p91; Yorkshire Dales p91

All other pictures supplied by Collins